LOS ANGELES RADIO PEOPLE

Volume 2, 1957 - 1997

by

Don Barrett

Published by

db Marketing Company

Los Angeles Radio People
Volume 2, 1957 - 1997

Copyright (c) 1997. All rights reserved
by Don Barrett

Printed in U.S.A.
1st Trade Printing
by db Marketing Company

Library of Congress Catalog Card Number: 95-092106
ISBN: 0-9658907-0-8

Inquiries, orders and correspondence should be addressed to:

    db Marketing Company
    PO Box 55518
    Valencia, CA 91385
    TEL: 888.Radio57
    FAX: 805.259.4910
    EMAIL: db@ecom.net
    WebSite: LARADIO.COM

Cover Design by Bundid Niyomtham
Graphics and Layout by Graphix Index

FOREWARD
by Gary Lycan, Radio-TV editor
Orange County Register

(Gary Lycan has been the Orange County Register's radio columnist for more than 25 years. In his 35 years with the newspaper, he has served in various editing and management capacities, including entertainment editor and assistant managing editor. Since 1987, he has worked in the newspaper's Information Services division, most recently as a Project Manager.

In 1991 he began producing The Pet Place television show, seen weekly in Southern California on KDOC/Channel 56. Gary and his business partner Missy Will have produced animal-themed tv documentaries, including "Why Don't You Love Me?," a 1994 program on uncaring pet owners, and anniversary videos for the group Actors And Others For Animals.

Gary is also active in The Ark Trust, an animal protection organization which monitors animal messages in the media and entertainment industry. The best of those works are honored each years with Genesis Awards.

His radio column appears every Sunday in The Register Show section. Gary was an enormous supporter of my first "Los Angeles Radio People" book. His E-mail address is glycan@link.freedom.com. We share a unique passion for chronicling the waves of radio change. I am grateful for his friendship, support and the industry is better for his quarter of a century perspective on radio. -db)

Southern California radio has changed dramatically in the 25-plus years I have been covering the radio beat for the *Orange County Register.* Stations have gone from full service to niche formats; big station groups have gobbled up small stations; and creativity has taken a back seat to the reality: bottom-line, it's a business, and if it's not making money, boot the talent and/or the format.

It's easy to get cynical, to wonder why sleaze replaced laughter and witty conversation in morning radio. Oh, to be sure, Howard Stern and Don Imus are talented radio personalities - their interviews are often penetrating, insightful and fun to listen to. But Stern, for one, can also step below the line of good taste when he detours into lengthy conversations about gratuitous, often explicit sex.

But, it begs the question: did Stern and Stern wannabes cross the line, or was the bar lowered to appeal to the changing tastes of the radio listener. It's a question with no clear answer, but it makes one wonder how low will it go before listeners say enough is enough. If TV talk shows can clean up their act, can radio's shock jocks do the same? I'm optimistic there will always be a place on the dial for the Sterns of the world, but the survivors will be those who never take themselves too seriously and know their strengths as well as their shortcomings.

As local radio moves forward into the year 2000, we can expect to hear more Spanish stations, a wider variety of music formats and, I predict, the emergence of children's radio as a viable, competitive format. At the same time, it's important to keep a perspective, and no one has done a better job at chronicling local radio than Don Barrett.

His first book, an A to Z listing of disc jockeys 1957-94, was well received and with good reason. It's a rich treasure of names, of people who woke us up, kept us informed, made us laugh and smile, and tucked us in at night. What a pleasure it was to remember why we did "Whittinghill" each morning or why Tom Dixon made classical music so pleasurable to listen to.

Barrett has updated his 1994 paperback to include news and talk radio people. If you're reading this now, I would bet this book will have dog-eared pages within a few hours as you leaf through it, re-discover an old favorite, and then another, and another. Barrett has painstakingly tracked down practically everyone who was in local radio, and his attention to accuracy speaks volumes about the kind of person he is - a true fan of radio whose books represent a labor of love.

So, sit back and travel through a time tunnel of memories. It's one of the happiest journeys you will ever take.

INTRODUCTION
by Don Barrett

When I embarked on the task of chronicling Los Angeles Radio People who have toiled in the "mind fields" of Southern California radio, I was totally unprepared for the daunting task of tracking over 3,000 personalities.

Who were these faceless men and, eventually, women who'd traveled from city to city as they perfected their craft in order to reach the nirvana of L.A. broadcasting?

The journey in putting together this "booktory" has been exhilarating. I grew up on the beach in Santa Monica in the '50s and '60s -- it seems like forever ago -- fascinated as radio made an often painful transition from "pop" to "rock" music. The date to begin this chronicle coincides with the debut of "Color Radio/Channel 98" at KFWB on January 2, 1958.

Having launched KIQQ ("psst, K-100-FM, pass it on") in the early '70s gave me another perch from which to view Los Angeles radio.

As I began this project I found myself less interested in awards acquired than in the vivid snapshot of each person's journey. If you read an entry and say "I didn't know that," or, "that's fascinating," then I've accomplished my task. The lines which define inclusion in

this volume continue to be blurred. The emergence of traffic networks to report not only freeway adventures but, sometimes, news and sports raises significant questions. As it turned out, this is an honest, full-scale attempt to include all those radio people who've spun records (45s, albums, floppies, CDs and/or from a hard drive), reported news and/or sports while employed by a station, hosted a talk show, programmed or ran a radio station. The size of the entry is in no way a reflection of contribution to Southern California radio. Some stories were fascinating, regardless of time spent on the air. Other personalities who may have deserved more space were unavailable, uncooperative or had passed away. The decision on which photos to include? Everyone who sent one is included.

What you are about to read in all its often-blinding detail could not have been done without the help, encouragement and remarkable generosity of many people. After the first edition was published, Gary Lycan of the Orange County Register devoted an entire column to the premier edition of Los Angeles Radio People published in 1995. He has been a constant source of moral support and a real friend. There are essential others as well. Nancy Plum was an initial researcher on the first edition. The foundation she created has allowed this second edition to grow. Mark Denis was the first to open his Rolodex and offer phone numbers. David Schwartz was so generous in providing names, dates and crucial phone numbers. Liz Salazar updated me on L.A. people who'd moved to the Bay Area. Greg Ogonowski who provided the technical wizardry in laying out both books. The folks at the Tournament Road post office, especially Mary Ann and Doris, were very helpful. John Bruno for his photographic recall of stations and dates. And thank you to so many who were generous in recalling fellow personalities and their possible whereabouts.

The proofreader's dispassionate eye -- four of them belonging to two people -- have provided an enormous, absolutely invaluable element for the project. My thanks to Sally Bartell and Alan Harvey.

It would be impossible to overstate the contribution of the individual so responsible for my growth in radio and life. His name is Earl McDaniel. Those who've had the good fortune to work with or for Earl know what kind of a rare jewel he is.

This book, finally, is a tribute to the men and women who've passed through the landscape of Southern California radio; where they came from, where they were when they were here and where they went when they went.

This labor of love has been 40 years in the making. Much of what you read comes from old radio surveys, in-house sales literature, local newspapers, trade publications and the radio people themselves. There was never an intent to vilify a personality with rumors, gossip, or behind-the-scenes scuttlebutt. The goal was to paint an accurate, positive picture of those who sat in an empty room talking to thousands of people, weaving a tale that kept the listener engaged and enthralled. It's a strange fraternity and this book is dedicated to those who feel at peace in the solitude of an empty building or studio with only a cup of coffee, a can of diet soda or a bottle of designer water as a friend. Do I hear, ever so faintly from the distance of the next millennium, calls for an eventual third edition?

Stay tuned....

A

AALVIK, Egil: SEE Swedish Eagle

ABADIA, Oscar: **KLVE**, 1989-97. Oscar works evenings and the Saturday night dance show at Spanish "K-Love."

ABCARIAN, Robin: **KMPC**, 1996-97. Robin joined Tracey Miller in the fall of 1996 in morning drive on Talk-formatted KMPC. She took a leave of absence from writing a twice-weekly column in the *LA Times Life & Style* section. In the early 1980s she was a columnist for the *Daily News*. She moved briefly to Detroit before joining the *Times*.

ABEL, Judy: **KIKF**, 1986-89; **KNX**, 1989-94; **KJQI/KOJY**, 1994-95; **KNNS**, 1995-96. Judy was born in Whittier and grew up in Hollywood. She worked in Providence and Boston before returning to the Southland. Judy is best known for her news and traffic reporting.

ABEL, Mark: **KTWV**, 1991-97

ACTOR, Allen: **KSRF**, 1977; **KOST**, 1978-82; **KBIG**, 1983-85. When Suburu of America launched its operation in the states, Allen was head of advertising and marketing. He filmed and voiced all the commercials. The native of San Antonio discovered his love for entertaining when he was in high school competing in oratory contests. After graduating from Trinity College, Allen found himself as the morning man on Armed Forces Radio Services in Okinawa. In 1954 following his service obligation, he started at WPAC-Long Island then on to WBUD and WTNJ-New Jersey. During a stint in Florida, Allen wrote and produced a movie, *Folks at Redwood Inn* that was renamed *Terror House*. "It seemed so easy at the time. Elvira aired the movie frequently." Suburu brought him to Los Angeles where he was very active at the Columbia School of Broadcasting, writing text and teaching. Beginning in 1989 he started doing voiceover work and teaching at Santa Monica City College.

ADAM, Leigh Ann: **KIBB**, 1996-97. Leigh Ann was hired for middays in the early weeks of KIBB's launch in the fall of 1996. The former poster girl for Coors Light was born in Wadsworth, Ohio. She started her radio career while still in high school in Alliance, Nebraska and was soon working in Dallas at KEGL and KHKS. In 1993 Leigh

Ann was selected as one of the most beautiful women of Texas for the "Women of Texas" calendar (she was November). In 1995 she moved to L.A. to pursue a radio and tv career and has appeared in *Walker, Texas Ranger*, *The Nanny*, *The Client* and *Hudson Street*.

ADAMS, Chris: **KEZY**, 1970s; **KIKF**, 1980-88, pd; **KEZY/KORG**, 1988-97. Born in Los Angeles in 1947, Chris was named pd of KIKF in 1985. He is production director and operations director for KORG.

ADAMS, Holly: **KOCM/KSRF**, 1989-92; **KACD**, 1996-97. Holly was part of the launch of the 15-month techno-alternative rock format called "MARSfm." Originating in the Pacific Northwest, Holly moved to Huntington Beach seeking sunshine and went to University of California Irvine and UC Santa Barbara where she started her radio career in 1988 at KTYD. After "MARS" changed formats, Holly went to KEDG-Las Vegas, KOME-San Jose and San Diego for a brief midday stint at "The Flash." She also has been working on syndicated programming with dance music guru and KACD pd, Swedish Eagle. Holly works middays at all-Dance format "Groove Radio" and hosts a weekly syndicated show called "The House Groove" on Saturday nights.

ADAMS, Joe: **KDAY**. Joe was an articulate '50s and '60s black dj specializing in tasty jazz. He was an actor who had a significant role in *The Manchurian Candidate*.

ADAMS, Sally: **KHJ**, 1977

ADAMSON, Jack: **KBIG/KBRT**, 1979-86, gm. Jack worked for Bonneville Broadcasting for 30 years. The former singer in the Mormon Tabernacle Choir was a senior vp at KMBZ-Kansas City, New York and KIRO-Seattle. He retired from Bonneville in 1994 and lives in Salt Lake City.

ADLER, Jodi: **KFWB**, 1995-97. Jodi is a news anchor at all-News KFWB. Her ubiquitous life includes being a math teacher and stand-up comic. The native Californian was a journalism and finance major at Cal State Northridge and UCLA.

AGUILAR, Alberto: **KALI**, 1987, nd

AGUIRRE, Jose David: **KVCA**, 1997

AIMERITO, Sylvia: **KNAC**, 1978-83; **KEZY**; **KHJ**; **KNOB**; **KNX/FM**; **KFI**, 1985-86; **KBIG**, 1987-97. Sylvia was teamed with "Bill" in morning drive at "K-

Big" for many years. Born in Springfield, Illinois, Sylvia grew up in Lakewood. She attended Cerritos College and Cal State Long Beach before starting her radio career in 1978. "I am a local girl who loves the beach, ping-pong and God. 'nuff said."

ALAN, Bernie: **KFAC/AM/FM**, 1971-72, pd and 1987-88; **KPPC/KROQ**, 1972-73; **KLVE**, 1973; **KVFM**, 1973; **KEZY**, 1976; **KOST**, 1979-82; **KZLA**, 1982-84; **KKGO**, 1990-91. "I knew when I was six years old that I wanted to be on the radio. I was listening to Don Wilson on a quiz show interview kids and when he inquired of a young guest what he wanted to be and he replied 'an announcer,' everyone laughed. I thought it was pretty neat!" Bernie has been the voice of PBS' KCET since 1984. He was born and raised in Trenton, New Jersey and graduated from Temple University with a B.S. in communications. Before arriving in the Southland, Bernie worked for radio stations in New York and Philadelphia. "At one stage I was working for two New York stations at the same time. I taped my classical show on WNCN while I was live at the same time at MOR WPIX." He started in the Southland in the fall of 1971 at KFAC. Through a series of ownership guffaws, Bernie was there for the flipping of KPPC and KROQ in 1972. He was on air with the launch of "Format 41" of Transtar service in the spring of 1984. Bernie is an active part of the rich history of Southern California radio.

ALAN, Magic Matt: **KIIS**, 1989-91; **KMPC**, 1996; **KIEV**, 1996-97; **KIIS**, 1996-97. Born Matthew Shearer in 1962, he grew up in the Northwest. At age 12, Matt was performing magic at fraternal organizations and at the Seattle Space Center. Through a magic performance  at an Everett, Washington radio remote, he developed a passion for radio. His magic led to a stint on the 1970s hit TV program, *The Gong Show*. His radio journey took him to a variety of radio stations. He worked in Seattle, Houston and WHTZ-New York. In the summer of 1989 Matt realized his dream of working in Los Angeles when he started in afternoons at KIIS. He told the *LA Times*, "I believe there's no reason you can't do a morning show in the afternoon." In October 1991, Matt's contract was not renewed due to "philosophical differences." Matt contended that the station cut him to cut costs. He told the *Times* that he had been seeking a raise of no more than 2%, his salary rumored to have been in the $500,000-a-year range. Matt kept his home in the hills of Encino when he went to KKLQ-San Diego and WYXR-Philadelphia. He said over lunch at the Magic Castle, "I will always consider Los Angeles my love." Speaking of another kind of love, a flight attendant from American Airlines attended one of his magic performances at the Magic Castle and performed her own magic, resulting in marriage in 1993. The former VH1 and MTV jock has been working with the owner of the Magic Castle, Milt Larsen, on a tv show. In the summer of 1996 Matt filled in on "710Talk KMPC." He hosts a cigar-lover's hour called "Lighten Up" on KIEV each weekend. In 1996 he returned to afternoons at KIIS and left a year later.

ALBERTS, Mal: **KHJ**. Mal was the sports director at KHJ and KHJ/Channel. He had heart surgery in the spring of 1997.

ALDI, Roger: **KMLA**, 1964; **KHJ**, 1964-72; **KRLA**, 1972-74; **KPOL**, 1974-75; **KDAY**, 1975-89, nd. The longtime news director of KDAY grew up in a radio family. Born in Brooklyn, Roger spent his youth in Scarsdale. At age 13 he decided that he wanted to be a tv director. He studied telecommunications at Columbia College and started his radio career at KMLA (100.3). Art Kevin was with KMLA and had known Roger's father. A year later Roger joined Art at KHJ. Roger has  received numerous awards. He won a Golden Mike award for conducting the first interview with Charles Manson after his arrest. Concurrent with his radio career, Roger studied for the ministry. In 1989 he left radio and became pastor of the Burbank Church of Religious Science. He is also married to a minister. Does he miss radio? "The only time I really missed it was during the 1994 Earthquake. I had nothing to do. I felt that I should be doing something, like phoning in a story."

ALEXANDER, Bill: **KGGI**, 1983-84; **KPWR**, 1987-93; **KYSR**, 1994-97. Born William Hulion in Monrovia, Bill grew up in Hacienda Heights and received a B.A. in communications from Cal State Fullerton. He started his radio career in 1986 at KENO-Las Vegas, where he stayed for six years. From there he worked in Oklahoma City, KSDO-San Diego and KACQ-Oxnard. When asked for a highlight of his work in L.A., Bill responded, "Being able to appear in the Hollywood Christmas Parade float every year." In March 1994, Bill moved to "Star 98.7," and handles the all-night shift.

ALEXANDER, Clark: **KGBS**, 1969-74. Clark was a newsman in Los Angeles radio. While Clark was on his shift at KGBS in 1974, he was discovered slumped in his chair. Program director Ron Martin administered mouth-to-mouth resuscitation, according to then-gm Ray Stanfield, while paramedics were called. Clark had died of a heart attack. He was a contract radio actor at CBS for many years before delivering "Minute Man News."

> "He's that wacky actor who doesn't know much about rock or classical music, but he mixes them pretty well."   - about Charles Laquidara

ALEXANDER, Dave: **KOCM/KSRF**, 1991. Dave was part of the "techno-Rock" format that was launched May 24, 1991. He came to the Southland from KRZR-Fresno.

ALEXANDER, Dixie: **KEZY**, 1987

ALEXANDER, Eddie: "Fast Eddie" was one of the more colorful sports broadcasting characters. A U.S. District Court judge in San Diego called Alexander "a con man" who could "sell refrigerators to Eskimos." According to the *LA Times* the one-time KABC/Channel 7 sportscaster was sentenced to two years in a federal prison. He spent five years of supervised probation for defrauding creditors and investors of $1.6 million. When he first arrived from San Francisco in the mid-1970s, he said he had been All-State in three sports as a high school athlete in Ohio. He also said he had done Ohio State football play-by-play for five years. It was later learned that none of this was true. (One of the most amazing cons revolved around a Dallas Cowboy cheerleader who flew to L.A. to interview with Eddie as the co-host of an ABC show to air opposite *60 Minutes*.) In 1985 the former sportscaster was convicted of fraud and served about one year of a two-year prison sentence, according to a 1985 story in the *Times*. In 1990 he was ordered back to jail in San Diego to await hearings on whether or not he violated his probation. In the *Times* story, Alexander's attorney said he would plead guilty.

ALEXANDER, Kermit: **KLAC**, 1984. The former San Francisco 49er and Ram and one-time president of the NFL Players Association broadcast the Los Angeles Express football games on KLAC.

ALEXANDER, Mark: **KUTE**, 1974-77. Mark worked morning drive at "Kute 102."

ALEXIA: **KWST**, 1976. Alexia Sokolov worked weekends at "K-West."

ALLEN, Bob: **KKGO**, 1986; **KSRF**, 1986-87; **KIKF**, 1989-90. Born and raised in Fresno, Bob has spent most of his career in country radio. He also worked for Transtar on their Special Blend and ACII formats from 1988 to 1990. Bob worked afternoons in the summer of 1989 at KIKF as Ken O'Connor. In 1990 he joined KFRG-San Bernardino. "In September 1986 I sat in on KKGO and was explained the controls and formatics by legendary jazz announcer Chuck Niles, whom I've admired for years." He currently works on WW1's Hot Country format as Bob McEntire.

ALLEN, Carol: **KPOL**, 1977

ALLEN, Dex: **KBLA**, 1961-62; **KDAY**, 1969-70. Born Claude Turner, he was best known for spearheading the "underground" movement at KPRI-San Diego. In the late 1960s, he drove to Southern California every weekend to work as a jock at KDAY, and eventually became gm of several stations in San Diego. Dex made one of those rare journeys from dj to station owner. Born in Ventura, Dex graduated from John Burroughs High School in Burbank and the University of Denver. His career can almost be broken down into decades. During the '60s Dex was a dj on KTLN-Denver, KQV-Pittsburgh, KOL-Seattle, and KCBQ-San Diego. In the '70s he moved into radio sales and gm positions in San Diego. By the 1980s he was ready for station ownership.

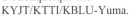

He created Commonwealth Broadcasting and KGGI/KMEN was his first purchase. He went on to own KROY-Sacramento and is the current owner of KMZQ-Las Vegas, KRST/KRZY/KOLT-Albuquerque and KYJT/KTTI/KBLU-Yuma.

ALLEN, Don: **KIKF**, 1985-96. Don worked afternoon drive for much of his time at the Country station and left KIKF in early 1996.

ALLEN, Don "Early": **KKTT**, 1983. When Don left the Southland he went to WWRL-Washington, DC. In the spring of 1995, the 27-year veteran returned to WBLK-Buffalo for morning drive.

ALLEN, "Hurricane" Gary: **KEZY**, 1986-90; **KCBS**, 1991-97. Born Gary Allen Belzman in Los Angeles, he grew up in West Hollywood and went to Fairfax High School. While attending Los Angeles City College and going to the Bill Wade School of Broadcasting, Gary interned at KHJ in 1972 and later at KKDJ. Gary, with an identity problem (he was "Hurricane" Allen at Westwood One, Sean Kelly at KACD and Marc St. John at "Arrow 93") started in Stockton at KSTN and KWIN. He brings to each job double duty since he is a strong engineer. After Stockton he joined KGOE, KACY-Oxnard and KDES-Palm Springs. In 1980 he worked at KFXM-San Bernardino. His last stop before arriving at KEZY was KPRZ-San Diego. Hurricane lives in the Santa Clarita Valley. At Westwood One from 1990 to 1994, he worked the 70's and Hot Country formats. He left "Arrow 93" in early 1997.

ALLEN, Keith: **KTWV**, 1991-97. The Los Angeles native returned to his home turf to work "the Wave" from "Love 94"-Miami.

ALLEN, Laurie: **KIIS**, 1982; **KNX/FM**, 1983-84; **KMGG**, 1984-86; **KPWR**, 1986-94.

The Morris, Minnesota-born jock got her first job in broadcasting as an 18-year-old weather person in Fargo. Her love affair with radio started early. "I loved to steal mom's radio up to my room at night and listen to the mysterious big city airwaves of WLS-Chicago and 'Beeker Street' in Little Rock. It opened up a whole new world for me." From Fargo, she moved to a small radio station, KCLD in Detroit Lakes, Minnesota, in 1975 where she met her husband-to-be, Bruce Vidal. They married in 1976. That trek took them from Princeton, Minnesota, to KSO-Des Moines and in 1978 to KOIL-Omaha. In 1979 Laurie worked in St. Louis, first for KMOX/FM and then KSD/FM. Prior to joining KIIS in 1982, she was at K1O1-San Francisco. She was often the first on-air woman hired. "Women have made such incredible strides in radio. There was a time when the only time slot for a woman was being tucked away late at night and sounding very breathy." Laurie got to Los Angeles before Bruce and started in the evenings at KIIS. Bruce joined as a part-timer. Laurie briefly went to KNX/FM, and after a format change, she returned to KIIS and read news for Rick Dees. She looks back fondly on the national attention she and her former-husband received in *People* magazine and on *Good Morning America*. The media was fascinated with the fact that the husband/wife team were on competing radio stations - occasionally in the same time slot. "We had our own careers plus each others to consider and with all our moving around it put a professional strain on us, but it had some fun advantages, too." Since 1987 Laurie has hosted a "classic rock" show on Armed Forces Radio. One of her career highlights was an AFRTS Tour of Europe in 1992. "I feel privileged to have been a part of the changes for women while working on some very high-profile stations."

ALLEN, Mark: **KWIZ**, 1977

ALLEN, Mike: **KFI**; **KMPC**; **KDAY**, 1974. Mike got his start in news at KXOA-Sacramento and KDIA-San Francisco. He was a network news reporter based in Washington, DC for NBC. He now lives in Phoenix.

ALLEN, Perry: **KRLA**, 1959-60; **KHJ**, 1962-63; **KFI**, 1976-77 and 1980. "Aardvark" was a familiar phrase during Perry's time in Los Angeles. Born Perry Gerstein in Scottsbluff, Nebraska, Perry attended Denver University on a broadcasting scholarship and worked at KTLN-Denver. While stationed in Tokyo for the Navy in 1952 he joined the Far East Network and fell in love with "the soul of the Japanese people." Perry arrived at KRLA from an enormously successful stint on Buffalo powerhouse, WKBW. He was almost one of the original "11-10 Men." Perry arrived two months into the new format in November 1959. KRLA ran a contest to "locate Perry Allen" with a $50,000 prize. KFWB knew that Perry hadn't left WKBW yet and dispatched newsman Charlie Arlington to Buffalo where he "found Perry Allen" and

KRLA had to pay their crosstown rivals $50,000. While he was working at KTLK-Denver, Perry hosted a children's program. "I brushed immortality by throwing up on camera." Perry was irreverent about the Top 40 format while in Denver. He stayed with KRLA until 1960 when there was a legendary switch of morning men with Wink Martindale, who did morning drive at KHJ. Perry wrote a very successful 3-hour salute to the "Magical World of Walt Disney." Perry worked the talk format on KFI. Perry hosted a KHJ/Channel 9 kid's show called *Cartoonsville*. "My own son wouldn't watch the thing. For which he's always held my deepest respect." He went to KCBQ-San Diego in 1979, then returned to KFI. He is currently writing *Good Luck, Disc Jockey.* Perry wrote from his home in Carlsbad: "Memory is a benevolent dictator. I've forgotten nearly all the sordid details. Currently, I labor under the umbrella misconception that I'm an actual writer, having finished a goofy tome on radio and drafting a novel which is neither goofy nor on radio." With tongue firmly in cheek, Perry went on, "I'm a spiffy dresser, can communicate with some competence in what passes as English and seldom violently kick small animals or sexually assault farm machinery."

ALLEN, Steve: **KNX**, 1946-48; **KHJ**, 1961; **KCBH**, 1969. The versatile entertainer, who excelled in television, wrote hundreds of published songs, starred in movies and wrote numerous books and worked morning drive at KHJ. Steve is well-known as the original star of NBC's *Tonight* show in the mid-1950s and of his own zany NBC comedy-variety series. In 1946 he did his first radio show working with Wendell Nobel for the Mutual Network. He eventually went solo at KNX. Steve continues to be a versatile entertainer, showing up as a spokesperson whenever the subject of tv talk-show hosts comes into vogue. He has written close to 6,000 songs. His best known songs are *This Could Be the Start of Something*, *Picnic*, *Impossible* and *Gravy Waltz*. Steve was born December 26, 1921.

ALLEN, Taz: **KIKF**, 1997

ALLEN, Terry: **KPPC**

ALLEN, Whitney: **KQLZ**, 1989-91; **KIIS**, 1991-94. Born in Los Angeles, Whitney's love affair with radio started at age 3 with a tiny transistor radio. She grew up in Eagle Rock. As she listened to the radio, she initially thought the Beatles were actually at the

radio station playing. "I could not figure out how they could be at KHJ and KRLA at the same time." Her only other career path consideration was to be a veterinarian, but then she found out that it took eight years of school. "I hated school so I set my sights on radio." There were no women on the air while she was growing up except for Sie Holliday and Kathi Gori. She spanned the state working for radio stations from Arcata and Eureka to San Diego. Whitney worked at eight radio stations in San Diego, before getting to Los Angeles. She was at "Q106"-San Diego when Scott Shannon called offering her a job. He would not tell her the format, but on blind faith she quit her job and was there for the high-profile launch of "Pirate Radio" on March 17, 1989. Two weeks after leaving KQLZ, she was on the air at her "dream-goal" station, KIIS/FM, working a weekend shift that eventually evolved into afternoon drive. Whitney left KIIS in the fall of 1994. She recounted that someone once said she was the best woman dj in the business. "When they drop the word 'woman' from the compliment, I'll be very happy." In early 1995, Whitney became the weekend host of the satellite country program "After MidNite With Blair Garner."

ALLISON, Hank: **KFWB**, 1968-74. "After covering the SLA shoot-out, I figured that I didn't survive Vietnam to be killed on the streets of Los Angeles." After the SLA shoot-out he was given a "safe" assignment covering a court hearing when he ended up in the middle of another shoot-out, this time a domestic quarrel. Hank and his wife bought a farm and moved to Montesano, Washington. He went back to  school to earn a clinical psychology degree. Born in New Jersey, Hank moved to the Southland with his parents when he was 6. After San Fernando High School and Woodbury College, Hank served two years in the Army with the 1st Cavalry Division. After the service he pursued journalism and became a writer for the *South Bay Daily Breeze* followed by the *Los Angeles Herald Examiner*. During the 1968 *Examiner* strike, Hank was driving his car when he heard that KFWB was going all-News. "I pulled my car over to the curb, called the station and applied for a job." He started as an editor and moved to outside reporter. "It was a fascinating time working for a news station. We covered the Manson trial, Bobby Kennedy's assassination and the Ellsburg trial. KFWB was on top of all of it." In 1974 Hank moved to Nashville and for the next twelve years worked for the CBS and ABC stations while attending law school. He is now practicing law in Nashville and living in Bell Buckle, Tennessee, a town of 350. "The 50 mile commute is worth it. Nothing has happened in Bell Buckle since someone drove off the interstate and robbed a convenience store 18 years ago."

ALLISON, Joe: **KRKD**, 1957; **KXLA**; **KFOX**, pd. Born in Texas in 1924, Joe started out in 1944 at KPLT-Paris, Texas. Known as "Uncle Joe," he distinguished himself in the world of country, jocking and writing hit songs. The Country station KRKD was one of the more active personality stations in the '50s. While at KRKD, Joe also hosted *Town Hall Party* on tv. He and his wife, Audrey, wrote *Teenage Crush* for Tommy Sands. As the former pd of KFOX, he joined the country music department at Liberty Records in the early 1960s. In 1976, Joe was elected to the Country Music Disc Jockey Hall of Fame Foundation. He wrote Jim Reeves' huge cross-over hit, *He'll Have to Go*. In a *R&R* salute to country, Joe reflected: "My best memory was having Tex Ritter as my mentor and father figure. He would take the time to show me things and teach me. He taught me to be fair and to give back to the business the things you take out of it. Tex was that way; he was probably the greatest man who was ever in our business. He was the wisest man I ever met. My worst memories are now. The business itself is beginning to forget the people who brought them here." Joe is a country radio consultant.

ALLISON, Randi: **KRLA**, 1983; **KFI**, 1986. Born Randi Singer, she was the screenwriter of *Mrs. Doubtfire*. Randi won the first annual Diane Thomas Screenwriting Award in 1987 for her screenplay *A 22 cent Romance*. Although still not produced, it brought her to the attention of Hollywood. Randi was raised in Palos Verdes. She studied political-science at the University of California at Berkeley and earned an M.A. in broadcast journalism from the University of Missouri. She pursued a newscasting career using the name Randi Allison while she began writing screenplays. When 20th Century Fox optioned the children's novel *Alias Madame Doubtfire* by Anne Fine, Randi was selected to adapt it to the screen. She has a deal at Fox, where she is working on several projects, including a remake of *The Ghost and Mrs. Muir* and was one of the executive producers of the Tony Danza tv show.

ALLISON, Steve: **KABC**, 1967-69. Steve worked at WPEN-Philadelphia and in Washington, DC before arriving in the Southland to work as a late evening talk show host. On the East Coast he was known as "The Man Who Owned Midnight." Steve died of brain cancer.

> *"Nobody understands baseball the way Vin Scully does. Scully is the world's best at filling the dull times by spinning anecdotes of the 100-year lore of the game. He can make baseball seem like Camelot and not Jersey City."* -syndicated columnist Jim Murray

ALLRED, Gloria: **KABC**, 1993-97. Nationally known

attorney and active feminist, Gloria hosted an early evening talk fest on KABC "TalkRadio." Born in Philadelphia, she earned her B.A. with honors in English from the University of Pennsylvania. She earned her M.A. from New York University and her JD cum laude from Loyola University School of Law in Los Angeles. Gloria has won countless honors from numerous organizations for her civil rights work on behalf of women and minorities and is well-known for her pioneering legal work in the area of women's rights. She contributes to KABC's morning show and is a regular commentator on KABC/Channel 7 *Eyewitness News*. She received three Emmy nominations for her television broadcasts. Gloria has a daughter, Lisa, who is an attorney and associate with Gloria's law firm.

ALMANEZ, Tino: **KALI**, 1993. Tino worked all-nights at Spanish KALI.

ALMENDAREZ-COELO, Renan: **KTNQ**, 1987-95;

KWIZ, 1995; **KKHJ**, 1995-96; **KWIZ**, 1996; **KSCA**, 1997. Renan worked morning drive with Humberto Luna and in early 1997 took over the morning chores at "La Nueva 101.9." He got his radio start in his native Honduras. An *LA Times* profile described his show: "He mixes scripted skits with improvisational humor in an eclectic format that is so fast-paced it's almost exhausting to listen to. But it's also witty and unpredictable, it's hard to turn off."

ALPERT, Lee: **KROQ**, 1986-89. Lee is an L.A. attorney who participated for three years in the "Loveline" show on KROQ, providing legal perspective.

ALVAREZ, Adrian: **KRTO**, pd. Adrian programmed Spanish-speaking formats in Miami and Los Angeles. Adrian had a long battle with cancer and died November 16, 1996.

ALVAREZ, Carlos: **KLVE**, 1996-97. Born in Puerto Rico in 1967, Carlos obtained a bachelor's degree in business administration in 1989 from the Institute of Technology in the Dominican Republic. After taking communication courses in Puerto Rico, he relocated to Los Angeles, where he worked in the banking industry. Carlos got his first dj opportunity at KLVE

in the fall of 1996 where he currently hosts the evening romantic show ("Romanticas").

ALVY, Ted: **KVFM**, 1967; **KPPC**, 1968-71. Ted was

known as Cosmos for some of his time at KPPC working with Les Carter. Ted is an L.A. native who worked behind the scenes with B. Mitch Reed. His current series of web pages and books include a "true fiction" cybernovel and paperback titled:

60's L.A. UNDERGROUND RADIO I was a Teenage Disc Jockey.

"When you do a show in Los Angeles, you experience an endorphin rush like a runner or swimmer. You open the microphone and there's an electricity that runs from the microphone switch, up your arm and to your brain."

-Joe Collins

AMADOR, Andrew: **KNX**, 1988-91. Andrew was a newsman for KNX.

AMBROSE, Mike: **KFWB**, 1965; **KRLA**, 1969. Mike  got his early start in radio at the age of 16 at a local station in Cleburn, Texas. While attending Arlington University of Texas he jocked at KLIF-Dallas. In 1964 he worked at KDEO-San Diego before arriving in the Southland. At KRLA he worked weekends. When Mike left L.A., he returned to San Diego in 1970 and did production at KOGO. For the past 25 years, "Captain Mike Ambrose" has been San Diego's favorite weathercaster. In the late 1980s he substituted for Spencer Christian on ABC's *Good Morning America*. His annual KGTV Christmas Toy Drive is the largest drive of its kind in San Diego's history. "This event has become the most meaningful event in my television career."

AMBROSINI, Michael: **KNX**, 1989-97.

AMES, Christopher: **KHJ**, 1970-72; **KRLA**, 1972-73; **KNX/FM**, 1973-80. Chris was born in Santa Monica and grew up in the San Fernando Valley. During KNX/FM's heyday, Chris was a news director/news anchor/public affairs director and morning drive personality. He also created the interview shows "Insight Out" and "After Midnight." He produced news and music documentaries for which he won numerous awards. Additionally, he was responsible for the station's "Sixty Seconds" feature. He participated in the "Odyssey File," one of the classic features on Los Angeles radio during the '70s. Chris is currently a screenwriter in Hollywood; with his wife Carolyn Shelby, he co-wrote the 20th Century Fox film *Class Action*, starring Gene Hackman.

AMIDON, Kim: **KLON**, 1982; **KUTE**, 1983-84; **KHJ**, 1984-85; **KRTH**, 1985; **KOST**, 1985-97. Kim has been teamed with Mark Wallengren in morning drive and their show was "rated #1 in the early '90s." Kim was born in Middletown, Connecticut, and worked at campus station KLON until her graduation from Long Beach State. Her first radio job after college was at "Kute 102" in 1983. "I love interviewing interesting people, especially those of whom I am a particular fan, like Linda Ronstadt." She's proud that she and Mark beat the 1980s' morning radio leader, Rick Dees. Kim was nominated for *Billboard*'s 1993 Music Director of the Year and AC Radio Personality of the Year (with Mark Wallengren) Awards.

AMOS, Famous: **KRLA**. Wally Amos, the famous cookie maker, was a semi-regular with Matthew "Doc" Frail in morning drive on KRLA. In 1988 he wrote *Wally 'Famous' Amos, The Power In You*. After trademark litigation following the sale of his cookie company in the late 1980s, he began selling cookies under the sardonic brand name Uncle Noname.

ANDERSON, Bob: **KMPC**, 1948-52; **KNX**, 1957; **KPOL**, 1958-59; **KLAC**, 1959-61; **KABC**, 1961-97. Bob is the most active voice in Southern California radio. "I have worked with some of the best broadcasters and personalities in the business." Bob was born in New York City and came to the Southland at the age of 11. After graduating from University High School, he joined the Navy and served three years in the South Pacific.

After the war, he attended the Don Martin School of Radio Broadcasting and Engineering. Upon graduation, he secured his first job with KXOB-Stockton and later joined KWBR-Oakland. He also attended the University of California, Berkeley. "I'll never forget receiving a telegram from KMPC saying I won an audition and they would pay me $80 a week to join the station." While hosting "Lucky Lager Dance Time," at KMPC, he attended UCLA. Since 1961, Bob has been a staff announcer at KABC. He hosted "Open Line," a talk show, and was the morning and evening news anchor. Since 1974, Bob has been doing news and commercials on Dodger baseball. "Some of the major news stories I've broken on Los Angeles radio was the firing of General Douglas MacArthur by President Truman and the assassination of John F. Kennedy. "I enjoy my work and am pleased to see that radio has a bigger connection in people's lives than ever before."

ANDERSON, Fred: **KFMU**, 1960; **KRHM**, 1960; **KGBS**, 1961-62; **KNX**, 1963-69. In the late 1960s, Fred was one of the original members of a then-revolutionary page in local tv news, KABC/Channel 7's *Eyewitness News*. His roots are in radio and they laid the foundation for his move into tv. "When *Eyewitness News* was launched, there were many seasoned tv news people who auditioned. Robert Irvine hired ONLY radio people for the first team of

Eyewitness News reporters. He believed the tv reporters of that day had developed lazy habits. They usually had all day to think about their story. Radio reporters, however, were used to meeting several deadlines a day, dashing to a phone to report a tight, coherent report and then rushing on to another story." Fred was born in Worcester, Massachusetts, and caught the radio bug at 15 after a visit to a local station. Two weeks after his 16th birthday he was working part-time at WAAB-Worcester, through high school. He really wanted to be a musician, playing the trumpet and later switching to string bass. He went to Leland Powers School of Theater in Boston and then the New England Conservatory of Music. As he worked in radio at Boston stations WEEI, WBOS and WCOP, he played bass after hours in nightclubs. In 1957 he was hired to be nd at WHYE-Roanoke and as a one-man news bureau for UPI. Before arriving in the Southland, Fred was nd of WJBW-New Orleans. His first job in L.A. in 1960 was, as Fred recalled, "A little FM classical music station in the Farmers Market on Fairfax, KFMU. We all lost our jobs when it became one of the first stations to be completely automated." In the early 1960s Fred was part of the ABC Radio series, "Weekend West" which led directly to his being hired by KNX in November of 1963 to take over a half-hour program called "Kaleidoscope." To survive in the early 1960s, he also did engineer work for ABC and was one of the regular engineers for acerbic-tongued Joe Pyne. At KNX, Fred covered increasing amounts of science, space and medicine and eventually became the science editor. During his six years with KNX he was also a regular reporter for the CBS network program, "Weekend Dimension." In the *LA Times*' listing of the best of 1968, Fred was named Announcer of the Year. The *Times* said: "Fred Anderson anchored numerous special reports for KNX over the years, handling every assignment with forcefulness and integrity." Three weeks before his death: "I have many fond memories of radio and its power to be the theater of the mind. I love being in tv...but I do miss radio a lot." Fred died June 23, 1996. A week before his death he suffered a heart attack and had triple bypass surgery. Fred had been in critical and unstable condition after the surgery and suffered a fatal heart attack. He was 59.

ANDERSON, George: **KMPC**, 1978-79. George was a newsman on the MOR station.

Favorite movie
Field of Dreams, **Charlie Tuna**
Tim, **Bob Hudson**
It's A Wonderful Life, **Rick Dees**
A Face in the Crowd, **Dick Whittington**
Treasure of Sierra Madre, **Bill Ballance**
Casablanca, **Dave Hull**
Rosemary's Baby Eats a Pamper!, **Gary Owens**

ANDERSON-POWELL, Lynn: **KHJ**, 1979, sales; **KIIS**, 1980-89, vp/gm. The former president and gm of KIIS was born in Detroit and earned a B.A. in business from Michigan State University. She was an intern at age 15 for WXYZ-Detroit. Lynn worked in sales in Chicago for the first half of the 1970s. In 1976 she joined Los Angeles Metro Radio Sales. Beginning in 1980, Lynn went from senior account executive to president and general manager at KIIS. Her broadcasting career includes vp/worldwide sales & marketing for Radio Express and president of her own consulting company, Broadcast Strategies. After a stint with Metro Networks, in the spring of 1996 she became nsm of KABL/KNEW/KBGG/KSAN-San Francisco.

ANDERSON, Paul Oscar: **KRLA**, 1970-71; **KROQ**, 1972. Don Page cited Paul's news reporting as the best of radio in 1970: "Paul Oscar Anderson's 'Fifth & Main, L.A.' ranks with the best, most touching efforts of any season." Paul spent time working for a number of stations in New York. He moved to San Antonio where he died.

ANDRES, Juan: **KFI**, 1996-97. Juan hosts a weekend talk show on KFI. He was the founder and host of the first Spanish radio network.

ANGEL, Bill: **KWKW**, 1955; **KFWB**, 1956-83. Born Angelo Fiorvanti, Bill was born and raised in Conway, just outside Pittsburgh. He started his radio career in 1938 at WJS-Pittsburgh and after serving four years in World War II, Bill came to the Southland with his Arkansas wife to work at KIEV. For two years Bill attended the Pasadena Institute for Radio and then worked in New Mexico and Wichita Falls. In 1955 he returned to the Southland and worked briefly at KWKW before joining KFWB as music director, freeway reporter and fill-in jock. He was assistant to Chuck Blore for the launch of historic "Color Radio/Channel 98" on

January 2, 1958, which ironically was Bill's birthday. Bill covered Vietnam for Westinghouse in 1967. "I went to Vietnam mainly because my son was wounded. He tragically died in the fall of 1996 from Agent Orange." In 1983 Bill turned 65. "I was making the most money of my life and I walked in and quit. I just walked away and retired." Bill is recovering from vascular bypass surgery. He lives in the San Fernando Valley.

ANGEL, Jack: **KMPC**, 1968-70; **KFI**, 1970-76; **KIIS**, 1972. Born in Berkeley, Jack arrived at KMPC from Gene Autry's sister station, KEX-Portland where he had worked since 1962. He sandwiched a year at KIIS between two stints at KFI. Jack has a very active voiceover career and was heard for years on KNBC/Channel 4.

ANGEL, Jill: **KODJ**, 1989; **KNX**, 1990-96. Born in 1957 in San Bernardino, Jill graduated from Cal Poly Pomona

in 1978. She started out as a teacher. Jill joined the Orange County Police Academy as a PE instructor. This led to her joining the California Highway Patrol in 1983. When multi-decade traffic and weatherman Bob Keene retired from KNX, Sergeant Jill was offered the job. In a 1993 interview, she told Gary Lycan of the *OC Register*, "I went back and forth. In the morning it was the Highway Patrol, in the afternoon it was radio. The head is saying stability, the heart is saying risk and go for it." She went for it. Her most coveted law enforcement award was being named "Toughest Cop Alive" (female) in 1988. By March 1996 Jill accepted a promotion with the California Highway Patrol and quit radio. "When I came in here, I really thought I knew what direction my career was going, but then doors started closing. Channel 2 canceled its morning news program (in which she appeared daily), and that cut my salary in half. I don't know where my life is going, but this is an opportunity I can't pass up." Jill is living in Lodi and working the health and safety section of the CHP in Sacramento.

ANGEL, Steve: **KFWB**; **KGIL**; **KNJO**, 1994-95, vp/gm. Steve died of leukemia on October 5, 1995, at 50. Born in 1945, he graduated from Dorsey High School and served in the Army in Vietnam. Steve's broadcast career spanned 20 years, including stints in sales at KFWB and KGIL before becoming vp/gm at KNJO. Jim Mergen, his longtime friend and fellow broadcaster for seven years at KGIL

delivered a warm, loving and amusing candid eulogy about Steve that captured this complex man. Part of this tribute, as follows: "Steve Angel was a different kind of man. You either loved him for what he was,...or...you probably couldn't stand him. I loved him. Steve was careless; and caring. He was compulsive, clever, compassionate, controversial, convincing, convivial and often complex. Most people were very fond of him, in spite of his eccentricities. Steve was frequently brash, feisty, impatient, selfish, impulsive, opinionated and stubborn. He was also very intelligent, stimulating, persuasive, enthusiastic, competitive, often sensitive, and sometimes emotional. He was always loving and caring to those he cared about. Yes, Steve Angel was a character. He was always a man - usually a <u>gentle</u>-man, and occasionally a supreme pain in the ass. Truly a great salesman...always my loyal friend...to the end, and I'll miss him a lot. May God bless Steve N. Angel."

ANGOTTI, Roberto: **KNAC**, 1982-85; **KROQ**, 1989. Roberto ran a cutting edge reggae show on Sunday nights.

ANITA: SEE Anita Gevinson

ANSILIO, Suzanne: **KLSX**, 1990-91; **KQLZ**, 1991-92; **KLOS**, 1993-97. She was Susie Who on KLSX and Suzy Cruz on "Pirate Radio," KQLZ.

ANSON, Bill: **KFWB**. Born in Chicago in 1908, he was discovered by Paul Whiteman. Bill was the first host of the old "Play Broadcast," a game show offered nationally by the Mutual radio network. He also was a composer and lyricist. Bill helped create the popular tune *When I Write My Song* recorded by Herb Jeffries and was also a lyricist for *The Man Upstairs* made popular by Kay Starr. He was one of the first members of AFTRA when it was formed in 1939. Bill worked Southern California radio in the 1940s and 1950s. The popular host of KTTV/Channel 11's *Glancin' with Anson* died in June 1983, of a heart attack. He was 75.

ANTHONY, Big Bob: **KIQQ**, 1974; **KHJ**, 1977-78. In the early 1980s he was working at KNBR-San Francisco. Bob has been running a Christian FM station outside Portland.

ANTHONY, Dave: **KODJ**, 1990-91, pd. In the early 1970s Dave hosted radio shows at KLAV, KBMI and KENO-Las Vegas, KRIZ-Phoenix and WZUU-Milwaukee where he was md and midday personality. By 1975 Dave had hit his first top 10 market working afternoons at KXYZ-Houston. During the second half of the '70s, Dave moved into management programming KRQ-Tucson and KLUC-Las Vegas. In 1981, Dave was promoted to program KZZP-Phoenix. "I received the highest ratings results in the history of the station." During the remainder of the 1980s Dave was affiliated with KHOW and KPKE-Denver, KLUC again, pd at KDWB-Minneapolis and in 1988 signed on Oldies formatted "Kool 108"-Minneapolis. "At KODJ I worked with classic talents like Charlie Tuna, The Real Don Steele, Machine Gun Kelly, Benny Martinez and Kris Erik Stevens." From L.A. Dave moved to KSFO and KYA-San Francisco. "In 1994 I had a chance at part-ownership of a group of stations which required a moved to WKQL and WIVY-Jacksonville." He continues to make Ponte Vedra Beach his home. Today, Dave consults radio stations, creates direct mail, telemarketing and tv campaigns as director of McClure Broadcast Promotions. He publishes custom magazines for various radio formats and is active in voice work for the PGA Tour, Delta Airlines and numerous other national clients.

ANTHONY, Ken: **KLOS**, 1991-92, pd; **KLSX**, 1994, pd. Prior to KLSX, Ken was operations manager of River City Broadcasting in Southern California. In the 1980s, Ken worked as pd of KLOL-Houston, KPNT and WFXB-St. Louis, KSJO-San Jose and KISS-San Antonio. In 1994 he joined Zoo Entertainment and three years later formed Radio Think Tank, an alliance of actively working programming specialists.

ANTHONY, Mike: **KFOX**, 1973. Mike arrived in Southern California from San Diego.

ANTHONY, R.: **KGFJ**, 1984-85. On-air as Marc Anthony, he worked morning drive at Urban KGFJ. When he left the station he went to New Orleans.

ANTHONY, Roger: **XTRA**, 1980. Born Roger Agnew, he was half of the Agnew & Felix Consultancy. The team attempted a "Boss Radio"-type format on XTRA in the fall of 1980.

ANTHONY, Ted: **KLAC**, 1975-76. Born Ted Nolan, he arrived in the Southland from WLS-Chicago in 1975 and left a year later. He is currently the booth announcer at WDIV/TV and evening jock on WLTI-Detroit.

ANTHONY, Tom: **KIKF**, 1985-90

ANTI, Don: **KFWB**, 1959-65. Don was an active part of the music presentation at KFWB.

ANTOINETTE, Karla: **KACE**, 1994-97. Karla arrived in the Southland from an Urban station in Richmond, Virginia. Her long-term ambition is to be become an actress. She has guested on *Martin*. In the spring of 1997 she moved into the midday slot at KACE.

ANZUR, Terry: **KABC**, 1997. The veteran L.A. broadcaster hosted America's Talking and filled in on the CNN Morning News. In the summer of 1997 she joined the KABC morning drive show. Terry is an assistant professor of journalism at USC.

APPLEGATE, Bobby: **KPPC**, 1971

ARBOGAST, Bob: **KMPC**, 1962-67; **KLAC**, 1967; **KFI**, 1968; **KGBS**, 1969. Bob struck a funny bone with those who enjoyed his unique brand of comedy. While

attending the University of Arizona on a tennis scholarship, he studied broadcast journalism. As part of a class assignment he broadcast the noon news over the campus P.A. system. "I could see out the window that no was paying attention to the news so I began broadcasting outlandish stories." This resulted in being offered a comedy show on a local station. The owner of WHB-Kansas City had a summer home in Tucson and in 1950 while vacationing was listening and was so impressed with Bob's comedy that Bob was soon headed for Kansas City. A year later he was working at WMAQ-Chicago. By the late 1950s Bob was in San Francisco working with Al Newman ("we had no chemistry") and Stan Bohrman at KFRC. In the middle of a show with Stan, the pd asked Bob to come into the hallway. "He fired me and it was my birthday. I must have offended him." Bob teamed with Jack Margolis for much of the '60s in Southern California, and released a best-selling album with KMPC's Dick Whittinghill. In the early 1960s he recorded *Chaos Pt 1 & 2* with Stanley Ralph Ross. "By 1969 I decided to leave radio for an even more insecure career in commercials and cartoon voice work." He was one of the first writers for *Sesame Street* and still receives substantial residuals for his voice work. Bob voiced 100 episodes of *Roger Ramjet* and hundreds of cartoons. "This year I received a residual check for 2 cents for my earlier work on *Jetsons*. From 40 cartoon shows I received a total of $25 in residuals." In 1992 Bob and his wife packed up for Mariposa and they now work and live on a 5-acre ranch. "I'm pretty good with a tractor. I'm a city boy who has adjusted to the country quite nicely. Our area is made up of either six-toed hillbillies or those who are sophisticated and funny. We haven't had a murder in our county for two years."

ARBOGAST, Pete: **KGIL**; **KFOX**; **KNX**, 1983-95; **KDAY**, 1984-85; **KFI**, 1985-86; **KHJ/KRTH**, 1986-87; **KNNS**, 1995-96; **KFWB**, 1997. Born December 5, 1954, Pete grew up in a broadcast family. His father was the humorous Bob Arbogast. Pete attended John Marshall High School and Los Angeles City College as well as USC. He worked sports for radio stations in Twin Falls, Victorville, Visalia, Fresno, Porterville and Riverside. Pete joined KNX as a news and sports anchor. While on KNX he called the play-by-play for USC football and basketball, did national sportscast for CBS Radio Network and was the CBS network reporter from the 1988 Seoul, Korea Olympics. At KFI and KHJ/KRTH Pete was the sports director and morning drive news anchor. From 1984 to 1989, he was the play-by-play announcer for the Los Angeles Clippers NBA Basketball team. At Dodger Stadium, Pete was the public address announcer from 1989 to 1993. He has appeared in the sports-themed films *Cutting Edge*, *Blue Chips* and *Rookie of the Year* along with many commercials. In 1995 Pete joined KNNS (formerly KGIL and KJQY) and by late 1996 he left with a format change to an all-Beatles format and joined KFWB. He is married with children and lives in Valencia.

> **KXEZ** (100.3FM) changes to Rhythm **KIBB**
> -August 30, 1996

ARCHERD, Army: **KABC**, 1972. Army has spent a  half-century in show business, most of which at *Daily Variety*. He has introduced the stars on their arrival at the Academy Awards for 30 years. Army's Star on Hollywood's Walk of Fame is in front of the Chinese theater where he has emceed dozens of movie premieres. He broke one of Hollywood's biggest stories on July 23, 1985, when he printed the Rock Hudson story on AIDS despite denials from all quarters. Army was born and raised in the Bronx. He graduated from UCLA at age 19 and started work in the mail room at Paramount Pictures. A few months later when World War II was declared, Army joined the Navy. After the war, Army and Bob Thomas opened the AP bureau at the *Hollywood Citizen News*. Army covered Hollywood. His first local tv show in the '50s was *Heart of Hollywood* on KNXT/Channel 2. He talked about the tv show: "I'd call up Bob Hope and Bing Crosby and say, 'Come on down and be on my TV show tonight' - and they'd say, 'Why not?' and come on the show." Over the years Army has appeared as himself in over 100 movies and tv shows. He has been honored by every major press group in the Southland. On April 15, 1996, Army was saluted by the Museum of Television and Radio with "An Evening With Army Archerd," celebrating his showbiz coverage for 50 years.

ARCHULETA, Jr., Alfred: **KFWB**, 1973; **KJOI**, 1973-75. Al worked the all-night shift at "K-Joy" during the height of the Beautiful Music station's success. After graduating from Los Angeles City College and California State University Los Angeles, Al started his radio career at KSEE-Santa Maria and was "Big Al" in the early 1970s. When he left KJOI, he joined the *Glendale Ledger* then returned to work for Lucky Stores, Inc.

ARDOLINO, Dr. Danielle: **KACD**, 1996-97. The doctor worked morning drive with the Poorman during the segment, "The Love Doctors" until the spring of 1997. Danielle performed similar chores on Poorman's Channel 56 TV show.

> *"I don't love baseball. I LIVE baseball."*
> -Traffic reporter, **Denise Fondo**

ARENAS, Juan Manuel: **KTNQ**, 1997. Juan is Spanish KTNQ's ombudsman. His early afternoon program provides listeners with help in dealing with matters ranging from use of credit, buying a car and job discrimination. "La Respuesta" assists listeners with relationships with the police and other government authorities. His Saturday night show,  "Extranos en la Noche" is KTNQ's answer to late-night loneliness. Juan performed for many years with one of California's premier tour bands.

ARGUELLO, Roberto: **KWKW**, 1993-95; **KTNQ**, 1995-97. The *LA Times* called Roberto "the star of Latino talk radio station KWKW, yet he didn't learn Spanish until age 7." He was born in California in 1939 and his family moved from San Francisco when he was 7 to be with his uncle, Leonardo, who had just become president of Nicaragua. Forty-seven days later Leonardo was forced from office. According to the *Times* profile, Roberto spent an additional 10 years in Nicaragua, Costa Rica and Mexico before returning to the United States. He attended boarding school in Mississippi, where he got a first-hand view of racial segregation and discrimination. He joined the Los Angeles Police Department and eventually became press liaison to the Latino community for police chiefs Tom Reddin and Ed Davis. He retired after 23 years with the police force and worked afternoon drive talk on KWKW until joining KTNQ.

ARLINGTON, Charlie: **KBBQ**; **KLAC**; **KFWB**; **KMPC**. The forty-year veteran of Los Angeles radio and tv died in 1989 at the age of 74, following surgery. One of his quiet pass times was repairing grandmother and grandfather clocks in his San Fernando Valley garage. One of his peers said of Charlie: "He was always meticulously dressed. He wore a shirt, tie and jacket as he popped out of his mobile unit, bullets at his feet! Somewhere in the early '40s he made his name as the feds closed in on an illegal gambling ship off the Southern California coast. With bullets flying Charlie did a live broadcast of the incident and the arrests that followed." Charlie graduated from Syracuse University. During World War II, he voiced hundreds of news broadcasts to the entire Pacific Theatre of Operations from the Office of War Information Headquarters in San Francisco. For many years he voiced *The March of Time* and *Pathe Newsreel*. In 1965 Don Page of the *LA Times* chose Charlie as announcer of the year. Charlie rode a motorcycle and in addition to his work as a newsman, he had a pool cleaning business. During his stay in the Southland, Charlie worked news on the Mutual Network. He had a way of phrasing that set him apart, e.g., "Among the halls and walls of Sacramento...."

ARMSTRONG, Dave: **KWIZ**, 1981-87, vp/gm; **KYMS**, 1987-91, vp/gm; **KKLA**, 1994-97, vp/gm. "I had done everything I wanted to do in secular radio and wanted to apply successful principles to Christian radio." The leader of Salem-Broadcasting-based Christian formatted KKLA was born and raised in Jefferson, Ohio, about 60 miles east of Cleveland. He started his radio career as a dj at a daytimer in Ohio. Once he saw that sales people made more money than announcers, Dave moved into sales. During the 1970s he worked in Erie, at KFJZ-Ft. Worth and KLOK-San Jose. He arrived in the Southland at KWIZ from sister station KLOK. "What we do in Christian radio at KKLA is to teach rather preach. We're not church or a replacement for church but we certainly support the church." Between KYMS and KKLA, Dave worked for the Orange County news channel. "I like to think that at KKLA we reinforce faith."

ARMSTRONG, Jack: **KTNQ**, 1978-79; **KFI**, 1979-81; **KNX/FM/KKHR**, 1984-86. Jack arrived in the Southland from WNBC-New York, where he was known as "The Unknown DJ." In 1982, Jack traveled to San Francisco and worked at KFRC for two years. When he left L.A. for the last time, Jack went to Cleveland and Fresno. He was a.k.a. "John Larsh" or "Big Jack." A Prodigy contributor recalled, "While attending Kent State University in 1967, I remember Jack shouting 'Your Lead-Dah!' on WKYC." A co-worker at "the new Ten-Q" said, "Jack had a 'gorilla' character voice that he used as an alter ego to get outrageous." Jack is currently working at WQMX-Greensboro/Winston Salem.

ARNOLD, Ed: **KNBB**, 1962; **KNOB**, 1963; **KOCM**, 1964-68; **KDAY**, 1968-69; **KOCM**, 1970-74, pd; **KHTZ/KRLA**, 1984-85; **KMPC**, 1986-88. Ed is one of

the most familiar faces on local television, but his heart has always been in radio. He started his radio career at age 14 at KOSY-Texarkana in 1954. "They had these new things called 45 rpm records that were replacing 78s and I was hired to create a filing system." Less than six months later he had his own show called "Rockin' with Eddy." His first live remote was from the local theater showing *Rock Around the Clock*. He helped host a weekly country jamboree with huge stars like Johnny Cash, Hank Thompson, and "this new kid from Memphis named Elvis Presley." In 1958 he enlisted in the U.S. Marine Corps and came to California where he stayed. In the Marines he was offered a football scholarship at Santa Ana College which he took. While in school he secured a job at KNBB. A few months later he moved to "The Jazz Knob." Ed received his B. A. degree in speech/radio/tv/film in 1968 from Long Beach State. After graduation he was hired by Tom Clay at KDAY. It was soon after that he began doing the on- and off-camera announcing for Dr. Robert H. Schuller's *Hour of Power* telecast from what is now known as the Crystal Cathedral. Their service is internationally syndicated and Ed has continued to be the volunteer announcer for over a quarter century. In the late '60s and early '70s Ed was a KTLA/Channel 5 booth announcer and in 1974 he replaced the legendary Tom Harmon on KTLA's *News at 10*. A year later he moved to KABC/Channel 7 and spent a decade with the station while jointly serving as the voice of KCET. Ed has been given every prestigious award imaginable for his community work. He has served on various civic boards and continues to be active in the KCET pledge drives. At KMPC Ed worked with Jim Lange and Robert W. Morgan in morning drive. When asked if he missed radio, Ed replied, "You bet!"

ARNOLD, Lee: **KLAC/KZLA**, 1987

ARTHUR, Bob: **KNX**; **KABC**, 1969-90. Born Joseph Arthur Prince in Kansas in 1921, Bob was one-half of the popular "Ken and Bob Company" morning news block on KABC. He studied journalism in college and began his career on tv in Wichita. He came to the Southland in the mid-1960s and worked for KTLA/Channel 5. After two years at KNX, Bob started at KABC in 1969 as a newsman. Beginning in 1973 and for the next 17 years "EGBOK" was Ken Minyard and Bob's catch phrase for "everything's gonna be OK." There was a spontaneous chemistry between the two. Ken was the more talkative of the two, would comment about news events or quirky happenings, while Bob, the more authoritative newsman, would provide wry one-liners and snappy observations. Bob retired in 1990. He explained the success of the team to the *LA Times*: "I've heard it said that it was like eavesdropping on a poker game where the stakes weren't very high." Bob died March 25, 1997, at his home in Albuquerque at the age of 75. According to former KABC partner Ken Minyard, his body was cremated and the ashes were spread off the Southern California coast. Half a bottle of Chivas Regal was poured over the ashes. "He didn't want to waste a full bottle," according to Ken. His wife said: "His nickname was 'Mr. News.' The thing he was most proud of was he interviewed John F. Kennedy twice."

ARVIN, Steve: **KMPC**. Steve was the entertainment editor for the Gene Autry station.

ASHER, John: **KMPC**. During the 1960s and 1970s John was the marketing director who created the "Did You Whittinghill This Morning?" billboard/bus campaign. He wrote "Helen Trump" episodes for Dick Whittinghill.

ASHLEY, Lorelei: **KOCM**; **KOST**, 1991-92. Lorelei hosted the popular "Love Songs" show on the weekends as well as other fill-in shifts. She and her husband run a video production company in Orange County.

ASHMAN, Chuck: **KABC**, 1976-77; **KMPC**, 1981; **KFI**, 1990; **KBLA**, 1991-92; **KNNS**, 1996. Chuck was a news anchor and investigative reporter for KTTV/Channel 11, the Ashman Files. Born in 1938 Chuck has had a varied life, to say the least. He's been a lawyer, a law professor and a public affairs director. He's authored a series of biographies about Henry Kissinger, Billy Graham, Martha Mitchell, Jimmy Hoffa and Angela Davis. He replaced Bill Ballance at KABC and Gary Owens at KMPC when that station was giving up MOR and turning to Talk radio. Simultaneously with his radio career, Chuck became a marketing executive at Casablanca Records and 20th Century Fox Pictures. He co-hosted KABC's "NewsTalk" for a short time and co-anchored Channel 11's irreverent *Metro News, Metro News* with Ken Minyard. He currently produces and hosts inflight audio programs on American, Delta, America West, Northwest, US Air and TWA airlines.

ASTOR, Art: **KDAY**, 1972, gm; **KHJ**; **KIKF**, 1980-97, gm. Art is one of the principals of KIKF/KYKF.

ASUNA, Bernardo: **KPWR**, 1997. Bernardo reports sports on "Power 106's" popular morning show with the Baka Boyz. He is the sports anchor for KMEX/TV.

ATKINS, Ted: **KHJ**, 1970-72, pd; **KIIS**, 1973. Ted  started in radio while attending the University of Denver. His first job was doing weekends at KLAK, a country station. Within months he was working at three stations on-air simultaneously under three different names: all night, weekends and news. Leaving Denver Ted returned to his hometown, Kansas City, and took over afternoons at KCKN and later KUDL and WHB. After time-out for the Air Force he was named pd at KDAB-Denver and then KBTR. Hired away by KIMN it was the beginning of Denver's greatest Top 40 battle. In 1967 Ted became om at WOL-Washington, DC, which led to teaming up with Bill Drake and RKO as pd of CKLW-Detroit and KFRC-San Francisco. At KFRC he was involved in the production of the 48-hour "History of Rock and Roll." Ted joined Chuck Blore as pd at KIIS in 1973. When he left the Southland Ted joined WTAE-Pittsburgh as gm and WXKX where he remained for 12 years. In 1985 he became a partner in a group that bought KROY-Sacramento and KSJQ-Modesto. Selling to Great American he returned to Pittsburgh and tried, unsuccessfully, to buy a local station. In 1989 he became gm at WWSW and in 1991 a consultant to WMXP. Today, based in Pittsburgh, Ted is a sales/marketing consultant in the East. He and his partner conduct two-day seminars. In 1996 he was also involved with Las Vegas attorney, Bob Massi, in the national syndication of a law program, call-in show heard in over 160 markets. Classic radio promotions in his career include giving away a Denver record store with just one listener phone call, giving away an entire used car lot over a weekend and the infamous turkey from a helicopter, later recreated on *WKRP*. "A great thrill was visiting the Rock and Roll Hall of Fame in Cleveland and hearing Morgan, Steele and 'Humble Harve' in the radio museum."

ATTACK, Jack: **KIKF**, 1992-94. Born Jack Scalfani in 1968, Jack became part-dj, part-psychologist, dispensing music and advice during the all-night shift at KIKF. Where did his radio name come from? "In high school my friends used to tease me because I'm very heavy. They said I would have to be 'Jack Attack' as the only way to get a date. I used the name to show them." Jack grew up in his hometown of Buena Park and became a club dj while attending Cypress and Fullerton Colleges. "I did a 'radio show' in the clubs so when I got on radio I brought all the energy from the clubs." His teacher at Fullerton was the pd at the time at KIKF. "Craig Powers taught me everything. He was the BEST teacher!" Jack left KIKF for KEWB-Redding and has since returned to the Southland awaiting his next radio assignment.

AUSTIN, Harold: **KKBT**, 1993-97, pd. As md and assistant pd at "the Beat," Harold worked with pd Keith Naftaly at KMEL-San Francisco before joining sister station, KKBT. He was upped to assistant pd in the summer of 1995 and to pd in early 1996. Harold was awarded the 1995 *Billboard* magazine R&B Music Director of the Year. In 1996 he was *BRE Magazine* and *Billboard*'s pd of the year.

AUSTIN, Paul: **KROQ**, 1977. The Firesign Theatre actor was part of KROQ's Nightshift show on Sunday nights.

AUSTIN, Tracy: **KIIS**, 1995-97

AUTRY, Gene: Gene Autry's career spanned more than sixty years in the entertainment industry. He is the only entertainer to have five Stars on Hollywood's Walk of Fame, one each for radio, records, movies, television and live theatrical including rodeo performances. Beginning his  radio career in 1928, by 1937 he was America's Favorite Cowboy. His CBS radio show "Melody Ranch" ran for

16 years. He has produced and starred in close to 100 television shows. Gene has appeared in 94 feature films and has made 635 records including *Rudolph the Red-Nosed Reindeer* which has sold over 30 million copies. In 1961 he acquired the California Angels. His Western Heritage Museum opened in November 1988 and has attracted millions of tourists. He owned KMPC AM&FM for decades and recently sold the outlets.

AVENATTI, Jeff: **KNAC**, 1984; **KOCM**, 1990. Avo's first break was when he appeared briefly on KNAC as "Manny Pacheco" when Manny was working overnights.

AVERY, Mark: **KLOS**, 1993-94

AVEY, Dan: **KWIZ**, 1978; **KFWB**, 1976-86; **KFI**, 1986-89; **KFWB**, 1989-97. Dan has won 11 Golden Mike Awards and has been decorated with a long list of industry nods matching his military service in Vietnam as a green beret captain. He was born in Spokane and raised in Whittier. "I spent my high school years hanging out at (ironically) KFWB, going in at night to pull records and referee fights between B. Mitchel Reed and Bill Ballance." Dan went back to Spokane for college and law school at Gonzaga University. His first radio job was at KXLY-Spokane in 1960 where for the next seven years he was dj, pd and tv talk show host. From 1969 to 1976 he managed the Los Angeles Forum for Jack Kent Cooke, negotiating player contracts and all the building's business and sales. During the 1970s and '80s, Dan worked as a sports announcer. He was the sidekick to L.A. Kings announcer, Bob Miller. He worked morning drive news at KFI with Geoff Edwards and Gary Owens. Dan also hosted a sports talk show on KFI. In the early 1990s, he was om at Metro Traffic Control. Dan has taught broadcasting at USC and Cal State Northridge. He continues as an anchor for all-News KFWB.

AVILA, Tom: **KMNY**. Tom worked at "Money Radio" and is the son of Jim Simon and brother of tv reporter Jim Avila.

KMPC/FM becomes KEDG	
	-March 1989
KEDG becomes KMPC/FM	
	-August 1989

AXE, Lisa: **KACD**, 1996. Lisa grew up in Columbus, Ohio and graduated magna cum laude from Ohio State University in 1994 with a B.A. in English literature. While in college Lisa worked in Columbus at WWCD, WSNY and WCOL. She also served as an airborne

traffic reporter. After working the summer of 1996 at KACD, Lisa became an instructor at the Academy of Radio Broadcasting in Huntington Beach. Since early 1995 she has been hosting the morning show at KCXX-Riverside.

"ARROW 93"
launched
at 93.1FM with
Old Time Rock and Roll
by
Bob Seger

Mornings: Gary Moore
Middays: Mary Price
Afternoons: Bob Guerra
Evenings: Dave White
Late Eves: Kevin Machado
Overnights: Verna McKay

-September 10, 1993, 3 p.m.

B

B, Christian: **KSRF**, 1991-92. Christian worked weekends and overnights during the techno-rock "MARS/fm" period. He left for "the Point" in St. Louis.

B!, Tony: **KIIS**, 1991-92; **KPWR**, 1992-96; **KACD**, 1996-97. Born Anthony Bennett in Virginia, Tony was asked if he had a highlight while working in Los Angeles? "It was standing before 6,000 people at the two-year anniversary Power Party." He now works evenings at "Groove Radio."

B, Willie: **KTNQ**, 1976-77. Born Robert Naftel, the 20-year-old rookie started mid-afternoons on "the new Ten-Q" on December 26, 1976. Prior to joining KTNQ, he was known as Willie B. Goode. When the "Ten-Q" format ran out of steam, Willie went to WBSB-Baltimore and achieved "big star" status until a controversial incident caused him to leave Maryland. In the 1990s Willie programmed a Sacramento station, worked at KHFI-Austin and WHHY ("Y102")-Montgomery. He's currently at KHOM-New Orleans.

BABCOCK, George: **KFWB**, 1961; **KABC**, 1973. George was part of management in the news department when the "Seven Swingin' Gentlemen" went off the air in support of the striking newsmen. George jocked the all-night shift. In 1962 he went to KMEN-San Bernardino as a jock. In 1973 he co-anchored the KABC news block with Bob Arthur.

BABCOCK, John: **KDAY**, 1955-57; **KFWB**, 1957-59; **KMPC**, 1959-61; **KLAC**, 1961-63; **KABC**, 1963-73. In 1970 Don Page of the *LA Times* named John newscaster of the year saying: "John Babcock is one of radio's premier commentators and a leading documentarian." John was born the day of the 1933 earthquake and started life as an orphan. He was shuffled between foster homes until he was adopted by the Babcock family. While he was in his delinquent teen years, John was sentenced to two years in the Boys Republic of Chino. Many years later, he became the president of Chino's Board of Directors. "I am the first ex-student to be elected president of this risk school." After graduating from the University of Texas, John started out in the newspaper business and WOAI-San Antonio. He came to the Southland and began with KDAY. For part of his stay with KABC news he hosted a morning talk show. John was the California press director for Vice President Hubert Humphrey in 1968 and 1972. In 1973 John joined KABC television as a writer/producer and eventually went into news management. "When I was at Channel 7's news assignment desk I could get the reporters to do four stories a day. Then it was 3, then 2 and now they think they're doing a favor by covering one story." John retired in 1995 and was active writing and running the Boys school. His wife of 17 years is principal of the Dubonoff School for "kids at risk." Their daughter attends the Peabody Music Conservatory in Baltimore. John died February 1, 1997, at the age of 63. Former KFWB newsman Al Wiman said unequivocally that John "was the best news person EVER!"

BABCOCK, Sam: **KDAY**, 1962

BACKUS, Jim: **KLAC**, 1959-60. The voice of the bumbling, nearsighted Mr. Magoo was part of KLAC's attempt to resurrect the "Big Five" personality era from the forties and fifties. Jim played the self-indulgent millionaire Thurston Howell III on *Gilligan's Island* for three seasons beginning in 1964. One of his movie roles was playing James Dean's father in *Rebel Without A Cause*. He is also remembered as the pitchman for a light bulb commercial imploring "Don't be a bulb snatcher!" Jim died July 3, 1989, of pneumonia at the age of 76. He had suffered from Parkinson's disease for many years.

BAD GIRLS CLUB: **KLSX**, 1995-96. A naughty Saturday evening talk show hosted by Kathlyn Kinmont and Kimberly Hooper.

BADE, Dennis: **KUSC**, 1982-89 and 1991-95

BAILEY, Carl: **KBIG**, 1952-79. Carl started work for KBIG by given over one and a half tons of his personal record collection to establish a working music library for the then new station on Catalina Island. He broadcast for five years as "Mr. Big of KBIG" from Catalina. Beginning in the summer of 1957 he broadcast from the upper deck of the "Big White Steamer" that crossed the channel from San Pedro to Avalon. *Life* magazine carried a photo of Carl's broadcast and he was made a "Commodore of the Port of Los Angeles." He has a commemorative plague on Avalon. In the mid-1960s he switched to news. He had to retire from broadcasting just shy of his 50th anniversary following a stroke that damaged his motor reflexes.

BAILEY, Duane "Doc": **KLIT**, 1989-94, pd; **KEZY**, 1996-97; **KBIG**, 1997. Originally from Zumbrota, Minneapolis, "Doc" worked for Transtar 41 for a number of years, when it was based in Colorado Springs. He transferred from Transtar's A/C network to KLIT. In the fall of 1994, he left the Southland to program KKLI-Colorado Springs. "Doc" returned in late 1996 to jock at KEZY.

BAILEY, Lee: **KMPC**, 1975-79; **KDAY**, 1975-76; **KGFJ**, 1976; **KUTE**, 1977-79. Lee, born in 1947 in Moreland, Georgia, was fascinated by radio since childhood. Growing up in Pittsburgh, he began visiting local radio stations handling odd jobs and learning about radio. He befriended the area djs who helped him refine his skills in production and broadcasting. In 1966, Lee joined the U.S. Air Force and relocated to Sacramento, but his love for radio remained.

Unable to deny his aspirations, Lee left the Air Force in 1970 and began his radio career at KPOP-Sacramento. His various stints included WAMM-Ann Arbor and KSTN, KJOY-Stockton. From 1973 to 1975 Lee worked in Washington, DC. He moved to Los Angeles and began working simultaneously at KMPC and KDAY. In 1978, he transferred from KDAY to KGFJ (while still working at KMPC) and then later to their FM frequency "Kute 102." In 1979 he formed a production company specializing in radio commercials. In 1983 Lee launched his flagship program "RadioScope: The Entertainment Magazine of the Air." Lee debuted "RadioScope" in 35 markets "providing Infotainment - a successful formula, working on both sides of the brain, covering all bases." His programming is heard in more than 250 U.S. markets, 3 British radio markets, and in 70 countries via the Armed Forces Radio & Television service. His company is based in Los Angeles.

BAILEY, Steve: **KMPC**, 1951-95. Steve was director of the Golden West sports operations. Born in Logan, Utah in 1925, he was a color commentator and producer of sports projects at KMPC for decades. He started at KMPC as a record librarian. Steve worked with such popular sportscasters as Bob Kelley and Dick Enberg, and produced game broadcasts of the Pacific Coast League L.A. Angels, California Angels, Rams and UCLA. He was briefly the announcer of the California (now Anaheim) Angels but his strength was behind the scenes. He began his career in 1946, moving right out of college to go to work in his hometown of Logan. When he joined KMPC in 1951, he immediately was taken under the wing of the late Bob Kelley - the sports voice of Southern California and play-by-play man for the Rams. In 1995 Steve produced an award-winning documentary on the broadcasting career of the late Jim Healy. He died November 24, 1995, of complications following treatment for lymphoma. He was 70. Sports announcer Dick Enberg reflected for Larry Stewart in the *LA Times*: "Steve was a producer before there were producers. He worked behind the scenes, but he was a real giant in the business."

What was your darkest moment?
"When I was grabbed by the neck and tossed through the swinging doors of broadcast history in late 1977 - the day Dr. Toni Grant (whom I'd introduced to radio, as I did Dr. Laura Schlessinger) was given my KABC show and I was compelled to slink OUT of the big time and down to San Diego."
            -Top Ten personality Bill Ballance

BAIN, Jim: **KWIZ**, 1965-69 and 1974-79 and 1981-85; **KIQQ**, 1973; **KEZY**, 1988. Jim is an example that you can do anything you want to, as long as you are willing to pay the price. Jim turned his love for radio into a career of inspiring young people by teaching at Fullerton College and running its FM station. He started a comprehensive program at Fullerton in 1981 and realized that he needed to enlarge his own academics. While running the program, he worked weekends at KWIZ and Unistar's AM Only channel AND went back to school. From 1969 to 1973, Jim was "the Mighty Quinn" at KMEN-San Bernardino. He received a B.A. degree in business management from the University of Redlands in 1988 at the age of 50 and didn't stop there. Three years later he received his M.S. degree in career and college counseling. His students fill 27 shifts per week on KBPK-Fullerton. His vocational advisory committee includes some of the most respected names currently working in Southern California radio. Jim talked about his love for radio: "This wonderful, sometimes frustrating business, ever challenging but the greatest of all industries and definitely the mistress that owns us all - radio."

BAKA BOYZ: **KPWR**, 1993-97. "It's the Baka/It's the Baka Boyz/In the morning/In the morning/It's the Baka Boys/ And we're gonna wake your ass right up/Because we're two fat Mexicans." In early 1994, Nick and Eric Vidal moved to the coveted morning drive slot at "Power 106" while still in their early 20s. Their on-air persona consists of sending "shout-outs" to friends and listeners, giving "props" to people they like and good-natured "dissing" to certain other people -- including each other. They started at KPWR in 1993 with a two-hour Friday night hip-hop show that was so popular they were soon moved to all-nights, then late-nights and by early 1994, mornings. In an *OC Register* interview in 1994, Eric said, "We dj on the radio, but we don't consider ourselves radio djs. Everything we know is self-taught. We came from the streets." Their father owned a teen club in Bakersfield where they grew up, which explains their moniker. Former "Power 106" pd Rick Cummings justified the unusual morning team: "In a market like Los Angeles, you'd better do something that's a breakthrough kind of thing, or you'll get lost in the shuffle." The station's charity event for 1995 was titled "The Baka Boyz Thump 'n Quick Mis's" CD with proceeds going to the Knowledge Is Power foundation.

BAKER, Dave: **KMGX**, 1990-92
BALDWIN, Bob: **KNX**, 1965-66
BALDWIN, Mel: **KNX**, 1951-66 and 1980-91; **KNX/FM**, 1971. Mel was one of the ubiquitous personalities at KNX taking on a number of long-running positions. "I made a quantum leap from managing a little station in Tillamook, Oregon to replacing Steve Allen at KNX." During Mel's time at the CBS O&O, he hosted "KNX Food Hour" with Jackie Olden and later Melinda Lee. He joined the "Food Hour" when Olden's original partner, Don Fitzgerald, died unexpectedly of a heart attack. At the time Mel lived aboard a boat in Los Angeles harbor and never really cooked until he began working on the show. He had a

talk show called "Opinion Please" and hosted American Airlines' "Music 'til Dawn" program for over two decades (including four years based at WBBM-Chicago). During the 1970s Mel took a break from radio and was a building contractor and writer. He has retired to his native Portland where he got his radio start at KEX.

BALLANCE, Bill: **KNX**, 1952-55; **KFWB**, 1955-65; **KGIL**, 1966; **KGBS**, 1969-73; **KABC**, 1974-77; **KWIZ**, 1977. Born Willis Bennett Ballance, "Billo" is uncertain about his birth date because "My records were

lost at Valley Forge." Bill distinguished himself as a Marine officer in World War II before making his mark in radio. A graduate of the University of Illinois, Bill worked for a total of six years at KOA-Denver and WBKB/TV in Chicago in the early 1950s. One of the original Chuck Blore "Seven Swingin' Gentlemen" when KFWB went "Color Radio" on January 2, 1958, Bill worked mostly evenings, except for a brief morning drive stint in the early '60s. A Civil War historian, Bill went to Denver and San Francisco following KFWB. He had equally impressive success. He also went to Honolulu, where he worked at KHVH and was pd of KGMB. "The success story of 1971 is the phenomenal return of Bill Ballance," wrote Don Page in the *LA Times*. "Once a baron of Top 40 radio, Ballance hit hard times and was even forced out of town to begin again." After returning to the Southland from KNBR-San Francisco, Ballance suddenly skyrocketed when he converted the routine rock-jock formula into the "Feminine Forum." His most lasting claim in Southern California radio was that he was the very first to openly address sexuality, issues of sexual intercourse and sexual preference. The program became one of the most discussed shows in town. His philosophy was always a little off-center but whimsical. Some of his observations included, "Anyone who says that money cannot buy happiness has had very little experience with either one." In a 1971 trade publication interview, Ballance claimed the idea for "Feminine Forum" came from an idea developed by Chuck Blore and Ken Draper. The idea was for Bill to pose a question of interest to female listeners, tape the answers and play them back the following day in 20- to 90-second segments. By 1972 his "Feminine Forum" was being syndicated in a number of major cities and simulcast in San Diego. He won the *Gavin* award that year. Ballance gave the phone lines over to the ladies and listened. He wouldn't even call them housewives. They were women in Bill's mind -- educated and intelligent -- and he treated them that way. Between calls, he played the hits. Bill described his audience to Burt Prelutsky in a 1974 interview: "The main thing I have concluded is that women are brighter than men, and that they're lonely. My average female listener, I've surmised, married her husband right out of high school, and she's bored with him and bored with being surrounded by shrieking toddlers. Her husband was, more often than not, a high school jock whose life peaked at the age of 16 or 17. Now in his late 20s or early 30s, he's still out shooting pool with the boys and getting loaded on beer at the local tavern. That's why I'm constantly trying to reassure my doll babies and urging them to go back to school, even it it's just to take a class or two. For no matter how bright they are, after living all that time with a gruntbrain, they can't help losing their self-confidence and self-esteem." Bill was profiled in every major publication in the country, as well as the *London Times* and a *Cosmopolitan* cover story. *Time* magazine said, "Bill has many imitators, but no rivals." In March 1973, a front-page story in the *Times* reported that Executive VP of Storer Broadcasting, Peter Storer, felt that the image of Bill's program had been "colored and damaged by less-restricted imitators." Bill's company caved and announced that the program was dropped. By the time the FCC announced that his show was "not obscene," it was too late. For all the attention his show attracted, Bill did it with taste. He knew the line not to cross, but his copycats didn't, and Bill got the blame. He never got true credit for his bold, sex-oriented broadcasting. Ballance commented in a 1987 *Times* interview: "The mistake most station managers made was to assign some beardless, 19-year-old, opaque-eyed, slack-jawed oaf to do my type of show, and these kids weren't mature enough. They were much too young to have any information on things like love, marriage and divorce, so what they started to do was get dirty. His

brilliant command of the language prevented his KGBS show from being dirty. His show was a lot like the old girlie magazines. It wasn't total nudity - it showed just enough to make it tantalizing. He wrote a number of nifty books with nifty advice, for example: "A kiss should never be planned. It should be spontaneous - like a coronary." His tome, *Bill Ballance Reveals How to Cope*, is in its fifth printing. In 1978 he moved to KFMB-San Diego, where he worked until departing in the summer of 1993 on a year-long Civil War Battlefield tour with his uncle, General Bob Ballance, age 90. In the summer of 1994, he told *OC Register*'s Gary Lycan: "Being a lifetime broadcaster, not to be heard is to be dead! I'm a city-bred and coin-fed communicator who yearns to be back in the mainstream media." As far as his own relationship with women is concerned, he has been married twice. In an interview in the *Los Angeles Radio Guide*, Bill said, "I'm auditioning for my third and final wife with the requirements that she owns cotton skivvies and has five good, serviceable teeth, preferably in front." Bill is exploring a number of options to return to the airwaves.

BALLANCE, Lance: **KOST**, 1989-97. Born in Venice, Florida, Lance considers Sacramento his "hometown" since he grew up and graduated high school there. He did much of his early radio work in Northern California. Lance started in Marysville at KRFD and went on to KYBB-Stockton. Lance commutes from Rancho Cucamonga to KOST, and recalled the scariest part of his L.A. radio tour was "being on the air during the riots when everything was burning around the station." He has being doing overnights since November 1991. "My greatest thrill was when my wife, Brenda and I welcomed our daughter, Daryn Elisabeth, into the world." Lance is a computer "freak" and designed his own web page. "I really enjoy it when people ask if I'm Bill Ballance's kid. Yes, that is my real last name, and no I'm not."

BALTER, Sam: **KLAC**, 1940s-61 and 1967. Sam was one of the most popular sports broadcasters in Los Angeles radio history. He was the former captain of the UCLA basketball team and a member of the gold medal-winning U.S. basketball team in 1936, when the sport was introduced to the Olympics for the first time. He left KLAC in 1961 and returned in 1967 while in his fifties.

BANDA, Tom: **KXEZ**, 1993-95; **KYSR**, 1996; **KIBB**, 1996-97. Tom first appeared on "Star 98.7" in January 1996. In late 1996 he moved to all-nights at KYSR's sister station KIBB and left in early 1997.

BANKS, Bill: **KNAC**, 1986-88, nd. "Private Dick" Bill Banks was part of the morning drive show on KNAC.

BANKS, Doug: **KDAY**; **KHJ**; **KFI**, 1978-82. Born in Philadelphia, Doug grew up in Detroit. While still in high school he did weekends and fill-in at WDRQ-Detroit. Doug studied law at the University of Michigan while working a part-time shift. When the lure of Hollywood came calling, he headed for KDAY. He left KDAY for KMJM-St. Louis and then came back to L.A. In 1980 he went to WBMX-Chicago, Las Vegas, KDIA-Oakland and then back to WBMX. He joined WGCI-Chicago in 1987. He was *Billboard* magazine's 1995 r&b Air Personality of the Year. Since the mid-1980s, Doug has been one of the top personalities in Chicago. In early 1996 he started afternoon drive for ABC Radio Networks.

BANKS, Robin: **KNX/FM/KODJ/KCBS**, 1989-97. Robin works weekends on "Arrow 93."

BANISTER, Raymond: **KROQ**, 1980-96, pd. From KPRI-San Diego, Raymond came to KROQ in the fall of 1980 to work middays. In the early 1980s, he was part of the morning drive show, Raymondo & Evans, and in 1982 he teamed with Richard Blade on the popular morning show, "Raymondo and the Blade." In December 1983 he moved into the pd slot. Raymondo has been production director and weekend dj since 1990.

BANOCZI, Jeannette: **KNOB**, 1966-87. Born in Dracut, Massachusetts, Jeannette was the lead trumpet player with Phil Spitalny's world famous all-girl orchestra in 1938. She also played with the Ina Ray Hutton group. In 1961 she started her first radio station, KGGK-Garden Grove. In 1966 Jeannette acquired KNOB and sold it for $15 million in 1987. She also built stations in Las Vegas, KCKC-San Bernardino, KBON-Lake Arrowhead and KUNA AM&FM-Palm Desert.

BARBER, Andy: **KTNQ**, 1978; **KWST**, 1981-82. Born in Glendale on April 21, Andy was raised in Hollywood and got into acting at the age of eight through his dad who worked at Universal Studios. In 1971, he was working at KUDL-Kansas City. Andy arrived at "the new Ten-Q" from KING-Seattle to do fill-in. Between KTNQ and KWST, Andy worked at KASH-Eugene and did radio/tv. Once he left the Southland, Andy spent the 1980s working at KAFM-Dallas, KHTT-Seattle, KAYI-Tulsa, KCPX-Salt Lake City, WRKA-Louisville and since 1993 he's been doing mornings at KHTT-Tulsa. Andy's long-term goal is "to keep the morning show dominating the Tulsa market so that my wife Sherri and I can go on cruises!"

> "I feel that everything I have gone through, from being a child prodigy to overcoming drug addiction to pastoring a church, has contributed to my ability to relate to people on a 'heart' level."
> -Warren Duffy

BARKLEY, Roger: **KLAC**, 1961-67, pd; **KFWB**, 1967-68; **KFI**, 1968-86; **KJOI**, 1986-89; **KABC**, 1990-96. Roger grew up in Odebolt, Iowa, and dreamed of being

either a radio announcer or preacher. "I guess the ham in me needed to have a stage." His brother appeared on a high school forum on a Yankton, South Dakota radio station. "I watched the broadcast and knew that this is what I'm going to do." After high school he attended the American Institute of the Air in Minnesota and was a page boy at WCCO-Minneapolis. "I was educated so well in Odebolt that I didn't have to go to college." He started his radio career at KYSM-Mankato, Minnesota. Two years later he was pd of KSUM-Fairmount, Minnesota. "My goals came in small steps. I figured that I would be a success if I could get to WHO-Des Moines by the time I was 45." He moved on to KALL-Salt Lake City. He served in the U.S. Army and returned to the microphone at KBOX-Dallas followed by KIMN-Denver. As director of programs at KLAC, Roger hired Al Lohman for the morning show. When the station was sold to Metromedia, the new owners began a search for a two-man morning team. "We figured we were all going to be fired so Al and I thought perhaps we should do the morning show as a team. This way we could buy some time to look for another job." The partnership lasted a quarter of a century. They stayed at KLAC until 1967. Next came one year at KFWB, until it went all-News, then they joined KFI for a very successful and long-running morning show. They were voted 1970 and 1980 Personalities of the Year in the *LA Times*' "Best of" listing. One of the highlights of their morning silliness was the impromptu "Light of My Life" soap opera. "We put organ music on a continuous loop, created a mythical town and made up the stories as we went along. All the character voices were Al's. My job was to tie everything together." They taped the soap opera and replayed it the following morning. "We did this so we could remember where we had left all the characters." Their 1976 tv variety show went into syndication. The *Times* described the 1986 break-up with Al Lohman as "abrupt and bitter." "Al and I have not talked since the day we parted. In 25 years of being together I guess we said everything we had to say to each other. It was painful, the breakup." At the start of his KJOI assignment, Roger commented, "I hope we attract a large enough audience with a new form of personality driven easy listening FM radio. It is, however, those hours again - the death-dealing ones in the early morning. Going solo will be a fun new bag." In the fall of 1990, he joined Ken Minyard for a KABC morning news block program called "Ken & Barkley Company," which was consistently rated one of the top five morning shows. Roger has a busy schedule of speaking engagements and he serves on the boards of many civic organizations. He owns ten restaurants primarily in the Pasadena/La Canada/Flintridge/Glendale area. Four of them are called, "The Barkley." His hobbies are writing and collecting anything to do with the American eagle. Roger has completed his <u>un</u>authorized autobiography, *...maybe, someday.* Roger left KABC in the fall of 1996. Ownership of many stations in a market is a problem. "When I left KABC, the logical place to look for a new job would be KMPC. The problem is they are owned by the same company."

BARNARD, Bill: **KHJ**, 1965; **KBLA**, 1966
BARNES, Hoss: **KBBQ**, 1968-70
BARNES, Ken: **KRLA**, 1959. Ken worked in Des Moines and Kansas City radio before joining KRLA.
BARNETT, Russ: **XTRA**, 1960-62; **KMPC**, 1963-72, pd; **KABC**, 1972-73. When Russ's voice changed in

junior high and he was moved to the bass section of Boy's Choir, someone said he should think about going into radio. He was born in Toledo and grew up in Jackson, Michigan. After attending the University of Texas, Russ started as a jock in 1950 on WAND-Canton followed by WFAA and KLIF-Dallas. He arrived in California in 1957 and worked at KPRO-Riverside and KSBW-Salinas where he jocked in the morning and did tv news in the evening. His mid-1950 association with KLIF paid off when Gordon McLendon tapped Russ as manager for the launch of the world's first 24-hour all-News operation. He built a 25-person news staff at XTRA that became the model for today's all-News formats. "Each man did a seven minute newscast and was then off for about 30 minutes to re-write and update his material for his next air shot. We obviously stole our traffic reports and were so good at it that we would have a report on the air within a minute of hearing it on monitors." Russ said that the owner of KMPC, Gene Autry, called him in Mexico to complain about the station break: "This is XTRA News over Los Angeles, just to the left of KMPC." He started as pd of KMPC on New Year's Day 1963, and won the *Gavin* Award as Program Director of the Year. KMPC also won the Radio Station of the Year award during his last year at the station. During the 1980s he worked on his voiceover career and built his retirement home near Auburn. In 1995 he was asked to host the mornings on KIDD-Monterey. "Isn't it strange? I'm playing the same music today that I was when I started out in radio." In 1971, Russ suffered a heart attack in New Orleans during the Bill Gavin Conference. Russ described the times at KMPC as being very "tense" and he needed to change his lifestyle. He said from his home in Monterey, "Outside of having an artery roto-rooted, I have had no heart problems since 1971. In fact with my tv production and voiceover career, I've never felt better. I'm anxious to let others know that life can go on and be productive if you make some lifestyle changes and keep the faith. From the time I was a young guy, I felt that if I could go on the air and add a few smiles to the lives of my listeners through my rather corny sense of humor and make enough money to support my family, I'd be well pleased with my contribution to life. Know what? I am."

BARON, B.B.: **KEZY**, 1975-76. Born Buddy Baron, he used the moniker "B.B." only once in his career, and that was at KEZY. He began his radio career in the back of his best friend's house in Jacksonville with used electronic parts and a rooftop tv antenna. While in the service from 1969 to 1972, he worked part-time at several Atlanta stations including WQXI. Prior to his arrival at KEZY he had done three years at WSAI-Cincinnati. "The thought of an early escape from those cold Ohio winters kept me going as I packed everything I owned in my Blazer that conked out twice on the desert before ever arriving in California." Buddy talked about his year at KEZY as being the best fun he's ever had in radio. "Everyone on the air staff drove some kind of flashy sports car (I blew half my pay on a used 450SL), and young ladies hung around us like a rock band. The pd's idea of jock talent fees was making certain we all had unlimited bar tabs at every disco we appeared at. A lot of my tenure there is a blurred memory because of this." When Rick Carroll arrived at KEZY, the entire staff was wiped out and five months later Buddy found himself doing mornings at KIMN-Denver. He went back to Atlanta for a while and then spent a year as a craps dealer in Las Vegas. In 1979 he worked afternoons at KFRC-San Francisco. Buddy stayed a year and moved on to "other opportunities." In 1989 he returned to the Bay Area and did mornings at Country KSAN. During this time Buddy was writing for Phyllis Diller, Jay Leno and the Premiere Radio Networks. In the summer of 1995 Buddy moved to morning drive at KYCY-San Francisco and left in the summer of 1997..

BARON, George: **KSRF**, 1986, gm

BARONE, Don: **KIEV**, 1972. Don was at KIEV for the Oldies format.

BARRAGAN, Jaime: **KYMS**, 1993-95; **KLOS**, 1995-96. Jaime started as an intern on the Christian station and eventually became a dj until the station changed format.

In the fall of 1995 Jaime did fill-in at KOLA-San Bernardino and part-time at KLOS.

BARRETO, Pepe: **KALI**, 1977-85; **KLVE**, 1985-97. Pepe anchors the very successful Spanish morning drive slot on "K-Love."

Born in 1947 to Peruvian parents, he and his wife moved to California in 1972 and started as a dj in San Francisco. He came to the Southland in 1985 to work at KLVE and KVEA/Channel 52. He went on to KMEX/Channel 34 as a news reporter while continuing the morning drive shift. A late 1995 profile in the *LA Times* described him as "a cheerful, good-natured man and decent Christian." Pepe talked about his success: "Well, ratings go up and down, you can't always be on top. But my purpose in the morning has always been to entertain the audience that wakes up in Southern California. But entertain them with class. My characters are my audience." He is teamed with Lupita Pena.

BARRETT, John: **KRLA**, 1961-69, gm. "We were all backstage at a 1963 Hootenanny charity show at the Pasadena Civic Auditorium. We were trying to figure out who we should invite for next year's concert when Casey, or Emperor Hudson, or maybe Reb suggested a group from Liverpool. It was actually Bob Eubanks who got through to a Brian Epstein who told us that his group had no intention of coming to Los Angeles and they were having a hard enough time getting out of Liverpool." A half-year later the Beatles exploded and when a tour to Los Angeles was explored, Epstein called KRLA to see if there was still interest. He said the boys were attracted to the Hollywood Bowl and was that a possibility?" John reigned over a crucial period in rock radio history at KRLA during the '60s. Don Page of the *LA Times* named John Executive of the Year in 1968 stating: "John Barrett introduced so many unique and imaginative changes at KRLA." John was born and raised in Omaha and after graduating from the University of Nebraska he worked for Don Burden as a dj, pd and in sales at KOWH-Omaha, WTIX-New Orleans and WHB-Kansas City. Before arriving in the Southland John managed WKBW-Buffalo radio and tv. When he left KRLA in 1969 John produced *The Smothers Brothers* and *Glen Campbell Hour* tv shows. John formed his own production company and produced tv specials for Bob Hope, Linda Ronstadt, Kris Kristofferson and John Denver among others. In the late 1980s and ready for semi-retirement, longtime radio friend Norm Epstein asked John to join him in a travel-related marketing firm. Eight years later he and Norm have revolutionized the marketing of travel companies and destination locations.

BARRETT, Rona: **KFWB**, 1985. Rona aired a 2-minute entertainment report on all-News KFWB. In the 1970s she gained national fame as the entertainment reporter on ABC's *Good Morning America*. In the early 1980s she had a similar stint on NBC's *Today* Show.

BARRI, Barbara: **KZLA**, 1979-93. Originally from

Southhampton, Long Island, Barbara thought she would pursue an acting career at Onondaga College in Syracuse where she remembered, "The seasons are July, August and winter (the sun never shines)." She landed and launched her radio career near Cape Canaveral at WCKS-Cocoa Beach and WLOF-Orlando. After a brief stop at WLEE-Richmond in 1978, she joined KZLA. "During the next 15 years I saw 2 locations, 3 sets of call letters, 3 corporate owners, 4 formats, 5 general managers, 11 program directors (I stopped counting the morning men), 3 shifts and I never changed jobs." During this time at KZLA, Barbara hosted *Top 40 Videos* on KCOP/Channel 13 and was the announcer on the syndicated *Singles Magazine* tv show. She left the station after the combo sale with KLAC. Barbara is heard on a number of syndicated shows, "Music Matters," "Coast to Coast" and "L.A. to Nashville, Backstage." She does character voices and has been master of ceremonies for shows at the Universal Amphitheater, The Forum and other major venues. "I love sitting alone in a room, playing music and talking out loud to myself. I think I may be spending too much time alone, but radio seems to be good therapy for me."

BARRY, Bill: **KMPC**; **KZLA**; **KOST**; **KGIL**, 1984-92. Bill hosted *The Channel 5 Theatre* on KTLA from 1971 to 1981 and the weekly *Pinbusters* show. Bill was a reporter with Shadow Traffic in Los Angeles at the time of his death in October 1993. He was 50.

BARRY, Thom: **KLAC**, 1987-93. Thom started his radio career in his hometown of Cincinnati and was one of the few black djs doing Country. He left KLAC in late 1993 when the Country outlet shifted formats to Unistar Satellite's AM Only Nostalgia format. He is currently a successful on-camera commercial actor.

BARTH, Paul: **KWIZ**, 1971, pd. Paul went on to own an advertising agency and then bought an Oldies station in Redding.

BARTHOLOMEW, Casey: **KFI**, 1991-97. In 1991 Casey was 21 years old and a Fulton College student. He was the board-op at KFI for Laura Schlessinger. In late 1995 Casey joined co-host Scott Hasick for an evening weekend talk show. During the O.J. Simpson trial Casey provided regular updates to KFI's "John and Ken" afternoon drive show. Casey and Scott have a regular weekend show. In the summer of 1997, the team went to the Cox station in Orlando, WDBO for afternoon drive.

BASS, Dick: **KMPC**, 1976-87. The former Ram running back who wore jersey No. 22 joined the Rams broadcast team in 1976. Dick was a speech and drama major at College of the Pacific (now University of the Pacific) in Stockton. During the time he broadcast color on the Rams games, Dick was a customer relations executive for a trucking firm, ICX.

BASTIEN, Brian: **KPOL**; **KFWB**, 1968-77; **KBIG/KBRT**, 1977-80; **KFWB**, 1980-83. Brian was a longtime respected news anchor at KFWB. He joined KBIG to oversee a new public affairs department. In 1983 Brian embarked on a free-lance career. For many years he was the voice of Murata Pearls and Martin Cadillac.

BAUER, Jacque: **KWIZ**, 1980-82; **KIQQ**, 1981-82; **KBRT**, 1982. Jacque was 18 years old when she started the late evening shift on KWIZ. She later went to work for a Christian record label, returning to her home in Denver. Jacque is now with AMFM Promotions in South Bend.

BAUGH, Jeff: **KFWB**, 1986-97. As the reporter in

KFWB's "Jet Copter 98," Jeff was born November 15, 1942, and he grew up in Coney Island, Brooklyn. He graduated from Mineola High School in 1959. Jeff enlisted in the U.S. Marine Corps in 1960 and was honorably discharged with decorations in March 1966 after two tours in Vietnam. After spending six years in the automobile business in New York City, he started working as a dj in some of New York's underground dance clubs, which soon came to be known as "discos." Jeff moved to Los Angeles in 1978 and became the dj at trendy Carlos and Charlie's El Privado room in West Hollywood. "I stayed there for too many years, accumulating enough personal experiences to write two books, a movie script and several soap operas, but, chose not to." He "survived" the club business and in 1986 attended the L.A.B. Broadcasting school in Hollywood and then interned at "Power 106." He was hired at KFWB as a part-time traffic reporter which progressed to full-time and both drive times. He has won seven Golden Mikes and has covered every breaking story in Southern California for the past decade.

BAUTISTA, Rafael: **KSCA**, 1997. "El Primo Rafa."

BAXTER, Danny: **KDAY**; **KRLA**, 1964-65; **KHJ**, 1968; **KGBS**, 1969. At KRLA his sports show was called "Inside the KRLA Book" which offered sports predictions and sports commentary. Off-the-air, his colleagues marveled what a marvelous handicapper Danny was, especially at baseball.

BAXTER, Frank: **KRLA**. Frank was a news commentator for many years in Los Angeles.

BAXTER, Gene: SEE Kevin & Bean

BAYLEY, Lee: **KIQQ**, 1978-80, pd. Before coming to L.A. Lee started radio at the age of 15 in Arkansas. He was the morning man for Armed Forces Radio and TV in Panama. Upon leaving the Army he became pd and worked morning drive for KAKC-Tulsa, where he first met Bill Drake. Beginning in 1971, Lee moved to L.A. as vp of programming for Bill Drake and Drake/Chenault. "The company programmed over 300 stations across the country with five different formats." Lee joined KIQQ in 1978 as pd and left for Dallas to be gm of Disney's TM Programming in 1980. He formed his own consultancy in 1981. "I just celebrated my 15th anniversary with my first clients, sister stations WAMZ/WHAS-Louisville." Lee has been involved with more than 600 stations over the last two decades, including several California stations. He is based in Irving, a suburb of Dallas.

BEACH, Sandy: **KDAY**, 1970-71. Sandy was born Howard Rogers. When he left the radio business he founded Rogers Sound Labs.

BEACH, Sandy: **KROQ**, 1977. Sandy was born Brad Sobel. In 1971, at age 19, he and his wife Jessie put KPOT on the air without FCC permission operating out of a closet. The FCC shut him down but he began to broadcast on local Theta cable.

BEAN: SEE Gene Baxter

BEASING, Dave: **KXEZ**, 1993-95, pd; **KYSR**, 1995, pd; **KYSR**, 1996, pd. Before arriving in the Southland, Dave programmed KMZU-Carrollton, Missouri, KLIN-Lincoln, KRMG-Tulsa and spent three years with WLTI-Detroit where he had been appointed pd in 1990. He joined KXEZ in the summer of 1993 and added pd responsibilities of KYSR in late 1995. Dave left the Viacom station in late summer 1996 when KXEZ switched to KIBB and he joined Jacobs Media Consulting staff.

BEASLEY, Dave: **KGFJ**, 1973-74. Dave worked the all-night shift on Urban KGFJ.

BEASLEY, Greg: SEE Captain G

BEATON, Fred and Bill: **KIEV**, 1961-97, owner and gm. Fred Beaton, with his father William and brother Ronald, have owned and operated KIEV since 1961.

BEATTY, Margaret: **KYMS**, 1993. Margaret worked middays at the Christian station.

BEAUBIEN, Andy: **KLOS**, 1971; **KNX/FM**, 1987-88. Born in Woonsocket, Rhode Island, Andy worked at his college radio station at the University of Rhode Island. After graduation in 1969, he went to work for WBCN, the very successful AOR outlet in New England. Two years later, Andy arrived in Los Angeles and within a year found that "L.A. was not to my liking." He returned to Boston and WBCN and WCOZ where he was pd. Andy joined KNX/FM as pd in the early summer of 1987 from KKHT and KSRR-Houston. He said that KNX/FM would be "a combination of soft album rock and AC." The on-air promos promised no hard rock and invited listeners to place suggestions on a "programmer hot line." In 1988 he was out as pd of KNX/FM and he joined WCXR-Washington, DC as pd. In the spring of 1994, Andy returned to Houston to program KLOL. In the spring of 1997 Andy joined Australia-based Broadcast Programming & Research. He is based in Sydney.

BEAVER CLEAVER: **KIQQ**, 1974; **KEZY**, 1976; **KGIL**, 1976; **KTNQ**, 1976-77; **KMPC**; **KFI**. Born Ken Levine in Los Angeles, the native Californian has taken an exciting radio career and built additional success as a tv writer/producer of such shows as *M*A*S*H*, *Cheers*, *Frasier* and *The Simpsons*. Ken is the winner of one Emmy and two Writers Guild Awards. He worked at KYA-San Francisco before returning to his hometown. "At KTNQ my show received a 4.2 rating when the station's overall number was a 1." During the 1990s he has been the play-by-play announcer for the Baltimore Orioles, Seattle Mariners and San Diego Padres. Ken was the executive producer of *Almost Perfect*.

BECERRA, Martin: **KALI**, 1965

BECK, Fred: **KLAC**, 1957

BECK, Ken: **KIQQ**, 1976-78; **KMPC**, 1978-82; **KFWB**, 1988-92, nd. The former news director of KFWB was

---

KRTH - The automated sound is metallic and uncomfortable at first, but once those records start spinning off the assembly line, reminding us of boulevards cruised during the '50s and '60s - all is forgiven. For some of us, these were the "golden days of radio."
-James Brown, LA Times, 1975

born October 4, 1952, in Santa Monica. Ken grew up in Taft and went to UC Davis. His first job as a jock was in 1974 at KSFM-Sacramento. In 1982 Ken went to KGO-San Francisco as assistant nd. When he left KFWB he rejoined KGO as news director. In 1995 Ken became program director of KPIX-San Francisco where he continues.

BECK, Thom: **KRLA**, 1966-70; **KIIS**, 1970-72; **KBBQ**, 1972; **KGFJ**, 1972; **KRLA**, 1974-76; **KFI**, 1980. Thom was one of the founding members of the nationally acclaimed and highly innovative satirical news group, "The Credibility Gap" in 1968. He narrated the popular "Pop Chronicles" in 1969, a weekly series that chronicled popular music from the mid-1950s to 1969. In the early 1980s, Thom worked evenings at KIIS when it was MOR. He also hosted a midday jock show at KRLA. He returned to his roots in Texas and taught acting. Thom died a few years later of a heart attack.

BEE, Ron: **KRTH**, 1980-89; **KLAC/KZLA**; **KBLA**. Ron was an engineer and part-time jock. He is now with the Asian station in L.A.

BEE, Tommy: **KBLA**, 1957-64; **KBCA**, 1966-84. Born Tom Braverman, Tommy worked afternoon drive during the KBCA glory days of the mid-1960s. In 1967 *Billboard* magazine voted Tommy most popular jazz personality. During his time in L.A. he presented jam sessions at the Hillcrest, Renaissance, Larry Hearn's Memory Lane, Parisian Room and the Rubiayat Room. He partnered with Les Carter for "Monday Night Soul Society" gatherings at local clubs. In Tom Reed's book, *The Black Music History of L.A. - Its Roots*, Tommy talked of his broadcast break: "You know how all this happened was strange. My assistant Jack Rose was to be the disc jockey and I was to sell advertising time, but Jack 'froze' on the mike, so I began as the 'Voice of Jazz.'" Before Tommy's death he was working in a Westside delicatessen.

BEEBE, Richard: **KRKD**, 1958-59; **KRLA**, 1959-70, nd; **KPPC**, 1971-72; **KRLA**, 1981-85 and 1991-94; **KGIL**; **KMET**; **KABC**; **KMNY**. Best remembered as a co-founder and member of the nationally acclaimed and highly innovative satirical news group, "The Credibility Gap," Richard had a relationship with KRLA that lasted over five decades. Richard was born in Pasadena and raised in Alhambra. He started his radio career in 1949 working as a dj/newsman in Santa Fe and then went to Globe, Arizona before joining the Air Force. He was  assigned to the base radio station at Barksdale Air Force Base in Shreveport. Following his discharge, Richard attended Pasadena City College and the Pasadena Playhouse and graduated with a B.A. in theater arts. One of his classmates was Dustin Hoffman. While waiting for his "big break" he worked in the freight yards of downtown Los Angeles and did relief work at KRKD. He was in a repertory company with Dyan Cannon when he was hired by KRLA. It was 1959 and KRLA had just been bought by Canadian millionaire Jack Kent Cooke. Richard remembered his instructions from Cooke when he started doing morning drive news: "I want it as fast as you can go and make it exciting." Morning man Emperor Bob Hudson syndicated "The Emperor" idea and soon there were "Emperors" in cities across the country. Each station received custom promos featuring Richard as Colonel Splendid and Casey Kasem as Lt. Cavendish. As a news alternative, the award-winning "Credibility Gap" was an irreverent presentation reflecting the volatile political landscape of the late '60s and early '70s. In June 1971, the "Gap" group moved to KPPC. They went on to record four albums (*An Album of Political Pornography* on Blue Note; *Woodschtick and More* on Capitol, *A Great Gift Idea* on Reprise, and *The Bronze Age of Radio* on Warehouse) with Richard as co-writer/performer/producer and they toured college campuses. The group broke up in the mid-seventies and Richard returned to radio news. He lives in Southern California and continues to do commercial and industrial voiceovers.

BEIGEL, Les: **KFWB**, 1967; **KBIG**, 1968; **KLAC**, 1969; **XPRS**, 1973; **KGBS**, 1974-78. Les is the son of Glenn Miller's trumpet player Leslie Beigel and their travels took them to Seattle when Les was starting the 6th grade. After graduating from school, Les was working at Boeing Aircraft while doing weekends at KOL-Seattle. "I was told that I was never going to be a good quality control inspector so I moved into radio full-time. I also did utility work at KVI-Seattle." At some stage Les became bored in Seattle. "I needed to move to the next level and I looked at the map and L.A. seemed to be all down hill." At KFWB he called his midday show the "Beigel Bash." He is a part-time engineer and owns his own production studio.

BEILER, Ed: **KWIZ**, 1973; **KABC**, 1973-76; **KIEV**, 1976; **KGOE**, 1978-79; **KGIL**, 1986; **KABC**, 1989-90; **KIEV**, 1994-96; **KWNK**, 1996. Ed was known as "Superfan" and was a cliche. He was a spouting bar owner when he was given a coveted drive time spot on the ABC O&O. Ed became a champion of the people but his hard-hitting opinions resulted in his firing at KABC in 1976. Larry Stewart of the *LA Times* reported: "George Green, the station's gm, fired Beiler because of too many threatened lawsuits." In 1974 he was sentenced to a year in prison for defrauding the federal government in 1969, when he was in the trucking business. He served 4-and-a-half months, then returned to his old job at KABC. After a brief stint at KIEV, he went to work for WFAA-Dallas. In an attempt to get back to the Southland, he bought part interest in the Thousand Oaks station KGOE, but the show never caught fire. In the early 1980s Ed was doing a general talk show at KSDO-San Diego. When he returned to Southern California in 1986, he commented on his old spot at KABC: "I think since I left the show at KABC, it has had the impact of a snow flake on the bosom of the Pacific."

BEIRNE, Brian: **KRTH**, 1976-97. When Brian Beirne, "Mr. Rock 'n' Roll" arrived at "K-Earth 101" on April 1, 1976, it was the end of a long journey that began 30 years and 12 stations before. Brian, who was born in San

Mateo in 1947, spent much of his youth in Oregon, where he got his start as a broadcaster on KBZY-Salem. Brian described his early radio job in Oregon: "It was a real mom and pop operation. It was great training ground because you got to do everything. You read the news, you did your show and you had other duties. We even had to feed the cows out in back and water the lawn." He went on to work in Sacramento, KFRC-San Francisco, Cleveland and Chicago. At "K-Earth 101" Brian has earned his reputation as one of the top modern music historians in the United States and in 1991 was awarded a Star on the Hollywood Walk of Fame. "I wanted to tell the history of rock 'n' roll on my shows and pass on the music to new generations." As a historian, does he collect records? "I have 40,000 in my collection including my first record, *Goodnight Irene*, by Gordon Jenkins and the Weavers. I keep some at home, some are in vaults, but none are ignored." A self-described Hopalong Cassidy fan, Brian attends the "Hoppy" festival each year in Cambridge, Ohio.

Tony Richland - Winner of Best Independent Record Promotion Executive
-Billboard, 1973

BELL, Mike: **KROQ**, 1988-89. Born in Bakersfield in 1958, Mike started as a "go-fer" in 1974 at KERN-Bakersfield. By the late 1970s, he was working part-time at KERN and KBAK/TV-Bakersfield. Mike moved to

mornings at KMGN-Bakersfield and in 1981 became pd of KLYD until 1983. During the mid-1980s, he worked mornings in Seattle at KYYX, KPLZ and KISW. When Mike left Southern California he went to do mornings in Palm Springs. In 1991, he returned to his hometown of Bakersfield to be production director and creative director at KRAB/KKXX. He continues in the same capacity, adding creative for KDJK-Modesto.

BELLAMY, Sam: **KMET**, 1975-83, pd; **KNX/FM**, 1987; **KUTE**, 1987; **KMPC/KDGE**, 1987-88, pd. Samantha started in radio in 1975. A year later she was the assistant to the pd at KMET and by the end of 1976 was made pd. In 1986 she was in Houston at KSRR, returning to program KNX/FM and, later, the radical new rock format called "The Edge." She debuted "Niche 29" on October 5, 1987. Sam abruptly left KMPC/FM in the summer of 1988 and went to WCXR-Washington, DC. She is now out of radio and working as a paralegal in a law office in Southern California.

BELLMAN, Joel: **KBIG**, 1987, nd. Joel was born in 1956. He was fired from KBIG on January 16, 1987, the same day he picked up a prestigious Golden Mike award for a documentary on the late Orson Welles. He has won six Golden Mike Awards.

BENDER, Marty: **KROQ**. Marty worked weekends at KROQ. In 1985 Marty was made pd of WSKS-Cincinnati. He is currently pd of WFBQ-Indianapolis.

BENEDICT, Chuck: **KLAC**, 1963-69. "I never got to be great, but I sure was fortunate to have worked with great people!" That's the way the folksy conversation started with the man who was "Joe Pyne on Fridays." (Joe worked a four-day week for a reported $2,000 a week and Chuck worked the fifth day.) Born April 17, 1919, in Woodside, Maryland, he grew up in South Carolina. Chuck was the son of a talented family. His mother worked in the early days of radio and his father was a poet and athlete. He was around some of the greats like Arthur Godfrey which sparked his fascination with radio. Chuck started in 1934 while in high school at WIS-Columbia, South Carolina. During and after World War II, he was active in Armed Forces Radio. "I got fired from more jobs which was beautiful. I got to travel and meet more interesting people as a result of moving around. I had a ball." Through a varied career Chuck has been a sports commentator, associated with the L.A. Rams for 40 consecutive years, wrote 23 sports annuals for Petersen Publishing during the 1970s, free-lanced with the 700 Club and Christian radio, represented the Heisman Trophy Award for the 11 Western states and worked with Tom Harmon. Chuck has embarked on a series of one-man shows. He is a master story teller and he always seemed to be in the right place. Chuck was in the underground Summa headquarters the day Howard Hughes died. Chuck broke the story.

BENNER, Michael: **KNAC**, 1976; **KWST**, 1976-77; **KLOS/KABC**, 1977-87; **KLSX**, 1990-95; **KPFK**, 1995-97. A graduate of Michigan State earning a B.A. in television and radio management, Michael spent time in Detroit radio before arriving in the Southland. He is best known for his popular talk radio programs. Some excerpts from local press on Michael's show: "...a kind of Norman Vincent Peale of the Left." "...a no-cream-please burst of enlightenment and inspiration." "...I have never heard a more enlightening, informative program." When Michael left KLOS, he told Gary Lycan of the *OC Register*: "It was a layoff, or reduction in force. They said, 'We're firing the afternoon news guy, and that was me, and as for my own program, it continued but I didn't. Radio is going into narrowcasting. It's the result of deregulation, which is just another 50-cent word for eliminating public service programming." Michael kept his radio ties but emotionally went in a different direction. In 1987, he started a stress management consulting service for businesses. He also provides personal development seminars to business people and private counseling to individuals and couples. "I'm teaching people to have faith in their dreams. I want to show how it's better to dream up your solution rather than worry about your problems." He left his Sunday show on KLSX when the station changed format in late summer 1995. About the same time he began a weekly show on KPFK.

BENNETT, Beau: **KIIS/AM**, 1997, pd. Beau joined the all-Sports station from KRFX-Denver.

BENNETT, Chuck: **KFI**, 1968-69. Chuck did sports commentary for KFI.

BENNETT, Frank: **KWST**, 1979-80; **KROQ**, 1980-82. Originally from Arizona, Frank made his mark in Southern California radio. When KROQ experienced financial difficulties, Frank became an engineer for Watermark, the production house for such successful

shows as "American Top 40." From there, Frank spent a decade in afternoon drive at KOME-San Jose. He was let go in 1994, ironically due to the addition of several syndicated shows. Frank moved to the tiny island of Saipan, near Guam, "to take in the tropical island life while doing radio," according to a radio friend. He returned to the states for afternoons at KSJO-San Jose and moved crosstown to KUFX soon after his arrival.

BENNETT, Matt: **KFOX**, 1982. Matt was a sports broadcaster.

BENNETT, Mike: **KFI**, 1984; **KIKF**, 1985-88 and 1992-93; **KYSR**, 1993-96; **KBIG**, 1996-97. Born Mike Carlucci in San Francisco, he grew up in the East Bay. When he moved with his parents to Orange County in the mid-1970s "there was nothing but orange groves." Mike started his radio career at KSON/KNTF-Ontario and moved to KGGI-Riverside. In the early '80s he jocked at KDES and KPLM-Palm Springs. His last radio spot before joining Southern California radio was at "91X"-San Diego. At KIKF he was known as Mike West. From 1988 to 1995 he worked at Unistar/WW1 Country format. Since the spring of 1994 Mike has been

the public-address announcer at Dodger Stadium. "When I was growing up my idol was Vin Scully. I used to imitate him as a kid and to think that I now work a couple of booths away from him at Dodger Stadium is great." When he was at KYSR, after the home games, he would rush to the station for the all-night shift. As part of his triple-threat, Mike is also a staff announcer at KDOC/TV in Orange County. In 1995, he added Anaheim Mighty Ducks P.A. announcer duties and numerous voiceovers to his busy schedule. One of his voiceover accomplishments includes Sony Interactive Video Games and Sony Playstation. He has also been a radio instructor at Fullerton College.

BENNETT, Myron: **KABC**, 1960. Myron was one of the early talk show hosts in Southern California.

BENOIT, Steve: **KNNS**, 1995-96. Steve worked weekends at the all-Bloomberg news operation until the station turned to an all-Beatles format on the last day of 1996.

> *"When I was 13, my folks gave me a little Sony tape recorder. It fired my imagination and opened up a whole new world."*
> *-Michael Sheehy*

BENSON, Don: **KIIS**, 1981-82, vp/op. In the late 1970s, Don was pd of WQXI-Atlanta and later became vp of programming for Western Cities. His legacy in Los Angeles radio was hiring Rick Dees to do mornings on KIIS. Don left February 22, 1982, to rejoin WQXI and later became a consultant with the Burkhart/Douglas firm working with various CHR, Hot AC and AC stations. In late 1994 he joined Jefferson-Pilot as vp of operations and programming.

BENSON, Gordon: **KGIL**, 1965-66; **KEZY**, 1966

BENSON, Sam: **KLAC**, 1947-84. For almost four decades, Sam was the only constant through management, ownership and format changes. He saw it all from the legendary "Big 5" djs to Joe Pyne to "Future Fonic Sound," Haynes at the Reins and the transition to a Country format. Sam was director of publicity, public affairs, and promotion. The native Angeleno has spent his entire life in California except for a stint in the Air Force (where he met his wife Dorothy). After Los Angeles City College, Sam worked for KIEV and KVEC-San Luis Obispo and after his military commitment, he returned, ironically, to both KVEC and KIEV before joining KLAC. In 1984 Sam was editorial director for KTTV/Channel 11 and retired in 1987.  For the past 20 years Sam has worked public relations every September for the Los Angeles County Fair. How did he survive for almost 40 years with KLAC? "I was the only guy willing to do the job. Before deregulation, there was plenty of public affairs material that had to be prepared at license renewal time. I bobbed and weaved. I always had a pencil behind my ear and I moved down the hallways on my way to a 'very important meeting.' It was difficult to hit a moving target." His days are filled with "plenty of golf."

BENSON, "Uncle Joe": **KLOS**, 1981-94; **KLSX**, 1995-96; **KLOS**, 1996-97. An AOR legend, for 12 years he was the host of Sunday night's "7th Day" on KLOS which highlighted a specific year each week. In 1968, Joe was working for a small station in Dubuque. Over the years, he has written several volumes of discographies, *Uncle Joe's Record Guide*. Joe, a race car enthusiast, covered auto races whenever KLOS let him. He was let go in late 1994 as part of a major station housecleaning. In early 1995, the "classic rock" station, KLSX, hired Joe to reprise his popular Sunday night show offering albums in their entirety as well as doing fill-in. In late summer 1996 he returned to KLOS to host "7th Day" and by early 1997 was working afternoon drive.

BENTI, Joseph: **KJOI**, 1987. The longtime television broadcaster and newsman, dispensed commentary on "K-Joy."

BENTLEY, Jason: **KCRW**, 1991-97; **KROQ**, 1996-97. In the fall of 1995 Jason was listed in *Buzz Magazine* as one of L.A.'s 100 "coolest": "L.A.'s best late-night dj, KCRW's Bentley mesmerizes listeners with his narcoleptic delivery and dry wit. His Quango Records specializes in music as curious and smooth as Bentley himself." Jason got his start at Loyola Marymount University's KXLU in 1990 and soon became an editor at L.A.'s *Urb* magazine. He dropped out of college and *Urb* to spend more time at KCRW. For two years he worked as A&R director at independent dance label Planet Earth Recordings. His nightly show on KCRW is called "Metropolis" and he hosts a KROQ techno-meets-rock show, "Afterhours," on Saturday nights.

BERGER, Ed: **KEZY**, 1979; **KWIZ**, 1980-85; **KFI**, 1995-97. Ed was born in Torrance and grew up in Lancaster. He listened to Antelope Valley radio and remembered, "Gosh, I can do that. But, of course, it was Lancaster radio." Ed went to Antelope Valley City College and Fullerton College. At KWIZ Ed was part of the morning drive team with Ronni Richards and Ed Nix. "The fact was I did a bit of everything. I did the news, fill-in, remotes and even morning drive." In 1985 there was a major personnel change at KWIZ and Ed made a decision. "I didn't want to bounce around from radio station to radio station, so I got out." For the next decade Ed worked at Creative Media in Cypress. In addition to weekend news work at KFI, Ed is a full-time radio broadcasting instructor at Fullerton College.

BERGER, Hal: **KMPC**; **KHJ**. Hal was one of the early baseball announcers in Southern California.

BERGER, Stew: **KWIZ**, 1990. Stew worked evenings.

BERNADETTE: **KRTH AM/FM**, 1980-90; **KKBT**, 1990; **KJLH**, 1991-94; **KKHJ/KBUE**, 1994-97. Born Irma Molina in the San Gabriel Valley, Bernadette went to Citrus College and graduated with a degree in communication from Cal State Fullerton. During her senior year she started a ten-year  relationship with the RKO/Beasley outlet. She began at KHJ when it was a Country format. She was Bob Hamilton's assistant when he was national music director for RKO. Bernadette worked under Phil Hall during the KRTH call letter and format change staying with the stations during the RKO-Beasley-Liberman days. Bernadette was programming coordinator for KRTH AM&FM from 1986 to 1990 and was the first and only female on Smokin' Oldies/"K-Earth," when she hosted the "All Request and Dedication Show." She moved on to "the Beat" in 1990 to work as promotion coordinator with Liz Kiley and later to KJLH.

After three years as the marketing director for Spanish KKHJ/KBUE/KWIZ, in early 1997 she joined KUPR-San Diego.

BERNAL, Vicente: **KALI**, 1986-87. Vicente worked afternoon drive at Spanish KALI.

BERNARD, Joe: **KFWB**, 1965-66, pd

BERNARDINI, Tony: **KROQ**, 1987-90. Tony has been with WBCN-Boston since 1978 and from 1987 to 1990 he was the gm of 'BCN and KROQ. He would spend two weeks a month at each station. Tony was born and raised in San Diego. "I majored in partying for my first two years at San Diego State and finally settled in making the dean's list in my junior year." In 1969 he started graduate school at San Francisco State and began his radio career as a "free-form" jock on KTIM. When Tony got to WBCN as a jock and music director there were only three Infinity stations. As the company grew Tony became pd and gm. He skipped the normal process of sales leading to gm. With WBCN becoming a legend, Tony took on the added duties of running KROQ. "It became increasingly apparent with stations becoming fragmented that I couldn't manage two stations 3,000 miles apart. I had been longtime friends with Trip Reeb, who was operations director of '91X' in San Diego. Trip moved to KROQ and a few months later I gave him the keys."

BERNHART, Bruce: **KNX**, 1986-92. Bruce broadcast the evening news on "KNXNewsradio."

BERNSTEIN, Bob: **KMEN/KGGI**, 1995-96, vp/gm. Bob arrived in the Southland from WALK-Long Island. Born in Great Neck, New York, he graduated from Bradley University in 1978 with a B.S. in broadcast journalism and radio/tv. Why sales and not programming? "The salesmen all drove nicer cars." He spent three years in Little Rock and in 1981 he went to KNIX-Phoenix until 1988 when he joined KAZY/KLZ-Denver as gsm. Bob was gsm of KOY-Phoenix in 1989 and then spent four years at WALK as gsm.

BERNSTEIN, Sheryl: **KTWV**, 1993-94. The comedian/actress was part of an 8-month experiment with two females hosting the morning drive show on "the Wave." Born and raised in Buffalo, Sheryl graduated from Buffalo State with a degree in art/education and a minor in theater. "I was planning to be a teacher." In 1973 she started at a 1,000 watt daytimer in Niagara Falls, WJJL. In 1975 she joined WKBW-Buffalo as production director writing and producing commercials. "In the evenings I did stand-up comedy with six others in Buffalo, when someone who was visiting from L.A. suggested I think about working there." She came to the Southland for a "look-see" and got accepted at the Comedy Store and secured an agent. While working as "Wonder Woman" at kids parties and going on voiceover auditions, she met her eventual KTWV partner, Keri Tombazian. "I loved doing the morning show. If we had been able to stay, I think we would have been really great. I sure learned a lot about working as a team. We did something unique, very real.

My only regret is that there was no time to say good-bye to our audience." Sheryl continues a very active voiceover career...doing commercials, narrations and animation.

KNX POWER

KNX Broadcasts 5 watts
-1920
KNX Broadcasts 30 watts
-1922
KNX Broadcasts 500 watts
-1923
KNX Broadcasts 5,000 watts
-1929
KNX Broadcasts 10,000 watts
-1932
KNX Broadcasts 25,000 watts
-1933
KNX Broadcasts 50,000 watts
-1934

BIE, Peter: **KIQQ**, 1987, nd. Peter worked morning drive with Jim Carson.

BIG BOY: **KPWR**, 1994-97. Born Kurt Alexander in Chicago, he moved to Culver City at age 2. The 400-pound, 6-foot-2 dj was a bodyguard for rap artists before hanging out at "Power 106." After high school he formed a mobile dj business and a hip-hop hot line, "Wudd-Up?" In the summer of 1995, Big Boy moved from evenings to afternoon drive.

BIGBY, Tom: **KFI**, 1982, pd. Tom arrived in the Southland from programming stops in Philadelphia and Detroit. Currently he is director of programming for sports radio WIP-Philadelphia.

BIG KAHUNA: SEE Bill Drake

BIG WATUSI: SEE Mark Mendoza

BILL, Brother: **KACE**; **KUTE**; **KGFJ**; **KEZY**; **KIIS**, 1979-93. William "Brother Bill" McKinney filed suit against KIIS, alleging that he lost his job as a result of racial discrimination, and sought $2 million. The station claimed McKinney wasn't "hip" enough when he was dismissed after 14 years on the radio station's graveyard shift. According to published reports, his attorney said, "Our view is that as soon as he began insisting on a daytime spot instead of the graveyard shift, that's when they started to make up a reason to fire him." The attorney for Bill said white disc jockeys were promoted to better time periods while McKinney was not. Bill started his broadcast career at WEEN in Alabama. He worked at KDES-Palm Springs and in San Bernardino before starting in the Southland.

BILLY the KID: **KIKF**, 1995-96

BINGENHEIMER, Rodney: **KROQ**, 1976-97. "There

was nothing about him that wasn't 'on.' Rodney single-handedly cut a path though the treacle of the '60s, allowing all we 'avants' to parade our sounds of tomorrow, dressing in our clothes of derision." This from David Bowie in July 1992 *Details* magazine. Rodney "on the Roq" Bingenheimer has been a longtime weekend jock. He was a fixture on the local rock scene who always seemed a step ahead of various trends from the English invasion to glitter to punk rock. He was born December 15 in San Jose and grew up in Mountain View. Rodney sat in on an album, performing a one-note piano solo with Joan Jett on *I Wanna Be Your Dog*. In 1966 he appeared on the Monkees' tv show as a regular guest and was Davy Jones's stand-in on the show. He hung around with Sonny and Cher and Sal Mineo dubbed him "Mayor of Sunset Strip." According to a profile in Art Fein's tasty book, *The L.A. Musical History Tour*, he opened Rodney Bingenheimer's English Disco club in 1972 (his previous club, the E Club was at 8171 Sunset) during the second "British Invasion" of the early 1970s. According to Fein, "It was *the* place to commingle with Queen, Bowie, Suzi Quatro, Joan Jett, Sweet, Led Zepplin and T. Rex." His movie credits include *Up In Smoke*, *Rock 'n' Roll High School* with the Ramones, *Back to the Beach* with Frankie Avalon and Annette Funicello and *Repo Man* among many others. He is a syndicated columnist for the national publication *Yeah, Yeah, Yeak* and appears in *Flipside Magazine*. His single record *I Hate the '90s* featured artists from Hole and Sonic Youth. On KROQ he plays music you can't hear anywhere else - local L.A. artists, punk, imports, and psychedelic '60s music.

BINGO, Mike: **KSRF**, 1985

BINN, Stacy: **KABC**, 1986. Stacy was the Metro traffic reporter in afternoon drive at KABC. She moved to Metro in Washington, DC where she's also part of the morning drive show on WRQX. Stacy also appears on tv providing traffic reports for several local stations.

BIONDI, Dick: **KRLA**, 1963 and 1965-67. Born in New York, Dick spent three months with KRLA in 1963, while waiting for a job with Mutual Broadcasting and rejoined the Pasadena station in 1965, from Chicago (he was the original nite jock on WLS). He billed himself as the "ugliest and skinniest disc jockey in the world" and "The Wild Italian." In 1961, Dick won the *Gavin* Top 40 Disc Jockey of the Year Award. Perry Allen wrote of Dick: "Some of us endured the music as we focused primarily on tripping over our own ego devices. Others held the music at arm's length and attempted to make it into some kind of unemotional reference point. Dick Biondi merged with the music. And, by doing so, he solidly coalesced with the listener. No walls. They simply shared. He and his listeners were Siamese twins...joined at the nerve endings of integrity. This, when bullshit was radio's most important product. He and a precious few rare others maintained a valid personal posture. Through it, radio itself was protected." During the KRLA 30-year reunion, host Casey Kasem introduced him: "Dick was one of the most beloved personalities to ever open a mike on KRLA." In 1966, *Billboard* published that Dick was the most popular late evening dj. In 1967, he returned to Chicago and worked the midnight-to-dawn slot on WCFL. Dick is currently working at WJMK-Chicago; in fact, he's rebounded to Chicago radio three times.

BIRCHUM, Mr.: SEE Adam Corolla

BIRD, Bob: **KRKD**, 1962-70. One of his colleagues at KRKD said he was so disappointed with his radio experience that Bob "threw in the towel" and left the business. He was last seen living in Hacienda Heights.

BIRDFEATHER, Barbara: **KPPC**, 1971-73; **KMET**, 1971-72. Barbara worked all-nights in the early years of AOR in Los Angeles radio.

> **KWST changes to AOR**
> -December 31, 1974

BIRRELL, Harry: **KFWB**, 1968; **KNX**, 1968-97. When Harry arrived in the Southland, he came with 19 years of experience at radio and television stations across the country - from Beaver Falls, Pennsylvania (beginning in 1949) to San Diego. Harry has won nine Golden Mike awards and several L.A. Press Club awards. In 1975 he told the *LA Times*: "It had always been my ambition to be a newscaster. I used to listen to Morgan Beatty, one of the old-time news people, and I suppose that convinced me." Born and raised in Steubenville, Ohio, Harry graduated with a liberal arts degree from Miami University of Oxford, Ohio. He was a dj for many years before he became a news anchor. During his jock journey, Harry had an interesting experience in Dallas. "In 1957 I was offered a job at KLIF. I sold my house in Ohio, packed up my things and moved my family to Dallas. When I arrived the pd who hired me was gone and no one knew who I was." He spent a month doing all-nights before they transferred him to another McLendon station, WNOE-New Orleans. "It was quite intimidating working the evening shift at KLIF knowing that Gordon McLendon was just down the hallway." At KCBQ-San Diego Harry worked as Jerry Walker. Harry retired from KNX in 1993 but continues to be a stringer for "KNXNewsradio" from Ventura.

BISHOP, Don: **KIQQ**, 1975; **KMGX**, 1994. Before broadcasting at "K-100" Don worked in Utah, Washington and Chicago. He now works mornings at WW1's Bright AC format.

BISHOP, Jerry: **KLAC**, 1965; **KFI**, 1969-74; **KKDJ**, 1975; **KIIS**, 1975-79; **KGIL**, 1983-85. After five and-a-half years with KFI, the Cleveland-born jock commented to *LA Times*' James Brown: "I'm not flashy on the air and people tell me that I'm self-deprecating. But I don't believe that everything you say or do has to be fantastic." In the early 1960s, Jerry worked afternoon drive at WDRC-Hartford. In between KLAC and KFI, he jocked at KFMB-San Diego. Jerry was named MOR disc jockey of the year in 1970. *Times*' radio reporter Don Page said he is "whimsical, pleasant and with good taste." In the 1970s, Jerry hosted a local tv variety show in Chicago. Preceding Dodger games on KFI, Jerry co-hosted "Sports Phone" in 1973. For part of his time at KIIS he worked morning drive. At KIIS he teamed with Tom Murphy for the "Tom and Jerry Show." In 1979, Jerry was the off-camera announcer on NBC/TV's *Dick Clark's Live Wednesday*. At the end of the decade, Jerry went to San Diego and hosted the *Sun-Up Show* on KFMB/TV and worked afternoon drive on KCBQ. By 1983 he was back in the Southland on KGIL. He currently has a very successful voiceover career and can be heard on the NBC network. Since the mid-1980s Jerry has been the voice of the Disney Channel.

BISHOP, Robert: **KPPC**, 1969. Born in Dallas in 1948, Robert arrived in the Southland from KNUS-Dallas. He left for San Diego in the early 1970s to work on KPRI and KGB in 1972.

BLABON, Duffy: **KBLA**, 1966, gm

BLACK, Tre: **KKBT**, 1995-96. Tre joined "the Beat" for evenings in early 1995 from stops in New York and WJLB-Detroit. He represented KKBT at the 1995 Million Man March in Washington, DC. He left KKBT in early 1996 and returned to Detroit.

BLACKBURN, Dan: **KFWB**, 1968-70

BLACKBURN, Michael: **KBCA**, 1976. Michael started in the summer of '76 from WJZZ-Detroit.

BLACKWELL, Mr.: **KABC**, 1972-74; **KIEV**, 1975-81. Born Richard Sylvan Selzer, the popular fashion observer, who made famous the yearly list of Top 10 Worst Dressed celebrities, worked in talk radio during the 1970s.

BLACKWELL, Richard: **KGFJ**, 1993-96. Richard is now with Continental Cable. He worked as a club dj before joining KGFJ for the evening shift.

BLADE, Richard: **KNAC**; **KROQ**, 1983-1997. Richard, born Dick Sheppard in 1952, started on BBC radio in the 1970s. He came to the United States in 1976, and his British accent became his trademark and virtually the essence of his livelihood. Some listeners insisted that he was from Australia. It was difficult to get a job in the beginning, so he ran a mobile disco company for a while, playing music for everything from Hollywood parties to bar mitzvahs. In the late 1970s he found radio work in Bakersfield and San Luis Obispo and finally arrived at KNAC. He picked his last name from the popular movie, *Blade Runner*. He offered his services to KROQ for free, which eventually led to his decade and a half of work. Richard made several appearances on CBS' *Square Pegs*, and he was "Mr. Doughnut" in a Japanese television commercial. He was half of the popular morning team of "Ramondo and the Blade" in 1983 and later did mornings with the Poorman for a period. In the mid-1980s he was also the Monday night dj at the 321 Club in Santa Monica and a veejay on the cable tv show *L.A. Music Guide*, which was carried on 35 stations. He has produced six compilation CDs of AOR rock from the 1980s that he features on his "Flashback Lunch" segment. "Radio is everything I've ever dreamed of. I was like every 12- or 13-year-old kid who's ever stood in front of a mirror with a hairbrush and dreamed of being a rock 'n' roller. I couldn't sing so a disc jockey was the closest I would come." He's currently the midday jock on KROQ.

BLAKE, Barbara: **KTWV**, 1990 and 1997. Barbara hosts an NAC show for KYOT-Phoenix as well as working part-time at "the Wave." Between assignments at KTWV, Barbara was living in Seattle. She produces, hosts, and syndicates "Citizen Planet," a two-hour show of international contemporary jazz, world fusion music and global cultural information. The show began its international syndication in France, Mauritius and Vietnam.

BLAKE, David: **KFI**, 1989, nd

"It has been a long and fun ride since the pioneering Rock stations in the Inland Empire. It's been an E ticket ride and I'm still on it and loving it." -Lyle Kilgore

BLANCHARD, Red: **KABC**; 1956; **KXLA**, 1956; **KPOP**, 1957-58; **KFWB**, 1959-60; **KNX**, 1960-65. Born in Gardner, Massachusetts, Richard Blanchard grew up in Southern California. As a little kid he was  fascinated with building crystal sets and became a ham operator. He loved music and played trombone during the era of "swing music." Red (nickname came from his shock of red hair) started his radio career after a stint in the Army and joined KPRO-Riverside in December 1945. He started the "14-40 Club" and it was his first association with teen fans. In 1950 he went to KCBQ-San Diego and a year later was working at KLAS-Las Vegas. While toiling in the back yard of his Sherman Oaks home and talking on a cellular phone in 1996, Red recalled about his stop in Vegas: "I was there during the atomic bomb testing and I recorded the sound of the blast and fed it to the networks. I was called a heroic, brave reporter for taking on this assignment." With a laugh, Red said, "The fact of the matter was that all I did was hang a microphone out the window of the radio station. Hardly brave or heroic, but nonetheless." He recounted his early fame: "I had my greatest radio success in San Francisco. I worked at KCBS from 1951 to 1955 and was written up in *Life Magazine*, *Time* and other major publications. By 1955 it had run its course and I returned to Los Angeles." He went to KPOP to do mornings and while he was there Red recorded *Cape Canaveral, Pts. 1 & 2* on Pirate Records. A year later on the very day he was let go from KPOP, he was hired for the "graveyard" shift on KFWB. In 1960 he became a staff announcer at KNX for five years. "I was fired due to illness. The boss got sick of me." Red had always been interested in the technical side of radio and was hired on as an engineer at KHJ/Channel 9, working there for 15 years until his retirement in 1980 at age 58. Red misses "the contact with the public" from his radio days but "enjoys the way things are." Red's wife died in 1986 at age 60 after a long illness with breast cancer. "I love retirement, playing with my computer and motor home. I'd like to meet some nice woman and spend the rest of my life with her, but, so far, nothing!"

> "We'll be right back with more music after the news."
> -KFWB, March 10, 1968. Gene Weed's last words before the format change from Top 40 to all-News.

BLASE, Neale: **KKDJ**, 1972-73; **KGBS**, 1975-76; **KDAY**, 1977-78; **KWST**, 1979-80; **KNX/FM**, 1983. Born in St. Louis and growing up in Sacramento, Neale started his radio career at the age of 19. Before arriving in Los Angeles, Neale worked for some of the Rock giants - KOMA-Oklahoma City, KGB-San Diego, WIBG-Philadelphia and CKLW-Detroit. He met his former wife, Christine Blase (now Christine Brodie, pd of KTWV), while working in Sacramento, and they worked together at KKDJ. In between radio and voiceover assignments, Neale was a studio location driver at all the major movie studios. He also has designed and produced a collection/series of innovative promotional, merchandising and marketing products based on his love of radio and music (SweetMusic, ShirtMusic, SleepMusic, SeatMusic and SleetMusic). Since 1971, Neale has worked mostly morning drive. When he sold his home in L.A. in late 1986, he returned to Northern California and worked at KFOG-San Francisco. For many years, Neale was part of the morning team at  KMGG-Santa Rosa. He candidly reflected in a 1995 interview, "Even after 20 years in major markets and having worked for 39 stations so far, this current position is my chance to recapture the 'fire in my belly' that I once had for radio. However, the sad reality is that this market only pays $7.50 an hour. I regret leaving L.A., even though it's like working the high wire without a net. So, I'm looking forward to returning!" In early 1997 Neale joined KWNR-Las Vegas. "I instantly stumbled into the vast wasteland of the liner-card mentality. In April I fired myself from station #40 for 'felonious sense making' and for security reasons. I'm living in seclusion in a radio re-hab retreat in an un-marked location in the Santa Monica Mountains."

BLASKE, Art: **KFWB**, 1968-71; **KHJ/FM**, 1971-72; **KLAC/KZLA**, 1972-93. "I started in radio during a really fun era." Art was one of the booming news voices that proclaimed we were about to hear "20/20 News." He was born and raised in St. Cloud, Minnesota and started working on a St. Cloud radio station while still in high school. In the beginning, Art alternated between jocking and news at KDWB and KTCR until he settled on news at WDGY-Minneapolis/St. Paul in 1963. "We had stolen the '20/20 News' theme from the Drake/Chenault people. Someone in their organization thought they might just as well hire me to do it on the real thing and that's how I got to KFRC-San Francisco." Technology was limited in Art's early news days. "We made up for the lack of actualities with dramatic writing and a dramatic delivery. At one station we had to write every story in the first person to give the sense that it was going on right now." In 1993 Art joined the world of voiceover. "Most stations would never allow a news person to do commercials. I'm having a great time doing voice work."

BLATTNER, Buddy: **KMPC**, 1962-68. Buddy was part of the California Angels announcing team. He was a former Major League infielder with St. Louis. When he left the Angels he joined the expansion club Kansas City Royals. Buddy went on to sell real estate in the Ozarks.

BLEU, "True" Don: **KHJ**, 1978-80. "I was the morning meat between the Charlie Tuna/Rick Dees slices of bread." That's how Don describes his year-and-a-half stint in Los Angeles radio after arriving from a decade in afternoons at KDWB-Minneapolis. He used various names like R. Thomas Thumb and Rick Kelleher. Born in East Grand Forks, Minnesota, in 1946,  Don worked morning drive at KHJ and later moved to middays along with md chores. In 1980, Don left "Boss Angeles" for KYUU-San Francisco, where he spent a decade. In 1982 he was acknowledged for outstanding achievement by the National Academy of Television Arts and Sciences for his program, *Record Reviews*, on KPIX/TV's *Evening Magazine*. Don has been working at K101-San Francisco and hosting the *Know Zone*, an entertaining look at science and technology, on the Discovery Channel. He is an ordained minister who has performed many on-air marriages.

BLINOFF, Mark: **KMPC**, 1968-79, pd. Mark was made pd at KMPC in 1972. After major changes to the format in early 1979, he commented on the firing of some high profile personalities: "We're not running a museum here. Radio is a living, breathing organism and we owe it to our listeners to try to reflect a contemporary lifestyle, to let them know what's going on in the real world." KMPC wanted Mark to broadcast more Frank Sinatra and less Beatles. "Can you believe? The new gm commanded me to fire Ron  Rodrigues, who was then our fine music director, and I refused. So, he fired us both. Smart move. KMPC has never been in the top 20 since. It must have cost them tens of millions." Mark joined Merv Griffin Radio as vp/gm and three years later bought KWIP-Salem, Oregon with Roger Carroll. "We sold the station in 1989 for a lot more than we paid for it." Before joining KMPC, Mark was pd of KEX-Portland and assistant pd at KSFO-San Francisco. He has retired from radio and now teaches sixth grade in Alhambra. Mark is also the PR guy for the school district and writes about 30,000 words a year. "I love listening to the radio, and am still known to scream at it when stupid things are aired. I still have occasional nightmares about the business, even though I've been out of day-to-day operations for 17 years." Mark is writing a novel. "It is based on many of the characters that I met in the 38 years that I spent in the business, but that's tough work. Look for it around the year 2002."

BLOCK, Susan: **KIEV**, 1985-87; **KFOX**, 1987-93. For years every weekend, Susan ran a singles connection show on a program called "Saturday Date Night" and later "Match Night." Her first show was sponsored by the *L.A. Weekly*. She began guesting on television programs plugging her book and suggesting how singles could meet someone of the opposite sex. The self-described "hostess of the most personal show on the airwaves" went to Germany to broadcast her dating formula overseas.

BLOOM, Andy: **KLSX**, 1991-93, pd. Before moving to the Southland, Andy was pd of WQFM-Milwaukee, WYSP-Philadelphia and a consultant for Jacobs Music. He has been given primary credit for bringing the syndicated Howard Stern show from New York and making it work. In the fall of 1993, Andy was promoted to vp/programming of Greater Media. He relocated to the company's East Brunswick, New Jersey, headquarters. In the spring of 1995, he joined Coleman Research as executive vp and two years later was named om of KTCZ ("Real Rock 100")-Minneapolis.

BLOOM, Howard: **KLAC/KMET/KTWV**, 1977-87, gm. Howard started out as a screener for Arbogast and Margolis at KLAC. He worked part-time after his work at a liquor store. Howard worked his way up through the sales ranks at Metromedia and was there for the end of "the Mighty Met."

> *"If you don't promote, a terrible thing happens - nothing!"*
> *-Earl McDaniel*

BLORE, Chuck: **KFWB**, 1958-63, **KIIS**. Born in Los Angeles, Chuck worked in Texas radio before programming one of the most successful personality-formatted stations in the early history of Los Angeles Rock radio, "Color Radio/Channel 98." Chuck claims he added "showmanship - the dash, the flash" - to KFWB. In an *LA Times* interview, Chuck said: "It's always been my theory that radio is an entertainment medium...and

what we did was bring entertainment back to the medium, but in a totally different way." When he left KFWB, he had a non-compete clause and was unable to work in radio for 18 months, so he decided to give commercials a try. He built an office in a little shack on his garage. His first expenditure was $13 for a file cabinet. Only eight months into his venture, he entered his first competition - the international broadcast awards - and he won in every single commercial radio category. Chuck has become a much bigger name in advertising than he was in radio, but it was his enormous success in radio that guided him into advertising. In 1961, he won the prestigious *Gavin* Award as The Radio Man of the Year. Twenty years later he was known as "The King of the Radio Commercials." In 1963 Chuck formed a business with his partner, the late Don Richman (a former tv writer and also the co-founder and former general manager of the NBA Seattle SuperSonics), writing and producing radio commercials. During the '70s, his commercials captured close to 20% of all annual awards for radio advertising excellence. A Chuck Blore commercial is the one you don't turn off, because you think it is part of the station's regular programming. In a rather unique advertising twist, Blore/Richman started creating tv spots for radio stations in the late '70s. Their most successful campaign, tagged "The Remarkable Mouth" series, visually illustrated the sounds of the client radio station originating from an attractive model's...uh... mouth. It was an audio picture of a radio station's on-air day. The commercial was created for a friend of Blore's at a station in Pittsburgh. He had just done a spot for the Hollywood Bowl showing two men talking. One said, "Guess what I have in my mouth?" The other man shrugs his shoulders. "I have the orchestra, the entire season and the audience." The second man says, "I don't believe it." The first guy opens his mouth and shows him. The other man says, "That's a remarkable mouth!" That commercial won the 1979 Australian Golden Reel Award -- the first commercial to win in 15 years. Women appearing as "The Remarkable Mouth" include Bree Walker in 1979, Kelly Harmon (sports legend Tom Harmon's daughter), 'Tic Tac' girl on tv and Deborah Shelton of *Dallas*. Other memorable campaigns include the family of chimpanzees who argue incessantly over hubby's infatuation with the station and "The Janitor Fantasy," where Richman played a radio station's night janitor, who was trying to imitate the various djs on the station. When KIIS radio was floundering in the '70s, Chuck consulted and created a unique sound that melded music, words and commercials into one flowing output. He has won every conceivable broadcast advertising award and continues to run his own company in Hollywood. SEE Charlie Brown.

BLOW, Kurtis: **KPWR**, 1995-97. Kurtis received a speech and broadcasting degree from City College of New York. In the 1980s he co-hosted Mr. Magic's "Rap Attack" show on WBLS-New York. In 1995 he started a Sunday night "Old School Show" on "Power 106."

BLUE, Bobby: **KNAC**, 1972-76; **KMET**

BODINGTON, Dave: **KFI**, 1968-69; **XPRS**, 1970-80; **KIEV**, 1977-78

BOHRMAN, Stan: **KHJ**; **KNX**; **KGIL**, 1985; **KFWB**, 1990-94. Born on November 9, 1930, Stan was raised in Van Nuys and studied at the Stanford University journalism school. He worked at KFRC-San Francisco in the late 1950s and early 1960s. Stan abandoned his disc jockey days to do news and was part of the Voice of America in New York. He started in the Southland at KHJ and went on to be a fixture on local tv news as an investigative reporter and anchor. He won Emmys for his newscasts in Los Angeles and San Francisco and accolades for his presentation of guests opposing the Vietnam War. He also won the duPont Award for investigative reporting in Philadelphia. In the 1960s, he co-hosted *Tempo II* on KHJ/Channel 9 with Regis Philbin and Maria Cole, widow of Nat "King" Cole. The show featured celebrity guests and those opposing the War when dissent was not popular. He also did Talk radio on KGIL. Stan had a substantial role in *China Syndrome* playing a newsman opposite newswoman Jane Fonda. His son, David, produces specials for NBC/TV. Stan retired in 1990 from KFWB. He had a heart attack on October 13, 1994, and died at the Tarzana Medical Center at the age of 63.

> **Largest ever broadcast sale when Infinity buys KROQ for $45 million -1986**

BOIVIN, Paola: **KMPC**, 1992-93. The *Daily News* sportswriter joined all-Sports KMPC in 1992 and co-hosted a show with Brian Golden.

BOLAND, Katie: **KTZN**, 1997

BOLLES, The Real Don: **KSRF**, 1990-92. As an obvious parody of legendary The Real Don Steele, Don chose the similar moniker for the techno-rock era at "MARS/fm." He worked the all-night "truck driver" show and when his shift ended at six a.m. and Don May came on, they made a big deal out of its significance of "dawn to dawn." He was a drummer for the group, Germs, and has had many musical projects under assumed names. He is also an agent for hard-to-find records. His by-line is seen frequently in the *LA Weekly.*

BOLLINGER, Russ: **KIKF**, 1987. Russ hosted "Sports Rap."

BOND, Lyle: **KHJ**. Lyle was sports director of KHJ in the 1950s.

BONES: **KNAC**, 1991-92. Bones worked morning drive at the "Pure Rock" station. He was last heard working in Las Vegas radio.

BONK, Thomas: **KMPC**, 1992. The *LA Times*' writer teamed with Fred Wallin as part of all-Sports programming at KMPC.

BOOGERMAN: **KROQ**, 1994-95. Boogerman was a utility person who helped on KROQ remotes. For a brief time he did all-nights.

BOOGIE, Captain: SEE Gary Cocker

BOOKASTA, Gary: **KROQ**, 1973-78, pd and gm. Gary was last seen working as a lobbyist in Washington, DC.

BOOKER, Levi: **KJLH**, 1979-84 and 1986; **KJLH**, 1994-97. Born and raised in Los Angeles, Levi did morning drive at KJLH and moved up from md to pd in 1983. During this time he was made director of singles and 12-inch records for Radiovision. He currently does evenings at KJLH.

BOONE, Pat: **KPZE**, 1988; **KJQI**, 1993-94. For most of his life, Pat has prided himself on a "squeaky clean" image. He once considered changing the title of his 1955 cover hit *Ain't That A Shame* to *Isn't That a Shame*. His singing career in the 1950s was second only to Elvis Presley's in record sales. He stayed atop the music charts for an astounding 200 consecutive weeks. His recording of *Love Letters in the Sand* stayed on the pop charts for 34 weeks. In late 1993, Pat started on the Beautiful Music station doing a three-hour weekend show and left a year later. His 1996 album of hard-rock cover songs, *Pat Boone: In a Metal Mood* was received with curiosity. Pat was born in 1934. He married Shirley Foley, the daughter of country music star Red Foley.

> *"I had a lot of wonderful years at ABC, but this is more fulfilling than anything I've ever done."*
> -the late Chet Forte upon joining XTRA

BORGERS, Helen: **KLON**, 1981-97. Helen does afternoons and is the sister of Ken. Helen left for EuroJazz, a cable radio service in Holland, early in 1994 and returned in the late summer for the midday shift on the Long Beach mainstream Jazz station. Her brother Ken said of his sister: "I wish I could bottle her laugh, put it on a cart and use it whenever I need it."

BORGERS, Ken: **KLON**, 1978-97, pd. Born in 1950, Ken has been pd of KLON. For many years he worked morning drive on the non-commercial Long Beach station.

BOTULA, Mike: **KNOB**, 1966-67; **KFWB**, 1968-71; **KRLA**, 1971-72; **KMPC**, 1972-77. Mike was born and raised in the East end of Long Island. He started his radio career at age 15 on his hometown radio station in the late 1950s. In 1961 he went to WTFM-New York and two years later was working for KRFM-Phoenix. He started on KNOB part-time while securing an FCC 1st Class License from the Don Martin School of Broadcasting. In 1967, Mike went to KFOG-San Francisco and returned to the Southland to join KFWB when they went all-News. "I always had an interest in news. I had been doing a little of this and a little of that and my three years with KFWB solidified my new direction in news." In 1971 he joined KRLA until the newsroom was shut down in 1972 and he went briefly to KSDO-San Diego. Mike returned to L.A. in the summer of 1972 and spent five years at KMPC doing the news for Gary Owens. In late 1977 he made the transition from radio to tv and spent the next decade as a field reporter and producer for every local station, including eight years at KTLA/Channel 5. He has won numerous major awards including four Emmy award nominations, two AP Awards and a Golden Mike. During this time, Mike was a regular on *The Redd Foxx Show* appearing in sketches and doing voiceovers. Auto racing has been a life-long interest of his and he was the race announcer, interviewer and master of ceremonies at the Riverside International Raceway. In the fall of 1989, Mike became the news secretary to Los Angeles County District Attorneys Ira Reiner and Gil Garcetti. Mike lives in Orange County with his wife of more than 30 years. He has two children in their twenties. Mike is currently assigned to the DA's bureau of family support operations as community outreach coordinator reporting to the bureau director on matters dealing with the media.

BOWER, Jayne: **KFWB**, 1990-93. Jayne moved to morning drive in 1990, joining Charlie Brailer and John Brooks.

BOWKER, Bill: **KNAC**, 1970; **KYMS**, 1972-74, pd; **KWST**, 1975-77; **KROQ**, 1978-79. Born in Passaic, New Jersey, Bill grew up in Glendora and worked as Bill Phoxx at KNAC and KYMS. He said he loved working in Southern California when he did because "FM was still creative and somewhat unstructured. I'm glad I'm out. I became less infatuated with radio when the tight playlists started surfacing." At "K-West" Bill had an opportunity to conceive a blues music show, "Blues with Bowker," that he was able to take with him to Santa Rosa, where he has been living and working since 1979. The show with its "roots music" is in its 15th year. Bill owns a production company in Santa Rosa and has been a concert promoter in the area for the past decade. In addition to his concert production company, Bill is md and does air work on "the Crush," KRSH-Santa Rosa.

BOWMAN, Don: **KBBQ**, 1970. Don gained fame as a country artist singing for RCA Victor records and starring in a number of country-oriented films. One of his RCA albums was *Funny Folk Flops* produced by Chet Atkins. The album liner notes noted: "He is a man who can make chills of fear go up and down the backbone of a composer." Born August 26, 1937, in Lubbock, Don has been dubbed "The World's Worst Guitar Picker." He learned to sing in church and his early goal in life was "not to be run over by a truck." In the 1960s he worked at KDEO-San Diego, KEWB-San Francisco, Minneapolis and WKDA-Nashville where Chet Atkins signed Don to the RCA label in 1964. He was in the same league as Homer & Jethro. Don was a jock in Los Angeles when KBBQ was a Country station. He was last heard working as a country jock in Austin.

BOWMAN, Lisa: **KABC**, 1983-87; **KLAC**, 1990. In 1983 KABC conducted a much-publicized talent search for a host to work with Bud Furillo and Tommy Hawkins on "SportsTalk." Lisa was runner-up; however, one month later the winner, Merrie Rich, was fired and Lisa was offered the job. Lisa, from La Canada, was a television actress. As the second-place finisher, she won a trip to Puerto Rico. She also got the afternoon drive "SportsTalk" job on KABC and co-hosted the "Sports Nut" show on KLAC with Gabe Kaplan. She lives in Flagstaff raising her son as a full-time mom. Lisa is married to Chuck Bowman, director of *Dr. Quinn, Medicine Man* and *Stingray* among others.

BOWMAN, Paul: **KFOX**, 1986. In afternoon drive, his bogus traffic reports were broadcast by "Sage Brushy," an imaginary character who hovers over imaginary freeway tangles.

BOXER, Larry and Jack: SEE Joe Terry

BOYD, Donnell: **KKTT**, 1979; **KGFJ**, 1980. Donnell moved into sales at KLAC.

BOYD, Ed: **KKDJ/KIIS**, 1973-79, gm. Ed became gm of KKDJ in the spring of 1973. He is now a consultant in Miami Beach.

BOZZI, Dick: **KRTH**, 1974, pd

Spanish KRTO (98.3FM) starts simulcasting with KACE as KPRO

-April 19, 1997

BRACKEN, Dennis: **KNX**, 1963-77. Dennis was described as a generalist in the world of radio. He worked 14 years at KNX in a variety of assignments from news to horse race color to co-hosting the "Food News Hour." At the time of his early death, the *LA Times*' James Brown described Dennis: "Bracken was quietly unique. He had the capacity, shared by too few of his contemporaries, of talking with rather than at an audience. There were none better at it. He had a million-dollar voice. It was a calm crescendo to tonal hills and valleys - a casual, folksy, comfortable presence." A native of New York City, he graduated from Fordham University and was a student sportscaster. He moved to KSON-San Diego in 1959 as a news reporter and joined KNX in 1963. Dennis collapsed and died at his home in Orange shortly after returning from Santa Anita racetrack in the spring of 1977 where he had done the "color" for the KNX radio broadcast of the Santa Anita Derby. He was 45.

BRADBURY, B.R.: **KIQQ**, 1974-75; **KHJ**, 1977. At the 1973 annual *Billboard* Radio Programming Forum, B.R. was voted best newsman. He left radio for a while and made jade jewelry. B.R. is now back broadcasting news in Seattle.

BRADLEY, Bill: **KLAC**, 1956-57; **KDAY**, 1958-60; **KLAC**, 1960. Born Bill Silbert in Detroit, he used his birth name while working at WMGM-New York. Milton Berle gave him his professional new name. Bill originated a tv dance show for teens from Palisades Park in New Jersey. While working in L.A., he was also on KTLA/Channel 5 and guest appeared on *77 Sunset Strip* and *Hawaiian Eye*. Bill had retired to Palm Desert and died July 4, 1997.

BRADLEY, Wayne: **KMGX**, 1992-94. Born in Boston, the Granada Hills resident came to Southern California from WNHQ-New Hampshire. Late in 1994, the station changed formats and began simulcasting country music with KIKF. As a result, Wayne lost his morning shift.

BRADY, Jim: **KLAC**, 1987-88. Jim grew up in Canada and worked radio in Toronto before joining Country KLAC. He worked morning drive when Eddie Edwards departed. Jim left KLAC in 1988 to do Country radio in Dallas and later joined KLUV-Las Vegas until 1990.

BRAGER, Stan: **KLON**, 1997. Stan hosts weekend show, "Jazz Scrapbook."

BRAILER, Charlie: **KFWB**, 1969-93. Charlie was a longtime reporter/anchorman for all-News KFWB. Charlie was born and raised in Silver Spring, Maryland and was a journalism major at the University of Maryland. "I wrote for the campus newspaper and the administration was offended by an editorial I had written and wanted me to retract it. I refused and lost my position on the paper. I went to the campus radio station that had no news department and started one and that's how I got into broadcast news." After graduation he served as a Voice of America producer for the Far East. Charlie went into the Army and was stationed at Fort Huachuca in Tombstone, Arizona and was editor of the post newspaper. After the service he joined Mutual Broadcasting as an engineer and eventually joined

Westinghouse in their Washington, DC bureau. That assignment brought him to Southern California. "Broadcast news changed in 1963. When I got into broadcast journalism it was not entertainment and was not to titillate. I was standing in Arlington cemetery watching a man dig a hole where they would bury John Kennedy. President Kennedy personified a mood of optimism. With his assassination I knew things would never be quite the same again. Americans became disillusioned." Charlie and his wife are now retired, living in the Antelope Valley and running a "very successful" pet-sitting service. "I bought land in Northern Nevada and in a couple of years I want to put a home on it. I feel fortunate to have been a reporter on some historic events over a four-decade period."

BRAND, Ed: **KMPC**, 1987; **KLAC**. Ed is currently heard on KLAC via the syndicated Adult Standards format from WW1.

BRANDON, Leah: **KYSR**, 1995-96. Leah joined Rick Stacy in afternoon drive at "Star 98.7" from a traffic reporting service. She followed Rick in the summer of 1996 for mornings at KWMX-Denver.

BRANDT, Gary: **KPOL**; **KIIS**, 1970-71, pd. Gary was a newsman during his stay in the Southland. When he left KIIS he joined KRLD-Dallas and later the Dallas Cowboy organization.

BRANDT, Michael: **KROQ**, 1983, pd

BRANSON, Bob: **KFI**, 1969

BRATTON, Corbett: **KRTH**, 1991-92

BRAVO, Luis Alberto: **KWKW**, 1984-97, nd. Luis is news and sports director for the Spanish language station.

BRAZELL, Carl: Carl is the former president of Metromedia.

BRECKOW, John: John was part of the jazz scene in Southern California.

BRENEMAN, Betty: **KLAC**; **KFWB**, 1954-58; **KHJ**, 1958-73, md.

While still in high school, Betty started working in the record library at KLAC. "Each 'Big 5' personality had a music programmer and I was trained on how to put a show together." She followed Peter Potter to KFWB and worked with him on his tv show, *Juke Box Jury*. Betty was a radio/tv major at UCLA and following graduation joined KHJ as music librarian. She married Tom Breneman in 1960, moved to Denver and returned to KHJ in 1961. In 1965 Bill Drake came to consult KHJ. "Under his direction I compiled the "Cavalcade of Hits," which was the lead-in to the now legendary 'Boss Radio' format." She was asked to stay on working with pd Ron Jacobs. As the first music director of "93/KHJ," Betty wielded enormous power because if a record went on KHJ, it went on everywhere. In 1967 she became national music director for the RKO Radio group and all Bill Drake-consulted stations. In 1990 she brought together the original "Boss Radio" team and produced the Silver Anniversary Reunion gala in Los Angeles. "The event was the hottest ticket in town. The souvenir book and CD produced for it have become collector's items." Betty is president of Breneman Radio Services and produces *The Breneman Review* audio magazine.

BRENEMAN, Tom: **KBLA**, 1958. Congressman Sonny Bono, initially a record promoter, sponsored a radio show on KBLA hosted by Tom. The show was broadcast live from various colleges around the city. He also hosted a live show from a local nightclub called "Bren's Den." Tom helped put KNEZ-Lompoc on the air and then launched KBLU-Yuma and later moved to KTKT-Tucson and KTLN-Denver. In the 1960s Tom was pd of KACY-Oxnard and worked at KCOP/Channel 13. "I was literally born into radio. My mom and dad met at KFWB in the 30's, she was a singer and he was an announcer." Tom, Sr. created and hosted "Breakfast in Hollywood" in the late 1940s. "It was the biggest daytime radio show of the time. My dad was in the initial group of entertainers to be selected for a Star on Hollywood's Walk of Fame." Today Tom is CEO of Breneman Radio Services.

BRENNEN, Tom: **KRKD**, 1958. He was known on-air as "Tennessee Tom-Tom."

BRENNER, Carol: **KWST**, 1976; **KZLA**, 1977-79, pd; **KMPC**, 1979-80. In the late '70s, Carol left her on-air work to study for her M.B.A. at Pepperdine University in order to prepare for the business side of the radio industry.

BRESEE, Frank: Frank was a radio performer and broadcasting archivist. Born in 1930, Frank began in radio as a child actor. He produced for KFI and KGIL the "Golden Days of Radio" in the early 1980s. The series was carried on Armed Forces Radio for more than two decades and has reached an estimated weekly audience of two million people. Frank played Little Beaver on *Red Ryder* for about a year as well as other radio dramas. He invented the board game "Pass Time." The game came out in 1961 and his first year's royalty check was for $2.50. By 1969 his royalties amounted to $46,000 so he invented more games such as Gulp 'n Giggle, Sip 'n-Go Naked and Sip & Strip. His ubiquitous jobs included heading a company that arranged prizes for tv games shows. In 1984 he launched KMDY (formerly KGOE) as a full-time comedy station.

> *"Despite all the hardships, there's a wonderful richness in black culture that I prefer. It was just the kids in my neighborhood that I played with, they were of the African American culture. We were raised together and I didn't care to leave."* —*Johnny Otis*

BRESHEARS, Carol: **KPFK**; **KFWB**, 1978-81, nd. "Sensationalism in news reporting is here. The fear is that it will take over. Legitimate news has become the enemy." Carol was the first woman nd at an all-News station and she is passionate about the roots of news reporting. "I was raised on Edward R. Murrow, Walter Cronkite and Eric Sevareid. You might not have liked the news but you knew that sources for each story were checked and double checked." Born in Cleveland, Carol came to the Southland at age 12. She went to the University of California Berkeley, Glendale College and UCLA studying to become a teacher and ended up falling in love with broadcasting. At KPFK she was nd and later became general manager. When she left KFWB, Carol became nd at KEYT/TV-Santa Barbara. In the mid-1980s she worked as a coordinating producer for the tv show *Newscope* and later assignment editor at KHJ/Channel 9 and KTLA/Channel 5. For the past eight years Carol has been assignment editor at KTTV/Channel 11. She has two daughters who have followed in her steps. Her youngest is an anchor at the NBC/TV station in Milwaukee and the middle daughter produces a show for the CBS/TV station in Indianapolis. Carol is the president of the Radio and Television News Association and is very outspoken about the state of news reporting. "I want to preserve journalism the way it used to be!"

BRETT, Ken: **KMPC**, 1987-91. The former Dodger pitcher was one of the California Angels announcers. During his career he played for ten teams. In 1991 he moved to tv broadcasting for the Angels.

BREWINGTON, Ron: **KLON**, 1982-87; **KGFJ**, 1992-94; **KJLH**, 1992-97. Ron has been the bureau chief of American Urban Radio Networks since 1983. He is an entertainment guru whose reviews appear frequently in advertisements for major motion pictures. Ron was born and raised in New York's Harlem area. He retired from the U.S. Navy in 1984, where he served for almost two decades as a journalist covering worldwide assignments. He worked at a number of stations in Corpus Christi and Seattle before settling in Long Beach in the early 1980s. In 1987 Ron earned a B.A. in broadcast journalism from Cal State Long Beach. He was instrumental in leading a worldwide campaign on behalf of the late Marvin Gaye for a Star on the Hollywood Walk of Fame. Ron is a stringer for UPI radio and has written for *Crisis* magazine and *Black Diaspora*.

BRIDGES, Gene: **KLAC**, 1989-93, pd. Gene worked afternoon drive at Country KLAC until a format change in late 1993. Formerly of Omaha, he was responsible for bringing the St. Jude Radiothon to KLAC and KZLA, which raised thousands of dollars for the children's cancer hospital and research center.

570AM KMTR becomes KLAC -1947

BRIDGES, Jim: SEE James Hill
BRIDGES, Scott: SEE Roy Elwell
BRIEM, Ray: **KGIL**, 1953-54; **KLAC**, 1960-67; **KABC**, 1967-94; **KIEV**, 1995-97. Ray was best known as the all-night host of talk radio's millions of night-owls for several decades. Born in 1930, Ray began his radio career as a 15-year-old in his hometown of Ogden. He and his buddies hosted a radio drama called "The

Adventures of Vivacious Vicky." During the Korean War, Ray was heard on Armed Forces Radio and in 1953 he became a dj at KGIL. A year later he hosted "The Breakfast Club" on KLUB-Salt Lake City for four years. In 1958 he was part of radio and tv at KING-Seattle, where he hosted a Seattle Bandstand-type show. "They called me the Dick Clark of Seattle." Ray returned to the Southland in early 1960 to jock at KLAC. When KLAC started Talk radio with Joe Pyne, Ray resisted. He told Claudia Puig of the *LA Times*: "I went into it kicking and screaming. I liked playing the music. I realized what a dumb head I was. I knew very little about politics or the workings of government, and the first year I was an embarrassment." He was hired at KABC on July 4, 1967. He initially got a percentage of the advertising during his all-night shift, but that perk was eliminated during a recession. For eight years his show was carried nationally on the ABC network. In an *OC Register* interview with Gary Lycan, Ray said he was most proud of his 10-year association with commentator Vladimir Posner from the former Soviet Union: "I started calling Radio Moscow in the fall of 1977. He would use our phone calls as basis for commentaries. Nobody else was doing it." Ray is a ham-operator and received a Freedoms Foundation George Washington Medal for information he helped supply after the seizure of the U.S.S. Pueblo in 1968. Over 1,000 listeners paid $50 to attend his retirement party in late 1994. His favorite artists - Mills Brothers, Frankie Laine and Tony Martin - performed. Asked if he would miss the all-night vigil, Ray said: "After 27 years on the graveyard shift, my body says staying up all night ain't the right thing to do. Your biological clock, your circadian rhythms are always upset." In late 1995 Ray started an afternoon drive talk show on KIEV.

BRIGGS, Eddie: **KBBQ**, 1968
BRIGGS, Lynn: **KJLH**, 1989-91, pd; **KACE**, 1991-92. Lynn served as md/asst. pd and became pd of KJLH in 1990 and worked middays. When she left KACE, Lynn joined Motown Records briefly and then to Detroit and WRKS-New York.

BRILL, Bob: **KNX**, 1987. Bob did sports on the all-News station.

BRILL, Charlie: **KFI**, 1975-76. Charlie teamed with Mitzie McCall on KFI. He was a frequent guest on tv's *Tattletales*. The pair has been seen in several tv sitcoms. He has a recurring role on USA Network's *Silk Stockings*.

BRINK, Scotty: **KHJ**, 1965-66 and 1968-70. Born Don L. Brink in Williamsport, Pennsylvania, Scotty started radio at age 16 when he was a high school senior in Williamsport. At 19 he was on the legendary WIBG-Philadelphia from 1961 to 1965. When he got to KHJ, the station already had a "Don" so he became Scotty for much of his career. He left "Boss Radio" the first time when he was drafted into the Army and saw Vietnam. After his tour of duty, Bill Drake put him on WOR/FM-New York as JJ Jordan. Why JJ Jordan? Scotty, from his home in Seattle, replied, "Because Drake liked the name." After his second tour with KHJ, in 1970 he went to the "Voice of Labor," WCFL-Chicago and later that year went crosstown to WLS. In 1971, Scotty joined KJR-Seattle and his love affair with the Northwest was born. "I'm an outdoor freak and really didn't appreciate what ultimately I hope will be my last home." He was pd of WRKO-Boston in 1972, then returned to Seattle in 1974 for two years. In 1976, Scotty was pd of KUPD-Phoenix. While in New York on WNBC in 1978, Scotty did the morning show with comedian Richard Belzer. In 1980 he was made pd of KHOW-Denver. A year later he worked morning drive Talk at WCAU-Philadelphia. Scotty went on to WKTU-New York. His first wife was from Nashville so his career includes WLAC, WSIX, WGFX and ownership of a recording studio for seven years beginning in 1983. "Radio was only a side interest in Nashville. I really wanted to be near my daughter." Once she left for college, Scotty sold his recording studio. In 1989 he went to KSDO-San Diego as pd. For two years Scotty was om of KOAI ("Oasis")-Dallas. In 1994, he had "nature withdrawals" and left KOAI for KXRX-Seattle which became KYCW ("Young Country & Western"). He was also the pd of KGON-Seattle. Following an ownership change at KYCW, Scotty started his own business providing custom voice tracks.

BRINKLEY, Amanda: **KYSR**, 1997. Amanda joined the "Star 98.7" morning show in early 1997 from Shadow Traffic.

> *Who are your heroes?*
> *"I have met my hero and he is ME. Every morning, I stand in front of my bathroom mirror, recite self-caressing anecdotes & murmur: "Bill, I will NEVER leave you...my affection & admiration for you will NEVER waver...sensitivity is now in session & YOU may depend upon my CONSTANCY."*
> *-Top Ten personality Bill Ballance*

BRITTON, Boyd R.: **KKDJ**; **KIIS**; **KTNQ**, nd; **KWST**; **KHTZ**; **KNWS**; **KROQ**, 1987-97. Born in Boston in 1947, Boyd went to Princeton University and Emerson College. He was a sergeant and reporter in Vietnam. Boyd is best known for his contribution to the presentation of the news and, often times, for his warped, cynical commentary. Boyd claims he was first heard on KROQ when he slipped past the guards to annoy Frazer Smith. He arrived in Los

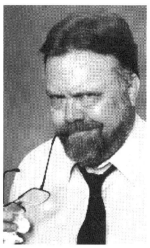

Angeles in 1974 and started his radio journey at KKDJ as part of Charlie Tuna's morning team for eight years. In 1981 he received a Golden Mike for his Anwar Sadat obituary. Boyd is currently "Doc on the Roq" on Kevin & Bean's popular morning show. "I created KROQ's first regular news features, combining rock beat, comedy skits, effects and commentary." He was the Fox/TV announcer in 1993. He is a former Sumo editor and was a travel writer for the now-defunct *The Los Angeles Reader*. His first news director job was in Lynn, Massachusetts when he was 17. For nine years Boyd has emceed the AIDS Walk Orange County. He considers his best work was done on KROQ in 1988. His motto: "Be semi-informed, it's better than nothing."

BRODEUR, Gene: **KMPC**, 1971-80; **KUTE/KGFJ**, 1982-84, nd. The former alternate White House correspondent for Golden West Broadcasters during the Nixon years, Gene grew up in New Jersey and studied English at St. Vincent College in Latrobe, Pennsylvania. He started his broadcast career as a journalist in San Francisco in 1967 and tracked the student protest movement from Berkeley to Santa Barbara. "The late Hugh Brundage hired me in February of '71, where I was doing news and programming in Santa Barbara. I was hired as a field reporter and anchor. As the trend of corporate downsizing accelerated in the late seventies, I was caught up in a newsroom cutback in '79." Gene landed at KCET as field reporter/producer for *28 Tonight*, which Clete Roberts anchored. After the funding ran out, Gene joined "Kute 102" as news director. During this same period he started doing field reporting and anchor work for NBC Network News in Burbank. From 1984 to 1986 Gene was the radio bureau chief in Paris for NBC News. In 1986 Westwood One bought NBC radio and Gene said, "That was enough for me."

His wife Jerolyn and Gene visited his old radio friend

Scott Shurian who was living near Bozeman. A local station offered Gene a job and the family has been there ever since. "Jerolyn paints water colors of the domestic animals on our small farm which lies about 18 miles north of Bozeman (Belgrade). I produce a bi-monthly series on political and social issues for Montana Public Television." He also produces educational videos and writes for a Bozeman-based newspaper. "We are proof that there is life after the city."

BRODIAN, Laura: **KUSC**, 1987-88; **KFAC**, 1989; **KKGO/KKJZ**, 1990-97; **KGIL**, 1997. Laura started as the host of "Music Through The Night" on KUSC which was syndicated. She works morning drive for KKGO's sister station in San Francisco, KKHI, which is broadcast

from KKGO. Laura works weekends on the Classical station. Born in Newark, Laura grew up in Union, New Jersey. She has three degrees in music from the Indiana School of Music. While Laura was working on her Ph.d she bugged the campus station, WFIU-Bloomington, for mispronouncing so many of the classical artists and selections. "They told me if I was so smart, why didn't I come down to the station. I did and they put me on for two years." She always had a love for music. Laura started playing the piano at seven. After graduation in 1982 she spent five years at KQED-San Francisco. Laura is a fan, big time, of science-fiction. She loves to read sci-fi books and recreate the costumes. In the sci-fi environment she met her husband Kelly Freas. For seven years Kelly was the artist for the front, back and inside cover of *Mad Magazine*. He has drawn over 1,000 covers. Laura is an illustrator in her own right. Her first nationally published illustrations appeared in *Weird Tales*, *Analog*, and *MZB's Fantasy Magazine*. For the past eight years Laura has been the host of "Delta Symphony" on Delta Airlines. "Not only have I always loved classical music, but being on the radio is the only job in which I feel competent, confident and comfortable. I love it!" She is also a part of all-Beatles format on sister station, KGIL.

```
BOSS to HOSS
              KHJ's switch to Country
```

BRODIE, Christine: **KTWV**, 1986-97, pd. Chris, a fifth generation Californian, was born, raised and went to school in Sacramento. She was working in Sacramento with Michael Sheehy (now production director at "the Wave") when she met her husband-to-be, Neale Blase. They both worked at KKDJ,

Neale as jock and Chris as md. In 1978 Chris was a vp of Goodphone Communications, which published an AOR-targeted trade publication. That trade included a section called "Triple Z Jazz" - almost a decade before the launch of "the Wave," it was a precursor to what is now NAC. Chris was part of the embryonic days of *R&R* with Bob Wilson. She became the third pd of KTWV, following Frank Cody's departure in 1988. Chris has always been known as a "bold" programmer who is willing to take risks. When the morning ratings were languishing, she installed a two-woman team to bolster the numbers. The experiment was unsuccessful, but the fact that she tried got her high marks.

BROOKLER, Rob: **KIQQ**, 1984-85. Rob was an intern answering phones when the gm gave him a periodic weekend shift.

BROOKS, Foster: **KHJ**, 1962. Foster had been a big MOR jock in Buffalo before arriving at KHJ. His comedy career skyrocketed after radio.

BROOKS, John: **KFWB**, 1979-97. John is part of the three-person morning drive team at "news radio/98." The New York native began working for KFWB as a news

editor in 1979 and for five years was a general assignment and investigative reporter. He has been awarded four Golden Mike awards and recognized by numerous organizations. John moved to the position of KFWB anchor in 1985 and in 1987 was co-anchor for KFWB's first Best Newscast award from the Los Angeles Press Club. John has been the calming voice after the Northridge earthquake, traveled to Saudi Arabia with Vice President Dan Quayle, reported on the total eclipse from Hawaii and in 1994 broadcast live from Woodstock II. John started in radio at Allegheny College in Pennsylvania in 1969. He moved to the Southland in 1970 where he met his wife Frances. They have a daughter and live in the Ojai Valley.

BROOKS, Monica: **KPWR**, 1987-89. Monica was part of Jay Thomas' morning show delivering the news. She is now out of radio living in Chino and running a gardening supply business.

BROWN, B. Bailey: **KDAY**, 1970-72. He worked the all-night shift at KDAY.

BROWN, Bill: **KMPC**, 1961-65; **KHJ**, 1965-74; **KRTH**, 1974. Bill was the youngest newsman at KMPC and he was there for the launch of "Boss Radio" at KHJ. Born in Paris, Illinois, he got started in radio in his hometown while a junior in high school. Bill went to Indiana State and worked for two Terre Haute stations. In 1960 Bill followed his brother who was in aerospace to Southern California and attended the Don Martin Broadcast school. The school had a placement service and Bill was hired as an apprentice to work the Angels baseball games. "The biggest thrill of my life is when I flipped the switch for my first newscast at KMPC. My adrenaline pumped for the next three years." Bill and his wife purchased a station in Lexington and eventually returned to Paris where he managed a station for years. Bill has designed a custom weather service on the Internet that he is marketing.

BROWN, Bobby: **KGFJ**, 1985. Bobby (no relation to the singer) left morning drive for acting, writing and tv sports. In 1989, he was back in radio doing mornings at WAMO-Pittsburgh. Currently Bobby is working for the ABC network.

BROWN, Burt: **KZLA**, 1987-97. The Mississippi native has been a longtime weekend regular at the Los Angeles Country station.

BROWN, Charlie: **KFWB**, 1961. Charlie was part of the management team that went on-air during the personality strike in sympathy with the newsmen. He appeared on only one KFWB survey and had an uncanny resemblance to pd Chuck Blore. Charlie used to bring his pre-teen daughter into the studio with him, and she voiced one of the most identified slogans, "My mommy listens to KFW-B."

BROWN, Charlie: **KGFJ**, 1972; **KIQQ**, 1975. Charlie arrived at KGFJ from WWRL to do the all-night shift.

BROWN, Don: **KHJ**. Don has since passed away.

"I'm very concerned about this current thinking that news has no place on a Rock station. Remember, FM stations were the first in the 1960s to talk about Vietnam. We wouldn't have heard about the huge herpes epidemic had the story not broken on an FM station."
-Larry Jacobs

BROWN, Jim: **KPOL**, 1962-64. Jim is the longtime entertainment reporter at the *Today* show. Born and raised in Los Angeles, following graduation from Pasadena City College Jim started at KSON-San Diego hosting a nightly classical music concert. During the next 8 years he worked at KFSD (now KOGO) and

KGB-San Diego, first as a dj and then making the transition to news. At KPOL he was a member of the news staff before joining the "Big News" at KNXT/Channel 2 where he specialized in aerospace. In 1972 Jim became a street reporter at KNBC/Channel 4. "I was always interested in the process of movie making and wanted to be the entertainment reporter." By 1974 his old boss had gone on to the *Today* show. "I pitched him on doing a behind-the-scene piece with John Wayne and Katherine Hepburn for *Rooster Cogburn*. Channel 4 let me do the network feature on the condition that it run in the local news." In 1984 Jim was fired by new management at Channel 4 and he moved to full-time *Today* assignments. "I always wanted to be in this business. Radio was the beginning of the evolution of my career. At KPOL I'll never forget that the music announcers broadcast from the transmitter site while we delivered the news from an old house on Wilshire Boulevard."

BROWN, Laura: **KROQ**, 1990; **KABC**, 1993. Laura was the producer-sidekick to Kevin & Bean when they arrived in the Southland. She went on to be a producer and on-air personality with the "Ken and Barkley" morning drive show.

BROWN, Stan: **KBBQ**, 1967; **KGIL**, 1967-76; **KBCA**, 1976. Stan was nicknamed "The Animal" by Dick Whittington. He did sports for the Valley station and was described as the locker room W.C. Fields. In 1968 Don Page, radio writer for the *LA Times* named Stan Sportscaster of the Year: "Stan Brown is the fastest-rising sports commentator in town, in the old Bob Kelley style." Stan is a graduate of Iowa State and he started as a newsman in Boone, Iowa. He made stops in Odessa, Denver and San Diego before arriving in Southern California.

BROWN, Steve: **KRLA**, 1972-74. Steve arrived as assistant pd, and during KRLA's brief experiment with the team concept in 1973, he was paired with Russ O'Hara. He went on to work as announcer for KCOP/Channel 13. Steve founded American Video Service in Irvine.

BROWN, Tom: **KGIL**, 1970-85; **KJOI**, 1989; **KNX**, 1973-97. Born in 1938 in Evanston, Illinois, Tom attended the University of Washington and graduated from the University of Illinois in 1960 with a degree in journalism. After he was discharged as 1st Lieutenant in the Army, Bill first worked for a series of Illinois stations before joining KCMO and WDAE-Kansas City, WHN and WNEW-New York and KNBR-San Francisco. The *LA Times*' Don Page referred to him as having "a certain X-plus that makes you visit his program regularly." Page called him the "biggest new star in the big town. He's witty and has his own style." Tom's afternoon drive show on KGIL was called "The Thomas Brown Affair," a take-off on the Steve McQueen movie, *The Thomas Crown Affair*. He did mornings on "K-Joy." He has been overnight news anchor on "KNXNewsradio" during much of the 1990s.

BROWNING, Bill: **KIIS**, 1975-76, nd. Bill was a longtime newsman starting his career in the 1940s. He was the news director at KIIS.

BROWNING, Chuck: **KHJ**, 1970; **KGBS**, 1972; **KFI**, 1980. "Shotgun Tom" Kelly of San Diego legend produced a classic one-hour video tribute to one of the best loved rock jocks. You could get laughter whiplash watching Chucker's friends tell outrageous stories about a much-loved man. The storytellers included Charlie Van Dyke, Frank Terry, Bruce Vidal, Jimi Fox, Joe Nasty and many more. "Shotgun Tom" intersperses each story with Browning broadcasting one of his air shifts, along with home movies provided by his wife, Melanie. His radio journey began on a Christian station in Oak Grove, Louisiana. He continued with stops in Knoxville, Birmingham, West Palm Beach, Memphis, Ft. Worth, Louisville and Indianapolis, before his "big break" came at WFIL-Philadelphia in 1966. A year later he was at CKLW-Detroit. He was frequently hassled by the border guards between Windsor, Ontario, and Detroit. On one particular crossing, when the guard asked the Chucker if he had anything to declare, he said, "Yeah, war. If you don't stop hassling me I'm gonna shoot holes in the Windsor Tunnel and turn it into a car wash." In 1968, he became a WMCA-New York "Good Guy" and then went on to KFRC-San Francisco. Between 1970 and 1974, he worked for KRUX and KUPD-Phoenix, KCBQ and KGB-San Diego and WMYQ-Miami. At KGB, one of the storytellers recalls a cart machine malfunctioning, and Chucker giving it away to the fourth caller. For the next five years he worked promotion/marketing for Warner Bros. and Capricorn Records. Between 1980 and 1986, Chucker jocked at KFI, WHBQ-Memphis, K101 and KFRC, and KTSA-San Antonio, his last station. He returned to San Francisco, his favorite city, and died March 3, 1988, leaving a wife and four children.

BROWNING, Reed: **KABC**, 1960-61. The KABC staff announcer was an early talk show host during the transition from Music to Talk at the ABC O & O. His program was called "Open Line." Reed gave listeners a chance to sound off on any subject. He would just listen without giving too much comment.

BRUCE, Larry: **KMET**, 1974-75 and 1986, pd. Larry was on the air during the heady days of "the Mighty Met." In 1980 he became pd of KGB-San Diego, returned to become pd of KMET in January 1986 and left seven months later. Larry owned a radio consulting firm on the Central California Coast and in early 1997 became pd of KFSD-San Diego.

BRUCE, Tammy: **KFI**, 1995-97. The highly vocal former president of the Los Angeles chapter of the National Organization for Women (NOW) was born in Northridge in 1962. In an *LA Times* interview in the fall of 1995, she said she never met her father, "who disappeared a few months before I was born. I'm not sure he ever knew about me." She grew up in Northridge and said she was a

good student until she entered Ventura High School, where she lasted only two weeks. She passed the California Proficiency Exam, left her formal education behind at 15 and moved to Illinois. In her late teens, she worked for actress Brenda Benet, featured on

Days of Our Lives, until Benet committed suicide. Tammy worked various electronic publicity jobs until she joined NOW in 1988. She became president of the organization in 1990 at the age of 27 which made her the youngest president in the L.A. chapter's 28-year history. The *Times* story went on: "Although she ran for office 'as an open lesbian,' she said she has always considered herself bisexual, and was engaged to be married at 19." She works all-night at all-Talk KFI. "This work is so satisfying that I have, uncharacteristically, no words to adequately describe how I feel. Let me just say that I may not be getting rich, but if I get hit by a Mack truck tomorrow, at least I'd know that I've done something with my life." Tammy was very vocal during the O.J. Simpson trial, proclaiming loudly her contempt for Simpson - based on his history of abusing his former wife Nicole Brown Simpson. In the spring of 1996 she abandoned her role in NOW and founded Women's Progress Alliance.

BRUNDAGE, Hugh: **KDAY**, 1957; **KMPC**, 1965-72, nd. Hugh died in 1972.

BRUNDIGE, Bill: **KEZY**, 1969. Chattanooga-born Bill Brundige is as prominent in the glass business (he claims

you can see right through him) as he was for 40 years in broadcasting until his retirement in 1975. He was the solid, no-frills sports broadcaster. Bill was the "color man" for Chick Hearn in the very first simulcast after the Lakers moved from Minneapolis. He started his broadcasting

career in 1937 at WAVE-Louisville. During World War II, Bill was the West Coast sports director for Armed

Forces Radio Services broadcasting to the Pacific Theater. He was discharged in 1946 and moved to Washington, DC to broadcast for Mutual Broadcasting System. While in DC he worked with Ted Husing on the "College Game of the Week" for Mutual. In the late 1940s and early 1950s he broadcast sports for Yale, Princeton, Philadelphia Phillies, Detroit Lions and Chicago Cubs. In 1952 the Cubs sent him to Southern California to work their Pacific Coast League affiliate, Los Angeles Angels. In the same year he joined Bob Kelley on the Los Angeles Rams broadcast team until 1960. He covered sports for all the local tv stations. In 1964 he founded "Bill Brundige Glass," which grew to a three-store chain. Bill retired from broadcasting in 1975 upon removal of his left lung. He has won two Golden Mike Awards, and on February 1, 1995, he was inducted into Southern California Sports Broadcaster's Hall of Fame, the day before his 80th birthday. He married in 1935 and they have three children and seven grandchildren.

BRYANT, Willie: **KDAY**; **KALI**. Known as the "Mayor of Harlem" when he was a New York dj, he started out as part of a dance team playing the "original" Apollo, strip joints and nite clubs. He loved to help up-and-coming talent. Willie died in 1964 at the age of 56.

BUBBA, the Love Monkey: **KQLZ**, 1989. Various personalities would sit in as "Bubba the Love Monkey" or "Russell the Love Muscle" during the early days of "Pirate Radio."

BUCHANAN, Buck: **KRLA**, 1985-86; **KRTH**, 1989-93. Son of actor Edgar Buchanan, who gained fame on the *Petticoat Junction* tv series, Buck worked with Bob Hudson as a team in early 1980 in Hawaii. They teamed briefly in 1985 on KRLA in morning drive. Buck was the voice of John Lennon's ghost in bits with Emperor Hudson and the experiment ended in early 1986. Buck started his radio career in 1965 working in Hawaii, Pennsylvania and West Virginia.

BUCKLEY, Richard: **KGIL**. Richard was president of Buckley Broadcasting in the 1960s.

BUDNIK, Buddy: **KDAY**, 1969; **KRLA**, 1972-73. In the mid-1960s, Buddy (real name Ron) worked at KFXM and KMEN in the Inland Empire and KACY-Oxnard. He now sells business real estate in Hollywood and the Valley areas.

BUELL, Bruce: **KFAC**; **KUSC**; **KPOL**. For four decades Bruce was a famous voice in Los Angeles classical radio. At KFAC he originated the program "Crossroads of Music." He was one of the pioneer announcers of television, but his real love was classical music radio. Bruce passed away April 23, 1996. He was 77.

BUHLER, Rich: **KBBI**, 1964-69; **KFWB**, 1968-72; **KNX**, 1972-74; **KFWB**, 1974-76; **KBRT**, 1980-90. Rich got started on the air at the age of 17 for a local FM station and after graduating from college was "salivating" with the opportunity to get into news. He was part of the embryonic days of all-News at KFWB and later originated the design of a system in which stories were written in triplicate to streamline the rewriting process. "I had a powerful spiritual renewal in the mid-1970s that changed my direction to a career in ministry." Although Rich continued working in media as a free-lancer and consultant, he became an ordained minister and served on the staffs of several churches including being the senior pastor of a church in Long Beach for seven years. In 1980 he was asked to help put

together a competitive news department for Christian formatted KBRT when they had people like Johnny Magnus and Clark Race spinning Christian records. When the station changed format a year later Rich proposed doing a commercially aggressive, drive-time talk show and brought "Talk From the Heart" on the air. It is credited with having introduced a new era in Christian Talk radio. Later, the program was nationally syndicated as "TableTalk" and was heard on KGER and KKLA. In 1995 Rich stepped down from hosting 15 years of live, daily talk radio and now owns Branches Communications, a production company in Orange. He has become a nationally known speaker and author with several best selling books and won numerous awards including an honorary doctorate from Biola University.

BULL, Frank: **KFWB**, 1950s. Frank hosted "Strictly From Dixie," a weekend Dixieland jazz show. He was the P.A. announcer for the LA. Rams for three decades.

BUNCH, Don: **KNAC**, 1967-70

> *What was your darkest moment?*
> *"When my mom had a heart attack and my dad was hospitalized with Alzheimer's symptoms within the same week in 1995."*
> *-Top Ten personality Charlie Tuna*

BURCHETT, Dave: SEE Dave Randall

BURDETTE, Bob: **KBOB/KGRB**. As owner and manager of these two stations, he worked for years in the 1970s and '80s to convince the listeners that KMPC was not the only Big Band format in town. He worked as an audio engineer from 1936 to 1950 and much of that time was spent doing big band remotes. In 1962 he bought KBOB and in 1967 he acquired controlling interest in KGRB.

BURDETTE, Gloria: **KBOB/KGRB**, pd

BURKE, Billy: **KIIS**, 1996-97. Billy joined KIIS from an afternoon drive slot at KSFM-Sacramento. He had been pd at XHTZ ("Z-90")-San Diego and worked at WIOQ and WCAU-Philadelphia. Billy has been seen on MTV's *Beach House* and was picked by *Playgirl* magazine as one of America's "sexiest DJS." He is a native of Hawaii and a 4th degree black belt in Korean karate.

BURNETT, Larry: The former Prime Sports anchor worked the L.A. Lakers pregame show on radio.

BURNS, Don: **KVFM**, 1963; **KNJO**, 1964; **KRLA**, 1970-72; **KROQ**, 1973; **KRLA**, 1974-75; **KIIS**, 1975; **KIQQ**, 1976-77; **KOST**, 1978-80; **KUTE**, 1986-88; **KTWV**, 1988-97. Born in Santa Monica, Don spent most of his radio career in Southern California. He was on Armed Forces Radio and Television from 1964 to 1968. While stationed in Vietnam in 1967 and 1968, he hosted *Good Morning, Vietnam* in Saigon.  The Venice, California resident worked on KKUA-Honolulu and KOL and KJR in Seattle before joining KRLA in 1970. Don worked at KROQ, then went back to KRLA from 1974 to 1975. He did morning drive for a portion of his Pasadena tour. Don is currently heard in afternoon drive on KTWV, "the Wave."

BURRELL, Larry: **KBIG**, 1959. Larry went on to do television announcing.

Sincerely and *Maybeline*
-composed by Alan Freed

BURSON, Jim: **KFWB**, 1972-97, nd. Jim has spent three decades with the all-News station. At KFWB he has covered major stories, from quakes to fires to flooding as well as the 1992 Los Angeles riot. Jim grew up in East Liverpool, Ohio, and started in radio in 1954 during his senior  year of high school. After graduating from Youngstown University with a degree in public relations, he joined KYW-Philadelphia in 1965. Since 1972 Jim has been with KFWB in a variety of capacities, including news anchor, sports anchor, reporter, editor, writer and news director. "Thirty years ago when we started the all-News radio format, the pace was hectic but exciting, and remains so today. I can't imagine anyone enjoying a lifetime of work as much as I have."

BURTON, Alan: **KLOS**, 1972. Alan worked the all-night shift.

BURTON, Michael: **KROQ**, 1990-95. "The Maintenance Man" was a real-life janitor who doubled as a fearless prankster on the Kevin & Bean morning show. According to radio lore, the morning team asked Burton to do an impromptu weather report as he was tidying up the studio. His "weather time" rap became a regular feature, along with an extension of responsibilities. When news broke out that the ducks in the Venice, California canals were infected with herpes, he chased the ailing fowl with his trademark bullhorn. Michael pulled another prank after Denny's restaurants was fined over discriminatory service. He went to a Denny's and shouted into his microphone, "Can't a black man get some coffee in this damned restaurant!" He left the morning team and the station in the fall of 1995 and filed a wrongful-termination suit charging the station with racial and religious discrimination. The suit was settled in late 1996 with both parties prohibited from revealing financial details.

BUSH, Birdie: **KRLA**, 1978; **KIIS**, 1979-86. Birdie grew up in Rialto. From tv modeling in St. Louis, she joined KSOM-Ontario in 1975. Birdie was a staffer at KNBC/Channel 4 before joining the Pasadena station. KRLA pd Bill Pearl hired Birdie to be one of the "Hitmen" in a major promotion in 1978, where she stopped cars with a station bumper sticker. If the car radio was tuned to KRLA, they were awarded $100. At KIIS she worked fill-in in production. Birdie is now a housewife and mother of four living in Valencia. She and her husband, Rex Bagwell, currently run a successful closed-captioning company, "Line of Sight," in Burbank.

BUSKETT, Larry: **KLAC**, 1961-62, gm. Larry also ran stations in Sacramento and Las Vegas. In the mid-1980s he went to Hawaii.

BUTLER, Jerry; **KHJ**, 1970-73; **KIQQ**, 1973-75; **KGIL**, 1975-76. Born in Cleveland, Jerry arrived at KHJ on October 15, 1970, from WRKO-Boston. Drake/Chenault bought KIQQ in 1973, and Jerry was one of the original jocks at their "K-100." Immediately after Drake/Chenault sold the station, Jerry's next stop was KGIL, which he left in the summer of 1976. Not long afterwards, he committed suicide.

BUTTA, PJ: **KKBT**, 1995-97. "Everyone told me that I would have to start out in some small hick town in the middle of nowhere making peanuts...I guess I showed them." Born on October 23, 1973, PJ was raised in San Diego as an only child in a single parent household by his Filipino mother. "I always knew that I would be involved with music and that I wanted to get the hell out of San Diego." He left San Diego to study broadcasting at the University of La Verne where he got involved on the campus radio station. In 1995 he received his degree and started at KKBT. "I always wanted to get my degree for my mother and for everyone who said that I couldn't do it." PJ is involved in the community making regular visits to children in juvenile halls, child placement homes and Boys & Girls clubs. "My whole thing is that I want to make a difference. That why I got into this, to make a difference." He appeared in the tv show *Moesha* and eventually wants to become a music history teacher. PJ works overnights at "the Beat" and has a voice that is *smooth like butta*.

BUTTERWORTH, Gary: **KIQQ**, 1987; **KLIT**, 1990. Gary did the all-night show on "K-Lite."

BUTTITTA, Joe: **KGIL**, 1975-80 and 1984-87; **XTRA**, 1995. "After I graduated from San Fernando Valley State (now CSUN) in 1964 I became the sports information director for the school and I was in hog

heaven. For a journalism major who loved sports I thought I would have this job through the rest of my life." Joe got a taste of broadcasting while in college when the owner of KVFM, located in the Valley's Porter Hotel, needed a student on Thursday evenings to spin records. "I volunteered with my hand up so fast that I almost broke my arm." In college Joe was the sports editor of the campus paper and played baseball. He played in the Dodger minor league organization for two years. At KGIL he broadcast the high school football game of the week. "When John Elway and Anthony Davis were playing, our ratings were incredible." In the late 1970s Joe got the bug to try tv. "A freelance cameraman I hired from one of the local stations taped me faking a sports report. At least I had a three and a half minute tape I could send around to the different stations." The tape worked. During the holidays in 1979 Joe sat in for Lynn Shackelford on KHJ/Channel 9 which led to a five-year job with KTLA/Channel 5 calling Angels baseball, UCLA sports and doing the nightly sports. In 1985 he joined KTTV/Channel 11 for three years. For 23 years Joe wrote a golf column for the *Daily News* and is a card carrying member of the PGA. Joe was born in 1942 in the Bronx and came to the Southland when he was 8 years old. "I still consider myself a New Yorker, even after all these years." In 1992 he became sports director at KADY/TV-Oxnard and a teaching pro at Westlake Golf Course. Joe freelances on UPN/Channel 13 and covered the 1997 L.A. Marathon.

BUTTRAM, Pat: **KGBS**, 1966; **KMPC**, 1989-93. Pat was the sidekick to Robert W. Morgan for almost five years and to Gene Autry for almost five decades. Born Maxwell E. Buttram in Alabama, he was the son of a circuit-riding minister and studied theology at Birmingham Southern College. He rode at Melody Ranch with Autry, portrayed a shrewd landowner on tv's *Green Acres* (he played Mr. Haney) and was an omnipresent master of ceremonies for many Los Angeles organizations. He and Gene first met in the 1940s in Chicago when both were appearing on the "National Barn Dance," the nation's first hillbilly radio show. He appeared in more than 40 films, most as Autry's constantly amazed partner, and played himself on Autry's radio shows from 1940 to 1956. Pat died January 8, 1994, of kidney failure. He was in his 80s.

BUTTS, Mike: **KIQQ**, 1972-73. Mike did morning drive on the launch of "K-100-FM." Originally a Motor City baby, he got his start in the mailroom at KLIF-Dallas, while he grew up in nearby Denton. In the 1970s, Mike worked in Detroit at WWWW and WKNR. His next stop was KDWB which, according to Mike, was rated #1 out of four CHR stations in the Twin Cities. He spent four years in Salt Lake City, as the first morning man that

helped put KKAT ("The Cat") on the air. Mike broke the Guinness Book of World Records for the Most Handshakes -- 16,615 to be exact, in seven hours. The event raised $17,000 for the Utah United Way. Mike is driven to perfection. During a five-year stay in Austin, he originated the gun buy-back campaign, plus married his pd, Lisa Tonacci, live on his radio show. Mike is now an ordained minister, who made his big debut marrying couples at the McDonald's drive-thru window, while taking his show on the road Valentine's Day morning for WPRO/FM-Providence. His relatable commitment to the community shows. He appeared as a guest on the *Maury* show after helping two young girls who had been wronged by the IRS. Another effort was raising 82-thousand pounds of food and supplies to assist a hurricane relief effort. "Tuesday's Friend," a regular WPRO feature, has found thousands of homes for homeless animals and has earned Mike the "Man of the Year Award" from the Humane Society. His local efforts help the Children's Hospital in Providence. He has authored the book, *Air Personality Plus*, an excellent comedy tool he has made available to fellow broadcasters worldwide. *Billboard* magazine has twice named Mike Air Personality of the Year. His secret wish? "I would like to win Powerball, so I can buy Maui from the Japanese!"

BYNUM, Roland: **KGFJ**, 1967-74, pd and 1984-85. Born in Detroit in 1940, after working at the Motor City's WCHB and WABX, Roland arrived in Los Angeles to replace the Magnificent Montague. By 1970 "the Soulfinger," as he was known, was the assistant pd and pd a year later. He was at KGFJ until Gene West arrived in 1974. In 1985, Roland did a show on Armed Forces Radio Network.

BYRON: **KFI**, 1980-85; **KBIG**, 1985-87. Born Byron Paul in New York City in 1946, his family moved to

Long Island shortly after his birth. Byron's father, a tv and movie director, moved his family to L.A. in 1961 to be close to the work. His father managed Dick Van Dyke and directed many episodes of *Have Gun Will Travel* and *Gunsmoke*. Byron was part of the very first graduating class of Palisades High School. He went to L.A. City College and graduated from what is now Cal State Northridge in 1969 with a degree in broadcasting.

He went to Don Martin Broadcast School to get his FCC 1st Class License, which was important for his early work at KIXF-Fortuna, KAFY-Bakersfield, KIST-Santa Barbara and in 1972 at KDON-Salinas. It was at KDON where he met his eventual partner Tanaka, who was doing morning news. "We were together but we didn't play off each other until 1975 when we worked at KROY-Sacramento. In 1977 Steve Rivers (then KROY pd) was hired to program WIFI-Philadelphia and he took 80% of the KROY staff." In October 1980 pd John Rook hired Byron and Tanaka to do overnights on KFI and to fill-in for morning legends, Lohman and Barkley. "Since Lohman and Barkley had earned about six weeks vacation every year, this gave us a great opportunity for exposure." In 1981 Byron and Tanaka started working afternoon drive. A year later Tanaka left the station and Byron continued solo. Subsequent pd's bumped Byron's shift around from afternoons to middays to overnight. He left the station in May of 1985. Within a month or so, Byron joined KBIG for mornings and worked there for "a week longer than two years." Since 1987 Byron has been doing a wide variety of freelance commercial and corporate voiceover work, including narrations for blue-chip companies such as IBM, Honda and Xerox. Any interest in returning to radio? "For my 20-year career, I enjoyed radio immensely. Tanaka and I had a ball performing for the 8 years plus that we were together. It was also great doing mornings with Phil Reed at KBIG. But it finally became time to make a change. I didn't want to wait too long and become one of the guys you feel sorry for when he begins to slide backwards through the markets he worked on the way up. I always had the idea to branch out into voiceover work." Byron has been living in Santa Monica for many years and is still good friends with his former on-air partners.

> **"I programmed against Jacor Broadcasting and it was very tough. Now, I'm very happy to be programming a Jacor station."**
>
> **-Bryan Schock**

C

CABRANES, Bill: **KWNK**, 1996, gm

CABRERA, Joe: **KWKW**, 1986-89, gm

CADELAGO, Hugo: **KTNQ**, 1996-97. Known as "El Gordo" to his afternoon drive Spanish audience on KTNQ, Hugo co-hosts "Contacto 10-20" with Antonio Gonzalez. This is an "issues" program dealing with gangs, racism, assimilation, societal matters and topical questions.

CADELL, Ava: **KLSX**, 1995. Ava auditioned on-air for a sex-relationships show for "Real Radio," KLSX.

CADWELL, Clyde: **KPOP**, 1957-58. Clyde had a "tele-request" show. He would talk to the listener for up to five minutes and then play their request.

CADY, Bob: **KWIZ**, 1982-85. Bob started out in sales at KWIZ and eventually went on-air. When he left the Orange County station, he joined "Format 41" at Transtar. In the early 1990s, Bob was doing a morning show in Palm Springs with Doug Ray.

CAGLE, Gerry: SEE Gerry Peterson

CALCOTE, Gordon: **KIEV**, 1966.

CALDER, Bill: **KHJ**, 1962-64. Bill worked morning drive, and one of his "shticks" was to blow an Army bugle every morning to wake up his listeners. His crosstown rival, Bruce Hayes, would play taps signifying "lights out" for his competition. In 1967 Bill was at WEMP-Milwaukee and KWK-St. Louis. He is in his late sixties, almost deaf and working for a talk station in Ft. Lauderdale, according to a colleague

CALDERONE, Tom: **KLSX**, 1996; **KLYY**, 1997. Tom hosted the "Modern Rock Live" show on "Real Radio" weekends. In early 1997 he joined "Y-107."

CALA, Joe: **KFWB**, 1983-97. Joe reports sports on all-News, KFWB.

CAMACHO, Victor: **KTNQ**, 1992-97. Victor has worked all-nights at Spanish KTNQ for the past five years. His talk show is described as truly "A little about everything." The open phone subjects range from the occult and superstitions to items in the day's news.

CAMAS, David Raul: **KLVE**, 1997. David works evenings.

> "Some gal got me drunk and I woke up the next morning as an NBC page."
> -Dave Garroway

CAMERON, Myles: **KHTZ**, 1985; **KBZT**, 1986. A fourth-generation San Franciscan he grew up in Belvedere. His high school years were spent in Santa Barbara where he was pd of the school station. After graduating from the University of Oregon in broadcasting/journalism his radio path led to news anchor at KIDD-Monterey and then air personality at KYTE-Portland, KLIF-Dallas, KQKT and KMPS-Seattle and in San Francisco at KSAN, KABL and K101. "The year 1986 contained the zenith and nadir for me as a broadcaster hosting Hands Across America and then on the air live when the space-shuttle Challenger exploded." In the late '80s, Myles returned to the Bay Area after acting in various tv sitcoms and industrials. While in the Southland Wolfman Jack emceed a Greater Media client party at the Hollywood Palace. "After introducing all the '11-10 Men', then KHTZ' Charlie Tuna, the Wolfman looked at me quizzically like, 'who the F**K are you,' and gazed at my name on his list and said, 'let's give a big hand for our 'K-Hits' midday man, Myyy, Myyyyyyy, Myyyyllllll, Myyyyyyllllleeeessss Camm, Myles Cameron, everybody!" Myles is back on K101. "You can usually find me sailing my boat on the bay; that is, when I'm not trying to find work to pay for it."

CAMPAGNA, Vince: **KFWB**, 1969-97. Vince has been a longtime newsman for KFWB and contributor to the history of Southern California radio. He began his radio career in 1953 in the Army's AFRS in Fairbanks, Alaska. "After the service I cut my teeth and paid my

dues in several major markets." Before joining KFWB Vince produced and directed tv programming as well as programming an L.A. tv station. During his 44 years in broadcasting, Vince has accumulated a library filled with awards for meritorious achievements including a dozen years as KFWB's entertainment critic.

CAMPBELL, Gary: **KHTZ**, 1983; **KZLA**, 1983-97.

After graduating from UCLA where the Bay Area native studied on the college radio station, KLA, Gary started working in the Inland Empire. From KDUO-Riverside, he arrived at "K-Hits." Gary brightened the overnights at KZLA for over a decade. One of his co-workers commented, "Gary's friendly personality has made him popular among his listeners and his fellow co-workers." He continues living in Riverside and has made the long commute every day for the past 12 years. In 1995, he signed on with Metro Traffic in addition to weekends and fill-in at KZLA. Gary hosts a Country show on WW1.

CAMPBELL, John: **KHTZ**, 1983-86; **KBZT**, 1986. John is a part-time actor.

CAMPBELL, Lori: **KYMS**, 1990

CAMPBELL, Stan: **KLAC**, 1989-93, pd. "I want to be the man on the radio when I grow up," Stan Campbell told his mother when he was 5. Stan was born and grew up in Nova Scotia. He joined the Canadian Army for 10 years and entered the radio business "through the back door," according to Stan in a 1995 phone interview from his home in Traverse City. He worked for Toronto radio stations for 10 years and was the "Ed McMahon" on Canada's longest running country tv show on the CBC. Stan quit radio to start a record label. "It was one of the worst decisions I've ever made." The record business took Stan to Nashville, which eventually got him back on the air and to WBVE-Cincinnati (known as "The Beaver"). He was hired at KLAC to be the morning man and pd. He created many characters to be the brunt of his jokes, such as Travis, a cranky weatherman, and Guru from Agoura, a wacko with a crystal ball. Stan left with the format change as the Country station went to Unistar's Nostalgia AM Only. He moved to a radio

station about an hour from Traverse City in Michigan. Good decision? "I'm not sure yet. My wife wanted a house and a quieter way of life. The stress of being morning man and pd is just as intense here as it was in Los Angeles. It IS beautiful in Michigan. Maybe I'll be back. But, then again, maybe not."

CAMPBELL, Wendell: **KGBS**, 1965, gm. Wendell is deceased.

CAMPOS, Roberto: **KALI**, 1965

CAMPOS, Tonya: **KNX/FM**, 1988; **KCBS/FM**, 1991-94; **KZLA**, 1994-97. The California native from Dinuba joined the Country outlet after working two years at Unistar's ACII. Tonya worked for three years at KCBS/FM as assistant pd. Before arriving in Southern California, she worked at KSDO-San Diego.

CANNING, Lisa: **KDAY**, 1986-90; **KJLH**, 1990; **KKBT**, 1993-97. Lisa was the leggy announcer on ABC/TV's late night show, *Into the Night Starring Rick Dees*. In late 1995 she became an entertainment reporter for *Entertainment Tonight*.

CANSELA, Eddie: **KXMG/KLAX**, 1997, gm. Eddie was promoted to gm in the spring of 1997.

CAPPARELA, Rich: **KUSC**, 1980-83; **KFAC**, 1987-89; **KJOI**, 1989-90; **KKGO**, 1990-91; **KUSC**, 1993-96; **KKGO**, 1996-97. Much of Rich's time in Southern California radio was spent in the Classical format. From 1989 to 1991, he hosted a Classical Top 25 Countdown show that was syndicated. In an *LA Times* story on his syndicated show in 1991, he commented on his experience at KJOI: "I stunk as a pop deejay. I was awful. I tried it and went `oops.'" On the Countdown show, Capparela said, "I want to reach people who would like to listen to classical music but are kind of put off by the way it's presented." Rich is one of the hosts on KCET public tv's fund-raising drives. Born in 1952, he learned his music appreciation from taking courses on his own in Upstate New York.

CAPPUCCI, Francesca: **KIQQ**, 1984. Francesca started out in the public affairs department at "K-100" and later teamed with Jay Coffey in morning drive. She went on to be the entertainment reporter for KABC/Channel 7.

CARDENAS, Rene: Rene was the original Dodger broadcaster to the Spanish community and has been 15 years behind the microphone.

CAREY, Kathleen: **KMGX**, 1994; **KNX**, 1994-97. Kathleen has been working at Shadow Traffic.

CARLISLE, Dan: **KWST**; **KROQ**, 1979; **KLOS**, 1981-83. Dan arrived in Southern California from KSAN-San Francisco and left in the fall of 1983 for WNEW-New York. He currently works weekends at Westwood One's Adult Rock 'n' Roll format.

CARLOS, Juan: **KLAX**, 1993-96

CARLSON, Bill: **KFAC**, 1953-83. Bill spent three decades with Classical music station KFAC before retiring in 1983. He started his radio career at the University of Wisconsin campus station. After graduation he went to KMBC-Kansas City. World War II took five years of his life but he returned to the states speaking three languages, which contributed mightily to his hiring because he could pronounce the composers and pieces flawlessly.

CARLTON, Russ: **KMGG**, 1984; **KFI**, 1984-85. Russ did news on KFI for two years when he left "Magic 106." He died November 5, 1985, of a brain tumor at the age of 38.

CARLUCCI, Mike: SEE Mike Bennett

CARNEGIE, Jack: **KKDJ**, 1972, gm

CAROLLA, Adam: **KROQ**, 1995-97. Adam is one of the co-hosts of "Loveline," an evening program dealing with love, sex and relationships. For three years he was part of the comedy group, the Groundlings. The part-time boxer and former construction worker was known as the comedic character Mr. Birchum for Kevin & Bean's morning drive show. Since late 1996 "Loveline" is also seen nightly on MTV.

CARPENTER, Scott: **KLAC**, 1984-87. Born Pat Bergin, Scott came to the Southland following a very successful run in Baltimore. When Rick Dees slammed Country music as "the music of the underachiever," Scott went ballistic. Rick bellowed: "Let's go out and drink and have cirrhosis. Be a moron and, you know, kick tail." Scott, a member of Mensa, responded in the *LA Times*: "It's just not a fair portrayal of people who enjoy this kind of music. Country music is America's folk music." When he left Los Angeles, he went to WYNY-New York, then to morning drive at KIIM-Tucson and finally to Washington, DC where he currently resides and does voiceover work.

CARPENTER, Scott: **KNX/FM**, 1988; **KABC**, 1988-89. Scott grew up in upper Wisconsin and worked at legendary rockers KDWB-Minneapolis and WIFE-Indianapolis. His real fame came in the early 1980s at KCBS-San Francisco. "It was great for a while. We brought in radical, son-of-a-bitch rock 'n' roll." After his stint at KABC, he followed Carl Brazell to KRLD-Dallas for a couple of years. From his home in Portland, where he's working on investments and writing a book, he said in a 1995 interview, "I'm ready to come back. But, you know, L.A. is not a radio market. They make movies down there. It's lucky there's radio at all."

CARPER, Carol: **KGFJ**, 1978-84. Carol broadcast news on Urban KGFJ. She is now the editor of *Urban Network Magazine*.

> *"I've been a disc jockey since 1937, and I've taken pride in being able to play the best in music. Top 40 programming is an inadequate service to the public."*
> -Peter Potter, early '60s

CARROLL, Larry: **KJLH**, 1970-71; **KIIS**, 1971-72; **XPRS**, 1972. The longtime television newsman from KABC/Channel 7 and KCAL/Channel 9 got his start at KJLH as news editor in June 1970. Larry grew up in Chicago and came to California to attend Pomona College in Claremont and be pd of the campus station in the late 1960s. He graduated from Pomona College with a B.A. in economics. At KIIS he worked evenings and was assistant nd at XPRS. In the spring of 1972 Larry worked at The White House as the California director of broadcast relations for President Richard Nixon and served there until a few days after Watergate. In the same year a number of jobs overlapped; he worked as assistant nd at XPRS, was the West Coast bureau chief of Mutual Black Network and started at Channel 7 on October 30, 1972, and stayed 17 years with the station. By the end of 1972, he was devoting full-time to tv. In 1989, Larry became the principal anchor for Channel 9's *Prime Nine News, Weekend Edition,* which included anchoring the station's prime-time coverage for the duration of the Persian Gulf War. In 1993 he was a correspondent for NBC's *Nightly News with Tom Brokaw* and a regular contributor to the *Today* show. He has won numerous awards including two 1992 Golden Mike awards. In 1996 he won an Emmy as anchor of the best daytime 30-minute newscast. Larry currently anchors the noon and 5 o'clock news on KCBS/Channel 2. He and his wife Roman and their two children live in Los Angeles.

CARROLL, Rick: **KKDJ**, 1973-75, pd; **KEZY**, 1975-78; **KROQ**, 1978-85, pd; **KEZY**, 1986-88, pd; **KROQ**, 1988-89. At age 14, Rick would hitchhike to KLIV-San Jose after school to hang out and help in any way he could. By 1970 he was the pd of two San Francisco stations. His significant contribution to Los Angeles radio is that during the 1980s and 1990s, he was most closely associated with the success of "New Music" radio. His formula was based on a passion for the music. Rick was described in the *LA Times* as "a stocky, intense man with a wild growth of hair." At KROQ, he found himself at the helm of a station that had for years been beset by a myriad of legal and financial problems. In fact, KROQ had actually gone "dark" to try to straighten out its entanglements. Some called it the flagship station of "madhouse rock." At one point the debt-ridden station used room 1228 of the Pasadena Hilton as its studio. A decade later Rick encouraged the perception. "We've managed to create the illusion that the station is non-structured. Actually, it's probably the tightest programmed format in the country, where the pd chooses all the songs by hand." In 1983 he took his "New Music" ideas into the consultant world, which even included MTV. His company, Carroll Schwartz & Groves, scored the film *Surf II*, but the company was less than successful. It was neither as glamorous nor as lucrative as Rick had imagined, and he triumphantly returned to KROQ. When Rick launched "Rock of the '80s" format, he attracted enormous interest from the AOR world. However, in 1983 when KROQ's ratings dipped while KIIS was beginning its strong ascent, the *Times* asked, "Has the fabled 'Rock of the '80s' already bitten the dust?" The death of his format was, indeed, premature. KROQ's programming was a more radical "free-form" version of AOR when Rick arrived. When he started, KROQ was the only station playing "New Wave" music. When Rick instituted some structure to the format and music selection, the jocks picketed and advertisers pulled out, resulting in a compromise. He described the new rock listener: "A KROQ listener may be carrying a skateboard or a briefcase." Rick was plagued by a troubled personal life. He had two attempts at rehabilitation for a drug problem. He was unable to spend much time on his last return to KROQ as a consultant in the summer of 1989. Rick died on July 10, 1989, of complications of pneumonia at the age of 42. When he died, KROQ personality Richard Blade gave this on-air testimonial: "I've lost a friend. In fact, everyone lost a friend who loves music. You might not have known his name, but you surely felt his influence." In *R&R*'s 1993 special edition of "Twenty Years of Excellence," Rick was cited as a "pioneer." Rick's contribution was noted with this reference: "His balance of carefully researched music and anarchic on-air attitude has built a heritage any station would envy...and it still may not have reached its mass-appeal peak." His philosophy: "The more you loosen the format, the lower the ratings are going to be. It's just a fact of life." A tribute to Rick appears elsewhere in this book.

CARROLL, Roger: **KABC**, 1948-58; **KMPC**, 1959-79.

Born Coleman Carroll Rutgen III in 1930 and growing up half-way between Baltimore and Washington, DC, there was never another thought but pursuing a career in radio. His older brother was an announcer at WCAO-Baltimore and at the CBS network in New York. Rog's brother left for World War II and never returned. Roger became the announcer in the family. His first job in radio was WFMD-Frederick, Maryland at the age of 15. In a 1995 interview, he remembered his first dance remote in Maryland, "I was so scared that I pooped in my pants." He became the youngest staff announcer in the history of the ABC network at the age of 18. During his two decades during the glory years at KMPC he was the tv announcer on *The Smothers Brothers Comedy Hour*, *Bing Crosby*, *Perry Como*, *Tony Orlando and Dawn*, *Redd Foxx* and *Pearl Bailey*, as well as hundreds of commercials. In the early 1970s, Roger ran a nightly five-minute feature called "Golden Days of Radio," which he considered "one of the most successful segments I've ever featured." In the mid-1970s, Roger did a live remote broadcast before the sports events at the Los Angeles Coliseum. "I chatted with baseball players from the standpoint of a fan, not like a sportscaster." He loved to broadcast from unusual venues. A promotion co-sponsored by United Airlines was the broadcasting of Roger's show live from a 747 en route to Hawaii. Long before the accessible of satellite transmission, KMPC leased transmitter equipment from NBC to beam the radio signal from the airplane off a satellite stationed in the Pacific. Once he got to Honolulu, he broadcast four one-hour shows live from the beach at Waikiki in the evenings preceding KMPC's coverage of Angels baseball. He was the announcer on NBC's *Bobby Darin Show* and the nationally syndicated *Mancini Generation*. In 1979, Roger moved to evening talk as the station was slowly moving out of its MOR/full-service status. When KMPC changed formats on January 1, 1980, Roger was made head of a new Golden West Syndication Features wing. In 1981, he resigned from Golden West to become executive producer of the "Lawrence Welk Radio Show" and owner of KWIP-Salem, Oregon, which he sold in 1991. He has hosted concerts at the Greek Theater, Hollywood Bowl, Santa Monica Civic, Pasadena Civic and the Waikiki Shell with all the top acts in America. Roger claims the enormous success of KMPC was a direct result of "management of attitude. The station manager treated each of us like a professional and we in turned performed like professionals." For all of his voiceover success, he maintains that he never made an audition tape. Roger was one of two announcers who was represented by William Morris and he attributes much of his work to the agency. "I believe you get assignments because of relationships. I lived a quiet life in South Pasadena with my wife and five children. When I performed or was on-air, I was Roger Carroll, the announcer." He is currently a fill-in announcer for ABC Television and pursuing a unique satellite opportunity.

CARRUTHERS, Mike: **KPSA/KLVE**, 1972-75; **KIQQ**, 1979-80; **KHTZ**, 1981-85; **KBIG**, 1987-93.

A common thread that is weaved through Mike's career is his association with network and syndicated programming. In the 1970s he worked on national programming with Robert W. Morgan ("Record Report") and Steve Lundy ("Hitbound from *Billboard*") among others. In 1982 he was the voice of *The Best of the Midnight Special* and narrated a series of "Spotlight Specials" for the ABC Radio Network. For over 15 years, Mike has been producing a daily 90-second feature called "Something You Should Know." Born in Columbus, Ohio, he grew up in Connecticut where he started his radio career at WJZZ-Bridgeport. Mike is a graduate of the USC Journalism School. While in college Mike began his L.A. radio career at KPSA. When the station became KLVE and changed format to Spanish, Mike was the last English announcer on the station. "That night we all left the station, out of work and headed to a Mexican restaurant where we hoisted a few margaritas!" He currently is president of Strand Media Group, Inc., in Los Angeles, which produces national radio programming.

CARSON, Jim: **KBLA**, 1965-67; **KBBQ**, 1967; **KIIS**, 1973; **KHJ**, 1973; **KIQQ**, 1973-89; **KEDG/KLIT**, 1989-94; **KRTH**, 1994-97. Born Vic Gruppie in LaCanada, Jim is one of those strong, solid personalities who fits nicely with a number of formats. The native Southern Californian was a journalism, radio/tv major at Pasadena City College. Jim also went to the Don Martin Broadcast School. He served in Panama and Korea twice as part of American Forces Radio, Korean Network and Southern Command Network in Panama. Jim had a very successful run in morning drive at KFRC-San Francisco and KGB-San Diego. At KBLA he was known as Vic Gee, then at KBBQ as Vic Grayson, working the Country format noon to three shift. Jim's time on KHJ was limited to one week in the mornings before Charlie Van Dyke arrived. He did mornings at "K-Lite." Jim's done voiceover work on a number of tv shows. He left Gene Autry's "K-Lite" when the sister station, KMPC, was sold to ABC/Capital Cities. In late 1994, Jim started fill-in and weekends at "K-Earth 101" where he continues. Jim and his wife Susan have a son named Kit.

CARTER, Big John: **KEZY**, 1969; **KHJ**, 1975; **KEZY**, 1976-79; **KHJ**, 1984-86. Born Johnny Yount, the Bill Wade School of Broadcasting graduate was known as "Spanky Elliott" at KACY-Oxnard and KEZY in the late 1960s. He got started at KNAK-Salt Lake City. Johnny's response to a request to track his career resulted in a three-page letter. The following excerpts reflect on some of his stops: "1967: Ogden 1st Phone was the only thing I ever did that amounted to anything. 1967, KSTN: first crack at mornings. 1969, KEZY: Replaced, or more correctly, succeeded Emperor Hudson for a month. Too young! 1969, KYNO: My call to the Big Time. Named 'Big John Carter' over the phone by programming genius Bill Watson. 1970-71, KGB: Charlie Van Dyke hired me and was the reason I got the big jobs. If it weren't for him, no one would have ever heard of me. I quit unceremoniously when some of my friends got fired. My heroism got me nothing but a lot of bad press. 1972, KCBQ: Jack McCoy was talked into hiring me by some well-intentioned but foolish friends. I screwed up mornings for a couple of months. Jack was always nice to me. I can't imagine what I was thinking. 1972, KFIG: My one and only turn at bat at FM "underground." Lasted a month. 1973, KCPX-SLC: It was the one and only time I got a woman in trouble. Some sort of chastity record for a dj. 1974, KPOI: Hired to do mornings as Maxx Mahimahi, and I victimized the Islands with the notorious election day gag of 1974. I got fired for my trouble. 1975, KHJ: Charlie hired me again. After some months I began to feel extremely unwelcome and bailed. 1976, Eugene: I thought I'd try the small time, and I hated it. I hung around a few months and managed to meet the woman I married, a wonderful gal who nearly killed me a few years later. If she calls, I'm not in. 1976, KEZY: No boss was ever more of a radio person than Rick Carroll, God bless him. 1986-present: I'm on the beach. I have the distinct misfortune of sounding like and looking like Rush Limbaugh." Johnny lives in Central California, working on his hobby of computers.

CARTER, Christy: **KROQ**, 1996-97. Christy works weekend fill-in at "the Roq." Christy was born and raised in a Detroit suburb. She enrolled at the college radio station at St. Clair County Community College in Port Huron. Christy went on to Wayne State College in Detroit to study radio and journalism communications. She spent 8 years at WRIF-Detroit, first as an intern and then working her way up to an on-air shift. "Along the way I was also working evenings at WWGE-Flint and then driving an hour and a half for the late all-night shift at WWDX-East Lansing." After almost a decade at WRIF she made a big decision. "I packed up my horse and dog and moved to California." Christy's first air shift at KROQ was on her birthday, November 20, 1996.

CARTER, John: **KMPC**; **KYSR**; **KFWB**; **KCBS**; **KLIT**, 1989-94. Born in La Crosse, Wisconsin, John grew up in Dallas and got his radio break on KVIL-Dallas in 1973. In 1989, John became part of Transtar Satellite. In 1992, he joined Shadow Traffic and has been traffic or news anchor on a half-dozen Southern California radio stations.

CARTER, Les: **KBCA**, 1963-67; **KPPC**, 1968-71, pd. Growing up in Detroit, Les had "some vague idea about being in show business." Born in the Motor City on February 3, 1943, he wrote a music column while in high school. Les went to college in Kansas where he got the itch to pursue his "vague idea" and headed for Southern California. Starting at World Pacific Jazz Records as a producer and national promotion man, he initiated a once a week air shift on Jazz station KBCA. It evolved into a full-time job where he was able to combine jazz and his love for r&b. A *Billboard* magazine survey listed Les the #1 jazz dj. He joined Tom Donahue in the embryonic stages of "underground radio" at KPPC and soon found himself part of an unsuccessful strike against management. On April Fools Day 1970, Les was hired as pd at KPPC. "Sometimes the pd's would last months, but mostly it was only weeks or days. I made KPPC an alternative to alternative formatted radio. Others were too serious and too political. I wanted the listeners to have fun." He hired the Credibility Gap to do the news and assembled a staff that included Outrageous Nevada, Dr. Demento and Steven Clean. His wife Susan, a.k.a. radio personality Outrageous Nevada, said: "He infused radio with humor, energy and taste. Les was the master of the seamless segue. Artistically blending musical styles and erasing the boundaries that dictated format, he created a bold new sound in radio. He recognized the commonality of great music, no matter what genre." Les, along with Outrageous Nevada and the Credibility Gap covered the Rose Bowl Parade. It was an unprecedented simulcast. He rejected ad agency produced spots and his production staff reproduced the commercials to reflect KPPC's "sensibilities." The *L.A. Free Press* proclaimed: "KPPC...sounds like a miracle, but it isn't." The "miracle" ended in 1971. Word had leaked out that the staff would be terminated and the djs chronicled the news as it unfolded. Listeners made a pilgrimage to the station, waiting for the historical moment. Les told his audience: "We don't know when they're going to pull the plug, but we know they will." And they did, right in the middle of his show during a Roland Kirk track. Static. The county marshal's arrived and the entire staff was fired. Les left radio. "I never felt bitter about leaving KPPC or radio. For me I did what I wanted to do. I loved radio more as a fan. It was time to go." He was writing an article for *New West Magazine* when he was given his first job in television, a script for *Charlie's Angels*. In 1976 Les began a successful career writing and producing for television and movies. Some of Les and Susan's writing credits include: *Homicide: Life On The Street*, *Cagney & Lacey*, *L.A. Law*, and *Almost Grown*. They also wrote the song *Good Old Acapella* which was recorded by the Persuasions and the Nylons. Les was working on a novel when he died of a heart attack at his Ojai home on August 26, 1996. He was 53. His wife asked that in lieu of flowers, "Please listen to the album *Kind of Blue* by Miles Davis and think of Les."

CARUSO, Maryann: **KLSX**, 1997. Maryann works the AAA weekend format.

CARYL, Joni: **KHJ**, 1984; **KMGG**, 1984-86; **KBZT/KLSX**, 1986; **KNX/FM**, 1987-88; **KRTH**, 1994-97, nd. Joni was the morning drive sidekick and news announcer to Robert W. Morgan at "Magic 106," after he hired her away from middays at KHJ. She then moved to KBZT to work mornings with Charlie Tuna. At KNX/FM Joni was the female half of a team that included Warren Williams and Jim Chenevy as news anchor. In the early 1990s, Joni left L.A. to program and be on-air at KMGQ-Santa Barbara. She appeared in *Playboy's* 1986 issue, "Women of the Airwaves," and in the same year she hosted a syndicated special, "Women in Rock." Joni and her ex-husband, Guy Davis (former KBIG dj) met  while working at her first radio job in Yuma. They jocked together as a husband and wife morning team at KERN-Bakersfield. Late in the summer of 1994, Joni returned to the Southland as nd of "K-Earth 101" and morning sidekick once again to Robert W. She is quick to praise her legendary mentor and friend for the past 12 plus years. "I am so lucky to work with the best morning show personality on Earth! Robert W. is truly one of the top radio broadcasters of all time!" Joni can also be heard on the in-flight music system at American Airlines West.

CASE, Dwight: **KHJ**, 1972-81, vp/gm. Born in Modesto in 1929, Dwight is a fourth generation Californian. Dwight started in 1948 as a copywriter for KFRE-Fresno. He worked up and down the coast and arrived in the Southland from KROY-Sacramento in 1972. He was appointed president of RKO Radio Division in 1975 and stayed until 1981. Dwight founded the Transtar Satellite Radio Network in 1981 and was president of Sunbelt Communications. He was publisher and CEO of *R&R* between 1983 and 1987. In 1988 Dwight was president of Networks-America and where he launched all Asian KAZN

(1300AM). Since 1989 Dwight has been president of Motivational Incentives Group and an officer of Western International Media Corporation. He earned his B.A. cum laude from the College of the Pacific (now University of the Pacific) and is an AMP graduate of the Harvard Business School.

CASEY, Steve: **KHJ**, 1977. Steve left the Southland after his stint with KHJ and programmed WLS-Chicago and MTV. He is currently with Critical Mass Research in Carefree, Arizona.

CASEY, Tom: **KZLA**, 1980-83, pd. Tom was working at in Dallas when he was dispatched to Los Angeles to turn KZLA into a Country station to upstage KHJ's premature announcement they were going Country. Many feel that KZLA's aggressive format switch took much of the steam out of KHJ's move from Rock to Country. After 21 years in radio, the nine-year vet of Cap Cities came back from a Thanksgiving vacation to learn that he had been let go from KZLA. Tom went on to program Transtar's Country format for several years. He now owns Research Partnership in Sunnyvale.

CASHMAN, Peter: **KLON**, 1985

CASSANDRA: **KROQ**, 1983. Known as "Mistress of the Roq," Cassandra worked weekends.

CASSIDY, Paul: **KFWB**, 1968-71; **KHJ**, 1971-72, pd and gm; **KLOS**, 1972, gsm; **KGBS/KTNQ**, 1974-79, pd/gm; **KWST**, 1979-81, gm. Paul started his radio career at KDKA-Pittsburgh in 1961 in the sales department. He'd been in hotel management at the Pittsburgh Hilton and arranged details so well for a Westinghouse Public Service Conference that the radio chain hired him. He spent 10 years with Westinghouse, working later at WIND-Chicago, then going to KFWB in January 1968 when it was still a music station. In August 1971, Paul went to KHJ and two weeks later was named manager. The RKO position lasted about a year, then he joined KLOS in sales before being moved to ABC sister station, KSFX-San Francisco. In October 1974 he moved back to L.A. to run KGBS AM&FM. When KTNQ took the AM band to Rock in 1976 and KGBS/FM retained the Country format, he became titular head of both new full-time operations. He was named vp in 1977. Paul helmed the beginning of "the new Ten-Q" radio format. He was active in getting KGBS/AM's signal on 24 hours a day rather than just a daytimer. Paul was let go shortly before the station was sold to the Liberman Brothers in 1979. He managed KOLD/TV-Tucson for a while in the 1980s and then was appointed gm of WKBW/TV-Buffalo. Paul now lives in Dallas.

CASSIDY, Thomas: **KFAC**, 1947-87. Thomas spent four decades with the Classical music radio station as an announcer and left in 1987. "Luncheon at the Music Center" debuted in March of 1965 hosted by Thomas until 1976 and the arrival of new host Martin Workman. Thomas also hosted the "Evening Concert" series sponsored by the Southern California Gas Company. He is retired and currently writing a book.

CASTRO, Daniel: **KPCC**, 1984-97. Daniel gave up a lucrative real estate career in 1984 to work with Mexican-American children. He used music to talk to the kids about staying in school. He goes by the name "Sancho" (Chicano slang for "other guy") on his Saturday evening show. He sends special certificates to youngsters who get good report cards. Daniel works at East Los Angeles College, where he is associate dean of student activities. He also created the Chicano Music Awards with proceeds going to a scholarship fund named for his son, killed at age 8 in an auto accident. Sancho told Gary Lycan in the *OC Register*: "School has to be made a family affair. We as parents should go to school as well."

CAT, The: **KNAC**. El Gato, the Cat, was from Bakersfield. She was on air in the mid-1980s. When she left, she returned to Bakersfield.

CATE, Ira D.: **KMPC**, 1955-60. Ira delivered the morning farm report on Dick Whittinghill's show. He was famous for his "flatulating cows" report.

CATRON, Bob: **KFI**, 1960s; **KROQ**, 1972. Bob was sports director at KFI.

CECIL, Chuck: **KFI**, 1952-73; **KGIL**, 1973-86; **KPRZ**, 1986-88; **KPCC**, 1988-97. Born in 1923, Chuck grew up on a farm in Enid, Oklahoma playing 78 rpm records after school and doing daily chores. When he was 12, catastrophic dust storms sent many thousands of Midwesterners fleeing from their homes and farms. His family migrated to California. He listened to some of the early Southern California radio personalities like Al Jarvis, while he was taking radio courses at Los Angeles City College. His first radio job was on KVEC-San Luis Obispo. He joined the Navy for three years, and when he

was discharged as a carrier pilot, he enrolled in what was then the Broadcast Network School. One of his classmates was Dick Whittinghill who had just left the singing group, the Pied Pipers. Following school, he got radio jobs in Klamath Falls, Oregon and Stockton before landing at KFI in 1956. It was at KFI that his syndicated series, "The Swingin' Years," was developed. At first it only aired for three hours on Saturday mornings. It evolved into a Saturday "Party Time," where his music was played in periods between live remotes of bands from the Ambassador's Coconut Grove, the Palladium and other venues playing Big Bands. The program ran from 1960 to 1968. Over the years, Chuck has conducted and collected a Who's Who of interviews with band leaders and sidemen. His listeners have helped him out by providing rare records. "The Swingin' Years" continues to be the quintessential program of this musical niche. Chuck sends out more than 100 hours of taped shows to some 30 stations across the United States. He's also heard on the Armed Forces Radio Network. In the early 1990s, he rerecorded more than 2,000 hours of Big Band programs, because the old tapes were deteriorating. He has a library of 50,000 records and more than 300 interviews with greats like Louis Armstrong, Woody Herman and Benny Goodman. Asked if he planned a full retirement, he said, "No, I'll be on the air as long as someone is listening."

CHAMBERS, Lee: **KWIZ**, 1990-91; **KEZY**, 1991-92; **KLAC**, 1991-93; **KYSR**, 1992-96. The Buffalo native worked at WNBC-New York prior to arriving in Southern California. Lee was the last jock on KWIZ on March 9, 1991, when the station went Korean. He also does part-time on the Oldies Channel at Westwood One.

CHANDLER, Ben: **KMPC**, 1958-62. Born Ben Morris, he was one of the big voices of radio. In 1961 the *LA Times* named Ben Newscaster of the Year.

CHANDLER, Bob: The former Trojan played 12 seasons in the NFL, eight with Buffalo and four with the Raiders. He retired before the 1983 season due to a knee injury that caused him to miss most of the 1982 season. In the first game of the 1981 season, Bob ruptured his spleen and almost died. It was so severe that he was given a transfusion on the playing field. For eight years during the off-season from football, he attended law school and earned a degree but he preferred announcing. Bob was the radio announcer for the L.A. Raiders. He learned about cooperating with the media from O.J. Simpson: "During our lean years in Buffalo, I'd see him over there at his locker surrounded by reporters. No matter how bad things were going, he'd talk to all of them. O.J. is in a class by himself," he told the *LA Times* in 1985. Bob became a sports reporter for KABC/Channel 7 and co-host of the *2 on the Town* show with Melody Rogers. Bob died in January 1995.

> *"I prayed that the all-night man wouldn't show up so I could be on the radio six more hours."*
> *-Tom Clay*

CHANDLER, Bruce: **KEZY**, 1973-76; **KIQQ**, 1976-85; **KRTH**, 1996-97. Born in Englewood, New Jersey, Bruce moved with his family to Southern California when he was 7. He was given his first transistor radio in the early 1960s. "I think the fact I could take the radio station with me was important. KFXM was the station that influenced me in my early teens and then on March 10, 1962, KMEN went Rock and now the Inland Empire had two stations. I listened to Lyle Kilgore doing weekend news at KFXM and said, 'I want to do that.'" And he did. Bruce started on KMEN in 1967 doing weekend news and then a year later he was a weekend jock. By October 1970, he was working the evening shift. A year later he crossed town to work afternoon drive on KFXM. "It was the first time someone went from KMEN to KFXM." At KIQQ he did mornings with Tony St. James for five years. In the late 1970s, he moonlighted on KWOW-Pomona as Jeff Robins and syndicated a show for many years called, "Romancing the Oldies." In 1982, Bruce started a voiceover career with ICM that has continued with successful campaigns. He was the voice for the Fox/TV show, *Front Page*, and did the 1994 national Mazda campaign. "I spent a few months at KRTH. I'll never forget, I got blown out the same day as the space shuttle blew up and in another way my career in local radio blew up." Since 1986 Bruce has been doing morning drive on what is WWI's Oldies Channel. His format is the second most listened to from all the satellite services WWI offers. He returned to KRTH in August of 1996 for part-time fill-in duties.

CHANDLER, Ed: **KMGG**, 1983-84. Ed arrived in Southern California from KSON-San Diego to replace the morning duo of London and Engelman. In early 1984, Ed went to Transtar satellite Country for three years. He left Southern California for Texas radio.

CHANDLER, Len: **KRLA**, 1968. Len was KRLA's resident songwriter-musician who was part of the legendary "Credibility Gap." He wrote fifteen new songs each week that parodied the news of the day and then sang them within the newscasts. Two days after he arrived at KRLA, Robert Kennedy was killed. Len rushed to the station to sing one of his first original songs: "Let us grieve for all men who are felled by/The violence that sweeps through the land like a death motorcade." He was last seen judging a song writing competition in San Diego in the early 1980s.

CHANEY, David: **KMET**, 1979; **KLOS**, 1979-81; **KEZY**, 1981; **KNX/FM**, 1983; **KMET**, 1985. The mountains of Santa Rosa are a world apart from the glitz, glamour and neon of Hollywood. For David Chaney, he chose the refuge of familiar territory. Born in Australia, he grew up in the Monterey/Salinas area. "I loved the mountains and as a kid would split my time between Big Sur and Lake Tahoe." In the late 1970s, David was visiting his recording engineer brother in Los Angeles and ended up doing the all-night show at KMET. It is impossible to talk to David about his Southern California radio experiences without hearing about B. Mitch Reed. David referred to his B.M.R. relationship in almost reverent terms. "The time was far more important than I realized at the time. It was larger than life." He talked about the volume of mail with photos and drugs that would arrive daily for all of the jocks. After leaving Southern California radio, he hooked up with the "most amazing thing in my life." In 1984, David became a jock on the Pirate ship Laser558. The ship was anchored between England and Holland and was the most listened-to commercial station in Europe, playing a mix of American r&b and European Rock. After a year of amazing stories of being chased on the high seas by different governments, David returned to California working in Santa Barbara and San Francisco. In 1988, he moved to Lake Tahoe to work at KTHX; pursue non-radio projects such as writing technical manuals and articles for outdoor sports publications; and enjoy the mountains. Would he return to Southern California radio? "Nope, I was anxious to get out. I loved the creative buzz, but I just didn't have the temperament. I'm where I belong, in the mountains."

CHAPMAN, Alan: **KUSC**, 1996-97. Alan works morning drive at KUSC.

CHAPPE, Jeanne: **KROQ**, 1978. Jeanne married Zack Zenore and they now live in New Mexico.

CHAPPEL, Bill: **KGFJ**, 1975-84; **KJLH**, 1984. "Dollar" Bill worked late evenings at KJLH. He is now in the computer field.

CHARLES, Chris: **KBLA**, 1965; **KGBS**, 1969-70. On January 1, 1997, "The Original Magic Christian" celebrated 40 years in radio. Born in Chicago in 1943, he moved with his family at age 13 to Whittier. "When I got to L.A. I listened to Bill Ballance on KFWB in the early 1960s and I wanted to be like him in every way." When he was 14 he called every station in the phone book and KDWC in West Covina invited him to the station. "I got a weekly shift playing Arthur Lyman music and my mom had to take me to work and pick me up after my shift." At 17 he began his career at KLAS-Las Vegas. "I was on my way! I was blessed with great pipes, good looks, a great sense of humor, gallons of testosterone and made big money playing poker." His next stop was KUTY-Palmdale. "I got my first taste of concert promotion. The Beach Boys came up for a four-hour show for $500. I got the rest of the money." Chris went on to work at KMEN-San Bernardino as Chuck Christensen, WCFL-Chicago, KYNO-Fresno, WMEX-Boston (he replaced Larry Lujack who was on his way to Chicago), KTAR-Phoenix and KCBQ-San Diego. At KYNO, the md was Al Casey. "I married Al's ex-wife and adopted his daughter. She works as Kelli Casey in Houston radio and I'm very proud of her." Influenced by his experience with the Beach Boys concert, Chris did rock concerts, "happenings" and hootenanny's. "I had briefcases full of sock-hop money...wrinkled 1, 5, 10 and 20-dollar bills." In the early 1970s "The Magic Christian" moved to Canada and worked at two Rock stations. "I was paid the same as Prime Minister Treaudeau." At one of the Toronto stations, Rick Moranis was his board-op. Chris is now working mornings at the Country format from the Jones Satellite operation out of Colorado. "Thirty years ago, Helen Gurley Brown looked me in the eyes and said, 'You should write a book!' If I ever get the time, I will. Folks have told me that if I did write one, it would make Howard Stern's book and movie look like a warm-up act. I've been truly blessed all my life and it's <u>FAR</u> from over."

CHASE: **KLYY**, 1997. Chase works the all-night shift at "Y-107."

CHASE, Eric: **KIQQ**, 1974-75; **KHJ**, 1975, pd; **KFI**, 1975-81. Best-known as Paul Christy, he was Eric Chase during his stay in Los Angeles radio. Born Paul Stelgus, he started his on-air radio career in his hometown of Lewiston, Idaho at the age of 16. He made up his mind to go for a career in radio during the summer of 1965, while studying at the Ogden Engineering School in Burbank for his FCC 1st Class License. Prior to Southern California radio, he worked at KUDL-Kansas City, KYNO-Fresno and KFRC-San Francisco. After KHJ, Eric worked afternoon drive at KFI, where he called himself "El Chasero," and got fired in 1981. "The firing took some of the cockiness out of my system." Eric was the dj on Cheap Trick's album, *Heaven Tonight*. He left L.A. for Seattle and KJR in 1981 and went on to KRBE-Houston in 1983, never to return to Southland radio. "Something I've learned is that people who want to be djs want to be the best they can. And, to an extent, you can train people. I was kind of a natural talent, so that took me a while to figure out." Eric is currently at KHMX-Houston as Paul Christy.

CHATTERTON, Larry: **KHJ**, 1964-65. Larry did afternoon drive shortly before the switch to "Boss Radio."

CHAVEZ, Julia: **KFWB**, 1980-84. Julia was a beat reporter for "news/98," KFWB. She has returned to Hawaii.

97.1FM

KBZT ("K-Best")
January to September 1986

KLSX ("Classic Rock")
September 26, 1986

CHEESE, Jack: SEE Billy Pearl
CHEN-SPRING, Mimi: **KSCA**, 1994-97. Born Mimi 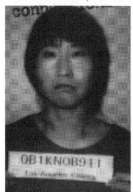 Madeleine Chen-Spring on August 10 in Chicago, she was influenced by two leading New York female djs. Mimi started in radio as a teen on WPST-Trenton which led to WMMR-Philadelphia. As a singer-songwriter she studied piano and violin at Juilliard and studied voice with the woman who coached Barbra Streisand. Mimi joined KSAN-San Francisco and stayed when the format changed to Country. She arrived in the Southland in 1994 from KRQR-San Francisco. Originally married to Chris Isaak in the 1980s, Mimi now lives in Glendale with her second husband and worked evenings on KSCA until the station was sold in early 1997. Currently she is working a&r at 911 Records.

CHENEVEY, Jim: **KKHR/KNX/FM**, 1984-88. Jim was part of the morning team at KKHR and the format/call letter switch to KNX/FM. He was also news and community affairs director and hosted a weekend public affairs program called "Free Form." Prior to joining L.A.'s CBS O&O, Jim worked at WHYT-Detroit, WGAR-Cleveland, KIMN-Denver and WFMJ/TV-Youngstown, Ohio. He attended Kent State. Jim is now with the CBS radio news network in New York and is married with no kids.

CHERIE: SEE Cherie Sannes

CHERRY, Hugh: **KFOX**, 1960-68; **KGBS**, 1968-73; **XPRS**, 1974-75; **KLAC**, 1976. Born in 1922, Hugh's first radio job was WKAY-Glasgow, Kentucky, in 1946 for $40 a week. His first break came when he started in Nashville on WKDA. While still in the Midwest, he appeared on ABC/TV's *Bourbon Street Beat* in 1959. He was a longtime performer on NBC/TV's *Midwest Hayride*. Hugh was voted the #3 most popular country dj as published in *Billboard* in 1967. When KGBS changed from Country to Hot 100 in October 1968, Hugh moved from dj to the news department, and then to all-nights. In 1970, he co-wrote and narrated a 36-hour documentary on the history of country music. Out of the Bill Wade studios, Hugh daily taped for XPRS a country program, which was trucked to Tijuana for airing. When his daily on-air career ended, he became a college instructor and lecturer on country music. His is the voice on Johnny Cash's album, *Folsom Prison*. In 1977, Hugh joined *R&R* as the Country editor and, in the same year, was elected to the Country Music Disc Jockey Hall of Fame Foundation. During the 1980s, Hugh wrote and narrated many country radio specials, including "Country Report Countdown." He penned over 300 album liner notes. The avid bicyclist said in a recent *R&R* interview that survival was his greatest achievement. In 1996 he moved to Nashville.

CHERRY, Marvin: **KBCA**, 1976-78. Marvin arrived in the summer of 1976 from WJZZ-Detroit to work the all-night shift.

CHESTER, Lloyd: **KFWB**, 1968-69. Lloyd was part of the early days of all-News at KFWB.

CHLOWITZ, Allan: **KNX/FM**, 1972; **KHJ**, 1973; **KRTH**, 1974-85, vp/gm; **KTWV**, 1987-92, vp/gm; **KRLA/KLSX**, 1993-95, gm. Born in Newark, Allan started his career at Compton Advertising in New York in 1966 followed by two years at Ogilvy & Mather. His radio career began in 1968 with CBS Radio Sales in New York. At KNX/FM Allan was the director of sales. In the fall of 1995 he was named vp/gm of  KNEW/KSAN-San Francisco and in April 1995 KABL and KBGG-San Francisco were added to his responsibilities and he left in the summer of 1997.

CHONGA, Jimmy: SEE Scotty Wilson

CHRISTIAN, Roger: **KRLA**, 1960; **KFWB**, 1961-65; **KBLA**, 1965; **KHJ**, 1965-67; **KBLA**, 1967; **KFWB**, 1967-68; **KGBS**, 1969-71; **KDAY**, 1971, pd; **XPRS**, 1971-72; **KIQQ**, 1973-74; **KRTH**, 1974-75; **XPRS**, 1978-79; **KRLA**, 1983-84; **XPRS**, 1985-86. There was a gentleness to Roger Christian that conveyed to his listeners an instant ease and a sense of warmth. Some thought he was aloof, but it was his busy schedule that kept him juggling ideas, thoughts and creativity. More often than not, he showed up for his shift after his first record had already been started. Rochester, New York  was where Roger started his radio career on WSAY. He worked as Mike Melody for a couple of years in Buffalo. His inspiration was Guy King on WWOL-Buffalo. Guy was actually Tom Clay. During the summer of 1960, Roger started the noon-to-three shift at KRLA. In 1961 he worked the all-night slot as part of the strike breakers at KFWB. Roger was always active in music. In 1964 his *Beatles Story* album was in the top three on the charts and earned a Gold record in sales. He was one of the original KHJ

"Boss Jocks" during the format's debut in April 1965, working the nine-to-noon slot. Roger returned to KFWB and was on the air when the station went all-News in March of 1968. Someone who was present on the last day of KFWB saw Roger "in tears." He was one of the original jocks (noon-3) when "K-100 FM" debuted. He wrote many of the surf songs popularized in the '60s by the Beach Boys and Jan and Dean. Many called him the Cole Porter of the teens. He wrote *Dead Man's Curve* and *Little Old Lady From Pasadena*. During one particular week while on KFWB, songs that Roger had written were #6, #7 and #8. Because of the payola scandals of the late 1950s and early 1960s, he couldn't play any of his songs until they hit the Top 5. Roger appeared in 17 movies, including *The Carpetbaggers*. In 1975, Roger and Jim Pewter launched Rock Shop with the 6-hour radio special, "The Beach Years." He was also a music consultant to the movie industry and in 1975 worked on *Return to Macon County*. He produced a Denver group called the Moonrakers that eventually became Sugarloaf. At his funeral in June 1991, Roger's brother told KRLA historian, Bill Earl, that Roger had committed suicide. Roger's show close seems somehow prophetic: "That's all she wrote - sleep warm - later, lover."

CHRISTIANSEN, Chuck: SEE Chris Charles

CHRISTENSEN, Ken: **KFI/KOST/KACE**, 1992-95, gsm; **KYSR/KXEZ/KIBB**, 1995-97, vp/gm. Ken worked at sales positions at WBCK-Battle Creek and WYAI and WYAY-Atlanta before joining Eastman Radio and Katz for eight years.

CHRISTIE, Ann: SEE Dr. Leslie Pam

CHRISTENSEN, Todd: **KMPC**, 1992. A native of Oregon, his father was a professor at the University of Oregon. The former Raider tight end graduated from BYU. In 1986, Todd led the NFL in receiving with 95 catches for 1,153 yards and eight touchdowns. In 1988, his totals were 15 catches for 190 yards and no touchdowns. Then, during the off-season, he had his gall bladder removed and came into the 1989 training camp about 30 pounds lighter. They cut him after 10 seasons, five All-Pro seasons and two Super Bowls. After his playing years, he became a football analyst for NBC for two years. In 1992 he joined KMPC for the launch of the all-Sports format and worked middays with Joe McDonnell. Their show was called "Monsters of the Midday." Todd left five weeks later and returned to his home and family in Alpine, Utah. Todd and his wife have four sons. One of his boys has spina befida, a partially open spinal column, which may have prompted his return to Alpine. Todd heads the Athletes for Youth Foundation.

> *"I would love to be remembered as someone who made people laugh and feel a little better...a person who was not as stupid as he looked."*
> —Top Ten personality Rick Dees

CHRISTOPHER, Brian: **KIBB**, 1997

CHRISTOPHER, Jimmy "the Saint": **KNAC**, 1978-87, pd. Jimmy grew up in Northern California. When the former pd left L.A. for KISS-San Antonio, he said, "I've been at KNAC almost one-third of my life - so it's kind of weird." After San Antonio he worked at KZEW-Dallas and in Las Vegas. He has since returned to the Big Sur area.

CHRISTOPHER, Mark: SEE Joe Daniels

CHRISTY, Bill: **KRTH**, 1982

CHU-LIN, Sam: **KFWB**. Sam was an outside reporter during the early days of the all-News station.

CHURCH III, George: **KFWB**; **KLAC**. George eventually went into syndication. He joined the Creative Factory and voiced in-flight programming for the airlines.

CILIANO, Paul: **KEZY**, 1991-92. Paul arrived in Orange County from Knoxville to team with Chris Little in morning drive.

CIPRIANO, Joe: **KHTZ**, 1980-83; **KKHR**, 1983-85; **KIIS**, 1985-90. Joe joined "K-Hits" from WRQX ("Q107")-Washington, DC, where he held down afternoon drive during that station's rise "from #18 to #1 in less than a year." He began his L.A. voiceover career doing the movie trailers and spots for *Porky's II - The Next Day* and *Fast Times At Ridgemont High*. He hosted "Concert Magazine" for the Creative Factor in the early '80s. While at KKHR he was known as Dave Donavan. On camera he was in a Prego Spaghetti national commercial and a co-star in *Knight and Daye*, which focused on two radio personalities from the '40s who are reunited at a San Diego radio station. The sitcom aired during the summer of '89 and starred Jack Warden and Mason Adams. In addition to being known as The Voice of Fox, Joe has a busy voiceover career. He is the image voice of many radio and tv stations and is the co-host (along with Adrienne Walker) of "World Chart Show," produced by radio legends Tom Rounds and Ron Jacobs, heard on over 300 stations around the world.

CISCO, Frank: **KIKF**, 1994-97, pd. For almost three years Frank held down three jobs at KIKF. He was Engineer Frank on the "Charlie Tuna Morning Show." Then at 10 a.m. he became the public service director. On the weekends, Frank turns into "The Cisco Kid" as an on-air country personality. Born in New York he fell in love with music at an early age. After serving in the Marine Corps, he opened his own hobby shop in Southern California while waiting for his music break.

After KIKF broadcast several remotes from his hobby store, he decided to pursue radio. He enrolled at the Academy of Radio Broadcasting in Huntington Beach and then joined KIKF. In late 1996 he was promoted to pd.

CLARK, Carolyn: **KBIG**, 1993

CLARK, Don: **KGIL**, 1973-75. Don was the associate producer of ABC/TV's *In Concert* series and wrote and produced the syndicated weekly *Music Scene U.S.A.* show hosted by Wink Martindale.

CLARK, Gloria: **KFWB**, 1959-63, md. Gloria was the music director for Chuck Blore's "Channel 98." A singer herself, she had a great ear for music and was instrumental in the musical sound of the legendary Top 40 station. She died suddenly in 1963 of a cerebral hemorrhage. Gloria was part of a famous Los Angeles radio family. She was the daughter of Tom Breneman, host of "Breakfast in Hollywood." Her younger brother, Tom, and sister-in-law Betty are profiled elsewhere in this book.

CLARK, Jay: **KRLA/KHTZ**, 1985, om; **KLSX**, 1996-97, pd. Jay was an East Coast executive with Greater Media who was dispatched to Southern California to improve the ratings of KRLA and KHTZ. Much turmoil followed his arrival with the departures of such staples as Dave Hull, Mucho Morales and Emperor Bob Hudson. Jay programmed WABC-New York, WLLZ-Detroit and WTKS-New Orleans before his return to L.A. in the summer of 1996.

CLARK, John: **KBLA**; **KNAC**, 1972-76. John was born in Los Angeles in 1947 and worked at KDON-Monterey and KISN-Portland among other stations prior to joining KNAC.

CLARK, Mel: **KBIG**, 1971-74

CLARK, Mike: **KFI**, 1996-97. Mike works in the news department at KFI.

CLARK, Richard: **KBLA**, 1966. Rick did production at KDEO-San Diego before arriving in Burbank. By 1970 he was working at KLOA-Ridgecrest. His life took a downward turn in recent years, and he died in early 1994.

CLARK, Shirley: SEE Shirley Strawberry

CLARK, Steve: **KHJ**, 1966-67; **KEZY**, 1981-82; **KUTE**, 1982-84; **KMPC**; **KTWV**, 1988-97.

Steve is one of those radio people who truly loves radio. "I was the class clown, a popular kid and president of the senior class in high school in my hometown of Brooklyn. I wanted to be a jock since junior high, figuring it would be a great way to meet girls, and I was right." At 17, Steve served two years in the Army and then two years at NYU. He started his radio career in Albany, then went on to New Haven and Cincinnati. While at WQAM-Miami, he sent a tape to KHJ pd Ron Jacobs. "He liked it, so I came to Los Angeles as a weekend 'Boss Jock' at age 24." Steve stayed a couple of years and was offered a job at his dream station, WMCA-New York. When Bill Drake took over WOR/FM, Steve followed his old RKO bosses and worked nine to midnight. His journey from "OR" took him to WCBS/FM, WRNO-New Orleans, WCFL-Chicago, WQXI-Atlanta and KSTP-Minneapolis. He returned to the Southland in the early 1980s after a stop at KYA-San Francisco. "In 1984 I got tired of all the moving and craziness, became a commodity/stock broker, got married, had two sons and decided to only do radio as a hobby." Steve went to Transtar in the late 1980s and is currently with Westwood One Radio Network, in addition to his on-air role at "the Wave."

CLARK, Wally: **KIIS/KPRZ**, 1982-85, vp/gm. Wally arrived in the Southland from KSD-St. Louis with new pd Gerry DeFrancesco and started as general manager on March 30, 1982. In a major *LA Times* profile in 1983, Wally talked about the success of KIIS. He said it stemmed from community contact and charity work. He said: "It's the willingness to go out and meet the public, shake their hands and get direct feedback on the station - that's the real secret to being No. 1."

CLAUS, Chris: **KFWB**, 1988-92, vp/gm; **KFWB/KTWV**, 1992-96, vp/gm. Born in Evanston, Illinois, in 1949, Chris graduated from Indiana University in 1971 with a Bachelor of Science degree in public administration. He started his radio career at WOWO-Fort Wayne in 1975 as a comptroller. Three years later he was a financial analyst and in 1982 moved to Group W Radio in New York. Prior to joining KFWB, he was vp/gm of KJQY-San Diego for three years. In 1996 Chris was elevated to vp of station operations for CBS Television & Radio. In late summer of 1996 he moved to WOGL-Philadelphia as vp/gm. Chris is married to Judy and has two sons, Max and Nathan.

Subscribe to the quarterly Los Angeles Radio People newsletter. Up-to-the-minute news about changes in the lives of your favorite radio personalities. Call 1.888.Radio57 for a complimentary copy.

CLAY, Tom: **KDAY**, 1960-62; **KBLA**, 1965; **KDAY**, 1966-67, pd; **KGBS**, 1971; **KPPC**, 1971-72; **KIQQ**, 1973; **KWIZ**, 1975; **KZLA**, 1979-80; **KPRZ**, 1980-85; **KMPC**, 1988-89. Wherever Tom played on the air, he left a legacy of stories. Beginning in the 1950s as Guy King in Buffalo, he truly has been one of the most interesting personalities in radio. In Detroit he worked for WJBK, CKLW, WWWW, WQTE and WTAK. At WJBK he was one of the voices of the "Jack the Bellboy" character. His inspirations and pixieish ways would often get him in trouble. In the early 1960s Tom was hired to replace the legendary Alan Freed at KDAY. After a month on the air, Tom announced that Elvis Presley was a very close friend and was in town. "I told the audience that I had just spoken to him and he, because of our friendship, agreed to take phone calls from the fans. I gave explicit instructions to the audience not to try to hold him on the phone, so that more people could have a chance to talk with him. 'Just say, Hi Elvis. I love you.' I then gave out the number of our competitor, KFWB. I thought that if I could impress KFWB with how many listeners I had, they would hire me. The promotion tied up the phone lines at KFWB for two days, and they couldn't make outgoing calls. They were going to sue KDAY for lost revenue, but a public apology was accepted. Needless to say, I was never hired by KFWB." Tom was a visible victim and critic of the payola scandal of the late 1950s and early 1960s. He wrote a letter to the trade publications about the payola confusion and lamented: "What's happened to the day when we were really deejays and would make rounds of distribs for new records, get excited and predict overnight smashes, make the charts instead of following them, play a record seven times in a row, get people to buy records the same day? So we had a little trouble in our biz. Are we going to crawl up in a shell and sit on our fat fannies and let the deejay die?" In the summer of 1960, Tom had a newsletter and commented on payola: "So now they're [distribs and manufacturers] complaining that they have to wine and dine and romance deejays -get them tickets to shows, etc. Don't we even deserve this? Is this also forbidden? If taking a deejay to dinner is romancing us, then they have a lot to learn about love." In between his on-air jobs in Los Angeles, he played Oldies on WCBS-New York and worked at KDEO-San Diego. He frequently returned to the source of his biggest success and greatest frustration during the payola scandal, Detroit radio. In 1971 Tom wrote and recorded a compelling voice version/sound collage of *What the World Needs Now Is Love* that was one of the fastest climbing songs in record history to hit #1 and stayed on the *Billboard* charts for seven weeks. Tom's son, Ron, following in his father's footsteps, became a very successful dj and died of cancer at age 41, leaving a wife and two kids. Son Ron was the number one dj in Louisville for 8 years, and when Tom would visit, he would go on the air with his son. Cancer struck Tom in late 1995 and died the day before Thanksgiving. On a last visit to the hospital before he died, Tom enthused: "I loved radio so much. About an hour before my shift was to end, I would pray that the all-night person wouldn't come in so I could work another six hours." He was 66.

CLAYTON, Linda: **KLOS**, 1987. Linda worked all-nights.

CLAYPOOL, Les: **KRHM**, 1957-65. Les' late night show on KRHM was called "Concert Hall." The retired record executive was an early player of music by Bob Dylan and Peter, Paul and Mary.

CLEAN, Steven: **KPPC**, 1968 and 1970-71; **KMET**, 1971-76. Born Steven Segal, he worked the AOR format throughout his Southern California broadcasting career. Born and raised in Buffalo, he started at a radio station housed in a garage, WNIA-Cheektowaga.  "After the University of Michigan, I went to Berkeley with all good hippie drop-outs in 1968. I heard that Tom Donahue was starting a station in Los Angeles so I bought a Corvair for $100 and drove to L.A. I ended up an engineer for Tom and when Tom didn't make it back from his San Francisco commute, I went on the air." Steven left to program WBCN-Boston and returned a year later to KPPC. In the early 1980s, Steven worked in Boston at WCOZ and WBCN and WMMR-Philadelphia. By 1986 he was on KZEW-Dallas. Ace Young called Steven, "The Lenny Bruce of radio." KMET gm L. David Moorhead said about Steven: "He is one of the finest five air personalities of all time...going back to Dave Garroway." Since 1987 Steven has been living in Milwaukee raising his now 10-year-old son, Alex. "The birth of my son has been the defining moment in my life. I'm attempting to resurrect my sagging radio career at WZTR-Milwaukee. I enjoy it a lot."

CLENARD, Val: **KRKD**; **KMPC**, 1955-72. Val was host of Lucky Lager Dance Time, and music director for the *Gavin* newsletter. In 1972, Golden West Broadcasting made Val news director of KMPC. Val went on to be a news reporter for KNXT/Channel 2. He retired to Las Vegas in the late 1980s. He was born on Valentines Day in 1928 and thus the name Val. He died December 2, 1996, at age 68.

CLEWER, Brian: **KRHM**, 1962; **KFAC**, 1969-72 and 1974-81. The transplanted Englishman arrived in the States in the early 1960s. He's hosted "Cynic's Corner." The former advertising man treated his long-running show strictly as an avocation. His principal work was in the travel business. During the turbulent times at KFAC in the early 1970s Clewer took over *Classics West* and the Listeners' Guild, shortly after both were founded in early 1971.

KKDJ (102.7FM) switches to Top 40 format with Rick Carroll as pd.   **-March 10, 1973**

CLIFFORD, Chuck: **KYMS**, 1969; **KPWR**, 1987-88; **KLAC**, 1988-93. Chuck was "Chopper Charley" at

"Power 106" and was the airborne traffic reporter in both drive times. Born Clifford Foote, a native Angeleno, Chuck's early career included KFXM-San Bernardino and KYMS in the late 1960s, and then stints in Portland and San Francisco. When KLAC dropped the 23-year-old Country format in the fall of 1993, he joined Mainstream Country format at WW1 where he continues in morning drive. While he was a traffic reporter at Metro, Chuck met and married another popular L.A. radio voice, Lisa May. An early musician, Chuck learned to play saxophone and guitar completely by ear. His band "The Tanagers" won a battle of the bands and the group played at a Teen Fair in Hollywood. His met some of the original KHJ "Boss Jocks" and got the "on-air bug." Chuck has a music/computer room set up at home. "This satisfies my musical cravings when I'm not on the Net. It has been a very interesting and extreme 30 years, but I wouldn't have it any other way."

CLIFTON, Charles: **KRKD**, 1965. Charles hosted a program called "Sports Dial" every afternoon. He is noted for race recreations from Santa Anita Park.

CLYDE, Buddy: **KWIZ**, 1965-66 and 1967-73 and 1974. Buddy worked morning drive on the Orange County station three times. For part of his stay he teamed with Fran Marion who was discovered by the gm while singing at the Five Crowns nightclub in Corona del Mar.

COBURN, Bob: **KMET**, 1977; **KLOS**, 1980-94; **KLSX**, 1995; **KZLA**, 1996; **KCBS**, 1996-97. Born in 1948, Bob is nationally known for being the voice of "Rockline" for 12 years. *Billboard* magazine recognized "Rockline" as the best syndicated show for five years. In 1972 Bob worked for Ron Jacobs at KGB-San Diego. Bob joined KLOS in the summer of 1980, from WMET-Chicago, where he was pd. In 1981, he was named assistant pd. Bob was part of the ABC Rock Radio Network and Global Satellite Network but gave up the assignment in the fall of 1993. He left KLOS as part of an overall housecleaning in late 1994. Bob told the *LA Times*: "In a nutshell, they wanted to take the station in a different direction, and we were not part of that direction. We were perceived as part of the past, part of the old. I'd like people to know we're not dead and buried. After all, it's the only thing I know how to do. I'm completely unqualified for anything else." In early 1995, Bob started afternoon drive at the "classic rock" station and a few months later left with a format change to Talk and "Real Radio." In the summer of 1996 he hosted "A Very Special Evening With Crosby Stills & Nash" for the Global Network. At the same time he joined KZLA for weekends and moved to afternoons in the summer of 1996. By the end of 1996, Bob had joined "Arrow 93" in afternoon drive. In the spring of 1997 he returned as host of "Rockline."

COCKER, Gary: **KIQQ**, 1975; **KTNQ**, 1978; **KFI**, 1978. After a brief stint at KIQQ, Gary went to KYA-San Francisco as Captain Boogie and then returned to Southern California on "the new Ten-Q." Gary's now working in San Diego doing weekend production at KCBQ, and since 1991 he has been the voice of San Diego's Channel 6.

CODY, Frank: **KLOS**, 1977-79, pd; **KMET**, 1986-87, pd; **KTWV**, 1987, pd. Frank is the CEO of Princeton-based Broadcast Architecture. Following his first job in Los Angeles at KLOS as the station's second pd, Frank returned to KBPI-Denver as pd and in 1980 was named Sandusky Division pd. He had been the director of programming for NBC's Source Network and NBC Radio Entertainment where he produced concerts and specials. He directed the development of Dr. Ruth's "Sexually Speaking," "Live from the Hard Rock Cafe" and "The Jazz Show with David Sanborn." He came back to the Southland as pd of KMET in September 1986. He made the transition from "the Mighty Met" to "the Wave." Frank fired the KMET staff and a story in the *LA Times* described why the call letters were given up: "I pulled out a bottle of Heinz catsup which I emptied the night before and refilled with a bottle of French's mustard. Everyone looked at the bottle of catsup with the mustard in it and realized that listeners wouldn't accept the same station with completely new music. The whole thing had to go." He was the architect of "the Wave" format. In early 1988 he and his partner Owen Leach formed Broadcast Architecture, a research/consulting firm serving radio, television and other entertainment industries.

> *"To me, KMET wasn't just any job - it was a mission from God, something we really believed in. That's what made all the stuff, later, so depressing."*
> -David Perry

COFFEY, Jay: **KHJ**, 1977; **KIQQ**, 1977-85; **KRTH**, 1985-97. Born in San Francisco, Jay has been heard on the radio in California since 1973 when he gave up a short career as a garage band bass player. Jay worked in Modesto, Yuba City and KMBY-Monterey before coming to the Southland in 1977, where he enjoyed success in afternoon drive. He has studied acting and his tv credits include roles on *General Hospital* and *Capitol*. The Encino resident was the runner-up in a sexiest voice contest. His credits include on-camera tv commercials for Taco Bell, Maxell, Walt Disney Productions and Computerland. In addition to evenings at KRTH, Jay is the music director.

COHEN, Sherman: **KGBS**, 1970; **XPRS**, 1971-72; **KRLA**, 1976-77, pd; **KIIS**, 1977-80; **KRLA**, 1980-82, pd. Sherman's career has been about taking over "broken radio stations and fixing them." Born in Los Angeles, he grew up in Westchester and was influenced by the early Rock days of KFWB and KRLA. Sherman was the first non-campus dj on KXLU at Loyola Marymount College. He had a love for music that was inherited from his late father. After KGBS, Sherman headed for KSTN-Stockton. At XPRS he was part of the "soul x-press" and developed a working relationship with Wolfman Jack. This led to a three-year assignment with a record distributor. Programming stints at KHYT-Tucson, KKLZ and KOMP-Las Vegas, and KRZZ-Wichita followed. During the '90s Sherman programmed XHRM and KUPR in San Diego.

COLE, Bob: **KRLA**, 1959-60. Bob worked noon-to-three in the early days of KRLA. When he left, he went to WHB-Kansas City.

COLE, Bob: **KBCA**, 1978; **KUTE**, 1986; **KMPC/KLIT**, 1988-94. Bob arrived at the Jazz station, KBCA, from rocker KQMQ-Honolulu. At KUTE, he worked all-nights at "the Quiet Storm."

COLE, Nadia: **KLAC**, 1966. The widow of Nat "King" Cole worked the overnight shift on KLAC.

COLEMAN, Jay: **KZLA**, 1981. Born Jay Fritz, he left the Country station to do weekend weather on KNBC/TV. He has become part of the very successful news team as Fritz Coleman.

COLEMAN, Pat: **KBLA**, 1976. Pat left radio to pursue construction in Montana.

COLES, Tony: **KXEZ/KIBB**, 1996-97, pd. Tony arrived at the Soft AC station, KXEZ, from a tour at WLTW-New York. He orchestrated a format change in late summer 1996 to a Rhythmic AC format and call letter switch to KIBB. He was involved in a number of stations in Columbus, Ohio: WVKO, WBBY and WCOL. Tony also programmed WFWI-Ft. Wayne.

COLLETTE, Pat: **KNOB**, 1961. Pat was Buddy Collette's brother. He hosted a gospel show on Jazz-formatted KBCA.

COLLIE, Biff: **KLAC**, 1959; **KFOX**, 1960-63; **KLAC**. Aside from Dick Haynes, Biff was probably the best-known of all country jocks in Southern California during the 1950s and 1960s. Born in San Antonio in 1926, he got his announcing start "broadcasting" between movies at the local drive-in theater at age 13. He was Houston's first country dj. Biff started on KLAC in the late 1950s and moved to KFOX on May 2, 1960. He later returned to KLAC. Biff married Shirley Caddell, who went from publicist for many C&W record labels to cutting a single in 1960 as Shirley Collie. Biff worked at KFOX when *Billboard* reported that Biff was the #1 country dj. He moved to Nashville in 1969 and held various record jobs. In 1973 he syndicated "Inside Nashville" while he was the national promotion director for country product at UA Records. Biff emceed a live album recording by Tex Williams at the Mint Hotel in Las Vegas. In 1976, he edited a book listing Country music radio stations across the country and sold it at truck stops. He was *R&R*'s first Nashville editor and was inducted to the Country Hall of Fame in 1978. During his career, he helped establish the Academy of Country Music. Before his death in 1992, Biff earned the Ernest Tubb Humanitarian Award for his contributions.

Los Angeles Radio People, 1957-97

5 Day's and 5 Knight's

24 Kelly or Kelley's
16 Smith's
14 West's
12 Edwards's
12 Jones's
11 Thomas's
8 Hall's
1 Oogie Pringle

COLLINS, Al "Jazzbo": **KMET**, 1968; **KFI**, 1969-71; **KGBS**, 1970. Al was a high school swimmer from Far Rockaway, New York. He drove to Florida because he heard scholarships were more easily available at Miami University. His big chance came when someone was needed to sign on and sign off for a college professor on the University radio station. Later, there was WIND-Chicago where "Jazzbo" was created. In the 1950s, Al originated the "Purple Grotto" program on WNEW-New York, which stirred the imagination. "I am down there with Harrison [the Tasmanian owl], who, by the way, has been fitted with purple contact lenses to shield his bright orange eyes." Al described the "Grotto" as being three mythical stories beneath the studio, portraying all of its accouterments as though they were real, thereby giving the whole idea a semblance of existence. His trademarks became his characteristic mustache, goatee and jump suit (he owned 150 of them). In 1960, he left WINS-New York for KSFO-San Francisco. In 1968, Al participated in the automated taping of "underground" music for KMET, along with Tom Donahue and B. Mitch Reed. In 1972 he went to WTAE-Pittsburgh and then KMPX-San Francisco. He recorded a successful single, *Little Red Riding Hood*, while working in San Francisco. Al went back to WNEW before returning to the Bay Area on KGO in 1977. In 1981 he was again on WNEW with a show called "Collins on a Cloud." In a *Billboard* interview, he described his love affair with the after-midnight listener: "I feel we are on a one-to-one basis after midnight. I am talking to them and I like to hear them talk back." He currently does a jazz weekend show on the San Francisco Peninsula, at KCSM-San Mateo.

COLLINS, Jesse: **KKBT**, 1994-97. Jesse was brought in for all-nights from WPGC-Washington, DC. He also co-hosted a Saturday night show on "the Beat" with the late Easy-E. Jesse's "official" bio from KKBT tells his story: "Three days after Christmas 1969, his father forgot to give his mother a Christmas present. To make up for this, his father took his mother out for a romantic

evening at their favorite restaurant, IHOP. After tantalizing her palate with the best in cheap waffles, he could see the passion in her eyes and quickly rushed her to 'Ray Ray's Love Shack Motel' and Jesse was born in September of 1970." Jesse was discovered while enjoying a career as a professional game show contestant. Pd Keith Naftaly said: "Craig Wilbraham (gm) and I were amazed at how well he handled the Plinko Game on *The Price Is Right*." Jesse traveled to D.C. in late 1995 for the "Million Man March." He left "the Beat" in early 1997.

COLLINS, Joe: **KMET**, 1974-75. Born Joe Sullivan in 1946, he grew up on the Central California coast. As a youth Joe could tune into stations in San Francisco AND

Los Angeles and was influenced by the early rock and roll radio djs from both markets. But it was a dial twisting experience at age 16 that led Joe to radio. "It was late in the evening and I was driving back from a battle of the bands at Pismo Beach that featured several surf bands when the car radio in my '54 Ford landed on KFWB. Suddenly I realized that there was something very special happening. The guy was more than the typical time and temp, happy horse-shit, smiling good guy. He was saying some really funny, far out, but rather deep stuff for 1962. As he spoke, I felt myself being drawn closer and closer to that radio light behind the dial in my dashboard. Once I heard Bobby Dale, I realized we weren't in Kansas anymore. Bobby inspired me to get into radio." Joe started at KSLY-San Luis Obispo in early 1964, shortly after his 18th birthday. From KSLY he went to KNEZ-Lompoc and then to KFRC-San Francisco as a board op and producer of the morning show, which quite coincidentally starred his idol, Bobby Dale. He stayed at KFRC for seven years and worked with 38 jocks. Beginning in 1972, Joe started moonlighting at the underground FM station in San Rafael, KTIM, as an evening jock and fell in love with the new music. Joe went to KQIV-Portland as pd and in 1974 joined KMET doing weekends and fill-in. "When you do a show in Los Angeles, you experience an endorphin rush like a runner or swimmer. You open the microphone and there's an electricity that runs up your arm and to your brain. I was in and out of various levels of a marijuana buzz. What can I say, it was the '70s." In the late 1970s, Joe went to Fresno where he has programmed various AOR and "classic rock" stations, owns his own production company and is a successful account executive with a tv station. During his career, drugs and alcohol took their toll. Joe entered a rehab program and now lives a life clean and sober.

No Rock! No Bach!
24 Hours a Day
Easy Listening
-KWST, 105.9FM, 1972

COLLINS, Larry: **KOCM**, 1987; **KJOI**, 1987-88. Larry worked weekends at "K-Joy."

COLLINS, Robert: **KFI**, 1969

COLLINS, Roger: **KFI**, 1978-83; **KUTE**, 1983-87; **KLIT**, 1989-90. While at KFI Roger was md and assistant pd. Born Paul Lancaster in Winslow, Arizona, he started his radio career in 1963 in Winslow followed by jobs in Holbrook and Odessa, Arizona. From 1971 until arriving in the Southland, Roger worked in Tucson. He was the sports director of KGUN/TV, pd of KTKT and KRQQ. Roger was director of instruction at the Los Angeles Broadcasters School during much of the 1980s. He was also the om of Breneman Radio Services and the *Breneman Review*. After returning to Arizona, Roger produced video workshops for school kids and was a consultant to Native America education radio for the Navajo Nation. He programmed KAFF AM&FM and KMGN-Flagstaff. He now functions as om of KVNA/KZGL-Flagstaff working under his birth name.

COMB, Bill: **XTRA**, 1967; **KKDJ**, 1971-72. The Lincoln, Nebraskan arrived in the Southland from WUBE-Cincinnati and did noon-to-six for most of his stay on the L.A. rocker, KKDJ. Bill moved into real estate in Victorville.

COMPTON, Paul: **KIEV**; **KHJ**, 1962-65; **KMPC**, 1965-68; **KGIL**, 1969-71; **KFI**, 1971-75; **KRLA**, 1975-76. Frank Sinatra's favorite disc jockey and the host of "Sinatra, Compton and Strings," Paul died April 17, 1996, at the age of 79. During his time on KGIL, Don Page of the *LA Times* awarded him the 1969 MOR radio dj of the year honor. On June 12, 1971, Paul departed KGIL. At his farewell he said, "I hated to leave that beautiful club. They were so great to me. They gave me complete freedom in the selection and sequencing of my music." Page was an enormous fan of Paul's, describing his style as "the original Mr. Cool, a voice like aged Scotch and the ever-present shades." Don said that Paul was the "acknowledged expert on the musical life and times of Frank Sinatra. Each considers the other the leader of the clan." During Paul's stay at KFI, Page said, "Paul Compton is the best disc jockey in the business. No one has better presence than Compton." Paul was on the air the day before Bill Drake launched "Boss Radio" on KHJ. It is rumored that he had an opportunity to be a "Boss Jock" but declined. Born Paul Compton Abbot in Ontario, he grew up in Long Beach and majored in journalism at Los Angeles City College and San Diego State. Paul had a brief career as a club jazz singer.

CONDYLIS, Paul: **KNX**, 1960; **KHJ**, 1963. Paul was partnered with Bob Grant in the early '60s on KNX.

CONIFF, Jim: **KKOP/KAPP**. Jim, the son of Ray Coniff, was a jazz dj at the Redondo Beach station. He started his career in the early '60s at rock stations KHOT-Madera, KFXM-San Bernardino and KAFY-Bakersfield.

CONIN, Al: **KMPC**, 1983-92. Al was one of the California Angel baseball announcers. During the 1994 baseball season he was heard doing fill-in for the San Diego Padres.

CONLEE, Don: **KEZY**, 1985-86. Don worked middays at the Orange County outlet.

CONLEE, Jim: **KTNQ**, 1979, pd; **KHTZ**, 1979-80, pd; **KKHR**, 1983; **KMGG**, 1985. Before joining Southland radio, Jim worked at WKOX-Framingham and in Texas. While at "the new Ten-Q," Storer Broadcasting made Jim national production director. He put together the jingles, promos and bumpers for all stations in the chain. In 1993 Jim was pd of KWFM-Tucson and doing afternoons. In 1995 he went to KLDE/KODA/KLTR-Houston.

CONLEY, Dave: **KTNQ**, 1976-77; **KHJ**, 1978-79. In the late 1960s, Dave worked at KACY-Oxnard as "The Clean Living Kid." Arriving from KSEE-Santa Maria and KCBQ-San Diego, he was one of the original mid-morning jocks on "the new Ten-Q" that premiered on December 26, 1976. KAVR-San Antonio was Dave's home in 1983, and in 1985 he was heard in Portland.

CONNORS, Al: **KHJ**, 1979-80; **KORG**, 1980; **KRTH**, 1986-93. Al was at KHJ during the experiment with "car radio - all traffic, all the time." During the summer of 1993, he went to be pd of KBZS-San Diego. Al is now the production director of Bonneville stations KMBZ/KLTH-Kansas City. He worked at WING-Dayton and in Cincinnati radio prior to arriving in the Southland. "From the moment I got my first transistor radio, I knew I wanted to be a disc jockey."

CONRAD, Rod: **KOCM/KSRF**, 1988. Rod teamed with Cindy Davis in morning drive.

CONRAD, Sean: **KHJ**, 1973, pd. Sean left WDAI-Chicago to program KHJ. When he left the Southland, he worked as pd at KSFX-San Francisco. Sean programmed KCBS-San Francisco during its AOR/Oldies days in 1979 and 1980. He is living in Santa Cruz.

CONWAY, Jr., Tim: **KLSX**, 1997. Tim teams with Doug Steckler in afternoon drive at "Real Radio."

COOK, Charlie: **KHJ**, 1981-82, pd; **KLAC**, 1982-83, pd. Charlie's contribution to Los Angeles radio was in the programming arena. Born Robert Catalano and growing up in Detroit, Charlie has programmed WWVA-Wheeling, WHN-New York, WGBS and WMXJ-Miami. He was *Billboard* magazine's Air Personality of the Year in 1977. Charlie hosted a number of nationally

syndicated shows, including "Country News," "Country Music's Top Ten" and "Solid Gold Country." Charlie's currently hosting Westwood One's "Country Six Pack." He was nominated for 1983 CMA DJ of the Year. Charlie has served on the board of directors of the Country Radio Broadcasters since 1984 and is currently the secretary of the organization. He organized the Organization of Country Music Broadcasters convention in 1984. Charlie is also the former president and chairman of the board of the Academy of Country Music. Charlie lives in Los Angeles with his wife Erica Farber, COO of *R&R*. After 12 years as head of the country format division of McVay Media Radio Consultants, in late 1996 he joined WW1 as vp of programming/formats.

COOK, Del: **KGFJ**; **KLON**, 1988-90. Del was a former Hanna-Barbera writer-producer. He died in 1991.

COOK, Ira: **KFAC**; **KABC**; **KMPC**, 1949-71; **KVFM**, 1972. Ira started his Los Angeles career at KFAC, but his success and long-term longevity came at KMPC. He began at KMTR as a record librarian and sometime announcer. He had just graduated from Stanford with a degree in basic medical science. His love affair with radio started at age 8 on a visit to a local station with his father. After World War II service, Ira hosted Lucky Lager Dance Time on KFAC. He also had a fascination with being a songwriter. In a 1957 *Newsweek* story connected with a payola probe, Ira made the following comment about being a dj: "It's safer than stealing, more legal than gambling, easier than loafing, and it beats working!" He made a career out of his association with Hawaiian music. He played one Hawaiian song an hour and brought Don Ho to the Mainland at the height of Ho's career. Another popular feature was "Star of the Day," in which Ira featured one track from one artist every half-hour. Between 1960 and 1972, Ira hosted over 3,000 AFRTS programs "It was really fascinating getting letters from servicemen in Iceland asking about Hawaiian music. It seemed to be as popular there as country music." He had an extraordinary relationship with sponsors. Wallichs Music City sponsored his program for 20 years and Felix Chevrolet for 10. In 1968 Ira appeared in the Gene Barry tv series, *Incident in Berlin*. About the same time, he was broadcasting a show called "Lunch With the Stars," from Universal Pictures' lot, each day at noon.

"The Big X over Los Angeles featuring Negro deejays"
-*XERB slogan, 1966*

COOK, Jay: **KIIS**, 1979-80, vp/gm. Jay was also the Gannett Radio Division president/gm.

COOK, John: **KIIS**, 1996-97, pd. John spent a year at the helm of one of the country's most successful stations, KIIS. He worked worked earlier in his career at KIIS in 1984 as research director and went on to program KHKS and KKBQ-Houston. John also programmed WYXR-Philadelphia. He left KIIS in the early summer of 1997 and joined KKPN-Houston.

COOK, Jonathan: **KLSX**, 1995. Jonathan was heard during the transition from "classic rock" to Talk radio in the summer of 1995.

COOK, Lou: **KABC**. Lou was a longtime KABC announcer. He was one of the original hosts of the popular Sunday night program, "Religion on the Line."

COOKE, Dave: **KHJ**, 1977-78; **KABC/KMPC/KTZN**, 1996-97, pd. Dave joined the Talk combo, KABC/KMPC as pd in the summer of 1996. He started his radio career in 1970 as news anchor at WFAA-Dallas and later as nd of KNUS-Dallas. Between 1973 and 1977 he was nd of WHDH-Boston and worked at KFRC-San Francisco. At KHJ he was news and public affairs director. In 1979 he was vp/nd of RKO Radio Network. For the past decade he was part owner of a consultant company. He has been a consultant to KIRO and the "Buzz" in Seattle, KXL-Portland, KRLD-Dallas, KCMO/KMBZ-Kansas City and KMOX-St. Louis. Dave holds a B.A. in journalism from the University of North Texas. He and his wife Landy moved to the Southland from San Francisco.

COOLEY, Brian: **KKBT**, 1994. Brian was part of the morning "House Party" broadcasting sports and news.

COOPER, Alex: **KXLA**; **KLAC**. Alex "pick up a couple of bucks" Cooper was one of the KLAC "Big Five" djs in the fifties. He died within a few years of leaving KLAC.

COOPER, Bill: **KRLA**; **KFWB**, 1990-97. Bill is one of the news reporters for all-News KFWB.

COOPER, Bob: **KABC**, 1958, pd. Bob was from KONO-San Antonio.

COOPER, Brandt, **KMPC/FM**, 1988. Brandt worked overnights at KMPC/FM from KPLX-Tucson.

COOPER, "Cajun" Ken: **KFI**, 1983-84; **KZLA/KLAC**, 1989-93; **KYMS**, 1994-95. Ken arrived in the Southland from a five-year million dollar contract at WEZB ("B-97")-New Orleans. Six months later he joined WFYR-Chicago. During his six months at KFI, he was known as C.K. Cooper. He told the *LA Times*: "They were nice

enough to let me out of my contract." He said he was "displeased with the very fast lifestyle of Los Angeles." Ken returned to Southern California for mornings at KZLA in 1989. When he was let go, he turned to the public in an effort to get his job back. His ad in the *Times* and *LA Daily News* read. "**WHERE'S KEN COOPER?**" - and included copy offering a phone number. His phone message: "Hi! This is Ken Cooper. I wanted to let you know that it was not my idea to leave KZLA. Now, if you're mad or upset about it, write to the gm of KZLA in Burbank and tell him `Bring back Ken Cooper.' Your one letter can make a big difference." In 1990, a KZLA listener, apparently distraught over marital problems, called the station and threatened to shoot himself if Ken didn't take the call and talk to the caller's wife. Ken was unreachable and the man shot himself. During a tv interview, Ken recalled that in 1992, when he and his wife had faced a personal tragedy in the death of their first child, he received hundreds of messages of concern and condolences and couldn't turn his back on the fans. Ken was the om and did mornings at Christian music station, KYMS until the spring of 1995. In the fall of 1995, Ken started mornings at WRBQ-Tampa/St. Petersburg.

COOPER, Marc: **KCRW**. Marc reported news on KCRW and was a writer for the *L.A. Weekly* and is a syndicated writer for *Nation Magazine*.

COOPER, Mark: **KWST**, 1976-78, pd. Mark left "K-West" to do promotion for Motown Records and eventually became music director of KMEL-San Francisco.

COPPOLA, Marc: **KLOS**, 1977. Marc is the nephew of *Godfather* director Francis Ford Coppola and sister of Carmine. He appeared in *Apocalypse Now* and *Cotton Club*. During the 1990s he worked fill-in for WKRS-New York and is currently with WAXQ-New York.

CORRALES, Jay: **KRLA**, 1994-97. Born and raised in Southern California, Jay became infatuated with radio listening to Huggie Boy. "Huggie Boy sparked a major interest in radio for me and I went to the Columbia School of Broadcasting in Hollywood. I worked afternoons at their station, AM1000, that could be heard for an 8-block radius. And now I follow him." Rick Diego was Jay's mentor. Jay started as an intern and pd Mike Wagner put him on the all-night shift where he continues.

CORDIC, Rege: **KNX**, 1966; **KRLA**, 1981-82. After a very successful run at KDKA-Pittsburgh, Rege arrived at KNX when longtime morning man Bob Crane left the CBS station to star in the tv show, *Hogan's Heroes*. When Rege left KNX he turned to acting and became a voice mechanic. The stately-looking actor frequently played the judge in tv courtroom dramas. He had a featured role in one of Darren McGavin's *Outsider* episodes on NBC. Rege worked morning drive at KRLA.

CORNELL, Skip: **KIQQ**, 1975

> *"We figured we'd be here awhile, then return East, but we liked it and stayed."*
> -Charlie Sergis

CORY, Bob: **KNOB**, 1966; **KEZY**

COTTON, King: **KIEV**, 1992; **KWIZ**, 1992-93. Former Bonedaddys front man, King Cotton's White Blur Show provided an oldies alternative.  The program blended vintage r&b with edgy comedy. King Cotton's show eventually was heard on the Cable Radio Network. Born in Houston, King Cotton is a band leader working in Southern California with a nine-piece r&b vocal group. He is an actor, a session singer, does commercial voiceovers and compiled CD reissue paks.

COUSSEY, Russell: **KJLH**, 1995. Russell hosted a reggae music show on KJLH.

COWAN, Brian: **KIKF**, 1995. Brian is known on-air as "Bubba." He got his stint at KIKF after interning while at Cal Poly Pomona. Brian received a B.S. degree in human resources management.

COX, Chris: **KEZY/KORG** 1991-97, pd. Chris arrived in the Southland from programming chores at WVEZ-Louisville and WLLT-Cincinnati. The mid-morning on-air pd is married to KFWB news anchor Vicki Cox. In early 1995, Chris was promoted to station manager for KEZY and co-owned Fairfield Communication outlet, KORG.

COX, Daryl: **KGFJ**, 1990. Daryl worked middays.

COX, Don: **KHJ**, 1977-78. In the mid-1980s, Don was the subject of an investigative series on payola in the music industry in *Rolling Stone* magazine and NBC reports by Brian Ross. His whistle blowing almost cost him his life when he was kidnapped and left for dead in a Florida swamp. He lives in Florida, works at WPOW-Miami and hosts a local tv show.

COX, Doug: **KRLA**, 1968-69, pd; **KPPC**, 1970-71, gm. At the age of 29, Doug took over the helm of KRLA from being the regional promotion man for Atlantic Records. He came out of nowhere, and when Doug left KPPC he never worked in radio again. His brief stay, however, had a career-changing impact. Doug was born in Hollywood, grew up in Pasadena and lived for a time in Santa Barbara. From the road, where much of his time is spent as a motivational trainer and counselor, he said, "I was talking with KRLA's news person Cecil Tuck and he thought I would be perfect for radio. He offered to help if I ever wanted to pursue a job in radio. He told me this the day I was fired from Atlantic." Cecil introduced Doug to the station's gm and he was hired. Doug wanted to move the station in a new direction and his first job was to convince the sales team that dollar volume could be increased by, as he said, "playing large records with small holes instead of small records with big holes." It flew in the face of what the station was doing. With the theme of the times reflected in music like *Get Together*, Doug created "a sensual, long-play weekend." He said that he learned music from Johnny Hayes and spiritual growth from Dick Moreland. Doug took the automation out of KRLA and returned the station to personality radio, including Jimmie Rabbit in the evenings. "Rabbit would challenge his audience with respect and admiration." For a brief time, his sister Sue ran the station. Doug recorded as J.P. Raggs for World Pacific Records, wrote a Bobby Goldsboro top five song and did the theme to David Wolper's movie, *If It's Tuesday, It Must Be Belgium*. "I was profoundly affected by radio. During my time at KRLA I spoke to a group of educators on the subject of why young people would listen to the radio instead of the teacher." That experience influenced his decision to spend the next quarter of a century as a motivational trainer to such corporation as Redken, Wells Fargo Bank and the Trump empire. Doug is based in Las Vegas.

COX, Kelly: **KLOS**, 1994-97. Kelly joined KLOS as a part-timer from KCQR-Santa Barbara. She got her first  job in Texas at Country KSPL. Having spent her teen years in Mexico, Kelly had very little exposure to country music and thought she would hate it. "I was having a blast at KSPL and moved to middays and production duties in just three short months." She spent her formative rock years at KOME-San Jose from 1979 to 1983. She dropped out of radio for a return to Puerto Vallarta, then she returned to school and in 1991 earned a B.A. with honors in political-science from the University of California Santa Barbara. While in college Kelly worked at KCQR. "In late 1994, upon returning from a ten-day vacation in Kauai, my boyfriend and I tuned in at the top of the Conejo Grade on our way home from LAX and discovered a format switch to Spanish on KCQR." Kelly is ubiquitous at KLOS doing vacation fill-in, assisting in production and hosting the "Local Licks" show every Sunday night.

COX, Tony: **KFWB**, 1969-84. Tony started as a writer while in college. He later went on to television news.

> "Asian programming is in its infancy, just like Spanish radio 20 years ago, and Asian is going to be huge."
> -Dave Sweeney

COX, Vicki: **KFWB**, 1989-97. Vicki is a news anchor, editor and reporter with KFWB. Vicki started her broadcast career doing high school news on, as she called it, "an itty bitty station in Southern Illinois." From  Evansville, Indiana, Vicki worked for a decade in Cincinnati at WLW and WKRC. She is married to KEZY pd Chris Cox. "Chris had always wanted to live in California, so when the opportunity arose, we packed up and moved kids, cats and U-Haul. We left the cold hot, humid Midwest arriving a month before a sizable earthquake that really initiated us." Vicki truly became acclimated to Southern California when it dawned on her, "that I wouldn't have to do school closings on snow days anymore."

COYLE, J.: **KALI**, 1967, vp/gm

CRANDALL, Brad: **KFI**, 1974. Brad passed away in the early 1990s.

CRANE, Bob: **KNX**, 1956-65; **KMPC**, 1972-73. Bob is best known for his starring role as Col. Robert Hogan in *Hogan's Heroes*. He played the rakishly handsome leader of a merry band of World War II Allied airmen in a German POW camp for six years beginning in 1965. His nine-year radio career on KNX was like a late-night tv variety show, only on radio. He was brash, irreverent, quick-witted and the master of the innocent insult. Initially, his contract forbade him to do tv. He loved to act and spent a number of years in dinner theater. When his tv exclusion clause expired, Carl Reiner put Bob on *The Dick Van Dyke Show*. He played Dave Kelsy on the *Donna Reed* series. His morning competition was KMPC's Dick Whittinghill, with whom he developed a feud that raged for nine years; they were contemptuous of each other. When Bob returned to Southland radio briefly on KMPC, he said, "I want to go out like Nelson Eddy, you know, die while I'm working." His tv show was in an era when contracts did not allow series stars to get rich from residuals. After a quickly canceled 1975 sitcom, *The Bob Crane Show*, and some tv guest shots, Crane had settled into the nomadic limbo of Sun Belt dinner theater. On June 29, 1978, Crane was beaten to death as he slept in a Scottsdale, Arizona, apartment. According to a coroner's report, his face, bloodied and swollen from beatings, was unrecognizable. He had an electric cord tied around his neck in a bow. In 1994 a Phoenix jury acquitted a man accused of killing Bob. The accused had been a longtime friend of Crane's.

CRANE, Charlie: **KLAC**, 1970

CRANE, David: **KLAC**, 1965-69, pd. David went from news director to pd at KLAC and then to KGO-San Francisco. He started his broadcast career while attending New York University, first at WINS-New York. After graduation with a B.A. in communication arts, he joined WDEV-Waterbury, Vermont. In the early 1960s he worked at WPTR-Albany, WCKR-Miami and WIP-Philadelphia. David bought a station in St. Augustine, Florida.

CRANE, Frank: The advertising and radio executive was the former president of the Southern California Broadcasters Association and a campaign manager for the March of Dimes. During the Bicentennial celebration, Frank traveled with the Freedom Train. A colleague remarked: "Frank was always promoting." He died of cancer in July 1992. Frank was 77.

CRANE, Fred: **KFAC**, 1947-87. Born in 1919, Fred was a classical music announcer for four decades. Fred came to Los Angeles in the late 1930s from New Orleans and wanted to be an actor. He auditioned for and won the role of one of the Tarleton boys in the classic film, *Gone With the Wind*. In fact, Fred's line is the opening line in the first scene of the film. After his film debut, he became a radio announcer for KFAC, where he held forth for well over 40 years as the morning drive time announcer until being dismissed on New Year's Day 1987. Fred successfully sued the station for $1 million for punitive damages and reinstatement of his job when he was dismissed and replaced by younger announcers. Occasionally, Fred is cast in soap operas like *General Hospital* and other tv shows.

CRANE, Les: **KLAC**, 1969-70. Born Les Stein, he started his radio career at KONO-San Antonio in 1958 and later worked at WPEN-Philadelphia. He became very popular in San Francisco radio as Johnny Raven. In 1961, Les was working at KGO and KYA and was awarded the *Gavin* PD of the Year award. In 1965 Les was the host of an unusual late night ABC/TV talk show that lasted only 14 weeks. His identity gimmick was going into his studio audience with a shotgun microphone. He also sat perched on a high chair above his guests. Les was married to Tina Louise of *Gilligan's Island*. He recorded the hit talking single, *Desiderata*. Les went on to an enormously successful career in computer software.

> "Orange County needed me more than I needed them. I was trying to fill a void."
> -Dr. Timothy Leary

CRANN, Tom: **KUSC**, 1991-92 and 1994-95. Born in New Jersey in 1965, Tom grew up in the New York area listening to some of the classical music greats. He earned a degree in English literature from Providence College and has worked in broadcasting since his graduation. He arrived in the Southland from WNED-Buffalo. Tom left KUSC to be production manager at WNED. In a 1992 *LA Times* profile of KUSC, Tom commented on the subtle changes to the classical music presentation: "There's a certain element who thinks that if we open the music up to anyone, it will no longer be their domain. They think that if people aren't appropriately serious enough, it won't be for the elite or the intellectuals anymore. That scares me a little bit." Tom returned to KUSC for the second time from Buffalo and worked morning drive. He left KUSC in late 1995 for a new post with Minnesota Public Radio. (As part of "Classical 24," Tom is heard in Los Angeles through Public Radio International.) Tom remembers his experience in the Southland: "Despite earthquakes, riots, mud slides, fires and sig-alerts, I look back fondly on my L.A. stints; and the opportunity to work alongside such impressive talent, both at KUSC and the L.A. market at large. In hindsight, it was a great experience for me."

CRAWFORD, Jean: **KCBH**. Jean Crawford owned KMGM (later KCBH) in Beverly Hills and programmed classical music from the stock of Crawford's, the family music store. A favorite feature of the station was "Concerto From Coldwater Canyon." Her husband A. Arthur Crawford was the gm. They sold the station in the mid-1960s and it became KJOI and, in 1990, KXEZ. Jean died in September 1991 at the age of 84.

CRAWFORD, Dick: **KFAC**, 1948-83. Dick hosted a light classical music show in the afternoons called "Continental Varieties."

CREAGH, David: **KLON**, 1981-85, gm. David was responsible for turning the Long Beach State station into a jazz outlet. Before his arrival he produced "All Things Considered" for NPR. He left in the mid-1980s to program a new public radio station in Baltimore.

CRIDLAND, Diane: **KABC**, 1992-94, pd. Diane joined the ABC O&O from Florida radio. When she left KABC in 1994 she programmed KDKA-Pittsburgh and has since moved to all-Sports radio in Pittsburgh.

CROCKER, Frankie: **KGFJ**, 1968-72; **KUTE**, 1979-80. Frankie first started working at WBLS-New York in 1971 when it was known as WLIB/FM and programmed it until 1976. Two years later, he returned for a second programming stint in L.A. Frankie was brought in to duplicate his success with the "New York disco sound." Failing to make his mark, he returned to New York and WBLS. He was named vp of entertainment and programming of Inner City Broadcasting a year later. He left Inner City again in March 1994. In the mid-1980s, Frankie was hosting *Friday Night Videos* and was one of the original VH-1 veejays. In 1987, Frankie became a consultant to WRXR-Chicago and also programmed WGCI-Chicago. He was on-air at WWRL-New York and WMCA-New York. In early 1994 he was hosting the "Quiet Storm" show via satellite to WBLS from his home in Coldwater Canyon. In late 1995 Frankie rode back to New York as "the Sheriff" and rejoined WBLS for the fourth time.

CROFFORD, George: **KPOL**, 1960-72. The Los Angeles native worked evenings at KPOL.

CROSS, Lee: **KGFJ**, 1968

CROSS, Tom: **KGFJ**, 1968-74. When the Memphis-born deejay arrived in Los Angeles, he was called "Cross the Boss." In addition to his midday jock duties, Tom operated Cross-Trax tapes, a 2-track recording studio specializing in production of commercials for albums. He also wrote a music column for *Singles Register* and *Hollywood Music News*. He left radio to join Revered Ike. One of his fellow jocks saw him many years after his radio career driving a Rolls-Royce.

CROSSWHITE, Paul: **KJOI**; **KNX/FM**; **KWST**, 1970s; **KFWB**; **KEZY**, 1980; **KNX**; **KRTH**, 1985; **KFI**; **KHJ**, 1988; **KFWB**, 1990; **KTWV**, 1990-97. Paul did news during most of his tenure in Southern California radio and has received Golden Mike Awards for documentary, feature and best newscast. He did news during the glory years of KNX/FM. During the Gulf War, he won the Associated Press Award for best newscast. When he moved to "the Wave," he gave

up news to become a deejay, originally in the evenings and, later, mornings after the abortive female morning drive team collapsed. In the summer 1995 *Wave Newsletter*, Paul talked of his morning assignment: "There's something almost magical about the music we play on 'the Wave.' From the moment I became morning host, I felt that soothing effect. It can elevate one's mood - even before the sun comes up - into something really positive and good-feeling."

CROWE, Daniel: **KMQA**, 1995-96, vp/gm; **KRTO**, 1996-97. Daniel worked Spanish-language media at Telemundo, KVEA/TV and Galavision TV network and was gsm of KWHY/TV before joining KMQA in late 1995.

CROWE, Deana: **KFI**; **KLAC**, 1982; **KMPC**, 1982-83; **KHTZ**, 1985; **KTWV**, 1987. At the launch of "the Wave," Deana was the only live voice performing news duties in morning drive. She worked the all-night shift at KMPC and left radio for television. Deana also worked as Carrie York. She briefly hosted one of the home shopping networks.

CROWE, Jim "The Cutter": **KLSX**, 1990. Born in San Francisco, Jim grew up listening to KFRC. How did he become "The Cutter"? Jim said that not many people know but, "I was ready to go on a new station, and the pd was concerned that the name Jim Crowe could be misunderstood as racist. He told me to come up with a list of possible names. My girlfriend came up with a list of 15 names. I was really farting that night, and she said, 'you really know how to cut them. You are a real cutter.'" So on a lark, Jim put Cutter on the list. The pd loved the name, and Jim has been known as "The Cutter" ever since. Jim arrived at the "classic rock" station from KSDO-San Diego. When Howard Stern took over the morning show on KLSX, schedules had to be juggled and Jim left. He eventually was offered an opportunity to program and work at WAQX ("95X")-Syracuse for a year. He has given up radio and since July 1991, he has worked as a promotion manager for Mercury/Polygram Records.

CROWELL, George: **KHJ**, 1959; **KPOL**, 1960s. George was a newsman during his stay in L.A. radio.

CROWELL, George: SEE George Wilson

CROWLEY, Mort: **KHJ**, 1963. The funny morning man arrived in Southern California from WKNR-Detroit, WLS-Chicago and KXOK-St. Louis. He was honored by UCLA for hosting the school's annual Mardi Gras for underprivileged children. Mort has since passed away.

CRUMMEY, Joe: **KFI**, 1988; **KMPC**, 1994; **KFI**, 1994-95; **KMPC**, 1995-96; **KLSX**, 1996; **KMPC/KTZN**, 1996-97. Born Edward Joseph Crummey III in Loudonville, New York, in 1954, Joe hosts the Crummey talk show. He started his radio career at WAAF-Worcester and moved on to WCOZ-Boston and WNBC-New York. When he first started on KFI, he worked weekends. In the early 1990s Joe worked live tv talk in San Diego. In 1993 he lost the hearing in his left ear when the removal of a benign brain tumor required severing the auditory nerve. "Sometimes it's like being in the middle of a very bad drunk that won't go away," he told Gary Lycan of the *OC Register*. "I was looking up at one of those kites at Huntington Beach and almost passed out. This totally destroys your notion of

invincibility. You think you've got so much time, when in fact every day you're alive you're damn lucky." Beginning in 1995, Joe worked early afternoons on "710Talk KMPC" until the spring of 1996. During the summer of 1996 he worked fill-in at "Real Radio," KLSX. He returned to KMPC in the fall of 1996.

CRUZ, Alfredo: **KLON**, 1997

CRUZ, Dennis: **KKBT**, 1991-97. Dennis was born in San Francisco on June 12, 1956. He went to Riordan High School and graduated with an A.S. in criminology (he wanted to be a cop) from San Francisco City College. "I was a Teamster truck driver in the Bay Area. My last job before John London brought me into the radio biz was with a rendering company, where my duties were to pick up used frying grease and dead animals, and bring them back to the plant, where they would be rendered into different products such as the base for soap and lipstick." He started his radio career when he called in to London's show at KKBT's sister station, KMEL-San Francisco with an Elvis impression. Dennis pestered John for years on the request lines while doing his regular job as a truck driver and was finally offered the position of sports director. He followed London's "House Party" to KKBT in 1991 as producer and also does character voices and hourly sports reports.

CRUZ, Suzy: SEE Suzanne Ansilio

CUERVO, Dan: **KIIS**, 1996-97. Born Sean Lynch, Dan hosts the KIIS Saturday night retro show. He is the director of national promotion for Priority Records.

CUETT, Peter: **KJOI**, 1987-88. Peter worked weekends at "K-Joy."

CULVER, Howard: **KLAC**, 1965-69; **KGIL**, 1969-74. The former newsman started as a radio actor acting in the drama, "Straight Arrow." He had a recurring role as "Howie" on CBS/TV's *Gunsmoke*. Howard traveled to Hong Kong and contracted spinal meningitis. He died in the early 1990s.

CUMMINGS, Brian: **KIIS**, 1975-76. Brian worked all-nights at KIIS.

CUMMINGS, Rick: **KPWR**, 1991-97, pd. Rick has been with Emmis Broadcasting since 1980 and was the third employee hired. He was made programming vp in 1984. After serving three years as pd of Emmis powerhouse KPWR, he was promoted to head of programming over eight company stations. He is now a vp at KPWR.

CUNNINGHAM, Darby: **KPPC**, 1986, gm

CURELOP, Carey: **KLOS**, 1989-91, pd; **KQLZ**, 1991-92, pd; **KLOS**, 1992-97. From stops in the 1980s at KFMG-Albuquerque, WABX-Detroit, WSUN-Tampa/St. Petersburg, WLLZ-Detroit, WYNF-Tampa and WRIF-Detroit, Carey arrived in the Southland as pd of KLOS in October of 1989. In 1991, he briefly served as pd of KQLZ, "Pirate Radio." When hired by "Pirate," Curelop told Gary Lycan in the *OC Register*: "KQLZ made some 'textbook mistakes' during the year Shannon was at the helm, and we'll have a chance to turn things around." He was back at KLOS within a year and stayed until early 1997.

CURTIS, Benson: **KRHM**, 1957-65, gm; **KBCA**, 1973-76. Benson grew up with Dixieland jazz in a sleepy Missouri River town 60 miles from Sedalia, where Scott Joplin once played at the Maple Leaf Club and traditional New Orleans jazz could be heard on the big river boats that paddled up the Missouri. He has a collection of dixie music acquired over 50 years. "Funny, it was originally known as jass," he told the *LA Times* in 1973. "It is a music which has defied simple explanation or description." Benson began his radio career in Los Angeles in the late '20s, during the pioneer stages of AM radio and did dance remotes from the Coconut Grove, Roosevelt Hotel, the Montmartre and Sebastian's Cotton Club.

CURTIS, Mac: **KLAC**, 1971; **KBBQ**, 1971; **KFI**, 1973-74. Mac was a full-time singer when he joined KLAC. He worked briefly for Alto Fonics Production facility in 1973. Mac lives in Dallas and produces the syndicated Evans and Harmon Show.

CURTIS, R.J.: **KDUO**, 1978-80, pd; **KLAC/KZLA**, 1980-85 and 1993-95, pd. When R.J. left KLAC in 1985, he had survived two gms and three pds in a half decade. In 1993, he returned to KZLA, where he once worked as a weekend announcer to be om. In between his two stays at KZLA, he was pd at KNIX-Phoenix. In 1994 he was nominated for *Billboard*'s program director of the year. R.J. left KZLA in late 1995. In January 1996 he joined After MidNite Entertainment as om. Since the fall of 1996 he has been pd of KCYY-San Antonio.

CUSTER, Fred: **KPOL**, 1955-65, gm. Fred is retired and living in Glendale.

CUTTING, Dick: **KFWB**, 1968-70. Dick played "Manners the Butler" on tv. The former KFWB anchor died in the Motion Picture Home. A colleague remembered: "One of the nicest guys I've ever worked with. He had a voice that mad the studio glow when he walked through the door."

"Listen to KIIS for 30-minutes and you'll feel better about being alive."

-Ads and billboards in 1970 when KRKD became KIIS/AM

A LOOK UP FROM "UNDERGROUND" RADIO
by
Billy Juggs (from Hong Kong)

I moved to Haight-Ashbury in 1967 during the "summer of love." I remember the day someone told me, "There's a new radio station playing all kinds of music. Jazz, rock, country and folk. It's weird." That was KSAN in its first days. I wanted to work there, and I did, although not until years later.

My first Rock station job was KPRI-San Diego. Mike Harrison was the program director. I walked in off the street and he hired me. He was my mentor and friend, and I often wonder what direction my career would have taken, if any, without his interest.

I drove to KMET from San Diego for my first Sunday night fill-in shift. Before I got into the station I was held up by a drunk with a riflebarrel against my head. He was staggering, with his finger on the trigger. When he saw that I had only 8 dollars, he gave it back and asked instead for a light for his cigarette, and let me go. I was a basket case by the time I arrived at KMET on what was the most important night of my life.

"The mighty MET" was on Wilshire Boulevard across from the La Brea tar pits. The building was old and the front door lock jammed one night. Mary Turner couldn't get in to do her show. She had to climb onto some trash cans, up the fire escape to the third floor and in through the men's room window to get in. This was at a time when she brought her big dog to work with her because some fan or someone had been waiting for her in the dark there a few times.

The urinal partition in the KMET men's room had the autographs from every famous radio, music and drug personality I'd ever heard of. We were going to enshrine it, but no one would touch it.

KMET moved to Metromedia Square, and began its rise to great success. It was the single most fun and satisfying radio experience I would ever have. The cohesion between all these different temperamental people was amazing. We were apparently all the right people in the right place at the right time. One thing that really pulled everyone together was the fact that our gm, L. David Moorhead, didn't trust us. He sensed rebellion in the air from a bunch of drug-crazed longhairs (us), and ruled that no meetings were to take place without his presence. So, we had our meetings in secret, every time at a different person's house. We'd whisper the meeting place among the staff, pass notes, make hushed phone calls. We'd gather, have our staff meeting (serious, organized planning and strategy) and then get stoned, and party. It made us all pull together, united in adversity. We really liked each other.

At KMET I was music director and associate program director. I was only doing weekends on-air and filling in for virtually everyone. I was putting in 50-60 hours a week. Then KLOS offered me my dream job...a full-time on-air job for lots more money. It was heartbreaking to leave KMET. I agonized. I cried. And I think Sam Bellamy (pd) never forgave me for it.

KLOS was a big stop. Damion was there. Jim Ladd, J.J. Jackson. Larry Jacobs was the news director and is now the national voice of ABC Radio Network News in New York. I did mornings for a while, then Frazer Smith took over that spot and I moved to evenings putting in several good years. Jim Ladd went to KMET. Shana came to KLOS. But KMET continued to beat KLOS. A change of pd's occurred, and I got fired.

I left for KSAN which Metromedia eventually sold and it turned into a Country station. Someone pulled the brass plaque off the entrance that said "KSAN, ace of the airwaves." I heard it eventually was given to Raechel Donahue, whose husband Tom was responsible for the format on KSAN that eventually spread across the country. A mob of people loudly protested the changeover, and someone dumped 50 pounds of horse shit on the front doorstep, but KSAN was gone forever. The audience that listened to KMET and KSAN was a little like deadheads: loyal till the end. The problem is the Dead can tour. The audience, loyal or not, couldn't support the stations.

I returned to KLOS. Bob Coburn had moved from KMET to KLOS and was hosting "Rockline." B. Mitch Reed had come to KLOS and was <u>supposed</u> to be the host of "Rockline," but the first day of the live show, he fell ill in the middle of the show and couldn't continue. The producer grabbed Bob, who was strolling down the hallway, and he stepped in and saved the day.

Bored at KLOS, I returned to KMET, to find it struggling in decline. A succession of at least five pd's couldn't pull KMET out of its dive. One of them fired me, but I was re-hired by yet another one.

A brand new station, KLSX, was experimenting with a new format called "classic rock." I went there, and two weeks later, everyone at KMET got fired and the station changed to "the Wave." KMET was gone forever! I felt like a man who had just sidestepped a speeding bullet. Many of the KMET personalities joined KLSX. Then a new pd arrived and fired the three highest paid jocks, including myself. It was during the recession, and I was making huge house payments. People were hanging onto their jobs for dear life. I freelanced around for a while and even did flying traffic reports to five different radio stations, using several different names.

Then I got a call from Hong Kong. I'd traveled through here twice before and liked it. At night, it can look like a scene from Blade Runner - all rain and steam. I half expect Peter Lorre to step out of a dark doorway and offer me opium. It's exotic and fascinating. I work for NBC Asia as the network announcer.

Rock radio was not the first thing in my career, nor is it the last. It occupied my life for a good 15 years, a <u>great time</u> for me, one that will never be equaled in its own way. But big rock radio of the '70s and '80s is gone, or at least changed. Even if I could go back, I might be inclined to say "fuck being being an oldie but a goodie."

D

D, Gary: **KDAY**, 1986-90. Gary Lynn Dillard passed away in 1994. He started at KDAY as an intern. When he left the station he went to XHRM-San Diego.

DAHL, Steve: **KPPC**, 1972-73; **KKDJ**, 1973. Most Los Angeles disc jockeys achieve their greatest fame in L.A. Steve is almost an asterisk in the history of Southern California radio compared to his very successful run in Chicago radio. And it started at a baseball game. The catalyst for the death of Disco radio, Steve's "disco sucks" event attracted national attention when it was staged between a double header at the Chicago White Sox' Comiskey Park in July 1979. Dahl blew up an outfield filled with 20,000 disco LPs. The "disco inferno" turned into a fiasco when 7,000 fans rushed the field resulting in cancellation of the second game and White Sox owner Bill Veech's threat to ban Dahl from the park for life. His "disco demolition derby" started a very successful run in Chicago radio, mostly on WLUP where he teamed with Garry Meier. Steve was born in Pasadena in 1954 and commented on his brief stay in Los Angeles: "With so much creative radio around like 'Firesign Theatre' and the 'Credibility Gap,' I realized that radio could be more than time, temp, and playing the music." During the 1970s, Dahl also worked in Bakersfield, San Diego and Sacramento. In 1973 Rick Carroll was in Bakersfield remixing the KKDJ jingles at the Buck Owens Studios and heard Steve on KAFY. One of the KKDJ djs (T. Michael Jordan) remembers, "Rick asked Steve to do weekends at KKDJ and did for a very

short time. He froze and sounded like crap. Rick wanted to axe him, but we all got the ax first and Steve went off to do big and wonderful things." He went to Detroit and made headlines when he faked a suicide attempt which prompted the arrival in the studio of several fire rescue units. In early 1981, Rick Carroll brought him to KROQ from WLUP-Chicago, and the Pasadena outlet was to be the flagship for a nationwide network. "I was fired from WLUP and never started on KROQ." He also worked for WDAI (the call letters stand for Detroit Auto Industry) and in Milwaukee. The roly-poly morning jock/performer also worked at WLS-Chicago and has been a major force in the Windy City radio wars. In the mid-1980s he commanded as much as $20,000 per appearance for his satirical live concerts. He played a dj in *Grandview USA*, starring Jamie Lee Curtis. In 1989, he was given the Father of the Year Award following an on-air vasectomy. Sometimes Steve's routines flirted with bad taste. In his nightclub act, he would sing an Elvis parody, *Heart Attack Hotel*, ending the number by collapsing on stage. He left WMVP-Chicago in the spring of 1996. Steve is married with three sons. Steve is now working afternoons at WCKQ-Chicago.

DALE, Bobby: **KFWB**, 1961-63; **KRLA**, 1964-65; **KGBS**, 1970. Bobby was born Robert Dale Bastiansen in Minneapolis in 1930. After a series of "weird jobs," he started in radio at age 25 in Glendive, Montana. From the very beginning, Bobby knew he had an uncanny knack to pick hit records and he loved music. From his home in San Rafael, he talked about discovering *To Know Him Is to Love Him*, by Phil Spector's Teddy Bears: "I was down in Minneapolis and had just been arrested for drunk driving, and I needed $100 to get out of jail. I didn't want to call my mother, so I called a local record distributor, who serviced the Fargo area. He bailed me out, and as I was recuperating from a terrible hangover on his couch, I was listening to his new 45s. As soon as I heard *To Know Him*, I told him that he had a smash." Bobby went on to KOIL-Omaha, where he replaced Gary Owens and then to KDWB-Minneapolis. In 1961, the disc jockeys at KFWB went out on strike in sympathy for the newsmen. Management and Crowell-Collier sister station jocks were called. Bobby worked his 6-to-9 p.m. shift, got on an airplane to Los Angeles and was on the air in B. Mitch Reed's shift the next night. (Reed flew to Minneapolis to replace Dale.) Bobby had high praise for KFWB pd Chuck Blore: "He was the sharpest, most open program director." His relationship with the next pd was not as endearing, and Bobby left for another C-C station, KEWB-San Francisco. Reb Foster hired Bobby for the all-night shift at KRLA. "That was the biggest I ever was in L.A. I played the Rolling Stones like the others were playing the Beatles, and I was huge." According to Bobby, he left KRLA in early 1965 because of burn-out. "I wanted to stay in L.A. because I was having so much fun, but I had to do six nights, six hours. I asked them either for five nights or more money. They said they could do without me." At KFRC-San Francisco he worked morning drive. "I just didn't like mornings. It had to be dark before my confidence would rise. Tom Rounds was the pd. I loved that cat, one of the best guys ever, but I hated the format. It was a living hell. I never had trouble talking up to a vocal until I had to do it. Talking up to *Reach Out I'll Be There* was ridiculous." He also worked at the legendary MOR station, KSFO-San Francisco, in the late 1960s and for four years beginning in 1971, and could play all his favorites. During his years in San Francisco, he hung out with Tom Donahue in North Beach. In the early 1980s he worked at KKCY ("The City")-San Francisco. He gave up radio as a full-time profession in 1985. From time to time he appears on the University of San Francisco campus station, KUSF. In 1992 he lost his voice and an operation on his nodules was required. In preparation for the operation, it was discovered that he had diabetes, a heart problem and cirrhosis of the liver. "The doctor told me that if I had one more drink or one more cigarette, I would die." He answered an ad in a local Marin County newspaper looking for a "grandfather." He now works for a pre-school as a crossing guard and helper. "It's very stressful trying to reason with 2 1/2-year-olds. I'm doing fine. The school gives me a room. I don't think I could do radio full-time anymore. But it was a blast."

DALE, Sharon: **KFOX/FM**, 1979-80; **KMGG**; **KOST/KFI**, 1983-97. While attending the University of Maine in 1970, Sharon visited the campus radio station during an open house, and thus began her love affair with radio. She started in Bangor and is generally recognized as one of Maine's first women broadcasters. She was the news/public affairs director at KFOX and joined "Magic 106" as part of the morning team of London and Engelman. Sharon is currently at KOST, where she is part of the morning team with Mark & Kim. In her spare time, Sharon is active at The Braille Institute and reads "talking books" for the blind. "After more than 20 years on the radio airwaves from coast-to-KOST...for me, radio is still #1."

DALTON, Bill: **KLAC**, 1970-71, gm. Bill arrived in the Southland from another Metromedia outlet, WASH-Washington, DC. He was the designer for the switch to a Country format at KLAC. Born in Lincoln, Nebraska, he grew up in Lincoln and the DC area. He graduated from Duke University in 1957 with a B.A. in business administration and accounting. Bill started his career in the summer of 1957 working for Kluge Enterprises. He went on to WHK-Cleveland and WIP-Philadelphia in sales. In late 1965 he was named vp/gm of WEEZ-Philadelphia and two years later went to WASH. When he left KLAC in the summer of 1971, he returned to WASH until early 1977 when he moved to run another Metromedia station, WNEW-New York. In 1981 he and his wife Susan bought WXTR-Washington, DC and sold it in 1987. He currently runs The Dalton Group, Inc. and owns WGRR-Cincinnati and WWMG and WEND-Charlotte.

DALTON, Don: **KFI/KOST**, 1982-84, gm. Don suffered a brain aneurysm the same day that the station's airborne traffic reporter Bruce Wayne's plane went down. (Read a stirring remembrance of that day from Jhani Kaye in this publication.)

DALTON, Rich: **KWST**, 1976-80. Rich arrived at "K-West" from Kansas City and spent much of his time working the all-night shift.

DALEY, Carson: **KROQ**, 1996-97. Carson joined evenings at KROQ in the summer of 1996. He came from afternoons at KOME-San Jose.

DALY, Larry: **XERB**, 1967. Larry worked in New Orleans before climbing aboard the "soul express."

DAME, Dave: **KIKF**, 1989-90. Dave worked all-nights at KIKF and then joined KOWF-San Diego. In 1993 he left for Arista Records in Chicago. Dave moved to Nashville in the fall of 1996 as the director of national promotion. He married the daughter of KIKF gm, Art Astor.

> *"wraparounddribbledrivefallawayprayer!"*
>
> *-L.A. Lakers broadcaster Chick Hearn*

DAMION: **KLOS**, 1969-80, pd; **KMET**, 1980-86; **KLSX**, 1986-94.  The Hartford native has spent his career in AOR radio. Before arriving in Los Angeles, Damion Bragdon was at WDAI-Chicago as the station evolved from "free-form" AOR to the "Rock 'n Stereo" format. He moved to Southern California to join KLOS in 1969 at the "home of rock 'n' roll radio." Damion partnered with Jim Ladd to produce the early "InnerView" shows. In a 1994 interview, he recalled his Southland radio highlights: "Being part of the California Jam in April 1973, and conducting four Led Zeppelin interviews and concerts. In the mid-'70s, KLOS was #1 and won *Billboard* magazine's Station of the Year." He was pd in the late '70s and gave up those duties in 1980 to join KMET. Damion joined KLSX and was a part of the original "classic rock" team. When his contract came due in the summer of 1993, it was not renewed -- a major surprise to Damion. He joined Unistar's Adult Rock & Roll network for the overnight shift and returned to KLSX in early 1994. In 1995 he went to the Hawaiian Islands, and on his first day he met a radio station owner who made Damion pd of his AM&FM operation.

DANIEL: **KHTZ**, 1979-82; **KABC**, 1982-96. He was born Daniel Ohse in Oregon City and grew up in Ventura listening to the leading rock stations in Los

Angeles. Daniel graduated from Ventura High in 1965 and was voted student most likely to succeed Wolfman Jack. "Unfortunately, it never happened." He went to KNDE-Sacramento in 1972 and KRUX-Phoenix for five years beginning in 1973. KHTZ pd Bobby Rich recalled the circumstances of Daniel's move to L.A. radio: "The day Greater Media took over, we let the staff go except Charlie Tuna and Jim Conlee. I really hadn't given this enough thought and realized I had NO air staff, and there was nobody for overnights. I went through the tapes that were on my desk and started calling people who sounded decent. Daniel was one of them. He was working at KACY-Oxnard/Ventura at the time. I called him and said, 'Here's the deal, I need someone starting TONIGHT. If you can be here by 10 p.m., you've got the gig; otherwise I've got to find someone else!' He called back 20 minutes later, quit his job and started driving to L.A.!" He worked afternoon drive at the end of the CHR format and continued after the change to "soft rock" as the evening jock. Since 1982, Dan has been a production engineer at KABC. His post dj career high: "Being B. Mitchel Reed's engineer on KLOS. Here was a man I had listened to as a child and I had the honor of being his engineer." Tough making the transition from jock to engineer? "You feel bad for about a week. Then you start having fun and the money, benefits and people you get to work with make up for your loss. At KLOS the jock sat in the studio and slipped albums through a slot in the wall. The jock had no controls, just a mike switch. There was no door between the studio and control room, so if the jock wanted to kill you it would take so long to get from the studio to the control room that he or she would have a chance to cool off." Daniel works the controls for KABC's popular morning show.

DANIELS, Bill: **KFWB**, 1957-58. Bill left with the change of Chuck Blore's "Color Radio" on January 2, 1958.

DANIELS, Dan: **KRLA**, 1993

DANIELS, David B.: **KWIZ**, 1976

DANIELS, Jim: **KLSX**, 1996-97. Jim arrived at "Real Radio" to replace Susan Olsen and Ken Ober. He grew up in the Southland. "The only place I was going to be happy on the air was L.A.," he said shortly after his arrival at KLSX.

"After 10 years of doing morning 'rim shot' radio in KHYT-Tucson, KYRK and KOMP-Las Vegas and KGGI-Riverside, I took off to cut my teeth in talk radio." He quit the morning show at KGGI to take the overnight shift on new Talk outlet WOWF-Detroit where he moved to evening host and then to mornings in less than six months. He arrived at KLSX from "B97 The Buzz"-New Orleans. "Now I'm working with one of my radio role models Frazer Smith. What a ride!" He left KLSX in the spring of 1997 for Houston.

In 1983 KABC conducted a talent search to find a co-host to Bud Furillo and Tommy Hawkins and the "SportsTalk" show. From 2,000 applicants, New Yorker Merrie Rich won. Within a month she was fired.

DANIELS, Joe: **KIIS**, 1977-83; **KHTZ**, 1983-84; **KRTH**, 1984-91. "If it wasn't for the Beatles, I wouldn't be in radio." Born Joe Dazzo in Chicago, he first got

interested in radio while listening to WLS-Chicago. His family moved to the Southland in the early 1960s and Joe was greatly influenced to follow radio as a career by listening to the journey of Beatlemania. "I would come home from school and be glued to the radio hearing about how Dave Hull had stowed away on the Beatles tour plane." Joe graduated from Arcadia High School in 1969 and went to the Bill Wade Radio school. In 1974 he spent two years working as the producer for Dick Haynes at KLAC. "My first on-air job was at KTIN-Casa Grande, Arizona, a station owned by Kevin Weatherly's father." Before arriving at KIIS, he worked at KKOK-Lompoc and KSOM-Ontario. While at KIIS he used the name Mark Christopher at KWOW-Pomona. In 1991 he joined WW1 and is now heard on the Soft AC format. "I miss local radio and hope to return to it some day."

DANIELS, Mike: **KRLA**, 1989-97. Born Mike Sirotzki, he does weekend fill-in work. He was The Real Don Steele's producer at KCBS/FM. Mike also does part-time work at WW1's Oldies Channel.

DANIELS, Roy: **KLON**, 1985-90. In the late 1980s, Roy worked morning drive at KLON, the Long Beach Jazz station.

DANIELS, Sky: **KMET**, 1985-87. Sky worked as a music critic and concert promoter in Cleveland before entering radio. From WYDD-Pittsburgh, WWWW-Detroit and WLUP-Chicago in the 1970s, Sky arrived in the Southland from KFOG-San Francisco. He joined KMET in the spring of 1985 to work afternoon drive and to be assistant pd. In a very candid interview in a summer 1995 edition of *R&R*, Sky talked about his experience at KMET: "Frankly my L.A. tenure was the worst time of my life. I remember standing on the roof of KMET, looking at the Hollywood sign, and thinking, 'How in the hell can a kid from Ohio have reached these heights and hate it so much?' It was the worst-managed station I've ever been associated with - nothing was done right. The personalities - as storied as they were - were dinosaurs with outmoded concepts. I went through five pds in two years. It was the nadir of my life and career, and I was miserable and a wreck. At the end of KMET, I decided never to create obstacles for myself again." After KMET he returned to KFOG where he won *Billboard*'s 1988 AOR Music Director of the Year Award and then to KISW-Seattle as pd. A year later he started a series of record company assignments at Epic Records, Island Records and LPG. He left Island in the summer of 1995 and became Alternative editor of *R&R*.

DARCEL: **KGFJ**, 1976-77; **KKTT**, 1977

DARIN, Dave: **KWIZ**, 1968-70. Born David Kleinbart Dave was one of two djs hired to convert KWIZ/FM from automated to its first live format in 1968. He moved to the AM in 1970. When Dave left the Southland he worked in the Bay Area and in 1982 joined CBS Radio Networks (now Westwood One) as Western Director of affiliate sales and account executive. Dave received a bachelor's in radio/tv/film from Cal State Northridge.

DARIN, Johnnie: **KIIS**; **KRLA**, 1968-71, pd; **KDAY**, 1971; **KROQ**, 1972-73, pd; **KNAC**, 1975; **KGOE**, 1975, pd; **KNX**, 1976; **KGIL**, 1976-83; **KJOI**, 1978; **KBLA**, 1989-92; **KGIL**, 1993. Born John Christian Miller in Rapid City, South Dakota, he grew up in Ventura.

When he was a youth watching a dj perform, John told him, "When I grow up, I want to be a disc jockey." The dj responded, "You can't do both!" Johnnie arrived at KRLA in December of 1968 from KGB-San Diego with earlier stops at KACY-Oxnard and KMEN-San Bernardino where he was md. He started as a production man and was the character Filbert E. Yarborough (Bill Drake's name at KYA-San Francisco) on Dave Hull's morning drive show. Within a few months, Johnnie had his own show in late 1968 and a year later became pd. "It all happened very quickly." In 1972, John started a decade of programs for Armed Forces Radio. He was the original pd at KROQ/AM. After "the Roq," John went to San Francisco to be gm of KSOL and orchestrated a Disco format. In 1975, he returned to the Southland and spent a summer month at KNAC and was pd of KGOE in Thousand Oaks for six months. John's father gave him prophetic advice about the "dj business," telling him to prepare for a life after being a jock. John began to make a transition into the world of business reporting on Channel 22 while doing business reports on KNX and playing music on KGIL. In the mid-1980s, John was an anchor on KCOP/Channel 13, field reporter on KHJ/Channel 9 and did reports for cable news. John and Chuck Ashman produce audio, video and web sites for clients on nine major airlines under the banner "Flight Talk Network." He has been reporting business news on American Airlines' audio channel for years. He launched KBLA as a full-time Business station in 1989 when realtor Fred Sands bought the station. John operates a full-service ad agency specializing in infomercials and industrial video work. "There is life after radio if you are creative, ambitious...and DESPERATE!!!!"

DARK, Danny: **KLAC**, 1963-66. Danny has been a very successful voiceover announcer for decades and the voice of NBC. "When I wanted to pursue a voiceover career I took a tape to Chuck Blore. He said it was the worst thing he'd ever heard. Chuck offered to help me put together an audition tape and we spent a Saturday working on the presentation. Ever since then, he has been my mentor. Everything I know, I learned from Chuck." Born in Oklahoma City, Danny was brought up in Tulsa. He started

at KICK-Springfield, Missouri while working his way through Drury College. Before arriving in Southern California, Danny jocked at KAKC-Tulsa, WERE-Cleveland, WFUN-Miami, WTIX-New Orleans and WIL and KXOK-St. Louis. He hosted evenings at KLAC. Danny's blue-chip clients have included the announcing chores on *Bonanza*, Budweiser and Mazda. "I have had a wonderful career."

DARLING, Bob: **KJOI**, 1986-88, pd. Bob is a broadcast consultant to several California stations in the area of sales, sales training, marketing, programming and overall management. He graduated in the top 10% at Fresno State University where he was a business administration major. In the late 1950s, Bob started his radio career at KPEN-San Francisco. During the 1960s he was the program director or general manager for KHFR-Monterey, KPGM-Los Altos and KNNU-Tulare. In 1971 he became owner and manager of KKNU. In 1977 he was 45% owner and president of KBAI-Morro Bay/San Luis Obispo. During the 1980s, before and after KJOI, he continued with KBAI and became part owner of KKCW-Portland. In 1989 he was gm of KMYX-Bakersfield. He is now a partner in a group that owns seven radio stations in California. He is gm and pd of all stations.

KKDJ (102.7FM) becomes KIIS/FM -October 1, 1974

DARRELL, John: **KMNY**. John was from Texas and worked for the Financial News Network.

DARREN, Dangerous: **KNAC**, 1989-95. Born in San Luis Obispo, Darren Silva went to Cuesta Junior College in SLO majoring in telecommunications. He started his radio career in his hometown on KSLY. "It was great playing Madonna and Michael Jackson songs over and over. Yeah, right! I was in hell, although it was a good experience." At KNAC he worked the all-night show. He left the Long Beach Alternative station with an owner and format switch to Spanish in early 1995. Darren moved to KEGL-Dallas.

DAVIS, Ann: **KACE**, 1985, gm

DAVIS, Bill: **KEZY**, 1984. Bill worked morning drive in Orange County.

DAVIS, Cindy: **KNOB**, 1987; **KOCM**, 1988-89; **KLIT**, 1991-94; **KLSX**, 1995. Cindy currently works at KOLA-Riverside.

DAVIS, Dick: **KGFJ**, 1980. Dick was a community leader who worked part-time at KGFJ.

DAVIS, Gina: **KGGI**; **KZLA**; **KPWR**, Born Theresa Tran, Gina was killed while base jumping when her parachute failed to open. She died in January 1996. Broadcaster Laurie Allen remembers her dear friend: "Gina was a beam of energy. After work which started at 3 a.m. she would usually polish off the day trail-biking or bungie jumping. Her passion was organizing charity events for needy children, eventually raising hundreds of thousands of dollars. She was the epitome of someone who lived life to the fullest. I never realized what a comfort that would be to those of us who miss her."

DAVIS, Gordon: **KFWB**, 1968-72, gm. Gordon worked for Radio Liberty in Europe and WINS-New York before joining the all-News station. He left for a corporate job dealing with the Pacific Rim.

DAVIS, Guy: **KHTZ**, 1985; **KBZT**, 1986; **KLSX**, 1986; **KBIG**, 1986-95; **KNJO**, 1996-97.

Guy grew up in the San Luis Obispo area and worked the central California area, including Bakersfield, KCUB-Tucson, KISS-San Antonio, KBST-San Diego before arriving in Los Angeles. Guy was married to Los Angeles dj Joni Caryl. He left KBIG in late 1995 and has been active in voiceover work and developing a syndicated cigar talk show. Guy is an auctioneer specializing in fund raising and charity auctions. In the fall of 1996 Guy started working at KNJO.

DAVIS, Jay: **KEZY**, 1961-71; **KNX**, 1965-67; **KGER**, 1971-92, gm. Jay's career started as a dj at KRAM-Las Vegas and KAFY-Bakersfield and when he retired in 1992 he was gm of KGER. Jay was born John Ellsworth Jason "Jay" Davis in Cameron, Missouri on August 27, 1927. After Jay was discharged from the service in 1952 he completed radio and tv training at the Don Martin Broadcasting School. After KAFY Jay worked at KRBO-Las Vegas and KBUC-Corona. He joined KGER as news and public affairs director and after a series of promotions was made gm in 1988. Jay has taught theater at Cal State Fullerton and Long Beach Community College. Jay retired to Las Vegas.

DAVIS, Jay: **KEZY**. Jay hosted the morning news with Craig Powers.

DAVIS, Jeff: **KNX/FM**, 1988; **KRTH**, 1988-91; **KYSR**, 1992-95. Jeff is the imaging voice for over 50 radio stations. He hosts a syndicated show, "On The Radio," for WW1 that is heard on over 200 stations around the world. Born in Apex, North Carolina, Jeff grew up in the Raleigh/Durham area. While attending Virginia Commonwealth College majoring in communication arts and design, he got the radio bug working at the campus radio station. His first job was working overnights for $100 a week on WAAB-Mobile. A gm from Washington, DC was in Mobile listening to Jeff and offered him middays at WEAN. During his seven months he worked every shift. "We joked about the swinging door at WEAN. We would need Kennedy Stadium to hold all the former workers from the station." After WGH-Newport News/Norfolk, Jeff started a 14-year odyssey at WLS-Chicago. From 1974 to 1988 he lasted longer than any other personality. Ironically he is the imaging voice of WLS today. While at WLS he started planning for a career change. "I saw some of the big WLS names having difficulty finding jobs, and I said that I was not going to be like that." In 1991 he started collecting equipment for his eventual move into full-time production. Jeff and his wife had a small apartment in Studio City. "I was doing voice work out of a clothes closet. The damp clothes would deaden the sound and create a perfect studio. People wondered where my studio was." Jeff admits to being very lucky. "In over 25 years I've never been without a job. I live in the Hollywood Hills under the Hollywood sign. The equipment in my studio adjacent to my house is better than most radio stations." Jeff worked afternoon drive at KYSR until the summer of 1995.

DAVIS, Jeff: **KRTH**, 1986-88; **KPWR**, 1988-89; **KQLZ**, 1990-93; **KMPC**, 1993-94; **KCBS**, 1993-94; **KFWB**, 1994. Originally from Iowa, Jeff Whittle was part of the morning drive team on "Pirate Radio," where he also hosted the "All Request Lunch Hour." Prior to working with Scott Shannon, Jeff was a morning drive producer for KRTH's "Steve Morris Show." At "Power 106" Jeff was weekend jock Johnny Marrs. He is currently the sports director for Shadow Broadcast Services and works as a weekend jock for "The Flash," an album alternative station in San Diego.

DAVIS, Jim: **KHJ**, 1976-77; **KMPC**, 1979-81, pd. A native of Buffalo, Davis is a second generation and life-long broadcaster. Following in the footsteps of his mother, who was a singer on WKBW-Buffalo, Jim began his career as an air personality in the western New

York area. He worked at WOR-New York, CKLW-Detroit (Big Jim Edwards) and WLS and WDAI-Chicago. His other stops included WPEZ-Pittsburgh, KIMN-Denver, WXYZ-Detroit and KLIF-Dallas. While working at RKO General Broadcasting, Jim was twice nominated for *Billboard* magazine's "Major Market Air Personality of the Year." Jim was named pd of KMPC in the summer of 1979. He has authored a book entitled *The Sales Success Spectrum - A System of Radio Sales*. In his spare time, Jim is an owner/operator of a twin engine Aero Commander and a rated pilot. He has been executive vp and gm of WZVU-Mommouth/Ocean-New Jersey.

DAVIS, Ken: **KUTE**, 1986; **KOST**, 1994. Ken worked mornings with Brooke Jones and evenings while at KUTE.

DAVIS, Krickett: **KYSR**, 1992-93; **KMGX**, 1993; **KCBS**, 1993-97. Krick's autobiography suggests a budding writer: "Krickett Davis' circuitous radio career has taken her from the cornfields of Iowa to the star-filled boulevards of Los Angeles. The journey began in 1982, playing heavy metal on the Iowa State University campus radio station KPGY ('K-Piggy' to the locals)." After a few jobs in Des Moines radio, she packed up an air-conditioned U-Haul and headed to Los Angeles. She worked peripheral markets such as Ventura and Lancaster before joining Metro Traffic and Shadow News. While at Shadow, Krickett worked weekends and fill-in on KYSR. Following that, she did weekends at KMGX. Krickett worked at "Arrow 93" for two years as a fill-in. During this time she did evenings on WW1's syndicated '70s Channel. In early 1996 "Arrow 93" moved her to early evenings where she "hangs-out" and also hosts a weekly Led Zeppelin show called "The Zepp-Zone."

DAVIS, Laura: **KNAC**, 1976; **KLOS**, 1976-80. During her nine years in radio, Laura experienced four AOR-formatted stations during the seventies. Born and raised in Pittsburgh, she graduated from Cornell University. It was during her senior year that radio attracted her interest. "Cornell's student-run station, WVBR, was one of the best anywhere. It was advertiser-supported and treated like a real station. We probably had the lowest grade point average on campus from working regular shifts." After college she joined WCMF-Rochester, stopping briefly in Detroit at WABX, before heading to L.A. During her four years with KLOS she worked for four program directors. In 1980 she joined NBC's Source Network where she hosted "Screen Scenes." This experience led in 1983 to an opportunity to produce electronic press kits for Universal Pictures

and to start a new career that now encompasses film production. "I loved radio for the music, concerts, parties and to think you could get paid for it all. At 28 I reached the point when I realized I had nothing left to say about *Stairway to Heaven*, and I got out."

DAVIS, Nawana: **KMET**, 1975. Nawana hosted weekends and did fill-in work.

DAVIS, Philip: **KOCM**; **KWIZ**. Philip was the former owner of KOCM and KWIZ. He died December 5, 1996, at the age of 60.

DAVIS, Willie: **KACE**. The former owner of soulful KACE was an All-Pro defensive end for Vince Lombardi's Green Bay Packers. Willie grew up in Texarkana and played college football for Eddie Robinson at Grambling. He earned a degree from the business school at the University of Chicago and bought a Schlitz Distributorship in South Central Los Angeles. On the football field he won six NFL championships, two Super Bowls and numerous awards and trophies. He bought KAGB in late 1976 and turned it into KACE and wanted the radio station to support Inglewood and the community. He still owns the 103.9FM frequency in the San Bernardino area.

DAWSON, Ted: **KLOS**, 1985. Ted broadcast sports on the KLOS morning drive show with Mark and Brian. He was best known as the sports reporter for KABC/Channel 7 during the 1980s. In 1987 Ted was replaced by Jim Hill, and he went to the CBS affiliate in Dallas and was the radio voice of SMU football. He left Dallas in 1992 for a news anchor assignment in Albuquerque.

DAY, Deano: **KLAC**, 1969-71 and 1980-82 and 1984-85. Born Ordean Moen, Deano was a station owner in Fargo while still in his 20s. He replaced the legendary Ken Dowe and Granny Emma in the morning drive slot at KLIF-Dallas in 1967. He left Big D for his first visit to Country KLAC in 1969. He was the morning drive host during part of this period. Deano's major success came in the Midwest where he did mornings on a number of Country stations in Chicago and Detroit. In 1975, Deano won *Billboard* magazine's Country Personality of the Year Award while working at WDEE-Detroit. He also worked at WCAR-Detroit. It seems Deano never met a radio station he wouldn't work for in Detroit...or Chicago. He returned to Detroit at WCXI in 1982, after 18 months at KLAC. In October 1984, Deano won the 18th Annual CMA DJ of the Year Award, and the ceremony was broadcast live on CBS/TV. Deano was nominated for CMA 1983 DJ of the Year. His fan club, unheard of in the 1980s, numbered over 5,000. He had enormous turnouts to his personal appearances. Deano left Los Angeles for the last time with Metromedia's sale of KLAC to Capital Cities Communications. He bought WACY-Flint. Deano is currently brokering mornings on WHND-Detroit, programming a mix of Country and Oldies. Deano talked about his WHND show: "We do a remote every day. One day we broadcast from a restaurant called Heaven. The next day we were in a tavern called Oar House, so the next day we went to Hell...Michigan. It's amazing, I'm still playing country music and I look just like Kenny Rogers."

DAY, Gene: **KGFJ**, 1974, pd. Gene went from all-nights to pd.

DAY, Howard: **KLFM/KNOB**, 1960-61; **KAPP**, 1962-63; **KKOP**, 1965; **KNAC**, 1966; **KFOX**, 1966; **KKOP**, 1968-74 and 1976-78. When Howard left the Southland he moved to Santa Rosa where he worked at KZST. He left radio in 1984 and works as an engineering tech for Optical Coating Laboratory of Santa Rosa.

DAY, Jerry: **KIEV**, 1972. Jerry was there for the Oldies format.

DAY, Steve: **KOCM/KSRF**, 1985-89, pd; **KXEZ**, 1989-91; **KLIT**, 1991-93; **KMGX**, 1994. Born in Washington, DC and raised in Rockville, Maryland,

Steve discovered his passion for radio while in his second year at Ashland College in Ohio. From a chance encounter with a programming executive from a station 30 miles from campus, Steve began his daily commute to WGLX-Galion, Ohio. He dropped out of college and during the 1970s worked at WSIR-Winterhaven, Florida, WDAE-Tampa, WDAT-Daytona and WKZL and WTOP-Winston-Salem. While in Winston-Salem he began broadcasting play-by-play sports and reporting sports for a local tv station. "We were doing okay but my wife wanted us to be more secure so I got out of radio and joined her father's insurance business in Rochester." The insurance job and the marriage ended in Rochester and Steve returned to radio in Rochester at WBBF and WWWG. "In 1979 I got the West Coast urge and packed up for San Diego." Steve worked weekends on KFMB-San Diego and broadcast sports on KGTV/TV. In the early 1980s, Steve joined the sports department at KTTV/Channel 11. In 1983 he partnered with Betty White for the tv game show *Just Men*. In 1993 Steve was the announcer for ABC's *Caesars Challenge* starring Ahmad Rashad. In 1994 he was part of Sony's Game Show Network and hosted several shows. Steve is now working the Bright AC format at WW1.

DAYTON, Bob: **KBLA**, 1966-67; **KRLA**, 1967-70 and 1972-73. Born in New York in 1934, Bob got his start on Long Island radio at WPAC-Patchogue. He worked in Dallas on McLendon's KLIF in the late 1950s and was known as "The Milkman." He was also on KBOX-Dallas. His radio journey eventually returned him to New York. In the early 1960s he jocked as Robin Scott in St. Louis. At WABC-New York he allegedly was fired on-air in 1965 when he dedicated the 20th Anniversary of the bombing of Hiroshima with the playing of *Happy Birthday* to the Japanese. He left WABC to start at KBLA. He joined KRLA in early summer of 1967 as vacation relief the day after KBLA folded. In 1972 he was on WPIX-New York and later that year went to KRLA, which was Contemporary/Oldies and MOR. The station was experimenting with teams in every time slot. Bob partnered with Reb Foster during the short-lived format. He departed KRLA and went to WCBS/FM-New York in 1974 and on Long Island's WGBB along with WGLI, WKJY and WHLI in the late 1970s. In 1982, Bob became part of ABC's Superadio. He wrote for Lohman and Barkley during their foray into television. He was living near Patchogue, where he originally started out, when he died of cancer April 28, 1995, at the age of 62. Paul Cassidy reported on Prodigy at the time of his death that he was told Bob had a stroke some time during the 1980s. For many years he closed his show with "I...gotta go now! Good-bye, world."

"Every great city has one great radio station that plays Beautiful Music. Los Angeles has KJOI stereo 99FM. Beautiful!"
— Slogan, 1972

DEACON, Squeakin': **KXLA**; **KFOX**. Squeakin' hosted a hard-core country show on KXLA with a studio audience. Beginning at nine each night he played records, interviewed guests and presented comedy sketches. He was from the Midwest where he was a big star with the song *Ding Dong Daddy from Dumas*. He has since passed away.

DEACON, Tom: **KUSC**, 1989-92, pd. A Canadian citizen, Tom was lured to the KUSC job with a promise of a housing stipend and help obtaining a work permit from the Immigration and Naturalization Service. He left the station in 1992. A lawsuit and legal response followed. According to a story in the *LA Times*, Tom hired on-air morning personality Bonnie Grice a few months after arriving at the station. The suit said that within one month of her coming to work at KUSC, Grice and station president Wallace A. Smith began a relationship that led to marriage about six months later. Tom charged that Smith "promoted his wife's career at the expense of other employees at USC" and that "Grice utilized her sexual and marital relationship with Smith to influence KUSC policy and to interfere with [Deacon's] supervision of her and the execution of his responsibilities as chief of KUSC programming." USC denied Deacon's charges, citing "economic factors requiring a reduction in force" as the reason for his dismissal. The case was settled out of court and Tom is living in Amsterdam.

DEAN, Jeff: **KEZY**, 1977-79; **KROQ**, 1979; **KLSX**, 1986-87; **KGGI**, 1987-93. Jeff has worked under the names Deaner and J.D. He got his start in the mid-1970s in Hawaii working at KPOI, KORL and KKUA. Jeff joined Michael Sullivan at KEZY for mornings and the team was known as "The Doctor and The Dean." In 1980 he went to KCBS-San Francisco for afternoons. His next stop was KPRI and KBZT-San Diego. In 1986 he worked morning drive at KMEN-San Bernardino while also working weekends and swing shift at KLSX. The Deaner & Daniels show was launched in morning drive at KGGI in 1987 and continued until 1993. While at KGGI he also worked the Oldies Channel at Transtar. He spent a year doing mornings at KSLX-Phoenix. Since 1994 Jeff has been doing afternoons as J.D. at KYCY-San Francisco. He lives in Walnut Creek.

DEAN, Joseph: **KTWV**, 1994-97. Joseph works the all-night weekend shift at KTWV. "If there's a more esoteric position in L.A., I'm sure it's my next stop." Born J.D. Coburn, Joseph arrived in the Southland from a successful career in Seattle. He started out as an event supervisor for the 3,000-seat Paramount Theatre in Seattle. In 1970 he joined KISW

and later worked afternoons at KZOK. During the 1980s he worked evenings at KOMO-Seattle. In addition to his work at "the Wave," Joseph teaches acting full-time at Playhouse West in North Hollywood. "I count myself as one of a very elite few who genuinely succeed in this business, though I've never made any splash. Every station I've worked for went to the top not long after I started there and never because of anything I did personally. I just drag good luck around with me."

DEARBORN, Bob: **KFI**, 1984-85; **KTWV**, 1989. Bob worked all-nights at the 50,000 watt clear channel station, KFI.

DeCASTRO, Jim: **KFAC**, 1989, gm; **KKBT**, 1989-90, gm. The former sm of KSFO-San Francisco and gm of WLUP-Chicago bridged the format switch from Classical to KKBT, "the Beat." Jim said at the time of the format switch, "I'm shocked that there weren't groups and pickets." Jim went on to be Evergreen president/coo and lives in Chicago.

DeCOY, Bob: **KGFJ**, 1950s; **KTYM**, 1960s. Bob was the writer, producer and narrator of KGFJ's award-winning, "This Is Progress." The program was the only daily radio documentary dedicated to the contributions of black culture and growth. Bob graduated from Yale University in 1951 receiving an M.F.A. degree. He died at age 54 in L.A. in 1975.

DEE, Lorna: **KIIS**, 1985-86. In 1986, Lorna was vacationing in Southern California from her on-air gig at KKRZ-Portland, when she was dared to try out for the job as Rick Dees's sidekick. She got the job.

DEES, Rick: **KHJ**, 1979-80; **KIIS**, 1981-97. It's not for nothing that cell phones flash the words *power on*. Arguably one of the top three morning personalities in modern Southern California radio history, Rick personifies *power on*. He is the Johnny Carson of

popular music radio. A survivor. It's ironic that his foray into late night television on the ABC network was up against Johnny Carson. No matter how many personalities the competition has thrown against him, Rick has been a major morning factor. Rick was born Rigdon Osmond Dees III in Jacksonville, in 1950, and raised in Greensboro, North Carolina. He worked weekends for a local station until starting at a campus radio station at the University of North Carolina, where he later got a degree in radio, television and motion pictures. Rick's first full-time radio job was with WKIX-Raleigh. He reached national attention in Memphis while working at WMPS, when he recorded the novelty hit that parodied the disco craze, *Disco Duck*. The song went platinum in 1976 and sold more than 4,000,000 records, earning him a People's Choice Award. The comedy hit remained on the *Billboard* magazine Top 100 list for 25 weeks. A number of novelty songs and albums followed, including a cover of Big Bopper's *Chantilly Lace* and the flip side, *Disco Brief*, which lasted only 45 seconds and was the world's shortest disco song. He has had appearances in tv and many movies, including the character of Rock Dees in *The Flintstones*, *La Bamba* and *Jetsons: The Movie*. When he arrived in the Southland from Memphis, he brought his cast of idiots to KHJ - John Revolting, Candy Plastique, Rex Rona, Groan 'n' Bear It, Road Hog Dees, Pelvis, Sparky and Chiquita and Willard Wizeman, many of whom were voiced by his wife, Julie. Before leaving Memphis, he married Julie McWhirter, who had developed a very successful character voice career. They met while taping a segment of CBS/TV's *Wacko* children's show. Julie was also a regular on *The Rich Little Show*. When Rick arrived at KHJ in April 1979, the gm enthused about Dees: "He's the hottest piece of radio talent in the business, one who we believe will help return KHJ to the dominance it held." Barely a year later on October 9, 1980, he left following a format change to Country, and was out of work for over a year. After he landed the morning show on KIIS in the summer of 1981, he dominated the mornings for more than a decade, truly the most successful morning personality of the 1980s. His popular features include "Spousal Arousal," "Dees Sleaze" and "The Battle of the Sexes." He hosted the syndicated series, *Solid Gold* in 1982 and 1983. In 1984, Rick released the Grammy-nominated album *Hurt Me Baby, Make Me Write Bad Checks* on No-o-o Budget Records. Other albums included *I'm Not Crazy*, *Rick Dees' Greatest Hit (The White Album)* and *Put It Where the Moon Don't Shine*. James Brown of the *LA Times* profiled Dees upon his arrival: "His style is a hybrid of various influences from Gary Owens and Don Imus to Jonathan Winters and Mel Blanc." Dees described his goal at the time: "We're trying to create *Saturday Night Live* for the radio. It took me 12 years to get out here [Los Angeles] and this definitely has to be the main thing for me." He talked about comedy limits in a *Billboard* magazine interview: "You can be risqué but there is a limit. We try to be middle America." On one program in 1987, Dees interviewed a ventriloquist and his wooden puppet over the telephone. When Dees asked about his family, the puppet replied, "My father is a birch, my mother is a pine and my sister is a piece of ash." Then Dees asked about the wood puppet's sex life. "It's scary," he answered. "My girlfriend has a new form of birth control." Dees asked what that was. "A pencil sharpener," said the puppet. Born-again Dees commented that he believed the couple's Christianity influenced and mediated their scope of humor. There is no denying that he has demonstrated staying power in an industry that leaves its youth for dead. Rick hosted a late-night ABC/TV show against Johnny Carson's *Tonight* show called *Into the Night, Starring Rick Dees*, which debuted in the summer of 1990. The show was billed as a cross between *Entertainment Tonight* and a variety show. In 1994, Rick reflected on why the network TV show didn't work: "I had the misfortune of being released to the public on late-night television in the middle of Johnny Carson's last year on TV and in the middle of the Gulf War. Our show didn't come on half the time until about 1:45 or 2 in the morning. It's very hard when Ted Koppel wants to just grab an extra 35 minutes to show people blowing up in Saudi Arabia. I'd love to have another opportunity, but who knows." His peers have recognized him with 12 consecutive Number One Radio Personality in America *Billboard* awards, and he has a Star on Hollywood Boulevard's Walk of Fame. His syndicated countdown show, "Rick Dees' Weekly Top 40," was originally aired on KIIS on September 1, 1983, as a local program, but evolved to being heard in 400 markets, including 50 countries worldwide. The show was voted Best Syndicated Top 40 Program of the Year by *Billboard* magazine in 1988 and 1993 and 1995's syndicated radio personality award. Rick beat two market rivals for the 1993 *Billboard* Top 40 Air Personality of the Year. In a 1995 *R&R* interview, he recounted his most memorable moment in radio: "We went through an earthquake on the air. We were 11 floors up in a building that looked like a knife cut it out from the bottom. All of a sudden it started shaking a little bit. Speakers started falling, and lights were falling on top of me. They say a human's most basic fear is fear of falling, being dropped, because that goes back to when you were born. So, being 11 floors up, you're in an earthquake and dropping at the same time. I could never forget that." In the same interview he listed as role models: Jackie Gleason, Jonathan Winters, Johnny Carson and Paul Harvey. Rick owns a production company, CD Media, with Wally Clark. Rick's words to live by: "There's no point in being stupid, unless you can prove it."

> *"I was available, the right age, the right sex and I happened to fit."*
>
> *-Mary Lyon*

DeFRANCESCO, Gerry: **KIIS**, 1982-86, pd and 1989-92, vp/gm. A native of Philadelphia, Gerry received a communications degree from Temple University in 1977. Beginning in April 1982, Gerry arrived from Gannett's KSD-St. Louis with Wally Clark. Gerry guided KIIS' initial good fortune until 1986. During his stay with Gannett Broadcasting, he was vp/programming in 1984 while retaining pd at KIIS. In 1986 he moved to Gannett's WDAE/WUSA-Tampa as vp/gm. He returned to KIIS in late 1989 to be president/station manager, a position he held through 1990. He left Gannett briefly to return home to Philadelphia as vp of WYXR. In August of 1991, he returned to KIIS as vp and executive vp of Gannett Radio. He made one of the rare moves from programming to general management as he eventually was tapped president and general manager of KIIS from 1991 to 1992. In 1992 he went to WSNI-Philadelphia and eventually became president of the Gannett Radio Division. Gerry is married to Carolyn and has two children, Katie and Gerry.

DELANEY, John: **KJLH**, 1984-85; **KMET**, 1985-87; **KEZY**, 1987-90. John worked with Rick Lewis in morning drive at KMET and KEZY. John grew up in the Bronx and always had a comedic edge. While providing comedy voices, sketches and song parodies for radio, he entertained his classmates at Cal State Long Beach while earning a degree in 1990. John has been doing voiceover work, looping and preparing for a new comedy act to go on the road and eventually get to Las Vegas. "I was born John Rossi and that is what I go by now, in fact, I'm working on a rap act under the name 'Rossi's Possi.'"

DELAVIGNE, Joe: **KTWV**, 1987

DEL RANCHO, Pancho: **KTNQ**, 1997. Born Francisco Avelar, Pancho is the evening talk host on Spanish KTNQ. His nightly show is issues-oriented and Pancho takes a hard-line conservative approach to his subjects. His approach has been described as "colloquial and peppery" which lends an element of humor to serious subjects. His Sunday night show is called "El Mundo de Avelar."

> *"It was love at first sight. The strange part about meeting her was that I had a cancellation on my show and she filled in. We haven't been separated since then and recently we celebrated 25 years of marriage."*   -Art Kevin

DeMARAIS, Adam J.: **KHJ**, 1964-65; **KRLA**, 1964-65; **KBLA**, 1966; **KRLA**, 1968-69; **KEZY**, 1970-81, nd; **KRLA**, 1988-91. Adam is one of the powerful, booming voices who reported the news in Southern California. Born in Montreal he originally studied to be an actor and toured with a company out of New York while still a

teen. "I decided to pursue Hollywood and the world would pave my way with palm branches and gold, not the myrrh and pyrite it turned out to be." Adam arrived in Southern California by bus in 1948 and stayed briefly in the old Bunker Hill section of Los Angeles. "I took the Angels Flight daily to catch a street car to go out on cattle call auditions." To make ends meet he worked on the loading docks of Coca-Cola while pursuing theater arts and communications courses at L.A. City College. When the draft board caught up with him he had a choice of returning to Canada or going in the service. "Since I had married an American woman and we were with child, I figured that I'd spend the rest of my life in the States so I went to Korea." He was promoted to combat platoon sergeant and received a Purple Heart for serious wounds suffered in action. He returned to the Southland, "but I had lost the directions to the yellow brick road and bought a beer/wine bar, graduated from the Don Martin radio school (The Real Don Steele was a classmate) and worked at the Bel-Air Hotel for four years." My first job was as a dj in 1960 at KACY-Oxnard but I soon ran out of Robert Orben one-liners." During the 1960s he worked at KFXM-San Bernardino seven times, KDEO and KSON-San Diego as well as KORK-Las Vegas and KGU-Honolulu. While in the Islands, he appeared in many episodes of *Hawaii 5-O*. For six years in the 1980s he worked as an announcer at KTTV/Channel 11. In 1991 he suffered a stroke that left him partially paralyzed. "Six months later, I was back to normal. It was amazing." Some of the highlights over the decades covering news in the Southland include being personally involved with police and a gunmen during a bank hostage situation, covering five U.S. presidents, Academy Awards and flying in the Blue Angels plane. "I'm having fun working as a bartender at Ghost Town at Knott's Berry Farm."

DEMENTO, Dr.: **KPPC**, 1970-71; **KMET**, 1972-87; **KLSX**, 1987-93; **KSCA**, 1994-97. His show has been the most successful AOR syndicated show of weird, off-beat, mostly homemade music, and it single-handedly resurrected awareness of Spike Jones. Born Barret "Barry" Hansen in Minneapolis in 1941, Barry eventually became known by the music he played while wearing a battered top hat and by his mad professor demeanor -- the undisputed King of Dementia. *Time Magazine* described him as looking "more like the skipper of the Yellow Submarine than a well-schooled

musicologist." While he attended Reed College in Portland, he worked on a 10-watt college radio station with a show called "Musical Museum." In 1963 he graduated with a bachelor's degree in classical music theory. He wrote his thesis on early 20th century opera: his master's thesis at UCLA was on the evolution of black music from blues to r&b from 1945-53. This led to his degree in folk music. He played records that he picked up at the local Salvation Army and junk record stores. Over the years, this early experience led him to obtain records for his show in thrift shops, flea markets and in old abandoned warehouses. He worked as a staff producer for Specialty Records, where he compiled numerous LP reissues of vintage blues, gospel and rock recordings. He was the road manager for the rock group Canned Heat. On a lark, he did a weekend show on alternative-programmed KPPC in 1970, and his career started there. A year later he had a regular show playing zany novelty tunes. He got his nom de plume by accident. While he was playing *Transfusion* by Nervous Norvus, the gm's secretary burst into the control room and said, "You've got to be demented to play that on the radio!" In February 1972, he went to KMET and started with a two-hour Sunday show, but public demand increased it to four hours. His music presentations include *Making Love in a Subaru*, *Pencil-Neck Geek*, *Boobs A Lot*, by the Holy Modal Rounders and the Roto-Rooter Goodtime Christmas Band. James Brown, in the *LA Times*, described his program as "providing its listeners with Dementia's endless safari for the lost gems of recorded mutation, mistakes, novelties, nostalgia, satire, sickness and the serious work of untalented people." Barry started syndicating his show nationally in 1974, and Westwood One took it on in 1978. "I am probably best known in the biz as the guy who discovered Weird Al Yankovic; I started playing his songs on the air when he was a high school student, in 1976." In 1975, *Dr. Demento, Volume 1* was released. He created a series of albums on Rhino and Specialty Records, including *Dementia Royale*. His on-air choices avoid songs that are exclusively concerned with human sexual functions, defecation or urination. "Obscene language, overt racism or ethnic slurs are other no-no's," according to the Doctor. He once described himself as "the straight man to the records I play." His description of his syndicated show seems simple: "The show is funny, it's light, it's comic relief, and you don't get much of that on the radio anymore. Most of radio is pretty damn serious." He estimates that his collection totals 250,000 recordings, dating back to 1897.

DEMETRIOU, Pete: **KLAC**, 1978-84; **KFWB**, 1985-97. Pete has been where every news person worth his or her salt wants to be. Right smack dab in the middle of the action. On April 29, 1992, he was near the intersection of Normandie and Florence - at the flash point of the L.A. riots - taking rocks, bottles and a few other objects in 24 straight hours of coverage of the worst urban riot in American history. From October 26 thru November  4, 1993, he was on the fire lines as a seemingly endless fire marched to the Pacific Ocean and destroyed more than 350 homes. At 4:31 a.m. on January 17, 1994, he was on the 101 freeway in the Cahuenga Pass as the Northridge quake devastated L.A. and was the first field reporter on the air live with the story. He followed the pursuit and arrest of O.J. Simpson in 1994. He's covered the Academy Awards 8 times, 14 landings of the space shuttle at Edwards Air Force as well as spending 58 days covering Operation Desert Storm in the Persian Gulf War for all-News KFWB. A 1978 graduate from UCLA with a bachelor's degree in political-science, he interned during his Bruin days at KLA, KGIL, KPFK and KPCC. Born in Los Angeles on August 25, 1956, Pete has worked for AP radio network and ABC Radio News.

DEMORY, Shawn: **KEZY**, 1988-89

**KUTE 102FM presents
The Quiet Storm Concert
featuring
Rare Silk - Special EFX -
Skywalk
Universal Amphitheater, 11/14/86**

DENIS, Mark: **KFI**, 1969, pd; **KEZY**, 1969-83; **KHJ**, 1983-86; **KRLA**, 1986; **KFI/KOST**, 1986-97. Mark was born in Glendale on February 8, 1941, and grew up in Compton. During his time at Compton JC, he announced  the half-time activities at the football games. The show-business bug, however, bit him much earlier. Mark built a performing stage in his garage and put on variety shows. His first on-air experience was KFIL (later KYMS), and he pronounced the call letters "KFI LFM". Interviewed between traffic reports, he commented, "Isn't it ironic that I end up at KFI?" He got started in Hemet in the early 1960s and went to KFXM-San Bernardino in 1962 before spending "some time in the Air Force." After the service, he went to KMEN-San Bernardino to do overnights and production, which in 1966 led to KGB-San Diego where he spent three years and ended up pd. He made his transition from dj work to traffic during his time on KHJ, when it was called "Car Radio" and traffic reports were dispensed every 10 minutes. Mark is universally one of the most well-liked radio people in Southern California and makes over 300 calls a year wishing his peers "Happy Birthday!" KFI pd David Hall utilizes Mark as the "image voice" for the 50,000 watt giant, and he is currently the traffic broadcaster during middays on KFI/KOST. He has been a regular guest lecturer and has taught a course in telecommunications at USC. Mark was the voice of the monorail at Disneyland for half a decade and continues to enjoy a successful voiceover career. His key to success? "Be versatile! After all, at KEZY I survived five program directors and I was one of them." On September 1, 1996, Mark celebrated 35 years in broadcasting, making it one of the longest current running careers in Southern California radio. During his decade with KFI/KOST, he has broadcast more than 70,000 traffic reports. "I still love it, most of the time."

DERDIVANIS, Kent: **KMPC**, 1983-86. Kent, a former UCLA student, was one of the UCLA sports play-by-play announcers. He teamed with Joel Meyers on the basketball and football broadcasts.

DeROO, Doug: **KIQQ**, 1977. Doug arrived in the Southland from KERN and KAFY-Bakersfield. After his brief stay at "K-100" he returned to Bakersfield, where he works for KERN.

DeSAEGHER, **KPZE**, 1987: He co-hosted "Sportsnight."

De SANTIS, Frank: **KMET**, 1977-79; **KWST**, 1979-83; **KNX/FM**, 1983; **KLOS**, 1983-88. Born in Los Angeles, Frank grew up in La Habra. "It was at Cal Poly San Luis Obispo where I stumbled into radio. I noticed that the campus radio station programmed classical music with students who seemed classically clueless, so I volunteered figuring I could do as well or at least no worse." After college he worked at KZOZ-San Luis Obispo and in 1977 started at KMET where he did fill-in and weekends. In December of 1979 Frank moved to KWST where he did overnights and production. "After a short cup of coffee at KNX/FM in 1983," as he described it, Frank began his half-decade stint at KLOS where he did overnights,  fill-ins, news and the weekend talk show. While at KLOS Frank also began a different phase of his radio experience working at Westwood One where he dove into the world of national radio, handling affiliate relations, production, voiceover and interviewing assignments. In December of 1988, the newly married De Santis moved to New York and began his association with national radio syndicator MediaAmerica. He also does voiceover work. "I have performed in four plays off and off-off Broadway, and still occasionally nurse old wounds accumulated from seven years of playing rugby." Frank, his wife Margo, and their two children live in New Rochelle, New York and "are one happy bunch."

DeSANTIS, Gia: **KROQ**, 1993. Gia worked the swing shift at KROQ.

DeSILVA, Walt: **KPPC**, 1965-66; **KFWB**. Walt was a jazz dj who went on to broadcast news on KFWB.

DeSOTO, Dave: **KMPC**, 1965-82. The veteran newsman served as Orange Country bureau chief for KMPC and was also part of the Robert W. Morgan morning drive team. In late 1980 Dave suffered a heart attack that affected his speech. From his hospital bed he began reading magazines aloud. In the beginning it was only a sentence at a time without stumbling or slurring. Within a month he was back to work at KMPC.

DETZ, John: **KWST**, 1975, gm
DEVANEY, Ken: **KHJ**, 1965, gm

Metromedia buys 94.7FM for $400,000. Call letters changed to KLAC/FM. -March 17, 1965

DEVEREUX, Nicole: **KMET**, 1984-85; **KJOI**, 1986-89; **KTWV**, 1987-97.

Nicole grew up in Colorado. "I really began my dj'ing when I was 7 years old. My mom and dad would sit by and listen as I would work our hi-fi, changing selections as fast as I could. Knowing they enjoyed my 'show' was exhilarating." After studying at the KIIS Broadcasting Workshop she worked in the early 1980s in Colorado at KLMO-Longmont, KLIR and KPKE-Denver. Nicole joined KMET as a production assistant and then to "K-Joy" where she was an announcer and morning show engineer for Roger Barkley. Nicole has been at "the Wave" since 1987. "Now, it's faith in knowing there are people listening and enjoying the music I get to play. That makes it the best job in the world. I love it!"

DEVINE, Bob: **KRHM**, 1957

DeVOID, Phil: **KNAC**, 1984-85

DeWITT, Paul: **KLSX**, 1995

DEXTER, Jerry: **KMPC**, 1959-63; **KLAC**, 1963-64. "I

was lucky to work at the very last of one of the great American radio stations, KMPC." Born in San Francisco, by age 15 Jerry was already appearing on local TV shows. At age 20, he opened his own publicity office. As famed *San Francisco Chronicle* jazz columnist, Ralph J. Gleason noted: "Dexter is the nation's youngest night club press agent, yet not old enough to be in a bar." His first account was "Fack's," a famed San Francisco nitery where he was befriended by KSFO morning giant, Don Sherwood. In 1957, Jerry took a job with the CBS/TV affiliate in Las Vegas working as a staff announcer and on-camera personality. At KENO-Las Vegas an on-air stunt to save the doomed fictional character Tom Dooley (Jerry claimed Dooley was being held in a Las Vegas jail) attracted not only local coverage but a full-page story in *Newsweek*. Don Sherwood followed Jerry's career and urged Golden West Broadcasting to hire Jerry for the morning drive slot at KVI-Seattle. Within months, KMPC programming vp Robert Forward moved Jerry from Seattle to KMPC becoming, at 24, the youngest on-air talent ever hired at the station. *Movie Mirror Magazine* named him one of "America's great radio performers" and the *LA Times*' Don Page named Jerry as host of "The Best Popular Music Show of 1963." Jerry started acting when he reached the Southland and appeared in *Gomer Pyle*, *Dragnet*, *McHale's Navy* and a host of other tv shows. His voiceover work included featured voices on cartoons including *Josie and the Pussycats*, *Aquaman* and *Gulliver*. In 1968 he hosted his own early morning daily variety/interview show on KABC/Channel 7 called *Good Day L.A. with Jerry Dexter*. Jerry was featured in one of 1969's biggest films, Robert Redford's *Downhill Racer*. Jerry wrote and produced a syndicated tv special, *Words & Music by Bobby Troup*. For a year he was encased in a black bag as KTTV/Channel 11's morning movie host. The gimmick attracted much national attention. Jerry was the announcer on Alex Trebec's first American show, NBC's *Wizard of Odds*. In 1976 he formed a program syndication company and for the past 20 years has been distributing tv shows all around the world including *The Wolfman Jack Show*, *Johnny Cash Ridin' The Rails* and the *Willie Nelson Special*. "If it had not been for Don Sherwood, I have no idea where I would be. I was so lucky to have been at KMPC in the last days of that legendary, really big time radio station. I will always remember that time in my life as being the most fun!"

DI, Lady: **KNAC**, 1986-87. Lady Di was an ex-Las Vegas dancer who wanted to change careers and work in radio. She was with a Baltimore station before arriving in the Southland. The South African born dj from Johannesburg married an account executive with the station. She has managed a comedy club in Long Beach.

DIAMOND, Dave: **KHJ**, 1965; **KBLA**, 1965-67; **KFWB**, 1967-68; **KRLA**, 1971-72; **KIIS/AM**, 1972-75; **KFI**, 1976-82. The Deadwood, South Dakota native born Sid Davison had early experience with Don Burden on Omaha's KOIL. He was pd of WKGN-Knoxville and WIL-St. Louis and had a radio and tv show in Denver before reaching Los Angeles. Dave became one of KHJ's original "Boss Jocks" when the new format was launched in April 1965, but he lasted only a couple of months. Dave went to KBLA where he launched the "Diamond Mine" and started playing long LP cuts. According to the book *Can't Get Out of Here Alive*, Dave is credited as the founder of The Doors. In 1966, he was signed to emcee the *Miss America Go-Go Contest*. He also worked the Crescendo Night Club on the Sunset Strip and Hollywood's The Action. In 1967,

Dave starred in an ABC/TV pilot called *Helpmate*. Dave published *Incense & Peppermint* by the Strawberry Alarm Clock which reached #1 in 1967. In 1968, he appeared in an episode of ABC/TV's *Outsiders*. Then he went to San Francisco's KFRC, where he worked from 1968 into the '70s. In  1971, besides his work on KRLA, he hosted a daily tv show called *Headshop* on KDOC/Channel 56. He produced *Acapulco Gold* by the Rainy Daze. In 1972 Dave was the pd of KCBS/FM-San Francisco and briefly did middays at KTLK-Denver. He returned to the Southland a year later and went to KIIS morning drive, moving to evenings in 1974 and staying at the station until 1975. He also recorded *Hobo John* for Claridge Records in 1976. In 1976 he signed on at KFI for music and talk shows. Dave is currently manager of KBHU/FM in Spearfish, South Dakota and teaches communication at Black Hills State University.

DIAMOND, Jim: **KYMS**, 1969. For the past two-plus decades, Jim has been working radio in Bakersfield.

DIEGO, Rick: **KHTZ**, 1985; **KBZT/KLSX/KRLA**, 1986-93; **KBIG**, 1993-97. A native of San Antonio, Rick started his radio career in 1974 at KTSA while attending San Antonio College majoring in radio/tv/film. He was working at KFMS-Las Vegas as pd and morning man before joining KHTZ. At KRLA Rick worked the all-night shift and in 1991 moved to assistant pd. For many years at KBIG he hosted a popular disco show on Saturday nights as well as working afternoon drive. He currently hosts "KBIG After Dark." Rick lives in the San Fernando Valley with his wife Ellen and two sons.

DIGBY: **KWST**, 1978-80. The British dj's real name was Welch.

DILLS, Elmer: **KABC**, 1977-96; **KMPC/KTZN**, 1996-97; **KIEV**, 1997. Born in 1928, Elmer has provided

Southland listeners with tips on where to go for a romantic evening, a birthday celebration or a wedding anniversary. He also has done food and travel reports for KABC/Channel 7 in addition to his radio show. He came to broadcasting after more than 20 years with the State Department, where his primary function there was to wine and dine dignitaries. His notoriety forced him to make restaurant reservations under an assumed name to avoid preferential treatment. In the fall of 1996 he took a table at sister station KMPC, now KTZN. Elmer left the station in the summer of 1997 for KIEV.

DINERO, Al: **KPPC**, 1968

DION: SEE Dion Jackson

DiPRIMA, Dominque: **KKBT**, 1994-97. Dominque hosts

the community action show, "Street Scene." She was born in Manhattan and raised in San Francisco. She was influenced by her "beat generation" parents (mother is poet Diane DiPrima, father is playwright/poet Amiri Baraka, aka LeRoi Jones). Dominque hosted her own magazine/talk show "Home Turf" in San Francisco which lasted seven years and earned her five local Emmy awards. She graduated from San Francisco State University's drama department. "Street Science" was chosen as 1994's radio talk show of the year by *L.A. Weekly*.

DITTY, Bill: **KFWB**, 1959-63; **KRLA**, 1963-65; **KFWB**, 1965-75. Bill was an engineer who worked weekends and fill-in at KRLA. He used *Do-Wah-Ditty* as his on-air name. At KFWB Bill was an engineer. "I was a farm boy in Minnesota and after serving in World War II I came to the Southland. At KRLA I did hops in the outlying areas where kids couldn't afford much more than fifty cents to attend a dance. I took over roller rinks and brought great acts like the Beach Boys to these depressed areas. I had six kids of my own, so I knew how tough it was." In 1975 Bill retired to a ranch in Sylmar where he raised horses. He has been very active in the American Lupus Association and has helped raised millions of dollars for the organization. In 1987 Bill fully retired and moved to Ukiah.

DIX, Mike: **KFWB**, 1964

DIXON, Diane: **KMPC**, 1994. Diane was Peter Tilden's first co-host on KMPC Talk radio.

DIXON, Glen: **KDAY**, 1974

DIXON, Mason: **KHJ**, 1977. In 1978, Mason left KHJ for WRBQ-Tampa/St. Petersburg and achieved longtime success. Scott Shannon had major success there with Mason, prior to Shannon's move to New York. In 1993, Mason won four *Billboard* awards for his work at WMTX-Tampa/St. Petersburg. In the spring of 1995, Mason saved several men who were capsized in Tampa bay while piloting his cruiser, The Radio Waves. He was upped to station manager of WMTX in the spring of 1995.

DIXON, Tom: **KHJ**, 1939-43; **KFAC**, 1946-87; **KUSC**, 1987-89; **KKGO**, 1989-97. Tom was part of the classic music scene in Southern California for 50 years. He was born in Edmonton in 1915. His family moved to L.A. in 1922, and Tom has never left. He studied acting at Los Angeles City College and wanted to achieve a career in the theater. However, a two-year bout with his health persuaded him to seek a steadier career. He landed a job at KHJ when it was part of the Mutual Network. He worked as a transcription file clerk and as a member of the sound department and, after a year as an apprentice, he was promoted to the "announce" staff. He announced newscasts, dramas, dance band remotes, live broadcasts and game shows. He also emceed audience shows and

filled in for Jack Bailey on *Queen for a Day* while Jack was on vacation. He left KHJ and for three years was a free-lance performer. He heard that KFAC wanted an announcer with a Classic Music background. He intended to stay six weeks, but, as Tom said over lunch during the holidays in 1994, "I was like the man who came to dinner and stayed 41 years." The highlight of his five years at KKGO was the opportunity to host the "Evening Concert" series which was sponsored for decades by the Southern California Gas Company. Tom is a frequent lecturer on his favorite composer, Mozart. His car bears the bumper sticker "WAMOZRT," which stands for Wolfgang Amadeus Mozart and advertises his addiction. "You have no idea how many people ask, 'What's a WAMOZRT?' And half the time, when I tell them it stands for Mozart...they ask, 'What's a Mozart.'" Tom lives in Burbank, he still loves the classics, has a marvelous sense of humor and feels blessed that he has the opportunity to continue to play and listen to his favorite music.

DOC ON THE ROQ: SEE Boyd R. Britton

How would you like to be remembered?

Charlie TUNA: "As somebody who did the best show I could every time on the radio and cared about kids with my 20 years of coaching youth sports."

Dave HULL: "As a man who tried to do his best."

Bill BALLANCE: "As the beloved founder of R.O.M.E.O - RETIRED OLD MAN EATING OUT. And as the first to realize that ENVY is the FRIENDSHIP that ONE performer has for ANOTHER and that there's NO DEODORANT like SUCCESS. And always be POSITIVE: anytime you're filling out a form for a new gig, in the space following "POSITION IN LIFE," print "ENVIABLE." I was the FIRST to discover that SPEECH is conveniently located midway between THOUGHT & ACTION - where it OFTEN SUBSTITUTES FOR BOTH...and the SECRET for long DECADES as a TALKSHOW COMMUNICATOR is to grow ANTENNAE INSTEAD OF HORNS. AND, that WHATEVER HAPPENS, NEVER HAPPENS BY ITSELF. At What He Did, He Was The Best There Was."

Bob HUDSON: "As a man who kept his word, and kept it on time. A man who never succumbed to Bill Drake and his disciples who erased story telling from radio while cutting lyrics from songs in order to play more records per hour. I want to be remembered as a man who forty years after the fact is still being quoted by doctors and lawyers and successful businessmen and women who were late for high school classes because of waiting in the school parking lot for the end of one of my stories. And last but not least, I want to be remembered as a man who lived with a lady who kept her word, and kept it on time, remaining soft and smelling good while she kept it."

DOEBLIN, Peter: **KIQQ**, 1987

DOGGETT, Jerry: Born in 1917, Jerry was one of the original Dodger announcers along with Vin Scully who followed the team from Brooklyn to Los Angeles. He retired in 1987 after 32 broadcast seasons with the Dodgers. He called more than 5,000 major league games plus about 2,500 in the minor leagues. Jerry began his broadcast career in 1938 at KFRO-Longview, Texas, where he announced minor league baseball and high school sports. For 15 years he was the play-by-play announcer for the Dallas Rebels of the Texas League. Jerry was part of Gordon McLendon's Liberty Network sports broadcasts. He announced SMU basketball games from 1946 to 1856, and handled play-by-play for the Dallas team in the U.S. Hockey League. Jerry's first Dodger game with Vin Scully was in September of 1956 at the Polo Grounds. Tom Hoffarth of the *Daily News* had memories of Jerry: "He was like your favorite uncle, the one who never knew exactly what was going on but was nonetheless entertaining even with that light-blue checkered sportcoat. Doggett could turn a simple 6-4-3 double play into a Chinese fire drill. He once described the fans at Dodger Stadium during Fernandomania as "a large Latin-speaking crowd." In 1996 he was elected to the Southern California Sports Broadcasters Association Hall of Fame. He died in July 7, 1997 at the age of 80.

DOLAN, Cindy: **KNX**, 1997

DOLAN, Joe: **KHJ**, 1964-65. Joe was one of the early talk-show hosts. When he left the Southland he moved to KCBS-San Francisco.

DOLL, Jonathan: **KRTH**, 1986-91. The former *Star Search* winner won the 1984 *Billboard* magazine

Personality of the Year Award while working at WZPL-Indianapolis and in 1979 while at KMGK-Des Moines. In the 1970s Jonathan was at WIVY-Jacksonville, "G-100"-Mobile and "96KX"-Pittsburgh. In 1981 he won the Drake/Chenault Top 5 Talent Search Award. Born and raised in New York City he's always been around comedy. Since the mid-1980s Jonathan has been doing stand-up and opens for Jay Leno, Jerry Seinfeld and Garry Shandling. He worked mornings at Westwood One Radio Network's Hot Country format for many years before joining mornings at KKRW-Houston in the summer of 1995. He now lives in Las Vegas.

DOMAS, Pete: **KRTH**, 1979-88. Pete started as an intern and went on to win 2 Golden Mike awards for sports reporting.

DOMINO: **KIIS**, 1993-96. Born Tony Lini, in 1990 Domino worked nights at WPLJ-New York. The party jock joined KIIS for frantic evenings in the late summer of 1993 after a similar post at KHKS-Dallas. He hosted a nightly feature, "Desperate And Dateless." In the summer of 1996, he went to KHKS-Dallas.

DONAHUE, Raechel: **KMET**, 1968-76; **KPOL**, 1977; **KWST**, 1978-83; **KROQ**, 1984-86; **KIIS**, 1984-87; **KLOS**, 1986; **KSRF**, 1988; **KMPC/FM/KEDG**, 1988-91; **KOCM/KSRF**, 1991; **KCSN**, 1996-97. Raechel

Hamilton was born in National City, California, and arrived on Southern California airwaves from KSAN-San Francisco. Raechel started at KMET as md, in 1968, with her husband, Tom "Big Daddy" Donahue. Jim Ladd described Raechel in his book *Radio Waves* as "a being who was never at rest. Her brain seemed to work something like a pinball machine. What passed for her attention span was really more akin to a speeding silver ball, unleashing a different idea every time it bounced off a new synapse bumper." At KIIS, she worked with #1 rated personality Rick Dees in the morning. Raechel appeared in a 1981 *Oui Magazine* article titled *Ladies of the Airwaves*. She has produced a local tv show and done voiceovers for 150 films, as well as local and national commercials. She was the narrator of ABC/TV's *Hail to the Chief*, starring Patty Duke, in 1985. In the same year, she drove in the Toyota Celica Pro Celebrity race at the Long Beach Grand Prix. In 1990 she spent a year working on an offshore radio station near the French Riviera. At "K-Surf" she worked morning drive and was part of the launch of "MARS/fm" on May 24, 1991. She did overnights briefly at KMPC and then joined Gene Autry's brief experiment with AOR on "the Edge." By 1990, Raechel was heard on KCQR-Santa Barbara. Living in Venice, California, Raechel is the feature editor for a group of five local newspapers. She has published books in a series called *The Golden Rules: Romance, Modern Etiquette* and *Single Parenting*. She writes for an English magazine called *Xpose* and is working on a new book provocatively titled *Jock Itch*. In the mid-1990s, Raechel worked at Unistar's "Adult Rock & Roll" format for weekend duty along with a Saturday show on Cal State Northridge's station.

DONAHUE, Tom "Big Daddy": **KPPC**, 1967-68; **KMET**, 1968. Tom left an important, indelible mark in the annals of radio in California and in the industry. Born in 1925, the 350-pound hippie changed the sound of radio on April 7, 1967. Frustrated with the Top 40 presentation, he recognized the convergence of a generational/societal/economic environment - the Vietnam War, drugs, the Richard Nixon presidency, hippies, and distrust of those over 30 years of age. His radio revolution involved playing sets of songs with no interruptions and no talk over the beginnings or endings of songs. At the end of each set, he would talk about how the music related to what was going on in the community or the world. Recognized as the "Father" of Progressive radio, Tom started his radio journey in Charleston, at WTIP in 1949, and a year later he worked at *Washington Post*-owned WINX-Rockville, Maryland. Before the end of 1950, Tom was in Philadelphia at WIBG with a show called "Danceland." He stayed for a decade. In 1961, Tom traveled to San Francisco and worked at KYA until 1965 when he and Bob Mitchell put together a record business. He produced shows at the Cow Palace and did the Beatles' last live performance in 1966. In April of 1967, Tom joined KMPX, where he introduced the "music sets" format, and in May of 1968, he moved over to KSAN. In 1967, Tom came to Southern California to work his evolving magic on KPPC in the basement of the Pasadena Presbyterian Church with his wife Raechel. By the summer of 1968 he was consulting the launch of Progressive radio on KMET and also did on-air work. He died on April 28, 1975, at the age of 48. He was winning at backgammon when he suffered a heart attack. He said, "At least I go out a winner." In Jim Ladd's book, *Radio Waves*, tribute was paid to Tom's contribution: "Tom Donahue was our generation's first town crier. He gathered the villagers together and introduced them to the music of a new breed of wandering minstrels. It was here, in this electronic town square, that we first heard the music and danced to its message. He was the first to strike the tribal drum, and his departure would mark a dangerous turning point in tribal history."

DONALDSON, Lorri: **KABC**, 1967-70. Lorri was one of 300 young women who answered full-page KABC ads, seeking two Ladybirds to become the first female helicopter traffic and weather reporters. She won the afternoon slot and was called "Eve O'Day." For more than two years, Lorri and her morning counterpart, Kelly Lange, in their tight-fitting silver lame jump suits, paved the way for today's less-exploited women deejays and announcers. Lorri remembered that her response to the ad started out as a college gag. "They ran huge ads showing a lady in a spacesuit with a helmet," she told the *LA Times*. "I was working at 20th Century Fox at the time and I thought it was the funniest thing I ever saw." Lorri and Kelly started on Valentine's Day 1967 and remained KABC sweethearts until 1970. Lorri went back to being an executive secretary with a Hollywood film production firm. "Maybe we helped pave the way for other ladies in radio."

DONAVON, Dave: SEE Joe Cipriano

DONEGAN, Mike: **KLAC**, 1986-87. Mike was sidekick to morning drive award-winner Gerry House during his brief stay in Los Angeles. Born and raised in Nashville, Mike graduated from the University of Memphis law school. He arrived at KLAC from doing the morning show at WSM-Nashville where he was also a writer for country tv shows on WTBS and TNN. Mike has been working as the morning show host at WKDF-Nashville since 1989.

DONOHO, Todd: **KLOS**, 1988-97. The Indiana native was born in 1956 and graduated from the University of Missouri in 1977 with a bachelor's in journalism. He did tv sports in Grand Rapids and Cincinnati and NFL play-by-play. Prior to joining the morning team with Mark and Brian in 1988, Todd hosted a national sports trivia show for the FNN/Score network. His trivia expertise is emphasized with a daily "Stump the Commissioner" segment on "Sports Snorts." Todd started double duty with KABC/Channel 7 as a member of the *Eyewitness News* team. He also hosts a post-Monday Night Football show. The Valencia resident lives with his wife and three boys. Todd has earned four Emmys.

DONOVAN, Bo: **KDAY**, 1970-71; **KLAC**, 1971-72; **KBBQ**, 1972-73. Bo began a broadcast career in 1964 at KXO-El Centro (his hometown). He went on to KBLU-Yuma and KDES-Palm Springs as morning personality and pd. In 1968 Bo joined KROY-Sacramento when *Billboard* named it Contemporary Station of the Year. From Sacramento he moved to KMEN-San Bernardino. When he left the Southland in 1973 he was appointed director of programming for all nine SRO stations. Three years later he joined Tuesday Productions and spent eight years. "We became the largest producer of musical IDs and promotional campaigns for radio and tv." In 1984 he formed his own company, Silvertree Productions, where he has won numerous awards. Active in the San Diego community, Bo has served as live announcer for the PGA Buick Invitational golf tournament for over a decade. Bo and his high school sweetheart recently celebrated their 29th wedding anniversary. They have 2 children and live in San Diego.

DONOVAN, Michael: **KCBS**, 1996-97. Since early 1996 Michael has been working the swing shift at "Arrow 93." Born and raised in Vancouver, Michael has voiced over 40 animation projects. He arrived in the Southland to pursue his animation voiceover career from five years at CKLW-Detroit.

DONOVAN, Sheri: **KROQ**, 1995-96; **KLYY**, 1996-97. Sheri was the first personality hired by "Modern Rock Y-107." She was born in Scarborough, Ontario, Canada and grew up in Farmington, Michigan. Prior to joining KROQ for weekends, Sheri worked in Michigan radio. She started in 1983 at WTCM-Traverse City as a news person and midday jock. Two years later she was in Flint first working at WWCK and then WKSG-Detroit. In 1988 Sheri joined WLLZ-Detroit and spent over six years working every shift but mornings and overnights. She hosted an Aerosmith concert in Brussels and Guns 'n Roses event in Paris for WW1. Sheri is married to Darren Eggleston of Maverick Records.

DOOLEY, Tom: **KHJ**, 1974. Tom worked at WQAM-Miami, WSAI-Cincinnati and KRUX-Phoenix in the early 1970s before arriving at "Boss Radio." Tom didn't last long. He accused President Richard Nixon of being the one behind John Kennedy's assassination and was fired on the air in 1974. Tom played guitar, drums, and piano and performed with the Mar-Keys, Bill Black's Combo and Ace Cannon. In 1983, he worked at KLIF-Dallas. His voiceover career includes the Billy Graham Evangelistic Association. Tom owns Master Media in Hurst, Texas.

DORNAN, Robert K.: **KLAC**, 1966; **KABC**, 1971. The former talk show host was a U.S. Congressman from Garden Grove. He served nine terms in the U.S. House of Representatives from the 46th Congressional District. Born in New York City on April 3, 1933, he graduated from Loyola High School in 1950. He attended Loyola University until 1953 when at age 19 he volunteered for service in the United States Air Force. Bob produced and hosted radio and television public affairs programs from 1965 to 1976 and was awarded Emmys. In addition to his radio work in Los Angeles, he spent 1970 hosting a talk show on KGO-San Francisco. Active in domestic civil rights during the 1960s, he marched with Martin Luther King and registered black voters in the South. He originated the POW/MIA bracelet worn by more than 12 million Americans during the Vietnam War.

DORTON, Joe: **KBIG/KBRT**, 1973-79, gm. Joe arrived in the Southland from Bonneville's WCLR-Chicago to run KBIG. When he left L.A. he moved to New York to be president of Bonneville's Torbet-Lasker agency. In the fall of 1995 he became marketing manager for Metro Networks in Detroit and is now gm of WWBR-Detroit.

DOUCETTE, Eddie: **KMPC**, 1990. Eddie was the voice of the Rams. He was the play-by-play announcer for the Milwaukee Bucks for 16 seasons, and moved to the San Diego area in 1980 to "provide a better climate" for his son, Brett, who was suffering from leukemia. Eddie continued to work for the Bucks through 1984 and has since been an announcer for the Indiana Pacers, the Denver Nuggets and SportsChannel, doing Dodger telecasts. He was originally hired to do Angels fill-in for Bob Starr but got the full-time job when Starr went to do radio with the Boston Red Sox. Eddie has also done college football for the USA Network and the 1985 Clippers.

DOUD, Chuck: **KLYY**, 1996-97. Chuck is the production director of "Y107" and also works middays.

DOUG the SLUG: **KROQ**, 1992-96. Doug Roberts arrived at "the Roq" from KZZP-Phoenix. In the spring of 1996 "Sluggo" joined WXRK-New York

DOUGLAS, Chet: **KBLA**, 1965; **KFWB**, 1968-80. Chet anchored morning drive news at KFWB for over a decade. He was also an actor during these years and was featured or co-starred in several major motion pictures for Columbia and Paramount Pictures. In

January of 1981 Chet joined ABC in New York where he anchored morning drive news for the Entertainment Network until late 1992. He then retired to Scottsdale where he and his wife currently live. "I keep my hand in the business by doing media consulting and training."

DOUGLAS, Gary: **KACD**, 1995-96. Gary worked weekends at "CD 103" and moved to middays in early 1996. When the format switched to "Groove Radio," Gary left the station and went to WW1. He arrived in the Southland from New Jersey and has worked at KCRW and has done production at KABC.

DOUGLASS, Dave: **KLAC**, 1981-84; **KMNY**, 1987; **KFWB**, 1985-97. Dave is a writer and part-time sports reporter for all-News KFWB. He also worked for "Money Radio." At KLAC Dave was an assignment editor and filled in as sports anchor and dj. In the late 1970s he was nd of Cal State Northridge's campus station, KCSN. In 1981 Dave spent three years working as a weekend news anchor at KVEN-Ventura. In addition to his work at KFWB, he is a news writer at KCOP/Channel 13.

DOURIDAS, Chris: **KCRW**, 1991-97. Chris is the host and md of KCRW's "Morning Becomes Eclectic." Born in 1963, he arrived in the Southland after working as host of a similar music show at a Dallas public radio station.

DOWER, Dona: **KNX**, 1983-90 and 1993-97. Dona, a native of Fitchburg, Massachusetts, graduated with an engineering degree from Rensselaer Polytechnic Institute in Troy. In 1993 Dona rejoined "KNXNewsradio" with Jim Thornton and Jill Angel for midday traffic from a stint at Metro Traffic. She was part of Bill Keene's (30-year KNX vet) replacement team. Dona is also active in voiceover work.

DOWLING, John: **KJOI**, 1989, pd; **KXEZ**, 1990. John arrived in L.A. from Viacom's Country station, WMZQ-Washington, DC, to be pd and work on-air in middays.

DOWNES, Steve: **KWST**, 1978-81; **KEZY**, 1981-82; **KLOS**, 1982-91; **KLSX**, 1994.

Steve grew up in Columbus, Ohio and graduated with a B.A. from the University of Dayton. He began his radio career in Ohio in 1969 at one of the Midwest's first progressive rock stations. In 1974, he became pd of WYDD-Pittsburgh. He was operations director of KWST in 1979. He spent the better part of a decade at KLOS. In the mid-1980s for a half-decade, Steve was the voice for many of the top syndicated rock shows produced by the Westwood Radio Network including "The Superstar Concert Series," "The Rock Chronicles" and "Rock and Roll Never Forgets." In 1986, he was flown to Japan to do a series of radio shows for "FM Yokohama" which was a new radio station. "In 1991 I was seeking a change in lifestyle and a desire to return to radio management and accepted a position of pd and afternoon drive at WRXK ('96K')-Ft. Meyers. No sooner had I unpacked my bags on Tranquil Sanibel Island, I was asked to transfer to WYNF-Tampa as pd." He was lured back to the Southland in late 1993 to host "Rockline." He joined afternoon drive at KLSX in the spring of 1994 and left before the year was out. He continues a successful voiceover career working with many record companies, movie studios, Toyota and Delta Airlines. Steve started morning drive at KTYD-Santa Barbara on February 13, 1995.

DOWNING, Al: **KABC**, 1983-87. The former Dodger pitcher hosted KABC's "SportsTalk" show and post-game shows following Dodger road games. Al was also affiliated with Chicago White Sox, ABC and CBS. He is now in industrial real estate.

DOYLE, Enos: **KMET**, 1973-75. Enos worked the all-night shift at "the Mighty Met."

DRAKE, Bill: **KHJ**, 1965-73; **KIQQ**, 1973-74. The architect of the legendary "Boss Radio" format along with pd Ron Jacobs, in April of 1965.

Charlie Van Dyke worked for Bill in Boston, San Francisco and Los Angeles and tells the Drake story: "Bill Drake had been working as pd of KYA-San Francisco and ran into the now-often-experienced 'philosophical differences.' He decided that he should quit KYA and find a station to program that would give him more room. Gene Chenault offered him the opportunity to program a station in Stockton and KYNO-Fresno. Drake said, 'Chenault gave me complete creative freedom, two salaries and a brand new Cadillac. Not bad!' Drake pulled off a quick 'worst to first' featuring a classic radio battle with KMAK, which was being programmed by Ron Jacobs. It is reported that the battle featured all the dirty tactics possible...going through the other station's trash, secretly recording conversations and more. When the battle ended, Drake and KYNO were strong winners. KYNO had more audience than the other 17 stations combined. Excited by the success, Chenault talked with a friend of his, Willet Brown, who owned another ratings disaster, KGB-San Diego. Chenault wanted to buy the station. Brown decided that he wanted to keep it and made a deal for Drake to come to KGB and work his Fresno magic at the San Diego property. Again, it was a quick win. KGB went from last to first in 63 days. Meanwhile, Brown was talking to a friend of his, Tom O'Neil, who was head of RKO. The conversation was about this whiz kid from Fresno who turned Gene's station around, then rolled into San Diego and did it again. O'Neil was well aware of the poor position of most of the RKO stations at that time. So, the decision was made to see if Drake could pull it off again. KHJ was given over to the team of Bill Drake and Gene Chenault. Chenault dealt with the ownership and Drake made the programming plans. Drake began running practice shows in a KHJ production room, getting ready for the debut of 'Boss Radio.' During this period, a newsman at KHJ was fired and, in reaction, took much of the material and tapes in his possession to then market champ KFWB. KFWB attempted to beat KHJ to the debut of the new format. Drake and KHJ responded by popping the format immediately and ran promos on KHJ inviting listeners to sample KFWB and KRLA and then come back to '93/KHJ' to hear the real 'Boss Radio.' The pd's job at KHJ was especially important and Drake selected his former Fresno competitor, Ron Jacobs, for the job, having been impressed with Jacobs' battle skills during the 'Fresno War.' The a capella jingles, reduced commercial load, tight format, high profile promotions and unique djs all worked together, and KHJ was another 'worst to first' for Drake. Detractors said that his was a West Coast style that could not work anywhere else. Drake and Chenault decided to test the format elsewhere and went to work at KAKC-Tulsa. So the friendship of Gene Chenault, Willet Brown and Tom O'Neil, which was really three guys operating radio stations that were 'dogs,' provided an opportunity for the birth of a new format. Drake said, 'Getting cooperation on the format was really pretty easy -- they had nothing to lose.' The reduced commercial load wasn't a problem, Drake notes: 'Most of the stations didn't have any commercials anyway.' Another factor was that all the stations, while performing poorly when Drake came on board, had good signals. The necessity for a strong signal was a position also held by Top 40-pioneer Gordon McLendon who said, 'it doesn't matter how good you are if the people can't hear you.' O'Neil recognized the potential of KFRC-San Francisco and handed it over to Drake. Within about a year, RKO also delivered CKLW-Detroit, WHBQ-Memphis, WRKO-Boston and WOR/FM-New York to be remade in the image of their winning sisters. Anyone who worked a Drake station knows that it wasn't just the spot load and jingles that made the Drake sound unique. Drake has been described by Bill Watson, a long-time programming associate, as having the kind of 'listener ear' that programmers often don't have. Watson said that he once went into a gas station, and the attendant made a comment about his station that went right to the point. 'Why didn't I think of what that gas station guy said,' Watson commented. 'That's the kind of feedback Drake would give all the time.' Drake also set up the station in a way that put air people directly under the pd, who was essentially the only one who could deal with the air staff. The pd's, in turn, were coached on style and morale techniques, and a real attitude developed that grew into pride. It was kind of the Marine Corps of Radio. Programmers were in constant contact with the air staff via the famous 'Batphone.' Drake pd's all had car phones long before they became so popular. And Drake and his team were available to the pd's 24-hours-a-day to talk through any sudden change in the market. So it was in Los Angeles that the nation really first noticed a new air product that received life primarily through the friendship of three radio executives who shared their frustrations with each other and decided to give it a try." Bill started as a jock in Northern California. In December 1973, he took over KIQQ and brought along Robert W. Morgan and The Real Don Steele to wage battle against their alma mater. In his definitive book on the history of radio and pop music, *Music in the Air*, Philip Eberly described the "Drake formula" this way: "He declared dead air a felony. He decreed more rapid-fire talk by disc jockeys. He dropped the traditional 40-song play list down 10 to 30 (that is, 'Boss 30'). He reduced the allowable 18 commercials per hour (the FCC quota) to an ironclad 12." During the first half of the early 1990s, Drake played a pivotal role in the success of "K-Earth 101."

DRAKE, Bill: **KDAY**, 1974. The "other" Bill Drake.

DRAPER, Ken: **KFWB**, 1975-78, nd. Ken was a key ingredient in the all-News format at KFWB. "You give us 22 minutes; we'll give you the world." Ken told the *LA Times*: "Even driving 40 minutes on the freeway, from Woodland Hills to downtown, you'll be distracted by traffic or by your own thoughts. The same news story may come on the radio two or three times, but you'll really only hear it once." Ken worked at KYW-Cleveand and WCFL-Chicago on his way to Los Angeles. He is retired and living in Illinois.

DREW, Bill: **KWIZ**. Bill worked overnights at the Orange County station.

DREW, Paul: **KHJ**, 1973, pd. Paul was a consultant to the RKO chain for many years. He achieved much success with CKLW-Detroit and KFRC-San Francisco. In the 1950s worked at WDET-Detroit, WHLS-Port Huron and WGST-Atlanta. During the '60s Paul worked in Atlanta at WAKE and WQXI, CKLW, WIBG-Philadelphia. Paul currently runs USA Japan Company and Paul Drew Enterprises.

DRISCOLL, John: **KTNQ/KGBS**, 1976-78; **KFI**, 1978; **KZLA**, 1987-89. Born John Moore in San Francisco, John grew up in Santa Monica and started as a dj at Santa Monica City College station KCRW. Prior to starting in the Southland, John was pd of WMYQ-Miami (using the name Bob Shannon), WCFL-Chicago, and Ram Research in San Diego. He has also used the on-air name John Moore. His first assignment in the Southland was to program and jock at "the new Ten-Q" when the station debuted on December 26, 1976. He arrived from doing evenings at WCFL. He did morning drive and programming as John M. Driscoll, perhaps because of Robert W. Morgan. When John left Los Angeles, he went to Denver to program KYGO and KPPL. Through the 1980s, until he returned to Southern California in 1987, John programmed KMJC ("Magic 91")-San Diego, WZUU and WLZZ-Milwaukee, KSAN-San Francisco, Malrite Communications group (where he was national pd), KRXY ("Y108")-Denver and KDKB-Phoenix. When he took over the new assignment at "Ten-Q," he said, "The major problem with Rock radio is that the stations don't create any magic on the air." His comments about programming in Los Angeles: "Peer group pressure affects people in Los Angeles faster than any other market. Fads, the Hollywood film scene, and the record industry here are catalysts." During his stint at KZLA, John said he achieved "the highest ratings for the morning show in the station's history, moving it from 18th to 9th." In 1989 he started John Driscoll Productions, "The New Voiceover America." His voiceover work has been heard on all networks. He has been the exclusive promo voice of tv and radio stations all over North America, Mexico, Japan and the United Kingdom. In 1992 and 1993, John worked afternoon drive on KSON-San Diego and was rated #1, according to John.

DRISCOLL, Mark: **KTNQ**, pd; **KLVE**, pd. Mark was the group vp for Brandon Communications in 1981. He held a similar role for H & G in 1984. In 1987 he was the pd of KHYI ("Y-95")-Dallas. During Scott Shannon's "Pirate Radio," Mark was the voice of KQLZ. In late 1993, Mark became vp/op of Pyramid Broadcasting and worked at WAQQ-Charlotte. His 28-year radio career includes KSTP-Minneapolis, WBBF-Rochester, WIOQ-Philadelphia and WAPE-Jacksonville. In 1994 Mark started Planet Creations, a production and voiceover facility. In late 1996 *R&R* reported a narrow escape from death for Mark. He was golfing in Santa Barbara when he pulled his golf cart to the edge of a cliff in order to snap a shot of the ocean view. The ground gave way and Mark and the golf cart plunged 120 feet down the rocky cliff. A four-foot ledge kept him from falling another 100 feet into the Pacific Ocean.

DRUMMOND, Mark: **KGFJ**, 1988-89; **KACE**, 1989-97. Born Markovic Drummond in Greenwood,

Mississippi, Mark arrived in the Southland from Urban KATZ-St. Louis. He's a songwriter and guitarist who has produced numerous jingles for stations in Los Angeles, the mid-South and West Africa. He produced the debut release for E. Harris. "The bright spot of working in L.A. was being involved with 'V103.9 Jam for Peace,' held at Irvine Meadows in 1993." Mark is the production manager and assistant pd at KACE.

DRURY, Theresa: **KABC**, 1970s. Theresa was the consumer affairs reporter for the all-Talk station.

DRYSDALE, Don: **KMPC**, 1973-81; **KABC**, 1987-93. The Hall of Fame former Dodger became a broadcaster for the Angels and Rams in 1973. By 1980 Don wanted to do the Angels AND work for ABC. KMPC didn't want to share him. In 1981 he left for Chicago to broadcast the White Sox games and was able to freelance with the ABC network. In 1987 he replaced Jerry Doggett on the Dodger broadcasts. Don was with the Dodgers from 1956 to 1969. His pitching record was 209-166 and he had a 2.95 earned run average. Don appeared in five World Series, won the Cy Young Award in 1962 and played on the All-Star team 10 times. On June 17, 1968, Don pitched an unprecedented six consecutive shutouts and a total of 58. On July 3, 1993, Don was on a road trip in Montreal. He failed to show up for the baseball broadcast. After a check at the hotel, it was discovered that Don had died of a heart attack. His surviving wife is broadcaster Ann Meyers who was the first four-time All-American basketball player - male or female - while at UCLA. In 1987, she was the first woman inducted into the UCLA Sports Hall of Fame. In 1979, she was the first - and still only - woman to sign a free-agent contract with an NBA team.

DUARTE, Jorge: **KBUE**, 1996-97. Jorge joined Spanish KBUE for mornings in February 1996 and left in the spring of 1997.

DUFF, Willis: **KLAC**, 1965-68, pd. When Willis left the Southland he became pd of WHDH-Boston. In the mid-1970s he teamed with Sebastian Stone and operated a research firm called Entertainment Response Analysts in San Francisco. Warren was one of the first to use galvanized skin tests to gauge reaction to new records. He is now a tv consultant.

DUFFY, Patrick: **KABC**, 1973-91; **KRTH**, 1991-97, vp/gm. Pat spent 18 years as general sales manager of KABC before arriving at "K-Earth." He started his career in the mail room at KNX and KNXT/Channel 2 and steadily moved up to sales.

DUFFY, Warren: **KMET**, 1970-71, pd; **KDAY**, 1973-74; **KKLA**, 1994-97. Warren began his career by singing on the radio in his hometown of Baltimore. At 10, he was starring in a weekly television show. Graduating from high school at 15, he went on to a long and varied career in broadcasting, including Washington, DC, where, according to Duffy, "I literally ruled the roost." Warren reflected on his first radio venture in Los Angeles: "KMET was a melting pot for some pretty talented people. To give us some validity with ad agencies when we were but a fledgling operation unable to afford 24-hour-a-day jocks, we were one of the first 'automated' music stations in the country. We hired Mitch Reed to host our afternoon drive-time show, so the agencies would recognize us." In 1974 Warren was the national album promotion director for 20th Century Fox Records. A year later he was the promotion director for the Beach Boys and engineered their worldwide tour celebrating their 15th anniversary. Along the way Duffy picked up a serious drug problem which he kicked in the late 1970s. This, according to Duffy, led to his religious conversion experience through Robert Schuller Ministries and renewed his faith. In the early 1980s, Duffy joined the staff of Crystal Cathedral in Garden Grove, where he served as executive administrative assistant to Dr. Schuller. He went on to become a pastor of a church in Kauai, Hawaii. He counts all his experiences as positive: "I feel that everything I have gone through, from being a child prodigy to overcoming drug addiction to pastoring a church, has contributed to my ability to relate to people on a 'heart' level." He opened his own marketing and consultancy agency, and one of his clients became Salem Communications, owners of 30 Christian stations around the country. He currently hosts an afternoon drive talk show on Christian KKLA that is syndicated as "Duffy and Company - Live From L.A."

DUGGAN, Tom: **KBLA**, 1965; **KLAC**, 1965-69. Tom was a very original talk show host who worked afternoon drive during the Joe Pyne talk radio days on KLAC. He also hosted tv shows on KTTV/Channel 11 and KCOP/Channel 13. Tom fell out of a window in the early 1970s and circumstances of his death caused much speculation.

DUMPSTER, Clete: SEE Dave Hume.

DUNAWAY, Mike: **KHJ**, 1976-77; **KIIS**. Mike was in Dallas and Kansas City before arriving in Southern California. He returned to KCMO-Kansas City and in the mid-1990s he joined WTIC-Hatford for mornings. He has also used the name Ray Dunaway.

DUNCAN, Jim: **KFOX**; **KHJ**; **KLAC**; **KZLA**, 1988-97. Born on a naval base on Mare Island in Northern California, his Navy father gave him a transistor radio from Japan. It was love at first hearing. His first job was on the campus radio station at San Diego State. At one time, Jim worked for four San Diego radio stations at the same time under the names Jim Chandler, Jim Morgan and Jim Duncan. At KSON-San Diego, Jim moved into morning drive at the age of 19, and he later became pd. Bob Wilson hired Jim to be the Country editor in the early days of *R&R*, a position he held for a decade. Being on the air became a hobby as Jim started hosting and producing many of the Westwood One shows, including "Live From Gilley's" and "The New Faces of Country." After a 14-year association, he still does production and engineering for the Network, including all their rock concert shows and much of their voiceover work. He works morning drive at WW1's Hot Country format. Besides radio, Duncan owns his own successful production company. In 1994 he produced the "Radio Across America" video to open NAB's Programming Convention in Los Angeles. He is active with the CMA, serving as a vp. Duncan married his college sweetheart 25 years ago and has two children. His early influences were the "Boss Jocks" and production masters Terry Moss and Bobby Ocean.

DUNCAN, John: **KLOS**, 1997, pd. John joined KLOS in the spring of 1997 from two years at KYYS-Kansas City. Earlier in his career he worked at WRDU and WTRG-Raleigh, WLZR-Milwaukee and WMAD-Madison, Wisconsin.

DUNCAN, Lee: **KDAY**, 1968-69; **KRLA**, 1969-70. Lee grew up in Ventura and Ojai. He started his radio career in 1958 in his hometown at KUDU. That led to KAFY-Bakersfield, where he became pd. During his stay in Bakersfield, he hired a young man by the name of Bob Weiner as his all-night personality. Since the Mayor of Bakersfield was named Weiner, Bob used the name Wilson. After a stint in the armed forces, Lee joined Gene Chenault's operation at KYNO-Fresno and "lived with the Indians." He got to Jerry Clifton's KDES-Palm Springs the day of the "hippie uprising." In 1978 Lee's former all-night man in Bakersfield, Bob Wilson, was the pd of KDAY and brought Lee to Southern California. He left a year later and worked nine to midnight at KRLA, replacing Jimmy Rabbit. When Rabbit came back, Duncan moved into afternoon drive. When he left Southern California, Lee followed his love for skiing and became part owner of stations in Mammoth, Sun Valley and Colorado Springs. He then spent 10 years in Aspen at KSPN, where he also started the local newspaper, the *Daily News*. After Aspen, Lee went to KOMO-Seattle from 1985 until 1992. In 1994, Lee said, "I live in the foothills of the Cascades, work part-time at KRWM-Seattle and trade in the commodities market."

DUNGEE, Ron: **KACE**, 1979-87, nd; **KGFJ**, 1995. Ron is currently the sports editor for the *Los Angeles Sentinel*.

DUNKIN, Greg: **KYSR**, 1993-94, pd. Born in 1961 in San Diego, Greg was in the third grade when he left with his family to live in Kansas. Greg started his radio career at the age of 12 at KUDL-Kansas City. "There was a pilot program for sixth graders to development career education. The only booklet left when I got to the counselor was on broadcasting." At KUDL Greg did everything, including phones, being a side-kick, and production for syndicated shows. He went to William Jewell Baptist College in Liberty, Missouri and produced an irreverent show. "I would call the president of the college at 6 in the morning. They didn't know what to make of me." After college he was assistant pd and md at

KLSI-Kansas City, WNSR-New York and pd of WMMX-Baltimore. Greg looked back fondly of his two years with "Star 98.7": "I just loved being in L.A." He left in October 1994, when his contract expired, for om at WENS/WNAP-Indianapolis.

> "Biggie Nevins was cremated in L.A. and his ashes were flown to New York but never arrived. Through some mishap they found him in Milwaukee. Biggie would have roared!" -John Rook reminiscing about his good friend

DUNNE, Carrie: **KIKF**, 1989-96, pd. In addition to middays, Carrie has been the air traffic reporter, asst. pd/md, and host of the weekly KIKF country countdown. In late spring of 1995 she became pd following the resignation of Craig Powers. She closes her show with the line, "I'm Carrie...and I'm done."

DURAN, Gina: **KIBB**, 1996-97. Gina hosts a weekend "Romance After Hours" show on Rhythm "B-100."

DURKIN, Jason: **KNOB**, 1966-69; **KOCM**, 1969-80; **KWVE**, 1980. Born and raised in Westfield, Massachusetts, Jason graduated from the University of Connecticut with a B.A. degree in communication. "I always knew I wanted to be in radio!" He was a boy dj in New England and hosted record hops when he was barely two years older than the kids at the hop. He spent two years at KGB-San Diego from 1963 to 1965. He arrived in the Southland to work at KNOB and moved to KOCM which, according to Jason, "was the best station I ever worked for. The benefits, the salary. They treated you like a real pro. It was a home away from home." When KOCM automated in 1980, all the djs were let go. Jason went to KWVE-San Clemente and a year later came home and told his wife, "If I ever see another microphone or cart machine, I'll vomit." He quit and got out of radio. He still lives in Orange County and works with his interior designing wife. Would he get back into radio? "I would for $300,000 a year, a three-hour shift and a station located next door."

DURLING, Lin: **KODJ**, 1990; **KABC**, 1990. Lin was part of the "Breakfast Bunch" with Charlie Tuna and Dean Goss at KODJ and broadcast traffic on the popular KABC "Ken and Bob Company" morning drive show. Lin is the morning traffic anchor at KGO-San Francisco.

DUROCHER, Leo: **KABC**, 1964. Leo hosted the "SportsTalk" show on KABC for nine months before being asked to become manager of the Chicago Cubs. Born July 27, 1905, in West Springfield, Massachusetts, the volatile infielder played for the famed early '30s "Gashouse Gang" St. Louis baseball Cardinals. Leo was temporarily banned from baseball in 1947 by Commissioner A.B. "Happy" Chandler for allegedly consorting with gamblers. On the brighter side, the "Lip," who once said he'd walk over his grandmother to win a game, was married to actress Laraine Day. He played for the Brooklyn Dodgers and New York Giants, and had a lifetime batting average of .241. When his baseball playing days were over Leo managed the Chicago Cubs, Houston Astros and was a coach for the L.A. Dodgers. While managing the New York Giants in 1951, Leo led the team to both National League and world championships. He died October 7, 1991, of natural causes. Leo was 86.

DVORAK, George: **KFI**, 60s; **KFWB**, 1970-77; **KGRB**, 1977.

DWYER, Danny: **KZLA**, 1992-96. "I was a tile man before starting as Shawn Parr's producer at KZLA." Born in Burbank, except for three years in Northern California, he has been in Southern California ever since. He followed his father in the construction business. In 1989 he was the Club DJ at Denim and Diamonds which led to a career switch to radio. During his time on KZLA, Danny hosted the weekly "Z-Past Show," that featured classic country artists. In the summer of 1996 he joined KTPF/KVOY-Lancaster.

Call letter origination

KMPC (710AM): MacMillan Petroleum Company

KJLH (102.3): Owner John Lamar Hill III (his first studio was in a Long Beach mortuary)

KGFJ (1230AM): "Keeping Good Folks Joyful"

KCRW (89.9FM): "College Radio Workshop" or "Corsair Radio West"

KFWB (980AM): Owner Fox-Warner Bros.

KFI (640AM): "Farm Information"

KECA (790AM): Owner Earle C. Anthony

KFSG (1150AM): Four Square Gospel, operated by evangelist Aimee Semple McPherson

KGBS (1020AM): Owner George B. Storer

E

EAGLE, Swedish: **KROQ**, 1983-90; **KOCM/KSRF**, 1990-92; **KACD**, 1996-97. Born Egil Aalvik, he was md for several years at "the Roq." He worked the all-night shift and also worked with the Poorman doing the "Loveline" show in its embryonic days. By 1994, the Swedish Eagle broadcast his 100th "Groove Radio International Show" for the Independent Broadcasters Network. He was part of the "MARSfm" techno-rock format at KSRF, and in the summer of 1996 he returned to the same frequency (103.1FM) to program "Groove Radio."

EARL, Bill: **KPCS**, 1970-72. Bill is known as "The Official KRLA Historian" and was heard occasionally on KRLA between 1974 and 1989. He wrote two radio-oriented books in the late 1980s. Bill is currently doing research and development on a follow-up Volume 2 to "When Radio Was Boss."

EARL, Warren: The former gm is now retired and living in Ventura.

EASLEY, Victoria: **KFWB**, 1986-94 and 1995-97. The Illinois native is most proud of a series she did for KFWB in 1990 called "When the Bough Breaks." The story about drug babies prompted a campaign that continues today whereby women volunteer three hours a week to hold and rock neo-natal babies. The station has donated rocking chairs to the program. Victoria was born in Kewanee, Illinois and studied journalism at Northern Illinois University. She dropped out of school and "became a gypsy" during part of the '70s. When she arrived in the Southland she joined the broadcasting program at L.A. Valley College and Cal State Northridge. Following intern programs at KHJ/Channel 9 and KNX, Victoria started at KFWB in the spring of 1986 as a desk assistant. Before long she moved up to writer and on-air by 1988. "Right after the 1994 earthquake I was wined and dined by WBBM-Chicago and decided to return to Illinois. My boss turned out to be the anti-Christ and fired me three weeks before my year-long probation period was to end. I returned to KFWB and have pretty much been a news orphan filling in as needed." Victoria was the first KFWB staffer to appear in the Martin Luther King parade. She has earned more than 15 international, national and local news awards including 4 Golden Mikes.

EASY E: **KKBT**, 1994-95. The N.W.A. founder and Ruthless/Relativity Records owner/president/artist, Eric Wright, hosted a Saturday night hip-hop show on "the Beat" called "Ruthless Radio Show" co-hosted with Jesse Collins. Eric died of AIDS on March 26, 1995. He was 31. Following his death, his former lovers and business associates were haggling in Los Angeles Superior Court. Ruthless Records was the company that helped put Compton gangsta rap on the pop culture map. Shortly after his death, in an April 1995 story in the *LA Times*, reference was made to Ruthless: "Once a thriving independent firm, (it) has floundered in recent years and is saddled with more than $1.5 million in debts. Even so, former Ruthless employees speculate that the company could be worth as much as $30 million, but competitors doubt whether the firm's assets could generate more than half that. Sources on both sides of the battle believe that the estate could be deluged by a slew of paternity suits as well as litigation seeking funds from disgruntled recording artists and producers."

ED, EverReady, **KNAC**, 1989-95; **KLSX**, 1997. Ed Kelley started at KNAC, a station where most all the personalities had "strange" names, answering phones and progressing to production assistant, promotions and eventually on air. Born in Monterey Park, Ed went to a private Catholic school in San Gabriel. He was working as an engineer at Northrup when he heard a radio ad talking about a career in broadcasting. "I put everything aside. I told myself this is want I want to do." When KNAC faded to black and changed ownership in early 1995, Ed became a club dj. In late 1996 Ed joined KLSX in the promotions department and worked weekends.

EDELDAIRA, La India: **KKHJ**, 1996-97. La India is part of "El Manicomo de la Manana" morning show on KKHJ.

EDWARDS, Brad: **KGBS**, 1969-71; **XPRS**, 1971-73; **KUTE**, 1973; **KDAY**, 1974; **KGBS**, 1975-77; **KFI**, 1983. "When I left KGBS in 1977 after the station became automated, I went to Tehran to work at the National Iranian Radio & TV Network. They reneged on everything they had promised. I had to make a daring escape from the country." Born Claude Hooten, Brad was a graduate of Montebello High School. After his Tehran experience, he worked at KDIA-San Francisco and KLIV-San Jose at the same time. During the next decade he worked at KAGY-El Paso, "Magic 108"-St.

Louis and two stations in Houston, "Magic 102" and KKBQ. "During 1985 and 1986 my life could have made a great Movie of the Week. I joined mornings at 'I-95'-Miami. The gm and pd had a combined 18 years at the station and thought I could achieve some stability. Within 60 days both had left the station and I was gone 60 days later. I was splitting with my second wife at the time and she ran off with my $30,000 severance check leaving me penniless." He applied at WAIA-Miami and submitted to interviews with a consultant and a company shrink. Brad was told on a Friday that he got the morning job and on Monday the gm and pd were let go. Jobs in El Paso and Milwaukee followed. In 1988 he started a hot five-year run at "Hot 105"-Miami as half of the morning team of Mindy and Malo. In 1993 he was a partner in the purchase of KBOM-Santa Fe. "The station was actually in Los Alamos and we called it 'K-Bomb' because that's where the atomic bomb testing grounds were." Brad has since sold his interest in the station and now runs four stations in Santa Fe, works morning drive for one of them and owns a number of Albuquerque mountain tops for transmitter tower sites.

EDWARDS, Dick: **KHJ**, 1979-80

EDWARDS, Eddie: **KLAC**, 1987-88. Eddie belongs to the only threepeat family in Los Angeles radio history. The native Californian's dad was a dj, and his grandfather was a radio announcer. In 1987, Eddie was named dj of the year by the CMA. He left the Nashville Country powerhouse, WSIX, in the summer of 1987 to do mornings at KLAC and left a year later for family reasons to join KAJA-San Antonio, which he subsequently left. He is currently doing mornings and is acting pd at WNOE-New Orleans.

EDWARDS, Geoff: **KHJ**, 1964-65; **KFI**, 1966-68; **KMPC**, 1968-79; **KFI**, 1987-89. Born in 1931 in the

East, Geoff got into radio in the 1950s, at WOKO-Albany, where the station manager suggested he consider another line of work since he did not have a deep "radio voice." Geoff arrived at KHJ just prior to "Boss Radio" and worked as operations director. He had been at San Diego's KFMB where he had a jazz show in 1959 called "Jazz on the Rocks." One of his popular running characters was the Answer Lady. The bit was particularly unique because he did not use a female voice. The Answer Lady fielded questions from listeners, and Geoff attempted to provide the correct answers. Geoff went up the dial to Gene Autry's traditional all-service MOR station, KMPC, and left when the station went Talk in 1979. "I had to make a decision. I had become involved in some tv activities that had become as interesting or more interesting than the radio work." Geoff's new tv projects included a deal with Warner Bros. to develop daytime programming. He resigned from "news/talk" KFI in March 1989, following his suspension for refusing to run a promotional spot for evening driver Tom Leykis' Yusef Islam/Cat Stevens record-destruction party. He was replaced by the syndicated "Rush Limbaugh Show." Geoff's most visible fame came in television. He was the host of numerous tv game shows including *Treasure Hunt*, NBC's *Jackpot*, and *Hollywood's Talking* on CBS. He was a featured performer on NBC's *Bobby Darin Show*, and co-host with Meredith MacRae of *Mid-Morning L.A.*, which earned him an Emmy while on KHJ/Channel 9. For many years Geoff traveled to Sacramento every weekend to host the California Lottery's *Big Spin*. "Geoff wears the look of a guy who always gets lost in an office building," said the *LA Times*. "He knows where he's going, but isn't quite sure how to get there." Geoff lives on the beach in the Marina.

EDWARDS, George: **KKBT**, 1989-92; **KYSR**, 1995-97. His real name is George Mathews, but not the same Mathews from KEZY.

EDWARDS, Glen: **KEZY**, 1959-66. Glen went on to the Financial News Network.

EDWARDS, Greg: **KIKF**, 1990, pd. Greg's early radio stops were KOSO-Modesto and KNAX-Fresno. Greg is now working in Fresno.

EDWARDS, Mike: **KIKF**, 1984; **KOCM**, 1990. Mike worked morning drive while at KIKF.

EDWARDS, Pam: **KMET**, 1983-86; **KNAC**, 1990-91, pd. Pam started her broadcasting career as pd of WPGU-Champaign/Urbana. Pam arrived in the Southland the second time from KGB-San Diego, where she was md and assistant pd. She left radio for a series of record promotion assignments at Columbia Records, Chaos and Work Group.

> "He had to voice track his show between records during his relearning period." -about John Rydgren

EDWARDS, Rob: **KOST**, 1970-77, pd; **KBIG**, 1978-93, pd; **KACD**, 1995-96, pd. Rob started his radio career at

KNUZ-Houston while in high school. He worked as pd in Waco, WFAA-Dallas and national pd at Strauss Broadcasting before moving to Los Angeles as pd for Gordon McLendon's KOST. Rob started at KBIG in 1978 as om, becoming pd in 1980 and two years later was promoted to divisional vp/programming for Bonneville. In 1985 he changed KOIT-San Francisco to AC. In 1986 he moved KBIG to an AC format which was later known as "Big Mix 104." Leaving KBIG at the end of 1993, he formed Apex Radio Consultants with KACD as a client and featured Hot AC blocks from the '70s, '80s and '90s. "I was watching a *Time/Life* 'Greatest Hits of the 80s' tv commercial and realized that's how people think of and use music at home, work and in the car." Rob left "CD 103" in the spring of 1996 and continues as a senior partner in Apex.

EDWARDS, Steve: **KABC**, 1990-95. He hosted *A.M. Los Angeles* for seven years in the 1980s on KABC/Channel 7. He started his broadcasting career

reporting sports in the early 1970s. A New York native, Steve graduated from the University of Miami with a degree in history. He worked towards a masters degree in clinical psychology at the University of Houston. Steve started his radio career at KTRH-Houston and moved to the Houston CBS tv station followed by WLS/TV where he hosted *AM Chicago*. In 1978 he joined KCBS/Channel 2 to host *2 on the Town* with Connie Chung and *Live in L.A.* on KCAL/Channel 9. He served as entertainment editor for the station. In 1982 and 1983 Steve was the co-host of *Entertainment Tonight*. In 1984 he joined Channel 7 and hosted numerous variety/talk shows. In 1990 he returned to radio and hosted a variety of magazine-style programs including "SportsTalk." The *LA Times'* Larry Stewart wrote: "When radio station KABC tabbed Steve Edwards as its replacement for Superfan, the obvious reaction was: 'Why Steve Edwards? Why not Regis Philbin? Or Cristina Ferrare? Or Oprah Winfrey?' But Steve...has shown a great knowledge of sports and what's more important, his pleasing personality and class come across well." Steve has alternated between radio and TV for the past two decades. He started hosting KTTV/Channel 11's dawn patrol show *Good Day L.A.* while working afternoon drive on KABC. "I'm 11 years younger than whatever Regis Philbin says he is," he recounted in an *OC Register* interview. He and Eric Tracy left "SportsTalk" in the fall of 1995.

EDWARDS, Tommy: **KCBS**, 1992-97, pd. Tommy attended Washburn University in Topeka. He served in the office of Asst. Chief of Naval Operations (Communications) while in the U.S. Navy. In 1960 he started his jock career at KTOP and KEWI-Topeka and moved to WEAM-Washington, DC. In 1969 he was at WOR/FM-New York and then on to WLS-Chicago in 1972 where he was air talent, production director and pd. He was "Lil' Tommy" in the popular radio program "Animal Stories" which was made into three best-selling comedy albums of actual radio broadcasts with partner, Larry Lujack. He also was pd at WKQX and morning talent at WJMK-Chicago. Tommy was public address announcer for the Chicago Bulls of the NBA for 14 years and originated most of the game presentation used around the league today including *Rock and Roll Part II* and Alan Parson's *Eye in Sky* during games. In 1990 he

joined CBS as pd of WODS-Boston and was moved to the Southland in early 1992 to guide KCBS to the "Arrow" format. On "Arrow's" web page, Tommy said: "I can still remember when Dave Van Dyke and I first started talking about developing the 'Arrow' format. It was over chili dogs and root beer at Carney's." Tommy lives in Calabasas with his wife Mary Lou and three children.

EICHENTHAL, Gail: **KUSC**, 1977-88; **KNX**, 1995-97. Gail hosted the L.A. Philharmonic radio concert broadcasts on KUSC for over 10 years. Born in 1954, she fell in love with the Philharmonic while attending the orchestra's Saturday morning Symphonies for Youth concerts with her father. Gail began playing the piano at the age of 6. Her early voice training started at age 11 when she narrated *How the Grinch Stole Christmas* in a school play. Gail continued to study piano and just before graduating from UCLA, she accepted an internship at KUSC in 1977 and learned classical-music radio production. A year later, when she earned her B.A. in English and classical music, she was hired full-time. She covered the O.J. Simpson double murder trial for news KNX.

ELDER, Bob: **KORG**, 1991-92. Bob hosted a sports Talk show on KORG and was on KDOC/TV's *Sports on the Go*.

ELDER, Larry: **KABC**, 1994-97. Larry refers to himself as the "Sage from South Central," and describes his political ideology as "fiscally conservative and socially liberal." Born and raised in Los Angeles, Larry graduated from Crenshaw High School. He attended Brown University and earned a B.A. in political-science. He continued his education and received a law degree from the University of Michigan in 1977.  After graduation, he was recruited by the ninth largest law firm in the country and moved to Cleveland to work as a commercial trial lawyer. Three years later, he left to start his own company, an executive search firm specializing in attorneys. While in Cleveland, Larry hosted and produced for four years *The Larry Elder Show* on the Fox affiliate. He also hosted *Fabric*, a monthly issues-oriented PBS tv program, for five years. In 1994, Larry sold his business and moved back to Los Angeles to begin his career at KABC "TalkRadio," a program that deals with a number of diverse viewpoints. In the spring of 1997 Larry was the subject of a segment on *60 Minutes*.

ELDRIDGE, Sheila: **KKTT**, 1979; **KACE**, 1979-80. Sheila moved to New York and opened her own PR firm, "Orchid Promotions."

ELLIOTT, Bob: **KBLA**, 1967. Bob's fame was as K.O. Bailey in other markets, including San Diego. He was also at KYNO-Fresno and worked as K.O. Beachin at KEWB in 1964. Bob died in a car accident.

ELLIOTT, Don: **KBLA/KBBQ**, 1965-71, pd; **KIIS**, 1971-72, pd; **KROQ**, 1972; **KEZY**, 1973; **KIQQ**, 1974; **KKDJ**, 1975; **KIIS**, 1975-86; **KFI/KOST**, 1994-97. "Legendary" is one way Don's peers talks about his production prowess. "Don would wear this piece of tape around his neck and just know which was the front and the which was the end." Born Jack Schwab in Wilmington, Delaware (he was told to change his name because it might prevent him from working in Hollywood because of the famous drug store), Don bleeds radio. Just when one thinks he has figured out his career path, he offhandedly talks about going to law school to study copyrights and its use with intellectual products on the Internet. While going to the University of Missouri he was working at KCMO on AM, FM and TV. He spent the early sixties at KUDL-Kansas City and then Don Burden's Rock stations KISN-Portland and KOIL-Omaha. He has created a 21-CD package of 2,000 musical beds in a multi-media library called "Legends." He worked on a jingle package that had what Don called "a Chinese whole-tone scale. It fits into any key. A jock could segue with it or record sweeps." He was the last voice on KKBQ. "I used the name Red Herring when we played out last country song and Charlie Tuna took over." He was the production director for a decade at KIIS. From time to time, he would be forced on air as a jock. He taught radio at Fullerton and Saddleback Colleges. When his marriage came apart in 1986 Don put all of his energy into his production facility and freelanced for all the major companies. He had the Mervyn's radio account for over two years. The ham operator was almost ready to take a teaching assignment at Mt. Hood College in the Northwest when KFI called. In 1997 Don won the Gold Medal award from PROMAX International. Not many jocks are successful in doing national voiceover work. "The announcer has to use the microphone as an ear. Quit listening to your own pipes and communicate."

ELLIOTT, Don: **KIKF**, 1995

ELLIOTT, Jack: **KIKF**, 1985, nd

ELLIOTT, Lee: **KLSX/KRLA**, 1989-93; **KXEZ/KYSR**, 1993-96. Born Lee Elliot Glassman in Springfield, Massachusetts. Lee spent four years at KLSX/KRLA, before joining "Star 98.7." According to Lee, one of the highlights of working at KLSX was the time he produced and aired the Brent Mydland/Grateful Dead tribute.

ELLIOTT, Mark: **KHJ**, 1970-73; **KWOW**, 1974; **KIIS**, 1974-75; **KHJ**, 1975-77. Mark has been an enormously successful voiceover talent heard for years on CBS/TV and Disney projects. Born in Des Moines, Mark launched Pied Piper Productions, which was a subsidiary of Tuna/Alan Productions. He was involved with "Jock

Seasoning," which featured singers with a phrase or word, then Mark voicing the dj's name over a sustaining note. He worked afternoon drive at KFRC-San Francisco before joining KHJ.

ELLIOTT, Mark: **KMGX**, 1991-94 pd. Born Mark McCoy in Clarksburg, West Virginia, he is currently the pd of KBBY-Ventura/Oxnard.

ELLIS, Dave: **KEZY**, 1984

ELLIS, Steve: **KLSX**, 1989-91, pd. Steve started his radio career at KDWB-Minneapolis. He arrived in the Southland from being pd at WQHT ("Hot 97") and WAPP-New York. Since leaving radio Steve has worked for Curb/Atlantic Records and Mercury Records in various promotion positions.

ELLISON, Melinda: **KMGX**, 1990-92. Melinda is the producer of Rick Dees' "Top 40 Countdown Show." She was born and raised in Big Spring, Texas and started her radio career at KBYG-Big Spring. Melinda came to L.A. without a job and did production and afternoon drive at KMGX. She loves to create comedy and parodies.

ELLISON, Nancy: **KBCA**, 1978; **KKGO**, 1979-80

ELLSWORTH, Scott: **KFI**, 1969-72; **KGBS/FM**, 1973. "His literate interviews and deep respect for the music and its practitioners provide special entertainment for an audience often neglected in AM radio," wrote Don Page in a 1971 *LA Times* story. When Scott was terminated at KFI in 1972, he said he was stunned. "Usually, you hear rumors, but this was a total shock. I knew they weren't too thrilled with the jazz format." His show combined conversation with music, and he was consistently articulate and entertaining. In the 1980s he was a lead anchor with the Financial News Network. Scott is living in Palm Springs.

ELMER, Terri-Rae: **KFI**, 1983-97. Terri-Rae teamed with Tracey Miller for the "TNT" news/talk program. She is now part of the news team on KFI.

ELWELL, Roy: **KRLA**, 1959-63; **KLAC**, 1967-68; **KRLA**, 1968 and 1973-76, pd; **KGIL**, 1976-77. Roy was one of the original "11-10 Men," arriving in Pasadena for the nine-to-noon slot from KQV-Pittsburgh. When he left KRLA the first time, he went to KEWB-San Francisco as Scott Bridges. At KLAC, Roy worked the talk format in afternoon drive. He left radio to experiment with tv and hosted the *Tempo* Show on KHJ/Channel 9 with Bob Dornan.

EMERSON, Bryan: **KIKF**, 1987. Bryan worked all-nights at the Orange County Country station.

EMORY, Patrick: **KFWB**, 1968-70. Patrick was one of the original newsmen at the launch of the all-News format. "When I left KFWB I was 26 and filled in for Jerry Dunphy at KNXT/Channel 2." He went on to KDKA-Pittsburgh, KMOX-St. Louis and back to Channel 2 in 1976. Patrick's next assignments included news stops in Indianapolis, Philadelphia and at 10 years at CNN. "Looking back, I just wonder whether I would have been a lot happier staying in one town all my life. I don't think so. It's been inconvenient at times, but I have seen this country and met people everywhere." He's currently with WTOG-Tampa/St. Petersburg.

ENBERG, Dick: **KMPC**, 1966-78. The signature, "My, Oh My" instantly identifies Dick. He has been the radio and tv voice of the California Angels, the radio voice of the Rams, the tv voice of UCLA basketball, a play-by-play telecaster for tv's basketball games of the week and in the early 1970s hosted *Sports Challenge*. Born in 1935, he was a football quarterback, basketball center and baseball pitcher in high school in Michigan. Dick began broadcasting while a student at Central Michigan University in the mid-1950s. He started at WCEN as a dj for $1 an hour and within a month he was sports director covering Little League baseball, Golden Gloves boxing and basketball. He pursued post-graduate work at Indiana University, earning a master's and a doctorate in health sciences. Shortly after arriving in Bloomington, Dick applied at WFIU, and the receptionist eventually became Mrs. Enberg. In the early 1960s he started teaching health education and was assistant to the president at San Fernando Valley State College (now California State University Northridge). He pursued radio to augment his teaching salary of $5,800, according to a profile in the *LA Times*. In the summer of 1962 KGIL offered him $9,200 to be a dj, which he declined. For the next couple of years he worked part-time for KGIL, KNX and KLAC. In 1965 he left teaching to join KTLA/Channel 5 in the sports department and started out covering boxing. After 12 years as Ram play-by-play announcer, he left for the NBC network. During the past three decades, Dick has become a premier sports broadcaster.

ENGEL, Rene: **KCSN**, 1978-80; **KCRW**, 1980-88; **KPCC**, 1988-96; **KUSC**, 1996; **KCSN**, 1997, gm. Rene's public radio career came full circle in 1997 when he was named gm of KCSN, the station where he started in 1978. At KCRW, Rene created "Citybilly," a country music program that celebrated a decade and a half on-air during the summer of 1997. "Citybilly" has long been considered a model for the AAA format and certainly a pioneering program for the country side of AAA. "The show pays homage to the notion that folk music reflects the times in which we are living and such modern forms as rap and r&b would fit into the unique format." Born in Antwerp, Belgium, he was raised in Southern California. "My father was a cabinet maker and his shop was on Pico Boulevard near where all the one-stop record distributors were located. He made friends with the owners and brought home wonderful music. I'll never forget when my dad brought home my first musical memory, Dvorak's *New World Symphony*." Rene's musical training turned serious with violin lessons and his home was always filled with music, especially the rich musical heritage of the Jewish faith. As a youngster, he regularly listened to classical music on KFAC. Rene rode his bicycle the few blocks from his home to KFAC "to see what the inside of a radio station looked like." He also absorbed the art of on-air communication as a teenager hanging around KFWB during its Top 40 heyday. Rene has hosted some of the most successful concert series in the Southland including the Santa Monica Pier Twilight Dance Series for seven years and Jazz at the Wadsworth for five.

ENGELMAN, Ron: **KRTH**, 1979-81; **KWST**, 1981-83; **KMGG**, 1983. Ron was born in Denver and the radio bug bit in 1961 while attending Northeastern College in Sterling, Colorado. He started at KGEK-Sterling and moved on to KBOI-Boise, followed by a station in Helena, the call letters he could not remember. His next stop was mornings at KLAK-Denver and then KLIF-Dallas in 1973 where he met his eventual partner, John London. From Dallas, Ron went on to be nd at KUPD-Phoenix in 1975 and then to KHOW ("96KX")-Denver. When Ron moved across town to KTLK, he began as a team with John and stopped doing news. Their journey as a team took them to Portland, back to KLIF and then to KULF-Houston before joining KRTH in 1979. There, in their first week on-air, they had Eddie Haskell teaching the Beaver how to snort cocaine. In Denver, the duo admitted their act was a bit sicker than what they did on KRTH. "We thought nothing of giving out the first energy conservation award to Karen Ann Quinlan's parents." Strong mornings were mostly the purview of AM radio when the team joined the RKO/FM Oldies station. One of their stronger running features was "Dan Woman, Private Eye" which was voiced by Ron. When they left "Magic 106," they did some tv writing before joining WFLA-Tampa and then KMEL-San Francisco in 1986. During their stay in the Bay Area, which would be their last as a team, Ron was in the hospital twice - once for open heart surgery and later for an aorta bypass. Ron has always enjoyed restoring old cars as a hobby and he opened an auto upholstery shop in Marin County for upscale cars. The break-up of the partnership was, as Ron related in a telephone interview from his home in New Mexico, "real ugly." Ron went on to WZOU-Boston in 1990, followed by a return to the Bay Area at KSOL-San Francisco. In early 1993, Ron had gone to KGBS-Dallas to return to his roots in news and become a talk host. Shortly after his arrival all hell broke loose. "Waco hit and all of a sudden I and the station became a link with David Koresh and the Branch Davidians. Tapes of my show were being monitored and obtained by the FBI. I was on virtually every single press outlet. At one stage the Branch Davidians hung a banner from the fortress that said WE WANT RON ENGELMAN." The government would not let Ron approach the compound and controversy swirled. He makes an emphatic point that he did not agree with David Koresh, but, as Ron said, "POWs during the war were treated more humanely." After the Waco incident, he lost his job and has had "a real, real tough two years." While waiting for his next radio assignment, he restored a 1934 Rolls Royce and it is now in a Houston museum. Ron had purchased some land in New Mexico and moved there in 1994. In the summer of 1995, Ron was doing fill-in at KOB-Albuquerque and living in Edgewood, New Mexico.

ENSARA, Roger: **KDAY**, 1984

EPPS, Warren: **KGFJ**, 1978; **KKTT**, 1979. Warren currently works for Big State Music Distributing in the Carolinas.

EPSTEIN, Bob: **KLON**, 1981-95. As a USC student, Bob was programming a film series. He later moved to UCLA, where he began to lecture on film history in the late 1960s. The pioneering film archivist and radio jazz personality co-founded the UCLA film archive. He saved nearly all of Paramount's 35-millimeter nitrate prints from destruction and persuaded 20th Century Fox to donate its nitrate collection to UCLA. Bob was one of the original founders of Filmex, the influential though now-defunct Los Angeles film festival. He was the cornerstone that KLON was built upon in 1981. He left UCLA in 1983 to pursue his other great love, traditional jazz music at KLON, where he served as md for a time. Bob taught at Loyola Marymount University while continuing his weekly Sunday morning jazz show called, "Classic Jazz." Along with being an avid record collector, he had been employed by Ray Avery of Rare Records of Glendale. Bob died of an apparent heart attack on April 8, 1995, just hours before he was scheduled to do his radio show. He was 57.

EPSTEIN, Norm: **XTRA/KOST**, 1968-73, gm; **KPSA/KLVE**, 1973-75, vp/owner; **KMPC**, 1975-84, gsm; **KLAC/KZLA**, 1986-93, vp/gm. Norm developed Marketron, a computer radio reach/frequency system. He

developed the first AM/FM sales combo with XTRA/KOST. Born in Los Angeles in 1936, Norm spent the mid '50s at UCLA and USC, graduating USC in 1958 with a B.S. degree. In between his radio assignments, Norm has owned several companies, including TEETOTUM Enterprises, where he developed the BOMP, a highly successful promotional tool during the rock years of KFWB. Norm and his wife Sandra, married since 1956, have three children and one grandson. Norm is also a cartoonist who developed "Chickisms," a cartoon strip which featured quotations from the legendary Laker broadcaster, Chick Hearn. Norm is a past chairman of the SCBA and has been a board member of numerous companies including *Variety* Children's Charity. He is currently a principal in Travel Related Marketing, Inc., an advertising/marketing company specializing in the travel industry.

ERDMANN, Luz: **KAJZ**, gm; **KIIS**, 1993-96, national sales manager. Luz was a long-term gsm of KFI/KOST and left KIIS in late 1996 following an ownership change from Gannett to Jacor.

ERICKSON, Keith: **KLAC**, 1979-87. Keith was part of the L.A. Lakers' broadcast team. He was partnered with Chick Hearn for seven seasons. Keith got the job when Pat Riley vacated the chair in 1979. He had worked for CBS Sports for two years following his retirement from basketball in 1977. He quit the Laker broadcasts in 1987 to become president of Sports Fantasies. Born in 1947 Keith is a former UCLA basketball star and was a pro player for the Lakers and Phoenix Suns for 12 years. He was a member of the 1964 U.S. Olympic Volleyball team. Keith is the father of five.

ERVIN, Dave: **KBIG**, 1993-96, pd. Dave arrived from WQAL-Cleveland. He previously programmed KGON-Portland, WNIC-Detroit, WCLR-Chicago and WMYG-Pittsburgh.

ERVINE, Jeff: **KWIZ**, 1990-91. Jeff working morning drive with John Kobik.

ERWIN, Ron: **KGBS**, 1966-68, pd; **KROQ**, 1969; **KPPC**, 1970; **KGBS**, 1970-76; **KFWB**, 1992; **KFI**. In the 1980s, Ron became a news writer and reporter for KFWB. Ron owns an ad agency in Encino.

ESCONDON, Ernan: **KALI**; **KWKW**, pd. Ernan was a long-time broadcaster on KALI. He's now with "Radio Ranchito."

> "I just didn't like mornings. It was a living hell. I never had trouble talking up to a vocal until I had to do it. Talking up to *Reach Out I'll Be There* was ridiculous."
> -Bobby Dale

ESENSTEN, Barbara: **KFWB**, 1979; **KABC**, 1985-86. Barbara produced short features for many years at KABC and did news commentary at KFWB. She married *LA Times* radio writer James Brown and the couple began writing for television including the *Dynasty* series.

ESTRADA, Ed: **KSKQ**, 1983, vp/gm

ESTRICH, Susan: **KABC**, 1991-97. Susan hosts her own Sunday morning show on KABC "TalkRadio." Born in Lynn, Massachusetts, Susan earned her B.A. with highest honors from Wellesley College. She earned her J.D. magna cum laude from Harvard Law School. In 1988 Susan was the national campaign manager for the

Michael Dukakis Presidential campaign. She had been on the senior staff of the Mondale-Ferraro presidential campaign in 1984 and Ted Kennedy's in 1980. She was the first woman president of the Harvard Law Review. Susan has sat in for Michael Jackson since 1991 and was one of the morning drive commentators. She is married and has two children. In the summer of 1997 KABC moved Michael Jackson into her weekend time slot and forgot to tell Susan.

VOTE FOR YOUR FAVORITE PERSONALITIES BETWEEN 1957 and 1997

EUBANKS, Bob: **KRLA**, 1960-67. The popular host of tv's *The Newlywed Game* got started in radio at KACY-Oxnard before arriving in Southern California for the all-night shift at KRLA. He worked morning drive as well as other shifts hosting "Teen Toppers," playing the most popular songs from all the schools in the Southland. Bob  risked personal finances to bring the Beatles to Los Angeles. The gamble paid off and he ended up producing all of the Beatles shows for the three years they toured Southern California. Bob was also the promoter behind such acts as The Rolling Stones, Bob Dylan, Stevie Wonder, Barry Manilow, The Who, The Beach Boys and the worldwide Merle Haggard Tour. Promoting led to management. He managed such performers as Dolly Parton, Barbara Mandrell, The Everly Brothers and Marty Robbins. He owned teen nightclubs: The Cinnamon Cinder at the traffic circle in Long Beach and Main Street in Alhambra. For more than two decades, Bob asked the questions on *The Newlywed Game* that garnered some of the most memorable responses in television history. In 1995 he released a video tape of the classic moments from the show. He has also served as host for *Rhyme & Reason*, *Trivia Trap*, *Card Sharks*, *Dream House* and *Family Secrets*. Every year Bob hosts The Hollywood Christmas Parade and Tournament of Roses Parade for KTLA. The latter parade regularly attracts more viewers than all other station broadcasts combined. The Bob Eubanks Southwest Gallery featuring Native American handmade jewelry, kachina dolls, rugs and such are regularly featured on the Home Shopping Network. These days he can be seen hosting one of the most popular morning shows in Branson, Missouri, *The $25,000 Game Show*. He has also hosted TNN's *Prime Time Country*. Bob ended his show on KRLA with: "Love thy neighbor, but don't get caught."

EVANS, Darryl: **KBLA**, 1961-64; **KXFV**, 1966-67; **KGFJ**, 1968-69; **KUTE**, 1973 and 1975; **KROQ**, 1977 and 1980; **XPRS**, 1982-84; **KIEV**, 1992-96. Darryl has been a dear friend to the world of oldies and doo-wop. He graduated from L.A. City College and worked in Brownsville, Albuquerque and Winslow, Arizona before joining KBLA and working with Huggie Boy. Over the last two decades Darryl has become disabled with crippling psoriatic arthritis which has left him permanently disabled. He has undergone eleven joint replacement surgeries with more expected. Darryl remains dedicated to preserving the sound of Southern California oldies.

EVANS, Don: **KROQ**, 1978-79

EVANS, Frank: **KRHM**, 1957-64; **KHJ**, 1965; **KDAY**; **KFI**, 1973. "Frankly Jazz" was the title of his radio and tv show and ultimately his signature. Born and raised in New Jersey, Frank studied dramatic arts at New York University. He was an actor on Broadway and played drums in a combo before taking his passion for music to a career in radio. As a Quaker, Frank was exempt from serving in World War II and during the 1940s he worked at WFTM-Ft. Meyers, WDNC-Durham, KYW-Philadelphia and KSBR and KSFO-San Francisco. He brought his family to L.A. in 1951 to pursue radio and an acting career. While in San Francisco he worked with Jack Webb. When Jack started *Dragnet*, he offered Frank a continuing role on the successful series. Frank was a heavy smoker and he died December 27, 1973, at the age of 56.

EVANS, Mike: **KFWB**, 1964-65; **KABC**, early '70s; **KBIG**, 1972; **KNAC**, 1975-79; **KABC**, 1976-78; **KROQ**, 1979-89, nd. Born in Honolulu, Mike has been associated with progressive music radio and sports during his career. He teamed with Larry Woodside at KROQ in morning drive. He was affectionately called "the Hose" while on "the Roq," where he did three stints during the '80s, between consultant jobs. He was producer of KABC's "SportsTalk" during the "Superfan" era. Later Mike was part of the Ramondo and Evans era from 1984 to 1989. Mike left Los Angeles to do mornings at KHFX-Honolulu. He consulted several stations; e.g., WTRG-Raleigh, and stations in Charlotte, Austin and Birmingham. In 1991, Mike hosted "Non-Stop Sports Show," which was syndicated in 25 markets. In 1993, XHRM ("the Flash")-San Diego "offered me mornings. I signed a two year deal and got blown out five months later." He is back doing sports and traveling to all major sporting events. When interviewed in early 1995, Mike said, "Hi to all the great people I've met in radio - and go to hell to all the jerks - you know who you are!" Mike got combat radio experience during his stint in Vietnam.

EVANS, Monica: **KFI**

EVANS, Pat: **KKDJ**, 1974; **KEZY**, 1976; **KHJ**, 1979; **KHTZ**, 1979-80; **KRTH**, 1982-85. Before arriving in Los Angeles, Pat worked at KIST-Santa Barbara, KDON-Salinas and KXKX-Denver. At KEZY he was Beaver Stevens. At KHJ he worked as Terry Foster and later as Terry Moreno. In the 1980s he worked at KSFX, KSFO and KYA-San Francisco. In the early 1990s Pat was in Florida.

EVANS, Scott: **KLAC**, 1989-90. Scott worked afternoon drive at the Country station.

EVANS, Stan: **KDAY**, 1966

EVANS, Tony: **KTNQ**, 1976-77. Tony arrived in Los Angeles from KRIZ-Phoenix. He returned to Arizona to KOPA which has since become KSLX.

"If I ever see another microphone or cart machine, I'll vomit."   *-Jason Durkin*

ON CHRONICLING POP
by
John Gilliland

(One of my early memories of early Rock radio at KRLA was a delicious series called "The Pop Chronicles." In the midst of the latest songs from the "Tune-dex" survey, the station tuned out for an hour to chronicle the history of pop music and the sometimes difficult transition between rock and pop. I caught up with the creator of "The Pop Chronicles," John Gilliland, while researching the main body of this book. He regaled me with his journey in meeting the superstars and I asked him to share a highlight or two. -db)

    A cold day in early '68 it was, and I had somehow made my way alone (via two unfamiliar London undergrounds) to the Jones Recording Studio in suburban Morden. The world's second most popular rock group was going to rehearse there and would be expecting me. Their newly-hired executive secretary, Jo Bergman (formerly of KRLA), had set it all up. And so I watched as they appeared one by one -- Bill Wyman, Charlie Watts, Keith Richards, a "roadie" or two and, finally, a bearded Mick Jagger and a Brian Jones decked out in what they called "psychedelic" gear. The original Stones! By afternoon's end, I had all five autographs on the cover of their current LP (Their Satanic Majesties Request. Moreover, on tape exclusively were long interviews with Mick and Brian and a bit of the band caught (unbeknownst) in ragged improvisation.

    This remains, surely, a highlight in the series of face to face interviews (150 approximately) that were taped for inclusion in the first audio history of popular music -- eventually called "The Pop Chronicles." The meetings took place from 1967 to '72; the show premiere in L.A. in January 1969.

    I spied my first Academy Award statuette in 1971. It was for Best Actor and belonged to Bing Crosby. He kept it on a mantle in a wondrous room in his Burlingame mansion near San Francisco. We talked there for more than an hour; the "groaner" in characteristically casual top form; the interviewer, well, kind of like a trembling kid in the presence of a childhood super-star. By the way, as also noted in person, one of Crosby's (and Frank Sinatra's) favorite songwriters, Jimmy Van Heusen, kept <u>his</u> Oscars, four of 'em, on top of a tv set in Palm Springs. (His winners were Swinging on a Star, All the Way, High Hopes and The Second Time Around.)

    Then there was multi-award recipient Roger Miller. I found his numerous Grammies scattered about on the carpet in the other-wise barren living room of a Sherman Hills ranch-style. His wife had gone off and left him and taken all the furniture, Roger quipped. Such a genuinely funny man. "I feel like I got malignant ignorance," he said at another point. "But, hey, let's stop talking about me and talk about you. What do <u>you</u> think about me?" Turned out that we had grown up at the same time only a few miles apart, in Texas and Oklahoma respectively.

Janis Joplin and I talked Texas roots in a pair of L.A. nightclub dressing rooms. This interviewer (not exactly a mechanical marvel) botched-up the first tape, and Janis graciously agreed to make a second later on. (So did Frank Zappa and Beach Boy Mike Love, whose first takes turned out faulty.) Others caught backstage -- sometimes before, sometimes after concerts -- included Perry Como and Peggy Lee, Johnny Cash and Marty Robbins. Jimmy Reed and John Lee Hooker, the three men of Cream and Peter, Paul and Mary. A decidedly mixed bag.

One session with a pioneer rock and roller (who will remain nameless) took place in a small motel room on La Cienega. Also, throughout the meeting, an attractive young woman resided, under the covers, in a dominant double bed. That is, except for the times she got up to answer the door - to greet the star's manager, his accountant, the guy from Chicken Delight, et al -- and wore nothing more than a dazzling smile.

And what at first appeared to be a young boy in cut-off jeans, playing basketball with some other kids in the driveway of Berry Gordy's secluded Hollywood Hills home, was in reality one Diana Ross. It was her short-haired, pixie-like days. The ensuing conversation, a delight, was further spiced by Gordy himself playing background grand piano in a nearby room. Among other Motowners met and taped: Marvin Gaye, Smokey Robinson and Martha Reeves.

And, lastly, Stevie Wonder, a lively eighteen-year-old at the time (1968 again). It was he who had to pint out to the interviewer that the tape machine wasn't working. For Stevie, casually running one hand over the equipment, had determined by touch what the interviewer had failed to note with all his senses: some dummy had neglected to push RECORD.

Call it "malignant ignorance," --right, Roger? (Wherever you are.)

F

FAIN, Mary: **KFAC**, 1987-89. Mary worked at a Classical music station in Seattle before joining KFAC.

FAIRCHILD, Johnny: **KEZY**, 1959. In 1968, Johnny worked at KIST-Santa Barbara. He is now deceased.

FAIRLY, Ron: **KMPC**, 1982-86. The former baseball player was the play-by-play announcer for the California Angels with Bob Starr. In 1987 he joined the San Francisco Giants announcing booth. The *SF Chronicle* harshly reported on his arrival, "Replacing Hank Greenwald with Ron Fairly is like replacing Pavarotti with Howdy Doody." Ron played baseball for 21 years starting with the Los Angeles Dodgers in 1958 followed by Montreal, St. Louis, Oakland Toronto and California Angels. In 2,442 games, he compiled a life-time average of .266 with 215 homeruns and 1,044 RBI. Since 1992, Ron has been broadcasting the Seattle Marines games. He lives in Westlake Village with his wife Mary. The couple has three sons.

FAJITA, Anita: SEE Anita Gevinson

FALKENSTEIN, Glenn: **KGBS**, 1974. During KGBS's foray into all-Talk, Glenn, a mentalist, hosted a Sunday afternoon show. Born in Chicago, he received a B.A. from Illinois State and a master's in speech from Pepperdine. His career as a mentalist began in 1965 when he arrived in the Southland to work at the Hollywood Wax Museum and the Magic Castle. In 1972 he was awarded the Academy of Magical Arts' top prize for a stage performer.

FARRELL, Rod: **KPOL**; **KBIG**, 1967

FAULK, Marshall: **KOCM**, 1987. Marshall worked overnights.

FAUST, Lou: **KPOL**, 1965-67; **KIIS**, 1970, gm. The *LA Times*' Don Page named Lou Executive of the Year "for supervising and helping develop one of the most stylish music concepts heard here in many years." He is credited with coming up with the "KIIS" moniker. Lou was a longtime executive with CapCities, managing WPAT-Patterson, New Jersey for a time. One colleague who worked for Lou at KPOL said: "We would have walked through fire for him." Lou also headed Selcom Radio Reps in New York, gm of WKBW-Buffalo and executive vp of Blair Radio. He went on to KCMJ-Palm Springs and is now working at Jones Radio Network as regional sales manager of Western and Central states.

FAUSTO, Fidel: **KLAX**, 1992-94, pd;

KKHJ/KWIZ/KBUE, 1995-97, pd. Since 1993 Fidel has been the md and pd for Liberman Broadcasting's three Spanish stations. Born in Ameca, Jalisco, Mexico, Fidel graduated from acting school at Academia Andres Soler in Mexico D.F. After graduation he came to the United States. "I worked menial jobs such as cleaning and in farming fields." He joined different musical groups and found his way to KGST-Fresno in 1984 where he got his radio start. In 1990 he moved cross town to KOQO and a year later joined KOXR-Oxnard as pd. In 1992 he joined KLAX and won a programming award from *Billboard* magazine.

FEATHER, Leonard: **KBCA**, 1972-74; **KUSC**, 1979; **KKGO**, 1982. Leonard was a noted jazz critic of the *LA Times*. He authored several books on the idiom.

FEDDERMAN, Steve: **KMPC**, 1996. Steve hosted a general issue talk show on KMPC.

FEDDERSON, Jerry: KFWB, 70s. She was an outside reporter.

FEDEROFF, Nick: **KFI**. Nick has been the gardening expert of weekend talk shows.

FEELGOOD, Doctor: SEE Rich "Brother" Robbin

FEINSTEIN, Steve: **KLOS**, 1984. The AOR editor for *R&R* magazine between 1983 and 1987 had an oldies show on KLOS called "Rock and Roll Roots." He started his radio career doing overnights at WIOQ-Philadelphia. Steve arrived in the Southland in 1983 from a pd slot at WYSP-Philadelphia. In 1987 Steve went to program KKSF-San Francisco. On September 26, 1996, Steve jumped to his death from the 30th floor of the Westin St. Francis Hotel. He was 40.

FELIX, Eva: **KWIZ**, 1997

FELZ, John: **KMPC**, 1971-94, pd; **KMAX**, 1995-96, pd. For almost a quarter of a century, John was part of KMPC. He started as a sports producer when KMPC was carrying the California Angeles, L.A. Rams and UCLA sports. Mark went on to be assistant pd to Mark Blinoff, senior producer during the Talk era, and producer of Robert W. Morgan's morning show. During the 1980s he served as operations manager and briefly as pd. John left KMPC in 1994 when it was sold to CapCities. Born in Ladysmith, Wisconsin, he came to the Southland with his parents when he was one year old. "I consider myself a native." His best friend while growing up was Pat Kelley, son of the legendary sports broadcaster, Bob Kelley, the voice of the Rams. While attending Cal State Northridge, John discovered his "passion" for radio while working on the campus station. His grandfather owned a radio station in Ladysmith and his father was in the automobile business. "Perhaps there is a parallel with selling radio time and selling cars." He graduated with a political-science major. After a stint in the Army, John started his radio career at KCIN-Victorville and KGRB-West Covina before joining KMPC. He is now operations director of the "Music of Your Life" satellite service servicing over 70 stations with Nostalgia music and "heavy" personalities.

FEMINO, Tony: **KMPC**, 1992-94. Tony was part of the all-Sports format at KMPC. He grew up in Pasadena and wanted to pursue journalism. As a high school student he interned at the *Pasadena Star-News*. Tony went to Northwestern, a school that many consider to be the best telecommunication school in the country. While there he was a sports writer and got hooked on radio while working on the campus station. Following graduation in

1991, Tony returned to the Southland and worked briefly at KBET in the Santa Clarita Valley. He joined the all-Sports format at KMPC as a desk assistant which eventually led to the all-night shift. Before he left he was working middays. In 1994 he joined all-Sports KGME-Phoenix where he continues to work. He also broadcasts sports on the weekends for the Phoenix CBS/TV station. Tony hosts the pre- and post-game USC football radio shows.

FENNOY, Dave: **KACE**, 1992; **KAJZ/KACD**, 1992-94. Dave worked morning drive during 103.1FM's brief experiment with a Jazz-format. He is now very active in a voiceover career.

FERGUSON, Gene: **KPOL**; **KFWB**; **KPOL**, 1973-86, nd. When Gene left radio in 1986 he became the campaign manager for Congressman Dana Rohrabacher. Gene was from Akron, Ohio.

FERGUSON, Joe: **KFOX**, 1972-73. Joe worked afternoon drive when the station was playing country music.

FERGUSON, Ted: **KWST**, 1980-81, pd. Born and raised in Shreveport, Ted graduated from LSU. He started his radio career in 1967 at WABB-Mobile followed by stops in Baton Rouge and Knoxville. Ted was part of the original staff of the legendary WMMS-Cleveland. After Cleveland radio, he went to what was then ABC's WDVE-Pittsburgh and on to Norfolk. It was in Detroit at WDRQ that Ted moved from evening jock to pd. He credits Jerry Clifton with being a real teacher. From his home in

Shreveport, Ted said: "Sometimes we're lucky to have a teacher who not only teaches us the basics of radio, but how to deal with people and life. Jerry was very critical in my growth." Ted's next stops were WABX-Detroit and then "96X"-Miami. Century Broadcasting owned 'ABX and asked him to take hold of "K-West." Ted remembered: "It was a classic staff with Raechel Donahue in the morning with Gayle Murphy doing traffic, Steve Downes, J.J. Jackson, China Smith, Dusty Street and Radio Rich. It was one of the most rewarding times of my life and, at the same time, disappointing. For years Century marched a wide array of pd's and gm's through, none ever being able to achieve better than a .7 share. We moved it to 2.3 in a year and a half. Five weeks before the 2.3 ARB, ownership decided to pull the plug." In the summer of 1984 Ted met the owner of, as he calls it, "a teapot station in France." He went to Europe and for the next half decade consulted stations in Asia, New Zealand, Tahiti, Sweden and Germany. The big opportunity came in Paris just three months after private radio was made legal. His company was called NRJ and ENERGY. Ted would set up the stations. Get the programming right. Train the program director and general manager. Today NRJ has 320 stations and three networks in five countries. He learned many languages in his foreign travels. After starting up 4 NRJ stations in East Germany and 18 in Sweden and getting them to profitable, Ted returned to his hometown. Ted is the general manager of KTAL-Shreveport. "I make more money with '98 Rocks' than I ever could in Los Angeles. It doesn't take much to be successful if you stick with the basics that work. Give the people what they say they want."

FERRAR, Sim: **KIEV**; **KDAY**; **KROQ**, 1974

FERRARI: **KEZY**, 1989-90. She was a Miami vice cop in the 1980s.

FERRERI, Carmy: **KKBT**, 1989-90; **KRLA**, 1995-96; **KIBB**, 1996-97. Born Carmelo Ferreri in Los Angeles, Carmy worked at KXTZ-Las Vegas, KRXQ-Sacramento, KBAI-San Luis Obispo and WHYI ("Y100")-Miami, before returning home. He was part of the launch of "the Beat" in the fall of 1989, and his show was called "The Nightbeat" -- a "Quiet Storm" type of show. He joined KGGI/KMEN-Riverside in 1993 as pd until his appointment as pd of KRLA in late 1995. In the summer of 1996 KRLA changed formats to "Mix 11" and his position was eliminated. In the fall of 1996, he joined Rhythmic Hot AC, KIBB and left in early 1997 to be pd at KQPT-Sacramento.

FERRIS, Bob: **KMPC**; **KNX**, 1957-67. Bob broadcast in the evenings on "KNXNewsradio."

FERRO, Pio: **KTNQ/KLVE**, 1995-97, pd. Born January 3, 1973, Pio arrived in the Southland from programming chores at WXDJ-Miami. He grew up Miami and started at WXDJ when he was 15 years old and was promoted to pd when the format shifted from NAC to Spanish. He talked about his schooling: "It's amazing how quiet I was in school. I was never a big time athlete. Basically I stayed out of trouble. My

passion was for music. I had a high-end sound system when all my teen friends had boom boxes. Pio won the 1995 *Billboard* magazine award for Best Spanish Program Director of the Year. His Miami mentor Bill Tanner followed Pio to KLVE and "the Cuban and Gringo" as he described the tandem, had strong success in 1996. "We focused on the romantic music. We also focused the jocks on being personal and talking about things people wanted to listen to."

FIELD, Elliot: **KFWB**, 1958-64. On January 2, 1958,  Elliot began afternoon drive on the launch of Chuck Blore's legendary KFWB "Color Radio/Channel 98." When he left the station in the summer of 1964, he was working nine to noon. Elliot was born in Malden, Massachusetts in 1927. By the time he reached KFWB, he had perfected a cast of thousands with such characters as his sidekicks "Tex," Alfred Hitchcock, Arthur Asti of Shields, California, Lonesome George Gobelfield and Milton J. Double-Cross. His private New York correspondent was Father Winshield. As a teenager, Elliot worked as an actor on the CBS Radio Network. While at KFWB, he created the legendary-but-imaginary rooftop swimming pool. Prior to arriving in Southern California, he worked at a number of McLendon stations, including KTSA-San Antonio, KLIF-Dallas and KILT-Houston. When he left the Southland, Elliot did free-lance voice work for Hanna Barbera on *Quick Draw McGraw* and *The Flintstones*. He joined WJR-Detroit for five years, then went to Palm Springs where he was gm at KPSI for 11 years. Elliot currently heads up EF/MC, a full service marketing operation. During his 15 years in Palm Springs, he was elected twice to the Palm Springs City Council, and he was elected mayor pro-tem in 1981. He commented on the burdens of being a city councilman: "My pet peeve as a public official is public indifference." He considers his years at KFWB as the "highlight of my radio career."

FIELDS, Lady Fay: **KAGB**, 1975

FIELDS, Rich: **KKHR/KODJ/KCBS**, 1989-92. Rick kicked off KODJ Oldies format on March 2, 1989. On Sundays he hosted a call-in show with a different major oldies singer as guest.

FIELDS, Sam: **KBCA**, 1972-80; **KROQ**; **KMET**; **KLAC**; **KKGO**, 1980-89; **KKJZ**, 1990; **KLON**, 1990-97. Sam is one of the jazz music personality veterans, whose career spans three decades in Southern California radio. In the mid-1970s, Sam moonlighted at KROQ, KMET and KLAC.

FIELDS, Tony: **KACE/KEAV**, 1992-93, pd. Born Anthony Fields in Louisville, he earned a B.A. degree in mass telecommunications at the University of Louisville. Soon after graduation in 1982, Tony spent five years with WLOU-Louisville doing morning drive and assisting with the programming. He worked at two more Louisville stations until early 1989 when he became pd and worked morning drive at WBLZ-Cincinnati. A year later he was off to do mornings at KSOL-San Francisco. In 1991, Tony became national pd for the 24-station Willis Broadcasting chain out of Norfolk. After his first stop at WKKV-Milwaukee, Tony arrived in the summer of 1992 at KACE/KEAV to be pd and morning drive jock. In the summer of 1993, he returned to WKKV, where he was pd, morning show host and consultant. While he was at KACE, he was asked in a *Hits* magazine Q & A for advice to younger programmers: "Save your money...pray a lot. Take your time to learn people. That's been my key. I like to surround myself with good people. You may be the greatest programmer in the world, but sometimes your attitudes are so far off that not even the gm or the owner wants to deal with you. The better you manage people, the better off you'll be as a programmer. All the other things will come." In the summer of 1995, Tony was promoted to a corporate position at UNC Media as vp of broadcast operations for four UNC stations. In March of 1996 he joined Blue Chip Broadcasting as vp of programming. He presides over the programming of WGZB/WLSY-Louisville and WIZF-Cincinnati.

FILIAR, Ricci: **KIKF**, 1991-92; **KLSX**, 1993-94; **KMGX**, 1994; **KRLA**, 1991-97, pd. He is known as "Little Ricci" on KRLA and since the summer of 1996 has  worked morning drive. Born August 29, 1968, in Riverside, he was raised by his mother until he went off to the University of California Riverside and Cal State Fullerton. While he was growing up in the Inland Empire, he constantly listened to Rocker KFXM. "I was fascinated by the jingles, the production elements, the djs, and the overall presentation. I used to make my mom take me to the station (located at the Holiday Inn in San Bernardino) so that I could watch the djs through the window. I knew very early on that I wanted to be in programming." In the spring of 1997 he was promoted to pd at KRLA.

FINLEY, Larry: **KFWB**, 1957; **KGIL**, 1966. After a long on-air career in the 1940s and '50s, Larry moved to the music industry working for Dot, Tops and MGM Records. In 1968 he became president of ITCC and the company became a pioneer in the tape field.

FISCHLER, Alan: **KBIG**, 1966, gm. Alan ran KNJO for several years. He is now deceased.

FISHER, Steven: **KFWB**, 1986-90, gm. Steven arrived from Group W Cable. He was assigned to dismantle the cable operation and then was made gm of KFWB. He is no longer with Westinghouse.

FISTELL, Ira: **KABC**, 1977-95; **KKGO/KNNS**, 1996. Ira is a treasure-trove of interests. He loves opera, trains, the circus, maps, the White Sox, trivia, night baseball, classical literature, Americana, Midwest high school basketball, the Civil War and virtually anything historical. He made the perfect open-ended type talk show host. Ira was one of the many hosts of "SportsTalk." He's a former history teacher at the University of Wisconsin and has a law degree from the University of Chicago. Born May 31, 1941, Ira made headlines after a fatal traffic accident in which he was accused of leaving the scene and driving with an expired driver's license. He was eventually reinstated to his nightly talk show and left KABC in the fall of 1995. He departed the station the first time in the summer of 1992 and rejoined the station later that year. In the spring of 1996 Ira became the entertainment editor for KKGO and KNNS.

FITZGERALD, Don: **KNX**. Don was one of the hosts of the "KNX Food Hour."

FITZRANDOLPH, Chris: **KNX**, 1987-88. Chris worked middays on the all-News station.

FLANAGAN, John Mack: **KHJ**, 1975. The San Francisco veteran called his brief stay at KHJ "the single biggest event in my career. I had always dreamed of L.A., and Charlie Van Dyke asked me to assist and pull a couple of shifts." In 1978, while working in the San Francisco market, John was *Billboard* Jock of the Year finalist. He was glad he didn't win, saying: "Never climb to the mountain top - the only way is down." In the 1990s he was fired four times in two years due to duopoly sales. He left KYA-San Francisco during the summer of 1994. A family friend who owned KJOY-Stockton offered him afternoon drive in 1994, and John was delighted: "I love it! I'm out of the pressure cooker and having fun for the first time in many years. Please pray for radio, it needs it...never been harder to survive." John currently works at KBGG ("K-Big 98.1")-San Francisco.

FLAVIO, Silva: **KTNQ**, 1993-94. Silva is now doing voiceover work.

FLEMING, Jack: **KGIL**, 1964. Jack lives in Eugene and has worked for a number of area radio stations.

FLEMING, Kevin: **KGFJ**, 1984-89, pd; **KACE**, 1994-97, pd. An 18-year entertainment veteran, Kevin graduated

from Clark College. In 1981 he spent time in Georgia radio and tv and WWDM-South Carolina before arriving at KGFJ as an on-air pd. Kevin has had vp positions at a number of record companies, including Perspective, Third Stone, Atlantic and Island. Kevin, married and the father of a young boy, is currently the pd of KACE, owned by Cox Broadcasting.

FLETCHER, Gary: **KJOI**, 1987. Gary worked all-nights.

FLO and **EDDIE**: **KROQ**, 1973-74; **KMET**, 1974-75. Mark Volman and Howard Kaylan are the Turtles and they were "happy together" as hosts of the "Flo and Eddie By the Fireside Show" on KROQ and KMET. Mark was born in Los Angeles and Howard in the Bronx. They met while attending Westchester High School by the airport. After a string of international success, the Turtles folded in 1970. Due to contractual restrictions made early in their career, they were prevented from using the name, the Turtles, as well as their own names, in a musical context. They became Flo and Eddie. Mark and Howard joined Frank Zappa's Mothers of Invention, for one of the most entertaining incarnations of that ensemble. While with The Mothers, they appeared on four albums including *200 Motels*, as well as appearing in the film *200 Motels*. In 1984 they regained the rights to the Turtles. As the Turtles they perform 50-60 times a year. Mark, who is a graduate of Loyola Marymount College with a degree in communication is just finishing his master's in fine arts said, "We could do a lot more but we'd touring but we would rather be at home with our families." Mark teaches the business of music at Loyola. "Radio is like *Jurassic Park*, it's the lost world. Early Rock radio was true Americana. You turned it on and it was heavy on personality. You got to understand the dj's opinion." In the 1980s they worked as a broadcast team at WLIR and afternoons at WXRK-New York. Mark said: "I have a tremendous lack of respect for radio today. The Oldies format has kept the Turtles alive, but radio in general is lost." Howard lives in Missouri.

FLORES, Julio: **KWIZ**, 1984-89; **KLSX**, 1989-90; **KGIL/KMGX**, 1989-92; **KTWV**, 1990-94; **KRLA**, 1994-95; **KSCA**, 1994-96; **KLSX**, 1997. For most of his radio career Julio has held two simultaneous radio jobs, on-air and engineering. "If I ever get blown out of one radio station," he laughed, "I still have a radio job." Julio was born in Anaheim on Halloween 1964. His radio passion began at age 11 while listening to a transistor radio under his pillow. "Jim Ladd was my hero. I thought, 'can he really say that on the radio?'" While attending Anaheim High School Julio fiddled with transmitters. In 1985 while going to Fullerton Junior College and working research at KWIZ, he got his first on-air job at KSMA and KSNI-Santa Maria. "Every Saturday I would leave on a Greyhound bus at 10:30 in the morning and get to Santa Maria around 9:30 at night in time for the first of three weekend shifts that started at 10. I would leave Sunday night, just after midnight and get back to Orange County as the sun was coming up. With what they were paying me and the cost of the Greyhound and motel room, I lost $50 a weekend." He spent four years doing weekend work at KGMG-San Diego while on the air at KWIZ. Married since 1989, he and his wife have a son, Jason. Julio worked fill-in and weekends at KSCA and continues the AAA format on weekends at "Real Radio," KLSX.

FLOYD, Gary: **KNOB**, 1949; **KGER**, 1950-60; **KGGK**, 1960-65; **KLFM**, 1966-70; **KBOB/KGRB**, 1975-88.

Gary loved radio all his life. He was born in Paterson, New Jersey and grew up in Utica. As a boy he put together crystal sets and as a young man in high school he was the one everyone counted on to set up the P.A. system to broadcast music for lunch time and special events. He and his wife came to the Southland in 1947 where he pursued his radio career. He graduated from Frederick H. Speare's broadcast school. Gary fulfilled his dream of being a radio announcer working Jazz, Gospel and Big Band formats. At KGRB, where he worked until his retirement in 1988, he was known to his big band listeners as "The Beachcomber." Even after his retirement, Gary was active in big band events and wrote articles for music publications and was a member of several industry groups. Gary passed away in May 1995 at the age of 72.

FLYNN, Howard: **KMPC**, 1953-79. Howard delivered the half-hour morning newscast for Harris & Frank clothiers for a quarter century. He played Wheezing Upton Peter Dunkel on Dick Whittinghill's "Helen Trump" spoof for years.

FONDO, Denise: Denise has been guiding commuters through the freeway traffic snarls in Southern California for over 15 years. Originally from Pennsylvania, Denise has led a double life for most of her life. "I'm a writer of fiction and non-fiction and took a job in 1982 with L.A. Network Traffic to pay the bills while I wrote." She attended American University and Lycombie College in Washington, DC studying poly-sci and philosophy. Denise came to the Southland to work for the Hollywood Entertainment Radio Network and wrote radio dramas for a number of years. Over the years she has written tv specials for the Discovery Channel and feature films. "Usually when I sell something big, I travel until I run out of money, and then I come back home." Denise joined Metro Traffic in 1989 where she continues. She is working on her master's degree in archeology at UCLA and has a passion for baseball. "I don't love baseball. I 'live' baseball."

FORD, Ed: **KEZY**, 1985-97. Ed is an instructor at Fullerton College's radio station, KBPK.

FORD, John Anson: **KRHM**, 1959. John worked weekends at KRHM. He became a Los Angeles city councilman.

FORD, Judy: **KFWB**, 1986-97. The Hawaiian native was born Judy Mugford. She worked for Ron Jacobs' KPOI-Honolulu as Kai Kailia and followed him to Watermark where she produced, among other projects, Chuck Southcott's "Musical." Judy has been a longtime news anchor for "news/98" who has worked midday and afternoon drive.

FORGIONE, Pete: **KJOI**, 1989. Pete worked weekends.

FORMAN, Dave: **KYMS**, 1974; **KWIZ**, 1975; **KEZY** 1976-82, pd; **KFWB**, 1986-88. Born in South Carolina, Dave's family moved to New York a few months after his birth, and he grew up on Long Island. He attended Adelphi University and then came to the Southland to attend Cal State Fullerton. While in college, he began doing mornings at KYMS and remained until the entire staff was fired the week before Christmas and the format changed to Christian. In 1981, KEZY/AM went all-News, and Dave orchestrated the KNWZ format. During much of his career, the ubiquitous Dave has worked several jobs at the same time, making it difficult to segment when he did what assignment. During the 1970s, he was a contributor to UPI, NBC News and *Billboard*. At KFWB he was director of news and programming and orchestrated a unique 12-hour broadcast called "California Dreamin'" where dozens of guest hosts talked about their California dreams. Since 1988, Dave has been the executive producer and host of *On Scene: Emergency Response*, that is syndicated in 160 cities and 30 countries worldwide. The tv program has taken Dave into the cockpit with the Blue Angels, out to sea with the U.S. Coast Guard Search and Rescue Crews and into a burning crack house in Harlem. In addition to the continuing *On Scene*, he is exec producer of *Special Access with Dave Forman*, airing daily on KCAL/Channel 9. In the fall of 1996 he hosted and executive produced *Fire Rescue* for Kelly News and *Air Rescue* for Western International Media. Dave is married to Barbara and they have two children. Would he go back to radio? Dave said he would if there were a unique "talk format" environment.

FORTE, Chet: **XTRA**, 1991-96. Chet spent 25 years at ABC/TV and helped launch *Monday Night Football*. After he was forced out of his job by a gambling addiction, he joined all-Sports XTRA. He and Steve Hartman billed themselves as "The Loose Cannons." Chet was an All-American basketball star at Columbia University who beat out Wilt Chamberlain as NCAA player of the year in 1957. He won 11 Emmy Awards during his quarter century with ABC as a producer and director. His work also included the network's coverage of the Indianapolis 500 and the 1968 and 1984 Summer Olympics. When he left ABC in 1987 he had gambled away nearly $4 million and lost a million-dollar home in Saddle River, New Jersey, because he couldn't pay the mortgage. Chet told the *LA Times* shortly after taking the XTRA job, which paid $57,800 a year. "This is the most fun I've had in my entire life. I mean that. I had a lot of wonderful years at ABC, but this seems more fulfilling than anything I've ever done." Born Fulvio Chester Forte Jr., Chet died May 18, 1996, of a heart attack. He was 60.

FORWARD, Bob: **KMPC** 1956-61, pd; **KLAC**, 1961-64, gm; **KRLA**, 1978-82, gm. Multi-media talented, Bob was in on the embryonic days of television and many firsts in Los Angeles radio. "Bob was the sound of KMPC. He was so far ahead of his time and was the greatest leader of employees. He knew how to motivate people for the highest results," according to a former KMPC dj. Born and raised in San Diego, Bob graduated from Stanford University with a political-science degree. When Bob was asked where he grew up, he responded: "I don't know if I ever did." After graduation in 1937, he became the first jazz djs in San Francisco at KYA. "I got the attention of all the 'cats' in town." Two years later he joined KFRC-San Francisco and was the host of Mark Goodson's first game show, "Pop A Question." He transferred to the Mutual/Don Lee Los Angeles station, KHJ in 1941. The war came and Bob joined the Army AirCorps where he was a pilot for almost 4 years. He returned to KHJ as an announcer/producer/director. In 1949 KTTV/Channel 11 owned by CBS and the *Los Angeles Times*, hired Bob as pd. "We broadcast from the top floor of the Bekins building at Santa Monica and Highland. I brought in mostly movie people - some famous, some soon would be - to help give KTTV a 'movie look.' We were doing 1/2 hour live dramatic shows for $125 each, including everything." In 1950, the CBS/TV network hired Bob to function as associate to Ralph Levy who produced and directed the live broadcasts of "The Jack Benny Show," "Burns and Allen" and "The Alan Young Show." "We did the 'Benny' show twice, a live feed at 4 in the afternoon for the East Coast, then we went to Nickodell's with the writer to polish any material that didn't work, then did the West Coast feed at 7." Bob went on to be pd of KECA/Channel 7 which was owned by United Paramount theaters. "First thing we did was change the call letters to KABC/TV." In 1956 the gm of KMPC, Bob Reynolds, offered Bob an opportunity to "re-juvenate" the station. "Bob was the best boss I ever had. He let me do my job. During that period we bought the AirWatch system, canceled some of the short-form programs that interrupted the flow of the station and, with the help of Bob Kelley and Jim Healy, continued the emphasis on sports." KMPC was the first radio station to broadcast the Dodgers' games after they moved to Los Angeles from Brooklyn in 1958. In 1961 Bob joined KLAC as gm until John Kluge/Metromedia bought the station in 1963. He remained with Metromedia as a consultant for several years. In 1968, Bob became one of the first writers on *Adam-12*, then produced *The D.A.* pilots and series for NBC/TV. He was the hospital administrator on *Marcus Welby, M.D.* for two seasons along with a slew of featured roles in other series and movies. Bob became vp of Goodson-Todman Broadcasting, responsible for reviving KOL-Seattle. Then in 1978 Bob was appointed executive vp/gm of KRLA representing the merged group holding the Pasadena radio station license, Goodson-Todman having been one of the applicants. "In 1987 I re-married and moved to San Diego I thought, for evermore. Unfortunately, my wife developed Alzheimer's Disease and passed away in March 1997." Bob is back living in Los Angeles. "I loved the business. I had great rapport with the troops. I loved the people I worked with."

FORWARD, Dr. Susan: **KABC**, 1982-84. Susan is a psychologist who worked weekends and eventually afternoons on the Talk station. She received her masters in psychiatric social work in 1970 and then a doctorate in psychology. An on-air psychologist was her second career. As actress Susan Dorn she appeared on more than 50 television shows during the late '50s and early '60s. She appeared in *Bonanza* and *The Donna Reed Show* among others. Her bridge from acting to psychology began in 1964 when she became involved with a psychodrama workshop at UCLA. She stayed on for four years as an assistant. She was the director of the Balboa Therapy Center which at the time was the only private sexual abuse clinic in California. Her work, *Betrayal of Innocence*, was published. Susan credited Dr. Toni Grant with opening the doors and paving the way for programs dealing with psychological problems. She created new headlines during the O.J. Simpson trial as Nicole Brown Simpson's therapist. Susan has written a best-selling book titled *Toxic Parents*.

FORZONN, Pam: **KRLA**, 1963-65. Pam was the husky voiced sidekick heard during Emperor Bob Hudson's morning drive show.

FOSTER, John: **KACE**, 1970, pd

FOSTER, Louise: **KJLH**, 1979-80; **KGFJ**, 1989-94. In 1985, Louise was heard on Armed Forces Radio Network. She hosted a reggae show on KGFJ. Louise is now in travel promotion working for Eastern Airlines.

FOSTER, Reb: **KRLA**, 1962-65; **KFWB**, 1965-66; **KRLA**, 1967-69, pd and 1973 and 1982-83 and 1985-87.

Born James Bruton, he started in Texas radio in the mid-1950s working in Ft. Worth and Amarillo. Before Los Angeles he was heard at KYW-Cleveland, KCIN-Denver and at KISN-Portland, where he was known as Dennis James. He arrived in Los Angeles from KYA-San Francisco. Reb was pd for a time at KRLA. One of his famous characters was Maude Skidmore. He put on dances at the Retail Clerks Union

Hall Auditorium in Buena Park with the cry "Let's Wail at the Retail." Reb had his own nightclub in Redondo Beach imploring the kids to "Be There or Be Square." In 1967 *Billboard* listed Rebel as the best midday dj. Reb quit KFWB to affiliate with Ted Randal in consulting radio stations. He made a third return to KRLA in 1973, when the Pasadena station went to an MOR format from contemporary music and experimented with teams in every time period. Rebel worked the afternoon drive shift with Bob Dayton. In the '70s Reb managed Three Dog Night, the Turtles and Steppenwolf.

FOSTER, Rod: **KPCC**, 1986-97, gm

FOSTER, Ron: **KIIS**, 1977-80; **KPRZ**, 1980-85, nd. The former news anchor for KIIS AM&FM was born in Los Angeles in 1942 and grew up in the Southland. "I found out I was fascinated by radio as early as four years old while living with my mom in Eagle Rock. I would look behind the big Philco radio on the floor hoping to see little people inside the brightly lit tubes." Ron later became a fan of radio theater and comedy shows. He entered the Navy in 1961 and ran a shipboard radio station on the USS Oklahoma City. Ron played records going up the Saigon river and played the saxophone in a rock band at every port during the Vietnam War. Ron started his radio career in 1965 at KTLW-Texas City followed by KPLZ-Lake Charles, Louisiana, and KTLW-Santa Paula. In 1969 Ron switched careers from dj to news when he joined KAFY-Bakersfield followed by KFRC-San Francisco and KGEE-Bakersfield. In the mid-1980s Ron joined KTSA-San Antonio as a morning news anchor. Since 1986 he has

been working in Fresno, currently at KMPH/KFRE. "Working in Los Angeles was the best part of my radio career. I loved the people I worked with during that time."

FOSTER, Sean: SEE Don Murray

FOSTER, Terry: SEE Pat Evans

FOX, Al: **KNOB**; **KTYM**. The Jazz format on KTYM was pioneered by Al.

| *KMPC Goes into the "Zone," KTZN* |
| *-February 24, 1997* |

FOX, Charlie: **KWIZ**, 1975-77; **KFI**, 1977-79; **KHJ**, 1979-80; **KUTE**, 1982-84; **KMGG**, 1985; **KRLA**, 1992-93. Charlie was born James Martin in Santa Monica. "I

was thrilled to work at legendary stations like KHJ and KRLA. I wound up working with legendary jocks who, early on, were heroes of mine. Talent like Robert W., Dave Diamond, "Humble Harve," Wolfman Jack and Dave Hull. I never felt that I belonged in that company but maybe someday, in retrospect, I will." He did morning drive at "Kute." Charlie also worked at WRKO-Boston, CKLW-Detroit, and KDWB-Minneapolis/St. Paul. He worked many years for Transtar (now Westwood One). In 1993, Charlie moved to San Diego to do afternoon drive at KBZT, moving to '70s Oldies KKBH in 1995, which he left in early 1996.

FOX, Cynthia: **KMET**, 1977-87; **KMPC/FM/KEDG**, 1987-89; **KLSX**, 1993-95

FOX, Jim: Jim was the L.A. Kings announcer in 1991 with Bob Miller.

FOX, Jimi: **KTNQ**, 1976-77. Born Norbert Gomes, Jimi started his radio work on KDES-Palm Springs. In early 1970 he was pd and midday air personality at KENO-Las Vegas. A year later, Jimi went to KIKX-Tucson to be pd and evening jock. In 1973, he joined Buzz Bennett at KRIZ-Phoenix as md and evening personality and before the year was out had moved to KUPD-Phoenix. Late in 1974 Jimi helped Bobby Rich put KFMB ("B-100")-San Diego on the air. He did weekends and acted as pd for the debut of "the new Ten-Q" on December 26, 1976. After leaving KTNQ, Jimi went to KCBQ-San Diego as pd. He then joined Mercury Records as vp of national promotions and was the radio editor for *Cash Box Magazine*. When Jimi got out of his daily involvement with radio, he followed his hobby and second love -- orchids! He grows world class highly awarded orchids and has been responsible in setting new trends

in hybridizing. "I've registered countless plants using rock 'n' roll identities, such as 'Itchycoo Park,' 'Amos Nitrate,' and 'Electric Ladyland,' the last of which now graces the label of an international orchid fertilizer."

FOX, John: **KEZY**, 1993-97. Growing up in Fallbrook, John was fascinated by electronics and all things mechanical. "My first visit to a radio station was in junior

high when KCBQ-San Diego ran a favorite teacher contest. I not only got all his students to sign, I got his past students at the high school and Palomar College. The win got us 15 minutes of fame on KCBQ with Lee 'Baby' Simms. I had to drag the school's Wollensak recorder to the station since I couldn't get the station at night in Fallbrook." At 19 while studying telecom and journalism at San Diego State, John took on production duties at KFMB and stayed for 17 years working various shifts under five different pd's. In 1993 he joined Metro Traffic in San Diego putting his encyclopedic knowledge of every shortcut in San Diego to use on close to a dozen stations. In late 1993, John joined KEZY and started doing the morning show in January of 1994. His morning show on KEZY is pumped with energy. "You'll know I'm close to suicide if I ever stoop to giving concert tickets to the 10th caller." His "Name That Tune" feature is, according to John, "Orange County's favorite radio game show. The phones are jammed 10 minutes before the game is announced." He also does voiceover work for QIAD Productions.

FOX, Lisa: **KYSR**, 1997. Lisa joined the morning show at "Star 98.7" from KMEL-San Francisco.

KMPC kicks off All-Sports Programming -April 27, 1992

FOX, Michael: **KABC**, 1981-91, pd. Michael is operations director for Shadow Traffic.

FOX, Mike: **KNAC**, 1972

FOX, Norm: **KMPC**, 1994; **KABC/KMPC/KTZN** 1995-97. Norm hosts a weekend travel show on KABC. Born in Denver, Norm became smitten with travel at an early age when his parents took him and his three siblings on long automobile trips. He graduated from Harvard and the Columbia Graduate School of Business. He believes that it was during his term breaks in London that he truly developed his  passion for traveling with extended trips throughout Europe, the Middle East and North Africa. During a stint with ad agencies in New York, he traveled extensively to test market new products. He has written for a variety of travel and entertainment publications including *Performing Arts Magazine.* In the early 1990s he took his travel experience to radio with a travel show on KTMS-Santa Barbara. He left KTZN in the spring of 1997.

FOX, Rosalie: **KZLA/KLAC**, 1988-94; **KFI**, 1996. Rosalie got her radio career started in Bakersfield. At KLAC she began as a reporter and continued as morning drive news anchor until the station changed format in 1993 and the station picked up a syndicated service. She went to KNBC/Channel 4 as a news writer and video editor.

FOX, Sonny: **KHJ**, 1972-73. Sonny came to Southern California from KCBQ-San Diego. While at KHJ, the Grand Rapids native wrote a weekly column for the *Bob Hamilton Report*. When he left "Boss Radio," he and Lee Abrams started the Superstar Radio Network. He programmed WRNO-New Orleans and WYSP-Philadelphia during the remainder of the 1970s. Sonny was on the fast track. In 1973 he was part of the creation of "The Last Concert in Fantasy Park" that, according to Sonny, "was later borrowed by the McLendon family." By the end of the 1970s, Sonny burned out, and in 1980 he went to Miami where he has been for the past 14 years. He said in a 1995 interview from his home in Miami, "I had done it all. The drugs, the mentions in the trades, the limelight and I needed a rest." Sonny started doing mornings at WSAG-Miami and then mornings at WHYI ("Y-100")-Miami in 1989 and was suddenly let go. He filed a $300,000 lawsuit against Metroplex Communications claiming his departure was "wrongful, willful, malicious and...for the sole purpose of having a less expensive replacement." Sonny's suit was successfully settled out of court. He's currently working his magic at WMXJ-Miami, "staying out of the limelight" and enjoying a new life. He proudly put his young daughter on the phone and said, "She's truly the magic in my life today. I'm a lucky guy to have survived."

FOXX, Holly: **KSCA**, 1996. Born Terri Alexander in Los Angeles on February 25, 1965, she grew up in Tulsa. Holly worked swing at KSCA.

FOXX, Lisa: **KYSR**, 1997. "I studied radio and tv at Ohlone Junior College in Northern California. I immediately fell in love with radio because unlike tv, you're in a position to really 'let go' and show your true personality." Lisa was born and raised in Fremont and started as an intern at KWSS-San Jose. In the late 1980s she was a research assistant for the syndicated "Countdown USA with Dave Sholin." Before arriving in the Southland, Lisa worked for KDON-Salinas, KHQT-San Jose and KMEL-San Francisco. "I love Southern California - the market, the people, the celebs - it's the most exciting place for radio on the planet!"

FRAIL, Matthew (Doc): **KRLA**, 1974-76. Matthew had two strange runs on KRLA: one as Lee Simms and another as "Doc" Frail on mornings. *LA Times* reporter James Brown reviewed 1974's high and low spots on the radio: "KRLA's unusual morning man may seem a bit off-the-map to some of you, and possibly offensive to a few others - but, it is probably because he is so unlike anyone else in town. Frail rambles incessantly, often to no conclusions. We hear much of his life as a veterinarian in the Simi Valley, his wife named Twilight and of the demons that trouble him." Brown concluded, "In any form, Matthew 'Doc' Frail is an original and we could use a few more of them." Famous Amos of cookie fame became a semi-regular with Matthew and participated in the ramblings. When KRLA automated in early 1976 and "Doc" Frail was let go, James Brown wrote again, "He was unpredictable. And when one considers today's AM dial, overpopulated with voices in gray flannel suits, unpredictability was perhaps Matthew Frail's greatest attribute."

FRANCIS, Rob: **KOCM/KSRF**, 1991-92. Rob arrived in the Southland from KITS-San Francisco. He was part of the launch of the "techno-Rock" format on May 24, 1991. When "MARS/fm" folded, Rob returned to the Bay Area.

FRANK, Joe: **KCRW**, 1982-88. The *LA Times* called Joe "the most innovative radio dramatist in Los Angeles." His radio plays, "Work in Progress," aired weekly on KCRW. Joe was born in 1939 in Strasbourg, France, to a Viennese mother and Polish father who were in flight from the Nazis. He was raised in New York, where he spent much of his childhood recovering from leg operations to correct clubfeet. He attended the prestigious Iowa Writers Workshop and wound up employed by a private school in Manhattan. His radio career started in 1977 hosting a comedy show on WBAI-New York. After a brief stint in 1982, Joe did a number of shows for NPR and joined the Southland college station on KCRW in 1985. His show was broadcast on the NPR network.

> *"Her brain seemed to work something like a pinball machine. What passed for her attention span was really more akin to a speeding silver ball, unleashing a different idea every time it bounced off a new synapse bumper."*
> *-from "Radio Waves" about Raechel Donahue*

FRANKEL, George: **KFWB**, 1995. George was a news writer and in-house reporter for all-News KFWB.

FRANKLIN, Brenda: **KIKF**, 1992-93; **KACD**, 1993; **KEZY**, 1993-97. Brenda works evenings on KEZY.

FRANKLIN, Gary: **KFWB**; **KABC**, 1988. The German-born news reporter first gained fame in Southern California radio as a reporter for all-News KFWB reporting in "Car 98." For 40 years he has been in the business of electronic journalism as a network news writer/producer, news director, reporter and critic. "I was never happier than when I worked in radio. You are all on your own. It's between you and the product." Gary's passion in life is photography. He was a motion picture cameraman while in the Army in Korea and over the years his black and white photo work has been frequently displayed at various one-man shows throughout the Southland. From 1972 to 1980 he was the entertainment reporter for KABC/Channel 7 and popularized a film rating "on a scale of one to ten, ten being best." How did his ratings come about? "It started out as a joke when I was filling in for the entertainment report. I was kind of arrogant but the general manager liked it and it has since become part of the entertainment landscape." In 1980 he joined Channel 2 and five years later rejoined KABC broadcasting entertainment on the tv evening news and on radio's "Ken and Bob Company." In early 1991 Gary returned to Germany to work for the country's top-rated commercial web RTL owned by Bertelsmann AG. Within a year he returned to the Southland and dispensed entertainment news for KCOP/Channel 13 until 1995. Gary started out at WTAR-Norfolk and then went to John Hopkins University on a fellowship to study network news theory. A series of radio and tv assignments followed including WJZ-Baltimore, WGBH-Boston, KYW-Philadelphia, WIND-Chicago and KYW-Cleveland. In New York Gary worked for ABC as a radio writer during the day and tv writer in the evening. He produced the Jules Bergman space reports and the evening news with Peter Jennings. "I got out of entertainment because the product got so bad. I blame tv and the film industry for the plight of young people." He is writing an autobiographical novel complete with his own photo illustrations titled *Son of Frankenstein*. "My mother's maiden name was Frankenstein."

FRANKLIN, Peter: **KYMS**, 1969; **KPPC**, 1970-73, pd

FRANKLIN, Robert: **KFOX**, 1972, gm. Bob was from Huntington, West Virginia, and worked at WAKY-Louisville before arriving in the Southland. He retired to Fresno and passed away in the fall of 1996.

FRANKLIN, Tom: **KFAC**, 1970-87, nd. Tom is a classical music veteran announcer. He also was the news and financial reporter for KFAC.

FREBERG, Stan: In the '50s and '60s Stan helped define American humor with a radio series, clever ad campaigns and records such as *St. George and the Dragonettes*, *John and Marsha* and *Green Christmas*. He writes 90-second commentaries for stations across the country and is heard on Armed Forces Radio. Some have called the Beverly Hills resident the Andy Rooney of radio. Stan was the first to use satire to question the way we do things in our everyday life. Thirty years after his first volume, in 1996 Stan released *The United States of America Vol. 2* on Rhino Records. Stan was born in 1927 and grew up in South Pasadena.

FREDERICK, Miranda: **KIQQ**, 1980-81. Miranda worked at "K-100" as an intern and front desk receptionist. The gm put Miranda on weekends.

FREDERICKS, Paul: **KMPC**, 1979-81, nd. Born

Frederick Chenevey, Paul worked at KFRC-San Francisco and WOW-Omaha before joining KMPC. When he left L.A. he joined the RKO Radio Network (later Unistar Radio Network) in New York for a decade. In 1990 he became a news anchor at WCBS-New York. "After 11 years of commuting into mid-town Manhattan, we sold our house and returned to where I grew up in Ohio." He's now working at WZKL-Canton. "I'm trying to invent a better morning show, after playing second banana to some of the best. Pretty soon I'll want to try this out in a 'Big Town.'" His brother is Jim Chenevey.

FREDERICKS, Steve: **KPOL**; **KIIS**, 1970-71; **KDAY**, 1971-76, nd; **KRTH**, 1976-77, nd. Steve worked the news beat while in Southern California radio. He didn't pursue radio initially; he was a photographer for ten years. His radio start came as an announcer at a Classical music station in Florida. After two years in the Army, Steve worked on the West Coast and by the mid-1960s was in Nashville radio. He came to the Southland in 1968 with no job, and it took him two years to land a news job at KIIS.

FREE, Laurie: **KNAC**, 1989-94; **KIIS**, 1994-95. Laurie was a part-timer on KIIS and hosted "Klub KIIS" with dj Jimmy Kim. In the summer of 1995, Laurie joined KSJO-San Jose as md/middays. Born in Baltimore and raised in Denver, Laurie went to Colorado State University and worked at KBPI-Denver from 1984 to 1988. As a kid, Laurie recalled, "I was a big radio fan and loved the music."

FREE, Scott: **KEZY**, 1992-97. Born in Long Beach on December 19, 1956, Scott returned to the Southland to work afternoon drive at KEZY from K101-San Francisco. He was appointed music director in 1994. "I got the job because I had the key to the music office and no one else did." He began his broadcasting career at age 12 with a "120-watt blowtorch on CB ch.21, which went dark when my parents caught on." When not on the air Scott works as a crime scene investigator for a police agency in Orange County.

FREEBAIRN-SMITH, Ian: **KFAC**, 1987-89; **KKGO**, 1992-97. Ian is a Grammy winning composer/arranger. He won a Grammy for arranging *Evergreen* for Barbra Streisand.

FREED, Alan: **KDAY**, 1960-61; **KNOB**, 1964-65. Born in Ohio on January 20, 1922, he is credited with coining the term "rock 'n' roll." Alan grew up in Salem, Ohio where his father was a clothing store clerk and a composer and band leader specializing in swing music. During the two years he spent at Ohio State University, Alan played the trombone and led the Sultans of Swing, a band named after the one in Harlem. After two years in the Army he started his radio career in New Castle, Pennsylvania at a station that featured classical music. Alan was a musician and started working at WINS-New York in the summer of 1954. On WINS he called himself "King of the Moon Doggers" and stayed there until 1958. He also worked at WABC and WNEW/TV in New York. His abuses and notoriety were ultimately his downfall in the wake of a national payola scandal. Alan took the brunt of punishment for hundreds of gift - and money-accepting djs. He was charged with having taken bribes totaling $30,650 from six record companies for playing and plugging their releases on his radio program. In 1959 Alan pleaded guilty to part of the charge and received a six-month sentence, which was suspended, and a $300 fine. At the height of his career he made as much as $200,000 a year, according to *Time Magazine*. His popularity over the air was matched on stage during school holidays, when he took over large New York's Paramount Theater and presented rock 'n roll performers to mobs of youngsters. A critic once said that attending an Alan Freed stage show was "like having an aisle seat for the San Francisco earthquake. When he entered the stage in his checkered sport jacket, he was accorded the same shrieking welcome as the performers." In the wake of the payola probe, Alan arrived at KDAY on May 16, 1960, from WABC-New York. His contract, which became public, was for exclusive radio services and guaranteed him $25,000 per year. A clause in his contract was about the selection of disks. On his hiring, KDAY gm Irving Phillips said, "We feel he's a dynamic radio personality and any problems he may have had are a thing of the past. We did not do this to flaunt the Commission. Freed has full knowledge of the way we operate and will abide by our restrictions." Eventually he was let go from KDAY for plugging local concerts which was in conflict with station policy. He had roles in several motion pictures with such titles as *Don't Knock the Rock* and composed two extremely successful songs, *Sincerely* and *Maybeline*. Alan died January 20, 1965, of uremia at the age of 43. Alan was elected to the Emerson Radio Hall of Fame in 1988. His last on-air job was at KNOB.

FREEMAN, Dave: **KNNS**, 1995-96

FREEMAN, J.D.: **KNOB**, 1987; **KZLA/KLAC**, 1993-96, vp/gm. J.D. arrived in the Southland in 1993 from KMLE-Phoenix. He spent 18 years in Phoenix radio. In 1995 J.D. was elected chairman of the board of the Southern California Broadcasters Association. In 1993 when KLAC switched from country to syndicated adult format, J.D. told Gary Lycan in the *OC Register*: "We thought we could be very successful with a middle-of-the-road music format featuring such artists as Streisand, Sinatra and Bennett." J.D. left KZLA/KLAC in the spring of 1996 and joined KDMX-Dallas.

FREEMAN, Jim: **KHTZ/KLSX/KRLA**, 1979-93, gm. The Los Angeles native spent 13 years with KHTZ, KLSX and KRLA working up the sales ladder to become general manager. Jim was president of the student body at Loyola University and knew from an early age that he wanted to be in radio. "After college I spent two years in the Peace Corps where I met my Honduran wife." On his return from Honduras, Jim joined the sales staff at KBKB-San Diego (later became KGB/FM). He joined the Eastman Radio and worked at the rep firm until 1975. Before joining KHTZ Jim was national sales manager of KMEX/Channel 34, owned his own tv production company and worked at Cristal Radio. Since leaving KRLA he worked with Rich White promotion company and is about to embark on a major non-media project.

FREEMAN, Paul: **KEZY**, 1970-76; **KHJ**, 1976; **KIIS**, 1976-89; **KODJ/KCBS**, 1989-92; **KZLA/KLAC**, 1992-93; **KYSR**, 1993-96; **KBIG**, 1996-97. Born and raised in Spokane, the longtime survivor in Los Angeles radio started early. By the time he was 15 years old, Paul had built a small radio station in the basement of his parents' home. He arrived in the Southland from KNAK-Salt Lake City. Paul started at KIIS during the disco period and moved to middays for most of the 1980s before leaving in 1989. At the CBS Oldies stations, KODJ/KCBS, Paul

hosted the "all-request lunch hour." In 1992, Paul took over the morning show at KZLA. He reminisced for this Booktory, "The highlight of my two-and-a-half decades in Southern California radio? It was being part of a team that achieved a 10 share (12+) in the mid-'80s at KIIS/FM. I think that was the last time any station has had double digits in L.A." He left KYSR in the spring of 1996. He now reports the news on morning drive at KBIG with Sylvia Aimerito.

FREEZE, Sam: **KROQ**, 1979-85; **KNAC**, 1986-94; **KACD**, 1995. Sam started at KROQ as an intern He was known affectionately as "The Freeze Disease." In 1994 he went to KEDG-Las Vegas and in the spring of 1995 took over middays. By the summer of 1995, he had left KEDG and joined the sales staff at KACD for a few months.

FRENCH, Don: **KFWB**, 1961-65, pd. Don was working at KTSA-San Antonio in the late 1950s. In 1961 he left programming chores at KDWB-Minneapolis for sister Crowell-Collier station KFWB, working the nine-to-noon shift during the infamous strike that affected newsmen and the personalities. Don became the pd in 1964. Bobby Dale described Don as "the nicest guy." When he left Southern California, Don went to KJOY-Stockton, KNEW-San Francisco and to program WGR-Buffalo. In 1971 he was the manager of the San Antonio Columbia School of Broadcasting. By 1975, Don was in Anchorage radio. He died on November 28, 1982, in Minneapolis, after a prolonged illness. During his career he worked for Gordon McLendon, Crowell-Collier, WNBC-New York, WDAF-Kansas City and WTAE-Pittsburgh.

FRICKE, Jonathan: **KFOX**, 1973, pd

FRIEDMAN, Andy: **KFI**, 1989-95. Andy was the assistant nd at KFI and covered the O.J. Simpson trial for the Talk station. He left in the summer of 1995 for KFBK-Sacramento. He started his radio career at KALF-Red Bluff, moving next to KUIC-Vacaville. In 1996 he went to KTAR-Phoenix as nd.

FRIEDMAN, Sonya: **KABC**, 1986-87. A graduate of Wayne State University in Detroit, Sonya wrote a column for *Ladies Home Journal* and hosted *Sonya* on the USA cable network before joining KABC. She replaced Dr. Toni Grant as one of KABC's psychologists in January 1986.

FRIGHT, Mike: **KOCM/KSRF**, 1992; **KWIZ**, 1993. Born Mike Ivenk, he hosted "Renegade Radio" on KWIZ featuring rave, techno and alternative music.

FRITZ, John: **KGBS**; **KBIG**; **KRKD**

FRITZINGER, George: **KFAC**. George is the previous owner and general manager of KFAC and owned Group III, a communications investment company. In 1988 George and Dwight Case launched all-Asian KZAN (1300AM).

FROMSON, Murray: **KABC**, 1986. Murray had a brief stay at KABC while regular commentator Bruce Herschensohn was running unsuccessfully for the U.S. Senate. He is a veteran broadcast journalist who has covered the Vietnam War and the Far East for NBC News and CBS News. In 1978 Murray was deputy campaign manager for Governor Jerry Brown. In the mid-1980s he was a full-time journalism professor at USC.

FROST, John: **KROQ**, 1987-97. Born August 11, John grew up in Seattle and came from Anchorage to work at "the Roq" in the spring of 1987. He is responsible for the multi-award-winning jingles, promos and i.d.'s that image the station. John wrote, voiced and produced a series called "The New Detective," that ran in the Kevin & Bean morning show for three years. He is the recipient of numerous national creative radio awards from the Southern California Broadcasters and Promax. In a 1995 *R&R* feature story, he said, "You need to stand out and sound like nobody else on the radio. Kids' BS detectors these days are on overdrive. You can't do something that will come off as contrived or lame, unless you're making fun of yourself."

FRY, Donald: **KRLA**, 1979, gm

FUHR, Paul: **KNAC**, 1981

FULLER, Shelly: **KCBS**, 1997

FULLER, Sid: **KFI**, 1964

FULTON, Liz: **KIIS**, 1979-84 and 1987-90; **KOST/KFI**, 1990. Born in 1953, Liz was the morning sidekick to Rick Dees. In 1979 she started her first journey doing news. Liz became a part of the morning team when Dees arrived and was made nd in 1981. She left in 1984 to work for a small station in Northern California. Liz had her first child there. She returned to the highly rated morning drive show in 1987. In 1990, represented by attorney Gloria Allred, she filed a sex discrimination suit, seeking judgment on specified damages and charged Rick Dees and Gannett with breach of contract and invasion of privacy. She contended that she was often the object of Dees' on-air sexual jokes while employed at the station. Liz went on to say that she and Rick hardly spoke to each other unless they were on the air. She said she didn't complain to Dees or station management about the sexual jokes because she feared she would be fired. Rick referred to her as Liz "Rug Burns" Fulton.

FURILLO, Bud: **KABC**, 1973-75; **KIIS**, 1975-79; **KABC**, 1979-87; **KFOX**, 1988-90. Born in 1926, the ex-newspaperman hosted "SportsTalk" with Bud Tucker on KABC where he was described as "cheerfully bombastic." For 40 years "The Steamer" covered sports in Southern California and wrote a column ("The Steam Room") for the old *Herald-Express* and *Herald-Examiner*, where he was sports editor between 1964 and 1974. In the mid-1980s he had a series of hospitalizations for abdominal surgery. In 1992 Bud was working at KSAC-Sacramento. He is now hosting a sports talk show at KPLM-Palm Springs.

KFWB - 980AM

First signed on: March 25, 1925

KRLA Line-ups

6 a.m. - 9 a.m.	Dave Hull
9 a.m. - Noon	Casey Kasem
Noon - 3 p.m.	Johnny Hayes
3 p.m. - 6 p.m.	Reb Foster
6 p.m. - 9 p.m.	Bob Dayton
9 p.m. - Mid	Jim Wood
Mid - 6 a.m.	Bill Slater

-September 1967

6 a.m. - 9 a.m.	Perry Allen
9 a.m. - Noon	Roy Elwell
Noon - 3 p.m.	Bob Cole
3 p.m. - 6 p.m.	Jimmy O'Neill
6 p.m. - 9 p.m.	Sam Riddle
9 p.m. - Mid	Frosty Harris
Mid - 6 a.m.	Frank Pollack

-early 1960

6 a.m. - 9 a.m.	Bob Hudson
9 a.m. - Noon	Charlie O'Donnell
Noon - 3 p.m.	Casey Kasem
3 p.m. - 6 p.m.	Dave Hull
6 p.m. - 9 p.m.	Bob Eubanks
9 p.m. - Mid	Dick Biondi
Mid - 6 a.m.	Bobby Dale

-February 1965

G

G, Captain: **KKBT**, 1993-94. Born Greg Beasley in 1960 in Chicago, he was the youngest of 13 children. While working in St. Louis in the early 1990s, Greg produced a syndicated show called "Urban Mix" that ironically was carried on the station he would end up working for, KKBT. The midday jock died July 1, 1994, at the age of 33. He did his regular show on June 30 but on July 1 was rushed to Daniel Freeman Hospital in Inglewood, where he died shortly after his arrival.

G, Julio: **KDAY**; **KKBT**, 1995-97. Following the death of rapper Easy-E, Julio started co-hosting the weekend show, "The Mixmaster Show." Julio moved into the evening slot in early 1996.

G, Johnny: **KFWB**, 1965. Johnny Gilbert left Los Angeles in 1965 for KEWB-San Francisco. In 1967 he was working at KCBQ-San Diego.

GABLE, Bob: **KHJ**, 1973. Bob worked at KHJ in the spring of 1973; he was there for less than 60 days. His stints included CKLW-Detroit and WHBQ-Memphis. In 1984, Bob went from WLW-Cincinnati to WMTE-High Point, North Carolina. He programmed Toronto powerhouse CFTR in the 1980s and is currently working at WOCL-Orlando.

GAGE, Bob: **KBIG**, 1959-60

GAIVAR, Carlos: **KNX**, 1995-97. Carlos is an anchor on "KNXNewsradio."

GALINDO, Enrique: **KALI**, 1990-93. Enrique worked middays at Spanish KALI.

GALLAGHER, Fred: **KFWB**, 1971-80; **KNX**, 1980-97. Fred hosts "Sports Reports" on "KNXNewsradio." The three-decade sports broadcasting veteran was born in Syracuse. He graduated from Syracuse University in 1959 with a major in radio and tv. Fred was the sports director of his college station. His career started in 1951 at KWTC-Barstow as a dj and salesman. In 1964 he joined KIDD-Monterey as sports director. In 1967 he was an announcer with ABC Networks' "Tom Harmon Sports Show." Fred joined KFWB in 1971 and in addition to sports reporting he was the football play-by-play announcer for University of Nevada football. He joined KNX in March 1980.

GALLAGHER, Ken: **KJOI**, 1973-74; **KFI**, 1986-97. Ken was part of the "TNT" morning news magazine format on KFI. He broadcasts news on KFI.

GALLARDO, Fred: **KLOS**, 1977; **KLSX**, 1987-88. Fred is a third generation native of Los Angeles.

GALLEGOS, Julian: **KKHJ**

GAMBOA, Hipolito: **KTNQ**, 1997. Hipolito is part of the afternoon drive sports show, "Hablando de Deportes." He co-hosts the show with Rolando Gonzalez. They present news commentaries, interviews and listener interaction at the Spanish Talk station. Their stringers throughout Latin America present the latest news on soccer and other sports.

GAMACHE, Tom: **KPPC**, 1969; **KMET**, 1969-71. Tom was at the vortex of "underground radio." He was born and raised in Manchester, New Hampshire. Tom became good friends with Peter Wolf (later of the J. Geils Band) while attending Boston University's School of Communication. Tom was quoted in an *R&R* special edition on "The AOR Story" of Peter's influence. "Peter was responsible for getting me to sit down in front of the microphone for the first time. He and I used to sit around listening to our collections of Little Walter records." Peter told Tom about the MIT 30-watt FM off-campus radio station that reached practically every student in the city. Armed with a box of his own records, Tom set out "to make as much of a travesty of commercial radio as possible." He spent 2 years at MIT radio and two more years across town at Boston University's 50,0000 watter, WBUR. A few more months at WBCN-Boston and then

sold everything, bought his first new truck ever and headed West looking for any and all other "progressive" stations. He got to L.A. and took a late evening shift at KPPC and soon thereafter was one of the first three "live" jocks on KMET. "I believe that what we were doing on the radio in the mid to late sixties was exactly the opposite of what financially successful 'rock stations' (like KMET) would later become. Today the written history of the format picks up in the early seventies and sings the praises of profit rather than the early history of the creation of a culture." After radio Tom became involved with record production, management and radio syndication. During the past ten years he has become a master of outdoor photography working with many national parks, magazines and newspapers doing both landscape and wildlife work. From Arnold Passman's book, *D.J.'s*: "Tom is generally recognized as the first of the underground rock jocks." *R&R* concluded: "Tom was a radio revolutionary in the truest sense."

GANDELL, Al: **KTYM**. "The Bearded One" was part of the Jazz programming at KTYM.

KBIG increases power from 110,000 to 134,000 watts and adds stereo.   -January 1, 1967

GARABO, John: **KZLA**, 1993-95. In the summer of 1993, Country-formatted KZLA teamed John, who was known as "Johnny Jumpster" at KFRG-San Bernardino, with

John Murphy for morning drive. The pairing as a radio team was a first for both. John was born and raised in New York City and his first job was at NBC in Rockefeller Plaza. In the summer of 1995, John left KZLA and segued to WWYZ-Hartford for morning drive. "Having a great time, but I truly miss L.A.!"

GARCIA, Dominick: **KRLA**, 1986-97. Dominick grew up and went to school in Denver where he got his early broadcasting experience working as an assistant tv director and part-time booth announcer as well as doing weekends on radio. "I was always playing with tape recorders and listening to the radio. Growing up, one of my favorite radio stations was the 'Mighty 95,' KIMN. When the boys in the neighborhood were saving up for a new football, I was saving up for another new album." In

1974 and through the disco era, he jocked on KDKO-Denver. The station was cited as station of the year by *Billboard*. Later in the 1970s, Dominick worked in radio and acted in community theater in Santa Fe. He spent half of the 1980s back in Denver radio working on KBRQ, KDKO, KLSC and Magic Johnson's station, KRZN. He moved to Southern California with the sole purpose of getting a radio gig but ended up working as part of the crew for Hollywood Center Studios. Eventually Dominick joined KRLA in a behind-the-scenes capacity. From the all-night shift he spent three years doing middays. He now works weekends, public appearances and production for KRLA.

GARCIA, Jesus: **KLAX**, 1996. Jesus is part of the morning drive team on Spanish KLAX.

GARCIA, Jose: **KWIZ**, 1997

GARDNER, Bill: **KPPC**, 1988-97. The quintessential host of Southern California's long-standing doo-wop music show, Bill hosts "r&b Time Capsule" and "Rhapsody in Black" every Friday night. The tall historian is frequently seen supporting the Southern California Doo-Wop Society. By day, Bill is a supervisor of social workers who aid victims of child abuse in Los Angeles County.

GARDNER, Jay: **KRTH**, 1986-87. Jay moved to Los Angeles when he was 2. In college he studied theater arts. By 1973 he was working as a jock. Jay was in Idaho and Virginia before joining KRTH in morning drive. He has been doing voiceover work and is the national voice of CBS/TV.

GARDNER, Randy: **KGBS**, 1973-75; **KFOX**, 1975-76; **KGGI**, 1981-84; **KMGG**, 1984; **KOST**, 1984-85; **KRTH**, 1985-89. Born in L.A. in 1958, Randy got hooked on radio when he won the Beatles *White Album* from "Humble Harve" on KHJ. "It was a school night and past my bedtime, so I used the phone under the covers with a flashlight. At age ten, hearing my name over the radio was a magical thing." While being a "go-fer" for the jocks at KGBS in 1973, he landed a weekend job carting up phoned-in dog race results. After working in the mail room, traffic and production departments, the late KGBS pd Ron Martin gave the precocious 16-year-old his dj debut on a Sunday night when the 50k daytimer would sign back on. As Randy Moss, he made stops at KFOX and KGOE. He moved to Las Vegas in 1978, where he was on KDWN, KORK and KENO as Steve O'Neil. Returning to Southern California in 1981, he was md, then pd at KGGI. By 1988 he settled on the name Randy O'Neil and was doing middays at KRTH AM930. "It was a full circle thing for me, stepping into the very studio where Humble Harve announced my name 20 years earlier." That same year Randy's voice was selected to be a permanent part of the STAR TOURS attraction at Disneyland. On New Years Eve 1990, Randy moved his family to Portland where he is doing middays on KXL/FM and performs character voices on nationally released CD-ROM projects. "It was fun being a small fish in the vast L.A. radio waters, but I discovered that a smaller pond is much more to my liking."

GARLAND, Les: **KIQQ**, 1974-75, pd. Les was one of the founders of MTV. In 1980, he was appointed gm of West Coast operations for Atlantic Records. He joined The Box (Music Television YOU Control) in 1990 as executive vp and left in the summer of 1996. He also programmed KFRC-San Francisco and CKLW-Detroit.

**KIIS/AM becomes Gospel
KPRZ ("Praise of Los Angeles")**
-June 1980

GARNER, Anita: **KBIG**, 1984-88. "I was at KBIG during their switch from Beautiful Music to personality AC. They spent big bucks on promotions and a generally heightened profile. It was an exciting time working afternoon drive with a gold-plated lineup of on-air people." Anita came to KBIG from Bonneville's sister station, KOIT-San Francisco, where she wrote and recorded commentary called "First Impressions" and "The Way We Live." When KBIG asked her to move South, she was the spokesperson for Lucky Markets in the

northern region, as well as several other regular accounts. "For the first year at KBIG, I flew to San Francisco in the morning several times a week to fulfill voiceover commitments, return just in time to go on the air in the afternoon." While at KBIG, Anita co-hosted MCA/Universal's syndicated show, "The Great Starship," with Byron Paul. After leaving the station, she produced the syndicated show "Something Special." Her 90-second feature "The Way We Live" ran on KBLA until that station changed formats, and is still in production today, available to stations across the nation. Anita grew up on the radio. Her parents were gospel performers in the deep south, with their own radio show. Anita was the first woman on the air at KHSL-Chico. "At first the farmers objected to getting their fruit frost reports from a woman - but eventually we grew quite fond of each other." She spent time on tv news and features, then became KROY-Sacramento's "Lovely Nita." Anita still records station promos and enjoys filling in for Bernie Alan on KCET/TV. "I'm spending most of my time completing a book about my family's days on the gospel circuit."

GARNER, Blair: SEE Blair Michaels

GARR, Bill: Bill has been broadcasting race results for Southern California radio stations for close to 40 years. Born and reared in San Francisco, he was the manager of the UC Davis radio station and after graduation he became a newscaster in San Francisco. During the 1950s, Bill was a dj in Los Angeles until he began covering the thoroughbred racing circuit in 1959. "Bill has a gift for making a race come alive," explained a colleague, "so much so that your heart pounds as the field nears the finish line. Only the smell of the stables is missing when he's on."

GARRETT, Keli: **KORG**, 1978-80; **KUTE**, 1980-87; **KXEZ**, 1990-93; **KACE**, 1990-93. Much of Keli Garrett's career has been associated with Lawrence Tanter. "In 1985 I was hired by Lawrence because he could 'hear my smile' when I talked." Her name changed with the stations. At KXEZ she was Samantha James and Keli Mitchell at KACE. Born on Christmas day, at age 13 Keli delivered a birthday card to her favorite dj, Bobby Mitchell at KYA-San Francisco. "He invited me to sit in with him on-air and I knew from that moment what I wanted to do when I grew up." In 1977 she graduated from the first broadcast workshop at KEZY and started at KCIN-Victorville. In 1980 Keli worked the Dance format at KUTE. For a year she was the full-time voice for Viviane Woodard Cosmetics. She returned to KUTE with "the Quiet Storm," format. In 1993 she joined Shadow Traffic and later in the year Metro Traffic in San Diego. Before the year was out Lawrence asked her to do afternoons, assistant pd and md at KQBR-

Sacramento. In late 1995 she moved crosstown to KSSJ where she is md for the smooth jazz station and middays.

GARRETT, Pat: **KIQQ**, 1974-75; **KHJ**, 1979-80; **KWST**, 1980-81; **KMGG**, 1981-83; **KEZY**, 1984-85, pd; **KKHR**, 1985; **KODJ**, 1991. Born Mark Beauchamp and also known as Mark Thomas during a couple of stops on Los Angeles radio, Pat got his start in Palmdale radio. At KHJ he was known as "The Unknown Disc Jockey." When he left KIQQ, he went to his first pd job at KAFY-Bakersfield. He left the Southland to program an Oldies station in Salinas. He currently programs an Oldies station in Bakersfield.

GARROWAY, Dave: **KFI**, 1970-71. Dave was part of a historic day in tv. In early 1952 NBC opened a broadcast with a shot of Dave looking outside through the "Window on the World" in New York City. The *Today* show was the first that featured his signature sign-off with hand raised, uttering one word, "Peace." He hosted the show from 1952 to 1961. He was acclaimed for his calm, understated manner. His thick-rimmed glasses gave a whole generation of imitators that owlish look. His broadcast career began shortly after he got his college degree from Washington University in St. Louis where he majored in abnormal psychology. He was visiting New York City in 1937, as he told it, when "some gal got me drunk and I woke up next morning as an NBC page." He spent many years at WMAQ-Chicago. After his wife died a tragic death by jumping from a building in 1961, he felt compelled to quit the *Today* show. He went on to do local radio and tv shows in Boston and then to KFI. Dave committed suicide on July 21, 1982, in Swarthmore, Pennsylvania. He was 69.

GARVER, Gary: **KLSX**, 1993-94. Gary's role at the "classic rock" station was primarily production work with some on-air. He also produced the "Howard Stern Show" feed to the station.

GARZA, Joaquin: **KLVE**, 1989; **KSKQ**, 1992, pd; **KBUE**; **KKHJ**, 1996. Joaquin joined KKHJ in early 1996 from a similar position at Spanish KBUE and left during the summer. He hosted "El Manicom de la Manana."

GASKINS, Bob: **KTWV**, 1988

GASKINS, Yolanda: **KABC**, 1991-94; **KMPC/KTZN**, 1994-97. Yolanda hosts a talk show on "the Zone." She left the station when it was KMPC in late 1996 and rejoined the Talk facility in early 1997. Yolanda is a graduate of Georgetown Law School. In a profile in the *LA Times*, Yolanda related how she got interested in broadcasting. It was when she was 7, on the back porch of her grandmother's house in Washington, where she grew up, and saw a woman on tv. "I said I would like to be on television, and my mother said, 'You can't do that. You are black. White people look at white people.' That stayed in my mind." She graduated from Lincoln University in Pennsylvania and then went to law school. Yolanda hosted a magazine show for the Fox station in Washington and then to the NBC affiliate in Miami and Black Entertainment Television.

GASSMAN, John and Larry: **KPCC**, 1980-97. The identical twin brothers, born blind in 1955, host an early evening show of classic radio dramas called "Same Time, Same Station" on KPCC. John and Larry were raised in Whittier and graduated with communications degrees from Cal Poly Pomona. They provided unique coverage of the annual Pasadena Rose Parade to listeners of KPCC. They have over 20,000 old radio shows in their collection and "a ton of interviews." They have a company that acts as a clearing house for radio/tv audio clips and source material for old radio shows.

GATES, Daryl: **KFI**, 1992-94. Born in 1926, the former L.A. police chief was brought in to KFI on September 29, 1992, as a replacement for the departing Tom Leykis. He left office under the shadow of the Rodney G. King beating by LAPD officers. Within two months he was cut back from three hours a day to one in order to bring in a new talk-show team, Ken Champiou and John Kobylt. In an *LA Times* interview, KFI pd David Hall denied that the move was influenced by listener complaints that Gates had a monotonous on-air style. Hall said: "The criticism will always be there. Some think he's dull and some don't."

GATO, El: **KNAC**, 1986; **KWIZ**, 1988-95. The Killer Kat was there for the beginning of the Rock format at Long Beach's KNAC and worked morning drive on the Orange County outlet, KWIZ.

GEE, Vic: SEE Jim Carson

GEHRINGER, Jeff: **KKGO**, 1986-89, pd; **KACD**, pd. While Jeff was pd of Jazz KKGO, he called the format "Full Spectrum."

GELLER, Andy: **KODJ**, 1989; **KLOS**. Andy did afternoon drive during the launch of the new "Oldies 93" format on the CBS station in March 1989.

GENTRI, John: **KHJ**, 1965. John was there just before "Boss Radio" and left before the "Boss Jocks" arrived.

GEORG, Frank: **KNX**, 1968; **KFWB**, 1968-70. Frank was the original executive editor at KFWB. Don Herbert remembered: "Frank set the tone for the launch of KFWB as all-News. He was a genius. Frank towered over his staff at 6 foot 12 inches tall. He taught us what to feel about the product. Frank had come to the Southland from WCBS-New York. In 1970 he retired to Sedona and built a school where he taught history." In 1984 he returned to KFWB to assist in the station's coverage of the Summer Olympics. In the mid-1980s his feet had to be amputated due to diabetes and he died a few years later.

GEORGE, Wally: **KABC**, 1987; **KLAC**, 1987-90. The right-wing, flag-waving conservative hosted *Hot Seat* on the Orange County tv station for many years. He was an aide to former Los Angeles mayor, Sam Yorty. Wally hosted a talk show Monday nights on KABC. In the summer of 1996 he underwent surgery to remove a potentially fatal blood clot that had been pressing against his brain.

GEORGI, Bill: **KJLH**, 1991

GERMAIN, Ann: **KFI**, 1992-93. Ann was a news anchor at KFI.

GERONIMO, Don: **KIIS**, 1981-82; **KFI**, 1982. Starting his radio career at age 14, Don arrived in Southern California in September 1981, from WNDE-Indianapolis. He worked the evening shift and was replaced by Laurie Allen a year later. In 1982, he went to WLS AM&FM-Chicago as weekend and swing shifter. Don suffered a mild heart attack in 1984. In 1990 he was teamed with WAVA-Washington, DC production director Mike O'Meara for a "morning zoo show." One of their stunts resulted in a $50 million lawsuit. The suit was filed by the WWMX promotions manager who claimed invasion of privacy after the duo called her a lesbian during a live broadcast. The case was settled, and terms were sealed, according to trade reports. By 1993, Don was working for Unistar. A year later he and Mike O'Meara had a very successful syndicated morning show on WW1 based at WJFK-Washington, DC where they continue.

GEVINSON, Anita: **KLOS**, 1980-81; **KMPC/KEDG**, 1988-90; **KSCA**, 1993-96; **KMPC**, 1993-96; **KLSX**, 1997. Born March 25, Anita grew up in Levittown, Pennsylvania, and after graduating from Neshaminy High and Bucks County Community College, she went to Mexico for a couple of years. She started her radio career in 1977 at WCAU-Philadelphia's Disco format. In 1978 she worked at WMMR-Philadelphia and in 1979 went to WCOZ-Boston. After KLOS Anita returned to WMMR and moved across town to WYSP in 1983. In the mid-1980s, Anita was one of the most popular personalities at WCAU/AM with a talk show called "Ask Anita." She has used simply the name *Anita* for many of her jock stops. In 1994 Anita went to work anchoring news and traffic reports at Shadow Broadcast Services. She worked middays at KSCA and hosted a Saturday night KMPC talk show on relationships. With the demise of the AAA format on KSCA in the spring of 1997, KSLX, "Real Radio," adopted the Alternative format for weekends and Anita was one of the first hired.

GILBERT, Jack: **KMPC**, 1965; **KGIL**, 1966. In the early 1970s Jack went to do tv weather on KNXT/Channel 2.

GILL, Jeff: **KJLH**, 1990-97. Jeff was born Geof Gilstrap and known on-air as the "Music Doctor."

GILLILAND, John: **KRLA**, 1965-70. John created one of the bright spots in Southern California radio history, "The Pop Chronicles." The show was narrated by Thom Beck, John and Sie Holliday. John graduated from Texas Christian University with a B.A. in English. John worked at two Dallas stations, KCUL and KLIF. For two years beginning in 1959, John was a member of the multi-

award-winning news department at KILT-Houston and

then moved on to KOGO-San Diego until joining KRLA in 1965. Inspired by the Monterey Pop Festival of '67, John approached the station with the idea of an audio history of pop music. John tells the story from his home in Quanah, Texas: "The plan was to do interviews with, maybe, fifty of the most influential contributors to Pop music in the '50s and '60s and weave them into some 25 programs. Two years later, when "The Pop Chronicles" made its first appearance on KRLA, the interviews totaled more than 100, and the series clocked in at 55 hours." John worked briefly on "The Credibility Gap" but concentrated on his "Chronicles" commitment. In 1971 he joined Gene Autry's KSFO-San Francisco and spent most of the decade producing a 24-hour blockbuster series on the 1940s and working as an evening jock. "After KSFO I retired from the business in 1978 and came home to Quanah to be with my parents during a difficult time. At the same time, I began writing a long-planned comic novel about broadcasting." The book was never published and in 1985 John returned to radio at KRBE-Houston. "In '87 after my mother's death, I came back to Quanah intending to sell the family home, then ended up settling in." During the 1990s, John has been doing video production, local and regional industriales. In 1994 his *Pop Chronicles*: *The Forties* was published as an audio book by the Mind's Eye.

GILMORE, Doug: **KJLH**, 1984-86, pd. Doug left L.A. for radio in Ojai.

GJERDRUM, Tom: **KIIS**, 1994, md. Tom grew up in Winona, Minnesota and graduated from Winona State University with a B.A. degree in mass communication. Tom started out at KAGE-Winona and in 1987 was md and evening jock at WLXR-LaCrosse. Before joining KIIS Tom programmed KZOK-Rockford, KQKQ-Omaha and KKLQ-San Diego. When he left the Southland he programmed KFMB-San Diego and in the summer of 1995 he joined WZPL-Indianapolis where he is currently the pd.

Who had the biggest influence in your life? "Three women and Three guys. My mother encouraged me, my sister who whetted my appetite for reading and entertainment and my wife, Arlette who helps me every day. And Larry, Moe and Curly who shared their wisdom and twisted the noses of my mother, my sister and my wife!"
-Top Ten personality Gary Owens

GLADSTONE, Terry: **KLOS**, 1978-81; **KEZY**, 1981-83; **KNAC**, 1984; **KMET**, 1985-86; **KNX/FM**, 1986-88; **KLSX**, 1993-94; **KSCA**, 1994-96. Born and raised in Oak Park, Michigan, Terry began her love affair with radio while listening to the Beatles on WKNR and CKLW in Detroit. She was surrounded by eventual musical talents Don Was, Curt Sobel and Marty Lewis. She went to Michigan State and took a radio course from Fred Jacobs and later transferred to Wayne State. Terry tried acting until her acting professor commented on one of her scenes, "That was the most boring performance I have ever seen." In 1976 she moved to San Diego and got a job working at a recreation center for underprivileged Spanish-speaking children while begging the management

of KGB for a job that she eventually got. Terry followed her husband-to-be to the Southland. "I sat in my house - windows closed, no air-conditioning - making my simulated airchecks. I was determined to get a job at KLOS. I sent a tape to then-pd, Frank Cody every week and made sure that I was at every industry function so I could run into him." Eight months later Terry was hired. "I always tell that story to people who want to be in radio. I figure if I could get a job in L.A. radio with so little actual on-the-air experience, then anyone with talent can, too." Since 1993, Terry has been working the Adult Rock & Roll format at Westwood One and currently does middays. Terry is a songwriter/composer and a music therapist working with Down Syndrome clients. "Besides my family, music is my other love."

GLAZER, Ron: **KWNK**, 1985. Ron was part of the radio announcing team for the short-lived L.A. Express football team.

GLEASON, David: **KKHJ**; **KWIZ**, 1991-94; **KTNQ/KLVE**, 1995-97, pd. David is pd of Spanish KTNQ and corporate consultant to Heftel stations in Florida, Texas and Nevada. Born January 5, 1946, in

Cleveland, he worked weekends during high school at WJMO and WCUY. In 1963 while in Mexico City he interned at Organizacion Radio Centro. Four years later he applied and built Ecuador's first two FM stations and later he built two AM stations. In 1970 he was forced to make an emergency departure from Ecuador due to political unrest. He joined WERC-Birmingham and during the 1970s consulted KENO-Las Vegas, KTKT-Tucson, KRUX-Phoenix and WJIT-San Juan. In 1980 David was named gm of WHTT-Miami. A year later he established "Musica en Flor," a syndicated program based on Latin adult contemporary music. In the late '80s he ran WPRM-Puerto Rico and WTNT/WNCS-Tallahassee. While at KKHJ, David was named programmer and consultant to a joint venture between TM Century of Dallas and Radio Express, Inc. to produce a Spanish music version of the well-known "Hit Disk" series of weekly CD's.

GLICK, Patti: **KGBS**, 1973; **KLVE**, 1974-75; **KLOS**, 1976-78; **KPOL**. A graduate of University High School in West Los Angeles, Patti was at KGBS during the "Gentle Country" period. She was in the traffic department at KGBS and auditioned for a shift on the all-female Country station. Patti currently does voiceover work.

1973 *Billboard* Radio Programming Forum

Chairman	**Gary Owens**
Best Soul Station	**KGFJ**
Best MOR	**KMPC**
Best Country	**KLAC**
Best Progresstive	**KMET**
Best Country pd	**Hal Smith and Jonathan Fricke**
Best CHR pd	**Ron Jacobs (KGB)**
Best Top 40 dj	**Robert W. Morgan**
Best MOR dj	**Dick Whittington**
Best Country dj	**Sammy Jackson**
Best Newsman	**B.R. Bradbury**
Best Independent Record Promoter	**Tony Richland**

Quite a year for Los Angeles Radio People!

GODFREY: **KTYM**, 1965-68; **KALI**, 1965-68. Born Godfrey Kerr, his mentor was Huggie Boy. Godfrey promoted and emceed dances and shows in the East Los Angeles and Montebello areas. He currently works for City Hall Distributors, a wholesale record distributorship.

GODGES, Mary Jo: **KNAC**, 1980-88. Mary Jo was part of the "rock 'n rhythm" days at KNAC. She was called "Bloody Mary" during the "pure rock" format. Mary Jo is a musician and went to Europe to be part of the Diamond Claw musical group.

GOICH, Lisa: **KLSX**, 1997. Lisa is a comedian who was  briefly partnered with WJR-Detroit's Mitch Albom before joining Jim Daniels at "Real Radio." Her comedy club appearances have been at all the top clubs across the country including locally The Ice House, The Improv and The Laugh Factory. Lisa has appeared on *The Oprah Winfrey Show!*, *48 Hours* and *A Current Affair*. After her partner moved to Houston, Lisa took over the all-night talk show and left in the summer of 1997.

GOLDEN, Brian: **KMPC**, 1992-93; **KLSX**, 1996. The *Antelope Valley News* sports writer hosted a midday show with Paola Boivin during the short-lived all-Sports format on KMPC. Brian hosts "TrojanTalk" prior to USC football.

GOLDEN, Pat: **KRKD**, 1956-59. Pat hosted the "Princess Pat Motors" program on KRKD.

GOLDFARB, Bob: **KFAC**, 1986-87, pd. Bob spent two decades in Classical music radio.

GOLDMAN, David: **KMPC**, 1996. David hosted a weekend restaurant show on KMPC.

GOMEZ, Batman: **KQLZ**, 1989-91. Born Brian Shook, Batman worked evenings at "Pirate Radio." When the format ended, one of his colleagues commented how crushed he was. Batman packed up his things and said he was getting out of radio.

GOMEZ, Elio: **KLAX**

GOMEZ, Martine: **KWIZ**, 1997

GOMEZ, Salvador: **KTNQ**, 1986; **KSKQ**, 1988; **KWIZ**; **KKHJ**; **KTNQ**, 1995-97. Salvador was born in the town of San Buenaventura in the state of Usulutan in El Salvador. He immigrated to the United States at the age of 17. Salvador studied at the Columbia School of Broadcasting and became one of the best-known characters on the Humberto Luna morning show on KTNQ. Known  also as "Chava," he returned to KTNQ in 1995 to work afternoon drive. Salvador is now working at KLSQ/KWNR-Las Vegas.

GONIER, Kevin: **KIQQ**, 1984-85. Kevin was a "phone answering intern" who was given a weekend shift from time to time.

GONNEAU, Pierre: SEE Lucky Pierre

GONZALES, Jacque: **KOST**, 1994-97. Born and raised in Albuquerque, Jacque used the name Jacque James for her decade in the radio business before joining "Coast" for weekends. She has worked virtually every music format starting with her first job in 1985 at Urban KANW-Albuquerque. She moved next to crosstown KKSS and then three stations in Kansas City, KXXR, KBEQ and KKCJ. In 1993 she returned to KKSS until joining  KCAQ-Oxnard in 1994. Jacque also works at KHAY-Ventura and *Network 40 Magazine*. She left KOST in the spring of 1997.

GONZALEZ, Amalia: **XPRS**, 1978-85; **KTNQ**, 1985-90; **KSKQ**, 1991-92; **KKHJ**, 1992-95; **KTNQ**, 1995-97. Amalia was born Erika Amalia Gonzalez in the town of Tepatitlan in Jalisco, Mexico. She moved with her family to L.A. when she was 13 and it was at Los Angeles City College where she developed her passion for  broadcasting. After graduating from the Don Martin School she started at KMEX/Channel 34 when it was SIN as a newscaster and hostess for a daytime program, "Los Angeles Ahora." She has starred in a number of Mexican films which she described as a "good experience." She started her radio career at XPRS in the traffic department and went on the air for one hour every weekend. "I was very proud to be on the air." Eventually she had a full-time shift leading to her current assignment as midday host of all-Spanish Talk, KTNQ. "We talk about relationships, wife battering, unfaithfulness and drunk drivers. We talk about how we can be better citizens in America." Since 1994 she has been the co-producer of "Exitos Express," a weekly service of new music for radio stations in Latin America. Amalia is assistant to the pd.

> *"I would rather be doing overnights in Nashville than morning drive in Dallas." -Jami Mayberry*

GONZALEZ, Antonio: **KWKW**, 1978-84, nd; **KTNQ**, 1984-97, nd. Antonio teams with "El Gordo" in afternoon drive. They host "Contacto 10-20," an "issues" program dealing with gangs, racism, assimilation, societal matters and topical questions. Antonio has won several Golden Mike awards.

GONZALEZ, Arturo: **KALI**, 1986-89. Arturo was a newsman for the Spanish language station, KALI.

GONZALEZ, Luis Roberto: **KTNQ**, 1987-97

GONZALEZ, Paul: **KFWB**, 1984-86. Paul was a reporter/newsman for all-News KFWB. He went on to free-lance for ABC News.

GONZALEZ, Phil: **KJOI/KYSR/KXEZ**, 1989-96. Phil was head of production and promotion at the Viacom stations and did on-air fill-in.

GONZALEZ, Luis Roberto: **KTNQ**, 1989; **KWIZ**, 1989-90; **KTNQ**, 1994-97. Luis worked middays at Spanish KWIZ and now hosts a Saturday old-fashioned swap shop. "El Tigre," as he is known, insists that the caller tell a favorite joke before they can sell or buy something.

GONZALEZ, Rolando: **KTNQ**, 1987-97. Rolando is known as "El Veloz." He leads a six-person sports staff and hosts a nightly sports talk show on KTNQ with co-anchor Hipolito Gamboa. For ten years Rolando has presented news, commentaries, interviews and listener interaction. The station has stringers throughout Latin America who present the latest news on soccer and other sports.

GONZALEZ, Ramon: **KWIZ**, 1997

GONZALEZ, Steve: **KWIZ**, 1978-87; **KABC**, 1987-97. Steve worked evenings on the Orange County outlet, KWIZ. He now does weekend news on KABC.

GONZER, Jeff: **KPPC**, 1969-71; **KMET**, 1971-72; **KLOS**, 1972-76; **KMET**, 1976-86; **KLSX**, 1993-94; **KSCA**, 1995-97. Jeff was born in 1949 and grew up in Southern California attending Hamilton High School. He got started in radio at the campus station at Cal State Los Angeles. In 1978, an *LA Times* profile of morning men prompted this comment from Gonzer: "I consider myself an entertainer, someone who is destined to do stand-up comedy - if I ever have the guts." In January 1985, Jeff returned to KMET after a brief hiatus as vidiot on Ted Turner's short-lived Cable Music Channel. When the KMET job ended, Jeff worked at stations in Miami and Boston, where he branched out into Talk radio. In the summer of 1993, Jeff returned to the Southland doing part-time on KLSX. Upon his return, he told the *Times*, "Sometimes, in order to make progress, you have to take a side road. I really don't know what's going to happen. I'm up for everything and anything." In the spring of 1995 Jeff started on WWI's Adult/Rock and Roll service and in late 1996 became pd. Jeff worked weekends at KSCA until an ownership change and the station went Spanish. He has a wife and two boys.

GONZO, Greg: **KNAC**, 1986-89. KNAC was Greg's first job out of college. When he left the Southland, he went to Philadelphia, KRXX-Minneapolis and WTFX-Louisville. In the fall of 1995 he joined mornings at KCAL-Riverside and left in early 1997. He;s now working in Detroit radio.

GOOD, Tommy: **KFOX**, 1957-60

GOODMAN, Jon: **KNX**, 1968-96. The veteran newsman for KNX left the all-News station after almost 30 years on the job. He reported from City Hall and the criminal courts and was known for his coverage of the Sirhan Sirhan, Pentagon Papers and Charles Manson trials, as well as the 1993 Malibu wildfire. Jon graduated from high school in Tacoma in 1952 and attended the University of Washington. He is a former U.S. Marine Corps Sergeant. Before getting to the Southland he worked at KIMA-Yakima, KERG-Eugene and KFBK-Sacramento. He won numerous industry awards.

GOODMAN, Mark: **KMPC/KEDG**, 1988-89; **KROQ**, 1992-93; **KYSR**, 1996-97. The former MTV vj left L.A. in 1993 to join WKQX ("Q101")-Chicago; he was gone from the Windy City in 1994. Mark also jocked on WPLJ-New York and WMMR-Philadelphia. In the spring of 1996, he joined "Star 98.7" for morning drive and currently works swing.

GOODWIN, Hal: **KRLA**, 1959; **KFWB**, 1961-73. When KRLA went rocking in late 1959, Hal was with the Pasadena station as a weekender and lasted a short time before going to KFWB as a newsman. Hal was one of the first news voices heard on KFWB when the station went all-News. The Texas native was the spokesperson on tv for a company that sold sides of beef. Hal suffered a fatal heart attack in 1973 while on the air. In the 1950s he was on tv as "Happy Hal the Clown."

GORBITZ, Scott: **KFWB**, 1979-96, nd. The former news director of KFWB first became attracted to news when he was about 10. "I wondered about why so many people were killing one another, and was curious about the history of conflict." He never worked anywhere else in the industry. Scott started at KFWB in April 1979 as a part-time desk assistant. He got a sports writing break during the 1980 Lake Placid Olympics. His news writing break occurred shortly thereafter when the Pope was shot. He became a full-time writer in 1983 and an editor in 1988. Scott resigned from the KFWB news director post in late spring of 1996 and moved to Honolulu. "I'm ready to cool my brain and drive a bread-truck."

GORDO, El: SEE Hugo Cadelago.

GORDON, Eric: **KEZY**, 1987. Eric worked morning drive at the Orange County outlet.

GORI, Kathy: **KMPC**, 1972-75; **KIIS**, 1975-76; **KTNQ**, 1977-80, **KPFK**, 1996-97. Don Page of the *LA Times* described Kathy as "a fifth generation San Franciscan of Italian stock and she's as effervescent as California champagne and as likable as pasta." Just out of high school, Kathy started on KSFO-San Francisco at the age of 18. "I was the first female on the air in the Bay Area." She started on the all-night show called "Night Flight" on KMPC in June 1972, when she was only 22 years old. Kathy recalled the time like it was yesterday: "KMPC's gm flew my parents to Los Angeles to assure them that their daughter would be okay. Up until this point I had lived at home." She continued her voiceover work when she arrived in the Southland and received a Clio in 1972 for best commercial. In 1973, she was nominated for DJ of the Year. Her voice work included *Gidget* in an animated ABC/TV movie and NBC/TV's *Inch High Private Eye*. Her radio act included a little company of wackos all performed by Kathy. There was Lavern Rondell, a waitress, who wanted to make it big in Hollywood; Miss Sherry, ("an alcoholic chef who drinks a lot of Ripple"), a takeoff on Julia Child; and Jewel and Dave, America's Sweethearts, a takeoff on Julie and David Eisenhower. Kathy has a rich heritage. Her great-great uncle published one of the first newspapers in San Francisco in 1854. Her great grandfather was John L. Sullivan's sparing partner. And she had a great-grandmother who was a surveyor by day and streetwalker by night. For the past 15 years Kathy and her husband have been successful screenwriters and are working on scripts for theatrical release. Kathy was a role model for many women who followed in her footsteps. In the fall of 1996 she joined KPFK to co-host the morning show and comment on the news. "I'm having so much fun."

GORMAN, Scott: **KDAY**, 1965

GOSA, Jim: **KBIG**, 1964-67, pd; **KBCA**, 1967-78; **KKGO**, 1982-89. A major jazz figure for more than three decades, Jim was a broadcasting major at L.A. City College. When he went to work for KBCA, he was known for his feature, "Jazz Chronicles." He also loved to act and performed at the Shakespeare Festival at Chapman College every summer. He served as a judge at jazz festivals and for more than a decade broadcast the Monterey Jazz Festival to Los Angeles. In 1987, L.A. Mayor Tom Bradley designated February 13 as "Jim Gosa Day" in the city. Jim stayed on the air until he died of melanoma cancer on December 18, 1989, at the age of 58, in his home in Venice. A colleague said of him: "Jim was a great man who was loved by his fellow staffers." He was married to KKGO afternoon personality Laura Lee.

GOSS, Dean: **KRTH**, 1981-86; **KMET**, 1986; **KODJ**, 1989-91. Dean, born in Palo Alto, near San Francisco, in 1950, was a graduate of San Diego State where he majored in telecommunications and film. His trademark has been his celebrity voices, which he worked on in his first radio job in Lake Tahoe at KTHO. In 1976, Dean was doing all-nights at KCBQ-San Diego. In 1981, the KRTH morning team of London and Engelman left for KWST. The station embarked on a national talent search and the winner from 450 entries was Dean, who was working at KGB-San Diego. Pd Bob Hamilton said, "The thing that impressed me about Dean was his enthusiasm. A lot of the other applicants seemed to want us to pursue them." In fact, Dean's boss at KGB, who was preparing a format switch to cable news, showed the trade ad to Dean. Some of his antics included broadcasting from a billboard while a crew dumped a cupful of white goo on his head claiming a mammoth pigeon had just flown overhead. Dean did morning drive when KODJ became "Oldies 93" in March 1989. He teamed with *Police Academy*'s Michael Winslow in a morning drive experiment that didn't last a month for Winslow. Dean later teamed with Charlie Tuna. Dean's highlight in Southern California, he recalled, was "broadcasting from a tank on Sunset Boulevard that was pulled over by Hollywood police." Out of radio in the late 1980s, Dean worked as a tv game show announcer on *Let's Make A Deal*, *High Rollers*, *$100,000 Pyramid* and others. When his run in Southern California ended, Dean went to San Diego to do mornings at KRMX and was teamed for the first time with Erin Garrett. They took their act to KFRC-San Francisco. The team moved to KYA-San Francisco with a change in format to "Young Country" and call letters to KYCY. In the late spring of 1995 the Goss + Garrett "Big Show" was not renewed by Alliance. Dean has returned to KFRC.

GOTHE, Jurgen: **KUSC**, 1989. Jurgen arrived at the Classical music station from Canada.

GOTT, Jim: **KABC**, 1996-97. The former L.A. Dodger relief pitcher hosted the return of "SportsTalk" to KABC starting January 22, 1996. Jim began his baseball career with Toronto in 1982, followed by San Francisco. He was with

Pittsburgh from 1987 to 1989. In 1990 he joined the Dodgers wearing jersey #35. Jim was a pitcher and outfielder for the 1977 San Marino High School CIF 2-A champions and he was the player of the year. In 1993 he led the Dodger relievers with 25 saves. He retired from baseball at the end of the 1994 season. While dominating the opposition from the mound, Jim became a third degree black belt in Hapkido, a Korean form of martial arts. Jim and his wife Cathy have six children, including twins.

GOURLEY, Bob: **KPPC**, 1986, nd

GOVERNALE, Jim: **KGER**, 1987; **KYMS**, 1988-93; **KKLA**, 1993-97.

Jim got the radio bug while in high school. He studied at Fullerton College and worked at the campus station in 1986. He landed his first professional job at the Long Beach-based Talk radio station, KGER. Jim started on KYMS, Orange County's Christian station on New Year's Eve of 1988. He worked afternoon drive and middays along with assignments of md, production director and om. Since 1993, he has been hosting "AM LA" at KKLA. Connecting with the audience is of prime importance to Jim. In a *Glendale News-Press* profile, Jim said: "It's a responsibility none of us here take lightly. Some days I just pray that the words come out right." Jim lives in Chino Hills.

GOWA, Bob: **KPPC**, 1971; **KYMS**, 1971-72; **XEPRS/XHIS/XHERS**, 1974-75, pd; **KMET**, 1976; **KROQ**, 1976-77, pd; **KWST**, 1977-79. Bob was born in Brooklyn on April 16, 1952. "At age 7, I became determined to grow up and hang out in radio stations." He moved with his family to Los Angeles in 1967 and did

indeed hang around radio stations, pestering the engineers until he was hired as an engineer/producer for "The Credibility Gap" at KPPC. He worked evenings at "free-form" KYMS and was pd for the Tijuana outlets, "HIS" and "HERS." In 1975 he joined Shadoe Stevens at his production house, Big Bucks Creations. Bob helped put KROQ back on the air after it had been dark for two years. "I became midday dj and, briefly, pd. I fielded calls from collection agencies and the police, all of whom were looking for the owners." In late 1977 he joined "K-West" as md and afternoon drive. He left the Southland in 1979 and joined KMEL-San Francisco for mornings and two years later moved on to KSAN and KNEW. He also did jock work at K101, KFOG and KOFY in the Bay Area. In 1987 he became om/pd at KTID-Sam Rafael. Two years later he was hired as news and traffic anchor/airborne reporter by Metro Networks in San Francisco. In 1995, Bob joined AMI News as director of operations. He lives in Sonoma County and is a part-time dad of a 5-year old son. "I'm doing well and very happy! I'm eager to hear from old cronies." He's now doing afternoons at KFGY-Santa Rosa. "I'm also on-call in San Francisco for engineering at KGO, jock work at KFRC and news anchor/flying traffic reporter for Shadow Broadcast Services."

GRACIE, Carolyn: **KLIT**, 1989-91; **KBIG**, 1993-97. Carolyn works afternoons at AC-programmed KBIG. The oldest of six children, she graduated from Purdue University and started out in Indianapolis radio sales. At KLIT, Carolyn partnered with Jim Carson in morning drive. A collector of exotic birds, she has an active voiceover career with her husband, Eric Edwards, who is production director at KPWR. "I love to play the piano," she told *Radio AM/FM*. "I started at the age of 8 and by the age of 10, I was playing John Phillip Sousa marches."

GRAD, Steve: **KNX**, 1993-97. Steve is a sports anchor on "KNXNewsradio." While pursing a B.S. in

communications at Southern Illinois University, Steve was reporting play-by-play sports for the SIU Network. Following graduation in 1972, he anchored sports at tv stations in San Antonio and Portland. In 1981 Steve joined KBEQ-Kansas City for morning drive sports and four years later moved to KBEA-Kansas City. For the rest of the '80s he worked at K101-San Francisco and KCMO-Kansas City. Steve has called baseball, football, basketball, hockey and boxing for numerous networks. He has earned an impressive list of awards, including two Golden Mikes.

GRAHAM, Gordon: **KGFJ**, 1965, nd. Gordon is now with CNN's Headline News.

GRAHAM, Tony: **KFWB**, 1968, pd. Tony left Southern California for WBZ-Boston.

GRANDE, Rudy: **KYMS**, 1987-88; **KLIT**, 1989-91; **KLSX/KRLA**, 1993-97. For almost a decade Rudy has been directing traffic from the air for many radio stations. In 1988 he joined Metro Traffic. "A few months after joining Metro I started flying a 172 and a year later I was airborne in a Bell JetRanger." Rudy was born and raised in Albuquerque and was hooked on radio from the moment he won a local on-air contest. "I was 14 and my girlfriend and I rode our bikes 10 miles to the radio station to pick up my prize. The jock on-air asked if I wanted to see the studio. From that moment, I fell in love with radio." A year later he got his FCC license and has been working ever since. Rudy came to the Southland to work morning drive and promotions at KYMS. He was a part-time dj at KLSX, hosted a morning talk show on Sunday mornings at KRLA and did fill-in at KLIT. "I made a big mistake giving up the talk show at KRLA. I thought I was too busy. But I really miss it and want to get back into talk radio.

GRANNIS, Larry: **KUSC**, 1950-51 and 1953-54; **KALI**, 1954-55; **KWOW**, 1956-57 and 1960-61; **KDWC**, 1957-58; **KWIZ**, 1961-71; **KYMS**, 1971-73; **KNOB**, 1973-78. "I discovered computers while I was a dj and administrative assistant to Bill Weaver at KWIZ during the 'All Request Radio' days." Larry was in charge of station operations which included the traffic department. He was fascinated with the possibilities of using computers for the then complicated manual job of daily scheduling. "Today, just about every station is doing it." He finally got a chance to put his ideas to work as om at KNOB when they selected a San Diego company to supply the computers and software. He combined the computer with the music and commercial automation unit and KNOB became one of the first stations to operate totally automated. He joined his old boss, Frank Crane, at the computer company. "It was a great move at a terrible time. The recession hit and the new idea of computerized traffic was really low on stations' priority lists. A year later I became a headhunter and recruiter specializing in computer placement." Born and raised in Long Beach ("the hospital where I was born is now a parking lot"), Larry was bitten early by the radio drama bug. It only got worse when his parents gave him a mock up of a sound effects control board. Larry started his radio career while completing his B.A. in telecommunications at USC. During his radio journey he "got a chance to build KDWC-West Covina and sister station KDWD-San Diego from scratch." Larry is now retired. "I don't know what I'm doing."

GRANT, Bob: **KNX**, 1960; **KLAC**, 1968-69. Bob partnered with Paul Condylis in the early 1960s on KNX. He worked afternoons when KLAC was a Talk station. Bob went on to be a long-standing voice in New York radio and was eventually syndicated. After ten years with WABC-New York, he was fired in a controversy over the airline crash that killed Commerce Secretary Ron Brown. Within two weeks he was working at WOR-New York.

GRANT, Hank: **KNX**, 1965-90. Hank was the entertainment reporter at KNX for almost a quarter of a century. Hank penned the "Rambling Reporter" column for the industry paper, *Hollywood Reporter*. Born Henry Galante in New York in 1913, he majored in journalism at L.A. City College and UCLA. While in college, he began moonlighting as a singer and emcee, first at KHJ and later at the Coconut Grove, on the Orpheum theater circuit, in Las Vegas lounges and at other night spots. After West Coast successes, Hank began successful one-man shows on Chicago tv. He continued working for KNX right up until his illness prevented him from doing so. He passed away July 19, 1990 after a battle with cancer at the age of 77. A press agent wrote at the time of Hank's death: "Hank never wrote an unkind word about anyone, yet also managed to make you feel that you learned a lot about what was going on."

GRANT, Jim: **KABC**, 1986. Former major league pitcher Jim (Mudcat) Grant joined KABC to work "SportsTalk" and "DodgerTalk" shows. Jim played baseball for 14 years, the first seven with Cleveland, beginning in 1958. He also played for Minnesota, the Dodgers in '68, Montreal, Oakland and Pittsburgh where he finished his career in 1971 when the Pirates won the World Series. After baseball he became a tv commentator for the Cleveland Indians and he hosted a radio show in Cleveland.

GRANT, Johnny: **KGIL**, 1949-50; **KMPC**, 1951-59 and 1991. For almost a half-century, Johnny has been

synonymous with Hollywood. He started his radio career in Goldsboro, North Carolina at the age of 17. He received national recognition for his 1940 coverage of a notorious murder trial after persuading the judge to allow him to broadcast the trial's progress from the doorway of the courtroom.

Beginning in 1944, he worked at WINS-New York hosting a program aimed at the GIs stationed around New York. In the late 1940s, Johnny arrived in Hollywood, did Lucky Strike cigarette commercials on the "Jack Benny Show" and hosted a talk show from Ciro's nightclub on the Sunset Strip. Beginning in 1951, Johnny worked afternoon drive at the Gene Autry station for eight years. He created the "Freeway Club" and said, "I was the first dj in the nation to intersperse traffic reports between records and guest stars." As the honorary mayor of Hollywood, he has emceed more than 3,500 civic and charity events. He has raised millions of dollars for the USO, Boy Scouts, Arthritis Foundation and countless others. His Star is on the Hollywood Boulevard Walk of Fame. Beginning in the late 1960s, he hosted KTLA/Channel 5's *Johnny Grant at Universal Studios* and became a regular on Channel 5's *News at Ten* with his feature "Backstage in Hollywood." For many years he hosted the tv movies. His daily radio show had an audience of 500 million on AFRTS, heard in 40 countries throughout the world. Johnny made 13 trips to Korea, 14 visits to Vietnam and 39 overseas trips for the USO. He is a retired major general in the California State Military Reserve. While Bob Hope worked the hospitals and big bases, Johnny and his small entourage worked the sweaty

---

KFAC was owned for 25 years by E.L. Cord, of the Cord luxury automobile. He sold the station to Cleveland Broadcasting for $2 million.

fields and bloody boondocks of Vietnam. Johnny gave up his touring in 1971 to devote more time to Channel 5 public affairs and to take entertainment into hospitals for the GIs. He has interviewed legendary luminaries such as Babe Ruth, Jack Dempsey, Ty Cobb, Eleanor Roosevelt and Capt. Eddie Rickenbacker. In the late 1970s, he turned the Hollywood Christmas Parade into a nationally televised event. In late 1991, Johnny joined Robert W. Morgan on KMPC, handling the weather and traffic. Johnny is very visible at each Star-unveiling as chairman of the Hollywood Walk of Fame selection committee.

GRANT, Dr. Toni: **KABC**, 1972-86; **KFI**, 1986-90; **KTZN**, 1997. Dr. Toni Grant is a clinical psychologist and a pioneer in media psychology. Her radio career

began in 1972 with weekly guest appearances on the "Bill Ballance Show." In 1975, she went on to revolutionize her field and the broadcasting industry with the nation's first psychology call-in format. In 1981, her three-hour afternoon show was syndicated by the ABC network. In 1986, she was recruited by the Mutual Broadcasting System, and was syndicated in 180 markets until her departure in 1990. In 1988, Dr. Grant wrote *Being A Woman*, the best seller which urged modern women to reclaim their femininity, lay down their "Amazon Armor" and return to traditional moral and family values. She took her own advice and that same year married industrialist John Bell. In 1990, Toni decided to "live the book I wrote" and took a creative hiatus from daily broadcasting. She entered the world of corporate America, serving in an executive position at Bell Packaging Corporation. Toni missed radio and in the spring of 1997 she returned to daily broadcasting. Her show is now syndicated from Dallas and is carried locally on KTZN. Famous for her phrase, "Life is not a dress rehearsal," Toni has spoken with over 50,000 people; subject matter has ranged from the bedroom to the boardroom. Born in 1945, Dr. Grant was educated at Vassar College and earned her doctorate at Syracuse University. Her first love has always been radio. "I like the privacy, the intimacy, and the connection with the people." She has two daughters.

GRAVES, David: **KFWB**, 1986, gm. David arrived at KFWB from a sister Group W station in the East.

GRAY, Gary: **KBIG/KBRT**, 1970-80. Gary worked for the Bonneville stations for almost a decade. In the mid-1970s, Gary teamed with Ray Willes in morning drive. He is currently working in radio in upstate New York.

GRAY, Marv: **KFI**, 1967-72; **KABC**, 1972-73. The ex-CIA agent from Connecticut started in the opinion business as Joe Pyne's producer. Marv was a World War II hero, author, lecturer and columnist who was the distinctive conservative voice of early L.A. Talk radio. He died November 8, 1973. He was 53.

GRAYDON, Joe: **KDAY**, 1959-60. The former FBI agent was a singer in the 1950s. After his radio career he promoted big band events.

GRAYSON, Vic: SEE Jim Carson

GRDNIC, Joy: SEE Ron Stevens

GREASEMAN: **KLOS**, 1993-94. *Penthouse Magazine* described Greaseman's show: "It is a cartoon for the ears, a fast-paced barrage of ad-libbed songs, stories and jokes." Born Doug Tracht in the Bronx on August 1, 1950, the Greaseman grew up in the Bronx and graduated from Ithaca College with a B.S. in broadcasting. His jock travels took him to WENE-Binghamton, WAXC-Rochester, WWDC-Washington, DC, WPOP-Hartford, WXRK-New York, WYSP-Philadelphia and KOME-San Jose. In 1975, he went to Jacksonville. He went through the police academy in Florida and as a civilian carried a gun and a badge. He felt that being a cop was a great way to learn a town. He began to tell sordid tales of his law enforcement character. Other wacky flights of fancy included telling stories about being a surgeon in medical school, where he specialized in chain-saw surgery. By 1977 the Greaseman was working at WLUP-Chicago. He gained national attention at WWDC when he took to the air in 1986 on Martin Luther King's birthday and joked that if killing one black leader was cause for a day off, then killing "four more" would create a holiday "all week long." Beginning in 1993 his show was syndicated from Los Angeles, where he did the early evening show on KLOS until late 1994. How did his name come to be? While working at WENE-Endicott, New York, the jocks were using

the expression, "I'm cookin' tonight." One night he said he was so hot he was "cookin' with grease." He knew he had arrived when he picked up one of the trade publications and an advertisement solicited a "Grease-man type." He is syndicated on WW1. Doug and his wife Anita returned to Washington, DC in the spring of 1997.

GREEN, George: **KABC**, 1960-94, pres/gm; **KABC/KMPC**, 1994-96, gm. A native of New York, George is a graduate of UCLA with a bachelor's degree in education. He began his career as an NBC/TV page and joined ABC as a junior sales executive at KABC/Channel 7 in 1959. George joined KABC radio from the sister tv

---

Robert W. Morgan announces on KRTH that he has lung cancer.   -May 28, 1997

station in 1960 as a salesperson and was promoted to gsm in 1965. He was gm of WABC-New York before returning to the West coast. When longtime KABC gm Ben Hoberman transferred to New York as ABC Radio division president, in 1979, George was again promoted. George stepped down in the spring of 1996 to open a consultancy firm and now represents Jacor. He is the father of three and lives in Encino with his wife Mim.

GREEN, Herb: **KMPC**. Herb was the gm of KMPC's AirWatch. The Texan flew for over 50 years. He was Gene Autry's personal pilot for 27 years and daily aired "A Pilot's View of the Weather." During World War II, Herb operated a flight school. In a 1974 *LA Times* profile, Herb said: "I'm not a meteorologist. But in 47 years of flying, I should know a little bit about weather." Herb was an advocate of the twin-engine aircraft as the only fixed-wing planes for traffic coverage. The aviator's axiom is: "If an airplane loses its power, it becomes a glider. If a helicopter loses its power, it becomes a rock." Herb died in the early 1980s and was buried in his hometown, Waco.

GREEN, John: **KFAC**, 1975

GREEN, Phil: **KLAC**, 1965-70. Phil was a newsman at KLAC during the Talk radio days. He left the radio business and started an ambulance service that became the biggest in Carson. Phil sold it and moved to Phoenix.

GREEN, Sean: **XPRS**, 1982-84. Sean was one of the jocks who taped his show in Glendale and had it trucked to Tijuana. He hosted an Oldies request and dedication show.

GREENE, Scott: **KMNY**, 1986-89; **KDAY**, 1988-90; **KJLH**, 1990-92; **KXEZ/KYSR**, 1989-93; **KGFJ**, 1994-95; **KFI**, 1995-97.

"I wasn't flying the plane." That was Scott's first line when interrogated for five hours after his traffic pilot violated restricted air space during the Pope's visit to the Southland. "Our plane was forced down via two military choppers with an aimed 16mm-military cannon. Very scary." Born on Long Island, his postal inspector father was transferred to Illinois when Scott was eight. He started his radio career at WDGC-Downers Grove, Illinois when he was 14 years old. He earned a B.A. in radio/tv/film from Cal State University Northridge in 1981. After graduation Scott worked in the Antelope Valley and was the overnight news anchor at "Money Radio," KMNY, along with Metro Traffic. His show at KFI is described as "libberservatism - somewhere between hard-line conservatives and hard-end liberals." Scott lives in the San Fernando Valley.

GREENE, Tim: **KKBT**, 1990-92; **KJLH**, 1992-94; **KMPC**, 1995. The ubiquitous Tim is doing it all and he is not yet 30 years old. From Philadelphia where he is scouting locations for a comedy/horror production called *Creepin*: "If I wasn't doing it, somebody else would." Tim is a national Deans List graduate and Sony Innovators Award finalist at Shaw University. He recently produced a moving tribute song to Dr. Martin Luther King. Tim has produced, hosted and directed 3 tv shows and has written many top ten songs for other artists. "When I was working at 'the Beat,' I heard a lot of bad records. I have a knack for picking a hit. Even though I can't read music, I certainly can produce winning records." Tim is the producer and manager of Rappin' Granny. He also hosts the international "World Dance Trax from Los Angeles" and *Dance City From Hollywood* for the Japanese market. Born in Philadelphia, he grew up all over the country playing in over 125 tennis tournaments. "Between 1992 and 1994 I won every celebrity tournament I played in including the John McEnroe 'Love Match.'" Tim worked at WCKZ-Charlotte before joining KKBT. *Whew!*

GREENLEIGH, Tom: **KRLA**, 1976-77; **KIQQ**, 1977. A graduate of UCLA and active at KLA, Tom was a self-admitted "radio junkie" who spent some time as a tv production assistant, at an ad agency and in marketing research. Tom arrived in the Southland after stops at KDES-Palm Springs and KSEA-San Diego. He programmed KIKX-Tucson with Bill Pearl and they took their ideas to KRLA and later KIQQ. He and Bill created the "Hitman" concept for KRLA that was very successful. Tom went on to own stations in Ogden and Indio. He currently lives in the Midwest and deals in the China import business.

GREENLY, Ed: **KPSA**, 1972, pd. The Los Angeles native worked as pd and hosted an afternoon shift.

GRESHAM, Bob: **KBCA**, 1964-69. Bob was part-time at KBCA while working for a car dealership.

GRICE, Bonnie: **KUSC**, 1989-96; **KKGO**, 1996-97; **KSCN**, 1997. Bonnie joined the Classical music outlet, KUSC, from WKSU-Kent, Ohio to do mornings. She wrote a new opera, *Mrs. Dalloway*, that was performed in the mid-1990s by the Lyric Opera of Cleveland. At KUSC Bonnie worked both drive slots. She married the president of KUSC, Dr. Wallace Smith, within a year of arriving at the station. In the fall of 1994, Bonnie's book, *Z to A -- The Classical Lovers Alternative* was published. Her awards include the prestigious Susan B. Anthony Award for Communications from the Business and Professional Women's Association Hollywood Chapter. In the fall of 1996 Bonnie resigned from KUSC concurrently with KUSC president/gm-husband Wallace Smith. She joined

KKGO in November 1996. She's now with WPBX-New York.

GRIEGO, Christine: **KRLA**, 1995-97. In addition to working morning drive on KRLA, Christine reports for Metro Traffic. She previously toiled at KGGI-Riverside.

GRIFFIN, Booker: **KGFJ**. Booker was a graduate of Baldwin-Wallace College in Berea, Ohio, and in 1962 moved to Los Angeles, where he started with Motown Records and was a volunteer in the presidential campaign of Robert F. Kennedy. Booker was an African American activist who, after the 1965 Watts riots, wrote and helped design programs for the Westminster Neighborhood Association in Watts. Booker died July 4, 1993, after suffering a diabetes-induced stroke at the age of 55.

GRIFFIN, Joey: **KWIZ**, 1980-82. Joey worked mornings at the Orange County station.

After 11 years in the radio business she became a corporate paralegal. Born and raised in Woodland Hills, Joey started her radio career in 1977 in San Luis Obispo. Her journey took her to Topeka, Racine, Mobile and Milwaukee. Joey originally wanted to be an actress and radio seemed to make sense after she got out of school. "Every once in a while when I talk with an old radio friend, I think about radio."

GRIFFIN, Ken: **KGOE**, 1972; **KGIL**, 1970-75. Ken came to the San Fernando Valley from WDRC-Hartford, which was near his birthplace of Waterbury. When he left the Southland, he returned to New England.

GRIFFITH, Bob: **KLOS**, 1977-78; **KMET**, 1979-82; **KFI**, 1982-84; **KJOI**, 1984-89, vp/gm; **KYSR/KXEZ**, 1990-95, gm. The longtime sales executive for a number of L.A. radio stations got his start in Detroit where he was born June 6, 1947. He graduated from Wayne State University in Detroit with a major in mass communications. Bob went to work in Detroit for WDEE, Eastman Radio and McGavren Guild. Bob arrived in the Southland to work sales at KLOS. He had a series of gsm positions until KJOI, where he held the post of vp/gm. Bob left KYSR/KXEZ in the summer of 1995.

GRIFFITH, Herman: **KGFJ**, 1963-66. Herman's on-air moniker was "God's gift to woman." He worked afternoon drive. "Y100's" Scott Lowe from Philadelphia remembers hearing Herman in 1967 on AFN while in Germany.

GRIFFITH, Norman: **KGBS**, 1965

GROSS, Al: **KPZE**, 1987

GROSS, Laura: **KRLA**, 1980-81. Laura filled in for Art Laboe for a short time.

GROVES, Larry: **KKDJ**, 1973-76; **KEZY**, 1976-77; **KROQ**, 1979. Larry went to KROQ with Rick Carroll as music director. When Larry was in college in Sacramento he was associated with Rick at KNDE. Larry's no longer in radio and works in a record store in Longview, Texas.

GUEBERT, Tim: **KNOB**, 1981

GUERRA, Bob: **KLAC/KZLA**, 1986-93, pd; **KCBS**, 1993-94. Bob is from Omaha and attended the University of Nebraska before graduating from the Brown Institute of Broadcasting in Minneapolis. He arrived in the Southland from KNEW-San Francisco, where he was md/pd and afternoon drive, to become om and pd at KZLA/KLAC. Bob helped create the "Discover Country Music" television campaign that became the marketing thrust for many successful

Country stations. He spearheaded "Country Fest" and "Country Scene," the first major outdoor festivals, attended by three quarters of a million country music fans over two years. Bob received 5 nominations from either *Billboard* or the *Gavin Report* as the Operations/Program Director of the Year and won the highly coveted *Gavin* Award in 1987. He has been active in projects with the Entertainment Radio Network and the Premiere Radio Networks. In 1993, he helped launch the "Arrow 93" format and worked afternoon drive. Bob is currently the president of his own consultancy company. He is married to radio personality Anne La Voy.

GUEVARA, Jorge: **KALI**, 1990. Jorge worked afternoons at Spanish KALI.

GUIDE, Thomas: **KROQ**, 1994

GUNN, Johnny: **KBIG**, 1966; **KGIL**, 1983-85, pd. While programming KVEG-Las Vegas in 1967, Johnny won the world championship of wild burro races for the third time. In the mid-1970s he was syndicating programs. At the San Fernando Beautiful Music station, KGIL, Johnny worked evenings and was pd.

GUNN, Mark: **KACE**, 1994-95. When Mark left the Southland he worked in Boston and later Pittsburgh. In early 1997 he took over the morning shift at WIZF-Cincinnati.

GUTIERREZ, Alvaro: **KTNQ**, 1996-97. Alvaro works weekends at the Spanish language station.

GUTIERREZ, Humberto: **KALI**, 1986

GUZMAN, Rich: **KACE**, 1982-94, pd; **KSCA**, 1994-97, om. Rich worked the all-night shift at the AAA formatted KSCA until the station changed to Spanish in early 1997. Born February 3, 1957, in Racine, Wisconsin, Rich spent 12 years at KACE and was upped to pd in the summer of 1993.

GWYNNE, Michael C.: **KROQ**, 1977. The character actor was part of the Sunday night insanity on KROQ.

"I cherish fondly my days in Los Angeles radio, a market that is second to none in the quality of product and personnel." —**Dave McClelland**

H

HABECK, Ted: **KWST**, 1979-81; **KMET**, 1981. At "K-West," Ted was a jock and md. He went to KSHE-St. Louis.

HADDAD, Edmonde: **KPOL**, 1961-84. The former KPOL newsman became an executive of the World Affairs Council. Ed is retired and living in Port Hueneme.

HADGES, Tommy: **KLOS**, 1980-85, pd. Tommy arrived in the spring of 1980 from New England where he was in dental school and worked at WBCN and WCOZ-Boston. He left KLOS in 1985 to join Jeff Pollack Communications as executive vp. In 1989 he was elevated to Pollack Media group president.

He continues as a key executive in the Pacific Palisades-based company that consults stations internationally.

HAESSLER, Eric: **KLSX**, 1995-97. Eric teamed with Larry Wachs for afternoon drive as the "Regular Guys" on the launch of the non-traditional Talk format on "Real Radio," KLSX. They have worked in radio, individually and together, doing morning personality radio. They were in Hartford and Rochester before arriving in the Southland.

HAFEN, Steve: **KGOE**, 1972

HAGEN, Carlos: 1976

HAGEN, Don: **KLSX**, 1986, pd

HAGGLER, Mike: **KPPC**, 1971, nd

HAIM, Joey: **KMAX**, 1995-96; **KWNK**, 1996-97; **KIIS/AM**, 1997. Joey was one of the "Sports Gods" on a nightly sports program on KMAX. He left when KMAX dropped their all-Sports programming in the spring of 1996. Born in Brooklyn, Joey moved to the Southland when he was ten and eventually pursued acting. He met his radio partner, Dave Smith, at a gym where they worked out next to each other. He and Dave now host a show on all-Sports "XTRA 1150."

HAINEY, Chandler: **KYMS**, 1993

HALEY, Bud: **KPOP**, 1959; **KRKD**, 1960-63; **KLAC**, 1968-79; **KABC**, 1979. Bud was the all-night talk show host for part of his run on KLAC.

HALISON, Frank "Hot Dog": **XPRS**, 1971-72. The "Hot Dog" worked morning drive at the "Soul Express."

HALL, David: **KORG**, 1977; **KNX/FM**, 1979-83; **KKHR**, 1983, pd. Dave grew up in the Washington, DC/Baltimore area. He came to the Southland when he was 14. "I was a fan big-time of KFWB. The jocks were like little god-heads." After graduation from UCLA, his entrance into radio was almost a fluke. "Acting is an obsession, but I always knew I wanted to perform." He played music, loved music and was a musician. When he was 27, he was playing in an Orange County club when the owner of KORG asked if he had any radio experience. He fibbed and was soon doing overnights. A year later Dave was driving his Volkswagen when a drunken truck driver with two loads of cement crashed into his car, and the gas tank exploded trapping him in his car.

He lost both legs and within six months was walking on artificial legs. Hardly a year after the accident, KNX/FM pd Steve Marshall offered Dave the position of md, prompting him to say "Life Can Be A Dream...Sh-Boom," -- an example of how he punctuates his conversations. He talks warmly about the experience at KNX/FM. He called it an "odd radio station" that played music no one else was playing and sounded live even though it was automated. Dave appeared in *Deal of the Century*, with Chevy Chase, playing the part of a Vietnam vet. Christopher Ames, who worked with Dave on the CBS/FM station, went on to write *Class Action*, starring Gene Hackman, and David played the part of the double amputee. Dave also co-starred in *Dream Lover* and *Andersonville*, a TNT drama in which he played a Yankee POW. His tv credit list is long including *Love and War*, *Beverly Hills 90210*, the recurring role of Judge Swaybill on *L.A. Law* and Mr. Mott on *Life Goes On*. David's voice is heard on cartoon shows like *Batman*, *G.I. Joe*, *The Littles*, and *Ghostbusters*. "You keep the dream alive, whatever it takes."

HALL, David G.: **KFI**, 1989-97, pd. Born in Sacramento, David arrived from News/Talk KFBK-Sacramento. A friend from Sacramento remembered Dave's early days: "In March 1978 a bunch of us at Sacramento State on the old KERS did a live production of *Julius Caesar*. David, who was a teenager who hung around the station, worked the control board." He started his career in early 1982 at KRNY-Monterey as a part-timer, moved up to full-time and then into the news department. From Monterey he joined KFBK as a reporter/producer and eventually pd. He prides himself with "taking KFI from 26th to third."

HALL, Don: **KPPC**, 1968-71; **KMET**, 1972-73. Don started on all-nights in the early days of the "underground" station and moved to various shifts. While at KPPC, Michelangelo Antonio hired Don to do the music for his 1970 film *Zabriskie Point*. When he left radio he joined the a&r division of MGM Pictures. From there he became a projectionist for a theater in San Mateo because he loved movies. Don was last sighted in Santa Barbara as a projectionist for a drive-in theater.

HALL, John: **KMPC**, 1977-78; **KIKF**, 1994. For a half year in 1994, John provided early a.m. sports commentary at Country KIKF, and was a twice-weekly regular on the Scott St. James sports talk show at KMPC in the late '70s. He is better known for his four decades as sportswriter and columnist for the *LA Times* (1953-1981) and *OC Register* (1981-1993). "I loved my 28 years at the *Times* and particularly working with Jim Murray, but the *Register* made me one of those Godfather offers and so I moved." Born and raised in central Los Angeles, his first newspaper job after graduation from Stanford was with the *Hollywood Citizen-News*. Although he retired from newspapers in June 1993, he has kept busy as a consultant with a half dozen organizations and was director of special projects for three years with the Orange County Sports Association putting on the Freedom Bowl and Disneyland Pigskin Classic football games at Anaheim Stadium.

HALL, Mell: **KRLA**, 1965-67, pd. Mell worked at KDEO-San Diego in 1960 and was at Channel 6/TV in San Diego before joining the Pasadena outlet, KRLA. Mell returned to San Diego and built one of the most successful production facilities in the city. In addition to major spots for the San Diego Zoo, he produces national commercials.

HALL, Mort: **KLAC**, 1958-63, gm. Mort was the owner and gm of KLAC. When Mort changed the format at KLAC, *LA Times*' Don Page wrote, "What fools these Mort Halls Be." Mort sold his station to Metromedia.

HALL, Phil: **KLAC**, 1982-83, pd; **KHJ/KRTH/AM/FM**, 1985-90, pd. Phil was raised in Oklahoma and spent much of his youth in Little Rock. He was greatly influenced by a teacher to pursue radio as a career. "I saw the inside of a radio station and got hooked." Before arriving in the Southland, he programmed a number of stations in Tulsa and was director of consulting for Surrey Broadcasting Research. He arrived in the Southland from WTIC-Hartford. In addition to his duties at RKO, Phil was the executive producer for NBA Clippers Basketball Network. He went on to own two stations in Little Rock. He created "The Oldies Countdown" for MJI Broadcasting and is now managing Sports Fan Radio in Las Vegas.

HALL, Tom: **KABC**, 1978-97. After receiving a B.A.

degree in humanities, Tom started with KABC "TalkRadio" in early 1978 with a program featuring a wide potpourri of topics. He also worked for KNBC/Channel 4 as a public affairs reporter and appeared in the Marlon Brando movie, *The Formula*. Tom was part of a documentary team as an interviewer/writer/segment producer traveling to most continents and had credits in over 40 documentaries. Tom was a weekend and utility talk host at KABC and he ran a consulting group. Tom died April 12, 1997, of lymphoma and leukemia at the age of 57. He left behind a wife and four children.

HALLORAN, Mike: **KROQ**, 1988. Mike worked at WLLZ-Detroit before arriving at KROQ to work swing. When he left the Southland, Mike went on to program "91X"-San Diego. He left "91X" in the spring of 1996 and joined KUPR-San Diego and stayed till the end of the year.

HALLORAN, Tricia: **KCRW**, 1994-97. Tricia hosts

"Brave New World" on KCRW. Born in Fullerton, she grew up in Concord. Tricia graduated from UCLA with a degree in computer science. For the next decade she worked at Xerox. "During that time I became an avid fan of Deirdre O'Donoghue's 'Snap' program on KCRW. I volunteered during a pledge drive and eventually became an evening host. Why is her show called "Brave New World"? "Well, in Shakespeare's play *The Tempest*, a young girl who has lived her entire life on an isolated island suddenly encounters some fascinating strangers who will change her life forever. [Oh, Brave New World,] she exclaims loudly, [that has such people in't]! I discover the music that jumps, kicks, whispers and screams its way into your soul."

HAMBLEN, Stu: **KLAC**, 1976. Stu was one of the first singing cowboys. He was born on October 26, 1908, to a Methodist minister in Kellyville, Texas. His singing career started at age 18, and for the next two decades he was unparalleled as a singer and writer (he wrote Rosemary Clooney's million selling song, *This Old House*). His colorful past includes movies with John Wayne, Gene Autry and Roy Rogers; arrests for speeding and drunk driving; and running for President on the Prohibition Party platform against Dwight Eisenhower. His personal revival came when attending a Billy Graham revival in 1949. He stopped drinking and began to travel the country speaking to youth organizations and prison inmates. KLAC gm, Bill Ward, was the lightning rod behind getting him in radio during the 1970s. The country jock got the 1,168th Star on Hollywood's Walk of Fame in 1976. At the ceremony, as reported in the *LA Times*, Stuart said: "I've accepted Lord Jesus Christ, and what a difference Christianity can make in a man's life." Stuart died March 8, 1989, at the age of 90. He had lapsed into a coma after surgery to remove a malignant brain tumor.

HAMBLIN, Jim: **KRLA**. A native of Southern California, Jim began his radio career at KRLA, where he was a general assignment reporter. He later covered San Francisco City Hall for KCBS and the state Capitol beat for KCBS, KFBK-Sacramento and AP Radio. He worked briefly as a television newsman for KPIX-San Francisco. Jim died May 10, 1996, at his home in Roseville, where he had been confined to a wheelchair since 1995 suffering from diabetes. He was 59.

HAMILTON, Bob: **KHJ/FM**, 1977-79, om; **KRTH**, 1979-86, pd; **KHJ**, 1983-85, om. Born in 1947, Bob grew up in Philadelphia and started his first radio assignment at WBCB-Levittown, Pennsylvania, while still in high school in 1963. He owned Hamilton Communications, Inc. and was brought in from WIFI-Philadelphia, where he was pd, to change all-Oldies KRTH to Contemporary music. He was instrumental in bringing "K-Earth" to a "live" format after years of automation. In 1980 he added to his KRTH pd duties the responsibility of RKO national music coordinator. In 1981, he went on the air when London and Engelman left abruptly for KWST. In 1994, Bob became vp/gm of KSFO/KYA-San Francisco and in the summer of 1995 was upped to om of Crescent Communications' KYLD ("Wild 107")-San Francisco and KYLS/KSOL. Beginning in 1996, Bob took over the programming of KABL/KBGG. In a 1995 interview in *Gavin*, Bob reflected on his success: "Put research, ear and gut together along with a road map of where you want to go. Stop worrying about what's happening to the left or right of you and you'll reach your goal."

HAMILTON, Gary: **KMGG**, 1984-85. Born and raised in the San Fernando Valley, Gary attended Monroe High School, L.A. Valley College and Cal State Northridge. In the early 1970s he worked behind the scenes at KHJ and KFWB. He then moved to Bakersfield in 1973 to work at KBIS, KERN, KAFY and KUZZ. After a series of stations in Tucson (KHOS, KMGX and KRQQ), Gary moved to San Diego in 1979 and worked at KBZT and KFMB. While in San Diego, he did weekends and vacation relief for KMGG including vacation relief for Robert W. Morgan. Beginning in 1985 Gary worked for five years at WFYR and WTMX-Chicago. Since 1990 Gary has been working at Infinity's WLIF-Baltimore.

HAMILTON, Sean: **KIIS**, 1986-92; **KGGI**, 1993-95. Growing up in Nevada, he started his career as a teen with a makeshift studio in his bedroom. Sean combined Radio Shack equipment with his mom's stereo. He started professionally in Reno and then moved on to "Y107"-Long Branch, New Jersey and Florida. He started in New York at age 21. "Hollywood Hamilton" arrived at KIIS from WPLJ and WHTZ ("Z-100")-New York. He was a former regular on ABC/TV's soap, *One Life to Live*. He co-hosted *The Gong Show*. He got the "Hollywood" moniker not in Hollywood but while working in New York. He wore sunglasses and trendy clothes - thus the nickname. In 1988 he hosted *Flip*, a CBS Saturday morning kids show, with sidekick Dr. George Brothers. "Hollywood" got the Saturday morning tv job when the production executive was riding around town and heard him on the air at KIIS. In 1989 he was voted one of radio's sexiest voices by readers of *Radio Guide* magazine. In 1991, he got an opportunity to co-host ABC/TV's *Into the Night* and was the voice of Saturday morning Fox/TV. He had a live national show in the early 1990s. In late 1993, he headed for mornings at KGGI-Riverside where he stayed until late 1995. In the spring of 1996 he surfaced in the evenings at WKTU-New York.

HANCOCK, Bill: **KBCA**, 1968

HANCOCK, Hunter: **KFVD/KPOP**, 1954-57; **KGFJ**, 1957-66; **KBLA**, 1966. "Huntin' With Hunter" was the familiar cry every afternoon in the fifties and sixties. "Ol' HH" was born in Uvalde, Texas in 1915 and started in Los Angeles radio on KFVD in 1943. He started out playing jazz music, but after a record promoter persuaded Hunter to play two or three "race records" an hour, his popularity skyrocketed. From a daily half hour, he went to a peak of six hours a day, playing rhythm and blues and gospel music. In 1955 he hosted a television dance-party-type program called "Rhythm and Bluesville." It was the first time many -- maybe most -- of his fans realized something about him: the man who was turning on increasingly large numbers of white kids to the new black music was white. In a story by Harry Shearer in the *LA Times*, Hunter commented: "For a fellow from Texas, with a lot of Southern traditions instilled from birth, I was a little nervous when I started. I did get, on several occasions, shall we say, some adverse criticism from white people. They called me a nigger lover." In the 1950s, he started Swinging Records. Hunter would play tapes of local artists, and if the response was strong, he would release the song on his label. The first release was numbered 614 because he started in radio on June 14. He was one of the first to have a female on-air sidekick, Margi, and for many years, "Huntin' with Hunter" broadcast from his Hollywood office. Margi later became a local tv news anchor/reporter and married Tony Williams of the Platters. (Margi is now heard on KBIG as Morgan Williams.) During the '50s, he staged a talent show every Sunday afternoon at the Lincoln Theatre on Central Avenue in Los Angeles. In 1962 he was convicted on three counts of tax evasion. He was placed on five years' probation and given a suspended sentence of four years on each count. He had been accused of failing to report $18,000 allegedly collected from record distributors for giving air exposure to their discs. Hancock pleaded not guilty, claiming the amount in question consisted of cash gifts from the distributor and, as such, was not income, therefore not reported. In 1968, on the urging of his doctor, he retired. "I was taking three pills a day for my stomach and four tranquilizers a day, and I was living on antacids every third week. It was just too much for my poor ol' nerves." His pd at KGFJ called Hancock the "Lawrence Welk of r&b." Hancock successfully underwent a quadruple-pass heart surgery. He and his wife Dorothy bought a motor home and if they aren't traveling the country, they are at home in Fullerton.

> *"I am fulfilling a vicarious dream of probably hundreds of born-again Christians in radio. They're in news, announcing, Top 40...everywhere. But they've never had a place to call their own before, though I know they've all talked about. I spoke with many of them while researching this format."*
>
> *-Gary McCartie*

HANDEL, Bill: **KFI**, 1993-97. Born in 1952 Bill is a lawyer first, specializing in surrogate parenting, and a broadcaster second. Bill moved from evenings to morning

drive on KFI replacing Terri-Rae Elmer and Tracey Miller. His conservative view-oriented show is in contrast with most mornings filled with comedy, music and celebrity interviews. Each Saturday he hosts "Handel on the Law," two hours of legal advice. Bill is acknowledged as one of the leading reproductive legal experts in the world.

HANLEY, Jeff: **KLOS**, 1990. Jeff was a part-timer with the AOR station before leaving for Fresno. In the mid-1990s he worked middays at KTYD-Santa Barbara.

HANNING, Evan: **KRLA**, 1973-74. During a period of automation at KRLA, Evan and Johnny Hayes were the only personality voices.

HANSON, Mark: **KKHR**, 1983-86; **KEZY**, 1988. In 1987, Dancin' Mark Hanson was in El Paso before returning to the Southland on KEZY. When he left KEZY, Mark went to work in San Francisco radio (KXXX, KFRC and KYLD). In the 1990s, Mark had gone to KCBQ-San Diego as Mark Jagger.

HANSON, Patty: **KBIG**, 1995-96; **KOST**, 1996. Patty works middays at WW1's Hot Country format.

HARDEN, James: **KNAC**, 1972, gm

HARDWICK, Chris: **KROQ**, 1996-97. The host of MTV's *Singled Out* works the all-night shift at KROQ. Born in Louisville, Chris grew up in Southern California and was a philosophy major at UCLA. While at the Westwood campus he had a guest shot on *Studs*, which led to hosting MTV's *Trashed*. He's a master chess player.

HARMON, Jim: **KWIZ**, 1965, pd; **KDAY**, 1966, pd

HARMON, Pete: **KEZY**, 1982-83; **KNX/FM**, 1983; **KRTH**, 1984-85; **KNX/FM**, 1986; **KBIG**, 1994. Pete is currently a dealer at the MGM Grand in Las Vegas.

HARMON, Steve: Steve is the voice of UCLA football.

HARMON, Tom: **KABC**, 1968-69. The outstanding football player from Michigan dispensed sports commentary for a number of Southern California radio stations. He died in 1990. There were three who spoke at his funeral services: his blocker at Michigan; Al Davis; and Chuck Benedict.

HARRIS, Bob: **KPOL**, 1961-72. Bob worked morning drive at KPOL. He is deceased.

HARRIS, Doug: **KMET**, 1976. Doug did the all-night shift at "the Mighty Met."

HARRIS, "Frosty" Bruce: **KRLA**, 1959; **KIEV**, 1971-88. Frosty was one of the original KRLA "11-10 Men" on September 3, 1959, working the nine to midnight shift. He became an administrator at the El Monte Adult School and retired in 1992.

HARRIS, Gene: **KGFJ**, 1988. Gene was at XHRM-San Diego before coming to Los Angeles. He worked weekends at KGFJ.

HARRIS, George: **KMET**, 1985, pd. George arrived in February 1985 from pd of WMMR-Philadelphia. He resurrected some special features that were popular in the 1970s, including "Rock Wars," "Psychedelic Supper" and "Soul Patrol." George only stayed a few months before returning to Philadelphia to consult stations for Metromedia, which ironically would include KMET.

HARRIS, Gillian: **KJLH**; **KRLA**, 1984-91, nd; **KACE**, 1994-97. When Gillian worked at KJLH she experienced prejudice. The deep ebony-skinned dj was told that she would be pulled off the air "...if you don't sound more black. You sound white." She wondered, "How do you sound black?"

HARRIS, Michael: **KNOB**, 1986-87. Michael worked afternoon drive at KNOB.

HARRIS, Rahn: **KGRB**, 1975-77

Keith Olbermann received a $25,000 bonus from KCBS/Channel 2 for growing back his mustache. The station said it made him more recognizable to the masses.

He recalled how Jim Healy once reported that Keith had been "seen at Thrifty Drug in Hollywood buying cheap underwear." Keith responded by sending Jim an autographed pair of shorts.

The Big Show, co-written by Keith Olbermann

HARRISON and **TYLER**: **KGBS**, 1972. While Hudson and Landry performed their comedy act for Nevada Club patrons, the team of Harrison and Tyler worked the morning shift at KGBS in 1972. In the *LA Times*, Don Page commented, "We don't know how far they're setting women's lib back, but surely not as far as they're setting back radio. They have virtually no discipline and they are not funny." Page said they sounded like a couple of New York secretaries on a coffee break. Pat Harrison was a $50,000 a year high fashion model with spreads in *Vogue* and *Harper's Bazaar*. Robin Tyler was a singer in a New York nightclub. They met one night when Pat responded from the audience to something Robin said and they quipped back and forth. The audience loved it and a comedy act was born. Two women working together was unique for the time, "My measurements are 21-21-21-21...Oh yeah? What's the last 21 for?...My IQ!" After their try-out on KGBS they tried the college circuit and they were never heard from again.

HARRISON, Jeff: **KACD**, 1994-95. Jeff arrived in the Southland in late 1994 from KDIA-San Francisco and he did the all-night shift. Jeff is now working for an Urban station in Houston.

HARRISON, Jim: **KLAC**, **XTRA**; **KWOW**; **KFI**, 1971, pd. Jim was last heard at KOGO-San Diego.

HARRISON, Mike: **KMET**, 1975-85, pd. Since 1990 Mike has been the publisher of *TALKERS Magazine*, the leading publication for Talk radio. In the early 1970s,

Mike was morning man at WNEW/FM-New York. Prior to that he was the first pd and creator of the legendary Long Island underground rocker, WLIR. He has been credited with coining the phrase "AOR" while he programmed KPRI-San Diego. Mike was the first managing editor of *R&R*. While at KMET, he conducted a decade-long weekend two-hour talk show, "Harrison's Mike," which many consider to be one of the major forerunners of today's emerging "youth talk." He became president and director of Goodphone Communications, a production/publishing and consultancy company he formed in 1978, which is still the umbrella company at the center of his projects today. In the early 1980s he served as editorial consultant to *Billboard* helping the publication revamp its chart methodology and wrote a weekly radio column. In October 1983, he was made pd of KMET. In 1986, his Goodphone Communications began to develop a nationally syndicated Talk format called "Supertalk" to revive flagging AM stations. At this time he bought and operated WSPR-Springfield, Massachusetts. He is the host of the publication's nationally syndicated weekly radio spin-off, "The Talk Radio Countdown Show." Mike is regularly heard on his many visits to the nation's capital as a talk show host on WWRC-Washington, DC.

HART, Ed: **KHJ**, 1959; **KFWB**, 1978-86; **KNX**, 1988-94. Ed reported the local business reports on "news/98," KFWB. He broadcast the financial news free-lance from a local investment company. Ed died in the mid-1990s.

HART, John: **KPOL**, 1959-61. John was a newsman at KPOL who went on to the NBC network.

HART, John L.: **KKOP**, 1972-73; **KEZY**, 1973-75. John was born and raised in San Pedro. His love affair with radio began with an impromptu visit with his father to the KFWB studios in 1959 when he was 11 years old. Taking a tour of the station and seeing Elliot Field on the air fueled the excitement to enter radio. That same year, John received a Webcor tape recorder and started "playing radio." Since those early days, he has assembled a full-service in-home production studio, thousands of 45's and LP's. After a successful career in retail, John took the plunge with radio starting at KKOP after quiz master Jack Barry bought the station to reenter broadcasting. John's greater success came in sales at KEZY and station management at KUIC-Vacaville. After being sales manager at KMBY-Monterey, John left radio for a business franchise. For the past 15 years he has taught communication and business courses at Fullerton College. In the mid-1990s he joined the teaching staff at Saddleback College in Mission Viejo. "It gives me great pleasure in sharing experiences with students who have the passion to enter broadcasting." In 1989, John segued from radio to tv production working as an audio operator for Witt-Thomas Productions and has worked on *The Golden Girls*, *Empty Nest*, and *Blossom*. For the past three years he has been the sound recordist for TriStar working on *Mad About You* and *Ned & Stacey*. John still has a love

for radio and is presently working on a book about the history of Crowell-Collier Broadcasting Corporation with emphasis on the KFWB years, 1958-63. His mother formed the Joe Yocam fan club in 1962. He is always looking for friends or relatives who worked for Crowell-Collier to contact him.

HART, Tony: **KGFJ**, 1989-96, pd. The former morning man and pd at Urban KGFJ left for a sports job with WCNN-Atlanta and an FM jazz station.

HART, Tanya: **KACE**, 1996-97. Tanya reports entertainment news for KACE. She is a veteran television host and commentator. Tanya is a correspondent and substitute host of E! Entertainment's *The Gossip Show*. From 1990 to 1992 she served as host and senior producer of Black Entertainment Television's *Live from L.A. with Tanya Hart*. Prior to BET Tanya spent 11 years with WBZ/TV-Boston as host and contributing producer of a news magazine series. She started her career at WKAR-East Lansing while earning a B.A. in tv and radio broadcast from Michigan State University. Tanya went to the graduate school of education at Harvard University.

HARTMAN, Steve: **KFOX**, 1990; **XTRA**, 1990. Steve hosted sports shows during his time in Southern California radio.

HARVE, "Humble": **KBLA**, 1965-67, pd; **KHJ**, 1967-71; **KIQQ**, 1973; **KKDJ**, 1974; **KIIS**, 1975-76; **KUTE**, 1980; **KRLA**, 1981-82 and 1985-86, pd and 1988-91; **KRTH**, 1991-92; **KCBS**, 1992-93; **KZLA**, 1996-97. Born Harvey Miller, "Humble Harve" started his radio journey when he was 17. He arrived in Southern California from a Top 40 powerhouse, WIBG, in his birth city of Philadelphia. He started at KBLA where he was an on-air pd. While at KHJ, Harvey said, "I realized my greatest achievement of a 21.0 share doing 6 p.m. to 9 p.m." Harve underlined that it was a 21.0 and not a 2.1. By 1971, Harve was working on AFRTS. In 1974 he was part of the KKDJ launch. In October 1975, KKDJ became KIIS/FM. In 1983 he hosted the syndicated "National Album Countdown" show. Harve had a brief stay in 1985 at Oldies WFIL-Philadelphia. In 1986 he worked at KVI-Seattle. Harve was the dj in the 1991 movie, *There Goes My Baby*. In the same year he hosted the syndicated "Rock 'n Gold" for 350 WW1 affiliates. In a 1993 *LA Times* interview, Harve commented, "Life at KHJ in the '60s was like New Year's Eve every night. We played happy, fun music. The music was inspired. It was the poetry of a generation. They used real instruments, instead of electronic crap. Milli Vanilli could never have happened then." Since the mid-1990s, Harve has run a very successful mobile dj business. In the spring of 1996, Harve joined KZLA for weekends.

93.1FM	
1976-83	KNX/FM "mellow rock"
1983-86	KKHR "hit radio 93"
1986-89	KNX/FM "quality rock"
1989-92	KODJ "oldies 93"
1992-93	KCBS/FM "CBS/FM"
1993-97	KCBS/FM "arrow 93"

HARVEY, Alan: **KNOB**, 1959-61; **KPOL**, 1961-70; **KIIS**, 1970-72; **KPOL**, 1973-76; **KDAY**, 1978-81; **KPOL**, 1981-84; **KLON**, 1982-89; **KMNY**, 1987-88; **KPFK**, 1991-95.

A newsman and political commentator, Alan visited KPOL three times. Born Albert Hoefeld II in Chicago, October 8, 1927, he graduated from Northwestern with a speech major in 1948. He started out in Evanston and was a staff announcer for a Chicago tv station until he was blacklisted for helping organize the talent union, TVA (Television Authority which was the forerunner to AFTRA). Alan left the cold for sunny Southern California and stayed for the long haul. He hosted a jazz show on KNOB and moved into news on November 4, 1961, and anchored the news for over three decades. "'I am not about to go gently into that good night,' but I've probably come to an end in radio," Alan said during the summer of 1996. His love for political commentary and jazz (his dog is named Swing) is outstripped by a passion for movies. In the mid-1980s Alan worked for Dr. Armand Hammer at Occidental Petroleum. At KLON he hosted "Saturday Evening Jazz" with records from his own massive jazz collection. This movie buff comes alive when talking films, especially those of close friend William A. Wellman, the late motion picture director. Alan remembered a line from John Chancellor when talking about his radio career, "I have outlived my culture."

HARVEY, Bob: **KFWB**, 1984-96; **KIKF**, 1995-96, pd; **KZLA**, 1996-97. Bob joined KIKF in the fall of 1995 for afternoon drive from hosting the PBS/TV show *Country Connection*, a country music video show that airs in 50 markets. He is a 20-year veteran Riverside/San Bernardino personality, mostly at KCKC. In late 1995 he was promoted to pd of KIKF and left in the summer of 1996 and now works afternoon drive at KZLA. At KFWB Bob was a sports anchor. He has also done play-by-play sports on radio and television for Cal State Fullerton, San Bernardino Spirit of the California League and Little League Baseball Western Region radio network.

HARVEY, Boyd: **KNX**, 1966-96. After almost 30 years with KNX, the station didn't even throw a farewell party when Boyd left in early 1996. Perhaps the oversight is related to the environment of mergers and how people are treated. In this case Boyd left on his own. Born in 1926 the native Nebraskan worked at WKNX-Saginaw, KWBE-Beatrice, Nebraska, and WIND-Chicago before arriving at KNX which was all-Talk in 1966. An Orange County resident, Boyd began the KNX Orange County bureau in 1973. Gary Lycan of the *OC Register* profiled Boyd: "Crusty. Cantankerous. To many, he's old-fashioned. He writes his copy on an Olympia manual typewriter. KNX shipped him an Olivetti electronic typewriter. He never opened the box. He has never used a computer, either." His co-workers were in praise of the generous help he gave to new reporters. Why did he retire? "I just woke up one morning at 3:30 and said, 'Why am I doing this?' Now some people said I should have retired a long time ago. But really, it just got to me, going to work on weekends and at 4 o'clock in the morning two days a week. It was time." Boyd is divorced and the father of five daughters and said that he was looking forward to spending more time with his family and playing golf.

HARVEY, Phil: **KMPC/FM**, 1988; **KSRF**, 1991

HARVEY, Rudy: **KDAY**, 1965; **KGFJ**. Rudy had his own record labels, Dynamic and Titanic. He had one major hit, *Moments To Remember* by Jennell Hawkins.

HARWELL, Ernie: **KMPC**, 1992. Ernie, who spent 32 years with the Detroit Tigers, worked fill-in broadcasting for the California Angels.

HASICK, Scott: **KFI**, 1994-97. Scott joined KFI in February 1994. He teamed with Casey Bartholomew for an evening weekend Talk show on KFI. In the spring of 1997 the pair went to sister Talk station in Orlando for afternoon drive.

HASS, Karl: **KUSC**. For 30 years, Karl has hosted the syndicated "Adventures in Good Music" (he never called it Classical Music). He earned a Ph.d.

HATTEN, Tom: **KNX**, 1986-97. Tom was the popular host of the *Popeye* show on KTLA/Channel 5 and

entertainment reporter on "KNXNewsradio." Born in 1927 in North Dakota, he grew up in Idaho and joined the Navy just before the end of World War II. Tom attended the Pasadena Playhouse School for the Theatre on the GI Bill and graduated cum laude in 1950. During an appearance in one of tv's earliest shows, *Space Patrol*, Tom was discovered and joined KTLA as a "utility infielder" with Stan Chambers. He spent the next four decades on the local scene as a composer, announcer, commercial pitchman, writer and pop and jazz concert producer. From 1978 to 1991 every weekend Tom hosted the "Family Film Festival" on KTLA. He is a member of five industry unions.

HAULE, Tom: **KNX**, 1987-97. Tom is one of the morning news anchors at all-News KNX. He graduated from Northern Illinois University and started his broadcasting career at WOLI-Ottawa, Illinois. Tom worked for a couple of CBS stations, including WBBM-Chicago and KCBS-San Francisco before joining KNX.

HAVEN, Patty: **KEZY**, 1975

HAWKINS, Tom B.: **KGFJ**, 1965, pd

HAWKINS, Tommy: **KABC/KLOS**, 1970-85; **KKGO**. The Fighting Irish basketball Hall of Famer and one-time Laker worked tv sports in the early 1970s on

KABC/Channel 7. Tommy started as host of a teenage talk show called *Youth and the Issues* on KNBC/Channel 4 which he hosted during his last two years with the Lakers. For four years he was a sportscaster for Channel 4 working with Ross Porter, Jess Marlow, Tom Brokaw, Tom Snyder, Paul Moyer and Kelly Lange. When he left KNBC he succeeded Regis Philbin as host of KHJ/Channel 9's *Tempo Morning Show*. He also hosted Channel 7's *Day Break*. He was replaced in 1973 by Bryant Gumbel. In the mid-1980s Tommy was the tv announcer for the L.A. Clippers. During his time on KABC he was sports director and worked in morning drive with the "Ken and Bob Company." Tommy talked about his time at KABC: "I created 'Dodger Forecast,' 'Dodger Confidential' and 'Baseball Spotlight.'" He also hosted "Sports Talk" and "Dodger Talk." On KABC's sister station, KLOS, Tommy created and performed "Sports Snorts" with Frazer Smith which continued after Mark and Brian arrived. He left KABC in 1985 after a 15-year association. In 1987 Tommy hosted *Midmorning L.A.* on Channel 9 with Meredith McRae and later Stephanie Edwards. He also had a four-year stint as host of *Nine In*

The Morning show. Tommy is currently vice president of communications with the L.A. Dodgers. "I am the only person in Los Angeles broadcast history to have done television talk, sports and music on a weekly schedule basis."

HAWTHORNE, Darr: **KPFK**, 1971. The son of Jim Hawthorne hosted a "rock and stuff" show called "Mr. Saturday Night." He has been in the tv commercial production business since 1969 as a producer and sales representative. Darr's one-year radio stint was done simultaneously with his career in tv production.

HAWTHORNE, Jim: **KXLA**, 1943-48; **KECA**, 1948-49; **KDAY**, 1959; **KFWB**, 1960-63, pd; **KHJ**, 1962-63; **KIEV**, 1991. Jim started at KXLA-Pasadena (now KRLA).

His humor established him as a unique broadcaster in the early days of personality radio, yet his major success came from television. In 1950, he created, produced and starred in the Saturday night coast-to-coast radio program, "The Hawthorne Thing," which was the final network radio show to originate in NBC's Hollywood Radio City. At KLAC/Channel 13 in the early 1950s, he created the first late evening talk show on television, *This Is Hawthorne*. An article in the *LA Times* reflecting on early tv described the show as "predecessor of NBC's *Saturday Night Live*." On KNBC/Channel 4, beginning in 1952, he did a daily five-minute weather show. In 1958, Jim traveled to KYA-San Francisco and created "Voice Your Choice," which he brought to KDAY. In the early 1960s, while doing *Instant Weather* on KTTV/Channel 11, Hawthorne joined KFWB as assistant pd and mornings, and eventually became vp, national program manager for Crowell-Collier Broadcasting. While still at KFWB he joined Sherman Grinberg Productions as a writer, producer, narrator. He produced *Jim Hawthorne's Funny World*. In 1965, "ol Weather Eyes" moved to Honolulu to "retire" and ended up creating the *Checkers and Pogo* kids show for tv which ran for 11 years. He was also involved with programming KGMB -Honolulu and was creative consultant to morning legend Aku. As one of his bits, since the tv weather was so short, he would hold up cards and do a pantomime. He was elected president of the newly formed Disc Jockey Association in 1960. In 1970, Jim moved back to his hometown, Denver, to help his ailing mother. He stayed for 11 years and established a very successful career at KOA, eventually becoming gm. In the late 1980s, Jim returned to Southern California and currently is completing his autobiography, *Funny Stuff That Happened to Me -- by Hawthorne -- Jim, not Nathaniel*. He has been writing a weekly "at large" newspaper column for a group of San Diego North County papers. He is also preparing a pilot for a return to television and re-editing *Funny World* into half-hour programs for cable networks.

HAYDEL, Janine: **KJLH**, 1995-97. Janine co-hosts the morning show on KJLH with Cliff Winston.

She was born Janine Zenon in Los Angeles and attended local private schools. Janine obtained a degree in business administration and accounting from Cal State Dominguez Hills. From 1982 to 1994 she worked for various corporations as in internal auditor. In 1994 Janine decided to fulfill a dream and study broadcast journalism. She interned at Continental Cablevision while attending Santa Monica College. Janine and her husband Michael married in June 1996 following his proposal on the air during her radio show.

Bonneville International Corporation (owned by the Mormon Church) purchases KBIG AM&FM on March 11, 1969.

On December 1, 1971, the FM station call letters were changed to KXTZ.

On August 12, 1974, the FM call letters were changed back to KBIG.

KYMS' blend of personality radio and Christian music came to end with the final song, "Friends" by Michael W. Smith. There was a prayer, then silence.

HAYDEN, Zirn: **KVFM**; **KMET**, 1975. "Z" did weekend work at "the Mighty Met" and is now doing voiceover work.

HAYES, Bruce: **KFWB**, 1958-61; **KDAY**, 1962; **KHJ**, 1963-64; **KFWB**, 1965-67; **KFI**, 1969. Bruce was the original morning drive personality on Chuck Blore's KFWB "Color Radio" debut on January 2, 1958. "Bright-

eyed and bushy tailed Uncle Bruce" worked as one of the "Seven Swingin' Gentlemen" into 1961. His signature sign-off was "Excelsior." After being discharged from the paratroopers, Bruce attended radio school in his hometown of Dallas, worked as an announcer in Corpus Christi and as a dj on WRR-Dallas where Gordon McLendon heard him and hired him to do the night shift at KLIF. When Bruce substituted for a couple of weeks as the morning-drive man, his irreverent humor touched the funnybone of early morning commuters. The station's ratings shot up and Bruce remained on the morning shift until he left Dallas to become the morning man at KFWB. He and Bea Shaw, whom he had known since grade school in Dallas, married and moved to the Southland in 1958. Bea, who had her own tv show in Dallas, went to work at KFWB as "Tiger," the sexy-voiced traffic information girl, who would banter with Bruce during his morning drive show on KFWB. The two also worked together during the '60s and '70s on radio commercials Bea wrote and produced, including award-winning campaigns for the Plymouth Barracuda and Western Airlines. Bruce acted in episodes of *Hunter* and *General Hospital*. His tv commercials for Clorox, in which Bruce surprised housewives in a laundromat by saying, "I'll give you $50 for that t-shirt" (and then tearing it in half, washing one half in you-know-what) were so successful that standup comics all over the country did take-offs on it. Bruce died November 20, 1994, of cancer. *Excelsior, Uncle Bruce.*

HAYES, Casey: **KWIZ**, 1978-79; **KUTE**, 1979-80; **KJOI**, 1983-86; **KWVE**, 1989-90; **KLIT**, 1993. Born and raised in Anaheim, Casey attended Anaheim High School and Fullerton Community College. He started his disc jockey career at KERN-Bakersfield. Casey worked afternoon drive during his stint at "K-Joy." Between dj stops, he worked the satellite services including Soft AC format at WW1. He currently has a successful voiceover career in Los Angeles, Orange County and San Diego working mostly narrations for non-broadcast productions. Casey is a stage actor in local theater and has written two stage plays for church productions.

HAYES, Jack: **KFWB**, 1964-65. Born February 14, 1940, in Hinsdale, Illinois, his first radio experience was as a child actor at WOPA-Oak Park, Illinois. When Jack's voice changed in his early teens he became summer relief announcer at KGON-Portland and by 15 was a jock at KEX-Portland. In 1960 he joined KLIV-San Jose and stayed four years. "I quit because they wouldn't give me more money." When he left the Southland, he became King Jack Hayes at

KCBQ-San Diego. Along the way he married a *Playboy* bunny. In 1968 Jack was part of KNEW-Oakland followed by afternoons at KNBR-San Francisco. In early 1973 his wife died and Jack dropped out of radio until 1989 when he was hired to anchor the morning news and program XTRA-San Diego. Since 1991 he has been consulting sports/talk radio stations. In the summer of 1997 Jack returned to the Southland.

> *"If an airplane loses its power, it becomes a glider. If a helicopter loses its power, it becomes a rock."*
>
> —Herb Green

HAYES, Johnny: **KRLA**, 1965-68 and 1969-71; **KDAY**, 1971; **KRLA**, 1971-92; **KRTH**, 1992-97. Johnny was

born March 10, 1939, and grew up in Macon. He started his radio career in his home state and was known as Danny Daye. His first job was on WNEX-Macon. Bill Drake was programming WAKE-Louisville, and he hired Johnny on his 21st birthday. By the time he moved to California in the early 1960s, he changed his name to Johnny Hayes to work all-nights at KYA-San Francisco. Johnny arrived at KRLA in 1965 from San Diego, where he was #1 in the afternoons as a KGBeach Boy, while Drake was consulting the station. Johnny might have gone to KHJ in the embryonic "Boss Radio" days if not for an oath that Bill Drake took not to raid any more jocks from KGB-San Diego after stealing Gary Mack and Johnny Williams. For decades lunch was never lunch without Johnny's countdown show. In 1973, KRLA experimented with MOR and teams in every shift, and Johnny teamed with Lee Simms for morning drive. In 1984 he won *Billboard*'s Personality of the Year and was the only non-morning drive winner that year. Upon receiving the award he was quoted as saying: "I can function within any format. If they give me 20 seconds of my own personal time between records, I'm gonna try to make every word count and try to say something that touches somebody and has some meaning."

HAYES, Kate: **KLSX**, 1989-90. Kate grew up in the San Francisco Bay Area and worked for KTIM and KSAN before heading to the Southland. She teamed with David Perry on KLSX when Peter Tilden left the morning show. Kate was the sole female voice on KTLA/Channel 5 for many years. Her husband David Hayes plays bass for Van Morrison. Kate works with former Southern California personality Tom Yates for a station in the Santa Rosa area.

HAYNES, Dick: **KLAC**, 1945-58; **KXLA**, 1958; **KLAC**, 1959-66; **KFOX**, 1966-71; **KLAC**, 1971-80. "Haynes at the Reins" was part of the Southern California radio landscape for 34 years, mostly at KLAC. A specialist in the one-line joke, he was thought of as the Henny Youngman of country radio - the Thief of Bad Gags. "You're too bowlegged to round up cattle...you can't get your calves together," he'd say. He had a qualitative range of *Hee Haw*'s best and Milton Berle's worst: "Why, I use so much of that perfume that I once got arrested for fragrancy." Dick was born in Beaumont, Texas and never canned the country corn. In 1945 he joined KLAC the first of three times as one of the "Big Five." In 1958 KLAC reacted to "Color Radio" at KFWB with a similar change to "Formula Radio," and Dick went to Country KXLA, which was only a year away from a format change and call letter change to KRLA. His on-air philosophy was simple: "I never want to give the listener the impression that I'm a smart aleck. I want them to feel superior to me - I think they like you better that way." In 1969 Dick won the Top Country Air Personality Award from *Billboard*. In 1971 the pd of KFOX moved to KLAC and brought Dick with him. One of the consistent expectations in getting up each morning and listening to Dick was that the airwaves would be filled with dumb jokes: "I know a man so dumb he thinks Shirley Temple is a place to worship" or

"Chill Will's mother said when her son was born, 'I just had a chill'" or "Have you ever been to Wedlock, Texas? Yeah, well, Gumdrop was born a little out of wedlock." Some of his other regular characters included Sir Chester Drawers and Wilhemina Mildew. In 1976 he signed on as a regular on tv's *Hee-Haw*. Dick was called on for many personal appearances and newsman Art Blaske remembered: "Dick was a real pro and he had to rehearse his lines. He would come into the newsroom and go through his whole act." Dick played bit parts in a number of films, including *The Phantom Planet*, a low budget science fiction epic that is perhaps best known for being Francis X. Bushman's last starring vehicle. Dick played a space jockey. He left his on-air chores at KLAC in early 1980. In April of that year a testimonial dinner was held for Dick by his friends at the Hollywood Palladium, and it was announced that Metromedia was establishing a Dick Haynes Scholarship Fund for Radio Broadcasting. In August, he had a Star dedicated on the Hollywood Boulevard Walk of Fame. On November 24, 1980, he died of cancer at the age of 69 at the Motion Picture Television Country Home and Hospital in Woodland

Hills. As Gumdrop would say every morning, "What time is it?" It was a good time, Dick.

HAYS, Quay: **KROQ**, 1983

HEALY, Jerry: **KMPC**, 1987-88. Jerry and Ed Brand shared middays sandwiched between Robert W. Morgan and the Joel Meyers sports talk show. Jerry works the Adult format at WW1.

HEALY, Jim: **KBIG**; **KMPC**, 50s; **KLAC**, 1961-65; **KFWB**, 1969; **KABC**; 1969-84; **KLAC**, 1973-82; **KMPC**, 1984-94. A one-of-a-kind sportscaster in Los Angeles for 43 years, Jim died July 22, 1994, at age 70 from complications of liver cancer. He began at KMPC in 1950, fresh out of UCLA, writing for broadcaster Bob Kelley. Jim wrote for Bob for 11 years. He hosted "Here's Healy" on KBIG and also worked at KFWB, KABC and KLAC. Jim was the nightly sports reporter on KABC/Channel 7 with a team that featured former County Supervisor Baxter Ward and Rona Barrett. He returned to KMPC in 1984. The veteran sports commentator left the air May 1, 1994, when KMPC switched from Sports to Talk. His illness was a well-kept secret. His son Patrick is a field reporter for KNBC/Channel 4. Inspired by Steve Harvey of the *LA Times* a heavenly broadcast from up above. The show begins with the strains of a song...

Healy: How do you do? I'm Jim Healy on K-H-V-N, K-Heaven. Dateline Pearly Gates
Ray Charles: Georgia, Georgia...
Healy: Carroll Rosenbloom's heavenly Los Angeles Rams. Excuse me, St. Louis Rams.
Howard Cosell: Who goofed? I've got to know.
Unidentified voice: Yeah, I did.
Healy: No, I did, you twit. The fans at the Heavenly Bowl were ecstatic about the win.
Benoit Benjamin: I don't give (bleep) about the fans.
Healy: Yes, we know, Benoit. Anyway, when the team moved from Anaheim to St. Louis to Heaven...
Tim Conway: Get to the point will you, Jim?
Healy: All right, all right, I'm trying. When a team loses its popular owner, the fans become upset!
Charles Barkley: Bad team, man. Bad (bleeping) team.
Cosell imitator: Jim Healy, you've got a sick show.
Healy: Angels beat the Mariners by 10 points. Tagline. A press box comic quipped: They musta thought they were playing Bo Derek. Gave 'em a 10.
Cosell imitator: I don't think that's funny.
Healy: Me neither, but I promised my butcher I'd use it.
Vin Scully: I can't beee-lieve it.
Healy: Dateline Hollywood. Whatever happened to female sportscaster Jayne Kennedy?
Song: You've come a long way baby.
Healy: Stay tuned. Kennedy grew up near the river in San Antonio.
Superfan Ed Beiler: And of course, San Antonio has the river, the San, what is the name of the river that goes through...? The San Antonio River goes through the heart of downtown Los Angeles.
Cosell: Who goofed? I've got to know.
Johnny Carson: I thought it was (bleeping) brilliant.

Healy: Dateline Chavez Ravine. Was the circus in town or are the Dodgers that bad?
Jerome Brown: We didn't come here to act monkeys for everybody.
Lasorda: This job is not that (bleeping) easy.
Healy: Dateline Indianapolis. Bobby Knight has never had a monkey on his team.
Knight: I forgot more about this (bleeping) game than all you people combined are ever going to know.
Nixon imitator: That's just plain poppycock.
Voice: Riiiight!
Chick Hearn: We've got to get off the air.
Healy: You mean the dreaded 6 o'clock tone is coming up? Then let's pause to savor it.
(Sound of tone.)
Healy: Now we can relax again. Dateline Toluca Lake. At the monthly sportscasters luncheon the other day, Silver-Tipped Stu, the man who never met a meal he didn't like, was asked by Dodger coach Billy Russell "What do you think is under more strain, the cables on the Golden Gate bridge or the suspenders on Stu Nahan's pants?"
Cosell imitator: Jim Healy, that's your lowest shot ever.
Healy: You might be right about that. Jim Healy. Good night.

"Is it true?" became one of his trademark lines. His headstone at Hollywood Hills Forest Lawn reads: "Jim Healy, 1923-94, IT IS TRUE." KMPC gm remembered the day that Jim came to work and was so happy to have found a plot next to a sidewalk. He wanted people to see it! In 1997 he was inducted into the Southern California Sports Broadcasters Hall of Fame.

HEARN, Chick: **KLAC**. Since 1959, Chick has been the voice of the L.A. Lakers on radio and tv. The former host of *Bowling for Dollars*, he was inducted into the American Sportscaster Hall of Fame, was the third broadcaster elected to the Basketball Hall of Fame and he received a Star on the Hollywood Walk of Fame. "Put a game in the refrigerator," signifying when the game outcome was locked, came from his 83-year-old grandfather who misplaced things around the house and later discovered them in the refrigerator. Born Francis Hearn, Chick graduated from Bradley University. In the early 1950s he worked in Peoria alongside veteran tv anchor Jerry Dunphy. Sometime during the 1997-98 season, he will broadcast his 3,000th consecutive Laker game. Chick was a college and high school referee for about eight years before becoming a broadcaster. Who will ever forget his one sentence: "Wraparounddribbledrivefallawayprayer!" In 1997 he was named top radio play-by-play announcer by the Southern California Sports Broadcasters Association.

HEATHERTON, Dick: **KFI**, 1986; **KMPC**, 1987; **KJOI**, 1989, pd; **KOCM**, 1989-90; **KXEZ**, 1991; **KCBS**, 1992; **KACD**. Born in Manhattan, Dick was surrounded by a show business family. His father Ray was a band leader and singer and introduced *Where or When* and *My Funny Valentine* from the Rodgers and Hart Show, *Boys From Syracuse*. His father worked at WNBC and WOR-New York and was on the CBS Network hosting a children's tv show. During his schooling at Long Island University and after graduation, Dick worked on two Long Island radio stations. Dick went to WPOP-Hartford in 1968 where he was known as "Happy Dick" Heatherton. He later moved to WFIL-Philadelphia, KLIF-Dallas and then WCBS-New York where he worked for 14 years. In 1986, Dick concluded: "If I have to play *Will You Love Me Tomorrow* one more time..." He came to Southern California and had a series of jobs beyond his dj work. He was a cruise director, got into sales at KLOK-San Jose, worked at Transtar, was gm of a group of stations in Pennsylvania "200 miles from nowhere," ran a real estate business and sold cars. The brother of actress-singer, Joey Heatherton, Dick worked for WW1's ACII format and was the gsm for KACD.

HECKLER, Bob: **KABC**, 1995-96; **KMPC**, 1996. Bob worked evenings on the Talk facility, KMPC. He arrived in the Southland in 1995 from Denver where he was the host of the only secular talk show on Christian KNUS. He spent time in the Navy before getting into the business world. The conservative radio personality was a former chemical, magazine and cable company executive. In January 1996, Bob moved between sister Talk stations to join KMPC in the midday slot. He lives in the South Bay area with his teenage son. He is also a licensed airplane and helicopter pilot. Bob left KMPC in the summer of 1996.

HEFTEL, Richard: **KTNQ/KLVE**, 1994-97, gm. Richard worked at family-owned Hawaii legend KSSK before becoming president and gm of KTNQ/KLVE. He was born October 7, 1959, in Denver and grew up in Honolulu. Richard served a two-year mission for the Church of Jesus Christ of Latter Day Saints and graduated from Brigham Young University in 1983.

HEIDE, Tami: **KROQ**, 1991-97. Tami came to the Southland from KROQ's sister station WBCN-Boston. Born July 23 in New Kensington, Pennsylvania, she graduated from Framingham North High School in Massachusetts. Tami has an extensive history in Boston College radio at Emerson's WERS and M.I.T.'s WMBR, where she was music director. She managed and was the record buyer for Newbury Comics, Boston's alternative record store. Tami did the evening shift at 'BCN and was assistant music director. She works middays at "the Roq."

HEIFETZ, Louise: **KFAC**, 1986, gm

HELLER, David: **KLOS**; **KWST**, 1980-81, nd; **KMPC**, 1984

HELLER, Hugh: **KMPC**, 1961-63, pd

HELLMAN, Bob: **KLSX**, 1995. Bob teamed with Kato Kaelin for the launch of KLSX's attempt at non-traditional talk with a format called "Real Radio." He left a few months later.

> *Who were your heroes?*
> *"My late grandfather and uncle. Ted Turner, Mario Cuomo, Stanley Kubrick and Tori Spelling."*   *-Top Ten personality*
> *"Sweet Dick" Whittington*

HELTON, Lon: **KHJ**, 1980-83, pd. Lon was born on the south side of Chicago and grew up as a teenager in the 1960s listening to WLS and WCFL. He earned a B.S. in chemistry at South Monmouth College in Illinois. In between graduation and the start of graduate school, he joined a local Beautiful Music station, WVPC, for the 5 p.m. to midnight shift. This was the beginning of his radio career. He went to Galesburg, Illinois, where he worked four hours on the FM and then four hours on the AM. He very innocently entered *Billboard's* Personality of the

Year competition. He didn't win but one of the judges ended up hiring him at KLAK-Denver. It was in Denver that he met Charlie Cook who was on in the evenings as Bob Clayton. In 1975 he was working with Bob Pittman at WMAQ-Chicago. In 1980, Charlie Cook hired Lon to program KHJ from Rock to Country. The format was to kick-off in November 1980, but a premature announcement two months earlier resulted in confusion in the marketplace and KZLA made a switch to Country within 30 days, blunting KHJ's Country format debut. Lon was going to work afternoon drive at the start of the Country format in November, however, when Rick Dees left in September, Lon worked the mornings as Scott Jeffreys (his brother's first and middle names)."I wasn't about to replace Rick Dees on the air. He had a strong loyal audience and I didn't want to be the recipient of the hate mail, so I created Scott Jeffreys." Lon commented to *Billboard* after his first rating book, "We've changed the music. We're playing album cuts and music right out of the box, really early. We've brought the temp way up and we're a little bit more country. We're taking chances on records." After three-and-a-half years in Los Angeles, he went to Nashville and has been the *R&R* Country editor for almost a decade. He hosts two syndicated radio shows, "Country Countdown, USA" and "Country World" for SJS in New York.

HEMINGWAY, Carole: **KABC**, 1974-82; **KGIL**, 1986-

93. Carole started at KABC on August 8, 1974, the night Nixon resigned from the Presidency and flew off in the official U.S. helicopter. She was an evening talk host covering current issues on KABC while writing a bi-weekly column for the *Los Angeles Times* syndicate. In 1974 the *Times* ran a profile of Carole and described her as "intelligent, unhaltingly self-assured and possessed of a combustible laugh. She has a kind of unimposing chic - alternately reserved and gregarious, soft and commanding." At KGIL, she hosted a talk show in afternoon drive. In 1989 Carole started a media training and media consulting company. Carole discussed the talk radio listener in an *Times* Op-Ed piece in 1991: "Forget the stereotype of lonely people with nothing to do. They are active people with a lot to do." A native of San Francisco, Carole earned a degree in international relations from Stanford and worked as an actress at the American Conservatory Theatre. She moved to Phoenix with her husband in the early 1970s and started her radio journey at KPHX. In 1974, with her marriage on the rocks and KPHX switching to a Spanish-language format, she applied to KABC and was hired. Carole is the president of the Hemingway Media Group, based in Beverly Hills.

HEMINGWAY, Frank: **KABC**. When Don Page of the *LA Times* listed the best radio of 1968, he said: "Frank Hemingway is a constant reminder of how news should be handled and delivered in an authoritative and honest manner." He is remembered for his Folger's Coffee commercials: "Good to the last drop." One of his colleagues reminiscenced about what a great salesman he was while delivering White King commercials. Frank passed away in the early 1990s.

> Former KJLH owner, John Lamar Hill, also owned a funeral parlor

HENDERSON, Brother: **XERB**, 1968; **XPRS**, 1972; **KGFJ**, 1973. Brother Henderson was also head of Cadet Records.

HENDERSON, Jr., Steve: **KKGO**, 1989; **KKJZ**, 1990; **KACE**, 1992; **KJQI**, 1993; **KKGO**, 1993-97. "I was born May 26, 1946, by the river (near Philadelphia) in a little tent and just like that river I've been running ever since." Steve's father moved to New York to pursue a career in opera and Steve grew up in the Bronx graduating from Bronx Community College and Evelyn Neinken Drama School. He came to the Southland to attend Los Angeles Broadcasters School. Steve is a classically trained baritone and sang and played piano with contemporary bands in New York and California. He is working the overnight shift at Classical KKGO. Steve has written several commercials, industrial shorts and documentaries, including "Gangs, An American Nightmare." He conducts emcee workshops and lectures young people at risk.

HENDRIE, Phil: **KWST**, 1978-80; **KNX/FM**, 1982-83; **KLSX**, 1987-88; **KFI**, 1989-90 and 1996-97. Born in Pasadena, Philip spent 15 years in music radio before moving into Talk radio. He arrived in the Southland from WSHE-Miami for morning drive on "K-West." He also did mornings on KLSX, starting on Friday the 13th in February of 1987 with Mary Lyons, and was featured on *Entertainment Tonight* and *2 On the Town*. He was joined by Marshall Phillips later in the year. After KNX/FM, he went to KGB-San Diego. When he left KLSX, he went to

News/Talk KFI, which eventually led to KSDO-San Diego. In 1994, he went from WCCO-Minneapolis to WIOD-Miami. In a 1995 interview, Phil commented about his on air work in Miami: "I'm doing one of the most creative talk shows in America, featuring character voices and interactive improv comedy. If you hear anyone else doing it, they stole it from me." In the fall of 1996 he rejoined KFI improving on the formula that worked so well in Miami.

HENRY, Alan: **KLAC**, 1964-65, gm. Alan was the first gm after Metromedia purchased the station. He was from St. Louis.

HENRY, Gil: **KNX**, 1955-59; **KLAC**, 1965-69; **KGBS**, 1972-73. Gil hosted a nightly feature called "Private Line." A native Angeleno, on his 17th birthday he joined the U.S. Navy Amphibious Corps, participating in numerous Pacific Island actions. Gil started his broadcast career in 1945 at KUTA-Salt Lake City. In the late 1940s he joined Capitol Records. In 1950 he worked at KING-Seattle while majoring in psychology and philosophy at the University of Washington. Between 1959 and 1965 he served as pd of stations in Seattle and Denver. In 1965 he joined KLAC, originally to produce the "Lohman and Barkley Show," but debuting "Private Line" a few months later.

HENRY, Mike: **KFWB**, 1960-63. Mike now lives in Texas.

HENSEL, Dr. Bruce: **KFWB**, 1993. The former medical editor at KNBC/Channel 4 joined KFWB in the spring of 1993. Bruce is also an assistant clinical professor of medicine at University of California Los Angeles.

HERBERT, Don: **KFWB**, 1968-97. Don is the last

remaining member of the original all-News staff when KFWB made the switch in March of 1968. A native of Brooklyn, Don made his radio debut in 1955 on WABP-Tuscaloosa while attending the University of Alabama. His career took him to Birmingham, Mobile and Little Rock, as well as Palm Beach, Florida before arriving at WTOP-Washington, DC. In Washington, Don covered local and national news with frequent assignments to the Pentagon, State Department and Capitol Hill as well as being a fill-in reporter at the White House. After two years, Don moved to Los Angeles where he became a writer and producer for KNBC/Channel 4 news in Burbank. In 1968, when Westinghouse geared up for an all-News format, Don decided to return to the air. Now, married and with two grown children, Don lives in the San Fernando Valley.

HERGONSON, Bill: **KYMS**, 1971; **KRLA**, 1972. Born in Syracuse in 1948, "Cap'n Billy" worked at KACY-Oxnard, KGB-San Diego and Watermark before joining the Orange County station, KYMS. Bill returned to KGB in 1972.

HERMANN, Cleve: **KFWB**, 1952-89; **KGFJ**, 1972.

Cleve was the continuity glue to the sound of KFWB for almost 40 years through many formats wearing a patch over his left eye - the eye being blinded in an accident at birth. Born in Peoria, he came to the Southland with his parents when he was six. His mother was a teacher. Cleve grew up in South Central Los Angeles and was a

stringer for the *L.A. Examiner* when he was 14. "They paid me twenty-five cents an inch." He never wanted anything else but broadcasting. "For a brief time I thought about being a preacher or lawyer. Perhaps this influenced my on-air style." His broadcasting career started in 1948, writing an NBC radio series called "Jason and the Golden Fleece" that starred MacDonald Carey. In 1951 he became sports director at KNBC/Channel 4. He was involved in a number of local tv productions. Cleve spent three years with Tom Duggan, hosted a KABC/Channel 7 sports discussion series called *Press Box* and produced Oscar Levant's last local program. Cleve appeared in a number of tv shows. He retired at age 72, having worked at KFWB for 37 years with a brief nine-month stop at KGFJ. He was at both the *Los Angeles Herald-Express* and the old *Daily News* before moving into broadcasting. Cleve Herman's "Live Line to the World of Sports" was an integral part of the enormously successful KFWB, "Color Radio/Channel 98." From his home in Redding: "Chuck Blore was the best. When he left there was something missing from the radio station. I almost went to our sister station in San Francisco to be the all-night jock just to get away." He left KFWB in 1989. "I was bitter at the news business and wrote a book titled *Garbage Collector*. I never did anything with it but it was great for the thereaupetic process." Cleve has written a book, *Hollygood*, about his memories and experiences that he plans to have published in 1998.

HERMOSILLO, Xavier: **KMPC**, 1995-97. A life-long

resident of Los Angeles and the community of San Pedro, Xavier has worked as a radio news reporter, tv commentator, newspaper sports writer, editor and photographer. He is the State Chairman of the Republican National Hispanic Assembly of California. Xavier's news commentary airs each Thursday night on KCOP/Channel 13 which serves as the counter balance to Bill Press, who is a radio commentator and Chairman of the California Democratic Party. Xavier owns his own public relations and government affairs firm. He left his evening KMPC talk shift in early 1997.

HERNANDEZ, Joe: Joe was the voice of Santa Anita thoroughbred racing heard on KMPC among other Southern California stations. He broadcast in L.A. for three decades.

HERRERA, Rich: **KMAX**, 1995-96; **KWNK**, 1996. Rich was part of the all-Sports format on KMAX until the station dropped the format with an ownership change in the spring of 1996. Rich and co-host Bob Golic moved their sports show to KWNK. In early 1997 Rich joined KNBR-San Francisco.

HERRERA, Stew: SEE STEW

HERRIN, Jim: **KBCA**, 1965-72. Jim was in law enforcement during the day. He worked part-time at KBCA. One of his co-workers remembers Jim arriving at the station for his shift coming directly from the Sheriff's Department "wearing his piece."

HERSCHENSOHN, Bruce: **KABC**, 1986. Bruce provided right-wing commentary on the "Ken and Barkley Company" morning drive show. In early 1986 Bruce resigned from KABC radio and tv to unsuccessfully challenge Democratic Senator Alan Cranston. Bruce returned to KABC in the summer of 1986. He is participating in a Fellowship with an Eastern College and plans to return to the Southland after school ends.

HERSKOVITZ, Al: **KPOL**, 1972-75, pd. Al orchestrated the 1975 transition of eliminating the "older" beautiful music in favor of post-1960 music at KPOL.

HESS, Leigh: **KNNS**, 1995-96

HESSLER, Fred: **KMPC**, 1953-84. Fred was the "Voice of the Bruins" for 23 years and it came to an end in 1983 when an Eastern sports packager bought the radio and tv rights to UCLA sports. He was also host of KMPC's

"Sports at Six" where he won six Golden Mike awards. A native of Sheboygan, Wisconsin, Fred got his first job in radio in 1941 at WHBL-Sheboygan. The station was owned by the local newspaper where he originally applied, however, the only opening was at the station. He did University of Wisconsin football and basketball. While working, he got in three years of college. Fred is an ex-Air Force officer. He was a navigator for a while, then joined Armed Forces Radio Service. Discharged a captain after World War II, he moved to the L.A. market, catching sports assignments where he could. He joined KMPC in 1953, doing major league baseball re-creations and Rams football. He became the voice of the Bruins in 1960. He recalled his football highlight for Larry Stewart in the *LA Times* - it was the 1965 football season, when the Bruins, led by Gary Beban, came from behind to beat USC and then upset Michigan State in the Rose Bowl. Fred retired from radio on December 31, 1983. He passed away in 1993.

HEWITT, Hugh: **KFI**, 1990-95. Born in 1956, Hugh worked Sunday evenings at KFI until the fall of 1995. The lawyer-commentator resigned after a five-year run to prepare an eight-part PBS/TV series, *Searching for God in America*. He appears on the KCET/Channel 28 nightly show *Life & Times*.

HIAM, Joey: **KMAX**, 1995; **KWNK**, 1996-97; **KIIS/AM**, 1997. Joey teamed with Dave Smith for a show called "Sports Gods." The pair met at a fitness center.

HIATT, Amy: **KEZY**, 1982-84; **KTWV**, 1988-97. Amy was born and raised in Los Angeles and grew up listening to the "Boss Jocks" on KHJ. "Because of my strong love of music, I always knew I wanted to be on the radio. My father said, 'If you still want to pursue this after getting your college degree, you have my blessings.'" So that's what she did. Amy graduated from UCLA and started as an intern at KHJ. Her on-air career began at KDES-Palm Springs, and then she went on to Phoenix before arriving at KEZY to do mornings and be md. Her former Sunday evening show of new music on KTWV, the "Listening Room," won a medal at the New York Festival of Radio. Amy's been back to KDES a couple of times "because of my love for the desert where I hope to retire." A big animal lover with three rabbits and a cat, Amy has started pursuing a career in voiceover work.

HICKLAND, Jim: **KMPC**, 1966-73. Jim was the traffic helicopter pilot who replaced Capt. Max Schumacher, who was killed when two helicopters collided over Dodger Stadium on August 30, 1966. On April 2, 1973, Jim was killed in his stateroom aboard the cruise ship Princess Italia moments before the ship was to sail on a vacation trip to Mexico. He was killed by a crazed listener who told Jim he would kill him. Jim made the mistake of telling on the air where he was going on vacation. KMPC aired his funeral services live.

> *"There are four critical essentials for success: attitude, luck, sense of humor and a wife with lots of money."*
> *-Cliffie Stone*

HIDALGO, Juan Carlos: **KLAX**, 1992-96, pd; **KLAX/KXMG**, 1996-97, pd. Hidalgo is part of the very successful morning team with "El Peladillo." Born in 1965 in Tariacuri, Michoacan, Mexico, he arrived in the United States illegally in the late 1980s. He worked in the fields of Ventura County, picking fruit while studying broadcasting on the side. He paired with Garcia ("El Peladillo") on KTRO/KELF-Oxnard and then went to program KOFY-San Francisco before arriving in the Southland. The Spanish morning drive show on KLAX was #1 for three consecutive Arbitron books in 1993-94. Juan won *Billboard*'s Spanish Music Director of the Year and Spanish Local Air Personality of the Year. In late 1994, the team was working on a comedy/variety pilot for KCAL/Channel 9. In the same year he was named Music Director of the Year by *Billboard* magazine and *Radio y Musica*. Juan talked about his morning show in a 1994 *LA Times* story: "We want people to have pride in our race, so we put in some advice. We feel awful about gangs and people shooting each other. We talk about getting a good education. We don't do jokes that offend people. My job is to entertain people." In the summer of 1996 he took on the additional duties of programming sister station KXMG.

HIDER, Ed: **KDAY**, 1969-70; **KFI**, 1974-77. Ed arrived in the Southland from KYA-San Francisco. In 1973 he wrote *Take My Turntable - Please*. It was a 125-page book of comedy bits. Known as "Mr. Comedy" to his fellow jocks, Ed was one of the writers on the *Donnie and Marie Osmond Show*. Ed created the "Electric Weenie," one of the first comedy services.

HIGGINS, Haagan: **KMGG**, 1985-86; **KLAC**, 1989-90; **KZLA**, 1990-97. Born in Pawtuxent River, Maryland, Haagan left with his parents at the age of 2 weeks, and he's never been back. Working in radio, he is living out his high school dream. Haagan went to Don Martin's broadcast school in Hollywood in 1968 and every morning listened to Robert W. Morgan, who became his inspiration. In school he would use lines he heard Robert use earlier in the morning. When Haagan arrived to work at "Magic 106," he discovered that his idol was there, and his dream came full circle. Before he got to L.A., he worked at KFYE ("Y-94") and KYNO-Fresno. He spent time at Unistar for a year after KMGG changed formats. In 1987, Haagan got burned out with radio and became a headwaiter for a private club in Beverly Hills. He returned to radio in 1989 and currently is doing weekends at Country-formatted KZLA.

HILBURN, Lincoln: **KPOL**, 1965-68; **KLAC**, 1968-69. Lin was the evening host during the Joe Pyne Talk days at KLAC. He is now deceased.

HILDRETH, Howard: **KGIL**, 1973-75. Howard is now a top engineer with Armed Forces Radio and Television.

HILL, Austin: **KYMS**, 1987-93; **KKLA**, 1990; **KZLA**, 1993-97. Born in 1964, Austin began his radio career at age 17 at KVPR-Fresno. After his high school graduation he moved to KYNO-Fresno and KSLY-San Luis Obispo where he also earned his bachelor's degree in English at

Cal Poly State University. In 1987 he joined KHTY-Santa Barbara and later that year returned to his native Orange County to do mornings on Christian music formatted KYMS. In 1990 he co-hosted a talk show on KKLA. In addition to his work on KZLA, Austin is completing his master's degree in "The Philosophy of Ethics" at Biola University. He is busy in the voiceover world and commercial acting.

HILL, James: **KZLA**, 1986-91; **KYSR**, 1992-94; **KFWB**, 1995-96. Hailing from Idaho, James was the morning sports anchor on all-News KFWB until late 1996. He was educated at Gonzaga State, Boise State, Florida State and San Francisco State Universities. His father built and owned radio stations which influenced James to pursue a broadcasting career. He's been a dj in San Francisco at KFRC, K101, KPEN and KCBS. He was Jim Bridges at KZLA and KYSR. James has hosted national television shows for ESPN, TNN, E! and the Learning Channel. He spent eight years as the co-host for the motor sports-oriented *Truckin USA* on the Nashville Network.

HILLERY, Jeff: **KDAY**, 1973; **KFWB**, 1973-75; **KIIS**, 1981; **KABC**, 1981; **KRLA**, 1982; **KHJ**, 1982-85. "I can write!" His response to Lew Irwin's question moved Jeff from a $300 a week sports writer at the *Santa Monica Evening Outlook* to joining the news staff at KDAY. Born in Los Angeles, Jeff studied English at Venice High School, Santa Monica City College and Cal State Northridge. His association with Irwin at his first radio job led him to a six-year affiliation with Lew Irwin's Earth News Radio. "I was a writer, producer, interviewer and reporter. Lew was awesome. I learned from the best." When Earth News folded, Jeff worked as a newsman at KRLA, KABC and KIIS. A week of vacation fill-in as morning news anchor on KHJ led to a full-time offer at then-Country KHJ. "I was stunned. I grew up listening to 'Boss Radio,' and here I was actually working at KHJ." He was paired with "Sweet Dick" Whittington during KHJ's "The Boss Is Back" format. The former newsman was turned into a morning "info jock" for the launch of "Car Radio" on KHJ, doing news and traffic between records. In 1985 Jeff took off for Dallas and during the next nine years worked for two stations and the Hot AC format at ABC Radio Network. By 1994 he moved to KSDO-San Diego. "When Gannett sold to Jacor I thought I should start to control by own destiny." Jeff is now managing a four-station group in Santa Rosa. "I figured that I couldn't do any worse than some of the pd's I worked for. Radio should be fun."

HINES, Craig: **KIQQ**, 1973; **KGIL**, 1976-77; **KBIG**, 1988-90. Known as "Hurricane Hines" during some of his radio stops, Craig grew up along the Central California coast in Lompoc and Morro Bay. He started in radio at KNEZ-Lompoc at age 15. Between semesters at Cal Poly San Luis Obispo, Craig helped launch WDRQ-Detroit. In the mid-1970s, when he left Southern California the first time, he went to program KMBY-Monterey. He spent a few years programming WMBR/WSNY-Jacksonville, beginning in 1977. Craig came back to Southern California in 1984 to work for the Transtar Radio Network as director of programming/operations for the five satellite-delivered radio formats until 1987. Craig hosted several nationally syndicated radio shows for Westwood One and Transtar/Unistar. He started doing middays at KBIG and moved to afternoon drive, until he left radio in late 1990. Craig is currently a computer consultant and voiceover actor in the Los Angeles area.

HINSON, Don: **KDAY**, 1969-70; **KFOX**, 1972, md; **KLAC**, 1979-84; **KBBQ**, 1991; **KLAC**, 1991-93. In 1960, Don could be heard on KTLN-Denver. He was named "King of the Truckers." His "Phantom 5-70 Club" had more than 8,000 truck members in 1979, during his all-night shift. He commented at the time, "My audience enables me to play more traditional country music, and this is the time period when we focus on it." Don left KLAC in late 1993 with the format change from Country to satellite-fed Unistar's AM Only format. Don is a "country flavored" comedian who opens for various country artists and is frequently the "warm-up" for country-themed concerts. Don always wanted to live in Nashville, and that is what he now calls home.

HOBBS, Tally: **KIKF**, 1986

HOBERMAN, Ben: **KABC**, gm. Born Bernard G. "Ben" Hoberman in 1922, the native of Minnesota was the architect who put the Talk radio concept together for KABC. After graduating from high school he started at a small station in Hibbing as an announcer and salesman. When World War II broke out, Ben joined Armed Forces Radio in London, and was eventually commissioned. He was put in charge of the First Army's mobile radio station during the Normandy invasion. At the end of his military career, Ben was in charge of all Armed Forces Network outlets in Britain and France. Ben arrived in the Southland in 1960 from being gm of WABC-New York. When he retired as ABC Radio president, he had been with ABC for 36 years. In the early 1980s he lived in New York and ran the network's radio division which controlled ABC's six AM stations and six FM stations, as well as such syndicated programs as Casey Kasem's "American Top 40."

HOCKUM, John: 1965, pd

HODSON, Jim: **KYMS**, 1982-85. Jim grew up in Orange and developed his love for radio, acting and broadcasting in high school. He attended Orange Coast College and while in school was a TBN cameraman and "hung out" at KYMS until he was hired to do overnights. He eventually moved to morning drive at age 22. "I had a lot of fun doing morning drive. I was probably the first to do drop-in bits and voices on Christian radio." Jim went on to host *Real Videos* on TBN and then became a music video jock on the Family Channel. He's very successful acting and doing voice work. Back to radio? "I'm not pursuing radio now. I'm very busy with my commercial work and acting."

> *When Earl McDaniel was asked to give a speech to an organization, the person in charge asked, "How shall I introduce you?" Earl replied: "Here is a man with no past, only a future."*

HOFFMAN, Steve: **KLOS**, 1985-88; **KQLZ**, 1989-90. Steve grew up in Los Angeles and got started as gm at UCLA's campus station, KLA. When he left "Pirate Radio" in 1990 he went to KKBB-Bakersfield in afternoon drive and pd and later became pd of XHRM-San Diego. Prior to that he worked afternoons and om at KCKC/KCXX-Riverside. He was also on-air at KCAL-Riverside and KZTR-Ventura. Steve has been vp at *Hitmakers* magazine and associate editor at *R&R*. Following a brief stop at KLLC-San Francisco in 1996, he went to KEDG-Las Vegas in late summer as "Supreme Godhead of the Space-Time Continuum." Steve concluded, "As you can tell, we're not well here."

HOFFMAN, Walt: **KNX**, 1966-85. Walt was a newsman for KNX. He is now doing commercials and industrial voiceover work.

HOFMANN, Don: **KDAY**, 1968, pd. Answering a blind ad in *Broadcasting* magazine resulted in Don taking over KDAY from February to July in 1968. He had been at KMBY-Monterey for six years before arriving in the Southland. KDAY was owned by Rollins, a leasing and renting company that also owned Orkin Exterminators along with a small chain of secondary AM stations.  "Radio was their least successful enterprise and KDAY was probably their biggest loser. When I arrived, I was told that my job was to keep it on the air until the company engineers could complete the new full-time pattern that would allow the station a 24-hour operation. My claim to fame at KDAY was that I was operations manager between Tom Clay and Bob Wilson." Don moved back North to KJOY-Stockton for six years and then to KVI-Seattle which he programmed for five years. Before retiring, he programmed KSFO-San Francisco. He lives in Monterey.

HOGAN, Rich: **KIIS**, 1980-81; **KWST/KMGG**, 1981-85; **KBZT/KLSX**, 1986. "I got a part-time job at KIIS the day I got into town." Rich spent the 1970s working mostly in his hometown of Albany at a series of stations and in

Washington, DC. He arrived in the Southland from WMYQ-Miami. During his stay at "K-West," the call letters were changed to KMGG. "I saw tons of people come and go...jocks, news, sales, management, production...the works." Rich was the first jock when "classic rock" went on the air at KLSX. He currently operates his own photo studio and is a part-timer at WW1's Mainstream Country format.

HOGENRAAD, Carolyn: **KEZY**, 1996-97. Carolyn works all-night at KEZY. The Orange County native started at KSBR at Saddleback College and part-time promotions at KOST.

HOLIDAY, Dolly: **KMET**, 1967. Dolly was part of the all-female format at KMET. She hosted the all-night show for Holiday Inns.

HOLLAND, Brad: **KFOX**, 1982. Brad broadcasted sports.

HOLLIDAY, Doc: SEE Joe Nasty

HOLLIDAY, Sie: **KRLA**, 1962-76; **KMPC**, 1976-78. Sie was born in Giddings, Texas, and her first radio work was doing book reviews as a teenager in 1948. She received a degree in broadcasting from the University of Texas and worked in radio and tv on the Texas Gulf Coast and Rio Grande Valley before moving to California. Her first full-time Top 40 dj shift was at KDEO-San Diego in 1959. Sie

was one of the first woman voices spinning records. She arrived in the Southland from KDEO. During Sie's stint at KRLA, she had a Sunday night show and was the traffic supervisor. She played Daphney on all the Emperor Hudson skits as part of Hudson's commandos. Sie was an active participant on the award-winning "Credibility Gap News" and John Gilliland's "Pop Chronicles." Sie did the children's story spots for the L.A. Public Library and played "Programmer Number 9" on the "Oidar Wavelength" syndicated show. She went back to jock work in 1973 and worked morning drive with the distinction of not only being the first female jock in L.A., but also the first to work morning drive. When KRLA abandoned live personalities and went automated in early 1976, Sie and most of the other jocks were let go. James Brown of the *LA Times* wrote: "She was one of the first women to take any kind of broadcasting foothold on L.A. rock radio." She returned to the Lone Star State in 1978 and lives as Shirley Schneider in Wichita Falls, where she does acting and directing on the local live theater scene.

HOLLIER, Vincent: **KMPC**, 1995-96. Vincent was one of the "computer guys" doing a weekend talk show.

HOLLIS, Gary: **KJQI/KOJY**, 1993-94; **KKGO**, 1994-97. Gary is also an actor who is active in films and sitcoms.

HOLLISTER, Jim: **KABC**. The San Francisco native worked at KMPX-San Francisco in the '60s and beginning in 1970 at KEX-Portland after leaving Southern California.

HOLLOWAY, Lee: **KGIL**, 1987-88; **KABC**, 1992-97.

Lee has been the trusted counselor of a celebrated diverse group of clients from all over the world for more than fifteen years using a blend of her business experience and knowledge of astrology as unique tools to help others. Born in Illinois, Lee grew up in Utah. She came to the Southland in the 1970s after many years as senior vp of a large conglomerate that ranged from manufacturing private label products and textile machines to custom snap-out printing forms. In her motivational seminars, classes and speaking engagements her business experience and people skills help her encourage people to risk and claim their hearts desire. "When my daughter hit puberty and the teens, I went running to a shrink." Her therapist referred Lee to an astrologer and she was hooked by the insight it provided in the personality and the cycles in individuals lives. "Like nature, our lives are made up of cycles, and when people tap those cycles and take personal responsibility for their life, personal power and effectiveness increase." Lee is an internationally published author and currently at work on books to be published by Harper Collins. "The Lee Holloway Show" airs Saturday evenings on KABC where she helps listeners deal with their personal life and business concerns.

HOLMES, Richard "Groove": **KBCA**, 1967-76. Born Richard Arnold Jackson, in 1967 *Billboard* magazine listed Rick as the 3rd most popular L.A. jazz deejay. According to Tom Reed in his book, *The Black Music History of Los Angeles - Its Roots*, Richard recorded for Dick Bock's Pacific Jazz label. "Holmes was a swingin' and creative organist, who would carry his organ in a hearse to and from his gigs." He performed up until a week before his death on June 29, 1991. Richard was 60.

HOLSTON, Jim: **KPOL**, 1986, pd

HOLT, Jim: **KFI**, 1969; **KLAC**, 1969-70; **KGIL**, 1971-73. Jim worked all-nights at KLAC.

HOLT, Lynn: **KFAC**, 1985-88. During Lynn's program, "Luncheon at the Met," Lynn Warfel met Tony Holt. He was a member of an English singing group, The Kings' Singers, that was touring the States. She moved to England and their romance blossomed. They married and did mornings together on KFAC.

HOLT, Tony: **KFAC**, 1985-89. Tony hosted the "Evening Concert." He teamed in morning drive on KFAC with his new wife, Lynn.

HOOD, Dave: **KRTH**, 1993-94

HORN, Mike: **KBBQ**, 1971-72; **KROQ**, 1972; **KFOX**, 1973; **KFI**, 1973-76; **KRLA**, 1976-80; **KIEV**, 1985-93; **KFI**, 1994-95; **KIKF**, 1996. Mike was a jock at KBBQ and at the original KROQ. He was nd at KRLA and worked Talk at KIEV and KFI. He is currently gm at KYK/FM. Mike always dreamed of owning his own radio station. In 1980 his active radio career expanded. Mike started his own company providing dance music for clubs all over the Southland. In 1983 an opportunity surfaced. "A cable company in Phoenix was looking for audio to place on their local ad channel." More than a decade later, Mike owns the Cable  Radio Network/CRN servicing close to 10 million listeners in 27 states. Mike now also "designs" radio services for businesses nationwide. He was born in Pasadena and raised in the San Fernando Valley.

HOTLEN, Allan: **KJOI/KXEZ**, pd; **KYSR**, pd. Allan arrived in the Southland from KSFO-San Francisco. He started at KJOI in 1984 and programmed the switch from Beautiful Music to Adult KXEZ. When he left the Southland he went to KOIT-San Francisco. In the spring of 1997 he was named gm of KOYT-San Francisco (formerly KPIX). Allan had previously run WPEN-Philadelphia, KKSA-Sacramento and WAYK and WSWF-Ft. Myers, WWZZ-Washington, DC.

HOUSE, Gerry: **KLAC/KZLA**, 1986-87. Gerry is the recipient of ten Air Personality of the Year Awards from CMA, ACM, *Billboard* and the *Gavin Report*. He also won the 1992 Marconi Air Talent of the Year-All Formats. He worked on Premiere Radio Network. In the summer of 1987, Gerry moved to mornings at KZLA. That same year he was named Country Radio Air Personality of the Year and was lured back to "Twang Town" after the awards. He won again the following year while working for WSIX-Nashville. Gerry was the emcee for the 1993 *Billboard* Radio Awards. "I've published 20 songs through my new company, House Notes Music. A George Straight song went to #1."

HOWARD, Bob: **KGFJ**; **KFWB**, 1981-97. Bob is an anchor on all-News KFWB.

HOWARD, Greg: **KGFJ/KUTE**, 1980, gm. A graduate of Princeton in 1974, Greg worked in radio sales in Boston and Newark before joining KGFJ/KUTE. He also spent three years as an account rep at Merrill Lynch.

HOWARD, Marv: **KDAY**, 1956-62; **KBBQ**, 1963; **KHJ**, 1963-77; **KFI**, 1977-82; **KMPC**, 1982-94. Marv has been one of the premier news voices covering four decades in Southern California radio. Born Marvin Howard Fink and raised in Los Angeles ("I was born at Cedars of Lebanon Hospital which is now the Scientololgy building"), Marv went to the old L.A. City College. During his schooling he took many years of Spanish which served him well in the Air Force. "I was sent to language school during the Korean War and studied cryptoanaylsis. I listened to Russian broadcasts to break the codes for U.S. Intelligence." Marv had a friend in the service who had gone to the Don Martin Broadcast School and when Marv was discharged he joined the school on a G.I. bill. "It sounded like lots of fun and they seemed to have a strong job placement opportunity. I knew I didn't want to work for the government." In 1956, after graduating from Martin's and obtaining his FCC 1st Class License, Marv became dj Mark Ford at KBIS-Bakersfield. Six months later he joined KDAY. "We went Top 40, actually 35, and I was the first to make out the record list. I traveled to the different one-stop record distributors and compiled the list." Marv stayed with KDAY until Rollins Broadcasting bought the station in 1962. He joined KMEN-San Bernardino and KBBQ briefly and started part-time at KHJ in 1963. When "Boss Radio" was launched everyone was fired. "I was called back to KHJ a few months later to cover the Watts Riots and stayed until 1977." At KHJ his newscasts were sponsored by Rambler. "I figured it was as good a time as any to go into news." He dropped the name Mark Ford and became Marv Howard. "I left KHJ when a new pd came in and wanted to make the station more 'FMmy' and demanded that the news stories deal with concerts and activities of young people. I guess he felt I didn't fit in so he fired me." After five years as nd of KFI, Marv joined KMPC and worked with Robert W. Morgan and John McElhinney in morning drive. "This period at KMPC was the most joyful time. Mornings would just fly by." Marv is living in the San Fernando Valley. He has been doing voiceover work and selling cars as "something to do."

HOWARD, Robert M.: **KFWB**. Robert was a longtime KFWB newsman.

> *"Empowerment through knowledge is my motto but always with a smile."*
> *-Rodri Rodriguez*

HOWELL, Laurie: **KNX**, 1991-95; **KLOS**, 1995-97. Laurie was one of the weekend anchors on all-News KNX. In August 1995 she became the nd on KLOS's "Mark and Brian Show." Laurie grew up as a "military brat" living everywhere from Hawaii to Washington, DC where she attended high school. She went to Oklahoma State University "on a lark" and majored in communications.

"I majored in communications with no real direction until a radio news director told me I would never make it in broadcasting. I've been working ever since." Laurie studied political-science in graduate school at the University of Colorado. She drove to Los Angeles in 1991 from the nation's capitol with no money, no job prospects and everything she owned jammed in the back of a pickup truck. "KNX took a chance and hired me - within a month of my arrival. That's probably been my biggest break ever in the business." Laurie enjoys skiing, biking and roller blading.

HOYOS, Rodolfo: **KALI**, 1965; **KWKW**; **KTNQ**, 1974-80. The co-announcer of Dodger baseball games broadcast in Spanish died April 15, 1983. Rodolfo starred in a number movies such as *Villa!*, *The Brave One*, and *Return of a Gunfighter*. He appeared on the stage in Los Angeles and New York in Spanish language plays and broadcast Legion Stadium fights in Spanish. He was a founding member of Nosotros, a nonprofit organization promoting Latino participation in the entertainment industry. Rodolfo had suffered a stroke a few months before his death. He was 67.

HUBBS, Kraig: **KOST**, 1983. When Kraig left the AC station be became a flight attendant for Morris Air based in Salt Lake City. He is now working for Loma Linda Hospital in the Inland Empire.

HUDDLESTON, J. Paul: **KFWB**, 1961-65; **KHJ**, 1965-72; **KROQ**, 1972. John Paul was a newsman during the "Boss Radio" glory years. Paul worked in Canada for part of his news career. J. Paul was born in Searcy, Arkansas and started out as a Fuller Brush salesman. His Southern roots played havoc with his accent broadcasting news. Art Kevin remembers: "In the early days of the civil rights movement he had trouble properly pronouncing the word negro. It came out 'nig-rah' and we had some calls from upset local black activists. I taped him and his Arkansas ear couldn't hear it. I got him to agree that every time he'd see the word NEGRO on wire copy or did a re-write he could write KNEE-GROW. It worked!" In 1993, he was working in the financial business in San Antonio, where he died at age 62, due to complications of liver disease.

HUDSON, "Emperor" Bob: KRLA, 1963-66; **KBLA**, 1966-67; **KFWB**, 1967-68; **KEZY**, 1968; **KGBS**, 1969-74; **KRLA**, 1974; **KFI**, 1974-76; **KIEV**; **XPRS**, 1981-82; **KRLA**, 1985-86 and 1988. Born Robert Howard Holmes, Emperor Hudson led his Commandoes to mornings on

KRLA in 1963 to replace Bob Eubanks, who was spending more time with his concert business and arranging for the arrival of the Beatles. By 1966 *Billboard* ranked Emperor Hudson #1 in morning drive. He was at KFWB when the music died in March 1968, to make room for Southern California's second all-News station. By now Bob was working afternoon drive. His biggest success occurred in 1971 when he teamed in the mornings with midday jock Ron Landry. He was also known as "Beautiful Bob, handsome, beautiful, blue-eyed and hairy chested." His classic album with Ron Landry, *Ajax Liquor Store*, won a Grammy award. In citing the best of 1971, Don Page wrote in the *LA Times* that the Hudson/Landry team was "fresh, bold and far-out funny. They have bridged the generation gap in radio, appealing to youth as well as the over-30s." Other great bits included "Ajax Airlines," "Ajax Pet Store," "Charlie Chan," "Hollyweird Squares" and "Bruiser LaRue." The team went to afternoon drive at KFI. Bob teamed with fellow jock Dave Hull to do a single on Cream Records in 1978 that was an adaptation of *Who's on First*, the classic Abbott & Costello routine. The Emperor traveled below the border to work at XPRS by tape in 1981, and he marketed messages for a new electronic device, the telephone answering machine. He recorded *Hanging in There*, which in 1981 became the #1 comedy album. After a year in Seattle radio at KKMI, Bob returned to KRLA in 1985 and teamed with Al Lohman in the mornings in a very short-lived experiment. He left KRLA in 1986, after making a remark the station felt was thoughtless. Bob suggested that the U.S. Space Shuttle blew up because the crew was freebasing Tang. When he left KRLA, Bob was replaced by Charlie Tuna. In 1988, he returned to KRLA for weekends, hosting "Emperor's Gold" on Sunday nights. The Emperor has retired, lives in Monrovia and continues his love for horses.

HUDSON, Lord Tim: KFWB, 1965-66; **KFOX**, 1979-80; **KGOE**; **KWIZ**, 1976. Tim was English, knew the Beatles personally, wore his hair fashionably long and had a wardrobe that was the image of Carnaby Street mod. He was 23 years old in the mid-1960s, and for a brief couple of years, he owned the town. During the Beatles revolution, Tim Hudson took on the title "Lord" to take advantage of the publicity and attention surrounding the British rock invasion. He arrived in the Southland from KCBQ-San Diego. In 1966 *Billboard* magazine voted Lord Tim tied with Johnny Mitchell as top early evening dj in the Top 40 category. After his Southern California radio run, he stopped at KFRC-San Francisco in 1967, then left radio to manage the Seeds. By 1970 the Beatles fever was over, the "Flower Power" era had gotten nasty and the ride for Lord Tim was over. For a decade he renovated houses and assessed his next move. In 1982 he was airing a once weekly show called "Hudson's Theater of the Mind" on the Loyola Marymount campus radio station KXLU. In 1993, based in Carlsbad, he created a traveling radio show called "The British Invasion," capitalizing on his association with the Beatles and collection of British memorabilia.

HUERO, Charlie: KPWR, 1993-96. Charlie had been the assistant md and versatile fill-in on "Power 106" from the summer of 1993 until leaving in March 1996. Born July 4, 1966, in Milwaukee he was raised in the area and graduated from the University of Wisconsin with a mass communications major. He started his career at WLXR-La Crosse and in the late 1980s WLUM-Milwaukee. In the spring of 1990 and for three years Charlie was with ("Jammin' Z-90"), XHTZ-San Diego. Following a couple of months at KGGI-Riverside he went to KPWR. In the spring of 1996 he joined KTFM-San Antonio as md and afternoon drive.

HUFFMAN, Larry: KWIZ, 1966-69; **KEZY**, 1969-70.

"It's a bird...It's a plane...It's Supermouth." That's the way the *LA Times* referred to Larry's announcing style. Larry boasts, "I can speak over 300 words per minute, clearly and distinctly." A native Californian born in Corona, he has spent most of his life and career in Orange County. Starting his radio journey in Elko, Nevada, and Lewiston, Idaho, Larry spent time at KGMB-Honolulu. After his half decade in Orange County radio, his career got up to speed when he began announcing speedway motorcycle races. He has since announced every type of motorcycle off-road race in North America, England, Belgium, France and Japan. Larry developed his mark as a premier Motocross announcer by showing up in a tuxedo, screaming and shouting, while most of the crowd was donning tee-shirts and jeans. He spices his announcing with "Huffmanisms" like..."He went down faster than an Idaho thermometer in January." Larry has built a state-of-the-art studio in his San Clemente home for his active commercial and voiceover work. In 1996 he voiced over two dozen national Dodge spots.

HUFFSTEDER, Paul: **KROQ**, 1976-78.

HUGGIE BOY: **KRKD**, 1951; **KWKW**, 1954; **KALI**; **KGFJ**, 1955; **KBLA**, 1965; **KRKD**, 1965-66; **XPRS**, 1981-82; **KRLA**, 1983-97. Born in 1928, Dick Hugg has been associated with r&b music in the Southland for four decades. Born in Canton, Ohio, Dick was 15 when he and his divorced mother moved to Los Angeles at the end of World War II. Kirk Silsbee profiled Dick in a 1994 issue of *Los Angeles Reader Magazine* and described him: "Tall and delicately thin, Hugg comes across as a nonjudgmental grandfather when giving a child an

autograph for his mother or talking to teenagers who want to dedicate a song to that 'special someone' with whom they've just broken up." As a youth working in a theater, Dick was influenced by listening to "Dumas's Drive-In" with Bill Sampson, broadcast from Florence and Vermont and Art Laboe broadcasting from Scribner's Drive-In at Western and Imperial over KRKD. He initially brokered a show on KRKD broadcasting from the Golden Gate Drive-In on Whittier Boulevard. He went on to broadcast from Dolphin's of Hollywood record store at Vernon and Central Avenue. At midnight on KRKD in 1951 Joe Houston's record *All Night Long* would wail and Huggie Boy opened his show: "Keep alive and listen in. All night long. Keep alive and listen in. All night long. Hi! Huggie Boy Show! All night long, from Dolphin's of Hollywood. In the studio front window at Vernon and Central, Central and Vernon, Vernon and Central, Central and Vernon..." His theme song during this period was *Rock and Roll* by Chuck Higgins. Dick told reporter Silsbee how he got his nickname: "Charlie Clifton was a big newscaster and sportscaster in town and he had a show on KRKD. He was about to retire at 65, but for a month before he left, the station decided that he should give my introductions before my show. When I met Clifton, he took one look at me and said, 'Oh, my God! I thought you were black and you're white. And you're just a boy.' From then on, Clifton would say over the air, 'Girl, get down to Dolphin's and see this boy...he'll give each woman a kiss...this boy is really huggy...come down and see Huggie Boy.'" Times got tough for Huggie Boy in the mid-1960s, perhaps coincidentally with the arrival of the British music. He opened a couple of record stores and managed a nudie theater in Hollywood. But the times and the music changed. In 1982, Dick recorded his show in Glendale, and it was sent to XPRS, one of the classic border stations in Tijuana. His show on "10-90 X-press" was a request and dedications show. Dick's evening program currently has the highest ratings on KRLA. "Disc jockeying is a dead art; that era is over. What I'm doing [on KRLA] is getting away with murder. I've become the George Burns of oldies." A familiar signature from Huggie Boy: "Remember...Others imitate. But none can duplicate the sound found here...The Huggie Boy Show must be the best. It's outlasted all the rest."

HUGHES, Bob: **KWST**, 1972-75; **KSRF**, 1975; **KNJO**, 1977-80, pd; **KZLA**, 1982-85. "I saw a dj in a store window in San Diego when I was 13 and that's when I knew what I wanted to do." Born in Chicago, Bob grew up in Southern California and pursued his dream while going to school (graduating from CSUN in 1977), securing his FCC 1st phone from Don Martin school and teaching at Columbia School of Broadcasting (13 years). While in the Navy Bob was a communications technician working as a Chinese cryptoanaylist stationed in the Phillipines. His

radio career started at KDUO-San Bernardino in 1965 followed by KENO-Las Vegas, two years in Barstow radio, and KTMS-Santa Barbara. In 1968 he went to KVEN-Ventura and spent four years before joining KWST. Bob was the last voice of the Beautiful Music KWST before the AOR format was kicked off at 6 p.m. New Years Eve 1974. During his time on KZLA he remembered: "It was a very stressful time. I was doing the all-night shift and I had just gotten custody of my kids. They literally slept on the floor of the control room while I was on the air." Bob's life is much more balanced today. He is a stand-in for actors on major tv and movie productions. "I've stood in for Tim Robbins, Charles Grodin, Bill Paxton and Sean Connery. It's been a good life."

> *Who were your heroes?*
> *"Roy Rogers was my first hero, later Elvis and JFK. Lately, I've realized my parents for giving me the values I have today."*
> —*Top Ten personality Charlie Tuna*

HUGHES, Luther: **KLON**, 1990. A respectable bass player, he started a new career as a dj at the Long Beach Jazz station.

HULL, Dave: **KRLA**, 1963-69; **KFI**, 1969-71; **KGBS**, 1971-73; **KIQQ**, 1973; **KRLA**, 1974; **KFI**, 1974-76; **KMPC**, 1978-81; **KRLA**, 1981-85; **KHJ**, 1985-86; **KRLA**, 1992-93; **KRTH**, 1994; **KIKF**, 1996. The "Hullabalooer" was born January 20, 1934, and raised in Alhambra. "There were three cut-ups at Alhambra High School that covered a 14-year span. First it was Stan

Freberg, then the Credibility Gap's Richard Beebe. When Beebe left, the school administrator was relieved until I arrived." Listening to the radio as a youth, Dave most revered Jim Hawthorne. "Jim used to pluck his 'Hogan Twanger' and I thought it was great. Then to find out it was only a guitar. I also loved Dick Haynes." He started in radio in 1955 at KGFL-Roswell, New Mexico. From 1957 to 1960 he worked at WONE-Dayton, where his nickname originated. "A woman wrote me from a hotel outside Dayton to say she couldn't stand all that hullabaloo. Well, Webster's defined it as a tumultuous out roar, so I used it." He worked at WQTE-Detroit, before going to WTVN-Columbus from 1961 to 1963. Before becoming one of the "KRLA 11-10 Men," Dave did mornings at WFLA-Tampa/St.Petersburg, where he was the corniest jock in Florida, holding a corniest joke contest each morning on his show, with the winner receiving a silver dollar and a bag of popcorn. In 1966 *Billboard* magazine, Dave scored #1 in the Top 40 category. Dave was fired from KRLA for jumping the release date on a Beatles record, and the public outcry was such that he was almost immediately hustled back on the air. Dave was quick on the bandwagon of Beatlemania - dispensing rumors, general information and assorted mischief to the legions of believers. He represented the rampant, freewheeling innocence of the period - a personal style that persevered even as that innocence was lost with the introduction of drugs and free love into the society. But his heady rein on KRLA came to an end in early 1969. At KFI, Dave did vacation relief for Lohman and Barkley and fill-in until being hired full-time following Dodger baseball, where he worked nightly with Dodger first baseman Wes Parker. Dave was at KMPC from 1978 to 1980, doing the nightly "Lovelines" show which had been described as a kind of *Dating Game* for "the homely, the overweight and the very lonely man or woman." When he left KRLA for the third time in 1985, he was the last jock pictured on the weekly "Tune-dex" survey sheet. Between radio gigs, Dave developed tv shows and for two years in the mid-1980s had an office at Columbia Pictures, writing and developing a movie based on his "Lovelines" program. In the late 1980s he was selling real estate. He had been living in Pine Mountain, a sparsely populated area in Kern County near Frazier Park. Dave has four sons and one daughter, who was a Rams cheerleader for three years. Making the transition out of radio to real estate, the Hullabalooer reminisced: "Your worst day in radio is a million times better than your best day in real estate." In a 1993 *LA Times* interview, Dave said, "I would say my best times were in the '60s, because that's when I was really a giant in this town. They'll never be repeated. There will never be a time as great or as innocent or as fun as those days. We've lost our innocence." In 1994, Dave filled in vacation relief at KRTH and in 1996 was heard on KIKF weekends. He currently works at KWXY-Cathedral City/Palm Springs.

HUME, Dave: **KTNQ/KGBS/FM**, 1976-78. Born in Oxnard, Dave got his radio start at KOZN and KSON-San Diego. In the mid-1970s, he was on air and programmed KFAT-Gilroy. He was hired at KTNQ to be Clete Dumpster the sports anchor, hosting "short snort on the business of sports," as well as to be the costumed mascot, the infamous "Ten-Q Duck." He used his real name, Hume, doing weekends and fill-in at sister station, Country KGBS. When he left the Southland, he did jock work and sports at WIFE-Indianapolis. In the 1980s, Dave became part of John Lander's "Q-Zoo" on KKBQ-Houston and also did tv sports reporting. For eight years he was the tv announcer for the World Wrestling Federation. In 1993, Dave did morning drive during the short-lived Sports format on WOWF-Detroit. He returned to Southern California in late 1994 to pursue sports announcing.

HUMMER, Rick: **KIBB**, 1996-97. Rick left "B-100" in the summer of 1997.

> "I remember the mother of one of my high school buddies who worked at a radio station saying, 'there's nothing sadder than a 40-year-old disc jockey.' As I drove home from my last show on KMPC, the echo of her comment from a quarter century earlier jolted me. I was 40 and I was leaving radio behind."
> —Neil Ross

HUMPHRIES, Herb: **KFWB**, 1967-71 and 1972-74; **KABC**, 1971-72. Herb was the architect for the launch of all-News KFWB on March 11, 1968. "It's indisputable the launching of the all-News format on KFWB was among the most historic events in Los Angeles radio," commented Don Schrack who later became news director of the station. On "Day One" of the new format there was only one paid commercial, "Due almost exclusively to the genius of Herb Humphries, four months later, this, the largest radio staff in the nation and, subsequently, the most expensive format in radio, was operating at a profit. The ratings and the industry nationwide could not have been accomplished without the vision, direction and motivation of Herb Humphries," said Schrack. Herb was in the ninth grade when he got his first peek at journalism through the Gladewater, Texas High School newspaper. From that point in 1944 and for the next 50 years, Herb was working for a newspaper or broadcasting news. His

first radio job was at KGVL-Greenville, Texas, and he worked in Texas radio for the next ten years picking up several AP awards. He was one of the original newsmen at Westinghouse's all-News WINS-New York. When Westinghouse bought KFWB, Herb was named news director and was heavily involved in the conversion. Herb left radio in 1974 and spent his next 20 years at KMOX/TV-St. Louis. In 1995, a year after retiring to a fishing hole in East Texas, a newspaper poll still found him to be the sixth most popular reporter among those St. Louisans polled. (An essay by Herb appears elsewhere in this publication.)

HUMPHRIES, Steven: **KLAX/KXMG**, 1996-97, gm. Steven was vp of Spanish Broadcasting Systems' Western Region when in late 1996, gm duties of the L.A. outlets were added.

HUNDLEY, Hot Rod: **KLAC**. The former NBA basketball player worked with Chick Hearn on Lakers broadcasts.

HUNTER, Ben: **KFVD**; **KFI**, 1946-50s. Ben hosted the "Night Owl" program on KFI. It would not be unusual to tune into Ben's talk show and hear him talking with major celebrities like Elizabeth Taylor and Judy Garland. Ben was acknowledged as the pioneer of the Talk radio graveyard shift. Ben would talk and talk and then call people. The quality of the incoming phone lines was so inconsistent, he always called out to major celebrities. Ben was a native of Oregon and worked at KEX-Portland before arriving in the Southland. Waiting for his break in L.A. he sold china door-to-door. Ben died in the middle 1970s.

HUNTER, Greg: **KIEV**. Greg hosted a restaurant review show and writes a weekly column for *The Tolucan*.

HUNTER, Max: **KMET**, 1985. Max worked as Rich Anderson in Ft. Lauderdale.

HUNTER, Mikel: **KFI**, 1969; **KLAC**, 1970; **KRLA**, 1971-72; **KMET**, 1972-74, pd; **KGBS/FM**, 1975-76. The North Carolina native was born Mikel Harrington in 1938. He arrived in Southern California from KLIV-San Jose. He was at KLAC during the "chicken rock" format. When he got to KRLA for the "underground" format, he worked late evenings and called himself "Hot Rocks Hunter" and "Motorcycle Mikel." During his stint as pd of "the Mighty Met," the environment was as irreverent as the music. The jocks had a wall full of "nude" pictures of listeners, and the ceiling of the studio was a mural with the moon and stars on it. Mikel left KOME-San Jose in 1982. His voiceover career includes being the national voice for Sears.

HUNTER, Rick: **KLAC**, 1989-93. A veteran air personality from Toronto, Rick was on the air at Top 40 giants CFTR, CHUM and CKEY. Rick was inspired to become a jock by listening to the great personalities on WLS and WCFL-Chicago and CKLW-Detroit in the 1960s. He arrived in the Southland in 1988 and got a job with Westwood One's Oldies Channel. He also worked weekends at KLAC until the station joined the Unistar AM Only satellite service. Rick is working at WJIM-Lansing.

HURTES, Hettie Lynn: **KRTH**, 1979-81, nd. **KRLA**, 1985-86. Hettie was a news sidekick to London and Engelman at KRTH.

HURST, Wilson: **KRLA**, 1959. This could be one of the greatest trivia questions about the jocks who traveled the L.A. radio airwaves. Wilson was one of the original morning drive "11-10 Men" on KRLA in September of 1959. He was gone within a month and was never considered part of the official line-up at KRLA. Wilson arrived in the Southland from WKY-Oklahoma City.

HUSER, Joe: **KKGO**, 1985-90; **KKJZ**, 1990; **KLIT**, 1991-92; **KAJZ/KACD**, 1992-95. Joe worked both drive slots at Jazz, KKGO. He is now affiliated with WW1.

HUTTON, Rose: **KOST**, gm. Rose worked for Gordon McLendon for many years and ran KOST shortly after its purchase. When she left radio, Rose co-owned the entertainment industry insurance brokerage firm, Truman Van Dyke Company. She died January 24, 1997, of cancer. Rose was 61.

HYDE, Alan: **KIEV**, 1971; **KLVE**.

HYMAN, Herb: **KRLA**, 1959-61, pd. Herb was replaced as pd by Jim Washburne in late 1961.

Lightning Strikes Twice
by
Jhani Kaye

I was operations manager of KFI and KOST. Our traffic reporter was Bruce Wayne. The veteran pilot was considered the nation's "Dean of Flying Traffic Reporters" and just weeks away from celebrating his becoming the nation's first reporter to have flown 25 years. Bruce was a rare man who was loved by all at the radio stations. Such a lovely man...and a good friend.

On June 4, 1986, the stations attempted to raise Bruce for his first traffic report in the 6 a.m. hour. He didn't respond on the two-way. Since Bruce's radio had experienced down-time before, we assumed that perhaps he was having a technical problem. However, the more time passed, the more worried we became. Air talents from both stations were calling me at home expressing their concern. Then, our worst fears became reality. Someone quite near to Bruce's home base of Fullerton Airport reported seeing a cloud of black smoke rising just a couple of blocks away. Deep inside, I knew it was Bruce's plane involved in a crash. We were in shock. How could it be?

Our general manager, Don Dalton, had been assisting our Miami properties as an interim gm there for several months. It just happened to be this very morning that he was due to return to Los Angeles. I took a chance that he might be changing planes in Atlanta since he always flew Delta. As luck would have it, the Delta agent was able to locate Don. I told him the devastating news. Don reassured me that we would work through this and that when he arrived in Los Angeles he would drive directly to the station.

Don arrived at KFI/KOST and met with me for about 45 minutes. After that he did what he did best: walked the halls and spoke to every person there. He was a tower of strength in the midst of an unbelievable tragedy. I remember Liz Kiley saying that Don came up to her and said, "I missed my kids," (meaning the KFI/KOST staff).

Shortly thereafter I received a frantic call from Liz telling me to come to the parking lot immediately. "Something" had happened to Don. I bolted down the hallway and noticed Liz's shoes were in the middle of the carpet. Later she told me that she had kicked them off to run faster

Once outside the station I saw Don lying beside his car in the parking lot. It seems that as he was opening the door, he felt dizzy, and collapsed onto the pavement. It was incredible that his wife, Mary Ann, happened to be there at that particular moment. Don Dalton had suffered a brain aneurysm the same day that Bruce Wayne had perished.

A decade later it still seems like yesterday. An incredible air talent...reporter...mentor...and good friend. There are so many of us that miss you in our lives.

I

ICKES, Larry: **KXEZ/KJOI**, 1989-96. Larry worked morning drive at the easy listening music stations. He spent two decades in Bay Area radio before coming South. On his arrival, he said: "After 20 years in the 'Fog,' I'm ready for the L.A. sunshine." When he left the Southland he went to KKSF-San Francisco.

IMPEMBA, Mario: **KMPC**. Mario is the color commentator for the Anaheim Angels.

IMUS, Don: **KGBS**, 1972. The bad-boy of Cleveland and New York radio filled in for Hudson & Landry on KGBS in the summer of 1972.

INGLIS, Sheri: **KRTH**, 1987-89; **KFWB**, 1990-97. Sheri is a weekend news anchor on KFWB. At "K-Earth" she handled morning drive news. Sheri is also a free-lance public relations consultant and ghost writer. Her early career includes radio and television talk hosting, reporting, co-anchoring and writing in Palm Springs and San Diego.

IRWIN, Lew: **KPOL**, 1959-61; **KRLA**, 1968-70; **KIQQ**, 1979; **KRLA**, 1991. The veteran newsman with an affinity for troublesome issues, his early stories on Hollywood blacklisting and the John Birch Society earned him a reputation and cost him several jobs. Lew was one of the founding members of the legendary "Credibility Gap" on KRLA. In the mid 1970s he was owned Earth News Network. Lew wrote and produced a drugola documentary for KNBC/Channel 4.

IVENK, Mike: SEE Mike Fright

INOR, Ron: **KPPC**, 1970-71; **KMET**, 1972. He was born Ron Middag.

IRVINE, Jeff: **KWIZ**, 1988

IVERS, Irv: **KHJ**, 1969-72; **KIQQ**, 1972-73, gm. Born in Montreal, Irv started his radio career in Quebec and Bermuda. He came to the U.S. to work in sales at KFRC-San Francisco and KHJ where he was appointed station manager in 1971. In 1974, following the successful launch of "K-100," Irv joined Columbia Pictures as head of advertising. He spent the next 20 years in senior executive marketing jobs at MGM/UA, 20th Century Fox and Warner Bros. In the early 1990s Irv decided to return to his native Canada and moved to Toronto to head up Astral

Communications. He died in November 1996 at the age of 57. His death was due to complications following surgery to remove his spleen 10 days prior. The author of this book hired Irv to run KIQQ and when Irv joined the motion picture business, he offered a unique opportunity to follow him. There wasn't a sweeter, more decent human being than Irv. God bless him!

Order:
Additional copies of *Los Angeles Radio People*, Volume 2
***Los Angeles Radio People*, Volume 1**
***Los Angeles Radio People* newsletter**
Call toll free - 1.888.Radio57

J

JACK, Cadillac: **KQLZ**, 1990-91. He worked the all-night shift at "Pirate Radio."

JACK, Wolfman: **XERB**, 1966-71; **XPRS**, 1971-72; **KDAY**, 1972-73; **KRTH**, 1976; **KRLA**, 1984-87; **XTRA**, 1987. Wolfman Jack was born Robert Weston Smith in a gritty section of Brooklyn on January 21, 1938. His parents died when he was young, and he shuffled among relatives between stints in reform schools. Wolfman got his start below the border on radio stations with mega-million watts of power, which was an inspiration for Francis Ford Coppola's *American Graffiti*. In the film his role took on mythical proportions and catapulted his trademark guttural shriek to national prominence. "I'm not a gimmick," he told the *LA Times* in 1972. "I'm doing me. I wanted to perpetuate a mystique by not appearing in public but that's been over for some time." He once said of the movie, "It took the Wolfman from a cult figure to the rank of American flag and apple pie." While working on Mexican radio stations, the Wolfman did an incredible mail order business selling Baby Jesuses that glowed in the dark and sugar pills that supposedly helped with arousal problems. Wolfman owned the business end of the Tijuana-based station. "I ran the campiest radio station around; we programmed what no one else wanted - preachers and rhythm and blues." Before XERB, Wolfman spent 1959 to 1962 at XERF-Del Rio. Wolfman reflected on his style in a lengthy *Times* interview: "My regular voice sounded like a little kid's and I knew that if I was going to make it, I needed a far-out style." He traveled the small towns, selling the ads, fixing the transmitter and screaming into the mike in small towns. He was influenced by "The Hound" at WKBW-Buffalo, Alan Freed and Murray the K. In 1973 he went to WNEW and WNBC-New York. He had his own radio show syndicated to more than 2,000 stations throughout the United States and 53 other countries at his height of popularity. He was the announcer on NBC/TV's *Midnight Special* for 8 years between 1973 and 1982. Wolfman started at KRLA January 14, 1984. His shaggy hair was sculpted to look like what the well-dressed wolf was wearing. Wolfman appeared in such films as *Hanging on a Star* in 1976, *Motel Hell* in 1980 and *Mortuary Academy* in 1987. He appeared as himself in a two-part episode of tv's *Galactica 1980*. In the fall of 1984, he debuted *Wolfman Rock TV*, an ABC Saturday morning children's program that featured rock gossip, information and videos. During the late '80s and early '90s, he hosted an oldies tv show out of Florida called *Rock 'n Roll Palace*. He was immortalized in 18 songs including *Clap for the Wolfman* by the Guess Who, *Living on the Highway* by Freddie King and *Wolfman Jack* by Todd Rundgren. By the spring of 1995 his authorized biography *Have Mercy: The True Story of Wolfman Jack, The Original Rock 'n' Roll Animal* was published. Following a 20-city tour promoting the book, he collapsed after returning to his Belvidere, North Carolina home 120 miles east of Raleigh. He died July 1, 1995. He was a heavy smoker and overweight but had lost 40 pounds shortly before his death. At the time of his death he was syndicating a live four-hour weekly show to 70 stations from Planet Hollywood in Washington, DC. At his funeral in Belvidere, mourners heard the Wolfman blaring from a jukebox. His black, broad-brimmed hat with a silver band rested atop his gray marble headstone with the kicker, "One more time." His longtime publicist said of the funeral, "Wolfman wanted a party. He wanted a celebration. He's not gone; he'll be around as long as people are playing the music he loved." He was one of five nominees to the Museum of Broadcast Communications' 1995 Radio Hall of Fame, in the pioneer category. From his book: "I'm Wolfman Jack, the guy who used to wash cars in Brooklyn and got lucky."

JACKSON, Bill: Airport Radio 530AM. Born in 1933, Bill is the announcer who steers motorists through the maze of Los Angeles International Airport. The radio station was established in 1972 and Bill has been the voice of airport radio since 1978. He has had minor roles in *Cheers*, *Love Boat* and *Dallas*.

JACKSON, Bob: **KBBQ**, 1967-68; **KLAC**, 1972. Prior to Los Angeles radio, Bob was known in San Diego as Robin Scott at KDEO and Robin at KCBQ. He was previously pd at KRAM-Las Vegas.

JACKSON, Bubba: **KLON**, 1984-92. Bubba hosted the "Nothing But the Blues" program.

JACKSON, Dion: **KNAC**, 1972; **KLOS**, 1976-77; **KLSX**, 1988-95. Dion worked overnights at KLSX when the station was playing "classic rock."

JACKSON, J.J.: **KLOS**, 1969-80; **KDAY**, 1980; **KWST**, 1980; **KROQ**, 1987; **KMPC/FM/KEDG**, 1987-89, pd. J.J. worked afternoon drive when he arrived at KLOS from WBCN-Boston. In the early 1980s, he left to pursue a tv career and became an MTV jock. In 1986, he left WQXI-Atlanta for KSON-San Diego before returning to the Southland on "the Roq." He was part of the change from KMPC/FM to KEDG, "the Edge." In 1988, he hosted a Sunday show called "A Cut Above" and eventually became pd of the Gene Autry station. In 1989 he joined Richard Blade as host of a Movietime cable tv show. In late 1994 J.J. began hosting "The Beatle Years," a syndicated series airing on 200 stations nationwide. He currently works at WW1.

> *"The New 10Q" becomes Spanish "La Super Q"*
> *-KTNQ, July 30, 1979*

JACKSON, Keith: **KABC**. In the mid-1960s Keith was a young sportscaster from Seattle with a folksy approach. He was building a network radio and tv reputation for himself. Keith was never able to achieve longevity with KABC because of the increasing network commitments. He has been associated with college football on the ABC network for decades.

JACKSON, Michael: **KHJ**, 1963-65; **KNX**, 1965; **KABC**, 1966-1997. The former rock and roll dj was a midday mainstay at News/Talk KABC for over three decades. Michael always imagined himself in radio. His father owned several pubs in London, and when he was 11, the family moved to South Africa and Michael became fluent in Afrikaans. By the time he was 16 and finished high school, he was on the air in Johannesburg, having lied about his age. He trained with the BBC. Michael started his American radio career in Springfield, Massachusetts and moved quickly to the Bay Area where he played rock music at KYA and KEWB and had faint tolerance for the music. In San Francisco he was known as Michael Scotland, and his program was called "Scotland's Yard." In 1963, Michael hosted a two-hour Hootenanny show on KHJ. In 1965,

when the format switched to "Boss Radio," he moved to KNX. The same year he became a U.S. citizen and married into Hollywood royalty. His wife Alana is the daughter of the late actor Alan Ladd, the man who played *Shane*. He hosted KCOP/Channel 13's *The Big Question* series, for which he was awarded a local Emmy. In a 1974 *LA Times* profile, Michael was described: "He is of small stature, as compact as a lightweight boxer. His facial expression is one of bemused, continental curiosity - a man secure in all things intellectual but having too good a time to be excessively tweedy." He says he dreamed of being a "combination of Edward R. Murrow and Johnny Carson." In the spring of 1984, he suffered a minor heart attack at the age of 50 while riding horseback through Griffith Park. Journalist Norman Cousins advised Michael during his recuperation period and told him, "A heart attack is something to laugh at. It really is." Michael is the recipient of seven Emmys and winner of four Golden Mike awards for outstanding achievement in radio broadcasting. His various awards include being honored as Member of the Most Excellent Order of the British Empire (M.B.E.) presented by Her Majesty, Queen Elizabeth, along with being given the French Legion of Merit Award, presented by president Mitterand in 1988 and a Star on the Hollywood Walk of Fame in 1984. In 1992 he was off the air for almost two months following heart surgery. He is a regular substitute for Larry King on CNN. In the summer of 1997 Michael moved to weekends. He told his listeners: "The powers that be at KABC have decided on a programming change and they've decided they no longer wish to have me as the host of a daily talk show on their station." He moved to weekends.

JACKSON, Pervis: **KGFJ**, 1973

JACKSON, Sammy: **KBBQ**, 1968; **KLAC**, 1969-72; **KGIL**, 1973-75; **KLAC**, 1976-79; **KMPC**, 1982-83. The one-time star of television's *No Time for Sergeants* was born and raised in Henderson, North Carolina. Sammy was on ABC/TV in the early 1960s. A string of unsold series pilots followed, and he was dropped by Warner Bros. Sammy had roles in several 1960s movies including Disney's *Boatniks*. He commented on his move to radio: "TV is a great avocation. I still do four or five guest shots a year. I'd be dishonest if I told you that if someone offered me a regular spot in a series, I wouldn't take it." He described his radio talent: "I don't do voices or one-liners. What I do is emphasize the music - the writers of a particular song or the story behind it. I'm a friendly on-air companion." While at KLAC he featured mid-morning interviews with some of the biggest stars in Hollywood. Sammy was voted Best Country Jock of the Year at the 6th Annual *Billboard* Radio Programming Forum in 1973. In 1980 he was voted the CMA Country personality of the year. An *LA Times* critic noted in 1981 that Sammy "has quietly and efficiently established a reputation as one of the finest radio personalities in the country." He went to Las Vegas in the late 1980s to work for KUDA. Sammy died of heart failure April 24, 1995. He was 58.

JACKSON, Tommy: **KPWR**, 1996

JACOBS, Jake: **KNX**, 1976-91. Jake was a reporter for all-News KNX until his retirement in 1991. When he left KNX he worked briefly at a local PBS station. He suffered a stroke while in the studio and died shortly thereafter.

> *"I used to listen to Casey Kasem and record 'American Top 40' on my little cassette player and then talk into the microphone between songs and pretend to be the announcer. Now I'm hosting the replacement show for 'AT40.' Wild!"*
> *-Adrienne Walker*

JACOBS, Larry: **KLOS**, 1977-82. Larry was a mass communications and political- science major at the University of Denver and was concerned about the cutback in news at Rock-formatted stations. He commented at the time of KLOS's dominance: "I'm very concerned about this current thinking that news has no place on a Rock station. Remember, FM stations were the first in the 1960s to talk about Vietnam. We wouldn't have heard about the huge herpes epidemic had the story not broken on an FM station." Larry has been with the ABC Network Radio news division since 1984. He said he approaches the news differently: "I segue each story like a

jock does with records; I think bridging stories is very important. I've done it the same way my entire career." Larry was born in the Bronx and grew up on Long Island. After graduating from the University of Denver in 1970, he started in Tucson at KTUC and later KWFM. He returned to Denver to work for KBPI and before joining KLOS worked at KOME-San Jose. Larry laughed that the station was called, "the KOME spot on your dial." He also worked with NBC's Youth Network "The Source" before leaving the West Coast in 1984, bound for New York City. Larry and his wife Cynthia are the parents of two daughters, Danielle and Heather.

JACOBS, Ron: **KHJ**, 1965-69. A native of Honolulu, Ron began his professional radio career as a correspondent for NBC's "Monitor" at KGU. Two years later, at age 20, he worked at KHVH, where he met Elvis Presley and began a lifelong friendship with his mentor, the late Col. Tom Parker. In 1958, Ron became Hawaii's youngest pd, and worked with Mike Joseph and Bill Gavin. "They taught me the basics of Top 40 formatics." In 1959 Ron joined KPOI as pd and morning drive dj. He had much success in Honolulu. In 1962 his drive and eagerness to learn took him to the Mainland as the Colgreene Corporation vp of programming. Ron fine-tuned his programming concepts at KMEN-San Bernardino and KMAK-Fresno. His success came to the attention of radio consultant Bill Drake - a Fresno competitor. Joining forces in 1965, Drake hired Ron, then 27, to program KHJ and the "Boss" format achieved an industry pinnacle. While at KHJ Ron produced radio's first "rockumentary," the 48-hour special, "The History of Rock and Roll." In 1970, he left KHJ for a new role, co-founder and vp of Watermark, Inc. Ron and Tom Rounds, a KPOI alumnus, launched Casey Kasem's "American Top 40." During his time with Watermark, Ron also produced, "The Elvis Presley Story" and a "long-dreamed-of project" called *Cruisin': A History of Rock 'n Roll Radio*. Each album recreated the radio show of a dj who held regional dominance during the developing years of rock music. Ron recalled a *Cruisin'* highlight: "I've always felt that - in its heyday - 'Color Radio/Channel 98' was the most exciting Top 40 station of its era. My personal on-air style was influenced by the late B. Mitchel Reed. I was also fortunate enough to have worked with BMR on a *Cruisin'* album in 1970." Ron produced other albums at the Watermark "farm studio" (built by an actor/carpenter named Harrison Ford), including *A Child's Garden of Grass*. Before returning to Honolulu, Ron joined KGB-San Diego for a quick turnaround. He staged the KGB "Charity Ball" in 1972, the largest public service concert in California history. He conceived and produced what would become a series of *Homegrown* album projects - taking raw, young talent eager to record and allowing them to do so. *Homegrown* became the largest-selling album in San Diego's history, according to KGB. The liner notes were written by a teenage KGB listener, Cameron Crowe. The KGB Chicken - later known to the nation as "The San Diego Chicken" - also hatched from Ron's fertile imagination. In 1972 he was honored by *Billboard* as Program Director of the Year and two years later KGB was named Station of the Year. Twenty-one years after he began his career, Ron was again behind the microphone in Honolulu. He was doing morning drive and pd at KKUA. He introduced *Homegrown* to the Islands, earning the Hawaiian Grammy and a series of tv specials. In 1981 he launched KDEO as Hawaii's only full-time Country music station. In 1985, Ron conceived, wrote and produced a nation-wide radio promotion in conjunction with Hawaii's visitor industry. "The Hawaiian Chief" contest ran in all 50 states. During much of the 80s he was

a contributing editor to both *Honolulu* and *Hawaii* magazines. Then 35 years after they first began their professional association, Ron was yet again re-united with Tom Rounds as executive producer of Radio Express's "World Chart Show" in 1994. At the end of 1995, the show was heard on 360 stations in 54 countries with co-productions of the program in 27 different languages. "World Chart Show" debuted in the United States in early 1996. In the summer of 1997 Ron returned to Hawaii to program KGMZ and work afternoons. He has reunited with 40-year colleague Tom Moffatt.

JACOBS, Vic "the Brick": **KIIS**. Born in 1954 in Brooklyn, Vic is the son of Hungarian parents. He grew up in Queens and earned a communications degree from Cornell University, then went back packing through Micronesia. He started his radio career in Guam covering cockfights. He arrived in the Southland in the summer of

1988 as a sportscaster on KCOP/Channel 13. Vic had worked at a Fresno tv station, KMPH, for the two years prior to joining Channel 13. Larry Stewart of the *LA Times* called the sports editor of the *Visalia Times-Delta* at the time of Vic's hiring who said: "He's all show. He doesn't really tell you who won and lost. He'll take some obscure news item and blow it all out of proportion." The nd at the Fresno tv station said: "When you first see him, it's like jumping into cold water. It's quite a shock. I think he's terrific." His tv trademark was a fake red brick with "Vic's Brick" written on it, and he threw it at the camera as he feigned anger. He wore a tuxedo, wing-collared tuxedo shirt and a bolo or string tie with spiked hair. Before Fresno he toiled in Roswell and Austin tv. Vic joined Rick Dees as a sidekick sports partner during morning drive on KIIS. On KIIS' web site, Vic talked about his style: "American kids have got so sophisticated you can't just give 'em the score any more or they'll tune you out." In the spring of 1997 Vic started his own talk show on "XTRA Sports 1150," KIIS/AM.

JACQUES, Truman: **KABC**, 1995-97. The former host of KABC's "Religion on the Line," Truman has been a tv talk show host and producer in four contiguous decades. He was a familiar figure on CBS/TV for years and has been hosting a local series called "Area of American Influence" on KCOP/Channel 13. A graduate of Pepperdine University, he holds an undergraduate degree in communications. In addition to his tv and radio work, Truman serves as a director of communications for the City of Inglewood.

JAGER, Rick: **KHJ**, 1975-80; **KWST**, 1981-82, nd; **KNWZ**, 1983-84. The senior media relations executive for the Los Angeles Metropolitan County Transportation Authority started out his radio career as a news intern at KHJ. Rick was born in 1954 in Thermopoulos, Wyoming and grew up in the Inland Empire. His interest in radio developed at Chaffee College when he switched from a history major to speech and acting. By the time he got to Cal Poly Pomona he was active in starting the campus radio station. In his junior year he became an intern in the public affairs department at KHJ. After graduation in June 1976, Lyle Kilgore hired Rick as an assignment editor at KHJ and he was promoted to virtually every shift including doing the news with Rick Dees in morning drive. Rick went to KNWZ for the brief foray into all-News and by 1984 he was ready to get out of radio. Does he miss it? "I still miss the spontaneity of radio news. I miss the excitement of radio. I don't miss the instability of radio." Rick lives in Fontana and makes the daily commute to MTA headquarters in Los Angeles.

JAMES, Chuck: **KGIL**, 1964, pd; **KDAY**, 1965. Born in 1935, Chuck started out in the mid-1950s at WIL-St. Louis. When he left the Southland in 1966 he went to be nd of KYW-Philadelphia and in 1968 joined KCBS-San Francisco.

JAMES, Daphne: **KJLH**, 1994-96

JAMES, Doug: **KGIL**, 1966

JAMES, Keith: **KMAX**, 1994-95, gm. Keith worked for an ad agency in Denver before arriving at KMAX to run the all-Sports programming. Keith left the station when it was sold.

JAMES, Kevin: **KKBT**, 1991-92 and 1994-97. Kevin is known as "slow jammin' James" and has a best-selling CD compilation series of slow jams. Born in Punxsutawney, Pennsylvania, he grew up in the Philadelphia area. After a stint in the Army, he eventually joined WKYS-Washington, DC in 1977. Over the course of 13 years Kevin was with the station four times. Where did "slow jammin' James" come from? "Our crosstown competition, WHUR, originated the 'Quiet Storm'. Donny Simpson told me to come up with a moniker for my evening show and the name just worked." Kevin has moved to Tampa but continues his weekend show on KKBT. "I really hated leaving my core audience. I loved being in the community and working with the young people." Kevin is on Snoop Doggy Dogg's *Doggy Pound* album and has a business relationship with Snoop. His *Timeless Jam Collection* has sold over 160,000 units and his "Love Affair" show is syndicated across the country.

JAMES, Peter: **KROQ**, 1979-80; **KWST**, 1980-81. He was born Peter Spatz.

JAMES, Rollye: **KPOL**, 1979, pd; **KMPC**, 1980; **KHTZ**, 1980; **KGIL**; **KLAC**; **KMPC**, 1990; **KFI**, 1990-91. There is no mistaking Rollye for a Milquetoast female broadcaster. Within minutes of meeting this brash, smart and funny woman, you discover that she bleeds radio. Her passion for r&b music was the springboard for her interest in radio. "I was 10 years old and sick in bed scanning the radio dial and heard r&b music and it was just transforming. It had the power to take me places I couldn't go." Her Bolivian father (at age 37 she learned

that she was adopted) died in a commercial air crash when she was 10. She became emancipated at 12 and has moved through the interstate non-stop ever since. She graduated magna cum laude from the University of Miami. Even though she qualifies for MENSA membership she quips: "Before you leap to conclusions, Miami grades on a curve." Rollye started her radio journey at WQAM-Miami as production director. After a stint in Nashville managing Charlie Rich she returned to radio and "Radio Poland." She is a self-described nut about call letter origination and is planning a book on the subject. "KPOL actually stood at one point for K-Polka." Rollye teamed with Charlie Tuna in morning drive at KHTZ. "Eventually I thought of offering to take a pay cut if I could own the dead air. I figured while Tuna regained his composure with alarming regularity, I could have run a few spots." In 1983 she joined *Billboard* as the radio editor and a year later was chairman of the magazine's radio convention. Her nomadic life (worked in 32 markets) might explain her love for the interstate. "I've driven every inch of interstate in America." Rollye eventually made the transition to talk radio and worked KOA-Denver broadcasting to 41 states and 5 provinces. In the nineties she talked at KFMB-San Diego following Padre games and KLBJ-Austin. "Radio is ingrained in my cells. When I'm not talking on a clear channel frequency, I'm listening to early r&b." She has been behind the scenes for major developments in Los Angeles radio including the meteoric rise of KRTH. Rollye has adopted a goal for national nighttime talk radio. "Radio, local and national alike, ignores half of the broadcast day. There's a lot of untapped revenue here. And more listeners than you need to start the cash flowing. It just takes some out of the box thinking - my specialty, as no one's ever accused me of fitting in."

JAMES, Samantha: SEE Keli Garrett

JAMES, Victoria: **KMET**, 1967. Victoria was part of the all-female staff at KMET.

JAMISON, Bob: **KMPC**, 1991-92. Bob was a California Angels broadcaster. He spent 12 seasons in Triple A ball in Nashville and worked in Richmond, Anderson, South Carolina, Newport News and Utica before that.

JANISSE, James: **KLON**, 1992-96. Born in Houston in 1951, James credits his love for jazz and blues to loving  parents for instilling in him an enormous appreciation for this music. James and his parents came to the Southland when he was five. After a stint in the Army, he graduated from UCLA in 1977 with a degree in draftsman engineering. For the next seven years James worked for several aerospace companies. When aerospace industry took a bump, he got into construction in order "to stay alive." A friend complimented James that he had a "radio voice." James went to the American Radio Network training center and a year to the day later joined KLON working overnights and weekends. He also manages an alcohol treatment facility near MacArthur Park.

JANKOWSKI, Judy: **KLON**, 1994-97, gm. Judy arrived to manage the Long Beach Jazz station from a similar position at WDUQ-Pittsburgh, Duquain University's public radio station, where she worked for 24 years.

JANSSEN, Dick: **KLAC/KMET**, 1968-70, gm. The former president of Scripps-Howard Broadcasting ran KLAC and KMET in the late 1960s. Dick was responsible for bringing the late L. David Moorhead to KMET. Born May 19, 1936, in Cleveland, Dick started his radio sales career in May 1958 at WHK. Following a three year stint at Metromedia Broadcasting sales in Detroit, he returned to WHK as gsm and was promoted to vp/gm in 1967. Dick was gm for the launch of the legendary Cleveland AOR station, "the Buzzard," WMMS. In late 1970 he returned to Ohio as gm of WGAR and then became vp of operations for Nationwide Broadcasting. Dick stayed at Nationwide, eventually becoming the executive vp of the radio/tv division, until joining Scripps-Howard in July 1978. He ascended rapidly, becoming president in May of 1988. Dick retired to Scottsdale on December 31, 1992. "I get to improve my golf game living in Arizona."

JARRETT, Hugh: **KBBQ**, 1968-70, pd. A former member of the Jordanaires who sang behind Elvis, Hugh became pd of KBBQ. His group continued to back up country singers.

JARRIN, Jaime: **KTNQ/KLVE**, 1975-84; **KWKW**. Born in 1936 in Ecuador, Jaime spent more than a quarter century broadcasting in Spanish in Southern California. He broadcasts the Dodger games on a national basis. In the mid-1970s when he wasn't involved with the Dodgers, he hosted a midday show on "K-Love." He was the first Latino to win a Golden Mike award. Jaime is also vp of news and sports for KWKW's parent company. He almost died from injuries suffered in an auto accident at Vero Beach in the spring of 1990. Jaime had a lacerated liver, a ruptured spleen, broken ribs and a collapsed lung. He underwent surgery the night of the accident and again a few weeks later to clear an intestinal abscess.

JARRIN, Jorge: **KABC**, 1985-97; **KSKQ**. The son of Jaime Jarrin, the noted Spanish language broadcaster of the Los Angeles Dodgers, Jorge graduated from Pepperdine University in Malibu. He has been a helicopter reporter in "Jet Copter 790" on KABC since August 1985. He also broadcast traffic reports on Spanish KSKQ. In 1990, Jorge was named an honorary Captain of the California Highway Patrol resulting in the title "Captain Jorge."  He was on the public relations staff of the Los Angeles Olympic Organizing Committee, where he became the Hispanic community relations officer for the Coliseum and South Central Los Angeles. He is the co-creator and publisher of the monthly children's coloring/life lesson book entitled, *The Adventures of Captain Jorge and the Jetcopter Kids*. Jorge has run in the

Los Angeles Marathon as a reporter for KABC "TalkRadio." He and his wife Maggie live in San Gabriel with their three sons.

JARVIS, Al: **KELW/KFWB**, 1932-60; **KLAC**, 1960-62; **KHJ**, 1962; **KFWB**, 1962; **KEZY**, 1963; **KNOB**, 1967. "Wanted: Man to Talk on the Radio." A record store owner in Hollywood thought if he could get someone to play "records" on the radio, it would help sell them. Al became a jock after answering that ad in 1932 and he was a pioneer and long considered the originator of the "Make Believe Ballroom" on KFWB (station was owned by the Warner brothers, hence the WB). Al was born in Canada and went to Roosevelt High School in L.A. where he performed a speech from *The Merchant of Venice* to win a Shakespeare Contest and a stint at the Pasadena Playhouse. An article in the *OC Register* quoted Al on his beginning: "A few weeks after I got the job at KELW in 1932 I was hounding the owner-manager to let me air pop records instead of those electrical transcriptions. By using  commercial records, I figured, I would not only have a more diversified program, but I could present some of the world's great stars. It was the first time on radio, it was the first time any records were played. That's how the 'Make Believe Ballroom' was born." Al has been credited with the discovery of Nat "King" Cole, Jimmy Boyd, Frankie Laine and Gogi Grant. He was at KFWB for the launch of Chuck Blore's "Color Radio" on January 2, 1958, and worked nine to noon. He never totally accepted the music transition but acknowledged rock music: "Top 40 programming has apparently satisfied the needs of a majority of the music- and record-conscious audience." He once said of Elvis Presley: "If he were a Negro and performed as he does now, he would be put in jail. I know this is true, because it has happened to singers. But because Elvis has white skin, they let him get away with it." In the spring of 1960 he left KFWB and joined KLAC in the midday slot; he also hosted a local tv show with Betty White. In 1962 he became a vp at DRA Records (he owned a record store on Hollywood Blvd in the late 1940s). Later that year he teamed with his wife, Marilyn, to do a music and interview show with Hollywood stars on KHJ for an hour at midnight. In 1967 he worked his "Make Believe Ballroom" magic during morning drive on KNOB. Al died in 1970 and at the time was a sales executive with KLAC.

JAXSON, Tommy: **KFI**, 1984-85; **KOST**, 1985-91; **KYSR**, 1992-93; **KXEZ**, 1993-96; **KBIG**, 1997. A Southern California native, he came from Dallas radio to work at KFI under the name Thom O'Hare. He was soon hosting the popular "Pillow Talk" evening show, until moving to the overnight shift on sister station, KOST. He's currently working weekends at WW1's Mainstream Country format and weekends at KBIG.

JAY, George: **KHJ**; **KFWB**. Best known for his very successful newsletter, the independent record promoter first worked as a jock in the 1950s.

JAY, Lyman: **KGRB**, 1983; **KORG**, 1993. Born in 1945, Jay started as a dj in 1964. He got interested in big bands while volunteering at KCRW. Jay has a collection of 9,000 LPs, covering 1920-40s music.

JAY, Steve: SEE Jay Stevens

JEAN, Linda: **KIKF**, 1995-97. Linda was hired at KIKF after an intern program at Saddleback Community College. She was born in 1971 in Laguna Beach. She graduated from the University of Arizona in 1993 with a B.A. in journalism. It was through her internship with midday personality Carrie Dunne, that she was hired for weekend overnights and fill-in work. "The job is great, I like the music and the staff, and really what more could a dj want? O.K. Money, Money, Money. I am told that comes later...ha ha."

JED THE FISH: **KORG**; **KROQ**, 1978-84 and 1985-97. Born Edwin Gould on July 15, Jed the Fish grew up in Newport Beach, Laguna Beach and Casa Grande, Arizona. His first radio job was in Casa Grande at KPIN. He has had a controversial long run with AOR KROQ, beginning in 1978 as md and moving to the night shift in 1979. In 1985, he swam north to KQAK-San Francisco for three months and a brief weekend stint at KRQR-San Francisco, then returned to KROQ. In March of 1989, his arrest on heroin charges was covered by all the major media. There was so much shame about all the publicity that Jed sought treatment. As part of his rehabilitation, he created a two-hour program called "Clean and Crazy," with former KROQ jocks April Whitney and Chuck Randall. "We want to remind people that you can still have fun and be creative - and be clean. In the old days, I'd just shoot a bunch of dope, go on the air and do anything. I'd developed my crazy style as a result of getting high. But now it comes out of being me. I'm more clear-headed and more focused." His long run with "the Roq" makes him one of the most visible radio personalities spanning three decades. When asked about his career, Jed said, "If I have a gimmick, it is trying to be myself on the air." Jed lives in Pasadena.

> *"I loved radio for the music, concerts, parties and to think you could get paid for it all. At 28 I reached the point when I realized I had nothing left to say about 'Stairway to Heaven,' I got out."*
> *-Laura Davis*

JEFFREY, Don: **KIKF**, 1985-90, pd. Don is known as

Hopalong Cassidy on the Inland Empire's KFRG where he is music director. Born January 31, 1949, in Trona, California, he spent most of his youth in Muskogee, Oklahoma. He entered the USMC in 1968, spending 12 years on active duty including 2 tours of Vietnam. After leaving the Marines, Don re-trained as a stockbroker while doing part-time dj work in night clubs. He started his radio career at KECO and KKCC-Weatherford, Oklahoma. In the mid-1980s he joined KBBQ-Ventura and then went to afternoons at KIKF. He's been on the board for the Academy of Country Music and was named Radio Personality of the Year. Don loves country music and has discovered a local singer, Gary Allan, whose career he is now managing. Don lives in Corona with Karen, his wife of 12 years.

JEFFREY, Scott: **KHJ**, 1980. SEE Lon Helton

JEFFREYS, Dave: **KHJ/FM**, 1970-72, pd; **KRTH**, 1972. Dave had been doing voiceover tracks for Hit Parade '70 when he became pd of KHJ/FM. He was there for the transition with the RKO stations, calling "K-Earth" the "Classic Rock n' Roll Radio."

JEFFRIES, Jan: **KFRG/KHTX**, 1995, pd. Prior to joining the San Bernardino outlet, Jan worked at WMET-Chicago, KZBS-Oklahoma City and KLTD-Austin. Jan left "the Frog" in the summer of 1995 to join KDDK-Little Rock as pd. In the fall of 1995 Jan was named pd/md of WRMF-West Palm Beach and worked early evening. Jan is currently at the Fairbanks owned Country formatted WCLB-West Palm Beach doing afternoon drive and pd. Born in Cleveland, Jan graduated from Lakewood High School in 1968 and joined the U.S. Navy and worked in communications.

JEFFRIES, Jason: **KLSX**, 1993-94; **KKLA**, 1995-97; **KLTX**, 1997. Born Jason Lerner Beaton in Montreal, Jason and his family moved to Sherman Oaks where he grew up and graduated from Los Angeles Valley College with a degree in broadcasting. He has been fascinated with radio since age four. "My dad bought me a tape recorder and I used to record songs off the radio and play them back pretending to be a disc jockey." Following an internship at KRLA, Jason moved to sister station KLSX in 1993. At KKLA  he was the assistant om. "My greatest achievement at KKLA was working every on-air shift at the station." In early 1997 Jason was transferred to new sister station "K-Light" (1390AM), "The Light in Los Angeles," as station manager and morning host.

JEFFRIES, Ken: **KFWB**, 1989-97. Ken is an anchor at all-News KFWB.

JENKINS, Bill: **KGBS**, 1967-68; **KFWB**, 1970-71; **KGBS**, 1975-76; **KABC**, 1985. Bill started his own production firm in 1968 and continued with his on-air show. He did news on KGBS. In the 1980s, he was doing news on KABC and a "New Age" weekend talk show called "Open Mind." The subject matter frequently centered on psychics and UFOs. He retired in 1989 and lives in Granada Hills.

JENNRICH, Phil: **KLAC**, 1983-97, nd

JENSEN, Jeff: **KQLZ**, 1991-92. Jeff was from WYNF-Tampa. In 1992 he hosted the syndicated "Pirate Radio USA." He apparently returned to Tampa after "Pirate Radio" was sold.

JEREMIAH, David: **KMPC**, 1994. When KMPC changed formats to all-Talk, a contest was held to find talk show hosts. David was the winner and did fill-in.

JETER, Cindie: **KMPC**, 1982-83. Cindie went to work for one of the traffic reporting operations.

JILLSON, Joyce: **KABC**, 1979-89. The world-known astrologer was a regular contributor to "Ken and Bob Company" morning show and she had a weekend talk show on KABC in the late '80s where she dispensed astrological forecasts to callers. During her time at KABC

she subbed for Michael Jackson. Joyce's syndicated daily horoscope column is published in over 100 papers nationally and 50 internationally. Her astrological studies began in early childhood when she was chosen to be the only protégé of well-known Boston astrologer Maude Williams. By the age of ten she was charting predictions on events ranging from the stock market to politics. Joyce is a best-selling author, having ranked on the *New York Times* best-seller list for 28 straight weeks. She has been featured in every major publication and many major network tv shows.

JO, Mary: SEE Mary Jo Godges

JOBSON, Wayne: **KROQ**, 1992-97. Wayne hosts a Sunday reggae revolution on KROQ.

JOHN, Captain: **KHJ**, 1973-74. Born John Lodge, the Captain arrived at KHJ from WAYS-Charlotte.

JOHN, Doctor: SEE John Leader

JOHN and **KEN**: **KFI**, 1992-97. John Kobylt and Ken

Champiou work afternoon drive at KFI. They first teamed in 1988 at WOND-Atlantic City. Ken, born in 1956, graduated from State University of New York at Buffalo. After graduation he worked as a C.P.A. for a health company. John spent a year of college at Seton Hall and then worked as a sportswriter. His first radio job in 1983 was KAAD-Canton and two years later was at a station in Elmira while commuting to Canton. The pair worked at WKXW-Trenton before arriving at KFI and they were best known for masterminding a listener "tax revolt" in which they enlisted audience members to protest tax increases to the New Jersey legislature. They have an uncanny ability to mix and match topics during the drive home. The pair rode the O.J. Simpson trial like a bucking bronco. In 1994 they held a yard sale to raise money for the DA's prosecution of the Menendez Brothers at the Insight Shooting Range in Artesia. During a week-long broadcast at "free-speech" area at the Republican convention, they were ousted. On another day they enumerated the byproducts of a cow. They are apolitical. Politicians are openly referred to as "cretins," "wackos" or "geeks." John, born in 1961, is married to CNN entertainment reporter, Deborah Zara Kobylt.

JONATHAN, Peter: **KHJ**, 1965. Peter left KHJ with the arrival of "Boss Radio" and shuffled off to Buffalo.

JOHNSON, Bruce: **KFAC**, 1969-71; **KLAC**, 1971-72, gm; **KHJ**, 1972-75. A second generation Angeleno and a graduate of USC law school, Bruce started in radio at the age of 17 as an announcer on KUSC at the University of Southern California. He began his professional radio career in 1956 at KOOL-Phoenix working 18-hour days between the tv and radio. During military service in Falls Church, Virginia, he ran an advertising agency with some other recruits and was on the air at WFAX. After Bruce was discharged he went to work for Peters, Griffin and Woodward in Los Angeles. He became manager of the office at 24. In 1962 he went to AM Radio Sales, then owned by Group W and Golden West, and started law school at night at the same time. Classical KFAC had been running $100,000 in the red, and when he left, it was operating $300,000 in the black. He accomplished similar results at KLAC. The year he arrived, the station lost $785,000. The next year the station was $300,000 profitable. In 1972 Bruce joined RKO as vp and helped change KHJ/FM to KRTH. By 1975 he was president of RKO radio with offices in New York and Los Angeles. Starr Broadcasting, at the time owned by William F. Buckley, hired Bruce to be president in 1976. In 1979 he merged Starr with Shamrock. Two years later he went out on his own and began consulting and has since purchased two radio stations in Idaho. From his home in Palm Springs, Bruce was asked for his most exciting "turn-around" situation. "Actually it was in cable television. I was brought in to the cable health network in 1983. They had no ratings, no cpm. So I ran it like a radio station, became highly promotional and doubled the revenues." The venture evolved into the highly successful Lifetime Network. In 1987, Bruce wanted to end the incessant traveling, so he moved to Palm Springs where he is currently the gm of KCMJ and continues to run his Idaho radio stations.

JOHNSON, Charlie: **KMPC**, 1967-69. Charlie moved into talent management and worked with his wife who had the Smothers Brothers as a client.

JOHNSON, Chuck: **KTYM**

JOHNSON, Harry: **KOST**, 1977-82; **KBIG**, 1983-88. "One of the most exciting broadcast experiences was doing the announcing for 'The Home Show. There's nothing like live television to get the adrenaline going." Born November 10, 1944, in Kansas City, Harry dropped out of Baker University (he worked on the campus radio station) to pursue his love for music and radio. After a stint in the Army and radio assignments at KFEQ-St. Joseph, KWBB-Wichita and KVOR-Colorado Springs, he got hooked into beautiful music and "the Shulke format." Jobs at Beautiful music-formatted stations in Milwaukee, Atlanta and Seattle led to KOST and KBIG. In a 1977 *LA Times* profile, Harry was described: "Johnson, a tall, casually dressed man with one of those voices that seems to have arrived straight from the Burning Bush." Since 1985 Harry has been using that voice teaching broadcasting at Santa Monica City College and doing free-lance voiceover work.

Former poster girl for Coors Beer

-Leigh Ann Adam

JOHNSON, J.J.: **KDAY**, 1974-91, pd; **KMPC**; **KJLH**, 1992; **KKBT**, 1993-94; **KACE**, 1994-97. Born in Cleveland as James O. Johnson, J.J. hung out at the local

jazz station in Cleveland Heights. He was only 15 years old when one of the jocks asked, "Why don't you do this?" "He asked me if I had a social security card. I said, 'Yeah,' and he said, 'Then, you can do this.' And that was it. I started on WABQ in January of 1968 when I was 17 years old." He called himself Jimmy O'Jaye. In the summer of 1969 he had two job offers from stations in Houston and signed on with KYOK at $125 a week because it was $15 more than the other offer. "I started August 11, 1969. I remember the day because it was the day I left home." In 1971 he went to KFRC-San Francisco where consultant Bill Drake and pd Paul Drew gave him the name J.J. Johnson which he has used professionally ever since. It was at KFRC where Drew taught J.J. the mechanics of being a programmer. In the summer of 1973, J.J. took over the pd position at KFRC/FM which was automated and he lasted nine months. "I was grateful for the job and I'm glad to have had the experience, but I hated it." On July 1, 1974, Jim Maddox hired J.J. which started a 17-year association with KDAY. During this time he was pd twice and won virtually every industry and community award including *Billboard*'s black jock of the year in 1976 and best pd of black radio in 1977; *BRE* air personality of the year in a major market; NAACP Image Award; American Jewish Committee Institute of Human Relations Award; and L.A. Black Media Coalition Outstanding Technical Achievement Award. Along the way he started a production company, Too Lunar Productions (he and his partner Gary Jackson are moon children). J.J. voiced most of the Motown tv specials during the 1980s including *Motown 25*, *Motown At the Apollo*, *A Motown Christmas* and *Motown on Showtime*. J.J. was absolutely the last voice heard on KDAY. In 1992 he became the JAMS editor at *Hits* magazine for two years. J.J. has two mentors: "Mike Payne taught me how to be a personality. Paul Drew gave me a Harvard education in the mechanics of programming. I'm probably more of a mechanic - not to be confused with 'mechanical' - than a great personality. But a good mechanic can often beat superior talent." J.J. got actively involved in syndication beginning in 1982 and co-hosted with Lou Rawls the 24-hour radio special "The Music of Black America." In the mid-1980s he hosted WW1's bi-weekly "Budweiser Concert Hour" and "Fresh Traxx." In the early 1990s he produced "Countdown/Countdown" hosted by Russ Parr.

JOHNSON, Jayne: **KPWR**, 1993. Jayne co-hosted mornings with Jay Thomas at "Power 106." She was nicknamed "Jabber Jaws Jayne." Jayne replaced "Powermouth Patty." In the spring of 1995, she moved to mornings at WZOK-Rockford, Illinois.

JOHNSON, Paul: **KIIS**, 1969-72; **KUTE**, 1972-73; **KPOL**, 1973; **KFAC**, 1974; **KZLA**, 1975-83. In 1982 Paul joined Metro Traffic and was made om in 1987. The former opera singer went on to join KNBC/Channel 4 as a weather and traffic anchor in 1988. Paul studied music and drama at St. Olaf College in Northfield, Minnesota and earned at Bachelor of B.S. degree in law from Glendale University. He spent eight years as pd of WJR/FM-Detroit.

JOHNSON, Dr. Perri: **KGFJ**, 1986. Perry hosted an evening love song show on KGFJ and dispensed with advice on relationships. Dr. Johnson is a counselor in Santa Barbara.

JOHNSON, Robin: Robin worked at Metro Traffic, In 1991 she joined Shadow Traffic where she continues.

JOHNSON, Ron: **KPPC**, 1971

JOHNSON, Van: **KROQ**, 1986-91, pd

JOKER, The: SEE Joe Terry

JOLIFFE, John: **KTZN**, 1997

JOLLE, Frank: **KNAC**, 1970-71 and 1972-74, pd; **KHJ**; **KKDJ**, 1971-72, pd; **KROQ**; **KYMS**, 1972. Born in St. Louis, Frank has done news or jock work at 32 stations over a 20-year period. He was born Franke Clark on March 25, 1939, in Springfield, Illinois. In the late 1960s

he attended LSU and studied law at Golden West College in Huntington Beach. Frank's radio journey started in Maryland and Virginia and then Georgia. He spent time on WMAK-Nashville, WKBW-Buffalo and three stations in Dallas: KLIF, KBOX and KVIL (known as the Jolle

Green Giant). He also worked for WNOE-New Orleans (his alter ego was Count Down), KAFY-Bakersfield and KONO-San Antonio. Frank made his way to station ownership in Northern California with KPDJ and KKDJ-Eureka and KPAK-Redding. He has produced and starred in a number of independent films. In the story of John Wesley Hardin, Frank played Bill Hickok because "I look just like him." Frank owned and hosted a syndicated oldies show called "Sh-Boom." In the 1980s he was the regional manager for Drake-Chenault programming services. Frank is an active member of the Producers Guild of America and currently owns and operates an independent film company that produces movies for tv and theatrically released films. He's based in Citrus Heights.

JONES, Bill: **KLIT**, 1990-93. Bill works weekends at WW1's AM Only/Adult Standards format, broadcasting to over 200 stations including KLAC. Born in Nashville, he worked at a number of stations in and around Music City U.S.A. until moving to L.A. in late 1987 to pursue an acting career. While at WAMB-Nashville, Bill was voted one of Middle Tennessee's top ten air personalities in the *Nashville Tennessean*'s 1986 reader's poll.

"When I arrived in L.A. I pounded the pavement looking for acting work. While waiting I put together an aircheck for what was then called Transtar Radio Network [later Unistar; now WW1] and worked two formats until 1990." He joined "K-Lite" for the evenings, where he was "eventually fired due to budget cutbacks and replaced by a tape machine." He kept the WW1 weekend position. Bill has an active voiceover career and is the current host of American Airline's "Centerstage" in-flight audio program.

JONES, Bob: **KHJ/FM**, 1966. Bob was the voice of the automated "Cavalcade of Hits."

JONES, Brooke: **KUTE**, 1986; **KACE**, 1990-92; **KAJZ/KBJZ**, 1992-94. Brooke worked morning drive at KUTE.

JONES, Buster: **KGFJ**, 1971-76; **KMPC**, 1976; **KUTE**, 1977-85. Born in Paris, Tennessee, in 1943, Buster went on to a very successful voiceover career. In the early '70s he co-hosted *Soul Unlimited*, a Dick Clark-produced dance party show on ABC/TV. Buster started playing the drums when he was 10 and two of his high school teachers told him that if he excelled in school they would support a scholarship to Lane College in Jackson, Tennessee. He did excel, he went off to Lane and when he arrived, they had never heard of him. Ashamed and with no money Buster began to walk 75 miles home. "Whenever I was in trouble as a kid I would walk. And I knew I was in trouble." About 25 miles later he came across WJAK located over a veterinarian hospital which happened to be owned by Wink Martindale's father-in-law. "I knew a dj there and went inside. One of their jocks had just quit." He worked out a deal to work on-air while the boss paid for his tuition at Lane College. He has been plagued with a stammering speech impediment since a kid and went on to work on his master's degree in Chattanooga while working at WNOO. Due to an asthmatic condition he missed being drafted. Racism was prevalent at the NBC station in Chattanooga. "The station was in a hotel and I couldn't enter by the front door. I worked evenings and nobody was to know that I was black. I was paid by the janitor." He spent three years in St. Louis before coming to the Southland where he spent five years with Motown. Buster is saving the rest of his story for a book that he is actively writing. He can be heard each year as the announcer on the *American Music Awards* show.

JONES, Chuck: **KDAY**, 1965

JONES, Dana: **KPPC**, 1973

JONES, David K.: **KOST**, 1982-85. David was the first morning man when KOST moved from Easy Listening to an AC format. "I was on my way to a career in architecture. I loved to build things." As a kid he loved to win contests on the radio and eventually became a jock in his native Lubbock at KLLL at age 15. In the 1970s David ran KQEO-Albuquerque and KPLZ-Seattle. Just before arriving in the Southland he was pd at WCFL-Chicago. In 1985 David moved to KSLX and fell in love with Phoenix. In 1994, he was the morning man on WFLC-Miami. Two years later he returned to Phoenix and KBUC where he hosts the morning show on the Country station.

JONES, Geno: **KJLH**, 1990-92. Gene worked the morning drive shift at KJLH when he arrived in the Southland from WAMO-Pittsburgh. He is now working in Florida radio.

JONES, Johnny: **KDAY**, 1974

JONES, Ken: **KGFJ**; **KIIS**, 1976; **KIEV**. Ken died in the early 1990s.

JONES, Mike: SEE Mike O'Neil

JONES, Sam: **KPSA**, 1971-72; **KLAC**; **KJLH**. Sam was born in Chicago in 1935.

"In a nutshell, they wanted to take the station in a different direction, and we were not part of that direction. We were perceived as part of the past, part of the old. I'd like people to know we're not dead and buried. After all, it's the only thing I know how to do. I'm completely unqualified for anything else."
   -Bob Coburn, after leaving KLOS

JORDAN, J.J.: **KHJ**, 1975. Born Jay Durkin, J.J. was group pd of the Starr Stations. He left radio to join *R&R* as CHR editor. He went on to work in the record business and in the mid-1990s hosted a successful syndicated show, "Lone Star Fishing."

JORDAN, Steve: **KTNQ**, 1978. Steve arrived in Southern California from KYA-San Francisco and in the 1990s returned to the Bay Area working afternoon drive at KSAN and KFRC. He's currently at KYCY.

JORDAN, T. (Tom) Michael: **KMEN**, 1967-68; **KKDJ**, 1973-74; **KEZY**, 1976-77. Born Thomas Nefeldt, Tom grew up in Chicago. His radio career took him to stations in Tucson, Orlando, San Jose, St. Louis, Minneapolis and KROY-Sacramento four times. He was one of the original jocks at KKDJ on March 10, 1973, and was on the station until 1974, working the late night and overnight shifts. In the early 1980s he returned home to Chicago and decided to get out of radio. He eventually landed in Dallas, instituting software training programs for the Tandy Corporation. In 1985 he returned to the Southland, where he was the MIS Director at the Writers Guild of America.

JOY, Bob: **KWIZ**, 1969-72; **KDAY**, 1972. Born Robert Hill in Tucson, Bob came to Los Angeles after stints at KIKX and KHOS-Tucson and KLIV-San Jose. He worked afternoon drive until 1971 when he moved to the "graveyard" shift so he could go to law school during the day. He passed his bar examination and is practicing in Susanville.

JOY, Dick: KNX, late 40s-early 50s; **KFAC**, 1950s-70s, nd. Dick died in 1996. He was living in Talent, Orgeon.

JUGGS, Billy: **KLOS**, 1977; **KMET**, 1977-85; **KLSX**, 1989-91. Born Michael Brown in Los Angeles, Billy was one of the classic personalities during the Southern California's AOR period. He grew up on a farm in Fallbrook (between L.A. and San Diego) and left for the Bay Area when he finished high school. "I was living in Haight-Ashbury in 1967 during the 'summer of love' and remembering this new station playing all kinds of music. Jazz, rock, country and folk. It was KSAN in its first days." Billy's first rock experience was when he was hired by Mike Harrison. "Mike is my mentor and friend, and I often wonder what direction my career would have taken, if any, without his interest." His first shift in L.A. started auspiciously. "Before I got to KMET I was held up by a drunk with a rifle barrel against my head. He was staggering, with his finger on the trigger. When he saw I had only 8 dollars, he gave it back and asked instead for a light for his cigarette, and let me go. I was a basket case." Billy talked about KMET and his most satisfying radio experience that he would ever have: The cohesion between all these started as a part-timer at "the Mighty Met." In the mid-1990s Billy went to work for NBC Asia as the network announcer for both CNBC and NBC. He also does a daily music show for Star Radio that goes into 22 countries in Asia and the Middle East. Billy concluded his E-mail: "You'd be surprised how many people from the states come out here for fun and profit." An essay, "Looking Up from the 'Underground,'" by Billy appears elsewhere in this book.

KIIS/FM	
6 am	Bruce Phillip Miller
10 am	Brian White
2 pm	Mike Wagner
6 pm	Paul Freeman
10 pm	Steve Weed
2 am	John Lee Walker
	-Summer 1977

KIIS/FM	
6 am	Paul Freeman
10 am	A.J. Martin
2 pm	Bruce Phillip Miller
6 pm	Steve Weed
10 pm	Joe Daniels
2 am	Val Valentine
weekends: Don Elliott, Brother Bill and Mark West	
	-early 1979

KIIS/FM	
6 am	Lon Thomas
10 am	Paul Freeman
3 pm	Mike Wagner
7 pm	Val Valentine
Mid	Brother Bill
weekends: A.J. Martin, Joe Daniels, Jeff McNeal and Rich Hogan	
	-spring 1981

K

K, Bob: **KMPC**, 1994, pd; **KABC**, 1995, pd; **KMPC/KABC**, 1995-96, pd. Born Bob Klopfenstein, he left KABC/KMPC in the spring of 1996. Before arriving in the Southland, he was pd at KOWO-Ft. Wayne in 1976 and gm at KING-Seattle. In early 1997 he joined Creative Promotion, a tv and radio syndicator.

K, Ellen: **KIIS**, 1990-97. One of her Los Angeles peer group said of Ellen: "This is going to sound sexist, especially coming from another female, but Ellen is undoubtedly the prettiest radio personality who ever worked here." Ellen has been one of the most popular sidekicks to highly rated morning man Rick Dees. Ellen is a veteran of talk shows in San Diego (worked with Bill Ballance) and KXXX-San Francisco. Ellen K's real name is Ellen Thomas. She told Gary Lycan of the *OC Register*: "I used that name on the air before I came here. But there was already a Thomas (Jay), so I dropped the last name. Then we thought we'd use my middle initial, but it was J so we're back to the Jay Thomas problem again. So what did we do? We picked the next letter in the alphabet, a K. So I became Ellen K. That's a true story."  Besides KIIS, Ellen hosts fashion shows and does commentary two or three times a year at high profile events. She is also the hostess for a two-minute daily show, "Screen Test," featuring movie trivia, offered by CD Media and Radio Today. In the fall of 1994, Ellen was given her own two-hour show on KIIS. In the April, 1995 issue of *Playboy*, Ellen was featured in the "Girls of Radio" pictorial spread. In the fall of 1996 she started as host of *The Newlywed Game* which was part of the *Dating/Newlywed Hour*. Ellen is Miss February in the 1997 "Tantalizing Takeoffs" calendar and appeared in the July 1997 *Playboy*. In late 1996 she married KIIS gm Roy Laughlin.

K, Jeff: **KACD**, 1996-97. Jeff joined Dance "Groove Radio" in the summer of 1996 from KDGE-Dallas.

> **KLSX, "Pirate Radio," KLOS**
> **Move Over and Let the Big Dogs Eat**
> **Teaser billboard campaign**
> **-KKBT 1989**

KABC, Mr.: **KFI**, 1992-96; **KABC**, 1997. Born Marc Germain in Los Angeles on May 28, 1967, Mr. KLAC grew up in the San Fernando Valley. "I was a big fan of Talk radio in college and thought it would be fun to give it a try." While earning a political-science degree at the University of California at Santa Barbara, Mr. KLAC worked at KTMS.  He initially worked fill-in and weekend nights at KFI, then became full-time weekender who was later promoted to weekday evening host in the summer of 1995. He kept his real identity a secret and chose his name, Mr. KFI, "because it was easy to remember." He is married to Ann Germain and they have a young daughter. He left KFI in the fall of 1996 and joined KABC as Mr. KABC in early 1997.

KABRICH, Randy: **KQLZ**, 1989-90. Randy was part of the launch of Westwood One's "Pirate Radio" format. Prior to joining KQLZ, he programmed WZUU-Milwaukee and WROQ-Charlotte. He left L.A. for WRBQ-Tampa. Randy has been twice named *Billboard* magazine Top 40 radio programmer of the year. In 1991, Randy was station manager of KHYI ("Y95")-Dallas. In early 1994, he became group consultant for Beasley Broadcast Group's 19 stations.

KAELIN, Brian Kato: **KLSX**, 1995-96. Infamous house guest at O.J. Simpson's home at the time of Nicole Brown Simpson's brutal murder (along with Ron Goldman), Kato co-hosted an afternoon drive talk fest with the launch of "Real Radio." He was born in Milwaukee and attended the University of Wisconsin and Cal State Fullerton majoring in communications. One of those who were caught in the glare of "the trial of the century," Kato talked about his assignment with KLSX. "I'm not as shocking as Howard Stern," he told the *Times*. "I'm pretty much the guy next door who takes the dog for a walk. You can relate to me." In late 1995, according to a story in *The Hollywood Reporter*, KLSX gm Bob Moore had a showdown when Moore lambasted Kato for not delivering what everyone wants more of: the juice on O.J. An insider at the station said: "A big fight took place between Moore and Kato. Then Kato was unofficially fired." The dismissal was quickly retracted when KLSX's management realized how much they'd have to pay Kato for the eight months remaining on his contract. He eventually left before his contract time had been fulfilled. He was on *Playgirl*'s January 1996 cover and guested on *The Watcher* and other tv series.

KAESINER, Anne: **KNX**, 1976

KAGAN, Marilyn: **KFI**, 1991-96; **KMPC/KTZN**, 1996-97. Beginning in August 1991, Marilyn hosted an evening therapy show on KFI. She went on to host a local tv program on KCAL/Channel 9. Marilyn left KFI in late 1995 to devote more time to her tv show which she hoped to take into national syndication. She joined KMPC in the late spring of 1996 and left a year later. She was bumped to make way for the syndicated psychologist Dr. Toni Grant. Marilyn told Gary Lycan of the *OC Register*: "They were deceitful, noncreative and rude to talent. I was promised they would make my presence known, and it never happened."

KAHLEN, Brent: **KROQ**, 1978

KAHN, Larry: **KNX**, mid-1980s; **KFOX**, 1991; **KORG**, 1991; **KFI**, 1991-92; **KMPC**, 1992-95; **KLSX**, 1996. Larry has been a radio sportscaster for over two decades. A telecommunications major at USC, he began his career in the mid-1970s at age 20 with the Mutual Radio Network. He has worked for NBC, CBS and ESPN radio networks and has covered every major sporting event including Super Bowls and World Series. In 1985 he won the L.A. Press Club Award for best sports reporting. At KFI he was a talk show host on L.A. Raiders broadcasts. In 1992 he joined the new all-Sports format at KMPC and was the Dodger reporter. Since 1995, Larry has been the USC Trojan play-by-play announcer.

KALMENSON, Howard: **KWKW**, 1962-97. Howard acquired KWKW in 1962. The son of Warner Bros. film executive Ben Kalmenson, Howard attended Riverside Military Academy, NYU and UCLA. While attending Riverside he met a Cuban classmate who invited him to spend a summer where Howard learned the language, and he speaks it like a native.

KALMENSON, Jim: **KWKW**, 1991-97, vp/gm. Jim grew up in Woodland Hills and received a B.A. in history from Southern Illinois University. He completed his M.B.A. at Vanderbilt University. Beginning in 1981, he began his formal career in broadcasting sales at CNN Radio Network. Two years later he was the vp of sales for the Southern Carolina Radio Network. Jim returned to California in 1985 as gsm of KWKW. In 1990 he was appointed vp/gm of the Spanish language station. His father Howard owns KWKW.

KAMER, Steve: **KHTZ**, 1982-83. In 1984 Steve joined Transtar's AC format. He now lives in New Jersey and does voiceover work.

KAPLAN, Gabe: **KLAC**, 1990-92. The former star of the *Welcome Back Kotter* tv series hosted a one-hour sports program on Country KLAC in afternoon drive. Gabe said after two years he got "burned out on sports."

KAPLAN, Leon: **KABC**. Leon has hosted "The Motorized World of Leon Kaplan" for decades each Sunday morning on KABC. His early interest in auto mechanics while growing up in North Carolina led to a degree from Nashville Auto Diesel College. He came to the Southland and created a "Hydro Stick Transmission" that was very popular with auto racers. Leon has had his own automotive service company, Lancer Automotive, that repairs all types of cars from Rolls Royces to Pintos. He has appeared on most all national tv shows as an automotive expert. Leon is a regular contributor to KABC's morning show and Channel 7's *Eyewitness News*.

KARNATZ, Mia: **KPCC**, 1996-97. Mia hosts a roots alternative rock music show on KPCC.

KASEM, Casey: **KRLA**, 1963-69. Born in Detroit in 1932, Kemal Amin Kasem dreamed of being a baseball player or an actor. He once heard Eddie Chase's countdown show on CKLW-Detroit and thought: "What a great way to make a living that would be!" After graduating from high school, he worked as an intern at Detroit's public radio station, WDTR, in the summer of 1950, where he met his longtime partner, Don Bustany. Both attended Wayne State University, where Casey starred in the campus radio drama "Scoop Ryan, Cub Reporter." He found extra work as a radio quiz-show usher at WXYZ-Detroit, and eventually started acting in youth roles on its nationally-aired shows "The Lone Ranger" and "Sergeant Preston." Drafted in 1952, he went to Korea and, without missing a beat, set up a production house in a Quonset hut at Armed Forces Radio HQ ("Radio Kilroy") in Taegu. A

civilian again in 1954, he returned to Wayne State to finish college, meanwhile working as a newsman, board op, and part-time dj at WJLB. A year later, he switched to WJBK-Detroit and became a full-time jock. After graduation from college, he quit radio to tend the family grocery store a while, then headed to New York in 1958 in an unsuccessful try for stage acting work. In 1959, he hosted radio and tv shows (*Cleveland Bandstand*) at WJW for a year. After a brief stint in Buffalo, he moved to KEWB-San Francisco. There, in 1962, he developed the "teaser-bio" format, putting drama into the introductions. It became his trademark technique, a much-copied industry standard. In 1963 he joined KRLA bringing his old moniker "Casey at the Mike" with him, but dropped it after saying it just once. During the '60s, he acted in American International biker "epics" like *Glory Stompers* with Dennis Hopper and *Cycle Savages* with Bruce Dern. He also hosted the Dick Clark-produced daily syndicated tv dance show, *Shebang*, for three years and 650 hour-long programs. While he was on KRLA, Casey appeared on *The Dating Game*. Record exec Mike Curb advised him in 1968 to try voiceover commercials which resulted in landing the role of Robin in the tv cartoon series *Batman and Robin*, as well as Shaggy on *Scooby Doo*. In 1964 he received a letter from a listener

named Elaina, who remembered Casey from the Bay Area. The letter told how she hugged her favorite Beatle, George Harrison, at a Beatles concert. He struck the charts himself with a turntable hit, *Letter From Elaina*, when he read her letter to the accompaniment of an instrumental recording of *And I Love Her*. He played the character "Lieutenant Cavendish" on KRLA as Emperor Bob Hudson led his Commandoes through humorous skits. During the last year at KRLA, Casey worked weekends only, because of his desire to do other projects. In 1969 Casey called Ron Jacobs at Watermark, a radio production company, to talk about a new idea, "American Top 40." Watermark had just started the *Cruisin'* music album series, and they didn't even have a studio. The association between Watermark, Casey and producer Bustany was consummated at Art's Deli in Studio City and internally was known as the Bagel Agreement. "AT40" debuted on July 4, 1970, on WMEX-Boston--its first show produced by Jacobs and his associate, Tom Rounds. The show originally aired in only seven markets and was bartered, but it didn't work. Mike Curb and MGM Records were the first sponsors. The first commercial was a one-minute spot for the first record by the Osmonds, *One Bad Apple*. To make the show work, Watermark eventually sold it outright to the stations. Casey's industry fame grew steadily. A member of NAB's Hall of Fame, he received a Star on Hollywood's Walk of Fame on April 27, 1981. By then, he had begun hosting a syndicated tv countdown show, *America's Top Ten*, which ran from 1980 to 1992. He continued acting on the side appearing on *Charlie's Angels*, *Quincy*, and *Fantasy Island*. He also continued doing commercials, but the long list of the thousands of spots his famous voice has delivered gradually eliminated products that Casey believed to be harmful to his fans. He wouldn't advertise cigarettes. He used to smoke several packs a day until the Surgeon General in 1964 reported smoking hazardous to health. He also avoids advertising alcoholic beverages, Las Vegas, motorcycles, meat, fish, poultry, etc. Casey never shied away from the political arena. Although a longtime Democrat, he registered as a Republican in 1978 to work for Mike Curb's campaign for Lieutenant Governor of California. Eventually, he contributed $70,000 of his own money to Curb's election campaign. Following his election, Curb appointed Casey's first wife, Linda, to the state Commission on the Status of Women. Through the '80s, remarried to actress Jean (of *Cheers* and *The Tortellis*), Casey's activism grew. The couple supported Reverend Jesse Jackson's '84 and '88 bids for the presidency. Casey marched for peace and protested against nuclear arms. He advocated vegetarianism and aid for the homeless. In November 1989, he was arrested in Washington, DC during the Housing Now march and was led off with others in handcuffs. He promoted workshops in conflict resolution between Arabs and Jews. Casey has never used his syndicated show to further his causes: "I know that as soon as the public can pin a label on me, I lose credibility. The moment I use the show as a personal forum, I lose the trust of the listeners." After 18 years with the enormously successful, syndicated "American Top 40," Casey parted ways with Cap Cities/ABC Radio Networks. After six months, he was back on the air with another countdown, "Casey's Top 40, With Casey Kasem" on Westwood One. Even before the show debuted on January 1, 1989, over 400 affiliates signed up, which validated his great track record with "AT40." His well-known farewell at the end of every program: "Keep your feet on the ground and keep reaching for the stars. And until you get the one you want, I hope you'll stay with the station of the stars, KRLA."

KAT, Killer: SEE El Gato

KATCHEN, Sharon: **KFWB**, 1986-97. Sharon heads the Orange County news bureau of KFWB. A veteran of over 20 years in print and broadcast journalism, she joined Westinghouse Broadcasting in October 1986. She has been honored with several coveted Golden Mike awards and L.A. Press Club Awards for Excellence. One of her honors was for

broadcasting live reports running the 26.2 mile Los Angeles Marathon while carrying a four-pound backpack of electronic equipment. She earned a Golden Mike for repeating the accomplishment several years later while guiding a blind runner through the Marathon course. Sharon received a journalism degree from Metropolitan State College in Denver. While in Denver she worked for KOA, KIMN, KEG, KNUS and KWBZ. In addition to her broadcast work, for five years beginning in 1973 she worked in print journalism as a reporter for Denver's weekly business newspaper. She's married to Los Angeles personality and lawyer Bill Pearl.

KAUFMAN, Mike: **KMPC**, 1992; **KFWB**, 1995-97. Mike reports sports on all-News KFWB.

KAY, Ella: **KDAY**, 1965

KAYE, Barry: **KHJ**, 1972-74, pd. Barry left home at age 16 to begin his radio career on KIBL-Beeville, Texas and never looked back. On quitting high school, he never regretted his decision. "In those days if you were good on radio you just didn't need to go to college. You didn't need an education to scream and holler on the radio." His radio journey took him to some of the Rock radio giants, KNUZ-Houston, KTSA-San Antonio and KGB-San Diego before he got to KHJ. When he left the Southland he worked at KILT-Houston, KLIF-Dallas, KRBE and KKBQ-Houston, as well as programming KHFI-Austin between 1985 and 1992. Amidst all the industry conventions, Barry was nominated eight times as dj of the year and won the award at the 1974 *Gavin* convention. He loves his weekend retreats to his 300-acre ranch in Mason, Texas where he dons hunting garb. Barry would like to conquer the music world. In 1977 he remade the Commodores hit *Easy* which peaked at number 59. He plays the fiddle, piano and guitar and plans to have a hit record before he retires full-time to his ranch.

KAYE, Barry: **KRLA**, 1985-93; **KRTH**, 1993-96. The former KRLA dj and KRTH producer is now producing radio for syndication including The Dr. Demento Show.

KAYE, Harry: **KFWB**, 1957

KAYE, Jerry: **KROQ**, 1977; **KLOS**, 1978

KAYE, Jhani: **KUTE**, 1972-74; **KKDJ**, 1974; **KGBS AM/FM**, 1975; **KROQ**, 1973-74; **KFI/KOST**, 1982-97, pd. Jhani is the longest running program director of a Los Angeles music station. "KOST has never been beaten 12+ in the Arbitron ratings reports since the format debuted some 57 books ago!" Born John Kazaroff in Maywood, Jhani is proud of his American Indian heritage. He got into radio by accident: a friend asked him to fill in on a local high school station's radio show. He worked as talent on KFXM-San Bernardino before KUTE and KROQ and then his first programming assignment was KINT-El Paso for five years. Jhani was offered the assistant pd position at KFI when it was a Top 40 station. It is important to Jhani to be successful in his hometown of Los Angeles. A year later, he was named pd of sister station KOST when the format changed to AC. He also worked afternoon drive for a while. Jhani was the winner of the *Billboard* magazine Program Director of the Year award in 1987, 1989, 1990 and 1991. He also won *Gavin*'s Programmer of the Year honors in 1987 and 1990. He embraces the "continuous soft hits" concept and likens his success and string of Arbitron achievements to "the burgers-sold tally on the old McDonald's signs," according to a story in a trade publication. Jhani is a tough programmer, insisting that the jocks adhere to the format, which has resulted in solid, long-term success.

KAYE, Marc: **KIIS**, 1992-94, pres/gm. The former president and gm of KIIS is a native of New York and graduated from Ohio University with a bachelor of Science degree. Marc began his broadcast career in 1973 at WGBB-Long Island. In the early 1980s he was sales manager of WRBQ-Tampa and gm of KODA-Houston. In July of 1984 he began his journey with Gannett Broadcasting as sm of KKBQ-Houston and two years later was promoted to station manager. In August of 1987 he became gm of KNUA-Seattle and a year later took over WDAE/WUSA-Tampa. Marc left KIIS to return to WUSA/WDAE where he was the president and gm until leaving in late 1996 following an ownership change. In the spring of 1997 he was appointed vp of Sandusky Radio's five Seattle properties. Marc is married to the former Susan Wayman. They have one daughter, Jennifer, "and a house full of critters."

KAYLAN, Howard: SEE Flo and Eddie

KAZAN, Dick: **KABC/KMPC**, 1993-95. Dick hosted "The Road to Success" on all-Talk KMPC. He started in the 1970s when he began his own company as a one-man operation. His company eventually employed 300 people and became one of the nation's largest computer leasing firms. Dick is now at KOGO-San Diego.

KAZE, Irv: **KIEV**, 1991-97. Irv has hosted a sports talk show on KIEV since 1991. He is the only Los Angeles area sports broadcaster to have the distinction of wearing both a World Series and a Super Bowl ring. During his eight years with the Los Angeles Raiders as senior administrator, the team won the 1984 Super Bowl. Prior to joining the Raiders, he was media relations director for the New York Yankees in 1981 when they won their last pennant prior to 1996. While attending New York University, he worked for the *New York Post*. Upon graduation, he began

his baseball career with the Hollywood Stars of the Pacific Coast League, moving up to the parent Pittsburgh Pirates when the Dodgers moved from Brooklyn. Irv was the first public relations director of the Los Angeles (now Anaheim) Angels. When Al Davis became commissioner of the AFL, Irv joined his staff and later became business manager and assistant to the president of the San Diego Chargers for seven years. For the past two years Irv was named best radio talk-show host by the Southern California Sports Broadcasters Association.

KEARN, Richard: **KGIL**, 1965, pd

KEENE, Bill: **KNX**, 1957-93. Bill was the longtime weather/traffic reporter for KNX. For many years he did similar duties on KNXT/Channel 2 and was part of the highly successful *The Big News* with Jerry Dunphy and sports announcer Gil Stratton. Born July 1, 1927, Bill worked in a meteorology firm before joining KNX in 1957. He hosted "The Bill Keene Show," a  local variety show, and met his future wife, Louise Vienna, who was appearing as a singer. Bill gave flavor to the traffic reports using words like "cattywampus," "chrome cruncher" and "paint peeler" instead of "accident." He started his professional career in Scottsbluff, Nebraska winning an audition at his high school. After flying in the United States Air Force during World War II, he became nd at KBOL-Boulder. He went into the weather field after an unruly winter interrupted his private flying lessons. After a year retired in Tucson Bill said, "For the first year I woke up every morning at three. Now I'm able to sleep as long as I want."

KEENE, Scott: **KBRT**, 1983-84; **KFI**, 1986. Scott is the  stepson of Del Fi and Mustang Records owner Bob Keane. Scott was born in Hollywood and went to Fairfax High School. For two years beginning in 1961, he was the bat boy for the California Angels and pursued semi-professional ball after Los Angeles City College. Scott returned to his love for music, received his 1st Class FCC License from the Don Martin School and started his radio career in early 1972 at KUHL-Santa Maria. During the remainder of the '70s he worked at KGUY-Palm Desert, KDES-Palm Springs, KMEN and KCKC-Riverside/San Bernardino. In 1979 he returned to Don Martin as an instructor and started a mobile dj business that he continues today. He has worked under the names Scott Taylor, Scott Christopher and Scott Simpson. In addition to his mobile dj business, he is professional umpire, and a tv commercial actor. Scott lives in the Santa Clarita Valley.

KEFFURY, Bill: **KRLA**, 1961-63. Bill joined the Pasadena outlet from KACY-Ventura, where he was pd. In 1963 he left for a stint in the Army and was replaced by Dave Hull. In 1982, he was heard on KFOG-San Francisco. Bill lives in San Rafael and opened the first CD store in Marin County.

KEITH: **KLOS**, 1977

KEITH, Bobby: **KDAY**, 1967

KELLEY, Bob: **KMPC**, 1946-64; **KRKD**, 1964-66. Bob was regarded as one of the finest football announcers in the history of radio and television. Bud Furillo was even

more effusive, "Ol' Kell was the best football announcer I ever heard." Bob came West with the Rams in 1946, a position he had held since the inception of the pro football team in Cleveland in 1937. He won immediate fame for his vivid broadcasts. Bob announced the PCL's Angel games from 1948 to 1957. He was twice named the *LA Times* Sportscaster of the Year. He had a nightly controversial sports show on KMPC and was the sports director for the station. Jim Murray wrote: "His dinner-hour sports show made as many people gnash their teeth as cheer. But they listened. His mail was sulfuric. But they wrote." Bob was born in Kalamazoo and attended high school in Elkhart, Indiana and Western Reserve University where he graduated in 1942. After graduation from high school, Bob moved to South Bend and a job announcing the football games of the Fighting Irish of Notre Dame. He became director of sports for WGAR-Cleveland and began calling Ram games. In 1942 he joined WJR-Detroit where he broadcast the games of the University of Michigan, while commuting back to

Cleveland on Sundays to do the Rams. In the mid-1950s Bob became part of the Angels and Hollywood Stars at Wrigley Field and California Angels beginning announcing team in 1961. In 1964 Bob was carried out of the Coliseum during the Pro Bowl with a heart attack. The Voice of the Rams died September 9, 1966, at the age of 49. His son Pat, who was known as Paraquat Kelley, pursued a broadcasting career and was heard in the Southland on KMET and KMPC/FM. (Bob is pictured with his son Tim who was the assistant equipment manager for the Rams while in school.

KELLEY, Chaz: **KRTH**, 1991-97. When Chaz was getting into radio, her idol was Yvonne Daniels, a longtime Chicago icon at WLS. In 1981, Chaz was working at KOPA-Phoenix. She also spent time in Portland and arrived in the Southland from Texas radio. She was part of the successful satellite offering "Format 41" and currently works middays at WW1's 70's format and weekends at KRTH.

KELLEY, Gary: **KIQQ**, 1978-79. Gary currently works at KGTV/Channel 10 in San Diego as a traffic reporter. He also spent time in San Diego at "B-100."

KELLEY, Pat "Paraquat": **KMET**, 1977-87; **KMPC/FM**, 1988. Pat was born in Los Angeles in 1950. To develop a taste for showmanship, he never had to look past home. As a youngster he listened to his father Bob call play-by-play for the Los Angeles Rams. He visited

the radio station, befriended all the superstars on KMPC, and attended summer football camp at Redlands University. His godfather was the owner of the Rams, Dan Reeves. Late in his teens, Pat says he was the produce manager for a local Safeway when it struck him, "What the heck am I doing here?" He called his dad's friend Steve Bailey at KMPC, and started doing everything around the station that no one else wanted to do. Gary Owens was very generous in offering advice during this period and was a main influence in his radio career. He landed his first job at KATY-San Luis Obispo ("Your Sports Host for the Coast") doing the all-nights on FM. The Vietnam War was raging and Pat ended up in the U.S. Army Reserves Broadcast Services. After active duty he went to KPSI-Palm Springs and worked for former KFWB jock Elliot Field, before moving on to KIST-Santa Barbara. In 1974 he was sending out sports audition tapes, and NBC hired him to replace Bryant Gumbel as host of a three-hour live broadcast, "Prep Sports World." After the show was canceled, Pat was brokering a five-minute sports show on KGRB, "Parade of Sports." The "the Mighty Met" news director heard the show and hired him for the afternoon drive news. Pat talks fondly about the early days at KMET: "It was really the last vestiges of freedom before the research suits came along." He presented "Good News" and would report that "a 747 with 350 aboard landed safely at LaGuardia" or "the school bus from Sherman Oaks Elementary School has delivered all the students without incident." He was a longtime key player with "the Mighty Met" and was there on the last day of AOR broadcasting on February 6, 1987, playing the last two songs. When he was fired on Black Friday at the Sheraton Premiere Hotel, the gm and pd suggested to Pat that his nine years at the station had surely been financially profitable. Pat snapped, telling them, "You don't get it! I didn't work there for the money; I believed in what I was doing. I gave it my heart and everything I have." Pat is married to former host of *2 on the Town* Melody Rogers, and they have produced a series called *Tales of America* and many children's programs. In the sping of 1993 he joined WNEW-New York. He and Melody were living in Benny Goodman's old house in Stamford, Connecticut until returning to L.A. in 1995. Pat is very optimistic about the future and his original screen writing projects: "Life is about the little guy going the distance. There should be purity of purpose. I still believe in what I am and letting others decide if they like it." In early 1996 he started syndicating "Pat Kelley's News & Views" for Media America.

> *"I have a love-hate relationship with mornings. The part I love is that you're fresh and you're finished at 10. The part I hate is that you have to get up early in the morning."*
>
> -Bruce Phillip Miller

KELLEY, Sandy: **KYSR**, 1991-92; **KXEZ**, 1992-96; **KLIT**, 1997.

Sandy was born in New Haven and grew up in Connecticut. She went to Grahm College in Boston. It was at Yale University that she began her radio career, playing eclectic jazz. In 1979 Sandy started at WOMN-New Haven. While in Hartford with WCCC and later at WWYZ, Sandy was the first female dj ever hired by the station. She eventually moved to afternoons and became pd. In 1983 she moved to WKCI-New Haven for three years. Sandy left Connecticut radio in 1986 and joined WCSX-Detroit for the launch of a "classic rock" format. While vacationing in Los Angeles in 1989, she nailed down a new position at the Unistar Radio Network on the Adult Rock 'n Roll format and worked evenings for 18 months. In September 1991 she began working afternoons at KXEZ. A year later the station became "Star 98.7" and she did middays. When KXEZ resurfaced at 100.3FM, Sandy returned to afternoon drive. She is currently in business for herself as a "voicer" for several stations nationwide, doing their IDs and promotional announcements as well as working part-time at WW1's 70's format. She lives in Woodland Hills and loves animals and has trained and shown Golden Retrievers for a number of years. Her busy schedule also includes being a certified scuba diver, race car driver and skier.

KELLY, Ben: **KKBT**, 1990-97. Born Ben Chambers, the Los Angeles native arrived at "the Beat" after three years in San Francisco at KSFO and KYA. Ben's biggest surprise about working in Los Angeles is that "it's not as cut-throat as it is reputed to be. It's actually a whole lot of fun and new experiences all the time. A dream realized and a goal reached." In the fall of 1993, Ben moved from all-night to join the morning drive "House Party" where he currently works.

KELLY, Bill: **KEZY**, 1987. Bill worked evenings at KEZY.

KELLY, Chris: **KWST**, 1981; **KFI**, 1983; **KEZY**, 1985. Chris worked at KHFI-Austin and "Y-100"-Miami.

KELLY, Don: **KLAC**, 1982, gm

KWIZ becomes "Little Saigon Radio" -1993

KELLY, Evelyn: **KFI**, 1978-81; **KIIS**, 1986. A simple gift changed her life forever. In 1963 Evelyn received a transistor radio for Christmas, and to this day she can remember vividly the "Top 63 of 63" flowing from that tiny battery-powered box. Evelyn entered the radio business through a combination of unforeseen circumstances. In high school she worked at a steak house in Englewood, Colorado. In 1972 she wanted a job change and a former restaurant customer tipped her to a job at KTLK-Denver. Evelyn started as an assistant to the music director and it was at KTLK that she met Tim Kelly. "I fell madly in love with him." She and Tim went to Chicago. Evelyn worked at WGCI and Tim was at WPGC. When the air staff at WGCI went on strike, Ev recorded a few voice tracks which made her a scab. Tim received a death threat, she left the station and Tim joined

the picket lines in front of WGCI during a freezing Chicago winter. In 1975 they went to WPGC-Washington, DC. Two years later Evelyn worked WNSR and WRKO as Beverly Hudson. In 1978 they arrived in the Southland. She was Tim's sidekick at KFI. In 1981 they worked morning drive at WAKY-Louisville. They returned to L.A. and she did weekends at KIIS. During the last decade Evelyn has been working on various countdown shows at Premiere Radio. She handles the weekly interviews and co-writes the scripts for "Country Plain Rap Countdown." They have two children. Tim and Evelyn certainly defy the difficult odds of a married couple working together in the radio business.

KELLY, Jeff: **KLAC**, 1985-88; **KYSR**, 1993. Jeff handled the overnights on Country-formatted KLAC before jumping into television. He was a tv weatherman in Palm Springs, Las Vegas and Salt Lake City before returning to the Southland on "Star 98.7."

KELLY, Jim: **KFWB**, 1961; **KBLA**. Jim came aboard from KDWB-Minneapolis during the 1961 strike at KFWB. He was known as Professor James Patrick O'Neill in the Twin Cities, but there was already a Jimmy O'Neill in the market, Jim changed his name. He only worked a few weeks in the late evening slot and then went on to KJOY-Stockton and then the Cleveland market for many years. He returned to the Southland to teach at Fullerton College and worked briefly at "Money Radio."

KELLY, Kidd: **KFOX**, 1982; **KWNK**, 1985. Kidd Kelly was born Brent Nordhoff in Los Angeles on May 2, 1964, and was raised in Torrance where he attended high school. On his sixth birthday, his parents bought him a plastic record player with which he locked himself in his bedroom playing *Sugar Sugar* over and over imitating The Real Don Steele. As a teen he befriended many L.A. djs providing bits. While at Torrance High School he became a jock on KFOX at the age of 16. He used the moniker "Nordhoff in the Night Time." After a year in college, Kidd took on a series of radio stations in Santa Maria, Amarillo, Phoenix, Tucson, Las Vegas and Stockton. He returned to L.A. to work at Simi Valley's KWNK. In the mid-1990s he worked the all-night shift at KRAK-Sacramento.

KELLY, Kurt: **KLOS**, 1983-87; **KNX/FM/KODJ**, 1988-90, pd. As md in Chicago and Dallas, Kurt landed at KLOS as md and subbed on the morning show. He went to work for the satellite service "Niche 29" where he was pd in 1987. In September 1988, Kurt went to pd KNX/FM and continued when the call letters were changed to KODJ in 1989; he was gone in 1990. Kurt is now producing television shows and works weekends at Westwood One's 70s Channel as an announcer.

KELLY, Machine Gun (M.G.): **KHJ**, 1973-78; **KTNQ**, 1978-79; **KFI**, 1983; **KOST**, 1985; **KIIS**, 1987-88; **KODJ/KCBS**, 1989-92. Born Gary Sinclair in Long Beach, he grew up in Oklahoma.

While at East Central State college in Ada, Oklahoma, he worked for the college radio station and then went to KOMA for two years. M.G. arrived in Los Angeles from KSTP-Minneapolis to join KHJ. M.G. was very active in the 1970s with commercial voiceover work. He went across town to "the new Ten-Q" complete with blazing machine gun water pistols. The Real Don Steele introduced the newest member of the staff at a Hollywood speakeasy. In 1974, 1977 and 1978, he was voted Best Major Market Personality at the Annual *Billboard* Radio Programming Forum. In 1978, he announced his retirement from radio from the floor of the convention. "I wanted to go out on top." His retirement from radio lasted five years. From 1984 to 1987, M.G. hosted "M.G. Kelly's Top 30 USA" for CBS RadioRadio in New York. When he returned to KOST from the Big Apple in 1985, the mood in Los Angeles had changed, and violence and gangs dominated the daily news. He responded to the headlines, and M.G. dropped Machine Gun from his moniker. When he got to KIIS he told the *OC Register* that KHJ was the KIIS of the '70s. He said, "It's like being on stage between two Woodstocks." M.G. had a very distinguished acting career performing in such heavyweight productions as *The Enforcers* with Clint Eastwood, in which he played the role of a priest; *A Star Is Born* with Barbra Streisand and Kris Kristofferson in which he was the fourth-billed star; and *The Buddy Holly Story*. He has appeared on over 80 episodic tv shows. He said that he gets weird residual checks for $5.48 for a part on *Barnaby Jones*. Since the early '90s he has co-hosted the syndicated "Good Times Oldies" show with Charlie Tuna. In 1993 "The Gunner" went to "KOOL" Oldies in Phoenix. In the summer of 1995 M.G. and his wife Kelly traveled the world working for a time at London Capital Radio, broadcasting to over 1.5 million people. In the summer of 1996 he joined KBGO-Las Vegas to work mornings with his wife who is known on-air as "Good Golly Miss Molly Potter." He left a year later.

KELLY, Marc: **KIQQ**, 1972-73. Mark was briefly on KIQQ during the "K-100-FM" days and left when Drake/Chenault bought the station.

KELLY, Margie: **KWIZ**, 1976-78; **KYMS**. Margie was part of the all-female jock line-up at KWIZ. She went to become an author of books dealing with single Christians. Margie lives in Mission Viejo.

KELLY, Merilee: **KSCA**, 1994-96; **KYSR**, 1996-97. Born Skye St. Foxx in Boston, Merilee worked at WBOS and WFNX-Boston before joining "FM 101.9" for the launch of the AAA format on July 1, 1994. She was md and on-air personality. Merilee left KSCA in early fall 1996 and joined "Star 98.7."

KELLY, Pat: **KHJ**, pd; **KFI**, 1950-68, pd. In 1968, Pat was upped to vp of operations and programming.

KELLY, Sean: SEE "Hurricane" Allen

KELLY, Steve: **KIKF**, 1993-97. Born Tyler Devin Hinds in Woodland Hills, Steve grew up in Orange County and graduated from Newport Harbor High School. His interest in radio comes from his father who was with KHJ from 1965 to 1972. Steve graduated from the University of Akron. He augments his weekend work at KIKF working for Metro Networks in Los Angeles.

> **KNAC** changes languages, "Pure Rock" to Spanish. Final song in English, *Fade To Black* by Metallica.
> -February 15, 1995

KELLY, Tim: **KFI**, 1978-81; **KIIS**, 1983-88; **KKBT**, 1989-90. From an initial investment of $15,000, Tim's Premiere Radio Networks has skyrocketed to a $100-

million company. His success story from dj to $100 million company is something for dreams. Tim was born and bred for the entertainment industry. Both his father and mother worked as performers, producers and managers in the entertainment business. At the time of Tim's birth, his dad was the morning man at WJR-Detroit. Baby Tim debuted in media on-camera at the age of six weeks on his dad's daily tv show. He landed his first on-air job when he was 16. By age 17 Tim had taken over as pd of WYSL-Buffalo. Beginning in 1968 he moved to KTSA-San Antonio followed by WKBW-Buffalo, KTLK-Denver (where he met his wife-to-be, Evelyn), and WCFL-Chicago. In 1976 he moved to morning drive at WPGC-Washington, DC followed by pd at WRKO-Boston. Tim landed at KFI in 1978 as music director and worked middays with Evelyn. In 1981 he and his wife moved to the morning slot at WAKY-Louisville and in 1982 the team worked at KPPL-Denver. They returned to the Southland in 1983 for evenings at KIIS. During his tenure at KIIS, Tim opted to venture beyond on-air work and formed his own radio syndication company -- Plain Rap, Inc., rapidly building the company's first show into one of the top three-rated countdowns in America, clearing a network of 200-plus radio stations in less than 30 days. He took on financial and creative partners which led to the formation of Premiere Radio Networks. Tim ventured back on air as part of the morning drive team with Patty Lotz and comedian Paul Rodriguez on the launch of KKBT (formerly Classical KFAC) in the fall of 1989. By 1990 he was teamed in the morning with Diana Steele. He left in the early 1990s to concentrate on his duties as executive vp for Premiere Radio Networks. With senior partner Steve Lehman, Tim helped grow Premiere from a four-person, $300,000-a-year entity into a $100-million-a-year public company with offices in New York, Los Angeles, Chicago, St. Louis, Washington, DC, Raleigh and Philadelphia.

KELLY, Todd: **KKBT**, 1989

KELLY, Tom: **KNX**, 1961-66 and 1988. Tom's signature assignment came when he began covering USC football and men's basketball in 1961. In his 35 years with the Trojans, he has described the moves of four Heisman Trophy winners and recounted the exploits of five national championship football teams. For his dedication, he was presented the Tommy Trojan award in 1987, the

highest award given by the USC Athletic Department. Tom began his broadcasting career in northern Wisconsin at a small 250-watt station where he "did everything." He worked at KTTV/Channel 11 and KNXT/Channel 2 for five-year stints at each tv station as a sports reporter. From 1976 to 1982 he called play-by-play for the San Diego Chargers. He's called the action for the Los Angeles Lakers and Los Angeles Clippers. He has telecast 23 bowl games including 16 Rose Bowls. Born in Minneapolis, Tom graduated in 1951 from Northland College in Ashland, Wisconsin with a Bachelor of Arts degree in English. Since 1988 he has been broadcasting Trojan sports on Prime Sports Television, now known as Fox Sports West.

KEMP, Guy: **KNAC**, 1984-85; **KMPC/FM**, 1988. Guy was Chuck Roast on KNAC. At AOR KMPC/FM he started in morning drive, moved to all-nights and left the station, all in the same year. When he left the Southland Guy went to WBPR-Myrtle Beach and eventually became part-owner of a station in Oregon, KCNA.

KENNEDY, Alton: **KPSA**, 1972, gm

KENNEDY, Virgin: **KROQ**. Born Kennedy Montgomery in 1972, she confessed to Howard Stern in an interview with the "King of All Media" that he influenced her decision to get into radio. When she left KROQ she became a veejay on MTV, where she continues to work. In an *US* magazine interview, she described the KROQ people listening to her overnight show as "insomniacs, students, people from Kinko's and 24-hour supermarkets. And Satanic 14-year-old boys who would send me magic powder, lace and sexual faxes. I probably still have them. I saved everything from KROQ." In 1993 she was voted MTV's most unpopular veejay. In *People*'s 1994 year-end review of Fresh Faces, Kennedy said, "One reason they hired me was because I say - and do - whatever's on my mind." The story said that she is probably the only Kennedy with a GOP elephant tattooed on her hip. In 1995, *Spy* magazine listed Kennedy 19th in their list of "100 Most Annoying, Alarming, And Appalling People, Places, And Things."

KENNEY, June: **KMET**, 1967. June was part of the all-female line-up at KMET.

KENNY, Tim: Tim was gm and the first to anchor Metro Traffic from 1981 to 1983. He was last heard in Denver.

KENT, Tony: **KPOL**, 1961-69 and 1971-74, nd. A native of England, Tony interrupted his stay at KPOL to join sister CapCities subsidiary in Washington, DC as head of Fairchild Broadcast News. He bought a station in Pismo Beach that he has since sold.

KERBY, Ed: **KIIS**, 1971; **KROQ**, 1972-73; **KIIS/KWST**, 1973; **KDAY**, 1974-94, vp/gm; **KMAX**, 1995. The longtime executive with KDAY has been in sales from the beginning. Ed started at KXOA-Sacramento and knew radio was for him. "I really liked it because it was like having something no one else had. Success in the early days was completely dependent on your ability as a salesman." Ed was born in Willows. "Willows is near Chico. You know how small it is if the closest reference city is Chico." His sales journey took him to Blair Reps in the late 1960s and then McGavern Guild in Los Angeles. He joined KIIS (1150AM) in local sales and moved to KROQ for a few months. "I got out of KROQ just before the pay checks started to bounce." He joined K101-San Francisco before returning to the Southland in 1974, starting his two decades-long leadership at KDAY from local sales manager to general manager by 1981. When KDAY was sold, Ed and Jim Maddox started *L.A. View*, a new newspaper venture targeted to the black community. Ed chuckles, "I decided to finance it myself so I wouldn't have to give everything to the venture capitalists. Then with the riots and the recession, I got hurt." He joined KMAX for, as he said, "a cup of coffee" in 1995. Ed is now an executive with Tichenor Broadcasting, owners of 20 stations.

KERDOON, Randy: **KWNK**, 1990; **KFWB**, 1990-96. Randy was hired as morning sports anchor at KFWB from KWNK. In addition to sports reporting on all-News KFWB, beginning in 1993, Randy was a substitute sports anchor for KTTV/Channel 11. In the fall of 1995 he joined the Fox station as weekend sports anchor and weekday sports reporter.

KERR, Bob: **KFI**, 1960-76. Bob was a distinguished newsman on KFI.

KESTER, Howard: **KEZY**, 1966, gm. Howard was gm of KYA-San Francisco during the station's success with a CHR format. He was the executive director of the Northern California Broadcasters Association. Howard died in 1989.

KEVIN & BEAN: **KROQ**, 1990-97. Gene Baxter (Bean) and Kevin Ryder (Kevin) make up the Kevin & Bean team. They met while at KZZP-Phoenix in 1988. Gene was off-the-air md at the station and, when he went to KXXX-San Francisco, the two stayed in touch. Gene worked solo at WPGC and WAVA-Washington, DC.

Kevin described the process of teaming: "We thought it might be fun to try a morning show and we put together a tape that a friend played for KROQ pd, Andy Schuon." They had never worked together on air, but were teamed and started on "the Roq" on January 2, 1990. The rest was history, as they became one of the few successful AOR morning teams in the country. During their first summer, they did a number of ear-catching remote broadcasts, including one under water off Catalina Island's Casino Point and another from Camp Pendleton, where they fired M-16s and trained with the Marine Corps. An example of their antics: The day after Pete Rose was convicted, they called a Las Vegas bookie attempting to get odds on whether he would serve all five months or not. The team cruised Palm Springs during Easter vacation. They had a character dress up as a groundhog and climb out of an L.A. sewer manhole cover opened by fitness guru Jack Lalanne. One continuing promotion was a visit to personalities' homes and rummaging through their refrigerators for insights. Controversy, headlines and an FCC decision have followed the team. They developed a comedy bit called "Confess Your Crime," in which listeners were encouraged to reveal their transgressions. On June 13, 1990, "Doug the Slug" Roberts called Kevin and Bean and confessed on the air to beating his girlfriend to death. Over the next few days, several local television news crews descended on the Burbank radio station and interviewed Kevin and Bean, who said they were "stunned" by the call. The series *Unsolved Mysteries*, which aired nationally on NBC affiliates, broadcast the phone call on its program twice and was deluged with leads. The result was a 10-month criminal investigation overseen by the Los Angeles County Sheriff's Department. When it was revealed that the call was a hoax, management told the *LA Times*: "I think this was due to the pressures of being in L.A. and trying to get ratings. They made a mistake. We are not the kind of company that gives up on its people that easily. We feel they have been exemplary and that they deserve a certain amount of loyalty on our part as well." In 1991, the FCC issued a 4-page letter admonishing KROQ management for its "deliberate distortion of programming." The Commission said, "The hoax broadcast was a spontaneous, isolated event orchestrated solely by certain on-air personnel who subsequently engaged in a cover-up." Kevin and Bean offered restitution for the cost of the murder investigation by L.A. County Sheriff's deputies. They paid $12,170.98, and each was sentenced to 149 hours of community service. Every holiday season, the morning team compiles a Christmas cassette for charity. They sold 20,000 in 1993 and more than double that number in 1994. The cassette featured members of the morning show performing their favorite Christmas tunes. In early 1995, the duo was honored by the Starlight Foundation for their humanitarian efforts.

> *"Before I got to KMET I was held up by a drunk with a rifle barrel against my head. He was staggering, with his finger on the trigger. When he saw I had only 8 dollars, he gave it back and asked instead for a light for his cigarette, and let me go. I was a basket case."*
> -Billy Juggs

KEVIN, Art: **KEZY**, 1959-61, nd; **KFAC**, 1961; **KFI**, 1961-63; **KHJ**, 1963-72, nd; **KMPC**, 1972-78. Art served in three capacities while at KHJ: news director, public affairs director and national news correspondent for RKO

General Broadcasting. He was on the air to RKO outlets the night RFK was killed at the Ambassador Hotel in L.A. At KMPC he was chief investigative reporter. He was born Art Ferraro in the Bronx. "In my start days on radio ethnic names were not allowed, thus, Art Kevin was born." Art discovered his passion for radio while working at WAVZ-New Haven. (B. Mitch Reed was a jock at the same time.) "I was doing the all night dj shift and the owner sent me to cover some ship disaster in New York Harbor. It was the sinking of the Andrea Doria and I forever got bitten by the news bug." Before he joined KHJ he was the first West Coast correspondent for the UPI audio radio network and was the first news director at KEZY. Always passionate about news reporting, in a 1972 speech before L.A. Town Hall, he said: "If these assaults on the credibility of the news media continue...the day of the dictatorship will be at hand." In 1982 Art started KRRI/FM-Boulder City/Las Vegas, because "I always thought I could do it better." He ran an Oldies format until selling the station in 1995. Art and his author-broadcaster wife Jodi Lawrence own and operate a radio/tv website known as the Kevin Broadcasting System. While at KHJ, Art met Jodi while interviewing her on a book promotion tour. "It was love at first sight. The strange part about meeting her was that I had a cancellation on my show and she filled in. We haven't been separated since then and recently we celebrated 25 years of marriage." Art hasn't gotten the news out of his veins. "We forget so quickly and that is why history is doomed to repeat itself." Art and Jodi have built a house on a mountain top overlooking Las Vegas. It keeps his vantage point clear.

KEYS, Austin: **KLOS**, 1997

KFI, Mr.: SEE Mr. KABC

KHAN, Chaka: **KIBB**, 1997. Born Yvette Stevens, she picked her name while searching for her African heritage. Chaka Khan means, "hot, fiery." The evening dj on Rhythm "B-100" recorded *I Feel For You* in 1984 that peaked at #13 in the year-end charts. A 1997 *R&R* profile suggested a fortuitous promotional visit by the Reprise artist led to discussions for an on-air shift. GM Ken Christensen said the artist is being paid for her 10 p.m. - 1 a.m. shift what most morning personalities receive.

KIDD, Jr., Paul: **KNOB**, 1968; **KFWB**, 1969-87; **KGFJ**, 1969-87; **KDAY**, 1984-87; **KMAX**, 1987-88; **KACE**, 1988-94. Paul hosted a gospel music show for much of his on-air work. He was born and raised in Kansas City where he learned to play the saxophone. He went to Nebraska University and remembered, "My ambition was always to be in radio." He spent two years in the Korean War and when he was discharged in 1955, he moved West. His father was a minister and went to San Francisco while Paul entered the California Institute of Radio and Television. "I put so much into KGFJ and when the bottom fell out, it took a lot out of me. I went to work for Hertz rental cars at the airport." Over the decades Paul has been an engineer at KFWB and is now in sales at KIEV. His gospel show on Armed Forces Radio has played for over 20 years. Paul created the Touch of Soul barbecue sauce, later renamed Touch of the South.

KIELEY, Dan: **KIIS**, 1997, pd. Dan arrived from KDWB-Minneapolis.

KILEY, Liz: **KFI/KOST**, 1982-89; **KKBT**, 1989-90. Born in 1956, Liz grew up in New York City and was

influenced by some of radio's greats. After Endicott College in Beverly, Massachusetts, Liz worked at two Grand Rapids stations before becoming the pd at WIFI-Philadelphia and on-air at WPGC-Washington, DC. In 1979, she achieved the status of being the first female air personality at WABC-New York during its Top 40 era. In a 1979 *Billboard* magazine interview, Liz said, "I refuse to come off sexy. I don't want to come off like a guy or a girl, just me, friendly, informative and entertaining." She commented on the very popular "Love Songs on the Coast" program: "It eliminates the boring dedication and allows the program to be written by and for listeners. We don't go for the dirt. We go for stories that remind listeners that other people are going through the same things they are." Liz admitted that the program sounds corny sometimes, "but so can people." She was voted *Billboard*'s Music Director of the Year AC in 1987, 1988 and 1989. *Gavin* awarded her the same accolades for four consecutive years beginning in 1986. Liz reflected on the awards: "After 11 and a half years, it is great to be in a business where I'm still able to grow and learn something new." In 1988 she was promoted to assistant pd at KFI/KOST. She hosted the syndicated soft hits show "Best of Times." Liz was the pd for the launch of KKBT (formerly Classical KFAC) in the fall of 1989. KKBT was an eclectic mix of music that changed after a few months to an Urban beat on February 3, 1990. Liz was promoted to vp of programming and operations at Evergreen Media, Inc. in 1992. In 1994 she joined The Box (Music Television YOU Control) as director of radio affiliations. In late 1995 she moved to Nashville with her song-writing husband and in 1997 was promoted to vp of radio affiliates at The Box.

KILGORE, Lyle: **KHJ**, 1966-77, nd; **KDAY**, 1978; **KLAC**, 1983-90; **KFWB**, 1990-97.

For three decades, Lyle has delivered news in his famous dramatic style. Before arriving at KHJ he worked the legendary Rock stations in the Inland Empire, KFXM and KMEN. Lyle started at KHJ shortly after "Boss Radio" was launched. "Ron Jacobs told me that radio is like a roller coaster ride...first you're up then you're down...I worked the overnight. I emerged from the darkness as new operations director with a staff of 20. We covered riots, Charles Manson and the Hillside Strangler stories on 20/20 News." For a brief time Lyle went into the cookie business. He currently does weekend news on KFWB. "It has been a long and fun ride since the pioneering Rock stations in the Inland Empire. It's been an E ticket ride and I'm still on it and loving it!"

KILGORE, Ron: **KFWB**, 1996-97. Ron is an anchor at all-News KFWB. He joined KFWB from a news station in Phoenix. Ron is no relation to KFWB's Lyle Kilgore.

> "Radio was long on talent and short on time. Today radio is long on time and short on talent."
> -Don Page

KIM, Jimmy: **KIIS**, 1993-97; **KFOX/KREA**, 1994-97. DJ Jimmy Kim has become one of the most respected sources for dance and hit music in the radio and recording industry. He has been sought to perform at such high-profile private events as Prince's Gold Masquerade Ball and Lisa Marie Presley's birthday party. Since 1993 he has been a mixer and music producer for KIIS's "Klub

KIIS," a live mix show on Saturday nights from 10 p.m. to 4 a.m. The show is broadcast from the Palace nightclub in Hollywood. On FM Seoul, 93.5 KFOX/KREA, he blends Korean dance music with American on Sunday evenings from 8-10 p.m. He started playing music at fraternity/sorority parties while at UCLA and it just grew until he was guest DJ'ing at local clubs. In the late 1980s he was spinning music seven nights a week at the Captain's Wharf restaurant in the Marina, which was considered the number one Korean club outside of Koreatown. For four years, from 1989 to 1993, he was the director of dance music promotion for American TRAX in Beverly Hills, which served as a record pool for many of the club DJs in the Los Angeles area. Jimmy is currently entering the realm of producing and remixing for both American/European and Korean artists.

KIMBALL, Richard: **KMET**, 1970-74, pd; **KWST**, 1975-76. Born in Oakland in 1936, Richard grew up in Sacramento. His mother played piano in various bands. "I was exposed to all kinds of music. Every weekend we

listened to opera." At 14 he wrangled a job at the NBC station, KCRA. After some college, Richard joined the Army and spent much of his time in the Far East. "I loved the international travel." Before he arrived at "the Mighty Met," he worked in the Bay Area at KLIV, KDIA, KSAN, KSJO and KMPX. "When I left KMET I managed Emerson, Lake and Palmer. In 1975 a group from Detroit arrived to turn 'K-West' into AOR programming and I was the only local guy hired. Within 18 months I tired of a daily show. I envisioned myself splayed over some console mumbling something about Joni Mitchell. Plus the suits and the corporate mentality had arrived and the music was no longer free-form." Richard managed David Cassidy and other artists until joining Westwood One in 1980 in the rock concert division. He stayed until 1993 when he left to co-produce "Rockline" for Global Satellite. Richard owns AASK (Artist Acquisitions Service Kompany) which acquires musical artists for network programming. He also co-produces "The Road" which is syndicated in 250 markets and 29 countries. "I was sitting in Las Vegas waiting to record some artists for 'The Road' when a three-quarter slot machine paid a progressive jackpot of $41,000. That's the way my life has been."

KIMMEL, Jimmy: **KROQ**, 1994-97. Jimmy was born in Brooklyn and sounds like it as "Jimmy the Sports Guy" on Kevin & Bean's popular morning show on "the Roq." Jimmy arrived from KRQ-Tucson. Frank Murphy, the former morning show producer for Kevin & Bean, described Jimmy's checkered past prior to arriving in the Southland: "Jimmy quit KZZP-Phoenix, was fired from KZOK-Seattle, fired from WRBQ-Tampa, quit KCMJ-Palm Springs, fired from KRQQ-Tucson, and we're waiting to see what happens at KROQ." He participates in stunts as part of the morning craziness. Jimmy fought another personality on the Kevin & Bean morning team, "Michael the Maintenance Man," in "The Bleeda in Reseda" boxing exhibition. In early 1996 he wrote a daily soap opera called the "Cahhisons."

KINDRED, Steve: **KMNY**, 1987-89, nd; **KFWB**, 1989-97.  Steve covered both O.J. Simpson trials for the all-News station. He has won six Golden Mikes and the Edward R. Murrow Award. His previous assignments include a stint in the Persian Gulf during Desert Shield, the Northridge earthquake and the trial of officers accused of beating Rodney King. Steve received an A.A. in radio/tv from L.A. City College and a B.A. from Cal State Long Beach. He was nd at KRNK-Cheyenne, KNUU-Las Vegas and "Money Radio" in Los Angeles.

KING, Alan: **KBBQ**, 1960s

Spanish KALI sells for $5.75 million
-1994

KING, Bill: **KNX**, 1982-83. Considered by many to be the best pro football radio announcer in the country, Bill has broadcast over 500 Raider games, many with Rich Marotta. He grew up in Peoria and wanted to be a major league catcher. While he was stationed in Guam as an Army private following World War II, he started announcing for Armed Forces Radio. After the war he was a dj briefly. Bill broadcast the Nebraska football program in the late 1950s and in 1959 he moved to San Francisco without a job. After some free-lance work, he was hired to be the San Francisco Giants third announcer behind Russ Hodges and Lon Simmons. In 1962 he started with the Warriors and did the broadcasts for 21 seasons. He started with the Raiders in 1965 and became an Oakland A's announcer beginning in 1981. In the 1980s, preparing for retirement, his financial counselor swindled all his money.

KING, Dave: **XPRS**, 1972, pd

KING, Howard: **KHJ**, 1972. Howard broadcast news on KHJ.

KING, Jackson: **KFWB**, 1962

KING, Josh: **KLAC**, 1965

KING, Roy: **KGFJ**, 1978; **KKTT**, 1979; **KIEV**, 1981-97

KING, Tom: **KUTE**, 1981-87; **KNOB**, 1984-86. Since 1984, Tom has operated the Academy of Radio Broadcasting in Huntington Beach with his wife, the former Lindy Thurrell (they met working together at KLOK-San Jose). Born in Cincinnati, he grew up in Huntington Beach and after graduating from the KIIS Broadcasting School became pd of a station in Truckee. He and his wife bought KTHO-Lake Tahoe and the success of their own broadcast school has now branched out to Phoenix, Walnut Creek and Fremont.

KING EMZ: **KKBT**, 1995-97. King Tech has a Saturday night hip-hop and rap show on "the Beat."

KINGSLEY, Bob: **KGBS**, 1961-69; **KLAC**, 1970-71, pd;

KBBQ, 1972; **KFI**, 1973. Bob launched his radio career with the Armed Forces Radio Service in Keflavic, Iceland. Following a series of Southwest radio jobs, he arrived in the Southland to start at KGBS. In *Billboard*'s Radio Response Ratings in 1967 and 1968, Bob was voted most influential country personality. In October 1968, KGBS changed from Country to Hot 100 and Bob was part of the lineup. At KFI Bob did the all-night shift. He has been affiliated with ABC Radio Networks' "American Country Countdown with Bob Kingsley" since 1974 and has been the host since 1978. Bob has collected ten consecutive *Billboard* Radio Awards for Nationally Distributed Program of the Year. In a *Billboard* magazine profile, Bob talked about being enamored with the history and roots of country music. He tries to include that passion and knowledge into the show, while still balancing those elements to keep it focused on current country music. In addition to the "Countdown," he also produces "Bob Kingsley With America's MusicMakers," another ABC program. "I try to leave people with a real picture of the stars who make the music. Whether it's a chart newcomer or Garth Brooks, when the listeners hear their record I want them to think, 'That's the singer Bob Kingsley told us about.'"

KINGSTON, Lenore: **KFWB**, 1959-62. Lenore was the home affairs editor during the colorful days of "Color Radio." Her show "Purely Personal" aired for three years. Lenore was featured on *This Is Your Life* for her important contributions during World War II. Born Eleanor Bourgeotte in L.A. on October 14, 1913, during the thirties she acted in the radio drama "Ma Perkins" and later starred with McDonald Carey in the *Lock Up* tv series. But her real interest was being a ham radio operator. After Pearl Harbor she founded radio training courses for the American Womens Voluntary Service. She specialized in phone patches between servicemen overseas and their families. During her time with KFWB she aired over 6,000 programs that dealt with finding missing persons, or trading or selling something. Lenore retired when she left KFWB and has since passed away.

KIRKLAND, B.K.: **KGFJ/KUTE**, 1983, pd. B.K. was the pd of WHUR at Howard University and one of the originators of "The Quiet Storm" concept while at WBLS-New York. He became the Western regional pd for Inner City Broadcasting. A year later he returned to WBLS. In the mid-1990s he was the regional vp of WIKS-Greenville/New Bern and WXNR-Charlotte.

KIRCHEN, Diana: **KWIZ**. Diana was part of the all-female jock line-up at KWIZ. She's currently the music director of the Cal State Fullerton college radio station, KBPK.

KLEIN, Frank: **KPPC**, 1971. Frank arrived in the Southland from KPRI-San Diego.

KLEIN, Michael: **KRLA**, 1970. Michael was one of the newscasters on KRLA.

KNIGHT, Chris: **KWST**, 1982; **KMGG**, 1982-83. Chris arrived in the Southland from WEZB-New Orleans. Chris is currently working morning drive at KKMG-Colorado Springs.

KNIGHT, Gene: **KHTZ**, 1979-80. Born Jerome Peterson in Los Angeles, Gene worked for Bobby Rich at KFMB ("B-100")-San Diego. When Bobby went to KHTZ, Gene followed. He later returned to San Diego as md of "B-100" and eventually became pd. He was at KFMB for 18 years until leaving in early 1994. In the fall of 1994 Gene went to afternoon drive at KKBH-San Diego and became pd in the spring of 1996.

KNIGHT, Michelle: SEE Marina Wilson

KNIGHT, Steve: **KIEV**, 1972-97. Steve has been associated with the world of food during his years on Southern California radio and currently hosts "Steve Knight's Broadcast Bistro" on KIEV. He was raised in the San Gabriel Valley, graduated from Rosemead High School in 1959 and studied radio at Pasadena City College. He started his radio career at KWUN-Concord in 1964 and joined KKAR-Pomona where he was pd from 1967 to 1972. When the music format at KIEV changed to Talk in March 1976, Steve co-hosted a show with Paul Wallach who was then dining critic for *Westways Magazine*. He found the world of food and wine so interesting "that I took cooking classes at Ma Maison restaurant's Ma Cuisine school and wine classes with Robert Lawrence Balzer." When Wallach left KIEV, Steve took over full-time. He also publishes a monthly newsletter and writes a restaurant review column for the *Irish News*.

KNIGHT, Ted: **KGIL**; **KPRZ**. The former Emmy award-winning portrayal of the unforgettable Ted Baxter on *The Mary Tyler Moore Show* and star of ABC/TV's *Too Close for Comfort* did fill-in for Dick Whittinghill during vacations. Ted appeared as Judge Smails in *Caddyshack*. Prior to his tv career, Ted was in Hartford radio.

KNORR, Peter: **KJOI**, 1989. Peter worked weekends at Beautiful Music "K-Joy."

"These are the golden years and with my social security check and AFTRA retirement monies, I'm having a great time. I like to laugh a lot."
                                                                    -Dave Robinson

KNOTT, Leo: **KDAY**, 1979-83; **KFWB**, 1983-84; **KABC/KLOS**, 1984-85; **KJLH**, 1984-89; **KACE**, 1989-90; **KGFJ**, 1990-93; **KTYM**, 1995-97. After a decade-

and-a-half in mostly Urban radio since 1979, Leo became a young disciple of Christianity and joined KTYM. Born and raised in Chicago listening to WVON, WCFL and WLS, he was in his second year at Loyola University when he heard his calling to follow radio as a career. Leo was listening to Bill "Butterball" Crane. "Hey, he sounds like me. I thought I could do radio and saw my counselor." The counselor guided Leo to Southern Illinois University. He was active on the campus station. After graduation in 1972 Leo joined KOWH-Omaha and started his radio journey that took him to WNOV-Milwaukee, mornings at KDKO-Denver and KVOV-Las Vegas. "Steve Woods offered me overnights at KDAY and that got me to L.A." Reflecting on his current job at KTYM, "I believe that He led me here. All my other jobs were filled with negatives and I wondered when is radio supposed to be fun? I'm enjoying KTYM and have a long way to go."

KNUTSON, Ken: **KFOX**, 1971

KOBIK, John: **KOCM**, 1987; **KWIZ**, 1990-91. John broadcast news during morning drive at KWIZ.

KOHL, Ken: **KFI**, 1987-88, pd. In 1981 Ken was programming KOMO-Seattle. After KFI he went on to program KSTE-Sacramento and in the summer of 1996 added KFBK programming duties. He also was operations manager for the Air Traffic Radio Net.

KOLODNY, Warren: **KCRW**. Warren hosted "Stay Awake" on KCRW. He was also employed by Rhino Records where he worked in media relations. Warren was a graduate of Amherst College and held a masters degree in Spanish from Stanford University. He died August 23, 1996.

KONYSKI, Hank: **KNX**, 1938-48; **KABC**, 1967-83. Henry was part of the broadcast news landscape in Southern California for almost five decades. The longtime roving reporter for KABC worked the morning drive "Ken and Bob Company" show and "SportsTalk." He was known as Henry when he broadcast news and Hank when doing sports. Henry started his career with United Press in the 1930s while going to school and joined KNX in 1938.

"I worked at CBS until 1948, except for World War II when I flew B-17's in the 8th Air Force in Europe for four years." He returned to KNX in 1946 until he was hired to do promotion and PR for a company that handled the premier clients in the Southland including the L.A. Rams, Ice Capades, Riverside Raceway, the L.A. Golf Open and the L.A. Home Show. He helped promote the first ever Super Bowl football game which was played in the L.A. Coliseum in 1967. At KABC he covered many major stories. "I was there the night Bob Kennedy was shot, the following Sirhan Sirhan trial, the brutal Manson murders and the trial, the two Watts riots and earthquakes, including the 6.6 San Fernando disaster which claimed 65 lives." He won a national award for his coverage of the Black Panther shootout with L.A. police. In 1975 he won a Golden Mike award for a series on how badly Mexico treated Americans in the courts and prisons. When the Summer Olympics came to L.A. Henry hammered home the concept of a tax-free Spartan 1984 Olympic games long before anyone dared to challenge city officials on the issue. He also lobbied successfully against a group led by the mayor to charge admission to Griffith Park. Henry was born in Port Chester, New York. He retired in 1983 and lives in the San Fernando Valley.

KOON, W.L.: **KRKD**, gm

KOONTZ, Bob: **KXMG**, 1997, gm. Bob served in sales capacities at KMPC, KLIT, KRLA, KJOI and KEZY.

KORDUS, Marie: **KMGX**, 1985; **KPWR**, 1985-97, gm. Marie came up through the sales ranks at "Power 106" to be appointed gm in March 1996. She was in sales at

KMGX. She arrived in the Southland from WISN/TV-Milwaukee where she worked in sales. Prior to that she was a sales rep for two years at WMIL and WOKY-Milwaukee. Born and raised in Milwaukee, Marie graduated from Cardinal Stritch College in Milwaukee where she majored in fine arts. She moved to L.A. and first worked as an art director on feature films.

KRAMER, Rhonda: **KFOX**, 1979-80; **KHJ**, 1980-81. Born June 6, 1957 in New York, Rhonda grew up in New York and moved to Palos Verdes Estates for her last two years of high school. She started doing overnights at KFOX and by the time she got to afternoon drive she was offered the airborne traffic job at KHJ. Rhonda started LA Traffic Network in 1982 after a traffic-reporting career that included a few months at Metro Traffic. She boasts that her service worked with all the big stations including KROQ. "We made the traffic cool for the station. We always kept in mind the audience of the station when doing traffic. Our banter would reflect the listeners of a particular station." The Real Don Steele introduced Rhonda's traffic report with "Help me Rhonnnnnda, Rhonnnnnnda, Rhonnnnnnnda." Rhonda loved starting her afternoon shift with such energy. "He woke me up." When KHJ experimented with "Car Radio" they asked Rhonda to be a part of the new format. She recalled telling KHJ: "I am not in love with my car. P-lee-sssse. I was not going to take a car down the altar." In 1989 she rejoined Metro for three years and has been with Shadow Broadcasting ever since.

KRAYTON, Mitch: **KMET**, 1969-70

KRAZY KIDS: **KPWR**, 1996-97. Joey Boy and Johnny 5 worked the streets in the "Power 106" van. In the summer of 1996 they started doing evenings. They left KPWR in the summer of 1997.

KRIKORIAN, Doug: **KMPC**, 1992-93; **KMAX**, 1995. The *Long Beach Press-Telegram* sports writer hosted a program when KMPC experimented with all-Sports. He paired with Joe McDonnell in afternoon drive.

KRUSCHEN, Steve: **KABC**. "Mr. Gadget" provides consumer advice on electronic products, gadgets and new technology. A graduate of the school of Journalism at USC, Steve first began his broadcasting career as the "Automotive Ombudsman" for KABC.

KUCERA, Bill: **KJOI**, 1974-75. Bill was one of the Beautiful Music announcers who arrived from Santa Barbara radio. When he left the Southland he moved near Lake Tahoe.

KUFMAN, Kelly Whelihan: **KFWB**, 1992-97. Kelly is a news editor at KFWB.

KUNZELMAN, Christine: **KABC**, 1986. Christine was the fashion editor for the all-Talk station, KABC. She is currently the fashion coordinator on *Live With Regis and Kathie Lee*.

KYKER, Bob: **KFWB**, 1967-84. Bob was at KFWB for the transition from Contemporary music to the launch of all-News KFWB. He felt "lucky" being at KFWB because he was associated with IBEW as an engineer which gave him seniority when the changes were made. Bob was there in March 1968 when dj Gene Weed said, "We'll be right back with more music after the news" and the station has yet to play "more music." Born and raised in Porterville he started his radio career in 1957 at KAVL-Lancaster after serving in the Korean War and graduating from the Don Martin Broadcast School. From there he spent five years at KTTS-Springfield, Missouri and San Jose before joining KFWB. "My dream was to be the top jock in Los Angeles." When he left KFWB, he bought a bar/restaurant, the Mona Lisa, across from the Budweiser plant in the San Fernando Valley. He sold the enterprise in 1989 and is now semi-retired. Bob is living in Porterville where he takes care of his ailing mother.

TIRED OF THE "RUSH" HOURS?

In all of America's major cities, only one talk show host consistently beats Rush Limbaugh in the ratings:

RONN OWENS

This morning at 9, meet the man who is Rush's worst nightmare! Now he's bringing his compelling, entertaining style of talk radio to the Southland. We've got the thoroughbred to beat the one trick pony. Finally, the "Rush" hours are over!

Ronn Owens, 9:00 - 11:45 a.m. Weekdays, Only on TalkRadio 790 KABC... Where Southern California Comes To Talk!

-*LA Times* ad for launch of Ronn Owens show on KABC, July 1997

KYSR launches "Star 98.7"
-August 17, 1992

THE TOP 10

LOS ANGELES DISC JOCKEYS BETWEEN 1957-97

A ballot was distributed with all copies of the premiere edition of *Los Angeles Radio People* asking readers to vote for their ten favorite disc jockeys. Over 232 djs received votes. After the Top 10 was determined, each winning personality was asked to write a brief comment about the other winners. B. Mitch Reed died in 1983. The Real Don Steele wrote: "I feel truly honored to be in such distinguished company, and it's very gratifying to be in the 'tops!' As for commenting on my fellow poll winners, may I respectfully say that the molds were broken when these guys came onto the broadcast scene...they are definitely the best of the best." The remaining eight give us individual insight into their peers.

#10
DAVE HULL

A great hockey player. What an athlete! Who knew he would be so great on a radio show, too?! (*Dees*) Dave has a 450 horse power engine mounted on a chassis designed for 400 horse power. In other words, Dave is full throttle every minute - and funny in a way that defies explanation. He has a natural giggle that gets tripped into action by honest reactions on his part. People respond because there is no sense of anything being contrived. With Dave, it's right on his sleeve, punch the right emotional button and wham! It comes right off his sleeve. He is one of the very few entertainers, after "forty," who can trigger honest-to-god reactions from teenagers. In person Dave is a very conservative guy - ultra conservative if you want to know the truth. He is the only person in the world who could have successfully handled five and six phone lines covering one topic involving five or six participants, with each of them laughing harder than the other, with he himself laughing harder and more genuinely than any of the others. He did this unfailingly on several different stations over many years. He tossed words like "scuzzy" and "yuck" around like confetti while the young callers became more and more hysterically jubilant by the second - it was rapid-fire and totally delicious. I listened to his show on a return trip from San Diego one Saturday night years ago on my car radio - it seems now as though it was just last night. By the time I reached home, I was literally too weak to walk from laughing non-stop all those miles. I would give anything to be in that car again this very minute re-living every single one of those belly laughs. The "Hullabalooer" is a "Pro."(*Hudson*) "Phone master." A good friend and one of the nice people in this business. Always the first to call whenever I left a station wondering if he could help me line up another job. One of the best ever working the phones on the radio. (*Tuna*) One of the most decent people in the business. Always sounded like he enjoyed his work and it was infectious. (*Whittington*) Had a 30+ share in afternoon drive in Los Angeles. What else needs to be said? (*Morgan*) Always under-estimated, Dave is absolutely brilliant on the air and is a hungry observer of HOW THE WORLD REALLY WORKS. The WINDS OF RECOGNITION are about to blow HIS way & revive his STAR TURN - via SATELLITE, according to rumors now eddying & swirling forward in the corridors of entertainment power. (*Ballance*) The "Hullabalooer" is always fun to hear...his lovable audio smile and superb sense of timing are compelling. We were on the same iconoclastic broadcasting crew at KMPC. Dave and I learned how to speak English while reading Fleer's Double Bubble Gum comics. He was also the first person in the world to successfully compare the incomparable Hildegard. He's a solid part of L.A. (*Owens*)

#9
EMPEROR BOB HUDSON

A great "Character." Very funny just listening to him, period. His Hudson & Landry album bits are still some of the best! (***Tuna***) No one will ever surpass the humor and creativity of "Beautiful Bob." (***Hull***) A true radio original. The best thing that ever happened to my career was his leaving KRLA. (***Morgan***) When he really CONCENTRATES, he is in TOTAL COMMAND OF THE BATTLEFIELD. He combines a personal, energetic drive with strict guardianship of his CREATIVE GIFTS. When Bob's on a roll, he gives the listener a SENSE OF PERPETUAL RAPTURE. It was an honor to <u>follow</u> him on the air at KGBS. (***Ballance***) An extremely talented man who created a radio kingdom. (***Whittington***) The crown marks on his headboard say it all. (***Dees***) My initial "Bob" meeting was in the Bay Area, when he was a brilliant advertising copywriter. Whe he became a josh dickey...his non-stop hilarity made him a great name at KRLA. Bob's superb drollery is tantamount to the great French Entertainer, LePetomane. His albums with Ron Landry are played ubiquitously throughout the land. He's a naturally funny guy. (***Owens***)

#8
CHARLIE TUNA

Charlie has a great voice. I thought that he would get an ambitious voiceover agent and move exclusively into voiceover work. I never heard enough of his on-air work to form an opinion about his contribution to radio from a standpoint of style and creativity. (*Hudson*) Very nice man - but always seemed like he wanted to be somewhere else. (*Hull*) Charlie has certainly built a constellation of listeners for many years in L.A. His great voice and style are part of the tapestry in this region. He's a broadcasting mainstay. With his aka "Charlie Tuna," I told him to go into business with Abe Vigoda and Eric Estrada and have "Fish and Chips"! (*Owens*) One of the most versatile in the business. He could play classical music and still be Charlie Tuna. (*Whittington*) The best timing on radio. Never once stepped on the vocal of *A Theme From a Summer Place*. (*Morgan*) Never frightened by the screaming nightsweats or midnight fantasies of unforeseen disaster, CHARLIE always exudes cheerfulness and reveals titanic preparation and risky exercises of the imagination through the act of fearless broadcasting. His performance is the greatest play since WILLY LOMAN LOST HIS GRIP. (*Ballance*) I have so many tapes of Charlie Tuna on WRKO and KHJ. Charlie was the "Drake Model" for America. He's got such a fast mind and those "great pipes" as they say at CBS. (*Dees*)

#7
DICK WHITTINGTON

"Wildman!" This man has had the wildest personal life I've every heard or read about in radio. If you didn't know Dick, you would think it was fiction. It's gotta' be where he's come up with all the very creative bits over the years on the radio. Quite a mind! *(Tuna)* Probably should have accomplished more, but he never learned to play between the lines. *(Whittington)* One of the wildest minds in the business. *(Hull)* "Sweet Dick" is very deep - he's part poet and part moth. He is very poignant, extremely intelligent and never met an envelope that wouldn't push beyond the precipice. For all of his gusto and headline grabbing publicity stunts and his ability to be confrontational in search of scintillating (not titillating) program content. I remember him best after all these years for a wonderfully poignant bit of prose having to do with the life cycle of a butterfly. It was his own composition. It really moved me because it emerged on a Saturday amidst all kinds of tough edged humor. I remember being so moved by the piece that I asked if He would make me a tape copy. I'm happy to say that he did and I still have it somewhere among my souvenirs. The "moth" part of "Sweet Dick" was known to all his friends and employers - he simply could not keep away from the flame of peril...when everything was seemingly perfect job-wise, he would fly abruptly from the safety of the formation, directly into the flame of the forbidden candle. He is one of a kind. I love him. *(Hudson)* When I first heard "Sweet Dick" I said to myself, "Self...here's a guy with a mind as great as Lenny Bruce." And he's on the radio! Dick's parodisical "Strum and Angst" is just absolutely positively! He's been a definitive part of the City of Angels for many a moon. His longtime affiliation with KGIL was a true marriage. (Dick got custody of the VU meter.) *(Owens)* You talk about wild ideas, creativity, stunts, fun radio - <u>this</u> is the man! When "Sweet Dick" <u>married</u> the Queen Mary to the city of Long Beach, I was hooked! *(Dees)* He was <u>better</u> than the best and knew precisely when to retire. Dick always burned brighter than his rivals AND he never worried about CRITICS: after all, does the SOLAR system FRET about its reputation among asteroids? Is the MOON concerned about the BAYING OF HOUNDS? Is an EAGLE bothered by INSECTS as it SOARS ALOFT WITH OLYMPIAN INDIFFERENCE? As the Chinese proverb puts it so succinctly: THE DOGS BARK, BUT THE CARAVAN MOVES ON....*(Ballance)* Brilliant, creative mind. Re-defined "off the wall." *(Morgan)*

#6 RICK DEES

Rick is bright. He has a nifty edge of manipulation when it comes to the "funny bone." If it's funny and will build his audience, he uses it. Like Dick Clark, he stays forever young. (*Hudson*) Sometimes maligned, probably from envy. Rick not only endures; he knows and fulfills his audience better than anyone I've ever heard. (*Whittington*) My first contact with Rick was when I was pd and morning man at KIIS AM&FM and I added *Disco Duck* and interviewed him when he was still jocking in Memphis. He's been a major player ever since KIIS gave him the opportunity back in 1981. Ironically I turned that same job down since I had just signed a new deal with KHTZ. (*Tuna*) Never really had an opportunity to meet him personally - but one of the best L.A. personalities ever. (*Hull*) Has vast talent & is using it fully. Rick has earned a satisfaction and triumph that few performers ever know. His employers wisely realize that there's not much POINT in HIRING Rick's nimble IMAGINATION and then HARNESSING it. THE SUN NEVER SETS AS RICK DEES BEGETS.

(*Ballance*) Rick, highly lauded and talented, with his boyish charm and mischievous sense of humor, has consistently been one of the Top rated air personalities in L.A. We worked under the same roof at Gannett and shared many laughs and furtive hallway anecdotes with Buffalo Bob while he was Bobbing for Buffaloes. Rick's syndicated shows are all rating winners, also. (*Owens*) Broke the DJ salary barrier. Thanks, Rick! (*Morgan*)

#5
B. MITCHEL REED

B. Mitch didn't talk too fast, people simply listened too slow. He was "New Yorky." He was pushy...and he loved the Biz and the music that made it work. (*Hudson*) "Cool." One of the jocks who set the standard for what was "cool" in the late '60s and on into the '70s. His impact is measured by simply being on this list with 9 other guys who are still alive and working. (*Tuna*) I never met Mitch - but he was truly one of the best. (*Hull*) Mitch had a unique style. When Chuck Blore and Bob Purcell took over KFWB, B.M.R. was told to talk twice as fast as his usual pace (which was a laid back jazz deejay style), and he did and became very big because of it. At Mitch's funeral, Joey Reynolds and I were driving away from the Synagogue to the 405 Freeway and I spotted a camper truck with a license plate that came right out of Rod Serling's *Twilight Zone*. It was California plate "BMR 98" (the first two numerals of which, were KFWB's radio frequency). The truck had nothing to do with the cortege...it was just there! (*Owens*) His jazz background contributed style and intelligence to the first wave of Top 40 jocks. (*Whittington*) A punishing denouement for his life-drama occurred when he died FAR before his time. (We were both graduates of the University of Illinois). I followed him on the air at KFWB. He talked faster than Gabby Hayes with his beard on fire, thus setting the pace for his FABULOUS 40 DJ show. (*Ballance*) What a great talent! He made music come to life. I miss him! (*Dees*) A Top 40 pioneer. He showed us how to do it! (*Morgan*)

#4
BILL BALLANCE

The quickest wit on the air. He invented modern Talk radio. *(Morgan)* A lot of people have been credited with the popularity of talk radio. Bill Ballance was the man - he did it - he caused women to put down whatever they were doing, and listen, and call in by the thousands. Men listened too and loved it. Bill worked harder than anyone I ever knew in radio with the possible exception of Casey Kasem. (*Hudson*) "Revolutionary." His "Feminine Forum" changed everybody's thinking about how far you could go with sexual topics on the radio. He revolutionized midday radio across the county. (*Tuna*) One of the first great "titillating" communicators. *(Hull)* Billo is one of the supreme talents in our biz. He is one of the most entertaining and literate individuals I've had the good fortune to know. He created the "Feminine Forum," a milestone in talk radio. We became close pals when we were nurgling together at KFWB. He's a star for long time. Bill is now between triumphs, living in utter decadence in La Jolla's most preposterously vulgar beachfront mansion. (*Owens*) A gentleman. Without his initial testing of the 1st Amendment and non-stated FCC rules, Howard Stern and Rush Limbaugh would be playing "Supertramp" tracks today. (*Whittington*) An original. He really knows how to "touch the listener's nerve." (*Dees*)

#3
ROBERT W. MORGAN

Robert W. is quite similar to another talented radio personality of the same name, Henry Morgan. Deliciously cynical, possessing rapier like wit, capable of being "Peck's Bad Boy." Always funny, never boring - lifetime batting average - 350 with power.(***Hudson***) "Witty mind." Despite all the rumors over the years I've always had a great amount of respect for Robert W. and his talent, and I think he's felt the same about me. He has a very creative mind, quick wit and great timing for comedy! (***Tuna***) Not only does he have a beautiful voice, and a quick mind, but he's also the best bass fisherman of anyone in radio. A legend. (***Dees***) Robert is always PREPARED, PROFESSIONAL, PERTINENT & PLAYFUL - AND he's never failed in PRAISING the work of competitors. He is a man of FORMIDABLE CREATIVE INTELLIGENCE; let's all hope that the VELOCITY OF HIS FORWARD MOMENTUM IS NEVER IMPEDED by those above him in the broadcasting hierarchy, NONE of whom is TALENTED. (***Ballance***) A very complex man. A master of the well-crafted one liner. I've sometimes wondered if he always has the courage of his professed convictions. (***Whittington***) One of the most ambitious men in the business. (***Hull***) A major force in Southern California radio. He's performed meteorically at every station that has had the wisdom to employ him. Robert W. has a wild way with topical humor and a Voltaire-like delivery. We've been friends for many years and bop into each other at the Supermarket (between the artichokes and the underwear-straightening booth) frequently. Former L.A.P.D. Chief Daryl Gates told me if he didn't have a "Good Morgan" on the radio each day, he couldn't get to work! Robert W. is indeed something special! (***Owens***)

#2
THE REAL DON STEELE

Don found a few absolute winners (trademark sayings such as "Tina Delgado is alive!") and used them successfully for nearly a half century. His lungs are made of kryptonite, and his energy level is from DNA material yet undiscovered by the rest of us. (*Hudson*) One of radio's "originals." A lot of guys have tried to pull off what Don does on the radio, but they always fall way short. He's one of the few guys in radio who still has a "mystique" about him, even after all these years. (*Tuna*) Don is a wonderful talent with an amazing kinetic energy. He always makes rock and roll memories come alive with zest and zing (Don's accountants). Don's had super ratings wherever he's worked. Our friendship dates back to Don Burden and Omaha. (*Owens*) LOUD - BUT GOOD! *(Hull)* A radio ANIMAL! He's the absolute best at what he does. Sounds better now, than he did 30 years ago...if that's possible. (*Morgan*) Pure, raw energy and focus. And he still has it <u>everyday</u>. That's amazing! (*Dees*) A master of surrealist imagery, STEELE was a cunning swaggerer of astonishing talent, exploiting every OPENING and mastering every CRISIS. He used HUMOR to kneed conventional society in the GROIN. He is a durable long-distance runner IMPLODED with uncontrollable laughter at Implacable Fate.(*Ballance*) I've always enjoyed his uniqueness. An original. Thank god Tina Delgado is still alive. (*Whittington*)

#1
GARY OWENS

The Godfather. He's the one we all wished we could be. (*Morgan*) Gary is a goulash of everything and everyone that was important and successful in radio. He knew the type of voice intonations that were desired and he perfected those pear shaped tones, mixed them well with superb timing of *New Yorker Magazine* style wit and humor, and spooned that feast to his loyal audience long enough to become a legend. Never blue, always wholesome. He responded to every favor I ever asked of him. (*Hudson*) "Funny!" Just a pleasure to be around! Constantly twisting words and phrases into a whole new funny angle. Every lunch I've ever with Gary always leaves me laughing. A genuinely funny man! (*Tuna*) A great thrill for me to know him and to have worked with - a real gentleman! (*Hull*) G.O. is a dear friend and a genius. I fell in love with his antics the moment I heard *Superfun* with Mel Blanc. (*Dees*) The consummate professional. (*Whittington*) My beloved buddy of 36 years. Gary is now at the PEAK of his ENORMOUS STENTORIAN POWER, not only on RADIO but in countless VOICEOVERS. His tremendous SHARE OF ACCLAIM is not NEARLY enough. There should be an OWENS EQUESTRIAN STATUE (prancing position) erected on the grounds of GRIFFITH PARK as a salute to his inimitable TALENT. (*Ballance*)

L

LABEAU, Steve: **KFI**, 1982-87, pd; **KLAC**, 1987-89, pd.

Steve grew up in the San Fernando Valley and married his high school sweetheart. As a kid, he "played" radio in his bedroom and had his own little mock studio. Steve ended up in Detroit radio, then returned to his roots to work as assistant pd of KFI under Jhani Kaye. He became pd at KFI in 1985 and added game shows to the evening programming. He was at KFI during the "Super 64" and "Amazing AM" periods. If you listen carefully in the movie *The Night of the Comet*, you will hear Steve. He substituted for Lohman & Barkley when they broke up in 1986. From KFI, he crossed the street and programmed Country KLAC. During the 1990s he programmed KAMJ/KMXX-Phoenix, WMXN-Norfolk, WQAL-Cleveland and is currently pd at WLTF-Cleveland.

LABOE, Art: **KFWB**, 1954-55; **KXLA**, 1955; **KPOP**, 1955-59; **KDAY**, 1960-61; **KPPC**, 1970 and 1972-73; **XPRS**, 1970-71; **KRTH**, 1970-75; **KRLA**, 1975-79; **KFI**, 1983-84; **KRLA**, 1985-97. Born Arthur Egnoian,

Art entered the U.S. Navy and was assigned to Pan American Airways. He became a full-time Flight Radio Officer. He had assignments in Latin America, Africa and the Orient. In 1954 he achieved the rank of Captain, U.S. Army Reserve. Art arrived at KXLA (which later became KRLA) in the 1950s after stops in Reno, Pomona, Palm Springs and KSAN-San Francisco. His career has spanned an incredible five decades in Los Angeles radio. He mastered the most successful record series in history, a compilation titled *Oldies But Goodies*. (The albums are sold on QVC as well as record outlets.) During the 1950s, Art conducted the first live contemporary remotes from midnight to 4 a.m. from Scrivner's Drive-In Restaurant at Imperial & Western. The restaurant was continually jammed with men and women getting off work at aircraft plants along with musicians and teenagers out past curfew. He took the successful concept to the hugely huge Ciro's nightclub on the Sunset Strip, where he would interview major movie stars going in and out of the establishment. As rock 'n' roll was about to skyrocket, Art recognized its potential. Beginning in 1955 he broadcast on KPOP from Scrivner's Hollywood Drive-In restaurant. Here, after school, teens created traffic jams near the intersection of Sunset and Cahuenga. His KPOP show from Scrivner's generated 30 Hooper shares. During this time he produced and hosted over 300 live dance shows at the legendary El Monte Legion Stadium, Harmony Park in Anaheim and the Long Beach Municipal Auditorium. Every top-name act appeared at the El Monte facility, including Ray Charles, Jerry Lee Lewis, Jackie Wilson and Chuck Berry. Many local acts got their first break there, like "Handsome" Mel Carter. During the live broadcasts from Scrivner's, it dawned on Art that many of the requests and dedications were for oldies. In 1957, Art was the first to package an album featuring different artists.

Volume One was on *Billboard* magazine's Top 100 for a mind-boggling 183 weeks. His Original Sound Records' first hits were *Bongo Rock*, by Preston Epps, and Sandy Nelson's *Teen Beat*. He skipped numbering volume 13 and went to 14 due to superstition. He emceed a highly rated tv show on KTLA/Channel 5. When KRTH went with the Oldies format in the early 1970s, Art was on air and a consultant. In 1973, the station broadcast a nostalgia party every weekend from his nightclub, "Art Laboe's Oldies But Goodies" (formerly Ciro's, now the Comedy Club) on the Sunset Strip. In 1975 he took on the multiple tasks of pd, air personality and sales consultant at KRLA, and by 1979 he was senior vp at the station. Art was given a Star on the Hollywood Walk of Fame on July 17, 1981, at the southwest corner of Hollywood Boulevard and Highland -- in the heart of Laboe's favorite hangouts of the 1950s. He returned to KRLA in 1985, and has acted in various on- and off-air capacities. He is the founder of the Art Laboe Foundation, which presents annual scholarships to four East Los Angeles high schools. Art is an animal lover (he owns "Farrah" Ferret) and devotes much of his time to animal causes. His "Sunday Night Killer Oldies Show" went the syndication route in 1994 where it continues. Humble Harve paid Art an enormous compliment: "Art was the only one to communicate with people on their level." In 1996 he purchased KOHT/KXEW/KTZR-Tucson.

LACY, Jack: **KIQQ**, 1981-85. Jack had a long and successful career at WBAL-Baltimore and in New York at WCBS/FM and WINS before joining "K-100." Jack moved to Spain to live with his daughter and died on June 9, 1996, in San Sebastian.

LADD, Jim: **KNAC**, 1967-69; **KLOS**, 1969-75; **KMET**, 1974-87; **KLOS**, 1985-86; **KMPC/FM/KEDG**, 1988-89; **KLSX**, 1991-95. Jim, who was there for the birth of "underground" AOR, chronicled it in a book, *Radio Waves: Life and Revolution on the FM Dial*. Born in 1948 in a small farming community outside Sacramento, at age 21 he moved to Long Beach to work at KNAC. In 1980 Jim was cited as the Top Rock Jock for "the passion that he brings to both the songs he plays and the words that set the mood. Ladd cares and it shows." In 1974, he started hosting "The Every Other Sunday Stereo Special," an interview show described by Jim as "a cross between *60 Minutes* and a kick-ass hour of rock 'n' roll." It later became the ABC syndicated show, "Inner View," put together by Damion and a KLOS salesman. In 1984 he hosted "Live From the Record Plant" for RKO Radio Networks. Jim left KMET for a brief time in 1985, going to KLOS for a Saturday night show, which he left on

September 26, 1986. He returned to "the Mighty Met" and was there when the plug was pulled on February 6, 1987. Listen for Jim's voice in the MGM movie *Rush*. In 1994, producer Howard W. Koch, Jr., optioned his book to be made into a movie for Paramount Pictures. Jim was let go from KLSX when the station changed from "classic rock" to "Real Radio" Talk format in the summer of 1995. On his departure he told Gary Lycan of the *OC Register*: "The problem is not KLSX but radio in general. It's not run by people who know the music anymore. This decision was made 3,000 miles away, and all radio is like that. They try to pick a little narrow slot." Jim is a "classic rock" jock at WW1.

LaFAVE, Norm: **KFI**, 1994. Norm hosted an automobile talk show.

LaFAWN, Jim: **KWST**, 1976; **KPOL**, 1977; **KZLA**, 1979-80, pd. Before arriving in Southern California Jim was om of KXGM-Santa Maria. The pd was 33 years old when he died of a heart attack in the KZLA offices on January 31, 1980. His friend, Neil Ross, remembers Jim telling him about waking up in the middle of the night with his heart pounding hard for no apparent reason. According to the *LA Times*, he died of a heart condition which developed while he was serving in Vietnam.

LAINEZ, Omar: **KLVE**, 1995-97. Omar was born and

raised in Puerto de Tela in Honduras. At the age of 18, he received his Bachelor of Arts degree in letters and science. Following graduation he came to the United States in 1990 to pursue broadcasting by attending school at VOZ Broadcasting Productions in Hollywood. Omar hosts the overnight show on "K-Love." He lives in Fontana with his wife and three children.

LAING, Art: **KFWB**, 1968-78. Art worked for all-News KFWB specializing in human interest stories. Born in Nova Scotia, he grew up in many parts of North America as his parents were officers of the Salvation Army and traveled frequently. Art fell in love with radio during World War II. He broadcast numerous Navy shows overseas over the BBC. After the war, Art started his radio career in Timmins, Ontario in 1946 and worked for a series of Canadian radio and tv stations. When he left the Southland in 1978 Art returned to Toronto to assist his ailing mother. He worked at CKLW radio and tv. In 1980 Art had a massive stroke and it took his voice. His wife, Neilela, said that he had four surgeries prior to his death on May 26, 1994. "Art had hip replacement surgery on both hips and two colostomies. The first colostomy was loused up and they had to do it again."

LAIRD, Diana: **KGGI**, 1996-97, pd. Diana joined the Riverside station from pd for WW1's Adult Rock format. She started her career at KSTN-Stockton, then went on to do airwork on KYNO-Fresno, KSFM-Sacramento and WSHE-Miami. Diana has programmed KWBR-San Luis Obispo and KJFX-Fresno.

LAIRD, Jere: **KRLA**. 1962-63; **KNX**, 1968-97. Jere is the financial editor for "KNXNewsradio." Born in Topeka on

August 8, 1933, he graduated from the University of Nevada with a journalism degree in 1960. His father's Army travels took Jere to Hilo, Hawaii when he was 15. It was in the Islands where Jere got his radio start at KHBC-Hilo. While in the U.S. Army, he was attached to the American Armed Forces Radio Network in Germany. Before arriving in the Southland, he worked at KOLO radio and tv in Reno during the 1950s. Prior to joining KRLA Jere worked in Sacramento at KCRA radio and tv. After KRLA he became a reporter for KNXT/Channel 2 which led to KNX in April 1968, the year the station adopted an all-News format. He won an Emmy for coverage of the 1965 Watts Riots in Los Angeles while at Channel 2. He has taught at USC and Cal State Northridge. "Talking on the radio has been great all these years. It sure beats working for a living!"

LAITE, Reg: **KFWB**, 1971-73, nd. Reg arrived in the Southland from WINS-New York. He has also worked for NBC Radio and was nd at WOR-New York.

LAKE, Martin: **KNAC**, 1969-70

LAMA, Stephen: **KUSC**, 1994-97, pd. Born and raised in Los Angeles, from 1985 to 1989 Stephen was broadcast manager of KCET/TV. Until March 1994 he was an associate director for performance programming at PBS's headquarters in Alexandria, Virginia. Stephan is currently the pd of KUSC.

LAMB, Ken: **KJOI**, 1974-77, pd. Ken arrived in the Southland to program KJOI from WRFM-New York. He's currently heard on ABC/TV as a network announcer.

LAMB, Mike: **KFOX**, 1990; **KORG**, 1991; **KFI**, 1991; **KMPC**, 1992-93; **XTRA**, 1994-95; **KMPC**, 1995; **KLSX**, 1996. A graduate of USC, Mike was an offensive tackle during John Robinson's first tenure as head coach of the Trojans. He began his collegiate career as a member of USC's last unbeaten team - the 1979 squad that produced a #2 national ranking and a Rose Bowl victory. His broadcasting career began in 1990 as he co-hosted the "Sportsbeat" radio magazine with Larry Kahn. Mike moved to KFI and the Los Angeles Raiders broadcasts,

hosting the "Raiders 5th Quarter" post-game show. At KMPC he hosted the "Football Saturday" show as well as "RamsTalk" before and after each Rams game. In 1994, he moved to XTRA and then returned to KMPC as USC Trojan color football announcer. In 1996 the commentator-packager moved USC football from KNX to KLSX. In 1997 he won best radio color commentator from the Southern California Sports Broadcasters Association.

LAMBERT, Garrett: **KWST**, 1978-79

LAMBERT, Lynda: **KODJ/KCBS**, 1990-94. Lynda was part of the "Breakfast Bunch" with Charlie Tuna and Dean Goss. In the spring of 1995, Lynda became news director for Ameron Broadcasting's WERC/WMJJ/WOWC-Birmingham. She has since moved back to Louisville, her hometown.

LAMON, Emiliano: **KFI**, 1995-97. Emiliano works the all-night shift and swing at the 50,000-watt Talk station, KFI.

LAMPHEAR, Alpert: **KDAY**, 1966, gm. Alpert moved to Big Sur and runs an old-time radio store on the wharf in Monterey.

LAMPLEY, Jim: **KMPC**, 1992-93. Jim started working afternoon drive for the kickoff of all-Sports KMPC in February 1992. The former anchor for KCBS/TV moved to mornings on KMPC when Robert W. Morgan left the station. Jim anchors major tv sporting events.

LANCE, Christopher: **KRTH**, 1982-83; **KKHR**, 1983-86; **KIIS**, 1991. Born Lance Habermeyer, he grew up in his native San Diego. His decision to pursue radio was influenced by listening to Rich "Brother" Robbin and Bobby Ocean. Christopher came to the Southland from KFRC-San Francisco and remembered arriving in Los Angeles: "KKHR was an exciting

start-up situation in a major CHR radio war at the time. We forced 'K-100' to change format, but could not overtake KIIS." He did "Lunch L.A.! with Christopher Lance" at KKHR. When he left L.A., he spent time in San Jose and Phoenix. Christopher recalled the highlight of his time in Los Angeles: "In 1985 I was the first radio personality to emcee the Miss L.A. beauty pageant." His success at KMXZ-Monterey resulted in his being named *Billboard* magazine's program director of the week. In 1994 he returned to college to complete his studies at the University of Texas, El Paso. In the summer of 1995 he joined middays and is md at KPRR-El Paso. "I was thrilled to be part of the highest rated CHR in the country!" In early 1997 he moved to KTFM-San Antonio to do middays.

LAND, John: SEE John Gilliland

LANDA, Mike: **KNX**, 1976-97

LANDAY, Tip: **KOST**, 1988-94. Tip got to KOST while working with the then-Los Angeles Raiders. The native Angeleno was producing the Raiders weekly coach's show along with the radio broadcasts when the flagship station moved from KRLA to KFI (KOST's sister station). "I met pd Jhani Kaye and was hired to be the assistant pd and I did weekend work for a number of years. This experience prepared me for my current assignment as program director at sister station, WFLC-Miami." Tip graduated from Long Beach State with a degree in radio, tv and film, and interned at KLON in the mid-1980s. His parents owned Tip's restaurant in Valencia, known as where James Dean had his final meal before his fatal car crash.

LANDER, David L.: **KRLA**, 1968; **KPPC**, 1970-71. David was part of the legendary "Credibility Gap" on KRLA. He arrived in the Southland from New York where he was an actor. He went on to play Squiggy in the ABC series *Laverne and Shirley*, a top-rated show in 1978 and 1979. David has appeared in *Nash Bridges* and *Pacific Blue* as well as numerous tv shows.

LANDERS, Chase: **KJLH**, 1979-80

LANDIS, Lon: **KCBS**, 1993-97, nd. The morning drive news anchor for "Arrow 93" arrived in the Southland from mornings at WCBS-New York. Lon was promoted to nd in late spring of 1995. The Garden City, New York native graduated from Syracuse University. "As a kid, I was always fascinated with radio's use of my imagination, the sight of the unseen," he described on "Arrow's" Web Site. "I secretly wanted to be part of that world. A world that included Orson Welles, Lowell Thomas, Paul Harvey, William B. Williams, Jim McKay and Dan Ingram." In 1997 Lon was nominated for best newscast by Associated Press.

LANDOLPHI, Suzi: **KMPC**, 1995. Before Suzi's start at KMPC, she had a one-woman show she toured called "Hot, Sexy and Safer," which is also the title of her first book. Suzi started a nightly talk show at KMPC on sex, relationships and self-esteem in early 1995 and left in the fall of the same year. When she started she told Gary Lycan of the *OC Register*: "Half of my family is black and I have a gay brother. I'm going to tell you the truth about my sex life." Suzi graduated cum laude from Middlebury College and was involved in regional theater. She has been married four times and has a daughter in her twenties. She does benefits for AIDS support organizations and since 1990 has been part owner of the Condomania condom stores. In 1994 she co-produced her own late night talk show, *Late Date with Suzi*. Suzi has written her second book, *The Best Love, The Best Sex*. In 1996 she appeared on KCOP/Channel 13 as an entertainment reporter.

LANDRY, Leah: **KMGX**, 1993-94. Currently Leah reports traffic conditions for Metro Traffic. She was a music and English major at the University of Southwestern Louisiana. Leah got her radio start in 1989 while in college at KTDY/KPEL-Lafayette, Louisiana. In 1996 she co-hosted the L.A. Marathon for the official radio station, KACD.

LANDRY, Ron: **KGBS**, 1969-74; **KFI**, 1974-75. Ron was part of one of the most successful comedy albums of all time, *Ajax Liquor Store*. The album was recorded during the time he was partnered with Emperor Bob Hudson at KGBS. His early inspiration came from Bob and Ray and Jean Shepherd. He created voices and honed his storytelling skills at radio stations on the East Coast. Beginning in 1953 and during the next three years, Ron worked for three Virginia stations, WJMA-Orange, mornings at WBTM-Danville and WSLS-Roanoke. It was during his stop in Roanoke that he hosted an evening tv

show that featured his sketch comedy. Ron was drafted in 1958 and served his two years at Armed Forces Radio in New York. "What a powerhouse of a staff we had. Dave Neihaus, who worked at KMPC later and now the voice of the Seattle Mariners, was doing sports and Bruce Wayne, later to be known as KFI's Eye in the Sky did news and sports. All I had to do was cover all the premieres and Broadway openings for two years for the boys overseas." He did a very popular music comedy show on transcription which was heard over almost every armed forces radio station in the world, and over AFRS short-wave. "It was in New York that I met my wife Margo, a United flight attendant, and we married in 1960." In April 1960 Ron joined WDRC-Hartford. "The years at WDRC were tremendously successful. I'll remember it for the rest of my life, should I live that long. Big ratings." At the end of the 1960s he worked at WBZ-Boston before heading West to team with Emperor Bob Hudson on KGBS. Ron started in afternoon drive at KGBS and within six months he and Hudson had recorded their first album. The success of the albums led to appearances on all the major tv variety shows and night clubs. Ed Sullivan announced the team on the Grammys: "...And nowwww for the best comedy album of the year, Hudson and *Sanders*." In 1977 he sold a pilot to CBS called *Szysznyk*. Ron moved full-time into producing sit-coms that included *Flo*, *Give Me A Break*, *Benson*, and *The Redd Foxx Show*. With a very successful run in radio, comedy albums and tv, Ron and his wife decided to travel...and travel. They spent two and a half years discovering Europe, Asia and the United States. He has finished some spec scripts and expects to continue traveling. "Maybe we'll travel till the end of the century. God, what a feeling."

LANE, Chris: **KFOX**, 1970-72; **XPRS**, 1974; **KGBS**, 1975-79; **KHTZ**, 1979; **KLAC**, 1980-87; **KNX**, 1990-95. Chris began his career in McMinnville, Tennessee, after recording star Eddie Arnold lined up an audition for him. His career has taken him to Des Moines, KISN-Portland, KJR-Seattle, KYA-San Francisco, WOKY-Milwaukee, WJJD-Chicago and WIL-St. Louis. When at XPRS, he voiced his show at the Bill Wade studios and it was shipped south of the border. At KGBS, he teamed with Bobby Morgan for morning drive. In 1991, Chris joined the "KNX Food Hour" as co-anchor with Melinda Lee. His television credits include creating and hosting ABC's *American Swing Around* and appearing on such network shows as *Cheers*, *General Hospital*, and the tv movie, *Favorite Son*. The 33-year old "KNX Food Hour" was canceled in the late spring of 1995 and Chris began working on a radio syndicated project.

LANE, Kay: **KYMS**, 1988-92; **KEZY**, 1996-97. Kay spent four years at KYMS using the name Kay Poland and worked as evening air talent, nd, director of community and church relations. After a brief stint in Colorado radio, Kay is back in Orange County as a weekend jock on KEZY.

LANE, Randy: **KYSR**, 1994-95, pd. Randy arrived at "Star 98.7" in late 1994 from Vallie-Gallub and Morningmasters consulting companies. He also programmed WRQX-Washington and WKQX-Chicago. He left KYSR in late 1995 and in the spring of 1996 joined the Pollack Media Group.

LANE, Spanky: **KDAY**, 1976-79. Born Rick Torcasso, Spanky was group vp for Infinity Broadcasting based in Dallas. Rick is an M.B.A. graduate of Case University's Weatherhead School of Management. He programmed WYNY-New York, WBMX-Chicago, WDRQ-Detroit, KRSR-Dallas and KMJI-Cleveland. One of his accomplishments was creating the "Young Country" format, which he trademarked in 1991. Rick's company is currently merged with Eagle Marketing. He is providing services exclusively for Mel Karmazin in a variety of special projects.

LANGE, Jim: **KMPC**, 1970-71 and 1984-89. "Gentleman

Jim" gained national exposure as the tv host of *Name That Tune*, *The Dating Game* and *The $1,000,000 Chance of a Lifetime*. Jim spent over two decades in San Francisco radio, much of it at KSFO. He returned to the Southland when King Broadcasting bought KSFO from Autry's Golden West, and everyone was fired on December 12, 1983. "Picture a guy there in a hangman's hood, throwing the switch at midnight." During his second trip to Southern California radio, Jim worked middays between Robert W. Morgan and Wink Martindale. In the summer of 1994 he started hosting a weekend show on Big Band KKSJ-San Jose. Jim also spent time in Branson, Missouri hosting *$25,000 Game Show*. Born in St. Paul, he's currently working mornings at KABL-San Francisco.

LANGE, Kelly: **KABC**, 1967-70 and 1973. The longtime KNBC/Channel 4 news anchor was the "ladybird"

airborne traffic reporter in the early days of KABC's move to Talk radio. It was one of the biggest radio promotions in Southern California history. For two months a roving trailer moved from shopping mall to shopping mall while hopeful women read one minute of copy in front of the crowd. Out of the tens of thousands who auditioned, Kelly was one of two who emerged as winners. She became a Ladybird, one of the first female helicopter traffic and weather reporters. Morning drive was won by "Dawn O'Day," who was Kelly. For more than two years, she in her tight-fitting silver lame jumpsuit, paved the way for today's less exploited women deejays and announcers. She and her afternoon counterpart, Lorri Donaldson, appeared in sexy KABC ads and on billboards with ad lines like "Our traffic figures aren't dated." The pair started on Valentine's Day 1967 and remained KABC sweethearts until 1970. Kelly hosted a talk radio show on KABC and served as a field reporter with KABC/Channel 7 before joining Channel 4 in March 1971. From that visible start she has been a tv anchor in various time slots since 1975. Kelly was born in New York and grew up in Andover, Massachusetts, where she graduated from Merrimack College in North Andover before moving to Los Angeles in 1966. She and Gail Parent co-hosted Channel 4's live weekday morning program, *Kelly & Gail*, which premiered October 22, 1990. For more than nine years she co-hosted Channel 4's 90-minute live public-affairs magazine, *Sunday*. Kelly has also filled in as substitute host on *Today*, weekend anchor of *NBC Nightly News* and guest host on the late-night *Tomorrow* show. Kelly is also a novelist. Her first murder mystery, *Trophy Wife*, was published by Simon & Schuster in the summer of 1995.

LANGAEN, John: **KMET**, 1983. John partnered with Mike West in morning drive for one month.

LANGFORD, Bruce: **KUSC**, 1993-97. Bruce works part-time for Classical KUSC.

LANGFORD, Don: **KLAC**, 1977-79, pd. Don left the Southland to program KRAK-Sacramento for over a decade. He was vp of programming for the EZ stations. He dropped out of radio and worked in public relations for the State of California, specializing in the area of state and county fairs. In the spring of 1996 he became pd of KSSJ-Sacramento.

LANGSFORD, Mike: **KMPC**, 1990; **KEZY/KORG**, 1990. Mike was one of the voices of the Rams. In 1990 he worked "Sports Confidential" on the SportsChannel along with sports shows for the two Orange County stations.

LANTZ, Stu: **KLAC**, 1987-97. A nine-year NBA veteran who played for the Lakers in the mid-1970s, Stu joined Chick Hearn in 1987 on all L.A. Lakers broadcasts. Stu graduated from the University of Nebraska in 1968.

LAQUIDARA, Charles: **KPPC**, 1968-69. After

graduating from the Pasadena Playhouse with a bachelor's degree in theater arts, Charles sought acting roles in Hollywood. One of those jobs was as a classical music announcer at KPPC, at the time located in the basement of the Pasadena Presbyterian Church.

When KPPC switched formats and became one of the pioneers of "underground-rock," Charles worked the overnight shift. He combined rock and roll with other types of music including classical. One scribe said: "He's that wacky actor who doesn't know much about rock or classical music, but he mixes them pretty well!" In 1969 Charles was hired at WBCN-Boston to replace Peter Wolf who was leaving to devote more time to his new group, the J. Geils Band. Within a few years he established that FM "underground" could attract a strong morning drive audience with "The Big Mattress Show." In the spring of 1996 he left WBCN to join WZLX-Boston and said: "If the creek don't rise and the good Lord's willin', you ain't seen nothin' yet!"

LARDNER, Lonnie: **KABC**, 1996. Lonnie works for Metro Traffic.

LARGENT, Lewis: **KROQ**, 1985-92. While at KROQ, Lewis was producer of the "Loveline" show. He left "the Roq" to be music director of MTV. In the spring of 1995 Lewis was made a vp at MTV.

LARGO, Tony: **KOCM/KSRF**, 1990-92. Tony hosted the weekend Saturday night mix show during the "MARS/fm" period. He is now a club dj.

LARKIN, Carroll: **KLAX/KXMG**, 1997, gm

LARSEN, Bob: **KPZE**, 1987

LARSEN, Lee: **KAPP**, 1961-64; **KMPC**, 1964-65; **KHJ**, 1965-70 and 1972; **KROQ**, 1972-73; **KFI**, 1973-75; **KLOS**, 1975-83. The personable general manager of KOA/KTLK/KHOW-Denver had much success in sales while in Los Angeles, however, Lee started out as a dj at Redondo Beach's KAPP. In the early 1970s he was station manager at KFMS-San Francisco and national sales manager at KFRC and RKO Radio Reps. In 1966 Lee earned a B.A. and master's degree from Pepperdine University.

LASCANO, Edmundo: **KTNQ**, 1991-92, pd. Edmundo is working at KESS-Dallas.

LASH, Shelley: **KFWB**, 1992-97

LaSHAWN, Joy: **KGFJ**, 1994; **KJLH**, 1996-97. Joy arrived in the Southland from WCIN-Cincinnati. She worked the midday shift at KJLH.

LASZLO, Charles: **KNX**, 1991-97. Charles broadcasts market and business reports for "KNXNewsradio." A native of Detroit, he graduated from Wayne State University. Charles is a veteran stock broker and financial consultant broadcasting from the Pacific Stock Exchange.

LAUGHLIN, Roy: **KIIS**, 1991-97, pres/gm. In the summer of 1995 Roy was promoted to president/general manager of KIIS. Prior to joining KIIS, Roy held sales positions with KKBQ and KTRH-Houston. He also had been gsm of *Baton Rouge Magazine*. In late 1996 he married KIIS morning personality Ellen K.

LAURELLO, Johnny: **KRLA**, 1972-73. Johnny was at KRLA during the short-lived experimentation with dual jock shifts. He was also known as Johnny Michaels and would use Michaels one day and Laurello the next.

LAUREN, Dana: **KMGG**, 1982-85; **KLSX/KBZT**, 1986. Dana arrived from WHN-New York to join "Magic 106." Born in 1960, Dana assembled a loosely knit organization calling itself Broads in Broadcasting, which was an instant Old Girl Network. The group wanted to help other female broadcasters break out of the stereotypical all-night shift. Dana complained that she had no role models. "The first job I had in San Diego, I went on the air with this squeaky voice because I'd heard a woman deejay with a squeaky voice." When she left the Southland, she returned to San Diego.

> *"I'll never forget receiving a telegram from KMPC saying I won an audition and they would pay me $80 a week to join the station."*
>
> *-Bob Anderson*

LAVOY, Anne: **KLAC**, 1986-89; **KZLA**, 1989-95.

Originally from Montclair, New Jersey, and a graduate of Syracuse University in 1973, Anne has called the West Coast home since 1974. She moved to San Francisco and worked at KSFO, KSRO and KNEW as well as tv news anchoring. In 1986 she moved to the Southland with her broadcasting husband Bob Guerra and went to work at KLAC. Anne has co-hosted the syndicated "Countryline U.S.A." show featuring interviews with country stars such as Vince Gill, Reba McEntire, Alabama and Tanya Tucker. Anne has co-written several music specials for syndication, done voiceover work and appeared in several movies. She and Bob have two children.

LAW, Al Brady: **KLAC**, 1983-84, gm; **KABC/KMPC**, 1994-96. From 1976 until the early '80s Al worked at WHDH-Boston as pd. When he left the Southland the first time in 1984, he went to Tampa. He was the gm of WNYN-New York and KKBQ-Houston and also managed WHDH, KQAI-Dallas, WRQX-Washington, DC, WABC-New York and WQFM-Milwaukee. During his stay in DC, Al was given credit as the architect of the highly successful "Q107" format. He worked as om at KABC/KMPC from 1994 until the summer of 1996. Al is now in Las Vegas with the Sports Fan Network.

LAWLER, Ralph: **KMPC**. If Ralph worked in any other city, his name would be well known. He works for Los Angeles' other NBA team doing play-by-play for the L.A. Clippers. Ralph stands 6 feet 3 and was a basketball star at Peoria Central High. When his team went to the state tournament, the games were on the radio and the announcer was Chick Hearn. Ralph got a basketball scholarship to DePauw in Greencastle, Indiana, but did not make the team. After graduation, he worked for a Peoria tv station. He spent the early part of his career in Riverside and San Diego. He spent five years in the mid-1970s covering 76er basketball, Flyer hockey and Temple football. Ralph was sports director for the Philadelphia CBS tv station. He returned to San Diego in 1978 to do play-by-play for the San Diego Clippers and did not follow them to Southern California in 1984. He stayed behind to work in real estate, but rejoined the team as broadcaster a year later.

LAWRENCE, Jay: **KFI**, 1968-70; **KLAC**, 1970-78. Born on October 6 in Chicago, Jay started his career in Evansville, Indiana, before moving on to such cities as Peoria and the legendary KLIF in Dallas. He stopped in Tucson before going to Cleveland and worked with such Eastern personalities as Ken Draper, Jim Stagg, Jim Runyon and Specs Howard. He came to Los Angeles as a replacement for Dick Sinclair's Polka Party, which was an institution on the 50,000 watt station. When Jay went to KLAC, the station was MOR, but two weeks later the station went Country. "I really got rattled. I was really worried that I wouldn't be able to relate." The station was known as the Big Auto Racing station, and Jay's task was to build up a personal relationship with the race drivers. He did morning drive for part of the time at KLAC. In the late 1950s, Jay was in a folk music trio with Jerry Bishop and Larry Helfand called the Three Jays. He recalled a highlight while in Los Angeles: "I hosted an event in El Monte where 30,000 people showed up for a prune parade." Jay also walked through Death Valley to raise money for the Foundation for the Junior Blind. Jay left L.A. for morning drive at WNEW-New York. On the decision to leave, Jay said, "My 10 years in L.A. were the best in my life. I never should have gone to WNEW, but what the heck. It's the nature of the biz." Jay is currently doing Talk radio at KTAR-Phoenix and selling real estate.

LAWRENCE, Jay: **KOCM**, 1990; **KFI**, 1987-97. Jay covers Orange County news for KFI.

LAWRENCE, Jim: **KHJ**, 1965. Jim arrived from KMEN-San Bernardino to broadcast news in the early days of "Boss Radio."

LAYNG, Rodger: **KBIG**, 1967; **KFAC**, 1969-70, pd; **KNX/FM**, 1971; **KOST**, 1971, pd; **KPOL**, 1976-77, pd; **KKGO**, 1985-89. Rodger is a fourth generation Californian and grew up next to Cary Grant's house. He was at KBIG when there was a boost to stereo power in 1967 and the station programmed "easy listening/light jazz" as they threw out the automation from Santa Catalina Island. Rodger was part of the creative team that put together KNX/FM. In 1986, Rodger created the "Fusion Format" for AudioNet. He has lived an adventuresome life in Mexico and with the Indians. His entrepreneurial projects have taken him to Hawaii, the Pacific Rim and now Mainland China with talk radio.

1966 FM Call letters	
92.3	KFAC
93.1	KNX/FM
93.9	KPOL
94.3	KVGM
94.7	KLAC
95.5	KABC
96.3	KRKD
97.9	KNOB
98.7	KCBH
100.3	KFOX
101.1	KHJ
105.1	KBCA
105.9	KBMS

LEADER, Dr. John: **KHJ**, 1975-77. John started out at WGRD and WLAV-Grand Rapids in the mid-1960s. "While programming WGRD in 1966, I worked with China Smith (who was then Wayne Thomas) and hired Sonny Fox to do afternoon drive...he was great!" John arrived in the Southland from four years at WQXI-Atlanta. Scott Shannon had shortened John's name to Dr. John when he became pd at "Quixie." His first night on KHJ was in September 1975. John narrated the RKO radio-Drake/Chenault co-production radio special, "The Top 100 of the '70s." John left KHJ in 1977 to become the Top 40 editor for *R&R*. He worked at the trade publication for eight years, eventually becoming vp and executive editor. While editor he continued narrating the monthly RKO specials. John hosted the syndicated program "Countdown America." He left *R&R* in 1985 to pursue a full-time career in voiceover. "I have been lucky enough to make a nice living." John is heard on many major movie trailers and is the promo announcer for *Entertainment Tonight.*

LEARY, Chris: **KIIS**, 1992-94; **KZLA**, 1995-96.; **KIIS**, 1997. Arriving in the Southland from WPXY-Rochester and WTIC-Hartford, Chris was originally the high-powered evening personality known as "LearJet" on KIIS. In 1994, he became the syndicated host of "Fox Kids Countdown" and began doing voiceover work, including many movie trailers. In late summer 1995, Chris went to Country KZLA for evenings as Max Ryder and left in the spring of 1996. He rejoined KIIS in early 1997 for part-time work.

LEARY, Dr. Timothy: **KEZY**, 1980. The former Harvard psychologist, lecturer and drug guru had a brief experiment during the launch of AOR on the AM station. The ex-Jesuit, ex-West Point officer, ex-dj and ex-convict worked his brand of "love" during morning drive. For decades, Leary was known as "the high priest of LSD." While on KEZY he ended a truck commercial with, "Hey, you can get that dreamy, hallucinogenic, new Toyota truck." It was not the traffic bulletins warning of the disappearance of the San Diego Freeway or reports of big ice packs off Malibu that caused Leary's firing in less than a month. Complaints to the station held him responsible for all the kids who killed themselves on drugs in the '60s. After the firing Dr. Leary told the *LA Times*: "Orange County needed me more than I needed them. I was just trying to fill a void." Born October 22, 1920, President Richard Nixon dubbed him "the most dangerous man in the world." He was jailed in 1970 on a drug-possession charge. He executed a dramatic escape, was recaptured in Afghanistan in 1973 and finally paroled in 1976. Timothy became an ardent proponent of communication in cyberspace, however, he scrapped plans to take his own life and broadcast his suicide over the Internet. He died May 31, 1996, of prostate cancer.

LEAVER, Katy: **KKGO**, 1987, nd

LEE, Allen: **KFWB**, 1992-97. Russell Allen Lee is currently part of the award-winning morning drive news team at "news 98." He came from WINS-New York. The Texas native served as pd for Shadow Broadcast services in 1993 and 1994 before stepping down to devote his full time to KFWB as AM traffic reporter.

LEE, Ana: **KNAC**, 1986-94. Ana started in radio in 1984 at KZTR-Ventura, a Lite AC station, and at the same time worked weekends at Urban KMYX-Ventura. She loved working at KTYD-Santa Barbara. At KNAC she was known as "The Animal Ana Lee." She was at KNAC until the station's last day on the air, February 15, 1995.  "What a day that was. We had James Hetfield and Lars Ulrich of Metallica fly down to Long Beach from San Jose and spend our last day on the air with the entire air staff, including former jocks. It was really fun, but quite emotional. After 9 years together, we were really like a family." For the past few years, Ana has been working at Capitol Records as the executive assistant to the executive vp of Capitol. They were responsible for the recent "Beatlemania." Ana is also the host of "Progressive Rock" on United Airlines in-flight entertainment.

LEE, Beverly Ann: **KNX**, 1976

LEE, Bob: **KHJ**, 1965-72. Bob was primarily the all-night newsman during the early years of "Boss Radio." Bob retired to a farm/ranch in the desert.

LEE, J.J.: **KLOS**, 1989-94. Born Jane Cutolo in Tampa, J.J. worked at AOR station WYNF in her hometown before coming to KLOS in early 1989. When asked for the highlights of her L.A. career, she responded: "An interview with Keith Richards, going to lots of shows and meeting various rocker types." She departed the station in October of 1994.

LEE, Jerry: **KGIL**, 1965-66, pd. Jerry's last stop before joining the San Fernando Valley outlet was KOB-Albuquerque.

LEE, Laura: **KKGO**, 1986-90. Laura worked afternoons at KKGO and was married to Jim Gosa. She has moved to Hawaii.

LEE, Lauren: **KROQ**, 1978

LEE, Melinda: **KNX**, 1985-94; **KABC**, 1995-97; **KTZN**, 1997. A native Angeleno, Melinda attended UCLA and Columbia University. She hosted the "Food News Hour" on News/Talk KNX for over eight years. Melinda told Gary Lycan in the *OC Register*: "I met Mel Baldwin, (former co-host of KNX's 'Food News Hour') and we hit it off. I was a caterer in Malibu  for 10 years and I was sure I could talk. I called the pd, Bob Sims, and told him, 'I see a major error in your life and I am here to fix it.'" She filled in for one show. It took months to win the coveted spot on KNX. Since 1993 she has co-hosted a national show that does not air in L.A. In the summer of 1995, Melinda started a weekly food talk show on KABC and moved to sister station, KTZN in the summer of 1997.

LEE, Mike: **KROQ**, 1973. Mike is now head of Brown Bag Productions in Denver. The company is the leading provider of sounds and music for the entertainment industry. The promos for every episode of *America's Most Wanted* all from Mike's library. Major tv shows like *ER* and *Homicide* use Mike's facility for music and sounds. At KROQ, he was music director and midday personality. Born and raised in Kansas City, Mike has a doctorate in communications from the University of Denver.

LEE, Robert E.: **KIIS**, 1973-74. Robert had a busy career before arriving in the Southland. In the 1960s he worked at KTKT-Tucson, KISN-Portland and managed Paul Revere and the Raiders.

LEEDS, Mel: **KDAY**, 1960, pd; **KMET**, 1968-69, pd. Mel arrived in the Southland from WINS-New York, where he was pd. Prior to WINS he had been a road manager for Tommy Dorsey and other big band leaders. After a highly publicized payola probe, the gm of KDAY, Irv Phillips, commented: "Leeds was just a fall guy in the investigation, and we are pleased to have him on our staff." After his radio career he joined Executive Car Leasing for 10 years and in the early 1990s he retired to Carlsbad.

LEGRAND, Chris: **KNX**, 1997

LEHMAN, Steve: **KIIS**, 1984-87. Steve graduated from the University of Nevada magna cum laude with a communications degree. He spent much of his career building networks prior to his on-air work at KIIS. Steve was on the ground floor in starting Premiere Radio Network in January 1987, as the president/ceo/chairman of the board. He continues in that capacity.

LEICHTER, Nancy: **KMET**, 1974-87 lsm; **KTWV**, 1987-89, lsm; **KQLZ**, 1989-93, gm; **KZLA/KLAC**, 1993-94, gsm; **KKBT**, 1994-97, gsm. Born and raised in Philadelphia, Nancy graduated from Penn State with a degree in journalism. After working in a Philly ad agency, Nancy came to Los Angeles for the embryonic days of KMET. She started in the sales department, eventually becoming sales manager. Nancy was the local sales manager for the transition from KMET to KTWV. She is currently the general sales manager of "92.3/The Beat."

LEIGHTON, Jerry: **KCBH**, 1968

LEISHER, John: **KFWB**, 1992-93. John was an evening anchor on all-News KFWB.

LEONARD, Jeff: **KHTZ/KBZT/KRLA**, 1985-87. Jeff has been with Metro Networks since 1995. During the early 1990s he produced and wrote a radio program for Buckley Broadcasting heard exclusively in Japan. Prior to that, he had a stint as a promotion administrator for the L.A. Dodgers. In the early '80s Jeff served double-duty for ABC/Watermark: first, as production coordinator for Casey Kasem's "American Top 40," then later as associate producer for Gary Owens' "Soundtrack of the '60s." In the mid-1980s Jeff worked with dick clark productions and Rick Dees' "Weekly Top 40" and was also md for KBZT and KRLA. He lives in the San Fernando Valley with his wife Denise, a son and a daughter.

LEOS, Richard: **KBCA**, 1967-76. Richard played Latin music on weekend evenings at the Jazz station. During the week Richard worked as a county probation officer. He graduated from Cathedral High School in 1954 and went on to East Los Angeles College as a music major. Richard wanted to be a singer. After a stint in the Army he graduated from Arizona State University with degrees in architecture and art design. While in college he joined a Latin Jazz station, KYND-Tempe followed by KCUB and KABT in the same city. Richard returned to his home in Los Angeles. He struggled as a musician and eventually fell into the KBCA job.

LERNER, Lori: **KPOL**, 1973; **KKDJ**, 1973-76; **KLVE**, 1975; **KIIS**, 1976-81; **KHJ**, 1981-82; **KRTH**, 1983-85; **KMET**, 1985-86. Lori grew up in Monterey Park and graduated from Cal Berkeley. She has been news director at virtually every station she's worked and won 6 Golden Mike Awards along the way. Her fortuitous luck with news began at her first station, KRE/KBLX-
Berkeley, which was owned by NBC's Chet Huntley. Lori broke the Patty Hearst kidnapping story. Part of her daily routine was to talk with the Berkeley police, and one of her friends on the force gave her the inside track. She fed the story to ABC Contemporary radio network and to various stations all over the country who called for updates. One of the stations calling was KPOL, which eventually offered her a start in Southern California doing weekend news. In addition to breaking the Hearst story, "I simulated an earthquake for a half hour in morning drive at 'K-Earth.' People still remind me today how harrowing that broadcast sounded." Lori started Radio Links almost by accident. She noticed that John Travolta was making a personal appearance for his new movie, *Perfect*. "I called the distributor, Columbia Pictures, and somehow got the right person. I told them they should pay me to cover Travolta, and I would service radio stations all over the country. I had great credentials and made lots

of friends over the years, and the piece got incredible usage." The simplicity of that idea has turned into a unique publicity corridor for movie studios, and radio stations get access to top Hollywood celebrities week after week. Radio Links has worked on over 500 movies. In addition to Radio Links, Lori also writes, produces and voices "Movie News" radio spots for Buena Vista Pictures (Disney, Touchstone, Hollywood).

LESLIE, John: **KLOS**, 1980

LESOURD, Maureen: **KABC/KMPC/KLOS**, 1996-97, president/gm. On May 1, 1996, Maureen became president of Walt Disney Co.'s Capital Cities/ABC stations in Los Angeles. Born in 1950 Maureen grew up in the New York/New Jersey area. According to a profile of Maureen in the *LA Times*, at 21 she found herself separated from her husband and a single mother with a year-old son. She started her radio career in the traffic department at WJLK-New Jersey. She became om and eventually moved to WHN-New York. In 1978 Maureen was an AE at Grey Advertising. She began her career with ABC in 1981 working in sales for WPLJ-New York which led to a promotion of vp/gm in 1988 at WRQX-Washington, DC. Following a stint running WQCD-New York, she rejoined Cap Cities/ABC in 1993 as senior vp of affiliate relations for ABC/TV. Maureen is an alumna of Monmouth College, West Long Branch, New Jersey.

LESTER, Shirley: **KYSR**, 1996-97. Shirley arrived in the Southland from a stint at K101-San Francisco where she was "Shirley the Stunt Girl" with morning host Don Bleu.

LEVI, Titus: **KUSC**, 1993-97. Titus hosts the "Gone  Global!" show on KUSC. He was born at Sunset and Vermont. "There are three hospitals on that corner and one is the Church of Scientology." Titus fell in love with music at home in South Central and later in Long Beach. His father enjoyed Romantic Period classical music and his mother listened to country music. His Sundays included substantial doses of black hymn/gospel music. Titus initially volunteered as a consultant on non-traditional classical music at KUSC. His program "Songs of the Earth" premiered October 3, 1993. He received a B.A. in economics from California State University Dominguez Hills. A former Long Beach elementary school teacher, and currently a teaching assistant at University of California Irvine, he is studying for his doctorate degree in business administration.

LEVIN, Harvey: **KMPC**, 1981. Harvey hosted a Sunday night program on KMPC called "Legal Line." Beginning in 1985 he spent a decade with KCBS/Channel 2 as a reporter and won nine Emmy awards. In 1997 Harvey was named co-executive producer and on-air legal anchor of a new tv version of *The People's Court*.

LEVINE, Ken: **KGIL**, 1976. SEE Beaver Cleaver

LEVINE, Saul: **KBCA/KKGO**, owner/jock/gm. Saul is the longest functioning station general manager in Southern California. Born in Cheboygan, Missouri, his schooling included University of Michigan, Cal Berkeley where he was a general liberal arts major, USC Graduate School of Social Work and the University of California School of Law. "In order to start up KKGO (KBCA), I managed to borrow a modest amount of capital to build the station. These limited funds were assisted by the purchase of the FM transmitter from a company in Massachusetts that had gone off the air and agreed to accept $1,500 for the equipment." A home-built FM antenna was built in a garage for $300. His pole at Mount Wilson was traded for advertising. "The offices and studio consisted of a 20 foot by 20 foot room divided in half." Saul went on to say that the station broadcast a Classical format which he thought was "the world's greatest." However, KFAC AM&FM was giving away the FM time with the purchase of AM time. Advertisers refused to buy FM advertising when they could receive it free, so less than a year later, KBCA changed to Jazz music.

LEVINSON, Marcy: **KLAC**, 1989-90. Nancy was part of the morning drive team.

LEVY, Arny: **KMEN/KGGI**, 1995. Arny arrived from WALK-Long Island in the summer of 1995 to become general manager of the Gold/CHR combo. Before his year at WALK, Arny worked in sales management at the Interep Radio Store.

LEVY, Jeff: **KFI**, 1995-97.  Jeff hosts a KFI weekend talk show "On Computers." Jeff described his show: "The show is a safe place for non-techies to jump in and participate. I get calls from 'computer creampuffs,' 'Windows wienies' and 'keyboard curmudgeons' who all hear the message that it's okay to be a beginner." Many of his Sunday morning shows originate from a live remote booth at the Pomona Fairplex, home of "Computer Marketplace."

LEVY, Stu: **KLAC**, 1959-79, gm. Starting out in the mail room, Stu was there during the end of the legendary "Big 5" djs and acerbic Joe Pyne and the beginning of Talk radio.

LEWIS, Bob: **KGGI**, 1996, pd. Bob arrived in the Southland from programming KWIN-Stockton and seven Silverado stations. He also worked for WLXR-LaCrosse, KKXL-Grand Forks, KRND-Des Moines and KGGG-Rapid City. He left KGGI in the summer of 1996.

LEWIS, Brett: **KLAC**; **KFWB**, 1997. Brett co-hosts with Doc Harris a weekly sports show on KLAC. In 1988, Brett began reporting sports for KNBC/Channel 4. He is developing a new syndicated sports show. During the 1996-97 Lakers season, Brett hosted the postgame show on KLAC. In the spring of 1997, he joined KFWB for weekend sports.

LEWIS, Chris: **KJLH**, 1992-97. Chris works early evenings at KJLH. Born and raised in Oakland, Chris grew up loving music and playing the drums in junior high school. After high school he started a mobile dj business. "One night while having fun with the crowd a short, fat guy told me I had great pipes and suggested radio." The "fat guy" turned out to be top Bay Area dj Roy

Lee Freeman. "From that night on my life changed. I ate, drank and slept radio." Chris started at KZEN-Monterey and then a series of stations in Berkeley, KPFA, KRE and 10 years at KBLX. He developed an evening show called "Fireside Chats" surrounded by romantic music. "I came to the Southland a few months before the L.A. riots and worked various shifts. It feels good to make listeners feel good through the music you play and the things you say. As long as there is music and a radio station to play it on, the saga continues!!!"

LEWIS, Johnny: **KWIZ**, 1965-70. Johnny donated 5,000 records to the station. During his half decade with KWIZ, he worked every shift.

LEWIS, Mitch: **KLIT/KMPC**, 1989-93; **KJQI/KOJY**, 1991-94; **KKGO**, 1993-97; **KRTH**, 1993-97. Born in Brooklyn and raised in Granada Hills, Mitch worked many small radio towns (Visalia; Stubenville, Ohio; Weirton, West Virginia; Golden Meadow, Louisiana; Provo and Salt Lake City) before returning "home." In 1989 he started at Unistar Radio Network and KLIT as weekend personality and md. It was at the Gene Autry station that he met Robert W. Morgan and the relationship has lasted since then. Mitch produced Robert's morning show at KMPC and followed him to KRTH. While producing Robert's show he worked weekends at other stations including the "Music of Your Life" satellite offering.

LEWIS, Rick: **KLON**, 1985-91, gm. Rick is a veteran of public radio and arrived as gm from a similar capacity at Minnesota Public Radio. Prior to that he was director of the news operations for NPR.

LEWIS, Rick: **KWVE**, 1981; **KEZY**, 1982; **KMET**, 1983-86; **KPWR**, 1986; **KMET**, 1986-87; **KEZY**, 1987-90. Rick grew up in Detroit. "I would go to sleep at night with a transistor radio under my pillow listening to CKLW in the Motor City." As his friends were playing sandlot sports, he drove them crazy doing non-stop play-by-play chatter. Rick never thought about a career in radio until college. He floundered at a number of colleges before giving Hollywood a try and appeared in numerous tv commercials, shows and movies. "One night in 1979, while working at a convenience store in Anaheim, something happened that convinced me to go back to school, get a degree and get my life together. While working in convenience stores to pay the rent between acting gigs, I was held at gun point by two men. I was fired because I gave the bad guys too much money." He went back to school and earned a bachelor's degree in radio/tv from Long Beach State in 1981. Rick started his radio career doing mornings at KWVE-San Clemente. A year later he went up the coast to KEZY, and two weeks after starting there was a format change and he was fired. "I thought maybe my radio career was over before it began, but Sam Bellamy hired me at KMET." He did evenings at "the Mighty Met" until he was fired on "Black Friday" in 1986. While at KMET, Rick was voted one of "America's Favorite Djs" in the February 1986 issue of *Playgirl*

magazine. "I thought my time at KMET was going to be the pinnacle of my radio career but it was just the tip of the iceberg. Even though I kept getting my heart broken over and over again by KMET management, I look fondly on my days with Jim Ladd and Paraquat Kelley and the rest." In 1988 he hosted a tv dance party on KDOC called *Zzapp*. He was also a guest host on *PM Magazine* as well as appearing in numerous tv commercials, movies and ABC's *Makin' It*. He has hosted the in-flight entertainment programs for United Airlines along with nationally syndicated radio shows for Westwood One and the NBC Radio Network. He returned to KEZY for three years until new management fired him. Rick left the Southland when Jacor hired him to do mornings at KRFX-Denver. The Lewis and Floorwax Show has been the #1 morning show in Denver since 1991, according to Rick. One of his female co-workers described Rick: "Not only is he a doll, very sexy, but one of the nicest people in the business." For many years Rick and his partner, Michael Floorwax, have played to sold-out audiences on the Budweiser Comedy Tour. Their show is considered by many people to be one of the top morning shows in the country. They are working on several movie projects. "When I was in L.A., movie and tv producers would blow me off on a regular basis. Now they're coming to Denver to see if we can get something going. I never dreamed that could happen." His experience in Southland radio? "I worked for some of the best pd's in the country in L.A., like Jeff Wyatt at 'Power 106,' and some of the worst...and, you know who you are."

LEWIS, Robert Q.: **KHJ**, 1961-62; **KFI**, 1972-75; **KRLA**, 1975. Robert Q. was a comedian actor who was a regular panelist on such popular quiz shows as *What's My Line*, *To Tell the Truth* and *Call My Bluff* in the 1950s and '60s. He was born April 25, 1920, in New York City. Bob Lewis got his entertainment start at the age of 7 as a boy soprano who appeared on the "Horn and Hardart Children's Hour" in New York. While in college, he worked for WTRY- Troy for $100 a month. The job came because his uncle owned the building that housed the station. To keep from being bored, he cleverly dropped in sound effects of horses, cows, cars crashing, etc. When he was hired at WNEW-New York, he was suddenly on a station with legends William B. Williams and Martin Block. It was during this time that he discovered many Bob Lewises on the air, so he added the Q to set himself apart from the others. Ted Ashley gave Robert Q. his first major break at the NBC network with a five-day-a-week program, *Listen to Lewis*. He also replaced Arthur Godfrey during vacations and sick time. He arrived in Southern California on KHJ in 1961 and, during his morning drive tenure, he teased his primary competition Dick Whittinghill on KMPC. He would frequently announce that the booby prize in one of his contests would be lunch with Dick Whittinghill. Lewis admitted that his first go-round in Los Angeles was "a big, beautiful bomb." He left KHJ in 1962 to do network tv and host NBC's *Play Your Hunch*. In the mid-1970s, he was the entertainment editor for KRLA. He formed Ouagga Productions, which was devoted to packaging tv shows. Robert Q. died December 11, 1991, of emphysema in a hospital in Los Angeles. He was 71.

LEWIS, Ron: **KKDJ**, 1973-74. Ron teamed briefly with Jay Stevens doing automated programming services. He and Jay were working together on some syndication projects at the time of his death in March 1994.

LEWIS, Tom: **KBIG**, 1965, pd

LEYKIS, Tom: **KFI**, 1988-92; **KMPC**, 1994-96. Born in 1957, Tom grew up in the Bronx and on Long Island and started his talk radio career in 1970 when he was 14. His father Harry worked his whole life at the *New York Post*, where he was also the Newspaper Guild's shop steward. He had become a touchstone for Tom. Harry was laid off when Rupert Murdoch bought the paper and, facing a mortgage and mounting debts from a struggle with cancer, he eventually got a mere $6,700 for his 43 years of service. Tom bounced around from cable tv columnist to stand-up comic and even sold real estate over the telephone. He joined afternoons at KFI the first time for a reported salary of $400,000. He had been working at KFYI-Phoenix and in Miami. A story in the *LA Times* profiled Tom's show as "verbal combat" and described Tom: "Leykis resembles a grown-up Spanky from *Our Gang* - dough faced, pot-bellied and surprisingly unthreatening." Tom shrewdly called his show the only one "not hosted by a right-wing wacko or a convicted felon." It was in 1981 in Albany that he came up with his "blowing up" gimmick to get people who were abusive off the air. He gained national attention when he burned Cat Stevens' records to protest the singer-songwriter's professed support of the Ayatollah Ruhollah Khomeini's order to kill Salman Rushdie, author of *The Satanic Verses*. In between his two stints in Los Angeles, Tom worked at WRKO-Boston. While in Boston he was returning home from an office Christmas party and he and his wife got into a drunken screaming match that turned into a shoving match. Susan Leykis called the police and Tom was arrested and held overnight. The D.A. dropped the case when she declined a protective order and filed an affidavit correcting the charges in the police complaint. A 1995 profile in *The Nation* described him: "One who likes to wear black clothing and listen to loud music. Tom Leykis is pro-labor, pro-choice, 'pro-homo' [his producer is openly gay], pro-drug legalization, anti-death penalty. He voted for Bill Clinton but now has no hope for him, thought the Gulf War was an oil war." In 1994 Tom joined all-Talk KMPC and in 1995 his program became syndicated and has grown to over 130 stations. "People who really know me - not people who sat at a desk down the hall from me - know that I get out whatever rage I have on the air and that in real life I'm really kind of a mellow, laid-back person," Tom said in the *Times* interview. "Sarcastic and cynical, but not angry." His show was taken off KMPC in the spring of 1996 while continuing in syndication.

LIBERMAN, Jaime: **KTNQ/KLVE**. Jaime and his brother Julio bought KTNQ and changed format to Spanish in the summer of 1979. They successfully accomplished a similar scenario with the purchase of KLVE.

LIEBERMAN, Carole: **KYPA**, 1996-97. Carole, a Beverly Hills-based psychiatrist, hosts "Media on Your Mind" on KYPA. She has written a book entitled, *Bad Boys: Why We Love Them, How to Live With Them and When to Leave Them*.

LIGHT, Joe: **KIQQ**, 1979 and 1984. Joe worked at KICN-Denver and afternoon drive at KRIZ-Phoenix before arriving in the Southland. He teamed with comedy writer Jeff Thomas for the "Joe and Jeff Show." After "K-100" Joe went to San Diego to be in radio sales and was last heard from in Omaha. Joe grew up in Indianapolis.

"I was given a certified check in the amount of $100,000 and flew to Memphis. I hung out with Elvis for four days at Graceland. Colonel Parker wasn't sure if Elvis would perform, but we had a good time."
  -Ted Quillin's quest to secure Elvis for KFWB event

LIGHTBODY, Andy: **KNX**, 1991. The all-News station's military and aerospace editor, Andy left KNX abruptly in the spring of 1991 following a profile in the *LA Times* that raised issues about his credentials. The *Times* reported that Lightbody had claimed to be a graduate of Loyola University, a former Air Force officer and an ex-fighter pilot. "His records show that Lightbody did not graduate from Loyola (he has two degrees from the now-defunct, never-accredited University of Beverly Hills), never was an Air Force officer, and his highest flight certification was student pilot." Andy responded to the *Times*: "The excellent relationship I have with the defense high-technology industries, as well as the military, was never based upon where I went to school or my military background." Andy also reported for KTTV/Channel 11 and the Financial News Network and was the American editor of the Geneva-based *Aerospace World* magazine.

LIGHTFOOT, James: **KLAC**, 1964-67, pd; **KFWB**. James followed gm Allan Henry to KLAC as John Kluge's personal choice. Al Lohman gave Jim credit for the Lohman/Barkley team, saying: "Jim sensed there was a chemistry that would work." He was looking for a match to Metromedia's New York team at the time, Klaven and Finch. Jim eventually moved to a similar post for Group W in 1968. Born in Bonham, Texas, he was raised by Speaker of the House, Sam Rayburn. It was not unusual to have have Harry Truman and Lyndon Johnson visit his home. One of his friends remember Jim saying, "I wished I paid more attention to who was in the house when I was growing up." Jim was overweight and had a heart condition. He died while still in his thirties.

LIGHTNING: **KROQ**, 1995-97. Originally an intern with "the Roq" he started working with Kevin & Bean after Kennedy left for MTV. In an *R&R* 1995 interview, Bean described Lightning's role: "He's a charity case, a catch-all for whatever job is too degrading for normal people to do."

LINDSAY, Steve: **KNOB**, 1981

LINDSTROM, John: **KSRF**, 1990-91. John worked the all-night shift at "K-Surf."

LIPPINCOTT, Ric: **KHTZ**, 1983-84, pd. Ric used the name Dave Denver until reverting to his birth name in 1983. He worked radio in the Midwest and was pd of WLS-Chicago and WISN-Milwaukee before joining "K-Hits" in June 1983. In the summer of 1984, he departed for KYUU-San Francisco. "When I started out, pd's were guys who wandered into the station in a tee-shirt at 11:30. Then they became businessmen in three-piece suits. The pd of the future will be someone with business sense who can see the big picture, but still be creative. He'll have to give the station something more than 300 researched records." In the 1990s, Ric worked promotion for Morgan Creek Records, Zoo Entertainment and Curb Records.

LISCOMB, Ken: **KDAY**, 1966

> "I wanted to be a jock since junior high school, figuring it would be a great way to meet girls, and I was right."   -Steve Clark

LISKA, A. James: **KFAC**. Jim hosted a long-running weekend jazz program on KFAC.

LITTLE, Chris: **KEZY**, 1989-91; **KFI**, 1991-97. Chris was teamed in morning drive with Rick Lewis. Chris does news at KFI.

LITTLE, Milt: **KJLH**, 1994-97

LLEWELYN, Doug: **KNNS**, 1996. Best known for his role on tv's *The People's Court*, Doug joined all-News KNNS as weekend anchor in February 1996. Doug left "K-News" when the station went to an "all-Beatles" format in late 1996. Doug was a reporter for CBS News.

LOCKWOOD, Scott: **KIKF**; **KUTE**, 1982; **KOST**, 1995

LOCO, Pito: **KWKW**, 1981-97. Pito is part of "Pina in the Morning" wake-up show on Spanish KWKW.

LODGE, John: **KHJ**, 1976. When he left Southern California, he headed for WDAI-Chicago. John left mornings at WXTU-Philadelphia in the summer of 1995.

LOGAN, Lee: **KLAC**, 1987, pd. Early in his career, Lee was pd of WMYQ-Miami. He programmed WUSN-Chicago for five years before joining KLAC. Lee left the Southland for San Francisco to program KSAN and KNEW and left in late 1994. In early 1995, Lee joined KFRG/KOOJ-Riverside as om. In the fall of 1996 Lee joined South Central Communications as group head of programming.

LOGAN-THOMAS, Monica: **KTWV**; **KACD**, 1994-95, pd. Prior to joining "the Wave," Monica worked at KBLX-San Francisco, WNUA-Chicago and KOAI ("the Oasis")-Dallas. After a format change at KACD in early 1995, she returned to Dallas as an NAC consultant under the Smooth Sounds banner and joined ABC Radio Networks. In early 1996 she was named pd for its Urban AC format, "the Touch."

LOGIC, John: **KROQ**, 1983-85; **KMPC/FM/KEDG**, 1988-89. John worked all-nights at "the Edge."

LOHMAN, Al: **KLAC**, 1963-67; **KFWB**, 1967-68; **KFI**, 1968-86; **KRLA**, 1986; **KWNK**, 1987; **KFI**, 1987-89. Born in Iowa in 1933, Al started radio work in Omaha, making his way through Wichita, Denver, Dallas and WABC-New York before joining KLAC. The team of Lohman and Roger Barkley got together in 1963 when Metromedia took over KLAC. Metromedia wanted to replicate their East Coast two-man team success. Al and Roger thought they should team. Roger thought they could buy some time while looking for a job. The teaming clicked big-time for a quarter of a century. Al started writing a daily "Gunsmoke" spoof and invited pd Roger Barkley to help fill out the cast of characters. Al claims his greatest pleasure in the partnership was derived from "watching Rog's personality disintegrate from pd to jock." Many make reference to Lohman and Barkley's humor as being reminiscent of the old "Bob and Ray Show." They stayed at KLAC until 1967, at which time they joined KFWB, and were on the air until the station went all-News in March of 1968. Lohman and Barkley have been at the end of many Southern California experiences. They were the last-ever act booked into the Coconut Grove, and they appeared on one of Ed Sullivan's last programs before he was canceled. In the fall of 1968, the team joined KFI while the station was experimenting with a blend of Country and Easy Listening. They did a tv variety show on KNBC/Channel 4 from 1968 to 1970 and the daytime quiz show *Namedroppers* over the NBC/TV network in 1969. One of their longest running bits was a daily soap called "Light of My Life." They stayed together until 1986 when Al teamed briefly with Emperor Bob Hudson on KRLA. Before rejoining KFI, Al worked afternoon drive at KWNK-Simi Valley. At KFI the second time, he attempted to recreate earlier magic, this time teamed with long-time friend Gary Owens on "L.A.'s Morning Show" in the same studios he shared with Roger. The show lasted for almost two years. Al had a stable of 46 whimsical characters with names like farm reporter Maynard Farmer, Ted J. Bologna and W. Eva Schneider Bologna. His characters also included food authority Leonard Leonard, "staff freak" Eglit ("four-eyes") Fullwood, the ever popular Roscoe Boscoe, "Choreographer and Good-Tooth Fairy," Dominick Longo and Cecil Hudspith. In 1978 *Billboard* described the duo: "Al was the more disciplined of the two, who led the slide into the silliness. None of their silliness was ever scripted in advance, never written down or discussed before the spontaneous instant of their invention on the air." Team player Roger Barkley recalled, "Every time we had a new boss, he'd ask us, `Why don't you guys plan some more?' But we've always worked this way. We have absolutely no file, we don't keep track and we don't prepare anything in advance. It's probably dumb that we've done it that way, but it just works better for us." And work it did through numerous format and management changes. Al works for KCMJ-Palm Springs and lives in nearby Rancho Mirage.

LOHR, Alan K.: **KROQ**, 1979-81. Alan hosted the "International Experience" on Sunday evenings and was the first to interview Oingo Boingo, Phil Collins and others.

LOMAX, Louie: **KLAC**, 1966-68; **KDAY**. Louie was one of the first black broadcasters to work an all-Talk format. Known as one of the major interpreters of the integration movement, he did not hesitate to criticize both sides. "You must have the guts to stand up and tell a black student 'no' when he is wrong." But he was tough on those who delayed integration efforts. Louie was a newspaperman from 1941 to 1958 and wrote a number of books including *The Reluctant African*, his first book and *The Negro Revolt*, an analysis and history of the drive for integration, in 1962. Other books were *When the Word Is Given*, a report on Malcolm X and *To Kill a Black Man*. He was born in Valdosta, Georgia, on August 16, 1922, and graduated from Paine College in 1942. He received a master's degree at the American University in Washington. He obtained a master's in philosophy from Yale in 1947.

In the 1960s he hosted a local tv talk show. Louie was killed July 31, 1970, when he lost control of his car while traveling near Santa Rosa, New Mexico. His car skidded across the highway, overturned three times and stopped on the right shoulder of the highway. He was thrown from the vehicle. At the time of his death he was working on a three-volume history of the Negro and was a professor of humanities at Hofstra University in Hempstead, New York. He was 47.

LONDON, Bob: **KFOX**, 1972-78; **KFWB**. Bob worked the all-night shift at KFOX, the Country station, for much of his stay in the Southland.

LONDON, Dave: **KROQ**, 1974-75

LONDON, John: **KKBT**, 1991-97. John is the anchor host of the morning "House Party" on "the Beat." John started his career while in college listening to what he thought was the world's worst disc jockey in Nacogdoches, Texas. He went to that station, applied for the announcers job, and got it. "It's hard to believe, one moment I'm in the dorm room doing calculus problems and the next I'm doing all night radio and picking up bus station waitresses. You can't just be funny. You have to be able to realize when there's a serious need in the community and use the power of what we do to help."

LONDON, John & **ENGELMAN**, Ron: **KRTH**, 1979-81; **KWST**, 1981-83; **KMGG**, 1983. Arriving for morning drive from KULF-Houston, London and Engelman were hired in October 1979, after three years as a team in Denver, Portland, Dallas and Houston. "K-Earth" was a semi-automated "Oldies/Contemporary" station when they were brought in as a live comedy team. They brought with them such sketches as "The New Leave it to Beaver" and "Bad News Junior Executives." The team came together in 1976 when London was the morning man at a station in Denver, and he started improvising comedy routines with Engelman, who was then an atypically madcap newsman. James Brown in the *LA Times* called them the "wildest radio comedy [duo] to come down the road since Lohman and Barkley. Their irreverent, *National Lampoon*-style humor, fantasy phone calls and outrageous sketches established them as the clown princes of L.A. Radio." John recalled, shortly after starting at KRTH: "Some lady called in and said we were jerks and asinine. We usually just got that from program directors." In June 1981 the team headed for KWST, which became KMGG. CBS/TV signed them in 1982 to write a pilot based on one of their popular radio bits, "Dan Woman, Private Eye." They also appeared in a Steve Martin special. During their stay at "Magic 106," the SPCA got riled up when one of the team's bits talked about taking a drill to a little dog. In mid-1983 they got caught in a format change and took out an ad in the local trade publications: "London and Engelman. Formerly with KRTH and `Magic 106' Los Angeles looking to relocate." The ad resulted in a move to KMEL-San Francisco. John is now with KKBT. Ron lives in Albuquerque.

LONGDEN, Jerry: **KEZY**, 1964 and 1966; **KNAC**, 1969-72; **KLOS**, 1972-77; **KWST**, 1977-80; **KEZY**, 1978-79;

KROQ, 1980; **KGIL/FM**, 1986-88. A Southern California native, Jerry graduated from Norwalk High School and went to work at Bethlehem Steel. While still a teen, Jerry recalled his schedule: "It was crazy. I ran an indoor bay crane during the day and interned at KEZY all night long." Before he was out of his teens, Jerry went to the Bill Ogden Broadcasting School to secure a 1st Class FCC License. After graduation he became a combo operator in Clovis, New Mexico, and before long the 20-year-old was playing rock 'n' roll as the only English language program on Spanish KPER-Gilroy. The station took advantage of his 1st Phone, and Jerry had to "dodge bulls" to get to the transmitter site for meter readings. A series of California stations in Riverside, Santa Ana, Ontario and Garden Grove followed. Jerry and Jim Ladd created The National Association of Progressive Radio Announcers (NAPRA). They produced a series of albums featuring anti-drug messages from all the top rock artists of the day. In the early 1970s, Jerry won *Billboard*'s Progressive Rock DJ of the Year; *Billboard* also named KLOS station of the year while Jerry was there. He was the voiceover announcer on Don Kirschner's *Rock Concert*. After KROQ, Jerry got "fed up with the noise," as he described his life in Southern California, he sold his Hollywood home and bought a lot on a lake near Fresno. He built his dream house and left Southern California, he thought, for good. Following a series of radio jobs in Fresno and Modesto, Jerry returned to Los Angeles in 1986 to produce several national public service projects while working at KGIL. He currently lives in Santa Rosa, does freelance voice work and teaches voiceover and narration for Voice Media in San Francisco. He recently released Speaking Mechanics, a speaking improvement course distributed via his company Dialogue Publishing. Would he return to Los Angeles radio? "If I could do my own show, you bet, but I'd want a bulletproof house."

LONGMIRE, Ted: **KPPC**, 1971. Ted was one of the first blacks working L.A.'s "underground" radio format. His father was a minister.

LOPEZ, Adrian: **XEGM**; **KROQ**; **XPRS**; **KTNQ/KLVE**, 1980-96, pd; **KMQA/KRTO**, 1996, pd. Born in Argentina, Adrian launched Radio Ritmo (which means rhythm in Spanish) in the summer of 1996. He had successfully worked production, PR as well as programming for many Spanish outlets. Adrian was made pd of KLVE in 1988. He died in 1996 of cancer at the age of 51.

LOPEZ, Dan: **KNX/FM**, 1983; **KKHR**, 1984-86. Dan arrived in the Southland from WKZL-Winston-Salem. In 1986 he went to Salt Lake City and Dallas.

LOPEZ, Manuel: **KUSC**, 1974. Manuel was known as "El Sabroso Oso."

LOPEZ, Mario: **KSKQ**, 1992, pd

LORIN, Bill: **KAPP**; **KNX**, 1987-97. Bill primarily reports Orange County news for KNX.

LOTZ, Patty: **KPWR**, 1986-87; **KKBT**, 1989-90; **KIBB**, 1996-97. As "Powermouth Patty," she worked morning drive with Jay Thomas at "Power 106." She became a VH-1 veejay for awhile. When KKBT was launched with comedian Paul Rodriguez and Tim Kelly in morning drive, Patty was part of the team. She joined KIBB in late 1996 as nd and morning co-host for the "Breakfast Jam."

LOUIS, Dave: **KIIS**, 1975; **KTYM**, 1976; **KEZY**, 1976-81. Born in Gary, Indiana, Dave grew up in Lansing, Illinois listening to WLS. In 1968 at the age of 16, he moved to the Southland and went to Rio Hondo JC as an art major and worked on the campus radio station. After attending the KIIS workshop in 1976, his first radio job was at KKOK-Lompoc. Before the year was out, he was back working at KTYM and later at KPSI-Palm Springs. Since 1981 Dave has been the owner of Audio Images Media recording studio in Irvine. He is a character voice on many projects. Miss radio? "Not at all. My commercials are on the air at dozens of L.A. radio and tv stations."

LOVE, Jeri: **KNX**, 1982-83; **KFWB**, 1984-86, nd. Jeri was born in Detroit. She started her news career in 1975 at WAUP-Akron. Jeri moved to the Southland in 1977 and received a degree in journalism from Cal State Los Angeles. Before joining KNX she worked for the Wave newspapers, *City News* and was a producer of two shows at KCET/TV. In 1986 Jeri was promoted to assistant news director at WINS-New York; nd in 1987. She left WINS in 1991 to work on her master's of fine art at New York University. Jeri returned to the Southland in 1994 to head the public relations department at the Southern California Gas Company. She is the director of corporate communications for The Gas Company's parent company Pacific Enterprises.

LOVE, Lorna: SEE Lorna Dee

LOVE, Mark: **KKBT**, 1994. Mark worked all-night at "the Beat."

LOVE, Mother: **KFI**, 1990; **KLSX**, 1995-96; **KACE**, 1996-97. Mother Love worked early evenings at the launch of the non-traditional Talk format on KLSX called "Real Radio." Born Jo Anne Hart, her character came to life at a bridal fair in Cleveland. She was the relationship expert on ABC's *The Home Show*. At KFI she was known as the "Queen of Advice." Mother Love has appeared in *Fresh Prince of Bel Air*, *Murphy Brown* and *Married...With Children*. On her return to L.A. radio at KLSX, Mother Love told the *LA Times*: "I'm so pumped and excited. I feel like a prodigal daughter returning to her roots, her radio babies [the audience]. I'm trying to stay calm so I won't just be babbling...We are going to have so much fun. It's going to be a blast." She has written a book, *Listen Up, Girlfriends! Lessons on Life From the Queen of Advice*. She left KLSX in early 1996 and by summer she was co-hosting morning drive on KACE with Rico Reed. A profile in *Buzz* magazine describes the size 18 personality as committed to plus-size women. In early 1997 she hosted the first Regal Empress Showcase and Pageant. "Just because I am a large person does not mean I have no fashion sense. I figured I'd give these little skinny one-bone chicks a run for their money." She left KACE in the summer of 1997.

LOVE, Walt "Baby": **KHJ**, 1971-72; **KKTT**, 1978-80; **KFI**, 1980. Walt's roots are firmly planted in Creighton, Pennsylvania, where he was raised by his great-grandparents. His great-grandmother told Walt that he would always have to do things 10 times better than the other fellow. Walt played football at Gannon University in Erie, while majoring in sociology. He left college to join the Army and served two tours of duty seeing combat with the 82nd Airborne division in Thailand, near the Laos/Burma border. After six years and 11 months and just before making a decision to join officers candidate school, he decided to pursue a radio career. He started on KILT-Houston. "I didn't know racism. My little town of Creighton was made up of 400 families who were Polish, Hungarian, Italians and probably five who were black. Many came from interracial families, including my great-grandmother, so I thought I could go anywhere to get a job." Paul Drew hired Walt for CKLW-Detroit. "I was the first black hired in the RKO chain which was comprised of 14 stations. I always took pride in my work. I wanted to prove a point that the consumer didn't care what color you were. All they were interested in was if I entertained them." His picture did not appear on the 'CK survey for 90 days. Once it was, he broke down the racial barriers, blazing the way for other blacks to work for stations other than Urban. Walt began working the RKO circuit moving to WOR/FM-New York. After KHJ, Walt returned to New York to work at WXLO and WNBC in the mid-1970s and KSD-St. Louis in 1976. For 15 years he has hosted Westwood One's "The Countdown with Walt Love," which won a number of *Billboard* magazine network syndicator category awards as best black radio program. The show is carried on 175 stations in 30 countries. In 1980 he became editor of the Urban Contemporary division of *R&R* where he continues. He was honored at the second annual *R&R* Salute to Excellence Awards for his contributions to radio. In recent years he has been instrumental in reaching young people in detention centers and prisons with a message of, as Walt says, "being kind to other people. It's all about what is in your heart." Since the summer of 1995, Walt has been hosting a second syndicated series called "Gospel Traxx" for Superadio Networks.

LOWE, Buddy: **XERB**, 1966-68. Buddy now works for Jazz KRML-Carmel.

LOWE, Keith: **KLVE**, 1974-75; **KLOS**, 1977; **KLSX**, 1988-94. Keith worked morning drive at KLVE and part-time at KLSX, the "classic rock" station.

LOWE, Paul: **KFWB**, 1991-97. Paul is a reporter/anchor at all-News KFWB.

LOZANO, Frank: **KPWR**, 1989-94 and 1996-97. "While watching the Hollywood Christmas Parade when the 'Power 106' entry went by, as sappy as it may sound, I actually got choked up. I made a promise to myself that night that next year I would be on that float." Frank, who grew up  in the San Gabriel Valley, worked in Fresno and San Antonio for nine years before it finally happened. "Jeff Wyatt was the one who hired me initially to work weekend overnights. I was successful by saying 'yes' to every shift offered." In the fall of 1993, Frank moved to morning drive on "Power 106" after Jay Thomas left the station. In early 1994 he moved to afternoons. In the summer of 1994, Frank became the first and only jock to quit. He moved to KYLD ("Wild 107")-San Francisco. In January of 1996, he returned to Los Angeles to pursue an acting career and opened his own commercial production company "Graphically Speaking." Frank was also asked to re-join the "Power 106" staff for weekends.

LUCK, Evan: **KKBT**, 1993-95. Evan left "the Beat" in early 1995. An ad in R&R read: "Living the life in Costa Rica. Beautiful babes, killer waves, muchas cervezas. Available via tape, digital, satellite?

LUCRAFT, Howard: **KLON**, 1989

LUDLUM, Andy: **KABC/KMPC/KTZN**, 1996-97, pd. Andy joined the talk combo on April 1, 1996. He had been regional director of Metro Networks. A graduate of San Jose State with a bachelor's in journalism, he started his career as a traffic reporter at KXRX-San Jose. In 1979 Andy went to KIRO-Seattle and six years later was pd of KMBR/KMBZ-Kansas City. From 1987 to 1994 he was a vp of news and programming at KIRO AM&FM and TV and KING-Seattle. Born in Trenton, he grew up in New Jersey and Virginia. He moved to Los Angeles in 1965 and went to junior and senior high schools in Palos Verdes. Why radio rather than journalism? "Radio is less anal and better suited to my short attention span."

LUNA, Humberto: **XEGM**; **KTNQ**, 1979-97. Humberto  has been described as "the Spanish Rick Dees." Born in Zacatecas, he graduated from Mexico's National School of Broadcasting. He moved to L.A. in 1970 to study English. At XEGM he recorded his show in L.A. and the tapes were trucked to Tijuana. On his KTNQ radio show he has a stable of "Lunatico" characters and was the first zoo-type morning show ("Humberto en la Manana") in Spanish. Humberto was the first Spanish radio announcer given a Star on the Hollywood Walk of Fame. He hosts a noon national daily variety show, "La Hora Lunatica," on Telemundo.

LUNDY, Mike: **KFI**, 1968; **KGBS**, 1968; **KDAY**, 1971-74, pd; **KFWB**, 1977-78; **KGIL**, 1979-80 pd; **KFI/KOST**, 1982-83; **KGIL/KMGX**, 1983-92, pd. Mike was born in Minneapolis and raised in Alhambra. He graduated from Pasadena Junior College and worked briefly at KDWC-West Covina. "My first real radio job was in Merced at KYOS." In 1964 the owners of KYOS bought KRIZ-Phoenix and Mike went with them. For two years in the mid-1960s he was at KAFY-Bakersfield. In 1966 Mike went to UCLA and graduated two years later with a political-science degree. He hired Bob Wilson at

KAFY which led to other opportunities of working together. Mike worked morning drive for a time at KDAY as well as programming chores. From 1974 to 1977 Mike was the general manager of Ted Randal Enterprises, one of the earliest consulting companies. Since 1992 he has operated Lundy Media Group. The company produces radio programs for Japan and monthly English language conversation CD's for use by students in Japan.

LUNDY, Steve: **KROQ**, 1972-73; **KRTH**. Steve was born in Tyler, Texas, and worked at WLS-Chicago, KILT-Houston and KFRC-San Francisco before joining KROQ. He walked with a wooden leg from an accident and his sign-off was: "Don't forget to smell the flowers - cause we're only here for a short visit."

LUPO, Tony: **KBRT**, 1980, gm. Tony ran the "born-again Cheeradio" with on-air personalities Clark Race, Chuck Southcott, Johnny Magnus and newsman Brian Bastien.

LURIE, Rod: **KMPC/KTZN**, 1995-97. The resident film critic hosts a two-hour Saturday movie show on "the Zone." In his mind, there are only two opinions that matter: his own...and his listeners. Rod's influence is so far reaching that Martin Landau and Mel Gibson acknowledged Rod during each of their respective Academy Award acceptance speeches. Among other publications, he writes about movies in *Buzz* magazine and *Los Angeles Magazine*.

LYMAN, Jay: **KGRB**, 1983; **KORG**, 1993. Born in 1945, Jay started as a dj in 1964. He got interested in big bands while volunteering at KCRW. Jay has a collection of 9,000 LPs, covering 1920-40s music.

LYNCH, Sean: **KIIS**, 1996-97. Sean, aka Dan Cuervo, joined KIIS in the summer of 1996 to host the Saturday night retro show. He was EMI director of national promotion.

LYNES, Bobb: **KCSN**, 1975-78; **KCRW**, 1982-92; **KPCC**, 1995-96. Born in Oklahoma in 1935, Bobb took a hobby of collecting old-time radio shows and built a career. For more than two decades he has been involved with old radio drama and served as president of SPERDVAC for five years. Bobb has been a consultant to *Entertainment Tonight* and *Jeopardy*.

LYON, Mary: **KFWB**, 1975; **KNAC**, 1975-76; **KLOS**, 1976-77; **KHJ**, 1977-79; **KRTH**, 1982-87, nd; **KLSX**, 1987. Mary grew up in West Los Angeles and attended Marymount High School and graduated from UC Irvine in 1975. She soon got a job as an editor's assistant at all-News KFWB, and an impressive career in Southern California news unfolded. The mood at the time - combined perhaps with pressure from the FCC - was to hire women. Mary considers herself "lucky" that the time was right. "I was available, the right age, the right sex and I happened to fit." Mary was the first female news director at KNAC and was the first woman to conduct a talk show on KLOS. Mary's enthusiasm for the news business is evident within minutes of talking with her. "I was always the new kid at these stations. All these veterans were most gracious, more than they had to be, and I was so appreciative." At KHJ, she was the first woman news director and she survived three format changes. In 1979, Mary was one of the first to be hired for the NBC Source Network and spent three years with them. She was teamed with Phil Hendrie to do morning drive on KLSX. From 1987 to 1995, she was the West Coast entertainment reporter for Associated Press Broadcast Services in Los Angeles and has a young daughter and son. "I've really had a career climb and had better luck than most. I've worked steadily for almost 20 years in L.A. radio." Mary has retired from radio and is designing exquisite bead jewelry and has won several awards for her creations.

LYONS, Dick: **KBLA**, 1962; **KUTE**, 1965; **KGBS**, 1969-72; **KLOS**, 1972; **KROQ**, 1972; **XPRS**, 1973; **KOCM**, 1987-89; **KACD**, 1994-95, gm; **KZLA/KLAC**, 1995-96; **KBIG**, 1996. Born Richard Poppers in Burbank, if Dick was not a jock on the radio, he would be selling radio. His father built an amateur radio station in their backyard guest house with a 55-foot tower and talked to people all over the world. Dick's first radio experience was buying a half-hour of KBLA time for $25 on Sunday nights and then solicit sponsors along Ventura Boulevard. As a result of KFWB airing talk on Sunday nights, his program became very popular with young people and before long he purchased multiple hours and resold it. "At Los Angeles City College I was fortunate enough to get a good education from an articulate radio guy from Mutual, Don McCall." During Dick's schooling he helped Bob Eubanks with publicity during his launch of three Cinnamon Cinder teen night clubs. He went to Ogden's Broadcast school to get a 1st Class FCC License. The lady who administered the test at the FCC was Mrs. Lyons and that's how he picked his radio name. After securing his license, his first job was at KAFY-Bakersfield and then he went to "Tiger Radio," KFXM-San Bernardino. "What a great radio station with Al Anthony running a radio battle with KMEN." Along the way he befriended Charlie O'Donnell who got him into KGBS. The station was one of the first to simulcast AM and FM. "I worked on the AM from 4 to 6 p.m. which we were simulcasting with the FM. At sundown, because the AM was a daytimer, we encouraged everyone to switch to FM and I came back to work nine to midnight. In between I hung out at Nickodell's with all the 'Boss Jocks.'" He got into sales at KVFM (later KGIL), selling produced "Funny Facts" to local retailers. His success took him to retail sales manager posts with KSRF, KRTH (he won RKO's Sales Person of the Year award), KSCI, KOCM and KACD, where he was gm. He met his wife of 13 years during a brief stint at Channel 18. "I just didn't like selling tv, I'm a radio guy, but the good thing was that I met my wife there." They have two children, ages 12 and 10. In spring of 1995 Dick joined KZLA/KLAC as new business development manager and a year later became director of new business at KBIG.

M

MACHADO, Kevin: **KCBS**, 1993-96. Kevin grew up in Eureka and graduated from Santa Barbara High School. He played in the same backfield at Santa Barbara as Randall Cunningham. "I was a slow footed fullback, but a tough blocker." While working on an oil rig in Texas, Kevin saw a broadcasting ad in the *Houston Post* and thus was born his radio career.  After graduation he paid his dues beginning in 1984 at KBLF-Red Bluff, KOSO-Modesto, KYOS-Merced and KREO-Santa Rosa. "I was in my Santa Rosa apartment reading a book written by Rick Sklar, the legendary pd of WABC-New York, and the phone rings. It's Rick offering me an opportunity at Braiker Satellite Radio Service in Seattle." Braiker didn't make it. "My opinion of Rick Sklar didn't change one bit. In fact, if anything my respect grew for the man." After the Seattle experience, Kevin joined United Broadcasting in Washington, DC and Cleveland and then went on to KZXY ("Y-102")-Victorville and KJFX-Fresno. His last move before arriving in the Southland was KGBY ("Y-92")-Sacramento. Kevin got a call from KCBS pd Tommy Edwards and thought it was a cruel joke. "It turned out to be legit and believe it or not I took the job not knowing what the format would be." Kevin worked the evening shift on "Arrow 93." He has returned to KZXY.

MACHADO, Mario: **KRLA**, 1981-83 and 1985-87; **KABC**, 1994-96.  The Emmy-winning Portugese-Chinese broadcaster hosted the very popular "KRLA Connection." Mario was seen in *Rocky III*, *St. Elmo's Fire*, and all three *Robo Cop* films. One of his passions in life is soccer. He has combined his experience as a former league soccer player in Asia with his broadcasting skills to become an internationally known soccer commentator. Mario's now the host of several tv talk shows and infomercials. He was hosting a minority-themed show on Saturday nights at KABC.

MAC, Don: **KDAY**, 1974-75; **KKTT**, 1977-78, pd. Don launched KKTT's ("The Katt") new format changing the call letters from KGFJ. "The difference is that our emphasis is on music. Almost anyone can sit behind a microphone. We found people 18-35 don't want to boogie all the time. They don't want to be assaulted by radio. We take the best of AM radio and FM and mix and blend them. In that way we can soothe our audience." Don was born in Omaha and worked at KOIL in his hometown before getting to the Southland. When he left L.A. Don became a teacher at a black college in the South. He is now a minister in Oklahoma City.

MACK, David: **KNAC**, 1981

MACK, Gary: **KRLA**, 1964-65; **KHJ**, 1965-67; **KLAC**, 1970. Gary came to KRLA in 1964 from KYNO-Fresno, where he was pd under Bill Drake. When "Boss Radio" was launched in April 1965, Drake hired Gary away from KRLA and made him the first of the original "Boss Jocks" on "Boss Radio" in "Boss Angeles." Gary worked noon to 3 p.m. until 1967, then briefly worked overnights prior to joining Drake/Chenault as a national program director. He helped set up the Drake Format at KFRC-San Francisco, CKLW-Detroit, WRKO-Boston and WOR/FM-New York. Gary went on to program WIP-Philadelphia, was om at WNEW-New York and was group pd for the FM division of Susquehanna Broadcasting in 1977. His last assignment was director of network operations at WSB-Atlanta, where he built the largest radio network in Major League Baseball for the Braves (166 stations). Born Gary McDowell in Cedar Falls, he grew up in Chicago and attended the Illinois Institute of Technology. Gary retired July 1, 1997 and lives in Atlanta.

MACK, Greg: **KDAY**, 1986-90; **KJLH**, 1990-92. Greg worked morning drive while in Los Angeles radio and currently co-owns a station in Oakland. Prior to arriving in the Southland he worked at KEYS-Corpus Christi.

MACK, Terry: **KYMS**, 1990

MacKINNON, Don: **KABC**, 1960; **KLAC**, 1963-64; **KFWB**, 1964-65. Don worked at KEWB-San Francisco between L.A. jock assignments. He was killed in an automobile crash in Malibu in June of 1965. His brother Doug was contacted by the management of KFWB and was offered Don's noon-to-3 shift in order to perpetuate a popular broadcasting name; Doug declined. Chuck Blore remembered Don: "The best one of all and there's no question about it. He had an incredible brain, you never ever heard him say anything that didn't matter. He was very, very funny about things which mattered."

MacKRELL, Jim: **KFI**, 1974. In 1974 Jim hosted the game show *Celebrity Sweepstakes* on NBC/TV. He went on to be the announcer on several tv game shows including *Sweethearts*. Jim is now a tv news anchor in Dallas.

MacLEAN, Spider: **KWIZ**, 1957-89. Jean MacLean was a native of Santa Ana and spent his broadcasting career in Orange County. He did it all for 30+ years at KWIZ. In the late 1980s, Spider reported traffic updates for Air

Traffic Communications. He was attracted to broadcasting because of the friendly way of communicating to listeners, according to *OC Register*'s Gary Lycan. Spider died in 1990 at the age of 62. MacLean's wife recounted the funeral to Lycan: "At the end of the service, a helium balloon filled with Scriptures was released into the air. It would have been his wish for the Scriptures to fall into hands of people who need that kind of comfort."

MADDEN, Chuck: **KMPC/KABC/KTZN**, 1993-97. Chuck reports news on KABC's "Minyard and Tilden" morning drive show. Born in Rochester, he grew up in Dallas. He graduated with a chemistry degree from a college in Alabama. Before coming to the Southland Chuck worked in Louisiana, Joplin, Dallas, Huron, South Dakota, Monterey and San Jose. He hosts a Sunday sports show on KABC from Trophys in Newport Beach. He is a bachelor living in Long Beach.

MADDOX, Jim: **KRLA**, 1971; **XPRS**, 1972; **KIQQ**, 1973-74; **KDAY**, 1974-77, pd; **KJLH**, 1984-85, gm. Born in 1948, Jim was a business administration major at Fordham University. As James Maddox, he did the news on KRLA. After an initial stint doing overnights at KIQQ, Jim did mornings with Mike Butts. Jim was the on-air pd with the new Urban format at KDAY that debuted in January 1974. "We went the `clean routine' and as far as I know, no station that has tried it has lost listeners or ratings. We use no reverb or echo or talk over the music. Previously, black radio stations were a laughing matter. I tried to find personalities and announcers who liked the music and respected it." While still on the air at KDAY in 1975, Jim and Walt Love from WXLO-New York formed a programming and engineering consultancy called Professional Radio Programs, Ltd. In 1976, Jim was the recipient of the Program Director of the Year award from the John Gambling Radio Dynasty International Radio Programming Forum. Jim's philosophy regarding programming was outlined in a *Billboard* interview in 1976: "In response to tune-out, I think that people listen to a radio station for a given thing and when you give the audience something it doesn't expect, they turn the dial." In 1977, Jim left KDAY to become gm of KMJQ-Houston. He later became an executive with a number of stations, including WBMX-Chicago and KJLH. In 1987 he was the executive vp/coo of All-Pro Broadcasting. In 1994 Jim joined DMX as vp of programming. He is in charge of 90 individual channels that are served by home and business cable outlet satellite dishes.

MADDOX, Tony: **KHJ**, 1979-80. Growing up in Memphis, Tony worked at WHBQ. He arrived in Southern California from KZBS-San Diego. After leaving "Boss Radio," Tony was the morning man at KOKE-Austin. During his tour in San Diego, Tony programmed XHTZ, KOGO and jocked at KCBQ. In the spring of 1994, Tony joined KZST-Santa Rosa.

MADRID, Charles: **KIQQ/KLIT**, 1977-86. Charles was one of the "phone interns" who, with no radio experience, was given a weekend shift on KIQQ. He served in various capacities including production and promotion. Born January 27, 1958, in Los Angeles, Chuck grew up in the San Fernando Valley. He currently teaches at the Academy of Radio Broadcasting in Huntington Beach.

MADRIGAL, Edgar: **KWKW**, 1974-85, pd; **KALI**, 1986-88, pd; **XPRS**, 1988-97, pd. The longtime Spanish talent and programmer was born in Michoacan, Mexico and worked at Radio Centro in Mexico City before arriving in Southern California. He started in San Francisco radio in 1965 at KOFY and KBRG. In 1985 he joined Lotus Communications in Chicago and programmed WTAQ. Edgar is programming a regional "Ranchero Mexican" format at XPRS.

MAGIC, Bobby: **KUTE**, 1972-80, pd. Bobby started his radio career in 1964 at WLCY-Tampa/St. Petersburg. During the rest of the '60s he worked at WIXY-Cleveland, WEAM-Washington, DC, KTSA-San Antonio and KYA-San Francisco. When he left the Southland, for much of the '80s he was in Cleveland, Philadelphia and was the national pd for the Beasley Group. Since 1995 he has been with Chancellor Broadcasting overseeing KNEW/KSAN/KABL/KBBG-San Francisco.

MAGNUS, Johnny: **KGFJ**, 1957-63; **KMPC**, 1963-73; **KAGB**, 1973-75; **KRLA**, 1975-76; **KGIL**, 1976; **KBRT**, 1980; **KIQQ**, 1981; **KPRZ**, 1981-84; **KMPC**, 1984-94; **KJQY**, 1994-95. Born near Frankfurt, Germany, "the host who loves you most" fled Hitler's Germany at age 10 and came to America speaking no English. Radio was his English teacher as he sat for hours listening to series like "The Shadow" and "Green Hornet." While in New York,

he auditioned for a job as the Dodgers announcer and lost to Andre Baruch. The Dodgers broadcasts inspired his great interest in sports. At 16, he did fill-in at WWRL-New York. Johnny broadcast from Harlem with "Dr. Jive" (Tommy Smalls) doing a live remote on WOV from The Baby Grand nightclub. Dr. Jive presented r&b, while Johnny played Sarah Vaughan, Duke Ellington and Count Basie. At WABC he did broadcasts from New York's Birdland with "Symphony Sid." A year later, he was producing and emceeing United Cerebral Palsy Association telethons across the country before moving West. While it was still MOR, Johnny started at KGFJ, which evolved into "Negro" music and, years later, r&b. He went to MOR KMPC in 1963 as, he said, a "professor of sorts, delivering lessons in popular music." He coined the traveling forecast bit "weather with a beat" done to a background tune by Count Basie. Johnny explained its origin: "I'm watching television - *Peter Gunn*. I heard the rhythm-section opening, which plays while you're seeing the commission of the crime. And I thought, 'what can I do that will give me a voiceover effect with some traveling music?' I didn't want to do news or sports, but weather is kind of harmless. Relatives want to know if they're freezing in Buffalo. So I used a rhythm track with Harry James, and it clicked right away. Then Neil Hefti and Count Basie created this form called 'Cute,' which left some holes in it for me to give the weather. I now have different versions." In 1963, Quincy Jones wrote a personal composition called *Nasty Magnus*, which showed up on Count Basie's album *Little Ol Groove Maker-Basie*. Johnny's love for music, which you can hear come through his broadcasts, resulted in a find. The *LA Times* called Johnny the "Prince of Darkness," a title originally given to him by Gary Owens and that eventually proved to be his undoing; he wanted desperately to work days. Johnny commented at the time, "I got so tired of getting up from the dinner table and going to work. I wanted more out of life than that. I wanted to be able to go out with a girl at night. I never saw in all those years a prime time tv show." In *Billboard*'s 1966, 1967 and 1968 Radio Response Ratings Johnny was voted #1 Pop LPs disc jockey. He also scored in the Jazz category as 2nd most influential. In 1974, Johnny left KMPC for KAGB, an eclectic mix of jazz, r&b and MOR music. In 1975, he was a tv guest host on locally produced KTLA/Channel 5's *Calendar* show. In 1978, the self-proclaimed "baseball nut" went to KDWN-Las Vegas, a place Johnny described as "that habitation of fallen angels," for two years and returned to Bonneville's brief journey into contemporary Christian music at KBRT. Johnny was a West Coast announcer for ABC/TV. "I'd like you to picture me as a disc jockey spinning a record. I'd like you to picture the singer in a ballroom or in a nightclub. I present sounds by orchestras and singers. I don't give dates because I don't want to monkey with people's memories. I'd rather deliver an anecdote than a stat." Johnny is now with Music of Your Life Radio Network.

MAHLER, Kurt: **KROQ**, 1979-80. Kurt worked weekends on "the Roq."

MAIER, Bill: **KFI**, 1985-86; **KBIG**, 1987-91. Bill started on KFI from "Y-94"-Fresno and KPLZ-Seattle. In late 1987, he joined KBIG as part of a morning team with Sylvia Amerito. He left the radio business in 1991 and returned to school to pursue a graduate law degree.

MAJHOR, John: **KLAC**, 1989-90; **KZLA**, 1991; **KCBS**, 1991. "From the time I saw the early television shows starring Arthur Godfrey, Ed Sullivan, Jack Parr, Steve Allen, Ernie Kovacs and others, I knew I would end up in television," John said from his home in Toronto. "I'm grateful to have been able to achieve that goal through radio." Born in San Bernardino John started his radio career at KVRA-Vermillion, South Dakota. He went on to KKLS-Rapid City and WAPE-Jacksonville. In 1975 he joined CHUM-Toronto and stayed for more than a decade. John's television credits include hosting 400 episodes of *Toronto Rocks*, 135 episodes of *After Hours* for Fox TV and was the original anchor/producer at the launch of E! Entertainment. Since the early 1990s John has hosted a live daily show on CITY-TV called *Lunch Television*. "I'm happy to have dual citizenship, as my Sioux ancestors were citizens of North America, as I wish to be. And if my ancestors knew I was a MacHead, they'd be laughing mighty loud."

MALAY, H.K.: **KNNS**, 1995-96. Hugh joined the all-News station in 1995 and stayed until a format change to all-Beatles in late 1996.

MALKIN, Phillip: **KALI**, 1970-80, gm. When Philip left KALI he retired to San Juan Capistrano and eventually moved to Marina del Rey.

MALONE, Sunny: **KWIZ**, 1976. Sunny was part of the all-female dj staff on KWIZ.

MALORUS, Farley: **KFOX**, 1984-93. In the mid-1980s Farley hosted the "Astrology Hour" on KFOX. He left the station for the Cable Radio Network. From an *LA Times* profile on Farley: "He claimed to be a skeptic who worked pushing paper in his parents' business. During a severe personal crisis in 1976 that included a death in the family and a bleeding ulcer, he walked into a metaphysical bookstore and from just his birth date, an astrologer zeroed in exactly on all his troubles." Farley was born in 1950. During his stay in Southland radio he also briefly appeared on Friday mornings on KROQ in the 1980s dispensing astrological forecasts. At KFOX, even though the time was brokered, he has been one of the few to have a daily show continually for years. He expounded on world politics and the impending Armageddon along with metaphysical topics such as reincarnation, vegetarians and mankind's destiny.

> *"Waco hit and all of a sudden I and the station became a link with David Koresh and the Branch Davidians. Tapes of my show were being monitored and obtained by the FBI."*
> *-Ron Engelman*

MANN, Ed: **KUTE**, 1982-83; **KIIS**, 1983-87; **KEZY**, 1988-89; **KBIG**, 1993-95. Ed was born in New York City in 1957 and came to California and grew up in Saratoga. He graduated from UCLA in 1979 and has been with Premiere Radio Networks since its inception in 1987 as senior vp of affiliate marketing.

MANN, Mike: **KJLH**, 1984-89; **KACE,** 1989-92; **KKBT**, 1992-97. "Since 1984 I've been involved with three

Urban stations. Each has been the leader while I was there. As the production direct at 92.3/'the Beat,' I teach each host how they can better communicate when delivering commercials." Born in Brownsville, Tennessee, Mike traveled to Clinton, Iowa, when his father went to work for U.S. Steel. Mike graduated from the University of Northern Iowa with a degree in speech. "I fell into radio getting free credits at the campus radio station. I was originally going to be a teacher." His radio journey started at KWWL-Waterloo followed by KLWW-Cedar Rapids, WCLY-Tampa, WIBG-Philadelphia and three stations in Houston (KULF, KFMK and KMGQ) before joining KJLH. The musician did morning drive during the KACE "Quiet Storm" programming. Mike is leader of America's premier Black Cowboy band, "Mike Mann and the Night Riders." The group performs original blend of country and soul which Mike has dubbed "Cowboy Soul." He is married to KOST personality Antoinette Russell.

MANN, Tony: **KHJ**, 1974-75. Born John Mitchell, Tony worked at WHBQ-Memphis in 1971 before coming to the Southland. When he left he went to KUPD-Phoenix.

MANNERS, Zeke: **KDAY**, 1959-61; **KFWB**; **XEG**, 1975. Zeke was at WINS-New York before joining Southland radio. In the 1950s he played the cover versions of r&b hits and eventually slid into playing the original songs. He called them "rhythm and happy's" because he wanted nothing blue or down on his show.

MANNING, Bruce: **KFI**, 1996-97. Bruce is in the news department at KFI and also works at the Orange County NewsChannel.

MANNING, Knox: **KDAY**, 1959-61. Knox worked for CBS news during World War II and was a narrator for many war films. He later developed a medical problem with his jaw.

MANNING, Phil: **KLYY**, 1996-97, pd. Phil joined the new Odyssey Communications station (billed as "Y-107") in the summer of 1996. Before arriving in the Southland he had programmed WNRQ-Pittsburgh, WENZ-Cleveland and WOXY-Cincinnati. In early 1997 Phil left Southern California to program KNDD-Seattle.

MANON: **KCRW**, 1982-83; **KSRF**, 1984-91; **KSRF/KOCM**, 1991 and 1992; **KBIG**, 1993; **KLSX**, 1994-95; **KAJZ**, 1992-95; **KACD**, 1995-97, pd. Manon (Ma-noh) Hennesy was born in Malibu and grew up listening to KHJ, KMET and KLOS. Her father was an actor and her French mother was a singer/actress which explains Manon's love for music. She started her radio career as a news reporter at KCRW while graduating from Santa Monica College with a liberal arts degree in radio and television. Her longest affiliation has been with the 103.1FM frequency ("K-Surf," "MARSfm," "Jazzfm," "CD 103.1"and "Groove Radio").

For almost a decade and a half Manon has held virtually every on and off-air position including operations manager and program director. In the spring of 1989 she was promoted to pd. "I value having programmed one of the country's first ever AAA formats on 'K-Surf'." Manon also does nationally syndicated radio news reporting and national television voiceovers. Currently, Manon is on-air and om at "Groove Radio."

MANOR, Katie: **KROQ**, 1983-89; **KQLZ**, 1989-91; **KROQ**, 1990. From "91X"-San Diego, Katie worked mornings with Scott Shannon for part of her tour with "Pirate Radio." She was briefly at "the Roq" before returning to KQLZ. She is no longer in radio.

MANTLE, Larry: **KPCC**, 1983-97, pd. Born in 1959, it wasn't long before he was toying with radio. In a 1994 *LA Times* profile, Larry recalled: "When I was 5, the first thing I bought with my own money was a transistor radio. I took my radio everywhere. I was a real verbal child and it was my constant companion." Larry received a bachelor's degree in psychology from Southern

California College, a Christian liberal arts school in Costa Mesa, in 1979. He studied for the Presbyterian ministry

and then psychology in graduate school before learning of his calling. He interned at KPCC, went to a Riverside station and returned to KPCC in 1983 as nd. In 1985 he developed and became the host of "AirTalk" which airs daily in afternoon drive. He told the *Times*: "Hosting 'AirTalk' is the best job in the world. I get to talk with literally the most interesting people in the world." Larry has been the pd and nd of KPCC and has won numerous awards.

MARANZ, Randy: **KNAC**, 1991; **KQLZ**, 1991-92; **KLOS**, 1993-97. Born in San Bernardino in 1958, Randy grew up in Orange County. By the time he reached junior high school, he knew he wanted to be a dj. He received an A.A. degree in communication at Santa Ana Junior College and attended the Orange County Broadcast Headquarters. He worked for Jerry Longden in Fresno and Modesto before going to "91X"-San Diego. He got out of the business, working for a time as a process server. His uncle is president of Macy's West Coast operations. Randy was on KNAC for a couple of months before hooking up with "Pirate Radio." When "Pirate" pd Carey Curelop returned to KLOS, Randy moved with him. He worked part-time and progressed to a full-time shift when three longtime personalities were let go in November of 1994 as part of a station house cleaning. Randy lives in Santa Ana with his wife and they spend their free time outdoors hiking and mountain biking. He volunteers at the Tucker Wildlife Sanctuary in Modjeska Canyon. Randy left KLOS in the summer of 1997.

MARCH, Jeff: **KVFM**, 1969; **KIEV**, 1970; **KBBQ**, 1970. "For a person who loves radio as much as I do, I had an inauspicious and disappointingly short career in broadcasting." As a child his earliest brush with radio was with a ham operator buddy. "I've been quite nearsighted and I may have been drawn to this aural medium as the increasing severity of my myopia inexorably reduced the diameter of my world." In 1970 earlier encouragement from the late-Tom Clay came full circle. "At KBBQ I was sitting at the same console where Tom had, five years earlier, told me I would work one day." When Jeff left the Southland he programmed KAHI-Auburn and KROY-Sacramento. He's currently a partner in EditPros, a marketing communications firm in Davis providing writing and editing services to corporate and institutional clientele. Jeff and his wife Marsha have two "wonderful" kids. "As far removed from radio as I am, the echoes from those distant days on the air in L.A. still resonate strong in my memory."

MARCH, Luz: **KWIZ**, 1997
MARCOS, Tina: **KIBB**, 1996-97
MARENA, Robert: **KKBT**, 1993
MARER, Carl: **KIQQ**, 1984-85. Carl worked as a "phone intern" and was given a weekend shift.
MARGI: SEE Hunter Hancock
MARGOLIS, Jack: **KMPC**, 1962-67; **KLAC**, 1967; **KMET**, 1970-71; **KGBS**, 1973. Jack teamed with Bob Arbogast as a comedy team. When he left radio he got into a real estate career amassing a fortune before the market fell apart.
MARIANO, Carolyn: **KIQQ/KLIT**, 1981-89; **KQLZ**, 1989-93. Carolyn grew up in Orange County and graduated from UCLA with a degree in sociology. She started as a request operator moving into music research and board op which evolved into a weekend on-air shift. When WW1 bought KIQQ she continued part-time at KQLZ and went to work at the parent company where she is currently the affiliate relations manager.
MARIE, Jan: **KWIZ**, 1977-78; **KEZY**, 1979-81; **KUTE**, 1982; **KRTH**, 1982; **KOST**, 1982-85, md; **KYMS**, 1993-94. CRASH! The closing day of the Los Angeles Olympics, August 11, 1984, at 7:30 p.m., a drunk driver smashes head on into a car driven by the air personality known as Jan Marie who "lives" in a coma for four months. She was born Jan Marie Tamburelli in Inglewood and spent much of her growing up in Orange County. From her home in Huntington Beach, she talked about how much she loves music (she studied the piano) and radio. "It's a bonus to be paid for loving your hobby." She started her broadcast career in the fall of 1976 in King City and a year later was working part-time at KWIZ. Her enthusiasm for radio is contagious. "I love radio soooo much! I love it as much today as I did when I started out." KEZY was looking for a hook in the late 1970s and Jan became "Strawberry Jan" which carried through "Kute 102." She got KRTH pd Bob Hamilton's attention when she sent him a beach towel with a HUGE strawberry. During this time she taught broadcasting at local schools. When KOST changed formats to AC in 1982, Jan became an integral part of the programming as music director and the evening host. And then the crash. Her miraculous progress in therapy recovery causes one to pause. Her parents were told that if she survived, she would be nothing more than a vegetable. For two months she was unconscious and for another two months she was incoherent.

They pumped KOST music into her room with recording stars like Lionel Richie giving words of encouragement to Jan Marie over the intro to their songs. "I am greatly blessed after being horrendously handicapped that God has restored me." She is in her 13th year of recovery from the near-fatal car crash. She still works out three times a week at the Sporting Club in Irvine with a personal trainer. She once taught young people how to read and now has had to teach herself how to talk again. If you didn't know about the accident, it would be impossible to know of her challenge: "My spontaneity on the radio is back! My goals and expectations are limitless."

MARIE, Jan: **KMGX**, 1990-92; **KMAX**, 1995. Born Jan Marie Zito in Rhode Island and half Canadian Indian, Jan Marie studied insurance and finance in New Hampshire. While a teen, she became the spokesperson for a department store and got the entertainment bug. In the late 1980s, she worked in Rhode Island on WWKX and WWON. By the end of 1990 she had arrived at KMGX. In November 1992, her car was hit by a truck resulting in permanent nerve damage, a broken nose and a stutter. Since the car accident she has been working at Metro Traffic and did mornings at KMAX in early 1995.

MARIN, Lina: **KLVE**, 1975

MARINO, Larry: **KPCC**, 1996-97. Larry, a native of Pasadena, hosts the "Talk of the City" show.

MARK the SHARK: SEE Mark McKay

MARK "the Whiffle Boy": **KROQ**, 1991

MARK and **BRIAN**: **KLOS**, 1987-97. One of the most popular Los Angeles morning teams became a market factor very quickly. Mark Thompson and Brian Phelps

had very different backgrounds before meeting professionally at WAPI-Birmingham. Born in 1956, Mark attended the University of Northern Alabama and started as a janitor at a radio station near his hometown of Florence, Alabama. Brian was born in 1959 and is a native of Cambridge, Illinois. He went to Illinois State University and then toured the Midwest with a comedy improv group before turning to radio. Mark had some experience with morning radio in Savannah but did solo jock work throughout the South. Mark and Brian were paired together at WAPI-Birmingham in 1985. Brian arrived from WKQX-Chicago and Mark moved cross town from WHHY-Birmingham. In the fall of 1987, they started their Los Angeles radio skyrocket. Less than two years later, they were #1. Since then they've been named Air Personalities of the Year twice by *Billboard* magazine and won the NAB's Marconi Award. Their first major on-air stunt was being dipped into a vat of chocolate on Valentine's Day. The stunt cost $5,000. In a 1989 *LA Times* interview, Mark said, "People call us shock jocks. We're not into shock. We'll do some gentle locker room humor. But we're not into shock. We'll get on the phone with a listener and we'll badger them a little bit, but they're laughing harder than we are." In that same interview, Brian said, "We're not there to get in their faces or to be jerks. We laugh at ourselves more than we laugh at anybody. We are average, everyday kind of guys. Human scum." Phelps continued, "We still make each other laugh. That core, that original thing the show's all about is the relationship of two guys, two buds, havin' a great time together." Mark added, "I think we both agreed a long time ago that we weren't going to do anyone else's type of radio. I'm very proud of our show, because it's a family atmosphere." They have been deeply involved in the annual Pet Fair and Adoption event. In 1990, the duo attempted to deliver the head of Elvis to Graceland in Memphis. A running feud with Graceland has been a part of their heritage and is resurrected every year on Elvis' birthday. They have presided over a "mega-marriage" of some 200 couples and tied the knot themselves at a marriage ceremony at a Las Vegas chapel. "It was our two-year anniversary, so we thought it was the thing to do," Phelps told the *Times*. "All right, we had to get married, ok? We just lost interest in the sex thing - mainly because we're both heterosexual." Special events over the years include the "Mark and Brian Day Before Thanksgiving Day Parade," "At the Drive-In," "Birthday Shows," and the star studded, hot-ticket, annual Christmas show. Bachelor Brian dated popular singer and dancer Paula Abdul in the early 1990s. Mark lives in the Santa Clarita Valley with his wife and three children. Their NBC/TV series *Adventures of Mark and Brian* ran for 13 weeks on Sunday nights against *60 Minutes*. Phelps joked, "My parents watched *60 Minutes* and taped us." In October 1993, an indecent broadcasting complaint was filed against the show. The same self-styled radio crusader who has made Howard Stern's life miserable with complaints to the FCC cited the shows called "The Big O Olympics" in which women called with faked orgasms. Mark and Brian have appeared in a number of movies, including *Escape From L.A.* and *Rocky V* and were cowboys in Fox/TV's *The Adventures of Brisco County, Jr*. In a 1994 interview with Fred Shuster in the *LA Daily News*, Brian talked about the competition while in Southern California: "We never cheapened the show or lessened it and we never hit back at what others said about us. We're not going to get into the ring with these other morning shows." In the spring of 1995, Mark made headlines when he went to bail out a friend. He innocently leaped a barrier at the sheriff's station to retrieve some personal belongings and found himself facing a ring of revolvers with safeties being clicked off. Once explained, he was cleared. The duo is scheduled for a Star on the Hollywood Walk of Fame in 1998.

MARKAS, Rory: **KNX**, 1987-97. Rory does sports

reporting for "KNXNewsradio" and is the voice of the NBA L.A. Clippers. He was born and raised in the San Fernando Valley and graduated from Cal State Northridge. Rory was a big fan of KRLA while growing up. His first radio job was at KLYR-Clarksville, Arkansas. How in the world did he get to Arkansas? "I put an ad in the trades and that was the station that responded." A year later he was doing news at KNUU-Las Vegas. He moonlighted as a jock, Alias Smith, at Urban formatted KCEP. "One day there was a knock at the back door of the station and a skinny kid is standing there. He said, 'ah, man, you're not a brother.' I told him that I was but with white skin. He wanted to thank me for playing his first record. It was Prince." In 1977 Rory was a morning dj at KUTY-Palmdale before going back to Las Vegas at KLAV working with Johnny Magnus. He got involved with play-by-play sports doing hockey at KTUC-Tucson. By 1981 he was broadcasting baseball for the Triple A Gulls in Salt Lake City. In the off-season he was a dj in Las Vegas. Triple A ball in Vancouver followed and in 1987 he returned to the Southland to work at KNX. In 1990, he took on tv chores at KCBS/Channel 2 as well as KTLA/Channel 5. He has won two Golden Mikes in the past two years.

> "When we were flying to San Francisco for Thanksgiving, I was about 7 and terrified. As we sat at the end of the runway at Burbank, the plane was shaking and noisy. I was wondering what was going on. As the plane got about 15 feet in the air, I realized that something incredible was going on. I fell in love with airplanes at that exact moment."
> -Mike Nolan, air traffic reporter, KFI/KOST

MARKHAM, Steve: **KFAC**, 1958-77

MARKOE, Merrill: **KTZN**, 1997. Merrill, the ex-writing partner for David Letterman, co-hosts afternoon drive on all-Talk "the Zone."

MAROTTA, Rich: **KNX**, 1981-82; **KRLA/KBZT**, 1983-90; **KFOX**; **KFI**, 1990-97. The former Raider radio commentator was part of KFI's morning news magazine. Born in 1949, Richard was a 1967 graduate of Notre Dame High in Sherman Oaks. He studied broadcasting at Cal State Northridge. After college he spent three years in Colorado doing football and basketball for the Air Force Academy and hockey for the University of Colorado. Rich spent two seasons as Bob Miller's partner on the Kings broadcasts and was the USC football commentator for Prime Ticket. He followed the Raiders broadcast team from KNX to KRLA. At one point in early 1990 he was the Raider commentator on KFI, worked mornings on KRLA and hosted an afternoon sports show at KFOX. He loves boxing and announced that sport for the USA network with Allan Malamud.

MARQUEZ, Al: **KSRF**, 1991; **KXEZ**, 1995-96; **KIBB**, 1996-97. Al worked weekends at KXEZ until late 1996 when the station changed call letters and format and he moved to new Rhythm KIBB.

MARQUEZ, Sue: **KFWB**, 1992-93 and 1995-97. Sue is a news writer and in-house reporter for all-News KFWB. She left the station briefly to take a news director position in Flagstaff and returned in 1995.

MARQUIS, The Young: **KROQ**. The Young Marquis (Doc Nemo) hosted a Sunday night show on "the Roq" in the early 1970s.

MARR, Bruce: **KABC**, 1973-81, pd. Bruce is a veteran of over 30 years in broadcasting including a long stint at KABC as program director. A graduate of New Rochelle High School in New York, Bruce attended USC. In 1980 he established a broadcasting consulting firm specializing in news and information programming. He was a principal in the syndication of the Rush Limbaugh radio program. Prior to KABC, he served as operations director at KVI-Seattle and earlier as marketing director at Group W's KFWB. In 1995 he established Lone Wolf Television Productions in Reno.

Los Angeles Radio People who became game show hosts:
Jim Lange: *Name That Tune, The Dating Game, The $1,000,000 Chance of a Lifetime*
Wink Martindale: *Gambit, High Rollers, Tattletales, Tic Tac Dough, Debt*
Bob Eubanks: *The Newlywed Game, Rhyme & Reason, Trivia Trap, Card Sharks, Dream House, Family Secrets*
Clark Race: *The Parent Game*
Geoff Edwards: *Treasure Hunt, Jackpot, Hollywood's Talking, Big Spin*
Dave Hull: *Match Maker*
Source: *Encyclopedia of Game Shows*, David Schwartz, co-author

MARRS, Johnny: SEE Jeff Davis

MARS, Andy: **KNX/FM/KKHR**, 1983-87; **KWIZ**, 1990-97, gm. In early 1996 Andy was promoted to Liberman Broadcasting corporate VP of sales representing KKHJ, KBUE and KWIZ. Born in Pittsburgh, he graduated from Syracuse University in 1977. In 1987 Andy became director of sales at WODS-Boston. He returned to Southern California in 1990 to manage KWIZ.

MARSH, Roger: **KYMS**, 1985-92, pd/vp/gm. Roger started his radio career in the summer of 1983 at KIQO-Atascadero and a year later was at KQLH (now KFRG)-San Bernardino while working on a bachelor's degree in accounting from Cal State Fullerton. In the summer of 1985 he moved to weekends at the Orange County Christian station and soon was promoted to pd. By 1991 Roger was gm of KYMS. In the fall of 1992 he moved to Fox television to do voice work and is currently the commercial billboard announcer for FBC. In 1993 he was pd of KPRZ-San Diego. Roger hosts the nationally syndicated program "Ambassador Express Talk" that airs in over 100 markets.

MARSH, Tobie: **KFWB**, 1997

MARSHALL, Andi: **KFWB**, 1997

MARSHALL, Chuck: **KPPC**, 1973; **KWST**, 1976. After KWST Chuck went to WRIF-Detroit.

MARSHALL, Claudia: **KFWB**, 1984-86; **KRTH**, 1986-91, nd. Born in 1961, Claudia worked for five years at KRTH as news director. While attending Western Michigan University, she changed her major to broadcast journalism after hearing someone on the radio "mutilate the news." The day after graduation, Claudia drove to L.A. without a job or any money. She began her career in news broadcasting at KFWB, first as a news writer and then on-air. When Claudia joined KRTH there was a news staff of seven. By the time she left in 1991 she was the news director and lone reporter. When the station added phony teletype sounds to her newscasts, she left for KXL-Portland. She told the *LA Times*: "I'll miss L.A. It's a wonderful, horrible place and it was home for six years." Claudia now lives in New York and broadcasts the CBS evening radio network news.

KKDJ (102.7FM) becomes KIIS/FM	
6 a.m.	Charlie Tuna
10 a.m	Jay Stevens
2 p.m.	Jerry Bishop
6 p.m.	Jerry Mason
10 p.m.	Danny Martinez
2 a.m.	Brian Cummings
(one month later "Humble Harve" replaced Jerry Mason)	
-debut line-up, October 1, 1975	

MARSHALL, Gary: **KRLA**, 1969-70; **KEZY**, 1970-75; **KWIZ**, 1975-83; **KUTE**, 1984-85; **KSRF**, 1985-86; **KRLA**, 1985-92; **KRTH**, 1992-97. Gary was the "morning Marshall" at KFXM-San Bernardino and worked at KYNO-Fresno before joining KRLA to do weekends, fill-in and production. He started his Southern California career in the summer of 1969, hosting a Sunday evening show on KRLA called "Heaven Is In Your Mind." The show, a mix of music, hip, spiritual comments and poems reflected the "underground" times. "Doug Cox, the pd, asked me to come up with a show directed to young people, but open to comments and input from all faiths, rather than just Christian. I chose 'Heaven Is In Your Mind' as the title because Traffic and Three Dog Night had versions of that song on their latest albums. The program was done live Sunday mornings for an hour and a half, and played back on tape Sunday nights." In November 1969 Gary commemorated the sixth anniversary of the JFK assassination by incorporating actualities from that day with Dion's song, *Abraham, Martin and John*. "Tom Clay's hit *What The World Needs Now* came out a year later and I like to think it was inspired by the 'Heaven Is In Your Mind' program. Brother John reworked the show when he joined KRLA." Gary was born in Los Angeles and grew up with KFWB and listening to Hunter Hancock, Bob Crane and Art Laboe. Gary began with Armed Forces Radio and Television in 1959 at age 18 while in the Marine Corps.

MARSHALL, John: **KFWB**. John was one of the early news voices at KFWB during the all-News period. He now has a biplane service working out of Whiteman Airport.

KRLA	
5 a.m.	Al Lohman/Bob Hudson
9 a.m.	Mike Wagner
Noon	Johnny Hayes
4 p.m.	The Real Don Steele
8 p.m.	Wolfman Jack
Mid	KRLA Jukebox
	-September 11, 1986

MARSHALL, Lee: **KHJ**, 1970-71; **KDAY**, 1976-78; **KHJ**, 1979-81; **KABC**, 1980-91, nd; **KDAY**, 1990-91; **KBLA**, 1991. Lee has been a booming news voice in

Southern California for decades. Before arriving in the Southland, he worked at legendary Rock radio stations such as KCBQ-San Diego and CKLW-Detroit. Lee's work has been featured in New York's Museum of Broadcasting and is also used as a teaching tool at the University of Illinois. He has been honored with Golden Mikes and an Emmy. In 1979 Lee was nd at KHJ as well as Western regional bureau chief for the RKO Radio Network. He joined KABC in 1980. For better than a decade he served as nd and part of that time as co-host of "SportsTalk." He also handled the Western regional bureau for the ABC Radio Networks. In the early 1990s he was syndicating a Notre Dame football pre-game radio show and a syndicated sports-entertainment program called "SportsAmerica." On April 17, 1991, Lee launched KBLA's business morning show, "California Drive." He is currently the executive vp of news and sports programming for Shadow Broadcast Services. Lee has always been active in broadcasting high-profile traditional sports; in 1969 he started providing play-by-play commentary for professional wrestling. For over a year Lee has been splitting his week between L.A. and the CNN Center in Atlanta doing the commentary for World Championship Wrestling. He is seen and heard on *TNT Monday Nitro*. Former Los Angeles Dodgers manager Tommy Lasorda said of Lee: "If God ever wanted to make a speech, Lee Marshall would get the call!"

MARSHALL, Steve: **KUTE**, 1966; **KBIG**, 1966-67; **KOST**, 1967-70; **KNX/FM**, 1971-79. Steve achieved much recognition for creating the first Soft-Rock format in the country, known as "The Mellow Sound," on KNX/FM. He began in 1971, remaining with the CBS-owned station until 1979. During that period, Steve

began consulting for other stations in the CBS/FM group, including KCBS-San Francisco, WEEI-Boston, KMOX-St. Louis and WBBM-Chicago. In 1979, he left radio to write for the hit comedy *WKRP in Cincinnati*. He also executive produced *Gloria* with Sally Struthers and co-created two other ABC comedies, *Off the Rack* and *Just the Ten of Us*. He enjoyed a long run as executive producer and writer of *Growing Pains*. He also created and executive produced *Live Shot*, a one-hour comedy-drama that aired on UPN. Most recently, Steve has written and directed a short dramatic film, *Insomnia*, which was an entry in the 1997 Sundance Film Festival. It featured a vocal performance by his former colleague at KNX/FM, Christopher Ames.

MARSHALL, Toby: **KFWB**, 1993-96. Toby was a fill-in and weekend news anchor at all-News KFWB.

MARSHALL, Tom: **KNAC**, 1987-89, pd. Born in Orlando on December 15, 1955, Tom grew up with a father who was a career Air Force Officer and lived in many cities. His first radio experience was at KGOU in 1976 while attending college in Norman, Oklahoma. In 1979 he started an eight-year run with KFMG-Albuquerque. After leaving KNAC Tom programmed WYNF-Tampa, WKLQ-Grand Rapids and KIOZ-San Diego. Currently Tom is pd/om for WKLQ/WBBL/WLAV-Grand Rapids.

MARTIN, A.J.: **KIIS**, 1979-82; **KNOB**, 1982-84; **KIQQ**, 1987. A.J. was Jason Williams at KNOB. He was part of the launch of Transtar's "Format 41." A.J.'s currently with the Bright AC format at Westwood One.

MARTIN, Alex: **KGFJ**, 1965-68; **XPRS**, 1971. Alex worked middays at KGFJ.

MARTIN, Chet: **KROQ**, 1972. Chet was a newsman at KROQ.

MARTIN, Chuck: **KHJ**, 1977-80, pd; **KWST**, 1981-82, pd. Born in New York City, Chuck successfully programmed WAVZ-New Haven, "Y103"-Jacksonville, KISN-Portland and WIFE-Indianapolis before arriving at KHJ. He was named 1972 Program Director of the Year in *Billboard* magazine for his work at WIFE. As pd of

KHJ in 1979, he created the 20-minute music jams and the acclaimed "Million Dollar Minute" contest. "During a time of mass exodus from AM to FM, KHJ's ratings increased 1.6 to 3.2," according to Chuck, "and represented the highest percentage of increase in KHJ's history. The industry trades labeled this feat as 'The Great L.A. Turnaround.'" When RKO made the decision to switch KHJ to Country, Chuck became the last rock 'n' roll pd of this L.A. Rock radio institution. He then went to KFRC-San Francisco and returned to the Southland to program "K-West." Without management support, Chuck chose not to renew his one-year contract. After Los Angeles radio, Chuck taught broadcast journalism courses for six years at Chapman College, "a prestigious Southern California college offering superior broadcasting and arts courses." On his decision to teach, Chuck said, "Radio had been so good to me, I wanted to give something back to the broadcast industry through teaching." Chuck now lives in Diamond Bar and owns a full service advertising agency and production/recording studio. His voice is heard on many radio and tv commercials. Aside from his many Gold and Platinum record awards, Chuck is also the recipient of four Telly awards, two Vision awards, and the coveted Clio award for outstanding creative achievement.

MARTIN, Elise: **KNOB**, 1986. Elise hosted "Love Messages" in the evenings on KNOB.

MARTIN, George: **KNX**, 1968-86. Born May 2, 1917, George is retired and living in Napa.

MARTIN, Jim: **KGIL**, 1975. Jim worked evenings on KGIL when the station had a Talk format.

MARTIN, Pat: **KMET**, 1986-87. Pat grew up in Anaheim and graduated with a B.S. degree in telecommunications

and film from San Diego State University. His first professional job was briefly at KZIQ-Ridgecrest before starting at KGB-San Diego in late 1977. For the next seven years Pat moved from part-time to full-time evenings, to middays to assistant pd and then as "Shotgun Tom" Kelly said, "Pat was the BIG night voice at KGB." Pat said he was "washed out" of KMET in late 1986 when the station changed format to "the Wave." He returned to KGB for a year, departing for KRXQ-Sacramento in 1988, where he started as midday host and held a number of programming assignments including pd. He is the lead singer of a local band Animal House. He is also the voice of the professional indoor soccer team the Sacramento Knights. Pat listed his Top Five radio experiences: 1. Raising $75,000 during Leukemia Cure-A-Thon; 2. KMET live broadcasting from Van Halen's dressing room at L.A. Forum; 3. Interviewing and riding in limo with Pete Townshend; 4. Traveling to London to cover Live Aid; 5. Singing with Ozzy and REO Speedwagon.

MARTIN, Roger: **KCBH**, 1968. Roger worked at KORL-Honolulu before landing in the Southland. He went on to host a cable access show on Continental.

MARTIN, Ron: **KLAC**, 1969-71, pd; **KGBS/KTNQ**, 1972-79, pd. Ron is a North Carolina native who came to Southern California to program KLAC. Under Ron, KGBS enjoyed healthy ratings with the "Bill Ballance

Show." He changed the FM format to "Gentle Country" and featured female announcers, which was unique at the time. Two years later, he dropped the "Gentle" part and the station became a mix of popular and "golden oldie country hits" as well as some country album cuts. In 1975, radio rebel Jimmy Rabbit mixed Rock and "progressive" country, a sound that became known as "Outlaw Country." Ron let Jimmy go after he played Charlie Daniels's *Texas* incessantly and rambled for hours. By 1976, the AM became "the new Ten-Q" and on the FM Ron continued to program a mix of eclectic popular country and album cuts. Ron left the Storer facility when it was sold in 1979 and started a syndicated radio show company called Weedeck. He hosted a daily feature called "Country Report." He and Nancy Plum, using the name Nancy Jordan, hosted a weekly "Country Report Countdown" show. Ron served a few terms as president of the Academy of Country Music. He was one of the founding members of the Academy and was instrumental in getting the Awards show televised. Ron had a heart attack and died playing golf, a sport he cherished, in the late 1980s.

"I feel we are on a one-to-one basis after midnight. I am talking to them and I like to hear them talk back."

-Al "Jazzbo" Collins, from the Purple Grotto

MARTINDALE, Christine: **KIKF**, 1985-87. In 1986 Christine covered the boxing matches at the Irvine Marriott. She now works part-time at WW1's Soft AC format.

MARTINDALE, Wink: **KHJ**, 1959-60; **KRLA**, 1960-61; **KFWB**, 1962-67; **KGIL**, 1968-79; **KMPC**, 1983-86; **KJQI/KOJY**, 1993. When Johnny Carson wanted to get a laugh at the expense of game shows in general -- and game-show hosts in particular -- more often than not,

Wink was the target. He personifies the tv game show host with a white toothy smile and frothy personality that worked so well on *Gambit*, *High Rollers*, *Tattletales* and *Tic Tac Dough*. The Winker, nicknamed by a neighborhood friend, was born Winston Conrad Martindale in 1935 in Jackson, Tennessee. His first radio job was at WBLI in his hometown at age 17. "They gave me a job at $25 a week, and for that you did everything." Next was WHBQ-Memphis when he also hosted a tv show called *Wink Martindale's Mars Patrol* and earned a speech and drama degree at Memphis State. Before the game shows, Wink was an enormously popular disc jockey. Wink did mornings on KHJ in the late 1950s. When Perry Allen, morning man at KRLA, wanted to stop playing rock music, an ingenious marketing move had Wink, who was doing mornings at MOR KHJ, switch stations with Perry. When Wink went to KFWB he replaced Gary Owens in morning drive. While at "Channel 98," Wink regularly broadcast from POP (Sea Circus Arena at Pacific Ocean Park pier in Santa Monica). He voiced one of the most popular "talk" records, a million-seller called *Deck of Cards* that resulted in an appearance on *The Ed Sullivan Show*. He worked as national program director at DOT Records. In 1966, *Billboard* voted the Winker the #1 midday personality. In a 1971 interview, Wink said: "I try to be humorous, but I'm not funny. I have a good sense of humor, but I'm not funny like Gary Owens." In 1972, Wink won the *Gavin* Radio Programming Award for "his good taste and showmanship in presenting musical portraits of featured artists." In 1973 he syndicated a three-hour show called "Those Were the Days." One of his most successful specials, the "Elvis Presley Story," came in 1975. In the early 1980s he returned to his native Memphis and after sitting in for Ken Minyard and Bob Arthur he got the itch to get back on the air. His return to the Southland was for the rebuilding of MOR on KMPC in 1983. KMPC's gm Bill Ward commented, "Bringing Wink back was simply another step in re-establishing this station to what it used to be. You can't rebuild overnight. We had to wait for Wink. But I think now our patience is beginning to pay off." How did he get into game show hosting? "My roots were in radio, but I thought it'd be fun to do something else. I thought, 'I love games, why don't I start auditioning and see if I can get a job as a game show host?'" He hit pay dirt with his very first audition, *What's This Song?* Before his successful run of hosting game shows, Wink hosted tv dance shows on three Los Angeles stations. Wink is part of the syndicated "Music of Your Life" format heard on 100 stations nationally. He hosts the game show *Debt* airing on Lifetime Cable. Wink heads his own production company and lives in Calabasas with his wife Sandy and five chihuahuas. He has four grown children and seven grandchildren.

MARTINEZ, Benny: **KDAY** and **KIIS** in the 1970s; **KUTE**, 1980; **KFI**, 1981; **KWST**, 1981-82; **KHTZ**, 1984-85; **KIIS**, 1985-86; **KCBS**, 1992; **KRTH**, 1993-94; **KIBB**, 1997. In 1993, Benny moonlighted at KGGI-Riverside and left his weekend work at "K-Earth." He has appeared in *Married...With Children* and the Motown movie, *The Last Radio Show*. In 1994, he went to Westwood One and is currently doing afternoon drive on the 70's format and weekends at "B-100."

MARTINEZ, Bill: **KWIZ**, 1970-72; **KDAY**, 1972-74; **KIIS**, 1975-80; **KRLA**, 1980-81. It is believed that Bill is the first Hispanic in L.A. radio to use his real last name. At KIIS, in addition to his evening shift, he was the assistant pd. It was also during this time that Bill directed the radio advertising for several Southern California retailers. Bill lists Waterbed Warehouse, Waterbed Gallery and The Woodworks as companies  he made household names. He was born in Oxnard in 1950 as the third of nine children. After leaving KRLA in 1981, Bill concentrated his efforts at BMEI, an ad agency he founded that focused on retail production, media placement and video/film production. He has recently graduated from bible college and returned to Orange

County radio at KIKF as a senior account executive. Bill is married to Mona and has five children.

MARTINEZ, Danny: **KHJ**, 1973-75; **KKDJ**, 1975; **KIIS**, 1975-76; **KFI**, 1977-78; **KWIZ**, 1979; **KHJ**, 1980-85; **KBZT**, 1986; **KRLA**, 1986; **KTWV**, 1988; **KRTH**, 1990-92; **KCBS**, 1992-93; **KYSR**, 1993-95; **KCBS**, 1996-97. Born in San Diego in 1946, Danny worked in the early 1970s at KACY-Oxnard, KCBQ-San Diego and WXLO-New York before arriving in the Southland at KHJ. He has the distinction of being the last pictured jock on the last "Boss 30" folder in 1980. During morning drive he had characters "Cousin Cochina" and "Juan Moretime." He stayed at the RKO outlet, where he solidified the Mexican-American listenership, until 1985. Danny was working at KBZT in 1986 and moved over to sister station KRLA where he did mornings for a brief time. He left KCBS when the station switched from Oldies to "Arrow 93" with an emphasis on music of the late '60s and '70s; moved to "Star 98.7," and returned to KCBS in early 1996. Danny has written several screenplays, one about radio, and he is hopeful it will be produced by a Canadian film company.

MARTINEZ, JL: **KMDY**, 1986; **KGFJ**, 1993-94. Jorge Lopez worked mornings at KGFJ. He now has a mobile dj business in Valencia.

MARTINEZ, Patty: **KWIZ**, 1973-88; **KOCM**, 1988.

Patty's first impression of radio was at KROY-Sacramento watching her father, longtime KWIZ owner Bill Weaver. After graduating from Corona Del Mar High School in 1973 she started her own radio career taking "instant requests" from people in malls and shopping centers. Patty went on to be music librarian and in 1976 started doing the weekend all-night shift. A year later Patty was part of the innovative "all-female dj staff" at KWIZ/FM which was located in South Coast Plaza Village. "The genius behind this unheard of move of all-female announcers was Bill Weaver," she proudly said of her father. From 1978 to 1986 Patty worked the midday shift on KWIZ. In 1987 she was promoted to station manager. After a brief sales stint at KOCM, Patty opened her own advertising agency. Not only was Patrice Weaver born into radio, she married radio people. Patty has two sons, Mike and Bryan, from her first marriage to L.A. dj Bill Martinez and in 1988 she married Dean Rathbun, grandson to Jeannette Bacozni, owner of KNOB and KBZT-Palm Desert. "I've been so fortunate to learn from the best."

MARY, Bloody: SEE Mary Jo Godges

MASON, Gordon: **KNX**, 1952-62, gsm; **KBIG**, 1968-74, vp/gm; **KJOI**, 1974-84, vp/gm. Gordon Mason spent 30 years selling and/or managing for Los Angeles-based radio, tv and print media. He ran his own promotion and advertising firm prior to joining The Southern California Broadcasters Association as executive director in April of 1986. He was elected president in December of 1988. Gordon started out as vp of sales of *MAC* (now *AdWeek*) and then in 1964 he was vp sales for KTLA/Channel 5.

MASON, Greg: **KRLA**, 1959. Greg was one of the "11-10 Men" in the late summer of 1959 but lasted only a few months. He arrived in the Southland from WNOE-New Orleans.

MASON, Jerry: **KNAC**, 1968-70, pd; **KIIS**, 1970-76; **KPRZ**, 1980-85. Jerry was born in Parks, Nebraska, in 1935. He worked at KIRO-Seattle before arriving at KNAC. At KIIS Jerry worked afternoon drive.

MASON, Pamela: **KABC**, 1960-67. The former wife of actor James Mason, Pamela was one of the early talk show hosts at KABC. The daughter of a British mill owner who was also in the movie business, Pamela left school at 9 and was married to a cinematographer when she was 16. She met James Mason while they were making a movie called *I Met a Murderer*. She divorced the cinematographer and wed Mason. The Mason's and their 12 cats moved to Hollywood in 1946. They acted together on Broadway in 1947 in *Bathsheba* and she appeared on her husband's 1950s tv program, *The James Mason Show*. Pamela wrote several books, including an advice book about men, and a movie industry column. She became a U.S. citizen in 1959. Pamela and her husband, a three-time Oscar nominee, divorced in 1964 after a 16-year marriage. She died June 29, 1996, at the age of 80.

MASON, Scott: **KKDJ**, 1974-75; **KIQQ**, 1975-76; **KGBS/KTNQ**, 1976-79; **KROQ**, 1979-97, om. When Rick Carroll's format at KKDJ was dumped, Scott was an intern and moved to "K-100" where he "button pushed" and did overnight IDs. At "the new Ten-Q" Scott did engineering and was given a weekend shift. When Storer Broadcasting sold KGBS/KTNQ in 1979, Scott's old friend Rick Carroll asked him to help establish a new format at KROQ. Scott's position was chief engineer and weekend jock, and he was known as "Spacin' Scott Mason." In 1981 he was made assistant pd and moved up to om in 1985. When asked for his most memorable moment, he recounted being on the air during the January 17, 1994, Northridge earthquake: "I just grabbed the console, opened the mike, and said 'we're having an earthquake, stay calm.'" Scott has been hosting KROQ's "Openline" talk show for nearly 10 years. Scott also participated in the successful evening show on KROQ, "Loveline." He claims his life is balanced because of his volunteer work with the American Red Cross for which he has been acknowledged by Mayor Richard Riordan.

MASTERS, Roy: **KGIL**, 1985

MASTREY, Tawn: **KNAC**, 1986-89; **KQLZ**, 1989-92; **KLSX**, 1994. After graduation from Ron Bailey's School of Broadcasting in the late 1970s, Tawn worked at KSJO-San Jose and KMEL-San Francisco. She then took five years off from radio to pursue rock-related posts in various media, only to return to radio in Southern California. At KNAC she was known as "The Leather Nun." One of her ventures was hosting a syndicated show, "High Voltage" as well as "The Tawn Mastrey Show" and "Rockzone." In late 1996 she joined morning drive at KUFO-Portland.

MATHERS, Jerry: **KEZY**, 1980-81. "Sometimes when a grown-up is mad at you, you can get in trouble by saying 'hello.'" The words were said in 1957 by Jerry "The Beaver" Mathers, and for almost four decades the character has become an American institution. He started his television career at age two and started his film career in 1955 with the Alfred Hitchcock film *The Trouble with Harry*. Two Bob Hope and two Alan Ladd movies followed. It was in 1957 that Jerry entered the hearts and homes of America with the debut of *Leave It to Beaver*. "This role has totally changed my life; it has led to world travel, meeting many intriguing people and best of all, to the continuance of the 'Cleaver' traditions." *Leave It to Beaver* ran for six seasons, and the top rated show produced 234 episodes. After the series ended, he pursued a recording career with Atlantic Records for his group, "Beaver and the Trappers." Following his high school graduation, Jerry spent six years in the Air Force National Guard and then graduated with a bachelor's degree in philosophy from University of California Berkeley. Jerry's made-for-television movie *Still the Beaver* was one of the top ten movies of the week for 1982 and led to a new series entitled, *The New Leave It to Beaver*, for which 108 episodes were filmed, some directed by Jerry. He loved radio and got an FCC license which led to his stint on KEZY. Jerry was the ABC radio interviewer for the 1994 Grammy show in New York. He and his wife own "Cleaver's Catering," which services the active tv and film industry in their hometown of Santa Clarita. In addition to voiceover and commercial work, he is constantly on the lecture circuit talking about '50s television and the difference in working in the industry today as opposed to working as a child. In 1995, a "Leave It to Beaver" collection was launched selling signed decorative ceramic plates for $125, autographed figurines for $195 and even an unsigned school lunch box for $9.95 made to look like one that he carried on the show.

MATHEWS, Hal: **KRLA**, 1973-76, gm. Hal was the station manager during KRLA's experiment with two-man teams around-the-clock and later with automation. He went on to work in San Diego radio.

MATHEWS, Pat: **KWIZ**, 1988-89, pd. Pat did mornings and was pd at KWIZ. He came from WAJY-New Orleans for a sales job in Orange County. After several months he returned to radio claiming "life was too short to have to work for a living." In 1992, he became a news anchor at KDOC/Channel 56.

MATTHEWS, George: **KEZY**, 1993-95; **KRLA**, 1994-95. He was George Matthews on KEZY and George Flores on KRLA.

MATTHEWS, Paula: **KIQQ**, 1980-85, pd. In 1984, Paula had her disc jockeys play the first single off Michael Jackson's new album *Victory* for 24 continuous hours. She and her gm George Wilson complained to Dennis McDougal in the *LA Times* that KIIS copied almost everything KIQQ had thrown on the radio. They got sick and tired of KIIS' copying coupled with being unable to match the massive daily cash giveaways. The *Victory* air play was something they felt could not be copied. Paula left with the format change to Transtar 41 and is currently living in Albuquerque.

MAULE, Tom: **KHJ**, 1967; **KDAY**, 1969-71. Born October 29, 1939, Tom started working at KMAK-Fresno in 1962 and two years later went to KGB-San Diego. Between KHJ and KDAY, Tom worked at KFRC-San Francisco. In the 1970s he moved to Fresno and worked at KARM, KFRE and eventually did tv weathercasts. Tom passed away of pancreatitis in early 1993.

MAVER, Mark: **KKBT**, 1989; **KMGX**, 1992. Mark was the image voice of both stations.

MAXEY, Deedee: **KGFJ**, 1985. Deedee worked middays at the Urban station.

MAXWELL, Cyndee: **KLOS**, 1991-92; **KQLZ**, 1992-93. Born in the California desert, part Chemehuevi Indian, Hispanic and Caucasian, and raised in the shadow of the pink El Monte Legion Stadium building, Cyndee set out to be a screenwriter. After time at Long Beach State in the late 1970s, Cyndee became disillusioned with the movie business. She worked for a time selling books door to door in the Southeast when she heard "the call of the wild" and headed for Alaska. The call turned out to be her new calling. On a lark, Cyndee called a local radio request line  to talk about music with the dj. After a short conversation she suddenly asked, "Do you have any openings?" To this day she doesn't know where the words came from, "but I got the job and on my first day of training, I just knew that radio was for me. I felt a destiny with radio in the form of a peace I had never known before. Radio was my calling." Five years and two radio stations later, having worked up from all-nights to pd, she got claustrophobic and left Alaska without a job. She ended up at KIOZ ("Rock 102")-San Diego, and in the summer of 1991 came to the Southland for a part-time shift at KLOS. She went to KQLZ with her former San Diego boss Greg Stevens, when he took over after Carey Curelop's exit. Cyndee - along with most of the staff - left when Viacom bought the station and changed format. She applied to be editor of the Rock section in *R&R* and a month later was back at work. Cyndee is the Webmaster for "Radio Transmissions," a radio web site on Prodigy.

"If you ain't crankin' it, you must be yankin' it"
-Cry of "Pirate Radio" launch in 1989

MAXWELL, Remy "The Max": **KSRF**, 1991; **KLIT**, 1991; **KNAC**, 1992-94; **KLOS**, 1994-97. Remy was born Remy Doega and raised in New Orleans. He started his career as a professional musician at age 17, singing,

playing guitars, bass and drums. He began his radio career in 1988 in Morgan City, Louisiana. Within the year he moved to "Hot 107"-New Orleans. In 1989, Remy attended a recording arts school in Orlando and following graduation in 1990 moved to L.A. to start a recording career. He worked with Great White, Motorhead and Blind Melon. Remy continued to do radio working part-time on "K-Lite" and "MARSfm." In the fall of 1992 he started all-nights on KNAC later moving to middays. Remy moved from Orange County's KNAC to evenings on KLOS in November of 1994. "I was most suited for nights on KLOS." Remy left KLOS in early 1997 and joined KEGE-Minneapolis for afternoons.

MAY, Brian: **KPFK**; **KXLU**; **KPCC**. Born in 1950, Brian was only 5 and growing up in Pacific Palisades, when he was one of 79 children in the U.S. to receive a polio shot from a batch of improperly manufactured vaccine that actually spread the poliomyelitis virus. He was rendered almost completely paralyzed and spent 16 months in an iron lung. Brian required 24-hour care and could breathe only through a respirator. The quadriplegic overcame his disability and created "Malibu Folk" which was a two-hour program of songs and interviews that he mailed to 40 public radio stations each week. In 1990, he won a national Victory Award for the disabled. In 1994, *Acoustic Guitar* magazine praised Brian, without mentioning his disability, as "one of acoustic music's true angels." On July 5, 1995, he died at his Malibu home of complications of polio and paralysis.

MAY, Don: **KSRF**, 1988-92. Don figured out why he hates to move. It's because he was born on the road in 1966 while his parents were traveling through Moorhead, Minnesota. Don grew up shuttling between Lake Geneva, Wisconsin and Southern California. He started at KSRF as an intern while attending classes at Santa Monica City College. Four years later he had worked practically every shift and was the production director. Don was part of the transition from KSRF to the techno-rock experiment, "MARSfm." When the experiment ended after 15 months, Don joined his mother's business, the Sheila May Permanent Make-Up company. He has opened Signal Core Studios, for voiceovers, "On-Hold" enterprises and recording Books on Tape.

MAY, Fred: **KPOL**, 1965-68. Fred was a news anchor with KPOL. He is now active with voiceover work.

MAY, Lisa: **KLAC**, 1993; **KROQ**, 1991-97. The Southern California traffic reporter for many stations worked weekends at KLAC. She started at Metro Traffic in 1987 and moved to Shadow in 1992. Born in Inglewood, Lisa grew up in Costa Mesa. Lisa is married to another popular L.A. personality, Chuck Clifford. Lisa has been an integral part of the Kevin & Bean show on KROQ since 1991, while doing traffic and news for other area radio and tv stations.

MAYBERRY, Carleton "Corky": **KBBQ**, 1969-71, pd; **KGBS**, 1974-75; **KLAC**, 1974 and 1976; **KFOX**, 1975-77; **KLAC**, 1977-83. Born in 1939, Corky was pd during his time at KBBQ. In 1971 he won the Academy of Country Music's Disc Jockey of the Year Award. The same year he was voted *Gavin* Country D.J. of the year - the first time an announcer won both awards in the same year. In 1974 Corky went to WMAQ-Chicago. In August of 1985, the former KLAC Country all-night man was convicted of pandering charges. A native of Amarillo, Corky said he was "just playing along and had no intent to commit a crime." Corky is living in the San Fernando Valley and is employed by Denver Pyle.

MAYBERRY, Jami: **KYMS**, 1983-88. Jami talked about coming to the Southland in an *OC Register* interview: "It was the first time away from my family in Texas, and I had never been treated so warmly by listeners. I would get flowers, teddy bears and books. I felt like I was a part of their lives." Born and raised in Amarillo, she got her radio start while attending Texas A&M

University and she originally intended to become an elementary school teacher. Jami started on a station in Bryan, Texas and moved on to a contemporary Christian

music radio station in Oklahoma City for two years. At KYMS she set history by becoming the first female on satellite radio in the format of Contemporary Christian Music. Her father is Corky Mayberry who won numerous awards for his work at KLAC. "As far as I know we are the only father and daughter to both work in L.A. radio." She moved to WSIX-Nashville in 1990 for overnights. Jami is the narrator of the Patsy Cline Exhibit at the Grand Ole Opry Museum. The station is located on Music Row. "I would rather do overnights in Nashville than morning drive in Dallas."

MAYHEM, Peter: **KEZY**, 1975-77; **KROQ**, 1979-80. Peter started out at KEZY doing production and was the all-night board operator.

MAYNE, Bill: **KZLA/KLAC**, 1983, pd. Bill arrived from KVET-Austin to work middays and be pd. He is now a record executive with Warner Bros. records in Nashville.

MAYO, Butch: **KACE**, 1979-80. Butch went on to program WKRS in New York.

MAZARIEGO, Sandro Erick: **KSCA**, 1997

McADAM, John: **KLAC**, 1975

McARTOR, Gene: **KIKF**, 1990-92. Gene grew up in Culver City and from his front lawn he could see the blinking tower lights at KABC, KFWB, and KHJ. In the 1970s he worked at KOSO-Modesto and KELP-El Paso as "Big John Carter." In a 1995 interview, Gene said: "I borrowed the name Big John from the original and believe me it was a compliment to him that I felt worthy of using his name." When he left KIKF, Gene joined a duopoly in the Inland Empire where he is "B.J." at KOOJ-Riverside and "Davey Croakett" on KFRG-San Bernardino. Gene is very active on the Prodigy BB.

McBRIDE, Norm: **KYMS**, 1973-79; **KNAC**, 1979-81; **KWIZ**, 1988. "Zany Norm" grew up in Arizona.

McCALL, Don: **KPOL**, 1961-63. Don taught radio for many years at Los Angeles City College.

McCALL, Mitzi: **KFI**, 1975-76. Mitzi teamed with Charlie Brill.

McCARTIE, Gary: **KBRT**, 1973-79; **KZLA**; **KBIG**. In 1979, Gary took KBRT all-Christian to take advantage of the "Born Again" movement. In a *Billboard* magazine interview that year, he said, "One thing we looked at was the growing popularity of contemporary Christian concerts at Disneyland and Knott's Berry Farm." Gary envisioned the new format as an alternative for young, energetic and active Christians seeking "an up, positive music station." Gary arrived in the Southland in May 1973 from the Northwest, where he worked at KOL and KETO. Gary concluded his 1979 interview, "I'm fulfilling a vicarious dream of probably hundreds of born again Christians in radio, they're in news, announcing, Top 40...everywhere. But they've never had a place to call their own before, though I know they've all talked about it. I spoke with many of them while researching this format." During the 1990s Gary programmed WMZQ-Washington, DC and in early 1997 joined WXTU-Philadelphia.

McCLATCHEY, Arnie: **KWIZ**, 1966; **KEZY**, 1967-75, pd; **KYMS**, 1975-83. Arnie started his radio career at the age of 15 at KVAN-Portland. After the military he went to Orange County where he worked in radio for almost two decades. In March of 1975, "I became general manager of KYMS in Santa Ana and put on the first Contemporary Christian Music station in the nation," he said in a 1995 interview from his home in El Paso. He eventually bought KYMS along with stations in Phoenix and Denver and kept them until 1983. "I took some time off and then I bought KELP/AM in El Paso in 1984, and I commuted from Southern California to El Paso for eight years until we moved here permanently in the early 1990s." Arnie still does commercials and voice work for "The Word for Today," a national radio ministry heard on 200 radio stations daily and Horizon Radio, another nationally syndicated program.

McCLELLAND, Dave: **KLAC**, 1975-85; **KFWB**, 1975-79. Dave was the racing voice of KLAC serving as reporter and anchor person for Formula One, Nascar, Indycar and short track stock car events. He also subhosted for Jim Healy. At KFWB, he worked weekends and vacation relief. Born in Kansas City and raised in nearby Liberty, Missouri, he pursued football until he was exposed to a microphone as part of an experimental course at Central Missouri State College. After success in broadcasting motor events in the South, Dave moved to Glendale in the fall of 1971 working for the National Hot Rod Association. "I fulfilled a life-long dream in 1985 building my own radio station in Kernville, California." Dave continues to announce all NHRA racing events and does their radio and television commercials. He also operates a 900# results line while anchoring and doing play-by-play hosting chores for 27 ESPN shows. "I cherish fondly my days in Los Angeles radio, a market that is second to none in the quality of product and personnel."

McCLOUD, Doug: **KLON**, 1997

McCLOUD, Jim: **KLAC**, 1984. Jim left the Southland to be pd and morning man at KHOZ-Harrison, Arkansas where he stayed until the summer of 1994.

McCLURE, Holly: **KBRT**, 1992-94; **KKLA**, 1995-97.

The ubiquitous midday hostess on Christian KKLA writes

a family entertainment column that is syndicated in over 355 newspapers, including the *OC Register*. She was born in Coffeyville, Kansas and grew up in Dallas listening to the giants on KLIF and KVIL. Following graduation from school in 1972, Holly flew with Braniff Airlines based in Minneapolis. In between flights she did voice work for many agencies and stations in the Twin Cities and Chicago. A marriage took her to Albuquerque where she continued her commercial voice work. In 1987 she wrote her first column featuring family film reviews. In 1989 she moved to Orange County and continued the family entertainment column for the Irvine World News which led to syndication. At KBRT she hosted an entertainment show called "Holly on Hollywood" and "For Women Only." At KKLA she hosts many midday shows and "Saturday Night with Holly McClure." Her busy schedule includes a weekly entertainment show on OCN (Orange County Network).

McCONNELL, Matt: Matt is the radio voice of the Mighty Duck hockey team.

McCORMICK, Larry: **KGFJ**, 1958-63; **KDAY**, 1963-64; **KFWB**, 1964-68; **KGFJ**, 1968, pd; **KLAC**, 1969-70;

KMPC. Larry made the most successful transition from radio to television news of any disc jockey who passed through the radio landscape. Larry grew up in Kansas City and left his first job at KPRS to work morning drive at KGFJ. "In the spring of 1963 I left KGFJ to join KIIX/TV, Channel 22 for an experiment in [all-black] tv which failed in four months." After a brief stay at KDAY, "I integrated KFWB in early 1964." When KFWB went all-News in 1968, he returned to KGFJ as pd and to work afternoon drive. In the spring of 1967, *Billboard* announced that Larry was voted 4th most popular r&b disc jockey. He hosted a weekend talk show on KLAC for a year. "While still on KGFJ, I started co-anchoring the weekend KCOP/Channel 13 newscasts with an old radio friend, Chuck Cecil." Before long Larry was anchoring a midday newscast and hosting *Dialing for Dollars*. Soon after, Larry was anchoring the nightly news on KCOP followed by weekend weatherman on KABC/Channel 7. "In April 1971 I joined Golden West Broadcasters at KTLA/Channel 5 as the weekday weatherman and KMPC as a news reporter. Larry's on-air presence at KTLA on health and consumer affairs segments as well as the station's weekend newscasts has contributed to its success. In the spring of 1994, Larry was the recipient of the Governor's Award from the Academy of Television Arts and Sciences, saluting his career achievement in Los Angeles television. In 1996 he received the "Mal Goode Award" for lifetime achievement from the Minorities in Broadcasting Training Program and the "Torchbearer" award from the Black Journalists Association of Southern California.

McCOY, G.W.: **KIQQ**, 1980-85. G.W. worked evenings and afternoon at "K-100," which was managed by his father, George Wilson. In the 1990s he went to work for a Jeep/Eagle dealership in the San Fernando Valley.

McCOY, Hugh: **KNX**. Hugh was a highly rated noon newscaster on "KNXNewsradio." He was known affectionately to his colleagues as "Yuma Coy" after a fan letter he received. Hugh died in the mid-60s.

McCOY, Ron: **KLAC**, 1958-60; **KFI**, 1961-79; **KGIL**, 1979-80; **KPRZ/KIIS**, 1981-84; **KGIL**, 1984-86; **KIEV**, 1986. As a kid, Ron dreamed about being a performer. When he was 13 years old, he did live drama as a kid actor. At age 16 while still in high school, he worked for KFEL-Denver. He stayed there nine years, helping to start the first tv station in Denver and earning a bachelor's degree at the University of Denver. His next stop was Salt Lake City where he worked for KALL, KMUR and KLUB for many years. At KFI, Ron worked all-night as the host of "The Night Owl Show." After 40 years in broadcasting, Ron said, "It was time to make a change. I had done everything I wanted to do and wanted to get into another field of consciousness." He became interested in religious science in the late 1970s. In the 1980s he did news fill-in on KPRZ and KIIS. By 1987, he was given the pastorship at a Sherman Oaks congregation. He continues an active role in pastoring for the Santa Clarita Church of Religious Science.

McCOY, Ronny: **KNAC**, 1968-79, pd. Born in Dallas in 1944, Ronny worked for Dallas/Ft. Worth stations WRR, KCUL, KXOL and KVIL, before arriving in the Southland. He is currently in the recording business in Los Angeles.

McCOY, Sid: **KFI**, 1968; **KGIL**, 1971-72. From WCFL-Chicago, Sid arrived in the Southland as relief man for the 50,000 watt station. In 1985, Sid joined Westwood One as vp of Black and Urban programming. He had the nationally syndicated radio show, "Special Edition."

McCULLOCH, Don: **KMPC**, 1982-93

McCULLOCH, Tom: **KFOX**, 1992, gm

McDANIEL, Earl: **KRVD/KPOP**, 1953-58; **KLAC**, 1958; **KDAY**, 1958-61, pd; **KFWB**, 1961-63. One of the

early pioneers when popular music was making a transition between pop and rock 'n' roll, Earl worked morning drive on a station that featured Hunter Hancock and Art Laboe. His morning characters, who included "Tilly the Timekeeper" and "Willie the Weatherman," made him one of the giants in the 1950s. While other jocks would check *Billboard* and *Cash Box* to see what the "happening" records were, Earl went to the juke box operators and record stores to find out what songs people were buying and wanted to hear. His "record of the week" and "sleeper of the week" were new to music shows. The accompanying photo of Earl with Elvis Presley was an event that catapulted Earl to national recognition. RCA's Steve Sholes and Ben Rosner sent Earl to Las Vegas to present the first gold record for *Heartbreak Hotel* on stage. Earl was credited with breaking the song nationally. Earl produced and presented live stage shows with just about every major rock star of the era. He also had the first record hop/dance show on L.A. television. Earl broke *The Chipmunks Christmas Song* and lost his job for a few days. Over a Thanksgiving weekend he was playing it twice an hour and the station owner threatened to fire Earl if he played it one more time. Earl played it and was fired, however, by Monday it was the hottest record at Wallichs Music City and Earl was rehired. While still a jock in L.A. he switched shifts with Hawaii's biggest dj, Aku. The first record Earl played on Aku's show was *Nel Blu Di Pinto Di Blu*. Earl announced the next record as Patti Page's *Old Cape Cod* and played *Nel Blu* and continued to play the song with different song introductions all morning long resulting in much press. He moved to San Francisco to program KEWB and has the distinction of hiring Robert W. Morgan and The Real Don Steele and having them on the air at the same time long before they arrived in Southern California for "Boss Radio." Earl left for the Hawaiian Islands and spent two decades with Senator Cecil Heftel as pd and eventually gm of the legendary KGMB (later call change to KSSK). He took Aku to new heights, capturing an unprecedented audience of over 50% of the listeners in morning drive. Earl was the first to give away $1,000,000 to one person. When he was running KGMB the population of Hawaii was about 700,000. The million dollar contest drew over 4 million entries. He believed in promotion, "If you don't promote, a terrible thing happens - nothing!" Another promotion was "A Car A Day In the Month of May." The promotion culminated at Aloha Stadium where 30 new cars were placed on the field and 200 finalists were given a key with the hope that it would unlock one of the cars. As Heftel's broadcasting empire grew, Earl became president and was involved in WLUP-Chicago, KTNQ and other successful ventures. Earl is retired from radio, lives in Gig Harbor, Washington, and travels extensively. An inspirational byline essay from Earl appeared in the premier edition of this publication. When Earl was asked to give a speech to an organization the person in charge asked, "How shall I introduce you?" Earl said: "Here is a man with no past, only a future." He's always felt that way. He lives by the credo: "Whatever you did yesterday doesn't count. It's the future that counts."

McDONALD, Jiggs: Born John Kenneth McDonald, in 1967 he became the first play-by-play man for the NHL Kings. He was working the Orillia Terriers of the Ontario Hockey Association when fellow Canadian Jack Kent Cooke hired him. It was Cooke who convinced John to find a nickname. According to a profile by Tom Hoffarth in the *Daily News*, Cooke said his brother had a nickname, his sister had a nickname, he had a nickname and his announcer was going to have a nickname. Jiggs was selected because of the popular comic strip at the time. Jiggs is considered one of the best hockey announcers. He has been doing the NHL on a continuous basis since the 1967 expansion, when he was the first voice of the L.A. Kings. He moved to Atlanta when the Flames were founded in 1972 until they moved to Calgary. He was the voice of the Avalanche, Islanders and Toronto Maple Leafs. Jiggs is heard on the Fox network.

McDONNELL, Bruce: **KFWB**, 1968, nd

McDONNELL, Joe: **KGIL**, 1975-82; **KFI**, 1988-91; **KMPC**, 1992-94; **KMAX**, 1994-96; **KWNK**, 1996-97; **KABC**, 1997; **KIIS/AM**, 1997. Born in 1956, Joe started in radio at KGIL in 1975, when he was 19 and attending L.A. Valley College. He left KGIL in 1982 and became a free-lancer, working for AP radio, UPI radio, Mutual radio, NBC radio and Unistar. In the summer of 1988, he went to KFI to become a producer for his close friend Chris Roberts, who did a nightly sports talk show. "Joe's the godfather," says Chris. "The Godfather. He is who he is on the air. There's no BS." By the end of that year Joe hosted a weekend show and did fill-in work. Joe started on KMPC January 11, 1992, with the debut of the all-Sports format on KMPC. During part of his stay he teamed with Todd Christensen and later with Doug Krikorian. When he teamed with Krikorian the show was called "McDonnell-Douglas" (referring to the aircraft plant in Santa Monica). *LA Times*' Larry Stewart said about Joe: "He has been described as a Howard Cosell without brains - or worse." Joe says he broke the Shaq-to-the-Lakers story and had a 3-hour in-studio interview with

Wilt Chamberlain, who hadn't done a talk radio show in 20 years. "I'm known as a talk show host who is a journalist as well. Most of my colleagues can't say the same." The *Daily News* listed the top 10 sports-talk radio hosts and Joe was #1: "McDonnell's strong-headed beliefs, passionate approach and pursuit of the truth have always been there." As far as the Stewart comment? "His comment was in jest, just his way of tweaking me! He sometimes thinks I'm too controversial, and that's his way of telling me." In early 1997 Joe joined KABC's "SportsTalk" and in the summer moved to "XTRA Sports, 1150."

McELDOWNEY, Kate: **KGIL**, 1986-87

McELHINNEY, John: **KMPC**, 1973-82 and 1987-92. "Big John" has had numerous careers but cherishes the time when he was part of the KMPC morning drive team with Robert W. Morgan and Marv Howard. Born in 1925 in Oakville, Iowa, John moved to the Southland when he was a youth. "Oakville had 500 souls." After serving in the military, he was discharged in 1946 and went to work in a gas station. "I was pumping gas and changing oil. Two L.A. cops came to the station every day and they encouraged me to take the police examination. I took the test at Hollywood High, was hired and spent 20 years as part of the helicopter unit of the Los Angeles Police Department." After a midair collision that took the life of KMPC's Max Schumacher, it was a very "unsettling time" for John. He left the police department and became general manager of Bell Helicopter's Van Nuys Center before going airborne for full-service KMPC. He left KMPC in 1982 after undergoing open-heart surgery. "I ran away to Salem, Oregon. I knew my flying career was over and I was feeling sorry for myself. I needed an escape vehicle." John worked in radio and was a tv weatherman in Oregon. In 1987 he returned to KMPC and experienced his happiest times. "For a while Marv and I did a one-hour show together each morning before Robert started his shift." John and his wife Doris live in Wofford Heights, between Kernville and Lake Isabella. "Our cabin sits on the side of a hill and it looks over the lake."

McELROY, Leo: **KNX**, 1960-63; **KFI**, 1963-69, nd; **KRLA**, 1969-71, nd; **KFWB**, 1971-72; **KABC**, 1972, nd; **KROQ**, 1972-74, nd. The former news executive with many Southern California radio stations was born in Los Angeles in 1932. He grew up in Baldwin Hills and graduated from Loyola University. "I wanted to be an editorial cartoonist but I turned out to be a better writer. At Loyola I started as an English major with an emphasis on journalism, but was advised that a radio and television major might serve me well when the industry discovers it needs real journalists. Four years at the campus station sealed my fate." After a stint in the Air Force, he started his radio career in 1956 at KAVR-Apple Valley followed by KBVM-Lancaster and KMJ-Fresno. In 1960 he won a job at CBS Network as a staff announcer. "I voiced the last network cue for the 'Amos and Andy Show.'" At KFI Leo was the first news director. At KROQ, he was vp of news and public affairs. "Joining KROQ was the worst decision of my life. There were management revolts and I was the only person not fired but I begged to get out of my contract." In 1974 Leo started a public relations firm in L.A. but a few months later was asked to temp at KABC/Channel 7. "I stayed until October 1981. Pretty long temp job." During his stint at Channel 7 he made frequent visits to cover Sacramento news and became engaged to a legislator. When he left KABC he moved to Sacramento, where he has resurrected his PR business specializing in political consulting.

McENTYRE, Debbie: **KNX**, 1992-93

McEWAN, Doug: **KGIL**, 1972. Doug hosted a weekly comedy hour. He was Dick Whittington's resident critic, Cincinnati Armory - KGIL's answer to Cleveland Amory.

McEWEN, Bob: **KDAY**, 1966

McFLY, George: **KPWR**, 1992-93. George was a Minneapolis broadcasting school student in the early '80s. By 1987, he was working in DeKalb, Illinois. High energy was George's trademark during his brief stay in L.A. He arrived at "Power 106" from WBBM-Chicago and a year later left. George claims he received his inspiration from cartoons to keep his show fresh. By 1988, George was voted one of America's sexiest deejay's as profiled in the April issue of *Playgirl*. Unhappy living in Los Angeles, in May 1993, the then 31-year-old put a find-a-job classified ad in the trades that said in part, "More than just a rhyme, get me outta the city of slime." He was nominated for 1993 *Billboard* magazine Top 40 Radio Air Personality of the Year. Advertising works. Since 1993, George has worked morning drive at WVIC-Lansing, rejoined WBBM, WWZZ-Washington, DC and in the fall of 1996 moved to KHHT-Denver.

McGARVIN, Dick: **KKGO**, 1980-89. Dick's first L.A. radio experience actually occurred when, at the age of 6,  he was one of kids who appeared on the *Art Linkletter Show*. "It was the first time I ever talked into a microphone and I immediately became anxious for my voice to change." It was a love for music that guided Dick to the world of radio, and later to acting. He was the first drummer for Paul Revere and the Raiders and an actor in *Die Hard 2* and *Fletch Lives*. Born in Los Angeles, his family moved to Caldwell, Idaho when he was 7. While in high school he worked at the local music store where the pd of the Caldwell radio station would frequent. "One day the pd came in and asked if I wanted to test my voice for radio." So, in his junior year Dick started on KCID-Caldwell doing weekends and eventually worked full-time. He got his FCC 1st Phone from Ogden's in 1957 and began working at KGEM and KIDO-Boise and KIMN-Denver, but always his eye was to work at KSFO-San Francisco. An active musician, his heart was in jazz and, at one point, he put his radio career on hold and went on the road with a band, but when they broke up he returned to radio. In 1965 he joined KVI-Seattle and a year later was one of the personalities on KSFO. He worked in the Bay Area from 1966 to 1974 during the days of the legendary Don Sherwood, Al Collins, and Jack Carney. In 1974 he was cast as the emcee in *Smile* which prompted him to move to Los Angeles and pursue a freelance career of music, voiceovers and acting. Among his many movie and tv credits are roles in *The Rockford Files*, *Dallas* and *WKRP In Cincinnati*. "The day I arrived in L.A., I found the jazz station on the dial (KBCA, later called KKGO) and they were playing a track from an album I'd recorded! What an omen, I thought." Dick called the "hot line" and developed a telephone friendship with the announcers. He got his own show on KKGO in 1980 and stayed until the end of 1989 when the station changed formats from Jazz to Classical music. Dick still lives in the Southland doing voiceovers, composing and appearing with his jazz group.

McGEARY, Richard: **KWKW**, 1950-52; **KHJ**, 1952-57; **KNX**, 1961-67; **KHJ**, 1973-80, gm; **KGIL**, 1983-93, vp/gm. Richard has not lost his New England accent which was evident as he talked about his retirement from a long career in the radio business. He lives a handful of miles from the beach in Vista in a house overlooking the third fairway at the Shadow Ridge Country Club. Born in Brockton, Massachusetts, Richard was a pre-med student at Western Reserve University in Cleveland and graduated from Kent State. Richard started his career as an account executive at KWKW in 1950 and two years later landed a coveted sales job with Mutual Radio's KHJ from 1952 to 1957. "I had been out of school for only two years and the man I was interviewing with wanted someone with more experience. I said 'how do I get experience if you won't hire me?' He did and I stayed there five years." In 1957 Richard went to NBC spot sales in Los Angeles and San Francisco and then to Katz tv Representatives. In between KNX and his return to KHJ he was at KABC/Channel 7. After running KHJ he was Western division VP sales of Mutual Radio Network. Richard retired in 1991. "While I have many pleasant memories of my broadcasting career, retirement has enabled me the time to travel more frequently, enjoy the fantastic weather here in Vista, and to get out on the course more often to bat the ball around."

McGLAUGHLIN, Tom: **KNOB**, 1965

McGOVERN, Terry: **KWST**, 1980; **KRLA**, 1982-83.

Terry was the nasty man who fires Robin Williams in the opening scene of *Mrs. Doubtfire* and the anesthesiologist in *Nine Months*. Born in Pittsburgh, Terry worked in his hometown at KDKA and had a successful run in San Francisco at KSFO and KSAN before arriving in the Southland where he worked mornings at "K-West" and KRLA. For 12 years he made hundreds of tv appearances including guest star roles on *Cagney and Lacey*, *Happy Days* and *St. Elsewhere*. He was a season regular on the CBS series *Charlie and Company*, starring Flip Wilson and Gladys Knight. He created the voice of Launchpad McQuack for Walt Disney's *Ducktales*. Launchpad has since spun off to become second banana in *Darkwing Duck*. Terry returned to San Francisco to enjoy much success at K101 and KYA. Since 1994 he has hosted *Bay TV* morning show on the local NBC station. He's an ardent supporter of the Muscular Dystrophy Association. He lives in Marin County with his wife, Molly, and their sons, Brendan and Anthony.

McGOVERN, Tim: **KRLA**, 1982. Tim was Terry's brother and did sports on his KRLA morning drive show.

McGOWEN, Jewel: **KACD**, 1994-95

McGREW, Rod: **KJLH**, 1973-78, pd. Rod joined the Stevie Wonder station in early 1973. The station was mixing jazz, mellow soul and contemporary MOR. In 1978 he hosted "Jazz Album Countdown," produced by Orcas Productions. At the height of its popularity, the three-hour weekend show was carried by 101 stations and 300 Armed Forces Radio Network stations around the world. In 1974, Rod was pd, manager and air personality at KJLH. His philosophy with his on-air staff: "We don't want a playlist which has to be adhered to. Whatever they want to spin within the format of the station is fine with me. Their only guideline is to communicate kindness, joy, love and happiness."

McILVAINE, Red: **KLAC**; **KHJ**, 1964-65; **KFI**, 1968. Born in Trenton, Red began his career as a 16-year-old radio announcer in Wilkes-Barre. He returned to his hometown in Trenton, where he met radio man Ernie Kovacs. Kovacs, who went on to become a renowned comedian and tv star, encouraged Red to audition for band leader Horace Heidt's network program, and at age 17 he became the youngest announcer on network radio. He spent six years touring the world with Heidt. Las Vegas became his home after short radio stints in Southern California. In Vegas he quickly became a hit as host of a morning radio show that dominated the Southern Nevada airwaves for decades. Over the years he wrote a twice-a-week column for the *Las Vegas Sun*, hosted a television show, was a tv news anchor and a casino publicist. As he fought brain and lung cancer, his humor was evident when he joked in a 1992 column about undergoing so much chemotherapy and radiation that on very dark nights he glowed. He died of cancer on January 11, 1993, at the age of 64. The head of marketing at the Stardust Hotel said of Red, "He unquestionably was the most popular broadcast personality to ever work in Las Vegas. His golden voice, wit, humor and talent to produce a radio show so popular Las Vegas probably will never see its match."

What was the last book you read?
"John Grisham's 'A Time To Kill' - however, you must understand I've read all his books, but not in any particular order."
-Top Ten personality Dave Hull

McINNES, Linda: **KLOS**, 1980-84. Linda hosted a syndicated 30-second show called "Radio Active" on London Wavelength. She did weekend work in the mid-1980s on KSFO/KYA-San Francisco. Since 1992 she has been holding down the evening shift at KFOG-San Francisco.

McINNES, Pamela: **KGIL**, 1978-79; **KMPC**, 1979; **KMPC/KEDG**, 1987. Born in New Zealand in 1948, Pamela has worked traffic helicopter reporting for a number of L.A. radio stations.

McINTYRE, Doug: **KMPC**, 1996-97; **KTZN**, 1997; **KABC**, 1997. Doug hosts an evening talk show at KABC. His program has been described as an entertaining, off-the-cuff style talk show. Doug is a tv writer by trade. He has worked for all four major networks. Born and raised in New York, Doug has lived in L.A. since 1985. He started his career as an advertising writer and producer.

McINTOSH, Richard: **KPRZ**, 1980-81, gm; **KWIZ**, 1996, gm. Richard arrived at KWIZ in early 1996 from a similar post at KFRG/KOOJ. He is now consulting a station in Arizona.

McINTYRE: **KLAC**, 1959-60

McKAY, Dan: **KLIT**, 1990-91, pd. Dan was from Lafayette, Indiana and worked at Transtar before seguing into "K-Lite." He returned to Lafayette where he is programming WGLM.

McKAY, JJ: **KIIS**, 1984. Born Jordan James "JJ" McKay in Washington, DC, he grew up listening to "Good Guys Radio...WPGC." His dream was to work at 'PGC. "My dream was fulfilled when Steve Kingston hired me in 1980." JJ graduated from La Sierra High School in Riverside in 1973 and worked for his father, Chuck Sullivan, who was gm of KREL-Corona. JJ began his career at WOHN-Herndon, Virginia in 1978. Some of radio stops include KHKS and KHYI-Dallas, WAVA and WRQX-Washington, DC, WYXR-Philadelphia, WZOU-Boston and WROQ and WBCY-Charlotte. He is the public address announcer for the Washington Bullets and is the image voice of over 80 radio and tv stations. His company, JJ McKay Productions produces local and national commercials.

McKAY, Larry: **KHJ**, 1974-75; **KKDJ**, 1975; **KIIS**, 1975-81; **KFI**, 1981-82; **KMPC**, 1982-92; **KRLA**, 1992-96; **KFWB**, 1996-97; **KRTH**, 1997. Born in Detroit as Larry McCabe and growing up with polio, Larry never let his handicap handicap his three decades as part of the Los Angeles radio landscape. Larry came to Los Angeles from WERK-Muncie, Indiana where David Letterman worked part-time and weekends. As part of Larry's afternoon drive show on KIIS, he teamed with Gary McKenzie to send up the news with the "Lar-Gar Report." Larry was the voice at the Fabulous Forum for three years during the L.A. Lakers' "Magic" years, which included two NBA championship seasons. Larry considers two highlights during his stay in Los Angeles radio as working at "Boss Radio" and for a decade at the "Old Cowboy" Gene Autry's 50,000 watt radio station, KMPC. He does voiceovers on *Married With Children*, *Blossom*, and *Fresh Prince of Bel Air*. Larry currently does fill-in at KRTH and KFWB and is one of the tv booth announcers on KTLA/Channel 5. He also works part-time at WW1's Oldies Channel.

McKAY, Ed: **KNX**, 1993-97. Ed does vacation fill-in and overnights at KNX.

McKAY, Maggie: **KSRF**, 1987-89; **KMGX**, 1992;

KXEZ, 1993-96; **KIBB**, 1996; **KCBS**, 1997. Born in the Southland, Maggie grew up in Brentwood and went to Marymount High School. She graduated in 1984 from USC with a degree in communications. "I have two passions in my life, photography and music. I figured that it was so hard to make a living as a photographer, I had no idea what I wanted to do when I got out of USC." Maggie started in the programming department at KBZT/KRLA/KLSX and found radio fascinating. Her first on-air job was at KSRF. Between 1989 and 1994 she worked the Country format at Unistar (later WW1). Short stints at Oxnard and KMGX led to a three-year run at KXEZ. Maggie now works all-nights at "Arrow 93."

McKAY, Mark: **KEZY**, 1986-93; **KIKF**, 1993-95. Born Mark Highleyman, he grew up in Orange County and graduated from Chapman College in 1990. In his freshman year of college he started his radio career as Mark the Shark doing mornings with Rick Lewis providing voices and characters on KEZY. He eventually got his own show. In 1993 he moved over to the Orange County Country station as "Mustang" Mark. Mark is focused on becoming an actor and while pursuing his dream he manages Lew Webb's Irvine Nissan dealership.

McKAY, Tom: **KDAY**, 1972-73; **KNX/FM**, 1973; **KWST**; **KNX/FM**, 1979-82. A graduate of Notre Dame, the Buffalo-born jock worked at WKBW, the big AM powerhouse in the '60s, before he shuffled off to KDAY. At KNX/FM he did the "Odyssey File" featurettes. He's currently living in Maine where he is writing.

McKAYE, Verna: **KCBS**, 1992-95. The Philadelphia native got started at WUSL and WSNI in her hometown. She joined KCBS when it was an Oldies station and stayed with the format change to "Arrow 93" in September of 1993. Verna held down the overnight shift through both formats and departed the station in the summer of 1995. She works the overnight shift on Westwood One's 70's format and does voice work for Premiere Radio.

McKEAN, Michael: **KPPC**, 1970-71. Michael was part of the nationally acclaimed "Credibility Gap" that spoofed the news at a time when it needed spoofing. He has gone to much success in Hollywood where he acts, writes and directs. Michael has appeared in such films as *Radioland Murders*, *Airheads*, *Coneheads*, *Man Trouble*, *The Big Picture* (also screenwriter) and *This is Spinal Tap* (also screenwrier, music and lyrics writer). He is in his second season in the cast of *Saturday Night Live*. He received Best Actor in a Comedy Series Cable ACE nomination for *Dream On* and *Sessions*. He also directed several episodes of *Dream On*. He first gained national recognition playing Lenny Kosnowski, teamed with Squiggy (David Lander) in the hit tv series *Laverne and Shirley*. David grew up in Manhattan and attended Carnegie Mellon Institute and New York University.

McKEAN, Rod: **KRKD**, 1965-70, nd; **KIIS**, 1970-75. Born in Riverside in 1932, Rod started at KRKD doing jazz and the station eventually became "the album station." After KIIS Rod got out of radio, he moved North and followed his passion working with horses.

McKENZIE, Gary: **KIIS**, 1977-79, nd. Gary's radio career began as an 8th grader helping his father build the transmitter for the family radio station WJRM-Troy, North Carolina. By his sophomore year in high school he returned home to Lynwood where he broadcast the high school football games. His idols were the "Boss" jocks and "20/20" newsmen at KHJ. From his home in Vienna, Virginia, Gary said, "When I grew up I wanted to be J. Paul Huddleston." Gary went into the Army and served briefly with Armed Forces Radio in Germany. In 1969 he started his radio journey in Big Bear, moving on to Corona, Riverside and Bakersfield. In 1973, he became news director for WXLO-New York. In 1977, Gary realized his dream of working in his hometown becoming the Golden Mike award-winning nd of KIIS. Network radio called in late 1979 and Gary became a charter newscaster for the RKO Radio Network and he stayed for nearly 15 years through the purchases by United Stations-Dick Clark and Unistar. In 1990 the network operation moved to the Washington, DC area. Two years later Gary expanded his horizons and, preparing for the inevitable closing of the network news operation started Ask The Expert Media. The company produces radio and Internet programming and operates an ad agency which specializes in radio and Internet banner advertising. It's Digital Dominion Partners Division builds and maintains radio station websites. "It's been a great ride, especially since I've never worked for a living...just having a ball and getting paid for it."

McKEON, Jim: **KWST**, 1974-76, pd. On New Year's Eve 1974 at six, L.A.'s newest AOR blasted off with Elton John's *Funeral For A Friend*. Helming the new operation was Jim, who had distinguished himself in Detroit at WCAR, WRIF (Jim was the first jock ever to be hired by an 18-year-old Lee Abrams) and "W4." Jim and his seat mates (David Perry and John Detz) on American Airlines Flight #41 from Detroit to Los Angeles the day after Christmas 1974 had never been to California. Arriving at KWST with no cart machines nor the right music, in less than a week the station was launched with Jim as pd and morning man. Born in Springfield, Massachusetts, he grew up in Detroit. Jim attended Holy Cross College in Massachusetts and graduated from the University of Detroit. During the 1980s Jim held various promotional positions with Epic, Columbia and RCA Records. In the 1980s, he and John Detz formed Visionary Radio and owned a series of small market radio stations. In 1992 Jim became part owner and president of KTYD-Santa Barbara and hired his buddy from Detroit, David Perry, to run the day-to-day operation. They now own three stations in Santa Barbara. Jim is president of M3 (McKeon Music Marketing) and lives in Seattle. He married the ex-wife of Steve Dahl in the 1970s. As for living in the Northwest, Jim commented, "I have no intention of ever living anywhere else."

McKEOWN, Kevin: **KROQ**, 1976-78, gm. While attending Yale University, Kevin worked at the campus station as md and dj. After college he worked for a series of Hartford/New Haven stations. After he left KROQ Kevin was a voiceover talent, creative director of JAM Advertising and owned L.A. RadioWorks studio in Santa Monica. He was executive producer of "Hollywood Niteshift" radio show with Phil Austin and Frazer Smith. Kevin produced the "History of San Francisco Rock" with Raechel Donahue for KFOG-San Francisco. He is currently a computer communications consultant working with businesses, L.A. County government, Santa Monica/Malibu Unified School District and local social service agencies.

McKINNEY, Bill: SEE Brother Bill

McKINNEY, Jeff: **KNX**, 1992-94. Jeff was one of the weekend news anchors on KNX, the CBS all-News station. He now works for WCCO-Minneapolis.

> *"I'm teaching people to have faith in their dreams. I want to show how it's better to dream up your solution rather than worry about your problems."*
> *-Michael Benner*

McLAUGHLIN, Bob: **KFWB**; **KLAC**. Bob was one of the power "Big Five" jocks at KLAC during the 1950s. His signature was a garage full of recorded interviews that he ran, simulating a broadcast from a night club, the "5-70 Club" (KLAC's dial position). He had every major star on disc, talking about his or her career. An alcohol-related incident on the roof of a Hollywood Boulevard building led to his rapid decline. After Southern California, he headed for KBAB in San Diego and, in the mid-1960s, was working afternoon drive in Lompoc. He died in 1977 at age 63.

McLAUGHLIN, John: **KOCM**, 1991, gm

McLEAN, Hal: **KFOX**, 1973. Before Los Angeles, Hal worked at KULF-Houston.

McLEOD, Reid: **KWIZ**

McMILLAN, Bill: **KRLA**, 1959-66, nd; **KABC**, 1966; **KNX**, 1967. Bill was news director during the glory years of Rock KRLA. Bill was cited by the *LA Times* as announcer of the year. The paper said although KRLA was a rock and roll station, the station covers the news like no other. "When John F. Kennedy was assassinated, we were the only station in Los Angeles to offer 24-hour news coverage until after the funeral. I had every stringer and available newsman working around the clock. We had built a bank of actualities that back-to-back ran 7 straight hours. KRLA was the last station to revert to regular programming." Bill was born in California and raised in Alhambra and worked for Armed Forces radio from 1945 to 1953. "When I got out of the service I had no idea where I wanted to work so I joined an Army buddy in Erie, Pennsylvania and started my commercial radio career." Bill went on to KVOO-Tulsa, WKY-Oklahoma City and WHB-Kansas City before joining KRLA. "I knew Jimmie O'Neill from Oklahoma City and he helped me get the job at KRLA." During Bill's time at KRLA, over a four-year period he produced 200 half-hour documentaries and won a Golden Mike for a story on drug addiction. After KNX, Bill got out of radio. "I was 40 and wanted to do something different." His "something different" was returning to Oklahoma City and opening up an advertising agency specializing in PR and production services. Bill returned to the Southland, currently runs a similar agency in Orange County and is active in commercial voiceovers.

McMURRAY, Jeff: **KLOS**. Jeff is currently pd of KYYS-Kansas City. He has worked at KRXG/KSEG-Sacramento, KZTR-Ventura, Palm Springs and Jackson, Wyoming.

McNAMARA, Shaune: **KHJ**, 1977-80, md; **KHTZ**, 1980-84; **KHJ**, 1984-86; **KRLA**, 1987-90, md; **KLSX**, 1990-92, md; **KRTH**, 1992-93, md; **KCBS**, 1993-94, md. Shaune was music director for all the major contemporary stations over a two-decade period. In the mid-1980s she was the assistant to the publisher of *R&R*. Shaune works with her husband, The Real Don Steele, on various projects.

> **"The Day the Music Stopped"**
> **-KABC, August 1, 1960**

McNEAL, Jeff: **KUTE**, 1979; **KHTZ**, 1979; **KIIS**, 1979-82, **KGGI**, 1981-82; **KRTH**, 1991. Jeff was born and raised in Pasadena, listening to the '60s personalities on

"Boss Radio," KFWB and KRLA. He decided at age 13 that he wanted "to become a dj as a way to have fun and entertain in a great way. I wanted to rekindle the interest in foreground personality that shaped the radio I grew up with." At 15, Jeff set a goal of being a dj in L.A. by the time he was 25. He was off by a number of years starting at KUTE when he was only 19 years old. Prior to "Kute 102," he attended Pasadena City College and served an internship at KRLA as music research and promotion assistant. Jeff got his FCC 1st Class License while attending Don Martin School of Communications in 1978 and started his career at KIDD-Monterey. Within five months he was offered a job at KACY-Oxnard. En route to his new job, the Oxnard pd who hired him was fired. It was an auspicious start; however, within a few months Jeff's goal had been attained. After only nine months in radio he was hired by Bill Stevens to work part-time at KUTE. He then flip-flopped back and forth with KIIS, going back to a full-time job at KUTE working evenings and middays before leaving for a brief evening stint at KHTZ and then back to KIIS for two years. During his last nine months at KIIS, he doubled as morning man for Chris Roberts at KGGI in San Bernardino. In 1982 Jeff moved to San Francisco to work afternoon drive at KYUU where he remained until 1988. After leaving KYUU, Jeff started his own production agency while working at KKIS-Concord. Lured back to radio in 1990, Jeff moved to San Diego and struggled to survive the vagaries of the business while trying to build a larger customer base for his production agency. After less than memorable stints with "Y95," KCBQ and KFMB-San Diego, Jeff left radio to focus entirely on his business with successful results. Today, Jeff serves hundreds of clients in over 40 states, owns two homes in San Diego and works from a studio in one of them. "I'm one of the most fortunate people I know. I'm independent, very happy with how my life has turned out and I'm grateful that my career in radio helped prepare me for what I do now." Would he go back to radio? "I never want to say never, but it's very unlikely. I had a great time for the first ten years, but I recognized my limitations and made the choice to move on. Besides, I never liked working on the weekends. I'd rather spend them with my wife, two sons and daughter, doing what I want to do."

McNEAL, Pete: **KHJ**, 1970-72. Pete never jocked outside of the state of California. Before arriving in the Southland, he worked at KEAP and KYNO-Fresno and KYA-San Francisco.

McQ, Lon: **KJLH**, 1990-97. Born Lawrence Williams, Lon has worked virtually every shift at Urban KJLH as well as om duties.

McROBERTS, Earl J.: **KDAY**, 1958-60; **XTRA**, 1961-66; **KFWB**, 1967-72. "In 1960 I established the Broadcast Journalism Company and put together the first all-News station in Southern California for Gordy McLendon. XTRA news debuted May 6, 1961." Earl grew up in Wisconsin and while attending the University of Wisconsin, World War II came along and Earl joined the Marine Corps. After the war he worked on his family farm until he realized that he could never make a living farming. Earl went to a broadcast school in Minneapolis and started his radio career in Ely, Minnesota. "I made 30 dollars a week. I worked seven days a week, which was no problem because there was nothing else to do in town. When the temperature hit 51 degrees below zero one day, I moved on." By 1953 he was pd of KCBQ-San Diego. In 1958 Earl initiated "formulated radio" at KDAY. At KFWB Earl was the military affairs director for Westinghouse Stations. In 1973 he bought a station in Boise and turned it into the 15th all-News operation in the country. In the late 1970s Earl was diagnosed with multiple sclerosis and he returned to San Diego. "I was in a state of denial about my MS, but once I accepted it, I lived life the best I could. It never stopped my spirit." Earl is 75, lives in San Diego.

McSHANE, John: **KMPC**, 1954-59. John was a popular all-night dj at KMPC. He eventually went into politics serving on the city council of Downey. John passed away in the 1970s.

McVAY, Mike: **KTNQ**, 1978. Mike was born in Youngwood, a suburb of Pittsburgh, and began his radio career at WHJB-Greensburg, Pennsylvania. A series of on-air and programming stints in Pennsylvania and West Virginia eventually brought him to "the new Ten-Q" as assistant to Storer national pd Ed Salamon. Mike programmed KTNQ for 10 months before moving on to program KBZT-San Diego in 1980. After only three days in San Diego he moved to WAKY-Louisville and later Cleveland as pd. He served as gm in Mobile and later returned to Cleveland as vp radio for Robinson Broadcasting and gm of Robinson's WMJI/WBBG. In the last decade, he has become one of America's most influential and successful radio consultants. His Cleveland-based company has hundreds of clients worldwide in all formats. Mike has also been involved in the ownership of radio stations in Florida, Michigan and Hawaii. Despite all of his success, he remembers, "To this day, I still treasure an air check where I filled in for legendary talent Charlie Tuna."

McWHIRTER, Robert: **KBLA**, 1967, gm

MEANS, Michael: **KIKF**, 1985-95, vp/gm; **KLOS**, 1995-97; **KABC/KTZN**, 1997. "I wanted to get into medical sales but couldn't land a job so I looked for sales experience in radio." Michael was born and raised in Houston. He graduated from Chaminade College with a degree in marketing. In the late 1960s Michael joined the Navy and was a corpsman specializing in trauma medicine. Michael started his radio career as a salesman in 1982 at KGU-Honolulu. In 1985 he joined the sales department at KIKF and by 1990 had worked his way up to general manager. Michael is on the sales team at KABC/KTZN.

MEANS, Pat: **KACE**. Pat conducts a public service program each week on KACE.

MEDINA, Enrique Gonzalez: **KUSC**, 1996-97. *!Bienvenidos a Nuestra Musica!* Enrique is the co-host of the weekly "Gone Global" program on KUSC. He received a Bachelor of Arts in composition from New York's Mannes College of Music in 1987, the year he moved to Los Angeles.

MEDINA, Oz: **KQLZ**, 1993; **KROQ**, 1993. In the mid-1980s, he was with KZEW-Dallas and joined "91X"-San Diego in 1986. After his L.A. run, Oscar moved to KBCO-Denver and took over morning drive in early 1995.

MEDRIANO, Joel: **KEZY**, 1985-95

MEEKER, Jim: **KWIZ**, 1967; **KEZY**, 1968-70; **KRLA**, 1970-71; **KEZY**, 1975-76. Jim worked afternoon drive at KEZY. He was at the Pasadena Rocker KRLA as production chief and weekend jock on Sunday evenings. In the mid-1970s he worked afternoon drive at KEZY and then went on to the Inland Empire. Jim is retired and living in Oregon.

MELENDEZ, "Slim" Jim: **KYMS**, 1989-95. "I lost 26 pounds in 7 weeks in an on-air promotion for Jenny Craig's Weight Loss program and they nicknamed me 'Slim' and it stuck." That's how Jim, ah, "Slim" described his on-air moniker at Christian KYMS. Born in Santa Monica, Jim got interested in radio while attending Rio Hondo College. He started as a board op at KYMS and eventually worked afternoon drive and was

assistant pd. He's currently hosting weekends at KOLA-San Bernardino.

MELENDEZ, Kiki: **KRLA**, 1996-97. Kiki hosted  mornings at KRLA for seven days before returning to late evening after a program director change. Born Christian Melendez in New York she was nicknamed Kiki by her grandmother. Her first experience with radio was at age 3 when Kiki won first prize in a local station promotion. As a child the family relocated to North Miami Beach and Kiki graduated from Florida Atlantic University in Boca Raton with a major in psychology and a minor in communication. After college she studied to become an actress at the Lee Strasberg Theatre and Film Institute and the Herbert Berghoff Studios. She appeared in many off-Broadway productions and her television credits include *Miami Vice*, *Naked Truth* and *Jeff Foxworthy Show*. Prior to arriving in the Southland she worked the morning show on WNWK-New York. "KRLA was preparing me for the morning show. Management changed and I was back on late night." Kiki left KRLA in early 1997. She is philosophical about her next step. "I always told my friends I wanted to be on radio because I've got so much love to give, God will take care of the rest. Just like I told our audience every night, take a leap of faith."

MELENDREZ, Sonny: **KIIS**, 1972-73, pd; **KMPC**, 1973-80; **KFI**, 1981; **KRLA**, 1983; **KMGG**, 1984-85.

Raised in San Antonio, Sonny majored in radio/tv at the University of Texas at El Paso. He worked Texas radio prior to joining KIIS. The *LA Times*' James Brown wrote about Sonny in the 1974 year-end review of radio ramblings: "Due applause at long last for KMPC rescuing Sonny Melendrez from the weekend catacombs and giving him a regular weekday program...even if it is from 1 a.m. - 6 a.m." In 1979 his midday show was a magazine format. He created a children's version of *We Are the World* to benefit the starving children of Africa and won a Grammy nomination. As a nationally syndicated radio personality, Sonny hosted such top-rated shows as CBS Radio's "The Spirit of Summer" and Drake/Chenault's "Christmas at Our House." He has guest-hosted "American Top 40." He was twice named *Billboard* magazine's Radio Personality of the Year and was also named Nosotros Hispanic Personality of the Year. Sonny has been seen nationally as the host of 130 episodes of Disney Channel's *You and Me, Kid*, a show he eventually took on the road. He appeared in an episode of *The Fall Guy* and as a reporter in *Rocky II*. He often appeared as a comedian on *Love Boat*. While working Los Angeles radio, Sonny was doing stand-up comedy at The Laff Shop and the Comedy Store. Sonny has developed literally hundreds of different voices for tv shows, movies and commercials such as the panicky roach that yells, "Oh, no! It's Raaaaid!" *Baretta's*" talking cockatoo Fred, gremlins in Steven Spielberg's movie *Gremlins* and countless Saturday morning cartoons, like *The Jetsons*. During *Archie Bunker's Place*, every time Archie turned on his tv, the voice the viewers heard was Sonny's. In 1988 Sonny was commended by President Reagan for his efforts to fight the war on drugs. During the Year of the Child, he was named Los Angeles chairman and created "Sunshine Day" as a national celebration of children. Sonny is frequently seen hosting children's shows on cable outlets. He began shuttling from San Antonio to Los Angeles in 1985 to do his continuing free-lance work. In 1995 Sonny was included in the "Dedicated to the One I Love" radio exhibit in the Rock and Roll Hall of Fame.

MELLEN, Johnny: **KNOB**, 1954-57; **KGLA**, 1957-60; **KLFM**, 1961-63; **KEZY**, 1963. "I was drafted the day before Elvis. He got to go to Europe. I got to go to Eniwetok and besides I'm still alive." Johnny worked at Armed Forces Radio in the late 1950s and when he was discharged, he programmed KLFM (later became KNAC) in Long Beach. He sold time at KEZY until the station was sold for $950,000 in 1963. John lives in Hawaii. "Even after thirty five years I still miss those good old days of starving, being unemployed, ownership changes, and management changes. Oh, do I miss it."

MELTON, Jeff: **KEZY**, 1987. Jeff worked afternoons at the Orange County station.

MENDELSON, Barry: **KFI**, 1973. Barry co-hosted "Sports Phone" with Jerry Bishop prior to Dodger games.

MENDES, Victor: **KWIZ**, 1990-96. Victor handles middays on the Orange County Spanish station as "El Bon Bon Chocolait."

MENDOZA, Mark: **KKHR**, 1984; **KUTE**; **KMGG**; **KQLZ**, 1989-92; **KIIS**, 1993-94; **KLOS**, 1996-97. Mark worked at KFXM-San Bernardino before making his way to Southern California radio. He worked at Unistar before replacing long-time overnight jock Brother Bill at KIIS where he was on the air as "Big Watusi" and left in the fall of 1994 to join KCXX-Riverside.

MERCER, Bill: SEE Rosko

MERCER, Gary: **KSRF**; **KALI**, 1985-97, gm. "I discovered a love for radio in Iceland, of all places." Gary quit college to join the Air Force and became part of Armed Forces Radio in Iceland. Since his years in the service he has worked for 24 stations. His career took him to WAYK-Ft. Meyers, WFLA-Tampa, WNDR-Syracuse and WSNY-Schnedtady. Gary spent eight years in Kingston, Ontario from 1972 to 1980 hosting "Mercer in the Morning." In 1981 he joined United Broadcasting and has served in various capacities over the years culminating with being appointed gm of KALI in 1995. Along the way the ubiquitous broadcaster who was born in New York City worked weekends at "K-Surf" and was an instructor at the old Columbia School of Broadcasting from 1988 to 1991. Gary lives in Glendale.

MERCER, Michelle: **KPWR**, 1993-97, pd. Michelle was born in 1967.

MERGEN, James F.: **KLAC**, 1959-71, gsm; **KGIL**, 1971-83, gm. Currently a partner with Ray Stanfield & Associates Media Brokers, Jim joined KLAC as a salesman in 1959. When Jack Kent Cooke bought the L.A. Lakers in 1965, KLAC became the "flagship" station and Jim sold the entire 81-game broadcast package to one sponsor, Sears-Roebuck. He broke new ground since Sears had traditionally been only a print advertiser and the package brought a half-million dollars of additional revenue to KLAC. Jim became gsm in 1969 and worked for eight gms at KLAC over 12 years. The inside joke, according to Jim: "The boss wants to see you." Reply: "Oh ya, who is he?" Jim went on to KGIL and originated the "Ballads, Blues and Big Bands, Too" music format. Jim and Ray Stanfield have been involved in several Southern California radio brokerage transactions. "Where else but in Los Angeles could a small town guy from Fennimore, Wisconsin (pop. 2,222 wonderful people and 4,444 friendly dairy cows) have had breakfast with Duke Ellington, lunch with Arthur Godfrey, brunch with Jack Benny and dinner with Woody Herman and Count Basie." Jim is now "Papa Jim" at home to his six children and ten grandchildren. He has worked with some of the giants in L.A. radio. "For controversy and knowledge, Joe Pyne; for pure creative talent, Al Lohman and Roger Barkley; for pain-in-the ass genius, "Sweet Dick" Whittington, my friend for over 40 years."

MERIS, Alan: **KLSX**, 1994

MERKELSON, Lew: **KJOI**, 1973-74. Lew was originally from the Virginia area and returned to WGAY when he left the Southland.

MERRILL, Adrienne: **KHTZ**, 1985-86; **KGIL/KMGX**, 1989-1990. Adrienne worked for Metro Traffic until 1996.

MESSER, Brad: **KMET**, 1975-77, nd. "Y'know that stage kids go through where they keep asking 'Why This and Why That?' Well, I never grew out of that stage - and it got me the best job in the world." Brad works afternoon drive at News/Talk KTSA-San Antonio. He has made a full circle growing up in San Antonio and now returning to his hometown after a journey that has taken him around the world. After high school, Brad joined the Army and served in the Far East as an interpreter and translator (Chinese language specialist). He started his radio career in Galveston, where his father was a newspaper editor.

He always had a way of capturing the "people" aspect to the news and Brad continued that tradition. Brad began as nd of the legendary Gordon McLendon stations in Texas, KILT-Houston and KLIF-Dallas. By age 30, he was nd of KYA-San Francisco during its #1 days toward the end of the "Flower Period." Brad was next in San Diego. "KGB was the most fun I ever had. The station became a legend under the brilliant guidance of pd Ron Jacobs." Ron teamed Brad and Brent Seltzer for a noon news-and-comment show. "At times it was the highest-rated 15-minutes in San Diego radio." He hosted "Brad Messer's Day Book" which was among the first shows syndicated by Westwood One. For 13 years he wrote a weekly column for *R&R*. Brad is the owner and publisher of "Prep," a show-prep sheet since 1988. He and Carole recently celebrated their 20th wedding anniversary. "We love our golden retriever, Pumpkin, and our uppity cat. In my spare time I love flying my open-cockpit aerobatic airplane."

NBA Basketball Star, Magic Johnson, promoted KMGG (105.9FM), "Magic 106" radio on tv

1984

MEYER, Dave: **KBCA** 1978-80; **KOST**, 1980; **KJOI**, 1980; **KBIG**, 1980-83; **KZLA**, 1983-89; **KKGO/KKJZ**, 1989-90; **KLIT/KMPC**, 1992-94. Dave is a free-lance voiceover talent living in Santa Barbara. He worked in his native Santa Barbara at KTMS and KOVA-Ojai before starting on KBCA. "Although a big jazz fan, I was by no means a jazz snob which worked for KBCA since they were attempting to broaden their audience. I'd like to think that I helped pave the way for stations such as KTWV." Dave's father was in radio time sales in Santa Barbara.

MEYERS, Jack: **KABC**, 1960-80, pd. Jack was the pd for the launch of the new Talk format at KABC in 1960. During his two decades with the station, his passion was overseeing the Dodger broadcasts. Born on the East Coast, Jack graduated from a business school. A colleague said: "Jack was one of the greats. He had this uncanny knack to mentally add a list of multiple numbers and consistently come up with the right totals." In the early 1980s Jack was involved in a serious automobile accident. Some time after the accident he died suddenly.

MEYERS, Joel: **KMPC**, 1983-87. The versatile sports broadcaster is a St. Louis native and studied broadcasting at the University of Missouri. He worked in Detroit for a while and was at KMOX-St. Louis for about a year. Joel joined KMPC to host the "Sports at Six" program from KSFO-San Francisco where he was the sports director. He was the UCLA announcer during the 1980s. In his first year he did color while Ken Derdivanis did the play-by-play. Next year they split the duties and the following year Joel was the play-by-play announcer. By the 1990s Joel was everywhere broadcasting network sporting events. He worked Angels baseball for SelecTV with Rick Burleson and did NFL football for the Mutual Radio Network. His "Sportsline" show on KMPC was dropped in 1987. He told the *LA Times*' Larry Stewart: "Baseball is my true love. Hooking on with a major league team would be the ultimate."

MICHAELS, Al: **KLAC**, 1967. Al was Chick Hearn's first broadcast partner for the L.A. Lakers. According to Larry Stewart he was originally hired to be the Kings' commentator with Jiggs McDonald but Al was switched to the Lakers. He didn't last long. "Chick really didn't want a commentator." A baseball and football player at Hamilton High School, he majored in radio and tv and minored in journalism at Arizona State University. In 1968 Al began broadcasting games of the Hawaii Islanders in the Pacific Coast League. He also called football and basketball play-by-play for the University of Hawaii Rainbows. Since 1976 Al has been part of ABC Sports and play-by-play announcer for NFL's *Monday Night Football*.

> *"When I left KABC, the logical place to look for a new job would be KMPC (now KTZN). The problem is they are owned by the same company."*
> -Roger Barkley

MICHAELS, Bill: **KFI**, 1985. Bill is at WW1's Oldies Channel as pd and on-air as well as off-air pd at Westwood One's 70's format. He met and married Tracey Miller, while working together at KFI. They divorced in 1993.

MICHAELS, Blair: **KIIS**, 1992-93. Blair worked at WPLJ-New York before arriving in the Southland. He started part-time and briefly moved to afternoon drive. Blair left KIIS to concentrate on country formatted-satellite services and the "After MidNite Show" under the name Blair Garner. In the spring of 1997 he began hosting the syndicated "The Country Chart."

MICHAELS, Dave: **KEZY**, 1974; **KDAY**, 1974 and 1977-82; **KUTE**, 1983-84; **KLAC**, 1983-84; **KRTH**, 1986-88; **KIQQ**, 1988-89; **KIIS**, 1989. Dave worked at KMAK-Fresno while in high school and before arriving in the Southland at KYNO-Fresno. He has also worked in Seattle and Tampa. In 1990 Dave became pd of WKQL-Jacksonville. He is now pd of Jacor's WXLY-Charleston.

MICHAELS, David: **KACE/KEAV**, 1992-93. When David left the Southland he went to WLUM-Milwaukee.

MICHAELS, Ford: **KIKF**, 1985-86. Ford worked overnights the Orange County station.

MICHAELS, Johnny: SEE Johnny Laurello

MICHAELS, Lee: **KDAY**; **KJLH**, 1994-95, pd. Lee was from Chicago. He worked at WXLO-New York, WDIA-Memphis, WGCI-Chicago and KMEL and KBLX-San Francisco. He's currently programming WBLS-New York.

MICHAELS, Pat: **KWIZ**, 1976, pd. Pat was head of programming when KWIZ was a soft hits/MOR station.

MICHELLINI, Geno: **KLOS**, 1984-94; **KFI**, 1995-96. Geno joined the "home of rock 'n' roll" in the fall of 1984 from KMEL-San Francisco where he was md. He hosted "Power Cuts" on the Global Satellite Network. In the February 1986 issue of *Playgirl* magazine, Geno was voted one of America's Favorite DJs. A popular feature on his afternoon drive show was "5 O'Clock Funnies." Geno parted company with KLOS in October of 1994 after a decade with the station. In the summer of 1995, he started a Sunday morning talk show on KFI. He told the *OC Register*, "I'm trying to develop some hard news skills. So far, it's gone extremely well." Geno left in the late spring of 1996. KFI's pd described the reason for Geno's leaving: "He doesn't fit KFI. We're like KOST and he's Led Zeppelin." In the summer of 1996 Geno joined KCAL-Riverside for mornings.

MIDDAG, Ron: **KPPC**, 1969-70; **KMET**, 1970-71. Ron was part of the "underground" movement in Southern California. Born in Minnesota, he grew up in San Diego and studied broadcasting at San Diego State. Ron was pd at KPRI-San Diego before joining KPPC. In 1970 he transferred to Metromedia's KSAN-San Francisco and worked there three times. "I was at KSAN under Thom O'Hair, Bonnie Simmons and Tom Donahue." He joined music promotion at Stax and Elektra Records until the early 1980s.. Since 1982 Ron has been an audio engineer at KRON/TV-San Francisco.

MIKKI: **KNAC**, 1992-95. The first time Michelle Parisi heard a tape of KNAC at her home in Madison,

Wisconsin, she screamed: "Oh, my god! The station plays everything." From the airchecks that a girl friend continually supplied and seeing the KNAC posters on MTV's *Headbanger's Ball*, Michelle made it a goal to work at the "Pure Rock" station. Born in Madison, she worked briefly at "93QFM" in Milwaukee and then decided to make the move and as she put it, "I followed the music." In 1991 she got a job at *R&R* and a year later the staff at KNAC gave her the on-air name of Mikki and her dream of working at KNAC came true. When the station changed ownership, Michelle got a job as affiliate relations with Global Satellite. She's determined to get back on the air. And who can argue with her determination? Mikki now works in rock promotion at Geffen Records.

MILES, Bob: **KBBQ**, 1972; **KKDJ**, 1972-73. The native Californian was born in Long Beach in 1941.

MILLER, Alonzo: **KAGB/KACE**, 1975-86, pd. Alonzo spent eight-and-a-half years at KACE, working morning drive, pd and md . He briefly went to MCA Records as a consultant. and in 1985 he returned to radio as pd of KACE. A year later, Alonzo was back at MCA as the director of black music. Alonzo lives in Riverside.

MILLER, Arlen: **KIEV**, 1972; **KBBQ**, **KEZY**; **XPRS**; **KWOW**; **KGIL**. Arlen was Dick Whittington's fill-in at KGIL. He is now a voiceover coach in Hollywood.

MILLER, Bob: **KPCC**, 1984, gm

MILLER, Bob: Born in 1939, Bob is to the Kings what Chick Hearn is to the Lakers and Vin Scully to the Dodgers. The Chicago native has been the announcer for over 23 years and 2,000 L.A. Kings games. There has only been one other announcer in the NHL who has been with one announcing team longer than Bob. He started his career in Oelwein, Iowa and was soon working in Milwaukee. Bob was the voice of University of Wisconsin sports before coming to the Southland in 1973.

MILLER, Bruce Phillip: **KWIZ**, 1973-75; **KKDJ**, 1975; **KIIS**, 1975-80. Born in Chicago, Bruce was a communications major at Southern Illinois University. Before he arrived in the Southland he worked at WLW-Cincinnati. In 1978, Bruce completed his 200th "coffee time" show for Armed Forces Radio. He participated in the radio drama "Alien Worlds" in the late 1970s playing a leading character in the Watermark series. In 1979, he emceed the 50th Anniversary of the Avalon Casino Ballroom on Santa Catalina Island. For one night, the Big Band Avalon turned into a disco. Bruce was the winner of the 1979 top radio personality award given by the California Town Meeting Organization. At the time, Bruce announced he wanted out of radio. He felt it was becoming increasingly difficult to do creative radio. "I have a love-hate relationship with mornings. The part I love is that you're fresh and you're finished at 10. The part I hate is that you have to get up early in the morning." During his tenure at KIIS, he survived three owners, four general managers and seven program directors. In the early '80s, Bruce was the in-flight music host on Continental Airlines. In the late '80s Bruce was teaching at a broadcast school.

MILLER, Harvey: SEE "Humble Harve"

MILLER, Ken: **KMPC/KTZN/KABC**, 1978-97; **KIIS/AM**, 1997. In 1978 Ken became gm of KMPC and in 1983 segued to director of sports marketing. In managing the Los Angeles Dodgers and Anaheim Angels radio package, he is responsible for all Dodgers and Angeles sales activities, and merchandising. Ken is the former senior vp of the Western Region of Blair Radio. During his 37-year career, Ken has had sales responsibilities for the Angels, L.A. Rams, UCLA football and basketball as well as the Dodgers. He is a member of the advisory committee for National Baseball Radio Network. In the summer of 1997 he moved to "XTRA 1150 Sports."

MILLER, Larry: **KLOS**

MILLER, Mark: **KQLZ**, 1991-93. Mark was the utility air personality during "Pirate Radio." He grew up in Michigan and went to Saint Clair County Community College in Port Huron. Mark was trained in journalism to be a writer but happened into WSMA-Marine City, Michigan and started his radio career. His next stop was WHLS-Port Huron and then WWWW-Detroit where he was named *Billboard*'s Program Director of the Year in 1981 and 1982. Before he got to "Pirate Radio" he worked at WWCK-Detroit. When he left KQLZ he continued his voiceover career and has been providing artist management services including radio promotions and publicity. His company, Connections Artist Management, is based in Los Angeles.

MILLER, Stephanie: **KFI**, 1994-95; **KTZN**, 1997. Stephanie's father, William E. Miller, was Barry Goldwater's running mate in the 1964 presidential

election. Born in 1961, she was the youngest of four children in a politically-minded family. Stephanie grew up near Buffalo and was only 3 when her father lost the election. She studied theater at USC, then fell into radio at WCMF-Rochester, WCKG-Chicago and WQHT-New York. When Stephanie arrived in the Southland she was fresh from doing a New York morning drive radio show, stand-up comedy and performing in her own one-woman off-Broadway show. Stephanie's show aired on KFI from January 1994 until June 1995, when she left to do a syndicated late-night tv show. She told Claudia Puig in a 1995 *LA Times* interview: "I never thought about doing talk radio. To me talk radio was like old gray-haired guys talking about the budget." She described late-night tv as the last door that women haven't gone through. "I keep going from one boys club to another: stand-up, talk radio, late night. I keep wanting to get into that boys' locker room. Women deserve the same chance to fail miserably on late-night and embarrass themselves on national television as men do." In a *People Magazine* issue of the 25 Most Intriguing people, her tv show was described: "Sketch collides with talk." The tv show was canceled in late 1995. She returned to radio in the summer of 1997 with a show on "710Talk," KTZN.

MILLER, Tracey: **KFI**, 1982-93; **KABC**, 1994-95; **KMPC/KTZN**, 1995-97. "It's a problem being a woman in morning drive. When you're irreverent, you're perceived as loud, pushy, tough or sleazy. Men can get away with it, but women have to maintain a certain image," Tracey told Gary Lycan in the *OC Register*. She spent over a decade at KFI, first as a news anchor and then as co-host of the morning "TNT" show with Terri-Rae Elmer. She has won four Golden Mike Awards and was honored with numerous prestigious awards. In January 1994 she joined Peter Tilden for afternoons on KABC. In May 1995 they moved to KMPC, where they co-hosted the morning drive program through August 1995. Since the departure of Peter Tilden to sister station KABC, Tracey now co-hosts the "Two Chicks on the Radio Show" at KTZN with Robin Abcarian. Tracey writes humorous articles for the *LA Times Life & Style* section. The single mother of two girls received an on-air marriage proposal in the spring of 1997. Tracey lives in Glendale.

"...but isn't it quiet when the gold fish die?" —*Jim Washburne*

MILNER, Cal: **KHJ**, 1962-63; **KGFJ**, 1965-76, pd; **KKTT**, 1977, gm; **KACE**, 1973-84; **KKGO/KKJZ**, 1984-92. Cal worked at WPEN-Philadelphia and WGBS-Miami in the 1950s and moved to Hollywood in 1959 to be coordinator of radio productions for the five RKO AM stations. He hosted a show on KHJ with Foster Brooks called "Top Star." They would concentrate their entire show on one particular artist. In the early 1960s he did play-by-play for the Lakers. In 1968, Cal was named manager of group operations for Tracy Broadcasting, which included KGFJ. He is now retired.

MILNER, Tom: **KLFM**; **KNAC**, 1963-64; **KEZY**, early 70s, gm. Tom is now living in Hawaii.

MINCKLER, Bill: **KNX/FM**, 1986-87, pd. Bill arrived in the Southland from programming KYA and KSFO-San Francisco. He is currently pd of KKCW-Portland.

MINCUCCI, John: **KPPC**

MINEO, Sal: **KABC**, 1973. The actor in such classic movies as *Rebel Without a Cause* briefly hosted a talk show on KABC. He appeared in close to 50 tv shows and movies including *Giant*, *The Longest Day*, *Exodus* and playing Gene Krupa in the *Gene Krupa Story*. Sal was slain in the parking garage of his apartment complex on Holloway Drive in Hollywood.

MINK, Sue: **KNAC**, 1981-85. Known as "Marie the Minx," she did fill-in work at the "rock 'n rhythm" station, KNAC. Sue went on to work at a "classic rock" station in Las Vegas.

MINNICK, Jim: When Bob Miller arrived to broadcast L.A. Kings games, Jim was his first sidekick but didn't last long.

MINTZ, Elliot: **KPFK**, 1966-68; **KLAC**, 1968-69; **KMET**, 1969; **KPPC**, 1970; **KLOS**, 1970-71; **KABC**, 1973-74. Elliot was born and raised in Manhattan and arrived in the Southland in 1963. When Elliot was on KMET, an article in the *LA Times* referred to his sound as "psychedelic rock or thinking man's rock." A popular feature of Elliot's at KMET was "The After Dinner Mintz." During the time he was on KABC hosting a talk show aimed at attracting a youthful audience, he was also on Channel 7's *Eyewitness News* reviewing rock groups and doing contemporary features. In the late 1970s, Elliot became a "media consultant." Interviewed by phone in 1995, he said, "I advise individuals and CEO's about their relationships with the media." He was guarded on whom he represents. "Publicly I have had a long-term relationship with Melanie Griffith and Don Johnson, and I have represented the John Lennon Estate since 1980." He has been friends with the Lennons since 1971. Other high-profile personalities he has been associated with include Diana Ross and Bob Dylan. His series, "The Lost Lennon Tapes" aired on over 200 stations weekly during the early 1990s. He told the *Times*: "Lennon wasn't an act. He wasn't show business. He was real big. He was real!" In late 1994, Elliot started a new series called, "The Beatle Years."

"Radio is like *Jurassic Park*. It's the Lost World." -Mark Volman

MINYARD, Ken: **KABC**, 1969-97. EGBOK! The morning drive cry for decades that Everthing's Gonna Be Okay! An integral part of that success, Ken was born and raised in McAlester, Oklahoma. He started his radio career in his hometown at the age of 13. Before arriving in Southern California, Ken worked as a dj at KSRO-Santa Rosa, KJOY-Stockton and KSAY-San Francisco. He made the transition to Talk in 1967 at WLOL-Minneapolis. At the same time he did commentary for KMSP/TV and wrote a column for the editorial page of the *St. Paul Dispatch*. He joined KABC "TalkRadio" in November 1969. The director of news and programming transferred Ken to morning drive in 1973 to co-anchor with network veteran Bob Arthur. He was made managing editor. In the mid-1970s Ken was one of the anchors on KTTV/Channel 11's irreverent look at the day's happenings with *Metro News, Metro News*. He appeared as a regular guest host with Dinah Shore on *Dinah & Friends*. Along with his former co-host Bob Arthur, Ken was named "Radio Personality of the Year" by the *LA Times*. The pair's quest for immortality included being honored with a "Starfish" on the Redondo Beach Walk of Fame. On October 1, 1990, Ken was joined by Roger Barkley to co-host the "Ken and Barkley Company." In a 1994 interview in the *Times*, Ken described the success of his long-running top-rated morning show: "We never get bogged down. We find it very easy to switch gears between silly and serious. On any given day, in any half-hour, in the conversation, we can go from screwing around to getting into serious topics." In the summer of 1996 Roger Barkley left the morning show and Peter Tilden joined Ken from sister station KMPC.

MIRABAL, Lee: **KMPC**, 1996-97. Raised as a "Navy brat," Lee was prepared for the "gypsy" world of a radio announcer. Her career began in 1965 at a small radio station in Jacksonville, North Carolina. Her three-decade career in radio took her from receptionist, bookkeeper and traffic person to news anchor, dj and syndicated advice talk show host. As a pd, Lee created a format called "Blues, Ballads & Jazz." She has won 16 Addy awards for her copywriting and her voice has been heard on over 4,000 radio commercials. Lee left her evening talk slot at KMPC in early 1997.

MIRANDA, Reuben: **KALI**, 1986-87. Reuben worked morning drive at Spanish KALI.

MISSMAN, Fred: **KBIG**, 1988-97. Fred works the all-night shift at "K-BIG."

MITCHELL, Bernie: **KPPC**, 1970-71

MITCHELL, Dan: **KEZY**, 1964-83, gm. Dan's uncle owned KEZY and Dan ran the operation. He has since moved to San Juan Capistrano and sells commercial real estate. Dan also has a new radio license in Palm Desert.

MITCHELL, Ed: **KPPC**, 1967-68. Ed was part of the "underground" KPPC sensation of the late 1960s. He arrived with Tom Donahue from KMPX-San Francisco. Earlier in the '60s he worked at the rock powerhouse in San Francisco. Ed moved to Denver and became a cab driver. In a dramatic end to his life, he drove his cab onto the tarmac at Denver Airport and committed suicide.

MITCHELL, Jim: **KFWB**, 1972-78. Born in Pennsylvania, Jim was a part-time news anchor at KFWB. In 1978 he joined KNXT/Channel 2 for 8 years. He is now a tv news reporter in Oregon.

MITCHELL, Johnny: **KHJ**, 1965-67. Born Ed Phillips, one of his goofy stunts early in his career was setting a world record of 195 "stay-awake" hours while on WYDE-Birmingham. He worked for four years in the early 1960s as Johnny Holiday at KCBQ-San Diego before becoming a "Boss Jock." He was also known as Sebastian Stone. In *Billboard*'s 1966 polling of djs, Johnny was one of the leading early evening Top 40 personalities. He left for KFRC-San Francisco to be pd in February 1967. Mitchell worked with the Dave Clark Five during his Northern California stay. He died in his sleep on November 11, 1987.

MITCHELL, Keli: SEE Keli Garrett

MITCHELL, Lenny: **KWIZ**, 1968; **KEZY**, 1969. Born in Brooklyn in 1941, during the 1960s Lenny worked at KAFY-Bakersfield, KDON-Monterey and KMEN-San Bernardino before joining KWIZ. In 1970 he went to KCBQ-San Diego. Lenny now works for the bus company in San Diego.

MITCHELL, Steve: **KIQQ**, 1973-74 and 1979; **KHTZ**, 1980; **KFI**, 1981-82. Born in Greensboro, North Carolina, Steve arrived at "K-100-FM" from WMYQ-Miami. When he left Los Angeles the first time in 1975, Steve worked for two years at KYA-San Francisco and then did ABC record promotion in North Carolina until he returned to L.A. radio. When he left the second time, Steve went to Southern powerhouse WKLS-Atlanta for five years as part of the morning team of "Mark & Steve." They were recruited for KSHE-St. Louis. In 1990, the team broke up and Steve went to WYAY-Atlanta. In 1992, he became the morning producer of WKHX's morning show and coordinates the feed to the ABC Satellite Music Network.

MOBLEY, Candida: **KJLH**, 1986. Candida now runs her own production company and produces short-form radio programs.

MOLL, Alan: **KHJ**

MOLLICONE, Cheryl: **KUSC**, 1984, pd. Cheryl resigned from KUSC in the summer of 1984.

MONDAY, Rick: **KABC**, 1993-97. The former baseball player hosted KABC's "DodgerTalk" show. In 1982 he worked fill-in for other sports announcers on the station. He was part of DodgerVision in the mid-1980s. In 1989 he went on to do play-by-play for the San Diego Padres and returned to be part of the Dodgers broadcast team when Don Drysdale died. Rick led Arizona State to the 1965 NCAA championships and earned All-American and college player of the year. The Kansas City Athletics chose him as the first player ever in the initial major league draft. He spent six seasons with Kansas City and five with the Chicago Cubs before joining the Dodgers in 1977. Rick compiled a .264 career batting average with 241 home runs. Rick began his active broadcasting career as a sports anchor at KTTV/Channel 11 from 1985 to 1988. He's best remembered for two special moments: An April 25, 1976 at Dodger Stadium while playing center field for Chicago, he ran into left field to rescue the American flag from a possible burning by a pair of protestors. In 1981, Rick delivered the game winning-home run in Game 5 of the National League championship series to send the Dodgers to the World Series.

MONDS, Big John: **KKBT**, 1990-93, pd. Before he arrived in Southern California, John was on WQHT-New York and was music director at WUSL ("Power 99")-Philadelphia. He was nominated for *Billboard* magazine's 1993 r&b Radio Air Personality of the Year. He was made pd at "the Beat" in late 1992 and stepped down in the fall of 1993. He left the Southland in 1993 to do mornings at WVAZ-Chicago.

MONROE, Rick: **KUTE**, 1979

MONTAGUE, Magnificent: **KGFJ**, 1965-67; **XERB**, 1968; **XPRS**, 1972. Mention the inflammatory words, "Burn, Baby, Burn" and anyone around Los Angeles in the mid-1960s will mention the Watts Riots and KGFJ dj the Magnificent Montague. In an *LA Times* interview on the 20th anniversary of the Watts Riots, he reflected: "I didn't know nothing about Watts. I had never been to the South Side. I was only in town for six months - I lived in Bel Air. I didn't know what Watts was all about." When he saw "Burn" scribbled on the sides of burning buildings, "it didn't even dawn on me then what it represented." He reluctantly dropped his slogan three days into the riot and never considered using his prominence to rally against the rioting. "I didn't know what the impact was until later. I'm not a social reformer. I'm an entertainer. You can't get me to make statements." In 1967 he left radio for the record business. Within a year, he was back on the radio. While at XERB, he popularized the phrase, "Keep the Faith, Baby." In 1971 he was the national promo manager for Kent Records. Claude Hall in a 1974 *Billboard* magazine article described him as "one of the world's most-heralded and most-copied air personalities, more than the world realizes." He has one of the world's greatest collections of rare books and memorabilia, ranging from movie stills to letters by George Washington Carver and Booker T. Washington to a children's book called *Ten Little Niggers*. His collection is priceless, belying his image of a wild man who yelled "Burn, Baby, Burn" during the Watts riots. Born in 1928, Monty became the Great Montague while working in Houston. During his variegated career, he did remotes with the Big Bopper from a black restaurant in 1953, sold time, recreated baseball games like Gordon McLendon and Ronald Reagan and opened up a record company and an advertising firm. In 1966, and for two consecutive years, Montague was voted the #2 r&b dj in *Billboard* magazine. He claimed that he worked for 80 stations in 50 markets, including WAAF and WAIT-Chicago in the late 1950s. There is much contradiction as to where Montague actually started in radio and there was a period when he moved every few months because he was the original rebel: "The dates and places are all screwed up because I was always getting fired for moving my mouth...trying to bring in unions, things like that." He helped put together the original National Association of Radio Announcers, later known as the National Association of Television and Radio Announcers. In 1976 he opened Montague's Gallarie on La Cienega Boulevard. It was devoted to black culture, and contained rare pictures, books, posters, prints, coins, cards, records, letters, paintings, etc. Over the years, he worked at radio stations in New York, Chicago and Houston. In 1985, he had a big band show on a Palm Springs radio station. The Magnificents, featuring Johnny Keyes, named their group as a tribute to Montague. They were a one-hit wonder with *Up On the Mountain*.

MONTIONE, Joe: **KHJ**, 1979-80; **KUTE**, 1980-81;  **KIIS**, 1992-93. "I was 13 years old and had a 'studio' in my basement growing up in Wilkes-Barre. I would spend hours playing disc jockey and listening to WFIL through the static." At age 16, Joe took a reel-to-reel tape to WFIL-Philadelphia and waited in the lobby for three hours to talk with pd Jay Cook. "He listened to the tape and said, 'I hear something.' He encouraged me to get on a daytimer or any kind of a station in Wilkes-Barre." A dream was encouraged. On the way out of the station, he met his night time idol, George Michael. Innocent and filled with youthful enthusiasm, Joe told George that he would replace him when he left. Joe did as Cook suggested and worked on WILK while a theater arts major at King's College in Wilkes-Barre. During the 1970s, Joe worked at KTLK-Denver, WHYI-Miami, WFIL-Philadelphia (replacing George Michael), WMJX-Miami, CHUM-Toronto and WLOF-Orlando. He has been known as "Banana Joe." Where did the moniker come from? "I was 18-years-old and working for John Rook and Big Ron O'Brien at KTLK. John said there were no Italians in Denver and changed my name to Joe Bradley. In the hallways, he called me 'Joe Bananas' like the underworld figure. Eventually Rook wanted me to be 'Banana Joe' on the air. I thought it was stupid. But it stuck." When "Banana Joe" got to "Y-100" in Miami, owner Cecil Heftel got him a monkey (with diapers) and a white safari suit for his appearances. It worked and his show was the "first FM show in the market to become #1," according to Joe. He arrived in Southern California to work afternoon drive and be assistant pd at KHJ. He won the 1979 Air Personality of the Year Award from the Bobby Poe Convention. During the 1980s he went on to successfully program stations in Wilkes-Barre, Harrisburg and Albany including the purchase of two stations, one in his hometown, and the other in Harrisburg. "I was standing there with my mother and father when the tower went up. It was pretty exciting." He was nominated for National Program Director of the Year for three consecutive years starting in 1983 and won the Broadcast Executive Excellence Award. For three years beginning in 1990, he worked for Premiere Radio Networks as the marketing director. Joe left his pd'ship of WDAE/WUSA-Tampa/St. Petersburg with a new bride, Kris Boyd of Gannett. Joe has studied acting for many years and appeared in a play with Vic Tayback for almost a year in 1989. At KIIS he originated the retro "Banana Joe Flashback Show." When he left KIIS, Joe joined *R&R* as an account executive followed by mornings at WMGK-Philadelphia, SJS Entertainment in New York and currently is pd and morning man at WWGR-Ft. Myers/Naples. "Give it a go, Banana Joe!"

MONTOYA, Dave: SEE Sky Walker
MOOR, Doug: **KTYM**
MOORE, B. Harold: **KGIL**, 1976
MOORE, Billy: **KKDJ**, 1972; **KRTH**, 1972-73; **KGIL**, 1974-75; **KIQQ**, 1974; **KUTE**, 1975-76. Born in 1942 in Chattanooga, Billy came to the Southland to work morning drive at Rocker KKDJ from Don Burden's KOIL-Omaha where he was Bobby Noonan. Under KKDJ pd Bill Combs, Billy produced, wrote and voiced a "British Are Coming" promotion. "I never forgot my promo line - 'get IN the way. The British are coming to KKDJ." Billy was the production director at KRTH and spent five years as the in-house voice for Drake-Chenault syndication on their AC, Rock and Oldies formats. Simultaneously, Billy appeared as the voice for and producer of Redken Laboratories' training modules, national seminar shows and audio visual presentations. He did some fill-in at KIQQ and worked morning drive at "Kute 102." During his time in L.A., he attended the Lee Strasberg Theatre Institute in Hollywood and was active at the Glendale Centre Theatre. In 1979, Billy left the Southland and went to KIDD-Monterey. He talked about that period in his life: "Now that was a job - om, morning man and pre-recording my show for my Monday morning plane trip to L.A. to cut tracks for Drake/Chenault, returning that evening for my duties and the next morning's show at '63KIDD.'" In 1981 he headed to Chicago as the ad campaign manager and copywriter for a local agency and then moved to Zionsville, Indiana. He built an in-home studio where he performs his voiceover work, station imaging liners and promos for radio and tv stations as well as Moore On Hold, an on-hold message service for business telephone systems.

MOORE, Bob: **KEZY**, 1972, sales; **KKDJ**, 1973, sales; **KFWB**, 1974, sales; **KHTZ**, 1980-86, gm; **KLSX/KRLA**, 1986-93 and 1994-97, gm. Born in Appleton, Wisconsin in 1946, the vp/gm of KRLA/KLSX graduated from Wisconsin State University with a major in marketing and business administration. He started his radio career in sales in 1968 for WISM and later WLVE-Madison. In 1991 Bob was executive vp of Westwood One. In 1994 he was made vp/gm of KIKK/KILT-Houston. In the summer of 1995 Bob turned KLSX into a non-traditional Talk station calling the youth oriented format "Real Radio." In an *OC Register* interview with Gary Lycan talking about the new Talk format: "The bottom line - callers will make or break 'Real Radio.' When you factor in commercials, traffic breaks and personality chat, you're left with about 27 minutes per hour for callers." On the KLSX format change he told the *LA Times*: "KLSX will deal with getting to work, the remote control on the VCR-why can't they make one that really works?...Everyday life, relationships."
MOORE, Del: **KLAC**, 1956

> *"Star 98.7 management thought about playing the same songs as the most successful stations in Southern California. After all, it worked for them. But, instead, we decided to try something different. Why? We know they'd kick our butts in. Can't fight back! It's all because we're pathetic weenies. You get to hear a music mix that the other stations won't play. This is 'Star Music.' Don't hesitate to try something new, 98.7."*
> *-KYSR promo*

MOORE, Gary: **KFI**, 1986-88; **KNX/FM/ KODJ/ KCBS**, 1988-97.

Gary is the morning man at "Arrow 93." He has been there for three call letter/format changes. "Can you believe I survived all those incarnations? Must have angels looking out for me." Gary was born July 23, 1958, in Evansville, Indiana and he grew up in Murray, Kentucky. In 1980 he graduated from Western Kentucky College in Bowling Green with a B.A. in theater arts and speech. In 1972 he got started on the Murray State public radio station. "I ran five-hour operas and odd Scandinavian hootenannies." For the next decade Gary worked in Kentucky radio at WDXR and WKYX-Paducah, and WBGN-Bowling Green. In 1980 he worked at WVLK-Lexington where, in addition to his air shift, he wrote and produced "award-winning commercials" for the flagship station for University of Kentucky sports. He spent four years at WRKA-Louisville before joining KFI in 1986. "Nice guy Steve LaBeau hired me for weekends/swing and then to afternoons." In the early fall of 1993, KCBS/FM underwent another change and Gary moved to mornings replacing Charlie Tuna. "It was difficult because Charlie and I were partners in the syndicated show 'The Goodtime Oldies Magazine.'" Gary's hobbies? "I love French and British travel, writing, most all music, occasionally acting, collecting old toys and passionately following Kentucky basketball and the Atlanta Braves." Does he like working morning drive? "Who the hell enjoys waking up at 3:50 a.m. for ANYTHING, aside from sex?"

MOORE, George: **KKTT/KGFJ**, 1978-85, pd; **KPWR**, 1986-88; **KSRF**, 1988-89; **KJLH**, 1989-93; **KMPC**, 1992-94; **KACE**, 1994-97. For over two decades, George

has been an active producer, program director, production manager, voice talent and personality. He was born in Detroit on March 1, 1957, and grew up in the Motor City listening to legendary personalities like Martha Jean the Queen, Butterball, J.P. McCarthy and the CKLW "Big Eight" giants. George was influenced by Walt "Baby" Love, the first African American at the then-powerful RKO General chain, broadcasting on 'CK. "From that point, I wanted nothing more than to be an air personality and I took every communications class in school." While going to Wayne State University in Detroit, he interned at WDRQ which eventually became his first gig. He later moved to WMJC-Detroit. In 1977 George went to KMJQ-Houston until he was hired by his childhood inspiration Walt Love at KKTT. The station eventually returned to its longtime call letters, KGFJ. At KMPC George was there for the Sports/Talk format and worked as talk host, field reporter and sportscaster. In 1992 George had two commercials that he produced, voiced and co-wrote that were nominated for the Southern California Broadcasters Association SUNNY Awards. One of his entries was judged Best in the Radio Station Produced category.

MOORE, Michael: **KHTZ**, 1983-85; **KHJ**, 1985; **KRTH**, 1987; **KBIG**, 1990-97. Michael moved to Orange County when he was age 3. He started doing stand-up in Palm Springs. He is currently doing news on KBIG.

MOORE, Michael "Mixin'": **KCRW**, 1991; **KKBT**, 1994. At the Santa Monica College station, he was known as "Militant Master Mixx".

MOORE, Pat: **KRLA**, 1966-69. Pat grew up in Long Beach and attended Wilson High School. Following graduation in 1957, he enrolled at Don Martin School of Radio and Television, obtaining his first radio job in Winslow, Arizona, before moving on to KACY-Oxnard in

1959. "KACY was perhaps the best of my radio days, working with the likes of Bob Eubanks, Bill Keffury, Bill Wade, Dick Moreland, Jim Steck and others who went on to do some terrific things in the industry." Pat was drafted into the Army in 1961 for a two-year period. While stationed at Fort Bliss (El Paso), he worked evenings and weekends at KELP. Upon discharge, he returned to KACY for a short time before moving to KLIV-San Jose and then on for "two quick cups of coffee" at KDEO-San Diego and KVEN-Ventura, before Moreland hired Pat for the all-night shift at KRLA in 1966. Automation arrived at the station in 1969, and he moved to off-air positions engineering Lew Irwin's "Credibility Gap" news programs and producing commercials and automation voice tracks. In 1970, Pat relocated to Sacramento for 10 years to work for a number of radio and tv stations before returning to Long Beach where he now heads the State Department of Fish and Game's Southern California public information office. In the process of night school and weekend classes, he acquired a business management degree at American River College. "There's little I miss about radio; the dreadful hours, insecurity, the lack of vacation days and holidays off, six days a week and the sad paychecks most of us received in those days. I watched a wealth of very fine air talent work long, sweat-shop hours to make other folks rich. There is one aspect of radio I do miss terribly. The people. They are my kind and perhaps it is the belief that they are a somewhat special kind of person willing to risk it all on the fickle whims of a listening public."

MOORE, Rex: **KGRB**, 1975

MOORE, Rick: **KUTE**, 1980

MOORE, Robert: **KPOL**, 1967-73. Robert's career in the entertainment business started when he was a child member of the singing group, the Mitchell Boys Choir. At KPOL he was a newsman/commentator. When he left radio in 1973 he pursued a career in singing and music. Prior to his death in 1995 he had been remodeling homes. A colleague remembered Robert: "A nicer man you would never meet."

MOORE, Vicki: **KFI**, 1996-97

MOORHEAD, L. David: **KFI**, 1968; **KLAC**, 1969, pd; **KFI**, 1969, pd; **KMET**, 1969-79, gm; **KIIS**, 1981, om. L. David Moorhead was affiliated long-time with Metromedia Broadcasting. Before he arrived in the Southland, David's on-air name was Guy Williams. In Phoenix he was known as Johnny Wallace. One of his early assignments was working at WMMS-Cleveland. At one time David produced the *Arthur Godfrey Show*. In fact, he started his career in 1952 on WSRS-Cleveland. He also was pd of WOKY-Milwaukee and was national pd of Bartell Broadcasting. David was gm of KMET in the mid-1970s and hosted the Sunday night forum "Mangle the Manager." He was also senior vp of Metromedia radio and vp of CBS radio. In the 1990s David moved to Las Vegas and consulted radio stations. He died July 7, 1996, at the age of 62.

MORAGA, Pete: **KNX**, 1969-72 and 1988-93. Pete was an active part of the Hispanic/Anglo broadcasting community for a quarter of a century, one of the first Hispanics in mainstream broadcasting in Los Angeles. Born and raised in Tempe, he graduated with an advertising degree from the University of Arizona in 1949, the same year he started with Arizona's first Spanish-language radio station in Phoenix.

In 1957 he joined the Voice of America in Washington, DC, broadcasting in Spanish and English to Latin America. Five years later he was assigned as assistant press attaché at the U.S. Embassy in Mexico City and in 1967, reassigned as press attaché at the Embassy in Lima, Peru. "It was such a difficult period in Lima that my family had to be evacuated from the country. I remained there for an additional 5 months." Resigning from the Foreign Service, he joined KNX in late 1969. Two years later he became news director of KMEX/TV, a position he held for 18 months before returning to KNX. "With my wife and son, we started our own PR business in 1978. When my 15-year-old daughter died in 1980, it was such a difficult time for us that I returned to KMEX as nd, occupying that post until 1988 when I returned again to KNX." For much of the late 1980s Pctc did a weekly commentary on the Sunday evening news at KNXT/Channel 2. Pete retired in late 1992 and returned to Arizona where he now lives in Mesa. What does he do all day? "I'm doing whatever I damn well please!"

MORALES, Dave: **KPWR**, 1993-97. Dave did morning drive for a couple of months, following Jay Thomas's departure from the station in the summer of 1993, before moving to evenings, afternoon drive and eventually middays.

MORALES, Diane: **KKHR**, 1984, pd; **KLOS**, 1984-87; **KROQ**, 1988. Diane was pd at KKHR before moving in 1984 to KLOS, where she was assistant director of creative services. She was selected 1987 *Billboard* AOR Promotion Director of the Year and is currently doing promotion work.

MORALES, Mucho: **KHJ**, 1977-80; **KRLA**, 1980; **KGFJ**, 1981-82; **KRLA**, 1983-85; **KMGG**, 1985; **KPWR**, 1986-90; **KKBT**, 1990; **KRTH**, 1991-92; **KGFJ**, 1993; **KRLA**, 1993-96; **KIBB**, 1997. Born in 1953, Mucho was working in Tucson when he was 20 years old. He came to the Southland from KFRC-San Francisco, which won the *Billboard* magazine Major Market Station of the Year all three years he worked there. At KHJ he was known as Nick Morales. "I worked all day-parts except mornings." Mucho recounted his success with each station: "When I was at KRLA, I had the highest ARB numbers in the history of the station. At KGFJ working afternoon drive and assistant pd, this dead AM station skyrocketed from a .8 to 2.4. While at 'Magic 106' one book went from .6 to 2.2. At 'Power 106' I was consistently #1 for nearly five years in the 12+ and 18-34 demos. In the 1988 spring Arbitron, I pulled the highest afternoon drive-time number since 1971. In 1989 and 1990, afternoon drive was the only day part that was #1 in the market on KPWR." He was one of the original jocks at KPWR when "Power 106" signed on in January

1986. In late summer of 1993, Mucho replaced Dave Hull in morning drive at KRLA and left in the summer of 1996 when the station switched from Oldies to "Mix 11" format. He now works swing at Rhythm "B-100."

MORALES, Nick: SEE Mucho Morales

MORAN, Bill: **KABC**, 1975-78; **KIIS**, 1979; **KABC**, 1980; **KIIS**, 1981-82; **KGIL**, 1986-88; **KFI**, 1988-90. The Southern California talkmeister was also a 14-year veteran with *Billboard* magazine. All of his weekly talk shows have been entertainment oriented with major artists from film and music except for his 1981 stop at KIIS which was more issue related. Concurrent with his talk shows, for decades Bill has been head of advertising and sales for The Grammy Awards Program Book, The CMA Program Book, Publicists Guild Directory and the Paul McCartney Tour Brochure. Since 1992 he has been director of advertising for the Golden Mike Awards for the Radio and TV News Association of Southern California. Beginning in September 1993 Bill has been hosting a live weekly call-in entertainment show on the Business News Network.

MORAN, Gussie: **KFAC**, 1972. The former international tennis star broadcast sports news over the Classical station, KFAC. She garnered press during play at Wimbledon for wearing "lace panties."

MOREE, Lisa: **KRTH**, 1986-91. The San Francisco native worked on the all-night shift at "K-Earth." Eventually replaced by Nancy Plum, Lisa went to Metro Traffic, where she did reported for KABC and other stations. She returned to the Bay Area with her husband who is the advertising director for a sporting goods firm. Lisa is out of radio and travels the country representing a pharmaceutical company. Lisa started her career in 1981 following graduation from San Francisco State University with a degree in broadcasting.

MORELAND, Dick: **KRLA**, 1961-69. Dick and his wife Pat started the very successful Music + record chain. In 1966, *Billboard* named Dick the most cooperative music director, program director or music librarian in exposing new music. In a 1966 interview, the gm of KRLA credited Dick's musical tastes as the key to his success. Every day Dick ended his show: "This has been a Desert Rose Production. Bye Bye, Buy Bottled in Bond. Bye Bye." Dick died of cancer in the summer of 1988.

MORENO, Raul: **KHJ**, 1980; **KIIS/KPRZ**, 1981-86; **KFAC**, 1987-89; **KKBT**, 1989; **KQLZ**, 1989-90; **KKGO/KKJZ**, 1989-91; **KMPC**, 1990-93; **KUSC**, 1991-93; **KEZY**, 1994-95. Raul is one of those ubiquitous young radio broadcasters who started at the age of 16 answering the request lines at KHJ. He followed Rick Dees to KIIS and became his assistant producer. In 1983, Raul became Bruce Vidal's producer and on-air side kick. He did a weekend air shift on sister station KPRZ. In 1987 he went to KFAC as announcer and production director. When the station became "the Beat," Raul produced the morning show with Paul Rodriguez. When Paul left a few months later, Raul went to KQLZ "Pirate Radio" and produced Scott Shannon's "Pirate" morning show and was one of the many people who was "Russell the Love Monkey." Many of Raul's assignments and radio stations overlap. At KMPC he was studio producer for the California Angels broadcasts. In the late summer of 1994, Raul started at KEZY and coordinates the Mighty Ducks Hockey radio broadcasts along with production and promotion assignments. Raul is an avid collector of *Dragnet* memorabilia which he has donated to the LAPD historical society.

MORENO, Terry: SEE Pat Evans

MORETTA, Mohamed: **KACD**, 1996-97. Mohamed joined Dance "Groove Radio" in the summer of 1996 from the power mixer at WPOW-Miami.

MORGAN, Bob: **KHOF**, 1960-63; **KGBS**, 1968-79; **KHTZ**, 1979; **KRLA**, 1986. "The best experience in my life was the 11 years at KGBS. I stayed through a mishmash of formats including being the only male on the air during the all-female 'Gentle Country' format in 1974." Born in Los Angeles and raised in Glendale, his family photo book has Bob holding a microphone as early as four years of age. "During high school my father used to drop me off at KFWB where I was a 'go-fer' for Bill Ballance and Red Blanchard. When Bill and Emperor Hudson arrived at KGBS, I never dreamed I would be working with some of my early heroes." Bob started at KHOF (99.5FM) after school, and in 1963 joined KAVR-Apple Valley, followed by KCIN-Victorville, KSEE-Santa Maria and KUTY-Palmdale. "Don Imus replaced me at KUTY when I left." In 1979 Storer sold KGBS AM&FM. "I was shattered. I had planned to retire at KGBS. I guess I was naive. When I looked around I realized that the industry was changing." Bob returned to KAVR and summer fill-in at KRLA before getting out of radio all together. While working evenings at KGBS, he had the opportunity to take on other jobs. Bob worked part-time as a paramedic, reserve police officer for the South Pasadena police department and drove a school bus. For many years after leaving radio he drove German tourists between New York and Los Angeles. Since 1989 Bob has fulfilled another passion, working with trains. He is now a locomotive engineer with Amtrak. Bob does all of Amtrak's commercials and is the voice announcing arrivals and departures at the train stations in the Western states. "Radio was the best. Every once in a while I meet an Amtrak passenger who remembers me from KGBS. I'm really lucky. I got to work in radio for 20 years, be a cop, drive an ambulance and be a railroad conductor. I've been able to do everything I ever wanted to do."

MORGAN, Charles: **KABC**; **KPFK**. Charles was an award-winning National Public Radio broadcaster known locally for his call-in show "Talk to Me" on KPFK. He joined KPFK in 1974 as a commentator and was heard Monday and Friday evenings. He won two AP awards and a Golden Mike. His early career involved such disparate tasks as working as a bank clerk, writing for *Bank News* magazine and announcing for small radio stations in the Midwest, occasionally for a young Lawrence Welk. He worked in television and newspapers in San Francisco in the late 1950s and '60s and then returned to the Southland. He died August 7, 1991. Charles was 78.

MORGAN, Dirck: **KFWB**, 1982-97

MORGAN, Larry: **KIIS**, 1984-86; **KSCA**, 1994-96; **KYSR**, 1996-97. Larry is the creative director for Premiere Radio Networks. He oversees production and coordination of all programming, including comedy services, syndicated networks and writing bits. Larry was born in Brownwood, Texas on July 27, 1962. He described his evening slot at KIIS as "loud, screaming, flame-throwin', shotgun, teen-idol jock." After working at KIIS in the mid-1980s, he went to KSFM-Sacramento, KWSS and KHQT-San Jose and KHMX-Houston. In early 1997 he started morning drive at "Star 98.7." Larry earned a B.A. in cinema production from USC, is married with a child and living in Acton.

MORGAN, Mark: **KDAY**, 1983-90. He was born Mark Morganella. He is now in the video editing field.

MORGAN, Melody: **KMGX**, 1994

MORGAN, Ray: **KDAY**. Ray was a newsman when the station boasted an Urban format.

MORGAN, Robert W.: **KHJ**, 1965-71 and 1972-73; **KIQQ**, 1973-75; **KMPC**, 1975-84; **KMGG**, 1984-86; **KMPC**, 1986-92; **KRTH**, 1992-97. Robert W. has burrowed his way into a magical place as the quintessential morning man over the decades in Los

Angeles radio, beginning in the mid-1960s. It wasn't always that way. "I decided that being a disc jockey was a lot more fun than spending the rest of my life in a courtroom." The world may have lost a lawyer, but it gained arguably one of the top three morning jocks during the second half of this century. Robert, born in Galin, Ohio on July 23, 1942, was the original morning "Boss Jock" at the Drake/Chenault-consulted "93/KHJ." He arrived in Southern California from KEWB-San Francisco. In 1967, *Billboard* published that Robert was voted 5th most popular disc jockey and the best in morning drive. During this time, he and his fellow jocks were surprised by a poll taken at one of the Teenage Fairs. "They asked the kids who they were most influenced by. Disc jockeys came in third behind parents and teachers. It stunned all of us. My job had always been a question of just having fun. After that, I became more responsible. I think it placed subconscious pressure on us." Robert hosted ABC's *In Concert* series, the *Helen Reddy Show* and KHJ/Channel 9's *Groovy* program. His morning signature at KHJ was "Zap, You're Morganized," which meant that one belonged to a very exclusive club. Even adults found it exhilarating to be "Morganized" as some kind of rite of passage. He made a personality out of his engineer "Fail Safe," manipulating him to the cover of a weekly "Boss 30" survey. In 1970, Robert left KHJ for an opportunity at WIND-Chicago. Wolfman Jack, who was hotter than a pistol at the time, was a guest on his last show. Robert called Wolfman Dick Whittinghill in obvious tribute to the long-running KMPC morning man. The irony of his reference to Whittinghill wouldn't be felt immediately. When he signed off he thanked Bill Drake, the Big Kahuna, and played Frank Sinatra's recording of the Rod McKuen song *A Few More Cities*. After the Windy City experience, Morgan returned to KHJ in 1972. In October of 1975, a once-in-a-generation job opened at KMPC, and Robert took it. His first assignment was a split shift on Sundays, as well as back-stopping KMPC sports events and filling in for the weekday staff. His move to KMPC seemed strange on the surface. There must have been a hidden agenda or a promise of a shift in order for the superstar morning man to settle for a Sunday split shift. Robert told James Brown of the *LA Times* that there were no promises when he joined KMPC. A few people did wonder how he'd handle the situation, but he said that he adjusted before he got there. To signal the new era, after 30 years of "Whittinghill in the Morning," Robert became the new morning drive personality on August 6, 1979. He started his first morning with Gene Autry blasting out *Back in the Saddle Again*. "I've worked every shift known to radio at KMPC but I like this the best. I've always thought of myself as a morning man." Robert has also hosted a number of syndicated radio shows, including "Record World" and "Robert W. Morgan's Special of the Week," which was syndicated by Watermark. While at "Magic 106" his morning partners were Joni Caryl and St. Louis sports guy Scott St. James, who moved to "Magic" from KMPC. By 1992, all the "Boss Radio" fans were listening to "K-Earth 101" and Robert's morning move to the Oldies station seemed like a seamless decision and a very comfortable fit. In early 1994, Robert was inducted into the National Broadcasters

Hall of Fame. In 1993 he received a Star on the Hollywood Walk of Fame. "Unfortunately the Star is in storage until MetroLink finishes construction on Hollywood Blvd." In late May 1997, Robert announced that he had lung cancer, perhaps due to being a two-pack-a-day smoker for 35 years before quitting in 1996. In an emotional on-air statement he said he was taking some time off work to fight the disease full time.

MORGAN, Scott: **KEZY**, 1969-76. Born Neal Christopher, Scott arrived in the Southland from KENO-Las Vegas. On his departure from KEZY, Scott said, "We can't compete with Los Angeles stations. We have to relate to the community more." For the past decade Scott has been a principal in the Morgan/Frey Advertising Agency of Fountain Valley. They have been responsible for all the advertising for the Cerritos Auto Square.

MORLEY, Russ: **KEZY**, 1991, pd

MORRIS, Barney

MORRIS, Felicia: SEE Poetess

MORRIS, Gary: **KLAC**, 1985

MORRIS, Hal: **KRHM**, 1959. Hal hosted a weekend show, "Brunch with Hal."

MORRIS, Johnny: **KGFJ**, 1983-95; **KACE**, 1994-97; **KYPA**, 1996-97. Born in Fresno, Johnny grew up in the Bay Area and graduated from San Francisco State. While in high school he started his radio career doing the all-night shift at KSOL at the same time Sly Stone was a jock at the station. Johnny moved to KDIA where he spent 14 years as on-air, md and chief engineer. His love for engineering ensured longevity at KDIA and KGFJ. "My day job is engineering at motivational radio KYPA, and I work overnights at KACE."

MORRIS, Mark: **KMDY**, 1983; **KNAC**, 1983-84; **KKLA**, 1984-88; **KACE**, 1990-92; **KMPC**, 1991-92; **KLSX**, 1992-97. Mark is the production director for "Real Radio, KLSX." The native Los Angeleno grew up near Baldwin Park. He got the radio bug while working on Loyola Marymount University's college station, KXLU, where he was gm for two years. With a sparkle in his voice, he proclaimed his school the "Marines of God." Mark did morning drive news and production at KKLA and then between 1988 and 1990 he worked at SI Communications. Mark was part of the morning drive team at KACE. In addition to his duties at KLSX he is the host and producer of a syndicated NAC show "Night Songs" that is heard on over 20 stations.

> *"What a day that was. We had James Hetfield and Lars Ulrich of Metallica fly down to Long Beach from San Jose and spend our last day on the air with the entire air staff, including former jocks. It was really fun, but quite emotional. After 9 years together, we were really like a family."*
> -Ana Lee, February 15, 1995, KNAC

MORRIS, Steve: **KRTH**, 1986-90; **KKGO/KGIL**, 1996-97. Born in Lynn, Massachusetts, in 1957, Steve got into radio as a result of the attention he received as a comedian while attending Cornell University. He was a comedian first and then a radio performer. "My role models were not other djs, but, rather, Johnny Carson, Jack Benny and Steve Allen. I treated my stand-up comedy work like a variety show." Steve started his radio career in Ithaca and from there worked in Rochester, Long Island and Hartford before landing in the Southland. Some of his features while doing mornings on "K-Earth" included "The Art of Dating" and "Moonlighting in the Morning" among others. "I put together my show based on whatever was happening in town. When Mike Tyson knocked his opponent out in 90 seconds, I played all short records that morning, music that could be played during the length of the fight. I felt like we were in touch with Southern California. I had Jonathan Doll, who is also a stand-up comic, doing traffic and Claudia Marshall doing news." On one April Fools' Day, Steve announced upcoming major roadwork on selected freeways that would close portions of the 10, 5, 101 and so on. He claims CalTrans was not happy with the April Fools Day prank but his audience loved it. "We announced we were going all-news one year. The pranks are a lot of fun." He appeared on *Moonlighting*, *Murphy Brown*, *Matlock* and *Frank's Place*. Steve was seen regularly at the Ice House, Evening at the Improv, the Brea Improv and other area comedy clubs. He went to KQQL-Minneapolis after he left L.A., and then to Florida. "I liked the Southern California audience and I liked making friends with them." Steve returned to the Southland in the summer of 1995 to star in a two-person original play called "The Forbidden Dance of Love." He worked morning drive at all-Beatles format, KGIL.

MORRISON, Bob: **KHJ**, 1977-78; **KIIS**, 1978-79. Bob was one of the newsmen at a time when KHJ was de-emphasizing news. In the late 1960s he worked his way up at KLIF-Dallas from request line operator to news anchor in only two short years. He went on to work for ABC/FM Radio and RKO Radio Network. After KHJ and KIIS, Bob left the Southland and returned to Dallas and worked for KVIL-Dallas for fifteen years. He earned "best major market newscast in Texas" award from UPI four out of the last five years. He is now news director at all-News KRLD-Dallas.

MORRISON, Mike: **KSCA**, 1994-97, pd; **KCRW**, 1997. The former program director of AAA KSCA was born on Long Island, May 19, 1961. He came to Pacific Palisades when he was 11 and returned to the East to attend the University of Pennsylvania. He discovered his fondness for radio while in college and he became pd of the campus radio station, WXPN. This was a paying position and he continued running the station long after graduation until he was 33 years old and got the call to start KSCA. Mike launched the AAA format on July 1, 1994, as pd and on-air at "FM 101.9." He was in a band called the Johnsons. He stayed with KSCA until it was sold in early 1997 that led to a format change to Spanish broadcasting. In the spring of 1997 he joined KCRW for a weekend show.

MORROW, Bruce: **KGBS**, 1965, nd

MOSHER, Tom: **KIQQ**, 1984-89, vp/gm; **KGIL/KMGX**, 1991-92, gm. Tom began his new position in Los Angeles at KIQQ with a new station format "K-Lite 100." He described the format at the time as "designed to appeal to an older audience." Tom was born in 1941 in Johnstown, Pennsylvania and was educated at Valley Forge Military Academy in Wayne, Pennsylvania. He began his radio career in sales in Detroit at WCAR, then became gm of WDRQ. After being gm at KVOR/KSPZ-Colorado Springs, consultant at KLBJ-Austin and gm at WSNE-Providence, Tom arrived in the Southland. Between KIQQ and KGIL/KMGX, Tom originated and implemented a new station in Orlando, WXXL. When KGIL was sold, Tom teamed up with Allan Barzman ("Barz") and formed a creative-driven advertising agency called Barzman & Mosher Advertising in Encino.

MOSHONTZ, Chuck: **KLOS**, 1982-95; **KSCA**, 1995-97.

The former nd for KLOS became an integral part of the morning "Mark and Brian Show" for eight years. He left KLOS in early 1995 and told Gary Lycan in the *OC Register*, "It was all very bittersweet. They said the company had decided not to renew my contract. I cleaned out my desk and left. I felt foolishly insulated from other changes because: A. I was doing news, and B. I was part of something that by any standards I might muse was a successful package. Subsequently, it clearly turned out Mark and Brian knew nothing about it, and they were devastated." Born Charles Moshontz in Los Angeles on June 11, 1948, he grew up in Southern California. He got the radio "bug" as a kid listening to Dick Whittinghill and Gary Owens on KMPC. Chuck worked at the campus station at the University of Santa Barbara, KCSB, and at KBMI and KLON/TV-Las Vegas, KZEW-Dallas, WCOZ-Boston and KZAM-Seattle before arriving in the Southland. Chuck joined former Mark and Brian producer Nicole Sandler for mornings at KSCA and left when the station changed formats from AAA to Spanish in early 1997. He has returned to school.

MOSS, Pete: **KEZY**, 1966; **KACE**, 1971, pd; **KGBS**, 1972-73; **KFOX**, 1975. Born Lester Leigh in 1938, Pete had been working at KTYM-Ladera Heights. He and Terry Moss (no relation) teamed together in the late 1970s as "the Dawn Busters" at KDWN-Las Vegas. He was last heard near Laughlin or Bull Head, Arizona.

MOSS, Ray: **XERB**, 1967-68. Ray Moss, "the Boss," arrived from Minneapolis radio when Johnny Otis was actively involved with the station; he returned to KUXL-Minneapolis.

MOSS, Terry: **KFOX**, 1975-76; **KHJ**, 1982-83. Born William Moss in Rochester, New York, Terry played the very last Top 40 record on KHJ before they went Country. During the 1980s Terry owned and edited *Galaxy*, a music and news tidbit sheet for disc jockeys. He also generated Cheap Radio Thrills, a personality production package. He spent time in Las Vegas on KDWN partnered in the morning with Pete Moss (no relation) as "the Dawn Busters." He also worked Country KSON-San Diego. In the mid-1980s, Terry was part of Transtar's Country format for a few years before moving on to Unistar and Westwood One. When he left the Southland he moved to a ranch in Durango, Colorado, then back to Las Vegas. Terry spent his final year in Dallas and passed away on October 15, 1994, at age 47. He asked for donations to AIDS research programs in lieu of flowers. Radio friend Dan O'Day said: "Terry was one of the best, most natural radio personalities ever. Wonderfully creative in the production room. Terrific guy."

MOTTEK, Frank: **KNX**, 1992-97. Frank is one of the anchors on "KNXNewsradio." Frank grew up in South Florida and remembers his start: "I got into radio when I was 16 at one of the top FM stations in Miami in 1978. While in high school I began doing the afternoon news on "96X"-Miami and by the time I graduated high school I was doing the morning news and was news director." At

the age of 19 Frank was hired as news anchor/reporter at the CBS radio affiliate WINZ-Miami covering space shuttle launches for six years. In the midst of his 11-year association with WINZ he earned a B.A. in liberal studies at Barry University. From Florida Frank filed stories for the *Nightly Business Report* on PBS. In addition to being weekend anchor at KNX, he is a reporter and frequently fills in for the morning drive anchors during the week. Frank has covered many stories for the CBS radio network including space shuttle landings, the 1997 mass suicides in San Diego and anchored hourly CBS Radio Network newscasts. Since 1992 Frank has also appeared on KCBS/Channel 2 News.

MOUNTAIN, Johnny: **KABC**, 1979. Johnny was part of the "Ken and Bob Company" morning drive show on KABC dispensing weather. He went on to be a fixture at KABC/Channel 7's *Eyewitness News*.

MOUNTAIN, Red: **KDAY**, 1972; **KROQ**, 1973 pd. Born John Schultz, he became pd when Johnny Darin departed KROQ. For a time he worked in Las Vegas and currently runs a chain of radio stations in East Texas.

MR. X: **KHJ**, 1975

MULHOLLAND, Russ: **KMPC**, 1948-49. Russ worked morning drive and was replaced by the "Clock Watcher," Dick Whittinghill.

MULHURN, Shawn: **KJOI**, 1976, pd. Shawn arrived in the Southland from Texas.

MUNDY, Greg: **KTWV**, 1993-94. Born Greg Partsch, he grew up in Rancho Cordova near Sacramento. Before "the Wave" Greg worked at KSJO-San Jose, KNDE and KFBK-Sacramento and programmed KPOI-Honolulu. In the mid-1970s he joined the David Forrest Agency promoting concerts. The production assistant and on-air talent died at age 39 on June 29, 1994, in a boating accident.

MURPHY, Bill: **KJOI**, 1974. After "K-Joy" Bill became a news anchor in Oregon and later in San Francisco.

MURPHY, Dave: **KIIS**; **KPWR**, 1986; **KKHR/KODJ/KCBS**, 1986-97. Dave started in San Bernardino with two Top 40 stations, KFXM and KMEN.

MURPHY, Duff: **KUSC**, 1995-97. Attorney by day, opera buff on Saturdays.

Duff trades depositions for divas as host of "The Opera Show" on KUSC. The Loyola Law School alumnus and magna cum laude undergraduate from USC can identify the precise moment he got hooked on opera. He was sitting with his parents in an Alhambra church as a second-grader, listening to a tenor singing an aria "in a huge voice." Reflecting on that memory, he accepts it as his "first operatic experience."

MURPHY, Frank: **KPWR**, 1992-93; **KROQ**, 1993-96; **KLOS**, 1996-97. Frank was the Kevin & Bean morning show producer during his time at "the Roq." K&B often referred to Frank as the "Realistic Plug 'n Talk from Radio Shack." He hosted "The Best of K&B." Before moving to the Southland, Murphy worked as morning show producer and air personality at WAVA-Washington, DC. He started there as an intern in 1984. At "Power 106," Frank produced the Jay Thomas show. Kevin & Bean considered Frank the best producer in radio. Kevin praised him in an *R&R* 1995 interview: "As a person, he's a freak of nature. We give him impossible tasks. He's excellent at detective/detail work. He also is a good idea person. Plus he's very organized - anal to the point where we want to beat him up." Frank left KROQ in the summer of 1996 and joined KLOS' morning team Mark and Brian.

MURPHY, Gayl: **KROQ**, 1977-80; **KWST**, 1980-81; **KLOS**, 1981-95. Gayl is the director of entertainment news for the Sony Radio Network. At "K-West" she worked morning drive with Raechel Donahue. When she left KWST the on-air staff participated in a dramatic spoof reporting that Gayle had been abducted by aliens and was leaving the station because of a higher calling. During her long reign at KLOS Gayl was the entertainment and backstage concert reporter. She covered all the larger music awards shows for the ABC Rock Radio Network. Gayl has been on tour with Bob Dylan, Van Halen, Guns 'n' Roses, The Rolling Stones and other major rock stars. For four years she hosted "Open Conversation." Gayl was born and raised in New York and came to the Southland as a teenager. Her goal was to be an actress (she appeared in *Revenge of the Lobster Man*) and comedian. She has performed at improv comedy clubs in Los Angeles and San Francisco.

MURPHY, John: **KIIS**, 1992-93; **KZLA**, 1993-95. Born in San Diego, John grew up in McCook, Nebraska. His father moved to the Cornhusker State with an executive promotion with JC Penney. John's love for radio started at nighttime. "I would lay in bed listening to these 50,000 watt giants like WLS, 'X-Rock' from El Paso and the blow torch, KOMA. When I heard a fan letter that I had written being read on the air, I was hooked." John attended the University of Nebraska as a broadcast journalism major until his junior year. In 1981 a part-time position at KQKQ-Omaha led to an offer of afternoon drive and he quit school, much to the chagrin of his parents. Eighteen months later, he left Omaha for morning drive at KLUC-Las Vegas. "It was my first morning drive job and I didn't know what I was doing and was fired nine months later, but I knew that my strength was in mornings." He traded up to mornings at KNBQ-Seattle and in 1984 spent two years at WBMW ("B-106")-Washington, DC. In 1986, John started at KKRZ-Portland and worked for four years in the mornings. In 1990, he moved to KKLQ ("Q106")-San Diego and had his first team experience where for six months he was part of the "Rumble and Murphy Show." By 1992, John wanted to pursue movies, acting and voiceover work, so he pulled up stakes and moved to the Southland. While doing infomercials and voiceover work, John wrote for Rick Dees and did fill-in at KIIS. At KZLA during the summer of 1993, John was hired to team with John Garado in morning drive. The team split up in the summer of 1995.

"The station wanted more music." In March 1996 John rejoined KKRZ.

MURPHY, Mary Ellen: **KYSR**, 1994

MURPHY, Tom: **KBLA**, 1967; **KFWB**, 1967. Tom arrived in the Southland from KCBQ-San Diego where he was Bobby St. Thomas. He replaced "Humble Harve" at KBLA. After his stint at KFWB, he went back to San Diego, where he was pd of KFMB. Tom was a time salesman at KCBQ in the 1970s.

MURPHY, "World Famous" Tom: **KRLA**, 1971; **KGIL**, 1976-77; **KIIS**, 1977-81; **KPRZ**, 1981-85; **KIIS**, 1985-86; **KFI**, 1987-88; **KJQI**, 1993; **KGRB**, 1994-95. Tom grew up in Portland and started his radio career on Don Burden's KISN in 1959 and stayed six years. In 1965, he moved to the legendary KJR-Seattle before arriving in the Southland in February 1971 for mornings at KRLA. Where did the "World Famous" come from? "It happened while I was at KJR. As a bit I called myself the Famous Tom Murphy. Then, I thought, what the heck, that wasn't big enough, so I called myself World Famous. After KRLA, Tom returned to Seattle for a year and then joined WCFL-Chicago for almost three years. In late summer of 1975, he went to WIXY-Cleveland. In 1993, Tom worked for the Salem Radio Network until the operation moved to Dallas in the summer of 1994. In late 1994, he joined KGRB in the East Valley until an ownership change changed the station to Spanish. He also produces 60- and 90-second "Humorous Commentaries" for several radio stations.

MURRAY, Don: **KIQQ**, 1980-84; **KHTZ/KBZT**, 1984-85; **KRLA**, 1985; **KYMS**, 1986-87, pd; **KNOB**, 1984-88. Born Grant Carlson, he grew up in Sacramento and started on KROY-Stockton in 1967. In the 1970s he worked in Medford, Oregon and KERN-Fresno before going to KFXM/KDUO-San Bernardino in 1978 for two years. Don spent four years at "K-100" during the George Wilson regime and then went to weekends at KHTZ in 1984. It was in 1984 that he started a four-year relationship with KNOB doing voice tracks as Sean Foster. In 1985 he went to KRLA and replaced "Humble Harve." A year later he joined the Orange County Christian station as pd. In 1987 he joined Transtar/Unistar for five years. In 1993 Don became the corporate pd for Shepard Communications and "K-Lord." In 1995 he established a voiceover workshop in Monterey and worked at KJMY, which is only a few blocks from Fishermans Wharf.

MURRAY, Hal: **KFWB**, 1961. With all of his old jokes and Orben books, Hal and his "Murray-Go-Round" show came to KFWB from one of Crowell-Collier's sister stations KDWB-Minneapolis. Hal was the morning man in the Twin Cities and took over similar chores at KFWB during the strike by the newsmen. In Minneapolis, Hal got his hair cuts from Charles Schulz' father. Bobby Dale described Hal as "an old Vaudeville guy. Always on." After the strike, he returned "kicking and screaming" to KDWB. In 1964, Hal went to mornings at KQV-Pittsburgh for three years. Hal has passed away.

MURRAY, Tom: **KMAX**, 1995. Tom has been a prime-time sports broadcaster on KCAL/Channel 9 for over eight years.

MYERS, Bob: **KJQI/KOJY**, 1993-94; **KGIL**, 1997. Born in Columbia, South Carolina, Bob grew up in Ashtabula, Ohio. He graduated from the University of Dayton in 1968 with a degree in chemical engineering. In 1973 he found himself between jobs. "Out of the clear blue I thought I would give radio a shot." He got a shot with WPCH-Atlanta and after quick stops at WEZW-Milwaukee and KEZK-St. Louis, Bob returned to WPCH and spent 15 years with the station. When "K-Joy" folded, Bob stayed with the parent company and broadcast Classical to sister station KKHI-San Francisco. In early 1997 he joined KGIL for the all-Beatles format.

MYERS, Chris: While growing up in Miami, Chris hosted a sports talk show at the age of 16. In early 1995 he took over ESPN's "Up Close" from Roy Firestone. Chris told Larry Stewart in the *LA Times*: "Roy's a tough act to follow. Roy shaped the show around his personality, and now I think it should be shaped around mine. He did the show for 14 years. It takes a while."

POP Expo '69

On stage performing:

Shades of Joy
Sir Douglas
Red Beans & Rice
Kaleidoscope
Alice Cooper
Jam

Pacific Ocean Park presented by KRLA

N

NADEL, Roger: **KNX**, 1976-89; **KFWB**, 1996-97, vp/gm. Roger arrived at all-News KFWB from the same post at WWJ/WYST-Detroit. Born October 31, 1950, in Washington, DC, he graduated from the University of the Pacific in 1971 with a psychology major. In 1974 Roger was a newsgatherer for Associated Press Audio News Service in Santa Barbara and in 1976 joined "KNXNewsradio" as a news writer/editor and in 1982 was promoted to executive news producer. Roger lives in Agoura Hills with his wife Debbie and two sons, Adam and Cory.

NAFTALY, Keith: **KKBT**, 1993-95, pd. Keith started as Bill Lee's phone person in 1980 at KFRC-San Francisco. He came to the Southland from KMEL-San Francisco where he had been pd. In the spring of 1995, Keith joined Arista Records and by the fall was promoted to vp/a&r for the label.

NAHAN, Stu: **KABC**, 1986-95. Stu has been a familiar face and voice in Southern California for decades. He has been in all five *Rocky* movies. Stu was the sports anchor on KABC/Channel 7 from 1966 to 1975 and moved to KNBC/Channel 4 in 1975 for a decade. In June 1987 he took over KABC's afternoon drive "SportsTalk" program. From 1986 to 1995 he was a part of KABC's popular morning drive show.

NAIMO, John: **KRKD**, 1962-70; **KIIS**, 1970-73; **KFAC**, 1973-76; **KABC**, 1976-97. Jack played albums and did the 6 o'clock sports on KRKD with Bob Kelley, Charlie

Clifton and Sam Balter. He was the first to say "KIIS" when the AM station changed call letters from KRKD. Jack was born in Chicago and attended Bowen High School on the South Side and spent some time at Indiana University before starting a string of play-by-play sports and sportscasting jobs in Kentucky and Indiana. "After 10 years of fun at KRKD and KIIS, the real fun began when I started a 21-year run at KABC." Jack got involved with KABC's "SportsTalk" and was the engineer for Dodger games. "I yearn some day to get back on the air, even if it's just weekends with either sports or music." Jack and his wife Adelina have been married 40 years and their three children all graduated from USC. "We now have three little Trojan grandsons."

NAJERA, Alfredo: **KTNQ**, 1996-97. Alfredo is the evening personality for the Spanish language station.

NARDONE, Mike: **KBIG**, 1970-71; **KKBT**, 1994-96

NASH, Kevin: **KKBT**, 1997. Before taking over the late evening slot on KKBT, Kevin worked for three stations in San Francisco, KBLX, KDIA and KMEL.

NASTY, Chuck: **KIIS**, 1994-96. Born Chuck Zimmerman, the master scuba diver worked at WBBM-

Chicago in 1985 and spent four years doing afternoons at "Q104"-Kansas City. Chuck did specialty programming for Armed Forces Radio Network serving Micronesia, Japan, Korea and the Philippines. In 1993, Chuck left SMN's "classic rock" format to join KZGZ ("Power 98")-Agana, Guam and KPXP-Saipan as pd/md and afternoon drive. He was the first in the world to broadcast underwater off Guam. Until September 1994, the "Nasty One" had never been in California. Chuck worked afternoon drive at KIIS until the summer of 1996. By the end of the year he was working morning drive at KHOM-New Orleans.

NASTY, Joe: **KTNQ**, 1976-78; **KPWR**, 1987-88. Joe was hired from Phoenix to be one of the original jocks on "the new Ten-Q" when it debuted December 26, 1976. In 1988 Joe went to WQHT ("102-Jamz")-Orlando, and in 1992 to XHTZ-San Diego. In 1994 he worked at KTFM-San Antonio and the following year went to WPOW-Miami.

NATHANSON, Geoff: **KFOX**, 1982 and 1984-87; **KLAC**, 1990; **XTRA**, 1990-92; **KNNS**, 1996. The  graduate of UCLA loved sports first. Geoff went into broadcasting as a way to be "involved" with sports. He started out at KFOX as associate producer of "Sports Forum" with Fred Wallin and went on to be the co-host. In 1990 he co-hosted Gabe Kaplan's "SportsNuts" show on KLAC. Geoff spent a few years in Las Vegas hosting SportsFan Radio Network which was syndicated on over 100 stations. He is the color commentator for the live action-video game Sportactive TV Football. Geoff was a local news anchor while "K-News" was broadcasting the Bloomberg news service.

NAVA, Maria Elena: **KLVE**, 1985-97; **KSCA**, 1997, pd. Maria has won the *Billboard* magazine Spanish md of the Year. In early 1997 she was named pd of Heftel's new Spanish station, "La Nueva 101.9."

NAVARETTE, Reuben: **KMPC**, 1994-95. Born in 1967, Reuben came to the attention of KABC while guesting on Michael Jackson's show discussing his book *A Darker Side of Crimson: Odyssey of a Harvard Chicano*. He was asked to sit in for Dennis Prager and then was teamed with Tavis Smiley who had been doing commentaries on the morning drive "Ken and Barkley Show." They started a late evening talk show called "Twentysomething Talk" on sister station KMPC.

NAVARRO, Rafael: **KLAX/KXMG**, 1997

NAVARRO, Richard: **KNOB**, 1981

NAVE, Milt: **KALI**, 1965

NAYLOR, Jerry: **KLAC**, 1979

NEAL, Howard: **KFI/KOST**, 1987-97, vp/gm

NEIL, Nasty: **KMET**, 1983-86; **KNAC**, 1986-95. Born Neil Katara, "Nasty Neil" started out as a production assistant at the legendary KMET. Moving to KNAC at its inception in 1986, "Nasto" continued doing production for three years before moving to the all-night shift and eventually 7 to midnight. One of his peers said that Neil was "one of the best production men and made the metal station sound right on the money." Teaming with voice impressionist and KNAC chief engineer Ron Russ, the duo created spots that won "SUNNY Awards" by finishing in first place three years in a row from 1989 to 1991. The KNAC building in Long Beach housed a physical fitness center and Neil became a personal  trainer while working at the station. Born and raised in Seattle, Neil came to the Southland in 1980 seeking "climate, fame and fun." Since KNAC folded in early 1995, "Nasty Neil" has been partnered with Tracy Barnes, the creator of "Z-Rock," a world-wide Internet radio station, playing similar music to KNAC's hard rock format.

NELSON, Art: **KFWB**, 1961-62; **KLAC**, 1973-82; **KMPC**, 1982-87. Art started in radio as a 16-year-old broadcaster at a small 250-watt station in Corsicana, Texas. Art got major experience at KLIF-Dallas during the McLendon glory years. In 1959 he was doing his show from McLendon's Inwood Theatre. Art also worked at WJJD-Chicago. During the personality strike of KFWB newsmen in 1961, Art became one of the strike breakers. He was assessed a $2,500 fine by AFTRA, which was to be paid by Crowell-Collier, but never was. A year later in 1962, Art went to sister station KEWB-San Francisco. After the Kennedy assassination, when he was at KEWB, FBI agents interviewed Art because he hung out at Jack Ruby's bar when he worked in Dallas. In a 1979 article about the changing music scene, Art said, "Not only has the music changed but the performers have as well. The big stars of a few years ago aren't there today. The sound has been upgraded and country has visibility it never had before." Called the "Silver Fox," Art specialized in remote broadcasts from Universal Studios and Santa Anita during his years as afternoon personality on KLAC.

NELSON, Carl: **KJLH**, 1980-97, nd. Carl hosts an early morning talk show on KJLH called "The Front Page." The show mirrors concerns of the African American community and played an important role in deflecting anger and calming fears during the 1992 L.A. Riots. In 1996 he was named nd of the year by *Black Radio Exclusive* magazine.

NELSON, Don: **KMGG**, 1985-86, gm. Don is currently the director of marketing for San Diego-based Directions in Radio.

NELSON, Robert: **KKHR/KNX/FM**, 1973-88, gm

NELSON, Sandy: **KIEV**, 1959. The "Teen Beat" drummer hosted a show with Dean Torrance.

NELSON, Terry: **KFI**, 1979. Terry grew up in Modesto and attended Yosemite JC and Delta College in Sacramento. Prior to arriving in Southern California, he worked in Modesto, Stockton, KROY-Sacramento and WXLO ("99X")-New York where he worked both drives. While at "99X" he was nominated for Disc Jockey of the Year. He had previously won the award for small market radio. Terry left the 50,000-watt giant for KFRC-San Francisco. He eventually moved to Sacramento with his wife and daughter and currently works at KYMX.

NELSON, Tyrone "Boogie": **KKTT/KGFJ**; 1977-85, pd. Born Tyrone Peppers in St. Louis, he got his radio start in 1974 at KOWH-Omaha. During the next three years Tyrone worked at WAMM-Flint, KSOL-San Francisco, KATZ-St. Louis and WPDQ-Jacksonville. "KGFJ hired me to be part of a new team. The station wanted a new image, a new format and new voices which became 'the Kat.'" In 1985 Tyrone joined "K-100" in Sacramento as pd. Wanting a break from radio, Tyrone joined Circuit City as a sales rep and is currently working for the Good Guys in the Beverly Center. "I desperately miss radio and am looking to make a return to broadcasting after a decade in retail."

NEMO, Doc: **KROQ**, 1977-78. Doc was the "Young Marques" for two hours each night on KROQ.

NESBITT, Bill: **KWIZ**, 1984-86; **KEZY**, 1990-93; **KYSR**, 1993-95; **KACD**, 1995. Bill was born in Brea, and lives in nearby Irvine. His radio career is part-time on air and he is a full time music producer. Between 1986 and 1991, he worked for Unistar. Bill is the voice of Disneyland: "Please keep your hands inside the vehicle." He also is the announcer for the various Disneyland shows, including the Electric Light Parade and Fantasy in the Sky. Bill is currently director of programming for the Entertainment Radio Networks in Malibu. The company syndicates 20 regularly scheduled shows and special events, including "Fight Back with Dave Horowitz" and "The Weekly Top Thirty Country Countdown with Charlie Tuna." Bill lives in Woodland Hills.

NEVADA, "Outrageous": **KPPC**, 1970-71. Susan Carter, a.k.a. Outrageous Nevada, was part of the embryonic launch of "underground radio" in Southern California. During this revolutionary period in L.A. radio, she received more fan mail than any other personality on the station. She started on the alternative station "discreetly at midnight" and soon moved to middays which preceded her husband/pd Les Carter. Susan is a singer who recorded albums produced by her husband. Married to Les for 30 years they have had a very successful writing and producing career in movies and television. Together their writing credits include: *Homicide: Life On The Street*, *Almost Grown*, *L.A. Law* and *Edna Buchanan: Miami Deadline*.

NEVINS, Biggie: **KFI**, 1973-84. Biggie was born and raised in Brooklyn. When Cox Broadcasting bought KFI in 1973, he was brought in to program the station. Biggie  was a winner of the *Gavin* Award for program management. When he arrived at KFI, he told Don Page of the *LA Times*, "We're very research minded. We intend to find out exactly what our audience likes. Basically, I can tell you that KFI will remain middle-of-the-road." He was elevated to national pd and then abruptly fired in 1984. Within a few months of leaving KFI, Biggie was moving into a new residence in Malibu when he suffered a fatal heart attack. John Rook talked about Biggie in a 1995 interview: "God, I miss him. He's still one of my closest friends, even though he's been dead for 10 years. Shortly before his death, he told me, 'If I die, I've done all that I've wanted to do.' How prophetic. He was a lovely person. He was cremated in L.A. and his ashes were flown to New York but never arrived. Through some mishap they found him in Milwaukee. Biggie would have roared!"

NEWELL, Peter: **KPOL/KZLA**, 1972-79, gm. Peter was CapCities third general manager at KPOL which became KZLA. In 1979 he was transferred to a cable franchise in Plymouth, Michigan.

NEWMAN, Harry: **KBLA**, 1965-66; **KBBQ**, 1967-68; **KLAC**, 1970-84. Harry was associated with country radio during his stay in Los Angeles. He was a rock jock at KBLA and survived the call letter/format change to Country KBBQ. At KLAC he was a performer and worked afternoon drive. Harry was the auto racing expert at KLAC, and he conducted the local pre- and post-race show interviews. In a 1979 interview he talked about the country music on KLAC: "I see a parallel between the growth of modern jazz from Dixieland and the emergence of contemporary country music from traditional." He had a show, "Harry Newman's Country Gold," that was syndicated and aired on AFRN. In 1983 he created syndicated radio shows aired on over 100 stations and was also involved with Country Radio's weekly magazine. Harry has been the main announcer at KCOP/Channel 13 for the past 15 years and retired in late 1995.

NEWMAN, Jim: **KFWB**, 1984-97. Jim is the financial editor at all-News KFWB and *KTLA/Channel 5 Morning News*. He came to KFWB from ABC/Group W's Satellite News channel where he was *Business Week Magazine*'s tv correspondent. Prior to that he was heard on both the NBC and CBS Radio Networks. In the early 1970s he started the first all-news television programming on a UHF station. "It laid the ground work for CNN, which prospered over cable a few years later." Born in Oklahoma, Jim received his B.A. from Westminster

College in Fulton, Missouri and attended the London School of Economics. He has become a great friend and promoter of the Los Angeles Philharmonic. The ubiquitous "Gentleman Jim" is also a collector of fine art and a wine connoisseur. He is the voice of African Wine. He's working on a book entitled *Taiwan...the Economic Revolution.*

NEWMARK, Phil: **KPWR**, 1986-91, vp/gm. The former gm of "Power 106," Phil came up through the ranks of radio rep firms. He was born in 1946 in Brooklyn and was a business major at William Penn College in Iowa.

NEWPORT, Mike: **KLON**, 1992-1997. Mike was born in Long Beach on November 29, 1962, and raised just a couple of miles from the studios of KLON. He joined the Air Force in 1984 to take advantage of the educational opportunities and became a radio and television broadcaster after basic training. Upon graduation from the Defense Information School, he spent the next several years in Japan, the Azores and Norway. In late 1993, a growth on each vocal chord was discovered that blocked about 80 percent of his airway. He had no other choice but surgery. "The doctor told me there was a good chance my voice would be damaged or ruined altogether. I waited eight weeks before I uttered a sound, and within five more weeks, I was back on the air at KLON." Mike continues to work at KLON and his education.

NEWTON, Todd: **KIIS**, 1997. Todd hosts E! Entertainment's *Coming Attractions*. He is active doing the voice work at E! and participating in other original programming. Todd is currently studying improv with The Groundlings and The Harvey Lembeck Comedy Group.  In the spring of 1997 he appeared in HBO's *Weapons of Mass Distraction* in which he portrayed a sleazy tabloid television reporter. Originally from St. Louis, he worked in his hometown for eight years, most recently at WKBQ and in local tv. Todd works weekends at KIIS.

NIAGARA, Joe: **KPOP**, 1959; **KBIG**, 1960-62. Joe is best known for his success on the East Coast. While in Southern California, he worked at KPOP from WIBG-Philadelphia. In 1960 he moved to KBIG for morning drive. In 1962 Joe returned to WIBG and never returned to L.A. Born on the fourth of July 1927, Joe was raised in South Philadelphia. "As a kid I listened to the radio and thought broadcasting was exciting and knew it was something I wanted to be connected with." Philly personality Leroy Miller at WFIL told Joe to be persistent. At 18, Joe served in the U.S. Army in Panama.
Affectionately known as "The Rockin' Bird," he started his career in 1947 on WDAS-Philadelphia and recently celebrated six decades of working on Philly radio. In 1980 he spun into the Guinness Book of World Records for playing 500 consecutive versions of *Stardust*. Joe currently works for WPEN-Philadelphia and lives with his wife Evelyn in the Philly suburbs. "I'm looking forward to the year 2000 when I will have spanned seven decades in broadcasting."

NICHOLAW, George: **KNX**, 1967-97, gm. George, the longest-tenured general manager of a news formatted radio station in the United States, has been one of the most visible radio executives in Southern California for the past three decades. He started as a dj and pd in 1953 at KDON-Monterey. In 1955, he joined CBS as assistant director of promotion and publicity. He earned a Bachelor of Science degree from Cal Berkeley and completed graduate studies for his foreign trade degree from the American Gradate School of International Management at Phoenix. George had been working in the promotion  department at KNXT/Channel 2 when the station implemented its first hour-long newscast with anchors Jerry Dunphy and Ralph Story. Soon after arriving at KNX in August 1967, he simply applied what he'd learned in television. He tried to replicate a daily newspaper on the radio with news, sports, a number of unique news features, including being the first radio station in the U.S. to simulcast CBS/TV's *60 Minutes*. KNX is one of only a handful or radio stations to do daily editorials, which he airs himself.

NICKSON, Nick: Nick was one of the sidekicks to long-running Kings announcer Bob Miller. He also worked as the P.A. announcer for the L.A. Dodgers.

NICOLE, Lauryn: **KPWR**, 1994; **KACE**, 1994. Lauryn worked part-time at "Power 106."

NIEHAUS, Dave: **KMPC**, 1966-76. The former California Angel broadcaster went on to the Seattle Mariners. It was figured that between the Angels and Mariners, Dave broadcast more losing seasons than any other announcer. He has been a Mariners broadcaster since the club's inception into the American League in 1977. While Dave was recovering from his second angioplasty surgery in three weeks, a local Seattle radio station sent Dave 3,077 autographed baseballs wishing him well. The number was how many Mariners games he had called. Dave was born and raised in Princeton, Indiana, and is a graduate of Indiana University, where he worked for the campus radio station. After leaving Armed Forces radio and tv service handled New York Yankee baseball as well as basketball and hockey from Madison Square Garden. While in the Southland he called the Angels action with Dick Enberg and Don Drysdale. He also broadcasted UCLA football and basketball. Dave lives in Bellevue, Washington with his wife Marilyn. They have three children.

NILES, Chuck: **KFOX**, 1956; **KNOB**, 1957-65; **KBCA**, 1965-79, pd; **KKGO**, 1979-89; **KKJZ**, 1990; **KLON**, 1990-97. Born in Springfield, Massachusetts, in 1927, Chuck began with an early interest in jazz and became one of the premier djs in Southern California radio history. On air he was frequently mistaken for a black man because of his be-bop patter and soulful delivery. Leonard Feather, the respected music critic for the *LA Times*, described Chuck as "the city's perennially eloquent voice." He began his jazz interest by studying with the same clarinet instructor as woodwind specialist Phil Woods. He was influenced by his actor father, who played trombone, and his mother, a pianist. He played alto sax when he was 11 years old and played his first gig when he was 14 at a hotel which actually was a house of ill repute. He studied clarinet, then alto and tenor sax, playing in school bands. Chuck got his start in radio in 1950 through a friend of a friend of his father's who knew the owner of a radio station in Springfield. He studied at the American International College, and after serving in World War II, he received his bachelor's degree in psychology and sociology. His first trip to California didn't last long and Chuck drove to Florida, where he says a "guy pumping gas" turned out to be a bass player who mentioned an opening at a Daytona Beach radio station. Chuck did a tv sports broadcast every night and a daily radio show in West Palm Beach. He admitted that "I was a big fish in a small pond, but I wanted to find a bigger pond." His next trip to Southern California resulted in a job as the afternoon movie host on KHJ/Channel 9, and he worked part-time at KFOX, where he met Jim Gosa and the legendary "Sleepy" Stein. He started the Jazz KNOB with Gosa and Stein while doing summer stock acting. In 1965 he went to KBCA and was pd for a long stretch. The station eventually became KKGO in 1979. In the early 1980s, Chuck hosted a series of jazz concerts. He is scheduled to receive a Star on the Hollywood Walk of Fame in 1998.

NIX, Ed: **KVOE/KWIZ**, 1950-62; **KEZY**, 1962-73, nd; **KWIZ**, 1973-86, nd. Ed worked morning drive in Orange County during the '70s and '80s with Bob Shannon, Ronni Richards and Spider MacLean. He was born and raised in Chicago and studied drafting in school. His first radio job was in Kankakee, Illinois. Ed followed a radio friend to California in 1949 and worked for a Fresno radio station located in the farmer's market. When the station got into trouble, Ed took a job as a draftsman in Riverside to support his wife and two boys while waiting for his next radio assignment. He didn't wait long. In 1950 he joined KVOE (Voice of Orange Empire) which later became KWIZ and for four decades Ed was *the* news voice of Orange County. One day in 1986 he woke up and said, "That's it, I'm finished with radio" and retired. Ed lives in Anaheim and is an avid golfer.

NIXON, Joe: **KXLA**; **KRKD**; **KGBS**, 1966-67; **KIEV**, 1967-74; **KFOX**. Born in 1924, Joe started his radio career in his hometown at WIBK-Knoxville in 1949. He was very inventive in getting to Southern California, according to an interview in *R&R*. While working in Ft. Worth, he would ask all artists appearing in the Dallas area to tout "The Great Texas DJ" when they got to L.A. One day the owner of KXLA offered him a job. "I looked at him, looked at my watch, and told him, 'I couldn't possibly start until 1 o'clock.'" He appeared in hundreds of local commercials and had his own show on KTTV/Channel 11 from 1959 to 1961. In 1967 *Billboard* magazine Joe was voted 5th most popular country jock. He built KVRE-Santa Rosa. Joe owned a music publishing company and wrote 25 songs for leading country artists such as Kenny Rogers (including songs for his gold record *Mother Country Music*), Waylon Jennings, George Jones, Dean Martin and Ann-Margret. He wrote Freddy Hart's Top 10 hit *The Pleasure's Been All Mine*. After his retirement, he taught broadcasting courses at L.A. City College until 1991. He died February 2, 1995, of leukemia at age 70.

NOBLE, Kenny: **KZLA**, 1978-79; **KFOX**, 1980-81; **KWST**, 1981; **KHTZ**, 1981-85; **KFI/KOST**, 1985-86; **KLSX**, 1986-87; **KACD**, 1995-96; **KOST**, 1996.  Growing up in Houston, Ken almost became an Air Force pilot. He was honored as an outstanding military cadet in high school R.O.T.C. and went to the USAF Academy in Colorado Springs in the mid-1960s. He elected to go into radio and graduated from the Columbia School of Broadcasting. Ken started at KTFM-San Antonio in 1974. He then went to KLOL-Houston and WLUP-Chicago before KZLA in the summer of 1978. In 1977 *Billboard* magazine saluted Ken as Top Major Market Album Personality. Between

KZLA and KFOX, Kenny went to the Northwest for the first time to work for Jay Blackburn at KZOK-Seattle. His voiceover career includes many movie trailers. He ran a dj critique service for 15 years and touched many young broadcasters. Oh, his love for flying? He's a private pilot. In 1985 he was a full-time production manager at KFI and KOST with a weekend air shift and fill-in at KOST. From 1987 to 1993, he worked during the week in San Diego and weekends in L.A. Before returning to the Southland to work at KACD in 1994, Kenny worked at KAFF-Flagstaff ("great station, great environment, lousy pay") and KRWM-Seattle. He moved from weekends at "CD 103" to morning drive when pd Rob Edwards turned the station into a Hot AC format in the spring of 1995. He contributes regularly to the "Punchlines" column in the *LA Times*. What's next for Kenny? He responded in a 1995 interview: "Don't know what the Lord has in store for me. It sure has been interesting so far!" In the spring of 1996 he left KACD and worked at KOST until the fall when he moved to Seattle. In the spring of 1997 Ken joined WFLC-Miami.

NOBLE, Wendell: **KABC**, 1960-61. Wendell was one of the early talk show hosts on KABC.

NOLAN, Mike: **KFI/KOST**, 1986-97. Born in October 1949 in Van Nuys, he graduated from North Hollywood High in 1967 and two years later from Fullerton College. As a youth growing up in the San Fernando Valley, he was inspired by KMPC's Captain Max Schumacher and occasionally rode with him. Mike remembered the moment his love for flying took wing. He was about seven. "We were flying to San Francisco for Thanksgiving. I was terrified. As we sat at the end of the runway at Burbank, the plane was shaking and noisy. I was wondering what was going on. As the plane got about 15 feet in the air, I realized that something incredible was going on. I fell in love with airplanes at that exact moment." He became a pilot in 1969. Mike's radio career started in 1974 at KTRT-Truckee. All the while he combined flying and radio and in 1980 he joined KXRX/KSJO-San Jose as the traffic pilot/reporter. He went to KOY-Phoenix for almost five years. When KFI/KOST's Captain Max died in a plane crash, Mike applied for the KFI/KOST traffic job and started in August 1986. He broadcasts traffic reports from his fixed-wing plane in both drive times. No one in Mike's family had ever been in aviation, but now, his brother is an air traffic controller in Phoenix.

NORBERG, Eric: **KMPC**, 1972-75. Eric runs a music research firm for Adult Contemporary radio stations and publishes the weekly *Adult Contemporary Music Research Letter* from Portland. Born and raised in Carmel in 1943, he graduated from Pomona College in 1964 with a B.A. in English writing. The part-time teacher has

written a weekly column for *The Gavin Report* since September 1978. At KMPC he was assistant pd and weekend personality. Eric was transferred in 1975 to Golden West station KEX-Portland, a position he held till 1979. In the 1980s Eric was gm/pd and personality at KWIP-Salem and pd of KPNW-Eugene. In the summer of 1996 his book *Radio Programming Tactics & Strategy* was published by *Broadcasting*'s Focal Press.

NORELL, Adrienne: **KLIT**, 1992-94; **KXEZ**, 1995-96

NORMAN, Gene: **KFWB**, 1944-52; **KLAC**, 1952-58. Gene was one of the "Big Five" jocks on KLAC during the 1950s. He left KLAC over the format switch to what he called "formula radio." "Formula Radio" was an attempt to combat the impressive launch of "Color Radio" on KFWB. Gene has operated successfully in every form of musical presentation. Besides radio, he had his own tv show on KHJ/Channel 9 and owned two famous nightclubs, the Crescendo (later became the

popular teen hangout, Tiger's Tail) and Interlude on the Sunset Strip. His interest in jazz inspired his first "Just Jazz" concert, featuring Benny Goodman, Peggy Lee and Erroll Garner. The concerts continued for two decades. Since the sale of the nite clubs in the mid-sixties, Gene has devoted most of his time to the development of his GNP Crescendo and Creative World record labels. He has five publishing companies and several of his albums have been nominated for or won Grammies. Born in New York, he was trained as a classical violinist. He played saxophone and clarinet in college dance bands, graduating from the University of Wisconsin at 18. "I was the first announcer at WPAT-Patterson, New Jersey in 1941. Before arriving in the Southland he worked at KMJ-Fresno, KLX-Oakland and KGO-San Francisco. Gene lives in West Los Angeles.

NORMAN, George: **KLAC**, 1959. George was the director of operations at KLAC.

**KNX/FM to KKHR (93.1FM)
-August 25, 1983**

NORMAN, Pat: **KRTH**, 1985-91, gm. Pat ran KFRC-San Francisco in the 1970s. He died of a brain tumor.

NORMAN, Phil: **KNX**, 1959; **KBIG**, 1968-69

NORRIE, David: **KMPC**, 1991-93; **XTRA**, 1994-95. The former Bruin football quarterback worked the UCLA games on the radio. Before starting in 1991, his only experience was a week at Roy Englebrecht's sportscasting camp. As a QB, David helped the Bruins to three Rose Bowl championships and one Fiesta Bowl championship. He led the Pac-10 in passing in 1985. He was quarterback for the New York Jets in 1987. David was promoted for the UCLA announcing job by former Bruin football coach Terry Donahue. He also hosted a sports show with Joe McDonnell during KMPC's experiment with all-Sports radio. David also works in real estate for CB Commercial. David is the color commentator for Fox Sports Pac-10 football regional syndication telecast package.

NORRIS, Jane: **KFI**, 1991-97. Jane was an early evening talk host. In 1991 she swirled in a whirlwind of controversy following an aggressive interview with KCBS/Channel 2 anchor Bree Walker. Bree was pregnant and doctors claimed there was a 50% chance that her ectrodactylism, a rare genetic condition that results in fused fingers and toes, would be passed on to her child. Jane asked listeners to call in with comments on whether she should conceive a child. She works part-time news at KFI.

NORTH, John: **XTRA**, 1960-65; **KLAC**, 1965-70; **KNX**. Born John North Edy, he worked during the early stages of McLendon's all-News operation out of Tijuana that covered Southern California. John is heard doing relief at KFWB.

NORTON, Duke: **KLAC**, 50s, 60s; **KBIG**, 1967, pd; **KLVE**. Duke was one of the "Big Five" djs at KLAC. He broadcast the all-night show from a window at Wallichs Music City at the corner of Sunset and Vine.

NOVAK, John: **KFOX**, 1973-75; **KWIZ**, 1975-89. Born in Missouri, John grew up in Washington. While attending Eastern Washington State in Spokane, he had a roommate in radio and decided to pursue a similar career. After college, John worked in Spokane, Michigan and Iowa. His last stop was KLAK-Denver before arriving in the Southland. He has been the voice of Orange County's PBS/TV station KOCE for the past decade. John currently does voiceovers and works with Hunter-Barth ad agency in Orange County.

NOVAK, Lisa: **KWST**, 1979. Born Lisa Epstein, she left the Southland for KSJO-San Jose and in the mid-'80s performed on KRQR-San Francisco. She returned to law school in 1985.

NOVAK, Mike: **KIQQ**, 1973-74. Mike was born and raised in Modesto and has worked exclusively in California. "I got into this business totally as an accident. During my sophomore year in college I was a bio-chem major and needed an elective, and a friend said, 'take radio.' And I said, 'take radio where?' And the rest is history. I've never been back in a lab since. Dreams do come true." His first station was in Turlock doing nights while in college. After college he did afternoons at KYNO-Fresno. His third job was KFRC-San Francisco, first as the all-night guy and then middays. "I knew the Drake/Chenault people, so when they bought KIQQ, they asked me to be part of the on-air staff." He got the programming bug and returned to KYNO to do mornings and programming. Later in the 1970s, Mike returned to do afternoons at KFRC for Les Garland, who happens to be his son's godfather. He spent time at KYUU-San Francisco before going to San Diego, where he has worked since 1983. He was first pd of "B-100," and then pd of KWLT. In 1991 he moved to KSON-San Diego. He also does voiceover work in San Diego and Los Angeles and hosts a tv movie every week.

NOVAK, Mimi: **KXEZ**, 1990-92; **KODJ/KCBS**, 1993-97. Mimi is part of the morning drive team on "Arrow 93." Mimi was born July 6 in Wallingford, Connecticut. She graduated from Boston Conservatory of Music with a theater major. She spent a year in New York taking acting and voice classes before moving to the West Coast. Mimi joined a band and "sang that new wave crap," Mimi laughed. She's done on-camera commercials for McDonald's and other national clients. She got her start in radio at Metro Traffic. Between

KXEZ and KCBS Mimi was a traffic reporter for Shadow Broadcast Services. When KODJ changed

formats to "classic rock" and became "Arrow 93," Mimi was part of the transition. Mimi lives in the Hollywood Hills and has been active in the local Big Sister program. In 1997 she was nominated for Best Newscast by Associated Press.

NUCKOLS, Joe: **KYPA**, 1996-97, gm. As co-founder of the motivational format, Joe launched 1,000-watt KYPA in 1996. Joe was programming a Big Band station in Florida during the mid-1980s when he was introduced to a tape by Zig Ziglar. Joe was struck by the idea to run 24-hours of motivational speakers like Anthony Robbins, Deepak Chopra and Leo Buscaglia. WWNN (Winners News Network) in Ft. Lauderdale became the flagship station.

NUELL, Joy: **KFWB**, 1969-84. Joy was raised locally and received her degree in languages and art. She loved Al Jarvis' "Make Believe Ballroom" long before she had

any thoughts of KFWB in her professional future. As a matter of fact, she resisted Herb Humphries repeated attempts to hire her as a newsroom secretary, probably, she thinks, because she may have been the only applicant to not ask about possible on-air opportunities. Also, Joy told Humphries that if it made him more comfortable during the job interview, he should feel free to say "f...". Joy's reservations about news disappeared after one day in the KFWB newsroom on Hollywood Blvd. Although Humphries moved on within weeks of hiring her, Joy went to a fifteen year on-air career. Joy was L.A.'s first full-time female radio news reporter, a fact which, she says, makes her feel old, but which she feels proud of since the trend continued to the point that women make up at least half of most news staffs. Highlights of her on-air career include network coverage of the Pentagon Papers Trial and being sent to cover Pope John Paul's visit to Mexico, his first to the Western Hemisphere (AP sent seventeen reporters, Westinghouse sent Joy and did an ad campaign featuring "Joy to the Pope"). When Joy left KFWB she became president of a communications company that provided media training for executives and spokespeople. In 1991 she was press deputy for L.A. City Councilwoman Joy Picus. Since 1995 Joy has been director of marketing for APA Travel Center in Beverly Hills.

NUNEZ, Linda: **KNX**, 1990-97. Linda is morning drive co-anchor at all-News KNX. A Southern California native, Linda graduated from Long Beach Polytechnic High School, then attended UC Berkeley, where she double-majored in mass communications and sociology. While in college, she interned at KBLX-Berkeley and KQED-San Francisco. After graduation she worked as an anchor/reporter for KTMS/KHTY-Santa Barbara. She joined "KNXNewsradio" in May 1990.

NUNEZ, Rick: **KGFJ**, 1986. Rick worked mornings at the Urban station.

NYE, Louis: **KLAC**, 1959-60. Louis was one of the funnymen from the Steve Allen tv show who worked weekends during one of the resurrections of "The Big 5" djs. He appeared on Broadway in *Charley's Aunt*.

If I didn't pursue radio:

Bob HUDSON: "I most likely would have been involved with sales. I would have enjoyed being a trial lawyer."

Rick DEES: "Psychiatry and maybe Amway on the side."

Dick WHITTINGTON: "Probably writing bad essays for obscure magazines."

Gary OWENS: "I'd probably be a cartoonist."

Charlie TUNA: "Writing in some form. My English teachers had all encouraged me."

Dave HULL: "Secret service agent - protecting the life of the president.

Bill BALLANCE: "Civil war writing."

O

O, Steven: SEE Steven-O Sellers

O'BRIEN, Jim: **KBBQ**, 1967; **KHJ**, 1969-70, pd. Born in Galveston, Jim arrived in the Southland from KCBQ-San Diego where he was pd and a jock. Between KBBQ and KHJ, he worked at WOR/FM-New York. At KHJ Jim replaced the legendary Ron Jacobs as pd. His first move was to loosen air personalities. He described the change: "It's like a rebirth within the framework of a Drake station." Jim later went to Philadelphia. While working at WFIL, Jim started doing tv work on WPVI which included part-time sportscasting and hosting *Dialing for Dollars*. He was best known in Philadelphia as a tv weatherman. During a station promotion in 1983, he parachuted out of a plane with another guy, and their cords became tangled. Jim cut his own cords and fell to his death thinking that the two jumpers could not both survive. It was his 814th jump.

O'BRIEN, Ron: **KFI**, 1979-81; **KROQ**, 1981; **KIIS**, 1982-87, pd; **KKBT**, 1989-91; **KOCM/KSRF**, 1991-92; **KIIS**, 1992-93. Born in Des Moines, Ron was the md at WFIL-Philadelphia before coming to Southern California. His earlier stops included WCAR-Detroit, WRKO-Boston, WCFL-Chicago, WPGC-Washington, DC and WNBC-New York. In the summer of 1981 Ron worked as Eugene Oregon at KROQ. Ron commented that he was "#1 rated for 14 consecutive ARBs during the glory years at KIIS." In 1988 he went to WKBQ-St. Louis. For seven years he hosted the nationally syndicated CHR show "On the Radio," which was heard on over 200 stations coast to coast. In the fall of 1989, Big Ron was part of the launch of "MARS/fm" and KKBT as afternoon drive personality and stayed through 1991. In the '90s Ron worked for KZDG-Denver and KKBH-San Diego. In the summer of 1996 he went to afternoon drive at WYXR-Philadelphia.

O'BRIEN, Scott: **KORG**, 1973. Scott was last heard on KXDC-Monterey.

O'CONNOR, Ken: SEE Bob Allen

O'CONNOR, Mike: **KGBS**, 1975

O'CONNOR, Pat: **KNAC**. "Pounding Pat," as he was known on KNAC, is now selling CDs and records.

O'DONNELL, Charlie: **KRLA**, 1964-67; **KGBS**, 1968-69; **KLAC**, 1969-71; **KBBQ**, 1971; **KLAC**, 1984-89. Charlie has been one of the versatile booming voices that endures with each project in which he engages. In addition to an on-air career in L.A. radio for over two decades, Charlie was the sidekick to Dick Clark on *American Bandstand* for decades. He has hosted local tv dance shows (*Bash* and *Hollywood Discotheque*), was the announcer on *Everybody's Talking*, *Wedding Game*, *TV Bloopers* and *Wheel of Fortune* for 22 years and *American Music Awards* for 24 years. Known as "The Jolly Lean Giant" at KRLA because of his lanky height, Charlie did morning drive for part of his tenure. For 16 years he was a news anchor at KCOP/Channel 13. Born in Philadelphia, he started his career in Chambersburg, Pennsylvania while still a teen. After working in Baltimore, he returned to Philadelphia and hosted an all-night movie show on WFIL/TV. By the time he was 26 he was an ABC network announcer.

O'DONOGHUE, Deirdre: **KKGO**, 1979; **KCRW**, 1980-86; **KMET**, 1983-87; **KNX/FM**, 1987-88; **KLSX**, 1988-97. The longtime host of "Breakfast With The Beatles" and "Snap" claimed in a 1996 *LA Times* profile: "These two shows represent my four favorite hours of the week." Born in 1948, Deirdre started her radio career in 1974 at WBCN-Boston, a station that she maintains "may still be the best radio station in the world." Beginning in 1983, Deirdre was heard on two FM stations - non-commercial KCRW and KMET. She was with corporate giant KMET until 1987 when the station changed format and call letters. Her show "Snap" (acronym of "Saturday Night Avant Pop") on KCRW aired three nights a week with anything considered on the cutting edge of contemporary Pop. In 1986, she was one of the five finalists in the best-deejay category of the 1986 New Music Awards. Since 1988 she has been hosting KLSX's Sunday morning show "Breakfast With The Beatles."

O'HAIR, Thom: **KMET**, 1975-76; **KFI**, 1984. His early success was in the Bay Area at KSAN and KMEL. He was the pd under gm Tom Donahue at KSAN (during the days in which Tom was known as the only vice president of a major American corporation to sport a full length pony tail). Thom was named major market program director of 1975. As 1977 rolled around, the time had come to start something new, and he returned to San Francisco to launch KMEL. His personal life began to spiral, but after his AOR experience, Thom worked in Portland in 1980 at KQFM. Off the air he worked at various audio, video and computer firms. He developed training programs for the Intercollegiate Broadcasting System. In 1985, he started a syndicated radio news service called "Rip 'n' Read." At KOFY in 1988, he called his new format AS ("Adult Smoking"). "If it smokes on the air, we'll play it. We're looking to portray the spirit of San Francisco." He has been producing Mountain Blue Grass Festivals for many years.

Chuck Cecil has a library of 50,000 records and more than 300 interviews with greats like Louis Armstrong, Woody Herman and Benny Goodman.

O'HARA, Russ: **KGFJ**, 1968; **KRLA**, 1969-72; **KKDJ**, 1972-74; **KEZY**, 1975-77; **KROQ**, 1979; **KRLA**, 1981-82; **KRLA**, 1992-93. Born Russell Neileigh in 1946, the California native from Glendale spent time at many California stations from KSEE-Santa Maria to KMEN-San Bernardino. In 1968 he worked at KFIF-Tucson.

Russ spent part of his time at KRLA working morning drive. In 1973, the station went MOR from a mix of contemporary/oldies, and jock teams were set for every time period. Russ was teamed with Steve Brown. His last assignment in Southern California was doing afternoon drive at KRLA. "Russ O'Hungry," as he frequently called himself, went to do mornings at KEZN-Palm Desert.

O'HARA, Steve: **KFWB**; **KCBS**

O'KEEFE, Walter: **KHJ**, 1962. Walter did remotes from the Hollywood Brown Derby and later at the Villa Capri restaurant. The former movie actor spun records and interviewed Hollywood celebrities.

O'LEARY, Jim: **KBIG**, 1960; **KFI**, 1965-68. Jim also worked as John Patrick. He spent some time in San Diego. Jim worked the all-night shift at KFI. He died in the late 1960s.

O'NEAL, Don: **KIIS**, 1990-94. Born Donald McDonald in Glendale, Don grew up in Bakersfield and achieved his boyhood goal of working at KIIS. His first on-air job was at KERN-Bakersfield when he was 14 years old. He was doing the all-night shift while in high school. After graduation, Don went to KDON-Monterey and in 1986 he was at KBOS-Fresno. His last stop before landing at KIIS in December 1990 was WCKZ ("KISS 102")-Charlotte.

He's currently pd at KFRR-Fresno, now known as "K-104 In-A-Row." "KIIS is a wonderful radio station. It is the epitome of all radio entertainment!" Don is currently pd at KFRR, KJFX and KYNO-Fresno and consults KDJK-Modesto.

O'NEIL, Garvey: **KLAC**, 1959

O'NEIL, Mike: **KHJ**, 1969-71; **KWIZ**, 1972-73; **KUTE/KGFJ**, 1974-76; **KIQQ**, 1975-77; **KUTE**, 1977-78; **KIIS**, 1978-83; **KLAC**, 1983-86; **KRTH/KHJ**, 1986-87; **KMPC**, 1989-90. Born and raised in Santa Monica, Mike worked in television as a child on *Leave It To Beaver*, *Ozzie & Harriet* and *The Donna Reed Show*. During the mid-1960s he played guitar in a couple of rock groups. In late 1969 Mike worked weekends at KHJ and became hooked on radio. "I worked every format from Rock to Bach and back." He used the name Mike Jones at KWIZ and KGFJ. Mike started a voiceover career

in 1989 and has done promos for all networks and trailers for Paramount Pictures and Universal Studios. In 1990 he built a home in Las Vegas with a 32-track digital studio. In 1996 he went back on the air in Las Vegas at KBGO. "I consider myself the luckiest guy in the world, as I have a gorgeous wife and wonderful family and have been able to make a living all these years by shooting off my mouth...which I love to do."

O'NEIL, Randy and Steve: SEE Randy Gardner

O'NEIL, Scott: **KNX/FM**, 1965-71, pd; **KGIL**, 1971-74; **KPRZ**, 1983-85; **KKLA**, 1985-86; **KMPC/KLIT**, 1985-92, pd; **KJQI/KOJI**, 1995. Scott was born in 1942 in Raleigh and graduated from the University of North Carolina with a broadcasting journalism degree. He arrived in the Southland from WKRG-Mobile to work at KNX/FM and within two years was appointed pd. He replaced one of the legendary voices on KGIL, Paul Compton. At KKLA he hosted an afternoon drive show, "Music on Faith." At KMPC Scott was the midday host. When KMPC's sister station KLIT joined the Lite AC format battle, Scott was deejay and pd. When the all-Sports format was attempted on KMPC, Scott "was brought in and asked to save a sinking ship," according to Larry Stewart of the *LA Times*. "O'Neil did the best he could. He immediately lifted morale and brought in upbeat Charlie Tuna to host the important morning drive shift." Scott is now part of the syndicated "Music of Your Life" format and broadcasts from a studio in his Las Vegas home. He also works at "Sunny 106.5."

O'NEILL, Erin: **KACE**, 1979-80

O'NEILL, Gary: **KGFJ**, 1983-84; **XHRM**, pd. When Gary left radio he joined Warner Bros. records in urban promotion.

O'NEILL, Greg: **KSRF**, 1988-90; **KXEZ**, 1990-96. Born in Seattle, Greg lost his home in the 1994 California earthquake. He praised KXEZ's parent company in an open letter to *R&R*: "When my wife and I lost our home during the January earthquake, Viacom came through for us with psychological and financial assistance - immediately. Our memories of how the people came to our aid will last a lifetime." He got the radio "bug" while in college. "I spent more time in the campus station than I did in class." Greg arrived in the Southland from "C-Fox"-Vancouver, B.C. He moved to mornings at KXEZ in late 1992. Greg is also a writer for comedians and has had two films produced (as a writer) as well as episodic tv shows.

O'NEILL, Jimmy: **KRLA**, 1959-62; **KFWB**, 1963-67; **KDAY**, 1969-71; **KRLA**, 1984-85 and 1990-93. Jimmy was the host of one of the earliest network (ABC) tv rock shows, *Shindig!* when he was only 22 years old.

The program regulars were Leon Russell, Darlene Love, and Billy Preston, and one of the dancers who frugged and twisted was actress Teri Garr. In the mid-1960s the show brought some of the greatest names in rock 'n' roll into America's living rooms. Born in Enid, Oklahoma, Jimmy worked three times at KRLA. He arrived in Southern California from KQV-Pittsburgh. Jimmy was one of the original "11-10 Men" when the Rock station debuted on September 3, 1959. In 1960, at the age of 20, he became the youngest deejay ever to be rated #1. In 1962, Jimmy opened the first Los Angeles teenage nightclub, Pandora's Box, a former coffee house on the Sunset Strip. He opened two other teenage nightclubs in Los Angeles: The Showboat on Melrose (partnered with Phil Everly and Sam Riddle) and the Chez Paree on La Cienega. Jimmy's first tv exposure was *The Jimmy O'Neill Show* on KCOP/Channel 13. It was a 1962 youth-oriented talk show. Rhino Records released *Shindig!* on home video in 1992. *People* magazine chronicled Jimmy's journey: "In 1966, unable to find steady work in showbiz, he began a downward journey that would take him through several careers, three marriages and years of drug and alcohol abuse." When his first wife, Sharon (*Poor Little Fool*) Sheeley, left him the same month *Shindig!* was canceled, the stress was too much. *People* reported that one night shortly after the show's demise, a drunken O'Neill tried to set Sheeley's house on fire. When police and firefighters arrived, he says, they took pity on the obviously troubled former star and told him to go home and sleep it off. Since he couldn't burn the house down, he took a sledgehammer to it. He was taken to a psychiatric hospital for observation but was quickly released without treatment. He then went to radio jobs in Albuquerque and Omaha, where he met and married the sister of actor Troy Donahue. Jimmy found a 12-step recovery group and gave up drinking. He spent the seventies selling stocks and cars and managing nightclubs. He ended the *People* piece: "I have walked through every nightmare you can imagine and come out okay."

O'SHEA, Michael: **KPOL**, 1979, pd; **KMPC**, 1979-80. The former midday jock at KLIF-Dallas in the late 1960s has carved great success out of the Great Northwest. He joined KPOL in 1979 from KVI-Seattle where he was pd. Within the year he was national pd for Golden West Broadcasting. He's currently president of New Century Management, Inc. in Seattle.

OAKES, Robert: **KFWB**, 1967, pd. In 1980 Robert was pd of KSTP-Minneapolis.

OAKES, Royal: **KPCC**, 1983-88; **KFWB**, 1988-97; **KABC**, 1994-97. During the "trial of the century," Royal was one of the resident legal voices heard on KFWB and KABC describing the O.J. Simpson proceedings. Royal's interest in radio started in the early 1970s while attending UCLA and working as a newsman and dj on campus station KLA. He went on to get a law degree and became a partner in the firm of Barger & Wolen, where he specializes in business litigation,

employment law and media law. In 1983, Royal started broadcasting a one-minute spot, "Focus on the Law," on KPCC. The feature wound up being syndicated on 55 NPR stations. KFWB hired Royal in 1988 to be the on-air legal adviser. In addition to his "Focus" feature, he has been there for analysis during highly visible trials. His legal expertise and on-air skills have evolved to talk show work on many California stations.

OBER, Ken: **KLSX**, 1995-96. Ken, a graduate of the University of Massachusetts at Amherst, worked in Boston radio before moving to New York to pursue comedy and acting. He appeared in the tv sitcoms *Parenthood* and *Fresh Prince of Bel Air*. He hosted MTV's *Remote Control* and teamed with former *Brady Bunch* star Susan Olsen as part of the launch of "Real Radio," a non-traditional Talk format. He and Susan left KLSX in early summer 1996. Ken is currently hosting a new tv version of *Make Me Laugh*.

What is the quality you like most in a man? "The ability to shave his chest hair so he can run faster."
-Top Ten personality Gary Owens

OCEAN, Bobby: **KHJ**, 1975-80; **KWST**, 1980-82. Born Ray Lenhart in Las Vegas, Bobby is arguably the best

production man in Contemporary radio. The seventh generation Californian started in radio as Ray Farrell on KMBY-Monterey. In 1968, Bobby was Johnny Scott on KYNO-Fresno before becoming Bobby Ocean at KGB-San Diego in March 1968. He joined KCBQ-San Diego in 1971. Bobby debuted on KFRC-San Francisco in September 1972 and on May 2, 1975, joined KHJ. He left "Boss Radio" in March 1980 to successfully pursue voiceover work in Los Angeles and also joined "K-West" that same year. He left KWST in the spring of 1982 to return to his native San Francisco. He joined K101 but was soon heard again on KFRC beginning February 10, 1983. Fourteen years later he continues to be KFRC's image voice. Though no longer a dj, his voice and production talents are heard all over the country. Bobby describes his promos: "...3-D: Dimensional, Dynamic, and Diverse...that's what keeps our clients coming back for more."

OHSE, Dan: SEE Daniel

OLBERMANN, Keith: **KNX**, 1985-92. The puckish sportscaster worked on KNX providing sports reports and commentary ("The Sports Column") in both drive periods. He co-anchored KNX wire-to-wire coverage of the L.A. Marathon for four years. Born in New York in 1959, Keith graduated in 1979 with a

B.S. in communications from Cornell University. Always in sportscasting, he started as a commentator for UPI Radio Network in 1979, moving to RKO Radio Network a year later. Assignments for WNEW-New York, WCVB/TV-Boston, CNN and ABC Radio preceded his journey to Southern California. While on KNX, Keith was a sportscaster for KTLA/Channel 5 and later KCBS/Channel 2. Larry Stewart of the *LA Times* reported his salary went from $80,000 to $250,000 when he joined Channel 2. In 1992 he became a part of ESPN and three years later he won the Cable Ace Award as the best sports host on cable tv. Keith left ESPN in the summer of 1997 and planned to join FOX Sports in the fall.

OLDEN, Jackie: **KNX**, 1978-86; **KABC**, 1986-87; **KGIL**, 1988-92; **KABC**, 1992; **KNX**, 1994. Born in 1934, Jackie hosted the "Food News Hour" on KNX. The native Nebraskan has co-authored countless cookbooks, is a community activist, appeared as a regular on ABC's *Home Show* and is the mother of three. She earned her chef certification at Los Angeles Trade-Tech. For 10 years she ran Just Ask Jackie, an Orange County catering company. Angry that she could not secure a contract at KNX, she bolted for KABC. During her second stint with KNX she hosts a weekend food show. Jackie's signature greeting to her listeners is a cheery "Come On Into The Kitchen."

OLDEN, Paul: **KMPC**, 1990-91. Paul announced play-by-play for the UCLA Bruins basketball and football games. In 1990 he replaced Joe Torre as KTLA/Channel 5's Angel play-by-play announcer and also hosted a baseball show called "Sportsline." In 1991 he started covering the L.A. Rams and moved from UCLA to the Rams, replacing Eddie Doucette. Before arriving in the Southland Paul was a radio announcer for the Cleveland Indians for two seasons.

OLIVA, George: **KFI**, 1989-91, pd. George left the station in June 1991. He is now writing.

OLIVER, King: **KJLH**, 1979-86; **KACE**. King is now retired.

OSBORN, Jamie: **KQLZ**, 1989-91. Jamie did production and on-air work at "Pirate Radio." He sounded so much like Shadow Steele that when he sat in for him, he called himself Shadow. He became a production engineer at Westwood One. In the fall of 1995, Jamie started doing mornings at KEDG-Las Vegas.

OLNEY, Warren: **KCRW**, 1992-97. The longtime tv news reporter and anchor hosts "Which Way, L.A.?" The program became a regular feature as an outgrowth of the Los Angeles civil disturbance of 1992. Between 1966 and 1991, Warren served as news reporter and anchor for a half-dozen tv stations in California, including four in Los Angeles. He has covered local, state and national politics, including presidential nominating conventions of both parties. He taught broadcast journalism at USC from 1976 to 1982. A graduate of Amherst College in Massachusetts, he earned a B.A. in English, magna cum laude, and was Phi Beta Kappa. His list of extraordinary awards is long and includes the Sigma Delta Chi's Broadcast Journalist of the Year. His daily show on

KCRW consists of guest interviews and listener call-ins on the future of Southern California and has earned 17 local, state and national awards.

OLSEN, Susan: **KLSX**, 1995-96. The former *Brady Bunch* tv star was best known for her role as Cindy Brady. She teamed with Ken Ober during the launch of "Real Radio" in the summer of 1995. Susan attended the American Academy of Dramatic Arts and worked as a graphic artist. She co-executive produced CBS' *Brady Bunch Home Movies*. She left KLSX in early summer 1996.

OLSON, Stu: **KVFM**, 1969-74; **KWST**, 1971-72; **KWNK**, 1987. Stu became an actor who appeared on such shows as *Punky Brewster*. He went on to the Creative Radio Network.

ORDUNIO, Doug: **KFAC**, 1973-86; **KKGO**, 1991. In addition to a weekend air shift, Doug was music director of Classical station KFAC. Born in Glendale in 1950, Doug attended UCLA, Glendale College and Cal State Northridge. Close to graduation in 1973, he got the job at KFAC. He sings professionally as a tenor in various churches around Southern California. Doug performed in the chorus with the New York City Opera at the L.A. Music Center and was in the chorus in a production of *The Barber of Seville*. In 1987 Doug translated about six turn-of-the-century German plays by Frank Wedekind and Carol Sternheim. He is currently the senior music programmer for AEI Inflight, which is the largest provider of audio programs for over 30 airlines. Doug designs web sites for users of the Internet. For over a decade he hosted a classical music program for Armed Forces Radio.

OREGON, Eugene: SEE Ron O'Brien

ORNEST, Laura: **KFWB**; **KNX**. Laura's father owned the St. Louis Blues hockey team.

ORR, Vern: **KZLA/KLAC**, 1982-85, gm. While KHJ and KLAC were battling each other for Country format leader, KZLA quietly slipped through the noise and became number one. "Most of us in radio take ourselves so seriously, but let's face it - we're not building the MX missile here. We're trying to entertain people."

ORTAL, Raul: **XPRS**; **KALI**, 1971-95, gm; **KVCA**, 1997. From Mexico, Raul started with KALI as an announcer and moved methodically up through the ranks until he became vp/gm of the Spanish station. He joined Fonovista and worked afternoon drive for Radio Express. In the spring of 1997 Raul became om of "Radio Centro America," KVCA.

ORTEGA, Sam: **KRLA**, 1996-97. Sam was born and raised in the San Gabriel Valley. He grew up listening to the sounds of KRLA, KDAY and KUTE. In the early 1980s Sam lived in Phoenix. He graduated from the Academy of Radio Broadcasting in Huntington Beach. Sam formerly worked at KMEN-San Bernardino. He now works swing at KRLA.

> *"Magnificent Montague was one of the world's most-heralded and most-copied air personalities, more than the world realizes."*
> *-former Billboard editor Claude Hall*

ORTIZ and LOMELI: **KTNQ**, 1996-97. Juan Carlos Ortiz and Marta Lomeli are a psychologist and marital counselor respectively. They host an evening talk show on KTNQ dealing with intimate subjects in a manner that is both professional and understanding.

ORTIZ, Ricardo: **KLVE**, 1991-94. Ricardo worked the all-night shift on Spanish "K-Love." He is now doing voiceover work.

OSBORN, Lisa: **KKLA**, 1995; **KFI**, 1996. Lisa hosted "The Information Highway" each afternoon on Christian KKLA. She works weekend news on KFI.

OSCAR, Carlos: **KLSX**, 1995-97. Born in New York City, Carlos was raised on the streets of East Los Angeles. He worked late evenings during the launch of the "Real Radio" format in the summer of 1995. Carlos trained to be a physical therapist before he got into comedy and his television appearances include Comedy Central and an HBO special. He was featured in Eddie Murphy's *Vampire in Brooklyn*. Oscar left the Talk station in early 1997.

OSHIN, Steve: **KBIG**, 1983-97, vp/gm. Steve started his career as a media buyer for Esaman, Johns & Laws Advertising. In 1983 he joined KBIG as a sales person and moved through the sales ranks. In the fall of 1995, Steve was promoted from vp of sales to vp/gm of KBIG.

OSTER, Ron: **KWIZ**

OTIS, Don: **KHJ**, 1965. From a local advertising agency, Don became pd for a short time prior to the launch of "Boss Radio."

OTIS, Johnny: **KFOX**, 1958; **XERB**, 1967; **KPPC**, 1968-69; **KPFK**, 1975-89. Born John Veliotes on December 28, 1921, of Greek parentage in an integrated section of Vallejo, Johnny decided early on to live in the black community. In a 1979 *LA Times* interview, he confirmed, "Despite all the hardships, there's a wonderful richness in black culture that I prefer." He reflected on his childhood in a 1995 *OC Register* profile: "It was just the kids in my neighborhood that I played with, they were of the African American culture. We were raised together and I didn't care to leave and go anywhere else." How did he get to L.A.? Johnny was interviewed by Billy Vera and told this story: "I was working with the Love Otis Band at the Barrelhouse in Omaha. Jimmy Witherspoon and Nat Cole, before they were big stars, came to Omaha. They said that Harlin Leonard was looking for me because the great drummer Jessie Price was going in the Army and wanted him to play drums. At first I thought it was too good to be true, but that's how I got to L.A." In the early 1940s when Johnny first moved to Los Angeles, he was making $75 a week as a drummer at the Club Alabam. It was all big band music. By the late 1940s, swing and big bands were dying, r&b

was beginning to take hold, and Johnny was on the ground floor. He was one of the forerunners of the r&b music of the 1950s, leading his band to a #1 single, *Willie and the Handjive*. Johnny hosted a local tv "musical show" that had guests like the Moonglows, Everly Brothers, Sam Cooke, Drifters, Little Richard and Ray Charles. He was a regular at the El Monte American Legion Stadium. As a writer he scored hits with *Dance With Me Henry, So Fine* and *All Night Long*. He produced early hits for Little Richard, Johnny Ace and Etta James, and he discovered Jackie Wilson, Little Willie John and Hank Ballard & the Midnighters. He was a record producer and talent scout before touring with his own revue. With the 1960s in full gear and the advent of the Beatles, r&b suddenly died. Johnny then became involved in the civil rights movement, wrote a sociopolitical column for the *LA Sentinel* and was a dj south of the border on XERB in 1967. He twice lost the Democratic nomination for a California State Assembly seat and was chief of staff for former Lt. Governor and Representative Mervyn Dymally. Johnny had a jazz show on KPFK. In the early 1990s, he tired of living in L.A. and bought a farm near Sebastopol. Outside the front window of his sprawling ranch-style house are life-size sculptures of three women, nude except for togas. His barn has been converted into a recording studio. In 1995 he was selling his likeness on bottles of Johnny Otis Apple Juice in San Francisco health food stores. He celebrated his artwork in a new book from Pomegranate Artbooks, *Colors and Chords: The Art of Johnny Otis*. Johnny and his wife Phyllis have been married for over a half century.

OWEN, Ray: **KPOL**, 1961-69, nd. Ray taught radio broadcasting at Valley College in Van Nuys and is retired and living in Aqua Dulce.

OWENS, Buck: **KBBQ**, 1967. The legendary country singer once worked as a dj. By 1970 Buck owned four radio stations, four ranches, a travel agency, a recording studio, a million-dollar publishing company and a syndicated tv show that was shot in Oklahoma City. Buck was born on August 12, 1929, in Sherman, Texas. The son of a sharecropper, he left school in the ninth grade to work in an Arizona nightclub. His first big hit was *Under Your Spell Again* in 1959. A big break came in 1963 when his song *Act Naturally* was recorded by the Beatles. The single that launched his singing career was *Tiger by the Tail*.

> "I'm Wolfman Jack, the guy who used to wash cars in Brooklyn and got lucky."
>
> `-from his autobiography`

OWENS, Gary: **KFWB**, 1961-62; **KMPC**, 1962-81; **KPRZ**, 1982-84; **KKGO**, 1985-86; **KFI**, 1986-89; **KLAC**, 1992; **KJQY/KOJY**, 1993-95. Nationally known for holding his cupped hand over his ear while announcing the comedy breakthrough show *Laugh-In*, Gary has become one of the most decorated broadcasters in Los Angeles radio history. Sifting through the voluminous chronicles of his existence, it becomes clear that economy of verbiage with a wry twist of words heightened his comedy. Gary was born Gary Altman in Plankenton, South Dakota (pop 600). He went to school

in Mitchell, South Dakota. Gary's first job in radio seems prophetic in retrospect - he started on KORN radio. Gary worked on KMA-Shenandoah, Iowa, and then went to Burden's KOIL-Omaha. It was at KOIL that Gary changed his name to Owens from his birth name that he had been using. He recalled for the *LA Times*: "We had six turntables and we'd stand while doing the show. And we had two Magnacord recorders, so we were always running around like octopuses while on the air. I went home with tears in my eyes and stood there at the front door of my not-too-lavish apartment thinking I wanted to go back to South Dakota." Some of his stops before California included KIMN-Denver, KILT-Houston and KTSA-San Antonio. In 1957, at WNOE-New Orleans, Gary came out with the first adult coloring book to be used as a giveaway. Other humorous giveaways included a two-piece Gary Owens jigsaw puzzle that still looked wrong after being assembled. Gary's next stop was WIL-St. Louis, followed by KEWB-San Francisco. He moved to sister station KFWB in 1961 and immediately a strike of newsmen took place. Gary honored the strike but went broke not being able to work. Five and a half months later, the strike ended and "G.O." became the morning man at KFWB where he garnered number one ratings. A year later, he accepted an offer from KMPC, where he stayed for two decades becoming the top afternoon broadcaster in Southern California. Gary went on to do tv and commercials. He has made over 1,000 national on-camera tv appearances, been on over 10,000 radio shows, nearly 3,000 cartoon episodes, 35 videos (that have sold over 500,000 copies), 20 albums and CDs (six have garnered Grammy nominations), 12 books on tape, thousands of commercials (he has won over 50 Clio awards) and been in 12 motion pictures. His first was Disney's *The Love Bug* which was one of the top-

grossing films of 1969. As a member of the star-studded cast of *Laugh-In* for all six seasons on NBC/TV, Gary did every episode of the Emmy award-winning comedy variety show. He made famous the phrase "Beautiful Downtown Burbank" which he had been using for years on his radio show. He has been called "a legend" by *R&R* and *Billboard* magazine. *Advertising Age* and *Adweek* called him "the most decorated man in broadcasting." One magazine described Gary as being "as much a part of the L.A. tapestry as the beautiful sunset in Santa Monica." Gary's Star on the fabled Hollywood Walk of Fame is next to Walt Disney's at 6743 Hollywood Boulevard. In 1971 Dan Rowan and Dick Martin stood on Gary's head at NBC and an impression of his ear was placed in cement as the *Laugh-In* cast cheered him on. One of Gary's most human characteristics is his willingness to help young people. David Letterman, while at Ball State, wrote Gary asking for advice about creative comedy writing. He started comedian/actor Albert Brooks in the business as well as a number of producers, writers and comedians. He was the emcee for the 1969 Grammy ceremony. He was also the nighttime host of *The Gong Show*. Gary's comedy writing included *Bullwinkle* and *Fractured Flickers*. He was the voice of Roger Ramjet. The *Times* awarded Gary 1968 Disc Jockey of the Year. In making the announcement the *Times* said: "Gary plays music for the middle ground, with an accent on youth, and works especially hard making traffic-time listening a lively and thoroughly entertaining experience. He's the master of the put-on." In a 1971 *Billboard* magazine interview, he explained his radio show as being "filled with non sequiturs." Despite Gary's obvious aural gifts, it was the world of art which first attracted the young Gary. At age 12 he received a scholarship from an art school in Minneapolis. By 18 he had amassed a collection of 2,500 comic books. In the summer of 1980 Gary closed the "Zootmeister Broadcasting Network." He became the creative director for the parent company, Golden West Broadcasting. Upon his departure from on air at KMPC, the *Times*' James Brown said, "He was the best of them all." Gary could hardly stay off the air and away from his first love, radio. In 1982, he was part of the "Music of Your Life" format on KPRZ. When he left, the *Times* described Gary as "the man who apologizes for inhaling his tie on the air...who can recall the sequel to 'Rosemary's Baby' entitled 'Rosemary's Baby Eats a Pamper'...who claims to have whoopee cushions sewn into each of his suits. Gary is leaving the airwaves at the same time the toilet chain is pulled on the station." He had been off the air a year when he recalled: "I discovered that I still had the desire to be silly on the radio." So, on September 23, 1985, Gary joined the market's Jazz station, KKGO, and stayed on with Gannett Broadcasting as vp of creative services. Gary teamed with longtime friend Al Lohman at KFI for two years. "This is the first time we will have been together since we were raised by apes as children in Omaha." In a *Billboard* interview, Gary offered this advice: "For those starting out in radio, I recommend a journalism background for better on-the-air structuralization. Many people in radio don't phrase the way they should and don't know when a punchline is coming. When you're pointing out something, there should always be a punchline." Gary was inducted into four Halls of Fame in one fiscal year: The National Broadcasters Hall of Fame, The National Radio Hall of Fame, The NAB Hall of Fame; and The South Dakota Hall of Fame. In 1979 Gary was the first radio personality to be inducted into the Hollywood Hall of Fame (along with George Burns, Monty Hall and Herb Alpert). He was the winner of the NAB Radio Award for lifetime achievement. At KLAC he hosted the "Sportsnut" program. He worked morning drive on "K-Joy" and in the early fall of 1995 the station changed format to all-News. Gary has joined the original creators of "Music of Your Life" syndicated nostalgia format doing mornings to 75 syndicated markets. In late 1995, Gary was listed in *Vanity Fair*'s TV Hall of Fame as one of the legendary voices in the history of television, joining Don Pardo, Dennis James, Johnny Olson and Ed Herlihy. In early 1997 Gary became the announcer on the *Rosie O'Donnell Show*. "Without sounding like a coffee break Thomas Aquinas, the apothegm that every person is his own Pygmalion may be correct. I have tried to enrich my life by performing, reading, writing, creating and belching, and helping others whenever possible. I try to stand up for what I believe in - humor has helped protect me from the bruises of life, in addition to a daily supply of fantasy, illusion and talcum powder."

OWENS, Ronn: **KABC**, 1997. Ronn worked at KGO-San Francisco for 22 years before replacing Michael Jackson at KABC "TalkRadio" in the summer of 1997. Ronn started as a Talk show host at age 23 in 1968. He worked in Atlanta, Miami, Cleveland and Philadelphia before joining KGO in 1975. He continues simulcasting his show at KGO alternating each week between cities. Ronn graduated from Temple University where he studied sociology and communication.

OXARART, Frank: **KFWB**, 1968-69 and 1977-84, gm. Frank started as gsm when KFWB went all-News in 1968. In 1969 he ran the Westinghouse station in Philadelphia. He has since managed WNEW-New York and for the past decade has been the vp/gm of KCBS-San Francisco.

"Give Me 22 Minutes and I'll Give You the Start of All-News KFWB"
by
Herb Humphries

(Herb Humphries is the only person to have been a "first day" pioneer in both electronic news gathering in television and all-News radio in the United States. He was there at ground zero for the launch of KFWB as an around the clock news facility. Herb filed this report from his retirement home in East Texas. -db)

I was working at KNOW radio in Austin when President John Kennedy was assassinated. The President's next scheduled stop on the Texas tour was Austin, where he was to meet with every political big-wig in the state in an effort to patch a split in the state Democratic Party. Consequently we at KNOW were responsible for a great deal of side bar coverage of the assassination. I loved covering the Texas White House and President Lyndon Johnson for UPI Audio, Fairchild Newspapers, ABC and numerous other news organization.

Partially because of this exposure I was hired by Westinghouse Broadcasting to be one of the original on-air staff of all-News WINS in New York. During the two years there I covered everything from the Great Northeast Blackout to the Mass Transit Strike during the first two weeks of 1966 to the Texas Tower Massacre by Charlie Whitman.

I had just completed my third on-air cycle at WINS and walking into the newsroom when the editor asked, "Herb you know what the Texas Tower is?" I did and I began an eight hour stretch on the phone to police and others involved in stopping the tragic slaughter of sixteen. I knew almost every cop on the Austin Police Department on a first name basis. My experience in Austin had taught me who and where to call to get the story. All the phone conversations went on the air "live" usually as soon as telephonic contact was made. This proved somewhat awkward when some of my old buddies on the Austin PD greeted me with a less than complimentary sobriquet. But it also proved to be fantastic radio.

At one point I was talking to Lt. Harvey Gann who was in an office on the University campus. I asked him for a description of the scene from Harvey's vantage point. The Lieutenant was telling me and the WINS listening audience what he could see below him, including the way armored cars were blocking Whitman's view from the fallen wounded and dead. Then how rescuers would jump from the armored car, grab the victim, and amid Whitman's withering fire load the wounded into the cars and speed away. During this description Harvey blurted into the phone, "Hold on a minute Herb, the shooter is coming around on my side." Then...the staccato burst of the officer's revolver. Bam...bam...bam. Six times. He emptied it. A few minutes later, after two heroic Austin policemen calmly faced the mass killer and killed him, I was talking to the Chief of Detectives, Major K.R. Herbert, who at the time was at the hospital where all the victims were being brought.

The conversation went something like this. "Major, have you been able to get an identification of the killer?" "Not yet, Herb...No, wait a minute...they're bringing him in now. Hold it fellows, I want to get his billfold." A couple of seconds of background sounds, then, "Herb, he's got a Texas Hunting license and a Florida drivers license. Both show his name as Charles B. Whitman." And all this went directly to the WINS listeners.

Westinghouse decided to buy a Top 40 station in Los Angeles and change it to an all-News operation. I was named news director and was heavily involved in the conversion. We interviewed almost five hundred applicants. Two weeks before all news went on the air, the new people began a school that taught them everything they needed to know about their new careers. Following a week of formal schooling, the newly trained news people began the all news operation...in every way...except one. The on-air product didn't go on the air. It was piped into a hotel room and station offices so that management types could listen and hone the product. After a week of that, the switch was thrown and "All News" ceased to be heard through the pipeline. Now it was on the air.

KFWB was an instant success in the L.A. market. On the day it went on the air there was only one client advertising on the station. That just happened to be Westinghouse Electric. KFWB was out of the red in three months...the fastest time any all-News station had gone into the black. Ratings were high from the beginning and during the coverage of a 160-thousand acre brush fire that raked across much of L.A. and L.A. County, KFWB's share went to a thirteen. That was the highest any station in the market had received since the earliest days of rock and roll more than a decade earlier.

The coverage of Bobby Kennedy's assassination earned the station several awards. That coverage was carried by all Westinghouse radio stations from beginning to end. The publisher of the Boston Globe wrote an editorial in which he lauded the coverage as "the very best" broadcast journalism. I was part of a four-man team that covered the SLA shoot-out that earned the most prestigious Columbia University-Dupont Award.

After forty years in the business my philosophy is simply tell the people. Don't put any spin on the story you're telling. Always give the facts and nothing but the facts. I don't tell the truth because the truth to George McGovern is not the truth to George Wallace. The truth of Jesse Helms is not the truth of Jesse Jackson. I just give the facts and then the Georges and Jesses can determine their own truths.

P

P-FUNK: **KKBT**, 1993-97. Born Paul Ramirez, P-Funk is an integral part of the morning drive "House Party" show. He grew up in Northern California but spent a lot of time in Los Angeles. In July of 1990 he moved to Southern California to get into the music industry. While going to city college, P-Funk worked at Wherehouse Records and was a student intern with BMG Records.

Every morning P-Funk establishes instant remotes in the neighborhoods. "I have been with Prince Charles and President Clinton. I had the most fun when I put a KKBT sticker on Johnnie Cochran's back in front of the courthouse during the O.J. trial."

PACHECO, Manny: **KRLA**, 1980-81; **KDAY**, 1981-84; **KNAC**, 1982-85; **KRLA**, 1985-89; **KKBT**, 1989; **KOCM**, 1990-91; **KIKF**, 1991-92; **KMGX**, 1991-94, pd; **KGIL**, 1993; **KRLA**, 1993-97. Born in 1957,

Manuel is a native Angeleno and graduated from UCLA in 1980. A heart-pounding diagnosis during his junior year of college changed the entire direction of his life. Manny was studying political-science and was headed in the direction of being a lawyer. "I was in my late teens when I was diagnosed with cancer in my kidney. While I was in the hospital awaiting the results of tests, I wondered if my life was to be cut short was being a lawyer what I wanted to do?" At that moment he realized that he wanted to entertain. It turned out that he had an abnormally shaped kidney and there was no cancer. He changed his major, got involved with KLA, the campus radio station along with other classmates who work in radio, Amy Hiatt and Maggi Ross. Manny became the gm of the station. A few months before graduation, the pd of KRLA, Jack Roth, called Manny looking for, as Jack put it, "A young, Hispanic radio major who understands oldies." Manny suggested three candidates including himself. "Mucho Morales got the job but Art Laboe liked my personality and hired me as promotion coordinator which eventually led to on-air work and two decades of great admiration for Art." For many years, Manny was the station's link to the Mexican American audience at Mexican fairs. Beginning in 1988, Manny co-hosted a KCOP/Channel 13 Saturday morning tv show, *In Studio*, for two years. His on-camera tv commercial work includes Miller Lite, Pacific Telephone Directory and a spot running in the U.K. In the fall of 1989, he was offered the all-night shift during the launch of KKBT. Manny has appeared in many episodes of the soap opera *Santa Barbara*. He has supported the KCET fund-raising telethon as a co-host for years. Even though Manny has been away from KIKF for a number of years, he's still active in their bowling league. For almost two decades, he has never been off the air in Los Angeles for more than eight weeks. Manny's enthusiasm for every facet of life is evident with the diversity of formats he's worked as a jock. His management skills acquired at "Magic 94" have led him to be director of network operations for Royal Programs, Inc. Royal was launched in 1993 with the premiere of Art Laboe's "Killer Oldies" syndicated show. He currently works afternoon drive at KRLA.

PADDEN, J. Ray: **KLAC**, sm; **KIIS/KPRZ**, 1981-82, gm. Ray was appointed gm of KIIS/KPRZ in March 1981. Prior to that he worked for Metromedia as sm of KLAC.

PAEN, Alex: **KMPC**. Alex gained national attention for his reports on the hostage crisis in Tehran. He also worked for the ABC Network and broadcast on KTLA/Channel 5. Currently Alex can be seen hosting the syndicated tv series, *Emergency with Alex Paen*.

PAGE, Don: **KLAC**, 1962-63 and 1968-76; **KGIL**, 1974-75; **KFI**, 1974-75. Don distinguished himself as the radio critic and tv sports columnist for more than two decades at the *Los Angeles Times*. At KLAC he hosted a 15-minute commentary called "Saturday Sports Page" and was the creator and host of "Inside Radio," a 2-hour Sunday show featuring industry guests. At KGIL Don provided color commentary for the High School Game of the Week. He was born "a driver and nine-iron from Dodger Stadium" and grew up in the San Fernando Valley. Don went to Van Nuys High, L.A. Valley College and the "University of the *L.A. Times*." On KFI he aired "Don Page's Notebook," which included stories of the human condition. His variegated career includes writing for Jack Webb, book editor for Steve Allen, co-author of *Did You Whittinghill This Morning?* and presiding as past board member of the Pacific Pioneer Broadcasters. He

considers the quarter-century from 1950 to 1975 the Golden Age of Southern California Radio. "Radio was long on talent and short on time. Today radio is long on time and short on talent." He believes the "star factor" is missing in today's radio. "There are too many chairs and not enough talent." Don looks back at his experience in covering radio and sports for the *Times* as his greatest experience. "I'm lucky I got in very young and got out young. It had its marvelous moments." Don is working on his third career as president of Page Media Services. "I get to pick and choose my projects." Don writes a general interest column that is syndicated in the 11 Western states. Don and his wife live in Toluca Lake.

PAGE, Jimmy: **KQLZ**, 1989. Jimmy was part of the embryonic "Pirate Radio" experiment when Westwood One bought KIQQ and brought in Scott Shannon. He came to the Southland from KCAQ ("Q105")-Oxnard and stayed one weekend.

PAIGE, Molly: **KWNK**; **KABC**; **KIBB**. Molly is one of the traffic reporters who has been active as part of the morning shows at KABC and KIBB. She was born in Greenwich Village and raised in Corvallis, Montana. "I hit the wide open trail and in a series of strange and unusual circumstances of mastadonic  proportions ended up in Las Vegas at the age of 10." On her own by 16, Molly won a radio contest to travel in the "Magic Bus" to see a Who concert in Los Angeles. She studied theater and broadcast communications at the University of Las Vegas and interned at KLSX and KRLA. "My first radio paycheck came from being a morning news side-kick at KWNK. Molly went to Santa Barbara and worked at KSBL, KTYD and KMGQ and returned to L.A. to pursue acting.

PALANT, Gary: **KDAY**, 1960. Gary was born in Catskill, New York on May 2, 1941. He grew up in Poughkeepsie and Riverdale and attended Horace Mann prep school for boys. He moved to Tucson in 1958 and started his broadcasting career while still in high school. He graduated with honors from the University of Arizona in the spring of 1964 with a government major. "As with most jocks, I traveled from town-to-town in search of ultimate fame and fortune." He toiled in Wichita Falls, Augusta, Charleston, Niagara Falls, Ontario, Albuquerque and two stations in Tucson. In the late 1950s he was at KPOI and KORL-Honolulu. When he left the Southland he joined WMEX-Boston, CKFH-Toronto and WNEW-New York. By the time he got to Toronto in 1968 he was in programming and no longer on the air. Gary concluded his broadcasting career at WNEW in January 1971 to join his folks' real estate firm in Tucson. He became a broker and is now retired in Tucson. "My time is limited due to my needing to tend to my wife of 28 years. She was seriously injured in Sicily in late April 1996 when struck by a bus."

PALEY, John: **KNX/FM**, 1970-71, gsm; **KWKW**, 1971-97, vp/gm. John is vp of Lotus Communication Corporation which is the parent company of KWKW. Born July 24, 1929, he completed his B.S. and M.B.A. in 1953 at UCLA. John started out in retail advertising and became a vp with Foote Cone & Belding and N.W. Ayer. From 1960 to 1968 he was the Western regional manager of ABC Radio Network. As part of his responsibilities at Lotus, he is the president of their satellite network.

PALMER, John: **KIIS**, 1972-73, gm. When John left KIIS he opened the KIIS Broadcast Workshop, which ironically had no affiliation with KIIS. He went on to purchase the Le Dome restaurant.

PAM, Leslie Dr. and Christie, Ann: **KMPC**, 1994-96. Psychotherapists Leslie and his wife Ann hosted a relationship talk show on KMPC. They have a private practice and are co-founders of Conflict Resolution Unlimited, where they specialize in crisis counseling.

They have been married for over 20 years. In January 1996 they told their listeners that they'd be back after a station break with a big announcement, which was: "We've been fired!" They finished their last hour, during  which callers in a reversal of roles comforted them with "Keep your spirits up, etc." They are doing a weekend show in Las Vegas.

PARK, Andy: **KMPC**, 1963-68; **KFWB**, 1968-69. "I was covering a jumper for the *Long Beach Independent* when I got a call from KMPC asking for a report of what was going on. I had no idea what to do. I was a newspaperman. So I described the scene for 45 minutes standing in a phone booth." That report resulted in a job

offer from KMPC and Andy became the Orange County bureau chief covering news and reporting traffic every morning with Paul "Panther" Pierce and "Captain Max" Schumacher with Dick Whittinghill. When KFWB changed formats to all-News, Andy was there at midnight on March 10, 1968. "Boy, did we have a ride." Andy was the first newsman to interview Charles Manson after his arrest. "No one knew where the police were holding the suspects or who they were. News organizations were scrambling and all leads were dead ends. On a hunch I went to the city audit bureau where employee travel vouchers were processed and discovered that 17 police officers had been to Independence in Inyo County in the past 48 hours. I was a private pilot so I rented a plane and flew to Independence. When I arrived at the jail, the sheriff thought I was just another L.A. detective. We didn't know it was Charles Manson or even who was the ringleader, so I asked to interview everyone in the jail. After taping each prisoner I flew back. I knew I had 'Manson' on tape but didn't know which one he was. News director Herb Humphries called the L.A. detective in charge and told him we had the interview and were going to run it on KFWB. They asked us to hold it until they could hold a press conference for the next morning and they gave us credit for breaking the story. Herb, still not knowing who it was, asked for a confirmation on the spelling of 'his' name. The detective spelled M-a-n-s-o-n. And he was on my tape." Andy was born and raised in Memphis, studied philosophy at St. Mary's College in Minnesota and law in Tennessee. He then joined the Navy and while doing public information work in Hutchison, Kansas, at the local naval air station, started moonlighting with the newspaper. His next newspaper job was in Wichita at the *Beacon* and he wrote tv program scripts and advertising in Atlanta and Chicago before coming to California and joining the *Independent*. Andy left KFWB after a stint in Vietnam for Group W and went on to KNBC/Channel 4 and KABC/Channel 7 as a reporter. Andy next joined two Bay Area tv stations as a prime-time news anchor. "How I got to San Francisco is interesting. I get a call from the nd who asks if I have a beard. I did. Apparently I looked like a successful bearded anchor at their East Coast tv station so I am all-of-a-sudden a tv news anchor." Andy is now living in Durham, retired as public relations director of the Duke University Museum of Art. He leads a very diverse life lecturing at local universities, doing wedding photography on weekends, and acting in numerous motion pictures at the Wilmington, North Carolina Screen Gems facility. He also edits a local magazine. "I'm having a ball."

PARKER, Gary: **KGIL**, 1966-69

PARKER, Norm: **KJOI**, 1972-74. When Norm left the Southland he moved to Round Rock, Texas.

PARKER, Ryan: **KDAY**, 1984

PARKER, Star: **KMPC**, 1996. The conservative commentator moved into the midday slot on Talk KMPC in March 1996 replacing Joe Crummey. In the early 1980s she was a welfare mother with two children. She removed herself from the welfare list and put herself through college. The founder of the Coalition on Urban Issues (a social think tank) hosted a talk show on KSFO-San Francisco before taking on the KMPC assignment. She and her family moved to Orange County when their business was destroyed in the Los Angeles riots. Star told Gary Lycan of the *OC Register*: "I also serve as a consultant to a minority task force that Newt Gingrich set up." She is in the process of writing a book titled, *I Can't Cry Racism*. By the summer of 1996 she had left KMPC.

PARKER, Steve: **KMPC/KTZN**, 1996-97; **KIIS/AM**, 1997. Steve is the "Car Nut" who reviews the latest trends in the automotive world. He joined "XTRA Sports 1150" for a weekend show in the spring of 1997.

PARKER, Todd: **KKHR**, 1983-86; **KNX/FM**, 1986; **KPWR**, 1986-93. Todd Parker McLaren grew up in New England and began his on-air career while still in school at Syracuse University. "I really wanted to be an actor, but to a kid growing up in New England that always seemed like too much of a dream." After moving to WFBL-Syracuse, WCAU-Philadelphia and KITS-San Francisco, Todd got closer to his dream. "I never really wanted to come to Los Angeles, I was having way too much fun at KITS. After turning them down several times, the lure of the "Big Time," and the (temporarily) deep pockets of CBS lured me here to do  afternoons at KKHR." A format and pd change followed and Todd left the CBS outlet in 1986. At the same time "Power 106" was being launched and Todd predicted a short run for the Urban/Disco hybrid. Todd not only ate his words but said, "Never tempt the gods." He started doing weekends at KPWR and filled in for the frequently vacationing morning man Jay Thomas which led to an afternoon shift. Todd talked about his departure from KPWR: "One day pd Rick Cummings called me into his office and said, 'Y' know, Todd, you're just too old and too white to work here anymore.' And while I immediately said to myself, 'Well, there's two lawsuits right there...,' I decided to put my energies elsewhere." Todd has a successful voiceover career, which includes work on *Roger Rabbit*; along with writing and producing for Fox Television. Todd created and produced the voiceover industry's first collection of talent on CD. The

"House Disc" has now become the industry standard. He is the principal in The Tellus Group, an international tv promotion and marketing firm with clients domestically, as well as in Great Britain and Germany. "I've got a beautiful wife and two terrific boys, and life couldn't be better. And, by the way, I still love radio!"

PARKER, Wes: **KABC**, 1987. The former Dodger first baseman replaced Al Downing on KABC's "DodgerTalk" in early 1987.

PARISI, Michelle: SEE Mikki

PARR, Russ: **KLOS/KABC**, 1978-85; **KDAY**, 1985-89. Born in San Antonio, Russell arrived in the Southland from Urban KLBS-Houston. "I loved working with Ken & Bob and doing a tv show with Frazer Smith." Russ left the Southland in 1989 and went to KJMZ-Dallas. Russ also hosts "On the Move," a syndicated Urban countdown show with co-host Alfreda. In 1995 he moved to KRBV-Dallas.

PARR, Shawn: **KIKF**, 1988-92; **KZLA**, 1992-97. At the Orange County Country station, Shawn worked morning drive. He was host for many "Kick" nights at the Crazy Horse in Santa Ana and Cowboy Boogie in Anaheim. He was the warm-up announcer on NBC/TV's *Hot Country Nights*. In 1990 he appeared on *Love Connection*. A fellow jock at KZLA said, "Shawn was hired for his upbeat personality, enthusiasm and energy." To promote the Disney film *Iron Will* in early 1994, Shawn led a seven-dog racing team down a snow-covered Hollywood Boulevard in sun-drenched California. Shawn works morning drive at KZLA.

PARRISH, Cathi: **KOST**, 1992; **KTWV**, 1994-97. Cathi graduated from Mundelein College in Chicago with a B.A. in English/communications in 1977. She spent her early broadcast days in the Windy City. She arrived in the Southland in 1989 and worked at KQLH and KFRG in the Inland Empire before joining "Coast" and then "the Wave" where she works evenings.

PARRISH, Gene: **KUSC**, 1984-97. Gene worked  middays at the Classical station. "On December 31, 1995, I left my day-job at KUSC to pursue a kind of laid back, free-lance career." He is in his 13th season as host and producer of "Worldwide Jazz" that is heard on 150 public radio stations. He co-produces "The First Art," a program of choral music syndicated to over 200 stations. In 1986 and 1987, he hosted and co-produced Los Angeles Music Center Opera productions of *Othello*, *Tristan und Isolde* and *La Boheme*, which aired live on KUSC. A graduate of Occidental College, he earned his degree in speech and broadcasting. Gene began his broadcasting career in 1973 as a staff announcer and engineer at KQED in San Francisco.

PARSONS, Fred: **KLAC**, 1965-70. When Fred left the Southland after doing news at KLAC, he returned to his home in West Virginia. One of his fellow broadcasters said, "Fred was an aristocrat in the noblest sense. When reporting a feature story, there was no one better at creating a word picture. Fred had mastered the English language."

PARSONS, Pete: **KFWB**, 1984-97. "When I finally realized that I wasn't meeting any old disc jockeys, I decided to get into the news business because there were lots of old newsmen." Pete has been a longtime anchor on all-News KFWB. Born in Upland, he was raised in the Bay Area. His father was a State Park Ranger based in the East Bay. After leaving the Army, Pete started as a dj at KMEN-Riverside in 1970. During the 1970s he worked for KHNY-Riverside twice, KHSJ-Hemet, KPSI-Palm Springs and a return to KMEN in 1980. "In 1984 I needed a change. I left the country and worked for 'Hit Radio 100' in Guam. When I came back later that year I started in production at KCKC-San Bernardino. The nd left on holiday and never returned so I became news boss for the next 11 years." Pete now works afternoon drive at "classic country" KCKC while at the same time taking on part-time anchor duties at KFWB. His wife, Connie, is a police officer for the city of Fontana.

PASCHALL, Benton: **KWIZ**. Ben was 49% co-owner of KWIZ until 1965. Prior to that time he had been executive vp and manager. Ben was born in Olney, Texas in 1913 and grew up in Fresno. He studied music and business administration at Fresno State where he originally wanted to be a teacher. After sales jobs with Union Oil Co., and Bekins Van & Storage, Ben joined the sales staff of KARM-Fresno. After managing a number of stations, Ben bought Western Radio Sales rep firm. In the early 1950s Ben was the vp of the Western division of Gordon McLendon's Liberty Network. In the mid-1950s Ben, along with Howard Tullis and John Hearne bought KAFY-Bakersfield and KFXM-San Bernardino. A station swap in 1959 gave Ben 49% ownership of KWIZ in exchange for his piece of KAFY and KFXM. He sold his interest in KWIZ in 1965. Ben is retired and is active in the Pacific Pioneer Broadcasting Association.

PAT, Waco: **KTYM**; **KFOX**; **KABC**, 1957-95. Born

Waco Patryla, Waco began his broadcast career as a dj while in high school in Waco. Before joining KABC in 1957, he worked as a jock in San Diego but always had a love for the technical side of broadcasting. He was with the successful KABC morning drive show as engineer since its inception until his retirement in October of 1995. Pat participated on the air with his own voice but was best known for his ability to speak through wild tracks and drop-ins. He also operated "Waco's," a country and western nightclub in Torrance.

PATRICK, Paul: **KPSA**, 1971-72. Paul worked for 20 years at small market radio stations before joining KPSA.

PATTERSON, Bill: **KFOX**, 1971-72; **KLAC**, 1972. Bill worked weekends and vacation relief at KLAC.

PATTERSON, Jack: **KHJ**, 1974, pd; **KDAY**, 1974-76 and 1981-91, pd; **KJLH**, 1991-97. Boston was Jack's home before being transferred from RKO's WRKO to be program director of KHJ. In 1974, he was a *Billboard* magazine award winner. In 1978 while at KMJQ-Houston, Jack was voted Unique Format Program Director of the Year at the 11th Annual *Billboard* Radio Programming Forum. Jack went to the Midwest in the early 1980s and worked as pd of WBMX-Chicago. He returned to the Southland as pd of KDAY in 1981. In a 1989 *LA Times* article on black music radio, Jack said, "Playing too many white artists would ruin our black identity and damage our standing in the community." At KJLH he works morning drive.

PATTERSON, Langley: **KAGB**; **KJLH**; **KKGO**; **KLON**. According to a story by Dennis McDougal in the February 22, 1985, edition of the *LA Times*, "Langley played be-bop. Swing. A little blues. He scoured old record stores for vintage records." Dave Randall recalled that Langley was late for his evening shift on KLON somewhere around Washington's Birthday in 1985. Dave said, "I was at the station doing some production when I was pressed into spinning some records until his arrival. About 6:30 his ex-wife called and melted into tears. Langley had been stabbed to death by some ne'er-do-wells who to this day have not been caught." His body was found in an alley behind a doctor's office about three miles from his home. Langley's longtime pal Lawrence Tanter said, "Langley was a guy who wouldn't hurt anybody. Whoever did it has really taken away a good cat. Langley wasn't a very high profile media broadcaster. He didn't get a lot of awards. He played music exposing an art form he believed in, like a policeman who's not on the force anymore but still walks a beat to protect the neighborhood." Langley was going to dental school part-time to try to supplement his earnings and was a lieutenant in the California National Guard on weekends. He died at age 35.

PATTIZ, Norm: Born in 1954, Norm was a one-time club bouncer and karate instructor before starting in tv sales. Norm was fired as KCOP/Channel 13 sales boss in 1974. He went on to launch what has become a mini-empire. In 1990 he owned Westwood One, the NBC and Mutual radio networks, radio stations and *R&R*.

PATTON, Jim: **KLOS**, 1972-73. Jim died of a heroin overdose in 1973.

PAUL, Long: **KNAC**, 1986-94; **KLOS**, 1994-97. Born Paul Long in Los Angeles, Paul grew up listening to L.A. Rock radio.

"When I was ten, I would sit on the floor with my little turntable and a stack of 45s doing weekly top 10 countdowns." He attended the University of La Verne and studied radio broadcasting at Mt. San Antonio College. In 1985 Paul started at KCAL-Riverside. A year later he went to KNAC and stayed for eight years. He hosts a syndicated show called "The Instrumentals of Rock" for Utopia Network. In November 1994, Long Paul joined KLOS when three longtime personalities were fired in an attempt to alter the demographics. He moved from afternoon drive at KNAC to the same shift at KLOS. He likened the opportunity to getting the call up to the majors. Paul is a self-professed "baseball freak." He lives in Upland with his wife, Mary, and their four children. Paul left KLOS in the summer of 1997.

PAULIE: **KHTZ**, 1979. Paulie came to the Southland from radio jobs on the East Coast for three years before joining "K-Hits." She worked the all-night shift.

PAULOS, Cindy: **KROQ**, 1978

PAYERLE, Teresa: **KKGO**, 1989-93; **KUSC**, 1993-94. Teresa worked in radio syndication sales and later in production and operations for Radio Arts, Inc. in Burbank from 1982 to 1984, after a number of years of on-air and board operator experience in college radio. She left the L.A. area in 1984 for a staff announcer position at commercial Classical station WFLN-Philadelphia, leaving after four years to return to Los Angeles. There she went to work for KKGO, doing afternoon drive and midday shifts and handling om duties for much of the four years she was there. Teresa then went to work for KUSC in morning drive doing both programming and announcing. After a year of getting up at 4:30 a.m., she moved on to Shadow Broadcast Services as an anchor for KFWB and other stations around L.A. In September 1995 she was offered a position as md for cable/satellite music provider DMX at its corporate headquarters in Los Angeles. After more than a year in the corporate environment, Teresa then went back to the freelance life, filling in at Shadow and KUSC and pursuing a few projects of her own including some work as a film extra. Teresa is thinking about starting a small business in the near future. Stay tuned!

PAYNE, Bruce: **KGIL**, 1969. Bruce was the "Skywatch" reporter for KGIL.

PAYNE, Mike: **XPRS**, 1972. Mike is working for a gospel station in Atlanta.

PAYNE, Ted: **KABC**, 1989-97. Ted handles the news on the "Minyard and Tilden" morning drive show on KABC. He won the 1994 Golden Mike Award for the best newscast in Southern California. Ted is an expert in radio money news and had a top-rated afternoon show in San Diego for KSDO for 10 years. Ted lives in Culver City with his wife Dorothy.

They are the parents of four successful sons. Ted retired in the spring of 1997.

PAYTON, Scott: **KMPC**, 1984-86; **KIQQ**, 1987. Scott worked evenings at KMPC.

PEABODY, Dick: **KFI**, 1971-72. Dick was a "moody" afternoon dj who also appeared in tv and movies. At 6-foot-nine, he was frequently cast as the bad guy.

PEARL, Bernie: **KLON**, 1980-85. Bernie was the decade-long host of "Nothing but Blues" and "The Blues Roll On" programs. He has been a leading figure in the annual Long Beach Blues Festival.

> KMPC (710AM) owned by MacMillan Petroleum Company is sold to Gene Autry/Partners for $800,000
>
> -1952
>
> KMPC (710AM) bought by Disney/ABC/CapCities for $20 million
>
> -1993

PEARL, Bill: **KYMS**, 1969; **KWIZ/FM**, 1969; **KLAC/KMET**, 1971-73; **KKDJ**, 1971-72; **KIIS**, 1972; **KKDJ**, 1973; **KIQQ**, 1973-74; **KHJ**, 1974-75; **KRLA**, 1976-77; **KIQQ**, 1977; **KMPC**, 1981-82; **KABC**, 1982-84 and 1986-91. One of the most enthusiastic evening jocks in contemporary radio, Bill is a home boy. Raised in Hollywood, he went to Fairfax High School. "My father spoke six languages and I was a history major at UCLA. I wanted to teach American history, the period between the two world wars. When I walked into UCLA's radio station, KLA, my whole life changed." Bill is a magna cum laude, Phi Beta Kappa graduate of UCLA and also holds the degree of Juris Doctor from the UCLA School of Law. "It was a radio dream that paid for law school." Between KHJ and KMPC Bill became a lawyer. He joined KABC "TalkRadio" in 1982 and for the better part of a decade did air work for the market's then-top rated AM outlet. Bill hosted and produced his own newstalk programs and teamed as a commentator/debater with Bill Press (of CNN's *Crossfire*

and their show was called "Dueling Bills") and in an intervening period with the ACLU's Ramona Ripston, for a Point-Counterpoint show. In 1976, he became a consultant with Tom Greenleigh to help rebuild KRLA, and they created the "Hitman" concept that brought automation to life. The "Hitmen" looked for homemade signs of the KRLA call letters which were showing up in every Southland neighborhood. "We beat the assumed-unbeatable KHJ with a small budget semi-automated outlet." Bill celebrated the feat by doing a live show from KRLA's old Pasadena studios as "Jack Cheese." Bill is a published freelance writer, whose op-ed articles have appeared in the *Wall Street Journal*, *New York Times*, *Washington Times* and countless dailies across the country. He is married to KFWB Orange County

Bureau chief, Sharon Katchen, lives in Long Beach, has a small law practice and is completing his first book.

PEDROZA, Cecilia: **KFWB**, 1972-84. Cecilia and her

sister Inez (15 years a reporter for KABC/Channel 7) were the first successful Hispanic sisters in the broadcast media. "We looked at our mission as role models to encourage Latinos to join broadcasting. We spoke in East L.A., at UCLA, USC and Hispanic community groups." Cecilia was born in Detroit and grew up in the Southland. Along with her sister, Cecilia authored an entertainment column on the motion picture industry that appeared in over 80 international publications. In the early 1970s she served as an apprentice with Regis Philbin on KHJ/Channel 9's *Tempo Show* and worked at KTLA/Channel 5. She was a high school drop out who benefited from the affirmative action programs in the '70s. "KFWB gave me an opportunity and for 12 years I served as general assignment reporter covering such major stories as the Hillside Strangler. When new management arrived at KFWB in 1984 the outside news reporters were let go. The news organization was gutted to become a rip 'n read organization. After the bloodletting I realized I was burned out. My life had belonged to the radio station." Encouraged by some to file a wrongful termination lawsuit, she said, "I never considered it. I didn't know my head from a hole in the ground when I started and I became a household name. It was just too bad that loyalty was not a factor in who was let go from the station." Cecilia joined the family travel business and with her brother, sister and mother (who was a featured columnist for the Hearst newspaper chain) they own the 30-year-old Pedroza Travel in the Fairfax district of Los Angeles.

PELADILLO, El: **KLAX**, 1993-96. Born Jesus Garcia in Michoacan, Mexico, he said in a June 1994 *LA Times* interview that he idolized Cantinflas, whose early nickname was El Peladillo. Jesus has modeled his Peladillo after the lovable scoundrel "who talks a lot but doesn't say anything." He has been part of the KLAX morning team with Juan Carlos Hidalgo, and the Spanish-speaking morning drive show was #1 for three consecutive books in 1993. Jesus was twice caught trying to cross the border into the United States, but he refused to return to his home in Michoacan. In 1985, his third try was successful. He made his way to Santa Paula where he picked avocados and attended broadcast school at night. Juan and Jesus first teamed in San Francisco before joining KLAX.

PENA, Lupita: **KTNQ**, 1992-94; **KLVE**, 1987-97. Lupita is such an integral part of the Pepe Barreto morning show that when KLVE changed traffic services, she moved from Metro to Shadow. Born in Bellflower, she grew up in Downey, "the home of the Carpenters." When a family member of the longtime Spanish radio Escondon family heard her speak, they commented on what a "wonderful Spanish voice" she had when she was

working as a high school intern at KSKQ. In addition to her traffic reports on "K-Love" and other stations for Shadow, Lupita had a weekend dj show for two years on KTNQ. "It finally became too much. I worked five days at Shadow and then the weekends being a dj." She is very prideful when she talks of the morning show. "I've learned so much from Pepe. I'm very proud of the type of program we have. We are very respectful to the public." Lupita would eventually like to become a tv news anchor. Anglo or Spanish? "Whichever comes first."

PENA, Pepe: **KALI**, 1965

PENNINGTON, Liz: **KEZY**, 1994-97. Liz works the morning show with John Fox.

PEPPER, Choral: **KABC**, 1972. Choral was the travel editor for KABC.

PERELLI, Angela: **KYSR**, 1995-97, pd. Angela was born and raised in San Francisco and she arrived in Southern California from eight years of programming chores at K101-San Francisco to be assistant pd and md. In the spring of 1997 she was made pd of "Star 98.7, the first modern AC station in the country." She has been attending UCLA. In 1996 she won the *Gavin* award for music director of the year.

PEREZ, Carlos: **KTNQ**, 1989. Carlos worked the all-night shift at Spanish KTNQ.

"KLSX is the rock and roll station that forgot to play records."
-"Real Radio" slogan, 1995

PEREZ, Gil: **KEZY**, 1985-89; **KFI/KOST**, 1989-97; **KEZY**, 1994-97. Born in Long Beach, Gil grew up and went to school in Orange County. In 1985 he became

KEZY's first full-time live overnight dj. While continuing to do overnights at KEZY, Gil does production at KFI/KOST and special assignments with stations in San Bernardino and San Jose. In 1989 he joined KFI/KOST full-time in production. A half decade later, Gil returned to an on-air position at KEZY. "It's kind of nice but strange to hear from listeners who call the station and say they remember listening to you when they were growing up in the '80s." Gil lives in Orange County. He worked on Tony Danza's ABC series, *Hudson Street*.

PEREZ, Maclovio: **KNX**, 1979-96. KCBS/Channel 2's weatherman frequently reported the weather on sister radio station, KNX. He worked for the tv station for over 17 years and survived 13 news directors. In a cost cutting measure by Westinghouse, Maclovio was let go in the fall of 1996. He had been active in the Latino community and a *Daily Variety* story reported he earned "close to $400,000." His replacement was reported to be earning about $300,000 less. Maclovio was born in San Antonio and was planning to return to Texas.

PERLICH, Martin: **KMET**, 1972; **KFAC**, 1987-89; **KKGO/KKJZ**, 1989-91; **KUSC**, 1996-97. Born in 1937 in Cleveland, Martin's early work was in music. After studying with noted American composer Douglas Moore at Columbia University, he became at 24 the first intermission host of the internationally syndicated Cleveland Orchestra radio broadcasts. A pioneer in "experimental FM radio," Martin continued in the '60s and '70s with interviews for WMMS-Cleveland before arriving in the Southland. At "the Mighty Met" he interviewed such luminaries of that turbulent period as Attica prisoners, Phil Ochs and Frank Zappa, with whom he had eight memorable encounters. He worked morning drive with newsman Leo Rosenberg. When contacted for this book, Martin said: "How did you ever find Leo Rosenberg's name? We worked together for a period of weeks, I think - his instant tune-out, week-long series on 'crib death' got him replaced by Ace Young, if memory serves." In 1975 he became co-producer of NBC/TV's *The Midnight Special*. Martin developed, produced and hosted many projects for PBS. He did a Sunday air shift at KFAC and hosted an interview show with top classical artists. He had four production companies over the years. One of his three sons is actor Max Perlich, who appeared in *Rush*, *Georgia* and *Beautiful Girls*. In early 1996 Martin wrote, produced and directed interactive videos with Warner New Media.

PERRIN, Lloyd: **KNX**, 1972-76. Lloyd was one of L.A.'s "top mobile field reporters," according to Don Page. He died suddenly in the 1980s.

PERRY, David: **KWST**, 1975-76; **KMET**, 1976-82; **KLOS**, 1984; **KHTZ**, 1985; **KMET**, 1986-87; **KLSX**, 1989-92. David has taken the road less traveled by djs; i.e., from programming to ownership. In 1993 he embarked on a journey hardly imaginable two decades earlier. David was born in New York and grew up in Seattle. His love for radio was born out of a passion for the music. "I just wanted to be near the music. That's what it was." While his brother Wayne got in on the ground floor of the cellular explosion, David was sending tapes to every AOR station in the top ten markets. Only two responded, KOME-San Jose and WABX-Detroit. In 1972 he joined John Detz at WABX, one of the truly innovative stations on the launching pad

of the "underground" radio movement. Two years later Detz, David and crosstown competitor from WRIF, Jim McKeon, left Detroit for sister Century station, KWST. "It was the day after Christmas in 1974; John, Jim and I got off the airplane in Los Angeles, saw sunshine and palm trees and I said, 'this is home.'" Somewhere along the way David read a story from the NAB that 35% of all radio jobs will disappear. He tucked that information away to prepare for the future. During the 1980s David programmed and jocked stations for Greater Media and Metromedia. He spent a moment or two at KSAN-San Francisco and KISW-Seattle. The first time he left KMET, newly hired consultant Lee Abrams fired him. "I skipped a card and played a song out of order." David was at KMET for the finale of "the Mighty Met" on February 6, 1987, when the classic "underground" dominant station of the '70s and early '80s abandoned AOR. David joined two other jocks and filed a multi-million dollar suit against KMET's owners. They claimed they were induced to sign employment contracts by station officials who knew at the time they would be fired. They contended that the station vp misrepresented the station's position concerning their status at KMET by either thwarting the disc jockeys' attempts to be hired elsewhere or promising attractive positions and/or perks. At their 1987 press conference, David said, "The real blow to me was the cold calculations involved. To me, KMET wasn't just any job - it was a mission from God, something we really believed in. That's what made all the stuff, later, so depressing." The suit was settled in 1989. There was a secrecy clause in the settlement but informed sources suggest that the personalities received a year's salary. In 1989 he helped his friend Tom Milewski launch KLSX's sister station in Detroit, WCSX, when the station went "classic rock." In 1992 David knew he was at a crossroads: "I knew I always wanted to do more." His brother Wayne had been vice chairman of a cellular company that was sold to AT&T for $13 billion and the family talked about investments. A fortuitous phone call on the day they were discussing buying a radio station led to the purchase of KTYD-Santa Barbara. Jim McKeon, who traveled with David from Detroit to Los Angeles, joined the new company. David was excited about the new venture and the search was on for a gm. His other two partners voted David the gm. Apprehensive at first, he developed a simple philosophy: "Be sure the income exceeds the outgo." He has also acquired KSBL and an AM Talk station, KQSB. They bought the AM station for $300,000 which as David described it was "the cost of a slum house in Santa Barbara." He has been filling-in for Casey Kasem's syndicated shows for almost five years. David has a daughter who attends UC Santa Cruz.

PERRY, Ed: **KRLA**, 1961; **KDAY**; **KIEV**, 1969-76, pd. **KIKF**, 1990. At KRLA he was a newsman and worked Sunday mornings as a jock. Ed hosted a Top 40 program sponsored by Nartell Clothiers. In a 1976 *Billboard* story, Ed described KIEV's mostly bartered programming over the decades: "We are prolific. We carry race results, offer religion in the morning and in the afternoon Mr. Blackwell and George Putnam. You have to do a lot of things to keep alive." Ed is working part-time at WW1's Soft AC format.

PERRY, Jim: **KNX**, 1983. Jim was a commentator on USC broadcasts. He was also the Trojan's sports information director.

PERRY, Les: **KCRW**, 1967-69; **KPPC**, 1969; **KDAY**, 1970; **KVFM**, 1971-74; **KIEV**, 1972-81; **XPRS**, 1973; **KDAY**, 1973; **KROQ**, 1973-74; **KRLA**, 1975; **KLVE**, 1975; **XPRS**, 1978-81; **KRLA**, 1983-84; **KEZY**, 1987-88; **KWIZ**, 1992-94; **KMAX**, 1994-95. Born in Los Angeles, Les grew up on the beach in Santa Monica and would sneak off campus to surf between classes at Samohi until he graduated in 1967. After school he was filing records at KFWB for Roger Christian, B.M.R. and Joe Yocam. He was influenced by the music and djs in the early rock era, especially Elliot Field, and in the quiet of his home "pretended" to be a jock of the 1950s. In a 1995 interview over lunch, Les enthused about radio and his three decades in it: "To me, radio is a disease, it gets in the blood. You just can't get rid of it." At KPPC he played the Tom Donahue tapes that were being sent from San Francisco. During his almost decade at KIEV, he made the transitions from MOR to Country to Oldies. Simultaneously he recorded jock shows at Oldies-formatted XEMO and the "soul XPRS" in Rosarita Beach. During his off-air journeys he produced "Super Trax," the Gary Owens syndicated show, for two years and specials for Wolfman Jack at Premiere Radio Networks.  Les also served as a broadcast instructor at Los Angeles City College and Santa Monica City College. He has hosted "Surf Patrol Party" on a number of Southern California radio stations. He runs a series of surf band reunion shows featuring the Chantays, Surfaris and The Living Ones.

IT HAPPENED FIFTY YEARS AGO!

And Hilly Rose does it again...In 1922 KFI Radio listeners heard wedding bells over the air waves. History repeats itself as love is *Rose*-ier the second time around when Hilly weds another happy couple at midnight, Saturday, December 2, in the KFI Theatre. You could be the lucky pair, so start throwing rice at your radio and listen for the contest details on
    TOTAL SPECTRUM RADIO.

THE HILLY ROSE SHOW 12 Mid-4 AM

-LA Times ad, November 12, 1972

PERUN, Steve: **KIIS**, 1994-96, pd. Steve started afternoon drive in the summer of 1994 from consulting KIIS's parent company, Gannett. He was optimistic when he told *R&R*: "There's only one KIIS, and together we'll figure out what we must do to return KIIS to dominance." He previously programmed WZOU-Boston, WBSB ("B-104")-Baltimore, WHYI ("Y100")-Miami, KDWB-Minneapolis, KWK-St. Louis, KBEQ-Kansas City, WKEE-Huntington, West Virginia and WLS-Chicago. In the summer of 1995, Steve was named national pd for Gannett Radio. By the spring of 1996 he had resigned his position at KIIS and resumed his consulting company.

PESSINO, Mario Fernando: **KALI**, 1986. Mario worked all-nights at Spanish KALI.

PETERS, John: **KKDJ**, 1973-75; **KEZY**, 1976; **KUTE**, 1979-82; **KEZY**, 1982-83. John worked afternoon drive at the beginning of KKDJ on March 10, 1973, until the station went more adult-oriented. John changed identities and became Joe Green for KUTE and KEZY. It is believed that he has gone into real estate.

PETERS, Keith: **KWVE**, 1990-97, nd; **KKGO**, 1994-97. As a youngster growing up in Southern California, Keith always loved listening to radio remembering Joe Pyne and the day "Boss Radio" was launched. "I have been interested in classical music and news for as long as I can remember." He is fulfilling both passions. He has been the news director of KWVE since May 1990 and does the Saturday shift at Classical KKGO. Keith has performed leading roles with opera and musical comedy groups throughout California, particularly enjoying the patter roles in Gilbert and Sullivan. At home with his wife and three children, his hobby is Lionel trains.

PETERSON, Gerry: **KHJ**, 1974-75, pd. In the 1970s Gerry was pd of WRKO-Boston. After KHJ Gerry left the Southland to be pd at KCBQ-San Diego. In the late 1970s, Gerry ran for the 4th Congressional District in his home state of Mississippi; in fact, he was called the "Mississippi Hippie" and almost won. In 1980, he became pd of KFRC-San Francisco for four years. In 1988 he was pd at WAPP-New York and then programmed KWOD-Sacramento. He returned to L.A. in 1993 as editor of "Network 40" based in Burbank.

PETTI, Ralph: **KFI**, 1972, gm. Ralph is now living in Oregon.

Color Radio/KFWB debut
January 2, 1958

6 a.m.	**Bruce Hayes**
9 a.m.	**Al Jarvis**
Noon	**Joe Yocam**
3 p.m.	**Elliot Field**
9 p.m.	**Bill Ballance**
12 a.m.	**Ted Quillin**

PEWTER, Jim: **KMET**, 1970-73; **KRTH**, 1973-75, pd; **KRLA**, 1983-85, pd. A native of St. Paul, Jim attended the University of Minnesota. He developed an interest in rock 'n' roll when he interviewed Buddy Holly, Chuck Berry, Alan Freed and Fabian for the local newspaper. He graduated from Brown Institute of Radio Electronics in Minneapolis and later studied drama with Jeff Corey in Hollywood. A stint in the Armed Forces in the early 1960s cemented his interest and goals in rock oldies when he became pd and all-night dj of the Munsan-Ni station of the Armed Forces Korea Network. Jim arrived in the Southland in 1959. "KFWB was the best sounding and most fun station that I had ever heard. The 'Seven Swingin' Gentlemen' will always be a memory in the soundtrack of my life." He started out as a singer and had a Midwest regional hit. He wrote songs for Gene Vincent, Jan and Dean, Dick Dale and Bobby Fuller. In 1968 he formed Playground Records and reactivated the label in 1995. In the early '70s, KMET hired Jim on Sunday evenings to play music of the '50s and '60s along with interviews with singers from that era. Jim was a

consultant for the live "Rock 'n Roll Revival" shows in New York and was also heard weekends over WPIX-New York, via tape. He also did a weekend Oldies show at KRTH before he became pd in 1973. He was voted 1974 Oldies Program Director of the Year. During the 1970s he produced specials with Roger Christian and Dick Clark. With Roger they launched a syndicated special called "The Beach Years," and other specials included "The Legend of Buddy Holly" and "The Frankie Valli Story." Jim co-produced and co-hosted "Dick Clark's 20 years of Rock 'n Roll" which was syndicated on over 250 stations. He joined KRLA in August 1983 as pd and commented, "We'll be catering to the people who grew up with the music, and we'll bring back the fun." Jim stepped down as pd of KRLA in 1985 but continued with a weekend show. He produced his own roots albums which included Bo Diddley, John Lee Hooker and Little Walter. Jim moved to Ojai and continued on Armed Forces Radio with an oldies show he'd been doing since 1966. He acted as research consultant for Columbia Pictures' *La Bamba*. For three years beginning in 1988, Jim hosted a morning radio show for FM Yokohama in Japan. Jim lives in Ojai with his wife Judy and their two daughters. He is compiling and producing CDs. He writes liner notes for MCA Music, Varese Sarabande Records and GNP Crescendo, which include *The Best of the Surfaris*, *The Chantays*, *The Hilltoppers*, *Surf Party* and *Surf City's Greatest Hits*. In the fall of 1995 his new label, Playground Records released *Pulp Rock Instrumentals*.

PFLUG, Joanne: **KMET**, 1967. Joanne was part of the all-female line-up at KMET. She went on to star in *M*A*S*H*.

PHELPS, Brian: SEE Mark and Brian

PHILBIN, Regis: **KABC**, 1972

PHIL the THRILL: **KKBT**, 1994-97. Phil Hernandez is part of the scene at "the Beat."

PHILLIPS, Doc: **KMET**, 1985

PHILLIPS, Irving: **KDAY**, 1960-62, gm

PHILLIPS, John: **KBCA**, 1978

PHILLIPS, Marshall: **KLOS**, 1972; **KWST**, 1978-80, nd; **KLSX**, 1987. Marshall was the news director at "K-West" and hosted the mornings with Phil Hendrie at the "classic rock" radio station. After KWST he worked in San Francisco, San Jose and Seattle and settled in San Francisco once more in 1990. He's currently heard doing news at KNBR-San Francisco.

PHILLIPS, Mike: **KRTH**, 1990-97, pd. Mike started his broadcast career at KISN-Portland in 1960 and then went to KJR-Seattle for three years beginning in 1962. His first pd'ship was KNBR-San Francisco in the mid-1960s. Mike did mornings at KFRC-San Francisco from 1966 to 1972 and then went to RKO sister station WXLO-New York. After a half decade as pd and air talent at KGW-Portland, Mike was in San Francisco during most of the 1980s. He worked at KYUU and was vp of programming for the NBC/FM division before moving on to K101, KFRC and KOIT. After a two-year stint at the Research Group in Seattle in 1987, Mike became vp of programming for WTMX-Chicago. His successful strategy at KRTH was to drop hundreds of songs from the play list, tighten up the format with consultant Bill Drake's help, and hire former "Boss" jocks Robert W. Morgan and The Real Don Steele. The record price, $116,000,000, paid for the station attests to the success of that strategy.

PICKENS, Hal: **KFWB**, 1965; **KBLA**, 1966-67; **KDAY**, 1968-69. Hal arrived in the Southland from KDEO-San Diego, with a stop in Atlanta at WQXI in 1963. His on-air experience at KFWB lasted from early 1965 until Christmas of 1965. Who can forget his mantra, "The Coast Is Clear, Dear"? In 1972, Hal was on KNEW-San Francisco.

PICKETT, Bobby "Boris": **KRLA**. Bobby hosted a Saturday evening show. At most every Halloween, the singer of the enormously popular "Monster Mash" played classic haunted hits on KRLA.

PIERCE, David: **KPPC**, 1963-71. "My stint at KPPC began in 1963 when I walked across the street from the Pasadena Playhouse to the bottom of the Pasadena Presbyterian Church to play classical music, show tunes, big band, pop and jazz on KPPC. Every format they came up with; I played just to stay on the air." David was in the center of the "underground" hurricane in 1968  when Tom Donahue arrived. During the Les Carter regime, David worked middays and served as md. "At Les' suggestion, my kids John-David and Chelle and my wife 'Sister Kate' went on the air with me. We were billed as The Pierce Family. Their six- and seven-year old voices juxtapositioned with the sound of folk and heavy rock was one more of many facets that made KPPC's sound unique." After a year at KAUM-Houston, David "closed the microphone" on radio and joined tv sales in Lafayette, Louisiana. Born in Bayou Country, David grew up with "rock and roll on my mind." For the past 15 years he has been sales manager at Fox 15/TV in Lafayette. David has written a book on his radio experiences, *The Disc Jockeys*, due for publication in early 1998.

PIERCE, Paul "Panther": **KMPC**, 1960-80; **KRLA**, 1980. Paul was the aerospace editor for much of his time with KMPC. He won four individual Golden Mike awards and shared some 15 others with KMPC news people. He joined KRLA for the "Focus On" series. In 1985, Paul wrote a book of poetry, *A Baja Love Song*. At KMPC he was famous for his "odes" to the sunrise each morning as he was driving from the "beach" and it was usually his first "traffic report." Paul was one of the original scriptwriters for the original radio drama, the "Lone Ranger" series. He was from Detroit.

PIERRE, "Lucky": **KHJ**, 1961-63; **KGFJ**, 1968-74; **KUTE**, 1974-84, pd; **KACD**, 1996-97. Born Pierre Gonneau, "Lucky" was born in Chatellerault, France and came to the United States to attend Ithaca College of Theatre Arts when he was 17 years old. His first love was acting. "Even though I got started in radio, I always

had it in the back of my mind that I would end up acting." He spent seven years in Buffalo radio beginning in 1954 on WWOL, WHLD, WEBR and WBNY. Beginning in 1955, for two years he hosted a weekly show on Mutual Radio Network from WOR-New York. During his first visit to Los Angeles and two years at KHJ, "Lucky" hosted an afternoon children's program on KHJ/Channel 9. He drew cartoons and even gave the youngsters French lessons. "We didn't do very well because we were up against Soupy Sales on KABC/Channel 7, Tom Hatten and *Popeye* on KTLA/Channel 5 and Sheriff John on KTTV/Channel 11. But while hosting movies on the weekends I had the thrill of a lifetime when I interviewed Maurice Chevalier who was appearing at the Greek Theatre. He was 80 years old and I was the only one who got to interview him. I must have run that interview 20 times," he laughed. (College kids at Ithaca nicknamed him after seeing a production of the play *New Faces of 1952*. Robert Clary sang about Lucky Pierre - the man of the hour, the man of the year - and Ithaca College's Pierre became "Lucky" and it stuck.) In 1963, he went to WFEC-Harrisburg for five years, returning to the Southland as md of KGFJ in 1968. At KUTE he started as md and by the time he left was pd during "the Quiet Storm" format. The station exploded in the late 1970s when KUTE was the only Disco station in the market. "Lucky" left radio in 1984 and has been acting full-time and has appeared on *Cheers*, *Golden Girls* and the 200th episode of *Married...With Children*. He said of his *Married* appearance, "More people saw me than anything I've done in the past decade. Amazing!" He lives in North Hollywood and is still big with the Hispanic community from his Disco days at KUTE. Most weekends he appears at local dance nightclubs and hosts special party nights. He also hosts a Sunday evening show on "Groove Radio."

PIERSAL, Jim: **KABC**, 1965. KABC was in the second season of experimenting with "SportsTalk" and the author of *Fear Strikes Out* co-hosted the program during the off-season in 1965.

PIETRO, Don: **KOST**, 1977. Born Don Pietromonaco, he was known as Johnny Rabbit during his best days at KXOK-St. Louis and KRIZ-Phoenix. He grew up in L.A. and appeared as Little Beaver on radio's "Red Ryder." His acting career included *An Affair To Remember*. He delivered a telegram to Cary Grant. Don also worked at KAFY-Bakersfield. For the past two decades, Don coached a voiceover workshop. He died of emphysema in April 1997 at the age of 61.

PIGG, Tony: **KPPC**, 1972. Tony is the announcer on *Live With Regis and Kathie Lee*. He works weekends at WNEW/FM.

PINA, Jaime: **KTNQ/KWKW**, 1980-96. Jaime hosts the morning drive show on Spanish KWKW. Jaime is from Guadalara.

PINSKY, Dr. Drew: **KROQ**, 1983-97. In 1983 Drew was a medical student at USC when approached to join the fledgling "Loveline" call-in show at KROQ. The program deals with young people's problems from heroin to herpes to puppy love. In addition to the nightly airing on KROQ, in 1996 the show became a regular show on MTV. In a *Buzz* magazine profile, Drew said of the show: "Nothing surprises me since medical school, but I still am shocked and amazed every 10 minutes. It's like I'm inside the Trojan horse and I get pushed inside the gates and I get to pop out and start trying to impress my values on the kids." Dr. Drew is the medical director of the department of chemical dependency services at Las Encinas psychiatric hospital in Pasadena.

PINTO, Matt: **KFOX**, 1983-84. Matt co-hosted "Sports Forum" with Fred Wallin.

PIOMBINO, Rich: **KMET**, 1983-86, pd. Rich arrived in the Southland from Detroit. He became pd in 1985 and left "the Mighty Met" in early 1986 for a marketing directorship at Westwood One. When Rich left KMET, consultant and former KMET pd George Harris said: "Rich was caught in a down-time period for the station." In the late 1980s, Rich went to WMMS-Cleveland and left in early 1990.

PIOTROWSKI, Casey: **KORG**, 1979; **KWRM**, 1980-81; **KFOX**, 1981; **KWIZ**, 1981-88. Born April 25, 1950, in Buffalo, Casey got started in his hometown in 1966 at WYSL. He moved on to WKBW-Buffalo, KLOK-San Jose and WSAI-Cincinnati. He wrote for *WKRP in Cincinnati* and was twice nominated for *Billboard*'s Air Personality of the Year Award. In 1994 he went to work for KOLA in the Inland Empire.

PLATT, Jane: **KMET**, 1977-78; **KABC**, 1978-79; **KLOS**, 1979-80; **KRLA**, 1981-85, nd; **KNX**, 1994. Born in Flushing, New York, Jane grew up in New Jersey and Los Angeles. She graduated from California State University Northridge. When Jane left her news directorship at KRLA, she was a network correspondent for ABC radio news and the tv network's NewsOne. Jane is the winner of numerous awards, including the highly-coveted AP Mark Twain Trophy for Best Newswriting and the Greater L.A. Press Club Award for Best Entertainment Reporting. She is now a public information officer for the Jet Propulsion Laboratory in Pasadena.

Cox Broadcasting buys 50,000-watt KFI for $15.1 million.   -1973

PLUM, Nancy: **KYMS**, 1973-74; **KGBS/KTNQ**, 1976-79; **KHTZ**, 1979; **KMPC**, 1979-80; **KFAC**; 1984; **KFI**, 1984-88; **KLAC**, 1988-91; **KRTH**, 1991-92; **KYSR**, 1992-93; **KFWB**, 1993; **KRLA**, 1994.  Nancy was born Nancy Hurst in New York City and grew up in Miami and San Francisco. Her radio career started in the Windy City at an all-female air personality station, WSDM, in the late 1960s. After her Southland start in Santa Ana, she moved to KAFY-Bakersfield for the evening shift and was the first female jock on the legendary Rock station. When she returned to the Southland in 1976, she worked the overnight shift at "the new Ten-Q." In 1980 she became a promotion executive at Universal Pictures. Nancy was one of the recognizable female voices in Southern California radio long before female djs became acceptable. She's currently a full-time news anchor and traffic reporter with Shadow Broadcast Services and also works weekends at Westwood One's Adult Rock and Roll format. She's writing a book on her personal "adventures" in radio. As a three-decade pioneer and survivor of the Los Angeles radio wars, Nancy observed, "I'm lucky to be living in Los Angeles, the best radio market in the world as far as I'm concerned. Being on the air is almost always the most fun!"

PLUNKETT, Jim: **KFI**, 1991-94. The former Raider quarterback hosted the Raiders radio pre-game shows on KFI. Jim was a Heisman Trophy winner at Stanford, 17 years in the NFL, 11 surgeries, played with 3 pro clubs and in two Super Bowls. He was voted most valuable player at the 1971 Rose Bowl when he led Stanford past Ohio State. Jim was the number one pick of the New England Patriots. At Super Bowl XV he passed for 261 yards and 3 touchdowns and was voted MVP. Jim left football in 1988 at the age of 40. Mike Downey at the *LA Times* said of Jim: "Brave and bold and a winner more often than not."

POETESS: **KKBT**, 1994-97. Host of "Hip Hop Hop" agenda, Felicia Morris, known as "the Poetess," joined "the Beat" in the spring of 1994 for weekends and fill-in.

KGFJ switches from Urban Gold to Gospel-tinged "Sweet Inspirations"
-1994

POHLMAN, Tim: **KTWV**, 1993-97, vp/gm.  Tim was upped to vp/gm of "the Wave" in the spring of 1996 from a position of gsm at both KTWV and KFWB. Prior to arriving in Southern California he had been in sales at WCPT/WCXR-Washington, DC, WWMG-Charlotte, WFOX-Atlanta and WHIO-Dayton. Tim was born and raised in Lima, Ohio and received a B.A. in communications from the University of Dayton.

POLAK, Frank: **KMPC**, 1978-80; **KLAC**, 1980-97. Frank has been the producer of the Los Angeles Lakers broadcasts on KLAC for almost two decades. "At KMPC I wrote sports and news, assisted with freeway traffic reporting, produced Rams, UCLA football and basketball and Angels games. I was also the voice of the now defunct KMPC 'Sportswire.' Come to think of it, KMPC itself is now defunct." In addition to his duties as Lakers producer, he also produced auto race coverage, L.A. Express USFL football, the Kings and the Mighty Ducks of Anaheim. Frank attended Pierce College and Cal State Northridge.

POLAND, Kay: SEE Kay Lane

POLK, David: **KRKD**, 1965; **XPRS**, 1973

POLLACK, Frank: **KDAY**, 1958; **KRLA**, 1959-60.  Frank worked middays at KDAY and his on-air time was described on the weekly survey "Shopping Time - Frolic with Pollack." Frank was one of the original KRLA "11-10 Men" in September 1959, working the all-night shift. In the early 1980s Frank was working at Big Band KLFF-Phoenix.

POND, Bob: **KGBS**, 1968; **KPPC**, 1972-73. Bob arrived in the Southland after functioning as pd of KRDS-Phoenix.

POOLE, Gary: **KQLZ**, 1991; **KLOS**, 1995. Gary is the director of Revolution Records. He started out as a jock. Gary arrived in the Southland from stints at WWCD-Columbus, KCFX-Kansas City, KSJO and KOME-San Jose and KLOL-Houston. In late 1995 he joined Discovery Records as a promotion director. In the spring of 1995 he did weekend fill-in at KLOS.

POORMAN: **KROQ**, 1982-93; **KIIS**, 1995; **KPWR**, 1995; **KACD**, 1996-97. Jim Trenton, born in 1962, was a surfer living in Huntington Beach. He studied in Oxford and was a graduate of Loyola Law School, but never passed the bar. Between examinations, he started selling "Poorman's Guide to Gourmet Dining." The KROQ pd invited him to review restaurants on the air, and his performance eventually led to a jock shift. In 1983 he conceived and co-hosted the "Loveline" program along with Dr. Drew Pinsky, who was a resident in internal medicine at Huntington Memorial Hospital in Pasadena. Between 1986 and 1988, the Poorman produced 32 episodes of *Adventures With the Poorman* for KDOC/Channel 56. In the early 1990s, he successfully marketed a line of clothing called "Poorwear" with nothing above $20, and it sold through surf shops. An impromptu KROQ party resulted in being suspended for "violating station policies." By the end of 1993 he was still off the air. Jim said, "It was a prank. I'm a master prankster, and they know that." In an *OC Register* interview, Jim said, "Infinity president Mel Karmazin told me taking 200 listeners to Bean's home was worse than having two of their people breaking and entering my home. I don't understand it." In the summer of 1993, he was part of KTTV/Channel 11's two-hour morning magazine show, *Good Day L.A.* In early 1994, he filed suit against KROQ and Infinity Broadcasting alleging breach of contract, slander, fraud and copyright infringement. The suit contended that by continuing to run the popular late-night "Loveline" show, which he developed and hosted, the station was infringing on his creation. Randy Lewis of the *Times* referred to the Poorman as having a "Beaver Cleaver-on-testosterone personality." He paired up with Domino at KIIS for his "desperate but date less" segment during the summer of 1995 and later he went to "Power 106" in the evenings. Jim told the *Register*: "Pretty amazing, huh? The white guy playing the music of the inner city. I even have a 'white mix' segment in which the listeners have to guess the name of the white band." He left "Power 106" in early 1996. He hosted "Hollywood Trash Reports" for Australian radio. The Poorman took on mornings at "Groove Radio," KACD, in the summer of 1996.

POPEJOY, Jack: **KGOE**, 1972, pd; **KIIS**, 1972-75, pd; **KPOL/KZLA**, 1976-79; **KLOS**, 1979-80; **KFWB**, 1986-97. Jack is the morning drive anchor/reporter on KFWB. He is also the fill-in financial editor for KTLA/Channel 5. Born in Austin, Jack grew up in the Delaware Valley living in New Jersey, Delaware and Pennsylvania. He graduated from Amherst College with a B.S. in astronomy.  He worked as gm of the campus station as well as other area stations. After college and Army basic training to become a reservist at Ft. Leonard Wood, Missouri, he worked at WMEX-Boston. He next spent a year as a news guy at WPEN-Philadelphia. He moved to Southern California to be production manager for Joey Reynolds & Associates, a jingle company. At KIIS Jack was hired as weekend dj and weekday newscaster. He was the first national pd for the KIIS concept syndication under Chuck Blore before being named KIIS pd at age 24. In 1976 he started as newscaster for KPOL AM&FM and was named pd of the FM station in 1977. He changed call letters to KZLA (it was a soft album rocker, long before being sold and changed to C&W). In the early 1980s he was nd and anchor for a San Francisco tv station. In 1983 Jack joined KCOP/Channel 13 as a reporter and fill-in anchor. At KFWB Jack is the resident expert on earthquakes. He is very active in the community and his work has been acknowledged with 13 Golden Mikes and 8 Press Club Awards.

PORTER, Ross: **KABC**, 1976-97. Ross is a longtime part of the award-winning L.A. Dodger broadcast team. Born in 1940, he grew up in Shawnee, Oklahoma, dreaming of being a play-by-play announcer, and he started doing it when he was 14. Ross graduated from the University of Oklahoma in 1960 and eventually won the coveted spot of being a Dodger broadcaster in 1976 alongside Vin Scully. Ross joined KNBC/Channel 4 in 1967, broadcasting sports for 10 years and winning an Emmy. He broadcast the 1977 and 1978 World Series on CBS Radio. Ross is the host of KABC "DodgerTalk" pre- and post-game shows for which he earned the Tom Harmon Award for Radio Sports Anchors in 1992. He is the father of two sets of twins.

PORTER, Scott: **KSRF**, 1991

PORTER, Vivian: **KRTH**, 1974-77; **KHJ**, 1978-85; **KRTH**, 1985-97. Vivian was born in Los Angeles and went to John C. Freeman High School and Cal State Los Angeles.  After working for a State Assemblyman she joined KRTH as a sales assistant. Within a few months her interest in public service led to a job in the public affairs department. Twenty years later she remains one of the constant voices in Southern California radio. "The basic 'core' issues in our community really haven't changed significantly. However, the changes that do occur in the nature or aspects of the issues we seek to address in programming, require an ongoing assessment which provides the basis for the job I do." The joy in her job is finding problems and creating programs that address those problems. "It is particularly gratifying when listeners respond to the programming. It's very rewarding." She attributes her long-running involvement as director of public affairs to "hard work and loving what you do." In the face of deregulation, many stations abandoned their public affairs department, but not KRTH. "Much of the continuing success of KRTH is that there has always been a caring management team that wants to give something back to the community." Her numerous community service commendations and awards include AP's Certificate of Merit and Excellence in Best Editorial and Documentary categories. She's won The Black Women of Achievement Award as well as commendations from the NAACP, United Way, Martin Luther King Foundation and Black Achiever in Industry. Vivian is divorced and lives in the Windsor Hills area of L.A. with her 10-year-old daughter and young adult son. She enjoys classical music and loves to cook Chinese, Caribbean and California style cuisine.

POSKA, Al: **KFI**, 1958. Al hosted a nightly interview show at KFI.

POSTON, Ken: **KLON**, 1987-97. Ken is a concert

promoter and hosts "Portraits in Jazz" on KLON. He got his start in his native Kansas City, attending the nearby University of Kansas to study music. He became interested in the history of jazz and began working in the university's jazz research library. After graduation, Ken became involved with the Kansas City Jazz Commission to preserve the city's jazz heritage. He started a local jazz magazine and began teaching jazz history at area universities. In addition to his decade of work at KLON, he also teaches jazz history at UCLA. Ken is also the director of the Sarasota Jazz Festival.

POTTER, Peter: **KLAC**, 1945-50; **KFWB**, 1951; **KLAC**, 1951; **KMPC**; **KVFM**, 1972. Creator of the *Platter Parade* and *Juke Box Jury* radio and tv shows, Peter was born William Moore in Henrietta, Oklahoma, and worked Los Angeles radio for a quarter of a century. He was one of the legendary "Big 5" disc jockeys on KLAC along with Dick Haynes, Alex Cooper, Gene Norman and Bob McLaughlin. Peter broke into radio accidentally. He had come to Los Angeles during the Depression in 1934, after graduating from the University of New Mexico. While working in a furniture store, he wrote a radio script, and it was picked up by KNX. Peter appeared on all three major radio and tv networks. On May 15, 1950, he did his first tv show, the local *Peter Potter Platter Party*. In the early 1960s, during the explosion of rock music, Peter commented on the state of music in a *Billboard* interview: "I've been a disc jockey since 1937, and I've taken pride in being able to play the best in music. Top 40 programming is an inadequate service to the public. Top 40 limits the audience to kids and they don't buy the sponsor's product." He won Best Entertainment Emmys in 1953 and 1955. In the early 1970s, he was heard on KVFM. He was married to singer Beryl Davis. Peter died of a heart attack on April 17, 1983, at the age of 78. In poor health, he had been living in Palm Springs.

POWELL, Dave: **KJOI**, 1987

POWELL, Mike: **KBCA**, 1968

POWELL, Russ: **KNX**, 1971-81. For part of his stay at KNX, he was business and financial editor. He has retired to Grass Valley where he owns a radio station.

POWER, Will: **KSRF**, 1992. Will was part of the morning drive team during the "MARSfm" programming.

POWERMOUTH, Patty: SEE Patty Lotz

POWERS, Craig: **KUTE**; 1976-77; **KIIS**, 1977-82; **KFXM**, 1982-85, om; **KKHR**, 1983-85; **KEZY**, 1985-91, pd; **KIKF**, 1991-95, pd. On KIIS, Craig was known as L.A.'s youngest dj. He was the host of the "Craig Powers Breakfast Club" at KEZY and was made pd in 1988. "I hold the world record for remote broadcasting in the Orange County market. In the last 10 years I've done over 1,500 remotes and live broadcasts and over 500 personal appearances." Name the Orange County concert and chances are he was the emcee. In 1993, Craig was the P.A. announcer for the Anaheim Bullfrogs/Arrowhead Pond. In 1994 he was nominated by *Billboard* magazine for pd of the year. Craig worked afternoon drive and was pd at Country-formatted KIKF until spring of 1995 when he left to be director, Western regional promotions for MCG/Curb Records, a country label.

POWERS, Francis Gary: **KGIL**, 1973. The Southern California Big Red Skywatch pilot was shot down over Russia on a reconnaissance mission during the Summit Conference in Paris in 1960. In an unprecedented move, the United States traded spies with the Soviet Union, and Frank came home in exchange for master spy Rudolf Abel in 1962. When he grew weary of test piloting, around 1970, Frank moved with his wife and two children to Studio City and tried out as the backup pilot for Col. Bruce Payne on KGIL. He commented at the time of his promotion: "The higher you get, the greater the sense of detachment. It's indescribable, but it's the detachment." He died in a helicopter crash in the San Fernando Valley while doing traffic reports for KNBC/Channel 4.

PRAGER, Dennis: **KABC**, 1983-97. Dennis's show is

billed as "talk about social issues from an ethical perspective." For 10 years he hosted "Religion on the Line," a popular Sunday evening show on KABC that featured a Jewish rabbi, Protestant minister and Catholic priest. He did undergraduate work in political-science at Brooklyn College and the University of Leeds in England and graduate work as a fellow at Columbia University's School of International Affairs and Russian Institute. In 1969, at the age of 21, he was the national spokesman for the Student Struggle for Soviet Jewry and a delegate to the first Brussels World Conference on Soviet Jewry. President Ronald Reagan appointed him a U.S. delegate to the Vienna Review Conference on the Helsinki Accords to negotiate human rights with the Soviet Union. His on-air personality deals with moral issues. He is for moral revenge and for capital punishment as an instrument of revenge. In late 1984 an early evening slot opened up on KABC when Hilly Rose retired. Since 1985 Dennis has been the sole writer and publisher of *Ultimate Issues*, a journal with more than 20,000 readers worldwide which focuses on life's greatest political, social, philosophical and religious questions and events. The conservative talk show host on KABC started a half-hour talk show in September of 1994 on KTTV/Channel 11. He co-authored *The Nine Questions People Ask About Judaism* which is the most widely used introduction to Judaism in the world. Dennis authored *Why The Jews? The Reason For Anti-Semitism*. In 1994 he started a daily noon to three shift on KABC's "TalkRadio." He lives in Los Angeles with his wife and three children.

PRATT, Jim: **KROQ**, 1997

PRELL, Jon: **KIKF**, 1988-90. Jon was last heard working in the South at a Country station.

PRESCOTT: **KMET**, 1981

PRESHER, Dave: **KMEN/KGGI**, 1994-95, vp/gm; **KPWR**, 1996-97, gsm; **KTWV**, 1997, gsm. Dave left his Inland Empire post in the fall of 1995 for a tv slot in Chico/Redding. In the spring of 1996, he joined "Power 106" as gsm and a year later took on a similar post at KTWV.

PRESS, Bill: **KABC**, 1990; **KFI** 1991-96. Bill worked with Bill Pearl in afternoon drive at KABC and their show was called "The Duelling Bills." He left KABC in 1990 when he announced his candidacy for state insurance commissioner. As chairman of the state Democratic Party, he raised more than $5,000 in pledges on just two KFI shows for the Fred Goldman family after the verdicts in the O.J. Simpson case. Bill left KFI in February 1996 to join former vice presidential candidate Geraldine Ferraro as alternating co-host for the left on CNN's *Crossfire*.

PRICE, Gary: **KHJ/FM**, 1971-72, gm; **KROQ**, 1972-73, gm; **KDAY**, 1973-83, gm; **KNAC**, 1984-95, gm. Gary started as a jock, moved into sales and spent the bulk of his radio career running stations in his native California. Born and raised in Monrovia, he earned an FCC 1st Class License after a stint in the Korean War. In 1958 he started as the morning man at KPER-Gilroy. While at KFXM-San Bernardino doing evenings in the early 1960s, he tried sales. Crosstown KMEN hired Gary as sales manager while allowing him to work a weekend shift. His first gm assignment came in 1970 at KLYD-Bakersfield followed a year later with a sales assignment at KHJ/FM which quickly turned into gm responsibilities. When KDAY adopted an Urban format in early 1974, there was a prophecy of doom, but the format was a success. Gary talked about the format switch: "The only people who bought the idea were the audience. We tried something new - no screaming disc jockeys, no street jive." Did he ever regret the switch from announcing to management? "Sometimes I think it wouldn't have been so tough if I had stayed a jock." Gary is working as a sales consultant for Fred Sands.

PRICE, Gene: **KDAY**, 1966-67; **KLAC**, 1970-71; **KFOX**, 1972; **KIQQ**, 1973-74, pd; **KIIS**, 1974; **KLAC**, 1975-84; **KIKF**, 1985-90; **KLAC**, 1990-93. Born in McKinney, Texas, Gene started his radio career in Lubbock while at Texas Tech. He came to the Southland from KEWB-San Francisco and joined KIQQ as pd until Drake/Chenault bought the station. In 1980, he quietly replaced morning wake-up legend "Dick Haynes at the Reins" and stayed until 1981. In fact, he was greatly influenced by Haynes, and some of his own cornpone humor was only a record away. Gene won the 1981 *Billboard* magazine Award for Personality of the Year given out at the Country Radio Seminar in Nashville. He hosted an Armed Forces Radio program for years. He has voiced numerous national commercials and was one of the early pioneers of the "Music of Your Life" format at Unistar. When he worked for Country KIKF, he made the drive from his San Fernando Valley home to the city of Orange every morning for five years. Gene left KLAC at the end of 1993, when the award-winning station changed formats to satellite-fed Unistar's AM Only. Gene has always loved sales. While in Texas radio, before coming to California, he sold his own program. He was the general sales manager for Shadow Broadcast Services in Los Angeles and later went to Western International Media.

PRICE, Mary: **KWIZ**, 1978-81; **KGGI**, 1982-84; **KZLA**, 1984-89; **KRTH**, 1992; **KCBS**, 1992-97. Born December 2, 1958, Mary grew up in Anaheim and her first radio job was at Orange County's KWIZ. In 1985 she joined Unistar and worked there until 1993 while doing part-time work at KZLA and KRTH. Mary joined KCBS during the "Oldies 93" format and a year later stayed with the change to "Arrow 93" in September 1993, moving from weekends to middays. On KCBS' web site Mary remembered "mowing the lawn with my dad" as her fondest childhood memory.

PRICE, Tony: **KGFJ**, 1972

PRINCI, Carl: **KWKW**, 1952-53; **KFAC**, 1953-87, pd; **KKGO**, 1990-92. Born in 1922, Carl worked as a classical music announcer for four decades and for much of that time was pd. Each afternoon at three on KFAC, Carl hosted "World of Opera," a show he inherited three decades ago. He worked right up until his death in 1992. He was a legend at KFAC and loved by everyone. When he was 14 he appeared in a theater production that required him to run across the stage in a loin cloth. Once he heard the applause, he was hooked. He graduated from Boston University and started radio at a Salem, Massachusetts station. In 1953 he auditioned for Classical KFAC where he was told there were no openings. The next day one of the announcers dropped dead and he got the job. He had over 40 bit parts in tv and movie productions.

PRINGLE, Oogie: **KWIZ**, 1985-87. Oogie worked at WNBC-New York in the mid-1980s and Chicago before doing morning drive at KWIZ. He committed suicide in 1987.

PROPES, Steve: **KLON**, 1981-92. Steve is a radio archivist and record collector. Born in Berkeley July 21, 1942, he grew up in Long Beach and graduated from Cal State Long Beach in 1965. He remembers when his love affair with music began: "When I heard two competing versions of *Stranded in the Jungle* on the radio, I was fascinated." He hosted an r&b Sunday morning show at KLON. Steve has written three books that have set the standard for price guides to record collecting. He works with foster kids for Los Angeles County and lives in Long Beach.

PURCELL, Bob: **KFI/KECA**, 1942-45; **KFWB**, 1956-62, gm. While waiting for the curtain to rise on the Civic Light Opera presentation of *Man of La Mancha* starring Bob Purcell as Cervantes/Quixote, you would be aghast reading in the program about the career of the star. He was known in Southern California as the general manager during the launch of historic "Color Radio" on January 2, 1958. A month after the launch Bob wrote pd Chuck Blore, the djs and newsmen: "Our total broadcast week is composed of 585,000 seconds. Each one of those seconds must be full, alive, bright, and alert. None should pass by un-noticed, each single second shall carry a full complement of colorful programming. In every five minute period you are each responsible for as many as 300 seconds, each one of them is a definite part of the KFWB sound, never let them go by emptily or dully. P.S. Have you tightened up lately." Another phase of Bob's success in Southern California predated KFWB, when the 6 foot, 5 inch broadcaster was named the program director of KTTV/Channel 11 in 1949. Bob started his radio career as a singer at age 14 at WHAM-Rochester where he was born May 11, 1912. In the '30s he spent 8 years with WCFL-Chicago as staff announcer as well as hosting "Make Believe Danceland."

While in Chicago he suffered a street accident that canceled his Army 1-A status. When he arrived in the Southland in 1942 he acted in several films, notably *Forever Amber* and *The Bride Wore Boots*. In the mid-1960s Bob and his wife Jane moved to Yucca Valley where he made use of his real estate brokers license. For the next 14 years he participated in theater companies all over Southern California. In 1982 he retired to Laguna Hills. Bob was terminally ill for the last two years before his death on August 5, 1987. He was 75. A columnist who knew Bob well wrote: "Purcell was the inherently lazy type of hard worker, ambitious but not ridiculously so. He had humor and a sense of proportion, he was free from swank, inspired confidence and loyalty." His wife remembered, "Bob had an unquenchable curiosity; everything he pursued was a challenge. His hobbies or avocations included Japanese Sumi painting, lectures on Chinese calligraphy, classical guitar, flute, recorder, amateur radio (he ran 5,000 phone patches during the Vietnam crisis for our servicemen) and even piano tuning."

PUTNAM, George: **KFI**; **KIEV**, 1975-97. George was born in Breckenridge, Minnesota on July 14, 1924. In college, he was the president of the freshman class, champion orator, ran on the track squad and played basketball and football. In 1934, his family suffered severe financial reverses and George took a job with WDGY-Minneapolis on his 20th birthday. Next was KSTP-Minneapolis/St. Paul and then NBC in New York where he did 14 programs a week, concentrating on news and special events.

He shared the role of commentator for *Fox Movietone News* with Lowell Thomas. During World War II, he served as a first lieutenant in the Marine Corps, winning two citations during his three-year stay. After the war he was seen and heard on the Mutual Broadcasting System, BBC and the Du Mont Television Network. George moved to Los Angeles in 1951 and his program *George Putnam and the News* has been seen on every local independent broadcast tv station. He starred with Mort Sahl in a nationally syndicated tv show entitled *Both Sides Now*. He has been the recipient of over 300 awards and citations and in 1982 was awarded a Star on the Hollywood Walk of Fame. His "Talk Back" show has been a two-decade institution on KIEV. George lives on a ranch in Chino, where he raises thoroughbred horses. He has ridden in every Tournament of Roses Parade on New Year's Day for four decades. Walter Winchell said: "George Putnam's voice is the greatest in radio and television." During the summer of 1996 George appeared in the blockbuster film, *Independence Day*. His signature line: "And that's the up-to-the-minute news - Up to the minute, that's <u>all</u> the news! - See You Then!"

PUTNEY, Sam: **KJLH**, 1984-88; **KACE**, 1988-92. Sam was part of the KACE morning drive team broadcasting sports and news. He is now working in Houston radio.

PYE, Jr., Brad: **KGFJ**, 1955-73; **KJLH**, 1973-75; **KACE**, 1975-77; **KGFJ**, 1977-79; **KDAY**, 1979-90. For three decades, Brad was the award-winning sports editor of

the *Los Angeles Sentinel*. He broke down numerous color barriers at the newspaper, in radio and as an active participant in sports. His style was unique. "Two of my greatest idols in the radio field were the late Walter Winchell and Jim Healy, two of my dearest friends. Winchell used to use my typewriter at Angel games at Dodger Stadium and Healy made me more famous on his program than I was on my own show." Brad was an all-star member of the 1949 undefeated East Los Angeles College football team and was student director of public relations. He was considered the "Dean of Black Sportscasters." The *Sentinel* had an exchange deal with KGFJ and Brad alternated with the late Chester L. Washington, Jr. on a five-minute news/sports show. He hustled a sponsor for a weekly 15-minute show each Sunday. He secured Julius L. Hibler & Company, the city's only black stock broker firm at the time for sponsorship. In 1956 he began a 17 year association with KGFJ hosting "Sportsville L.A." He coined such phrases as "Overheard at Tommy Tucker's Play Room From the Lips of a Los Angeles Dodgers Star" and "Pretty Little Green Ones." During his pioneer stint with the *Sentinel*, Brad was credited with leading the campaign to make the late Emmett Ashford the first African American umpire in the history of major league baseball. He is given credit for integrating the L.A. Coliseum press box and other local press boxes. He served as the first African American PR rep for the L.A. Angels, the L.A. Chargers and as administrator assistant for AFL Commissioner Al Davis. Brad served as assistant Chief Deputy for County Supervisor Kenneth Hahn. Presently, he is the ADA Coordinator for the Los Angeles County Department of Children and Family Services. Today he is the lead sports columnist for the *New Pittsburgh Courier* and the sports editor for *Inglewood Today Magazine*. Who will ever forget, "Switch Reels," and "And That's All of My Time...Thanks For Your Time...This is Brad Pye, Jr. Reporting...Have A Ball."

PYLE, Ed: **XTRA**; **KFWB**, 1974-84; **KNX**, 1985-97.

Born in 1939, in Paramus, New Jersey, Ed was raised in Plant City, Florida. In 1990, he was named executive news producer at KNX. After being released from the service, Ed went back to Florida in 1960 where he worked for a variety of radio stations in Tampa/St. Petersburg as a dj and newsman. He came to California for XTRA in the last year of its all-News programming.

PYNE, Joe: **KABC**; **KLAC**, 1965-69. "No one conducts the straight, hard-hitting interview as well as Joe Pyne, the master showman of the talk realm," according to the *LA Times* in 1967. Born in Chester, Pennsylvania, he joined the U.S. Marine Corps upon graduation from high school. In World War II he won three battle stars and lost his left leg. Joe started his radio career at WCAM-Camden while studying at a Philadelphia dramatic school. He worked in Canada, Delaware and Arizona. By the time he arrived in the Southland it was estimated that he commanded $2,000 a week for four broadcast days. His competitors and critics called him "Killer Joe" and the "ranking nuisance of broadcasting." Marv Gray who got his start as Joe's producer talked to Harry Shearer for a 1972 talk radio feature in the *Times*: "Joe Pyne was such a peerless showman. He had such a great sense of how to get the public excited and talk radio needed that to get established as a medium. Then, as the years went by, the issues became more serious and people began taking them more seriously. In some cases, the old days were more fun, you know, just screaming at each other." He could be heard telling a caller he disagreed with to "go gargle with razor blades." At the peak of his career, in 1966, he had a syndicated television talk show on Metromedia stations and a syndicated radio show on 254 stations. A heavy smoker, he once said that although he realized cigarettes might cause cancer, he would "rather take a chance than be a fat neurotic." When he learned he had cancer, he stopped smoking. For a few months he began broadcasting from his home until he quit radio and tv in 1969 due to illness. Joe died of cancer on March 23, 1970. He was 44.

KFI founded by Earle C. Anthony
KFI broadcasts 5 watts, April 16, 1922
KFI broadcasts 50,000 watts, 1931
KFI original studios at Olympic and Hope Street

Q

Q, Leo: KIIS, 1988-97. The best way to describe Leo Quinones is "utility player." He is KIIS's recognized movie reviewer and announcer at station sponsored movie premieres. Leo hosts the KIIS "Cinema Sunday Night." He is also the head writer of the nationally syndicated "Fox Kids Countdown" radio show which boasts 215  affiliates. He appeared in 20th Century Fox's *Volcano*. Leo started out as an intern for the "Rick Dees Weekly Top 40 Countdown" in 1987. "I was a huge fan of Rick Dees. As a listener, my buddy and I took a Dees trip to Puerto Vallarta. I told Rick's writer a joke and five minutes later, Rick did the joke as Willard Wizeman. That was it. I was hooked."

QUEST, Johnny: KEZY, 1989-97. Johnny works the  overnight shift at Orange County's KEZY. He was born October 22, 1970, at The UCI Medical Center in Orange and grew up in Anaheim. After graduating from high school, Johnny started interning at KEZY. "I've never looked back." Following some assistant's positions, he got the call to go on the air in March 1990. "The overnight jock called because his wife was in labor and could not make it in that night. The pd called everybody on the air staff and could not get anybody to work, so it came down to either him doing it or giving me my big break. He chose the latter." Two years later he started full-time. Johnny collects baseball cards and is an amateur radio operator. He also manages a little league baseball team. "People might wonder why I'm still where I was four years ago, but I'm just happy to be making a living doing what I love to do and in my own hometown.

QUIGLEY, Lane: KUSC, 1969-73. Lane hosted the "Memory Lane Show" every Sunday night, playing music from rock's early years. The show was all-request and featured pre-Beatles oldies with lots of r&b from the early 1950s. Lane is now a practicing lawyer in Los Angeles.

QUIGLEY, Paxton: KMPC/KTZN, 1996-97. The self-  defense guru to 15 million women hosts a weekly show on KTZN. "The Paxton Quigley Empowerment Hour" deals with personal reliance and responsibility for women of all ages and the men in their lives who really and truly care. Her book *Armed & Female* is known as the "bible of women's gun self-defense." Born in Chicago, Paxton is a divorced mother of two with a master's degree in anthropology from the University of Chicago.

QUILLIN, Ted: KFWB, 1958-61; **KRLA,** 1962-64; **KEZY,** 1966-68; **KFI,** 1969; **KFOX,** 1969-71; **XPRS,** 1972. Look out for "Blue Skies and Green Lights" has been T.Q.'s mantra for decades. Born in Oklahoma City, Ted was part of the original "Seven Swingin' Gentlemen" at Chuck Blore's historic "Color Radio" launch at KFWB on January 2, 1958. Ted left Oklahoma City when he was 13 and lived in Denver, Lubbock and El Paso before graduating from the Texas College of Mines and Metallurgy (now UTEP). As one talks with T.Q. it is impossible to miss his quest for excellence, which is punctuated by his "sayings"; e.g., "attitude determines desired altitude." His communication motivation seminars have been successful for decades: "Learn one magic trick that will change your life, personally and financially, forever." During the 1950s, his "people-pleasing personality" took him through a number of Texas radio and television stations. It was at KELP-El Paso that his fortunes would leapfrog him to California. The pd at KELP was Chuck Blore. When Chuck got the call to program KFWB, T.Q. was the only personality he took with him to launch the new format. Ted worked all-nights and he loved it. From his home in Las Vegas, Ted explained, "During the all-night time, Chuck didn't care what I played, so I flavored the rock music with lots of blues; in fact, I  called it 'Blues for Breakfast.'" It was during this time that Ted and Ritchie Valens became good friends. "He used to visit me at my home and in the KFWB studios. I became sort of a big brother/consultant to Ritchie. He was a shy person and had a little trouble handling admiring throngs." When Elvis got out of the Army, KFWB wanted to bring him to the L.A. Coliseum, and they asked Ted to help since Ted knew Elvis. "I was given a certified check in the amount of $100,000 and flew to Memphis. I hung out with Elvis for four days at Graceland. Colonel Parker wasn't sure if Elvis would perform, but we had a good time in Memphis with Elvis." By 1972, Ted was, as he put it, "at the intersection of walk and don't walk. I had to get out of the fast lane." During his time in L.A. he appeared in many of the Warner Bros. tv series, such as *77 Sunset Strip*, and with Debbie Reynolds in *My Six Loves*. He said he still gets residual checks for $5. Ted settled for a slower lane in Las Vegas and immediately went to work at KORK, where he was the morning star on radio and host of the afternoon tv movie. He eventually opened his own advertising agency, which he ran for 20 years. He is about to launch an infomercial, while continuing his motivation seminars. He taught for years at Las Vegas City College. Always optimistic, T.Q. summed up his life with another "truism," saying, "The road to success is always under construction."

QUIMBY, Crys: **KNX**, 1985-94; **KFWB**, 1996-97, nd. The news director at all-News KFWB has been in broadcast news since 1981. She started as a freelancer at KNX moving to a full-time position in 1991 as a producer/editor and writer. In 1995 she went to WBBM-Chicago as a producer/editor, writer and reporter. Crys also did freelance writing for KCBS/Channel 2 and KTLA/Channel 5. She was a segment producer/writer for *Crimewatch Tonight*, a syndicated television news magazine. As a tv news anchor, Crys hosted an hour long monthly news program for the Emmy nominated CityChannel News in Los Angeles. She joined KFWB in the fall of 1996.

QUINN, Louis: **KLAC**, 1963. Louis was the afternoon dj at KLAC. He was also an actor and played "Roscoe" on *77 Sunset Strip*.

QUINN, Tony: **KGFJ**, 1965

QUINTANA, Jorge Lopez: **KWKW**; **KALI**, 1993. Jorge worked afternoons at Spanish KALI. Jorge spent two decades at KWKW and is considered one of the pioneers of Spanish radio.

QUIRM, Herman, **KMET**, 1968-69. Herman worked morning drive at KMET.

QUIROZ, Francisco Javier: **KSCA**, 1997

"I knew I couldn't be a winner in L.A. by cloning the existing radio stations, so I started visiting record stores, talking with record distributors, and listening to juke boxes to hear what records were being worn out. This resulted in playing the Coasters, Bill Haley and Fats Domino when no one else was. The big break came when I introduced Elvis. RCA flew me to Las Vegas to present Presley with his first gold record for 'Heartbreak Hotel.' From there, the floodgates ripped open. I was an original; there were no Top 40 formatted stations in Los Angeles. I started my own fan newsletter, compiled a weekly hit list and took live shows to every high school that would let me in the front door." -Earl McDaniel

"I was the third female music director promoted by Larry Berger at WPLJ. Periodically within ABC, I'd read propaganda that would get circulated about the upper echelon of the company. I remember seeing a piece with a photo of 12 ABC execs. They were all white, middle aged, WASPY-looking men. No women! Today the prejudice against female executives, fortunately, no longer exists. So, if you're a woman, remember: Alice may have been the first female through that 'looking glass,' but through persistence and perseverance, I eventually followed. And women like Mary Catherine Sneed and Liz Kiley have done it as well, and have enjoyed tremendous success. You could be next!" -Lisa Tonacci-Butts

"On March 28, 1989, it was announced that demolition had begun on the Huntington Hotel and the adjacent 'Carriage House' annex, the beautiful landmarks where KRLA had held forth for so many years. With some trepidation, I visited the site of the old KRLA studios. The window in the lobby was still there. The 'man in the sun' sunface was still on the lobby floor, a reminder of past glories. We opened the door to the disc jockey booth. Debris. All that remained was the window, where so many times we had watched the '11-10 Men' for all those years. For a moment, I saw the 'Hullabalooer.' He turned and waved. The transmitter, the station, the music, the personalities and the porch people. I was just a kid then, with a dream. It seems like only yesterday." -Bill Earl

(Excerpts from the premier edition of Los Angeles Radio People)

R

RABBIT, Jimmie: **KFI**; **KRLA**, 1969-70; **KLAC**, 1971; **KMET**, 1971-72; **KBBQ**, 1972; **KHJ**, 1972; **KROQ**, 1972-73; **KMET**, 1975; **KGBS**, 1975, pd; **KLAC**, 1976; **KROQ**, 1977-78. Jimmie is one of radio's outlaw characters. Jimmie was born Dale Payne in 1941 and grew up in Tyler, Texas. He joined the Marine Corps and after serving in the military, he returned to Tyler and sold shoes until his first radio gig at KGKB. Jimmie's radio roots were planted and sprouted at KLIF-Dallas. As the music changed in the mid-1960s, KLIF pd Ken Dowe allowed Rabbit a Sunday-night-only show, featuring "psychedelic" music. Within no time, he was on nightly, and McLendon spent a fortune putting psychedelic lights in the KLIF studio windows that were visible to the outside. In 1968, he was off to KCBQ-San Diego. When the station tightened its playlist in 1969, Jimmie, looking for a way out, contacted his buddy Doug Cox, who was programming KRLA. The times were a-changing in 1969 when Doug put Jimmie on the air for a combination of "free-form" sprinkled with country music. He left the station less than a year later. In 1969, the *LA Times* named Jimmie rock dj of the year. When times got tough for Jimmie, he could always count on breaking horses in Topanga Canyon. He joined KMET for the first time on January 18, 1971, for the 11 a.m.- 4 p.m. shift. In May 1972, "The Rabbit" was on KHJ for three days. He was called to a meeting at Nickodell's (an industry hangout) with Ted Atkins and Bill Watson. According to Jimmie in a *Billboard* magazine profile, Watson said, "We don't want another Robert W. Morgan at night." Jimmie was suspended, not fired, but only because Bill Drake had hired him and Bill was in Hawaii; he was eventually fired after Drake approved it. Later in 1972, Jimmie joined *Bob Hamilton's Radio Report* publication as country editor. In 1975, he was back on KMET in the early evenings. When things didn't work out on KMET, management put him on sister Metromedia station, Country KLAC. One fellow worker marveled at Jimmie's ability to meld progressive music with the music coming out of Austin: "He'd mix classic country oldies with the Eagles and Linda Ronstadt." After playing *Texas*, by the Charlie Daniels Band, 16 times in a row, he abruptly left KGBS. Jimmie performed with his band, Renegade, at the Palomino Club. By this time he had logged 3,000 personal appearances. Jimmie had moderate record-selling success with *Positively/15 O'Clock* on Hanna-Barbera Records and with the Southern version of *Psychotic Reaction*. He cut records with Johnny Winters. Between radio assignments, he did a one-to-one voiceover workshop at Wally Heider Studios, up the block from local jock hangout Martoni's. Capitol Records released an album by Renegade with *Ladies Love Outlaws* as the first single. Jimmie dislocated his shoulder in 1977, and eased the pain by singing at The Palomino. In 1996 Jimmy had returned to Tyler, Texas and was working at KKUS.

RACCO, Al: **KLAC**, 1960-61, gm. Al moved from programming ranks to be general manager. He left the Southland to work at ABC in New York.

RACE, Clark: **KMPC**, 1971-77; **KBRT**, 1980. Following an enormously successful 11-year run at KDKA-Pittsburgh, the then-36 year-old Clark joined KMPC in 1971 as an heir apparent to the morning heavyweight Dick Whittinghill and lasted until 1977. In 1972 Clark became the host for ABC/TV's game show *The Parent Game*. At KMPC he worked mostly overnights and by 1978, Clark had failed to make an impression with Southern California listeners and turned to booze. Clark headed for KYUU-San Francisco and San Diego before returning briefly to the Southland in 1980 to work mornings on the short-lived contemporary Christian music station KBRT. On his departure, he sat with James Brown of the *LA Times* and said, "I'm an emotional person. So while I was going through this divorce, I began to let everything out. I was being unfair to my audience by subjecting them to my problems. I was being unfair to KMPC. I just wasn't entertaining." At the time of his return to "Born-Again" KBRT, Clark said that "the idea of a personality playing Christian music is that it's not just for people in the church, it's for everyone. You can't preach to people. It's nice to be able to run to a radio station that gives out positive messages." He was gone from the station by the fall of the same year. He reflected on the short-lived experience: "My closest friends are either happy Christians or ex-drunks...and they're the happiest people I know." In early 1981, Clark worked afternoon drive for five years at KYXY-San Diego. By the mid-1980s, he and his family were running a bed and breakfast inn outside of Pittsburgh.

RACHTMAN, Riki: **KNAC**; **KROQ**, 1993-96; **KLSX**, 1996-97. The former host of MTV's *Headbanger's Ball* and owner of a punk rock club called Radio Cathouse, Riki hosted the popular "Lovelines" program on KROQ. Riki, a recovering alcoholic and former drug addict (according to a profile in the *LA Times*), refers to his own experiences with much empathy as the host of "Loveline." His mind-altering drug abuse caused the manager of Guns 'N' Roses to ask him to stay away from the band because he was a bad influence on THEM! The San Fernando Valley-raised Riki is the lead singer in a punk band called Battery Club. In a 1995 issue of *Playboy* Riki was one of the participants in a feature on "sex talk radio." In January 1996 he joined "Real Radio," KLSX and refers to himself as the "triple R." He lives in Marina del Rey with six lizards, four cats and a bird. He snowboards, is a stock car racing fanatic and has a "43" tattoo for Richard Petty. Riki started hosting "Rockline" in early 1997.

> *"Holmes was a swingin' and creative organist, who would carry his organ in a hearse to and from his gigs."*
> —about Richard "Groove" Holmes

RADKE, Walt: Robert W. Morgan called his engineer "Failsafe" during the "Boss Radio" glory days. Walt's picture was featured on the cover of a "Boss 30" survey.

RAMIREZ, Al: **KROQ**, 1976-79; **KLOS**, 1979-97. The Los Angeles native started his radio career in San Francisco in 1971 at KSFX. Al started his long run at "The Home of Rock 'n' Roll," KLOS, on December 24, 1979. Looking back on his 18-year stay at KLOS, Al recalled some highlights: "I co-hosted morning drive with Frazer Smith in 1983. I also produced and announced 'The Hollywood Niteshift' hour on KROQ and KLOS, starring Phil Austin, Michael C. Gwynne and Frazer. I had the privilege of filling in as the host of 'Seventh Day' for two years in the absence of 'Uncle' Joe Benson." Since 1973 Al has been a free-lance motion picture and television recording engineer.

RAMIREZ, Robbie: **KLVE**, 1991. Robbie hosted middays at Spanish "K-Love."

RAMONDO: SEE Raymond Banister

RAMOS, Carol: **KFWB**, 1994-97. The Puerto Rican is the morning anchor on all-News KFWB. She was born

and raised in New York and worked for a decade in Chicago news before arriving in the Southland in June 1994. She worked in tv until 1986 when she joined WBBM-Chicago as afternoon drive anchor. Influenced by Geraldo Rivera at age 13 when she was a student in Brooklyn, Carol described herself as a "news junkie."

Carol started her broadcast career for the CBS affiliate in San Juan, Puerto Rico in 1979, moving next to WBDC-Huntingburg, Indiana and then to Chicago. "I had been waiting to move to California since 1987. I fell in love with the state after attending a professional conference here."

RAMOS, Richard: **KOST**; **KJOI**, 1973-75. Richard has a very active voiceover career. He was the longtime voice for Ford Motor Company.

RAMSAY, John: **KWIZ**, 1974-76. John worked weekends while at KWIZ. He became the stadium announcer for the Rams and Dodgers. John opened an ad agency in Orange County.

RAMSBURG, Jim: **KLAC**, 1965. Jim arrived in the Southland as assistant pd and worked a weekend show during the "two-way" Talk format. A product of the University of Minnesota School of Journalism, in the 1950s he started at WLOL-St. Paul followed by WDGY-Minneapolis and KWKY-Des Moines. Before arriving in the L.A. he worked at WPTR-Albany and KMBC-Kansas City.

RAMSEY, Tom: **KMPC**, 1991. The four-year QB starter for the UCLA Bruins between 1979 and 1982 went into broadcasting Bruin football. After UCLA he joined the USFL for two years, mainly with the Los Angeles Express and then the New England Patriots and Indianapolis Colts.

RANDAL, Ted: **KFWB**, 1961-62. Ted started as a dj on KASH-Eugene, in 1947 while attending the University of Oregon, majoring in radio and drama. He worked small market stations for about nine years. His success stories include CHUM-Toronto and KROY-Sacramento. Randal was one of the strike breakers during the relatively short-lived union dispute with the KFWB newsmen. He had his own tv show called, appropriately enough, *The Ted Randal Show*, before joining KEWB in the Bay Area where he was the pd. He worked at KDWB-Minneapolis before arriving in Southern California. He consulted KFI in the late 1960s and the "Soul Xpress," XPRS, in the early 1970s. Ted was editor of *Cash Box Magazine*.

RANDALL, Chuck: **KMET**; **KROQ**, 1979-80. During his time at "the Mighty Met", Chuck recalled in a 1990 *Billboard* magazine interview that "every night on my way to KMET, I would stop at the liquor store and buy a little bottle of cognac to go with my little container full of blow, and I was on my way." He ballooned up to 250 pounds and suffered a mild heart condition before he quit drugs and alcohol. In the early 1990s, he created a two-hour program called "Clean and Crazy" with his wife, Whitney Allen, and Jed the Fish. Chuck became a tour manager in the late 1980s and has spent time on the road with the Neville Brothers, Huey Lewis & the News, Kenny Loggins, Little Feat and Tonio K. He lives in Pasadena.

WAKE UP WITHOUT FACING THE MUSIC
KABC Talkradio AM 790
-1988 Advertisement

RANDALL, Dave: KLON, 1981-86; **KRTH**, 1994-97. Born Dave Burchett (which was his air name at KLON) on July 28, 1959, in Los Angeles, he graduated from Carson High School in 1977 and earned a B.A. degree in radio/tv at Cal State Long Beach in 1982. Dave was the first Cal State Long Beach student to earn an internship at KNX. He idolized Walter Cronkite and Vin Scully and thought he would pursue journalism. From August of 1981 to Halloween 1986, Dave did afternoon sports and a late night jazz show for KLON. He won a Golden Mike in 1983. The Real Don Steele's return to L.A. radio had a profound effect on Dave. "Steele had opened my eyes and shown me how to use my talents. It soon dawned on me that everybody doing CHR in the '80s owed him a debt of gratitude." Dave headed for KWLT/KKYY-San Diego and worked for Mike Novak for two years. In July 1988 he started at KCAQ ("Q105")-Oxnard and currently is doing afternoon drive. During this time he sold bits through the Burchett Bullshoy Players and free-lance work for Jay Thomas' morning zoo. Dave works weekend fill-in at KRTH. He enthused about working at "K-Earth": "To be working on a station I'd listened to for 20 years, to be working with Steele and Morgan, the very embodiment of [Boss Radio] and the best of Top 40 makes this job the crowning glory of my career...a career that is still blossoming."

RANDALL, Jeff: KMGG, 1983. Jeff joined "Magic 106" for weekends from KACY-Oxnard.

RANDOLPH, Jim: KGFJ, 1965-73, pd. In 1966 and 1967, *Billboard* voted Jim the #1 personality in the r&b category. He became pd at KGFJ in 1968. One of his colleagues at KGFJ said about Jim: "He never knew when to sleep." Jim died of a heart attack in 1973 and left behind a wife and six children. Jim grew up in Dallas where his folks owned a drug store.

RAPHONE, Mike: KROQ, 1978-79

RAPP, Joel: KFI, 1972. Joel billed himself "Mr. Mother Earth" and hosted a daily interview-talk show. He wrote tv scripts for *McHale's Navy* and *Here's Lucy*.

RASER, Jim: KNX, 1968-78. Jim broadcast sports commentary in the early days of all-News KNX. He has since passed away.

RATNER, Bill: KJOI, 1979-80; **KBIG**, 1980-85. "After five years of working morning drive at KBIG, I was still making scale. I told KBIG that I wanted double my pay or I was out. They offered 15% and I got the hell out of radio." Bill told this story with much enthusiasm. He realized that he was making three times his KBIG salary as a free-lance voiceover actor and knew he could make a living outside of broadcasting. He got into radio late at age 30. He was born in 1947 in Minneapolis and moved to San Francisco to pursue an acting career. At age 30 he joined a Walnut Creek/Pittsburg radio station selling ad packages on the condition he could voice the commercials. He got to "K-Joy" in 1979 and attempted to unionize the station which was owned by Coca-Cola. It was messy and unsuccessful. Bill joined KBIG in April 1980 and teamed with Phil Reed in morning drive. When he left KBIG to concentrate on a voiceover career, he chronicled the Mormon Church's influence on the station. As Bill told the story in an October 1985 piece, the station operates in the shadow of the church. "We had to stay away from religion clearly, and from sex and from alcohol jokes. Whenever I would mention Eastern religion or meditation fads or far-out cults - in any way - I would be spoken to. Whenever I would talk about male-female relations, either about dating between older couples or something else, I would be gently warned away." An officer at Bonneville headquarters responded with their corporate philosophy: "Our goal is to inform and entertain our listeners, not to offend their sensibilities. The company is in business to make a profit, not evangelize." Bill looks back on his radio career fondly: "I had a wonderful time." His voiceover career includes eight years with the ABC network voicing soap and MOV promos and four years as the voice of KABC/Channel 7 *Eyewitness News*. Bill did 50 episodes of *G.I. Joe* as the voice of Commander Flint. Every week he reads to elementary classrooms, teaches theater games at a kids camp every year in New Hampshire and reads Books on Tape for the Braille Institute.

RAVEN-STARK, Bruce: KLAC/KZLA, 1996-97, gm. Bruce had managed KDBQ-Santa Cruz, KDBK, KSRY-San Francisco and KBSG-Seattle before arriving in the Southland to run the Nostalgia/Country stations.

RAY, Bob: KSRF, 1967-68; **KMPC**, 1968-70. The native Californian grew up with the Rock radio stations of the early '60s. "I was highly influenced by 'Boss Radio/KHJ,' KRLA and KFWB. While I was going to school at Fairfax High, Los Angeles City College and Cal State Los Angeles I got to work in Southern California radio." He was on the air at KMPC the night Bobby Kennedy was shot and won accolades for his performance. When he left the Southland, Bob worked for KNCE-Riverside, WSAR-Fall River, Massachusetts and KLIV-San Jose. During the mid-1970s he was the color/analyst of the San Jose Earthquakes soccer team at KEEN-San Jose. In 1980 he was appointed operations manager at KSFO-San Francisco. "KSFO stole my soul.

I was only 30 years old and not prepared to deal with the politics and the egos in major market radio. When I was 17 I worked briefly for Chuck Barris as a contestant producer for *The Dating Game*. When morning man and *Dating Game* host Jim Lange learned I was to be his new boss, everything at KSFO went downhill from there." A year later Bob found himself at the end of a 14-year radio career. Since 1981 he has been operating a full-service advertising agency in Saratoga billing $3.5-4 million a year. "I still look back on radio as the major love of my life."

RAY, Byron: **KIKF**, 1984-85. Byron grew up in Concord and worked in Yuba City and San Bernardino before joining KIKF.

RAY, Doug: **KWIZ**, 1985-87. In the early 1990s, Doug was doing a morning show with Bob Cady in Palm Springs.

RAY, Steve: **KLIT**, 1991-93; **KMPC**, 1993-94; **KRCI**, 1993-94; **KGRB**, 1994-95. Steve started at WPGC-Washington, DC in the mid-1970s. In the early 1980s he arrived in the Southland to pursue a career in the motion picture business. When that didn't work out, he returned to radio and became pd of KIST-Santa Barbara. After a stint at KMPC/KLIT, Steve became gm of Radio Catalina, KRCI. He has spent time at WW1's Oldies Channel.

RAZOR: **KNAC**, 1994. Born Rey deCarolo, Razor started at KNAC working the request phone lines and being a prize van driver. He's currently working at WZTA-Miami.

REAGAN, Maureen: **KABC**, 1973-74. The former president's daughter was described by KABC pd Jim Simon as "our girl at large on the 'NewsTalk' station." She started with a weekly show and her first guest was then-Governor Reagan. The daughter of the governor and actress Jane Wyman made her movie debut at the age of 5 in *It's A Great Feeling*, which starred her mother. Maureen graduated from Marymount College at Arlington, Virginia. Prior to KABC she worked as a secretary, PR rep for an airline and supper club singer.

REAGAN, Michael: **KABC**, 1983-85. Michael became the third family member of the former president to work at KABC. The younger Reagan worked in sales and marketing and hosted a tv show in Canada and raced boats before getting into radio. It started in 1983 when he sat in for Michael Jackson and then hosted a Sunday evening show. He told Gary Lycan in an *OC Register* interview in 1995: "I saved tapes of every show I did and sent them to KSDO-San Diego." He sat in for ex-San Diego Mayor Roger Hedgecock and then, in January 1989, he read the news in morning drive. "I couldn't read the news, and they didn't believe me. I was terrible. They got me a voice coach. I would read the Bible into a microphone for two hours. They thought if I could put inflection in the Bible, I could read the news." He couldn't and they gave him a talk show. Michael was let go by KSDO in early 1992 to make room for Rush Limbaugh. He went on to talk show host positions in Milwaukee and Seattle, leading to syndication. Michael lives in Sherman Oaks with his wife, Colleen, and two daughters. By early 1996 his syndicated talk show was heard in over 100 markets.

REAGAN, Ron: **KMET**, 1984. The former president's son reviewed movies on "the Mighty Met." In 1985 he went to KABC/Channel 7 as a reporter. He's now part of a tv computer show.

REBENSTORF, John: In 1991 John became the radio play-by-play voice of UCLA football and basketball. Before the start of his second season (1992) with the Bruins, John died at the age of 41. He started out as the voice of Cal State Fullerton where he was a one-man show. He bought the rights, sold the commercials, served as engineer, did the play-by-play and swept up the broadcast booth. John had a history of heart problems according to Larry Stewart in an *LA Times* profile. John suffered his first heart attack at 28. In the fall of 1985, at 35, he had triple bypass surgery. He was looking forward to his second season at UCLA when he required another heart bypass. He died shortly after the operation.

REEB, Trip: **KROQ**, 1988-97, gm. Before starting his L.A. radio trip, Trip was pd at KISS-San Antonio, KAZY-Denver and XTRA ("91X")-San Diego. His philosophy was detailed in a *LA Times* profile in the early '90s: "We haven't succeeded by compromising or homogenizing the radio station. I believe that KROQ is one of the most challenging stations anywhere in commercial radio."

REED, B. Mitch: **KFWB** 1957-63; **KFWB**, 1965-67; **KPPC**, 1967-68; **KMET**, 1968-71; **KRLA**, 1971-72; **KMET**, 1972; **KLOS**, 1979-81. B.M.R. played an important role in two key, distinct format successes: Top 40 and AOR "underground." Mitch was born Burton Mitchel Goldberg in Brooklyn on June 10, 1926, and entered radio following a decision at the University of Illinois to forgo a career teaching political-science "for

the boogie and the glamour of broadcasting." In 1956, after a few months of doing late nights in Baltimore, he landed the all-night "Birdland Jazz Show" at WOR/AM-New York. He got to KFWB just before Chuck Blore went "Color Radio." Mitch produced his "Boy on a Couch" program, which interlaced modern jazz with stream-of-consciousness thoughts for the intrigued listener. He says he called it the "Boy on a Couch" because "I was undergoing analysis at the time." When the station went Contemporary music, Mitch asked, "What is Top 40? I mean, who knew? It had evolved in the Midwest and this was the first any of us had heard of it." He was one of the first "Seven Swingin' Gentlemen" of "Channel 98" when Chuck Blore's "Color Radio" debuted on January 2, 1958. Known as "The Beemer," he was hired to work the early evening shift. In a *Billboard* interview, he said, "We used the Robert Orben joke book a lot for one-liners." His trademark was high energy, using horns, bells and buzzers. He was called the "fastest tongue in the West." Mitch had a rapid delivery, and between breaths he would "toot on his magic zapping horn." When asked why he talked so fast, he responded, "I'm not talking too fast, you're listening too slow." In 1963 he was wooed back to his hometown to work at WMCA-New York as one of "the Good Guys." His adopted idol was Alan Freed. When Freed left New York radio, under a cloud of payola charges, and Murray the K's star subsequently began its ascendancy, Mitch became rankled: "When WMCA offered me the night slot - opposite the number one Murray over at WINS - I felt that position rightfully still belonged to Freed. So, I decided to go back and knock off Murray...plus I wanted to be #1 in my hometown." Within three months, Mitch reversed the K's shares. He spent a lot of time in London developing contacts with Brian Epstein, Derek Taylor and the Beatles. From 1963 through 1965, Mitch became inextricably entwined in the breaking of the Beatles in the New York area. He would bring back exclusive interviews and advance record pressings from his trips. At his final New York show on March 25, 1965, 4,000 well-wishers saw him off at the airport. He returned to KFWB in 1965 for the "Wide, Wide, Weird World of B.M.R." Something was happening to him during this period; the horns and buzzers became irrelevant. Mitch recognized a music explosion was beginning, and he slowly turned the evening hours into album-oriented rock programming. Mitch had met "Big Daddy" Tom Donahue at the 1967 Monterey Pop Festival and discovered they were equally frustrated at their respective stations. Donahue went to KMPX-San Francisco while Mitch found backers for a start-up FM station KPPC. Mitch and Donahue provided four hours of taped album rock. By 1971, the outlet had gone entirely live - with one dj being Guy Williams, also known as Dave Moorhead. At KRLA Mitch was originally hired for the noon-to-3 shift but eventually moved to morning drive, switching time slots with Don Burns. Syndicated countdown show host, tv actor and former radio jock Shadoe Stevens called Mitch "one of the three best disc jockeys in the nation." In 1972, B.M.R. was selected as one of the jocks in Watermark's *Cruisin'* series. He once did his radio show from a hospital bed in 1974 while he was recovering from corneal transplant surgery. The donor was a young kid who had been in a motorcycle accident. He died at midnight, and they started operating on the Beemer at 3 a.m. "It's a sobering thought to know that you're carrying someone else around with you." His health woes continued in 1978. He underwent successful coronary bypass surgery in 1978 and said at the time: "I had been walking around with a heart condition for three years without even knowing it. My heart was functioning, but just barely." B.M.R. was the original host of ABC's "Rockline" on May 4, 1981 and the guest was Joe Walsh. Mitch died at his West Los Angeles home in March 16, 1983, at the age of 56, of a lingering heart condition. In a Los Angeles tribute to B.M.R., *Times'* James Brown said: "To Mitch, good music didn't have a year, an artist or a name tag attached to it. It simply was. And he wasn't afraid to put his own credibility on the line to back it up." He also offered this insight: "You see, he had broken into radio during a time when disc jockeys were supposed to know their stuff - not simply read something from a color-coordinated file card. So choosing the right music and telling his audience a little something about it was important to him." Brown concluded, "I think many of us are saddened by B. Mitchel Reed's death, not only for the loss of someone we felt we knew, but for the loss of a priceless piece of our own past. Each succeeding generation of young people responded to B.M.R. because he never gave in to the advancing years. He kept his mind open and his spirit free. And if he never grew up in the conventional sense, we were all better off because of it."

REED, Donn: **KABC**, 1959-60; **KMPC**, 1961-81. In hushed tones: "Arriving at the scene...the suspect is coming out of the liquor store...police have half-circled the store...he's got a gun...(officer's shout) DROP THE GUN...the suspect stands frozen...he raises his arms while dropping his gun...LET'S MOVE IN...[dialogue of the arrest]...Donn Reed, Nightwatch." No broadcaster around Southern California radio in the sixties or seventies can forget the word pictures Donn created as he covered Los Angeles wearing a trench coat, mike cord down his sleeve and the microphone hidden in his flashlight. Donn pioneered AirWatch along with Captain

Max Schumacher. "I was always fascinated with planes having flown in the Air Force during World War II." After the war he worked for a producer of radio shows at CBS called "Nightwatch." In the late 1950s he was vacationing at Marine Land and he happened upon a helicopter sitting in the parking lot. "I went over to the pilot who was flying a Hollywood starlet to the tourist attraction. We started talking aviation and liked each other right off." The pilot was Captain Max Schumacher who had been a captain in search and rescue missions during the war. They huddled together to explore reporting the news airborne. The two attracted a business partner and they pitched KABC. "We bluffed our way and they secured our service. We bought a Bell chopper and began broadcasting every fifteen minutes from over the freeways of Southern California. We called it 'AirWatch.' The noise vibration of the aircraft was so intense that the tubes in the broadcasting equipment would constantly wiggle loose. "We knew we could broadcast about an hour before losing our equipment, so I strapped a walkie-talkie between my legs that had a range of 4 miles. Wherever we were we knew we had to get back into the 4-mile walkie-talkie range to make our reports." They took a lot of chances in the early years. "We really pushed the choppers beyond their limits plus doing live commercials under difficult conditions." Their first accident resulted in broken backs for both Donn and Max. As a result of his injuries, Donn could no longer sit in a stationary place for long periods of time and began covering the city from the ground. Donn bought out his partners and sold "AirWatch" to Gene Autry. The *LA Times*' Don Page described Donn: "What he really relishes is investigative reporting, and he does it with the dash and flair of a fiction writer's cop. Donn is quiet and serious and you sense he enjoys playing the role." In 1970 Donn was named announcer-reporter of the year by the *Times*. He retired from broadcasting in 1981 and began lecturing at local colleges on the legal aspects of news reporting, secrets of interviewing and "reading the interviewees eyes." During his illustrious career he won 16 Golden Mikes and 5 L.A. Press Corp awards. "I was most proud of the Edward R. Morrow award because it was national. It was for a documentary I did called 'Skid Row Merry-Go-Round.'" Donn was a stickler for the actuality. He learned during the war that when you are in a crisis, you stop, and speak slowly. "I never raised my voice. I was in the midst of the damnedest gun battle between two gangs. Listening to the guns, broken bottles and grunts and groans told it all." Donn was born Donnald in Los Angeles. Today he is a "mad fisherman." He bought a boat and heads for fresh water whenever the weather permits. Donn loves the lakes in the High Sierras.

REED, Eric "Rico": **KJLH**, 1974-93; **KACE**, 1993-97; **KOST**, 1997. Rico was presented the 1992 NAACP Humanitarian Image Award. He received a commendation from the L.A. City Council for playing a major role in calming the situation during the L.A. Riots. A graduate of Dorsey High, he attended CSUN, West L.A. College and Los Angeles Community College during the 1970s. His long association with Stevie Wonder's station, KJLH, allowed him to co-host with Stevie the King-a-thon. He has hosted the Lou Rawls Cavalcade of Stars Telethon along with numerous community events including the Magic Johnson UNCF fund-raiser. In 1992 he won the highest honor in radio, the Peabody Award. In 1993, his morning drive show, "Rico & Company," raised over $10,000 to help a family who lost their daughter during a Christmas tree fire. Over the years he has been known as "Rico on Your Radio." He was pd at KJLH from 1982 to 1984. Rico is married with three children. He restores classic cars and collects animation cels. In the summer of 1997 Rico moved to sister station, KOST.

REED, Larry: **KPOL**, 1965; **KMPC**. Larry was a newsman and on-air engineer.

REED, Leonard: **KDAY**

REED, Phil: **KFWB**, 1968-73; **KNX**, 1973-78; **KBIG/KBRT**, 1978-87, nd; **KNX**. When KFWB made the historic switch from Rock to all-News, Phil was the second voice on the air. Born in Los Angeles, he grew up in Pasadena. One of Phil's early influences was Bob Crane. "It was sometime around being a junior in high school when I stopped and thought about broadcasting. While I was attending the Don Martin school to get my FCC 1st Class License, I would deliver newspapers to earn a living. After I delivered the papers and before school I would hang at Columbia Square and watch Bob Crane on KNX." After knocking the needle off a disc, he thought he would never be invited back, but Bob continued to let him watch and encouraged him. KBUC-Corona was Phil's first stop in 1962 and then, six months later, KGRB-San Bernardino. He graduated with a psych major in 1966 from Pasadena Nazarene college. Before joining the news format at KFWB, Phil spent some time at KSOM-Ontario. Phil has worked morning drive during his on-air news days and was made nd of KBIG in 1979 which included work on the Bonneville AM station, KBRT. In 1987 Phil joined the world of voiceovers and teaching. He teaches at Pt. Loma Nazarene and Cal State Los Angeles. "Voiceover work is a very shaky way to make a living. You go in strings or runs of work and no work."

	FM format start dates		
92.3	KKBT	Urban	9/21/89
93.1	KCBS	"Arrow 93"	9/10/93
93.9	KZLA	Country	9/13/80
94.7	KTWV	New Age	2/14/87
97.1	KLSX	"classic"	9/26/86
97.9	KLAX	Spanish	8/1/92
98.7	KYSR	AC	8/21/92
99.5	KKLA	Religion	10/19/85
103.5	KOST	AC	11/15/82
104.3	KBIG	AC	11/5/86
105.1	KKGO	Classical	9/21/89
105.9	KPWR	Urban	1/11/86
107.5	KLVE	Spanish	Sept '75

REED, Tom: **KGFJ**, 1966-69; **KMET**, 1969-70; **XPRS**, 1971-73; **KDAY**, 1973-76. Born and raised in St. Louis, he arrived in L.A. in 1959 and was on the air at the Los

Angeles City College radio station. He also attended UCLA and Windsor University. While working in Kansas City he was the reporter for *Down Beat*. Tom tells the legend of his nickname "The Master Blaster": "While sitting in a Kansas City bar, O'G's, many years ago, a patron was taunting me, saying, 'You are gonna get blasted outta here.' I said, 'You can't; I am the Master Blaster.'" The next morning, in a calmer moment, his only recollection of the night before was the "Master Blaster" reference. He went on KPRS/AM&FM-Kansas City with the descriptive line, and the name stuck. In the mid-'60s Tom worked at WLIB-New York and WJLB-Detroit before blasting into the Southland in the little house on Melrose Avenue. In 1969 Tom was elected president of the Western States Chapter of the National Association of TV-Radio Announcers. Tom forwarded a 1973 Arbitron that showed KDAY was Number 1 in teens. "This was the first time in Los Angeles radio history - a black station or radio personality was No. 1." Between 1976 and 1979, Tom was assistant advertising manager and music critic for the *Los Angeles Sentinel* newspaper. In 1978, he went back to school and earned a master's degree in communications science at Windsor University. Tom has done doctoral work at USC's Annenberg School of Communication. He is a member of the National Academy of Recording Arts & Sciences and votes yearly on Grammy selections. His uncle, Walter Davis, the legendary St. Louis, Missouri bluesman and blues/gospel pioneer Vance "Tiny" Powell along with his godfather, Charlie Creath, the '20s and '30s trumpet great, have inspired his dedication to black music environs. He has completed a lifelong passion by documenting the rich history of black music in Los Angeles with the 1993 publication of a book called *The Black Music History of Los Angeles - Its Roots*. Tom credits his own firm roots to strong family values: "My father was a policeman and my mother was a school teacher. My cousin was the first black ball player for the New York Yankees, Elston Howard." Tom was the first African American to win an Award of Excellence from the Greater Los Angeles Press Club three years in a row for tv entertainment reporting. Since 1990 Tom has won five Angel awards for excellence in media for his program "For Members Only," the longest running locally produced African American program in L.A. television history now it its 17th year on KSCI/Channel 18.

REEVES, Dave: **KGIL**, 1968-69

REGAN, Dennis: **KGIL**, 1975-76. Dennis arrived at the San Fernando Valley station from KFMB-San Diego and left in 1976.

REID, Gary: SEE Gary Moore.

REILING, Joe: **KLOS**, 1977-81; **KMET**, 1982; **KNX/FM**, 1983; **KLSX**, 1988-90. Joe's jock and rock programming past prepared him well for his current task of producing over 30 shows each month for AEI, the company that provides in-flight music (with announcers) for over 30 airlines. Joe was born and raised in Dayton and was a double major at the University of Dayton. A psychology and communication arts combo led him to the local radio station. "One of my shows was a Sunday morning talk show and I quoted from a magazine report on a Masters and Johnson study and mentioned the word *penis*. The president of the Catholic university told me later he almost cut himself shaving when he heard the word." In 1974 Joe went to KFIG-Fresno for midday jocking, morning news and later he became pd. "I remember interviewing Jim Jones and I haven't sipped Kool-Aid since." Tom Yates hired Joe at KLOS in 1977. For almost a decade, beginning in 1984, Joe hosted a daily alternative rock show on Armed Forces radio. Since his divorce, Joe stayed in the Southland to be near his teenage daughter, Christa.

REITLER, Bill: SEE Bill Wright

REMY: SEE Remy Maxwell

RESNICK, Wayne: **KFI**, 1988-97. Wayne had a variety  of assignments at KFI including a stint as Joe Crummey's screener and supplier of character voices before he got his own show. He moved to early evening in late 1995 when Marilyn Kagan left the station. Born in Port Arthur, Texas, he graduated from West Virginia University with a degree in psychology. Wayne was a supervisor with the U.S. Probation Office and previously employed as the program director of a methadone treatment program.

REYES, Pepe: **KALI**, 1993. Pepe worked morning drive at the Spanish station.

REYNOLDS, Andy: **KFWB**, 1983-85. Andy was a reporter for all-News KFWB. "I am forever indebted to Ed Pyle and Frank Oxarart for allowing me to go to law school while working at KFWB." Born in New York, Andy grew up in Havana and after school worked news in New York and Miami before coming to the Southland. After KFWB he was a reporter at KTTV/Channel 11 for a year and a half. Andy is now working as a deputy DA in the Newhall office. "I'm just one of the grubs in the office."

REYNOLDS, Bo (Pat): **KZLA**, 1993-97. Bo arrived from doing mornings at KOY-Phoenix in late 1993 to do evenings. He has worked all shifts. In early 1996 he hosted the syndicated "Boot Scoot'n Party'n Nights."

REYNOLDS, Jack: **KGIL**, 1969. Jack left KGIL for a pd post at WIBG-Philadelphia.

REYNOLDS, Joey: **KMPC**, 1980-81; **KRTH**, 1981-82; **KMGG**, 1984. Joey started his career at KQAQ-Austin, Minnesota in 1960 and then moved to WNDR-Syracuse and WPOP-Hartford. In 1963 he worked nights at WKBW-Buffalo, the station that was powered by Niagara Falls, and his characters included the Count, General Shelby Singleton Silver, Jr., Esquire Yawl, wife Margie and dog, Pet. In the second half of the sixties, Joey worked in Cleveland at WDOK and WIXY, WXYZ-Detroit and WDRC-Hartford. During the 1970s he programmed "Banana Radio" at KQV-Pittsburgh and later worked at WIBG-Philadelphia. While at KMPC, Joey had a brief stint as host of "Satellite Live," a national call-in radio show. He went to WGAR-Cleveland in 1981 only to return to the Southland later in the year on KRTH. Between KRTH and his last return at KMGG, he worked at WHTZ-New York and WHYT-Detroit. Before the year was out Joey was off to WFIL-Philadelphia and then WNBC-New York. After his afternoon drive stint at WNBC, he was working with Morton Downey, Jr. in tv development. Joey had his own daily half-hour tv show in Miami, followed by a year of Miami morning radio. In the summer of 1995, Joey was named president of Cutler Productions, a new tv production operation. By late 1995 Joey was on the WOR network.

REYNOLDS, Steve: **KIBB**, 1996-97. Steve is part of the morning drive team at Rhythmic/AC "B-100."

RHINES, Howard: **KFAC**, '50 and '60s, pd

RHODES, Dusty: **KMET**; **KWST**, 1979. Born Melissa Townsend, Dusty became a paralegal in Northern California working for Law In Motion. She does weekend work at KFOG-San Francisco.

RHONE, Paul: **KRHM**, 1959. Paul worked weekends at KRHM.

What was the last book you read?
The History of Steam
Top Ten personality Gary Owens

RIALS, Beau: **KSRF**, 1988-89; **KLSX**, 1989-96. During Beau's seven-year stay at KLSX he worked every daypart. He came to the Southland from WCKG-Chicago. He's been with WW1 since 1990 working at the Adult Rock format. For a period in the early 1990s, Beau hosted "Rockline" and a weekly rock show broadcast in Japan. The actor/host has appeared in many national tv commercials and infomercials. Since the summer of 1993, the ubiquitous Beau has been the host at Hollywood's Laugh Factory. He can

also be seen on KWHY, the tv business channel.

RICCI, Little: SEE Ricci Filiar

RICCO, Paulie: **KLOS**, 1978; **KWST**, 1979; **KHTZ**, 1979-80. Paulie became a paralegal living in the San Fernando Valley.

RICE, Bill: **KNOB**, 1968; **KYMS**, 1968; **KNAC**, 1969; **KWIZ**, 1969-70. Bill fell in love with radio while touring with the Young Americans in the summer of 1967. The group appeared on *The Ed Sullivan Show*, *Andy Williams Show* and the *Tonight* show. "We did lots of radio and tv interviews. I just found the medium exciting." While

attending Fullerton Junior College and Cal State Fullerton, Bill started working part-time on Orange County stations. Born in Los Angeles in 1947, Bill left for KUUU-Seattle in 1970 and by the mid-1970s made a transition to news. He was nd of KPLZ-Seattle for six years. Since 1984 Bill has been the nd of KJR/AM&FM and KUBE-Seattle. He's done tv news in the Northwest and for eight years in the 1980s was the stadium announcer for the Seattle Mariners.

RICH, Allan: **KRHM**, 1959. Allan worked weekends at KRHM.

RICH, Bobby: **KHJ**, 1973-74; **KHTZ**, 1979, pd; **KFI**, 1981-83. Arriving from WAVZ-New Haven, Bobby started in June of 1973 at KHJ. Paul Drew was the pd and it was a volatile time. The Real Don Steele had just left and Robert W. Morgan would leave within weeks, to be replaced by Charlie Van Dyke. Drew was promoted to RKO national pd and brought in Sean Conrad who lasted six months, replaced by Gerry Peterson Cagle. Bobby left in early 1974 for KFMB-San Diego and created "B-100," which became, according to Bobby, "the first Contemporary music FM station in the country to capture overall #1 ratings." In 1978, he became pd of WXLO ("99X")-New York with Jay Thomas powering the mornings. Bobby returned to the Southland and joined "K-Hits" as pd and afternoon drive. He was Greater Media's first pd and was responsible for converting the station from Top 40 to Adult CHR. He left in less than a year. "Even though I was given less than a year under somewhat undesirable conditions, I built another winner, assembled a great staff and developed an excellent sounding station." He joined Drake/Chenault in 1981 as the director of specialized programming. In 1982, Bobby became assistant pd and night jock on KFI until Cox transferred him to program WWSH-Philadelphia. He returned to KFMB in 1984 as pd and morning host. There, he created the Hot AC format and the Rich Brothers morning show. In 1989 he gm'ed KMGI-Seattle. After investing in a new Tucson radio station, he is currently pd and doing mornings at KMXZ-Tucson.

RICH, Jai: **KBCA**, 1969-72. In *Billboard* magazine's Radio Response Ratings, Jammin' Jai was listed 2nd most influential jazz deejay. A year later he was listed as the major dj influencing jazz record sales.

RICH, Merrie: **KABC**, 1983. Merrie participated in one of the more bizarre promotions in Los Angeles radio, which is an answer to an excellent trivia question. KABC conducted a talent search to find a co-host to Bud Furillo and Tommy Hawkins and the "SportsTalk" show. Merrie, a New Yorker who was best known as a singer of the National Anthem before New York Knicks and Rangers games won out over nearly 2,000 applicants. Her move from New York where she was working for her father's public relations firm, was not paid for and she felt isolated once the publicity blitz died down. Within a month she was fired. She's now working in England.

RICHARDS, Barry: **KGFJ**, 1984-85, pd. Trying to repeat success achieved in Slidell, Louisiana, a city 35 miles from New Orleans, Barry was made pd at WAIL in 1980. He was dominant for three of his four years at the helm of WAIL. Barry became pd of KGFJ in the fall of 1984.

RICHARDS, Bill: **KIIS**, 1990-92, pd. Bill's first programming job was at KQWB-Fargo at the age of 21. His programming career has included KDWB-Minneapolis, KLUC-Las Vegas, WNCI-Columbus, KYUU-San Francisco and KKBQ-Houston. While programming KIIS, Bill was named *Billboard* magazine's Program Director of the Year in 1992. Bill's radio consulting brochure states: "Bill brought KIIS/FM back to #1 for the first time in five years. He did so in the face of a CHR format that was failing across the country." Bill owns his own consultancy firm and is based in Orlando.

RICHARDS, Grahame: **KFAC**, 1972, gm

RICHARDS, Lisa: **KACE**, 1990. Lisa was part of the morning drive show. She went on to WBLS-New York.

RICHARDS, Mark: **KGIL**, 1985; **KFI**, 1985. Born in 1942, Mark was weaned on game shows as a youth and appeared as a contestant on "Break the Bank" with Bert Parks when he was 12. He started his dj work at WZAK-Cleveland between 1966 and 1975. Alan Freed is his father-in-law. Mark created, produced and promoted "The Game Show" which was heard every evening on KFI in 1985. Before arriving in the Southland, Mark hosted *Starcade* on WTBS-Atlanta for 26 weeks before it went into syndication. In an *OC Register* interview with Gary Lycan, Mark recounted how he took his program first to KGIL in 1985. He said he was reading his contract in his KGIL office when he got a call from Steve LaBeau, pd at KFI. "The Los Angeles *Daily News* did a short story [about him joining KGIL] and Steve saw it. He said 'Don't sign it.' This was at 10 a.m. By 11:30 a.m. I was at KFI. The enticement to do the show at night was terrific. KGIL was miffed, so I did two weeks there before going to KFI."

RICHARDS, Ronni: **KWIZ**, 1981-87. Ronni was born back, "when God was a boy." She grew up in a swampy area of Florida now known as Cape Canaveral. After graduating from the University of Florida, Ronni worked for several years with WFLA and WIPC in Central Florida. As part of a two-voice radio comedy team, she and partner Dan O'Day won one of *Billboard* magazine's Top Jock Awards in New York City and promptly moved to the San Francisco area where she began a successful 13-year run with Davis-Weaver Broadcasting Company. At KLOK-San Jose, she became one of the first female morning drive personalities in the country and was seen nightly on KGSC/TV. She spent 15 years with the KWIZ organization, starting in 1974 with KLOK. She commented on her decade-and-a-half to Gary Lycan in the *OC Register*: "They were good to me, and the new owners asked me to come back, but since I started free-lance commercials, working every day was just too much. While on maternity leave from KWIZ, I tasted the sweet nectar of commercial voiceover work and residual pay." She owns Aubergine Productions and can be seen and heard across the country in tv and radio

commercials. She is active in the yearly Orange County PBS/TV station pledge drive.

RICHARDS, Stoney: **KIIS**, 1973-74; **KLAC**, 1980; **KHTZ**, 1981; **KLAC/KZLA**, 1981-94. From Jack Thayer's WGAR-Cleveland, Stoney (born Chuck) arrived at KIIS in 1973 and left the station a year later. In 1977 he was doing stand-up comedy at Catch A Rising Star in New York and the Paragon in Washington, DC, while working on the radio. Stoney said at the time, "It works out well, since it gets me out in the community." In 1979 he was cast in two productions of New Playwrights Theatre Dramathon in Washington. Stoney left WRQX-Washington, DC for a play in New York called, *Practice*. In 1981 he did weekends at "K-Hits" before returning to Country KLAC where he stayed until the 23-year format was abandoned for satellite generated AM Only nostalgia programming. Stoney played an intern in 1983 on *St. Elsewhere*. He was the voice, with Merlin Olsen, for FTD Florists. He appeared in Dudley Moore's *Best Defense* and was in a production of *Hamlet*. When KLAC changed formats the *LA Times* published a farewell from Stoney to the KLAC fans in an Op-Ed piece: "And all we of KLAC country have left are the feelings of the fun and games and gossip we shared and the words of all those great country songs. And no one can ever take that away from us. Thanks for the memories." Since 1994, Stoney has worked at WQKB, WXRB and WZPT-Pittsburgh.

RICHARDSON, Burton: **KMPC**, 1974; **KJOI**, 1978-89; **KBIG**, 1991-92. Burton worked as an actor and performed on KTLA/Channel 5 before joining the Gene Autry outlet, KMPC. He was the announcer on the *Arsenio Hall Show*.

RICHARDSON, Lisa: **KCRW**, 1994-97

RICHEY, George: **KGBS**, 1967. George arrived in the Southland from KAYO-Seattle. He was a singer on Hickory Records and a regular with the Foggy River Boys on the old Red Foley *Ozark Jubilee*.

RICHMAN, Don: **KIIS**, 1973-75. Don broadcast the "KIIS of Sports" during the Chuck Blore programming days. The vignettes were described in the *LA Times* as "an ironic collection of chuckles from the games people play." He was the gm of the San Diego Chargers and was one of those responsible for adding names to the back of football jerseys for tv.

> "Half of my family is black and I have a gay brother. I'm going to tell you the truth about my sex life."
> -Suzi Landolphi

RIDDLE, Sam: **KRLA**, 1960-63; **KFWB**, 1963-65; **KHJ**, 1965-70; **KDAY**, 1971-72; **KROQ**, 1972-73; **KHJ**, 1974. The highly regarded tv producer came to Los Angeles radio from KDEO-San Diego. Born in Fort Worth, he was there for the beginning of "Boss Radio" in April of 1965. His shift was nine to midnight, and he left the station in 1970, only to return in 1974. In the 1960s Sam hosted a nightly show on KHJ/Channel 9 called *9th Street West* and *Boss City*. He used to open his show with "Hello Music Lovers." Another on-air trademark was reference to eating  "peanut butter and banana sandwiches." In 1967, *Billboard* recognized Sam as the top late evening dj. He hosted an RKO TV show on Saturday nights at six called *Sounds of Now*. Sam hosted the *Hollywood A Go Go* tv show with the Gazzari Dancers. He was the longtime producer of tv's syndicated *Star Search*. For over a decade he produced the annual *Supermodel of the World* specials. Sam has also produced a variety of successful Latin series and specials.

RIEGLE, Barbara: **KNX**, 1967-69; **KFWB**, 1969-87. The former Orange County bureau chief for all-News KFWB was born in Los Angeles and grew up in Oakland. "I earned ten cents a word working for a daily newspaper in Marin County." Barbara followed her husband to Europe where she published a newspaper for U.S. Army dependents at Landshut, Germany. Returning to the states to Fort Benning, Georgia, an opportunity developed at the local tv/radio station where she became one of the first female broadcasters to cover hard-news. "My station had moved me to sales and I told the boss - if you want to go broke you will keep me in sales - how about news? It wasn't available right then but soon after there was a big story - nobody to cover and the nd came into the hallway waving keys and hollering who will go - I grabbed those keys and took off." In 1962 Barbara joined the staff at the *Los Angeles Herald-Examiner* where she was the political writer and columnist for four years. "It was terribly exciting to be on the cutting edge as someone covering politics with front page bylines. Barbe left the newspaper to write a book *Where's the Broad in Broadcasting*, which was excerpted in several publications, including one textbook. In 1966, she went to work for KNX as a full-time news reporter and Women's Editor - at the time the only woman news reporter on radio in Southern California. Barbara joined KFWB where she remained for 17 years as writer, reporter and finally, Orange County bureau chief. "I retired in 1987 after a three-year battle against management's purge of women broadcasters, a purge which took out Joy Nuell and Cecilia Pedroza." To boost her deflated ego, Barbara returned to college studying journalism, graduating from Cal State Fullerton in 1993 following study of art in Paris and international politics in Salzburg, Austria. She raised five children as a single parent and is now "Gram" to eight and "Gigi" to one great-granddaughter. Barbara has returned to an early love of sewing which has changed dramatically with the introduction of computerized machines. She serves on the board of the Southern California Chapter of the American Sewing Guild, which is the largest chapter in the United States.

RIGGENBACH, Jeff: **KFAC**, 1989; **KFWB**. Jeff was part of the all-News operation at KFWB. He is now a writer/commentator.

RILEY, Chuck: **KZLA**, 1979-80. From WIBC-Indianapolis, Chuck was part of the launch of Country KZLA. He now does voiceover work for the DAB-Row Agency and lives in Las Vegas.

RILEY, Dick: **KIKF**, 1985-90, pd. In addition to his programming chores, Dick worked morning drive at KIKF.

RILEY, Pat: **KLAC**, 1978-79. The highly successful NBA coach was the sidekick announcer with Chick Hearn on the broadcasts of the L.A. Lakers. Born March 20, 1945, and raised in Schenectady, he was the son of a strict Catholic homemaker and a one-time minor league baseball manager. In high school Pat was the quarterback on the football squad. In 1963 he turned down an offer to play football for Bear Bryant at Alabama, deciding instead to play basketball at Kentucky where he became a member of "Rupp's Runts" (no one on the team was taller than 6'5"). The San Diego Rockets, preparing for their first NBA season, selected Pat with the seventh overall pick in the 1967 NBA draft. During his 9-year pro career, Pat mostly played reserve including five seasons with the Lakers. He ended his playing career in Phoenix. Early in the 1979 season, Lakers Coach Jack McKinney was seriously injured in a bicycle accident and had to step down. He was replaced by assistant coach Paul Westhead, who asked Pat to become his assistant. He eventually was made head coach and no other NBA coach won 500 games so quickly. During nine years with the Lakers, the team went to the NBA finals 7 times and won 4 championships. Pat had amassed a 533-194 record. He went on to the broadcast booth at NBC and then coached four years with the New York Knicks. He is now head coach with the Miami Heat.

RIOS, Jesse: **KLAX**, pd. The former pd of Spanish KLAX programmed KXTN and KROM-San Antonio as well as KINT-El Paso and KCDI-Tucson. Currently Jesse is the pd of Spanish WYSY-Chicago.

Business Radio
Goes Into Business Full-Time
-KBLA, April 1991

RIPSTON, Ramona: **KABC**, 1990-91. The longtime executive director for the ACLU of Southern California worked at KABC. In the spring of 1990 Ramona joined Bill Pearl as co-host on the "Point/Counterpoint" show in afternoon drive. Born and raised in New York she reached her $90,000-a-year job as head of the Department of Public Affairs for the New York Urban Coalition through activist involvement. Ramona is the

daughter of an Orthodox Jewish mother and a physics professor who was Roman Catholic. She said she was raised to be aware of inequality and discrimination. She thought she was going to be an actress, a veterinarian or a teacher. Instead, she became a model after graduating from Hunter College in 1948, and soon married. She pursued volunteer work editing a newsletter for the New York Civil Liberties Union, raised funds and organized new chapters. Married five times she runs one of the 53 affiliates and chapters that make up the ACLU's national organization.

RIVAS, Chris: **KPWR**, 1995. Chris was part of the evening Ruffnex Show with Mr. Chocolate. Chris has left radio and is now working for a record company.

RIVERS, Mark: **KODJ**, 1989. J. Rose arrived at the launch of Oldies KODJ in March 1989 from WBSB ("B104")-Baltimore.

RIVERS, Steve: **KIIS**, 1986-89, pd. Steve started as a jock in 1972 at KCBQ-San Diego. He arrived at KIIS from KMEL-San Francisco and programmed the station until 1989. His major programming assignments started in 1974 at WZGC-Atlanta. He was a jock at WCJX ("96X")-Miami where he met his mentor Jerry Clifton, followed by WRBQ-Tampa/St. Petersburg, KOPA-Phoenix, WAPE-Jacksonville and KNDE/KROY-Sacramento. During Steve's watch at KIIS, some of his unusual programming innovations included the FM's zero-talk hours and the AM's Dance-Mix format. He also conceived the KIIS/FM "Star Cruiser," a $250,000 mobile broadcast studio. Steve left in 1989 for WZOU (now WJMN)-Boston where in addition to programming he could do outside consulting. In 1990 he was named *Billboard* magazine Program Director of the Year. Steve's wife Maureen Matthews was pd of Transtar's Niche 29. In 1991 Steve left WZOU and crossed town to rival WXKS ("Kiss108"), where he became vp of programming. In late 1994, he was promoted to the newly created post of chief programming officer for parent Pyramid Communications where he continues. In a two-part 1995 Q & A session in *R&R*, Steve was asked his strongest and weakest attributes and he responded, "Being persistent and not giving up on a win and probably spending too many hours at it." In the same article he discussed his programming principles: "First you've got to play the hits. The hits form the center of the radio station. The music has to be familiar, strong and show some passion. We also have to remember what business we're in. We're in radio, but in reality, we're entertainers."

RIVERS, Tom: **KIQQ**, 1975-76. Big Tom Rivers (he stands 6 foot 8 inches) has been a significant Contemporary radio jock during his career. He has worked for CHUM-Toronto, CKLW-Detroit and KFRC and KYA-San Francisco. During the nineties he returned to Canada to work at CJEZ and most recently in Edmonton. Tom is now working for a Talk station in Edmonton.

RIZO, Jose: **KLON**, 1990-97. Jose was born in Guadalajara and raised in Oxnard. During the 1970s and '80s, Jose was active in Santa Barbara radio working on KCSB and KIST. He has produced numerous Latin and

jazz concerts under his production company, "Brown Magic." In 1980 he produced the first concert in Santa Barbara at the Lobero Theatre, starring Los Lobos, Jorge Santana and Poncho Sanchez. For five years Jose produced the yearly Cinco de Mayo concerts for UCSB. He has written numerous articles on jazz music for jazz and Latino publications. In addition to the "Jazz on the Latin Side" program on KLON, the show is transmitted with the Playboy TV channel providing listenership in the Central and North American continent. "This coupling makes KLON the most listened-to jazz radio station in the world." Aside from music, Jose worked as an electrical engineer for Lockheed for about seven years before he changed careers and became a teacher, currently working for the Los Angeles Unified School District.

"*It's just the two of us and our managing partner and we did a million dollars last year!*"
-Stevens and Grdnic

ROADMAP, Dr.: **KABC**, 1990-95. Obsessed with

alternate routes to the maze of complicated freeways and roadways, Dr. Roadmap is a breath of clarity. David Rizzo, aka Dr. Roadmap, helped listeners to the KABC morning drive show navigate around trouble spots on the Southern California highways and byways. In the late 1980s he contacted every major radio station to offer his services. "I went to KABC with a demo tape and a proposal. I got nowhere, anywhere." Once his book *Freeway Alternatives* was published in 1990, within 13 days after appearing on the "Ken & Barkley Company" he was hired to be the alternative route expert on KABC. David has been a doctor of feet since earning a Doctor of Podiatric Medicine degree in 1976 from California College of Podiatric Medicine in San Francisco. He has become the "Dear Abby" of commuting. Making house calls forced him to find short cuts around Southern California to maximize his time. "The part I love is solving a puzzle in real time," he told the *LA Times*. In 1995 he became the answer man for L.A. Cellular and began working for Metro Traffic.

AM Format start dates

570	KLAC	Pop	12/5/93
640	KFI	Talk	7/11/88
710	KMPC	Talk	5/2/94
870	KIEV	Talk	1975
930	KKHJ	Spanish	4/1/90
980	KFWB	News	3/11/68
1020	KTNQ	Spanish	7/30/79
1070	KNX	News	4/15/68
1110	KRLA	Oldies	3/1/76

ROAST, Chuck: SEE Guy Kemp

ROBBIN, Rich "Brother": **KIQQ**, 1973 and 1975; **KKDJ**, 1974-75; **KGFJ**, 1975; **KTNQ**, 1976-77. He

was born Rich Werges in Rice Lake, Wisconsin and grew up under the shadow of WCCO's giant tower in Minneapolis. He arrived at KIQQ from KCBQ-San Diego and originated the idea of using dial position as a station identifier, named the station at 100.3 "K-100-FM." During late 1974 and early '75 this fiery redhead with an energy level to match lit up late nights at KKDJ, then moved to his second tour at "K-100" during the Drake/Chenault ownership. This was followed by a stint at KGFJ until December 26, 1976, when KTNQ went on the air and Rich became one of the original jocks on "the new Ten-Q." Since his L.A. days, Rich programmed KHYT-Tucson and KCMO-Kansas City before becoming president/gm of KFXX-Tucson. He later came full cycle, returning to San Diego to program Oldies "K-Best" and to introduce "Modern Oldies," the first '70s-based format (which inspired the popular "Arrow" and other '70s formats), on KCBQ in 1993. Rich returned to Tucson in 1994 and is doing afternoons at Oldies "COOL-FM."

ROBBYNS, Linda: **KACD**, 1994. Linda worked weekends at "CD 103."

ROBERTS, Art: **KFWB**, 1961. Art worked at WKBW-Buffalo before becoming a member of the KFWB strike replacement team in 1961. In the 1970s Art was at KNBR-San Francisco, WCFL and WKQX-Chicago and WOKY-Milwaukee. During the 1980s, he worked for WBCS-Milwaukee, KWKH-Shreveport, WLS-Chicago and KXTN/KBUL-San Antonio. In 1995 Art was sales manager and worked afternoon drive at KDOK-Tyler.

ROBERTS, Brian: **KDAY**, 1976-80; **KUTE**, 1980-83; **KMGG**, 1984-86; **KKHR**, 1986; **KZLA**, 1987-90; **KRTH**, 1990-93; **KCBS**, 1993-94; **KRLA**, 1996; **KZLA**, 1996. Born Jered Persten, Brian has spent three decades in radio, much of it working morning drive. In 1983 he spent a year-and-a-half doing Country at Transtar. Brian worked at KYA-San Francisco and KCBQ-San Diego before arriving in the Southland. In 1984 he graduated from law school only to fail his bar examination by a mere 11 points. "When I didn't pass it the first time, I decided I really didn't want to be an attorney. Maybe I'll take the test again." Brian works the Oldies Channel at WW1 every weekend.

ROBERTS, Chris: **KUTE**, 1973-79; **KGGI**, 1981-82; **KFI/KOST**, 1981-92; **KMPC**, 1992-94; **XTRA**, 1994. Born Bob LaPeer in Alhambra in 1954, Chris played football, basketball and baseball at Baldwin Park High and baseball at Cal Poly Pomona. He began his broadcasting career at KCIN-Victorville, KREO-Indio and KWOW-Pomona where he announced high school and junior college sports. He changed his named professionally in 1970 when there was a name conflict at KFXM-San Bernardino. In the late 1970s he announced Cal Poly Pomona baseball. For 10 years he called play-by-play for Cal State Long

Beach until the school dropped the sport in 1991. While on the air doing overnights at KOST, Chris prepared a sports report for morning drive live on sister station KFI. He eventually became sports director and covered the Los Angeles Raiders while KFI had the broadcast rights. He called his KFI and KOST sportscast "Athletic Briefs." When KMPC went Sports programming, Chris became an important part of the on-air presentation. He left KMPC when the station changed formats in 1994. He has been the play-by-play voice for UCLA football, basketball and baseball since 1992. Besides broadcasting, Chris has a second career in real estate. He owns income property and also works as a broker for a firm in Glendora.

ROBERTS, Dave: **KEZY**, 1976. Dave, who holds a doctorate in research from the University of Oregon, worked at KYNO-Fresno, KMEN-San Bernardino and KPOI-Honolulu. In the early 1980s he was at KYA-San Francisco as assistant pd, research director and afternoon drive. In 1983 he was named vp/director of programming for the RKO Radio Network.

ROBERTS, Craig: **KIIS**, 1991; **KRTH**, 1991; **KYSR/KXEZ**, 1992; **KIIS**, 1997. Craig was born in Lansing and started on a local radio station while in high school. His journey before getting to Southern California included WOKY-Milwaukee, WMET-Chicago and KXOK and KHTR/KMOX-St. Louis. By the mid-1980s he was in San Francisco working for KITS, KFRC, KYUU, and "X-100." He is currently the production director for Westwood One Radio Networks. He does voice work for many tv stations and part-time at KIIS.

ROBERTS, Joel: **KSRF/KOCM**, 1988-90; **KMPC**, 1990-91; **KFI**, 1991-92; **KABC**, 1992-94. Joel hosted an evening talk show on KABC and moved to afternoon drive with Steve Edwards. At KSRF he created "The Best of Health," an interview show which found its way to syndication very quickly. It was eventually headquartered on KMPC and carried on KNBR-San Francisco, KSDO-San Diego, KTAR-Phoenix and others. In the fall of 1991, Joel became a permanent fill-in host for KFI. A native of Maryland, Joel moved to the Silicon Valley area when he was five. He has a highest honors degree in politics from the University of California at Santa Cruz. Upon graduating from college he lived abroad for one year. In 1995 Joel experienced an explosion inside his head. "I lost a third of my hearing. My doctor said that I wouldn't be able to wear headphones for at least a year." Joel took advantage of the disability by opening the premier training and consultation company for Talk radio. He's based in Los Angeles.

ROBERTS, Ken: **KROQ**, 1972-86; **KSRF/KACD**, 1991-97. Born in Hoboken, Ken has a deep history with KROQ. In the mid-1970s with the station heavily in debt, he attained his first partnership meeting. He owned the station for almost 15 years before he sold it to Infinity Broadcasting Corporation for $45 million. According to a station profile in the *LA Times* in 1985, "KROQ's owners turned out to be a doctor, a pair of dairymen, a Sacramento lobbyist, a secretary and several other small investors who knew little or nothing about broadcasting. Roberts found himself president on the strength of his experience as a concert promoter - as close to actual radio experience as any of the KROQ partners had." On July 29, 1974, KROQ went off the air for two years. In 1976, Ken began to rebuild slowly. There was no more commercial-free broadcasting or million-dollar promotional gimmickry. In the article Ken said: "Rick Carroll liked to tell everybody he was the one who turned it around." Ken said he was responsible for making KROQ the first mainstream station in Los Angeles to regularly play Prince, an artist who had been consistently heard only on Los Angeles' four black stations until the early '80s. By 1982, Ken had controlling interest in the company that owned KROQ. In 1991 he bought KSRF and KOCM for $17.8 million. The two stations occupied the same dial position - 103.1- the former based in Santa Monica and the latter in Newport Beach.

ROBERTS, Nathan: **KDAY**, 1969-74. Nathan was born in 1944 in Atlanta, and worked at Atlanta's WGST before joining KDAY. In 1974, he went to KHJ/Channel 9, where he was a news anchor for many years.

ROBERTS, Rick "Jo Jo": **KJLH**, 1984. Rick arrived in Los Angeles from St. Louis and KMJM-Houston to do afternoons and music at KJLH.

ROBERTS, Stephanie: **KNX**, 1997. In the spring of 1997, Stephanie won a National Headliner Award for "Best Coverage of a Live News Event."

ROBERTS, Tom E.: **KYMS**, 1972-74. Tom hosted an innovative evening "progressive rock" show when KYMS was an AOR station. His features included: "Gusty Winds Do World Weather" and the "KYMS Late Movie." When the station changed formats to Christian, Tom turned to his other love in life for a career - breeding horses - which he currently does with his father; they also produce films on that subject.

ROBERTSON, Ron: **KRLA**, 1971. Ron was a newsman for KRLA.

ROBINS, Jeff: SEE Bruce Chandler

ROBINSON, Curtis: **KACE**, 1994; **KJLH**, 1995. Curtis is now out of radio.

ROBINSON, Dave: **KBIG**, 1971-86. Dave had a long career with Beautiful Music KBIG. Born and raised in Baltimore, Dave went into the Air Force in 1947 and was a radio operator working "photo-mapping platforms" with B-17 and B-29's. During pre-flight radar tests, Dave would call the tower and his engineer told Dave he had a nice voice and should work on the base radio station. Following a stint with Armed Forces Radio in Puerto Rico, Dave was discharged in 1951 and started his radio career at WASA-Havredegece, Maryland. For the next 15 years Dave worked at radio and tv stations in the Baltimore, West Virginia corridor. "In the mid-1950s I worked at WFBR-Baltimore, the station where Arthur Godfrey got his start." In 1965 he joined the Bonneville station in Kansas City, KMBZ. Six years later he transferred to KBIG. He brought his new wife, jazz singer Kay Dennis to the Southland. After his stay at KBIG, Dave became the admissions director at L.A.B. "For a shy kid who spent most of his life alone in a control booth, I really liked interacting with people." When the school folded, Dave took a similar position with the National Broadcasting School of Sacramento until 1992 when he retired. "These are the golden years and with my social security check and AFTRA retirement monies, I'm having a great time. I like to laugh a lot."

ROBINSON, Mark: **KMGG**, 1983-85; **KIKF**, 1991-97. Mark handles the all-night shift at the Orange County Country station.

ROBINSON, Marsha: **KACE**, 1980-89; **KGFJ**, 1989-95. Marsha arrived in the Southland from Cincinnati. When KGFJ folded, Marshal returned to Cincinnati to head promotions at WCIN.

ROBINSON, Pamela: **KACE**, 1979-80; **KJLH**, 1984-85; **KACE**, 1985-86, pd; **KACD**, 1995. Pamela graduated from Long Beach State with classmate Kim Amidon. Pamela's afternoon drive show on KACE was a mix of pop, soul, blues and jazz music. At KJLH she was md and acting pd. She is currently working at "Shadows and Light" video production company.

ROCCO: **KEZY**, 1971-85 and 1992-97. Born Mark Moceri, the L.A. native grew up in Whittier. Rocco started with the "kick-ass rock and roll" station as an assistant engineer and became the chief of technical operations. He ran the FM automation and was the voice on the overnight shift for years. Rocco left for an assignment with a consulting firm in Cleveland and returned to the Orange County station in 1992.

ROCHON, Lonnie: **KDAY**

ROCINNA, Joe: **KAGB**, 1975

ROCKOFF, Neil: **KNX/FM**, 1972, pd; **KGBS/KTNQ**, 1976-79, pd/gm; **KHJ**, 1979-82, gm. For two years, Neil struggled to convince Los Angeles listeners that they should "all grow up to be cowboys" and listen to KHJ. Later, Neil was part-owner of KBZT-San Diego and worked at WHN-New York before moving on to be Storer Broadcasting vp of the radio division. In the summer of 1995, Neil joined Jones Satellite Network as manager of special projects.

RODDY, Rod: **KGBS**, 1967; **KDAY**, 1967; **KOST**, 1972-74, pd. Since 1985 Rod has been the voice on *The*

Price Is Right that invites contestants to "Come on down!" He is a native of Ft. Worth and attended T.C.U. majoring in radio and tv. Rod was a wedding photographer while in high school and college and appeared as a regular on a local tv show, *Teen Times* with Pat Boone. He started as a dj in 1953 at KXOL-Ft. Worth. "During my lengthy broadcasting career I was pd for both true pioneers of format radio, Todd Storz and Gordon McLendon." His radio journey took him to WQAM-Miami, WABR-Orlando, KXLR-Little Rock, WTIX-New Orleans, KOMA-Oklahoma City, KQV-Pittsburgh, KYW-Cleveland, WJJD-Chicago WQXI-Atlanta, WKBW-Buffalo. In 1968 he returned to Dallas as morning man on KLIF and hosted a controversial talk show with McLendon. "Our show was the inspiration for Oliver Stone's *Talk Radio*." Rod returned to Southern California in 1972 to program KOST and he hosted a syndicated show "On A Clear Day" featuring guests from the world of the occult. In 1974 he initiated his new career in voiceover work. He was the voice of ABC's *Soap* which ran for four years. Rod was the announcer on a number of game shows including *Whew, Battle Stars, So You Think You've Got Troubles, Hit Man* and *Press Your Luck*. He was the announcer on *Love Connection* for the first four years before joining Bob Barker on *The Price Is Right*. Rod is in his 12th year as Bob Barker's sidekick "on camera" announcer for *The Price Is Right* which is the longest running game show in television history. He hosted *The $25,000 Game Show* for two seasons at the Roy Clark Theater in Branson, Missouri. Internationally, Rod is the official ambassador of Chaing Mai, Thailand and travels frequently to Southeast Asia to create his colorful Thai silk wardrobe featured on *The Price Is Right*.

RODRIGUES, Paul: **KKBT**, 1989. The movie actor, who appeared in *D.C. Cab*, joined "the Beat" as part of a new call letter/format change in morning drive. He left a few months later for tv's *Grand Slam*.

RODRIGUES, Ron: **KMPC**, 1979-82; **KMGG**, 1985, om. Ron is the managing editor of *R&R*. He was born in Japan. "I was a Navy brat. Before I was five I lived in Japan, San Francisco, Honolulu and Alameda." Ron was exposed to the radio experience when he was four and living in Hawaii. "My brother won a contest on KPOI and he took me to the station to pick up his prize and the jock on the air was Tom Rounds." Ron started his radio career in 1973 as a board-op for K101-San Francisco. "I fell in love with radio in the early '70s listening to KYA and KFRC. I loved the music and it made a connection with me. I resolved then to pursue radio." After graduation from San Francisco State with a degree in communications, Ron worked in the news department at KFRC. He met Mark Blinoff (then KMPC pd) at an industry convention and in 1978 was offered a music director position at KMPC. He was also om of KIDD-Monterey in the late 1970s. In 1982 Ron joined *R&R* and for the next three years was the AC editor. After a stint as om at KMGG, Ron returned to *R&R*. "I am just thrilled with the growth of the publication, especially in the last two years. It will only get better." In the summer of 1997 he was promoted to Editor-In-Chief of *R&R*.

RODRIGUEZ, Alfredo: **KWKW**, 1984-91, pd; **KLAX**, 1992-95. Born in 1948, Alfredo left KLAX in late 1995.

RODRIGUEZ, Joe: **KKBT**, 1995-97. Joe hosts the afternoon drive "L.A.'s Original 5 O'Clock Traffic Jam" on "the Beat."

RODRIGUEZ, Rodri: **KFI**, 1996-97. Rodri works weekends at all-Talk KFI. She owns an international live concert production company. Rodri has won countless awards and has been recognized by the White House and many charitable organizations. Her

philosophy is simply: "Empowerment through knowledge is my motto but always with a smile."

ROEBUCK, Jay: **KLON**, 1985-93, pd. The program director and on-air personality of the Long Beach Jazz station was also a reviewer of jazz recordings for the *OC Register*. Before joining KLON, he worked at the Saddleback College station. Jay died of a heart attack on March 17, 1993, at the age of 55.

ROGERS, Beach: **KFWB**; **KNX**, 1971-97. A native Californian, the former high school president graduated from USC with a degree in telecommunications. During the Korean War Beach was with Armed Forces Radio in Tokyo. Prior to joining "KNXNewsradio" in May 1971, he was a member of the Westinghouse Radio space team that covered the NASA space launches. Among his numerous awards, he has won two Golden Mikes. Beach is the overnight news anchor.

ROGERS, Dave: **KLAC**, 1967. Dave joined KLAC from KIMN-Denver.

ROGERS, Joe: **KPPC**, 1970-71; **KMET**, 1971-72. "Mississippi Fats" worked at WBCN-Boston before arriving in the Southland. He called himself "Mississippi Harold Wilson" at WBCN after the British prime minister. While in Los Angles he used the name Mississippi Brian Wilson. After two years in the Southland he returned to the legendary AOR New England station. Joe is now a restaurant broker in Boston.

ROHDE, Barry: **KNX**, 1965-97. In the 1980s Barry was the afternoon anchor and moved to middays in the '90s on "KNXNewsradio." Born in Rahway, New Jersey he started his radio career in Kansas and Indiana. He was the co-director of the Indiana Presidential Primary and General Election unit for the CBS Radio Network. Barry won the "Outstanding Young Man of the Year" award, and in 1965 joined KNX where he has worked as feature reporter, traffic, weather and sports editor. He has been part of the team that has won 22 Golden Mike Awards for Best News. Barry retired to Florida in the summer of 1997.

ROLFE, Cary: **KZLA**, 1994-96. Cary came to the Southland from KKNU-Eugene and KMLE-Phoenix. He also worked as a West Coast promotion rep for Giant Records. Cary was promoted to interim pd of KZLA in late 1995 until leaving for a pd'ship in the spring of 1996 at Country KUBL-Salt Lake City.

ROLL, Robert: **KROQ**, 1985-86. Robert worked afternoon drive with Raymond Banister.

ROLLER, Lori: **KEZY**, 1994-95. Lori left the Orange County station in 1995.

ROLLINS, Jeff: **KJOI**, 1989; **KIKF**, 1990. Jeff is the morning dj on WW1's Adult Standards format heard locally on KLAC. "I've been doing mornings for seven years which is the longest I've been anywhere." Jeff was born in Washington, DC and graduated from the University of Maryland in 1971 with a degree in theater. He originally wanted to be an actor and director and started two theater companies while working in Maryland and Northern California. He spent 10 years in San Francisco "performing as a dj on KNBR, KFOG and KEEN." He arrived at KJOI from KKSA-Sacramento to do the news with morning man Roger Barkley. Jeff also worked at WCHS-Charleston, West Virginia. At KIKF he did morning news with Sean Parr and worked at Unistar and Shadow traffic. "I love radio, creating the imagery and theater of the mind."

ROLON, Pepe: **KSKQ**, 1992, nd

ROMAN, Nick: **KLON**, 1997, nd

ROMAY, Lina: For a decade during the 1980s, Lina was the race track call girl for Hollywood Park. She translated racing information into Spanish for many Southland stations and made the calls for KNX. Born in New York City, a "true Latin from Manhattan," she was only 18 years old when she debuted as the vocalist for Xavier Cugat over a coast to coast radio broadcast that originated from the fabled Waldorf Astoria Hotel. MGM announced plans to do a remake of their Academy Award winning *Grand Hotel* and combine it with a musical version of a recently published novel titled *Weekend at The Waldorf*. Lina's performance was rewarded with a studio contract. "My contract guaranteed that I wouldn't be limited to just musical roles and for at least 10 years appeared in movies with Clark Gable, Mickey Rooney, Van Johnson, Ava Gardner, Fred Astaire and many other MGM luminaries." Lina also appeared for 39 consecutive weeks on Bing Crosby's "Kraft Music Hall" radio program. She guest starred in *I Love Lucy* and several tv shows with Bob Hope and Red Skeleton. She married in 1954 and left the entertainment business to bring up her growing family. "By 1980 I decided it was time to retire from retirement. When I was approached in 1980 by an official at Hollywood Park, I knew nothing about sports. They just liked my voice and the fact I was bilingual." Lina serves on the board of Southern California Sports Broadcasters Association and is active in the Pacific Pioneer Broadcasters Association.

ROMERO, Bobby: SEE Sky Walker

RONDEAU, Jim: **KOST**, 1993-94; **KCBS**, 1994-97; **KYSR**, 1997. Before arriving in the Southland, Jim worked at KJQY/KRMX-San Diego and KUBE-Seattle. In 1994 he went from part-time at KOST to afternoon drive at "Arrow 93." He left KCBS in early 1997 and joined swing at KYSR and projects at Premiere Radio Networks.

RONNI: **KIIS** weekends

ROOK, John: **KFI**, 1977-82, pd; **KABC**, 1988-89, pd.

The very successful radio programming consultant during the 1970s and '80s was born in Chillicothe, Ohio, and raised in Chadron, Nebraska. After high school he came to the Southland in the mid-1950s and studied acting at the Pasadena Playhouse with Sal Mineo and Natalie Wood. Following bit parts in several motion pictures, his best friend, Rock 'n Roll Hall of Fame legend Eddie Cochran, suggested John consider a career in radio. His first dj job in 1957 was at KASL-New Castle, Wyoming, followed by KOBH-Hot Springs, South Dakota, KALL-Salt Lake City and KTLN-Denver. By 1964, he was pd of KQV-Pittsburgh and from 1967 to 1971 he was pd of WLS-Chicago. In 1969, his peers named WLS "Station of the Year" and John Rook "Radio's Man of the Year." In the early 1970s, John teamed up with Chuck Blore and Ken Draper in a consultancy company. He started John Rook & Associates in 1974 with WCFL-Chicago as one of his first clients. Within weeks, the legendary Larry Lujack left WLS for WCFL saying, "I think John Rook is the greatest pd of our time or any other time. He's a real pro, super fair and up front and honest." As a consultant, John's impressive client list soon included WABC-New York, WIFI-Philadelphia, WHYI-Miami, WZGC-Atlanta, WBAP-Dallas/Ft. Worth, KIMN-Denver, KRBE-Houston and WGCL-Cleveland. In 1977 John was named "Consultant of the Year" and at the suggestion of Chuck Blore was named pd of KFI. Cox VP James Wesley and operations head Elliott "Biggie" Nevins backed John as he rocked KFI's 50,000 watts and took on RKO's KHJ. Within a year, KHJ went to a Country format, the end of an era. In 1983, John purchased KCDA-Spokane and started dividing his time between his Northridge residence and his horse ranch south of Coeur d'Alene, Idaho. In 1987, the Reagan White House named him a commissioner candidate at the FCC. In 1988, gm George Green persuaded John to return to Los Angeles as pd of KABC for two years. In 1994, *R&R* readers voted John, "One of the most influential programmers of the past twenty years." Today, John lives on his Idaho ranch and owns two Spokane radio stations.

ROOPE, Jim: **KWST**, 1980; **KFOX**; **KIEV**; **KRLA**; **KFI**; **KNNS**, 1995-96, pd; **KGIL**, 1997, pd. Jim began his radio career in Cincinnati in 1977 at WFIB followed by WCLU and WKRC. He spent most of his time in L.A. working as a dj or talk show host. In 1982 Jim helped develop and launch the Cable Radio Network. In 1995 he was hired to put all-News KNNS on the air for Mount Wilson Broadcasting. He served as operations manager, news director and midday anchor. Jim also worked as pd and morning jock for sister station, San Francisco Jazz KNOB. When "K-News" changed formats, Jim was kept on to develop the all-Beatles format, KGIL. He is the om, pd and afternoon drive personality at KGIL.

ROSE, Dianna: **KSRF**, 1989-91; **KLIT**, 1991-92; **KACD**, 1992-95. Dianna began her radio career in Los Angeles after receiving her master's in broadcast journalism from USC. After college she worked in London for Children's Television at the BBC. Dianna has been with Metro Networks since 1992 and is also producer/writer of the nationally syndicated show "The Countdown, hosted by Walt Love." She is a cousin to Hilly and Roger Rose.

ROSE, Doyle: **KPWR**, 1991-96, vp/gm. Since 1989, Doyle has been the president of Emmis Broadcasting. He graduated in 1972 from St. Cloud State University as a business/history major. While at University of Minnesota law school, he started in sales at WWTC and later at WCCO. In 1975 he returned to WWTC as gsm  and was promoted to gm a year later. Ligget Broadcasting hired Doyle in 1979 to manage WLOL-Minneapolis which was later acquired by Emmis. In 1984 he was promoted to regional vice president, overseeing KPWR and KSHE-St. Louis. In 1988 he assumed responsibility over all the Emmis radio stations and was named executive vp of operations. Doyle turned over the management of KPWR to Marie Kordus in March of 1996. He remains president of Emmis Broadcasting.

ROSE, Hilly: **KABC**, 1970-72; **KFI**, 1972-79; **KMPC**, 1979-82; **KABC**, 1982-84. Hilly was best known for his talk show "Open Phone Forum" on KFI, before satellites made national talk shows feasible. The KFI signal stretching across the country drew calls from all 48 states. Hilly was a child actor, performed in network radio soap operas in Chicago, ("Ma Perkins" and "First Nighter") and has made industrial films and commercials since 1961. In 1979 he joined KHJ/Channel 9  News to review restaurants. "I appeared live on tv and radio simultaneously through the wonders of tape." In the late 1970s Hilly demonstrated the power of Talk radio advocacy. "There was a lot of talk about tax relief for property owners and Proposition 13 was born as Jarvis-Gann. Problem was they weren't talking to each other an it looked like it might fail." Hilly surreptiously brought them together along with the L.A. County Tax Assessor Phil Watson. "I locked the studio doors while they worked out their differences on-air!" The result was a huge vote for Prop 13. In 1984 Hilly retired from radio and purchased a large housewares store in Santa Cruz. A year later he started a series of weekend radio shows on KGO-San Francisco that ran until 1992. He's done fill-in since then. He now travels widely for his own plasure and has created a series of radio shows for the Monterey Bay Aquarium.

ROSE, J.: **KNX/FM**, 1988-89; **KODJ**, 1989. "Big J" was doing late evenings during the launch of the "Oldies 93" format on KODJ in March 1989. In the mid-1990s he was doing work for an AC station in Washington, DC.

ROSE, Jim: **KZLA**, 1985-93. Born Dennis Brown, Jim left the Southland for Portland and owns a company called Digital On-Hold. He also owns his own studio in Grants Pass where he has an active voiceover career.

ROSE, Judd: **KFWB**, 1978-79. Judd has been with ABC News since 1982. His responsibilities have included reporting for *World News Tonight With Peter Jennings*, *20/20* and *Nightline*. Since 1989 he has been a correspondent for *ABC News PrimeTime Live*. His assignments at *PrimeTime* have ranged from providing on-the-scene coverage from Panama after the U.S. invasion and traveling to San Francisco to report on the aftermath of the earthquake. Judd was part of the award-winning investigation of the crash of Pan Am Flight #103 over Lockerbie, Scotland. In the fall of 1996, he and Sam Donaldson co-hosted a *PrimeTime Live* special edition on cancer in which each discussed his personal experience with cancer. Judd attended UCLA and New York University. Prior to joining all-News KFWB, he worked as a desk assistant at KHJ and a reporter for AP Radio in New York and Washington. Judd is Hilly Rose's son and brother of Roger Rose.

ROSE, Roger: **KMGG**, 1983; **KFI**, 1986. Roger is the son of legendary talkmeister Hilly Rose. Born in Highland Park, Illinois, he worked at the high school radio station and interned at WLS-Chicago. In the late 1970s Roger jocked at KFXM-San Bernardino. After KFI, Roger was an original VH-1 vj who now has a lucrative career doing voiceovers and celebrity voice impersonations. "I starred in *Ski Patrol* and have appeared in various other feature films as well as hosted two network tv shows on CBS and NBC. I currently am hosting a show for Brandon Tartikoff that is sponsored by AOL and am about to shoot a feature, *Dill Scallion*, it's a country-western *Spinal Tap*. Roger is married to longtime L.A. dj Maggie Ross.

ROSEFSKY, Bob: **KABC**, 1986. Bob was the financial reporter for KABC news radio. He hosted a financial show on PBS. Bob went to England to work and is now living in the East.

ROSEN, Sharone: **XPRS**; **KWNK**; **KLAC**. Sharone got her start doing voiceovers and character voices on Disney read-a-long records that includes *Bambi* and *Lady and the Tramp*. If you were a fan of *L.A. Law*, Sharone was the voice of the "fowl-mouthed" parrot on an early episode. Her early broadcast work was in Arcata and Napa. Sharone's first Southern California assignment was doing news and traffic in morning drive with "Sweet Dick" Whittington, and she later became KWNK's pd and midday jock. At KLAC she was one of the weekend jocks and special events producer. Sharone has sung the national anthem for the L.A. Kings, Dodgers and Angels. She moonlights as a synagogue cantor in the San Fernando Valley.

ROSENBERG, Hal: **KRTH**, 1972-74, gm. Hal was running KFSD-San Diego until his retirement in the summer of 1996.

ROSENBERG, Leo: **KMET**, 1972. Leo was part of the news team on "the Mighty Met." According to a fellow staffer, Leo "broke the Watergate story and gave it to Jack Anderson." After KMET Leo got out of radio and became a teacher in Long Beach.

ROSENBLOOM, Randy: **KWNK**, 1984-85. Randy was the sports director who brought the Clippers broadcasts to Southern California when the team arrived. He was one of the radio announcers for the short-lived L.A. Express football team.

ROSENBLOOM, Slapsie-Maxie: **KLAC**. The Las Vegas comedian, actor and former professional boxer, was part of KLAC's attempt to resurrect the "Big 5" dj personality sound. Art Kevin remembers: "He was the passing of an era. One of the greats! His material would not be allowed today due to all the 'protest' groups. Slapsie-Maxie used to do a vaudeville type 'dah dah dah dah' with a plaintive look that would be considered insensitive to folks with real afflictions. He did his shtick for so long that it really became his persona because that is what people expected."

ROSETTI, Hector: **KLVE**, 1994. Hector worked afternoon drive at "K-Love."

ROSKO: **KGFJ**, 1964-65; **KBLA**, 1965; **KMET**, 1971. Born Bill Mercer, "Rhymin' Bill Rosko Mercer" began the "underground" revolution in New York on WNEW/FM on October 30, 1967. Once a legend at WNEW, he was with WQIV in 1975 when the station went dark. Rosko is doing voiceover in New York and can be heard during the fund raising drives on WBAI-New York. He is the voice of CBS Sports in New York.

ROSS, Brenda: **KPWR**, 1987-92. Brenda joined Unistar's syndicated ACII series in the evening slot in early 1994. In 1995 she moved to KBLX-San Francisco for morning drive.

ROSS, Don: **KHJ**; **KNX**, 1966. Don left Southland radio for KFMB-San Diego and was a tv booth announcer for decades. He retired in San Diego and worked on his art work. Don has passed away, according to KNX nd Bob Sims.

ROSS, Eva: **KHJ**, 1974 and 1976-77; **KIKF**, 1980-90. Eva anchored the news at KHJ from 1974 to 1977 except for a year spent in Boston doing the news. At KIKF she reported "Orange County Closeup." Since 1995 she has been writing a column for the *OC Register*. "Lyle Kilgore was my boss at KHJ and I ended up marrying him! We've been married for 17 years and have a 12-year- old daughter named Paige."

ROSS, Frankie: **KJLH**, 1986-90; **KKBT**, 1990-92; **KJLH**, 1992-95, pd. Frankie worked afternoon drive during his first soul journey at KJLH and in 1992 returned as pd. He left KJLH in late 1995.

ROSS, Kevin: **KGFJ**, 1993; **KKBT**, 1993-94; **KACE**, 1994-97. Born and raised in Buffalo, Kevin grew up listening to Frankie Crocker and Gary Byrd. He went to the School of Performing Arts and in 1985 graduated from Buffalo State College. Did he get the interest in radio while in school? Kevin laughed in a 1996 phone interview, "I wasn't good enough to be on the college radio station. They turned me down, so I forgot about it." After college, Kevin moved to Atlanta for a fresh start and after watching a tv commercial for the Columbia School of Broadcasting, he went back to school and eight months later was working for WIGO-Atlanta. A year later in 1987 he moved to evenings and the "Quiet Storm" at WEKS ("KISS 104")-Atlanta. In 1988 he became md of WFXE-Columbus, Georgia. Kevin's first pd assignment came in 1990 at KDKO-Denver. A year later and in a quandary as to what his next career move should be, he was debating a job offer from Kansas City, returning to Atlanta or going to Los Angeles which had always been a dream. "One night I was channel surfing and came across the Psychic Network infomercial and decided to call. The psychic said that I already knew Atlanta, that I would hate Kansas City and I should go to Los Angeles. And that's how I got to L.A." He used his writing abilities upon arrival and worked for the Urban Network for two years before joining KGFJ in 1993. Kevin also writes a national newsletter called *Radio Facts*. His next career move? "KACE may be my last radio gig. I'm constantly looking for acting jobs. I want to be an actor!"

ROSS, Kevin: **KTZN**, 1997; **KABC**, 1997. The 33-year-old Los Angeles Deputy District Attorney talks about a variety of issues during his weekend program on KABC. After marrying his junior high school sweetheart in January 1995, Kevin organized and operated a grassroots political campaign for a seat on the L.A. City Council. Finishing a strong third out of an initial field of seven candidates, he received impressive endorsements including one from the *LA Times*.

ROSS, Lee: **KFOX**, 1962-63. Lee wrote *My Shoes Keep Walking Back to You* and *Heart-to-Heart Talk*.

ROSS, Lorri: SEE Lorri Donaldson

ROSS, Maggie: **KIQQ**, 1977-80; **KMPC**, 1980; **KHTZ**, 1980-82; **KLAC**, 1982-87; **KZLA**, 1989-94; **KCBS**, 1994-97. After graduating from UCLA in the class with fellow L.A. jocks Amy Hiatt and Manny Pacheco, the Oakland native landed her first on-air assignment at KIQQ doing the late evening shift. While doing part-time at KMPC, she handled the weekend shift at KOGO-San Diego. In 1986 Maggie moved to New York when her husband, Roger Rose, became a VH-1 vj.

ROSS, Neil: **KPOL/FM**; 1978; **KZLA**, 1979-80; **KHTZ**, 1981; **KNX/FM**, 1981; **KMPC**, 1982-85. Neil was born in London, raised in Montreal and arrived in Long Beach at the age of 11. When he got to the Southland he couldn't believe his ears. In Canada, there were only two

hours of rock 'n' roll with a dj who seemed uninterested. "I turned on KFWB, and I heard rock 'n' roll music 24 hours a day with great djs." He went to high school in San Diego and broadcast school in New York before attending Bill Ogden's school to prepare for the FCC 1st Class License examination at the time of John Kennedy's assassination. He started his radio career in Utah and Idaho. He then grew professionally when he worked in Honolulu for five years, much of that time for Earl McDaniel (who wrote an essay for the 1st volume of this book). He returned to the Mainland and worked with Gary Allyn at KCBQ-San Diego before taking on a couple of huge Tijuana outlets, XHIS and XHERS (his and hers) in early 1972. He was "Natural Neil" at KYA-San Francisco and KDEO-San Diego and Neilson Ross at KCBQ. Neil arrived in the Southland to work afternoon drive at KPOL/FM, which later became KZLA. He and pd Jim LaFawn created "News Roulette" at KZLA, which drew national attention on Tom Snyder's *Tomorrow* show. In 1985 Neil had done his last radio work. "I felt the tail wagging the dog and made a decision to try voiceover work full time. I remember the mother of one of my high school buddies who worked at a radio station saying, 'there's nothing sadder than a 40-year-old disc jockey.' As I drove home from my last show on KMPC, the echo of her comment from a quarter century earlier jolted me. I was 40 and I was leaving radio behind." In addition to his very successful commercial voiceover work, he narrates *Movie Magic*, now in its fourth season on Discovery Channel and voiced several *Biography* shows for A&E. He was the *21* announcer in Robert Redford's movie *Quiz Show* and he appeared in *Dick Tracy*. Would he go back to radio? "I'm not sure I want to sit in a room waiting for a CD to end. Maybe a morning newstalk show...maybe."

ROSS, Nicci: **KOCM/KSRF**, 1989-90; **KACD**, 1994-96.

In the early 1980s, Nicci (born Nicollette Ralles) attended Cypress College and eventually graduated with honors from Miramar College in San Diego. She was an intern at KEZY while in school and spent some time in Plainview and Huntsville, Texas, "paying my dues." For five years beginning in 1984, she worked in San Diego at "Y-95," "K-Lite" and KBZT. Prior to joining "K-Ocean," Nicci worked at Metro Traffic. When she left "K-Surf" she worked a variety of formats in San Jose at "Hot 97.7," "Mix 106.5," "The Fox" and for two years at KOME. For part of her stay at KACD she worked afternoon drive and middays. Nicci now works in artist management and promotion at Eventure Entertainment in Hollywood.

ROSS, Phil: **KYMS**, 1986-94. Phil started out as an intern at the Christian station prior to graduating from Cal State Long Beach in 1986. He worked his way from traffic reports to afternoon drive. "In 1990 when my first child was on the way, we had to make the choice between starving as a jock or eating as a sales person." Phil moved into sales and continued to write and voice spots on the air. In 1994, a year before KYMS was sold, Ambassador Advertising Agency, a producer and syndicator of Christian radio programs, hired him as program producer. Phil co-hosts a nationally syndicated, weekly half-hour radio program called Ambassador Express Talk. "My next goal is to do voiceovers in animated cartoons!"

ROTH, Jack: **KRLA**, 1976-83, pd. Jack was a graduate of Cal State Northridge with fellow classmates who got into L.A. radio, Michelle Roth and Johnny St. Thomas. While he was on the air at KRLA he was known as "Jack the Hit Man." In 1976 he was assistant to Art Laboe and filled in for him in morning drive. Jack was pd of KRLA beginning in 1979. Currently, he is doing voiceover work in Hollywood including LoJack.

ROTH, Michelle: **KDAY**, 1979-80; **KRLA**, 1983-85; **KBIG**, 1992. Before her arrival in Los Angeles, Michelle had moved from news to an evening shift at "underground" KMPX-San Francisco. She was one of the active women in radio when it was not easy to get on the air. After leaving K101-San Francisco in 1978, she called a Los Angeles pd inquiring about a job opening. She was dismissed with, "If you're ever down here, come see me." The pd was shocked when Michelle arrived and commented: "The only reason I talked to you at all is that we have to talk to you women and minorities. If we are not nice, you'll take us to the FCC!" Undaunted by such attitudes, Michelle prevailed and was the third female voice on KRLA when she joined the station in 1983. Michelle lives in Hollywood and is married to a police officer. She has been heard as an announcer on cable game shows.

ROURKE, Jack: **KABC**, 1957-58. Jack was a talk interview host on KABC. He is now in the advertising business.

ROWE, Bob: **KMPC**, 1966-94; **KMAX**, 1995. For almost three decades, the native Angeleno had been part of the sports scene at KMPC. Dubbed "Dr. Angel Fever" by Robert W. Morgan, Bob started with KMPC in 1966 working the "Sportswire." When fans called "Webster 8-3000," they got sports scores from around the country. Two years later Bob became the sports producer, coordinating the broadcasting's of the Angels, Rams and UCLA Bruins. "I was anxious to get on the air and the opportunity came in 1972." Bob did fill-in news and sports. "In 1979 my career really flourished when I was given the talk show following the Angel games. I did that right up until 1994 when the station was sold to CapCities. Despite my 28 years at the station, the new owners never game me the courtesy of an interview before they bought the station. But I was hired a month after the sale to continue my "AngelTalk" shows and teamed with my old boss, Steve Bailey, to do a memorial tribute to Jim Healy who died in July 1994." The project won a Golden Mike award for best documentary. "I was not re-hired for the 1995 baseball season. Nobody ever explained why." Bob played baseball at Poly High School in Sun Valley and was always interested in radio. After graduation he attended the Don Martin Radio School and started as a dj in 1961 at KUTY-Palmdale. After two years at KACY-Oxnard, Bob was drafted into the Army and he spent almost two years in Heidelberg, Germany. "At least it wasn't Vietnam." Bob is living in

Glendale and has recently completed a book about his time at KMPC.

ROWE, Red: **KFI**, 1968-69. Red was doing a one-hour morning variety show on KNXT/Channel 2 while working as a dj at KFI. In the 1950s he hosted a tv show called *Panorama Pacific*. Red has retired to Palm Springs.

ROY, Mike: **KNX**, 1965-76. Mike was one of the hosts of the long-running series, "Food News Hour." In the early days of tv Mike emceed *The Victory Parade of Spotlights*, *Duffy's Tavern* and *Abbott and Costello*. His first job was working on a newspaper as a teenager in his native North Dakota. He came to California in 1944 after working for a number of Midwest radio stations as an announcer. In 1950 he debuted "Mike Roy's Kitchen" on KTLA/Channel 5 which he did until 1957 when he took a turn at building and running restaurants. The rotund - about 350 pounds - chef clearly loved food and delighted in talking about it. He wrote over a dozen cookbooks. By 1960 he was back in radio. One survey indicated that 43% of his audience was men. The "KNX Food Hour" ran for 11 years until his death June 26, 1976. He was 63.

ROZ: **KLSX**, 1988-90. Born Jane Rozman in Chicago, she was raised in Detroit. While attending Michigan State University majoring in telecommunications, Jane worked at WFMK and part-time at WWCK-Flint. After graduation in 1982 she went by "The Roz" and worked middays and was md at WCKG-Chicago. She originally teamed with Peter Tilden at KLSX in morning drive and then went to evenings. Roz remembers being part of a wave of firings. "I came in to do my night shift and

found a memo in my box from the pd. It said 'Roz, I need to see you in my office at 1 p.m. tomorrow for a meeting. Please be prompt.' I showed it to Billy Juggs who I followed on-air at the time. The next day, in the meeting, I was fired. Exactly one week later, at home I get a call from Billy Juggs. He's got the exact same memo in his box! Only the name was changed! Sure enough the next day Billy gets blown out. This pd actually had a template in his computer for firing people!" While at KLSX, Roz had started her migration to the sales side of the radio business by sitting in on sales meetings led by the gsm Jim Freeman. "He was a great guy. He didn't have the common management misconception that programming and sales shouldn't mix." After KLSX, she debuted in sales at WJMQ-Lansing. Two years later in 1992 she moved back to her native Chicago and has been in sales at WXRT/WSCR ever since. Recently married, she's legally changed her first and last name to Roz Byrne.

RUBIN, Sam: **KNX**, 1994-97; **KMPC/KTZN**, 1995-97. Sam covers the entertainment news from theater to tv to movies and celebrity interviews. He is popular for his work on the *KTLA/Channel 5 Morning News* which he joined in 1991. Born in L.A., Sam attended Occidental College and in 1982 received a B.A. in American studies and rhetoric. In the fall of 1996 he and Dorothy Lucey

had a short-lived syndicated entertainment show. His show business reports air on KTVU-San Francisco as well as *Show Buzz*, a nationally syndicated show out of Canada. He has written articles for *McCalls*, *Home* and the *LA Times*. He was a regular contributor the *Joan Rivers Show*. The former KTTV/Channel 11 entertainment reporter was an intern at KHJ during the "Boss Radio" days. He and his wife Julie enjoy raising their daughter Perry who was born in the summer of 1995.

RUDNIK, Lee: **KMET**, 1971. Lee was the midday jock at "the Mighty Met."

RUIZ, Martin: **KALI**, 1986-93. Martin worked evenings at Spanish KALI.

RUSH, Andy: **KNX/FM**, 1987-88; **KMPC/FM**, 1988. "When I was 12 I wanted to go into acting. When I found out that somewhere along the line I'd have to wear tights and do Shakespeare in a public park, acting became just a fond fantasy." Two years later Andy discovered his passion for radio. "I came across an 'instant recording' exhibit at the Science and Industry Museum in Exposition Park. I spoke into a condensor microphone when the green light went on and stopped as the red one came on. Within 10 seconds, it played back for you. A visitor to the Exposition suggested that I

should get into radio broadcasting. That's all it took." Andy started at KOTE-Lancaster followed by KREO-Indio. He secured an FCC First Class License and in 1975 joined KUBA/KHEX-Yuba City for $400 a month. Following a return to Lancaster, Andy was hired by KROI-Sacramento. "And I didn't have to work Bakersfield or Stockton to get to the 23rd market." In 1982 Andy joined KFOG-San Francisco followed 2 years later with a job at KRQR-San Francisco. "After leaving KMPC/FM, I got hired at L.A.B., as a teacher. I spent two years there, earning half as much as I could being on the air, but getting more satisfaction from it." In 1994 Andy was hired to be the "Navigation Voice" for Amerigon. "Right now, I own rental property in West Los Angeles, Hollywood and Oregon and breed Dachsund pups. Along with everything else in life, the schedule is pretty full. Want to see pictures of my pregnant dog?"

RUSS, Ron: Ron worked as a jazz deejay over the decades.

RUSSELL, Antoinette: **KJLH**, 1987-89; **KACE**, 1989-97; **KOST**, 1997. Antoinette was born in New York to West Indian parents. She graduated from Washington State University with a degree in communications. Antoinette began her broadcasting career in Seattle which included jobs in both radio and television. In 1986, she moved to L.A. and joined KJLH in 1987

where she worked for two years before going to KACE. She remained there until March of 1997 when she moved across the hall to sister station, KOST. Antoinette is married to Mike Mann, "92.3/the Beat" production director and leader of America's premier Black Cowboy band, "Mike Mann and the Night Riders."

RUSSELL, Aundrae: **KJLH**, 1988-97. The Meridian, Mississippi, native worked in his hometown at WALT as pd and md from 1983 to 1988. In a recent interview, Aundrae recalled one of his thrills during his stay in Southern California was "doing my show live from Las Vegas." Aundrae is currently sports director in addition to his air shift.

RUSSELL, Bill: **KABC**, 1970-73 and 1982. Bill hosted KABC's "SportsTalk" show. He led the Boston Celtics through more than a decade of almost uninterrupted success. He led the Celtics to 11 championships in 13 years. In 1973 he joined the Seattle Supersonics. Bill was talked into the KABC job by Keith Jackson and others. Russell moved to L.A. after leaving basketball in 1969. There was no mistaking Russell's on-air cackle.

RUSSELL, Robby: **KWIZ**, 1995-96. Steve Harvey conducted a promotion for his "Only in L.A." column in the *LA Times* to find Southern California's Most Annoying DJ. Robby won and admitted that he stuffed the ballot box but Harvey gave the title to him anyway because he found him so annoying. Robby complained that the *Times* didn't run a photo of him.

RUSSELL, Lew: **KGFJ**, 1957-58. Lew arrived in the Southland from WJW-Cleveland, where he was known as "Moon Dog."

RYAN, Lori: **KEZY**, 1995-97. Lori works weekends at the Orange County station.

RYAN, Nick: **KWIZ**, 1977. Nick did morning drive on the Orange County station.

RYDER, Kevin: SEE Kevin & Bean

RYDER, Max: SEE Chris Leary

RYDER, Turi: **KMPC/KTZN**, 1996-97; **KFI**, 1997. The Chicago talk-show hostess joined KMPC in 1996 for the midday slot and left a year later and joined KPIX-San Francisco for fill-in. In late spring 1997 the *Hollywood Reporter* reported that Turi had been fired for inflammatory on-air comments she made about earthquake-stricken Iran. She reportedly said: "If the whole country of Iran is destroyed by earthquake, I'd say these are the people who hate us. I really don't care. If I had money I would have dropped an atomic bomb in Tehran."

RYDGREN, John: **KRLA**, 1972; **KRTH**, 1977-82; **KRLA**, 1985; **KRTH**, 1986-88. "Brother John" had a unique place in Southern California radio. Born in North Dakota, he grew up in Seattle. In 1958 John graduated with a divinity degree from Pacific Lutheran University in Washington. John was one of the first people to use rock music in religious radio programs. He began his radio work in Minneapolis when he taped a Christian rock show called "Silhouettes" from a church basement. The show became so popular that it was nationally syndicated, and he was chosen to direct the American Lutheran Church's national tv, radio and film department. John was the voice of ABC's pro-album *Love Format* in 1968. In 1970, John left WABC/FM to produce religious and socially slanted radio/tv programs. He moved to L.A. in 1972 and eventually hosted a program called "Heaven Is in Your Mind." In 1982, John suffered a debilitating stroke while on the air, which left him with a form of dyslexia, forcing him to relearn reading and speaking from the third-grade level. Doctors predicted that he would never be able to talk again. However, with therapy he rejoined KRTH in 1986. Randy Gardner talked about the opportunity to have worked with John: "What a dear sweet soul! He had come full circle. He had to voice track his show between records during his relearning period." John died in his favorite easy chair on the day after Christmas 1988, of a heart attack. He was 56. Beasley Broadcasting's Allen Shaw said that John "was unusual during the cultural revolution of the late '60s."

RYKER, Malcolm: **KNAC**, 1994-95. Malcolm came to the Southland from "Z-Rock" in Texas. In the summer of 1995, Malcolm joined KNRX-Denver for middays and by 1996 was at XTRA ("91X")-San Diego.

Rick Carroll, Life and Times
by
T. Michael Jordan

(Some have likened working at a radio station to "summer camp." There seems to be a sense of camaraderie during the time working together, however, when one leaves, their paths may never cross again. For some, "summer camp" has led to lasting and deep friendships. One such rich relationship was when Rick Carroll came into T. Michael Jordan's life. Join us for such a radio relationship. -db)

I have been looking for some way to memorialize Rick since his untimely death on July 10th, 1989. After his funeral a few of his friends got together to think of ways to commemorate him. The final decision was to get him a Star on the Hollywood Walk of Fame, Rick had the location of many of the stars memorized.

I called the Hollywood Chamber of Commerce, they told me that either it had to be done prior to a death, or you had to wait 5 years after a persons death. The cost was about $5,000. I put it on my calendar, and annually contacted the friends to remind them. As time passed, so did many of the friends. Some to death, some to relocation and/or career changes, others just "lost."

There is no Star, but when I walk down the Walk of Fame, many memories rush through my mind...

I first became aware of Rick Carroll in May of 1969. He was the evening jock/md at KXOA in Sacramento. I was evenings at KROY-Sacramento. We wouldn't meet until a year later, but we were very aware of each other. I took the on-air position that "Paul was truly dead," playing Beatles records backwards. Rick's position was it was all a hoax. Of course this competitive stance took place throughout the country. Even though the "death promotion" was not a factor I ended up with a 32 Arbitron share, and Rick had an 8. KROY was better promoted, the pd allowed a lot of flexibility and we were an "ensemble" staff. I was also fired 2 days before the ratings came out, not the first time and not the last.

There was a kid named Greg Partsch (eventually Greg Mundy) who wanted to be a jock, and Rick and I were his heroes. He used to hang out at each station and take messages back and forth between Rick and myself. He eventually brought Rick and I together. About 6 months and two stations later, I was in Orlando at WLOF (54 share by the way) and Rick was now pd at KLIV in San Jose.

Rick was born in Redding as Ricky Carroll and grew up in San Jose. He got his first job in radio at KLIV at about 15, answering phones and "go-ferring." His first air shift was back in Redding at KRDG.

Rick was really proud to now be pd at KLIV. After about a month, Greg got Rick and I together on the phone, and he offered me the all-night slot at KLIV. Even though I was having a good time in Orlando, I really missed California, and got to really know and like Rick from our phone calls. I took the job. Rick also hired a guy he had heard in Honolulu, Neale Blase. Greg was answering phones and "go-ferring," Dave Sholin was md and Scott St. James was doing middays. We were an AM'er doing an FM format, ratings were pretty good, but politics were not. Rick was off to KSJO-San Jose as pd and I returned to Sacramento at KCRA.

After the owners of KSJO bought KXOA in Sacramento, they changed the calls to KNDE ("Kandy"). Rick moved to KNDE, hired me for evenings, Neale Blase for mornings and John Peters for afternoons. Greg was still "go-ferring" and did some weekend all-night shifts. Christine Brodie (then Schriefer) was doing promotions and md chores. Larry Groves (later md at KROQ), was an "intern" doing a variety of things. At every station Rick was pd, he had an md, but it was Rick who made the final decision on the music. He always took the md's suggestions in mind, and he had some great md's, but ultimately he decided.

His uncanny ability to "pick the hits," was his greatest asset and contributed most to his success. He liked jocks with a "different sound," and was able to create exciting promotions for little money, but the music was the answer.

After more typical radio "bull shit," Rick landed the job at KKDJ in January 1973, after spending time working for Drake-Chenault Enterprises. U-Haul ran out of trucks in Sacramento as Rick hired all the above mentioned to come work in L.A. We had become a tight "family" in Sacramento, and couldn't wait to be in L.A. together. Russ O'Hara joined the "family" at this time. KKDJ became renowned for its technical sound and coverage. Low power (8k) at the most perfect location on Mt. Wilson, and a processing chain that made it the cleanest and loudest thing on the dial, all thanks to Chief Engineer Paul Wieman. KHJ was still top dog in the market, but we gave them a run for their money, we were their "death-knell" (they were about the last AM king in the country). We never took top spot overall, but by the Jan/Feb 1974 ARB we were the #1 FM in town cuming about 1,000,000 people 12 plus, Monday-Sunday, 6 a.m. to midnight.

At KKDJ we experienced some tragic personal/emotion upheavals within the "family" and in one way or another we remained friends. There was some other great talent at the station contributing to its success: Billy Pearl, Kris Eric Stevens, Jay Stevens, Steve Dahl, Jahni Kaye, and more.

New owners came in and fired most of the staff and changed call letters to KIIS. It took KIIS a couple of years to regain the numbers, and eventually newer owners turned the station into the giant it became.

Rick and I went off to Hawaii for awhile. When we came back I bought a pet shop, and went broke. Rick did some consulting and then landed at gig at KEZY/AM. Several of the "family" had moved on to other things, Chris went to work at Radio & Records, Neale promoted a great idea called "Sheet Music" (bedding with music to the hit songs on it) and Greg went to the David Forrest Agency promoting concerts.

Greg Ogonowski became the newest member of the "family" as Chief Engineer and made that little sucker sound like FM on AM. So it was Rick as pd, Larry Groves md, on-air was Big John Carter, Mark Denis (there forever and great guy), John Peters, Russ O'Hara, Jim O'Neal (another new "family" member), myself and Peter Mayem running the board all-night and Patty Haven on the weekends

We had great fun. The promotions (bicentennial year 1976) sounded great, we had decent ratings, but competing with L.A. signals was next to impossible in Orange County, at least then. We had the usual clashes with management, some personal problems and we were off again. I went back to Sacramento, Rick back to consulting.

In 1979 Rick landed the pd job at KROQ and asked me if I wanted to come back to L.A., being fearful of the reputation of KROQ at the time and declined. After about a year I decided to get out of radio for good and got myself into computers.

Rick went on to great success at KROQ as you all know. I have gone off to success and happiness in cyberland. We remained close friends, and in close contact during the years remaining in his too short of life. Most of the "family" remained in contact in one way or another, several of us still do.

Greg Ogonowski and I had dinner with Rick near his Malibu home about a month before his death. He was, as usual, in great shape and ready to party his ass off! We had a great evening, and planned on getting together again soon. We talked during the following month and everything was great with Rick. A little kitten named TC joined Rick's home. Being a cat lover TC and I became fast friends.

Then came the day! Jahni Kaye called to tell me he had heard that Rick had just died of pneumonia. He went into the hospital on a Thursday and was dead the next Monday. Fortunately he didn't have to suffer long. The "family" was devastated, as were his new friends and family from KROQ. Even though I'm happy with the choice I made in my life, a part of me wishes that I would have been with Rick for his last triumph, but he did share the experiences with me over the final few years.

We had a great "memorial bash" in Malibu, with friends, radio "family" and his blood family. Many kind words were said, some shocking and true, and all with love. After it was over, a couple of us tossed his ashes into the ocean.

TC now lives with me and often brings up many great memories. He loves to party and listen to rock and roll. I finish this with tears in my eyes, and love in my heart.

S

SAAVEDRA, Neil: **KKLA**, 1990-92; **KFI**, 1996-97. Neil hosts a weekend talk show at KFI. He started at the station in 1994 as an intern and left a year later to take a management position with the Kinko's Corporation. Neil was lured back to KFI in 1996 to join the promotion department which eventually led to his weekend shift. Born in Encino, he was  raised in Ventura County. Neil started at KDAR-Ventura with his partner Bob Lownsdale which led to a two-year stint at KKLA.

SABO, Walt: **KHJ**, 1983, pd. Walt is president of Sabo Media, a consulting firm that has worked with major Talk stations for 14 years.

SABOL, Bob: **KUTE**, 1979, gm

SACCACIO, Jeff: **KFI**, 1994-96. Jeff hosted a weekend talk show.

SAHL, Mort: **KLAC**, 1967-68; **KABC**. Mort has done it all. He is a political satirist, comedian and screenwriter. Mort always thought he knew what was ailing America and became the darling of the San Francisco coffeehouse liberal scene in the  1950s. He got his start in San Francisco's hungry i nightspot taking verbal shots at President Eisenhower and attacking the Establishment. He was allegedly let go from KLAC for espousing a conspiracy theory around the Kennedy assassination.

SAINT CLAIRE, Claudine: **KJOI**, 1986-89, nd; **KXEZ**, 1993-96. Claudine also did the news and afternoon drive at KJOI.

SAINTE, Dick: **KRLA**, 1969-71, pd; **KHJ**, 1971-72; **KIIS**, 1972. Born Dick Middleton in McMinnville, Oregon, he started out in his home state and worked at KISN-Portland and WIFE-Omaha and eventually teamed up with Johnnie Darin at KGB-San Diego. His next stop was KFRC-San Francisco in 1968. The Real Don Steele gave Dick his on-air name, and added "e" at the end of his name in 1970 following a suggestion by Dionne Warwick(e). Dick joined KRLA in late 1969 and became pd in 1971, replacing Darin. At the 30-year KRLA reunion, host Casey Kasem said of Dick: "He had an exciting style that can really only be equaled by Dick's long-time friend, The Real Don Steele." Before 1971 ended, Dick became a "Boss Jock" on KHJ. He worked at KEX-Portland in the early 1980s. Since 1993, Dick has been working Country on KFMS-Las Vegas.

"I would like to win Powerball, so I can buy Maui from the Japanese."   -Mike Butts

SAKELLARIDES, Mike: **KGFJ/KUTE**, 1976; **KPOL**, 1976-78; **KZLA**, 1979-82; **KFI/KOST**, 1982-97. Mike was born in the borough of Queens. "I was raised on the world's best pizza and great radio stations like WABC, WMCA and WNEW/FM with their legendary air talent." In 1968 he started his college career at State University of New York at Albany where he joined the campus station and became pd. Eager to start his broadcast career, "I graduated early with honors and a B.A." He worked in Albany-Schenectady-Troy area at WDKC, WTRY, WABY and WPTR. In the fall of 1972 Mike and his wife Barbara emigrated to KQIV-Portland. "I was inspired to move after reading Ken Kesey's *Sometimes a Great Notion*." His pd was Jim LaFawn. "Jim referred to me as 'the Crazy Greek' which caught on with listeners and we stayed friends until Jim's untimely death in Los Angeles." In 1974 he moved to KGW-Portland and flew a Cessna doing traffic reports. Mike became Mike Steele when he joined KGFJ/KUTE. "We left the wet Pacific Northwest because we felt the need to dry out, literally!" Within a year of arriving in the Southland he joined KPOL as production director and in 1977 won the prestigious Golden Mike Award for Public Affairs. At KPOL he produced the music library for the new "Rocking You Softly" format which debuted November 22, 1976. He became midday host and  voicetracked the automated late night show called "The Greek's All Night Diner." In 1978 KPOL became KZLA. "Thanks to md Rollye Bornstein, I had Murray the K as my special guest co-host one evening. How many nights had I listened to this man with my pocket radio hidden under the pillow? Not long after that show he died of cancer." Mike stayed with KZLA during its switch to Country music in the fall of 1980. On November 15, 1982, he joined middays at KOST and has been their one and only midday host for 15 years. In 1987 *Billboard* nominated Mike as "Best Major Market Air Talent." He has been the Grand Marshal of the City of Glendale's "Days of Verdugos" parade and has appeared annually in the East L.A. Mexican Independence Parade, the Chinese New Year Parade, the Montrose Christmas Parade and the world-famous Hollywood Christmas Parade.

SALA, Bob: **KPPC**, 1969-73; **KROQ**, 1978. John Detz, the pioneering AOR gm in Detroit and KWST, brought Bob to Santa Rosa, where he stayed. (Detz eventually bought five stations in Hawaii after open heart surgery.)

SALAMON, Ed: **KGBS/KTNQ**, 1978. While national

pd for Storer Radio, Ed had a short, but eventful tenure as interim gm of KTNQ/KGBS. When he left the Southland he returned to program WHN-New York. In 1981 Ed formed the original United Stations with Dick Clark. After the company merged with Transtar, Ed returned to L.A. and replaced its chairman to run Unistar's 24-hour satellite delivered formats. Unistar has now been absorbed into Westwood One and Ed serves as president/formats.

SALAZAR, Liz: **KWST**, 1978-82. Born in Boyle Heights in 1961, Liz broke into radio in 1978. While growing up in El Sereno she was inspired by KHJ's "Boss" jocks of the '60s, in particular The Real Don Steele, as well as by the jocks at KKDJ like Rich "Brother" Robbin. She earned her FCC 1st Phone. Hardly age 17, Liz started at KWST. Within a year she was public affairs director. In 1980, she added a weekend jock shift to her public affairs duties. When "K-West" went CHR in June 1981 she moved to overnights. In 1982 she worked at Metro Traffic and later that year married Bobby Ocean and moved to the Bay Area. She and her husband operate their own radio production studio in San Rafael. "I loved every minute of it. I accomplished it all before I was 20 *without* succumbing to the 'casting couch' or baring all to a girlie magazine."

SALAZAR, Ricardo: **KTNQ**, 1989-91, pd. Ricardo started his broadcast career in his home country of Mexico at age 16. He worked in Guadalajara, Monterrey and Mexico City before joining KXEW/KXMG-Tucson in 1984. He went on to program KRIA-San Antonio and in 1989 arrived at the Spanish station KTNQ. He also spent time at KVAR-Riverside. Ricardo was born in Sonora, Mexico and is now one of the leading Spanish radio consultants. How did he become a consultant? Ricardo laughed: "When you are totally unhirable, you call yourself a consultant. I've been doing pretty good." He is currently pd of Spanish KXBS-Oxnard.

SALGO, Jeff: **KRHM**; **KBIG**, 1970; **KLAC**, 1970; **KKDJ**, 1971-72; **KWST/KMGG**, 1982-84, pd; **KEZY**, 1985-89, pd. Born in 1951, the Los Angeles native went south to KBZT-San Diego in 1972 and returned a decade later as pd of KWST. In 1975 in between L.A. assignments he programmed "KU16" and "OK 102½" in Seattle. In 1982 he changed KWST to KMGG. Jeff described his new format at "Magic 106" as "KIIS with more kick." After his experience with "Magic 106," he bought KIVR-Cave Junction, Oregon, and went on to run KCMJ-Palm Springs. By 1989, Jeff had become vp of Anaheim Broadcasting. In 1990, Jeff joined KUFO-Portland as vp/gm. In the summer of 1994 he left a gm spot with KHTX-Riverside to run sister station KRQC/KDON-Monterey. By the end of 1995, he became vp/gm of KCTC/KYMX-Sacramento. He also continued to be responsible for the programming at the 16-station Henry Radio chain.

SALINAS, Josefa: **KPWR**, 1994-97

SALINAS, Salvador: **KALI**, 1965

SALVATORE, Jack: **KNX**, 1984-97. Jack is the late evening news anchor on "KNXNewsradio." Every week Jack broadcasts "KNX Citizen of the Week." The program salutes those who make selfless contributions to others and their communities. Jack worked in Louisiana and at WCKY-Cincinnati before arriving at KNX. He is a native of New Jersey and graduated from St. Vincent College in Latrobe, Pennsylvania with an English major. At age 7 Jack appeared on Broadway in *Damn Yankees*.

SAMUELS, Ron: SEE Johnny Soul

SANCHEZ, Elizabeth: **KFI**, 1992-93. Elizabeth was a news reporter on KFI.

SANCHEZ, Ernie: **KIQQ**, 1982-84. Ernie joined KIQQ fresh out of broadcast school.

SANCHEZ, Ramauldo: **KWIZ**, 1995-97. Ramauldo hosts the evening shift on the Orange County Spanish-language station.

SANCHEZ and **WALKER**: **KFI**, 1997. When asked by

callers to Talk KFI how they are, they respond, "We're bitchin.'" Maria Sanchez (l) and Glynnis Walker host a weekend talk show. Maria, mother of four children, started out as a producer for Mark and Kim on sister station KOST. She went on to host a public affairs show. Glynnis started her radio career at CKLS, "Canada's version of *WKRP*." She has been on five book tours.

SANCHO, Willie: **KKHR**, 1983; **KGFJ**, 1984. Willie worked all-nights at KKHR and one night didn't show. "He just disappeared," one of his fellow jocks remembered. "Three days later he called from Texas saying his wife was homesick and wanted to go home. Willie asked the pd if he was mad and was there still a job for him." They didn't.

SANDER, Dean: **KLAC**, 1961-97. Dean started his radio career in Liberty, Iowa. He was a veteran newsman at KLAC and survived 15 gms in 32 years through Talk, MOR and Country formats.

Jimmie Fidler was the most controversial of the Hollywood broadcasters earned at his peak in 1950 $250,000 a year. His gossip show was heard by 40 million people a week. He died in 1988 at 89.

SANDERS, Arlen: **KXLA/KRLA**, 1956-63; **KEZY**, 1964-65; **KIEV**, 1967; **KFOX**, 1972-77. Arlen was one of the "11-10 Men" during the Rock heyday of KRLA. Born in Roxburg, Oregon he grew up in Texas. Arlen worked in a number of markets prior to Southern California including Klamath Falls.  He joined KXLA in 1956 as an engineer and moved on-air when the station changed call letters to KRLA. During the eighties Arlen became a stage actor and consulted WWVA-Wheeling as well as stations in Oklahoma and Cincinnati. Arlen died of a stroke in 1994. He was 64.

SANDERS, Laurie: **KOST**, 1985-91; **KXEZ**, 1991-92. Laurie arrived in the Southland from Chicago radio. She replaced Liz Kiley on the very successful evening program "Love Songs on the KOST," and achieved enormous evening ratings. Laurie went to KOIT-San Francisco, where she hosts a similar "Love Song"-themed program.

SANDERS, Tommy: **KYSR**, 1996-97. Tommy arrived in the Southland from KFMA-Tucson where he was known as Ted Stryker. Born Gary Sandorf, he grew up in Los Angeles and in 1989 he graduated from Palisades High School.  While attending the University of Arizona his first radio job was at KJYK-Tucson where he did nights and eventually mornings as "The Sandman." His next Tucson job was at KKND as Ted Stryker and after graduation in 1994 joined KFMA.

> Art Laboe's compilation album, *Oldies But Goodies, Volume One*, stayed on *Billboard*'s Top 100 for a mind-boggling 183 weeks

SANDLER, Nicole: **KLSX**, 1987; **KNX/FM**, 1988; **KODJ**, 1988-90; **KLOS**, 1990-94; **KSCA**, 1994-97. Born on November 4, 1959, in New York, Nicole spent her teen years in Hollywood, Florida and attended the University of South Florida in Tampa. Her radio career began there at WUSF, WMNF, and WNSI. A year after graduation she moved back  to New York and spent the next three years at WMCA producing the highly controversial "Bob Grant Show" while simultaneously holding weekend airshifts at AOR WRCN-Long Island. She then moved to WPLJ to work with Jim Kerr and the Morning Crew. After two years she moved West. Her nine years in the Southland began in 1987 at KLSX as the morning show producer. She then moved on to KNX/FM as morning co-host and joined KLOS in the summer of 1990 to produce the "Mark and Brian Show." She left exactly four years later to be part of the start of AAA KSCA as midday personality. In April 1995 Nicole was reunited with Chuck Moshontz to co-host mornings. (Chuck was newsman for Mark and Brian while Nicole was at KLOS.) In the fall of 1996 she was promoted to music director and moved back to middays. When KSCA changed ownership, Nicole took a job as music director at *The Album Network*, a national trade publication.

SANDS, Steve: **KEZY**, 1971 and 1974-76; **KGBS**, 1971; **KROQ**, 1972; **KIIS**, 1973; **KGBS**, 1973; **KKDJ**, 1973; **KWIZ**, 1977; **XTRA**, 1983. Steve was born Stephen Sandoz in Ventura in 1947 and grew up in the area. He started hanging out at KVEN-Ventura at age 10 and found himself on the air from time to time. During his high school years, he went as a missionary to Haiti, where he helped set up a Christian station. He worked at KACY-Oxnard before entering the Army in the summer of 1967. Before his release he had been made staff sergeant E-6 and received four medals, among them the Army commendation medal. While in Vietnam he served with the psychological operations unit. He was involved in Armed Forces Radio. After the military Steve went to WSB-Atlanta before joining KEZY. In 1978, he went to KEZL-San Diego and eventually transferred to the Bonneville station in Milwaukee. In the early 1980s, Steve went to Chicago, working for a number of stations until his death in 1992. Steve's wife Cathy talked about the day he died: "He called me from the station to say he wasn't feeling well and probably wouldn't mow the lawn when he got home. I came home, and he had had a massive heart attack and was on the couch dead." Cathy remembered Steve: "He was an immensely talented man who always supported his fellow broadcasters. It was his passion at an early age. I always envied him for knowing what he wanted to do since he was 10. One of his big thrills was when his father took him to see Bob Crane do his show at KNX. Steve thought it was great that he had a drum set in the studio. He also had a passion for trains and his biggest thrill was when they allowed him to drive the train all the way from Chicago into St. Charles."

SANNES, Cherie: **KHJ**; **KRTH**, 1979-82; **KMGG**, 1982-83. Cherie was a registered nurse in the Bay Area and got on KMBY-Monterey by a fluke: she became their "token woman" on-air while she was holding down her nursing job. "It was a sought-after gig, and I'm sure it may have offended some people that I got the job with very little experience in the business. I took a chance and it paid off." Born in 1946, she told *Broadcasting* magazine, "I wanted to be a doctor and did what every middle class girl does, and that is become a registered nurse." When there was an opening at KFMB ("B-100")-San Diego, she auditioned on the air. "B-100" pd Bobby Rich remembered, "Cherie flew down from Monterey, and we drove around town for a couple of hours chatting. I really thought she had potential, so although she had no audition tape, I put her on the air for a live try-out. She did so well that the next morning on the way to the airport I offered her the job!" In 1983 she hosted a 90-second syndicated feature called "California Way of Life" on the California Radio Network and worked briefly for the L.A. Traffic Network. Cherie is currently a pr rep for a chain of hospitals in Northern California.

SANTANA, John: **KFAC**, 1984-89; **KKGO**, 1989-97, pd. John was the morning man on Classical KFAC in the mid-1980s. In the spring of 1996, John became pd of KKGO. He owns his own computer consulting company.

SANTIAGO, Richard: **KKHJ**, 1991-92; **KLVE**, 1992-97, nd. Richard is part of the very successful morning drive show "Barreto in the Morning." He is from Puerto Rico where he worked at WFID. Richard went to work for CRC, the Heftel Spanish operation in Hollywood.

SANTOS, Jose: **KKHJ**; **KLAX/KXMG**, 1996-97. Jose was the director of programming for Heftel Texas which he left in late 1995. He went to program KEYA-Houston and has returned to Los Angeles where he is operations manager of KLAX/KXMG.

SANTOYO, Oscar: **KOCM/KSRF**, 1991-92; **KWIZ**, 1987-92. In 1992, Oscar left the Southland for WEZW-Milwaukee and returned to Orange County in 1993. He's now out of radio and serving a four-year term on the board of the Newport-Mesa Unified School District. He's also involved in "Save Our Youth," a gang-intervention program in Costa Mesa.

| 94.7FM | KSUN | 1950 |

SARGENT, Kenny: **KQLZ**, 1991-93; **KLOS**, 1994-97. In 1996 the popular Los Angeles broadcaster was recruited from KLOS for entertainment reporter at KCOP/UPN-13. He remained at KLOS until late summer of 1996, then departed to dedicate full-time to his expanding UPN-13 Pop World segment that includes the youth-political beat as well as fill-in sports.

Originally hailing from Dallas, he first rose to fame as an all-state football kicker, turning down then-OSU coach Jimmy Johnson to attend broadcast-oriented Sam Houston State on an NCAA soccer scholarship. Upon graduation the "Sarge" joined KTXQ-Dallas and contributed to FOX/TV's entertainment programs. He demonstrated his promotional and sports versatility performing long-distance place kicking at KQLZ sponsored half-time shows at L.A. Rams games. After "Pirate Radio" sank, Kenny starred in the Coca-Cola-sponsored AX-WAVE tv music/interview program reaching over 20 million viewers on the Nippon TV Network in Japan. He remains AX-WAVE's U.S. correspondent. A social consciousness pervades all Kenny's endeavors. He has been an active participant in the Big Brothers program for six years. Kenny lives in the San Fernando Valley with the two surviving of three fat cats he rescued from the pound.

SARTORI, Maxanne: **KLIT**, 1994. Maxanne started her radio career in 1969 at progressive KLFM-Seattle. A year later she crossed the country to WBCN-Boston and stayed with 'BCN until 1977 when she joined Jazz outlet WRVR-New York. In 1983, Maxanne went to program WBOS-Boston and the following year joined WNEW as md and dj until 1987. Following her stint on the East Coast, Maxanne worked Seattle and Monterey radio stations. She currently lives in New York and is in the record business.

SAUNDERS, Art: **KZLA**, 1983. Art worked weekends before going to sister station WBAP-Ft. Worth to be assistant pd.

SAVAGE, Don: **KACE**, 1979-83; **KNAC**, 1984-85. Don is programming for AEI, the largest provider of in-flight music for over 30 airlines.

SAVAN, Mark: **KFWB**, 1968-80. Mark was part of the launch of KFWB's all-News format on March 11, 1968. Hired as a writer, he was quickly promoted to editor and then news supervisor. After an AFTRA strike against the station, Mark went on the air and stayed there, first as a general assignment reporter and then as a feature reporter, anchorman and investigative reporter. During most of his tenure at KFWB, Mark was also responsible for producing all the station's promotional announcements and for three years actually functioned in a dual capacity, with a morning drive shift on the air and the rest of the day heading up the station's three-person promotional department. In 1980, Mark was hired away from KFWB by KVI-Seattle to host a midday talk show. In 1983 he retired from radio. For the last several years, he's been working as executive vp of The Chuck Blore Company, creating radio and tv commercials, infomercials and consulting tv stations on promotion. He works just a few short blocks from KFWB, for many years home to Mark and Chuck Blore.

SAXON, Mike: **KRHM**, 1965-68

SCARBOROUGH, Ed: **KKHR**, 1983-86, pd. Ed started in radio while in college in 1970. He grew up in Hartford, and much of his early radio experience was in the Northeast at stations including WDRC-Hartford and WBZ-Boston. He moved into programming in 1979 at the CBS/FM station in St. Louis, KHTR. This led to his programming assignment at KKHR. When asked to reflect on his Los Angeles radio experience, Ed said, "The memories get fonder with time. We had a tough time up against KIIS at their very strongest. We went to war with rubber bullets." After he left Southern California, he spent five years at KLTR-Houston. He is currently the programming head of WMXJ-Miami.

SCARRY, Rick: **KEZY**, 1968-72; **KKDJ**, 1972-73; **KDAY**, 1973-74; **KGIL**, 1974-79, pd; **KMET**, 1979-81; **KRTH**, 1982-83; **KHJ**, 1984-85, pd; **KMET**, 1986-87; **KMPC/FM/KEDG**, 1988; **KLIT**, 1989-91. Rick grew

up in Delaware, Ohio, and while in high school he was a "go-fer" for Dave Hull, the Hullabalooer at WTVN-Columbus. Rick got his first job in 1963 at WDLR-Delaware. "I did everything including maintenance when the transmitter was off on Sunday nights." His passion for radio and acting "co-mingled"

sometime around high school. His Army career included stops in Frankfurt, Germany, and Ft. Lewis in Olympia, Washington. "The station was actually on a wharf, and I had to use another name so the Army wouldn't know. It was in Olympia that the acting bug bit when I was an extra in an Elvis movie filming nearby." After he was discharged, he headed for Ventura to "explore the acting action" and worked at KUDU as pd and p.m. drive. During his time on KUDU, he would drive to Hollywood three nights a week to take acting lessons. At KDAY he followed Wolfman Jack and eventually worked morning drive until the entire staff was fired when the station changed formats. In 1978, Rick acquired part ownership of KRLT-South Lake Tahoe. As part of his stay with RKO, he became pd of KHJ's experiment with "Car Radio." Rick explained, "It was every kid's dream to work at KHJ. AM radio in the 1980s was tough. You've got to have a reason for people to listen. Just having a great format wasn't good enough anymore. Every 10 minutes around the clock, we'd have a traffic report. If nothing was happening, we'd say that. Everyone scoffed at the idea but the irony is that it has become the mainstay for KNX and KFWB today." He did mornings at KMET during his second visit to "the Mighty Met." Rick and "Paraquat" Kelley were the last voices heard when "the Mighty Met" went dark on February 6, 1987. Rick commented on the KMET mass firings that became known as Black Friday in L.A. radio lore. He recalled being called to the Sheraton Premiere Hotel: "I'd been fired by the best. But I'd rather have someone say, 'Get out of here' than to walk into a room and have the gm say, 'The cancer was too deep. We just had to cut it out.'" He worked at Transtar briefly and then went to KMPC/FM. When his run at the Gene Autry station ended, he sold his first screenplay, *Fear*, which starred Kay Lenz. He admitted that he "never enjoyed radio during the last few years. All the fun had disappeared." Rick has concentrated on acting and writing in recent years. His acting credits now include *L.A. Law, Murphy Brown, Ellen, Murder, She Wrote* and *Star Trek - The Next Generation*. Two of his screenplays have been optioned, and his voiceover career is going at full steam; he voiced the 1994 Mazda campaign.

SCHAEFER, Mike: **KIIS**, 1982-86. A theater student at the University of Missouri, Mike worked in Jefferson City in 1976. In 1979, he was doing promotion in St. Louis at Elektra/Asylum Records, which led him to a small station in St. Louis in 1980 and later to Chicago. Mike landed in Southern California at KIIS as the md. When he arrived at KIIS, it was an "old disco station" that had a six share by the end of the year. Mike was elevated to acting pd in 1984. Upon his promotion he acknowledged that KHJ was the station of the '60s, KMET of the '70s, and his task would be to make KIIS the station of the '80s. "Radio has educated this town; they are very aware of it." He stopped briefly at Virgin Records for a promotion job, then became pd of KMAI-Honolulu in 1987. In 1988, Mike was pd of KHTY-Santa Barbara. He most recently was an account executive at *R&R* until late 1994. In 1995, according to *R&R*, Mike left Network 40 after 120 hours.

SCHELL, Russ: **KFOX**, 1979-81, pd. Russ was born in Pennsylvania and raised in Philadelphia where he listened to such legends as Dr. Don, George Michael, Hy Lit and Jerry Blavat. He was bitten by the radio "bug" while living in Europe listening to pirate radio stations Radio Caroline, Radio Veronica and Radio Luxenborg. In 1976 he graduated from Penn State with a B.A. in speech/communications. "I remember how frustrating it all was at KFOX/FM, but we have some fond memories of the place. It was a small station located on the second floor of a building at the foot of Pacific Coast Highway in Redondo Beach. We were understaffed but tremendously committed to making our little 3,000-watt station sound every bit as good as the big guys, and I worked with some wonderfully talented people." During his brief stay he had a number of personalities work for him - Kenny Noble, Sharon Dale, Lord Timothy Hudson and Rhonda Kramer (who went on to form the LA Traffic Network with her husband). When Russ left Los Angeles, he went on to WKJN-Baton Rouge, WFMS-Indianapolis, gm of WGH-Norfolk and pd of WYAY-Atlanta. In 1993 he became a consultant to 17 Country, AC and Oldies stations for Lund Consultants while continuing as operations manager for WKKX/WKBQ//KRAM-St. Louis. Russ lists career highlights as helping to design and develop Susquehanna's Information Exchange system on CompuServe. He also hosted "American Country Countdown" worldwide for ABC in 1988. He produced a country music concert series annually in Indianapolis which has attracted more than a quarter of a million fans. Russ lives in Nashville where he is vp of The Interstate Radio Network and The Road Gang Coast-to-Coast Network with his wife Marsha and two children, Ryan and Allison.

SCHLESSINGER, Dr. Laura: **KWIZ**, 1976-79; **KMPC**, 1980-81; **KABC**; **KWNK**, 1989; **KFI**, 1991-97. The enormously successful syndicated Talk show

host, got her start working with a number of local radio stations. A native of Brooklyn, born in 1948, Laura has many degrees including a black belt in the martial arts. She got the bug for radio following a call to the Bill Ballance Show in the 1970s. She worked at the Sun Radio Network before arriving at her current assignment at KFI. Laura is a state-licensed psychotherapist and family counselor. She has Ph.d in physiology and says she is not a therapist. Laura told Gary Lycan of the *OC Register* that she preaches, teaches and nags. She wrote *Ten Stupid Things Women Do To Mess Up Their Lives*. She has appeared in *Star Trek The Next Generation*. Laura's show is syndicated on over 400 stations in the United States and Canada. Her current book is *How Could You Do That?* In the fall of 1996 she assumed control of SBI Broadcasting, the program supplier that distributes her talk program. For her 50th birthday in early 1997, a '50s dance party was staged for charity.

SCHNABEL, Tom: **KCRW**, 1979-97. The longtime host of "Morning Becomes Eclectic" left the station in 1990 to work for A&M Records and returned a year later to host the weekend eclectic music show, "Cafe L.A."

SCHOCK, Bryan: **KNAC**, 1990-91 and 1993-95, pd. "The first impact that radio had on me was listening to KCBQ-San Diego in the late 1960s. We could also hear

KMET in San Diego and it sounded like a family." Bryan was born in Chicago and grew up in Las Vegas and San Diego. While attending San Diego State he was the first overnight jock at "91X" when the station went "Modern Rock" in 1983. He quit school because it became "too much" and pursued radio full-time. Bryan's radio journey took him to WHVY-Baltimore, WLZR-Milwaukee and KGB/XTRA-San Diego before arriving in Southern California. In the spring of 1995, KYBG-Denver switched from Talk to Rock KNRX ("92X") and Bryan programmed the change. In the spring of 1996 he was named om for Jones Satellite Networks' Rock Alternative format. A year later he returned to "91X" as pd. "I programmed against Jacor Broadcasting and it was very tough. I'm very happy to be programming a Jacor station."

SCHOFIELD, Dick: **KFOX**, 1965, gm

SCHOLL, Michael: **KSRF**, 1990

SCHORR, Arnold J.: **KHJ**, 1961-64, pd; **KGFJ**, 1964-79, vp/gm; **KUTE**, 1973-79, vp/gm. The longtime general manager of KGFJ was born in Philadelphia and followed his father, who was in radio sales, to many markets. As a teen Arnie worked at WFEC-Miami in 1950 and during the next decade programmed WRVM-Rochester, WBNY-Buffalo ("I hired Casey Kasem") and WBZ-Boston. Some of his fondest memories are from his time in Southern California. He created a MOR-personality format in the early '60s on KHJ. When Tracy Broadcasting acquired KUTE, Arnie brought the Disco-format to the Southland. "We were very successful for about 18 months to two years." When he left L.A. he bought WOKB-Orlando which he owned for eight years. Arnie now lives in Orlando and consults radio stations while in semi-retirement. His daughter works for an ad agency in Orlando.

SCHRACK, Don: **KNX**, 1969-72; **KFWB**, 1974-79, nd. Don was part of the embryonic decade of all-News KFWB and became nd in 1975. A third generation native of the Fresno County community of Selma, he majored in journalism at UCLA. After graduate work at New Mexico Highland University, he started his radio career in 1966 at KOAD-Lemoore. For the next three years he broadcast news at KBCH-Lincoln City, Oregon, KSLM-Salem and KEX-Portland. Don has been in general management and/or station ownership since leaving Los Angeles. He is based in Yakima.

SCHREIBER, Art: **KFWB**, 1969-77, gm. Art is credited by many who worked with him of tightening the all-News format at KFWB. "When I was a news director I always had a good rapport with program directors with whom I worked. They had a great sense of production and good editing skills. One of the best was Ken Draper. We worked together at KYW-Cleveland and WCFL-Chicago. I hired Ken to be executive editor at KFWB." The Westinghouse Broadcasting Company's director of research, Jim Yergin, discovered the average time a person listened to all-News radio was twenty minutes. Bob Kline of a local ad agency came up with the slogan, "Give us 22 minutes and we'll give you the world." Ken changed the 30-minute news cycle to 20 minutes. "Ken and I pushed the 20-minute cycles with A, B and C stories. The A stories ran three times each hour, the B's twice and the C's just once an hour." Art is a native of Ohio and grew up on a farm near East Liverpool. He attended a one room school. "I went through eight grades in one room, not one grade for eight years!" He received a B.A. from Westminster College majoring in bible, philosophy and psychology. "The major advisor told me to get out of the speech department and get into something you can make a living at." Consequently, he took the triple major. Art worked for Westinghouse for 17 years, joining Group W at KYW in 1960. Before reaching KFWB he was assistant gm at KYW-Philadelphia and before that headed the Group W national foreign news services as Bureau Chief in Washington, DC. In 1977 he became president of "Commuter Computer," the regional ride-sharing organization in Southern California which he founded in 1972. Art left L.A. for Hubbard Broadcasting's KSTP-Minneapolis and two years later Hubbard sent him to Albuquerque to manage KOB AM&FM which he did until 1990. He lost the sight of one eye in 1969 and went blind in 1982. After 16 eye surgeries he has some sight. He credits the National Federation of the Blind with "turning my life around. I have good mobility skills with my white cane and good independent living skills." Art ran for mayor of Albuquerque in 1993. "My three friends didn't vote often enough!" He served as Director of the New Mexico Commission for the Blind for two years and is now president of Schreiber Enterprises, a consulting company.

SCHREIBER, Carson: **KBBQ**, 1965-71; **KLAC**, 1971-76, md. Carson has been with RCA Records for 18 years, most recently in Denver. In 1994, he joined Mike Curb's record label, Curb AG.

SCROEDER, Ric: **KFWB**, 1988-97. Ric is a longtime street reporter and assignment editor for all-News KFWB. Born and raised in Milwaukee, Ric graduated from the University of Wisconsin with a business degree. He began his news broadcast career in his hometown at WRIT, WBCF and WOKY. Ric arrived in the Southland in 1984.

SCHRUTT, Norm: **KZLA**, 1980-81, gm. Norm was a 33-year veteran of ABC radio. He had been a Buffalo car salesman when he joined WKBW-Buffalo as a time salesman. He became 'KB's gm in 1977 and joined KZLA in 1980. In 1981 he joined WKHX/WYAY-Atlanta as gm and stayed until his retirement in the fall of 1996.

SCHUBERT, Bill: **KBIQ/KBIG**, 1961-65; **KPOL**, 1961-65; **KKAR**, 1965-68; **KFWB**, 1968-90. Bill was part of the launch of all-News KFWB and stayed for 22 years. He covered the assassination of Robert Kennedy, the 1971 Sylmar earthquake and election year campaigns of Richard Nixon and Jesse Unruh. Bill is a native Angeleno born August 31, 1926. He grew up in Alhambra and attended Pasadena City College and St. Lawrence University in Canton, New York. In 1949 he started his radio career at WSLB-Ogdensburg, New York. Bill returned to L.A. in 1951 and worked as public

relations director for the Southern California Edison Company. He returned to radio in 1958 at KDWC-West Covina and KDWD-San Diego. Bill took an early buy-out from Westinghouse and retired in 1990 and lives in Covina. He secured a real estate license but became the primary caretaker for his ailing wife.

SCHULMAN, Heidi: **KFWB**. Heidi was one of the early voices on all-News KFWB. She is now living in the Washington, DC area. Heidi is married to the politician who took over Ron Brown's job after he was killed in an airplane crash.

SCHULTZ, Edwin: **KXLA/KRLA**, 1959, gm. Edwin was from the Midwest and orchestrated the move from KXLA to KRLA. He left a few months after the launch of the "11-10 Men" programming following a fiasco involving a Perry Allen promotion.

SCHUMACHER, Max: **KMPC**. Capt. Max was killed when two helicopters collided over Dodger Stadium on August 30, 1966. His successor, Jim Hicklin, was slain in his stateroom aboard the cruise ship Princess Italia moments before the ship was to sail on a vacation trip to Mexico on April 2, 1973.

SCHUON, Andy: **KROQ**, 1989-92, pd. In 1989, Andy left the "Rock of Denver" to join KROQ. Andy was 25 years old when he arrived and his gm described him as a "radio fanatic, someone who'll help give the station a strong sense of on-air production." Andy is credited with teaming Kevin & Bean for morning drive. The pair had never worked together but had been friends since meeting at KZZP-Phoenix. Andy also worked at KISS-San Antonio, KAZY-Denver, KISW-Seattle and KOZZ-Reno. In 1993, he became sr vp at MTV, and in the spring of 1994 he became senior vp/music and programming for both MTV and VH-1.

SCHWARTZ, Edward "Buz": **KMNY**. Buz was the founder of "Money Radio" on April 1, 1987.

SCHWARTZ, Rick: **KMPC**, 1994. Rick was one of the UCLA sports broadcasters in 1994.

SCHWARTZ, Roy: **KGBS**, 1970, gm. Roy arrived in the Southland from an East Coast Storer Broadcasting station.

SCHWEINSBURG, Mike: **KROQ**, 1976-78. When KROQ resumed broadcasting in 1976 after a two-year hiatus, Mike joined the station.

SCOT, Charlotte: **KGBS**, 1975. Charlotte grew up in Maine.

SCOTT, Al: **KNOB**, 1965; **KGFJ**, 1965-66; **XERB**, 1968. Al worked the all-night shift at KGFJ.

SCOTT, Bill: **KROQ**, 1984-85; **KNAC**, 1985-86 and 1988-89.  "Wild Bill" Scott grew up in Los Angeles and San Francisco and went to high school in Lake Tahoe. His early radio influences were the early days of KFWB and KRLA. His first radio gig was in Truckee, near Lake Tahoe in 1961. In 1965 he spent a year at the Don Martin School of Broadcasting. His radio journey includes stations in Bakersfield and Reno, KUDL-Kansas City, KDKB and KUPD-Phoenix and WMYQ-Miami. At KMEL-San Francisco he was the first morning jock when the station became AOR. In Detroit he worked for WABX, WWWW and WLLZ. The Chicago stations included WLUP and WMET, WKLS ("96 Rock")-Atlanta and Houston followed. He worked nine to midnight at "the Roq." He left the Southland to help establish the Z-Rock Satellite in Dallas. In the 1990s, he jocked in San Francisco at KFOG, KSFO and KYA and KFRC. He currently hosts the "Dynamite Shack" on KDIA-San Francisco and is making plans to syndicate the show. His wife works middays at KRQR-San Francisco.

SCOTT, Bob: **KNX**, 1975-78 and 1984-97. Bob is an anchor/reporter on "KNXNewsradio" specializing in science and medicine. He has had two careers at KNX. He left KNX in 1978 "to give tv a shot" working in Fargo and Syracuse. In 1983 Bob was an anchor for CNN's Headline News. "Things were rustic and frustrating in the early days of CNN so I decided to return to KNX." Bob earned an A.A. in photography from Moorpark College and a B.A. in journalism from Seton Hall University in New Jersey. Beginning in 1965 he worked for the *Newark Evening News* and then WNAC-AM&TV, Boston. From 1968 to 1975 while working at ABC Network News, Bob taught at Moorpark College and Cal State University Northridge.

SCOTT, Dred: **KSCA**, 1996; **KLSX**, 1997

SCOTT, Ivan: **KABC**, 1971-72. Ivan arrived at KABC to replace Hilly Rose and ran into a buzz saw. He incurred the wrath of the John Birch-ers and openly criticized sponsors. In an *LA Times* interview he lambasted management. He got out of radio and returned to Washington, DC as the tv-radio director for the government's Environmental Protective Agency.

SCOTT, Jeff: **KIBB**, 1996-97. Jeff works all-nights at the Rhythm AC station.

SCOTT, Larry: **KBBQ**, 1967-68 and 1971; **KLAC**, 1971-82. Born in Modesto in 1938, Larry spent most of his childhood in southwest Missouri. His first radio job was in Neosho, Missouri for 75 cents an hour. He became the unofficial spokesman for those fans who decried the "modern" trend in country music. "I show the fans that I am still loyal to a sound they can relate to by the records I play." Larry's love affair with country music started while at Southwest Missouri State College. He became a friend of Chet Atkins while working at WAGG-Franklin, Tennessee in 1958. Before moving to Southern California, he worked at WIL-St. Louis and, beginning in 1961, spent four years at KUZZ-Bakersfield, where he befriended Buck Owens and Merle Haggard. He promoted records for a while, then became pd at KVEG-Las Vegas. In 1966 he worked at KBOX and KRLD-Dallas/Ft. Worth. A year later, his general manager moved to Los Angeles and Larry followed on June 17, 1967. In 1968, *Billboard* listed Larry the 2nd most popular country dj. The CMA voted him #1 DJ of the Year four times between 1968 and 1974. In 1971, Larry returned to KBBQ after a stint as pd in St. Louis. In 1973, he was working at KLAC and won his second consecutive DJ of the Year award from the CMA. Larry created the "Phantom 5-70 Club" for truckers only, and it boasted 8,000 members in 1975. Larry left KLAC in 1982 to host the "Interstate Radio Show" out of Shreveport. He was last heard on KEEL-Shreveport.

SCOTT, Morton: **KLAC**, 1965-67. Morton was the stockbroker who broadcast business news at KLAC. A veteran of motion pictures and tv, he has been the only stockbroker to be nominated for two motion picture Oscars. A graduate of Stanford University, he became a film studio local arranger and later president of Republic Pictures Television.

SCOTT, Rick: **KRTH/KHJ**, 1985-86. Born in 1960, he was let go when KHJ/FM became KRTH. "It's the end of an era, man. Half of L.A. grew up with `Boss Radio.'"

SCOTT, Robertson: **KPOL**, 1952-71, pd. Bob joined KPOL before the station went on the air in the summer of 1952 and programmed the station until 1971. Born in Birmingham on May 8, 1922, he considers Frankfort, Kentucky home. Bob spent three years in World War II piloting a B-24 bomber and flying 30 missions over Germany and occupied Europe. He graduated from the University of Kentucky in 1947. In 1971, with partners, Bob bought KDB AM&FM-Santa Barbara. In 1991 the partners took the AM (Spanish) and Bob kept the Classical music FM. "Although I'm not yet retired, my son, Roby, manages the business and does all the hard work. I do programming Mozart, Beethoven, Schubert and Brahms. KDB is a <u>great</u> radio station."

SCOTT, Steve: **KHTZ**, 1980-85, pd; **KRTH**, 1985-90. Born Steve Christiaens, he grew up in Helena, Montana and started his radio career in Deer Lodge, Montana. Steve went on to Albuquerque and programmed KLIF-Dallas before arriving in the Southland. Beginning in 1984 Steve was pd of "K-Hits" and he worked afternoon drive all five years at KRTH. Steve left the Southland to program a "classic rock" station in Santa Fe. "I left radio in 1995 and am training horses. I am building an Earthship (a tire house), about 45 miles Southeast of Santa Fe.

SCOTTY, Scorchin': SEE Scotty Wilson

SCULLY, Vin: **KFI**, 1959-72; **KABC**, 1972-97. Vinny is one of the most recognizable personalities in sports broadcasting. He has been the voice of the Dodgers since 1949, the longest consecutive service of any current major league broadcaster for one team. He began his broadcasting career at Fordham University announcing all school games over the campus radio station. For two seasons he was a Fordham outfielder. Just a year after graduating from college, Vinny joined the Dodger broadcasting team. He merged with Hall of Fame announcer Red Barber and Connie Desmond. In addition to his work on Dodger baseball, he announces the World Series for the CBS Radio Network and has worked for NBC covering baseball and golf. He considers his inclusion in the broadcast wing of the Baseball Hall of Fame, as the crowning accomplishment. In late 1994, Vin was inducted into the American Sportscasters Hall of Fame. Barber gave Vinny a piece of winning advice: "There's one thing you can bring to the booth that no one else can and that is yourself." Vinny is married to Sandi and they have three sons. Syndicated columnist Jim Murray paid tribute to Vinny: "Nobody understands baseball the way Vin Scully does. Scully is the world's best at filling the dull times by spinning anecdotes of the 100-year lore of the game. He can make baseball seem like Camelot and not Jersey City."

SEACREST, Ryan: **KYSR**, 1995-97. Born in 1976, Ryan moved to evenings at KYSR in March 1996 and afternoons in the fall of 1996. He is the host of tv's *Wild Animal Games*. In early 1997 Ryan left for afternoons at K101-San Francisco.

SEBASTIAN, Dave: **KEZY**, 1971-74; **KHJ**, 1974-77; **KFI**, 1978; **KTNQ**, 1978-79; **KIIS**, 1980; **KBRT**, 1981-82; **KIIS**, 1983; **KHJ**, 1985; **KRTH**, 1994-96. Born Dave Sebastian Williams, he grew up in San Jose. He started his broadcast career in 1967 at KYOS-Merced. From there Dave worked at KNGS-Hanford, KTOM-Salinas, KLOK-San Jose, KDON-Salinas and KNAK-Salt Lake City. In addition to an active radio career, Dave is in his 17th year of his own Voice Over "Workout" Workshops. He's also an actor having appeared in *Sisters*, *Picket Fences*, *Step by Step*, *Murphy Brown* and all 10 episodes of the FOX series *Hard Ball*. He was with the TranStar Oldies Channel from 1986 to 1990 where he was responsible for the first AFTRA contract. "I should have learned my lesson back in the '70s as a Shop Steward at KHJ. Two good jobs cut out from under me because of my humanitarian concern for The Greater Whole...Oh, well." Dave married his former agent in 1990 and now she manages his on-camera and voiceover career. They publish L.A.'s *Voice Over Guide* newsletter with a quarterly circulation of 7,000.

SEBASTIAN, Joel: **KLAC**, 1964-65. Born in Detroit, Joel was a big star at WXYZ-Detroit and many stations in the Windy City, including WLS-Chicago. He died January 17, 1986, after a long bout with pneumonia and prostate cancer.

SEBASTIAN, John: **KHJ**, 1978-79, pd; **KLOS**, 1981; **KTWV**, 1988-89, pd; **KZLA/KLAC**, 1996-97, pd. Born in 1949, John started his radio career in Portland in 1968. His claim to fame was in creating new formats and being a consultant to top stations all over the country. John has worked at just about every rock station in the history of Phoenix radio. From 1974 to 1978 John was the pd at KDWB-Minneapolis. John was one of the pioneers of call-out "passive research." In the late '70s John was brought in to KHJ to try to save the AM rock format. In an *LA Times* interview upon his arrival he said: "We're trying to aim toward a more FM-oriented direction. The announcers won't scream, they'll talk to you. We're playing the album version of hit songs. The approach is more mature. We aren't de-emphasizing personalities, but we do want our announcers to talk only when they have something relevant to say. No puns or corny jokes. We'd like to spotlight KHJ as a music station." John left KHJ in early 1979 for Phoenix and created the top tracks "kick ass rock and roll" format at KUPD. After "an explosive success" at WCOZ-Boston in 1980, John returned to Phoenix. In 1983 he launched EOR ("Eclectic-Oriented Rock"), which eventually evolved into the commercially successful "the Wave" in

1987. In August 1988, John became the pd of KTWV. John was a music consultant for MTV when it debuted. He claims the "fastest turnaround" for a number of stations including WCOZ-Boston, KTWV and KSLX-Phoenix. In the spring of 1996, John took the reins of Country-formatted KZLA and Nostalgia KLAC.

SEGAL, Karen: **KLSX**, 1994. Karen worked part-time at the "classic rock" station.

SEGEL, Steven: SEE Steven Clean

SEIDEN, Fred: **KBIG/KBRT**, 1973-80, pd; **KOST**, 1981-82. Fred was a longtime employee of Bonneville, starting at WFRM-New York in 1966. From the position of director of program services for Bonneville Broadcast Consultants, Fred joined KBIG in late 1973. He was credited with having a keen insight on promoting KBIG through other mediums. A colleague said of Fred: "He was the first to understand how to own a medium. He made a $250,000 campaign look like a million dollars. He was the first to roadblock television. He bought bus sides with such acute acumen that it looked like he was on every bus in the city." When his job at KBIG ended in 1980, Fred was devastated and attempted suicide by jumping from a building. He shattered a leg and was partially crippled. By 1985 he had rejoined Bonneville in their syndication operation based in Chicago. Five years later, when that job ended, he jumped from a bridge damaging his legs further. A year later, struggling with crippled legs and a diabetic condition resulting in failing eyesight, Fred successfully ended his life by jumping from another building. He was born and raised in Albany and graduated from Emerson College in Boston with a broadcasting degree. A colleague reflected on Fred's creativity: "When he wasn't able to create, severe depression set in." Fred started his broadcast career in San Francisco at KABL and KNBR.

SELLERS, Steven O.: **KQLZ**, 1992-93. Steven had been teamed with KQLZ pd Greg Stevens in morning drive for over a decade. They were known as "The Rude Boys" at KQLZ. Steven met Stevens at KISS-San Antonio and traveled with him to KCFX-Kansas City and KIOZ-San Diego. When Steven left the Southland he anchored the morning news on the Don Imus broadcast at KOGO-San Diego. He's worked many stations in his native San Antonio and has returned to KTSA with his wife and two children.

SELNER, Allen: **KABC**, 1984-94. Allen is a podiatrist in the San Fernando Valley who was a regular contributor to the KABC Saturday morning show.

"If we were lucky, we even got paid every couple of weeks if the water bed companies paid their bills."   *-Ace Young*

SELTZER, Brent: **KWST**, 1975-76; **KMET**, 1976-78; **KZLA**, 1979; **KNX/FM**, 1980; **KMPC**, 1981-82. "The death of John Kennedy changed my career path. I was a dj on WJBR-Wilmington when Kennedy was assassinated and I was so moved by my role in radio. People just wanted to touch a media person, it made them feel better. After all, for 96 hours tv babysat the nation." Born and raised in Wilmington, Delaware, Brent attended Ithaca College. After college he was off to New York and worked at ABC News and was a

writer/producer at Hartwest Productions working with *Mad* magazine and Joe Pyne. Brent worked for three years at KGB-San Diego and would feed KMET news stories. "When I arrived at KWST people would call and wonder why I had left KMET. I never knew that Ace Young was using so much of my feeds." Brent eventually worked the news at KMET and at the same time was the entertainment correspondent for CBC in Canada which he did for five years. "I used street-talk when doing the news. A suspect wasn't arrested, he was busted. The audience seemed to respond to familiar language." At KMPC he worked the Talk format from nine to noon. During this time, Brent worked closely with Watermark Productions as a writer and/or producer. "When Elvis died, I worked as associate producer/program coordinator of 'The Elvis Presley Story.'" In 1985 he realized that "nobody wanted me around. News had been eliminated at most stations and there didn't seem to be a place for me." Brent joined his wife who has a public relations firm that places clients on radio and does media coaching. His voiceover career includes the huge toys from movies: *Teenage Mutant Ninja Turtles*, *Power Rangers* and *Star Trek*. Brent also does per diem news at KABC and KNX.

SENDER, Jack: **KBIG**; **KBRT**, 1979

SERAPHIN, Charlie: **KNX/FM/KODJ**, 1989, gm. In 1964, at the age of 15, Charlie became the youngest announcer in the history of WOBT-Rhinelander, Wisconsin. During his college days at Lawrence University in Wisconsin, he worked at WAPL, WYNE, WISM and WOKY. In 1972 he was nd at WMYQ-Miami and two years later moved to KFRC-San Francisco as reporter and news anchor. For the next decade he worked news at K101 and later KCBS-San Francisco. In 1991 Charlie joined KRLD-Dallas and the

Texas State Networks as vp of programming. In the mid-1990s he was gm of KMYX-San Diego.

SERGIS, Charlie: **KFWB**, 1971-97. "I guess a newsman's natural curiosity is responsible for my being in radio and

in California." Charlie grew up in New York, graduated from Columbia University and earned a master's degree from the University of Missouri School of Journalism. After the Army, he worked for several newspapers including the *Louisville Courier-Journal* and then went to Associated Press. "When Westinghouse created all-News radio at WINS-New York in 1965, I was fascinated and began working part-time while still with AP." In 1967 he became a full-time editor, then assistant news director. "When offered the nd's job at KFWB, curiosity bit again: I had always wanted to see California. We figured we'd be here awhile, then return East, but we liked it and stayed." In 1974 Charlie returned to reporting. In 1990 he received the Broadcast Journalist of the Year Award from the Society of Professional Journalists. "There isn't a much better chance to cover everything than as a reporter for an all-News radio station." Charlie's wife Pilar is a registered nurse in the mental health field and they have three grown children.

Are you a writer? A collection of short stories and essays written by radio people is being prepared. Write Los Angeles Radio People, PO Box 55518, Valencia, CA 91385

SERR, Jeff: **KIIS**, 1982; **KMGG**, 1983-85; **KBIG**, 1986-88; **KODJ/KCBS**, 1988-97. The native Californian has spent his radio career in his home state. He started at age 15 at KBLF-Red Bluff. After high school he went to San Francisco for college and worked at KPEN and KSJO-San Jose. While in San Francisco from the mid-1970s to 1982, Jeff worked at K101 and KYA. He

started at KIIS doing weekend work. Less than a year later he was doing afternoons at "Magic 106." In 1985 Jeff spent a year on the Unistar satellite Oldies Channel. Living in the San Fernando Valley with his wife and three children, Jeff is the production director and works weekends at "Arrow 93," along with a heavy commitment to hosting charity events. His active voiceover work includes commercials for Nissan, CompUSA, El Pollo Loco and First Interstate Bank. His recent tv work includes announcer duties on the new game show *Switch-A-Roo*.

SERVANTEZ, Joe "The Boomer": **KPWR**, 1986-96; **KACD**, 1996; **KIBB**, 1996-97. The Garden City, Kansas, native arrived in Los Angeles from KEYN ("FM104")-Wichita. "The Boomer" was one of the original jocks at "Power 106" when the station switched from KMGG and stayed for almost a decade. He hosted the grand openings of Disney's Videopolis and Star Tours. "The Boomer" had high compliments for pd Rick Cummings: "He's great!" In the spring of 1996 Joe joined KACD and in late 1996 moved to new Rhythm AC, KIBB where he works afternoon drive.

SESMA, Chico: **KOWL**, 1949-57; **KALI**, 1957-67. Born Lionel Sesma in the Boyle Heights area of East Los Angeles, Chico attended Hollenbeck Junior High School and graduated from Roosevelt High School. He had studied classical music since he was ten years old. Chico was a trombone player who played with the popular East L.A. bands in the forties. He spent a year at Los Angeles City College and then dropped out to travel with some big bands including his own. Chico returned to California at the age of 23. In a 1975 *Latin Quarter* interview, Chico said, "I didn't feel I was going to make it. I really wanted to join the Los Angeles Philharmonic Orchestra because, though I loved jazz and the big bands, my love was in classical music. KOWL (later KDAY) was having success with the black market. When the station turned its attention to the Mexican American market, Chico debuted the first show for a Chicano audience in February 1949. He exposed music by Tito Puente and Perez Prado along with artists like Billy Eckstine and Duke Ellington. Chico stayed with KOWL until 1957 when the station changed its name to

KDAY and switched to Top 40. He moved to KALI until 1967. During the 1950s he produced a monthly series of musical presentations and dances called Latin Holidays at the Hollywood Palladium. In early 1969, Chico joined the State Employment Redevelopment Department as a job agent, which he did for many years. He said, "I'm working exclusively with disadvantaged youths, most of whom are from the barrio - drop-outs, some with arrest records, others with psychological hang-ups, or drug addiction, or alcoholism. It's the same old story: the perpetuation of poverty." Chico gave some advice to young Mexican Americans: "Prepare yourself for *mainstream* media - that is the key."

SEWARD, Bill: **KXLU**, 1976-80; **XPRS**, 1980-81; **KWNK**, 1987-88; **KGIL**, 1989; **KNX**, 1990-97. Bill was a sports anchor for "KNXNewsradio" and KCBS/Channel 2. Born in Sherman Oaks, he went to Notre Dame High School and Loyola Marymount University where he did play-by-play for basketball and baseball from 1977 to 1988. He was a former high school football "Coach of the Year" at St. Bernard High in Playa del Rey. Bill was a television sports anchor for stations in Eureka, Oxnard and New England before returning to Los Angeles. A thoroughbred race horse owner, Bill hosted *Inside Santa Anita* on KDOC/TV and *Santa Anita Today* on Fox Sports West. Bill was part of the KNX sports team that was named best in radio by the Southern California Sports Broadcasters Association. In the spring of 1997 he joined ESPNEWS as an anchor.

SEXTON, Miles: **KEZY/KORG**, 1990-95, gm

SEYMOUR, Ruth: **KPFK**, 1960s-70s; **KCRW**, 1980s-90s, gm. Ruth was pd of KPFK during its glory years. The *LA Times* said she "has achieved a rare balance of serving the local community, the network and her own eclectic interests." In an *LA Weekly* October 1996 story: "Much of the credit for KPFK's success in the early '70s goes to an intense, mercurial former New Yorker named Ruth Hirschman (now Seymour). Before leaving to live in Europe during the 1960s, she had been KPFK's drama and literary director, producing award-winning series on Shakespeare and Oscar Wilde. Returning to the station in 1971 as pd, Hirschman was, by all accounts, brilliant. Imaginative and organized, with a taste of culture and a visceral hatred of left-wing ideologues, she championed intelligent, well-produced programs and the hiring of intelligent, like-minded staffers." At KCRW she is gm and pd. The *Weekly* story praised her success at KCRW: "She'd taken over a no-watt, surfer-boy, community-college station and made it the hot place on the dial for all those '60s hippies turned '80s yuppies to tune in to as they cruised down the 405 in their shiny new Volvos."

SHACKELFORD, Lynn: **KLAC**. Lynn was Chick Hearn's sidekick during the L.A. Lakers broadcasts. He was on Coach John Wooden's 1968-69 UCLA basketball team that started Lynn with Lew Alcindor, Curtis Rowe and Sidney Wicks.

SHADE, Jeff: **KMPC**, 1992-94; **KLIT**, 1994; **KACD**, 1995-96. Born and raised in Dayton, Jeff started his radio career in his hometown. He went on to work in Providence, WMGK-Philadelphia and WPIX-New York. In 1985 Jeff began to shift his focus from on-air to production. He produced *Heartlight City*, a music video show on the USA Network. He helped launch a company that has become the largest supplier of in-store, point-of-purchase radio advertising and entertainment. In 1987 he joined WFAN-New York as the director of on-air production and worked with Don Imus in the morning. In April 1992, Jeff moved to Los Angeles to head up the production department of all-Sports programming at KMPC. In 1994 he went back on the air.

SHAFER, Don: **KNAC**, 1969-70; **KYMS**, 1971-73. Don left Southern California for CHUM-Toronto where he programmed and was on-air for over a decade at the Canadian powerhouse.

KHJ Line-up

6 a.m.	Charlie Van Dyke
9 a.m.	Dave Sebastian
Noon	Bobby Ocean
3 p.m.	Machine Gun Kelly
6 p.m.	Billy Pearl
10 p.m.	J.B. Stone
2 a.m.	Paul Freeman
weekends	Beau Weaver

-May 1975

SHALHOUB, Martha: **KLVE**, 1978-97. Martha is one  of the early women in Spanish radio. She also has a syndicated program on which she interviews Latino performers. She started out as the receptionist for the Liberman Brothers when they bought the station. They thought she had a pleasant voice and Martha eventually became a full-time personality on Spanish KLVE.

SHANA: **KHJ**, 1976-78; **KEZY**, 1978-80; **KROQ**, 1980; **KLOS**, 1980-86; **KLSX**, 1986-95; **KPCC**, 1996-97. Shana was born Margaret Reichl of German parents on April 10, 1953, at Camp LeJeune AFB in North Carolina. She was raised just outside of Detroit and began her love affair with radio while growing up in Kalamazoo. She learned English from cartoons like *Felix The Cat* and *Casper* and started her radio career at the Kalamazoo college radio station in 1971. She then moved to KWBB-Wichita. Programmer Paul Drew became Shana's mentor and in 1974 at age 21, she started on the all-night shift at KFRC-San Francisco, becoming one of the first female Rock jocks. It was actually KFRC pd Michael Spears who gave "Margo" her new professional name. Two years later, she came to the Southland to work at KFRC's sister station and become a "Boss Jock." During her stay at KLOS, she hosted *Rock ON-TV*. The over-the-air "cable" experiment was a rock series simulcast by KLOS and ON-TV. The 30-minute, magazine-style program ran twice a week. She did morning drive at KLOS, starting in the spring of 1984 when Frazer Smith left the station. In addition to hosting several nationally syndicated radio features, Shana's heart shows with her involvement in the community. She devotes considerable time to the Children's Hospital. In 1994 and 1995 the mother of three taught a course at UCLA. The pioneering class was called "Becoming a Disc Jockey: The Inside View." Before 1994 was over, Shana had pulled the ultimate radio "hat trick" and returned for a third time to KLSX, following the arrival of new management. In  early 1996 Shana joined KPCC as the assistant pd and md as well as evening on-air talent. "I lecture on campus and outside public speaking in the Los Angeles area. I am teaching the very first Southern California Regional Occupational Program for radio communications for the L.A. county board of education."

SHANE, Ed: **KKDJ**, 1971, pd. Ed was brought in from Atlanta to program the new Rock station.

SHANNON, Bob: **KWIZ**, 1975-76, pd; **KFI**, 1976-79; **KWIZ**, 1979; **KHJ**, 1980-82; **KLAC**, 1982. Bob was the last dj on KHJ before the station switched to country music. He was born in St. Catherine's, Ontario and grew up in Western New York near Buffalo. He started his radio career in Arizona working in Yuma and KRUX. From KUTY-Palmdale in 1965, Bob joined KDWB-Minneapolis for the first time. He went on to work mornings at WKYC-Cleveland, KXOK-St. Louis and KING-Seattle. In the early 1970s Bob was at KJR-Seattle, WIXY-Cleveland, KDKA-Pittsburgh and back at KDWB to be pd and work mornings. Bob worked morning drive as "BS in the Morning" with Ed Nix at KWIZ. At KFI he was hired to work the swing shift and ended up doing afternoon drive for two years. He left KFI for middays at KCBQ-San Diego and he returned to the Southland for KHJ. During the 1980s Bob started "The Actor's Workshop" in Orange County. Using his birth name of R.J. Adams he turned to acting. Bob has appeared in close to 100 episodic tv shows including a regular role on *Riptide*. He was seen frequently on *Hill St. Blues*, *Murder She Wrote* and *Hotel*. He appeared in *Rocky IV*. Bob lives in Mission Viejo and continues to act, coach at his workshop and produce documentaries. He is also exploring opportunities in talk radio.

SHANNON, Gregg: **XTRA/KOST**; **KDAY**, 1971-72; **KRLA**, 1972-73; **KROQ**, 1973-74. Born in 1949 in the Big Apple, Gregg was on a fast track, working for seven stations in his first three years in the business. His move from KDAY to KRLA was a transition as both stations were experimenting with "progressive" music. In 1973, Gregg appeared in *The Battle of the Planet of the Apes*.

SHANNON, Scott: **KQLZ**, 1989-91. Michael Scott Shannon's name is derived from two early influences: WABC's Scott Muni and CKLW's Tom Shannon. Scott is, first and foremost, a student of radio history. He collects airchecks the way some people collect baseball cards. He told the *LA Times* that he has over 2,000 hours of the original KHJ "Boss Radio" and 500 hours of the original KFWB "Color Radio" from the late 1950s and early 1960s. Scott's father was in the Army and the family moved frequently. He dropped out of high school in Indianapolis at age 17. He told the *LA Radio Guide*: "I wanted to get away from it all. I thought I was James Dean." Scott worked as a jock at WABB-Mobile and added pd chores at WMPS-Memphis and WMAK-Nashville. Before joining Casablanca Records in 1977, Scott was the national pd for Mooney Broadcasting and pd at WQXI-Atlanta. He also became a record executive with Ariola Records. In 1979 he returned to radio and joined WPGC-Washington, DC, as pd. He had much success at WRBQ-Tampa/St. Petersburg. In a *Billboard* magazine interview Larry Berger of WPLJ-New York reviewed the decade of the '80s and said of Scott: "I always thought of Shannon as a PT Barnum character. He was better than just about anybody at creating sizzle on a radio station, and quite a talented on-air personality." *WELCOME TO THE JUNGLE* was the greeting. In January of 1989, Scott left WHTZ ("Z-100")-New York, where he was 1987's *Billboard* magazine Program Director of the Year in the Top 40 category, to launch "Pirate Radio" for Westwood One. Scott signed a 5-year deal as vp of the network's radio station group. *Billboard* estimated the deal at $10 million - or $2 million per year. For the launch of "Pirate Radio" on KQLZ, Scott was on the air as "Bubba, the Love Sponge." In New York, his popular show was called the "Morning Zoo." Since Jay Thomas already claimed the use of the "Zoo," Shannon called his morning team the "Nut Hut Crew." In the beginning, the station sold only one spot per hour at $1,000 each, which was $300 to $400 more than KPWR. The immediate media attention to Scott and "Pirate Radio" was enormous. *USA Today* rarely covered a format change but they chronicled AC KIQQ becoming KQLZ. The produced spots between music boldly declared, "Don't Be a Dickhead." Another was, "When you're on the air in Southern California, you've got to be loud to cut through the crap." In an *LA Times* profile of morning men, Scott described himself: "One of the problems with people when they first meet me is they expect Eddie Murphy. I'm not a comedian that plays records. I don't always make you laugh. I'm a human being that has certain emotions and I run a passionate radio show. There's a tremendous amount of passion involved. Intensity." A year later, when the station stalled, Scott spoke of the competition: "There's no easy answer for building a station in Los Angeles." During this time, he constantly mocked his competition, talking about "Little Dickie Dees" and "Ol' Goat Lips," in a reference to KIIS gm Lynn Anderson-Powell. When the experiment with Scott eventually failed, Westwood One, feeling a $$ crunch as a hangover from the debt-riddled takeover craze of the '80s, let Scott go in early February of 1991. Scott reminisced, "Just about every dj who starts out in this business dreams of opening the microphone and speaking to Los Angeles, California. It has been a dream. I feel we had a plan and we were going to do it and they pulled the rug out at the last minute." In 1993, Scott was cited by *R&R* for excellence in programming during the past 20 years. Scott recalled his highlight during this period as being when he took WHTZ-New York from "worst-to-first" in 74 days, calling it "a thrill I'll never forget." Scott was one of the first vjs on VH-1. He hosted the nationally syndicated "Smash Hits Video Countdown " for three years and was the subject of a feature story on CBS's *48 Hours*. He has been doing mornings at WPLJ-New York and lives in Westchester, New York with his wife Trish and pre-teen daughter.

SHANNON, Steve: **KMPC**, 1978-80. The former California Angels broadcaster went on to the Milwaukee Brewers in the 1980s. He did fill-in for the Angels, but always wanted to do football. Steve was slotted to broadcast UCLA football when he left. He lives in St. Louis.

SHAPIRO, Ron: **KLIT**, 1997, pd. Ron arrived at trimulcast "Lite 92.7FM" from seven years as production director at KIIS. He also worked for Cutler Productions and ABC Watermark.

SHAPPEE, Michael: **KMNY**, 1988; **KFWB**, 1996-97. Michael is one of the anchors at all-News KFWB.

SHARISE: **KACE**, 1994; **KJLH**, 1995-96

SHARK: KROQ, 1994. A part-timer on KROQ Shark left the Southland for afternoons at KRQT-Houston. In 1996 he went to "Q101"-Chicago and in early 1997 he joined KOME-San Jose. Born Ric Sanders in Madison, he graduated from the University of Minnesota with a marketing and communication degree in 1986. He started his radio career at KDOG-Mankato followed by KFIV-Modesto and KDON-Salinas. Before he took the name Shark he worked at "Eagle 106"-Philadelphia and "B101"-Baltimore. "I was a sensitive kid when I was in school and took swimming lessons at the YMCA. All the other kids had macho names like Tiger but my father called me Shark and it stuck." He worked at KEDJ-Phoenix before joining KROQ for swing.

SHARON, Bob: **KFWB**, 1960-61, gsm; **KPOL**, 1960-66, gsm; **KIIS**, 1970-71, gm. Bob was part of KPOL when it was the "biggest grossing radio station west of Chicago." He made the comment in a lengthy 1996 interview. Growing up in the Midwest, he calls Joplin home. "I always had an appetite for radio. All I wanted to be was a sportscaster. I loved sports!" Bob went to University of Denver because he considered it "the best radio school in the country. Between my freshman and sophomore years, I joined the Navy where I was injured, which eliminated any hopes of participating in sports." After graduation he started his radio career in Craig, Colorado for $75 a week. Bob was a jock at KXEO-Mexico, Missouri. Three months later he went into sales because he discovered that salesmen made more money than jocks. Bob was in sales at WHB-Kansas City during the legendary years. He went on to station ownership at WPEO-Peoria and KQEO-Albuquerque. He got to the West Coast working at KDEO-San Diego and eventually consulted KFMB and KARO/TV-Bakersfield. Bob loved radio and joined KFWB in October 1960 as gsm and eventually ran the station for Bob Purcell until it was sold to Westinghouse. Bob was the first station manager at KIIS. When he left in 1971, he joined Ted Randal in San Francisco for a consulting role. A couple of years later Bob managed two stations in Portland and in the mid-1970s was the sales manager for Chuck Blore Enterprises. In the late 1970s, he managed KALK and KPPL in Denver and then KAJM and KJAZ-Seattle. In 1984 he became president of the Northern California Broadcasters Association. For the next decade he was head of the Nissan Dealers Association of Southern California. By 1994 he was facing many challenges. He had a successful cancer operation that opened his face from his ear to his throat, and during recuperation his Sherman Oaks home was destroyed in the earthquake. A year later he had regained his weight and energy and was managing a used car site on the Net. Between them from previous marriages, Bob and his wife have nine kids (he lost a two-year-old while living in San Diego) and live in North Hollywood.

SHARP, Bill: **KACE**, 1997. Bill joined mornings at KACE in the summer of 1997 from KQXL-Baton Rouge.

SHARP, Colin J.: **KDAY**, 1966

SHARP, Karen: **KWIZ**, 1987; **KOST**, 1988-97. Karen

hosts the high-rated evening show "Love Songs on the Coast." She got her start in Ventura radio and applied for a job with KQLH-San Bernardino. Her eventual husband Alex Tostado was the pd and remembered: "She really didn't have much experience but I knew I wanted to hire her. I told her that in six months she MUST send a tape to KOST because she would be perfect for the 'Love Songs' program." Karen moved on to KWIZ and Alex moved on. When Karen got a part-time job at KOST Alex called to congratulate his former employee. Another year went by and Karen saw Alex acting on television and she called with congratulations. Both were available and they started dating. Four years later they were married. "I didn't know that when I hired Karen in San Bernardino that I was hiring my wife."

SHARPE, Jim and Melissa: **KYSR**, 1993-95. Jim and Melissa met in Tucson in 1988, but how they got there was from two very different paths. Jim, born in 1964, grew up in Page, Arizona, and started in radio at age 16.

After school, he went to radio jobs in Flagstaff, Spokane, Albuquerque and Reno before ending up in Tucson. Melissa, on the other hand, was born in 1961, grew up in Stockton, attended the University of Pacific and then took odd jobs in San Francisco. She moved to Tucson, returned to school majoring in journalism and worked as a club dj at night. Local gm, Rich "Brother" Robbin, heard her tape and according to Rich said to pd Royce Blake, "Get her on the air tonight!!!" She was on the AM and Jim was working on the FM side. They fell in love and married on October 16, 1987, during a simulcast in morning drive that was carried on all the local tv stations. Two years later they were on competing stations and decided to team together and went to KXKT-Omaha. Less than a year later they were doing their morning show at KRSR-Dallas. When Westinghouse sold the station two years later, Jim had an opportunity to go into programming management at WMXZ-New Orleans. He worked morning drive. She was the news director. Melissa did not like Jim as the boss. She said, "He'll never do that again!" They arrived in the Southland from "The Big Easy" to work morning drive at Viacom's "Star 98.7." After five years of marriage Jim was anxious to have a child. While on the air in the summer of 1994, Melissa gave copy for Jim to read. When he opened the envelope, it contained the positive results of a home pregnancy test. He was left speechless by the news. They've made tv appearances together on *The Marilu Show* and *Baywatch*. In a 1995 *LA Times* interview, the Sharpes talked about a rocky period in their marriage when they first moved to Los Angeles. Sometimes the working together doesn't work. Melissa reflected, "We would drive together to work, we would do the show, we would get off the air, we would go to breakfast or lunch, we'd go to the health club together - it was like, argghhhhhh!" The separation made Melissa feel worse. "It's just because I'm so damned irresistible," said Jim. Melissa concluded, "We belong together. We're desperately in love." The couple left "Star 98.7" in the fall of 1995. In the spring of 1996 they moved to KZON-Phoenix. Jim works afternoon drive and Melissa joined sister station **KYOT** for mornings. "It's so much easier living in Phoenix. We have family here."

SHAUGHNESSY, Pat: **KIQQ**, 1973-79, gm. Pat was present at the launch of the Drake/Chenault era at KIQQ. He told the *LA Times*: "This will be the first time where FM, from a big personality standpoint, will have a chance to prove its viability and strength." Pat was born in Council Bluffs, Iowa on January 22, 1945, and was not yet 30 when he arrived in the Southland. He went to the University of Nebraska at Omaha and got started in sales at KOIL-Omaha in 1966. Pat was also the executive vp/gm of Drake/Chenault Enterprises. In 1980 he became president and ceo of TM Communications, which at that time, was the largest producer of jingles and production libraries. He took the company public in 1985 and in 1987 sold his interest and bought four radio stations. In 1991 he formed AVI Communications of Dallas. AVI is a broadcast services company specializing in new business development for tv and radio.

SHAUN, Jackye: **KNX**, 1976-97. Jackye has been an editor and on-air newscaster for over two decades at KNX.

SHAW, Dave: **KFI**, 1964

SHAW, Don: **KMPC**, 1992. Don hosted a late-night weekend show during the all-Sports programming at KMPC. He was let go in a media-covered event. A sketch by Don of a mock interview with a Japanese basketball player generated complaints from the Media Action Network for Asian Americans. They accused Don of making a racial slur. In an *LA Times* interview Don explained that he saw the sketch as funny and essentially harmless: "I'm not a racist. The whole thing was blatantly preposterous."

SHAW, Rick: **KEZY**, 1984; **KNX/FM**, 1986. Rick has been working at Westwood One Radio Networks.

SHAYNE, Bob: **KPFK**, 1959; **KVFM**, 1959-60; **KNOB**, 1961-63, pd; **KPPC**, 1967. Bob followed Tom Donahue on the all-night shift at KPPC. He was just coming out of jazz and getting used to "underground rock" when Tom fired him for playing a cut by Lambert, Hendricks and Ross. Bob left radio after his brief stint at KPPC to become a tv/movie writer-producer. He wrote about "every fourth episode of *Simon & Simon*." Bob wrote the feature length *Return of Sherlock Holmes*. Born in New Jersey, Bob was 7 when his father, who had a heart condition, moved the family to Southern California. Bob grew up in the San Fernando Valley. He is now teaching screenwriting and a course on the "History of Romantic Comedies" at UCLA and NYU which he hopes to turn into a book.

SHEARER, Harry: **KRLA**, 1965-70; **KPPC**, 1970-71; **KMET**, 1975; **KCRW**, 1987-97. Harry's radio career reached an early apex during the heady days of KRLA and the daily "Credibility Gap," an irreverent look at the news in the late 1960s. His diversity of accomplishments is staggering. He started out as a child actor in *Abbott and Costello Go to Mars*. He played the bass player Derek Smalls in *This Is Spinal Tap*. Harry has always been on the cutting edge of parody. He played the role of Eddie Haskell in the pilot episode of *Leave It to Beaver*. He quit the cast of *Saturday Night Live* twice and had a role in *The Right Stuff*. Harry was fired twice from KMET during the 1970s. He used to listen a lot to Jean Shepherd and Bob and Ray, whose influences are apparent in his free-form monologues and shrewdly paced comedy skits. His multi-faceted career has him doing a weekly radio program "Le Show" (an early version of this show aired Sunday afternoon's on KPPC called "Desintation Music") on KCRW on which readings from obscure trade journals alternate with slickly produced episodes of "Clintonsomething." He also does the voice of Mr. Burns (and 19 other characters) on *The Simpsons*. He's working on the first musical comedy about J. Edgar Hoover's relationship with his longtime assistant, Clyde Tolson. In the October 1996 issue of *Buzz* magazine, Harry was listed on the "*Buzz* 100 Coolest."

SHEARER, Licia: **KGFJ**, 1989-96; **KACE**, 1996. Licia worked morning drive with Tony Hart at Gospel/Urban KGFJ. She is a versatile entertainer, talented actress, singer and dancer. Licia portrays mad Sarah in the popular, nationally syndicated radio soap opera, "It's Your World" that airs on the "Tom Joyner Morning Show." She received a  best actress nomination by the NAACP Theatre Awards in the musical *A Little Meditation* and starred in Jayne Kennedy's long-running musical *The African-American* and *For Colored Girls*. Licia is featured in Bill Bellamy's movie *How To Be a Player*. She created Shearer Energy Productions, a communications/entertainment company that produced *The Holy Hook-Up* national gospel newsletter. From Ohio, Licia earned a master's degree in broadcast journalism and radio/television communications.

SHEARER, William: **KGFJ**, 1973-74; **KLOS**, 1974-77;  **KACE**, 1977-84, vp/gm; **KGFJ/KUTE**, 1984-85, vp/gm; **KGFJ**, 1986-96, vp/gm. Born in Columbus, Ohio, William was a human relations and organization behavior major at the University of San Francisco. He was part of the

M.B.A. program in business management at Pepperdine University. William started in radio sales and in 1977 he became vp/gm at KACE. He has been chairman and on the board of directors of the National Association of Black Owned Broadcasters. He is also the past chairman of the Southern California Broadcasters Association. William left KGFJ in February 1996 when the station was sold. In the spring of 1996 the Black Media Network bestowed on William a Lifetime Achievement Award.

SHEEHY, Michael: **KNX/FM**, 1976-83, pd; **KKHR**, 1983; **KTWV**, 1990-97. The quintessential production master, Michael developed a passion for music at a very young age. "When I was 13, my folks gave me a little

Sony tape recorder. It fired my imagination and opened up a whole new world." His early radio work was between Houston and Honolulu, and he arrived in the Southland from KGB-San Diego. He eventually became pd of KNX/FM. Michael remembered that the station "realized the highest ratings and revenues in its history, ranking as the 6th-most-listened-to radio station in the United States." While there, he was awarded 26 gold and platinum records for his early and enthusiastic support of developing new artists. In 1985, he was asked to create and develop a broadcast division for HLC/Killer Music, a respected music production company best known for its work with Levi's, Gatorade and Wheaties. His company earned a reputation as the country's premier broadcast jingle outlet. Michael produced Killer Tracks, a 40-CD production music library, that continues to serve as a favorite means of source music worldwide. In 1990, Michael joined KTWV heading up their creative/production department. His work earns international awards, most recently at the New York International Radio Festival, where his entry beat 13,800 other entries from more than 29 nations. He also produces all the KFWB news jingles. He was the director of programming for the Discovery Music Network on cable television. In 1992, Michael was doing mornings on "the Wave," and he moved to evenings in 1993 when the New Age station adopted a female morning drive team. Michael talked about production: "I don't care what the medium is...producing is a state of mind. It's not necessarily what tools you're using...it's what's in your head!"

SHEFF, Stanley: **KROQ**, 1977-82. Sheff was the "and Stanley" in the spoof-driven Sunday night show, "Young Marques and Stanley" on KROQ. Born and raised in Hollywood, Stanley graduated from Fairfax High School and pursued the movie business. He employed KROQ'er Doc Nemo, who was the "Young Marques," for one of his movies. They developed a friendship. "We had Adam West and Linda Blair come out to Pasadena to spoof their projects. The shows were half-scripted and half-improvised." Stanley went on to direct *Lobster Man from Mars* (a title inspired by a working relationship with Orson Welles). He's currently working on a number of film projects.

SHELBY, LaRita: **KGFJ**, 1990. LaRita was part of morning drive on KGFJ.

SHELDEN, Thom: **KJOI**, 1987-89. Tom broadcast news in morning drive at "K-Joy."

SHELDON, Harvey: **KFOX**, 1985. Harvey hosted a sports Talk program.

SHELTON, Iris: **KRLA**, 1981; **KFWB**, 1988. Iris was part of the public affairs department at KRLA and broadcast news at KFWB.

SHERMAN, Gene: **KABC**, 1969. Gene was an award-winning *LA Times* "Cityside" columnist who aired a nightly 10-minute program about the city on KABC.

SHERWIN, Wally: **KABC**, 1960-89, pd. "Adee Do!" Wally's tv commercial for a plumbing service called Adee Plumbing gave him as much notoriety as his decades-long role as pd of KABC. In the tv spot he appeared as a white-haired plumber who advertises the services of Adee Plumbing and Heating. At the end of the commercial he widens his eyes and proclaims, "Adee Do!"

SHERWOOD, Lee: **KIIS**, 1970-71, pd; **KHJ**, 1980-82. In 1970, Lee was pd of KIIS, and he left in 1971. From 1975 to 1980 he was at WMAQ-Chicago until he was called to do mornings for the new Country format at KHJ. In the summer of 1981, he lost control of his car on a narrow mountain highway and flipped over. He suffered a broken right leg, separated shoulder, broken rib, and blow-out fracture of the right eye. A miniaturized broadcast studio was built in his bedroom during his convalescence so he could broadcast his morning show. He commented to the *LA Times* that he was happy to be alive and, "besides this isn't the first time that someone in Hollywood made a living in bed." In 1982, he left for stations in New York, Washington, DC, St. Louis and Chicago. Lee currently hosts a widely syndicated country show.

SHERWOOD, Tom: **KRLA**, 1997

SHIELDS, Cal: **KAGB**, 1974-78, om; **KACE**, 1978-83, pd. Cal started out as pd of black-owned KAGB. He followed his uncle to Southern California to be operations manager. Cal created a series of specials devoted both historically and musically to leading black recording artists. One of his programs on Duke Ellington won honorable mention for a Peabody Award. "We were *that* close to winning." When KAGB was sold to Willie Davis, Cal stayed through the format and call letter changes. During Cal's tenure as pd and jock, KACE sponsored a summer of free concerts in the park, with artists like Les McCann and Abbey Lincoln performing. Born in Detroit, Cal grew up in New York City and after serving in Vietnam, he went to the New York Institute of Technology and studied communications. Cal has been working for a local cable company and is an active participant in Too Lunar Productions. Miss radio? "Yeah, it never gets out of your blood."

SHIELDS, Del: **KAGB**, 1974-78, gm. When Clarence Avon bought KAGB, Del joined the station as gm from similar posts in Philadelphia and New York. He authored the *Black Experience in Sound*. Del is now a minister in New York.

SHINDLER, Merrill: **KABC/KMPC/KTZN**. Merrill's

"Dining Out" restaurant show has been a Saturday fixture for many decades. A graduate of New York University with an M.A. in film criticism and aesthetics, Merrill has traveled extensively throughout Europe, Mexico and Central America. He landed in San Francisco where he began working for the *Bay Guardian*. Merrill wrote columns on entertainment for *San Francisco Magazine* and became the West Coast editor for *Rolling Stone*. He was the head writer for Casey Kasem's "American Top Forty" syndicated radio show for decades. In the fall of 1996 he moved his restaurant critic show to sister talker KMPC (now KTZN). He lives in a restored Bauhaus-style house in Cheviot Hills and to keep the weight off he runs five miles a day. He describes himself as "Just a big, old hungry boy who works for the fun of it."

SHIRK, Larry: **KPCC**, 1985, pd. Larry was the pd of the Pasadena City College station, KPCC.

SHOEN, Michael: **KFWB**, 1997

SHORE, Sandy: **KGIL**, 1984; **KTWV**, 1989. Sandy had a harrowing experience before arriving at the San Fernando station. She was working at a Monterey radio station when a listener came into the station and shot up all the equipment. Sandy has returned to Monterey and works for KPIG. Since 1990 she has been producing and hosting a series of smooth jazz concerts and music events in Monterey Bay. Recently she was named promoter of the year by the local Monterey newspaper.

SHURIAN, Scott: **XTRA**; **KMPC**; **KNX**. Scott was a newsman in Southern California radio.

SIDDERS, Carolyn: **KOCM**, 1986-87. Carolyn worked afternoon drive at "K-Ocean."

SIEGAL, Jack: **KJOI**, 1970-73, gm; **KPSA**, 1973, gm; **KLVE**, 1973. Jack made the first broadcast from Inchon beachhead in September 1950 that was carried by all radio networks. He was decorated for action with the 1st Marine Division Recon Company during the assault to liberate Seoul. The broadcast action during the war earned him a spot with Edward R. Murrow and the *See It Now* program. In the 1960s Jack worked for IBM and appeared on all three tv networks during coverage of the late Gemini and early Apollo space missions. Using computer animation he explained how rendezvous would be effected. In 1970, he put KJOI on the air, then KLVE and two stations in the Inland Empire. He has owned KSRF and KOCM. Jack was born in Philadelphia and raised in West Virginia. He began in radio as a dj in Philadelphia in 1944. He graduated from the University of Pennsylvania and went into the Navy as a radio/tv officer. He was the first person to ride Col. John Stapp's rocket crash-research sled at Edwards AFB, carrying a tape recorder along to record a description for broadcast. Jack has served in various executive capacities with the NAFMB and Southern California Broadcasters Association. He is the president and general manager of Chagal Companies, a multi-media investment/consulting firm dealing in broadcast ownership. KFOX, KREA and KYKF are part of Chagal.

SIEGEL, Joel: **KPPC**, 1970-71; **KMET**, 1971. Joel's

program, "Uncle Noel's Mystery Theatre" was heard weekly on KPPC during its "underground" radio period. A native of Los Angeles, where he graduated cum laude from UCLA, he was a book reviewer for the *LA Times*, freelance writer for such publications as *Rolling Stone* and *Sports Illustrated*, joke writer for Senator Robert Kennedy and ad agency copywriter responsible for inventing ice cream flavors for Baskin-Robbins. In 1972 Joel joined WCBS/TV-New York and four years later became the entertainment critic at WABC/TV-New York, a position he continues to hold. He has been a family member of ABC's *Good Morning America* since 1981, blending his unique sense of humor with his insights in the field of films and filmmaking. Joel wrote the book for *The First*, a musical play produced on Broadway in the 1981-82 season, that told the story of the legendary Jackie Robinson's breakthrough into major league baseball. For it, he was honored with a 1982 Tony Award nomination - the only drama critic ever to receive one. Joel is married and resides in Manhattan.

SIFUENTES, Karla: **KRLA**, 1996-97. Karla joined "Little Ricci" for morning drive at KRLA in the fall of 1996. The bilingual 28-year old was born in Madrid and arrived in the Southland when she was in her early teens. Originally hired for the promotions department, she quickly moved to an on-air position. She was "discovered" as the Spanish "hold voice" for Kaiser-Permanente's phone system.

SIGMON, Loyd: **KMPC**. Born in Oklahoma in 1910, Loyd created the SigAlert traffic system in the mid-1950s which revolutionized the idea of covering the growing traffic congestion in Southern California. He was with Golden West for 30 years with the exception of three years spent in Europe during World War II where he was officer in charge of radio communications for the European Theater. During this period Colonel Sigmon

directed the building of the world's largest mobile transmitter, 60,000 watts. Prior to selling his interest in Golden West, Loyd was the corporation's executive vp. He was vp of operations at KMPC and was part of the acquisitions of the California Angels with Gene Autry along with running a number of radio stations and KTLA/Channel 5. The son of a cattle rancher, Loyd was educated at Wentworth Military Academy and started his radio career at WEEI-Boston and KCMO-Kansas City. He devotes his time to private investments and community service and serves on numerous boards.

SIGNAL, Tori: **KFWB**; **KMPC**; **KYSR**, 1991-97. Born

Diana Finn-Stang in New York City, Tori grew up in New Jersey. She jocked on stations in New York and New Jersey starting in 1985. She came to Los Angeles via New York City's Shadow Broadcast Services, where she was the traffic reporter for all-News WINS. She was first heard in Los Angeles on KFWB and KMPC. The pd at "Star 98.7" decided Tori should be a part of their morning team doing traffic reports and news. In early 1997 she left the morning show but continues to host a Saturday morning program.

SILVA, Flavio: **KALI**, 1986-90; **KTNQ**, 1993-94

SILVIUS, Jon: **KRLA**, 1972. Jon was a newsman for KRLA.

SIMMONS, Brian: **KFWB**, 1963-64

SIMMONS, Bryan: **KOST**, 1982-97. The California native was born James Simmons in Castro Valley and grew up in Sacramento. As a teen, Bryan's main interest was in the martial arts and he competed in state tournaments. His life was forever changed when, at 16, his high school started a low power radio station. "It was a chance to get involved in something I had always fantasized about." As a college freshman he started in the research department at KROI-Sacramento and then went on-air with stops at KROY, KZAP and KXOA, all Sacramento stations. In November 1982, Bryan was chosen by pd Jhani Kaye to kick off the new KOST format and

has been doing afternoon drive since the spring of 1983. He's been the number one afternoon AC talent in L.A. for more than a dozen years. He has been rated number one in his time slot for more than three years straight in the early '90s, according to Bryan. *R&R* has named him consistently to their national list of Top 25 P.M. Drive Time Dominators. His personal on-air highlights include doing a remote show from the 1986 World's Fair in Vancouver, B.C. and satellite broadcasts from Disneyworld in Florida. Bryan also appears in the Hollywood Christmas Parade every year. He assessed KOST for this publication: "I love working at the Radio Station of the Year." Bryan lives in Glendale with his wife Minda and sons Bryan and Brandon.

SIMMONS, Jim: **KFWB**, 1958-59

SIMMS, Lee "Baby": **KRLA**, 1971-73; **KROQ**, 1973; **KMET**, 1973; **KRLA**, 1975. Lee was born in Charleston, South Carolina in 1944, and started his radio career in 1961 playing an Impressions song on WTMA-Charleston. He quit high school at age 16, thinking he could learn more about life by experiencing life. One of his early mentors was George Wilson. "George saved my life. George was my great inspirational guide. George taught me how to get people to listen to me; he taught me how to relate to them, and he taught me entertainment in radio." Lee got his nickname "Baby" from Woody Roberts, pd of WONO-San Antonio. "I was a kid and they were kids and we got off together." In 1965 he worked in Phoenix and traveled with the Beatles to Las Vegas. Lee worked at WPOP-Hartford from 1966 to 1968, followed by stops in San Diego and San Antonio and then went back to San Diego. He jocked at KCBQ-San Diego before arriving in the Southland. He first worked as Lee Simms and later with the nom de plume Matthew "Doc" Frail. His first night on KRLA was the day of the 1971 San Fernando earthquake. "I think about my show all the time, every waking moment. If anything happens that I think is interesting, or relatable, I'll tell it. If I think of some line, I'll write it down so I won't forget it. Good jocks are those that do good, unexpected things." In 1973, KRLA went MOR, and Lee was teamed with Johnny Hayes in morning drive. In the early 1980s he was working at KFOG-San Francisco and KDUF-Honolulu. In 1985 Lee joined the morning team at WLVE-Miami. He went to KYA-San Francisco in 1993 and left the station in early fall of the same year for mornings at KOOL-Phoenix.

SIMON, Cat: **KHJ**, 1972-73. He worked as Johnny Williams at WRKO-Boston, but had to change his name when he arrived at KHJ, since there was a long-established all-night man with the same name. His birth name was Clyde Mole, and he was originally going to use the name C.C. Simon before settling for Cat. When he left L.A., he went to WRKQ-Cincinnati as pd and worked afternoon drive. In 1978, he did evenings at KVIL-Dallas. In 1982, Cat was heard on KYST-Houston, and the following year he went to WHTZ-New York, Oklahoma City and Chicago's WMET. He was let go from his pd/md/morning drive slot at KAMZ-El Paso when the syndicated Howard Stern arrived in October 1993.

SIMON, Chris: **KNX**. Jim is the son of former L.A. newsman, Jim Simon and the brother of Jim and Tom Avila. Chris is now living in Czechoslovakia.

SIMON, Don: **KBIG**, 1985-96. Don worked weekends at AC KBIG. In 1989 he started a three-year relationship with WWI's AM Only channel. He's married to Jan Simon.

SIMON, Jan: **KKGO**, 1987-89; **KFAC**, 1989; **KKGO/KJQI**, 1989-97. Jan arrived in the Southland from KING-Seattle. She is married to KBIG personality Don Simon.

SIMON, Jim: **KABC**, 1970-76; **KFI**, 1976; **KGIL**, 1985-88; **KKGO**, 1991, pd; **XEKAM**, 1992. Jim pioneered news and talk radio at KABC in the 1970s and was co-anchor of the station's "NewsTalk" with Bob Arthur. He served many years as president of Mutual Broadcasting System and held on-air and executive positions at WBBM-Chicago, KCBS-San Francisco and KGIL. Jim was one of the last air talents on the old KYA-San Francisco. He was Gene Nelson's first newsman on his return to KSFO, according to Bob Balestieri, a follower of San Francisco radio history. Jim was part of an attempt to broadcast talk at XEKAM (950AM). The tapes were transported from Hollywood to the transmitter site near Rosarita Beach, Mexico. He retired in 1993. The Jehovah's Witness member died June 6, 1995, of complications from diabetes, an aneurysm and a stroke. He was 61.

SIMON, Lou: **KKHR**, 1983-86; **KNX/FM**, 1986. Born Lou Goldberg in Newark, Lou legally changed his name in 1984. He worked at KZZP-Phoenix before he arrived in Southern California. He worked both drive periods at the CBS/FM Rock experiment. While in the Southland, Lou hosted "Live From the Record Plant" and hosted and produced "After Midnight," which was a weekly interview show on KKHR and KNX/FM. In the late 1980s, Lou was heard on KZHT-Salt Lake City and was also pd. He lives in Basking Ridge, New Jersey, and was a major executive with RCA Records in New York until 1995. He's senior vp of programming for Music Choice, the digital cable radio network.

Mornings,	Christmas 1988
KLOS:	Mark and Brian
KMPC/FM:	Raechel & Rick
KROQ:	The Poorman
KNAC:	Thrasher
KLSX:	Peter Tilden
KBIG:	Bill and Sylvia
KEZY:	Rick Lewis
KLIT:	Jim Carson
KSRF:	Greg O'Neill
KTWV:	Danny Martinez
KABC:	Ken & Bob Company
KFI:	Owens & Lohman
KGIL:	John Swaney
KPWR:	Jay Thomas
KIIS:	Rick Dees

SIMON, Perry Michael: **KLSX**, 1995-96, pd. "I practiced law until I couldn't stand it anymore and had to go back to broadcasting." Perry uses his middle name to avoid confusion with Viacom's tv president. Perry was hired for the launch of "Real Radio" at KLSX. As the former pd of the highly successful John and Ken team (KFI) in Trenton, Perry was expected to replicate his past successes with WTKS-Orlando and WKXW-Trenton. From 1986 to 1991, Perry worked corporate management (programming, legal, marketing) for the Press Broadcasting Company with four stations on the East Coast. Born in Patterson, New Jersey in 1960 he was raised in New Jersey, then lived in Philly, New York and Los Angeles. Perry graduated from Haverford College and Villanova Law School. Why the three-name thing? "It has that charged-with-a-heinous-crime feel to it." His contract with KLSX was not renewed.

SIMS, Robert: **KABC**, 1967-68; **KNX**, 1968-97, nd. "I loved English, literature, writing...but I was also good at science and math so I figured I'd be an engineer." Bob was raised in Klamath Falls, Oregon. While he was in college he tutored high school students in geometry, algebra and trigonometry. He liked explaining things and for a time considered becoming a teacher or a science writer. So he took some journalism classes. "When I took a broadcast journalism course it really clicked. It was the perfect fit for me." In 1967 Bob interned for KABC News then worked for a time in the KABC newsroom. He joined KNX as a news writer shortly after the station went all-News in 1968. Bob became news director in 1982. How has the station changed over the years? "I think we're a little less stuffy now than we were in the 70's. We try to be pleasant, intelligent company in the car or the kitchen or wherever."

SINCLAIR, Dick: **KIEV**, 1950-54; **KFI**, 1954-68; **KIEV**, 1968-97, pd. Dick gained prominence in Southland radio as the host of "Polka Party." The show debuted during World War II on Guadalcanal Island. Private Sinclair, who was a pioneer in the creation of the Armed Forces Radio Service, first aired the show to an all G.I. audience over the island's military station. While at Guadalcanal he met George Putnam, who today airs his "Talk Back" program on KIEV. After the war, Dick enrolled and graduated from the University of Utah. He

started in Butte, Montana before coming to the Southland. A tv version of *Polka Parade* was syndicated in 65 markets and aired locally for two decades. While at KFI he served as staff announcer and financial editor. Since 1968 Dick has been the pd of KIEV.

SIRMONS, Tom: **KNX**, 1987-94. Tom arrived in the Southland from a news/talk station in Florida to become one of the morning news anchors at KNX. His father is head of labor relations for CBS. Tom now lives in Florida.

SKAFF, Ned: **KDAY**, 1968-70; **KFI**, 1970-79, pd; **KGIL**, 1979-92. When you drive near the Los Angeles Airport and tune in 540AM, you get Ned Skaff 24 hours a day giving traffic and parking conditions. In semi-retirement, the Charleston, West Virginia native has spent a half century in radio. After high school in Charleston, Ned went to USC and the Don Martin School of Broadcasting in the mid-1940s. He started his radio career at WTIP-Charleston followed by WATG-Ashland, Ohio and WKOY-Bluefield, West Virginia. In 1950 Ned began a 17-year career with WCHS-Charleston doing dj work on radio and being a news anchor on tv. He was JFK's announcer in the 1960 elections. In 1968 he followed his WCHS gm to KDAY as pd. "One day as I was leaving KDAY, a van full of scruffy kids pulled up to the station and begged me to play their record. Turned out it was Charles Manson and his group. Manson was from Charleston and lived a block away from my wife and across the street from my elementary school. Kinda scary." Ned spent a decade with KFI, first as a newsman then pd. He has always been fascinated by motorcycles, sailboats and airplanes. When he joined KGIL he opened a wholesale motorcycle accessory business which he ran for over a decade. Ned lives in the San Fernando Valley.

SKY, Bob: **KWIZ**, 1975-77; **KIQQ**, 1986, om; **KLIT**, 1990. Bob did afternoons at "K-Lite."

SKYLOR, Dave: SEE Bobby Romero

SKYLORD: **KLOS**, 1990-97. Scott Reiff was born and raised in San Diego. He graduated from San Diego State University in 1985 with a degree in business. Skylord moved to the Southland to pursue a career as a pilot reporter. He joined the morning team of Mark and Brian and was christened "Skylord." Scott is a physical

fitness enthusiast and lives in the San Fernando Valley with his wife, Lisa.

SLADE, Karen: **KJLH**, 1990-97, gm. The former cheerleader and homecoming queen at Kent State University is one of the few African American females to hold the post of major market radio vp/gm. Karen received her B.S. telecommunications degree from Kent State and an M.B.A. from Pepperdine University. She spent a decade working for the Xerox Corporation in various sales executive positions before joining Stevie Wonder's station. Karen is active in numerous local organizations and is a 1993 Peabody Award recipient.

SLATE, Allin: **KIEV**, 1950-62, gm; **KABC**, 1963-69; **KNX**, 1969-78. In 1964 Allin was sports director of KABC. He arrived at the station with the idea of doing an all-night sports show. Instead he captained KABC's maiden voyage in early evenings. He was told to "talk sports and make it interesting." Guests were hard to come by and it was strictly a raw experiment that developed into "SportsTalk." Born in Illinois, Allin grew up in L.A. "I was the kid who sat in the bleachers and called the game." He was a radio actor before World War II and worked in radio dramas with Jack Webb. "I was working in the sound and lighting department at the Biltmore Bowl while studying at the Pasadena Playhouse. A waiter suggested that I try radio acting." After the war he worked for three stations in Hawaii before arriving in the Southland at KIEV. Allin continued his radio acting and appeared in some tv series including *Dragnet*. In the late 1960s Allin came down with Parkinson's Disease and suffered a stroke in 1991. He is past president of the Southern California Sports Broadcasters Association. In the summer of 1997, Allin was planning to move to Seattle in order to be closer to his daughter.

SLATER, Bill: **KFWB**, 1964-65; **KRLA**, 1965-67; **KPPC**, 1969-70. Bill started out with McLendon Top 40 powerhouse KILT-Houston in 1960. He spent a year at WGR-Buffalo in 1963 before arriving for weekends at KFWB. In 1966, *Billboard* published the results of the Radio Response Ratings, and Bill tied for top all-night disc jockey in the Pop Singles category. Between KRLA and KPPC, Bill was pd and did the evening shift at Progressive KSJO-San Jose. After KPPC, Bill worked KZEL-Eugene, KZAP-Sacramento and KQFM-Portland. The University of Houston radio/tv graduate returned to his hometown of Victoria, Texas, in the 1980s, and he does radio and tv production. He also restores antique photos at "Custom Copy Photos by Bill Slater."

SLATTERY, Jack: **KLAC**, 1959

SLAUGHTER, Paul: **KBCA**, 1968. Born in 1938, he arrived in the Southland from jock work in Maui and Sydney, Australia.

SLICK, Vic: **KRLA**, 1984-87, and 1992. Born Vic Corral, he was a producer for KRLA morning and afternoon shows including Emperor Hudson, Danny Martinez, Mucho Morales, Manny Pacheco, Russ O'Hara and Charlie Fox. Vic did fill-in work and in between KRLA assignments he worked in the Riverside and San Bernardino markets. He has been with KOLA-Riverside since 1995.

SLIM: **KKHR**, 1985-86. Born Leslie Nelson.

SMALLS, Tommy: **KDAY**, 1958-59. Known as Dr. Jive in New York, Tommy owned an L.A. nite club called Smalls' Paradise West.

SMILEY, Tavis: **KGFJ**; **KJLH**; **KKBT**; **KABC**, 1994; **KMPC**, 1994-95. Born in 1964, Tavis co-hosted a late evening talk show on KMPC with Ruben Navarette billing itself "A Generation X Viewpoint." The show was launched in April 1994. He was a former aide to Los Angeles Mayor Tom Bradley and ran for a City Council seat against Ruth Galanter finishing third in a field of 15. Born in 1965, Tavis grew up near Indianapolis and is one of 10 children and the oldest of eight sons. He left Indiana University to work for the mayor of Bloomington. He began his radio career while running for the 6th Los Angeles City Council District in 1990. He felt a voice was needed to represent the African American constituency and started a series of commentaries, "The Smiley Report," that eventually was compiled into a book, *Just a Thought: The Smiley Report*. In the summer of 1996 he wrote *Hard Left: Straight Talk about the Wrongs of the Right*. Currently he is with Black Entertainment Television.

SMITH, Bill: **KGIL**, 1970-76; **KABC**, 1980-90; **KNJO**, 1996. An Army "brat" whose youth was spent globe-trotting with his U.S. Army parents, beginning school in Japan and finishing in Germany, Bill's entire broadcasting career has been in Los Angeles. Bill began as a news reporter at KGIL, became nd and eventually took over morning drive when Dick Whittington left the station after a long and successful run. During the "Whittington" years, Bill was the "mystery voice" of the character Harrison Hollywood, a popular parody of Hollywood reporters. As a licensed pilot, Bill often flew the KGIL Skywatch plane reporting on freeway traffic. This led to his first stint on KABC. Following KGIL, Bill spent ten years as reporter and anchor on KTTV/Channel 11, anchoring the station's "*Today*-like show" noontime newscast. During his decade at KABC, he worked as regular fill-in (with Eric Tracy) for the popular morning team, Ken Minyard and Bob Arthur. He also teamed with Wink Martindale for an afternoon drive program. After KTTV, Bill spent three years at KCBS/Channel 2 and currently reports for KTLA/Channel 5. "Even though I have won various awards for 'best TV reporter,' my heart remains with radio." At KNJO, Bill was teamed with co-host Kirby Hanson, billing themselves as a "low budget Regis and Kathie Lee" in an experiment to see if talk radio would work on a "very local" level. "All was proceeding well until gm Steve Angel (longtime friend from the KGIL days) died of leukemia and the station was sold." Bill free-lances for "KNXNewsradio."

SMITH, Bobby: **KGFJ**, 1973

SMITH, Calvin: **KFAC**. Calvin launched his first Los Angeles radio station in 1926 with a $200 investment and introduced KFAC's Classical music format. He and an L.A. High School classmate scraped up $200 and went on the air as station KGFJ. They broadcast only when they had something to say, then went off the air and spent the balance of their time trying to sell commercials so they could resurface the next day. According to the *LA Times*, Calvin went to work for KFAC in 1932 as chief engineer and became manager during a difficult Depression-era economy. He hit on the concept of using recorded classical music introduced by announcers who were classics-oriented. His first success was the ongoing Southern California Gas Co. two-hour evening concert. He retired to Hawaii in the mid-1980s and died in August 1991. He was 86.

SMITH, China: **KDAY**, 1971-72; **KRLA**, 1972-73; **KROQ**, 1973-74; **KMET**, 1974-75; **KLOS**, 1979; **KWST**, 1980-81; **KMGG**, 1983-84; **KUTE**, 1984-87; **KTWV**, 1989-91; **KAJZ/KACD**, 1992-96. Thomas Wayne Rorabacher was born in Grand Rapids in 1943. He used the name Wayne Thomas for his first four years in Michigan radio. In 1969, at KCBQ-San Diego, pd Gary Allyn gave him the name China. The name Smith was picked to give an ethnic balance of exotic and American. Bob Wilson brought China to the Southland to work AOR KDAY from KING-Seattle. After KMET, China had the urge to go back home to Michigan. "I was at the old KROQ with Rabbit and Lee Simms, and I left with the station owing me $12,000. So I went home to fish, water ski and get back near family." He worked for stations in Lansing and WWWW-Detroit. "I hated Detroit so much that I drove 90 miles each way each day to avoid living there." In the 1980s, he was the voice on tv's *Solid Gold* syndicated show. He is most proud of a syndicated program called "Fusion 40," which was heard on four continents. China described the program as "a combination Quiet Storm, jazz/NAC and World Beat." He did the show for almost five years. He was involved with the Academy Award-nominated music from *Young Guns II* and was thrilled to attend the awards ceremony. China hosted the afternoon and midday slot on KACD, "CD 103" until a format change to "Groove Radio" when he returned to Grand Rapids.

SMITH, Dave: **KIEV**, 1993; **KMAX**, 1995-96; **KWNK**, 1996; **KIIS/AM**, 1997. Dave gave up the security of a coaching and teaching job to pursue a radio career. He teamed with Joey Haim for a program called "Sports Gods" on KMAX. "It was not a logical thing to do. I had been at Canoga Park High School for four years as the basketball coach and another six years teaching physical education. My wife couldn't believe that I would give up the security of a job, a house and marriage." Born and raised in the San Fernando Valley, Dave grew up listening to sports talk shows. "I knew more than anyone I heard on the air." Dave combines comedy with sports trivia. Dave and Joey now host their "Sports Gods" program on "XTRA Sports 1150."

SMITH, Dennis: **KBCA**, 1969-76. Dennis left the Jazz station in the summer of 1976.

SMITH, Frazer: **KROQ**, 1976-79; **KLOS**, 1979-84; **KMET**, 1984-86; **KLSX**, 1986-97. Frazer's success is fueled by funniness. His zany brand of humor made an indelible mark on the Southern California landscape when he did mornings at KLOS. He was known as the "Party Animal." Born in Kalamazoo, Frazer graduated from Pioneer High School in the shadow of the University of Michigan stadium. In his home state, he did tv weather and sports and Top 40 radio. His reflector sunglasses and pseudo-cool image have been his trademarks during tv, concert and public appearances. After a brief stint in Chicago's Second City comedy troupe workshop, Frazer perfected his stand-up comedy, and while in Detroit, he opened for Phil Proctor and Peter Bergman of the Firesign Theatre. This collaboration led to KROQ, where he hosted a weekend program called "The Hollywood Nightshift," with Phil Austin and Michael C. Gwynne. The show mixed punk rock escapades with mock showdowns with the LAPD. In 1979, after he publicly lambasted KROQ management, he was fired. Later, when he left KLOS, management said that Frazer's outside activities were a factor in his departure. During his time with KLOS, Fraze noted a front-page photo in the *LA Times* of a

massive car pileup on Interstate 5. He roared, "Folks, everyone is lined up on I-5, waiting to see the Fraze's new film, 'Personal Worst,' starring Mariel Hemingway, Ernest Hemingway, Carole Hemingway - what a family." His roster of radio playlet themes included "Wild Frazedom," "Leave It to Frazer," "The Six Million Dollar Fraze" and "The Frazeford Files." At the height of the *Star Trek* craze, he created "Fraze Trek-The Motion Picture." He created bizarre technical jargon with Billy Carter as the captain of the dreaded gorgon spaceship, Frazerprise. When he joined KLSX, he hosted "Saturday Night Fraze." In 1980, Frazer headlined at the Roxy on Sunset Boulevard where he featured many of the characters from his morning radio show. In 1981, he appeared on the CBS series *White Shadow*. In February 1982, the Fraze starred in a film called *Tag* that was patterned after a James Bond-style spoof. After the "Party Animal" moniker played itself out, he started calling himself the Garden Weasel and Weed Molester. In the February 1986 *Playgirl*, Frazer was voted one of "America's Favorite DJs." Fraze went for triple entendres, so if you didn't get one reference, you'd get another: "We've got Bo Derek, Bo Belinsky, Bo Schembechler, Beau Bridges, not to mention Bobo Brazil. The only question is who'll win the Olympic-size toaster and who'll get stuck with the free trip to Poland." The Fraze has been broadcasting on weekends live from local comedy clubs.

SMITH, Hal: **KLAC**, 1972-76, pd. Hal joined the Country station from being the Southeast marketing director for Capitol Records. His time at KLAC included being the operations manager. At the 1973 *Billboard* Radio Programming Forum, he was awarded country music pd of the year. In 1976 he went to KNEW-San Francisco as gm. When Hal left the Bay Area he traveled to Philadelphia to manage WMMR and WIP. When the stations were sold, the president of Metromedia formed Encore Media. Hal was hired to manage an Encore station, KSYG-Little Rock.

SMITH, J. Thomas: **XPRS**, 1972. He worked the all-night shift on "the soul express."

SMITH, Jack: **KLAC**, 1957-59

SMITH, Jan: **KWIZ**

SMITH, Joe: **KFWB**, 1961. A major music industry veteran who retired as president and chief executive of the Capitol-EMI record label, Joe is also an accomplished pianist. Earl McDaniel remembers introducing Joe in Japan in 1947. He started as a dj in Boston before becoming a weekender at "Channel 98." Joe left KFWB in August 1961, refusing to cross the picket line. Only Joe and Ted Quillin did not return to KFWB after the strike. He commented on leaving his on-air career: "I felt an insecurity in the talent end of the business. The emphasis had shifted from individual personalities to a station's sound." Born in 1928, Joe rose through the ranks of Warner Bros. Music, beginning in 1961 when he was national promotion manager. He was responsible for signing and developing the careers of such artists as the Grateful Dead, James Taylor and Jimi Hendrix. By 1966, he was gm of the label. At Capitol he helped revive the career of Bonnie Raitt. He has served as president and ceo of Warner/AMEX Cable's sports entertainment. In 1975, Joe was made Elektra/Asylum Records chairman of the board. In 1993, he became executive producer of entertainment activities for World Cup USA 1994 - the world's soccer championship.

SMITH, Ken: **KGFJ**, 1986. "The Master K," as Ken was known, worked overnights at Soul KGFJ. He is now part of Bayley Productions.

SMITH, Milton: **KJLH**, 1992. Milton worked the all-night shift at KJLH.

SMITH, Pete: **KNX**; **KDAY**, 1956-58, pd; **KRKD**, 1958-61; **KNOB**; **KPOL**; **KMPC**, 1961-88; **KJQI/KOJY**,

1993-95. The native Californian, who was born in Orange, has spent his entire radio career in Southern California. He grew up in Laguna Beach and Newport Beach. "Ever since I was little kid I wanted to be an announcer. I liked the style of announcers on CBS and I was thrilled to work a summer at KNX." At 23 he was programming KDAY, an early pioneer Top 40 station. "Of all the stations I worked, my experience at KDAY was the best. The gm didn't interfere and I was able to hire and fire." At KRKD (now KIIS/AM) Pete worked morning drive and was the md. During his 40 years of radio employment, the longest journey was on and off KMPC, for three decades. Pete worked at Armed Forces Radio Services for 21 years. "For many years there was another Smith who followed me at Armed Forces Radio, Bob Smith. As the Wolfman he had a 'little' different style." In 1979 Pete became a station owner. A group of investors bought KWVE-San Clemente and ran it until 1985. Pete's five years at KNOB was because he loved jazz. "I taped the shows. There was no money, so mostly it was for a little barter and a love for the music." Pete is now on "The Music of Your Life" satellite-delivered program. He splits his time between living in Palm Springs and Rosarita Beach, Mexico.

SMITH, Wallace: **KUSC**, 1972-96, pres/gm. When Wally took over control of KUSC he decided that a university radio station should not have much to do with a university - outside of accepting its monies. He moved the station off campus, got rid of the students, switched to classical music and signed up with National Public Radio. He was KUSC's first general manager, and except for one year ('87-'88) in New York running WNYC, has served in that capacity until 1996. In a 1994 profile of

classical music radio in the *LA Times*, Wally described KUSC: "Our objective is to bring...classical music to a new public." He was born in 1936. He is a graduate of Waynesburg College and the Pittsburgh Theological Seminary, receiving his master's and Ph.d degrees in communications from the University of Southern California. Dr. Smith resigned in the fall of 1996, according to the *LA Times*, "amid a review by a USC task force of the station's finances and management structure and an analysis of its listenership and programming." The station experienced a $500,000 deficit in his last fiscal year. In the summer of 1997 he became gm of WPBX-New York.

SMITHERS, Ray: **KPOL**, 1978-79; **KMPC**, 1980-81. Ray arrived at KPOL as midday air personality and production director. He joined KMPC the following year as creative production director and also did weekend work and fill-in. In 1980 he conceived and produced a national public service campaign called *Energy 80* with Orson Welles, Henry Fonda, Martin Sheen and as Ray said, "a few other nobodies." The campaigned aired on over 5,000 radio stations. Ray has developed a new product that reaches over six million phone calls a year. "In 1983, former KPOL newsman Jerry Trowbridge and I invented the first touch-tone based radio/tv polling system called Touch-Vote. In 1985 we developed Touch-Map, the first automated telephone locator system. We do 100% of the automated ATM locating in North America for such companies as 1-800-GOODYEAR, Harley-Davidson and 1-800-WALGREENS. It is my voice on all of these locators. I never had such a big audience when I was in radio!"

SNAKESKIN, Freddy: **KTNQ**, 1977-78; **KROQ**, 1980-89; **KOCM/KSRF**, 1991; **KROQ**, 1990-93. The Arizona native first came to Los Angeles as a weekend/fill-in at "Ten-Q" as Dave Trout. When he went to KROQ, there was already a fish name (Jed the Fish), so Frederick J. became a snake. Freddy worked at KROQ for almost a decade and was pd for a while in 1983. He had an enormous drop-in collection and probably even more Jack Webb one-liners that he seamlessly integrated into his music and show. He launched the "MARSfm" techno-rock format on May 24, 1991. The format did not last long, and he returned to KROQ for weekend part-time work. In the late spring of 1994, Freddy left for morning drive and md at KEDG-Las Vegas, moving to afternoons during that summer.

SNOW, Jack: **KMPC**, 1993. Jack teamed with Chris Roberts briefly on the all-Sports KMPC.

SNYDER, Jack: **KEZY/FM**, 1973-77, pd; **KMET**, 1977-82; **KLOS**, 1984-85; **KMET**, 1985-87; **KLSX**, 1991-92. Jack was part of the legend of "the Mighty Met." Born in Cannonsburg, Pennsylvania, his parents brought him to Compton when he was one year old, and he grew up in the area. While at KEZY, Jack started on KMET as a community switchboard volunteer. At KEZY he eventually became assistant pd and afternoon drive personality. In 1980, Jack joined Westwood One as artists relations director. He returned to KMET in 1986 and was there when the AOR "underground" format was abandoned on February 6, 1987. Results in the settlement of a multi-million dollar suit against KMET's owners and operators coincidentally changed his life. Jack had not been on a vacation in years and took off for Cancun. A friend encouraged him to stop in New Orleans. He fell in love with the city, its charm, its pace and the deep roots of the music. "I couldn't believe it. Every day I learn things about music that I never knew." He came back to the Southland for a brief stay at KLSX and Unistar. "In early 1992 I knew that New Orleans was to be my new home. I packed my car; anything that didn't fit, I didn't take. I got there with no job but soon was working at WRNO and in early 1995 joined WZRH. The city is a living, breathing organism."

SOBEL, Brad: SEE Sandy Beach

> *"I enjoyed my two years at KABC more than anything else in my career. I was offered 'DodgerTalk' for the second time and insanely, for a few dollars and the matter of pride I turned it down. It was the worst decision anyone in my industry could ever make."*
> *-Fred Wallin*

SOBEL, Carol: **KFWB**, 1968-74. "As a reporter for City News Service, I was covering the news conference in early 1968 announcing the format change to all-News at

KFWB. I stayed at Perrino's for lunch that followed and was asked if I would be interested in applying for a job at the new operation. I was making $80 a week and vowed to take the job if they offered $100. To my amazement they offered $235. I also was the only woman hired on the news team." Born in California, Carol grew up in Highland Park, Illinois only to return to the Southland to attend UCLA. She graduated with a degree in English and started with the City News Service as a reporter. Carol quickly moved up the ranks at KFWB. "It was an exceptional team when we started out at KFWB. A very exciting time. We were like pioneers." She left the station in 1974 for the birth of her daughter. For the past 16 years Carol has been publishing with her husband a monthly 32-page magazine on the law of entertainment.

SOBEL, Ted: **KFWB**, 1995-96. Ted reports weekend sports from Shadow Traffic for all-News KFWB.

SOLARI, A.J.: **KMET**, 1968-69; **KLAC**, 1969; **KYMS**, 1970; **KPPC**, 1970-71. A.J. worked middays at KMET. He is now in the produce business in the Bay Area.

SOMMERS, Bill: **KHJ**, 1970-73; **KLOS**, 1973-96, gm. The longtime boss of Alternative-formatted KLOS was

born in Los Angeles and went to L.A. City College and Santa Monica City College with a pharmacy major. Bill started his radio career in 1963 as an on-air personality and newsman at KNJO. In the mid-1960s he worked in Oxnard, first at KACY and then as gm of KUDU. In

1968 he joined RKO Radio Reps and two years later became nsm of KHJ. Bill started his run with KLOS in 1973 as gsm and was promoted to gm in 1978. He has retired to Coeur d'Alene, Idaho.

SOMMERS, Karen: **KFI**, 1984

SOMERS, Steve: **KMPC**, 1981-82. The predecessor to Fred Roggin as KNBC/Channel 4's sports anchor, Steve worked sports at KMPC. He left the morning drive sports commentary show with Robert W. Morgan in 1982.

SONTAG, Frank: **KLOS**, 1985-97. Frank hosts two weekend Talk shows as well as news on the popular Mark and Brian morning drive show. He also does fill-in sports in Todd Donoho's absence.

SORKIN, Dan: **KHJ**, 1965. From 1951 to 1964 Dan worked at WJJD and WCFL-Chicago. He was a popular morning man who performed as the announcer on *The Bob Newhart Show*. A few months after his arrival in Southern California, KHJ went "Boss Radio," and Dan headed North to San Francisco where he spent many years on KSFO, KGO, KFRC and KKSJ-San Jose. In 1982 Dan was director of Synanon. He was an engineer major at the University of Wisconsin and graduated with a B.S. from the University of Illinois. Dan is a certified flight instructor and a captain and flight officer in the civil Air Patrol. He founded "Stumps R Us," a social club for amputees. Dan's currently with KKSJ where he demonstrates his love for jazz, blues and big band.

SOTO, Henry: **KKGO**, 1986-91. Henry hosted a Latin jazz show.

SOUL, Johnny: **KGFJ**, 1968-74; **KDAY**, 1974-76. Born Ron Samuels, Johnny arrived in the Southland from Texas. He worked the all-night shift at KGFJ and quickly moved to mornings. Johnny left KGFJ in 1974 to turn KDAY into an Urban station. When he left Southern California, Johnny went to San Francisco to work in "underground" rock as Ron Samuels.

SOUTHCOTT, Chuck: **KGIL**, 1962-75, pd; **KBRT**, 1980; **KPRZ**, 1983; **KMPC**, 1988-92, pd; **KJQI/KOJY**, 1992-95, pd. Born on the beach in Santa Monica, the California native began his stellar career at the tender age of fifteen in St. Thomas, Virgin Islands. Chuck and his family chartered their boat to American tourists interested in learning how to use an aqua lung, and other underwater gear. "I was spear fishing with a friend and he told me about an opening at WSTA paying 50 cents an hour and that started my radio career." Chuck worked at KAFY-Bakersfield before joining KGIL. He left after 13 years to launch a radio syndication firm. Chuck was named Disc Jockey of the Year in 1967, as reported by the *LA Times*, and was upped to pd in 1968. The *Gavin* sheet named Chuck Program Director of the Year in 1971 while still at KGIL. For the "Music of Your Life" format, *Billboard* awarded Chuck the Program Director of the Year in 1983. At KMPC, Chuck was pd and on-air talent when

the station won the 1990 Marconi Award for Radio Station of the Year. At KJQI ("K-Joy"), Chuck was pd. In 1993 the Digital Pop Standards Network launched Chuck's "K-Joy" Adult Standards format. When KJQI changed formats to all-news KNNS in the early fall of 1995, Chuck left to help design a revival of a syndicated "Music of Your Life" format. The programming is heard on over 75 stations. "Yes, a skin diving, spear fishing beach bum can make it in the tough world of broadcasting."

Who were your heroes?
"Like everyone, I have fewer as I grow older. As a child, my grandfather was definitely my hero. He worked hard, shared everything, cared vitally for every family member, told me great stories about sports figures and legendary people the world over, and asked me repeatedly about how I was doing, and assured me that everything would be 'hunky dory' - he ended every story with a warm smile. He lived for 96 years. Now, my hero is my wife, and has been for many years, she's there for me every minute, she thinks I am bright and well bred and speaks highly of me to all her friends and acquaintances...and of course, she's soft and smells good."   -Top Ten personality Bob Hudson

SPANGLER, Dick: **KFWB**, 1964-66; **KBBQ**, 1966-67, nd; **KGIL**, 1968-80, nd; **KBLA**, 1991-92. For a quarter of a century "Spangler's World" has been part of radio's landscape. In 1970 the *LA Times*' Don Page named "Spangler's World" the Best Interview Series: "A gem of an interview series provides in-depth profiles of extraordinary perception." Long recognized as "one of America's ten best interviewers," his series is produced under his Spangler's World Communication banner and is syndicated across the country. Dick was born at West Point Military Hospital in New York and as an "Army brat," attended 14 schools before graduating from high school. He then went to the University of Hawaii and, at 18 years old, began his radio journey by teaming with Don Berrigan for the "Dick and Don Show," a "minor sensation" on KHON. He moved solo to KORL-Honolulu. "I was America's stunt dj for a while. I set the world record for underwater broadcasting, a world bowling record, raced speed boats, flew planes, M.C.'ed 'Best Tan' contests on Waikiki Beach...all in the name of better ratings and advertiser promotion. I suppose the

craziest was broadcasting among 16 sharks (underwater kind) at Hawaii Marineland. I also did my show for two weeks dressed as an Indian Chief while living in a tepee." In 1960 at KELP-El Paso he set a trampoline bouncing record and in another stunt, as a cowboy, rode a horse from Mexico to the radio station. His world travels gave him the opportunity to learn a half-dozen languages and attending the University of Mexico in the 1960s. "While studying journalism and drama at the San Fernando Valley State College, I interned at KFWB and quickly became a special features reporter and anchorman." Dick later won just about every award in California radio, including give Golden Mike awards. His book, *Kung Fu: History, Philosophy & Technique*, is still selling as a trade paperback. His new book, in progress, is based on his provocative interviews with America's best authors. Dick has served as president of many local trade organizations. As a Financial News anchorman, he was part of the launch of all-Business KBLA on April 17, 1991. His communication company produces radio/tv business programming, commercials and infomercials.

SPARKES, Ken: **KGBS**, 1968. Ken was one of a handful of jocks from Australia to work in L.A.

SPEARS, Gary: **KYSR/KIBB**, 1996-97. Gary was hired for weekends at KYSR and doing fill-in at sister KIBB. He hosts "Cafe Hollywood," a Hot AC syndicated show from Superadio. In the fall of 1996 he joined mornings at "B-100" as part of the "Breakfast Jam."

SPEARS, Michael: **KHJ**, 1977. Michael was a longtime personality at legendary KLIF-Dallas, as Hal Martin, in the 1960s. When he left his on-air jock life for one of programming, "Hal Martin" disappeared. In 1975 Michael was voted *Billboard*'s Program Director of the Year while at KFRC-San Francisco. In 1977 he joined KHJ as pd and left before

Christmas. He went on to purchase with partners Tampa Bay's first all-Talk radio station, WPLP. He owned the station four years prior to joining the Fairbanks Group as national pd. In 1978, Michael launched New World Media, a radio programming service. He has programmed WYSL-Buffalo, KFRC, and KNUS-Dallas (first FM station in Dallas). As programmer at KKDA ("K104")-Dallas for eight years, Michael achieved enormous success with the Urban station. Michael was in the television business for two years syndicating two national programs: *The Beam*, a black entertainment and music show and *Youth Quake*, which was on the USA Network. In 1992, Michael left Dallas to program WPNT-Chicago, a Hot AC station. He left in the summer of 1994 and returned to the city of his greatest success to be operations director of News/Talk KRLD-Dallas.

SPEARS, Russ: **KHTZ/KRLA/KLSX**, 1983-93; **KSCA**, 1996-97. Russ broadcasts afternoon traffic from Shadow Broadcasting and lives in Santa Clarita. Born October 19, 1957, he grew up in Arizona.

SPERO, Stan: **KFAC**, 1951-52; **KMPC**, 1952-97, gm. Stan started his 40+ year career in sales at KFAC moving to KMPC two years later and staying 42 years. When Stan stepped down as gm in 1978, he took over as parent Golden West's vp in charge of sales for its sports division. He is past president of Southern California Broadcasters Association and the Hollywood Chamber of Commerce and is active in other community groups. In the mid-1990s he was senior sports consultant to KABC/KMPC. Stan was born and raised in Cleveland Heights and came to the Southland to study at USC. He received a B.S. degree in business administration.

SPIVAK, Joel A.: **KLAC**, 1965-68. Son of big band leader Charlie Spivak, Joel distinguished himself as a talk show host and news commentator. One of his fellow workers at KLAC said of Joel: "What a wonderful guy. He arrived in Southern California from the East. He got off the airplane with an umbrella, searing spats, a fedora hat, tight, close-fitting suit and narrow tie. He was a bit out of touch but within a month of his arrival, everyone loved him." His radio career began quite unintentionally when he took a temporary job at a local station while attending the University of North Carolina. He came to KLAC following five years at KILT-Houston and four at WPRO-Providence. When Joel left the Southland he could be heard over the next decade in Philadelphia and Washington, DC. His dry wit was reflected in one of his on-air promos: "Droll A, Here's Joel A." In the spring of 1997 an Internet correspondent said: "I've bumped into Joel on the public bike trail that runs behind our house so I presume he still lives near or in Bethesda."

SPOON, Marco: **KJLH**, 1980-90, pd. A few weeks after his arrival in Southern California from WGCI-Chicago, he became operations manager. He is now living in Chicago.

SPRINGFIELD, Dan: **KHTZ**, 1984. Dan arrived from KSDO-San Diego.

SQUIRLE, Julie: **KROQ**, 1978-79

ST. CLAIR, Dick: **KFI**, 1976

ST. CLAIRE, Chuck: **KCBH**, 1968

ST. JAMES, Scott: **KMPC**, 1979-82; **KMGG**, 1984; **KMPC**, 1991-92 and 1995; **KCBS**, 1995-97. The Walnut Creek native's name was a household word for four years at KMOX-St. Louis before he joined Robert W. Morgan at KMPC. In the '70s he worked at WPOP-Hartford, KLIV-San Jose and KSD-St. Louis. Scott hosted an early evening sports talk show on KMPC from 1979 until 1982 when the station dropped Talk for the "Hitparade" format from Drake/Chenault Enterprises. He was a sports reporter/anchor for a number of tv stations including KCAL/Channel 9. Scott was also a part of the brief KMPC all-Sports format experiment. At KMPC he did the post game "AngelTalk." In the fall of 1995 he joined "710Talk," KMPC for evenings. Currently he is heard doing the sports reports on "Arrow 93." Ultimately he strives for an acting career and had a role on *The Young and the Restless*.

ST. JAMES, Tony: **KYMS**, 1969-70; **KWIZ**, 1970-74; **KWOW**, 1974-78; **KIQQ**, 1978-85. The Philadelphian was born in 1946. At KIQQ he teamed in morning drive with Bruce Chandler for close to five years until the station changed format to "Lite-100," the Transtar 41 satellite-delivered format. In 1987, he went to work at Unistar and was the original night jock on AM Only. He had a very lucrative voiceover career and his campaign for Coors Extra Gold provided for the down payment on his house. Tony died April 22, 1990, at the age of 42 from complications following a perforated ulcer.

ST. JOHN, Geoff: **KPWR**, 1993-95. Geoff arrived in the Southland from the Bay Area. He now works for KYLD ("Wild 107")-San Francisco.

ST. JOHN, Gina: **KYSR**, 1993-95. Gina was the nighttime jock on a Cleveland station before landing the nighttime gig at "Star 98.7." Gina left KYSR in the late spring of 1995 to pursue a career in television. She's hosted C\Net Central that runs on USA Network and the Sci-Fi Channel. Gina is the co-host of *E! News Daily*.

ST. JOHN, Mark: SEE Hurricane Allen

ST. THOMAS, Bobby: SEE Tom Murphy

ST. THOMAS, Johnny: **KRLA**. Using his real name, John Newton, he worked Southern California radio during the 1970s and 1980s. Johnny became assistant pd to Jack "The Hit Man" Roth at KRLA in the early 1970s and he left in 1985. He now sells Farmers Insurance.

STACY, Rick: **KYSR**, 1995-96. Rick moved to afternoon drive at "Star 98.7" in the summer of 1995 from pd of KKFR-Phoenix, WINZ and WHYI-Miami and WNNX-Atlanta. He has spent 12 of his 18 years in radio in morning drive. He has subbed for Rick Dees on his national countdown show. In late 1995 Leah Brandon joined Rick to co-host the afternoons. One of their features was "The Battle Of Sexual Orientation." Rick left the Los Angeles market in the summer of 1996 for mornings at KWMX-Denver. In 1996 he was nominated for *Billboard* dj of the year.

STAGGS, Brad: **KGIL/FM**, 1987

STANFIELD, Ray: **KLAC**, 1966-69, gsm; **KGBS**, 1970-74, gm. Bill Ballance's "Feminine Forum" and the creation of the Hudson & Landry morning team was launched under Ray's watch. Ray grew up in Greenville, South Carolina and started his radio career in his hometown at age 16. After two years in the Navy, serving in the Pacific after the war, he returned to work in Greenville. In 1952 he joined WIS-Columbia, South Carolina, and moved from sports to nd, to pd and into

> *"Homesickness, lack of friends and no feeling of belonging in that most challenging and frightening of cities began to drive a wedge between my young wife and me. I loved L.A., no matter how much I hated living there."*
> -Dave Williams

sales. In 1956 he joined WIST-Charlotte for his first gm assignment. Ray joined a rep firm in New York between 1962 and 1965. Metromedia sent Ray to manage KMBC-Kansas City in 1965 and a year later the company made him gsm of KLAC. In 1969 he became the gm of WRNG-Atlanta and a year later he returned to the Southland to manage his last radio station, KGBS. After leaving KGBS in 1974, Ray became a radio station broker in Southern California. "Brokering is certainly far more rewarding than station management. I always had an adversarial relationship with my bosses, one of whom referred to me as 'our corporate rebel.' Now I don't have a boss and can only get mad at myself."

STARK, Mike: **KNAC**, 1990-94. Mike hosted KNAC's "Talkback" show on Sunday mornings. He is now an engineer for Cap Cities.

STARLING, David: **KFI**, 1940-71; **KFAC**, 1972-88. Born in Middletown, Ohio, David came to the Southland to attend UCLA where he graduated in 1936 with a pre-legal degree. It was accidental that he got into radio. While working in a little theater a fellow actor suggested he join his group doing radio shows. This led David to a three-decade run with KFI. Some twenty years later he hosted at KFI and KFAC over 2,000 90-second programs called "A Word on the Presidency," "Energy" and "A Word on Tomorrow." Since retiring he has worked quite a few Los Angeles County Fairs and has taught in a local radio school. "I have enjoyed the days spent, able to do what I liked, but I haven't forgotten it was tough going when trying to get a start."

STARR, Bob: **KMPC**, 1980-89 and 1993-97. Bob was the play-by-play broadcaster for the Rams and the Angels. He was brought in from KMOX-St. Louis where he had been the voice of the St. Louis Cardinals for eight seasons. He had two stints as the announcer for the California Angels. During his first tour he worked with Ron Fairly and then left to broadcast Boston Red Sox games, returning in 1993. Bob started his sports broadcasting career in the mid-1950s.

STEADMAN, Bill: **KNX**, 1957-60. Bill was a USC professor who hosted "Trojan Digest" and a Sunday cultural program.

STECK, Jim: **KRLA**, 1964-67. Jim arrived in the Southland from KACY-Oxnard and was a newsman during the era when KRLA brought the Beatles to L.A. conducting many of the interviews with the Fab Four. When he left the Southland he went to the Bay Area and worked for KCBS and KTVU/TV. Jim eventually spent time in Hawaii. In 1993, it was discovered that Jim had an inoperable brain tumor. A colleague noted, "He had humor all the way through till his death." Jim died in 1993.

STECKLER, Doug: **KLSX**, 1997. Doug works afternoons at "Real Radio" with Tim Conway, Jr.

STEELE, Diana: **KKBT**, 1989-97. Born Diane Matt in Chicago, Diana started her radio career as a traffic reporter from Chicago's John Hancock Building. She received double degrees in political-science and speech communications from the University of Illinois and the University of California Berkeley. Her first on-air radio shift was in Champaign, Illinois, and then to San Francisco to work at KMEL and K101. She arrived at KKBT from KMEL to work middays (her show is called

"Steele at the Wheel") at the launch of the new format and call letters (formerly KFAC). During her time in the Southland she gave herself high marks for lasting through three format changes and four program directors. Her dream is to be a television entertainment reporter, and she has worked with both *Extra* and *Hard Copy* on celebrity interviews. Diana gets involved with many organizations and serves as spokesperson for "My Friend's Place," an organization helping 4,000 homeless teenagers. She lives in Hollywood.

STEELE, The Real Don: **KHJ**, 1965-73; **KIQQ**, 1973-74; **KTNQ**, 1976-77; **KRLA**, 1985-89; **KODJ**, 1990; **KCBS**, 1992; **KRTH**, 1992-97. A California boy with a mouthful of energy, The Real Don Steele personifies all that is right about afternoon drive. When you think center stage, think the Real Don Steele. At the end of a school or work day, Don has lifted our spirits like no other over the course of three decades. He was born Don Revert and born for stardom in Hollywood on April Fools Day and attended Hollywood High School. Before making the round-trip home to Los Angeles radio, he worked at KOIL-Omaha, KISN-Portland and KEWB-San Francisco. Don was the original afternoon drive "Boss Jock" at "93/KHJ." He was the dj on the air when the station debuted in 1965 and was the first one to utter the now immortal phrases "Boss Radio" in "Boss

Angeles." He described the moment: "We were standing literally at ground zero, then it became a huge giant. It was like a mushroom cloud that went up - heavy on the mushroom." In 1967, he hosted a Canadian syndicated radio show called "CBC's Action Set," and in the same year he made his acting debut in ABC/TV's *Bewitched*. In 1967 and 1968 Don's popularity and influence were such that he was named *Billboard*'s #1 air personality influencing the sales of record singles. "Tina Delgado is Alive, Alive!" became his afternoon cry. He had his own weekly tv show, *The Real Don Steele Show*, which was the top rated rock-and-roll television dance show in Southern California from 1968 to 1975. Legendary film maker Roger Corman utilized Don to create movie versions of fast-talking, hip characters numerous times. He starred in movies with Sylvester Stallone, David Carradine and Ron Howard in cult classics such as *Death Race 2000*, *Rock & Roll High School*, *Grand Theft Auto* and *Eating Raoul*. In the early '80s, Don hosted "Music USA," a syndicated radio show for the Golden West stations. The late '80s saw a resurrection of his tv dance show on Orange County's KDOC/TV. "Live From the Sixties," a successful, nationally syndicated weekly radio show brought The Real Don Steele into over 300 markets coast-to-coast and is still heard in reruns in many places in the country. Additionally, Don's voice can be heard in films, tv shows and commercials, as well as on Capitol Radio in London, which has over six million listeners. He provides that "Top 40 American Sound" to the station promos, IDs and lines aired on England's #1 Oldies station. Philip Eberly, in his definitive book on the history of radio and pop music, *Music in the Air*, cites the following excerpt as an example of "Boss Radio" as delivered by The Real Don Steele between records: "It's three o'clock in Boss Angelese! hey hey, HEY, thitz me, The Real Don Steele! A billion dollar weekend there, and you're looking out of sidewalk call. I got nothing but groovy those groovy golds. We're gonna kick it out here on a fractious Friday boy, got to get a set outside that (unintelligible words resembling blowing bubbles in a glass of water) jumbo city! (Pause). Take a trip. When you chase'em daylight!" It took 11 seconds. In 1995 The Real Don Steele received his Star on the Hollywood Walk of Fame. He continues to be the definitive afternoon drive personality working his uninterrupted magic every afternoon on historic Oldies radio station "K-Earth 101."

STEELE, Gregg: **KNAC**, 1991-95, pd. Gregg was om/pd of KRXX-Minneapolis before arriving at KNAC to be pd in the spring of 1991. He left in early 1995 when the station switched to a Spanish format and joined WZTA-Miami as pd. Gregg has since been promoted to Paxson vp of programming.

STEELE, Mike: SEE Mike Sakellarides

STEELE, Shadow: **KQLZ**, 1989-91. Scott Wright, also known as Shadow P. Stevens, was part of Scott Shannon's "Pirate Radio" experiment and was operations manager. After KQLZ ended in 1991, he returned to program WEZB-New Orleans. He was heard on KROQ April Fools Day 1994. In 1995 he was writing for *Hits Magazine*.

STEELE, Sharon: **KEZY**, 1992-93. Sharon worked for the Unistar Hot Country format and evenings at KEZY.

STEIN, Les: SEE Les Crane.

STEIN, Mike: **KRHM**, 1959

STEIN, Sleepy: **KNOB**, 1957-64, gm. Sleepy was originator and gm of "the Jazz KNOB."

STEINBRINCK, Bob: **KMPC**, 1972-92, nd. Bob joined KMPC to broadcast UCLA games and was assistant pd. He commuted to the station every day from Riverside.

STERNBERG, Ira David: **KWIZ**, 1968-70; **KOST**, 1971-73. Born in Brooklyn, Ira grew up in the Boyle Heights area and spent his teen years in West Hollywood. "I used to sneak into KHJ on Vine Street on weekends and roam the hallways. I loved being around radio and television." Ira went on to L.A.C.C. and UCLA. At UCLA, he joined the campus radio station, KLA, became public service director and on-air personality, working with Larry Boxer, Bill Pearl and Gary Campbell. At the same time, he would call the Dick Whittington show, performing voice impersonations of Mort Sahl, commentator Louis Lomax, car salesman Ralph Willams and others. In the late 1970s, Ira moved to Las Vegas, where he worked as a writer, editor and public relations consultant. He jocked at KNUU and KDWN and became a stringer for several radio networks and a correspondent for *Billboard* magazine. Ira developed the character of Larry Las

Vegas, whose intro was: "This is Larry Las Vegas, Man About Town, Bon Vivant, Close Personal Friend to the Stars, and former Las Vegas showgirl, with my news, view, previews and reviews on what's happening in the 24-hour town." The character was heard on KGIL and KABC's "Ken and Bob Show." Ira is currently director of PR at Tropicana Resort and Casino. "I currently hold the title of longest-running PR director at one property on the Las Vegas Strip." The single father of three teaches comedy writing and is writing a book on casino publicity.

> *"My closest friends are either happy Christians or ex-drunks...and they're the happiest people I know."*
> *-Clark Race*

STEVENS, Andy: **KEZY**, 1988-93. Andy worked morning drive for part of his stay in Orange County.

STEVENS, Bill: **KUTE**, 1973-79, pd; **KKGO**, 1983-86; **KRTH**, 1991-97. Bill was born and raised in Montebello. He started his radio career in 1964 at KRFS-Superior, Nebraska, and went on to KODY-North Platte, KUDO-Riverside, KFXM-San Bernardino, KLOK-San Jose, KYNO-and KFIG-Fresno in 1971 as pd. He was pd of KUTE during the disco era and described the station at the time to the *LA Times*: "Although we identify ourselves as a Disco station, I think it's altogether

appropriate for us to play a ballad every once in a while. You have to break it up. You can't run on 140 beats per minute for 24 hours." In the early 1990s he sailed his small boat around the Pacific to Tahiti, Marquesas, Bora Bora, Samoa and Hawaii. In 1991 he worked as pd at a small island station, WVUV-Pago Pago. Bill has done many films and his tv credits include the part of Dr. Forbes on the CBS soap *Young and the Restless*. In 1992 when Brian Roberts left "K-Earth," Bill moved into the overnight slot. He relates well to the nocturnal hours. "Overnights on KRTH is the best job in radio!"

STEVENS, Bob: **KNX**, 1985-88. Bob reported news during the all-night shift.

STEVENS, Edwin J.: **KFAC**, 1965, vp/gm. Ed is deceased.

STEVENS, Greg: **KQLZ**, 1992-93, pd. Greg arrived at

"Pirate Radio" from KGMG ("Rock 102")-San Diego and replaced Carey Curelop. He teamed with Steven O. Sellers and they billed themselves "The Rude Boys." The "Guitar-Based Rock" format was beginning to see ratings success when Viacom bought the station in the spring of 1993 and changed it. Greg aired the last show on "Pirate Radio" with gm Bob Moore, and they played *Another One Bites the Dust* by Queen, The Traveling Wilburys' *End of the Line* and Guns N Roses' *Welcome to the Jungle*, which ironically kicked off the format in 1989. Greg was born in Buffalo and was exposed to not only the big personalities in Buffalo but at night he could tune in the Chicago voices. In 1975 Greg graduated from Ithaca College with a B.S. degree in radio and tv. He worked for a half dozen Buffalo stations while in college and after graduation he started at WBBF-Rochester followed by "13Q"-Pittsburgh. Greg shifted from Top 40 to AOR to work mornings at WQXM and WNYF-Tampa and KEGL-Dallas. His first pd job was in 1982 at KISS-San Antonio, where he met his 11-year morning partner, Sellers. They moved the "Rude Boys" show to KCFX-Kansas City in 1986 and a year later to KGMG. In the spring of 1993, Greg returned to San Diego and dropped his on-air work to program KIOZ. "My first interest in radio came when my dad took away my night-light (age 6 or 7) but still allowed the glow of the lighted radio dial. I pretended to sleep, but stayed up listening for hours." Greg has a wife and teenage son and says he hopes to retire in San Diego "in about 20 years from now if my luck hold out!" Following an LMA, Greg left KIOZ in early 1997 and joined KQRC-Kansas City.

STEVENS, Jay: **KRLA**, 1969-72; **KROQ**, 1972; **KIIS**, 1972; **KKDJ**, 1973-75; **KIIS**, 1975-77; **KGIL**, 1978; **KRLA**, 1986-87; **KMGX**, 1990; **KRLA** 1992-93; **KRTH**, 1993-97. Born Steve Janovick in Pittsburgh, he got the opportunity to own radio stations, a goal that most jocks only dream about. Steve grew up in Orange County and graduated from Anaheim High School. He started as Steve Jay at KFXM-San Bernardino, KMAK-Fresno and KGB-San Diego. In 1966 Steve went to KFRC-San Francisco where he spent three years. Morning drive was his first assignment at KRLA in June of 1969 with his companion Moby Duck and within months he was made md. During his stay at KKDJ he began a programming syndication business with Ron Lewis. He was briefly involved with a radio station in Bishop. During the mid-1980s he traded some programming for a radio construction permit in Klamath Falls. He built an AM daytimer and a Class C FM station. The economy, Gulf War and other financial factors eventually forced Steve to sell his stations. He has been the voice of the Wherehouse commercials and Paul's Big Screen Televisions. Steve is currently working fill-in at KRTH as Steve Jay and doing voiceover work.

STEVENS, Jackie: **KJLH**, 1989-97, nd

STEVENS, Julie: **KJOI**, 1989. Julie worked all-night at "K-Joy."

STEVENS, Les: **KKDJ**, 1974

> *"Our show was the inspiration for Oliver Stone's 'Talk Radio.'"* —Rod Roddy

STEVENS, Kris Erik: **KKDJ**, 1973-74; **KIQQ**, 1974-75; **KGBS**, 1975; **KIIS**, 1975; **KCBS**, 1991-92. Kris' success comes from his own company, which he started  in 1975 when radio became, for him, a "secondary and part-time thing." As president/owner of Kris Stevens Enterprises, Inc., he creates and produces radio/tv commercials and syndicated radio programs. Additionally, Kris is the voice of many major radio/tv commercials and network/cable television channels. He came to Los Angeles from WLS and WCFL-Chicago. While in the Windy City he appeared in a movie with Candice Bergen. In the summer of 1973, Kris started with KKDJ and a year later went on to brief stints at KIQQ and KGBS. In 1975, Kris moved to KIIS and was on the air until forming his own company. He played a disc jockey in NBC/TV's *Zuma Beach* in 1978. In the early 1990s, Kris did fill-in vacation and weekends at KCBS. His radio highlights include receiving *Billboard*'s Air Personality of the Year Award, plus working at CKLW-Detroit, WQXI-Atlanta and KQV-Pittsburgh. In 1985, he conceptualized, produced and hosted one of the first satellite-delivered weekly radio programs for the CBS Radio Network, "Entertainment Coast to Coast." The program won the Gold Medal Award for Best Entertainment Radio Program of the Year. In 1990, Kris added another dimension and dream for many broadcasters: station ownership. He bought his first radio station, WFXD-Marquette, Michigan. Other career highlights include hosting Drake/Chenault's "History of Rock-and-Roll," playing a deejay on *Roseanne* and doing character voices on *Wonderful World of Disney*, *The Smurfs* and *Scooby Doo*. In 1996, Kris updated "Christmas in the Air," "Christmas in the Country" and "Magic of Christmas" and digitally mastered these 12-hour specials to CD. Kris has been the voice of The Orkin Man for many years and is heard as the voice of Movie Tunes which plays between movies in over 7,000 theaters worldwide.

KHJ "Boss Jocks"	
6-9 am	Robert W. Morgan
9-Noon	Charlie Tuna
Noon-3	Bobby Tripp
3-6 pm	The Real Don Steele
6-9 pm	Sam Riddle
9-Mid	"Humble Harve"
Mid-6	Johnny Williams
	-November 1967

STEVENS, Richard: **KRTH**, 1989-91. Richard worked for "K-Earth" during the Phil Hall programmed days. Born in Jamestown, North Dakota, Richard followed his famous brother Shadoe to the local radio station. Prior to arriving in the Southland, he spent over six years in Palm Springs at KDES and KPSI. When Richard left KRTH, he moved his family to Dallas to work at KODZ and later at USA Overnight, KKDA and KPLX, where he did mornings. He's now developing a radio show for the Internet with his brother, Shadoe. How does he get along with his famous brother? "The entire family cheers for each other. We're all very close."

STEVENS and **GRDNIC**: **KWST**, 1979-80. Ron Stevens and his wife, Joy Grdnic have over 700 stations worldwide that subscribe to their comedy service. "I was standing in a parking lot at a high school party when someone got the bright idea to call the dj on KSHE-St. Louis and invite him to the party," said Joy. "The dj was Ron and by the time he arrived everyone was gone but me. We talked and then later in the  school year I was writing a story for the school paper and called KSHE to interview a personality. Ron answered the phone. We've been together ever since." Joy eventually joined KSHE as a dj and worked morning drive. At KWST Ron did morning drive during the week and Joy was morning personality on the weekends. When "K-West" ended, the couple wrote for tv. Some of their credits include *WKRP in Cincinnati*, *Facts of Life* and *Anything For Money*. They have written comedy books, *How To Make Love To Yourself* and *Should I Have a Baby Test?* They won a Grammy for their album *Somewhere Over the Radio*, which also was the theme of a two-hour KMET special. A second album was titled, *Retail Comedy at Wholesale Prices*. Ron and Joy launched a national talk show at the time of the O.J. Simpson trial. "The timing was awful." They teamed at "hot dance urban mix" WQHT-New York. "Can you imagine? We never worked as a morning team on a music station and we start in New York!" They took the show to AC "Y95"-San Diego. Joy and Ron have returned to their home in St. Louis and host the morning show at KIHT ("K-Hitz"). They are the most widely syndicated radio comedy team with their morning show prep sheet and over 3,000 produced comedy bits to date. "It's just the two of us and our managing partner and we did a million dollars last year!"

STEVENS, Shadoe: **KHJ**, 1970; **KRLA**, 1970-73, pd; **KROQ**, 1973, pd; **KMET**, 1974-75, pd; **KROQ**, 1977-78. The oldest of five kids, Shadoe was born Terry Ingstad in 1947 in Jamestown, North Dakota, and became a weekend deejay at age 11. He studied art at the University of Arizona and did on-camera announcing at a Tucson tv station. He worked at KIKX-Tucson and WRKO-Boston before arriving in the Southland. In addition to his activities at KRLA in 1972, Shadoe produced, narrated and syndicated "The Greatest Hits of

Rock 'n' Roll." By the end of the year he had stepped down as pd and remained as a jock. While at KMET in 1974, he was the pd and midday jock; he left in 1975. Shadoe described his station as being "for this age and beyond. Theater of the mind. No formulas. We are satirical in nature." He was *Billboard* magazine's Personality of the Year in 1975. He returned to KROQ to do weekends in 1977 with Sparkle Plentee and was a programming and production consultant in 1978 through his company Big Bucks. In the early 1980s, Stevens was Fred Rated, the bearded tv spokesman for the Federated Group, selling discount stereo equipment. One of his most celebrated tv spots for Federated stated, "Rabid frogs ate our warehouse, so we're passing the savings on to you." Fred Rated then announced "RabidFrog Bonanza Days" as hundreds of rubber frogs bounced around the tv screen. He started as the announcer on *Hollywood Squares* in 1986. The producers experimented with putting Shadoe in a celebrity square occasionally, and the appearances escalated, giving him national exposure. In 1988, Shadoe took over the "American Top 40" countdown show and became only the second host of the program. Watermark spent $1 million to promote Shadoe and by 1994, "AT40" had been discontinued in the United States. A profile in *People* magazine chronicled his 10-year first marriage, which ended in 1978 and produced his son who is now a chiropractor in Seattle. His three-year second marriage ended in 1984. His 14-year drug and alcohol-addiction ended the same year as his second marriage in 1984. Commenting on his current family, in a 1988 *Daily News* interview, Shadoe said, "My wife and daughter eventually would like a place in the country where we could spread out with our art collection and do some painting on our own." Shadoe became a regular on tv's *Dave's World*.

STEVENS, Woody: SEE Steve Woodman

STEVENSON, Al: **KTYM**. "Steve O" was considered one of the best jazz programmers. Al played football at Kansas University.

STEVENSON, Verne: **KCBH**; **KMLA**. Verne "Just A Little Jazz" Stevenson was hurt in a serious auto accident in the 1950s and resurfaced years later on KMLA.

STEW: **KNAC**, 1994; **KLOS**, 1994-97. Stew Herrera is KLOS's production director. On air he is known as Stevie Jam.

STEWART, Bill: **KMPC**, 1953-59; **KGIL**, 1965-66; **KRHM**, 1966; **KRHM**, 1969; **KGIL**, 1973-75. He was the Bill of the KMPC jingle..."Ira, Johnny, Bill and Dick!" In 1962, Bill was president of Albums, Inc. For Armed Forces Radio he hosted "A Quarter Century of Swing." In 1969, the 30-year veteran was honored with a concert at the Palladium. For 20 years he did in-flight airline music programming. Bill died in 1993 of congestive heart failure.

STEWART, Guy: **KDAY**, 1974-75

STEWART, Hank: **KBCA**

STEWART, Michael: **KKDJ**, 1971-72

STEWART, Rick: **KROQ**; **KNAC**, 1986. Rick returned to the Santa Cruz area and does fill-in on KYLD-San Francisco.

STEWART, Suzanne: **KLSX**, 1989; **KLOS**. Suzanne came to KLSX from WNCX-Cleveland.

STEWART, Zan: **KBCA**, 1977-80; **KCRW**, 1980-82. Zan is the longtime jazz writer for the *LA Times* and other publications.

STILES, Sue: **KFWB**, 1978-97. "I found an old high school paper recently where I wrote that I wanted to be a journalist. I don't even remember writing it." Sue, a Glendale native and resident, she originally studied theater arts in college. After two years she dropped out only to return at 25. "As a journalism major I wasn't sure what I wanted to do after graduating from Cal State Northridge. While working at the campus radio station, our instructor was working as a traffic scanner at KFWB. When he left I kind of inherited the job and have never worked anywhere but KFWB."

STONE, Bob: **KGRB**, 1965-67 and 1972-73; **KWST**, 1973-78; **KGRB**, 1978-89; **KKGO**, 1989-90; **KGRB**, 1990-93; **KJQI/KOJY**, 1993; **KGRB**, 1994-96. While Bob was in the U.S. Coast Guard School of Electronics in Groton, Connecticut, his commanding officer suggested that he had a voice for radio. Once out of the service in 1960, Bob secured his first radio job in his native San Francisco at KHIP. In the early 1960s he joined CBS Films in New York. Bob returned to California in 1963. He worked at KFMX-San Diego and KGUD-Santa Barbara before starting on KGRB. Between 1967 and 1972 he was at KCRA-Sacramento. During his career he remembered an unusual job: "I was the voice of Kmart for many years." Bob's last stop at KGRB was as transitional gm during the sale of the station.

STONE, Bonnie: **KBIG**; **KACD**, gm; **KSCA**, 1995-97. After an ownership at KSCA in early 1997, Bonnie joined Fox Sports.

STONE, C.J.: **KYSR**, 1992-95. Born in Montana, C.J. arrived in the Southland in September 1989 from XHTZ-San Diego, "91FM"-Auckland, New Zealand, and KPKE-Denver. He started on Unistar's Oldies Channel in 1989 and continues with WW1 doing all-nights. The Studio City resident said he loves "just being a part of the legendary L.A. radio experience! I've met some great people."

> *"It was an exciting time back then, because you didn't operate under any rules. You could play anything you wanted, say anything you wanted and who cared? FM at that time was a joke, especially to Top 40 people. We were the hippies, and they were the stars."*
> —*Mary Turner*

STONE, Cliffie: **KFVD**, 1940-44; **KFI**, 1950s; **KPAS/KXLA**, 1952-59; **KFOX**, 1959-65; **KLAC**, 1973-78.  Cliffie was born Clifford Snyder in 1917, and his primary success came from his association with the country music industry. Beginning at age 15 when he was discovered playing bass at Burbank High School, he performed with Stu Hamblen for 14 years on tv and radio shows. Cliffie hosted "Hometown Jamboree" for 10 years. The show started at the El Monte American Legion stadium which was a launching pad for a multitude of singers that included Johnny Cash, Eddie Arnold, Jim Reeves, Johnny Horton, Tex Ritter and many more. He produced over 14,000 tv and radio shows during his 50-year career in the entertainment industry. Cliffie played in the bands of Jan Garber, Gene Austin and Ken Murray. He started Lariat Records with $300 and produced records for Merle Travis, Stan Freberg and Mary Ford (before Les Paul). Cliffie managed Tennessee Ernie Ford for 20 years. In the early 1940s he was head of A & R for Belltone Records and a music producer at Capitol Records, where he was involved with Tex Ritter and Hank Williams. He is currently president of Showdown Enterprises, which includes book and song publishing, along with a record label. His awards include: Pioneer Award, Academy of Country Music/1972; Country Music Associations' Hall of Fame/1989; Hollywood Walk of Fame/1989; Walk of Western Stars/1990; Nashville's Country Music Disc Jockey Hall of Fame/1979. Cliffie is the official historian of the Academy of Country Music (previously serving as president and vp). He is still active in the C/W industry producing albums and running his publishing company from the Santa Clarita Valley. He has written two successful books, *Everything You Always Wanted to Know About Songwriting* and *You Gotta Be Bad Before You Can Be Good.* "I never planned on being a manager or anything else that came my way. In many ways I wish I were still playing the bass. You have to have a lot of luck in this business. There are four critical essentials for success: attitude, luck, sense of humor and a wife with lots of money."

STONE, Greg: **KLOS**, 1993-94. Greg hosted the program "Stone Trek."

STONE, J.B.: **KHJ**, 1974-77; **KGFJ**, 1980-81, pd; **KJLH**, 1982-84, pd/gm. Born John Barry Pleasant, J.B. arrived in the Southland from WHBQ-Memphis. Between KHJ and KGFJ, he worked at KDIA-San Francisco. At KJLH he was upped to vp/gm, and by the summer of 1984 he was out. In 1990 he became director of Taxi Productions. In 1993, he was head of Stevie Wonder's broadcast group. In 1995, J.B. was working at "Magic 97" in Albany, Georgia.

STONE, Jay: **KNX/FM**, 1971, pd. When Jay left the Southland he worked for WXLX-Pittsburgh, KZZP-Phoenix, KIKI-Honolulu, and three stations in Las Vegas. He is currently working at KXTZ-Las Vegas.

STONE, Jefferson: **KEZY**, 1976

STONE, Sebastian: **KHJ**, 1966. Sebastian was Johnny Mitchell at KGB-San Diego before he joined "Boss Radio." He was at KFOG-San Francisco in 1976 and was pd of KFRC-San Francisco.

STOREY, Roy: The former broadcaster for the California Golden Seals began as the announcer for the Los Angeles Kings in 1972. He was sports director of KYA-San Francisco and formerly "the voice" of the San Francisco 49ers.

STOREY, Tom: **KJOI**, 1974-81; **KOST**, 1977; **KMPC**, 1981-82; **KZLA**, 1981-87. "I love to fly over L.A. It's so beautiful, the sunrises, the sunsets and the weather."

Tom works for Shadow Traffic and the best part of his job is when he's "airborne" broadcasting live traffic reports for KFWB. Tom was born in Hollywood "near Sunset and Vine." He grew up in the San Fernando Valley and went to L.A. Valley College and studied anthropology at Cal State Los Angeles. "I trained for a year for a dig in Peru. Just as our team was about to leave we received a call from the consulate office warning us of Communist guerrilla activity in the mountains. We never went." Following a year at Don Martin's broadcast school, Tom joined KJOI. After a brief four-month stay at KOST in late 1977, Tom rejoined KJOI as operations manager. In the early 1980s Tom hosted a weekly talk show on KMPC and was the news director for KWHY, the financial tv station. He is active in voiceover work and appeared in *General Hospital* and with his older daughter in a local production of *Damn Yankees*.

"Music has always been thought of as the DNA chromosome of Zapoleon's station."
—**programmer reflecting on consultant Guy Zapoleon**

STRADFORD, Mike: **KKBT**, 1990, pd. Mike arrived from KMJQ ("Magic 102")-Houston.

STRATTON, Gil: **KNX**, 1967-84 and 1986-97. "I call 'em as I see 'em" has been the familiar signature from the versatile entertainer. Gil attended Poly Prep in Brooklyn and earned his B.A. from St. Lawrence University. During World War II he served as a bombardier in the Army Air Corps. After the service he appeared in a number of movies including *Stalag 17*, *The Wild One*, *Girl Crazy* and *Bundle of Joy*.

Gil was an actor on radio in the 1950s. He worked with Gale Storm on the hit series *My Little Margie* that was done in the same CBS Columbia Square where he's been doing his sportscasts since 1967. Gil entered the television broadcasting business in the mid-1950s as sports director of KNXT/Channel 2. He has covered virtually the whole spectrum of sports. He reported from the 1960 Summer Olympic Games in Rome and was the "voice" of the L.A. Rams for a time. Gil and his wife, singer-actress Dee, live in Studio City.

STRAW, Tom: **KMPC**, 1981-82, pd. Born in Baltimore, Tom came to the Southland very young and became fascinated by radio while listening to Gary Owens and the other personalities on KMPC. "You can imagine my thrill when I became pd of KMPC and worked with Gary." For a high school project Tom interviewed Gary and was invited to watch him on the air and then go to dinner. They have been friends ever since. Gary's advice to Tom was to join the radio club. "Birmingham High School had a closed circuit radio station which was basically playing music over the loud speaker at the lunch hour." By the time he was a high school senior he was working at KVFM and while a freshman at UCLA he worked afternoon drive at KGOE. From Thousand Oaks Tom leaped to morning drive at WYSP-Philadelphia followed by his first visit to KSEA-San Diego. In 1975 he joined evenings at KSD-St. Louis and became program director. During his four years in St. Louis he also broadcast the weather on tv. In 1979 Tom left for KVI-Seattle and was part of the shift from MOR to Talk. His Golden West affiliation at KVI opened the door for KMPC and Tom covered vacation schedules which led to his pd'ship. After KMPC he peripherally got involved with a station in Phoenix and the California Radio Network. At KSEA he hired a friend from high school, Ken Levine (Beaver Cleaver), who was making a mark in tv and was involved with *M*A*S*H*. Ken and Tom had always stayed in touch and Tom helped his old friend get writing experience on *After M*A*S*H*. Tom then wrote a *Benson* episode which led to a staff job and a position as story editor. He was involved in the pilot and 13 episodes of the new *Mary Tyler Moore* show and "two great years" with *Night Court* where he received two Emmy nominations. Tom joined Castle Rock Studios and sold four pilots which led to Fox's *Parker Lewis Can't Lose*, *Good and Evil* and *Nurses*, for which he was executive producer. He recently sold a pilot to NBC. In late 1996 he took over *Dave's World* as executive producer.

STRAWBERRY, Shirley: **KKBT**, 1990-97. Shirley arrived in the Southland as Shirley Clark from WGCI-Chicago and is part of the very successful morning drive House Party on "the Beat." A popular morning feature is Shirley dishing the Hollywood dirt. She married Michael Strawberry in early 1995 as an on-air event.

STREET, Commander Chuck: **KIIS**, 1983-97. Chuck has been the pilot for KIIS Yellow Thunder traffic helicopter for 15 years. In an *LA Times* profile of freeway traffic reporters in the sky, Chuck was quoted: "It is stressful. When I get down at the end of a shift, I need to sit down and unwind."

COMMANDER CHUCK STREET
SKY'S THE LIMIT!

KFWB launches all-News -March 1968

KNX launches all-News -April 1968

STREET, Dusty: **KWST**, 1977; **KLOS**, 1978; **KROQ**, 1979-86; **KMET**, 1986-87; **KROQ**, 1987-89; **KLSX**, 1990-94. Dusty Frances Street is her birth name! The native Californian was born in San Francisco and started

her career in 1967 in the Bay Area at KTIM-San Rafael and KSAN-San Francisco, where she became md in 1971. Dusty was one of the youngest female AOR rock djs. Her father's name was Emerson Street, and they lived on Emerson Street in Palo Alto. In 1979 she arrived at KROQ, where she worked until 1986, when she moved over to KMET for a year. Dusty was part of a radio/video production company that was launched in 1979. She was on the last broadcast of "the Mighty Met" on February 6, 1987. Dusty returned to the "Roq" in March of 1987 and stayed until 1989. She claimed she was fired from KROQ because she had "too strong of a personality." She told the *LA Times*: "DJs no longer have any voice. They might as well hire people with no ears. By the end of the year, I doubt seriously the station will resemble what KROQ used to be." Interviewed in 1994, she talked about the highlights of working in Southern California radio: "I loved the experience of interviewing Billy Idol, Wendy O Williams, Johnny Rotten, the Cult and Slash of Guns and Roses." Dusty commented on the state of women in radio. "A lot of ladies who got into radio decided that they had to do that bedroom thing, and not many of them developed an individual personality." She left KLSX in the spring of 1994. She told Gary Lycan of the *OC Register*, "It was like mini-purgatory working in "classic rock" radio. My background is free-form, progressive rock. I started with Tom Donahue and hopefully I'll be getting back into new music." In the fall of 1994, Dusty went to Las Vegas for middays at KEDG. In the spring of 1995, she moved to weekends at KXPT-Las Vegas.

STRODE, Tolly: **KBCA**, 1962-72; **KAJZ**. Tolly brought an East Coast flavor to his music presentation on Jazz KBCA. One of his trademark lines was, "If you want to get ahead, you got to get the bread." According to one of his co-workers, Tolly became a Black Muslim.

STURGEON, Wina: **KFWB**. Wina was a writer and consumer reporter type for all-News, KFWB. She is the former wife of science fiction writer Theodore Sturgeon. She is now a sports writer with the *Salt Lake Tribune*.

SUDOCK, Mark: **KLON**, 1975-78

SULLIVAN, Alex: **KNX**, 1976-97

SULLIVAN, Chuck: **KLAC**, 1973-80. Chuck worked evenings for much of his stay at KLAC and has since passed away in 1991. He had been living in Hot Springs, Arkansas.

SULLIVAN, G. Michael: **KEZY**, 1977-80; **KWIZ**, 1980-87. Michael

dreamed of either pursuing radio as a career or being a cop. After he got out of the Navy, he was involved in an auto accident and lost one eye. The decision was made for him. Michael started at KBRN-Bright, Colorado where he "did everything." His next stop was KAAT-Denver. Michael remembers the studio being in Hugh Hefner's old suite in the Radisson Hotel. "There was a sunken bath tub in the studio." How did he get to Southern California? "After KAAT was sold I had always wanted to work in California. So I packed my car until it was filled and gave away the rest and headed to Orange County." At KEZY he teamed with Jeff Dean for the "Doctor and the Dean" show in morning drive. Michael was born in Dallas and grew up in Salina, Kansas. When he was done with radio he joined the Orange County Fair in their radio/tv department. He had done many remotes from the fairgrounds and knew the people. "I spent three years doing that then decided to check out the management end and went to Victorville, San Bernardino County Fair for three years. Michael is now the manager of the Monterey County Fair. Miss radio? "Radio was great and yes I miss it at times."

SULLIVAN, Joe: SEE Joe Collins

SULLIVAN, Pete: **KZLA**, 1980

SULLIVAN, Paul: **KNAC**, 1976-78, pd. Paul arrived in the Southland from WWWW-Detroit.

KLAC Legendary "Big 5" during the 1950s
Dick Haynes
Peter Potter
Bob McLaughlin
Alex Cooper
Gene Norman

SULLIVAN, Tim: **KLAC**; **KHJ**, 1973-79, vp/gm; **KWST/KMGG**, 1981-82, vp/gm. Tim joined KHJ from a sales post at KLAC. He currently runs KCAL-Riverside.

SUMMERS, Karen: **KOST/KFI**, 1984. Karen arrived in the Southland from WUSN-Chicago for overnights. She now lives in Ventura.

SUMMERS, Scott: **KWST**, 1981. Scott arrived in the Southland from KFRC-San Francisco. In the 1990s he worked at Shadow Traffic services. He died in January 1995 of complications resulting from a kidney transplant.

SUMNER, Kevin: **KYMS**, 1995. Kevin worked weekends at the Orange County station.

SUPERFAN: SEE Ed Beiler

SUTTON, Ralph: **KGFJ**, 1984-86. Ralph was part of the news staff on KGFJ. He is now with the Urban League of Southern California.

SUTTON, Robert P.: **KNX**, 1953-68, gm. Born in Ogden, Bob started out as a vaudeville writer at the age of 7 performing with his parents. He later wrote for radio comedy shows. After a stint in the Navy during World War II, he worked at WCCO-Minneapolis before joining KNX in 1953 as pd. In 1961 he was named vp/gm. Following his retirement in 1968 he turned to sculpting and also built a yacht in which he cruised the world. Robert died April 18, 1996, at the age of 87.

SVEDJA, Jim: **KNX**; **KUSC**, 1978-97. Jim is "irreverent and savvy when it comes to Classical Music," according to Gary Lycan of the *OC Register*. In the summer of 1994, he completed his 600th show and marked his 12th year as host of his nationally distributed "The Record Shelf." Jim, who plays oboe and English horn, also reviews films for "KNXNewsradio" and the CBS Radio Network. At KUSC he worked on two weekly features, "The Record Shelf" and "The Opera Box" (both shows were syndicated by American Public Radio). He also recorded the intros for a nightly midnight show, "Music Till Two." Born in 1948, Jim grew up in Michigan and earned a master's degree from Syracuse University. After serving as the md of WONO-Syracuse, and a similar post at WCRB-Boston, Jim joined the staff of KUSC.

SWANEY, John: **KFWB**, 1968-78; **KGIL**, 1987-89. John was morning news anchor at all-News KFWB. In 1978 he left broadcasting to pursue a law degree and he passed the bar examination. John returned to radio to host a morning talk show on legal matters on KGIL. One of his colleagues at KGIL remembered: "John was one of the most professional broadcasters ever. And what a great intellect." John now runs his own legal service called Attorneys To Go. When a lawyer is unable to make a hearing, John's service provides a substitute lawyer.

SWAY: **KKBT**, 1996-97. Sway hosts a Saturday night hip-hop show with King Tech.

SWEENEY, Dave: **KEZY**, 1965-69; **KGBS**, 1969; **KBBQ**; **KFOX**, 1972-76, gm; **KALI**, 1996-97. David started his career in broadcasting almost four decades ago in his hometown of Kannapolis, North Carolina. He jocked in Charlotte before coming out to KEZY in 1965 to work in sales. KEZY was in the Disneyland Hotel at the time and Dave opened the Los Angeles sales office. While there, he and Emperor Bob Hudson broadcast high school and junior college sports at least three times a week. Dave was offered his first management position at KGBS in 1969. "I was very, very young, around 26 or 27, and KGBS was loaded with talent but we were a daytimer on the AM and full-time simulcast on the FM." After a brief sales stop at KBBQ before it was sold, Dave was gm of KFOX for almost five years. He became a diversified consultant, first establishing a presence within the local agency community for KMEX/TV. He ran the Chapman Brokerage firm in Atlanta and packaged a syndicated World Cup '86 broadcast for his old friend from KMEX, Danny Villanueva. He joined a group that bought two radio stations in the San Francisco Bay Area and turned them into successful Spanish outlets. In the summer of 1995 Dave became West Coast vp for United Broadcasting, owners of KALI. The FM programs all Asian. "Asian programming is in its infancy, just like Spanish radio 20 years ago, and Asian is going to be huge."

SWENSON, Steve: **KFWB**, 1980-85. Steve was a newsman at all-News KFWB and moved up to assistant pd. In 1985 he became pd of WINS-New York and a decade later vp/gm of WTOP-Washington, DC.

SYMONDS, Dave: **KEZY**, 1982-84, pd. Born, raised and educated in Oxford, England, Dave started his radio career in 1966 in New Zealand and before the year was over, relocated to London and joined the BBC. During the 1970s David worked both drive times on Radio One, Capital Radio and BBC Radio Two. Following his time in Orange County radio, David returned to London and currently does mid-mornings on Capital Gold. He also makes numerous tv appearances, frequent journalistic contributions and wrote the liner notes for a Moody Blues album. David reports from London for various U.S. tv outlets, including the old *McNeil/Lehrer Report*.

> *"I got my first taste of concert promotion. The Beach Boys came up for a four-hour show for $500. I got the rest of the money."*
> -*The Magic Christian*

T

T, Simon: **KQLZ**, 1989-90, vp/gm. Simon started "Pirate Radio" with Scott Shannon from a similar capacity at KCBQ-San Diego. He became president and COO of Beasley Broadcasting.

TABER, Jim: **KROQ**, 1973-75, pd. Jim started in radio at KOSI-Denver. From there he joined WSGN-Birmingham and WABB-Mobile. Jim returned to his hometown of Dallas and had a long stay at KLIF. Jim came to Southern California to program KROQ. In 1974 he purchased KINT AM&FM-El Paso which he retained until the early 80s. He then purchased a station in Roswell, New Mexico. Following that sale, Jim went to work for Century/TM Productions Dallas selling jingle packages. A tumor developed on his lungs which eventually resulted in a brain tumor. Jim died March 15, 1993.

TAGGART, Jill: **KGBS**, 1972-73; **KABC**, 1973-74. The Hollywood-born blonde was the host of "Male Call," that was the male counterpart to Bill Ballance's "Feminine Forum" on KGBS. Her program on KABC mainly covered entertainment news.

TALAYA: SEE Talaya Trigueros

TALBOT, Bud: **KOCM**, 1964-65; **KHJ/FM**, 1966. After graduating from Chapman College, the Korean war vet went to work at KOCM. After his brief stint in radio, Bud has been engaged in many entrepreneurial enterprises in Orange County.

TALBOT, Mario: **KWIZ**, 1990-91. Mario worked in morning drive on Spanish KWIZ as "El Gato."

TALLEY, Rick: **KABC**, 1980-82; **KGIL**, 1985-86. Rick was host of KABC's "SportsTalk," a program that went through many hosts. No matter who his partner was, Rick was always the calm host. In addition to his radio work, Rick was a columnist for the *Daily News*. He also wrote a book on Jay Johnstone. Rick was a commanding figure at 6'2" tall. He later went to work for a Las Vegas sports radio network. He died in 1995 after suffering with dementia.

TANAKA, T.N.: **KFI**, 1981. Born Ed Higashi in Santa Monica in 1951, he grew up along the San Francisco

peninsula. After receiving his 1st Class FCC License, he placed a trade ad that said, "Have Ticket, Will Travel." This creative marketing tool took him 15 miles from the Canadian border to KOJM-Haver, Montana. A few months later Tanaka joined KNEB-Scottsbluff where he was an on-air pd and earned a degree from Scottsbluff Junior College. "I lovvved Nebraska! It was just beautiful." In 1972 he was off to KCHY-Cheyenne and a half-year later he left for KDON-Monterey to do news. It was at KDON that Tanaka first met his eventual partner. "The first time I heard Byron, I was absolutely enthralled. I had never heard anything like him." They worked morning drive together but didn't really play off each other until pairing at KROY-Sacramento in 1975. They started on April Fools Day and Tanaka remembered, "It was like we had been together forever. He was on my back for 10 years." Consultant John Rook had much to do with many of their moves which included WIFI-Philadelphia from 1977 to 1980. "John brought us out to KFI to work all nights, Saturday mornings and fill-in for Lohman and Barkley." They eventually worked into afternoon drive before economic decisions split the pair and Tanaka left the station. In 1982 Tanaka started a series of part-time jobs, including booth announcer at KCET/TV, UPI Audio, teaching at the Columbia School of Broadcasting and doing part-time news at a number of stations. In 1985 he joined a family farm business in Port Hueneme starting at the bottom and now supervising two strawberry ranches and 350 workers. Miss radio? Tanaka quickly replied with conviction, "Oh, yeah. I really do! My son Matthew was born while we were in Philadelphia and ten years later I became a single father. There's a lot of insecurity in radio with a lot of moving and I wanted my son to have one place to grow up. My hours have been flexible so I could be his Little League coach for years." Byron happens to be Matthew's godfather. "My son turned 18 in late 1995. Once he's out of the house, I think I'll return to radio. Maybe a part-time gig. I've been toying with putting together an aircheck."

TANNER, Bill:

TANNER, Mike: **KMGX**, 1994

TANTER, Kirk: **KGFJ**, 1993-95; **KACD**, 1994-95; **KYPA**, 1996-97. Kirk is the production coordinator at motivational-formatted KYPA. His cousin is Lawrence Tanter.

TANTER, Lawrence: **KJLH**, 1979-84; **KUTE**, 1984-87, pd; **KOCM**, 1988-89, pd; **KLIT**, 1989, pd; **KACE**, 1990-92, pd; **KAJZ**, 1992-93. In the late 1970s, Lawrence was the creative force of the "Quiet Storm" format -- a successful integration of vocals and instrumentals -- calling it "360 Degrees of Music" at the Stevie Wonder station. He was the P.A. announcer for the Los Angeles Lakers at the Fabulous Forum, and a former basketball player. In late 1993, Lawrence joined two others in ownership of KQBR-Sacramento, where he is vp/md/pd. He told *R&R*, "I've always wanted to become involved with station ownership." He has been running KQBR since 1993. In 1996 he hosted a series called "The Immortals" for Urban stations to air during Black History Month. In February 1996 he resumed his P.A. duties as the Forum voice of the L.A. Lakers.

TANTUM, Greg: **KFWB**, 1992-97, pd. Greg programmed news and News/Talk stations for Gannett, CBS and KING Broadcasting in Cincinnati, Indianapolis and San Diego for 20 years before arriving in the Southland to run all-News KFWB. He has been an award winning reporter, anchor and writer.

TATE, Leed: **KRKD**, 1965

TAYLOR, Al: **KDAY**, 1966

TAYLOR, Alvin: **KLAC**, 1965-69. One of Alvin's fellow newsmen at KLAC remembered him as having a "booming, thunderous voice." Alvin is retired and living in Phoenix.

TAYLOR, Bill: **KFWB**, 1966-69; **KLAC**, 1969-70; **KGBS**, 1970-74; **XPRS**, 1973, pd, **KFOX**, 1975-78.

While growing up in his hometown of Milwaukee, Bill, born Bill Chimka, dreamed of being a night club comedian. "When I realized the only place for a comedian in Wisconsin was in strip joints, I turned to radio for a career with more security. I'm really a genius, eh?" He started his radio career in 1959 in Milwaukee, first at WISN followed by WOKY and WEMP. "I came to L.A. with my pregnant wife and landed a part-time news job at KFWB. I later became a disc jockey. When the station went all-News, I stayed on as a news anchor. In between newscasts, so to speak, I had a chance to perform as a comic impersonator at the Comedy Store and twice on ABC/TV's *Joey Bishop Show*." When he left the Southland Bill joined KDWN-Las Vegas and in the evenings was part of the Mickey Finn Review at the Union Plaza Hotel. "I finally got to be on stage as part of a large variety act." Saudi Arabia was one stop for the touring group. During the 1980s Bill worked in Houston, Tampa, Miami, Austin, Milwaukee and Phoenix, as well as being the voices of Johnny Carson, Rodney Dangerfield and President Reagan on hundreds of morning shows around the country, including "Z-100"-New York. When *Top Gun* was #1 at the box office, Bill commented on the air that he would love to fly in a jet fighter. An offer from the Texas National Guard put him in an F-4 Phantom. "It was the thrill of my life and I'm happy I didn't throw-up." In 1992 at KMLE-Phoenix, Bill seemed to finally find his place. He was nominated twice for CMA Country Jock of the Year and once by *Billboard* magazine. Bill was offered a 3-year contract at KIKK-Houston and the station was sold 8 months after Bill started. He moved to KSAN-San Francisco and eventually mornings at the Jones Satellite Network. He has returned to Wisconsin and is awaiting his next assignment.

TAYLOR, Bob: **KMGX/KGIL/FM**, 1989-90. Bob worked middays at KGIL.

TAYLOR, Bobby: **KPPC**, 1971. Bobby arrived at the "underground" station from KPRI-San Diego.

TAYLOR, Chris: **KNX/FM/KODJ/KCBS**, 1988-97. Chris joined the CBS outlet in 1988 as fill-in and eventually joined the production department and went through three format and call letter changes. During Oldies KODJ, he worked morning drive. He was born in Portland and raised in Seattle. While still in high school he worked for a 250-watt daytimer in Sumner, Washington. He studied advertising at Washington State University and worked for two Pullman stations. "My biggest break came in 1976 when I joined KISW-Seattle for evenings." A year later he joined afternoon drive at "98 Rock" in Tampa. Three years later the staff, en masse, crossed town to WYNS where he spent two years. His next stop was KZEW-Dallas and then to the Southland to pursue a voiceover career. He also worked as an associate producer at the Global Satellite Network. Chris is married to KNX reporter Diane Thompson.

TAYLOR, Doug: **KEZY**, 1972. Doug worked weekends at the Orange County station. He's currently raising orchids in Perris.

TAYLOR, Frank: **KCBS**, 1993

TAYLOR, Mark: **KIQQ**, 1976-77; **KFI**, 1977-88; **KBIG**, 1988-97. The native of Nacogdoches, Texas, attended Texas A&M and Stephen F. Austin State College. He worked in San Antonio and Honolulu. Mark arrived in Southern California from a pd'ship at KYA-San Francisco. While at KFI, Mark and Bruce Wayne, acknowledged as "The Dean" of America's traffic reporting for 25 years, filled in as a team when Lohman and Barkley were on vacation.  When "Bruce Wayne's KF-Eye-in-the-sky" airplane crashed, Mark has vivid memories of his on-air hours following the death of the traffic pilot on June 4, 1986. Mark resides in Simi Valley with his four children, and he continues to host the midday show on KBIG. He is active in the KCET Pledge Drives. Mark co-starred on an *Empty Nest* episode and featured on ABC's *Hudson Street*.

TAYLOR, Rick: **KOCM**, 1988-90. Rick worked evenings at "K-Ocean."

TAYLOR, Tony: **KLAC**, 1970. Tony left Southern California in 1971 to join Metromedia's sister station in New York.

TAYLOR, Zack: **KIBB**, 1996-97. Zack works part-time at "B-100" and at WW1's 70's format.

TEITEL, Joe: **KEZY**, 1996

TERRELL & KATZ: **KMPC**, 1996; **KABC**, 1996-97. The controversial pair was hired to host a weekend talk show on "710Talk." Preeminent civil rights attorney Leo Terrell represented the NAACP during the trial of the officers involved in the Rodney King beating and the O.J. Simpson case. Conservative retired L.A. Superior Court judge Burt Katz was a prosecuting attorney in L.A. Burt specialized in homicide cases, including his notable role as a lead prosecutor in the Charles Manson family murder trials. In the summer of 1996 their show moved to middays. In the fall of 1996 they joined sister Talker KABC for weekends.

TERRY, Frank: **KHJ**, 1965-68; **KFI**, 1969; **KGIL**. Born Terrance Crilly in Rapid City, South Dakota in 1938, when KHJ went "Boss Radio" in April 1965, Frank was working weekends. Before KHJ he worked at KMEN-San Bernardino and KMAK-Fresno. He went on to San Francisco and was part of the very successful KSAN morning team with Charlie Wilde. He's been with Country outlets KSAN/KNEW for the past 17 years.

TERRY, Joe: **KDAY**, 1968; **KGFJ**, 1971-75; **KHJ**, 1980-81; **KNX**; **KWNK**, 1985-86. Born Larry Boxer in Los Angeles, he grew up on the Westside and attended Los Angeles High School. His interest in radio was born between his junior and senior high school years. Joe took a public speaking course and the teacher had a program on Armed Forces Radio. His teacher showed him a small studio he had built in his home with a minimixer. Joe was so impressed that he built a "studio" in his bedroom and every afternoon after school, he "played radio." Prior to his graduation from Cal State Los Angeles in 1968, he co-founded the campus radio station. After college he sent out tapes and got a job as a weekender at KDAY as Dave Boxer. When Bob Wilson arrived to program KDAY, he was the first guy fired. "Bobby called me in and said, 'we're making some changes and you are one of them.' I'll never forget those exact words." His next stop was KSTN-Stockton. His new pd had slips of paper with names on them and he drew his new on-air name, Joe Terry. In 1970 he was hired as pd of KNOK-Dallas. "I was too immature for a market that size and left for KDON-Salinas." It was at KDON in 1971 that he met his wife-to-be over the request lines. Later in 1971, Joe returned to the Southland and started on the all-night shift at KGFJ. While there he was also known as "The Joker." In 1975 Joe traveled to San Diego and worked as J.L. Terry at KMLO and KDIG. In 1978 he got out of radio for two years working for his father's company, which rebuilt refrigerator components. In 1980 he got the "itch" to return to broadcasting and became one of the anchors as Larry Boxer on Channel 22, the financial news tv station. While at the tv station he worked KHJ morning drive news for a while with Lee Sherwood. In 1982 he started a country syndication company with Jim Brown Productions and opened one of his own called Mule Ticket Entertainment where "Country Traxx" was one of his offerings. After a year at Simi Valley's KWNK as Joe Terry, he joined Transtar (now WWI) and became the first personality to work on two different formats at the same time (a practice no longer allowed). He was Joe Terry on the Oldies Channel and Jack Boxer on the Country format. He continues at Westwood One doing afternoons at the Mainstream Country format.

TERRY, Ted: **KJLH**, 1979-81 and 1995-96. Ted grew up in Tulsa and in 1985 was the first black dj to work the country format in his hometown. Frankie Crocker was a big influence on Ted. He called his program the "music menu," an amalgamation of music and interviews with white and black crossover artists. He described it as not about being black or white. "It's about being."

THACKER, Tom: **KEZY**, 1966, pd

THAXTON, Lloyd: **KABC**, 1973-74. Lloyd had a long-running zany tv show on KCOP/Channel 13. He went on to be a producer for consumer activist David Horowitz.

THAYER, Gene: **KRLA**, 1971-72. Gene started his radio career in 1963 as Bill Thayer at KMBY-Monterey. He spent most of his career working radio in Honolulu and Tucson. He was "Bronco Birdbath" at KRLA. Gene has retired to cattle ranching near Sonoita, Arizona.

THAYER, Jack. **KLAC**. The stardom of Joe Pyne and Don Imus is traced back to Jack Thayer. He was the chief architect of KLAC's immensely successful two-way talk format. After leaving KLAC - the House That Pyne Built - he went on to WNEW-New York. In 1974 Jack was named president of the NBC Radio division. On June 18, 1975, he launched a new 24-hour "news and information service." The service didn't last long but was considered a forerunner of the full-service networks. Jack started as a dj in the Twin Cities and eventually became gm of WDGY-Minneapolis. From there he was gm at WHK-Cleveland, KXOA-Sacramento and WGAR-Cleveland where he generated national attention with the meteoric rise of Don Imus. In the early 1980s, he was gm of WNEW and in the early 1990s he was COO/exec vp of Gear Broadcasting of New England. He died over New Year's weekend 1995 at the age of 72. He had survived a stroke in the mid-1980s.

THEO: **KKBT**, 1994-97. "I love you, Theeeeo!" The callers to Theo's afternoon drive show on "the Beat" scream this love theme every day. Born Theo Mizuhara in San Mateo, his parents pushed him hard through gifted programs at school. He told *Buzz* magazine: "In my culture if you're not academically successful, you're really nothing." At 16, he dropped out of high school and a Filipino friend introduced him to the world of turntables and remixing. Theo originally started overnights at "the Beat" from nights at KMEL-San Francisco. He came to the attention of KMEL while making a name for himself as a club dj. The rumbling "Barry White bass voice" told *Vibe Magazine* in a March 1996 profile: "I'm an Asian on a black station in the No. 1 drive slot. But the support I've gotten has been staggering." Whitney Houston's movie *Waiting to Exhale* featured Theo's voice as the dj on the radio. In 1996 he won *Billboard*'s r&b dj of the year award. Theo has a recurring role on the *Dangerous Minds* tv series.

THOMAS, Ellen: SEE Ellen K

THOMAS, Jay: **KPWR**, 1986-92. The voice of Comedy Central is where you should find the ubiquitous Jay Thomas, if he would ever stay still long enough. The co-star of the surprise hit movie *Mr. Holland's Opus* was born in 1948. He attended the University of Tennessee. Jay spent three years at WAYS-Charlotte and eventually became pd. His wacky on-air sidekick characters started to emerge during this period: Mister Denise, the station hair dresser; Granny Glick, the oldest skin flick maker in the world; Dr. Henry the K; Rock, the inflation fighter; and Caleb Kluttz, the local redneck policeman. His first visit to the Southland was a two-season stint as a deli owner on ABC/TV's *Mork and Mindy* comedy series. His tap-dancing mother called him after each television appearance to tell him how proud she was. The third season of *Mork and Mindy* introduced Jonathan Winters, and five character actors hit the street. Jay recalled: "Winters said, 'I'm 58. I need the work.' What, and we didn't?" Before joining KPWR Jay did a number of tv shows, including *Love Boat* and *Spencer for Hire*, followed by dinner theater in North Carolina and Florida. He arrived at KPWR in October 1986 from a successful run doing morning drive at WKTU-New York. While there was much media attention directed toward "Pirate Radio," KIIS and "the Edge." KPWR captured NAB's first Marconi Award during the 1989 convention in New Orleans. Even though the award was new, it was being touted as the Oscar of radio. Jay commented on the station's award: "It's a great, fabulous honor. Marconi invented wireless transmissions. Unfortunately, if Marconi heard 'Power 106' he would probably die again. I don't think this is what he had in mind. But he's dead." In a 1989 *Los Angeles Magazine* article profiling morning personalities, Jay remembered an excellent piece of advice. A fellow actor encouraged Jay to relax, that the only competition was himself. One of Jay's bits early in his L.A. radio career included telling his audience that he was launching a condom helicopter drop to make Los Angeles safe for sex. Jay was a semi-regular on *Cheers*, playing Eddie Lebec, the hockey-playing husband of Rhea Perlman. He portrayed a dj on the short-lived tv show *Almost Grown* and was a pivotal plot character in Candice Bergen's *Murphy Brown* and won an Emmy. He's also appeared on *Family Ties* and *The Golden Girls*. In 1990, he was in the short-lived ABC/TV sitcom *Married People*. Jay starred with Susan Dey in *Love & War* in 1992, and with Annie Potts in 1993. When Jay was terminated from "Power 106" in 1993, he filed a $1,000,000 breach of contract lawsuit.

He was nominated for *Billboard* Top 40 Radio Air Personality of 1993. At the start of the second season of *Love & War*, Jay lamented about his firing from KPWR: "I'm having withdrawal symptoms. I had the rug pulled out from under me. It's very hurtful." Jay told the *LA Times* in September 1993, that KPWR fired him "because they became jealous of my tv show. They could not parlay my television popularity into what they wanted." His breach-of-contract lawsuit with Emmis Broadcasting was settled in late 1994. In addition to his variegated career, Jay is the promotion voice of Comedy Central.

THOMAS, John: **KHJ**, 1978-79. When John left the Southland he moved to Dallas and worked for a computer software company that provided music programming.

THOMAS, John: **KOCM**, 1987

THOMAS, Lon: **KUTE**, 1973-79, pd; **KIIS**, 1979-81. Lon survived a variety of format changes at KUTE, from Jazz to Disco to r&b. He worked mornings at KIIS. During his time on KIIS, Lon was one of those who subbed for Casey Kasem on "American Top 40." Before arriving in the Southland Lon spent a year in Germany as a dj. He was also a sports producer for the Armed Forces Network. When he left the Southland, Lon worked morning drive at WARM-Atlanta. In the 1990s he worked at WWMX-Baltimore as Mike McCarthy.

THOMAS, Mark: SEE Pat Garrett

THOMAS, Mark Austin: **KNX**, 1988-89; **KFI**, 1988-97, nd. Mark is the assistant to the pd of KFI as well as news director. In 1995 he was a per-diem news writer for KCAL/Channel 9. Mark graduated from the University of Illinois with a B.S. in radio and television. Following graduate course work in educational psychology, he started as a reporter/anchor for WIVK-Knoxville. In 1981 he went to WEEI-Boston and a year later to KSOL-San Francisco for five years as the news director. He is president of the AP Television and Radio Association for California and Nevada.

THOMAS, Marshall: **KWST**, 1978-80; **KNAC**; **KNX/FM**. Marshall was born Thomas Willets.

THOMAS, Randy: **KMET**, 1986-87; **KMPC/FM/KEDG/KLIT**, 1988-91; **KTWV**, 1991-93. Born in New York and raised in South Florida and Detroit, Randy set out for New York at age 18 with an enormous zest for life and confidence to be an actress. She studied acting while waiting tables. Her inspiration to pursue radio was spawned late at night  by listening to WNEW and the "Nightbird," Allison Steele. "I would lie in bed at night listening to Allison read poetry and play the Stones and segue into the original blues tune that inspired their music - she was amazing." Randy packed her bags and headed home to Detroit where she was hired right out of college radio on WWWW then WRIF. In 1974 an ABC executive took her to WPLJ-New York. Next was KZEW-Dallas, then "Zeta-4," WAXY and WSHE in South Florida before arriving in Los Angeles in 1986 with no job but a great resume. Tucked away on a boat in the Marina, Randy knocked on radio station doors until KMET hired her. "It was a dream come true to finally add those legendary call letters to my resume." Shortly thereafter the entire air staff was fired as KMET made way for KTWV, the first New Age radio station (that featured no djs). Inspired by the music and spiritual aspects of the format, Randy created Crystal Vision Productions with her husband, to produce a syndicated show. Then alternative radio knocked and Randy moved on to KMPC/FM which became "the Edge" to do middays. It was while Randy was at KMET that she became the commercial spokeswoman for the reading program "Hooked on Phonics." That association continues today and Randy has traveled to Paris to be part of an International Family Literacy conference with UNESCO and has conducted seminars. "They tell me that I have taught more people to read than almost any teacher." In 1991 Randy became the morning show host for "the Wave" and it was while she was there that her life changed dramatically. In 1993 Randy was chosen to be the first woman in history to be the announcer for the Academy Awards presentation and continued the honor for two additional years. Since then, Randy has gone on to announce The Miss America pageant. Currently, Randy and her husband Arnie Wohl have created Wohl 2 Wohl Productions where Randy does "voice imaging" for television and radio stations. Since losing their home in the 1994 earthquake, they are building a new home in Ft. Myers, Florida that will be equipped with a digital studio. The basic message of the Thomas philosophy is: "If you dream it and never give up - anything is possible." Spoken like a woman who fully expects to ride out all of life's tempests. Randy had her first child, Rachel Morgan, in the spring of 1997.

THOMAS, Rolle: **KFI**, 1963

THOMAS, Steve: **KHJ**, 1982, pd. Steve arrived in the Southland from a pd'ship at KIKF-Tucson.

THOMASON, Mark: **KABC**, 1991-96. Mark was part of the weekend news operation at KABC.

THOMLINSON, Larry: **KKGO/KKJZ**, 1986-90; **KJOI**, 1988. Larry worked overnights at "K-Joy." He is now in the mortuary business working with the bereaved.

THOMPSAN, Tracy: **KMGX**, 1994

THOMPSON, Bill: **KGBS**, 1965-68, pd; **KLAC**, 1970; **KBBQ**, 1972. Bill worked morning drive at KGBS in 1967. A year later, while continuing in morning drive, he joined Smothers Brothers Comedic Productions and eventually joined them full-time to deal with the *Smothers Brothers Show Featuring Glen Campbell.*

THOMPSON, Bob: **KIQQ**, 1984. Bob teamed with Joe Light to replace the morning team of Jay Coffey and Francesca Cappucci. This was Bob's first full-time radio gig coming from an acting and comedy background.

THOMPSON, Delores: **KGFJ**, 1994-95; **KJLH**, 1996-97. Delores grew up in Oakland and works part-time at KJLH.

THOMPSON, Diane: **KHJ**, 1980-85, nd; **KNX**, 1985-97. Diane has been a reporter/anchor for KNX and CBS Radio Network News covering every major news event in Southern California for over a decade. Born in Texas in 1957, Diane earned a bachelor of journalism with honors degree in 1979 from the University of Texas. She worked for radio and tv stations in Houston, Austin and Phoenix before joining KHJ as afternoon drive anchor/reporter in late 1980. Diane has won numerous awards for her news and feature reporting including eight Golden Mikes and five awards from the Los Angeles Press Club. In 1996 she was nominated for the "Outstanding Young Texas Ex Award" given by the ex-students of the University of Texas. "I don't have a prayer of winning, but it's nice to be nominated. That sounds so Hollywood." She is married to "Arrow 93" air personality Chris Taylor and they have two young sons.

THOMPSON, Eric: **KYSR**, 1993

THOMPSON, Frank: **KDAY**, 1967-69. Born in Canada, Frank learned his voice work from Lorne Greene. Frank was at KOGO and the "Mighty 690"-San Diego before arriving in the Southland. When he left, he became news director at KJR-Seattle and now lives in White Rock, British Columbia, where he does voiceover work and raises champion roses for which he has won many national trophies.

THOMPSON, Gary: **KLIT**, 1992; **KYSR**, 1993-97. Gary started at KYSR as the production director and now works middays. In the fall of 1995 he moved to morning drive. Gary worked at Unistar Satellite before joining KYSR. Gary is married with one son and lives in El Segundo.

THOMPSON, Mark: SEE Mark and Brian

THOMPSON, Ron: **KHJ/KRTH**, 1984-86, vp/gm; **KBLA**, 1991-97. "This is the best job I've ever had," Ron said of his involvement with Korean-formatted KBLA. For a man who worked for RKO and every legendary California Rock station in the fifties and sixties, his comment speaks volumes. Ron was born in Ottumwa, Iowa but moved to Southern California when he was 15. After a stint in the Marine Corps, Ron started his radio journey in sales in 1958 at KAFY-Bakersfield.

He quickly moved up the sales ladder to KROY-Sacramento and in 1962 became part owner of KACY-Port Huenene and then KMEN-San Bernardino. After a time at KARM-Fresno, Ron joined RKO in 1980 as gm of WHBQ-Memphis. He arrived at KHJ for the launch of "Car Radio." In 1986 he joined Kent Burkhardt as minority partner in a number of Southern radio stations. Ron started his Asian radio journey in 1988 with Dwight Case and George Fritzinger at KAZN and is currently running KBLA.

THORNBURY, Will: **KNOB**, 1961-65; **KCRW**; **KLON**. Will has been described as the "djs' dj." One of his admirers said, "He was the most brilliant human being and one of the most gracious. Will should have been Orson Welles." Will wrote liner notes for albums by jazz greats. Even though he toiled over each one for extended periods, often his work brought him $75 an assignment. Over the years he worked at KCRW. Will was married to Ruth Price. Will died of cancer in the early 1990s.

THORNTON, Jim: **KMGX**, 1988-91; **KNX**, 1993-97. Jim began his broadcast career in 1983 back in his

hometown of Huntington, West Virginia by working as cameraman at WOWK/TV. "In 1984, I moved my wagon West to California and within a year was reporting for Metro Traffic Control." After four years as "Thunder Jim Thornton" at KMGX working morning drive and another 4 years at WW1, he started at "KNXNewsradio" full-time. In addition to reporting traffic for KNX and KCBS/Channel 2, since the fall of 1995 he has been the staff announcer at KCOP/UPN-13. Jim, his wife Susan, and baby on the way live in "scenic Tujunga, where we spend time tending to our squirrels. They know I'm a nut."

THRASHER: **KLOS**, 1987-89; **KQLZ**; 1989; **KNAC**, 1989-95. Born Ted Prichard in Charlotte, the "Thrasher" worked at WKRL-Tampa/St. Petersburg before joining KLOS as "Engineer Ted" on the Mark and Brian show for a year-and-a-half. When asked about highlights while being on the air in Southern California, he said, "Any of the great talents who have co-hosted with me. Alice Cooper whipped out his big snake on the air, and Harry Shearer did some *Spinal Tap* stuff and berated me as `Mr. Burns' from *The Simpsons*." Ted had the tough job of being on stage at the Coliseum for the Monsters of Rock tour and had to quiet the crowd after Metallica's plug had been pulled due to the riots. He left the Long Beach Alternative station in early 1995 with a format switch to Spanish. Ted now works for a Korean tv station.

THURRELL, Lindy: **KHTZ**, 1982-83; **KWIZ**, 1984-86; **KNOB**, 1984-86. At "K-Hits" Lindy worked evenings. "I started out doing all-nights and when they moved me to evenings they told me not to talk. Then they ended up firing me because I 'had no personality.'" Born in San Diego, Lindy grew up in New Hampshire. She graduated from the University of the Pacific with a degree in classical music. "I played the bassoon and wanted to be a musician. But once I started hanging around the campus radio station, it was like a disease and I had it real bad." After graduation Lindy worked in Reno, New Hampshire and KLOK-San Jose in 1978 where she did afternoon drive. In 1984 she and her husband Tom King (they met at KLOK) opened the Academy of Radio Broadcasting in Huntington Beach. "We're now in our 14th year. We worked in the good part of radio and run the school from that same perspective. Casey Kasem sent both his kids to our school." They now have schools in Phoenix, Walnut Creek and Fremont. "We owned KTHO-Lake Tahoe for a while. It was just something we had to do."

THURSTON, Carlos: **KPWR**, 1995. Carlos was part of "Power 106's" evening Ruffnex Show.

TIGER: **KFWB**, 1958-61. A native of Dallas, where she starred in a popular tv show called *Miss Bea*, Bea Shaw came to the Southland with her husband dj Bruce Hayes. Bea was the voice of "Tiger," a sexy sounding personality, on Bruce's morning show on KFWB. "Tiger" stood for "Traffic Information Girl - Exclusive Report." Bea did the reports from home on a remote mike the station patched in at the house. "I would give a report on freeway traffic conditions in a seductive voice and add a quip, a flirtatious

remark, or maybe heckle the dj. In between reports, I'd go back to sleep. The groggier I was, the huskier and sexier my voice sounded. Thank goodness it was radio and the audience couldn't see me with my hair in curlers, no make-up and wearing a bathrobe and wool socks." Bea was also the voice of Connie the Computer, predicting football scores on a syndicated radio show, and a regular member of the *Steve Allen* and *Donna Reed* tv shows. In 1965 she started Bea Shaw Productions, writing and producing radio commercials and frequently used hers and Bruce's voices - as in the enormously successful "Backaruda" campaign. Bruce played the pompous Plymouth dealer who couldn't pronounce "Barracuda" and Bea as the lady who for five years tried to cajole, hypnotize, bully or seduce him into saying it right. Bea has been honored with numerous industry awards for her commercials.

TILDEN, Peter: **KLSX**, 1988-89; **KABC**, 1989 and 1991-94; **KMPC**, 1994-95; **KABC**, 1996-97. After growing up in Philadelphia and graduating from Temple

University with a Bachelor of Science in physiology, Peter worked in many major markets on his way to Los Angeles, where he started in morning drive at KLSX. After he was abruptly fired, there was a noisy picketing campaign to have Peter rejoin the "classic rock" station. He told Gary Lycan in the *OC Register*: "Hey, I got a shot. I was the new kid in town from Philadelphia. It wasn't perfect, but what is? They say it takes two years to make a dent in the morning ratings, and I only had eight months. But it was fun, and I enjoyed it." He left for New York, wrote *Over My Dead Body* and returned to work at KABC. He eventually replaced Steve Edwards in afternoon drive who said: "Peter is one of the funniest guys around. He is Woody Allen on speed, and he's kind of an Everyman exaggerated to an Nth degree." In 1991 he was voted Funniest Air Personality in L.A. by the *LA Daily News*. In the spring of 1994, he and Tracey Miller left for morning drive at the newly acquired KMPC, when it went to a Talk format. Peter's tv writing includes Howie Mandel's animated series, *Bobby's World*. He co-produced *Nurses* and was a writer for *Major Dad*. Peter joined Ken Minyard for KABC's morning drive show in the fall of 1996.

TOBIN, Joe: **KMGX,** 1992

TODD, Jim: **KFI**, 1964-74. During the middle of the night, Jim provided farm programming, music and news.

TOMBAZIAN, Keri: **KORG**, 1976-77; **KGIL**, 1977-81; **KRTH**, 1982-84; **KTWV**, 1988-94. In the fall of 1993, Keri moved from evenings to morning drive and teamed with Sheryl Bernstein for a dramatic format switch at "the Wave." Billed as the first morning drive female team, it was an experimental mix of politics, comedy and reduced music. Born and raised in the San Fernando Valley, Keri studied drama and acting. She went straight from high school to the airwaves. After much encouragement from industry friends she applied at KGIL. "I was naive enough to believe that I could stay in L.A. to start my career in broadcasting. Rick Scarry told me to get three months experience at a smaller station and he would hire me. My timing was good as stations all over the country were looking for on-air female talent." At KRTH Keri worked early evenings and counted down the Top 30. "It was an interesting moment in KRTH's history. Program director Bob Hamilton was going after KIIS, mixing oldies with his hot hits." Currently, Keri continues a very successful voiceover career and is happily married to screenwriter-actor, Thom Babbes. They have three children under six years of age.

TOMEI, Mel: **KLYY**, 1997. Mel works morning drive at "Y-107."

TOMELI, Martha: **KTNQ**, 1996-97. Martha hosts an evening talk show at Spanish KTNQ.

TOMLIN, Todd: **KIKF**, 1996-97

TONYA: SEE Tonya Campos

TOPETE, Fernando: **KTNQ**, 1991. Fernando worked the all-night shift at Spanish KTNQ.

TORRE, Joe: **KMPC**, 1989-91. The colorful manager of the World Champion New York Yankees in 1996 was the color man for the California Angels and filed reports for KTLA/Channel 5. He was the first Yankee manager born and raised in New York City to lead the team to a title. The former catcher with the Milwaukee Braves and Philadelphia Phillies from 1956 to 1963 was the co-winner of the 1996 American League Manager of the Year award.

TORRERO, Jesse: **KDAY**, 1987-93; **KJLH**, 1993-96; **KMPC**, 1995-96. Jesse hosted a weekend talk show on KMPC about computers.

TOSTADO, Alex: **KSRF/KACD**, 1989-96; **KGGI**, 1994; **KOST**, 1997. Alex was born in Calexico and his family left for Monterey County when he was five. In his senior year of high school, Alex began working at 1,000-watt KRKC in Salinas. He went on to KBAI-Morro Bay and KQLH-San Bernardino. Alex was out of radio 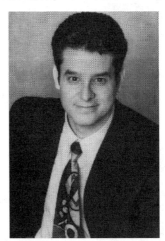 for a while and pursued his other passion, acting. Since leaving KACD when the format changed to "Groove Radio," Alex has co-written, co-produced and starred in his first feature film titled *Alvarez & Cruz*. "The movie is a homemade project not unlike *El Mariachi* or *Brothers McMullen*. We're looking for a distributor and pursuing film festivals." He's married to Karen Sharp, the host of KOST's "Love Songs on the Coast" program.

TOWNSEND, Ken: **KEZY**, 1976. Ken has left radio and is doing computer work.

TOY, Terrence: **KKBT**, 1994-95. Terrence was co-host of the "underground" beat, playing deep house music.

TRACY, Don: **KGFJ**, 1969-74; **KDAY**, 1976-90; **KGFJ** 1993-94, pd; **KMBY**, 1995, gm; **KABC** 1995-97.

Originally from Pittsburgh, he was born Don Malloy in 1941. After Schenley High School he graduated from Roger Williams Junior College in 1962. He started out at WEHW-Windsor, Connecticut and went on to WPOP-Hartford and WNHC-New Haven. He came to Los Angeles to work at KGFJ. Don started the first minority-owned-and-operated school of broadcasting. He said his goal was "cultivating a student's talent rather than merely cranking out a graduate. That may have sounded corny but that's the way I was raised." The school's curriculum ranged from newscasting to copy writing. Since 1975, Don has also been pd/md and afternoon drive on Armed Forces Radio/TV Network. In 1991 Don became director of radio for S.I. Communications, a radio syndication company. In addition to his career in radio, he was the international editor of *R&B Report*, wrote many songs for Freddie Hubbard and was a music correspondent for German and Japanese publications. Following a stint in sales at KABC, Don has open Malloy & Associates, an advertising agency in the San Fernando Valley. He's married with two children.

TRACY, Eric: **KMPC**, 1982; **KABC**, 1982-96; **KFWB**, 1997. "I won't beat round the bush. We've decided your style just won't fit our new morning show so we're letting you go." After 14 years with KABC, he wasn't able to say good-bye when he was let go in the fall of 1996. He did his farewell on the op-ed page of the *LA Times*. Born in Detroit in 1951, Eric grew up in the San Fernando Valley and worked in Montana, at WOKY-Milwaukee, WWL and WSGO-New Orleans and KSFO-San Francisco prior to starting in L.A. In the early 1980s, he was involved with the broadcasts of the Oakland A's and the San Francisco 49'ers. He talked of the spontaneity of radio: "Once I

commented on the air that I would be spending the holidays alone and did anyone know of any good parties? Well, within three hours, I got invitations to 174 New Year's parties - and I decided to 'crash' them - not telling them where I'd go - I hit a dozen parties." Eric was part of the launch of RKO's "American Overnight" in 1981. The launch was based on the overnight success of Larry King. He shared the six-hour talk fest with Ed Busch who was hosting from Dallas. In 1982 he went to KABC to work sports for the first time, which he did exclusively. He worked afternoon drive at KMPC in the fall of 1981. Eric has had various assignments reporting on the Dodgers, including pre- and post-game host. He co-hosted KABC's "SportsTalk" with Steve Edwards. He has several tv and theatrical credits. Eric is an active "Big Brother," drives a 1957 T-Bird and is an avid golfer. In 1997 Eric began broadcasting sports on KFWB.

TRAMMEL, Charles: **KGFJ**, 1954-60. C.T. ("the tall oak tree") worked the all-night shift at KGFJ. He hosted live broadcasts from Dolphin's of Hollywood for many years. He worked for a time in San Francisco. Charles died in 1983.

TREFF, Adam: **KSRF**, 1991. Adam worked mornings at "K-Surf."

TREMAINE, Larry: **KBLA**, 1960s. When he left the Southland, he went to Radio Nordsee International, a pirate station eventually silenced by the Dutch government. He was also a member of the Sunrays, who had a one-hit success single, *I Live for the Sun*.

TRENTON, Jim: SEE Poorman

TRIPP, Bobby: **KHJ**, 1967-68. Born Mike Guerra, he was Bobby Mitchell at KFRC-San Francisco before arriving at "Boss Radio." Bobby worked afternoon drive at KYA-San Francisco. He died of a chronic blood disease on July 19, 1968.

TRIPP, Peter: **KGFJ**, 1963-64. Peter was known as the "Curly Headed Kid in the 3rd Row." He was at WMGM-New York before his brief stay in Southern California. When he left KGFJ he joined WHN-New York. Peter has since passed away.

TRIGUEROS, Talaya: **KUTE**, 1984-87; **KNX/FM**, 1988; **KOCM/KSRF**, 1988; **KTWV**, 1988-97. The silky voice of "the Wave," Talaya was born in Albuquerque and worked in the broadcast community while attending the University of New Mexico and San Francisco State during the mid-1970s. Her first commercial job was doing a special Latin show called "Sabor y Salsa" on KRE-Berkeley. A change of ownership and of call letters to

KBLX allowed her to be part of the new "Quiet Storm." During her stay in the East Bay she was very active in community events, and she served as emcee for the first four years of UC Berkeley's Cinco de Mayo concerts. Fluent in Spanish and Portuguese, she acted as contributing editor to a Hispanic entertainment magazine called *Avance* and produced a variety music show on cable tv called *Entertainment Spectrum*. In 1984 the owners of KBLX asked Talaya to introduce the "Quiet Storm" on their L.A. station, KUTE. Talaya was the voiceover host for Turner Superstation WTBS' *Night Tracks* and hosted a cable tv show called *The Jazz Network*. In addition to her work on "the Wave," Talaya does a weekly one-hour Latin music show for AFRTS, is an in-flight programming host on United Airlines and does voice work for CBS and Fox. She also tapes a midday show for NAC-formatted KYOT-Phoenix. The mother of two actively participates in fund raisers for her children's school in Montebello.

TROTTER, John: **KABC**, 1959-60. When John left the Southland he joined WJJD-Chicago and KILT-Houston. In 1962 John worked at KEWB-San Francisco. In the early 1970s John was at KBOX-Dallas. He died May 21, 1976, in Abilene.

TROUPE, Curtis: **KDAY**, 1965; **XPRS**, 1971-73; **KGFJ**; **XERB**; **KDAY**, 1981-82. Curtis returned to KDAY as an account executive. Curtis had worked news at WJMO-Cleveland and KSOL-San Francisco.

TROUT, Dave: SEE Freddy Snakeskin

TROUT, Dick: **KTNQ**, 1977

TROUT, Earl: **KDAY**, 1969-70, pd; **KWIZ**, 1970. Born in Blythe, in 1945, Earl arrived in Southern California as pd of KDAY from KDWB-Minneapolis. One of his early stations was KFIF-Tucson. He called himself "Horrible Head." Earl went on to be one of the founders of L.A.B. or the KIIS broadcast school. He's currently working for Woodbridge Media in South Pasadena.

TROUT, Mike: **KBRT**. Mike is now living in Colorado Springs and running "Focus on the Family."

TROWBRIDGE, Jerry: **KUSC**, 1973, pd; **KLVE**, 1975; **KPOL/KZLA**, 1976-79. Born in Long Beach Jerry worked at KNAC and KFOX while in high school in the late 1960s. In 1975 he graduated with a B.A. from the USC School of Journalism. When KZLA was a soft rock/jazz fusion, Jerry produced "Street Talk" and "Jerry's Best Bets" as well as broadcasting news. After leaving radio, he and life-partner Ray Smithers founded Access Radio, providing telephone polling systems for major radio stations. They developed the Touch-Map system in use by national ATM networks to provide nearby cash machine locations. Today he and Ray own "Flying Pig Ranch," an independent video production company and are producing a documentary on border radio station XER.

> KFWB "Seven Swingin' Gentlemen' strike in support of newsmen.
> -1961

TRUITT, Steve: **KMPC**, 1995-96. Steve was born in 1966, grew up in Connecticut and arrived in L.A. in 1992. He appeared in several films and commercials. He did traffic reports on KMPC and was a sidekick to Suzi Landolphi's sex therapy show. In 1995 he appeared in a one-man show called "Walking Pneumonia." Steve continues to do traffic for Metro.

TRUJILLO, Silverio: **KWIZ**, 1997

TRUJILLO, Tammy: **KFI**, 1993; **KLAC**, 1986; **KEZY**, 1991-94; **KXEZ**, 1994-95; **KFWB**, 1997.

TUCK, Cecil: **KRLA**, 1963-68, nd/pd. Cecil was born in Texas and grew up in Piney Woods, near Houston. He roomed with Dan Rather at Sam Houston State and pursued a career in investigative journalism. While in college, Cecil not only worked for the campus paper but also the consumer papers. He was eventually fired from every newspaper in the Houston area for his crusading journalism. After a two-year stint in the Army, Cecil took his news skills to Galveston in 1957 followed by two years at KTSA-San Antonio, WKNR-Detroit and KILT-Houston. While at KILT he wrote and narrated many of the "mood intros" on Gordon McLendon's Beautiful Music stations, notably KABL-San Francisco. Shortly after arriving at KRLA the mood of the country was changing and Cecil innovated a new, satirical approach to the news with "The Credibility Gap." Instead of five-minute newscasts, Cecil and his team delivered a 15-minute newscast every four hours complete with skits and an original song. He and Bob Eubanks started the *KRLA Beat* which was a newspaper featuring music news that could be adapted to appear as if was locally produced. Near the end of his stint with KRLA, which would be the end of his involvement with radio, he doubled as the head writer on *The Smothers Brothers* tv show. He eventually made the move full-time into tv. He was hired as the head writer on *The Glen Campbell Hour* and breathed new life into the series. He went on to be the head writer for 53 episodes of the syndicated Kenny Rogers series. Cecil never seemed to be content with the status quo and wanted to continually push the envelope. He was the speech writer for Pat Paulsen's presidential campaigns. In a 1995 phone interview from his home in Phoenix he said: "I strapped on my six-shooter and became a hired gun. I went to KTVI/TV and with an aggressive approach to the news and took the station from a 3 to a 21 rating." Flushed with success his next stop was WLS/TV in Chicago where he was nd from 1978 to 1980. "I was pretty damned cocky and told the network executives they were raping the station and couldn't apply band aids any more and that more money would be needed to make their news operation more competitive. They didn't see it the same way and fired me." He was off to Phoenix which has been his home since 1980. "I took a woeful ABC operation on my arrival to #1 in three years." He left broadcasting in 1983 when he discovered a new gemstone. He co-ventured with Arizona savings and loans to establish this purple stone out of South Africa. When the savings and loans industry collapsed, so did Cecil's venture. After a bout with a neurological problem, Cecil is once again pushing the envelope into new areas. He is working with *Arizona Highways Magazine* and has created a series of travelogues and produced 25 videos. With 5 million visitors to the Grand Canyon each year, the tapes and other merchandise sell very well. "I am fortunate that I have dealt with new situations and have had the opportunity to revamp some old situations and turn them around. I've had fun with it. I've never been good when there were too many rules." His brother is Michael Tuck of KCBS/Channel 2.

TUCKER, Bud: **KABC**, 1975-76; **KWIZ**, 1977-81; **KMPC**, 1981-86. Bud started his career in 1967 with "Press Box" on KTLA/Channel 5 with Dick Enberg, Bud Furillo and Tom Harmon. During the 1972 season, Bud was the color man for Los Angeles Sharks hockey. In 1974 he hosted "SportsTalk" on KABC. During the mid-1970s Bud hosted the pregame and halftime activities at USC and Raiders games. In the spring of 1981 Bud started reporting sports commentary on KMPC's morning drive show with Robert W. Morgan. While at KMPC he hosted "Rams Report" and the pregame show for the Angels. In 1985 he purchased KIOT-Barstow and four years later put KXXZ-Barston on the air. "It's fun running a radio station, but just too much paper work with the FCC, lawyers and the tax man."

TUNA, Charlie: **KHJ**, 1967-72; **KROQ**, 1972-73; **KKDJ**, 1973-75; **KIIS**, 1975-77, pd; **KHJ**, 1977; **KTNQ**, 1978-80; **KHTZ**, 1980-85; **KBZT**, 1985-86; **KRLA**, 1986-90; **KODJ/KCBS**, 1990-93; **KMPC/KABC**, 1993-94; **KIKF**, 1994-97. Born Art Ferguson, Charlie grew up in Kearney, Nebraska, where

he was a high school athlete and sports editor of the local newspaper. He started on the radio in his hometown at the age of 16. He moved from KOMA-Oklahoma City, where he had a 10-state following, to WMEX-Boston. Charlie was noon-to-three on KHJ and moved to mornings in 1970 when Robert W. Morgan left for Chicago. He was voted rock dj of the year for 1970 by Don Page, radio editor of the *LA Times*. In 1972, Charlie went to KCBQ-San Diego. When he returned to the Southland, he was the first voice and morning personality on KROQ/AM. In 1973, Charlie was very active with numerous radio specials through his Alan/Tuna Production company. Some of the programs offered in syndication included "Dirtiest Show in Town for the Airlines," "Christ & Rock and Roll," "Summertime - 74," "Yes, Virginia, There Is a Charlie Tuna," "Rock-and-Roll Superstars," and "Do You Wanna Dance?" On October 10, 1973, Charlie joined KKDJ, where he became pd in 1975. In 1974, Charlie gave up his syndicated company with Alan. When KIIS AM/FM debuted on October 1, 1975, Charlie was the first morning man and was pd of both stations. Later, he resigned the pd'ship and stayed on as morning man. The station was simulcast on KIIS/AM in both drive times. Charlie always stayed active and in 1977, in addition to his on-air chores, he hosted "Record Report," a syndicated series from Gary Kleiman. Later in 1977, Charlie replaced Charlie Van Dyke at KHJ. Local tv station KTLA produced a magazine show called *Calendar*, and Charlie was one of its local hosts. Some of Charlie's favorite features that followed him from station to station included "Breakfast Serial" and the "Wake-Up Story." On January 10, 1990, Charlie was the first KHJ "Boss Jock" to receive a Star on the Hollywood Walk of Fame, ironically near KIIS morning star Rick Dees. He teamed briefly with Dean Goss when KODJ debuted on February 26, 1990. On September 10, 1993, KCBS became "Arrow 93" and Charlie was gone. His longtime market nemesis, Robert W. Morgan, declared the next morning, "This is the first time you can hear the oldies without a fish smell." Within a month Charlie started on all-Sports KMPC as the morning anchor. He had never worked for a non-music station, and it was a bit of gamble for both Charlie and KMPC. He has been active in Voice of America and AFRTS since 1971. He appeared in the Universal movie *Rollercoaster* and was the announcer on numerous tv shows including *The Mike Douglas Show* and *Scrabble*. In a 1993 *Times* interview with Claudia Puig, Charlie reminisced, "I love the business. It's very comfortable. It's not work. I'm much more regimented than I've ever been. It was a lot more unstructured then, and, to be honest, a lot more fun. Now there are a lot more bankers and accountants in it. It's not as fun, but you adapt." Charlie worked as 1994 summer fill-in on KABC and KMPC. Since late 1994, Charlie has been doing mornings at Orange County Country KIKF. He continues an active voiceover career along with hosting "Weekly Top 30 Country Countdown" syndicated show. Married in 1965, he and Shari have two daughters and two sons.

TUNNO, Fran: **KABC**, 1994. Fran reported traffic conditions on the morning "Ken and Barkley" show.

TUR, Bob: **KNX**, 1987-97. Born in 1960, the native Californian attended UCLA. In June 1988 Bob and his Aerospatiale 350-B jet helicopter "Chopper 10-70" were added to "KNXNewsradio." Prior to joining KNX, Bob was a paramedic but decided to find a healthier line of work after being shot at while on duty. The Portofino Inn in Redondo Beach was so seriously threatened during a savage storm that guests had to scramble to the roof. Bob braved the driving rain and high winds to make 13 heroic airlifts carrying 54 people to safety. His camera shots captured the beginnings of the infamous L.A. Riots as did his coverage of O.J. Simpson and his "slow chase" on L.A. freeways. Bob lives in the Pacific Palisades and he is president of LA News, specializing in providing freelance features for tv news use.

TURKINGTON, Bill: **KJOI**, 1983-88. Bill worked afternoon drive at the Beautiful Music station.

TURNAGE, Richard: **KMPC**, 1991; **KRTH**, 1992-97.

Richard is one of the featured players on KRTH's morning drive show starring Robert W. Morgan. Richard began his broadcasting career in 1987 on Cal State Northridge's college station, KCSN. After earning a bachelor's degree in radio and tv in 1988, he joined Metro Traffic reporting for a number of Southern California stations. He began as Morgan's traffic reporter/sidekick at KMPC in 1991 and followed him to "K-Earth" a year later.

TURNBULL, Bob & Yvonne: **KORG**; **KKLA**

TURNER, Mary: **KMET**, 1972-82; **KLSX**, 1993. Born in Baltimore in 1947, Mary was a tv/radio major at Indiana University in Bloomington. She wanted to be a television director and left for San Francisco after graduation. She got a local phone book and started dialing tv stations. Her first industry job was in traffic at Metromedia's KNEW/TV. She listened to KSAN and was influenced by the music and lifestyle of the "underground station," resulting in stints at ABC's KSFX and KSAN. She worked as an engineer for the legendary Tom Donahue before graduating to a weekend shift. Mary was a strong female voice for five years in the San Francisco area before coming to Los Angeles. Her real jump in exposure began with the taping of "Off The Record" for Westwood One, which was heard by an estimated 25 million listeners. Her second venture was the syndicated "Rock 'n' Roll Never Forgets." "The Burner" arrived at KMET in June of 1972 and left on the eve of her 10th year with "the Mighty Met." She did a daily program on Armed Forces Radio/TV, worked for Canada's CHUM group and "Music in the Air," a pre-recorded airline program on TWA. Her photo appeared in a 1981 edition of *Oui* Magazine as part of an article on "Ladies of the Airwaves." In the early 1980s, Mary married Westwood One founder and CEO, Norman Pattiz. In the summer of 1982, she left KMET to devote time to her national and international projects. She stayed on with Metromedia as special director of artist relations. Mary reflected on her early radio days: "It was an exciting time back then, because you didn't operate under any rules. You could play anything you wanted, say anything you wanted and who cared? FM at that time was a joke, especially to Top 40 people. We were the hippies, and they were the stars." On being a successful female: "I think being a woman helped more than anything else. The time was right for it, and I happened to be in the right place at the right time." Mary left Westwood One's "Off the Record" in late 1994 after 15 years to devote more time to her volunteer drug and alcohol counseling efforts.

TURNER, Michael: **KMET**, 1971-72. Michael worked late evenings at "the Mighty Met." He arrived in the Southland from ABC stations in New York and Detroit. When Michael left "the Mighty Met," he joined KDML-North Tahoe. He now lives in the San Jose/Monterey area.

TURPEL, Pete: **KNJO**, 1986

TUSHER, William: **KABC**, 1960. William hosted "Candid Session" in the evening for the launch of KABC Talk radio on August 1, 1960.

TYLER, Chuck: **KFI**, 1985-89. Chuck was the host of "The Game Show" during its brief programming run on KFI. When he left the Southland he headed for the Northwest working as om at KXL-Portland. Chuck is now working for Christian KPDQ-Portland. In the fall of 1995 he was laid off for the first time and the only stations that responded to his search were Religious stations. "God was leading me this way and Christian radio is what I was supposed to be doing."

TYLER, Dean: **KHJ**, 1965. Dean worked the first weekend of "Boss Radio" in April 1965.

TYLER, Joy: **KEZY**, 1996-97. Joy works weekends at KEZY and Shadow Traffic.

TYLER, Larry: **KBLA**, 1965

TYLER, Nick: **KKGO/KKJZ**, 1986-97. Nick is an actor who has appeared in films such as *American President* and a starring role in Showtime's soap opera, *Sherman Oaks*. He acts under the name Nick Toth.

TYLER-PEACH, Patty: **KWIZ**, 1985. Patty went on to work at Transtar.

TYNDALL, Karen: **KPZE**, 1989; **KORG**, 1993

"The new gm commanded me to fire Ron Rodrigues, who was then our fine music director, and I refused. So, he fired us both. Smart move. KMPC has never been in the top 20 since. It must have cost them tens of millions." —*Mark Blinoff*

U

UNKNOWN DISC JOCKEY: SEE Pat Garrett
UNRUH, Stan: **KYMS**, 1987-93, nd; **KNX**
UTLEY, Reginald: **KKTT**, 1979; **KGFJ**, 1980; **KMAX**, 1995, pd; **KACE**, 1996-97. When KMAX went from Asian to sports programming, Reggie became pd. He hosts a gospel music show on KACE.

V

VACAR, Tom: **KNX**, 1992-93. Tom was the consumer reporter for "KNXNewsradio."
VALDEZ, Tony: **KAGB**, 1975; **KGFJ**, 1979-86. Tony is working tv news on the East Coast.
VALENTINE, Mike: **KHJ**, 1973
VALENTINE, Sean: **KIIS**, 1996-97. Sean arrived from KHKS-Dallas in the summer of 1996 to work evenings. Sean jocked at KJMN and WZOU-Boston, WTIC-Hartford and WKCI-New Haven. Sean hosted SuperRadio's "Open House Party" and his own syndicated show "Party Online." He works part-time with the Bright AC format at WW1.
VALENTINE, Shawn: **KOST**, 1997
VALENTINE, Val: **KIIS**, 1977-82; **KRLA/KBZT**, 1984-93. The Whittier resident cruised into Southern California from KSOM-Ontario in 1977, after stops in San Bernardino, Palm Springs and Rexburg, Idaho. Born Val Valentine Jurado in El Paso, the Tique Indian attended Rio Hondo College and had a very unique experience: he was one of 18 students who toured radio stations in small and medium markets in nine states and Canada during a six-month school project. Val started at KIIS in 1977, and his bi-lingual Spanish/English presentation on-air at KIIS between 1980 and 1981 "propelled the early evening shift into the most-listened-to CHR station in Southern California," according to Val. He was the traffic anchor for Metro Traffic in 1991.
VALENTINO, Charly: **KKHJ**, 1996-97. Charly works mornings at Spanish KKHJ.
VALERIO, Ramon: **KWIZ**, 1990-97. Ramon does all-nights on the Orange County Spanish station.
VAN, Carolyn: **KOCM**, 1990-91, pd. Carolyn is also an actress and voiceover performer.
VANDERHURST, Fred: **KPOL**, 1965-72. The Los Angeles native worked afternoon drive at KPOL.
VAN deWALKER, Dave: Dave produced the L.A. Dodger radio broadcasts from 1968 until 1994. He died November 30, 1995, after undergoing surgery for a brain tumor.
VAN DYKE, Charlie: **KHJ**, 1972-77, pd. Arguably one of the purest examples of a strong morning man during the 1960s, '70s and '80s. Charlie, born Charles Steinle, started his on-air career at the legendary McLendon flagship station, KLIF-Dallas, at the age of 14. On his 21st birthday, he was appointed program director. Before arriving in Los Angeles, Charlie was on-air at CKLW-Detroit, KFRC-San Francisco and KGB-San Diego. He was appointed pd of KHJ in 1975. Charlie's first stop in Southern California was at KHJ in 1972 to work nine to noon, sandwiched between Morgan in the morning and Mark Elliott at noon. He moved to morning drive in 1973 and was made pd in 1975. In 1976, Charlie created the ultimate maintenance promotion called "The Great American Money Machine." He was gone before summer of that year and went to WLS-Chicago. He returned a summer later to work morning drive and be pd and stayed until March 1977. When he left the RKO outlet, Charlie said, "Charlie Tuna was right. It's difficult to be a pd and on-air at the same time." Charlie Tuna eventually replaced Van Dyke. In 1977 he returned to KLIF-Dallas. In 1979 Charlie went to the Northeast to work at WRKO-Boston and in 1980 guided WRKO from Top 40 to Talk as pd. In 1982 Charlie landed in Phoenix as pd of KOY; by 1984 he was working at KTAR-Phoenix. About this time, Charlie built his own recording studio in Scottsdale and became the voice of over 60 tv stations and 100 radio stations. He personifies the voice that lends identity to a radio station. In addition to his voiceover career, Charlie has returned to the school of ministry and is studying to become an ordained deacon.
VAN DYKE, Dave: **KHTZ/KCBS**, 1991-97, pd, vp/gm. Dave worked at WWWW-Detroit, WODS-Boston and WDAI-Chicago and programmed KTXQ-Dallas, KAZY-

Denver and KGON-Portland before getting to the Southland. He worked the transition to the '70s-based "Arrow-93" in the fall of 1993. The first Arbitron in January 1994 listed the station with a "dramatic full-point increase," according to Dave. Dave talked about the "Arrow" format on Prodigy: "When we started down this road in the fall of 1992, we had no preconceived notions of what a new '70s-based format should be. We only knew that this fertile decade that had such a variety to offer, had not been fully tapped. We spent eight months researching and proving what our guts were telling us and found, not another 'classic rock' format clone, but an entirely unique and different musical mix. Less than a third of our audience has come from the 'classic rock' station. We have attracted listeners from all over the dial. It was designed with L.A. in mind, and other stations that have cloned the concept without localization in mind, have failed." In 1996 he became chairman of the Southern California Broadcasters Association. He lives in Glendale with his wife Denise.

VAN HOOK, Rod: **KMPC**, 1972-78; **KFWB**, 1979-97.

Rod broadcasts sports on KFWB. In 1995 he won a Golden Mike for best sportscast and an AP award. Rod has been the recipient of 3 L.A. Press Club awards. He is married with a 7-year-old daughter.

VAN HORNE, Chuck: **KUTE**, 1979-80. Born in Fresno, Chuck Van Horne Dukeslaw, Jr. grew up in Arcadia. Chuck was bitten by the radio "bug" while serving overseas with the U.S. Air Force. When he left the military his family, who had been in the banking business for over 100 years, expected him to pursue a banking career. Instead, Chuck enrolled in the Don Martin School of Radio and Television Arts and Sciences in Hollywood. He started his first radio job on November 12, 1972. "It was my 25th birthday and what an unexpected surprise, it was the same day that KMET broadcast the KFWB recreation." In less than two years Chuck had worked at KTOT-Big Bear, KICO-Calexico, KPTL-Carson City, KTHO-So. Lake Tahoe and KONE-Reno. A network of radio friends began to pay off for Chuck with assignments at KDES-Palm Springs, KSTN-Stockton, KSOM-Ontario, KFXM and KUDO-San Bernardino/Riverside. In 1977 Chuck returned to college and also became an instructor at Don Martin's. After programming two Reno stations, Chuck started at KUTE in November 1979. Less than a year later, he was off to Albuquerque and by 1985 had left the radio business. He went to work producing and directing training videos for the City of Los Angeles' Department of Transportation, which led to a position as program manager for Ralph's Grocery Company's television department doing co-op and training videos. In 1992, he became director of operations for the American Video Network in Corona del Mar, which specializes in interactive media production. When asked if he ever thinks about radio, he replied lightning quick, "All the time. I'm a jock...always." While working at AVN, Chuck has returned to school for a master's at Cal State Long Beach.

VAN NUYS, Larry: **KBCA**, 1959; **KBLA**, 1960; **KNOB**, 1961-62; **KGFJ**, 1963-65; **KGIL**, 1964-66; **KFI**, 1969-70; **KGIL**, 1970-75; **KFI**, 1976-77; **KABC**, 1977-81; **KMPC**, 1981-84. Born in 1941 in Providence, Larry has spent his radio and tv career in California. Larry worked in the oil fields of Long Beach where his early interest in jazz music led him to KBCA. He did the morning show at the "Jazz Knob" for "Sleepy" Stein. "I clearly remember my first day on KGFJ as the day President Kennedy was shot." Larry has been very visible over the decades, hosting KTLA/Channel 5's *Help Thy Neighbor*, game shows, and the Arthritis Telethon, for which he has helped raise millions of dollars. "It's hard to separate parts of my career, since they've overlapped." Larry did weekend mornings on KABC and fill-in for "Ken & Bob" and was also the booth announcer for KTLA. He got weary of "format changes" and gave up radio in the mid-1980s. His voiceover career includes imaging for tv stations all over the country. "As busy as I am, I still miss radio. I'll be driving along and think of a great bit."

VANCE, Tommy: **KHJ**, 1965-66. The Brit arrived in the Southland from Seattle. Tommy returned to England in 1966 and worked for Radio London and BBC Radio 1. He is currently with VH-1 in London.

VARGAS, Gustavo: **KTNQ**, 1993-94. Gustavo worked afternoons at Spanish KTNQ.

VELING, Pat: **KWIZ**, 1985. Pat runs an ad agency in Orange County.

VENT, Peter: **KPZE**, 1987; **KFOX**, 1988. Peter co-hosted "Sportsnight" on KPZE and "Sports Time" with Bud Furillo on KFOX.

VERA, Billy: **KCRW**, 1986-92. *Yo!* The ubiquitous Billy Vera decided early on to have many projects going on at

the same time. "If you can do one thing well, then there's no reason that you can't apply that talent to other areas. Interests and abilities overlap." Born in Riverside, he grew up in Westchester County in New York. His father, Bill McCord, was one of the premier game show announcers (*21* and *Tic Tac Dough*) and was a staff announcer with NBC for 35 years. His mother sang with the Ray Charles Singers on the *Perry Como Show*. Billy loved music and at 16 he was performing with his own band. "A friend suggested that I change my name so it wouldn't be confused with my father. I had a school friend named Guadeloupe Vera and took her last name. It was cool and a total accident. And besides 'Vera' would look big on a marquee." During the 1970s Billy picked up gigs wherever he could and continued to write songs. His song writing successes included compositions recorded by Fats Domino, Nancy Sinatra, the Shirelles, Crystal Gayle, Robert Plant and George Benson. In 1979 Dolly Parton recorded one of his songs, *I Really Got The Feeling*, and based on that success, he moved to Southern California. The 1980s were good to Billy. The Beaters were born, an opportunity for his personal love affair with r&b to flourish. Hardly unpacked in L.A. his song *At This Moment* appeared on the highly successful *Family Ties* tv show and the song shot to #1 and stayed at the top for two weeks. Billy and the Beaters was the in-house band for ABC/TV's *Rick Dees Into the Night* show. Another of his songs appeared on Bonny Raitt's 5-million selling album, *Luck of the Draw*. Billy produced three successful albums for Lou Rawls. His diversity was reflected on screen. Billy's acting adventures included roles in films such as *Buckaroo Bonzai*, *Blind Date* and Oliver Stone's *The Doors*. On tv he appeared in *Wiseguy, Alice* and the recurring role of Duke on *Beverly Hills 90210*. He is the voice you hear singing the theme on the successful series, *Empty Nest*. In 1988 he received a Star on the Hollywood Walk of Fame. For six years Billy hosted a Saturday show on KCRW playing oldies from his 35,000 record collection (singles, albums and photographs pack two bedrooms). In 1989 a casting agent heard his radio show and thought Billy would be perfect for commercials. "He heard a sincerity in my voice. I'm not sure what he heard, but I'm not about to change it. I've been doing voiceover work since then." Billy has taught the history of American black music at UCLA and has produced over 100 compilation CDs. Every Thursday night since 1993, Billy carries a box of records from his own collection to a non-descript strip mall in Sunland and in a basement studio broadcasts two hours of the "Rock 'n Roll Party" on CRN (Cable Radio Network). "I get calls from all over the country." Billy regales his audience with stories of artists, record company owners and the colorful characters who make up the world of his special music.

> *"What we all need is another John Wayne...and as fast as possible."*
> *-Jon R.W. Wailin*

VERCELLI, Gary: **KBCA**, 1978. Gary worked weekends at the Jazz station.

VEZA, Pepe: **KTNQ**, 1991. Pepe worked middays at Spanish KTNQ.

VIDAL, Bruce: **KIIS**, 1982-96; **KNJO**, 1997. Bruce arrived at KIIS in the fall of 1982 from K101-San Francisco, replacing Laurie Allen who eventually became his wife. In 1984 he was going head-to-head against his wife who was on KMGG. Their rivalry was chronicled in *People* magazine and an appearance on *Good Morning America*. The media were fascinated with the fact that the husband/wife team were on competing radio stations, at times in the same slot. In the mid-1980s, parked in the duo's San Fernando Valley driveway were two cars: a sleek, brand-new red Corvette and a not-so-sleek dented Dodge Aries. His then-wife explained, "Whoever got the highest ratings got to drive the Corvette." Bruce moved to swing at KIIS in late 1996 following an ownership change from Gannett to Jacor. In the spring of 1997 he joined KNJO.

VILLANI, Mike: **KWIZ**; **KNOB**, 1986-87

VIOLETTE, Todd: **KIIS**, 1995-96. Todd was KIIS's

youngest air personality. Growing up in Rialto, he worked as a board op at KOST. His first on-air job was KPSI-Palm Springs and then KGGI, KDES-Palm Springs and KKBT. "Radio to me is like the air you breathe, and I can't live without it." Todd worked weekend all-nights at KIIS while doing afternoons at KRUZ-Santa Barbara. He left KIIS in late 1996 and in early 1997 moved to mornings at KRUZ-Santa Barbara.

VIRGIN, Tim: **KROQ**, 1995. Tim left "K-Roq" and his weekend work in the spring of 1995 to be md of KYNN-Omaha.

VISCOTT, David: **KABC**, 1980-93; **KIEV**, 1994-95; **KMPC**, 1995-96. David started as a substitute for radio psychologist Toni Grant and eventually got his own full-time shift. In 1989 the radio therapist left KABC for a few months in a dispute with then-pd John Rook. Born in Boston in 1939, the psychiatrist became a mini-empire unto himself. He wrote over 13 books, ran the David Viscott Center for Natural Therapy (a short-form confrontational treatment that stressed facing the truth). He created a line of greeting cards with inspiration/motivational messages. For those who didn't get enough of him on the radio, he sold audio cassettes through mail order. David traveled the world conducting "discovery weekends" with a combination of seminars and lectures. He went to medical school at Tufts University after graduating from Dartmouth in 1959. David taught at University Hospital in Boston, set up private practice in 1968 and moved to Los Angeles in 1979 where he was a professor of psychiatry at UCLA. Later in the 1980s he had his own tv show. For the last two years of his life, David was a semi-regular guest on the KIIS morning show with Rick Dees. David died October 12, 1996, at the age of 58. A friend of David's said: "He died of a broken heart."

VISSION, Richard "Humpty": **KDAY**, 1989; **KPWR**, 1990-97. Born Richard Gonzalez in Toronto, he started his radio career in Southern California. Asked if there were any highlights while living here, Humpty shivered, "I was on the air when the 7.8 earthquake hit!!!!"

VLASIC, Dominic: **KNOB**, 1982-87. Dominic, a native of Yugoslavia, married the KNOB owner's daughter, Madelaine and they became the morning drive team at KNOB.

VLASIC, Madelaine: **KNOB**, 1981-85, pd. Madelaine hosted the midday show. She has since moved to Hawaii. She was the daughter of the owner, Jeanette Banoczi. Madelaine met her husband Dominic when he applied for an announcing job at KNOB. They eventually became a marriage team and on-air team at KNOB. She lives in Maui and is doing voiceover work in the Islands.

VOGEL, Dick: **KJOI**, 1972-76

VON ARTERBERRY: **KRHM**, 1965. He hosted a jazz show.

VON, Stuart: **KBMS**, 1961-63; **KLAC**, 1965-68; **KABC**, 1968-70. Born Stuart von Rathjen in St. Louis, he graduated from William and Mary College, attended Georgetown University Law School and graduated from the California College of Law. Stuart was part of the volatile and embryonic days of talk radio in Southern California. At KLAC Stuart followed the outspoken Joe Pyne. TV Talk editor for the *LA Herald-Examiner* called Stuart "sort of a nice Joe Pyne." For many years he was the host of KHJ/Channel 9's *Tempo* show. Stuart lives in Pomona and is the voice image for a number of stations in the Midwest.

VONCE, Lee: SEE Michael C. Gynne

VOTAW, Jim: **KIKF**, 1985, pd. In 1985 Jim left for Fresno. Following a stint as gsm of "91X"-San Diego, he was promoted to director of sales at Jacor's San Diego stations.

VOXX: **KLSX**, 1995-96. Voxx's paternal great-great grandmother was a full-blooded Cherokee sorceress and her mother is a descendant of the witches of Arcadia, Italy. She is the resident psychic at the House of Blues. Voxx joined KLSX's new Talk format in the summer of 1995 billing herself "The Rock and Roll Psychic."

During AFTRA's strike against KFWB in 1961, the station published a full-page ad. Part of the ad listed weekly salaries.

Present AFTRA Scale	$155.00
AFTRA Demand	$200.00
Charles Arlington	**$230.75**
Cleve Hermann	**$199.62**
Mike Henry	**$173.00**
J. Paul Huddleston	**$173.00**
Bill Ballance	**$432.70**
Elliot Field	**$480.76**
Ted Quillin	**$376.00**
Joe Yocam	**$357.60**

W

W., Jeffrey: **KEZY**, 1986. Jeffrey was called "the boy with all the songs."

WACHS, Larry: **KLSX**, 1995-97. Larry teamed with his best friend Eric Haessler for afternoon drive at the launch of "Real Radio" in the summer of 1995. They have been in radio, individually and together in Hartford and Rochester. "The Regular Guys" follow Howard Stern on KLSX. Larry used to own a restaurant in Baltimore.

WADE, Bill: **KHJ**, 1963 and 1968-74; **KBRT**, 1980-81, pd. Born in Los Angeles on October 11, Bill spent his radio career in California. Bill worked for KHJ in 1963, KDEO and KGB-San Diego. In 1966 he was working at KFRC-San Francisco. He returned to KHJ, when it was "Boss Radio," in 1968. In 1973, Bill worked morning drive while waiting for Charlie Van Dyke to join the station. He had a different guest dj every morning with superstars of the day like Dionne Warwick, Diana Ross, the Carpenters, Glen Campbell and the Osmonds. In 1969 Bill ran the Bill Wade Broadcast School of Radio and Television. In 1975 Bill was the gm of KSOM-Ontario. He's now teaching at Lampson Business College in Mesa, Arizona.

WAGNER, Gary: **KLON**, 1992-97. Gary hosts "Nothing but the Blues."

WAGNER, Jack: **KNX**, 1947; **KGIL**, 1951-52; **KHJ**, 1952-57; **KBIQ**, 1957-58, pd; **KHJ**, 1958-62; **KHJ/FM**, 1967-68, pd; **KNX**, 1968, pd. Jack's show business career began at age 4 in Hollywood films as a French-speaking child actor. By age 17, he was a contract player at MGM. He became a radio personality at KHJ and the Mutual Network while performing in tv shows, including *Dragnet*, *Sea Hunt*, *The Ann Sothern Show* and 144 episodes of *The Adventures of Ozzie & Harriet* as "Jack in the Malt Shop." Jack

started an association with the Disney organization when he and his family were guests for the opening of Disneyland. Beginning in 1970 Jack handled the voice work at the park and production of over 40 master tapes that contained background music for the theme areas at Disneyland, Walt Disney World, Tokyo Disneyland and Disneyland Paris. His taped messages included "Keep your arms and legs inside the coach," "All aboard" or "Enjoy your stay." For many years, he supplied the authentic voices of some 20 various Disney cartoon characters that were heard at the parks. His radio career spanned a period of special programs to popular music. At KHJ in 1957, he hosted an all-night talk/music show with guest stars. During his first job at KNX, Jack was the announcer for a live music program featuring performances by his older brother, Roger Wagner. Jack was the last pd at KNX before the station switched to all-News. At KMPC and KABC, he was the guest host for Dick Whittinghill and Gene Norman. In the 1990s, Jack was a consultant to Las Vegas casino owner Stephen Wynn and produced the music for the Treasure Island Hotel and Casino. Jack's son, Mike, was pd of KRLA for a decade. Jack passed away after collapsing at a rest stop on his way to Palm Springs on June 16, 1995. He was 69.

WAGNER, Mike: **KEZY**, 1974; **KIIS**, 1976-82, pd; **KRLA**, 1984-94, pd. Mike started his show business career at the age of 3 when he first appeared on *The Adventures of Ozzie and Harriet*. He went on to appear in more than a dozen episodes. At age 6, he was featured

on an album cover of popular easy listening music. In the 1970s Mike appeared in *Happy Days* and *Ozzie's Girls*. His father, Jack Wagner, worked for a half-dozen radio stations in the 1950s and '60s. Mike's uncle was Roger Wagner, conductor of the L.A. Master Chorale and the Roger Wagner Chorale. His cousin Phil Volk was known as "Fang" as a member of the rock band Paul Revere & the Raiders. He started his radio career in 1973 at KDES-Palm Springs and in late 1974 joined KEZY. Mike became the KIIS all-night man on March 18, 1976. When the station went to a Disco format at noon on November 14, 1978, he was named pd. In a 1979 *LA Times* interview, Mike commented, "I really believe that disco is the most mass-appeal format there is. It's become a new life-style." Mike resigned KIIS as pd in the spring of 1981 and stayed on another year in afternoons. Between KIIS and KRLA, Mike was vp of programming for Alta Broadcasting. Mike joined KRLA in late 1984 and served as pd for over a decade. He has narrated countless video presentations, and his voice has been heard introducing guest performances and special parades at Disneyland and Walt Disney World. Mike was the voice at the Sony Game Show Network. In the fall of 1995 Mike joined Disneyland Paris as manager of marketing. He is the English language voice of the Eurostar train service between London and Disneyland Paris.

WAILIN, Jon R.W.: **KZLA**, 1979-80. Jon worked morning drive at Country KZLA during his brief stop in Los Angeles. "I was the first FM country jock in L.A. I was the first voice when the station changed format." Born in Winnipeg, he moved with his family to Minneapolis at an early age. After graduation from Brown Institute, he started his radio career in 1965 at KAUS-Austin, Minnesota. What happened between Austin and now? "Six wives, the Vietnam War and several presidential elections." Jon's humor is evident in everything he does. Before he joined KEWB-San Francisco in 1981 for a decade-long stay, Jon worked in Honolulu, Duluth, Nashville (twice), Indianapolis, Cincinnati and Evansville. "For the first ten years of my career I had no comprehension that radio was a business. I'm now making up for my sins. I work very closely with the sales department helping in every way I can." While in Cincinnati, John Baylis gave him life-long encouragement. "John told me that I had a God-given talent and I was obligated to use it in the proper way." In the 1990s Jon has consulted for stations in Illinois and Chattanooga. He now lives in San Leandro. "I've done it all. Life's a lot easier. What we all need is another John Wayne...and as fast as possible."

WAITE, Charles: **KNX**, 1968-69. Charles worked morning drive news and talk on the CBS O&O all-News station.

WALCOFF, Rich: **KIKF**, 1983. Rich was sports director at KIKF and the voice of the UC Irvine sports teams. He left in 1983 for a similar position at KMEL-San Francisco. Currently Rich is morning drive sportscaster at KGO and KGO/TV-San Francisco.

WALD, Ronnie: The former Southern California broadcaster is the voice of the Visalia Oaks.

WALDEN, Mike: **KNX**, 1966-69; **KFI**, 1970-73. Mike

has been prominent in sports broadcasting in Southern California for over 30 years. He's the only announcer in radio and tv to serve as both the voice of the USC Trojans in football and basketball, and later the voice of the UCLA Bruins in both sports. He's well known for his play-by-play work on NCAA football and basketball, including tennis telecasts for the Prime Ticket Network (now Fox Sports West). Mike has done seven Rose Bowl games and major league baseball for the Dodgers, Cardinals and Braves. He was born in 1931 and grew up in Springfield and graduated from the University of Illinois with a degree in journalism. He worked on the Illinois Sports Network while in school. After the Air Force, he spent 10 years in Milwaukee broadcasting Wisconsin football and basketball, the Green Bay Packers and Braves. From Milwaukee he went to CBS radio in Chicago. Then, in 1966, he got the USC job. In 1970, he became sports director at KFI. He has won four Golden Mike awards, an L.A. Press Club award and has served five terms as president of the Southern California Sports Broadcasting Association. Mike lives in Tarzana with his wife Nancy and has four grown children.

WALDOW, Mitch: **KFWB**, 1984. Mitch was a news reporter for all-News KFWB. He went to KCOP/Channel 13.

WALKER, Adrienne: **KOST**, 1993-95. Adrienne is the co-host of the syndicated "World Chart Show." She was born in San Jose and remembered as a little kid, "I used to listen to Casey Kasem and record 'American Top 40' on my little cassette player and then talk into the microphone between songs and pretend to be the announcer. Now I'm hosting the replacement show for 'AT40.' Wild!" Her parents moved to Chicago in 1978. Adrienne's radio career began at WILL-Champaign/Urbana when she was a 17-year-old freshman at the University of Illinois. She was hired as the youngest sports anchor in the station's history. She knew she had a problem with pronouncing sports names when her first fan mail stated: "It's WimbelDON, not WimbelTON." In 1984 she anchored both drive newscasts at WPGU-Champaign and eventually became nd. While in school she interned at WXRT-Chicago. She graduated in 1986 knowing, "where to find the best bratwurst on the westside." Adrienne headed for warmer weather and joined KLPX-Tucson. Her next job was morning host at KFMU-Colorado Springs, which the station proudly proclaimed "The World's Only Wind Powered Radio Station." When she joined KKLD-Tucson in 1988, Adrienne remembered, "I was the first female ever to host her own entertainment morning show in Tucson." She is referred to as "Ace" on "The World Chart Show."

WALKER, John Lee: **KIIS**, 1977

WALKER, Mike: **KLSX**, 1997. In the spring of 1997 Mike started hosting a morning talk show on "Real Radio." He writes the "Behind the Scenes" column for *The National Enquirer*.

> *"I'm looking forward to the year 2000 when I will have spanned seven decades in broadcasting."*
> —**Joe Niagara**

WALKER, Rhett: **KRLA**, 1967. Born in New Zealand, Rhett held several higher education degrees in music. He was a popular dj at KOL-Seattle. From KFXM-San Bernardino, Rhett arrived at KRLA in 1967 and left within the year. He's currently working mornings at WGKX-Memphis.

WALKER, Sky: **KTNQ**; **KHTZ**; **KIIS**, 1988-90 and 1991-92; **KKBT**, 1990-91; **KJLH**, 1992-93; **KRLA**, 1993-96; **KACE**, 1996. Sky was born and raised in Encino. It was evident from an early age that he would pursue radio. He started the first campus radio station at Mulholland Junior High in Van Nuys. Sky started his career at the age of 16 doing an overnight weekend shift at KTNQ. By the age of 18 he was doing overnights full-time at KHTZ while attending Cal State Northridge. After college Sky programmed KLAV-Las Vegas, XTRA and worked afternoons at KGGI-Riverside. Beginning in 1985, he was doing mornings at KPOP-Sacramento and later cross town at KWOD. While in Northern California he anchored local television news and hosted a game show. At "the Beat" he worked nights and became their promo voice and production director. At KRLA Sky worked afternoon drive as Bobby Romero. As Sky Walker he works at the WW1 Oldies Channel and is doing weekends and swing at KACE and KOLA-Riverside.

WALLACE, Gerry: **KFI**, 1990-93. Gerry was part of the "TNT" morning news magazine show.

WALLACH, Paul: **KIEV**, 1976-93. Paul was a popular talk show host and restaurant critic while associated with *Westways* travel magazine.

WALLENGREN, Mark: **KOST**, 1985-97. Born in Heber, Utah, the Studio City resident works morning drive with Kim Amidon. Mark arrived in Los Angeles from KBOI, a full-service AC station in Boise. In a 1989 *LA Times* article profiling morning personalities, Mark said: "The key to our success is that we haven't changed. We've been consistent. We're kinda mom and pop. People who listen to us are keeping their eyes on the interest rates, hoping the variable rates on their mortgages don't go up." A career highlight for Mark was interviewing Paul McCartney. His personal high was being present at the birth of his first child. Mark was nominated for *Billboard*'s 1993 Adult/Contemporary Radio Air Personality of the Year. When asked if Wallengren was his real name, Mark replied, "Would I change my name to Wallengren? You've got to be kidding."

London and Engelman leave KRTH morning show and move to same slot at KWST
          -June 25, 1981

WALLIN, Fred: **KIEV**, 1976; **KGOE**, 1978-79; **KPRZ**, 1981-82; **KWNK**, 1985; **KFOX**, 1982-87; **KABC**, 1988-89; **KMPC**, 1992-93; **KIEV**, 1995; **KWNK**, 1996; **KIIS/AM**, 1997. Fred's contribution to the Southern California radio scene has been sports reporting. He was one of the many who hosted KABC's afternoon drive "SportsTalk." He started hanging around KABC in 1975 doing odd jobs hoping for a shot. His first job out of Cal State Northridge, with a political-science degree, was as a producer. "Part of my morning newstalk responsibilities was to steal the traffic reports from KNX, since we no longer had a helicopter reporter." He followed Ed "Superfan" Beiler as a producer and got his first on-air experience filling in for Beiler on the weekends. In the mid-1970s, Fred worked as a sports producer in Boston at WEEI and WMEX. In 1985 he left the Southland to join KEX-Portland but was back in four months. In 1987 he did fill-in work at WFAN-New York and was back at KABC "I enjoyed my two years at KABC more than anything else in my career. It was there I made the worst decision anyone in my industry could ever make. After gm George Green brought in Beiler, I was offered 'DodgerTalk' again. Insanely, for a few dollars and the matter of pride I turned it down." At KMPC Fred started out doing all-nights during the all-Sports programming and then moved to mornings until Charlie Tuna arrived and Fred moved to weekends. At KIEV he hosted an evening sports show. In late 1995 he joined KMJI-Sacramento to host an afternoon drive sports talk show. Over the years he worked afternoons on the Sports Radio Network, was sports director of SelectTV and broadcast Los Angeles Lazers Indoor Soccer and the pre-game show for the Los Angeles Express. Larry Stewart profiled Fred in 1988 in the *LA Times*: "Wallin began dreaming about doing a KABC talk show of any kind while attending Culver City High School and lived only five minutes from the station." Fred used to go to the station after school and watch the talk shows. He graduated from Cal State Northridge in 1971 and planned to join his two brothers who were lawyers. He now works for "XTRA Sports 1150."

WALSH, Chuck: **KFWB**, 1968-79; **KABC**, 1979-93. Born in 1935, Chuck was one of the first voices when KFWB launched the all-News format in March 1968. In the early 1960s he was an actor who always loved the movies. At KABC he worked morning drive with the popular "Ken and Bob Company" team and has done movie reviews for years. In 1986 he co-hosted a new food show with Jackie Olden.

WALSH, George: **KNX** 1952-86. "When I was growing up in Cleveland in the 1930s, radio was magic. It was like being an astronaut today." In his junior year in high school, George had to give a speech on what he wanted to be when he grew up. "I had no idea. I said that I wanted to be on the radio and repeated some lines from radio shows. My instructor gave me a reasonable mark and asked if I would host a floor show and do some impersonations at the prom. They paid me $15 and two tickets to the prom." From that point George kept improving his act on local amateur shows aired on radio and won some contests. After high school graduation he joined the local steel mill and worked church socials at night. World War II broke out and George enlisted in the Army Air Corps and served for four years. "I froze in Munich and decided that when I got out I wasn't going to return to the Cleveland cold." In 1946 George became pd of KSWS-Roswell, New Mexico and stayed five years. In 1952 he decided to return to school for more education and enrolled in the Don Martin School of Broadcasting in Hollywood. On May 26, 1952, KNX offered a part-time job of vacation relief at $100 a week. He stayed 34 years. George was the announcer on *Gunsmoke* for three decades (10 years on radio and 20 on television). "By 1986 I was ready to retire. I had had a prostate cancer operation and a heart pace maker installed." George lives in Monterey Park.

WAMSLEY, Bill: **KLAC**, 1971, pd; **KFOX**, 1971-72, pd

WAPLES, Alvin John: **KGFJ**, 1972-77, pd; **KJLH**, 1984; **KGFJ/KKTT**, 1984, pd; **KACE**. Born in 1946 in St. Louis, Al worked at KATZ in his hometown before joining KGFJ. A radio peer cited one of Al's major contributions was being one of the first to play "hip-hop." When Grandmaster Flash and the Furious Five had a tough time getting airplay, Alvin supported their efforts. In 1977, he left KGFJ for KDIA-San Francisco and returned for morning drive on KJLH in 1984. Alvin is now working for ABC Radio Networks based in Dallas.

> "I was a Teamster truck driver in the Bay Area. My last job before John London brought me into the radio biz was with a rendering company, where my duties were to pick up used frying grease and dead animals, and bring them back to the plant, where they would be rendered into different products such as the base for soap and lipstick."
> -Dennis Cruz

WARD, Bill: **KBLA/KBBQ**, 1967-70; **KLAC**, 1972-79, pd; **KMPC**, 1982-93, pd and gm; **KLIT/KSCA**, 1993-97, vp/gm. Bill was born in 1939 in Italy, Texas. His first radio job at age 15 was in Waxahachie, a few miles from his hometown. He got an FCC 1st Class Radio License and did the all-night shift at WRR-Dallas while attending the University of Texas at Arlington in the late 1950s. Bill went to McLendon's WAKY-Louisville in 1959 to do the morning show and in 1962 moved to evenings at WPRO-Providence. His first programming job was at WPLO-Atlanta while doing mornings. Bill moved to KBOX-Dallas in late 1964 as morning man and became pd in 1966. In March 1967, he joined KBLA

as pd and changed the call letters and format to Country music. He became station manager in 1970. Bill was hired by Metromedia in the late summer of 1971 to program KLAC and within a year was promoted to manager. In 1979 he was promoted to executive vp of Metromedia and moved to New York. By the spring of 1980 he was elevated to president. He left Metromedia in the spring of 1982 and moved back to Los Angeles as president of Golden West Broadcasters, where he became manager of KMPC, in addition to his duties as president of the company. In 1985, Bill bought KUTE for Golden West, and the station adopted a Soft AC format with the call letters KLIT. Bill orchestrated the format change of 101.9FM to KSCA, Los Angeles' first AAA station. The station was sold in early 1997 and Bill retired.

WARD, Paul: **KBIG**, 1971-72

WARD, Rick: **KDAY**, 1962; **KBLA**, 1965; **KIEV**, 1973; **XPRS/XERB**, 1973-75; **KALI**. Born David Ricci, Rick started his Southern California run at KDAY. In 1975, after the theatrical success of *American Graffiti*, Rick guided the rebirth of the Mexican mega-watt stations XPRS and XERB which could be heard in 13 states on a clear day. At the time, XPRS was on tape with the voices of Art Laboe, Ted Quillin and Sam Babcock. Rick left for Macon, Mississippi, then returned to Los Angeles to work with Huggie Boy. He had brief stays at Spanish KALI, WQAM-Miami and WWSC-Cocoa Beach before spending time in the military.

WARD, William: **KNX**, 1958-62. William was known as the "laziest host on the coast" by the time he joined KNX. Bill, a Seattle native, began his radio career in 1939 at KOL-Seattle. After serving the U.S. Army Signal Corps. during World War II, he worked for various Seattle stations, KOIN-Portland and KFRC and KCBS-San Francisco. In the early 1960s he joined the writing staff of *The Tennessee Ernie Ford Show*. He established KIQS-Willows, north of Sacramento. Bill returned to the Northwest in 1970 and retired in 1972 following a stroke. He died December 13, 1996, of congestive heart failure at the age of 76.

WARE, Ciji: **KABC**, 1977-93. Born Corlis Jane Ware in 1942 in Pasadena, she moved with her family to Carmel in 1954. Her father was Harlan Ware, novelist and writer of the classic radio show, "One Man's Family." She attended Radcliffe and graduated from Harvard in 1964. Ciji majored in Renaissance History, but spent most of her time in musical comedy and ended up as the first female dance captain of the Hasty Pudding Club. She developed a career in radio and television, reporting and producing, often on consumerism or public affairs, and also wrote for magazines. In the early 1970s Ciji was the consumer reporter for three local tv stations. In 1984 she wrote her first book, *Sharing Parenthood After Divorce*, after her own marriage came apart. She also won a local television Emmy in 1977 for a program on children whose own parents kidnap them during custody disputes. Ciji worked with KABC's morning news team for decades as the health and lifestyle editor. She has published two historical novels, one titled *Island of the Swans* which was an 18th Century historical epic based on the life of the Duchess of Gordon, a Scottish woman and confidant of kings and queens. She also does voiceover work.

WARLIN, Jim: **KPSA**, 1972. Jim was born in San Gabriel and worked morning drive at KPSA.

WARNER, Steve: **KLAC**, 1993

WARREN, Bob: **KGBS**, 1970-74. The former announcer for the *Lawrence Welk Show* and *This Is Your Life* worked news at KGBS.

WARWICK, Stan: **KXLA**, 1957; **KMPC**, 1957; **KLAC**, 1957-64; **KGIL**, 1964-92, gm. "Your whole life changes after a stroke. I'm lucky I can still walk and drive but I can't write." That's the way Stan started a phone conversation in the spring of 1996 from his home on the Central California coast. He spent three decades with Buckley Communications, holding every job within KGIL (dj, newscaster, director of news, pd in 1967 and, finally, gm). He was the Announcer of the Year in 1961. From 1969 until KGIL was sold, Stan was the vp of West Coast operations at Buckley Communications. He was born in Tekoa, Washington and graduated from Washington State College with a degree in communications a few years after Edward R. Murrow went through the same program. Stan suffered two strokes in 1995. One side of his brain was affected. Every Thursday, five men in the Morro Bay area who have had recent strokes gather for group physical and emotional therapy. "I am thankful that the stroke was not worse and that I am able to get around."

WASHBURNE, Jim: **KRLA**, 1961-63, pd. Jim came to KRLA as the Pasadena outlet's pd and afternoon drive jock. Some of his best remembered on-air references included calling the L.A. basin the "Washbasin" and

saying "..but isn't it quiet when the goldfish die?" During his short two-year reign, Jim brought Emperor Bob Hudson to the station. In 1963, Jim left everything for San Francisco and KYA. In 1966 he fell asleep at the wheel of his car coming home from a weekend in Big Sur and died in the automobile accident.

WASSIL, Aly: **KABC**, 1972.

WATERS, Lou: **KFWB**, 1968. Lou spent a half-decade working early evenings at KDWB-Minneapolis before coming to sister station KFWB for the all-night shift. He was at the station the last night that rock music was broadcast along with Gene Weed, Roger Christian and Joe Yocam. Lou went to Tucson and Cleveland before ending up as a news anchor at CNN.

Coca-Cola buys KJOI for $3.9 million in 1976
KJOI sells for $18 million in 1983
KJOI sells for $44 million in 1986
KJOI sells for $79 million in 1989

WATKINS, Chick: **KMPC**, 1987-88. Chick is the pd of WW1's Adult Standards format, and he also hosts a program. The format is aired on KLAC. Born and raised in Akron, Ohio, Chick got his radio start at WCUE-Akron and stayed for 12 years. In 1972 he was the pd of WGAR-Cleveland during the Don Imus/Jack Thayer period. In 1982 he joined Transtar Satellite Network in Colorado Springs. Two years later he became pd of KOY-Phoenix. In 1988 he rejoined Transtar which had become Unistar and is now Westwood One. The Adult Standards format is carried on over 250 stations. "We were originally designed as an alternative for AM radio, and it just grew from there."

WATSON, Bill: Drake-Chenault Enterprises, 1965-72, national pd; **KHJ**, 1972-73, pd; **KIQQ**, 1973-74, pd; **KMPC**, 1975-78 and 1982-87, pd. "Bakersfield, KBIS and KAFY for a year or so. Next Spokane to try tv at KREM. Boring. Too cold. Missed radio. Auditioned for an afternoon drive opening at KXOA-Sacramento. Got the job. I also hosted an *American Bandstand*-type tv show on KXTV. After a great run of four years we left for hometown L.A. (Van Nuys High School 19--). I thought I had a job waiting at KRLA but the pd I had spoken with was replaced and the new pd had his own ideas. No job. That's when I met Ron Jacobs who was in town looking for talent for KMEN-San Bernardino and KMAK-Fresno. Ron convinced me to go to KMEN as pd and afternoon drive jock, 'Mr. Kicks 3 to 6.' KFXM was a huge number one. Less than six months later KMEN was number one, and stayed there. KMEN pd Hilite: Presenting the Rolling Stones for their first U.S. appearance at Swing Auditorium. Blew the roof off. Ask Mick. After four great years at KMEN, I left to consult a few California stations including KCBQ-San Diego and KDIA-San Francisco. Fast Forward: Bill Drake leaves KYA-San Francisco to consult KYNO-Fresno to do battle with Jacobs at KMAK. A great fight. Drake is hired to consult KHJ and hires Jacobs as pd, and is soon asked to consult programming for the entire RKO chain; KFRC-San Francisco, CKLW-Detroit, WRKO-Boston, WOR/FM-New York and WHBQ-Memphis. Drake hires me as right hand man national pd. Jacobs resigns KHJ, other plans. The Beat Goes On. A few years later KHJ slips to number three with a 3.8 ARB. Drake asks me to go 'in the house' at KHJ as pd in addition to my national chores. OK. Six months later KHJ is number one again with a 6.0. KHJ pd Hilite: The worlds greatest all time, all around rock and roll disc jockey. The Real Don Steele. Politics. Drake leaves RKO and purchases KIQQ/FM. Robert W. Morgan, Steele and Watson join him. We had some fun. Drake-Chenault sells KIQQ. I go to KMPC to work with top MOR personalities for three years. Politics. Hook up with Drake again to produce syndicated special features, new version of 'The History of Rock and Roll' and 'The History of Country Music.' Too much fun in Nashville. Drake-Chenault sell the company. Drake disappears to a dark cave until later when Gotham City needs him again at KRTH. I return to KMPC. They want a Big Band format. Can do. KMPC jocks and I take the station to number four in Los Angeles with a 4.2. The only and the last AM station in town, in the top ten, playing music. Big Band Boss Radio. KMPC pd Hilite: A cocktail party for the staff to celebrate the 4.2 in the General Managers conference room. I toasted and said a few words to the jocks. They will remember what I said. The gm will not. Enough! Sell Northridge home and move to Laughlin, Nevada. Blackjack. Craps. Sell Laughlin place and buy Carlsbad La Costa condo and also my favorite hide-out, an ocean front condo in Baja between Rosarito and Ensenada. Since 1967, I have been an aficionado de los toros, a bullfight fan. If you're looking for me, I'll be in the first row, dead center shady side at the Tijuana bullring every season Sunday at 4 p.m. That's it and that's that. Adios."

WATSON, Rich: **KUTE**, 1982-87; **KOCM**, 1988-89; **KJOI**, 1989; **KLIT**, 1989-90; **KIKF**, 1990; **KACD**, 1992-97. "I survived seven format changes during my stay at KACD. I'm not sure what it says." Rich was born in Maywood Bell and grew up in Garden Grove. He was a music major at Cypress College, but knew he would eventually end up in radio. "I was 12-years old when I won $11.10 in a KRLA contest. I told my mom that this wouldn't be the last time she would hear me on the radio." A chance meeting with Paul Freeman led Rich to attend the Orange County Broadcast Headquarters (run by Paul and Jack and Mike

Wagner). "I was so bad they let me go through the school a second time." He got his start in 1975 at KRCQ-Indio and later programmed KFXM-San Bernardino before joining KUTE. "I have friends who have worked for 20 stations in two years. I survive because I just keep working at it."

WATSON, Tom: **KKDJ**, 1972. Tom arrived in the Southland from KERN-Bakersfield.

WATUSI, Big: SEE Mark Mendoza

WAYMAN, Tom: **KMPC**, 1962-81, nd. At various times during his two-decade involvement with KMPC, Tom was news director. He was the news sidekick to both morning show veterans Dick Whittinghill and Robert W. Morgan. In early 1981 he hosted a one-hour cooking show as the station was heading toward an all-Talk format. Tom began his radio career at age 14 just after the outbreak of World War II. Most of the announcers at his hometown station in Logan, Utah, had been drafted. When he walked into a radio station with his booming voice, he got the job, despite being in his teens. He wrote a cookbook called *Chef Tom's Chicken*.

WAYNE, Bill: **KZLA**, 1983, pd

WAYNE, Bruce: **KFI/KOST**. Born in New Hampshire, Bruce was KFI's fixed-wing traffic veteran reporter whose single-engine Cardinal crashed shortly after takeoff from Fullerton Airport. He was considered the nation's dean of flying traffic reporters. He started in 1961 for a Boston station. He died exactly one month before his 25th anniversary as an airborne traffic reporter. Bruce reflected in an interview before his death, "I was in television and radio for 10 years before I ever had a flying lesson." He came to Los Angeles in 1968 and because of his media background was able to cover breaking stories from the air. In 1985 his wife talked about the dangers of traffic piloting, "It's very hazardous. Most people don't know that. It's stressful too. Heart attacks are very high among them."

WAYNE, Bruce: **KLOS**. Bruce left the Southland for XHRM-San Diego, which he departed in early 1995.

WAYNE, Daryl: **KROQ**, 1979-81. Daryl was pd and worked afternoon drive. In 1979 as the overnight death of disco prevailed, "Insane Daryl Wayne" buried disco albums at the beach as part of a funeral.

WAYNE, Sid: **KBLA**, 1965

WEATHERLY, Kevin: **KROQ**, 1993-97, pd. Born in 1963, Kevin started his career at age 12 working for his father at KPIN-Casa Grande, Arizona. He came to "the Roq" from KKLQ ("Q106")-San Diego. Before "Q106," Kevin was the md at KIIS and KMEL-San Francisco and on the air at KZZP-Phoenix. When he arrived at "the Roq," he immediately tightened the play list, reflecting his Top 40 background. In the summer 1993 Arbitron, KROQ catapulted to #5 in the market - ahead of all other rock stations including Top 40 KIIS. In a September 1993 story in the *LA Times*, Kevin attributed the success of the station to the fact that much of its direct competition had disappeared, and because KROQ was more reflective of the market instead of trying to lead the market. He was quoted in the *Gavin Report*'s 1993 year-end issue: "Basic Top 40 principles are the proven fundamentals of radio. They can be applied in many situations and are not exclusive to a format." In a 1995 issue of *Requests*, Kevin was listed among the "25 Most Influential People in the Music Industry." He was the honoree of the seventh annual T.J. Martell Industry Roast. *Entertainment Weekly*'s 100 Most Powerful People in the entertainment business listed Kevin #100. Kevin was named *Billboard*'s 1995 Rock pd of the year. In early 1996 his ever-expanding corporate role took on the format change of WXRK-New York. In late 1996, Kevin was promoted to vp of programming for Infinity Broadcasting's alternative stations.

Remembering Top Ten Personality
B. Mitchel Reed

"When I came to KFWB to introduce 'Color Radio,' Mitch was already there doing a jazz program. I told him we were going to rock and roll and he said he couldn't do that. He said that's terrible, I'm a jazz fan. I told him he could be the number one dj in the city. He said, 'I'll sacrifice for that.' And he became number one very quickly."
-*Chuck Blore*

"B. Mitch was a constant joy. He was a hambone and a hugger and a guy who could laugh and cry in public with no problem or embarrassment."
-*Cleve Hermann*

"His rock and roll voice was different from his jazz voice. Chuck Blore wanted Mitch to accentuate his voice and speak twice as fast."
-*Gary Owens*

"B. Mitchel Reed was the only student in the history of Brooklyn Boys High School to major in English as a foreign language."
-*Irwin Zucker*

"He was legend. There was no other disc jockey in the United States like him. That was why KFWB during the sixties was what it was because of gigantic personalities like B.M.R. That's exactly what he was. He wasn't just a time and temperature dj. He was one of a kind."
-*Sam Riddle*

"The Cruisin' Series was a tribute to the best disc jockeys of an era gone by. Disc jockeys had to go back in the studios and recreate. B. Mitch Reed being the fastest tongue anywhere just couldn't recreate those old Top 40 days. Producer Ron Jacobs ended up feeding 'Beemer' about 10 or 12 cups of coffee. They put him back in the booth and what you hear is the 'Cruisin' album as it stands today."
-*Bob Coburn*

From KLOS tribute to B. Mitchel Reed

WEAVER, Beau: **KHJ**, 1975-76; **KRTH**, 1990-94. Beau was on KHJ during the Charlie Van Dyke regime "at the time of the station's biggest numbers ever," according to Beau. Born in 1955, he has achieved much success as a freelance voice. Beau started in 1969 as Thomas Randall at KRBE-Houston. Before arriving in the Southland, he worked at KAKC-Tulsa, KILT-Houston and KNUS-Dallas. He came to the Southland from KFRC-San Francisco. "I did morning drive at age 21 for about 15 minutes before the arrival of Dr. Don Rose." Beau started hanging around radio at age 12 in Tulsa where local legend KAKC was under Bill Drake and Gene Chenault's control. RKO's Michael Spears discovered Beau in Tulsa on his way from CKLW-Detroit to KNUS. After KHJ, he joined KILT working under the name Beauregard Rodriguez Weaver. He was half of the popular Houston team, Hudson & Harrigan and eventually became pd in 1980. In the early '80s he joined his former RKO CEO Dwight Case in Colorado for the launch of the Transtar Radio Network. "During this time I was briefly a candidate for ordination in the Episcopal Priesthood, but that's another story." When Transtar moved to Los Angeles in 1984, Beau was in the advance party. He did morning drive on the Oldies Channel for three years. His voiceover career includes the syndicated oldies show "Let the Good Times Roll" and major national clients. Beau voices promos for *Jeopardy* and *Wheel of Fortune*, is heard on all the tv networks and on motion picture trailers. He's the lead character Dr. Reed Richards, "Mr. Fantastic" in Marvel's *Fantastic Four*. He was the voice of Superman for Hannah-Barbera/Ruby-Spears. Beau played the voice of God on *Duckman* and the fractured narrator on *Felix the Cat*. He is remarried to lyricist Aynne Pryce and lives in Santa Monica, where he services clients from a studio at home.

WEAVER, Bill: **KWIZ**, 1964-90, vp/gm. Bill is responsible for the very successful Oldies all-Request format that dominated the Orange County ratings for many years. He created the first male-female morning team, an all-female air staff and "yes/no radio." Born in Brooklyn in 1918, Bill was the son of a New York cab driver. His family moved to Los Angeles when he was only six. After graduating from Marshall High School and attending L.A. City College and Ventura Junior College, he served in the Navy during World War II. After the service, his first radio job was at KGFL-Roswell, New Mexico followed by KBST-Big Springs, Texas. Unable to lose his New York accent, Bill returned to California, where he became a salesman for the *Ventura Star Free Press*. In 1952 he joined the sales staff of KROY-Sacramento and was later promoted to general manager. "My father very rarely took vacations," his daughter Patrice remembered. "He often told me when putting the family on an airline that he loved what he did, and he looked forward to going into the station each day. It was never work for him, it was love. He ate, slept and lived radio." Bill passed away in January 1990. His daughter remembered that it was perhaps the greatest gathering of the biggest "Who's Who" in radio, "paying their respects to this genius. Bill Weaver who was often imitated, but NEVER DUPLICATED."

WEAVER, Bill: **KPOL**, 1967-70, gm. Bill followed Lou Faust and became the second CapCities gm at KPOL. He had been with Gordon McLendon in Texas.

WEAVER, Patty: SEE Patty Martinez

WEBB, Larry: **KRLA**, 1965-75, gm. When Larry left KRLA he joined the staff of FCC Commissioner Robert E. Lee in the position of engineering assistant and broadcast specialist.

WEBER, George: **KMPC**, 1995. George reported weekend sports on all-Talk KMPC.

WEBER, Pete: As one of the sidekicks to veteran hockey announcer Bob Miller, Pete broadcast the L.A. Kings games between 1978 and 1981. When Pat Riley left as Chick Hearn's colorman to be an assistant under coach Paul Westhead, Pete finished the broadcast season. Born in Galesburg, Illinois, he graduated from Notre Dame with a B.A. in modern languages and an M.A. in communications arts. He spent his sophomore year at the University of Innsbruck, Austria. Pete has done play-by-play for a number of sports. He has been connected with the Buffalo Sabres for better than a decade. Pete has also been associated with the Buffalo Bills pre- and post-game shows along with being a radio analyst. His baseball play-by-play assignments include the Buffalo Bisons since 1983. He did vacation fill-in for Fred Hessler on KMPC with Robert W. Morgan.

> **Lite KLIT (101.9FM) debuts AAA format with call letter switch to KSCA -September 1994**

WEED, Gene: **KFWB**, 1958-68; **KLAC**, 1971. Born in 1935, Gene started in Texas radio when he was 17 years old and attended North Texas State University. He went on to work in Dallas, Omaha and Miami before joining KFWB. The "Weedy One" worked weekends at KFWB at the age of 23 while assigned to Armed Forces Radio and Television Service in Hollywood. In early 1961, Gene was made assistant pd to Jim Hawthorne. He

moved to afternoon drive in 1961. Except for a month during the infamous personality strike in 1961, Gene stayed with the station until the very end, on March 10, 1968, having worked every shift. In 1966, he was voted top all-night dj in *Billboard* magazine's Radio Response Ratings. He created the nationally syndicated *Shivaree* tv rock show which ran for three years and aired in more than 150 markets and seven countries overseas. Before joining dick clark productions (dcp), Gene began producing and directing a new art form he called "Song Films," better known today as music videos. He produced and directed over 200 of the mini-movies for recording artists such as Glen Campbell, The Fifth Dimension, Creedence Clearwater and Debbie Boone. He has produced and directed over 300 tv commercials and numerous industrial and sales presentations. As senior vp of television at dcp, Gene has developed, produced and directed major television series, specials and annual events. Each year he produces and/or directs the *Golden Globe Awards*, *The Academy of Country Music Awards*, *The Soap Opera Digest Awards* and the *Sea World/Busch Gardens Party*. Under his supervision the CMA Awards show has won its time slot every year since it was first televised in 1974. In 1986 he hosted the album *Interviews from The Class of '55*, which was awarded a Grammy as the best spoken word album. In the early 1990s, Gene produced and directed the *Hot Country Nights* series for NBC which continues to air on The Nashville Network. His other specials include *Farm Aid III and IV*, *The Golden Globes 50th Anniversary Special*, *The Lou Rawls Parade of Stars* and *Prime Time Country* nightly on TNN. He also directed the three-hour *LiveAid* concert for ABC. His work as a producer/director earned him two first place awards for creative excellence at the International Film Festival in Chicago. Gene has four children from his first marriage: Kent, a tv director in L.A.; Kymberli, a graphics artist in North Hollywood; Julie, a hair dresser living in Indiana; and Adam, a highly acclaimed video editor, living and working in Nashville. He has three children, all under the age of 10, with his second marriage.

WEED, Steve: **KIIS**, 1977-79. In the spring of 1995, Steve left his pd slot at WKQI-Detroit for a programming assignment with WMXV-New York.

WEEDO, Charlie: **KPWR**, 1994-95

WEINER, Len: **KMPC**, 1992, pd. Len arrived at KMPC to launch the all-Sports format from a successful similar format at WFAN-New York. He attempted to model KMPC after WFAN, down to the idea that in the morning-drive period, a sports station needs "an anti-sports show" that appeals to a more general audience. Robert W. Morgan was kept in place during the format change. Len told Steve Weinstein in an *LA Times* profile that his goal was to draw women and casual sports fans which he felt could be done with the right personalities.

WEINTRAUB, Roberta: **KMPC**, 1981-82. Roberta, the controversial Los Angeles school board member who helped lead the fight against busing for school integration, had a general issues weekend talk show on KMPC.

WEISSMAN, Sharon: **KLON**, 1982-94, gm. Sharon left in 1994 to help direct the Richard and Karen Carpenter Performing Arts Center in Long Beach.

WELCH, Clarence: **KDAY**, 1965

WELCH, Pat: **KACD**, 1995, gm

WELLES, Dara: **KRTH**, 1979-80, nd; **KGIL**, 1989

WELLS, Don: **KMPC**, 1961-72; **KFWB**, 1972-87. Don was part of the original broadcast team for Gene Autry's California Angels in 1961 and spent 12 seasons with the team. Born in Sacramento in 1923, Don grew up in Salinas, where, as a kid, he could "tune in on our aging Atwater Kent radio" the play-by-play reports of the San Francisco Seals and the Oakland Acorns of the Pacific Coast League. After spending three years in World War II becoming a Corporal, Don went to the Hal Styles School of Radio and Television. "We didn't have tape recorders then but one of the school's facilities was a large studio turntable that enabled me to record an acetate disc for audition purposes." A recreated play-by-

play baseball game led to a job at KSBW ("Salad Bowl of the World") as sports and program director. At the Salinas station, he broadcast Class C ball games along with local college football and basketball. His next stop was KWBB-Wichita where he called the action for the Wichita Indians. In the late '40s and early 1950s Gordon McLendon created the Liberty Network which recreated games from wire services and Don would travel to various Major League cities to do the game-of-the-day broadcasts. When the Liberty Network collapsed, Don joined the White Sox broadcast team in Chicago where he worked for eight years. He also did Big Ten football and basketball plus the NFL Chicago Cardinals games before the franchise moved to Phoenix. As the first announcer for the Angels, Don's first broadcast partner was the "voice of the Rams," Bob Kelley. After the 1972 season, Don joined KFWB doing sports reports for the next fifteen years. When Don retired he and his wife moved to Switzerland to join his family. "We now have permanent residence in Switzerland and don't plan to return to the U.S.A." Don's son is a "valued employee" at the Village City Hall. Don and his wife have two grandsons in their 20s and Don owns a three-family chalet in the village that is surrounded by the Alps. "When we retired it was time for a restful climax to an oh-so-active 40 year career. I have never forgotten all those who were so helpful during that long span of time."

WELLS, Jack: **KABC**, 1963-67. Jack was a talk show host on KABC.

WELLS, Pam: **KACE**, 1987-89, pd. Pam arrived at KACE as pd from WHRK-Memphis and was the 1987 *Billboard* magazine Radio Award winner. Pam was pd until a family illness forced her to take a leave of absence. She returned on-air to the Willie Davis-owned station without the programming chores. Pam has since returned to Memphis.

WELLS, Paul: **KMET**, 1986; **KNAC**, 1986-88. Paul joined KMET from KQAK ("The Quake")-San Francisco and did not stay long. He started his career while at Stanford University on the Peninsula of San Francisco, polished his act at KSJO-San Jose and then swam South to KMET. Paul spent some time at KNAC in morning drive with the "Lobster Breakfast Show." He was best-known for his AOR journey in the Bay Area. In 1993, the "Lobster" was on KRQR-San Francisco. In the summer of 1995, Paul joined Ben Manilla Productions, a San Francisco-based digital production facility, as production director and stayed on weekends at KRQR.

WELLS, Scott: **KLON**, 1987-97. Scott hosts a weekend show featuring local jazz artists.

WELLS, Womina: **KACD**, 1996-97. Womina is billed as the "Godmother of House" on "Groove Radio" working early evening. Womina is a recording artist with Aqua Boogie Records in Los Angeles.

WELSH, Pat: **KROQ**, 1979-84, gm; **KACD**, 1996, gm

WENDELL, Bruce: **KDAY**, 1960, pd; **KBLA**, 1967, pd. The longtime Capitol Records executive and baseball fanatic came from radio, where he was md at WINS-New York and pd at KDAY. In the spring of 1995, Bruce joined Rotations promotion and marketing firm.

WENDI: **KIIS**, 1990-96. Born Wendi Westbrook in Shreveport, she arrived in the Southland from KHYI ("Y95")-Dallas where she had worked for two years. In a *Casting Call* magazine interview she described herself as "an ugly duckling and unpopular with the 'in crowd' in high school." She studied accounting in college but left to pursue a career in radio. Wendi worked the overnight shift while at KIIS. In addition to being a vj on MTV and no longer "an ugly duckling," Wendi was a Miller Genuine Draft poster girl while in Dallas and continued that role for two years after arriving in the Southland. Wendi has appeared in *Born on the Fourth of July*, *Silk Stalking*, *Beverly Hills 90210*, *Models, Inc.*, and *Renegade*. She left KIIS in late 1996.

WENNERSTEN, Robert: **KFAC**, 1981-90; **KKGO**, 1991-96, pd. Bob was the music director at Classical music-formatted KFAC throughout the 1980s. When it became "the Beat" in 1989, he moved to KKGO. In an *LA Times* profile on the classical music radio scene, Bob defined KKGO: "The programming philosophy at KKGO is highly structured and admittedly 'hit-oriented.' The station takes far fewer chances with its programming. It shies away from opera and vocal music." He left the station in the spring of 1996.

WERTH, Paul: **KRHM**; **KVFM**; **KNOB**; **KNAC**; **KFAC**. Paul was a knowledgeable, creative musical documentarian. On the KNOB his program was called "Werth Listening To." He brought Bing Crosby back to live performances with a concert at the Music Center. His career began in the 1950s in New York, where he produced concert performances for Harry Belafonte, the Weavers, Woody Guthrie, the Modern Jazz Quartet and Stan Getz. He moved in 1957 to the Southland where he produced concerts and theater shows for Dinah Washington, Herbie Mann and others. Paul produced many radio specials including "This Is Steve Allen" and "Johnny Green's World of Music." In 1972 Paul received a *Billboard* Air Personality award while working at KFAC. He wrote and directed the Leukemia Society radiothons for many years. Paul created an audio history of Harry Truman titled "A Journey to Independence." In 1992 he adapted and produced Neil Simon's *Sunshine*

Boys as the first in a series of Mark Taper Forum Theater of the Air radio programs. Paul died on December 20, 1996, of cancer. He was 69.

WESHNER, Skip: **KRHM**, 1957; **KNAC**, 1972; **KFAC**, 1984

WESLEY, Jim: **KFI**, 1973-80, gm. Jim arrived at KFI when Cox Broadcasting bought the station for $15.1 million. He was an 18-year veteran with Cox and was brought in from WIOD/WAIA-Miami. He was president of the Florida Association of Broadcasters, director of the Economic Society of South Florida, served on the NBC Radio Network executive affiliates committee. Jim commented to the *LA Times* at the time of his arrival: "KFI is a massive operation. Turning it around is like changing the course of the Queen Elizabeth - it will take time." In 1981 he was elevated to Cox Broadcasting executive vp of radio. Currently Jim is the pres/ceo of Patterson Broadcasting.

WEST, Andy: Jumpin' George West left for KPOI (440)

WEST, Bert: **KNX**, late 1950s, gm; **KRLA**, 1980-84, vp/gm. The former president of Golden West Broadcasting came out of semi-retirement to run KRLA. He is now retired and lives in Palm Springs.

WEST, Charlie: **KLOS**, 1987-89, pd. Charlie arrived at KLOS in April 1987 after a 10-year run at KWOD-Tulsa. In the spring of 1989, Charlie left KLOS to open his own consultancy firm.

WEST, Daniel: **KHTZ**, 1979. Born and raised in Los Angeles, Daniel spent 10 years in California radio before joining "K-Hits" in mid-afternoons.

WEST, Don: **KROQ**, 1977

WEST, Gene: **KIQQ**, 1972-73; **KGFJ**, 1975-76. Gene left when Drake/Chenault bought KIQQ in the fall of 1973. He worked in San Diego at KGB and KCBQ and worked the all-night shift at KFRC-San Francisco. In the late 1970s, Gene worked at KWOW-Pomona.

WEST, Joe: **KNX**; **KMPC/KTZN**. Joe anchors the news during morning drive in "the Zone." A graduate of North Carolina, Joe started his broadcast career at KYOU/KGRE-Greeley. In the early 1980s, he handled chores for the Denver Broncos and USFL Denver Gold. Joe interrupted his broadcast start by joining the Navy, where he became a highly-decorated serviceman during Operation Desert Storm. Following an honorable discharge, he joined KNX as a news writer and later worked at Metro Traffic. His voice is heard throughout the Southland delivering on-hold messages to thousands of businesses.

> *Who had the biggest influence in your life?*
> *"My grandfather who raised me not to be afraid of the truth, but fear the lie."*
> *-Top Ten personality*
> *"Sweet Dick" Whittington*

WEST, Mark: **KIIS**, 1979
WEST, Mike: SEE Mike Bennett
WEST, Phyllis: **KBZT**, 1986; **KNAC**, 1986-87. Phyllis worked the all-night shift at KBZT.
WEST, Randy: **KMGG**, 1983-87. Randy was apparently vaccinated at birth with a phonograph needle. "I was chapter president of WABC's Cousin Bruce Morrow fan club and audience regular at tv game show tapings while in high school." Randy started his radio career at age 17 working for a number of stations in New York including WRNW, WALL, WHVW and pd at WFIF-New Haven. In 1979 he arrived in the Southland and worked record promotion and at The Creative Factor. He joined KMGG as production director and later worked weekends and swing. "I appeared on

several tv games shows in the mid-80's and decided to break into the protected bastion of game show announcing and audience warm-up. While waiting for 'the' break during the tough years I made condo payments with the help of dj jobs at KCAQ-Oxnard, KWNK, KKUR and KGMX and KIEV." Randy also taught at Jimi Fox's L.A.B. He broke the tv barrier announcing *Hour Magazine* and *The Chuck Woolery Show*. During the '90s he worked a number of game shows including *Trivial Pursuit*, *Boggle*, and *Wild Animal Games*. Randy continues his tv voice work and is in his second year in looping and sweetening CBS's *The Nanny*.

WEST, Rod: **KZLA**, 1981. During the early 1980s Rod worked at KZLA. In the mid-1990s, he became the CEO of AfterMidNite Entertainment.

WEST, Roland: **KNAC**, 1983-85; **KROQ**, 1986. Roland was at KNAC working afternoon drive and md in the Alternative Rock era, prior to the station going Metal. He moved to KITS-San Francisco in 1987 where he is currently apd and midday personality. Born in Ohio, Roland grew up in California and earned a B.A. in radio and television from Long Beach State.

KIIS AM&FM discontinue simulcasting
-October 10, 1977

WEST, Scott: **KIKF**, 1984

WESTGATE, Murray: **KPOL**, 1963-69. Murray was the Sacramento reporter for KPOL providing a number of phone reports daily. He eventually joined the L.A. operation full-time. In 1969 Murray moved to Las Vegas where he broadcast news for a number of radio and tv stations. Eventually he became the longtime director of public affairs for Nevada Power and Light. He is now an independent entrepreneur with business interests in the Far East.

WESTHEIMER, Ruth: **KFI**, 1983-84. The former kindergarten teacher turned sex guru, "Dr. Ruth" broke new ground on talk radio. On her show she dispensed frank and sexually explicit advice. She borrowed from a Supremes song when she discussed premature ejaculation: "you can't huwwy love." Ruth was born in Germany in 1928, where she lost her parents and grandparents to the Nazi regime and grew up in a Swiss orphanage. She earned a B.A. degree in psychology at the Sorbonne and had a daughter by a French lover. She migrated to Israel and became a kindergarten teacher. Dr. Ruth came to America in 1956 knowing little English and three years later earned a master's in sociology from New York's New School for Social Research. Her doctorate is in the interdisciplinary study of the family, not sexuality. She has written 14 books, the latest called *The Value of Family: A Blueprint for the 21st Century*. The psychosexual therapist started sex counseling in the early 1970s.

WESTMAN, Dick: **KLAC**, 1959-60, gm. Dick went to work in PR unrelated to the entertainment world.

WESTWOOD, Denise: **KNAC**, 1977-80; **KROQ**, 1980-82; **KMET**, 1982-86; **KNX/FM**, 1986-89; **KEDG**,

1989; **KLIT**, 1990. The seed of Denise's radio ambition was planted in her Palos Verdes bedroom. She developed a passion for the voices who glued the music together. The P.V. peninsula was considered Denise's hometown even though she showed up there 18 months after her birth in Syracuse. The "Boss Jocks" were her constant friends and fascination. Denise's zest for life manifested itself by being elected class president at Rolling Hills High School. She followed those inner "voices" to Cal Poly San Luis Obispo, where she was a broadcast journalism major. By her junior year, Denise was working morning drive at KZOZ. After graduation she started her 13-year Southland radio journey at KNAC. From her newly adopted home in San Diego, she enthused: "I love rock 'n' roll music! Growing up I always asked for gifts of albums to improve my record collection. Part of my success as a performer is that I'm selling something I truly enjoy. Radio is a great medium because it's live, a spontaneous experience." While at KNX/FM, Denise and the station lobbied for a Star on the Hollywood Boulevard Walk of Fame for John Lennon, and when it happened, she hosted the event on the air. She presented the Star to Yoko Ono and remembered, "I felt Yoko's presence. It was pretty amazing." She got to meet the voices she listened to on "Boss Radio" and became a voice for a new generation. "It's really strange when someone comes up to me and says they listened to me in high school." Denise feels she got "lucky" with her radio assignments. "I'm a 20-year veteran Southern California Rock jock, and I've loved it." Denise has been doing mornings since the beginning of 1994 at KGB/FM-San Diego.

WEXLER, Paul: **KOST**; **KWST**. Paul was the voice of God in the movie *Ten Commandments*. He died of leukemia in the mid-1980s.

WHATLEY, Susanne: **KHJ**, 1981-85; **KFI**, 1986-97. A native Californian, Susanne has the unique distinction of spending her entire radio career in the Southland. She grew up in Pasadena with a mother who distinguished herself writing CBS radio dramas at "Gower Gulch" and her older sister, who became one of the early hosts of *Entertainment Tonight*. Susanne was editor of her high school newspaper and went to USC where she graduated with a B.A. in print journalism. Beginning in 1978, in her sophomore year, she interned with KIQQ, KNX/FM and KCOP/Channel 13 before graduating from college in 1981. Susanne spent four years with KHJ and was dismissed along with the entire news department on the day of the Challenger explosion. "I'll never forget. We were in a room listening to a dispassionate voice from New York on a squawk box. He had the audacity to suggest that the closure of the news department was not so bad when you 'think of the plight of the astronauts.'" In early 1986 Susanne started her career as entertainment reporter for AP News and her entertainment reports have been airing for years. She recently logged a decade with KFI news. "I like the immediate gratification of being on the air. I am the author of my own newscasts. We are also the springboard for topics on KFI." She hosts two shows on sister station KOST and her celebrity interviews are now heard around the world.

KDAY changes formats from progessive rock to r&b   -December 26, 1976

WHEATLEY, Bill: **KRLA**, 1959, pd; **KFWB**, 1965-66, pd. In the late 1960s he worked at WWOK-Miami.

WHEELER, Mark: **KMDY**, 1986-89; **KNJO**, 1989-96; **KSCA**, 1996-97. Mark is the program director for Shadow Broadcast Services. He joined Shadow in 1993 and was promoted a year later. Mark was born in Encino on July 13, 1965, and got his radio start at KSTR-Ventura. He anchors the news and traffic reports on various Los Angeles and Ventura radio stations. Mark is well liked among his peers and will be the first to announce that he is a staunch Republican. He did fill-in news at KSCA.

WHIPPING BOY: **KPWR**, 1994. John Wilbur worked in Arizona radio before arriving in the Southland. The part-timer left in the summer of 1994 for sister station KOME-San Jose. In the spring of 1996 he joined WXRK-New York and later in the year he was doing afternoon drive at KBPI-Denver.

WHITCOMB, Ian: **KIEV**, 1977-80; **KROQ**, 1980-84; **KCRW**, 1986-91; **KPCC**, 1991-96. Ian burst on the music scene in 1965 with the top ten hit *You Turn Me On*. He has produced numerous albums, recorded hundreds of songs and written ten books (his favorite is *After the Ball*, which is a history of popular music from rag to rock). Ian has written music for a Las Vegas revue and his songs have been used in many movies. He was the original tv host for the long-running BBC series *The Old Grey Whistle Test*. His list of accomplishments include writing and appearing in several documentaries. Ian was born in Surrey, England, in 1941. While an undergraduate at Trinity College in Dublin, *You Turn Me On* reached Number 8 on the music charts in July 1965. His life has been dedicated to early American and British popular music, especially Tin Pan Alley, Ragtime and British Music Hall. Ian left KPCC in late 1996. He lives in Altadena with his wife Regina and "a delightful mongrel I inherited from the late crooner Rudy Vallee."

LIFE COULD BE A DREAM

A rolling full circle came to an end in 1995 with the death of Jimmy Keyes. His life was more than just a dream.

Before there was Bill Haley, Elvis and a host of early rockers, there was the Chords led by Keyes. Sh-Boom was the launching rocket to the stratospheric sound of rock 'n' roll, the original crossover dream. The group had the first r&b song to crack the pop music Top 10. A doo-wop soul was born that day.

Sh-Boom was written in the back of a Buick convertible. It was a song about what could possibly be. The success of Sh-Boom opened doors but some got their fingers caught in the jam as record companies took the songs and repackaged them with matinee-idol white singers. From that beginning in 1954, the sound of rock was forever colored.

Jimmy Keyes sang till the end.

"Sweetheart hello, hello again."

His only disappointment was the lack of recognition from the Rock and Roll Hall of Fame.

At his funeral in the summer of 1995, they were all there for the last chorus - Cadillacs, Harptones, Tokens, Wrens, Chantels and Vocaleers. And they all sang. Their hair was grayed but, still wearing the Ban-Lon shirts, they crooned for Keyes and all to hear.

"Life could be a dream. If I could take you up to paradise up above."

WHITE, Brian: **KDAY**, 1976; **KIIS**, 1977. "When I was 7 years old I saw Scotty Day broadcasting from a picture window studio at KCBQ at 7th and Ash in downtown San Diego and I knew from that moment I wanted to be in radio." Born in New Rochelle, New York, Brian moved with his family to San Diego in 1956 when he was five. He started his radio career in 1970 at KREL-Corona, then moved to KAMP-El Centro and KSEA-San Diego. Prior to working the all-night shift at KDAY, Brian toiled at WDRQ-Detroit, WXLO-New York and KCBQ. When he left Los Angeles Brian programmed WEFM-Chicago, KGGI and WDRQ. During the 1980s he worked on-air or programmed at KKBQ-Houston, KITY-San Antonio, KSFM-Sacramento, WMXB-Richmond, KFRC-San Francisco and WMAS-Springfield, Massachusetts. Since the spring of 1996 Brian has been pd at KBGO-Las Vegas.

WHITE, Dave: **KCBS**, 1993-96. Dave was part of the new "Arrow 93" format in the fall of 1993, from WMMQ-Lansing.  "The 'Arrow' job started with a phone call from WLS-Chicago legend Tommy Edwards. He stressed the confidentiality of the conversation about an L.A. format change. After I hung up with Tommy I called all my friends to see if they were playing a joke on me." Dave flew out to Southern California. "Here I am 24 years old. They had a car waiting for me and they put me up in this French hotel in Beverly Hills. I kept asking myself, 'what's the catch?'" No catch. He got the job. Dave started his radio career in 1988 at WSMA-Marine City, Michigan. "You couldn't hear the station 10 feet past the fricken parking lot!" He went on to WKMF and WCRZ-Flint. In 1990 Dave received his bachelor's degree in communications from Michigan State and worked at WMMQ until his move to L.A. In 1996 he returned to the Detroit area and is now part-time at CIDR and CIMX-Windsor/Detroit. "I guess I'd like to return to Southern California radio. I'd like to see my name on the Hollywood Walk of Fame. Radio success is more important to me than anything else...imagine that!"

WHITE, Wood: **KDAY**, 1987

WHITESIDES, Barbara: **KFI**, 1980-93; **KFWB**, 1996. Barbara was a news anchor and talk show host at KFI. She left for morning drive at KMOX-St. Louis. By summer she was working at KSDO-San Diego. A year later she joined KOGO-San Diego doing an evening talk show.

WHITMAN, Don: **KXLA**, 1957. Don was from Oklahoma City and returned after his brief stint at KXLA.

WHITNEY, April: **KROQ**, 1980-92; **KEZY**, 1993-97. Early in her career, she was the house dj at Big Ben's record store in Van Nuys. In the March 1986 *Playboy*, April appeared in a 10-page feature spread on "Lady D.J.s." She was pictured in a seductive pose, reclining on a bed in pink lingerie with a Brian Ferry compact disc at her side - and it's clear that she left her underwear at home. She was afraid that a lot of kooks might come out of the woodwork after the *Playboy* appearance. "So far the only really weird call came from a guy in Dallas who wanted to send me a plane ticket to do some more photos." In a 1990 *LA Times* story by Patrick Goldstein, April talked about her life recovering from drug and alcohol abuse. "There was a time at KROQ when it was the inmates running the asylum." As part of her rehabilitation, she participated in a two-hour program called "Clean and Crazy" with KROQ jock Jed the Fish and her husband, Chuck Randall. April works middays at KEZY. She was born in 1961.

WHITTAKER, Debii: **KGFJ**, 1993-94. Debii worked middays at KGFJ. She left the Southland for overnights at KSOL-San Francisco.

WHITTAKER, Gary: **KBBQ**. Gary worked at KBBQ as Chuck Wagon. He is now at KHMO-Hannibal, Missouri.

WHITTINGHILL, Dick: **KIEV**; **KGFJ**; **KMPC**, 1950-79. For three decades, every morning Southern Californians were "Whittinghilled." In the 1940s, Dick was a singer with The Pied Pipers, a vocal ensemble from the Big Band years. He was born March 5, 1913, and began his radio career at KPFA-Helena, Montana, making a stop in Denver before arriving in the Southland to work at KIEV and mornings at KGFJ. He then had an incredible quarter of a century with Gene Autry's KMPC, beginning in 1950. His old morning rival Bob Crane said it best: "Whittinghill has likability." He was described as steady, honest and faithful to his audience. Crane continued, "Whit's a flag-waver. He likes golf and booze. He says so on the air and he's completely honest and likable." On his 25th anniversary, Dick commented: "What I'm doing is basically the same format that I've used since 1954.  We'll go with an instrumental, a boy vocal, then a girl vocal, up tempo...you just can't play the same type of music constantly." What he did do constantly was an hourly "Story Record," in which Dick told a joke that was punctuated by the lyrics from a song. Part of his morning ritual was his breakfast break during a half-hour newscast, when he would leave the station and walk two blocks down Sunset Boulevard to Norm's, where a plate was already prepared with a hamburger patty and tomato slices. His morning team included traffic reporter Paul "Panther" Pierce, Herb Green, Dave DeSoto, John McElhinney and news director Tom Wayman. In 1957, Dick was co-chairman of the high-profile Southern California Heart Fund drive. In 1966 *Billboard* published the Radio Response Ratings and Dick was voted #2 in the top dj in Pop LP category. Dick never made any bones about why he loved radio. In an *LA Times* profile, he said he enjoyed the money and did the morning show because "it's more money and I can get away early for golf every day." In the 1950s and 1960s, KMPC was "The Station of the Stars" - the personification of MOR radio - and Dick Whittinghill was the #1 star in the galaxy. He hung out daily at the Lakeside Golf Club in Toluca Lake. "The disc jockey," he once said, "is the lowest rung on the show business ladder. There's no talent required for this whatsoever. Believe me. I should know, I've been doing it long enough." In a 1972 front-page story in the *Times* written by David Shaw, he described Dick as "King of the ratings war for more than 20 years, with his easy, folksy humor, side-splitting double entendres and snide denunciations of hippies, pornographers, antiwar protesters and homosexuals." In a 1978 interview, Dick said, "I don't believe in ratings and surveys. The way you know you're doing well is to look at your log; if you have a bunch of commercials in there, you know you'll be back the next day." He valued the friendships with his sponsors and advertisers: "I play golf with some of the fellows. Cadillac has been with me about the longest." Dick made a commitment to never tease the sponsors. His show had something for everyone. He had a number of trademark features that his audience could always count on: soap opera lampoons of "Helen Trump," "On This Day in History," and he ended the show with a minute or so of an instrumental. When he retired from the morning show on KMPC in 1979, he said, "You keep saying to yourself that it has to happen sometime but when you finally make up your mind, it becomes kind of scary. I'm perfectly reconciled to the fact that I've been here long enough and have nothing more to prove." In 1976, he wrote his best-selling autobiography (with Don Page) *Did You Whittinghill This Morning*? He was immortalized in the Hollywood Wax Museum. In 1982, Dick went to KPRZ and got to sleep in by working afternoon drive. The "Music of Your Life" format was eventually abandoned and the station was renamed KIIS/AM. "The real tragedy was not my leaving the air but rather the city's loss of one more good music station." Dick was featured in hundreds of tv shows and movies. Whittinghill summed up his journey: "I just stumble through life."

Spanish KROQ/AM ordered to shut down by the FCC
        -November 3, 1982
KZLA (1540AM) becomes Spanish KSKQ
                    -1984

WHITTINGTON, Dick: **KNOB**, 1960-62; **KLAC**, 1960-63; **KGIL**, 1965-79 and 1985; **KABC**, 1966-68; **KFI**, 1975-77; **KIEV**, 1982 and 1988; **KHJ**, 1983; **KABC**, 1989-90; **KMPC**, 1990-91; **KNJO**, 1994-95. Born Karl Whittington in Philadelphia, he was raised in Odessa, Delaware. "Sweet Dick" carved a niche in morning radio with zany stunts for decades in Southern California. He personifies the theme that radio is "the theater of the mind." What would be an example of his zaniness? "When I married the Queen Mary and a tug boat. We did it for $22, and all three networks carried the promotion." He started in radio in his early 20s after

an abortive career as a featherweight boxer. His mother ran a radio station, and one of her disc jockeys was Joe Pyne. After six months, his mother fired him and Pyne for cutting up too much and playing too few records. For two years in the mid-1950s, Dick could not find a job in radio, so he washed dishes by night and got drunk by day. Then he found an opening with a station in Stockton before moving on to KSFO and KNOW-San Francisco. After San Francisco Dick came to Los Angeles to host a game show called *The Wedding Game* which lasted only four weeks. He worked for "Sleepy" Stein at the "Jazz Knob" and on the all-night shift at KLAC. After he was fired, he worked 18 months as a nightclub comic before landing a radio job in Phoenix, which he lost a month later after encouraging a traffic reporter who had been drinking a bit to report that a giant teapot was hovering low in the desert sky. Back in Los Angeles, "Sweet Dick" sold oil leases, then got hired by KGIL. After five months, he was fired and went back to night work until a management change resulted in his rehiring. He engaged in a succession of stunts which have since become legend. He occasionally opened his show by interviewing God. "Good morning, sinner Dick," God would say with an echo. Dick responded with, "Good lord...it's, it's the Lord." Then the two of them would discuss such topical, earthly problems as election-year politics (God's advice: "Vote Yes on Commandment 3"). During one of his other chats with God, the Lord says, "I saw the play 'Jesus Christ, Superstar,' but I liked the book better." He was the winner of the 1968 Personality of the Year honors from the *LA Times*. Radio editor Don Page wrote: "Even his competition agrees that Dick is the freshest, funniest and most original personality on local radio. He could play better music on his show, but this is a small price to pay." During the controversy surrounding *Last Tango in Paris*, "Sweet Dick" shot a homemade movie called "First Fox-trot in Fargo" about an old rooster and young hen with a premiere in Saugus. He was named *Times*' Radio Personality of the Year again in 1969. Page noted: "Until someone comes along who displays as much humor, creative drive, topical interest and imagination...he will continue to rule the personality scene." During the disco era, "Sweet Dick" went to a senior citizens home for a show. Dick set new standards for unpredictability. He led an invasion of Santa Catalina Island, with soldiers dressed "in the war of their choice." Dressed in full military regalia himself, he led an armada of small craft from Long Beach, Newport and Marina del Rey in the invasion, with an old B-29 circling overhead. He once conducted a paint-off in the KGIL parking lot, subsequently flying to Paris with the winner and hanging the winning painting in the men's room at the Louvre. During the early 1970s, "Sweet Dick" loved to tease "Tricky Dick" Nixon. After President Nixon met the Japanese prime minister, Dick did an imitation of Nixon offering him a job as White House gardener. In 1973 the industry recognized "Sweet Dick" by voting him the Best MOR Jock at the 6th Annual *Billboard* Radio Programming Forum. One of his proudest accomplishments was being awarded *Time-Life's* Radio Personality of the Decade during the 1970s. In 1981, Dick purchased an interest in radio station KAVR-Apple Valley, serving as general manager and morning man. This arrangement caused several radio insiders to speculate that this would give "Sweet Dick" the first opportunity to fire himself. And he did. "It just didn't work out." His biggest bit, "The Accident," was a real-life eye opener on St. Patrick's Day in 1982. He told the *Times*: "I was feeling old, defeated and very sorry for myself. I'd heard that I'd been blackballed in L.A. radio, my Apple Valley station was in trouble, a relationship was coming undone and CBS turned down a comedy pilot." He smashed his car against the retaining wall of the Tujunga Wash and suffered a broken nose that required surgery. Dick faced some of his demons and a year later went to work for an hour each morning on KIEV. In 1989 he was asked to sit in for Ken and Bob, and lasted only three days. He did a bit called "Ask the General Manager," impersonating KABC gm George Green, and said bizarre things about personalities, which the audience and George did not get. It would be difficult to list all the special bits orchestrated by Dick over the decades, however, one of the favorites followed the news that the government had dumped nerve gas into the ocean off the coast of Florida. Whittington flew a "mercy mission to Miami," determined to provide the Atlantic "relief from the discomforts of nervous gas." From a helicopter hovering over the "exact spot" where the gas was dumped, Whittington dropped three rubber ducks and two Alka-Seltzers into the ocean. "Sweet Dick" talked from his Thousand Oaks home and said he admires the on-air work of Howard Stern. He believes Stern has "pushed the envelope into the next dimension." Dick is currently writing a book "loosely based on my life, consisting of a trilogy of three cities in the Midwest."

WHO, Susie: SEE Suzanne Ansilio

WICKSTROM, John: **KWOW**, 1974, pd. John was responsible for the automated rock station in Pomona.

WIGGINS, E.Z.: **KACE**, 1977-97. E.Z. is the last surviving air personality from the original airstaff at KACE. "The station went on the air April 11, 1977, and with the exception of about a 10-month period I have been there from the beginning." He is most known for hosting E.Z.'s "Mood For Love" program. "I hosted this show from the late '70s and the decade of the '80s. I chose and played my own music." He was born Ezell in Cleveland and grew up in Des Moines where he studied theater arts at Des Moines Tech High. After a four-year stint in the Navy, he came to Hollywood and attended the Don Martin School of Radio and TV Communications. *Buzz* magazine listed E.Z. as one of the "Buzz 100 Coolest" and described him as "the Barry White of deejays."

WILABRAHAM, Craig: **KKBT**, 1995-97, vp/gm

WILCOX, Brent: **KCRW**, 1980s. Brent hosted the Saturday night "FRGK."

WILDE, Rita: **KEZY**, 1978-82; **KLOS**, 1983-97. Born Rita Ledbeter, she did mornings until Mark and Brian arrived. Rita is the music director of KLOS, hosts the daily "Rock Report" and is a fill-in jock.

WILDER, Chuck: **KIEV**, 1972-95; **KWOW**. Born Rod Fry.

WILDMAN, Diane: **KMET**, 1973. Diane reported news during the early days of "the Mighty Met."

WILLES, Ray: **KGIL**, 1966; **KBIG/KBRT**, 1968-77. Ray was pd at KOIL-Omaha and KDEO-San Diego before arriving in Southern California. He has a successful voiceover career and has been the voice of the *Barbara Walters Specials* over the past ten years. In the mid-1970s he teamed with Gary Gray in morning drive on KBIG.

WILLIAMS, Bill: SEE William F. Williams

WILLIAMS, Brad LaRay: **KACE**, 1981-87; **KKGO/KKJZ/KJQI/KNNS** 1989-97. Brad is a musician turned dj. In 1979 he attended the KIIS Broadcasting Workshop. He started at KACE as a weekend announcer and moved to middays and production director. Brad was talent coordinator and stage manager for the KACE Concert in the Park series. He's currently doing production and announcing duties for Mt. Wilson Broadcasters' stable of outlets including KKGO.

WILLIAMS, Charlie: **KFOX**, 1960-72, pd. Charlie moved to Nashville and built a home on a lake. He managed Bobby Bare and hosted a talk show on WSIX. Charlie passed away in 1995.

WILLIAMS, Chuck: **KHJ**. Chuck started in radio in the late 1960s in St. Joseph and in the 1970s worked CKLW-Detroit, WLS-Chicago and KHJ. During the 1980s he was heard on KRIZ and KOPA-Phoenix, WMYQ-Miami, WMAQ-Chicago and WFAA-Dallas. By the mid-1980s he was heard in Las Vegas and Kansas City. He also went by the name Greg Austin during the *Six Million Dollar Man* days.

WILLIAMS, Dave: **KRTH**, 1973, pd. Dave was born August 6, 1951, and lived in Sacramento before arriving at KRTH from KROY-Sacramento. In a lengthy message sent on Prodigy in 1995, Dave remembered: "At 21 years of age with a wife the same age, L.A. was a bit too much for me. We lived like tourists for six months and then became terribly homesick. It was the first time away from home for both of us." KRTH was automated during Dave's regime. He fondly remembers working with Bill Drake, Hal Rosenburg and Dwight Case. "When Drake left the company and Paul Drew was hired to be national pd, I was hustled off to Boston to chair a meeting of RKO FM pds to present strategy for replacing the Drake/Chenault oldies library and logos." Dave was charged with overseeing the production of the new oldies library, hired Chip Hobart to be the "voice" of the FM properties and created new jingles with Toby Arnold. He stayed at KRTH only nine months. "Homesickness, lack of friends and no feeling of belonging in that most challenging and frightening of cities began to drive a wedge between my young wife and me." He returned to Sacramento and in 1974 headed for WHBQ-Memphis. He has been programming KFBK-Sacramento since 1985. "I loved L.A., no matter how much I hated living there."

WILLIAMS, DC: **KEZY**, 1994

WILLIAMS, Dudley: **KGIL**, 1966-70

WILLIAMS, Eric: **KFWB**, 1972-97. Eric was unemployed for a year before joining KFWB, but now celebrates a quarter of a century with the all-News operation. Born in Marblehead, Massachusetts, Eric grew up in Salem. "My father worked at WBZ-Boston for 20 years and he would take me to the station to watch him work." Eric studied journalism at El Camino Junior College and San Jose State. At San Jose State he could waive an internship if he secured a full-time job. He walked into KXRX-San Jose in 1966 and was offered a job as a news reporter. A year later he joined San Jose's KNTV/TV and he worked in the news department for five years. "In 1970 I got caught in the recession and the station layed off half of the 18 person news team." At KFWB Eric has covered several national disasters and commercial airliner crashes. "During the MidEast War I wrote hours and hours of copy."

WILLIAMS, Gary: **KKGO**, 1994-97. Gary worked in Boston public radio before arriving at KKGO.

WILLIAMS, Guy: SEE Dave Moorhead

WILLIAMS, Hamilton: **KCBH**, 1966, pd. Hamilton hosted the "Concerto from Coldwater Canyon."

WILLIAMS, Jason: SEE A.J. Martin

WILLIAMS, Jeff: **KABC**, 1974-76; **KTNQ**, 1978-79, gm; **KFWB**, 1982-84; **KIIS**, 1984-87; **KTNQ/KLVE**, 1993-97. Jeff was born in Richmond, Indiana and grew up in many East coast cities. At Syracuse University, Jeff studied communications and wanted to be a play-by-play sports announcer. At the campus station he was director of sports and news director. "A dear friend told me that I would never make it on the air and encouraged me to get into sales and I did." After graduation in 1962 Jeff joined the Leo Burnett agency in Chicago. He then got into tv sales and arrived in the Southland in 1971 to be part of ABC Spot Sales. Three years later he joined the retail sales staff of KABC. After working in sales and sales management, Jeff went into consulting in 1987. A year later he joined the tv division of TAPSCAN. In 1992 he went to KFRG-San Bernardino and then vp of sales at Shadow Traffic. Jeff is now head of research at KTNQ/KLVE.

WILLIAMS, Johnny: **KRLA**, 1965; **KHJ**, 1965-74. Best known as the all-night man during KHJ's "Boss Radio" days, Johnny now lives in Hawaii. In 1962, Johnny worked afternoon drive at KISN-Portland hosting the "Fabulous Fifty Hit Parade." He was born in Fort Scott, Kansas and lived there until he was 5 years old. He came to the Southland from Denver where he was "Dapper Dan, the All-Night Man" via a stop-over as pd at KCBQ-San Diego. When Gary Mack left KRLA to join his old friend Bill Drake at the newly

formatted KHJ, Johnny was brought on to KRLA in the spring of 1965. Johnny only worked one weekend shift before becoming one of the original "Boss Jocks." He did nine to noon for a brief time in early 1967. In *Billboard* magazine's Radio Response Ratings of 1966, Johnny was voted top all-night jock. In 1975 he went to work for his old friend Ted Atkins at WTAE-Pittsburgh. In 1985 Johnny left WTAE and started a Pittsburgh advertising agency with his wife, Carol. It was during this time that Johnny developed an interest in computing and telecommunications. He started a bulletin board system in Pittsburgh. In late 1991 he and Carol closed the agency and moved to the Islands. "Hawaii is our most favorite location on earth." He worked for the two all-News stations in Hawaii until 1995. He has been surfing the Net and running the "best" radio web site.

WILLIAMS, Larry: **KUTE**, 1973-76, pd

WILLIAMS, Laurie: **KSCA**, 1995-97. Laurie worked weekends on the Adult Album Alternative station, KSCA until an ownership change in early 1997 that took the format Spanish. Born February 11, 1960, in Washington, DC, she worked in Baltimore and DC during the 1980s. Earlier in the '90s she broadcast Rock in Santa Barbara and was in radio syndication sales in Los Angeles. On KSCA's Prodigy site she said: "Love of music got me into the business. KSCA brought back my passion for radio."

WILLIAMS, Morgan: **KGFJ**; **KBCA**; **KRLA**; **KFI/KOST**; **KBIG**, 1984-97. Born Morgan in New York, she was known as Margi when she worked with Hunter Hancock. "Hunter thought his name was so unusual and not many women were named Morgan, so I became Margi." Morgan married the lead singer of the Platters, Tony Williams. Her love affair with radio began with a love for her grandfather. "When I was three or four I would sit at my grandfather's feet and listen to the radio news with him. I would say 'Papa Charlie what does the man mean'? And he would answer me like a grownup. He said if I was old enough to ask the questions, I was entitled to an answer. He never told me to hush." Morgan studied at USC and UCLA and in between radio assignments worked for seven years at KABC/Channel 7 and almost two years at KHJ/Channel 9. Morgan ended our phone conversation with, "I have truly been blessed in this life."

WILLIAMS, Rick: **KACE**, 1970-71; **KNAC**, 1977; **KSCA**, 1994.

"A Los Angeles native, I grew up listening to some of the best radio ever in L.A. in the mid to late sixties." Rick started his radio career at age 19 while in college working at KATY-San Luis Obispo. Charlie Fox gave him his break. "Charlie is still one of best jocks to ever walk the earth." Rick followed Charlie to KACE a year later. "I finished college and did afternoons at KZOZ-San Luis Obispo with Denise Westwood and Frank DeSantis." Before the '70s were over Rick worked at KNAC, back to KZOZ and then evenings at KKDJ-Fresno. During the 1980s he was pd of KTYD-Santa Barbara and signed on AAA KCQR-Santa Barbara. Rick is the A&R supervisor at DCC Compact Discs, an L.A. audiophile label. He's currently working on a CD entitled *The Golden Age of Underground Radio: Featuring B. Mitchel Reed*. "Radio remains in my blood."

WILLIAMS, Verne: **KABC**; **KFWB**; **KFI**. Verne was one of the original anchors when KFWB went all-News. Born in New York, he grew up in Texas and Massachusetts. He started out on WESX-Salem, Massachusetts and later spent two decades with WBZ-Boston. Verne's son Eric has been with KFWB for 25 years. When Verne left the Southland in 1971 he moved to Sacramento and San Francisco. While he was in the Bay Area Verne was the executive assistant to the mayor of San Francisco. Verne passed away in 1992.

WILLIAMS, Vince: **KFWB**, 1968-70. Vince (no relation to KFWB newsman Eric and Verne) was with the all-News operation as an outside reporter. He was also an actor who appeared in a number of tv series before and after his stint with KFWB.

WILLIAMS, Warren: **KNX/FM**, 1987-88; **KLSX**, 1991-96, pd. Warren arrived for his first visit in the Southland

from KSRR/KKHT-Houston for morning drive at KNX/FM. He left in 1988 to program WOFX-Cincinnati and returned in 1991 to be assistant pd at KLSX, later becoming pd in 1994. Born June 13, 1955, in Nyack, New York, Warren graduated from Penn State University with a B.A. in speech communication. While doing post-graduate work he produced Coach Joe Paterno's pre-game show that aired on the 80-station Penn State Football Network. In 1981 he programmed KATT-Oklahoma City and three years later became pd of KDKB-Phoenix. Warren has an active production company that is responsible for the writing and producing of all radio advertising for Fox Sports. He created the national radio launch campaign for the conversion of Prime Sports to Fox Sports Net.

WILLIAMS, William F.: **KDAY**, 1960; **KBLA**, 1965-67; **KBBQ**, 1966-67; **KRLA**, 1968-69; **KPPC**, 1971-72. William worked in San Bernardino at KMEN and San Jose's KLIV before arriving at KDAY where he spent his days at Martoni's with Alan Freed waiting for the format change. After KDAY, he returned to KMEN for three years. While at KBLA, he worked a live-concert booth at the first Teenage Fair at the Hollywood Palladium and was voted by the Fair's attendees "L.A.'s Coolest Jock." He left KBLA to be pd of KCBQ-San Diego. While at Country KBBQ, he was Bill Williams. His time at

KBBQ led to the formation of Canopy Music and Canopy Productions with Jimmy Webb. They co-produced *MacArthur Park* by Richard Harris for Dunhill/ABC Paramount Records. William described this period as "weird," and he lived on a mountain top until KRLA pd Doug Cox in 1968 coaxed him to morning drive. There, his "weirdness" prompted a memo from the gm which William read on the air. Another gm memo told him to refrain from airing internal memos. William read this memo on the air. The next memo was "you're fired," which he read on the air, before leaving the station. He played a Presidential advisor in the Peter Sellers movie *Being There*. After a return stint to the mountains, William's old friend Doug Cox was now gm at KPPC. "As jock/pd in 1971, I instituted the first and only truly 'free-form' radio station in Los Angeles. The country was in the throes of an unpopular war, and we reflected the restlessness of the times." By 1972, William got on his Harley and headed for Mexico. In 1976, he rejoined Jimmy Webb for another run at the music business, where he wrote tv specials for *Rolling Stone*, Ringo Starr, Olivia Newton-John and acted as music supervisor on a couple of feature films and a tv series. Since 1984 William has been living and writing in the mountains.

WILLIS, Scott: **KLON**, 1994-97, pd
WILLS, Maury: **KABC**. The former Dodger star was one of the hosts of afternoon drive's "SportsTalk" on KABC.
WILSON, Andy: **KRHM**, 1966; **KPPC**, 1966-68
WILSON, Bob: **KDAY**, 1969-72, pd. Born in 1946 in Providence, Rhode Island, Bob moved to California with his family in 1955. "I was a major radio and music junkie by age 5." Bob used to park cars in the Hollywood lot behind KFWB where he was befriended by Gary Owens. "Gary helped me get into radio and he also wrote a weekly column for me in the early years of *R&R*." He arrived in the Southland from a successful run as pd of KAFY-Bakersfield. On his arrival at KDAY, he told a trade publication that he was "putting show business back into radio." He put Wolfman Jack on L.A. radio. "I told him that it was time to make it in legitimate radio.

We extended him to television, with Wolf hosting *Midnight Special* and playing a key role in *American Graffiti*." KDAY played a major part in the promotion for both projects. "Wolf and I were partners in a company called Audio Stimulation - the logo was a radio with a lighted dynamite stick stuck in the side." Together they syndicated two versions of the "Wolfman Jack Show" (Hits & Gold), two weekly concerts from the KDAY series that ran Wednesday and Friday nights from the Troubadour and the Whiskey night clubs. KDAY was the first station to bring back "live concerts" since the early '50s, which have now become a staple of programming. They also produced a six-hour Beach Boys special, Jefferson Starship and Hank Williams specials. "The only other player of our size was a new company called Watermark and a show called 'American Top 40.'" Bob revolutionized the publishing business in the summer of 1973 with the launch of *Radio & Records* and virtually overnight the publication became the bible for radio and record people. During this period Bob was the co-creator of the long-running television show *Solid Gold*. He moved *R&R* into music entertainment productions for outdoor venues. They produced giant, multi-screen traveling shows like "The Great Rock & Roll Time Machine" that played at theme parks and state fairs. "*R&R* Conventions blew the industry away. We had major keynote speakers and events. They got so big we had to go every other year in order to plan them to be fresh and get the dynamic keynoters and music stars. We had the Eagles reunion two years before they toured." Bob sold *R&R* and is now running his own company. "I've been partnered for the last year with Jeff Pollack and Mel Karmazin developing a grand concept for what radio really could be like on the world wide web, now and in the future. I've also joined with former radio buddy, Sam Riddle, to manage major Latin-crossover acts."

WILSON, George: **KIQQ**. Born George Wilson Crowell, he made his marketing presence felt with the Bartell chain. (George used Wilson professionally and this entry should not be confused with George Crowell who worked at KPOL.) George was pd of WOKY-Milwaukee. In the early 1970s he was gm of WDRQ-Detroit. In a multi-part interview in *Billboard* in 1975, George, as the executive vp of Bartell Media's radio division commented: "Chuck Blore was always kind of like my hero. He used to have phenomenally great ideas and I would just find out what he was going to do next week, then I'd do it." During his time helming KIQQ in 1988, a federal grand jury investigating payola indicted George. In an April 31, 1990, front page story in *R&R* in the Joseph Isgro federal government investigation, George was the first of the payola witnesses to testify. From *R&R*: "[Crowell] agreed to testify against [Isgro] only after the prosecution lured them with the promise of reduced charges and no jail time. Crowell told the court he and Isgro came to an agreement 'sometime in 1980,' whereby Crowell would receive $750 for each Isgro record KIQQ added. According to Crowell, once the station's music committee decided the weekly adds each Tuesday, 'I would call Joe and tell him which of his records got on the air.' Later, 'One of [Isgro's] employees would meet me at Martoni's or the Jolly Roger restaurant and pay me...I'd meet them in the men's room, collect the money in a record envelope, and go back to the bar.' Crowell said he kept no record of the transactions. He said the station added between 'none and ten' of Isgro's records each week and figured he 'averaged a couple thousand a week' from the payments. He said most of the proceeds 'went to the racetrack.' The defense attorney used the cross-examination to portray Crowell as a gambling-obsessed, debt-ridden alcoholic. Crowell admitted he'd been a heavy drinker while at KIQQ. He said he'd been indebted to bookies for several thousand dollars and admitted to having judgments filed against him. Crowell had been facing charges of failure to file income taxes." George has since moved to Albuquerque.

WILSON, Marina: **KOCM**, 1988; **KIKF**, 1990-92; **KEZY**, 1992-96; **KLIT**, 1992-94; **KSCA**, 1994; **KOST**, 1995-96; **KACD**, 1996; **KZLA**, 1996-97. Marina was an art/history major in college. She worked in the Redlands/San Bernardino market at KCAL, KFRG and KQLH. Her voice work includes AEI In-flight programs and the Warner Bros. tv series *Hawk* and *Life Goes On*. Some of her commercial work includes Nissan, Mighty Ducks NHL and Woolite. At KACD she worked as Michelle Knight. She is the afternoon traffic reporter for KEZY and works weekends at KZLA.

WILSON, Mississippi Brian: SEE Joe Rogers

WILSON, Nancy: **KTWV**, 1987-95. "I joined 'the Wave' two weeks after it was launched. There were no announcers in the beginning but when John Sebastain arrived, he put me on the air." Nancy was born in Merced but grew up in Granada Hills. At 17 she was doing tv work and was an early female hire in the engineering department at KCOP/Channel 13. "As an editor we were still cutting tape with a razor blade." Nancy decided to pursue radio and started all over again. She was a dj in 29 Palms and the Antelope Valley all the while "begging" KFWB for a job. After working at KFWB, Nancy became an engineer at KABC but wanted to be on the air. While attending music school, she heard the promos announcing the change at KMET to KTWV, applied and got the job. "I had always wanted acreage and after the 1994 earthquake I started making plans to leave. I bought 10 acres in Idaho and moved in 1995." She has been working radio and doing on-camera commercial work in the Spokane area. Nancy's planning to return to the Southland. "The winters are brutal. We were buried in snow this year and now plan to use my Coeur d'Alene residence as a second home."

WILSON, Scotty: **KNAC**, 1984-88; **KIIS**, 1993-94. Born in England in 1959, Scotty became interested in radio while attending high school in London. He started a half-watt pirate radio station and broadcast to those living on campus. At 16 he put together a band to tour foreign military bases. When he got out of school, he joined the Navy. After the service, Scotty wanted to pursue a radio career. His first gig was at KPIG-Honolulu, where he got the job because he matched the height requirements for fitting into the pig mascot uniform. Scotty moved to mornings on KIKI-Honolulu for four years and wondered if he could make it in LA. He landed on the Mainland and started in the desert at KDES-Palm Springs. He bombarded KNAC with tapes and eventually landed the evening slot under the name Scorchin' Scott. He replaced Wild Bill Scott. Scotty was active in the community doing commendable volunteer work for the city of Lawndale and helping new bands. When he finished his "Pure Rock" tour on KNAC, he produced a Hard Rock tv show and eventually went to Fresno and Las Vegas. Late in 1993 he briefly did the all-night shift on KIIS as Jimmy Chonga. Scotty went on to KGBS/KEGL-Dallas and the Hard Radio, the first hard rock radio on the Internet.

WILSON, Warren: **KFWB**, 1968-70. Warren has been a longtime reporter for KTLA/Channel 5.

WIMAN, Al: **KFWB**, 1959-66; **KLAC**, 1966-69. Al had three incredible journeys reporting news in Southern California. He was at KFWB during the Chuck Blore/Jim Hawthorne rock years, the Joe Pyne talk era at KLAC and the early stages of the successful KABC/Channel 7 *Eyewitness News*. "I was at the Charles Manson murder site with my cameraman and sound engineer. We found the bloody clothes on a hillside six minutes and 20 seconds away from Sharon Tate's house. We got in the news van and traveled down Benedict Canyon. I was undressing in the station wagon and when I put on new clothes we

stopped the station wagon. We hiked down the hillside and found the bloody clothes. The detectives were flabbergasted. We filmed it but didn't touch the pile of clothes." Al joined KFWB doing traffic reports while he was in the Navy. Civilians were running Armed Forces Radio and were jealous of Al's involvement with KFWB so they shipped him out on the U.S.S. Topeka, a guided missile cruiser. "I took music on the ship along with a jingle package. We must have been the only ship with a set of jingles." Al grew up in Laurel, Mississippi, and has been working as the medicine and science editor for KMOV/TV-St. Louis for the past 20 years. When a photo of Al was requested from KMOV/TV, the marketing manager Mary Westermeyer wrote the following unsolicited words about Al: "Al is extremely humble and will never pat himself on the back. He's an outstanding reporter, St. Louisan, husband and father, but foremost he's an incredible human being. Al personally gives back to the community more than any other talent with the station. He has an impeccable reputation within the St. Louis medical community. Al has a terrific wit, caring attitude and he's adored in the community."

WINDSOR, Natalie: **KMGX**, 1990. Natalie worked afternoons at the Soft MOR station.

WINESETT, Barry: **KRLA**, 1984-92. The KRLA production man did sporadic fill-in as Barry Rhodes in the late 1980s. Born in Santa Monica, Barry went to Springfield College in Massachusetts on a swimming scholarship. After graduation he was the volleyball coach at Springfield. "My involvement with radio happened by accident. I started at KRLA as an intern and then became production assistant in 1986." During his stay at KRLA he moonlighted at KXPT-Oxnard and traffic at the L.A. Network. "I'm the engineer for three syndicated shows and I keep sending tapes out looking for another radio show."

WINGERT, Wally: **KTWV**, 1987-97. Born in Des Moines, Wally grew up in the Aberdeen/Sioux Falls area of South Dakota. How did he become interested in radio? "When I was 11 or 12 my best friend got a tape machine and microphone and we used to play dj." He spent 10 years on-air and programming stations in Aberdeen and Sioux Falls. He also had a keen interest in theater and acting. How did he get to L.A. from Aberdeen? "I used to send parodies to Dr. Demento, and when I made the decision to try Hollywood, he opened all sorts of doors for me. He was really terrific." Wally started at "the Wave" as a board op during the "no djs" period before John Sebastian brought in "voices," and he stayed during the transition. Wally did overnights and even mornings briefly in 1991. "I was laid off in July 1993, and became a performer full-time as 'BeetleJuice' at Universal Studios." He has done guest spots on *Murphy Brown*, *Vicki*, *Saved By the Bell* and *Fresh Prince of Bel Air*. Wally has done character voices on many CD-ROMs. "My true love continues to be my project for kids called 'Uncle Wally's Wacky World' - a rock and roll extravaganza." He returned to "the Wave" in late 1994 and is also a regular performer on the syndicated comedy services from Cutler Comedy Network.

WINNAMAN, John: **KLOS**, 1974-79, gm. John died on the baseball field during a KLOS promotional game.

WINRICH, Darrell: **KABC**, 1979. Darrell was a financial reporter on the morning drive "Ken and Bob Company" show.

WINSLOW, Harlan: **KMET**, 1975-76; **KMPC/FM/KEDG**, 1988-89. Harlan grew up in Southern California and got his radio start at KMET as the surf and weather reporter. In 1980 he joined KZOZ-San Luis Obispo where he served as nd, md, dj and pd. Prior to joining KMPC/FM he was at KTYD-Santa Barbara and KKDJ-Fresno. In 1990 he joined KKDJ-Fresno and since 1993 has been the evening personality at KSEG-Sacramento.

WINSLOW, Michael: **KODJ**, 1989. The sound effects actor in the *Police Academy* series teamed with Dean Goss in March of 1989. The morning drive experiment lasted less than two months, despite the station's five-week buildup that the pairing was designed for only a one-week trial.

WINSTON, Cliff: **KJLH**, 1986-90, pd; **KKBT**, 1990-93; **KJLH**, 1993-97, pd. Cliff grew up in Southern California and originally intended to be a sportscaster. He attended the University of Washington and started his radio career at KYAC-Seattle doing both drive times. He moved to KMJM-St. Louis, followed by a stint at WBMX-Chicago and was pd at WDRQ-Detroit. KRLY-Houston was his last stop before joining KJLH. He was "the Beat's" first morning man and public affairs director and in late 1993 rejoined KJLH in morning drive. In the summer of 1995 Cliff was appointed pd of KJLH. He has been recognized as air personality of the year by the Urban Network.

WINSTON, Kari Johnson: **KBIG**, 1978-82 and 1985-95, vp/gm. Kari began her radio career at Bonneville's Seattle stations in 1972. In 1978 she moved to KBIG as assistant station/business manager. She became KOIT-San Francisco gm in 1982, then moved back to KBIG in 1985 as gm. In the fall of 1995, she moved to KNWX/KIRO-Seattle as vp/gm.

WISDOM, Gabriel: **XHIS/XHRS**, 1972. Born in Manchester, New Hampshire in 1949, she worked at KPRI-San Diego. After the Tijuana stint, she returned to San Diego radio and KGB.

WISK, Al: **KMPC**, 1978-79. The former California Angel and L.A. Ram broadcaster went on to be an attorney practicing in Dallas. From Dallas he continued to be the voice for State Farm Insurance commercials, a longtime sponsor of UCLA broadcasts. Al's last broadcast was the Rams-Pittsburgh Super Bowl.

WITCHER, Geoff: **KGIL**, 1969-70; **KABC**, 1975-83; **KMPC**, 1992-94; **KABC**, 1995-97. Born in 1949 Geoff dreamed of becoming a sportscaster since he was 10. "I remember sitting at Dodger Stadium with my best friend and pointing to the broadcast booth declaring that I would be there one day." Geoff started at KGIL as a newswriter and then, from 1969 to 1973, he worked the Dodgers radio/tv wire. In 1975 he joined KABC and hosted "DodgerTalk," "Dodger Confidential," "LakerTalk," "Laker Confidential," "TrojanTalk," "NFL Sunday Preview" and "SportsTalk." ON-TV was his next assignment and for seven years beginning in 1977 he did

play-by-play for the Dodgers, Angels, USC basketball and the L.A. Lakers. In 1992 he joined KMPC and co-hosted "Baseball '92" and filled in for California Angels play-by-play when Bob Starr did Rams games. Geoff also did play-by-play for USC and UCLA games on Prime Ticket (later Prime Sports and now Fox Sports West) from 1985 to 1990. Geoff also called boxing for the USA Network, pro basketball for ESPN and USC football for the Lorimar Sports Network. Geoff grew up in the Southland and was Cal State Northridge's sports director for the school's radio station, KCSN.

WITHERSPOON, Jimmy: **KMET**. The blues recording artist hosted a Blues show on Sunday nights.

WOLF, Janine: **KHJ**, 1980-84; **KHTZ**, 1985; **KNX/FM**, 1988-89; **KODJ**, 1989-90; **KBIG**, 1993-97. Janine began her radio career in 1977 at KYTE-Portland. "I went on to work as the first female announcer ever on #1 KGW and KWJJ-Portland." In 1980 she joined KHJ and from 1984 to 1988 worked at Transtar Radio Networks. In 1985 she was holding down a weekend shift at "K-Hits" in addition to her satellite service duties. From 1983 to 1987 she co-hosted syndicated "Country Music's Top Ten" with Charlie Cook. "In the winter of 1990 I went to do mornings at Unistar Radio Networks (now WW1) and continued to work afternoons on their Soft AC format." In the early 1990s, she hosted a weekly show on KCAL/Channel 9 called *Our Planet* and was nominated for two Emmys for host and producer.

Beginning in 1993 Janine was the live announcer for KCAL's *Live in L.A.* morning show.

WOLFSON, George: **KXEZ**, 1995, gm

WOLT, Ken: **KTNQ/KLVE**, 1982-91, vp/gm. Ken was born November 5, 1938, in North Dakota. He majored in electronics engineering at San Diego State. Ken started his radio career with the NBC station in Washington, DC in 1971. Ken went on to run stations for Lin Broadcasting and Gulf Broadcasting. He started with KTNQ/KLVE when Cecil Heftel bought the stations in 1982. He now manages a group of Spanish stations.

WONG, Al: **KYPA**, 1996, gm

WOOD, Jim: **KBLA**, 1965; **KGFJ**, 1966-67; **KRLA**, 1967-68; **KGFJ**, 1970-72; **KROQ**, 1972; **KGFJ**, 1978-79; **XPRS**, 1982-83. Tyler, Texas-born "Big Jim Wood" spent time on black-formatted stations and was referred to as a blue-eyed soul personality on KGFJ. At KRLA he was known as "The Vanilla Gorilla." The latter off-air reference was dubbed during his KGFJ days when Jim was one of two white jocks on the r&b station. He was given the *Billboard* Leading Soul Music Air Personality award at the first annual ceremony in 1970 and for the next three years. He worked at KILT-Houston and WIBG-Philadelphia. Jim died at the age of 58 in 1990. At the time of his death he was a security guard and was suffering from emphysema. One of his friends remembered, "Jim was in the hospital and got a cough drop stuck in his throat and he choked to death."

WOOD, Jim: **KPOL/ KZLA**, 1979-80, pd. Jim was responsible for orchestrating the format change of KPOL/FM from Soft AC to KZLA Country in 1980. The diversified Nashville-based entrepreneur started his radio career in Rockford, Illinois and Chattanooga before joining KPOL in the late 1970s. When Malrite bought KZLA, Jim returned as the corporate vp of programming. He headed the Malrite team that created WHTZ ("Z-100")-New York, WEGX ("Eagle 106")-Philadelphia and KRXY-Denver. Recently Jim created the programming and marketing platform to launch Toronto's first Country FM station. "Broadcasting for less than 60 days, CISS-Toronto went from nonexistent to 7.2 share with a cume of 780,000 listeners." Jim juggles dozens of projects including consultant to 24 stations and owns several service related companies to the radio and marketing industries. "After I left Malrite I was determined to never be beholden to one company for my livelihood." In 1995, Jim created Fan Club Management Services, a company that manages the fan clubs of recording artists and other "fan" sensitive groups.

WOODS, David: **KPOL**, 1965-70

WOODS, George: **KJOI**, 1973. George was the all-night announcer during the Beautiful Music format. He is no longer in radio.

WOODS, J. Thomas: **KWIZ**, 1972. Thomas was from Durham, North Carolina.

WOODS, Steve: **KDAY**, 1974-85, pd; **KJLH**, 1985-89, pd; **KACE**, 1989-90, pd; **KBIG**, 1993-96. Steve hosted the "KOOL Jazz Festival." A 1989 *LA Times* story quoted Steve: "The identity of black radio is based on playing music by black djs." He is now working at KDKA-Dallas.

WOODS, Tom: **KPOL**, 1965-69; **KFWB**, 1969-86. Tom was the Sacramento bureau chief for all-News, KFWB. When new ownership took control of KFWB in 1984, Tom was asked to transfer to Los Angeles, which he declined. "I opened Capitol Newslink, a radio news service in Sacramento and KFWB was my client for two years." In the fall of 1986 Tom became the director of corporate communications for Sacramento-based Sutter Health system. In late 1989 he became director of publications for the School of Business and Economics at Cal State Los Angeles. Tom edits the quarterly business journal - *Business Forum*. "I'm still an all-news addict and have fond memories of my many years with KFWB. An inveterate pack rat, I still have a large box of audio tapes of many news events that I covered." Tom lives in San Bernardino.

WOODMAN, Steve: **KFWB**, 1965; **KDAY**, 1968. Steve never got into the starting line-up at "Channel 98" and always worked weekends. At KDAY he did morning drive as Woody Stevens.

WOODRUF, Fred: **KLON**, 1975-78

WOODSIDE, Larry: **KROQ**, 1980-81; **KLOS**. Larry had four tours of duty at KROQ. He remembered the early days at the "free-form underground" station when the jocks used an advertising trade-out so they could be assured of one square meal a day, because their pay was infrequent at best. Larry worked mornings during early 1980 with partner Mike Evans. He is currently a car salesman.

WOODSON, Valerie: **KRLA**, 1975-76; **KTNQ**, 1977-79. Valerie was with KRLA during the Soft Rock era until the staff was fired and the station went Rock-automated. She was working in the promotion department during "Ten-Q's" heyday.

WOOLERY, Chuck: **KLSX**, 1996. The former *Love Connection* host joined KLSX for an evening talk show in March 1996 and left shortly thereafter.

WORKMAN, Martin: **KFAC**, 1976-87. Martin hosted "Luncheon at the Music Center." He has performed as a professional violinist, a singer of light opera and oratorio and as an actor. Martin holds degrees in economics, sociology and a doctorate in abnormal psychology. In 1979 he suffered a heart attack but was back on the air after two months of rest.

WORLDS, Jamie: **KOST**, 1990; **KACE**, 1990-91; **KKBT**, 1992-93; **KTWV**, 1994-97. Jamie grew up in Pasadena with colorful thoughts of being on the Rose Queen's "court." Jamie was greatly influenced by her father, whom she described as, "real cool. He played the electric guitar and he gave me the love for music." Jamie attended Pepperdine University's school of business management and started as a financial analyst for Warner Bros. and Sony Pictures while doing some acting. Jamie's career path changed with an "intuitive" move to Hawaii in 1988 going to work for KRTR-Honolulu. She has thoughts of radio station ownership "down the line" but is willing to explore her options each day. "I still don't know what I want to be when I grow up."

WORTHINGTON, Cal: **KXLA**, 1950-59. The noted car dealer, who gained his fame in Southern California for his outrageous saturation tv spots, was a country jock in the 1950s. When the KRLA era began, Cal Worthington signed off the air. Immediately Jimmy O'Neill became the first voice on KRLA. Cal signed off his country show with: "Well, until we see you at Worthington Dodge today or get back with you on KXLA, we're gonna have to pick a wildwood flower bouquet." From 1965 to 1974 he broadcast traffic

conditions in the sky for KLAC, KFOX, KRLA and KEZY. He was born in Bly, Oklahoma, on November 27, 1920.

WORTHINGTON, Diane: **KABC**, 1989-95. Diane worked weekends at KABC and hosted "California Foods."

WORTHINGTON, Rod: Rod is Cal Worthington's son and like his dad has a real love of flying planes. He turned it into a career, using the handle "Captain Rod" and doing traffic reports from a Cessna 150 for various Southern California stations in the early 1970s. In the early 1980s, he bought his own station in Needles and set up the studios in a Ford dealership. He left radio for good in the late 1980s and again, like his dad, is in the car business in Northern California. He was born in Southern California in October 1951.

WRIGHT, Bill: **KPFK**, 1976-78; **KWIZ**, 1978-89; **KYMS**, 1990-91; **KBIG**, 1992-96. Bill was part of the successful "Bill and Sylvia Show" mornings on KBIG. Bill was born in Santa Monica and became involved with radio in high school and then in college at the University of California San Diego, where he received his B.A. degree in communications. He is a frequent guest lecturer at radio schools. Bill is married and has two sons, one daughter and two cats. He left KBIG in the fall of 1996.

WRIGHT, Charleye: **KLAC**, 1969-70; **KIIS**, 1970-75; **KPOL**, 1975-76; **KIIS**, 1981-90; **KKBT**, 1990-93; **KNX**, 1995-97. Charleye reported sports as "The Coach" alongside Rick Dees on KIIS for much of the eighties. Born in Inglewood in 1937, Charleye graduated from Lynwood High and Compton College. He graduated with an M.A. from Baylor University with plans to enter the ministry. He got into broadcasting while in college. When he was 21, Charleye (whose father's name was

Charles) changed the spelling of his name because he thought Charles was a sissy name. Charleye taught high school English for two years and worked in Waco and Dallas radio, then moved to Dick Clark's KPRO-Riverside before arriving at KLAC. He was Les Crane's newsman in afternoon drive. At KIIS, he worked under programmer Chuck Blore, who was attempting features such as mini-dramas and a series of mind-sputtering aphorisms called "Kissettes." Chuck encouraged his newsmen to converse with the audience instead of reading to them. "The time with Blore was a great benefit to me. He encouraged the personality approach. He taught me to look for the human aspect of the news." In 1982, Charleye won a third Golden Mike award. He had undergone dialysis three times per week for five years when the treatments began to fail. He was gradually deteriorating, to the point he became incoherent, could not speak plain English and couldn't remember the names of his wife and children. A successful transplant left him with one perfect kidney and two old ones that function less than ten percent of normal. His father died of the same ailment. "My father got it too young to take advantage of kidney transplants." In the summer of 1990, he left Dees for the successful "House Party" morning drive show with John London at KKBT, where he continued to perform as "The Coach." Since the summer of 1995, Charleye has been a member of the sports department at KNX. He writes poems and articles for publication and is completing the "Great American Novel."

WRIGHT, Jo Jo: **KEZY**, 1988; **KIIS**, 1997. Jo Jo arrived for the all-night shift at KIIS from four years at KYLD-San Francisco.

WRIGHT, Van Earl: **KFWB**, 1997. Van Earl is the morning drive sports anchor at all-News KFWB. From 1989 to 1993, Van Earl had a cult following at CNN. He popularized the phrase, "taking it DEEEEEEP." When Van Earl left CNN, he joined the NBC/TV affiliate in Detroit and hosted a call-in show on all-Sports WDFN. In the late 1980s he worked tv in Charleston, North Carolina, Tupelo, Mississippi and Beaumont, Texas. Tom Hoffarth of the *Daily News* described Van Earl's unique style: "Maybe it's like listening to a tape of Ted Baxter going through a Cuisinart. Or someone running a pocket watch through a knife sharpener." KFWB's pd said of Van Earl: "He is unafraid to call the 'bull' connected with many of the self appointed sacred cows of sports and everyday life. His style is a perfect fit for the 21st century." In addition to KFWB, Van works fill-in at KCBS/Channel 2.

WYATT, Jeff: **KPWR**, 1986-91, pd; **KIIS**, 1991-94, pd; **KACD**, 1996-97, gm. Jeff arrived in the Southland after being pd at WUSL-Philadelphia and assistant pd at WXKS ("KISS 108")-Boston in the late 1970s. He has a degree in political-science from Miami of Ohio. He moved to Boston to play guitar in local clubs - "a cool/jazz kind of thing." In 1986, Jeff powered KPWR and the arrival of morning man Jay Thomas. With an initial buzz in the ratings, Jeff said, "They do a great job over at KIIS, but I think Rick Dees is beginning to go south." Wyatt freely admitted that he was more of an assimilator than an innovator. "We're trying to reflect our listeners' tastes, not necessarily educate them." In 1987, Jeff was named Program Director of the Year (black format) by *Billboard*. From 1987 to 1991, he was host of Westwood One's "American Dance Trax." A year later *Billboard* placed "Power 106" in the Top 40 category and Jeff won the 1988 Program Director of the Year. He was recognized by KPWR's parent company, Emmis Broadcasting, in 1988 when he was made regional vp of programming. Wyatt feels that promotion "is an essential component of success. There's nothing scientific about rotating songs. But how you package it, how you create the sizzle around it, will make the difference." Even though KIIS was his primary competition while programming KPWR, Jeff left "Power 106" to go on-air in afternoon drive at KIIS. He became pd of KIIS in 1992 and left in the summer of 1994. In early 1996 he started Fair Air Communications. Jeff was born in South Bend, Indiana and is "a HUGE Notre Dame fan!" He lives with his wife Kathy and three children, Andrew, Spencer and Abby. In the summer of 1996 he was appointed gm of KACD during its "Groove Radio" format and left in early 1997.

WYATT, Marques: **KKBT**, 1994-95. Marques hosted the underground beat with down home music on "the Beat."

"It was an exceptional team when we started out at KFWB News. We were like pioneers." -Carol Sobel

X

X, Doctor: **KLSX**, 1997
X, Eddie: **KROQ**, 1985

Y

YARNELL, Bruce: **KCBH**. Bruce worked afternoons at KCBH and then moved to San Diego.

YATES, Tom: **KLOS**, 1971-77, pd; **KLSX**, 1986-89, pd. Tom is credited with taking KABC/FM and turning it into KLOS and a powerhouse AOR competitor, with the "Rock 'N Stereo" marketing campaign. In 1974 Tom shared some of his programming philosophy with James Brown of the *LA Times*: "The hard-core music freaks were listening, but we weren't taking anyone away from Top 40. Also, those people on the borderline who appreciated album cuts were put off by the "underground" presentation. We also discovered that the Bill Drake-programmed KHJ/FM had a greater audience than KMET, KPPC and KLOS combined. So we sat down and decided to do something about the format." KLOS retained the album cuts, but the music dwelled on the mainstream of Rock, rather than the fringe element, and the on-air personalities retained the low-key, whispered knowledge of traditional FM rock but were allowed to expand their individual approaches. Tom was quoted in a 1975 issue of *Time Magazine* in a story titled "Sex Rock." He left KLOS in the summer of 1977 to form Nova Broadcasting Services. In 1985, Tom was the consultant for KKCY-San Francisco when it changed format and call letters and became "the Quake." Before he returned to the Southland, he worked in St. Louis. Tom bought a station in Santa Rosa, where he currently lives.

YEAGER, Bill: **KFWB**, 1987-92, pd. Bill now works for Metro Traffic.

YEAGER, Steve: **KMPC**, 1992. The former L.A. Dodger catcher hosted a baseball show during the launch of KMPC's all-Sports format.

YNIGUEZ, Pepe: **KWKW**. Born in 1955, Pepe broadcast the Spanish pre-game show for the L.A. Dodgers.

> *"When I left KGBS in 1977 after the station became automated, I went to Tehran to work at the National Iranian Radio & TV Network. They reneged on everything they had promised. I had to make a daring escape from the country."*
>
> *-Brad Edwards*

YOCAM, Joe: **KVOE**, 1942; **KFWB**, 1942-68; **KLAC**, 1969. Joe was one of the original "Seven Swingin' Gentlemen," working noon to three on Chuck Blore's "Color Radio" KFWB during its debut on January 2, 1958. He was given credit for dubbing the music list "Fabulous Forty." Born and raised in South Bend, Joe started out in radio at WASP-Borger, Texas. He came to the Southland to attend Santa Ana City College and work at KVOE (later KWIZ) in Santa Ana. Joe spent a quarter of a century with KFWB. In early 1965, KFWB let Joe go and he filed a grievance with AFTRA. At one period he was president of the union. In December 1965, KFWB was forced to hire Joe back, and he stayed until March 1968, when the station went all-News. Joe was a staff announcer with PBS's KCET. He devoted much of his time as a volunteer with Rancho Los Amigoes Home for disadvantaged children. Joe retired to Balboa Island and died of cancer March 3, 1974. He was 55.

YORK, Carrie: SEE Deana Crowe

YORTY, Sam: **KGBS**, 1974. The former mayor for 12 tumultuous years hosted a morning drive show during KGBS's brief move into an all-Talk format. His producer, Wally George, told the *LA Times* at the time: "People see Yorty as filling the void of conservative commentary that has been left vacant since the death of Marv Gray." The ex-saxophone player from Nebraska, "Mayor Sam" started his show each morning with his theme "Sam's Song."

YOUNG, Ace: **KMET**, 1971-83 and 1985-87. Born Dennis Young in St. Louis, he grew up listening to KMOX and KXOK and the great voices of the Cardinals broadcasting team. He moved with his parents to Ojai when he was 12 and after school would hang out at KUDU-Ventura where he eventually got his first job while in high school. In his senior year his parents made a move to Northern California and Ace (Dennis called everyone Ace, so everyone called him Ace and it stuck) wanted to spend his last semester with his friends and KUDU. After two years at Ventura Community College where he was elected president of the student body, Ace moved to Sacramento State and became gm of the college station. The times, they were 'a changing. It was 1968 and Ace convinced the owner of KZAP to allow a group to change the station from Jazz to Janis Joplin, Jefferson Airplane and other music coming out of the Bay Area. There were two complete staffs at KZAP, each group working four days. One group would live in a downtown commune while the other lived on an 156-acre farm with collective farming. "If we were lucky, we even got paid every couple of weeks if the water bed companies paid their bills." It was the first time that news complemented the music and vice versa. Ace was part of the news dissemination to "underground" stations all over the country. In 1971 Ace became a key member of "the mighty Met" and was news director and worked morning drive. In 1977 in Santa Barbara he launched his own news network "Newspace." It served stations in all the major California markets. "Newspace" folded after two years, and Ace returned briefly to KMET. In 1984 he joined Turner's new CNN radio network in Atlanta and a year later went to WINZ-Miami. He rejoined

KMET in late 1985 in morning drive, only to see it go off the air. "I came back to nothing. The times had disappeared and finally KMET was gone." Ace did some syndication shows and managed a radio station near Yosemite Park where he moved to be close to his elderly parents. Ace lives in a home heated by wood and he gets his water from a ditch system that was built in 1850. "The times have changed. I'm looking out my window and I see a 200-foot redwood and pine trees. There is a deer wandering in the back of the house." Ace has developed a Web site servicing Yosemite National Park that is a rich resource for visitors from around the world. There are over 100 clients supporting his Web site. The times, they are indeed 'a changing for Ace.

YOUNG, Billy: **KACE**. Billy worked for KACE for eight years during the 1980s. He is now living and working in Milwaukee.

YOUNG, Clara: **KFI**, 1996-97. Clara works a weekend shift on all-Talk KFI. She was a "print reporter" for KNBC/Channel 4 and a production manager before joining KFI. Clara also hosted a tv show on KSCI.

YOUNG, David L.: **KPPC**, 1965-66; **KGLA**, 1966; **KDAY**, 1967

YOUNGBLOOD, Jack: **KMPC**, 1987-91. The former Ram was one of the radio announcers for the Rams. Jack played in the 1980 Super Bowl with a broken leg and never in his 13-year pro career did he play injury-free.

YOUNGBLOOD, Rob: **KIQQ**. Rob was also a vj on CNN's Cable Music Channel.

YURDIN, Larry: **KMET**, 1971-73, nd. Larry moved to the Bay Area and worked for KFAT.

Z

ZAILLIAN, Jim: **KABC**; **KNX**, 1966-78, nd. The Southern California Radio and Television News Association names its annual scholarship after Jim. He died of a heart attack.

"I still miss the spontaneity of radio news. I miss the excitement of radio. I don't miss the instability of radio."
                                                              -Rick Jager

ZAPOLEON, Guy: **KRTH**, 1973-75 and 1976-77; **KRLA**, 1977-78; **KRTH**, 1978-81. Born in Nashville, Guy grew up in Stamford, Connecticut and fell in love with radio listening to WABC-New York and Cousin Brucie. When his family moved to Los Angeles, he started listening to "Boss Radio," and Bill Drake became his biggest inspiration. He graduated from UCLA with a degree in psychology and started his radio career as md at KRLA. He worked  as pd at KRQQ-Tucson and WBZZ-Pittsburgh before returning to the Southland as md in 1978 at KRTH; he became the pd in 1980. In 1989, Guy was the national pd for Nationwide Communications. One programmer summed up Guy's talent: "Music has always been thought of as the DNA chromosome of Zapoleon's stations." Guy currently runs Zapoleon Media Strategies out of Sugar Land, Texas. In 1995 and 1996 *Billboard* named Guy Radio Consultant of the Year in two formats - Adult and Top 40.

ZEKE: **KROQ**, 1996-97. Zeke Piestrup started as a part-timer on KROQ. He moved to evenings in the summer of 1996.

ZELADA, Edgar: **KLVE**, 1989. Edgar worked all-night at Spanish "K-Love."

ZENON, Janine: SEE Janine Haydel

ZENORE, Zachary: **KPPC**, 1970-71; **KMET**, 1972. Zack was a groupie when KPPC first went on the air in 1967. Original all-night KPPC jock Bob Shayne remembered him as "this kid with long, dark floppy hair who wanted to be a disc jockey." He also worked the all-night shift at "the Mighty Met." Zack now lives in New Mexico.

ZIDER, Bob: **KMDY**, 1986, pd. Bob started the nation's third all-Comedy radio station.

In 1987, RKO sells KRTH to Beasley Broadcasting for $87 million

In 1994, Beasley sells KRTH to Infinity for $116 million

ZIEGENBUSCH, Ted: **KMGG**, 1982; **KOST**, 1982-97.

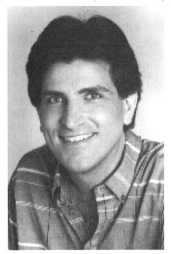

Born in Lima, Ohio, Ted interned at KMEN while he was going to high school in San Bernardino and later became md and utility jock in 1971 and 1972. "I decided on a career in radio after watching my 'idols' on KMEN. As luck would have it, the radio station was located directly behind the high school. Every day, on my way home, I would watch the masters at work, spinning their stories and playing the tunes. These were my mentors, to whom I owe so much respect and appreciation. It's mind boggling when you realize the talent that came out of one little AM station in San Bernardino." In the early 1980s Ted worked mostly mornings in San Diego at "91X," "The Mighty 690," KGB and KIFM. Prior to San Diego he was pd and morning drive at KLAV-Las Vegas. Ted started at KMGG in 1982 and stayed briefly until joining KOST. For several years, he did the late evening program on "the Coast" and was top rated with double digits. He has appeared in tv and motion pictures since 1984. Ted has been named to Who's Who in Entertainment and Who's Who in the West. He lives in Orange County with his wife and three children.

ZIEL, Ed: **KLAC**, 1965-71; **KRLA**, 1971-72; **KROQ**, 1973; **KFI**, 1973-76; **KGIL**, 1976-92; **KMGX**. Ed has been a premier newsman in Southern California for close to three decades. He was part of the morning team with "Sweet Dick" Whittington at KGIL and Lohman and Barkley at KFI. Ed was born in Indiana and received a Bachelor of Science degree in broadcast journalism from Indiana University. During his Army days he was a reporter for The American Forces Network while stationed in Berlin. When he left the Army he worked as a writer for the Associated Press in Milwaukee. His first job in the Southland was at KLAC when it was L.A.'s first all-Talk station. Joe Pyne did mornings while Bob Grant worked afternoons and Mort Sahl did the evenings. "It was a great station." He is now with the Ventura County Correction Services Agency working with juvenile offenders.

ZIFF, Sid: **KFWB**; **KRKD**. Sid was an L.A. sports columnist and editor for the now-defunct *LA Mirror* who aired commentaries in the '50s and '60s.

ZORN, Dave: **KNX**, 1981-97. Except for a brief stint in Detroit, since 1981 Dave has been an anchorman/reporter at "KNXNewsradio." He served as a corporal in the U.S. Marine Corps between 1964 and 1967 and was in Vietnam for two years. He married his college sweetheart, Carolynn Bauer, and has been a broadcast journalist for over 25 years. Dave has won 7 Golden Mikes including three consecutive best newscast awards. From the L.A. Press Club he has received 12 first-place awards in various categories including best newscast. His son David is a broadcast journalism major at Northern Arizona University. Dave and Carolynn live in Agoura Hills.

"The disc jockey is the lowest rung on the show business ladder. There's no talent required for this whatsoever. Believe me. I should know, I've been doing it long enough."
-Dick Whittinghill

VOTE FOR YOUR FAVORITE
LOS ANGELES RADIO PEOPLE!

Over 230 disc jockeys received votes for the Top 10 djs during the balloting in the first volume of *Los Angeles Radio People*. The second edition has not only updated the disc jockeys, but now includes news and sports people, talk show hosts, program directors and general managers.

Will you please vote for your 10 favorite Los Angeles Radio <u>People</u> between 1957 - 1997?

1._____ 6._____

2._____ 7._____

3._____ 8._____

4._____ 9._____

5._____ 10._____

Please send your ballot to:

> Don Barrett
> Los Angeles Radio People
> PO Box 55518
> Valencia, CA 91385
>
> or fax to: 805.259.4910

GLOSSARY

"Arrow 93"	KCBS (93.1FM)
"B-100"	KIBB (100.3FM) 1996-97
"the Beat"	KKBT (92.3FM)
"Big Five"	KLAC djs in the '50s
"Boss Jocks"	KHJ djs ('60s and '70s)
"Car Radio"	KHJ format
"CD 103"	KACD (103.1FM)
"Coast"	KOST (103.5FM)
"Color Radio"	KFWB format sound beginning 1958
"the Edge"	KMPC/FM
"11-10 Men"	KRLA djs (1959-68)
gm	general manager
"Groove Radio"	KACD (103.1FM)
KACD	simulcast with KBCD
"K-Earth"	KRTH (101.1FM)
"K-Hits"	KHTZ (97.1FM)
"K-Lite"	KLIT (101.9FM)
"K-Love"	KLVE
"KNXNewsradio"	KNX (1070AM)
""K-Ocean"	KOCM (103.1FM)
"K-100"	KIQQ (100.3FM)
"Kute 102"	KUTE
"K-West"	KWST (105.9FM)
"La Nueva 101.9"	KSCA (101.9FM, 1997)
"Magic 106"	KMGG (105.9FM)
"the Mighty Met"	KMET (94.7FM)
"the new Ten-Q"	KTNQ (during Rock era in second half of '70s)
nsm	national sales manager
OC Register	*Orange County Register* (CA) newspaper
om	operations manager
"Oldies 93"	KODJ (93.1FM)
"Pirate Radio"	KQLZ (1003.FM, 1989-92)
pd	program director
"Power 106"	KPWR (105.9FM)
R&R	*Radio & Records* trade publication
"Real Radio"	KLSX (97.1FM) talk format
"the Roq"	KROQ (106.7FM)
sm	sales manager
"Seven Swingin' Gentlemen"	KFWB djs (1958-65)
"SportsTalk"	KABC sports show for decades
"Star 98.7"	KYSR (98.7FM)
"underground"	a free-form approach to music and format in the late '60s and early '70s
vp	vice president
"the Wave"	KTWV (94.7FM)
WW1	Westwood One
"the Zone"	KTZN (710AM, 1997)

ABOUT THE AUTHOR

Don Barrett became the historian of contemporary Los Angeles radio history with the publication of his first book, *Los Angeles Radio People - a booktory of Disc Jockeys from 1957-94*, published in 1995. Growing up in Southern California, he graduated with a bachelor's degree from Chapman College and a master's in psychology.

Don started his radio career as a disc jockey and before he was 30 years old he was general manager of two stations in Detroit, WDRQ and WWWW. He spent five years with Gordon McLendon including a stint as national program director based in Dallas. In the early 1970s he launched KIQQ ("K-100"), the first successful AC station in Los Angeles.

He joined the motion picture business in 1974 and has held executive marketing positions at Columbia, Universal and MGM/UA Pictures.

Don never lost his passion for radio. He lives in Valencia, California with his wife Ulla, and three children, Don, Tyler and Alexandra and listens to the restless waves of Southern California radio.